Lloyd's Popular Edition

PUBLISHED BY THE PROPRIETORS
OF "THE DAILY CHRONICLE,"
LONDON

THE LIFE OF GLADSTONE

WILLIAM EWART GLADSTONE

From a Photograph by the London Stereoscopic Co.

THE LIFE OF

WILLIAM EWART GLADSTONE

BY

JOHN MORLEY

IN TWO VOLUMES—VOL. I

(1809–1872)

LONDON
EDWARD LLOYD, LIMITED
1908

THE LIFE OF

WILLIAM EWART
GLADSTONE

BY

JOHN MORLEY

NOTE

THE material on which this biography is founded consists mainly, of course, of the papers collected at Hawarden. Besides that vast accumulation, I have been favoured with several thousands of other pieces from the legion of Mr. Gladstone's correspondents. Between two and three hundred thousand written papers of one sort or another must have passed under my view. To some important journals and papers from other sources I have enjoyed free access, and my warm thanks are due to those who have generously lent me this valuable aid. I am especially indebted to the King for the liberality with which his Majesty has been graciously pleased to sanction the use of certain documents, in cases where the permission of the Sovereign was required.

When I submitted an application for the same purpose to Queen Victoria, in readily promising her favourable consideration, the Queen added a message strongly impressing on me that the work I was about to undertake should not be handled in the narrow way of party. This injunction represents my own clear view of the spirit in which the history of a career so memorable as Mr. Gladstone's should be composed. That, to be sure, is not at all inconsistent with our regarding party feeling in its honourable sense, as entirely the reverse of an infirmity.

The diaries from which I have often quoted consist of forty little books in double columns, intended to do little more than record persons seen, or books read, or letters written as the days passed by. From these diaries come several of the mottoes prefixed to our chapters ; such mottoes are marked by an asterisk.

The trustees and other members of Mr. Gladstone's family have extended to me a uniform kindness and consideration and an absolutely unstinted confidence, for which I can never cease to owe them my heartiest acknowledgment. They left with the writer an unqualified and undivided responsibility for these pages, and for the use of the material that they entrusted to him. Whatever may prove to be amiss, whether in leaving out or putting in or putting wrong, the blame is wholly mine.

J. M.

1903.

CONTENTS

BOOK I

(1809–1831)

Book I

(1809-1831)

INTRODUCTORY

I AM well aware that to try to write Mr. Gladstone's life at all —the life of a man who held an imposing place in many high national transactions, whose character and career may be regarded in such various lights, whose interests were so manifold, and whose years bridged so long a span of time— is a stroke of temerity. To try to write his life to-day, is to push temerity still further. The ashes of controversy, in which he was much concerned, are still hot; perspective, scale, relation, must all while we stand so near be difficult to adjust. Not all particulars, more especially of the latest marches in his wide campaign, can be disclosed without risk of unjust pain to persons now alive. Yet to defer the task for thirty or forty years has plain drawbacks too. Interest grows less vivid; truth becomes harder to find out; memories pale and colour fades. And if in one sense a statesman's contemporaries, even after death has abated the storm and temper of faction, can scarcely judge him, yet in another sense they who breathe the same air as he breathed, who know at close quarters the problems that faced him, the materials with which he had to work, the limitations of his time—such must be the best, if not the only true memorialists and recorders.

Every reader will perceive that perhaps the sharpest of all the many difficulties of my task has been to draw the line between history and biography—between the fortunes of the community and the exploits, thoughts, and purposes of the individual who had so marked a share in them. In the case of men of letters, in whose lives our literature is admirably rich, this difficulty happily for their authors and for our delight does not arise. But where the subject is a man who was four times at the head of the government—no phantom, but dictator—and who held this office of first minister for a longer time than any other statesman in the reign of the Queen, how can we tell the story of his works and days without reference, and ample reference, to the course of events over whose unrolling he presided, and out of which he made history? It is true that what interests the world in Mr. Gladstone is even more what he was, than what he did ; his brilliancy, charm and power ; the endless surprises ; his dualism or more than dualism ; his vicissitudes of opinion ; his subtleties of mental progress ; his strange union of qualities never elsewhere found together ; his striking unlikeness to other men in whom great and free nations have for long periods placed their trust. I am not sure that the incessant search for clues through this labyrinth would not end in analysis and disquisition, that might be no great improvement even upon political history. Mr. Gladstone said of reconstruction of the income-tax that he only did not call the task herculean, because Hercules could not have done it. Assuredly, I am not presumptuous enough to suppose that this difficulty of fixing the precise scale between history and biography has been successfully overcome by me. It may be that Hercules himself would have succeeded little better.

Some may think in this connection that I have made the preponderance of politics excessive in the story of a genius of signal versatility, to whom politics were only one interest among many. No doubt speeches, debates, bills, divisions, motions, and manœuvres of party, like the manna that fed the children of Israel in the wilderness, lose their savour and power of nutriment on the second day. Yet after all it·was to his thoughts, his purposes, his ideals, his performances as states-man, in all the widest significance of that lofty and honourable designation, that Mr. Gladstone owes the lasting substance of his fame. His life was ever '*greatly absorbed*,' he said, '*in working the institutions of his country*.' Here we mark a signal trait. Not for two centuries, since the historic strife of anglican and puritan, had our island produced a ruler in whom the religious motive was paramount in the like degree. He was not only a political force but a moral force. He strove to use all the powers of his own genius and the powers of the state for moral purposes and religious. Nevertheless his mission in all its forms was action. He had none of that detachment, often found among superior minds, which we honour for its dis-interestedness, even while we lament its impotence in result. The track in which he moved, the instruments that he employed, were the track and the instruments, the sword and the trowel, of political action ; and what is called the Gladstonian era was distinctively a political era.

On this I will permit myself a few words more. The detailed history of Mr. Gladstone as theologian and churchman will not be found in these pages, and nobody is more sensible than their writer of the gap. Mr. Gladstone cared as much for the church as he cared for the state; he thought of the church as the soul of the state; he believed the attainment by the magistrate of the ends of government to depend upon religion; and he was sure that the strength of a state corresponds to the religious strength and soundness of the community of which the state is the civil organ. I should have been wholly wanting in biographical fidelity, not to make this clear and superabundantly clear. Still a writer inside Mr. Gladstone's church and in full and active sympathy with him on this side of mundane and supramundane things, would undoubtedly have treated the subject differently from any writer outside. No amount of candour or good faith—and in these essentials I believe that I have not fallen short—can be a substitute for the confidence and ardour of an adherent, in the heart of those to whom the church stands first. Here is one of the difficulties of this complex case. Yet here, too, there may be some trace of compensation. If the reader has been drawn into the whirlpools of the political Charybdis, he might not even in far worthier hands than mine have escaped the rocky headlands of the ecclesiastic Scylla. For churches also have their parties.

Lord Salisbury, the distinguished man who followed Mr. Gladstone in a longer tenure of power than his, called him 'a great Christian'; and nothing could be more true or better worth saying. He not only accepted the doctrines of that faith as he believed them to be held by his own communion; he sedulously strove to apply the noblest moralities of it to the affairs both of his own nation and of the commonwealth of nations. It was a supreme experiment. People will perhaps some day wonder that many of those who derided the experiment and reproached its author, failed to see that they were making manifest in this a wholesale scepticism as to truths that they professed to prize, far deeper and more destructive than the doubts and disbeliefs of the gentiles in the outer courts.

The epoch, as the reader knows, was what Mr. Gladstone called 'an agitated and expectant age.' Some stages of his career mark stages of the first importance in the history of English party, on which so much in the working of our constitution hangs. His name is associated with a record of arduous and fruitful legislative work and administrative improvement, equalled by none of the great men who have grasped the helm of the British state. The intensity of his mind, and the length of years through which he held presiding office, enabled him to impress for good in all the departments of government his own severe standard of public duty and personal exactitude. He was the chief force, propelling, restraining, guiding his country at many decisive moments. Then how many surprises and what seeming paradox. Devotedly attached to the church, he was the agent in the overthrow of establishment in one of the three kingdoms, and in an attempt to overthrow it in the Principality. Entering public life with vehement aversion to the recent dislodgment of the landed aristocracy as the mainspring of parliamentary power, he lent himself to two further enormously extensive changes in the constitutional centre of gravity. With a lifelong belief in parliamentary deliberation as the grand security for judicious laws and national control over executive act, he yet at a certain stage betook himself with magical result to direct and individual appeal to the great masses of his countrymen, and the world beheld the astonishing spectacle of a politician with the microscopic subtlety of a thirteenth-century schoolman wielding at will the new democracy in what has been called 'the country of plain men.' A firm and trained economist, and no friend to socialism, yet by his legislation upon land in 1870 and 1881 he wrote the opening chapter in a volume on which many an unexpected page in the history of Property is destined to be inscribed. Statesmen do far less than they suppose, far less than is implied in their resounding fame, to augment the material prosperity of nations, but in this province Mr. Gladstone's name stands at the topmost height. Yet no ruler that ever lived felt more deeply the truth—for which I know no better words than Channing's—that to improve man's outward condition is not to improve man himself ; this must come from each man's endeavour within his own breast ; without that there can be little ground for social hope. Well was it said to him, 'You have so lived and wrought that you have kept the soul alive in England.' Not in England only was this felt. He was sometimes charged with lowering the sentiment, the lofty and fortifying sentiment, of national pride. At least it is a ground for national pride that he, the son of English train-ing, practised through long years in the habit and tradition of English public life, standing for long years foremost in accepted authority and renown before the eye of England, so conquered imagination and attachment in other lands, that when the end came it was thought no extravagance for one not an English-man to say, 'On the day that Mr. Gladstone died, the world has lost its greatest citizen.' The reader who revolves all this will know why I began by speaking of temerity.

That my book should be a biography without trace of bias, no reader will expect. There is at least no bias against the truth ; but indifferent neutrality in a work produced, as this is, in the spirit of loyal and affectionate remembrance, would be distasteful, discordant, and impossible. I should be heartily sorry if there were no signs of partiality and no evidence of prepossession. On the other hand there is, I trust, no im-portunate advocacy or tedious assentation. He was great man enough to stand in need of neither. Still less has it been needed, in order to exalt him, to disparage others with whom he came into strong collision. His own funeral orations from time to time on some who were in one degree or another his antagonists, prove that this petty and ungenerous method would have been to him of all men most repugnant. Then to pretend that for sixty years, with all 'the varying weather of the mind,' he traversed in every zone the restless ocean of a great nation's shifting and complex politics, without many a faulty tack and many a wrong reckoning, would indeed be idle. No such claim is set up by rational men for Pym, Cromwell, Walpole, Washington, or either Pitt. It is not set up for any of the three contemporaries of Mr. Gladstone whose names live with the three most momentous transactions of his age—Cavour, Lincoln, Bismarck. To suppose, again, that in every one of the many subjects touched by him, besides exhibiting the range of his powers and the diversity of his interests, he made abiding contributions to thought and knowledge, is to ignore the jealous conditions under which such contributions come. To say so much as this is to make but a small deduction from the total of a grand account.

I have not reproduced the full text of Letters in the proportion customary in English biography. The existing mass of his letters is enormous. But then an enormous proportion of them touch on affairs of public business, on which they shed little new light. Even when he writes in his kindest and most cordial vein to friends to whom he is most warmly attached, it is usually a letter of business. He deals freely and genially with the points in hand, and then without play of gossip, salutation, or compliment, he passes on his way. He has in his letters little of that spirit in which his talk often abounded, of disengagement, pleasant colloquy, happy raillery, and all the other undefined things that make the correspondence of so many men whose business was literature such delightful reading for the idler hour of an industrious day. It is perhaps worth adding that the asterisks denoting an omitted passage hide no piquant hit, no personality, no indiscretion; the omission is in every case due to consideration of space. Without these asterisks and other omissions, nothing would have been easier than to expand these two volumes into a hundred. I think nothing relevant is lost. Nobody ever had fewer secrets, nobody ever lived and wrought in fuller sunlight.

CHAPTER I

CHILDHOOD

(*1809–1821*)

I know not why commerce in England should not have its old families, rejoicing to be connected with commerce from generation to generation. It has been so in other countries; I trust it will be so in this country.—GLADSTONE.

THE dawn of the life of the great and famous man who is our subject in these memoirs has been depicted with homely simplicity by his own hand. With this fragment of a record it is perhaps best for me to begin our journey. 'I was born,' he says, 'on December 29, 1809,' at 62 Rodney Street, Liverpool. 'I was baptized, I believe, in the parish church of St. Peter. My godmother was my elder sister Anne, then just seven years old, who died a perfect saint in the beginning of the year 1829. In her later years she lived in close relations with me, and I must have been much worse but for her. Of my godfathers, one was a Scotch episcopalian, Mr. Fraser of ——, whom I hardly ever saw or heard of; the other a presbyterian, Mr. G. Grant, a junior partner of my father's.' The child was named William Ewart, after his father's friend, an immigrant Scot and a merchant like himself, and father of a younger William Ewart, who became member for Liverpool, and did good public service in parliament.

Before proceeding to the period of my childhood, properly so-called, I will here insert a few words about my family. My maternal grandfather was known as Provost Robertson of Dingwall, a man held, I believe, in the highest respect. His wife was a Mackenzie of [Coul]. His circumstances must have been good. Of his three sons, one went into the army, and I recollect him as Captain Robertson (I have a seal which he gave me, a three-sided cairngorm. Cost him 7½ guineas). The other two took mercantile positions. When my parents made a Scotch tour in 1820-21 with, I think, their four sons, the freedom of Dingwall was presented to us all,[1] with my father; and there was large visiting at the houses of the Ross-shire gentry. I think the line

[1] The freedom was formally bestowed on him in 1853.

6

of my grandmother was stoutly episcopalian and Jacobite : but, coming outside the western highlands, the first at least was soon rubbed down. The provost, I think, came from a younger branch of the Robertsons of Struan.

On my father's side the matter is more complex. The history of the family has been traced at the desire of my eldest brother and my own, by Sir William Fraser, the highest living authority.[1] He has carried us up to a rather remote period, I think before Elizabeth, but has not yet been able to connect us with the earliest known holders of the name, which with the aid of charter-chests he hopes to do. Some things are plain and not without interest. They were a race of borderers. There is still an old Gledstanes or Gladstone castle. They formed a family in Sweden in the seventeenth century. The explanation of this may have been that, when the union of the crowns led to the extinction of border fighting they took service like Sir Dugald Dalgetty under Gustavus Adolphus, and in this case passed from service to settlement. I have never heard of them in Scotland until after the Restoration, otherwise than as persons of family. At that period there are traces of their having been fined by public authority, but not for any ordinary criminal offence. From this time forward I find no trace of their gentility. During the eighteenth century they are, I think, principally traced by a line of maltsters (no doubt a small business then) in Lanarkshire. Their names are recorded on tombstones in the church-yard of Biggar. I remember going as a child or boy to see the repre-sentative of that branch, either in 1820 or some years earlier, who was a small watchmaker in that town. He was of the same generation as my father, but came, I understood, from a senior brother of the family. I do not know whether his line is extinct. There also seem to be some stray Gladstones who are found at Yarmouth and in Yorkshire.[2]

My father's father seems from his letters to have been an excellent man and a wise parent : his wife a woman of energy. There are pictures of them at Fasque, by Raeburn. He was a merchant, in Scotch phrase ; that is to say, a shopkeeper dealing in corn and stores, and my father as a lad served in his shop. But he also sent a ship or ships to the Baltic ; and I believe that my father, whose energy soon began to

---

[1] Sir William Fraser died in 1898.

[2] Researches into the ancestry of the Gladstone family have been made by Sir William Fraser, Professor John Veitch, and Mrs. Oliver of Thornwood. Besides his special investigation of the genealogy of the family, Sir W. Fraser devoted some pages in the *Douglas Book* to the Gledstanes of Gledstanes. The surname of Gledstanes occurs at a very early period in the records of Scotland. Families of that name acquired considerable landed estates in the counties of Lanark, Peebles, Roxburgh, and Dumfries. The old castle of Gledstanes, now in ruins, was the principal mansion of the family. The first of the name who has been found on record is Herbert de Gledstanes, who swore fealty to Edward I. in 1296 for lands in the county of Lanark. The Gledstanes long held the office of bailie under the Earls of Douglas and the con-nection between the two families seems to have lasted until the fall of the Douglas family. The Gledstanes still continued to figure for many generations on the border. About the middle of the eighteenth century two branches of the family—the Gled-stanes of Cocklaw and of Craigs—failed in the direct male line. Mr. Gladstone was descended from a third branch, the Gledstanes of Arthurshiel in Lanarkshire. The first of this line who has been traced is William Gledstanes, who in the year 1551 was laird of Arthurshiel. His lineal descendants continued as owners of that property till William Gledstanes disposed of it and went to live in the town of Biggar about the year 1679. This William Gledstanes was Mr. Gladstone's great-great-grandfather. The connection between these three branches and Herbert de Gledstanes of 1296 has not been ascertained, but he was probably the common ancestor of them all.

outtop that of all the very large family, went in one of these ships at a
very early age as a supercargo, an appointment then, I think, common.
But he soon quitted a nest too small to hold him. He was born in
December 1764 : and I have (at Hawarden) a reprint of the *Liverpool
Directory* for 178—, in which his name appears as a partner in the firm
of Messrs. Corrie, corn merchants.

Here his force soon began to be felt as a prominent and then a foremost member of the community. A liberal in the early period of the
century, he drew to Mr. Canning, and brought that statesman as
candidate to Liverpool in 1812, by personally offering to guarantee his
expenses at a time when, though prosperous, he could hardly have been
a rich man. His services to the town were testified by gifts of plate,
now in the possession of the elder lines of his descendants, and by a
remarkable subscription of six thousand pounds raised to enable him
to contest the borough of Lancaster, for which he sat in the parliament
of 1818.

At his demise, in December 1851, the value of his estate was, I think,
near £600,000. My father was a successful merchant, but considering
his long life and means of accumulation, the result represents a success
secondary in comparison with that of others whom in native talent and
energy he much surpassed. It was a large and strong nature, simple
though hasty, profoundly affectionate and capable of the highest
devotion in the lines of duty and of love. I think that his intellect
was a little intemperate, though not his character. In his old age,
spent mainly in retirement, he was our constant [centre of] social and
domestic life. My mother, a beautiful and admirable woman, failed in
health and left him a widower in 1835, when she was 62.

He then turns to the records of his own childhood, a period
that he regarded as closing in September 1821, when he was
sent to Eton. He begins with one or two juvenile performances,
in no way differing from those of any other infant,—*navita
projectus humi*, the mariner flung by force of the waves naked
and helpless ashore. He believes that he was strong and
healthy, and came well through his childish ailments.

My next recollection belongs to the period of Mr. Canning's first
election for Liverpool, in the month of October of the year 1812. Much
entertaining went on in my father's house, where Mr. Canning himself
was a guest ; and on a day of a great dinner I was taken down to the
dining-room. I was set upon one of the chairs, standing, and directed
to say to the company 'Ladies and gentlemen.'

I have, thirdly, a group of recollections which refer to Scotland.
Thither my father and mother took me on a journey which they made,
I think, in a post-chaise to Edinburgh and Glasgow as its principal
points. At Edinburgh our sojourn was in the Royal Hotel, Princes
Street. I well remember the rattling of the windows when the castle
guns were fired on some great occasion, probably the abdication of
Napoleon, for the date of the journey was, I think, the spring of 1814.

In this journey the situation of Sanquhar, in a close Dumfriesshire
valley, impressed itself on my recollection. I never saw Sanquhar
again until in the autumn of 1863 (as I believe). As I was whirled
along the Glasgow and South-Western railway I witnessed just beneath

me lines of building in just such a valley, and said that must be
Sanquhar, which it was. My local memory has always been good and
very impressible by scenery. I seem to myself never to have forgotten
a scene.

I have one other early recollection to record. It must, I think,
have been in the year 1815 that my father and mother took me with
them on either one or two more journeys. The objective points were
Cambridge and London respectively. My father had built, under the
very niggard and discouraging laws which repressed rather than
encouraged the erection of new churches at that period, the church of
St. Thomas at Seaforth, and he wanted a clergyman for it.[1] Guided
in these matters very much by the deeply religious temper of my
mother, he went with her to Cambridge to obtain a recommendation
of a suitable person from Mr. Simeon, whom I saw at the time.[2] I
remember his appearance distinctly. He was a venerable man, and
although only a fellow of a college, was more ecclesiastically got up
than many a dean, or even here and there, perhaps, a bishop of the
present less costumed if more ritualistic period. Mr. Simeon, I believe,
recommended Mr. Jones, an excellent specimen of the excellent
evangelical school of those days. We went to Leicester to hear him
preach in a large church, and his text was ' Grow in grace.' He became
eventually archdeacon of Liverpool, and died in great honour a few
years ago at much past 90. On the strength of this visit to Cambridge
I lately boasted there, even during the lifetime of the aged Provost
Okes, that I had been in the university before any one of them.

I think it was at this time that in London we were domiciled in
Russell Square, in the house of a brother of my mother, Mr. Colin
Robertson ; and I was vexed and put about by being forbidden to run
freely at my own will into and about the streets, as I had done in
Liverpool. But the main event was this : we went to a great service
of public thanksgiving at Saint Paul's, and sat in a small gallery
annexed to the choir, just over the place where was the Regent, and
looking down upon him from behind. I recollect nothing more of the
service, nor was I ever present at any public thanksgiving after this in
Saint Paul's, until the service held in that cathedral, under my advice
as the prime minister, after the highly dangerous illness of the Prince
of Wales.

Before quitting the subject of early recollections I must name one
which involves another person of some note. My mother took me in
181— to Barley Wood Cottage, near Bristol. Here lived Miss Hannah
More, with some of her coeval sisters. I am sure they loved my
mother, who was love-worthy indeed. And I cannot help here deviating
for a moment into the later portion of the story to record that in 1833
I had the honour of breakfasting with Mr. Wilberforce a few days
before his death,[3] and when I entered the house, immediately after the
salutation, he said to me in his silvery tones, 'How is your sweet
mother ? ' He had been a guest in my father's house some twelve years
before. During the afternoon visit at Barley Wood, Miss Hannah

---

[1] John Gladstone built St. Thomas's Church, Seaforth, 1814-15 ; St. Andrew's,
Liverpool, about 1816 ; the church at Leith ; the Episcopal chapel at Fasque built
and endowed about 1847.

[2] Charles Simeon (1759-1836) who played as conspicuous a part in low church
thought as Newman afterwards in high.

[3] See below, p. 80.

More took me aside and presented to me a little book. It was a copy of her *Sacred Dramas*, and it now remains in my possession, with my name written in it by her. She very graciously accompanied it with a little speech, of which I cannot recollect the conclusion (or apodosis), but it began, 'As you have just come into the world, and I am just going out of it, I therefore,' etc.

I wish that in reviewing my childhood I could regard it as presenting those features of innocence and beauty which I have often seen elsewhere, and indeed, thanks be to God, within the limits of my own home. The best I can say for it is that I do not think it was a vicious childhood. I do not think, trying to look at the past impartially, that I had a strong natural propensity then developed to what are termed the mortal sins. But truth obliges me to record this against myself. I have no recollection of being a loving or a winning child ; or an earnest or diligent or knowledge-loving child. God forgive me. And what pains and shames me most of all is to remember that at most and at best I was, like the sailor in Juvenal,

digitis a morte remotus,
Quatuor aut septem ;[1]

the plank between me and all the sins was so very thin. I do not indeed intend in these notes to give a history of the inner life, which I think has been with me extraordinarily dubious, vacillating, and above all complex. I reserve them, perhaps, for a more private and personal document ; and I may in this way relieve myself from some at least of the risks of falling into an odious Pharisaism. I cannot in truth have been an interesting child, and the only presumption the other way which I can gather from my review is that there was probably something in me worth the seeing, or my father and mother would not so much have singled me out to be taken with them on their journeys.

I was not a devotional child. I have no recollection of early love for the House of God and for divine service : though after my father built the church at Seaforth in 1815, I remember cherishing a hope that he would bequeath it to me, and that I might live in it. I have a very early recollection of hearing preaching in St. George's, Liverpool, but it is this : that I turned quickly to my mother and said, 'When will he have done ?' The *Pilgrim's Progress* undoubtedly took a great and fascinating hold upon me, so that anything which I wrote was insensibly moulded in its style ; but it was by the force of the allegory addressing itself to the fancy, and was very like a strong impression received from the *Arabian Nights*, and from another work called *Tales of the Genii*. I think it was about the same time that Miss Porter's *Scottish Chiefs*, and especially the life and death of Wallace, used to make me weep profusely. This would be when I was about ten years old. At a much earlier period, say six or seven, I remember praying earnestly, but it was for no higher object than to be spared from the loss of a tooth. Here, however, it may be mentioned in mitigation that the local dentist of those days, in our case a certain Dr. P. of —— Street, Liverpool, was a kind of savage at his work (possibly a very good-natured man too), with no ideas except to smash and crash.

---

[1] xii. 58—' Removed from death by four or maybe seven fingers' breadth.'

My religious recollections, then, are a sad blank. Neither was I a popular boy, though not egregiously otherwise. If I was not a bad boy, I think that I was a boy with a great absence of goodness. I was a child of slow, in some points I think of singularly slow, development. There was more in me perhaps than in the average boy, but it required greatly more time to set itself in order : and just so in adult, and in middle and later life, I acquired very tardily any knowledge of the world, and that simultaneous conspectus of the relations of persons and things which is necessary for the proper performance of duties in the world.

I may mention another matter in extenuation. I received, unless my memory deceives me, very little benefit from teaching. My father was too much occupied, my mother's health was broken. We, the four brothers, had no quarrelling among ourselves : but neither can I recollect any influence flowing down at this time upon me, the junior. One odd incident seems to show that I was meek, which I should not have supposed, not less than thrifty and penurious, a leaning which lay deep, I think, in my nature, and which has required effort and battle to control it. It was this. By some process not easy to explain I had, when I was *probably* seven or eight, and my elder brothers from ten or eleven to fourteen or thereabouts, accumulated no less than twenty shillings in silver. My brothers judged it right to appropriate this fund, and I do not recollect either annoyance or resistance or complaint. But I recollect that they employed the principal part of it in the purchase of four knives, and that they broke the points from the tops of the blades of my knife, lest I should cut my fingers.

Where was the official or appointed teacher all this time ? He was the Rev. Mr. Rawson of Cambridge, who had, I suppose, been passed by Mr. Simeon and become private tutor in my father's house. But as he was to be incumbent of the church, the bishop required a parsonage and that he should live in it. Out of this grew a very small school of about twelve boys, to which I went, with some senior brother or brothers remaining for a while. Mr. Rawson was a good man, of high no-popery opinions. His school afterwards rose into considerable repute, and it had Dean Stanley and the sons of one or more other Cheshire families for pupils. But I think this was not so much due to its intellectual stamina as to the extreme salubrity of the situation on the pure dry sands of the Mersey's mouth, with all the advantages of the strong tidal action and the fresh and frequent north-west winds. At five miles from Liverpool Exchange, the sands, delicious for riding, were one absolute solitude, and only one house looked down on them between us and the town. To return to Mr. Rawson. Everything was unobjectionable. I suppose I learnt something there. But I have no recollection of being under any moral or personal influence whatever, and I doubt whether the preaching had any adaptation whatever to children. As to intellectual training, I believe that, like the other boys, I shirked my work as much as I could. I went to Eton in 1821 after a pretty long spell, in a very middling state of preparation, and wholly without any knowledge or other enthusiasm, unless it were a priggish love of argument which I had begun to develop. I had lived upon a rabbit warren : and what a rabbit warren of a life it is that I have been surveying.

My brother John, three years older than myself, and of a moral character more manly and on a higher level, had chosen the navy, and went off to the preparatory college at Portsmouth. But he evidently underwent persecution for righteousness' sake at the college, which was then (say about 1820) in a bad condition. Of this, though he was never querulous, his letters bore the traces, and I cannot but think they must have exercised upon me some kind of influence for good. As to miscellaneous notices, I had a great affinity with the trades of joiners and of bricklayers. Physically I must have been rather tough, for my brother John took me down at about ten years old to wrestle in the stables with an older lad of that region, whom I threw. Among our greatest enjoyments were undoubtedly the annual Guy Fawkes bonfires, for which we had always liberal allowances of wreck timber and a tar-barrel. I remember seeing, when about eight or nine, my first case of a dead body. It was the child of the head gardener Derbyshire, and was laid in the cottage bed by tender hands, with nice and clean accompaniments. It seemed to me pleasing, and in no way repelled me ; but it made no deep impression. And now I remember that I used to teach pretty regularly on Sundays in the Sunday-school built by my father near the Rimrose bridge. It was, I think, a duty done not under constraint, but I can recollect nothing which associates it with a seriously religious life in myself.[1]

II

To these fragments no long supplement is needed. Little of interest can be . certainly established about his far-off ancestral origins, and the ordinary twilight of genealogy overhangs the case of the Glaidstanes, Gledstanes, Gladstanes, Gladstones, whose name is to be found on tombstones and parish rolls, in charter-chests and royal certificates, on the southern border of Scotland. The explorations of the genealogist tell of recognitions of their nobility by Scottish kings in dim ages, but the links are sometimes broken, title-deeds are lost, the same name is attached to estates in different counties, Roxburgh, Peebles, Lanark, and in short until the close of the seventeenth century we linger, in the old poet's phrase, among dreams of shadows. As we have just been told, during the eighteenth century no traces of their gentility survives, and apparently they glided down from moderate lairds to small maltsters. Thomas Gladstones, grandfather of him with whom we are concerned, made his way from Biggar to Leith, and there set up in a modest way as corn-dealer, wholesale and retail. His wife was a Neilson of Springfield. To them sixteen children were born, and John Gladstones (b. Dec. 11, 1764) was their eldest son. Having established himself in Liverpool, he married in 1792 Jane Hall, a lady of that city, who died without children six years later. In 1800 he took for his second wife Anne Robertson, of Dingwall. Her father was of the clan Donnachaidh, and

[1] The fragment is undated.

her mother was of kin with Mackenzies, Munros, and other highland stocks.[1] Their son, therefore, was of unmixed Scottish origins, half-highland, half lowland borderer.[2] With the possible exception of Lord Mansfield—the rival of Chatham in parliament, one of the loftiest names among great judges, and chief builder of the commercial law of the English world, a man who might have been prime minister if he had chosen— Mr. Gladstone stands out as far the most conspicuous and powerful of all the public leaders in our history, who have sprung from the northern half of our island. When he had grown to be the most famous man in the realm of the Queen, he said, 'I am not slow to claim the name of Scotsman, and even if I were, there is the fact staring me in the face that not a drop of blood runs in my veins except what is derived from a Scottish ancestry.'[3] An illustrious opponent once described him by way of hitting his singular duality of disposition, as an ardent Italian in the custody of a Scotsman. It is easy to make too much of race, but when we are puzzled by Mr. Gladstone's seeming contrarieties of temperament, his union

[1] One or two further genealogical *nugæ* are among the papers. A correspondent wrote to Mr. Gladstone in 1887: Among the donors to the Craftsman's Hospital, Aberdeen, established in 1633, occurs the name of 'Georg Gladstaines, pewterer, 300 merks' (£16 : 13 : 4 sterling), 1698. George joined the Hammerman Craft in 1656, when he would have been about 25 years of age. His signature is still in existence appended to the burgess oath. Very few craftsmen could sign their names at that period—not one in twenty—so that George must have been fairly well educated. Mr. Gladstone replied that it was the first time that he had heard of the name so far north, and that the pewterer was probably one planted out. At Dundee (1890) he mentioned that others of his name and blood appeared on the burgess-roll as early as the fifteenth century. As for his maternal grandfather, the *Inverness Courier* (March 2, year not given) has the following :—'Provost Robertson of Dingwall was a descendant of the ancient family of the Robertsons of Inshes, of whose early settlement in the north the following particulars are known : The first was a member of the family of Struan, Perthshire, and was a merchant in Inverness in 1420. In the battle of *Blair-na-leine*, fought at the west end of Loch-Lochy in 1544, John Robertson, a descendant of the above, acted as standard-bearer to Lord Lovat. This battle was fought between the Frasers and Macdonalds of Clanranald, and derived its appellation from the circumstance of the combatants fighting only in their shirts. The contest was carried on with such bloody determination, foot to foot and claymore to claymore, that only *four* of the Frasers and *ten* of the Macdonalds returned to tell the tale. The former family was well-nigh extirpated ; tradition, however, states that sixteen widows of the Frasers who had been slain, shortly afterwards, as a providential succour, gave birth to sixteen sons ! From the bloody onslaught at Loch - Lochy young Robertson returned home scaithless, and his brave and gallant conduct was the theme of praise with all. Some time thereafter he married the second daughter of Paterson of Wester and Easter Inshes, the eldest being married to Cuthbert of Macbeth's Castlehill, now known as the Crown lands, possessed by Mr. Fraser of Abertarff. On the death of Paterson, his father-in-law, Wester Inshes became the property of young Robertson, and Easter Inshes that of the Cuthberts, who, for the sake of distinction, changed the name to Castlehill. The Robertsons, in regular succession until the present time, possess the fine estate of Inshes ; while that of Castlehill, which belonged to the powerful Cuthberts for so many generations, knows them no more. The family of Inshes, in all ages, stood high in respect throughout the highlands, and many of them had signalised themselves in upholding the rights of their country ; and the worthy Provost Robertson of Dingwall had no less distinguished himself, who, with other important reforms, had cleared away the last burdensome relic of feudal times in that ancient burgh.'

[2] The other sons and daughters of this marriage were Thomas, *d.* 1889 ; Robertson, *d.* 1875 ; John Neilson, *d.* 1863 ; Anne, *d.* 1829 ; Helen Jane, *d.* 1880.

[3] At Dundee, Oct. 29, 1890.

of impulse with caution, of passion with circumspection, of pride and fire with self-control, of Ossianic flight with a steady foothold on the solid earth, we may perhaps find a sort of explanation in thinking of him as a highlander in the custody of a lowlander.

Of John Gladstone something more remains to be said. About 1783 he was made a partner by his father in the business at Leith, and here he saved five hundred pounds. Four years later, probably after a short period of service, he was admitted to a partnership with two corn-merchants at Liverpool, his contribution to the total capital of four thousand pounds being fifteen hundred, of which his father lent him five hundred, and a friend another five at five per cent. In 1787 he thought the plural ending of his name sounded awkwardly in the style of the firm, Corrie, Gladstones, and Bradshaw, so he dropped the s.[1] He visited London to enlarge his knowledge of the corn trade in Mark Lane, and here became acquainted with Sir Claude Scott, the banker (not yet, however, a baronet). Scott was so impressed by his extraordinary vigour and shrewdness as to talk of a partnership, but Gladstone's existing arrangement in Liverpool was settled for fourteen years. Sometime in the nineties he was sent to America to purchase corn, with unlimited confidence from Sir Claude Scott. On his arrival, he found a severe scarcity and enormous prices. A large number of vessels had been chartered for the enterprise, and were on their way to him for cargoes. To send them back in ballast would be a disaster. Thrown entirely on his own resources, he travelled south from New York, making the best purchases of all sorts that he could ; then loaded his ships with timber and other commodities, one only of them with flour ; and the loss on the venture, which might have meant ruin, did not exceed a few hundred pounds. Energy and resource of this kind made fortune secure, and when the fourteen years of partnership expired, Gladstone continued business on his own account, with a prosperity that was never broken. He brought his brothers to Liverpool, but it was to provide for them, not to assist himself, says Mr. Gladstone ; 'and he provided for many young men in the same way. I never knew him reject any kind of work in aid of others that offered itself to him.'

It was John Gladstone's habit, we are told, to discuss all sorts of questions with his children, and nothing was ever taken for granted between him and his sons. 'He could not understand,' says the illustrious one among them, 'nor tolerate those who, perceiving an object to be good, did not at once and actively pursue it ; and with all this energy he joined a

---

[1] In 1835 formal difficulties arose in connection with the purchase of a government annuity, and then he seems to have taken out letters-patent authorising the change in the name.

corresponding warmth and, so to speak, eagerness of affection, a keen appreciation of humour, in which he found a rest, and an indescribable frankness and simplicity of character, which, crowning his other qualities, made him, I think (and I strive to think impartially), the most interesting old man I have ever known.[1]

To his father's person and memory, Mr. Gladstone's fervid and affectionate devotion remained unbroken. 'One morning,' writes a female relative of his, 'when I was breakfasting alone with Mr. Gladstone at Carlton House Terrace something led to his speaking of his father. I seem to see him now, rising from his chair, standing in front of the chimney-piece, and in strains of fervid eloquence dwelling on the grandeur, the breadth and depth of his character, his generosity, his nobleness, last and greatest of all—his loving nature. His eyes filled with tears as he exclaimed: "None but his children can know what torrents of tenderness flowed from his heart."'

The successful merchant was also the active-minded citizen. 'His force,' says his son, 'soon began to be felt as a prominent and then a foremost member of the community.' He had something of his descendant's inextinguishable passion for pamphleteering, and the copious effusion of public letters and articles. As was inevitable in a Scotsman of his social position at that day, when tory rule of a more tyrannic stamp than was ever known in England since the Revolution of 1688, had reduced constitutional liberty in Scotland to a shadow, John Gladstone came to Liverpool a whig, and a whig he remained until Canning raised the flag of a new party inside the entrenchments of Eldonian toryism.

In 1812 Canning, who had just refused Lord Liverpool's proffer of the foreign office because he would not serve under Castlereagh as leader in the House of Commons, was invited by John Gladstone to stand for Liverpool. He was elected in triumph over Brougham, and held the seat through four elections, down to 1822, when he was succeeded by Huskisson, whom he described to the constituency as the best man of business in England, and one of the ablest practical statesmen that could engage in the concerns of a commercial country. The speeches made to his constituents during the ten years for which he served them are excellent specimens of Canning's rich, gay, aspiring eloquence. In substance they abound in much pure toryism, and his speech after the Peterloo massacre, and upon the topics relating to public meetings, sedition, and parliamentary reform, though by sonorous splendour and a superb plausibility fascinating to the political neophyte, is by no means free from froth, without much relation either to social facts or to popular principles. On catholic emancipation he followed Pitt, as he did in an enlarged view of commercial

[1] *Memoirs of J. R. Hope-Scott*, ii. p. 290.

policy.   At Liverpool he made his famous declaration that his
political allegiance was buried in Pitt's grave.   At one at least
of these performances the youthful William Gladstone was
present, but it was at home that he learned Canningite doctrine.
At Seaforth House Canning spent the days between the death
of Castlereagh and his own recall to power, while he was
waiting for the date fixed for his voyage to take up the
viceroyalty of India.

As from whig John Gladstone turned Canningite, so from
presbyterian also he turned churchman.   He paid the penalty
of men who change their party, and was watched with a critical
eye by old friends ; but he was a liberal giver for beneficent
public purposes, and in 1811 he was honoured by the freedom
of Liverpool.   His ambition naturally pointed to parliament,
and he was elected first for Lancaster in 1818, and next for
Woodstock in 1820, two boroughs of extremely easy political
virtue.   Lancaster cost him twelve thousand pounds, towards
which his friends in Liverpool contributed one-half.   In 1826
he was chosen at Berwick, but was unseated the year after.
His few performances in the House were not remarkable.   He
voted with ministers, and on the open question of catholic
emancipation he went with Canning and Plunket.   He was
one of the majority who by six carried Plunket's catholic
motion in 1821, and the matter figures in the earliest of the
hundreds of surviving letters from his youngest son, then over
eleven, and on the eve of his departure for Eton :—

SEAFORTH, *Mar.* 10, 1821.

I address these few lines to you to know how my dear mother is,
to thank you for your kind letter, and to know whether Edward may
get two padlocks for the wicket and large shore gate.   They are now
open, and the people make a thoroughfare of the green walk and the
carriage road.   I read Mr. Plunket's speech, and I admire it exceedingly.
I enclose a letter from Mr. Rawson to you.   He told me to-day that
Mrs. R. was a great deal better.   Write to me again as soon as you
can.—Ever your most affectionate and dutiful son,

W. E. GLADSTONE.

In after years he was fond of recalling how the Liverpool
with which he had been most familiar (1810-20), though the
second commercial town in the kingdom, did not exceed 100,000
of population, and how the silver cloud of smoke that floated
above her resembled that which might now appear over any
secondary borough or village of the country.   'I have seen wild
roses growing upon the very ground that is now the centre of
the borough of Bootle.   All that land is now partly covered
with residences and partly with places of business and industry ;
but in my time but one single house stood upon the space
between Rimrose brook and the town of Liverpool.'   Among his
early recollections was 'the extraordinarily beautiful spectacle

of a dock delivery on the Mersey after a long prevalence of westerly winds followed by a change. Liverpool cannot imitate that now [1892], at least not for the eye.'

III

The Gladstone firm was mainly an East India house, but in the last ten years of his mercantile course John Gladstone became the owner of extensive plantations of sugar and coffee in the West Indies, some in Jamaica, others in British Guiana or Demerara. The infamy of the slave-trade had been abolished in 1807, but slave labour remained, and the Liverpool merchant, like a host of other men of equal respectability and higher dignity, including many peers and even some bishops, was a slave-holder. Everybody who has ever read one of the most honourable and glorious chapters in our English history knows the case of the missionary John Smith.[1] In 1823 an outbreak of the slaves occurred in Demerara, and one of John Gladstone's plantations happened to be its centre. The rising was stamped out with great cruelty in three days. Martial law, the savage instrument of race passion, was kept in force for over five months. Fifty negroes were hanged, many were shot down in the thickets, others were torn in pieces by the lash of the cart-whip. Smith was arrested, although he had in fact done his best to stop the rising. Tried before a court in which every rule of evidence was tyrannically set aside, he was convicted on hearsay and condemned to death. Before the atrocious sentence could be commuted by the home authorities, the fiery heat and noisome vapours of his prison killed him. The death of the Demerara missionary, it has been truly said, was an event as fatal to slavery in the West Indies, as the execution of John Brown was its deathblow in the United States.[2] Brougham in 1824 brought the case before the House of Commons, and in the various discussions upon it the Gladstone estates made rather a prominent figure. John Gladstone became involved in a heated and prolonged controversy as to the management of his plantations ; as we shall see, it did not finally die down till 1841. He was an indomitable man. In a newspaper discussion through a long series of letters, he did not defend slavery in the abstract, but protested against the abuse levelled at the planters by all 'the intemperate, credulous, designing or interested individuals who followed the lead of that well-meaning but mistaken man, Mr. Wilberforce.' He denounced the missionaries as hired emissaries, whose object

[1] The story of John Smith is excellently told in Walpole (iii. p. 178), and in Miss Martineau's *Hist. of the Peace* (Bk. II. ch. iv.). But Mr. Robbins has worked it out with diligence and precision in special reference to John Gladstone : *Early Life*, pp. 36-47.

[2] Trevelyan's *Macaulay*, i. p. 111, where the reader will also find a fine passage from Macaulay's speech before the Anti-Slavery Society upon the matter—the first speech he ever made.

seemed to be rather to revolutionise the colonies than to diffuse religion among the people.

In 1830 he published a pamphlet, in the form of a letter to Sir Robert Peel,[1] to explain that negroes were happier when forced to work ; that, as their labour was essential to the welfare of the colonies, he considered the difficulties in the way of emancipation insurmountable ; that it was not for him to seek to destroy a system that an over-ruling Providence had seen fit to permit in certain climates since the very formation of society ; and finally with a Parthian bolt, he hinted that the public would do better to look to the condition of the lower classes at home than to the negroes in the colonies. The pamphlet made its mark, and was admitted by the abolitionists to be an attempt of unusual ingenuity to varnish the most heinous of national crimes. Three years later, when emancipation came, and the twenty million pounds of compensation were distributed, John Gladstone appears to have received, individually and apart from his partnerships, a little over seventy-five thousand pounds for 1609 slaves.[2]

It is as well, though in anticipation of the order of time, to complete our sketch. In view of the approach of full abolition, John Gladstone induced Lord Glenelg, the whig secretary of state, to issue an order in council (1837) permitting the West Indian planters to ship coolies from India on terms drawn up by the planters themselves. Objections were made with no effect by the governor at Demerara, a humane and vigorous man, who had done much work as military engineer under Wellington, and who, after abolishing the flogging of female slaves in the Bahamas, now set such an iron yoke upon the planters and their agents in Demerara, that he said 'he could sleep satisfied that no person in the colony could be punished without his knowledge and sanction.'[3] The importation of coolies raised old questions in new forms. The voyage from India was declared to reproduce the horrors of the middle passage of the vanished Guinea slavers ; the condition of the coolie on the sugar plantations was drawn in a light only less lurid than the case of the African negro ; and John Gladstone was again in hot water. Thomas Gladstone, his eldest son, defended him in parliament (Aug. 3, 1839), and commissioners sent to inquire into the condition of the various Gladstone plantations reported that the coolies on Vreedestein appeared contented and happy on the whole ; no one had ever maltreated or beaten them except in one case ; and those on

[1] 'A statement of facts connected with the present state of slavery in the British sugar and coffee colonies, and in the United States of America, together with a view of the present situation of the lower classes in the United Kingdom.'
[2] In Demerara the average price of slaves from 1822 to 1830 had been £114 : 11 : 5¼. The rate of compensation per slave averaged £51 : 17 : 1½, but it is of interest to note that the slaves on the Vreedenhoop estate were valued at £53 : 15 : 6.
[3] *Dict. Nat. Biog.*, 'Sir James Carmichael Smyth.'

Vreedenhoop appeared perfectly contented. The interpreter, who had abused them, had been fined, punished, and dismissed. Upon the motion of W. E. Gladstone, these reports were laid upon the table of the House in 1840.[1]

We shall have not unimportant glimpses, as our story unfolds itself, of all these transactions. Meanwhile, it is interesting to note that the statesman whose great ensign was to be human freedom, was thus born in a family where the palliation of slavery must have made a daily topic. The union, moreover, of fervid evangelical religion with antagonism to abolition must in those days have been rare, and in spite of his devoted faith in his father the youthful Gladstone may well have had uneasy moments. If so, he perhaps consoled himself with the authority of Canning. Canning, in 1823, had formally laid down the neutral principles common to the statesmen of the day : that amelioration of the lot of the negro slave was the utmost limit of action, and that his freedom as a result of amelioration was the object of a pious hope, and no more. Canning described the negro as a being with the form of a man and the intellect of a child. 'To turn him loose in the manhood of his physical strength, in the maturity of his physical passions, but in the infancy of his uninstructed reason, would be to raise up a creature resembling the splendid fiction of a recent romance,[2] the hero of which constructs a human form with all the corporal capabilities of a man, but being unable to impart to the work of his hands a perception of right and wrong, he finds too late that he has only created a more than mortal power of doing mischief.' 'I was bred,' said Mr. Gladstone when risen to meridian splendour, 'under the shadow of the great name of Canning ; every influence connected with that name governed the politics of my childhood and of my youth ; with Canning, I rejoiced in the removal of religious disabilities, and in the character which he gave to our policy abroad ; with Canning, I rejoiced in the opening he made towards the establishment of free commercial interchanges between nations ; with Canning, and under the shadow of the yet more venerable name of Burke, my youthful mind and imagination were impressed,'[3] On slavery and even the slave trade, Burke too had argued against total abolition. 'I confess,' he said, 'I trust infinitely more (according to the sound principles of those who ever have at any time meliorated the state of mankind) to the effect and influence of religion than to all the rest of the regulations put together.'[4]

[1] He took Follett's opinion (Aug. 5, 1841) on the question of applying for a criminal information against the publisher of an article stating how many slaves had been worked to death on his father's plantations. The great advocate wisely recommended him to leave it alone.

[2] *Frankenstein* was published in 1818.

[3] House of Commons, April 27, 1866.

[4] *Letter to Dundas, with a Sketch of a Negro Code,* 1792. But see *Life of W. Wilberforce,* v. p. 157.

CHAPTER II

ETON

(1821-1827)

It is in her public schools and universities that the youth of England are, by a discipline which shallow judgments have sometimes attempted to undervalue, prepared for the duties of public life. There are rare and splendid exceptions, to be sure, but in my conscience I believe, that England would not be what she is without her system of public education, and that no other country can become what England is, without the advantages of such a system.—CANNING.

It is difficult to discern the true dimensions of objects in that mirage which covers the studies of one's youth.—GLADSTONE.

IN September 1821, the young Gladstone was sent to Eton. Life at Eton lasted over six years, until the Christmas of 1827. It impressed images that never faded, and left traces in heart and mind that the waves of time never effaced,—so profound is the early writing on our opening page. Canning's words at the head of our present chapter set forth a superstition that had a powerful hold on the English governing class of that day, and the new Etonian never shook it off. His attachment to Eton grew with the lapse of years ; to him it was ever 'the queen of all schools.'

'I went,' he says, 'under the wing of my eldest brother, then in the upper division, and this helped my start and much mitigated the sense of isolation that attends the first launch at a public school.' The door of his dame's house looked down the Long Walk, while the windows looked into the very crowded churchyard : from this he never received the smallest inconvenience, though it was his custom (when master of the room) to sleep with his window open both summer and winter. The school, said the new scholar, has only about four hundred and ninety fellows in it, which was considered uncommonly small. He likes his tutor so much that he would not exchange him for any ten. He has various rows with Mrs. Shurey, his dame, and it is really a great shame the way they are fed. He and his brother have far the best room in the dame's house. His captain is very good-natured. Fighting is a favourite diversion, hardly a day passing without one, two, three, or even four more or less mortal combats.

'You will be glad to hear,' he writes to his Highland aunt Johanna (November 13, 1821), 'of an instance of the highest and most honourable spirit in a highlander labouring under great disadvantages. His name is Macdonald (he once had a brother here remarkably clever, and a capital fighter). He is tough as iron, and about the strongest fellow in the school of his size. Being pushed out of his seat in school by a fellow of the name of Arthur, he airily asked him to give it him again, which being refused, with the additional insult that he might try what he could do to take it from him, Macdonald very properly took him at his word, and began to push him out of his seat. Arthur struck at him with all his might, and gave him so violent a blow that Macdonald was almost knocked backwards, but disdaining to take a blow from even a fellow much bigger than himself, he returned Arthur's blow with interest ; they began to fight ; after Macdonald had made him bleed at both his nose and his mouth, he finished the affair very triumphantly by knocking the arrogant Arthur backwards over the form without receiving a single blow of any consequence. He also labours under the additional disadvantage of being a new fellow, and of not knowing any one here. Arthur in a former battle put his finger out of joint, and as soon as it is recovered they are to have a regular battle in the playing fields.'

Other encounters are described with equal zest, especially one where 'the honour of Liverpool was bravely sustained,' superior weight and size having such an advantage over toughness and strength, that the foe of Liverpool was too badly bruised and knocked about to appear in school. On another occasion, 'to the great joy' of the narrator, an oppidan vanquished a colleger, though the colleger fought so furiously that he put his fingers out of joint, and went back to the classic studies that soften manners, with a face broken and quite black. The Windsor and Slough coaches used to stop under the wall of the playing fields to watch these desperate affrays, and once at least in these times a boy was killed. With plenty of fighting went on plenty of flogging ; for the headmaster was the redoubtable Dr. Keate, with whom the appointed instrument of moral regeneration in the childish soul was the birch rod ; who on heroic occasions was known to have flogged over eighty boys on a single summer day ; and whose one mellow regret in the evening of his life was that he had not flogged far more. Religious instruction, as we may suppose, was under these circumstances reduced to zero ; there was no trace of the influence of the evangelical party, at that moment the most active of all the religious sections ; and the ancient and pious munificence of Henry VI. now inspired a scene that was essentially little better than pagan, modified by an official Church of England varnish. At Eton, Mr. Gladstone wrote of this period forty years after, 'the actual teaching of

Christianity was all but dead, though happily none of its forms
had been surrendered.'[1]

Science even in its rudiments fared as ill as its eternal rival,
theology. There was a mathematical master, but nobody
learned anything from him, or took any notice of him. In his
anxiety for position the unfortunate man asked Keate if he
might wear a cap and gown. 'That's as you please,' said
Keate. 'Must the boys touch their hats to me ?' 'That's as
they please,' replied the genial doctor.[2] Gladstone first picked
up a little mathematics not at Eton, but during the holidays,
going to Liverpool for the purpose, first in 1824 and more
seriously in 1827. He seems to have paid much attention to
French, and even then to have attained considerable proficiency.
'When I was at Eton,' Mr. Gladstone said, ' we knew very little
indeed, but we knew it accurately.' 'There were many shades
of distinction,' he observed, 'among the fellows who received
what was supposed to be, and was in many respects, their
education. Some of those shades of distinction were extremely
questionable, and the comparative measures of honour allotted
to talent, industry, and idleness were undoubtedly such as
philosophy would not justify. But no boy was ever estimated
either more or less because he had much money to spend. It
added nothing to him if he had much, it took nothing from him
if he had little.' A sharp fellow who worked, and a stupid
fellow who was idle, were both of them in good odour enough,
but a stupid boy who presumed to work was held to be an
insufferable solecism.[3]

My tutor was the Rev. H. H. Knapp (practically all tutors were
clergymen in those days). He was a reputed whig, an easy and kind-
tempered man with a sense of scholarship, but no power of discipline,
and no energy of desire to impress himself upon his pupils. I recollect
but one piece of advice received later from him. It was that I should
form my poetical taste upon Darwin, whose poems (the 'Botanic
Garden' and 'Loves of the Plants') I obediently read through in
consequence. I was placed in the middle remove fourth form, a place
slightly better than the common run, but inferior to what a boy of good
preparation or real excellence would have taken. My nearest friend of
the first period was W. W. Farr, a boy of intelligence, something over
my age, next above me in the school.

At this time there was not in me any desire to know or to excel. My
first pursuits were football and then cricket ; the first I did not long
pursue, and in the second I never managed to rise above mediocrity and
what was termed 'the twenty-two.' There was a barrister named
Henry Hall Joy, a connection of my father through his first wife, and a
man who had taken a first-class at Oxford. He was very kind to me,
and had made some efforts to inspire me with a love of books, if not of
knowledge. Indeed I had read Froissart, and Hume with Smollett, but

only for the battles, and always skipping when I came to the sections headed 'A Parliament.' Joy had a taste for classics, and made visions for me of honours at Oxford. But the subject only danced before my eyes as a will-of-the-wisp, and without attracting me. I remained stagnant without heart or hope. A change however arrived about Easter 1822. My 'remove' was then under Hawtrey (afterwards headmaster and provost), who was always on the look-out for any bud which he could warm with a little sunshine.

He always described Hawtrey as the life of the school, the man to whom Eton owed more than to any of her sons during the century. Though not his pupil, it was from him that Gladstone, when in the fourth form, received for the first time incentives to exertion. 'It was entirely due to Hawtrey,' he records in a fragment, 'that I first owed the reception of a spark, the *divinae particulam aurae*, and conceived a dim idea, that in some time, manner, and degree, I might come to know. Even then, as I had really no instructor, my efforts at Eton, down to 1827, were perhaps of the purest plodding ever known.'

Evidently he was not a boy of special mark during the first three years at Eton. In the evening he played chess and cards, and usually lost. He claimed in after life that he had once taken a drive in a hired tandem, but Etonians who knew him as a schoolboy decided that an aspiring memory here made him boast of crimes that were not his. He was assiduous in the Eton practice of working a small boat, whether skiff, funny, or wherry, single-handed. In the masquerade of Montem he figured complacently in all the glories of the costume of a Greek patriot, for he was a faithful Canningite ; the heroic struggle against the Turk was at its fiercest, and it was the year when Byron died at Missolonghi. Of Montem as an institution he thought extremely ill, 'the whole thing a wretched waste of time and money, a most ingenious contrivance to exhibit us as baboons, a bore in the full sense of the word.' He did not stand aside from the harmless gaieties of boyish life, but he rigidly refused any part in boyish indecorums. He was in short, just the diligent, cheerful, healthy-minded schoolboy that any good father would have his son to be. He enjoys himself with his brother at the Christopher, and is glad to record that 'Keate did not make any jaw about being so late.' Half a dozen of them met every whole holiday or half, and went up Salt Hill to bully the fat waiter, eat toasted cheese, and drink egg-wine.

He started, as we have already seen, in middle fourth form. In the spring of 1822 Hawtrey said to him : 'Continue to do as well as this, and I will send you up for good again before the 4th of June.' Before the end of June, he tells his sailor brother of his success : 'It far exceeds the most sanguine expectations I ever entertained. I have got into the remove between the fourth and fifth forms. I have been sent up for good a second time, and have taken seven places.' In the summer of 1823 he announces that he has got into the fifth form after taking sixteen places, and here instead of fagging he acquires the blessed power himself to fag. In passing he launches, for the first recorded time, against the master of the remove from which he has just been promoted, an invective that in volume and intensity anticipates the wrath of later attacks on Neapolitan kings and Turkish sultans.

His letters written from Eton breathe in every line the warm breath of family affection, and of all those natural pieties that had so firm a root in him from the beginning to the end. Of the later store of genius and force that the touch of time was so soon to kindle into full glow, they gave but little indication. We smile at the precocious *copia fandi* that at thirteen describes the language of an admonishing acquaintance as 'so friendly, manly, sound, and disinterested that notwithstanding his faults I must always think well of him.' He sends contributions to his brother's scrap-book, and one of the first of them, oddly enough, in view of one of the great preoccupations of his later life, is a copy of Lord Edward Fitzgerald's stanzas on the night of his arrest :

> O Ireland, my country, the hour
>   Of thy pride and thy splendour has passed,
> And the chain which was spurned in thy moment of power,
>   Hangs heavy around thee at last.

The temper and dialect of evangelical religion are always there. A friend of the family dies, and the boy pours out his regret, but after all what is the merely natural death of Dr. N. compared with the awful state of a certain clergyman, also an intimate friend, who has not only been guilty of attending a fancy ball, but has followed that vicious prelude by even worse enormities unnamed, that surely cannot escape the vigilance and the reproof of his bishop ?

His father is the steady centre of his life. 'My father,' he writes to his brother, 'is as active in mind and projects as ever ; he has two principal plans now in embryo. One of these is a railroad between Liverpool and Manchester for the conveyance of goods by locomotive steam-engine. The other is for building a bridge over the Mersey at Runcorn.' In May 1827, the Gloucester and Berkeley canal is opened : 'a great and enterprising undertaking, but still there is no fear of it beating Liverpool.' Meanwhile, 'what prodigiously quick travelling to leave Eton at twelve on Monday, and reach home at eight on Tuesday !' 'I have,' he says in 1826, 'lately been writing several letters in the *Liverpool Courier*.' His father had been attacked in the local prints for sundry economic inconsistencies, and the controversial pen that was to know no rest for more than seventy years to come, was now first employed, like the pious Æneas bearing off Anchises, in the filial duty of repelling

his sire's assailants. Ignorant of his nameless champion, John
Gladstone was much amused and interested by the anonymous
'Friend to Fair Dealing,' while the son was equally diverted by
the criticisms and conjectures of the parent.

With the formidable Keate the boy seems to have fared
remarkably well, and there are stories that he was even one of
the tyrant's favourites.[1] His school work was diligently supplemented. His daily reading in 1826 covers a good deal of
miscellaneous ground, including Molière and Racine, Blair's
Sermons ('not very substantial'), *Tom Jones*, Tomline's *Life of
Pitt*, Waterland's *Commentaries*, Leslie *on Deism*, Locke's *Defence
of The Reasonableness of Christianity*, which he finds excellent ;
Paradise Lost, Milton's *Latin Poems* and *Epitaphium Damonis*
('exquisite'), Massinger's *Fatal Dowry* ('most excellent'), Ben
Jonson's *Alchemist* ; Scott, including the *Bride of Lammermoor*
('a beautiful tale, indeed,' and in after life his favourite of them
all), Burke, Clarendon, and others of the shining host whose
very names are music to a scholar's ear. In the same year he
reads 'a most violent article on Milton by Macaulay, fair and
unfair, clever and silly, allegorical and bombastic, republican
and anti-episcopal—a strange composition, indeed.' In 1827 he
went steadily through the second half of Gibbon, whom he
pronounces, 'elegant and acute as he is, not so clear, so able, so
attractive as Hume ; does not impress my mind so much.' In
the same year he reads Coxe's *Walpole*, *Don Quixote*, Hallam's
Constitutional History, *Measure for Measure* and *Much Ado*,
Massinger's *Grand Duke of Florence*, Ford's *Love's Melancholy*
('much of it good, the end remarkably beautiful') and *Broken
Heart* (which he liked better than either the other or *'Tis Pity*),
Locke *on Toleration* ('much repetition').

There is, of course, a steady refrain of Greek iambics, Greek
anapaests 'an easy and nice metre,' 'a hodge-podge lot of
hendecasyllables,' and thirty alcaic stanzas for a holiday task.
Mention is made of many sermons on 'Redeeming the time,'

---

[1] Doyle tells a story of the boy being flogged for bringing wine into his study.
When questioned on this, Mr. Gladstone said, 'I *was* flogged, but not for anything
connected in any way with wine, of which, by the by, my father supplied me with a
small amount, and insisted upon my drinking it, or some of it, all the time that I was at
Eton. The reason why I was flogged was this. I was præpostor of the remove on a
certain day, and from kindness or good nature was induced to omit from the list of
boys against whom H. [the master] had complained, and who ought to have been
flogged next day, the names of three offenders. The three boys in question got round
me with a story that their friends were coming down from London to see them, and
that if they were put down on the flogging list they could not meet their friends.
Next day when I went into school H. roared out in a voice of thunder, "Gladstone,
put down your own name on the list of boys to be flogged."' Mr. Gladstone on this
occasion told another tale of this worthy's 'humour.' 'One day H. called out to the
præpostor, "Write down Hamilton's name to be flogged for breaking my window."
"I never broke your window, sir," exclaimed Hamilton. "Præpostor," retorted H.,
"write down Hamilton's name for breaking my window and lying." "Upon my soul,
sir, I did not do it," ejaculated the boy, with increased emphasis. "Præpostor, write
down Hamilton's name for breaking my window, lying, and swearing." Against this
final sentence there was no appeal, and, accordingly, Hamilton was flogged (I believe
unjustly) next day.'—F. Lawley in *Daily Telegraph*, May 20, 1898.

'Weighed in the balance and found wanting,' 'Cease to do evil, learn to do well,' and the other ever unexhausted texts. One constant entry, we may be sure, is 'Read Bible,' with Mant's notes. In a mood of deep piety he is prepared for confirmation. His appearance at this time was recalled by one who had been his fag, 'as a good-looking, rather delicate youth, with a pale face, and brown curling hair, always tidy and well dressed.'[1]

He became captain of the fifth at the end of October 1826, and on February 20, 1827, Keate put him into the sixth. 'Was very civil, indeed; told me to take pains, etc.; to be careful in using my authority, etc.' He finds the sixth very preferable to all other parts of the school, both as regards pleasure and opportunity for improvement. They are more directly under the eye of Keate; he treats them with more civility and speaks to them differently. So the days follow one another very much alike—studious, cheerful, sociable, sedulous. The debates in parliament take up a good deal of his time, and he is over-whelmed by the horrible news of the defeat of the catholics in the House of Commons (March 8, 1827). On a summer's day in 1826 'Mr. Canning here; inquired after me and missed me.' He was not at Eton but at home when he heard of Mr. Canning's death. 'Personally I must remember his kindness and con-descension, especially when he spoke to me of some verses which H. Joy had injudiciously mentioned to him.'

II

Youthful intellect is imitative, and in a great school so im-pregnated as Eton with the spirit of public life and political association, the few boys with active minds mimicked the strife of parliament in their debating society, and copied the arts of journalism in the *Eton Miscellany*. In both fields the young Gladstone took a leading part. The debating society was afflicted with 'the premonitory lethargy of death,' but the assiduous energy of Gaskell, seconded by the gifts of Gladstone, Hallam, and Doyle, soon sent a new pulse beating through it. The politics of the hour, that is to say everything not fifty years off, were forbidden ground; but the execution of Strafford or of his royal master, the deposition of Richard II., the last four years of the reign of Queen Anne, the Peerage bill of 1719, the characters of Harley and Bolingbroke, were themes that could be made by ingenious youth to admit a hundred cunning side-lights upon the catholic question, the struggle of the Greeks for independence, the hard case of Queen Caroline, and the unlaw-fulness of swamping the tories in the House of Lords. On duller afternoons they argued on the relative claims of mathe-matics and metaphysics to be the better discipline of the human mind; whether duelling is or is not inconsistent with the

character that we ought to seek ; or whether the education of
the poor is on the whole beneficial. It was on this last question
(October 29, 1825) that the orator who made his last speech
seventy years later, now made his first. 'Made my first or
maiden speech at the society,' he enters in his diary, 'on education of the poor ; funked less than I thought I should, by much.'
It is a curious but a characteristic circumstance not that so
many of his Eton speeches were written out, but that the manuscript should have been thriftily preserved by him all through
the long space of intervening years. 'Mr. President,' it begins,
'in this land of liberty, in this age of increased and gradually
increasing civilization, we shall hope to find few, if indeed any,
among the higher classes who are eager or willing to obstruct
the moral instruction and mental improvement of their fellow
creatures in the humbler walks of life. If such there are, let
them at length remember that the poor are endowed with the same
reason, though not blessed with the same temporal advantages.
Let them but admit, what I think no one can deny, that they
are placed in an elevated situation principally for the purpose
of doing good to their fellow creatures. Then by what argument can they repel, by what pretence can they evade the
duty ?' And so forth and so forth. Already we seem to hear
the born speaker in the amplitude of rhetorical form in which,
juvenile though it may be, a commonplace is cast. 'Is human
grandeur so stable that they may deny to others that which
they would in an humble situation desire themselves ? Or has
human pride reached such a pitch of arrogance that they have
learned to defy both right and reason, to reject the laws of
natural kindness that ought to reign in the breast of all, and
to look on their fellow countrymen as the refuse of mankind ?
. . . Is it morally just or politically expedient to keep down
the industry and genius of the artisan, to blast his rising hopes,
to quell his spirit ? A thirst for knowledge has arisen in the
minds of the poor ; let them satisfy it with wholesome nutriment and beware lest driven to despair,' et cetera. Crude
enough, if we please ; but the year was 1826, and we may feel
that the boyish speaker is already on the generous side and
has the gift of fruitful sympathies.

In the spacious tournaments of old history, we may smile
to hear debating forms and ceremony applied to everlasting
controversies. 'Sir,' he opens on one occasion, 'I declare that
as far as regards myself, I shall have very little difficulty in
stating my grounds on which I give my vote for James Graham
[the Marquis of Montrose]. It is because I look upon him as a
hero, not merely endowed with that animal ferocity which has
often been the sole qualification which has obtained men that
appellation from the multitude—I should be sorry indeed if he
had no testimonials of his merits, save such as arise from the
mad and thoughtless exclamations of popular applause.' In

the same gallant style (Jan. 26, 1826) he votes for Marcus
Aurelius, in answer to the question whether Trajan has any
equal among the Roman emperors from Augustus onwards.
Another time the question was between John Hampden and
Clarendon. 'Sir, I look back with pleasure to the time when
we unanimously declared our disapprobation of the impeachment of the Earl of Strafford. I wish I could hope for the same
unanimity now, but I will endeavour to regulate myself by the
same principles as directed me then. . . . Now, sir, with regard
to the impeachment of the five members, it is really a little
extraordinary to hear the honourable opener talking of the
violence offered by the king, and the terror of the parliament.
Sir, do we not all know that the king at that time had neither
friends nor wealth ? . . . Did the return of these members with
a triumphant mob accompanying them indicate terror ? Did
the demands of the parliament or the insolence of their
language show it ?' So he proceeds through all the well-worn
arguments ; and 'therefore it is,' he concludes, 'that I give my
vote to the Earl of Clarendon, because he gave his support to
the falling cause of monarchy ; because he stood by his church
and his king ; because he adopted the part which loyalty, reason,
and moderation combined to dictate. . . . Poverty, banishment,
and disgrace he endured without a murmur ; he still adhered
to the cause of justice, he still denounced the advocates of
rebellion, and if he failed in his reward in life, oh, sir, let us
not deny it to him after death. In him, sir, I admire the sound
philosopher, the rigid moralist, the upright statesman, the
candid historian. . . . In Hampden I see the splendour of
patriotic bravery obscured by the darkness of rebellion, and
the faculties by which he might have been a real hero and
real martyr, prostituted in the cause,' and so on, with all the
promise of the *os magna sonaturum*, of which time was to prove
the resources so inexhaustible. On one great man he passed a
final judgment that years did not change :—'Debate on Sir R.
Walpole : Hallam, Gaskell, Pickering and Doyle spoke. Voted
for him. Last time, when I was almost entirely ignorant of
the subject, against him. There were sundry considerable
blots, but nothing to overbalance or to spoil the great merit of
being the bulwark of the protestant succession, his commercial
measures, and in general his pacific policy.'[1]

As for the *Eton Miscellany*, which was meant to follow
earlier attempts in the same line, the best-natured critic
cannot honestly count it dazzling. Such things rarely are ;
for youth, though the most adorable of our human stages,
cannot yet have knowledge or practice enough, whether in life
or books, to make either good prose or stirring verse, unless by
a miracle of genius, and even that inspiration is but occasional.
The *Microcosm* (1786-87) and the *Etonian* (1818), with such

[1] Feb. 10, 1827.

hands as Canning and Frere, Moultrie and Praed, were well enough. The newcomer was a long way behind these in the freshness, brilliance, daring, by which only such juvenile performances can either please or interest. George Selwyn and Gladstone were joint editors, and each provided pretty copious effusions. 'I cannot keep my temper,' he wrote afterwards in his diary in 1835, on turning over the *Miscellany*, 'in perusing my own (with few exceptions) execrable productions.' Certainly his contributions have no particular promise or savour, no hint of the strong pinions into which the half-fledged wings were in time to expand. Their motion, such as it is, must be pronounced mechanical ; their phrase and cadence conventional. Even when sincere feelings were deeply stirred, the flight cannot be called high. The most moving public event in his school-days was undoubtedly the death of Canning, and to Gladstone the stroke was almost personal. In September 1827 he tells his mother that he has for the first time visited Westminster Abbey,—his object, an eager pilgrimage to the newly tenanted grave of his hero, and in the *Miscellany* he pays a double tribute. In the prose we hear sonorous things about meridian splendour, premature extinction, and inscrutable wisdom ; about falling, like his great master Pitt, a victim to his proud and exalted station ; about being firm in principle and conciliatory in action, the friend of improvement and the enemy of innovation. Nor are the versified reflections in Westminster Abbey much more striking :—

> Oft in the sculptured aisle and swelling dome,
> The yawning grave hath given the proud a home ;
> Yet never welcomed from his bright career
> A mightier victim than it welcomed here :
> Again the tomb may yawn—again may death
> Claim the last forfeit of departing breath ;
> Yet ne'er enshrine in slumber dark and deep
> A nobler, loftier prey than where thine ashes sleep.

Excellent in feeling, to be sure ; but as a trial of poetic delicacy or power, wanting the true note, and only worth recalling for an instant as we go.

III

As nearly always happens, it was less by schoolwork or spoken addresses in juvenile debate, or early attempts in the great and difficult art of written composition, than by blithe and congenial comradeship that the mind of the young Gladstone was stimulated, opened, strengthened. In after days he commemorated among his friends George Selwyn, afterwards bishop of New Zealand and of Lichfield, 'a man whose character is summed up, from alpha to omega, in the single word, noble, and whose high office, in a large measure, it was to reintroduce among the anglican clergy the pure heroic type.'

Another was Francis Doyle, 'whose genial character supplied
a most pleasant introduction for his unquestionable poetic
genius.' A third was James Milnes Gaskell, a youth endowed
with precocious ripeness of political faculty, an enthusiast, and
with a vivacious humour that enthusiasts often miss. Doyle
said of him that his nurse must have lulled him to sleep by
parliamentary reports, and his first cries on awaking in his
cradle must have been 'hear, hear!' Proximity of rooms 'gave
occasion or aid to the formation of another very valuable
friendship, that with Gerald Wellesley, afterwards dean of
Windsor, which lasted, to my great profit, for some sixty years,
until that light was put out.' In Gaskell's room four or five of
them would meet, and discuss without restraint the questions
of politics that were too modern to be tolerated in public
debate. Most of them were friendly to catholic emancipation,
and to the steps by which Huskisson, supported by Canning,
was cautiously treading in the path towards free trade. The
brightest star in this cheerful constellation was the rare youth
who, though his shining course was run in two-and-twenty
years, yet in that scanty span was able to impress with his
vigorous understanding and graceful imagination more than
one of the loftiest minds of his time.[1] Arthur Hallam was a
couple of years younger than Gladstone, no narrow gulf at
that age; but such was the sympathy of genius, such the
affinities of intellectual interest and aspiration spoken and
unspoken, such the charm and the power of the younger with
the elder, that rapid instinct made them close comrades.
They clubbed together their rolls and butter, and breakfasted
in one another's rooms. Hallam was not strong enough for
boating, so the more sinewy Gladstone used to scull him up to
the Shallows, and he regarded this toilsome carrying of an idle
passenger up stream as proof positive of no common value set
upon his passenger's company. They took walks together,
often to the monument of Gray, close by the churchyard of the
elegy; arguing about the articles and the creeds; about
Wordsworth, Byron, Shelley; about free will, for Hallam was
precociously full of Jonathan Edwards; about politics, old and
new, living and dead; about Pitt and Fox, and Canning and
Peel, for Gladstone was a tory and Hallam pure whig. Hallam
was described by Mr. Gladstone in his old age as one who
'enjoyed work, enjoyed society; and games which he did not
enjoy he left contentedly aside. His temper was as sweet as
his manners were winning. His conduct was without a spot
or even a speck. He was that rare and blessed creature,
anima naturaliter Christiana. He read largely, and though
not superficial, yet with an extraordinary speed. He had no
high or exclusive ways.' Thus, as so many have known in that

---

[1] Mr. Gladstone fixed on two of the elegies of *In Memoriam* as most directly conveying the image of Arthur Hallam, cviii. and cxxviii.

happy dawn of life, before any of the imps of disorder and
confusion have found their way•into the garden, it was the
most careless hours,—careless of all save truth and beauty,—
that were the hours best filled.

Youth will commonly do anything rather than write letters,
but the friendship of this pair stood even that test. The pages
are redolent of a living taste for good books and serious
thoughts, and amply redeemed from strain or affectation by
touches of gay irony and the collegian's banter. Hallam
applies to Gladstone Diomede's lines about Odysseus, of eager
heart and spirit so manful in all manner of toils, as the only
comrade whom a man would choose.[1] But the Greek hero was
no doubt a complex character, and the parallel is taken by
Gladstone as an equivocal compliment. So Hallam begs him
at any rate to accept the other description, how when he
uttered his mighty voice from his chest, and words fell like
flakes of snow in winter, then could no mortal man contend
with Odysseus.[2] As happy a forecast for the great orator of
their generation, as when in 1829 he told Gladstone that Tennyson promised fair to be its greatest poet. Hallam's share in
the correspondence reminds us of the friendship of two other
Etonians ninety years before, of the letters and verses that
Gray wrote to Richard West; there is the same literary sensibility, the same kindness, but there is what Gray and West
felt not, the breath of a busy and changing age. Each of these
two had the advantage of coming from a home where politics
were not mere gossip about persons and paragraphs, but were
matters of trained and continued interest. The son of one of
the most eminent of the brilliant band of the whig writers of
that day, Hallam passes glowing eulogies on the patriotism
and wisdom of the whigs in coalescing with Canning against
the bigotry of the king and the blunders of Wellington and
Peel; he contrasts this famous crisis with a similar crisis in
the early part of the reign of George III.; and observes how
much higher all parties stood in the balance of disinterestedness and public virtue. He goes to the opera and finds
Zucchelli admirable, Coradori divine. He wonders (1826) about
Sir Walter's forthcoming life of Napoleon, how with his ultra
principles Scott will manage to make a hero of the Corsican.
He asks if Gladstone has read 'the new *Vivian Grey*' (1827)—
the second part of that amazing fiction with which an author,
not much older than themselves and destined to strange historic
relations with one of them, had the year before burst upon the
world. Hallam is not without the graceful melancholy of
youth, so different from that other melancholy of ripe years
and the deepening twilight. Under all is the recurrent note of
a grave refrain that fatal issues made pathetic.

'Never since the time when I first knew you,' Hallam wrote

[1] *Iliad*, x. 242.   [2] *Ibid*. iii. 221.

to Gladstone (June 23, 1830), 'have I ceased to love and respect
your character. . . . It will be my proudest thought that I
may henceforth act worthily of their affection who, like yourself, have influenced my mind for good in the earliest season of
its development. Circumstance, my dear Gladstone, has indeed
separated our paths, but it can never do away with what has
been. The stamp of each of our minds is on the other. Many
a habit of thought in each is modified, many a feeling is associated, which never would have existed in that combination, had
it not been for the old familiar days when we lived together.'

In the summer of 1827 Hallam quitted Eton for the journey
to Italy that set so important a mark on his literary growth,
and he bade his friend farewell in words of characteristic
affection. 'Perhaps you will pardon my doing by writing what
I hardly dare trust myself to do by words. I received your
superb Burke yesterday; and hope to find it a memorial of
past and a pledge for future friendship through both our lives.
It is perhaps rather bold in me to ask a favour immediately on
acknowledging so great a one; but you would please me, and
oblige me greatly, if you will accept this copy of my father's
book. It may serve when I am separated from you, to remind
you of one, whose warmest pleasure it will always be to subscribe himself, Your most faithful friend, A. H. H.'

A few entries from the schoolboy's diary may serve to bring
the daily scene before us, and show what his life was like :—

October 3, 1826.—Holiday. Walk with Hallam. Wrote over theme.
Read Clarendon. Wrote speech for Saturday week. Poor enough.
Did punishment set by Keate to all the fifth form for being late in
church.

October 6.—Fin. second Olympiad of Pindar . . . Clarendon. Did
an abstract of about 100 pages. Wrote speech for to-morrow in favour
of Caesar.

November 13. — Play. Breakfast with Hallam. Read a little
Clarendon. Read over tenth Satire of Juvenal and read the fifth, making quotations to it and some other places. Did a few verses.

November 14.—Holiday. Wrote over theme. Did verses. Walked
with Hallam and Doyle. Read papers and debates. . . . Read 200 lines
of *Trachiniae*. A little *Gil Blas* in French, and a little Clarendon.

November 18.—Play. Read papers, etc. Finished Blair's *Disserta-
tion on Ossian*. Finished *Trachiniae*. Did 3 props. of Euclid.
Question : Was deposition of Richard II. justifiable ? Voted no.
Good debate. Finished the delightful oration *Pro Milone*.

November 21.—Holiday. . . . Part of article in *Edinburgh Review* on
Icon Basilike. Read Herodotus, Clarendon. Did 3 props. Scrambling
and leaping expedition with Hallam, Doyle and Gaskell.

November 30. — Holiday. Read Herodotus. Breakfasted with
Gaskell. He and Hallam drank wine with me after 4. Walked with
Hallam. Did verses. Finished first book of Euclid. Read a little
Charles XII.

February 27, 1827.—Holiday. Dressed (knee-breeches, etc.) and
went into school with Selwyn. Found myself not at all in a funk, and

went through my performance with tolerable comfort. Durnford followed me, then Selwyn, who spoke well. Horrors of speaking chiefly in the name.

March 20.—My father has lost his seat, and Berwick a representative ten times too good for it. Wrote to my father, no longer M.P. ; when we have forgotten the manner, the matter is not so bad.

March 24. —Half-holiday. Play and learning it. Walked with Hallam, read papers. Hallam drank wine with me after dinner. Finished 8th vol. of Gibbon ; read account of Palmyra in second volume ; did more verses on it. Much jaw about nothing at Society, and absurd violence.

May 31.—Finished iambics. Wrote over for tutor. Played cricket in the Upper Club, and had tea in poet's walk [an entry repeated this summer].

June 26.—Wrote over theme. Read *Iphigenie*. Called up in Homer. Sculled Hallam to Surly after 6. Went to see a cricket match after 4.

Gladstone's farewell to Eton came with Christmas (1827). He writes to his sister his last Etonian letter (December 2) before departure, and 'melancholy that departure is.' On the day before, he had made his valedictory speech to the Society, and the empty shelves and dismantled walls, the table strewn with papers, the books packed away in their boxes, have the effect of 'mingling in one lengthened mass all the boyish hopes and solicitudes and pleasures' of his Eton life. 'I have long ago made up my mind that I have of late been enjoying what will in all probability be, as far as my own individual case is concerned, the happiest years of my life. And they have fled ! From these few facts do we not draw a train of reflections awfully important in their nature and extremely powerful in their impression on the mind ?'

Two reminiscences of Eton always gave him, and those who listened to him, much diversion whenever chance brought them to his mind, and he has set them down in an autobiographic fragment, for which this is the place :—

To Dr. Keate nature had accorded a stature of only about five feet, or say five feet one ; but by costume, voice, manner (including a little swagger), and character he made himself in every way the capital figure on the Eton stage, and his departure marked, I imagine, the departure of the old race of English public-school masters, as the name of Dr. Busby seems to mark its introduction. In connection with his name I shall give two anecdotes separated by a considerable interval of years. About 1820 [1823], the eloquence of Dr. Edward Irving drew crowds to his church in London, which was presbyterian. It required careful previous arrangements to secure comfortable accommodation. The preacher was solemn, majestic (notwithstanding the squint), and impressive ; carrying all the appearance of devoted earnestness. My father had on a certain occasion, when I was still a small Eton boy, taken time by the forelock, and secured the use of a convenient pew in the first rank of the gallery. From this elevated situation we surveyed at ease and leisure the struggling crowds below. The crush was everywhere great, but greatest of all in the centre aisle. Here the mass of human beings, mercilessly compressed, swayed continually backwards and forwards. There was I, looking down with infinite complacency and satisfaction from this honourable vantage ground upon the floor of the church, filled and packed as one of our public meetings is, with people standing and pushing. What was my emotion, my joy, my exultation, when I espied among this humiliated mass, struggling and buffeted—whom but Keate! Keate the master of our existence, the tyrant of our days! Pure, unalloyed, unadulterated rapture! Such a περιπέτεια, such a reversal of human conditions of being, as that now exhibited between the Eton lower boy uplifted to the luxurious gallery pew, and the head-master of Eton, whom I was accustomed to see in the roomy deck of the upper school with vacant space and terror all around him, it must be hard for any one to conceive, except the two who were the subjects of it. Never, never, have I forgotten that moment.[1]

I will now, after the manner of novelists, ask my reader to effect along with me a transition of some eighteen years, and to witness another, and if not a more complete yet a worthier, turning of the tables. In the year 1841 there was a very special Eton dinner held in Willis's Rooms to commemorate the fourth centenary of the ancient school. Lord Morpeth, afterwards Lord Carlisle, was in the chair. On his right, not far off him, was Dr. Keate, to whom I chanced to have a seat almost immediately opposite. In those days at public dinners, cheering was marked by gradations. As the Queen was suspected of sympathy with the liberal government of Lord Melbourne which advised her, the toast of the sovereign was naturally received with a moderate amount of acclamation, decently and thriftily doled out. On the other hand the Queen Dowager either was, or was believed to be, conservative; and her health consequently figured as the toast of the evening, and drew forth, as a matter of course, by far its loudest acclamation. So much was routine; and we went through it as usual. But the real toast of the evening was yet to come. I suppose it to be beyond doubt that of the assembled company the vastly preponderating majority had been under his sway at Eton; and if, when in that condition, any one of them had been asked how he liked Dr. Keate, he would beyond question have answered, 'Keate? Oh, I hate him.' It is equally beyond doubt that to the persons of the whole of them, with the rarest exceptions, it had been the case of Dr. Keate to administer the salutary correction of the birch. But upon this occasion, when his name had been announced the scene was indescribable. Queen and Queen Dowager alike vanished into insignificance. The roar of cheering had a beginning, but never knew satiety or end. Like the huge waves at Biarritz, the floods of cheering continually recommenced; the whole process was such that we seemed all to have lost our self-possession and to be hardly able to keep our seats. When at length it became possible Keate rose: that is to say, his head was projected slightly over the heads of his two neighbours. He struggled to speak; I will not say I heard every syllable, for there were no syllables; speak he could not. He tried in vain to mumble a word or two, but wholly failed, recommenced the vain struggle and sat down. It was certainly one of the most moving spectacles that in my whole life I have witnessed.

1 I have heard him tell this story, and Garrick himself could not have reproduced a schoolboy's glee with more admirable accent and gesture.

IV

Some months passed between leaving Eton and going to Oxford. In January 1828, Gladstone went to reside with Dr. Turner at Wilmslow in Cheshire, and remained there until Turner was made Bishop of Calcutta. The bishop's pupil afterwards testified to his amiability, refinement, and devoutness ; but the days of his energy were past, and 'the religious condition of the parish was depressing.' Among the neighbouring families, with whom he made acquaintance while at Wilmslow, were the Gregs of Quarry Bank, a refined and philanthropic household, including among the sons William R. Greg (born in the same year as Mr. Gladstone), that ingenious, urbane, interesting, and independent mind, whose speculations, dissolvent and other, were afterwards to take an effective place in the writings of the time. 'I fear he is a unitarian,' the young churchman mentions to his father, and gives sundry reasons for that sombre apprehension ; it was, indeed, only too well founded.

While at Wilmslow (Feb. 5, 1828) Gladstone was taken to dine with the rector of Alderley—'an extremely gentlemanly and said to be a very clever man,'—afterwards to be known as the liberal and enlightened Edward Stanley, Bishop of Norwich, and father of Arthur Stanley, the famous dean. Him, on this occasion, the young Gladstone seems to have seen for the first time. Arthur Stanley was six years his junior, and there was then some idea of sending him to Eton. As it happened, he too was a pupil at Rawson's at Seaforth, and in the summer after the meeting at Alderley the two lads met again. The younger of them has described how he was invited to breakfast with William Gladstone at Seaforth House ; in what grand style they breakfasted, how he devoured strawberries, swam the Newfoundland dog in the pond, looked at books and pictures, and talked to W. Gladstone 'almost all the time about all sorts of things. He is so very good-natured, and I like him very much. He talked a great deal about Eton, and said that it was a very good place for those who liked boating and Latin verses. He was very good-natured to us all the time, and lent me books to read when we went away.'[1] A few months later, as all the world knows, Stanley, happily for himself and for all of us, went not to Eton but to Rugby, where Arnold had just entered on his bold and noble task of changing the face of education in England.

[1] Prothero's *Life of Dean Stanley*, i. p. 22.

CHAPTER III

OXFORD

(*October 1828–December 1831*)

Steeped in sentiment as she lies, spreading her gardens to the moonlight, and whispering from her towers the last enchantments of the Middle Age, who will deny that Oxford, by her ineffable charm, keeps ever calling us nearer to the true goal of all of us, to the ideal, to perfection—to beauty, in a word, which is only truth seen from another side?—M. ARNOLD.

GLORIOUS to most are the days of life in a great school, but it is at college that aspiring talent first enters on its inheritance. Oxford was slowly awakening from a long age of lethargy. Toryism of a stolid clownish type still held the thrones of collegiate power. Yet the eye of an imaginative scholar as he gazed upon the grey walls, reared by piety, munificence, and love of learning in a far-off time, might well discern behind an unattractive screen of academic sloth, the venerable past, not dim and cold, but in its traditions rich, nourishing and alive. Such an one could see before him present days of honourable emulation and stirring acquisition—fit prelude of a man's part to play in a strenuous future. It is from Gladstone's introduction into this enchanted and inspiring world, that we recognise the beginning of the wonderful course that was to show how great a thing the life of a man may be made.

The Eton boy became the Christ Church man, and there began residence, October 10, 1828. Mr. Gladstone's rooms, during most of his undergraduate life, were on the right hand, and on the first floor of the staircase on the right, as one enters by the Canterbury gate. He tells his mother that they are in a very fashionable part of the college, and mentions as a delightful fact, that Gaskell and Seymer have rooms on the same floor. Samuel Smith was head until 1831, when he was succeeded by the more celebrated Dr. Gaisford, always described by Mr. Gladstone as a splendid scholar, but a bad dean. Gaisford's excellent services to the Greek learning of his day are unquestioned, and he had the signal merit of speech, Spartan brevity. For a short time in 1806 he had been tutor to Peel.

36

When Lord Liverpool offered him the Greek professorship, with profuse compliments on his erudition, the learned man replied, 'My Lord,—I have received your letter, and accede to the contents.—Yours, T. G.' And to the complaining parent of an undergraduate he wrote, 'Dear Sir,—Such letters as yours are a great annoyance to your obedient servant T. Gaisford.' [1] This laconic gift the dean evidently had not time to transmit to all of his flock.

Christ Church in those days was infested with some rowdyism, and in one bear-fight an undergraduate was actually killed. In the chapel the new undergraduate found little satisfaction, for the service was scarcely performed with common decency. There seems, however, to have been no irreconcilable prejudice against reading, and in the schools the college was at the top of its academic fame. The influence of Cyril Jackson, the dean in Peel's time, whose advice to Peel and other pupils was to work like tigers, and not to be afraid of killing one's self by work, was still operative. [2] At the summer examination of 1830, Christ Church won five first classes out of ten. Most commoners, according to a letter of Gaskell's, had from three hundred and fifty to five hundred pounds a year; but gentlemen commoners like Acland and Gaskell had from five to six hundred. At the end of 1829, Mr. Gladstone received a studentship *honoris causa*, by nomination of the dean—a system that would not be approved in our epoch of competitive examination, but still an advance upon the time-honoured practice of deans and canons disposing of studentships on grounds of private partiality without reference to desert. We may assume that the dean was not indifferent to academic promise when he told Gladstone, very good-naturedly and civilly, that he had determined to offer him his nomination. The student-designate wrote a theme, read it out before the chapter, passed a nominal, or even farcical, examination in Homer and Virgil, was elected as matter of course by the chapter, and after chapel on the morning of Christmas eve, having taken several oaths, was formally admitted in the name of the Holy Trinity.

Mr. Biscoe, his classical tutor, was a successful lecturer on Aristotle, especially on the Rhetoric. With Charles Wordsworth, son of the master of Trinity at Cambridge, and afterwards Bishop of Saint Andrews, he read for scholarship, apparently not wholly to his own satisfaction. While still an undergraduate, he writes to his father (Nov. 2, 1830), 'I am wretchedly deficient in

---

[1] Charles Wordsworth's *Annals*.

[2] After Peel had begun his career, Jackson gave him a piece of advice that would have pleased Mr. Gladstone :—' Let no day pass without your having Homer in your hand. Elevate your own mind by continual meditation on the vastness of his comprehension and the unerring accuracy of all his conceptions. If you will but read him four or five times over every year, in half a dozen years you will know him by heart, and he well deserves it.'—Parker's *Life of Sir R. Peel*, i. p. 28.

the knowledge of modern languages, literature, and history ; and the classical knowledge acquired here, though sound, accurate, and useful, yet is not such as to *complete* an education.' It looked, in truth, as if the caustic saying of a brilliant colleague of his in later years were not at the time unjust, as now it would happily be, that it was a battle between Eton and education, and Eton had won.

Mr. Gladstone never to the end of his days ceased to be grateful that Oxford was chosen for his university. At Cambridge, as he said in discussing Hallam's choice, the pure refinements of scholarship were more in fashion than the study of the great masterpieces of antiquity in their substance and spirit. The classical examination at Oxford, on the other hand, was divided into the three elastic departments of scholarship and poetry, history, and philosophy. In this list, history somewhat outweighed the scholarship, and philosophy was somewhat more regarded than history. In each case the examination turned more on contents than on form, and the influence of Butler was at its climax.

If Mr. Gladstone had gone to Oxford ten years earlier, he would have found the Ethics and the Rhetoric treated, only much less effectively, in the Cambridge method, like dramatists and orators, as pieces of literature. As it was, Whately's common sense had set a new fashion, and Aristotle was studied as the master of those who know how to teach us the right way about the real world.[1] Aristotle, Butler, and logic were the new acquisitions, but in none of the three as yet did the teaching go deep compared with modern standards. Oxford scholars of our own day question whether there was even one single tutor in 1830, with the possible exception of Hampden, who could expound Aristotle as a whole — so utterly had the Oxford tradition perished.[2]

The time was in truth the eve of an epoch of illumination, and in these epochs it is not old academic systems that the new light is wont to strike with its first rays. The summer of 1831 is the date of Sir William Hamilton's memorable exposure,[3] in his most trenchant and terrifying style and with a learning all his own, of the corruption and ' vampire oppression of Oxford ' ; its sacrifice of the public interests to private advantage : its unhallowed disregard of every moral and religious bond ; the systematic perjury so naturalised in a great seminary of religious education ; the apathy with which the injustice was tolerated by the state and the impiety tolerated by the church. Copleston made a wretched reply, but more than twenty years passed before the spirit of reform overthrew the entrenchments of academic abuse. In that overthrow, when the time came,

---

[1] On the four periods of Aristotelian study at Oxford in the first half of the century see Pattison's Essays, i. p. 463.   [2] *Ibid.* i. p. 465.

[3] Reprinted from the *Edinburgh Review* in *Discussions on Philosophy and Literature*, pp. 401-559 (1852).

Mr. Gladstone was called to play a part, though hardly at first a very zealous one. This was not for a quarter of a century ; for, as we shall soon see, both the revival of learning and the reform of institutions at Oxford were sharply turned aside from their expected course by the startling theological movement that now proceeded from her venerable walls.

What interests us here is not the system but the man ; and never was vital temperament more admirably fitted by its vigour, sincerity, conscience, compass, for whatever good seed from the hand of any sower might be cast upon it. In an entry in his diary in the usual strain of evangelical devotion (April 25, 1830), is a sentence that reveals what was in Mr. Gladstone the nourishing principle of growth : ' In practice the great end is that the love of God may become the *habit* of my soul, and particularly these things are to be sought :—1. The spirit of love. 2. Of self-sacrifice. 3. Of purity. 4. Of energy.' Just as truly as if we were recalling some hero of the seventeenth or any earlier century, is this the biographic clue.

Gladstone constantly reproaches himself for natural indolence, and for a year and a half he took his college course pretty easily. Then he changed. ' The time for half-measures and trifling and pottering, in which I have so long indulged myself, is now gone by, and I must do or die.' His really hard work did not begin until the summer of 1830, when he returned to Cuddesdon to read mathematics with Saunders, a man who had the reputation of being singularly able and stimulating to his pupils, and with whom he had done some rudiments before going into residence at Christ Church. In his description of this gentleman to his father, we may hear for the first time the redundant roll that was for many long years to be so familiar and so famous. Saunders' disposition, it appears, 'is one certainly of extreme benevolence, and of a benevolence which is by no means less strong and full when purely gratuitous and spontaneous, than when he seems to be under the tie of some definite and positive obligation.' Dr. Gaisford would perhaps have put it that the tutor was no kinder where his kindness was paid for, than where it was not.

The catholic question, that was helping many another and older thing to divide England from Ireland, after having for a whole generation played havoc with the fortunes of party and the careers of statesmen, was now drawing swiftly to its close. The Christ Church student had a glimpse of one of the opening scenes of the last act. He writes to his brother (Feb. 6th, 1829) :—

I saw yesterday a most interesting scene in the Convocation house. The occasion was the debate on the anti-catholic petition, which it has long been the practice of the university to send up year by year. This time it was worded in the most gentle and moderate terms possible. All the ordinary business there, is transacted in Latin ; I mean such things as putting the question, speaking, etc., and this rule, I assure you, stops many a mouth, and I dare say saves the Roman catholics many a hard word. There were rather above two hundred doctors and masters of arts present. Three speeches were made, two against and one in favour of sending up the petition. Instead of aye and no they had *placet* and *non-placet*, and in place of a member dividing the House, the question was, '*Petitne aliquis scrutinium?*' which was answered by '*Peto!*' '*Peto!*' from many quarters. However, when the scrutiny took place, it was found that the petition was carried by 156 to 48. . . . After the division, however, came the most interesting part of the whole. A letter from Peel, resigning the seat for the university, was read before the assembly. It was addressed to the vice-chancellor and had arrived just before, it was understood; and I suppose brought hither the first positive and indubitable announcement of the government's intention to emancipate the catholics.

A few days later, Peel accepted the Chiltern Hundreds, and after some deliberation allowed himself to be again brought forward for re-election. He was beaten by 755 votes to 609. The relics of the contest, the figures and the inscriptions on the walls, soon disappeared, but panic did not abate. On Gladstone's way to Oxford (April 30, 1829) a farmer's wife got into the coach, and in communicative vein informed him how frightened they had all been about catholic emancipation, but she did not see that so much had come of it as yet. The college scout declared himself much troubled for the king's conscience, observing that if we make an oath at baptism, we ought to hold by it. 'The bed-makers,' Gladstone writes home, 'seem to continue in a great fright, and mine was asking me this morning whether it would not be a very good thing if we were to give them [the Irish] a king and a parliament of their own. and so to have no more to do with them. The old egg-woman is no whit easier, and wonders how Mr. Peel, who was always such a well-behaved man here, can be so foolish as to think of letting in the Roman catholics.' The unthinking and the ignorant of all classes were much alike. Arthur Hallam went to see *King John* in 1827, and he tells his friend how the lines about the Italian priest (Act III. Sc. i) provoked rounds of clapping, while a gentleman in the next box cried out at the top of his voice, 'Bravo! Bravo! No Pope!' The same correspondent told Gladstone of the father of a common Eton friend, who had challenged him with the overwhelming question, 'Could I say that any papist had ever at any time done any good to the world?' A still stormier conflict than even the emancipation of the catholics was now to shake Oxford and the country to the depths, before Mr. Gladstone took his degree.

II

His friendships at Oxford Mr. Gladstone did not consider to have been as a rule very intimate. Principal among them were

Frederick Rogers, long afterwards Lord Blachford; Doyle;
Gaskell; Bruce, afterwards Lord Elgin; Charles Canning,
afterwards Lord Canning; the two Denisons; Lord Lincoln.
These had all been his friends at Eton. Among new acquisitions to the circle of his intimates at one time or another of
his Oxford life, were the two Aclands, Thomas and Arthur;
Hamilton, afterwards Bishop of Salisbury; Phillimore, destined
to close and life-long friendship; F. D. Maurice, then of Exeter
College, a name destined to stir so many minds in the coming
generation. Of Maurice, Arthur Hallam had written to Gladstone (June 1830) exhorting him to cultivate his acquaintance.
'I know many,' says Hallam, 'whom Maurice has moulded like
a second nature, and these too, men eminent for intellectual
power, to whom the presence of a commanding spirit would in
all other cases be a signal rather for rivalry than reverential
acknowledgment.' 'I knew Maurice well,' says Mr. Gladstone
in one of his notes of reminiscence, 'had heard superlative
accounts of him from Cambridge, and really strove hard to
make them all realities to myself. One Sunday morning we
walked to Marsh Baldon to hear Mr. Porter, the incumbent, a
calvinist independent of the *clique*, and a man of remarkable
power as we both thought. I think he and other friends did
me good, but I got little solid meat from him, as I found him
difficult to catch and still more difficult to hold.'

Sidney Herbert, afterwards so dear to him, now at Oriel,
here first became an acquaintance. Manning, though they both
read with the same tutor, and one succeeded the other as
president of the Union, he did not at this time know well.
The lists of his guests at wines and breakfasts do not even
contain the name of James Hope; indeed, Mr. Gladstone tells
us that he certainly was not more than an acquaintance. In
the account of intimates is the unexpected name of Tupper,
who, in days to come, acquired for a time a grander reputation
than he deserved by his *Proverbial Philosophy*, and on whom
the public by and by avenged its own foolishness by severer
doses of mockery than he had earned.[1] The friend who seems
most to have affected him in the deepest things was Anstice,
whom he describes to his father (June 4, 1830) as 'a very clever
man, and more than a clever man, a man of excellent principle
and of perfect self-command, and of great industry. If any
circumstances could confer upon me the inestimable blessing
of fixed habits and unremitting industry, these [the example
of such a man] will be they.' The diary tells how, in August
(1830), Mr. Gladstone conversed with Anstice in a walk from
Oxford to Cuddesdon on subjects of the highest importance.
'Thoughts then first sprang up in my soul (obvious as they

[1] Tupper (*My Life*, etc., p. 53, 1886) mentions that he beat Mr. Gladstone for the
Burton theological essay, 'The Reconciliation of Matthew and John'; but Gladstone
was so good a second that Dr. Burton begged that one-fifth of the prize money might
be given to him as solatium.

may appear to many) which may powerfully influence my
destiny. O for a light from on high! I have no power, none,
to discern the right path for myself.' They afterwards had
long talks together, 'about that awful subject which has lately
almost engrossed my mind.' Another day—'Conversation of
an hour and a half with Anstice on practical religion, particularly as regards our own situation. I bless and praise God for
his presence here.' 'Long talk with Anstice; would I were
more worthy to be his companion.' 'Conversation with
Anstice; he talked much with Saunders on the motive of
actions, contending for the love of God, *not* selfishness even in
its most refined form.'[1]

In the matter of his own school of religion, Mr. Gladstone
was always certain that Oxford in his undergraduate days had
no part in turning him from an evangelical into a high churchman. The tone and dialect of his diary and letters at the time
show how just this impression was. We find him in 1830 expressing his satisfaction that a number of Hannah More's tracts
have been put on the list of the Christian Knowledge Society.
In 1831 he bitterly deplores such ecclesiastical appointments
as those of Sydney Smith and Dr. Maltby, 'both of them, I
believe, regular latitudinarians.' He remembered his shock at
Butler's laudation of Nature. He was scandalised by a sermon
in which Calvin was placed upon the same level among heresi-
archs as Socinus and other like aliens from gospel truth. He
was delighted (March 1830) with a university sermon against
Milman's *History of the Jews*, and hopes it may be useful as an
antidote, 'for Milman, though I do think without intentions
directly evil, does go far enough to be justly called a bane.
For instance, he says that had Moses never existed, the Hebrew
nation would have remained a degraded pariah tribe or been
lost in the mass of the Egyptian population—and this notwithstanding the promise.' In all his letters in the period from
Eton to the end of Oxford and later, a language noble and
exalted even in these youthful days is not seldom copiously
streaked with a vein that, to eyes not trained to evangelical
light and to minds not tolerant of the expansion that comes to
religious natures in the days of adolescence, may seem un-
pleasantly strained and excessive. The fashion of such words
undergoes transfiguration as the epochs pass. Yet in all their
fashions, even the crudest, they deserve much tenderness. He
consults a clergyman (1829) on the practice of prayer meetings
in his rooms. His correspondent answers, that as the wicked
have their orgies and meet to gamble and to drink, so they that
fear the Lord should speak often to one another concerning
Him; that prayer meetings are not for the cultivation or exhibition of gifts, nor to enable noisy and forward young men to

---

[1] Anstice was afterwards professor of Classics at King's College, and was cut off
prematurely at the age of thirty. See below, p. 99.

pose as leaders of a school of prophets ; but if a few young men of like tastes feel the withering influence of mere scholastic learning, and the necessity of mutual stimulation and refreshment, then such prayer meetings would be a safe and natural remedy. The student's attention to all religious observances was close and unbroken, the most living part of his existence.

The movement that was to convulse the church had not yet begun. 'You may smile,' Mr. Gladstone said long after, 'when told that when I was at Oxford, Dr. Hampden was regarded as a model of orthodoxy ; that Dr. Newman was eyed with suspicion as a low churchman, and Dr. Pusey as leaning to rationalism.' What Mr. Gladstone afterwards described as a steady, clear, but dry anglican orthodoxy bore sway, 'and frowned this way or that, on the first indication of any tendency to diverge from the beaten path.'[1] He hears Whately preach a controversial sermon (1831) just after he had been made Archbishop of Dublin. 'Doubtless he is a man of much power and many excellences, but his anti-sabbatical doctrine is, I fear, as mischievous as it is unsound.' A sermon of Keble's at St. Mary's prompts the uneasy question, 'Are all Mr. Keble's opinions those of scripture and the church? Of his life and heart and practice, none could doubt, all would admire.' A good sermon is mentioned from Blanco White, that strange and forlorn figure of whom in later life Mr. Gladstone wrote an interesting account, not conclusive in argument, but assuredly not wanting in either delicacy or generosity.[2] 'Dr. Pusey was very kind to me when I was an undergraduate at Oxford,' he says, but what their relations were I know not. 'I knew and respected both Bishop Lloyd and Dr. Pusey,' he says, ' but neither of them attempted to exercise the smallest influence over my religious opinions.' With Newman he seems to have been brought into contact hardly at all.[3] Newman and one of the Wilberforces came to dine at Cuddesdon one day, and, on a later occasion, he and another fellow of Oriel were at a dinner with Mr. Gladstone at the table of his friend Philip Pusey. Two or three of his sermons are mentioned. One of them (March 7, 1831) contained 'much singular, not to say objectionable matter, if one may so speak of so good a man.' Of another,—'heard Newman preach a good sermon on those who made excuse' (Sept. 25, 1831). Of the generality of university sermons, he accepted the observation of his friend Anstice,—'Depend upon it, such sermons as those can never convert a single person.' On some Sundays he hears two of these discourses in the morning and afternoon, and a third sermon in the evening, for though he became the most copious of all speakers, Mr. Gladstone was ever the most generous of

[1] Gleanings, vii. p. 141.   [2] Ibid. ii. p. 1.
[3] Purcell (Manning), i. p. 46) makes Mr. Gladstone say, 'I was intimate with Newman, but then we had many friends in common.' This must be erroneously reported.

listeners. It was at St. Ebbe's that he found really congenial ministrations—an ecclesiastical centre described by him fifty years later—under Mr. Bulteel, a man of some note in his day; here the flame was at white heat, and a score or two of young men felt its attractions.[1] He always remembered among the wonderful sights of his life, St. Mary's 'crammed in all parts by all orders, when Mr. Bulteel, an outlying calvinist, preached his accusatory sermon (some of it too true) against the university.' In the summer of 1830, Mr. Gladstone notes, 'Poor Bulteel has lost his church for preaching in the open air. Pity that he should have acted so, and pity that it should be found necessary to make such an example of a man of God.' The preacher was impenitent, for from a window Mr. Gladstone again heard him conduct a service for a large congregation who listened attentively to a sermon that was interesting, but evinced some soreness of spirit. A most painful discourse from a Mr. Crowther so moves Mr. Gladstone that he sits down to write to the preacher, 'earnestly expostulating with him on the character and the doctrines of the sermon,' and after re-writing his letter, he delivers it with his own hand at the door of the displeasing divine. The effect was not other than salutary, for a little later he was 'happy to hear two sermons of good principles from Mr. Crowther.' To his father, October 27, 1830 :—'Dr. Chalmers has been passing through Oxford, and I went to hear him preach on Sunday evening, though it was at the baptist chapel. . . . I need hardly say that his sermon was admirable, and quite as remarkable for the judicious and sober manner in which he enforced his views, as for their lofty principles and piety. He preached, I think, for an hour and forty minutes.' The admiration thus first aroused only grew with fuller knowledge in the coming years.

An Essay Club, called from its founder's initials the W E G, was formed at a meeting in Gaskell's rooms in October, 1829. Only two members out of the first twelve did not belong to Christ Church, Rogers of Oriel and Moncreiff of New.[2] The Essay Club's transactions, though not very serious, deserve a glance. Mr. Gladstone reads an essay (Feb. 20, 1830) on the comparative rank of poetry and philosophy, concluding with a motion that the rank of philosophy is higher than that of poetry : it was beaten by seven to five. Without a division, they determined that English poetry is of a higher order than Greek. The truth of the principles of phrenology was affirmed with the tremendous emphasis of eleven to one. Though trifling in degree, the influence of the modern drama was pronounced

[1] *Gleanings*, vii. p. 211.
[2] Sir Thomas Acland gives the names of the first twelve members as follows : Gladstone, Gaskell, Doyle, Moncreiff, Seymer, Rogers, two Aclands, Leader, Anstice, Harrison, Cole. Mr. Gladstone in a letter to Acland (1889) mentions these twelve names, and adds 'from the old book of record,' Bruce, J., Bruce, F., Egerton, Liddell, Lincoln, Lushington, Maurice, Oxenham, Vaughan, Thornton, C. Marriott.

in quality pernicious. Gladstone gave his casting vote against the capacious proposition, of which philosophers had made so much in France, Switzerland, and other places on the eve of the French revolution, that education and other outward circumstances have more than nature to do with man's disposition. By four to three, Mr. Tennyson's poems were affirmed to show considerable genius, Gladstone happily in the too slender majority. The motion that 'political liberty is not to be considered as the end of government' was a great affair. Maurice, who had been admitted to the club on coming to Oxford from Cambridge, moved an amendment 'that every man has a right to perform certain personal duties with which no system of government has a right to interfere.' Gladstone 'objected to an observation that had fallen from the mover, "A man finds himself in the world," as if he did not come into the world under a debt to his parents, under obligations to society.' The tame motion of Lord Abercorn, that Elizabeth's conduct to Mary Queen of Scots was unjustifiable and impolitic, was stiffened into 'not only unjustifiable and impolitic, but a base and treacherous murder,' and in that severe form was carried without a division.

Plenty of nonsense was talked we may be sure, and so there was, no doubt, in the Olive Grove of Academe or amid those surnamed Peripatetics and the Sect Epicurean. Yet nonsense notwithstanding, the Essay Club had members who proved in time to have superior minds if ever men had, and their disputations in one another's rooms helped to sharpen their mental apparatus, to start trains of ideas however immature, and to shake the cherished dogmatisms brought from beloved homes, even if dogmatism as stringent took their place. This is how the world moves, and Oxford was just beginning to rub its eyes, awaking to the speculations of a new time.

When he looked back in after times, Mr. Gladstone traced one great defect in the education of Oxford. 'Perhaps it was my own fault, but I must admit that I did not learn when I was at Oxford that which I have learned since—namely, to set a due value on the imperishable and inestimable principle of British liberty. The temper which too much prevailed in academical circles was that liberty was regarded with jealousy and fear, something which could not wholly be dispensed with, but which was to be continually watched for fear of excesses.'[1]

III

In March 1830 Gladstone made the first of two attempts to win the scholarship newly founded by Dean Ireland, and from the beginning one of the most coveted of university prizes. In 1830 (March 16) he wrote :—' There is it appears smaller chance

[1] At Palmerston Club, Oxford, Jan. 30, 1878.

than ever of its falling out of the hands of the Shrewsbury
people. There is a very formidable one indeed, by name
Scott, come up from Christ Church. If it is to go among them
I hope he may get it.' This was Robert Scott, afterwards
master of Balliol, and finally dean of Rochester, and the coadjutor with Dean Liddell in the famous Greek Lexicon
brought out in 1843. A year later he tried again, but little
better success came either to himself or to Scott. He tells his
father the story (March 16th, 1831) and collegians who have
fought such battles may care to hear it :—

I must first tell you that I am *not* the successful candidate, and after
this I shall have nothing to communicate but what will, I think, give
you pleasure. The scholarship has been won by (I believe) a native of
Liverpool.[1] His name is Brancker, and he is now actually at Shrewsbury, but had matriculated here though he had not come up to reside.
This result has excited immense surprise. For my own part, I went
into the examination *solely* depending for any hope of pre-eminence
above the Shrewsbury men on three points, Greek history, one particular
kind of Greek verses, and Greek philosophy. . . . It so fell out,
however, that not one of these three points was brought to bear on the
examination, though, indeed, it is but a lame one without them.
Accordingly from the turn it seemed to take as it proceeded, my own
expectations regularly declined, and I thought I might consider myself
very well off if I came in pretty high. As it is, I am even with the
great competitor, Scott, whom everybody almost thought the favourite
candidate, and above the others. Allies, an Eton man, Scott and I are
placed together ; and Short, one of the examiners, told us this morning
that it was an extremely near thing, and he had great difficulty in
making up his mind, which he never had felt in any former examination
in which he had been engaged ; and indeed he laid the preference given
to Brancker chiefly on his having written short and concise answers,
while ours were long-winded. And in consideration of its having been
so closely contested, the vice-chancellor is to present each of us with a
set of books. . . . Something however may fairly enough be attributed
to the fact that at Eton we were not educated for such objects as these.
. . . The result will affect the scholarship itself more than any individual
character ; for previous events have created, and this has contributed
amazingly to strengthen, a prevalent impression that the Shrewsbury
system is radically a false one, and that its object is not to educate the
mind but merely to cram and stuff it for these purposes. However, we
who are beaten are not fair judges. . . . I only trust that you will not
be more annoyed than I am by this event.

Brancker was said to have won because he answered all
the questions not only shortly, but most of them right, and
Mr. Gladstone's essay was marked 'desultory beyond belief.'
Below Allies came Sidney Herbert, then at Oriel, and Grove,
afterwards a judge and an important name in the history of
scientific speculation.
He was equally unsuccessful in another field of competition.

[1] His father was a Liverpool merchant, and had been mayor.

He sent in a poem on Richard Cœur de Lion for the Newdigate
prize in 1829. In 1893 somebody asked his leave to reprint it,
and at Mr. Gladstone's request sent him a copy :—

On perusing it I was very much struck by the contrast it exhibited
between the faculty of versification which (I thought) was good, and the
faculty of poetry, which was very defective. This faculty of verse had
been trained I suppose by verse-making at Eton, and was based upon the
possession of a good or tolerable ear with which nature had endowed
me. I think that a poetical faculty did develop itself in me a little
later, that is to say between twenty and thirty, due perhaps to having
read Dante with a real devotion and absorption. It was, however, in
my view, true but weak, and has never got beyond that stage. It was
evidently absent from the verses, I will not say the poem, on Cœur de
Lion ; and without hesitation I declined to allow any reprint.[1]

He was active in the debates at the Union, where he made
his first start in the speaking line (Feb. 1830) in a strong
oration much admired by his friends, in favour,—of all the
questionable things in the world,—of the Treason and Sedition
Acts of 1795. He writes home that he did not find the
ordeal so formidable as it used to be before the smaller
audiences at Eton, for at Oxford they sometimes mustered

[1] By the kindness of the present dean of Christ Church I am able to give the reader
a couple of specimens of Mr. Gladstone's Latin verse. The two pieces were written
for 'Lent verses' :—

(1829) Gladstone.   *An aliquid sit immutabile?*
                                        Affirmatur.
Vivimus incertum? Fortunæ lusus habemur?
  Singula præteriens det rapiatve dies?
En nemus exanimum, qua se modo germina, verno
  Tempore, purpureis explicuere comis.
Respice pacatum Neptuni numine pontum :
  Territa mox tumido verberat astra salo.
Sed brevior brevibus, quas unda supervenit, undis
  Sed gelidâ, quam mox dissipat aura, nive :
Sed foliis sylvarum, et amici veris odore,
  Quisquis honos placeat, quisquis alatur amor.
Jamne joci lususque sonant? viget alma Juventus?
  Funereæ forsan cras cecinere tubæ.
Nec pietas, nec casta Fides, nec libera Virtus,
  Nigrantes vetuit mortis inire domos.
Certa tamen lex ipsa manet, labentibus annis,
  Quæ jubet assiduas quæque subire vices.

(1830) Gladstone.   *An malum a seipso possit sanari?*
                                        Affirmatur.
Cernis ut argutas effuderit Anna querelas?
  Lumen ut insolitâ triste tumescat aquâ?
Quicquid in ardenti flammarum corde rotatur,
  Et fronte et rubris pingitur omne genis.
Dum ruit hûc illûc, speculum simulacra ruentis
  Ora Mimalloneo plena furore, refert.
Pectora vesano cùm turgida conspicit æstu,
  Quæ fuit (haud qualis debeat esse) videt.
Ac veluti ventis intra sua claustra coactis,
  Quum piget Æolium fræna dedisse ducem ;
Concita non aliter subsidit pectoris unda,
  Et propriâ rursum sede potitur Amor,
Jurâsses torvam perculso astare Medusam
  Jurares Paphiæ lumen adesse deæ.

as many as a hundred or a hundred and fifty. He spoke for a strongly-worded motion on a happier theme, in favour of the policy and memory of Canning. In the summer of 1831, he mentions a debate in which a motion was proposed in favour of speedy emancipation of the West Indian slaves. 'I moved an amendment that education of a religious kind was the fit object of legislation, which was carried by thirty-three to twelve.' Of the most notable of all his successes at the Union we shall soon hear.

His little diary, written for no eye but his own, and in the use of which I must beware of the sin of violating the sanctuary, contains in the most concise of daily records all his various activities, and at least after the summer at Cuddesdon, it presents an attractive picture of duty, industry, and attention, 'constant as the motion of the day.' The entries are much alike, and a few of them will suffice to bring his life and him before us. The days for 1830 may almost be taken at random.

May 10, 1830. — Prospectively, I have the following work to do in the course of this term. (I mention it now, that this may at least make me blush if I fail.) Butler's *Analogy*, analysis and synopsis. Herodotus, questions. St. Matthew and St. John. Mathematical lecture. *Aeneid.* Juvenal and Persius. *Ethics,* five books. Prideaux (a part of, for Herodotus). Themistocles Greciae valedicturus [I suppose a verse composition]. Something in divinity. Mathematical lecture. Breakfast with Gaskell, who had the Merton men. Papers. *Edinburgh Review* on Southey's *Colloquies,* [Macaulay's]. *Ethics.* A wretched day. God forgive idleness. Note to Bible.

May 13. — Wrote to my mother. At debate (Union). Elected secretary. Papers. *British Critic* on *History of the Jews* [by Newman on Milman]. Herodotus, *Ethics.* Butler and analysis. Papers, Virgil, Herodotus. Juvenal. Mathematics and lecture. Walk with Anstice. *Ethics,* finished book 4.

May 25.—Finished Porteus's *Evidences.* Got up a few hard passages. Analysis of Porteus. Sundry matters in divinity. Themistocles. Sat with Biscoe talking. Walk with Canning and Gaskell. Wine and tea. Wrote to Mr. G. [his father]. Papers.

June 13. *Sunday.*—Chapel morning and evening. Thomas à Kempis. Erskine's *Evidence.* Tea with Mayow and Cole. Walked with Maurice to hear Mr. Porter, a wild but splendid preacher.

June 14.—Gave a large wine party. Divinity lecture. Mathematics. Wrote three long letters. Herodotus, began book 4. Prideaux. Newspapers, etc. Thomas à Kempis.

June 15.—Another wine party. *Ethics,* Herodotus. A little Juvenal. Papers. Hallam's poetry. Lecture on Herodotus. Phillimore got the verse prize.

June 16. — Divinity lecture. Herodotus. Papers. Out at wine. A little Plato.

June 17. — *Ethics* and lecture. Herodotus. T. à Kempis. Wine with Gaskell.

June 18.—Breakfast with Gaskell. T. à Kempis. Divinity lecture.

Herodotus. Wrote on Philosophy *versus* Poetry. A little Persius. Wine with Buller and Tupper.

June 25.—*Ethics.* Collections 9-3. Among other things wrote a long paper on religions of Egypt, Persia, Babylon ; and on the Satirists. Finished packing books and clothes. Left Oxford between 5-6, and walked fifteen miles towards Leamington. Then obliged to put in, being caught by a thunderstorm. Comfortably off in a country inn at Steeple Aston. Read and spouted some *Prometheus Vinctus* there.

June 26.—Started before 7. Walked eight miles to Banbury. Breakfast there, and walked on twenty-two to Leamington. Arrived at three, and changed. Gaskell came in the evening. *Life of Massinger.*

July 6.   *Cuddesdon.*—Up soon after 6. Began my Harmony of Greek Testament. Differential calculus, etc. Mathematics good while, but in a rambling way. Began *Odyssey.* Papers. Walk with Anstice and Hamilton. Turned a little bit of Livy into Greek. Conversation on ethics and metaphysics at night.

July 8.—Greek Testament. Bible with Anstice. Mathematics, long but did little. Translated some *Phaedo.* Butler. Construed some Thucydides at night. Making hay, etc., with S., H., and A. Great fun. Shelley.

July 10.—Greek Testament. Lightfoot. Butler, and writing a marginal analysis. Old Testament with Anstice and a discussion on early history. Mathematics. Cricket with H. and A. A conversation of two hours at night with A. on religion till past 12. Thucydides, etc. I cannot get anything done, though I seem to be employed a good while. Short's sermon.

July 11.—Church and Sunday-school teaching, morning and evening. The children miserably deluded. Barrow. Short. Walked with S.

September 4.—Same as yesterday. *Paradise Lost.* Dined with the bishop. Cards at night. I like them not, for they excite and keep me awake. Construing Sophocles.

September 18.—Went down early to Wheatley for letters. It is indeed true [the death of Huskisson], and he, poor man, was in his last agonies when I was playing cards on Wednesday night. When shall we learn wisdom ? Not that I see folly in the fact of playing cards, but it is too often accompanied by a dissipated spirit.

He did not escape the usual sensations of the desultory when fate forces them to wear the collar. ' In fact, at times I find it very irksome, and my having the inclination to view it in that light is to me the surest demonstration that my mind was in great want of some discipline, and some regular exertion, for hitherto I have read by fits and starts and just as it pleased me. I hope that this vacation [summer of 1830] will confer on me one benefit more important than any having reference merely to my class—I mean the habit of steady application and strict economy of time.'

We can hardly say that these fragmentary items reveal the striking or impressive dawn of extraordinary genius. They bear no trace of precocity, and show little more than the dispersive and promiscuous interest of the common virtuous undergraduate. He kept up a correspondence with Hallam,

now at Cambridge, and an extract from one of Hallam's letters
may show something of the writer, as of the friend for whose
sympathising mind it was intended :—

Academical honours would be less than nothing to me were it not for
my father's wishes, and even these are moderate on the subject.   If it
please God that I make the name I bear honoured in a second generation,
it will be by inward power which is its own reward ; if it please Him not,
I hope to go down to the grave unrepining, for I have lived and loved
and been loved ; and what will be the momentary pangs of an atomic
existence when the scheme of that providential love which pervades, sus-
tains, quickens this boundless universe shall at the last day be unfolded
and adored ?   The great truth which, when we are rightly impressed
with it, will liberate mankind is that no man has a right to isolate
himself, because every man is a particle of a marvellous whole ; that
when he suffers, since it is for the good of that whole, he, the particle,
has no right to complain ; and in the long run, that which is the good
of all will abundantly manifest itself to be the good of each.   Other
belief consists not with theism.   This is its centre.   Let me quote to
their purpose the words of my favourite poet ; it will do us good to
hear his voice, though but for a moment :

> One adequate support
> For the calamities of mortal life
> Exists—one only : an assured belief
> That the procession of our fate, howe'er
> Sad or disturbed, is ordered by a Being
> Of infinite benevolence and power,
> Whose everlasting purposes embrace
> All accidents, converting them to good.[1]

Hallam's father, in that memoir so just and tender which he
prefixes to his son's literary remains, remarks that all his son's
talk about this old desperate riddle of the origin and significance of evil, like the talk of Leibnitz about it, resolved
itself into an unproved assumption of the necessity of evil.   In
truth there is little sign that either Arthur Hallam or Gladstone had in him the making of the patient and methodical
thinker in the high abstract sphere.   They were both of them
cast in another mould.   But the efficacy of human relation-
ships springs from a thousand subtler and more mysterious
sources than either patience or method in our thinking.   Such
marked efficacy was there in the friendship of these two, both
of them living under pure skies, but one of the pair endowed
besides with 'the thews that throw the world.'

Whether in Gladstone's diary or in his letters, in the midst
of Herodotus and Butler and Aristotle and the rest of the time-
worn sages, we are curiously conscious of the presence of a
spirit of action, affairs, excitement.   It is not the born scholar
eager in search of knowledge for its own sake ; there is little of
Milton's 'quiet air of delightful studies' ; and none of Pascal's
'labouring for truth with many a heavy sigh.'   The end of it

[1] *Excursion*, Book iv. p. 1.

all is, as Aristotle said it should be, not knowing but doing :—
honourable desire of success, satisfaction of the hopes of friends,
a general literary appetite, conscious preparation for private
and public duty in the world, a steady progression out of the
shallows into the depths, a gaze beyond garden and cloister, *in
agmen, in pulverem, in clamorem*, to the dust and burning sun
and shouting of the days of conflict.

IV

In September 1830, as we have seen, Huskisson had disappeared. Thomas Gladstone was in the train drawn by the
Dart that ran over the statesman and killed him.

' Poor Huskisson,' he writes to William Gladstone, ' the great promoter
of the railroad, has fallen a victim to its opening ! . . . As soon as I
heard that Huskisson had been run over, I ran and found him on the
ground close to the duke's [Wellington] car, his legs apparently both
broken (though only one was), the ground covered with blood, his eyes
open, but death written in his face. When they raised him a little he
said, "Leave me, let me die." "God forgive me, I am a dead man." " I
can never stand this." . . . ' On Tuesday he made a speech in the Exchange reading-room, when he said he hoped long to represent them.
He said, too, that day, that we were sure of a fine day, for the duke
would have his old luck. Talked jokingly, too, of insuring his life for
the ride.'

And he notes, as others did, the extraordinary circumstance
that of half a million of people on the line of road the victim
should be the duke's great opponent, thus carried off suddenly
before his eyes.

There was some question of Mr. John Gladstone taking
Huskisson's place as one of the members for Liverpool, but
he did not covet it. He foresaw too many local jealousies, his
deafness would be sadly against him, he was nearly sixty-five,
and he felt himself too old to face the turmoil. He looked
upon the Wellington government as the only government
possible, though as a friend of Canning he freely recognised its
defects, the self-will of the duke, and the parcel of mediocrities
and drones with whom, excepting Peel, he had filled his cabinet.
His view of the state of parties in the autumn of 1830 is clear
and succinct enough to deserve reproduction. 'Huskisson's
death,' he writes to his son at Christ Church (October 29, 1830),
' was a great gain to the duke, for he was the most formidable
thorn to prick him in the parliament. Of those who acted with
Huskisson, none have knowledge or experience sufficient to
enable them to do so. As for the whigs, they can all talk and
make speeches, but they are not men of business. The ultra-
tories are too contemptible and wanting in talent to be thought
of. The radicals cannot be trusted, for they would soon pull
down the venerable fabric of our constitution. The liberals or

independents must at least generally side with the duke ; they are likely to meet each other half way.'

In less than a week after this acute survey the duke made his stalwart declaration in the House of Lords against all parliamentary reform. 'I have not said too much, have I?' he asked of Lord Aberdeen on sitting down. 'You'll hear of it,' was Aberdeen's reply. 'You've announced the fall of your government, that's all,' said another. In a fortnight (November 18) the duke was out, Lord Grey was in, and the country was gradually plunged into a determined struggle for the amendment of its constitution.

Mr. Gladstone, as a resolute Canningite, was as fiercely hostile to the second and mightier innovation as he had been eager for the relief of the catholics, and it was in connection with the Reform bill that he first made a public mark. The reader will recall the stages of that event ; how the bill was read a second time in the Commons by a majority of one on March 22nd, 1831 ; how, after a defeat by a majority of eight on a motion on going into committee, Lord Grey dissolved ; how the country, shaken to its depths, gave the reformers such undreamed-of strength, that on July 8th the second reading of the bill was carried by a hundred and thirty-six ; how on October 8th the Lords rejected it by forty-one, and what violent commotions that deed provoked ; how a third bill was brought in (December 12th, 1831) and passed through the Commons (March 23rd, 1832) ; how the Lords were still refractory ; what a lacerating ministerial crisis ensued ; and how at last, in June, the bill, which was to work the miracle of a millennium, actually became the law of the land. Not even the pressure of preparation for the coming ordeal of the examination schools could restrain the activity and zeal of our Oxonian. Canning had denounced parliamentary reform at Liverpool in 1820 ; and afterwards had declared in the House of Commons that if anybody asked him what he meant to do on the subject, he would oppose reform to the end of his life, under whatever shape it might appear. Canning's disciple at Christ Church was as vehement as the master.[1] To a friend he wrote in 1865 :—

I think that Oxford teaching had in our day an anti-popular tendency. I must add that it was not owing to the books, but rather to the way in which they were handled : and further, that it tended still more strongly in my opinion to make the love of truth paramount over all other motives in the mind, and thus that it supplied an antidote for whatever it had of bane. The Reform bill frightened me in 1831, and drove me off my natural and previous bias. Burke and Canning misled many on that subject, and they misled me.

[1] It is curious, we may note in passing, that Thomas Gladstone, his eldest brother, was then member for Queenborough, and he, after voting in the majority of one, a few weeks later changed his mind and supported the amendment that destroyed the first bill. At the election he lost his seat.

While staying at Leamington, whither his family constantly
went in order to be under the medical care of the famous
Jephson, Mr. Gladstone went to a reform meeting at Warwick,
of which he wrote a contemptuous account in a letter to the
Standard (April 7). The gentry present were few, the nobility
none, the clergy one only, while ' the mob beneath the grand
stand was Athenian in its levity, in its recklessness, in its
gaping expectancy, in its self-love and self-conceit—in everything but its acuteness.' 'If, sir, the nobility, the gentry,
the clergy are to be alarmed, overawed, or smothered by the
expression of popular opinion such as this, and if no great
statesman be raised up in our hour of need to undeceive
this unhappy multitude, now eagerly rushing or heedlessly
sauntering along the pathway of revolution, as an ox goeth
to the slaughter or a fool to the correction of the stocks,
what is it but a symptom as infallible as it is appalling,
that the day of our greatness and stability is no more, and
that the chill and damp of death are already creeping over
England's glory.' These dolorous spectres haunted him incessantly, as they haunted so many who had not the sovereign
excuse of youth, and his rhetoric was perfectly sincere. He
felt bound to say that, as far as he could form an opinion,
the ministry most richly deserved impeachment. Its great
innovations and its small alike moved his indignation. When
Brougham committed the enormity of hearing causes on Good
Friday, Gladstone repeats with deep complacency a saying
of Wetherell, that Brougham was the first judge who had
done such a thing since Pontius Pilate.

The undergraduates took their part in the humours of
the great election, and Oxford turned out her chivalry
gallantly to bring in the anti-reform candidate for the
county to the nomination. 'I mounted the mare to join the
anti-reform procession,' writes the impassioned student to his
father, 'and we looked as well as we could do, considering that
we were all covered with mud from head to foot. There
was mob enough on both sides, but I must do them justice
to say they were for the most part exceedingly good-
humoured, and after we had dismounted, we went among them
and elbowed one another and bawled and bellowed with the
most perfect good temper. At the nomination in the town
hall there was so much row raised that not one of the
candidates could be heard.' The effect of these exercitations
was a hoarseness and cold, which did not, however, prevent the
sufferer from taking his part in a mighty bonfire in Peckwater.
On another day :—

I went with Denison and another man named Jeffreys between
eleven and twelve. We began to talk to some men among Weyland's
friends ; they crowded round, and began to holloa at us, and were
making a sort of ring round us preparatory to a desperate hustle, when

lo ! up rushed a body of Norreys' men from St. Thomas's, broke their
ranks, raised a shout, and rescued us in great style. I shall ever be
grateful to the men of St. Thomas's. When we were talking, Jeffreys
said something which made one man holloa, 'Oh, his father's a parson.'
This happened to be true, and flabbergasted me, but he happily turned
it by reminding them that they were going to vote for Mr. Harcourt,
son of the greatest parson in England but one (Archbishop of York).
Afterwards they left me, and I pursued my work alone, conversed with
a great number, shook hands with a fair proportion, made some laugh,
and once very nearly got hustled when alone, but happily escaped.
You would be beyond measure astonished how unanimous and how
strong is the feeling among the freeholders (who may be taken as a fair
specimen of the generality of all counties) *against* the catholic question.
Reformers and anti-reformers were alike sensitive on that point and
perfectly agreed. One man said to me, 'What, vote for Lord Norreys ?
Why, he voted against the country *both* times, *for* the Catholic bill and
then against the Reform.' What would this atrocious ministry have
said had the appeal to the voice of the people, which they now quote as
their authority, been made in 1829 ? I held forth to a working man,
possibly a forty-shilling freeholder, [he adds in a fragment of later
years,] on the established text, reform was revolution. To corroborate
my doctrine I said, ' Why, look at the revolutions in foreign countries,'
meaning of course France and Belgium. The man looked hard at me
and said these very words, 'Damn all foreign countries, what has old
England to do with foreign countries ?' This is not the only time that
I have received an important lesson from a humble source.

A more important scene which his own future eminence
made in a sense historic, was a debate at the Union upon
Reform in the same month, where his contribution (May 17th)
struck all his hearers with amazement, so brilliant, so powerful,
so incomparably splendid did it seem to their young eyes. His
description of it to his brother (May 20th, 1831) is modest
enough :—

I should really have been glad if your health had been such as to
have permitted your visiting Oxford last week, so that you might have
heard our debate, for certainly there had never been anything like it
known here before and will scarcely be again. The discussion on the
question that the ministers were incompetent to carry on the government of the country was of a miscellaneous character, and I moved what
they called a 'rider' to the effect that the Reform bill threatened to
change the form of the British government, and ultimately to break up
the whole frame of society. The debate altogether lasted three nights,
and it closed then, partly because the *votes* had got tired of dancing
attendance, partly because the speakers of the revolutionary side were
exhausted. There were eight or nine more on ours ready, and indeed
anxious. As it was, there were I think fifteen speeches on our side and
thirteen on theirs, or something of that kind. Every man spoke above
his average, and many very far beyond it. They were generally short
enough. Moncreiff, a long-winded Scotsman, spouted nearly an hour,
and I was guilty of three-quarters. I remember at Eton (where we
used, when I first went into the society, to speak from three to ten
minutes) I thought it must be one of the finest things in the world to

speak for three-quarters of an hour, and there was a legend circulated
about an old member of the society's having done so, which used to
make us all gape and stare. However, I fear it does not necessarily
imply much more than length. Doyle spoke remarkably well, and made
a violent attack on Mr. Canning's friends, which Gaskell did his best to
answer, but very ineffectually from the nature of the case. We got a
conversion speech from a Christ Church gentleman-commoner, named
Alston, which produced an excellent effect, and the division was favourable beyond anything we had hoped—ninety-four to thirty-eight. We
should have had larger numbers still had we divided on the first night.
Great diligence was used by both parties in bringing men down, but the
tactics on the whole were better on our side, and we had fewer truants
in proportion to our numbers. England expects every man to do his
duty ; and ours, humble as it is, has been done in reference to this
question. On Friday I wrote a letter to the *Standard* giving an account
of the division, which you will see in Saturday's paper, if you think it
worth while to refer to it. The way in which the present generation of
undergraduates is divided on the question is quite remarkable.

The occasion was to prove a memorable one in his career,
and a few more lines about it from his diary will not be
considered superfluous :—

May 16*th.* — Sleepy. Mathematics, few and shuffling, and lecture.
Read Canning's reform speeches at Liverpool and made extracts. Rode
out. Debate, which was adjourned. I am to try my hand to-morrow.
My thoughts were but ill-arranged, but I fear they will be no better
then. Wine with Anstice. Singing. Tea with Lincoln.

May 17*th.*—Ethics. Little mathematics. A good deal exhausted in
forenoon from heat last night. Dined with White and had wine with
him, also with young Acland. Cogitations on reform, etc. Difficult to
select matter for a speech, not to gather it. *Spoke at the adjourned
debate for three-quarters of an hour* ; immediately after Gaskell, who was
preceded by Lincoln. Row afterwards and adjournment. Tea with
Wordsworth.

When Gladstone sat down, one of his contemporaries has
written, 'we all of us felt that an epoch in our lives had
occurred.' His father was so well pleased with the glories of
the speech and with its effect, that he wished to have it
published. Besides his speech, besides the composition of
sturdy placards against the monstrous bill, and besides the
preparation of an elaborate petition [1] and the gathering of
770 signatures to it, the ardent anti-reformer, though the
distance from the days of doom in the examination schools
was rapidly shrinking, actually sat down to write a long
pamphlet (July 1831) and sent it to Hatchard, the publisher.
Hatchard doubted the success of an anonymous pamphlet,
and replied in the too familiar formula that has frozen so
many thousand glowing hearts, that he would publish it if
the author would take the money risk. The most interesting
thing about it is the criticism of the writer's shrewd and wise

[1] It is given in Robbins, *Early Life*, pp. 104-5.

father upon his son's performance (too long for reproduction
here). He went with his son in the main, he says, 'but I
cannot go all your lengths,' and the language of his judgment
sheds a curious light upon the vehement temperament of
Mr. Gladstone at this time as it struck an affectionate yet firm
and sober monitor.

In the autumn of 1831 Mr. Gladstone took some trouble to
be present on one of the cardinal occasions in this fluctuating
history :—

October 3rd to 8th.—Journey to London. From Henley in Blackstone's
chaise. Present at five nights' debate of infinite interest in the House
of Lords. The first, I went forwards and underwent a somewhat high
pressure. At the four others sat on a round transverse rail, very fortunate in being so well placed. Had a full view of the peeresses.
There nine or ten hours every evening. Read Peel's speech and sundry
papers relating to King's College, which I went to see ; also London
Bridge. Read introduction to Butler. Wrote to Saunders. Much
occupied in order-hunting during the morning. Lord Brougham's as
a speech most wonderful, delivered with a power and effect which cannot
be appreciated by any hearsay mode of information, and with fertile
exuberance in sarcasm. In point of argument it had, I think, little
that was new. Lord Grey's most beautiful, Lord Goderich's and Lord
Lansdowne's extremely good, and in these was comprehended nearly all
the oratorical merit of the debate. The reasoning or the attempt to
reason, independently of the success in such attempt, certainly seemed
to me to be with the opposition. Their best speeches, I thought, were
those of Lords Harrowby, Carnarvon, Mansfield, Wynford ; next Lords
Lyndhurst, Wharncliffe, and the Duke of Wellington. Lord Grey's
reply I did not hear, having been compelled by exhaustion to leave the
House. Remained with Ryder and Pickering in the coffee-room or
walking about until the division, and joined Wellesley and [illegible]
as we walked home. Went to bed for an hour, breakfasted, and came
off by the Alert. Arrived safely, thank God, in Oxford. Wrote to my
brother and to Gaskell. Tea with Phillimore and spent the remainder
of the evening with Canning. The consequences of the vote may be
awful. God avert this. But it was an honourable and manly decision,
and so may God avert them.

This was the memorable occasion when the Lords threw out
the Reform bill by 199 to 158, the division not taking place
until six o'clock in the morning. The consequences, as the
country instantly made manifest, were 'awful' enough to
secure the reversal of the decision. It seems, so far as I can
make out, to have been the first debate that one of the most
consummate debaters that ever lived had the fortune of listening to.

v

Meanwhile intense interest in parliament and the newspapers had not impaired his studies. Disgusted as he was at
the political outlook, in the beginning of July he had fallen
fairly to work more or less close for ten or twelve hours a day.

It 'proved as of old a cure for ill-humour, though in itself not
of the most delectable kind. It is odd enough, though true,
that reading hard close-grained stuff produces a much more
decided and better effect in this way, than books written
professedly for the purpose of entertainment.' Then his eyes
became painful, affected the head, and in August almost
brought him to a full stop. After absolute remission of work
for a few days, he slowly spread full sail again, and took good
care no more to stint either exercise or sleep, thinking himself,
strange as it now sounds, rather below than above par for such
exertions. He declared that the bodily fatigue, the mental
fatigue, and the anxiety as to the result, made reading for a
class a thing not to be undergone more than once in a lifetime.
Time had mightier fatigues in store for him than even this.
The heavy work among the ideas of men of bygone days did
not deaden intellectual projects of his own. A few days before
he went to see the Lords throw out the Reform bill, he made a
curious entry :—

October 3rd, 1831.—Yesterday an idea, a chimera, entered my head,
of gathering during the progress of my life, notes and materials for a
work embracing three divisions, Morals, Politics, Education, and I
commit this notice to paper now, that many years hence, if it please
God, I may find it either a pleasant or at least an instructive reminiscence, a pleasant and instructing one, I trust, if I may ever be permitted
to execute this design ; instructive if it shall point while in embryo,
and serve to teach me the folly of presumptuous schemes conceived
during the buoyancy of youth, and only relinquished on a discovery of
incompetency in later years. Meanwhile I am only contemplating the
gradual accumulation of materials.

The reading went on at a steady pace, not without social
intermissions :—

Oct. 11th and 12th.—Rode. Papers. Virgil. Thucydides, both
days. Also some optics. Wrote a long letter home. Read a chapter
of Butler each day. Hume. Breakfasted also with Canning to meet
Lady C[anning]. She received us, I thought, with great kindness, and
spoke a great deal about Lord Grey's conduct with reference to her
husband's memory, with great animation and excitement ; her hand in
a strong tremor. It was impossible not to enter into her feelings.

Then comes the struggle for the palm :—

Monday, November 7th to Saturday 12th.—In the schools or preparing.
Read most of Niebuhr. Finished going over the *Agamemnon*. Got up
Aristophanic and other hard words. Went over my books of extracts,
etc. Read some of Whately's rhetoric. Got up a little Polybius, and
the history out of Livy, decade one. In the schools Wednesday,
Thursday, and Friday ; each day about six and a half hours at work
or under. First Strafford's speech into Latin with logical and rhetorical
questions—the latter somewhat abstract. Dined at Gaskell's and met
Pearson, a clever and agreeable man. On Thursday a piece of Johnson's
preface in morning, in evening critical questions which I did very badly,

but I afterwards heard, better than *the rest*, which I could not and cannot understand. On Friday we had in the morning historical questions. Wrote a vast quantity of matter, ill enough digested. In the evening, Greek to translate and illustrate. Heard cheering accounts indirectly of myself, for which I ought to be very thankful. . . . Dined with Pearson at the Mitre. Very kind in him to ask me. Made Saturday in great measure an idle day. Had a good ride with Gaskell. Spent part of the evening with him. Read about six hours. *Sunday, November* 13*th.*—Chapel thrice. Breakfast and much conversation with Cameron. Read Bible. Some divinity of a character approaching to cram. Looked over my shorter abstract of Butler. Tea with Harrison. Walk with Gaskell. Wine with Hamilton, more of a party than I quite liked or expected. Altogether my mind was in an unsatisfactory state, though I heard a most admirable sermon from Tyler on Bethesda, which could not have been more opportune if written on purpose for those who are going into the schools. But I am cold, timid, and worldly, and not in a healthy state of mind for the great trial of to-morrow, to which I know I am utterly and miserably unequal, but which I also know will be sealed for good. . . .

Here is his picture of his *viva voce* examination :—

November 14*th.*—Spent the morning chiefly in looking over my Polybius ; short abstract of ethics, and definitions. Also some hard words. Went into the schools at ten, and from this time was little troubled with fear. Examined by Stocker in divinity. I did not answer as I could have wished. Hampden [the famous heresiarch] in science, a beautiful examination, and with every circumstance in my favour. He said to me, 'Thank you, you have construed extremely well, and appear to be thoroughly acquainted with your books,' or something to that effect. Then followed a very clever examination in history from Garbett, and an agreeable and short one in my poets from Cremer, who spoke very kindly to me at the close. I was only put on in eight books besides the Testament, namely Rhetoric, Ethics, *Phædo*, Herodotus, Thucydides, *Odyssey*, Aristophanes (*Vespae*), and Persius. Everything was in my favour ; the examiners kind beyond everything ; a good many persons there, and all friendly. At the end of the science, of course, my spirits were much raised, and I could not help at that moment [giving thanks] to Him without whom not even such moderate performances would have been in my power. Afterwards rode to Cuddesdon with the Denisons, and wrote home with exquisite pleasure.

I have read a story by some contemporary how all attempts to puzzle him by questions on the minutest details of Herodotus only brought out his knowledge more fully ; how the excitement reached its climax when the examiner, after testing his mastery of some point of theology, said : 'We will now leave that part of the subject,' and the candidate, carried away by his interest in the subject, answered : 'No, sir ; if you please, we will not leave it yet,' and began to pour forth a fresh stream. Ten days later, after a morning much disturbed and excited he rode in the afternoon, and by half-past four the list was out, with Gladstone and Denison both of them in the first class ; Phillimore and Maurice in the second ; Herbert in the fourth.

Then mathematics were to come. The interval between the two schools he passed at Cuddesdon, working some ten hours a day at his hardest, riding every day with Denison, and all of them in high spirits. But optics, algebra, geometry, calculus, trigonometry and the rest, filled him with misgivings for the future. 'Every day I read, I am more and more thoroughly convinced of my incapacity for the subject.' 'My work continued and my reluctance to exertion increased with it.' For the Sunday before the examination, this is the entry, and a characteristic and remarkable one it is : — 'Teaching in the school morning and evening. Saunders preached well on "Ye cannot serve God and Mammon." Read Bible and four of Horsley's sermons. Paid visits to old people.'

On December 10th the mathematical ordeal began, and lasted four days. The doctor gave him draughts to quiet his excitement. Better than draughts, he read Wordsworth every day. On Sunday (December 11th) he went, as usual, twice to chapel, and heard Newman preach 'a most able discourse of a very philosophical character, more apt for reading than for hearing—at least I, in the jaded state of my mind, was unable to do it any justice.' On December 14th, the list was out, and his name was again in the first class, again along with Denison. As everybody knows, Peel had won a double-first twenty-three years before, and in mathematics Peel had the first class to himself. Mr. Gladstone in each of the two schools was one of five. Anstice, whose counsels and example he counted for so much at one epoch in his collegiate life, in 1830 carried off the same double crown, and was, like Peel, alone in the mathematical first class.

It was an hour of thrilling happiness, between the past and the future, for the future was, I hope, not excluded ; and feeling was well kept in check by the bustle of preparation for speedy departure. Saw the Dean, Biscoe, Saunders (whom I thanked for his extreme kindness), and such of my friends as were in Oxford ; all most warm. The mutual handshaking between Denison, Jeffreys, and myself, was very hearty. Wine with Bruce. . . . Packed up my things. . . . Wrote at more or less length to Mrs. G. [his mother], Gaskell, Phillimore, Mr. Denison, my old tutor Knapp. . . . Left Oxford on the Champion.

December 15th.—After finding the first practicable coach to Cambridge was just able to manage breakfast in Bedford Square. Left Holborn at ten, in Cambridge before five.

Here he was received by Wordsworth, the master of Trinity, and father of his Oxford tutor. He had a visit full of the peculiar excitement and felicity that those who are capable of it know nowhere else than at Oxford and Cambridge. He heard Hallam recite his declamation ; was introduced to the mighty Whewell, to Spedding, the great Baconian, to Smyth, the professor of history, to Blakesley ; renewed his acquaintance with the elder Hallam ; listened to glorious anthems at

Trinity and King's; tried to hear a sermon from Simeon, the head of the English evangelicals; met Stanhope, an old Eton man, and the two sons of Lord Grey; and 'copied a letter of Mr. Pitt's.' From Cambridge he made his way home, having thus triumphantly achieved the first stage of his long life journey. Amid the manifold mutations of his career, to Oxford his affection was passionate as it was constant. 'There is not a man that has passed through that great and famous university that can say with more truth than I can say, I love her from the bottom of my heart.'[1]

VI

Another episode must have a place before I close this chapter. At the end of 1828, the youthful Gladstone had composed a long letter, of which the manuscript survives, to a Liverpool newspaper, earnestly contesting its appalling proposition that 'man has no more control over his belief, than he has over his stature or his colour,' and beseeching the editor to try Leslie's *Short Method with the Deists*, if he be unfortunate enough to doubt the authority of the Bible. At Oxford his fervour carried him beyond the fluent tract to a personal decision. On August 4th, 1830, the entry is this :—
' Began Thucydides. Also working up Herodotus. ἐξηρτυμένος. Construing Thucydides at night. Uncomfortable again and much distracted with doubts as to my future line of conduct. God direct me. I am utterly blind. Wrote a very long letter to my dear father on the subject of my future profession, wishing if possible to bring the question to an immediate and final settlement.' The letter is exorbitant in length, it is vague, it is obscure; but the appeal contained in it is as earnest as any appeal from son to parent on such a subject ever was, and it is of special interest as the first definite indication alike of the extraordinary intensity of his religious disposition, and of that double-mindedness, that division of sensibility between the demands of spiritual and of secular life, which remained throughout one of the marking traits of his career. He declares his conviction that his duty, alike to man as a social being, and as a rational and reasonable being to God, summons him with a voice too imperative to be resisted, to forsake the ordinary callings of the world and to take upon himself the clerical office. The special need of devotion to that office, he argues, must be plain to any one who 'casts his eye over the moral wilderness of the world, who contemplates the pursuits, desires, designs, and principles of the beings that move so busily in it to and fro, without an object beyond the finding food for it, mental or bodily, for the present moment.' This letter the reader will find in full elsewhere.[2] The missionary impulse, the yearning for some apostolic destina-

tion, the glow of self-devotion to a supreme external will, is
a well-known element in the youth of ardent natures of either
sex. In a thousand forms, sometimes for good, sometimes for
evil, such a mood has played its part in history. In this case,
as in many another, the impulse in its first shape did not
endure, but in essence it never faded.

His father replied as a wise man was sure to do, almost with
sympathy, with entire patience, and with thorough common
sense. The son dutifully accepts the admonition that it is too
early to decide so grave an issue, and that the immediate
matter is the approaching performance in the examination
schools. 'I highly approve,' his father had written (Nov. 8th,
1830), 'your proposal to leave undetermined the profession you
are to follow, until you return from the continent and complete
your education in all respects. You will then have seen more
of the world and have greater confidence in the choice you may
make ; for it will then rest wholly with yourself, having our
advice whenever you may wish for it.' The critical issue was
now finally settled. At almost equal length, and in parts of
this second letter no less vague and obscure than the first, but
with more concentrated power, Mr. Gladstone tells his father
(Jan. 17th, 1832) how the excitement has subsided, but still he
sees at hand a great crisis in the history of mankind. New
principles, he says, prevail in morals, politics, education.
Enlightened self-interest is made the substitute for the old
bonds of unreasoned attachment, and under the plausible
maxim that knowledge is power, one kind of ignorance is
made to take the place of another kind. Christianity teaches
that the head is to be exalted through the heart, but Bentham-
ism maintains that the heart is to be amended through the
head. The conflict proceeding in parliament foreshadows a
contest for the existence of the church establishment, to be
assailed through its property. The whole foundation of society
may go. Under circumstances so formidable, he dares not look
for the comparative calm and ease of a professional life. He
must hold himself free of attachment to any single post and
function of a technical nature. And so—to make the long story
short—'My own desires for future life are exactly coincident
with yours, in so far as I am acquainted with them ; believing
them to be a *profession* of the law, with a view substantially
to studying the constitutional branch of it, and a subsequent
experiment, as time and circumstances might offer, on what
is termed public life.' 'It tortures me,' he had written to his
brother John (August 29th, 1830), 'to think of an inclination
opposed to that of my beloved father,' and this was evidently
one of the preponderant motives in his final decision.

In the same letter, while the fire of apostolic devotion was
still fervid within him, he had penned a couple of sentences
that contain words of deeper meaning than he could surely

know :—'I am willing to persuade myself that in spite of other longings which I often feel, my heart is prepared to yield other hopes and other desires for this—of being permitted to be the humblest of those who may be commissioned to set before the eyes of man, still great even in his ruins, the magnificence and the glory of Christian truth. Especially as I feel that my temperament is so excitable, that I should fear giving up my mind to other subjects which have ever proved sufficiently alluring to me, and which I fear would make my life a fever of unsatisfied longings and expectations.' So men unconsciously often hint an oracle of their lives. Perhaps these forebodings of a high-wrought hour may in other hues have at many moments come back to Mr. Gladstone's mind, even in the full sunshine of a triumphant career of duty, virtue, power, and renown.

The entry in his diary, suggested by the return of his birthday (Dec. 29, 1831), closes with the words, 'This has been my debating society year, now, I fancy, done with. Politics are fascinating to me ; perhaps too fascinating.' Higher thoughts than this press in upon him :—

Industry of a kind and for a time there has been, but the industry of necessity, not of principle. I would fain believe that my sentiments in religion have been somewhat enlarged and untrammelled, but if this be true, my responsibility is indeed augmented, but wherein have my deeds of duty been proportionally modified ? . . . One conclusion theoretically has been much on my mind—it is the increased importance and necessity and benefit of prayer—of the life of obedience and self-sacrifice. May God use me as a vessel for His own purposes, of whatever character and results in relation to myself. . . . May the God who loves us all, still vouchsafe me a testimony of His abiding presence in the protracted, though well-nigh dormant life of a desire which at times has risen high in my soul, a fervent and a buoyant hope that I might work an energetic work in this world, and by that work (whereof the worker is only God) I might grow into the image of the Redeemer. . . . It matters not whether the sphere of duty be large or small, but may it be duly filled. May those faint and languishing embers be kindled by the truth of the everlasting spirit into a living and a life-giving flame.

Every reader will remember how just two hundred years before, the sublimest of English poets had on his twenty-third birthday closed the same self-reproach for sluggishness of inward life, with the same aspiration :—

> Yet be it less or more, or soon or slow,
> It shall be still in strictest measure even
> To that same lot however mean or high,
> Towards which time leads me and the will of heaven.
> All is, if I have grace to use it so,
> As ever in my great taskmaster's eye.

Two generations after he had quitted the university, Mr. Gladstone summed up her influence upon him :—

Oxford had rather tended to hide from me the great fact that liberty is a great and precious gift of God, and that human excellence cannot grow up in a nation without it. And yet I do not hesitate to say that Oxford had even at this time laid the foundations of my liberalism. School pursuits had revealed little ; but in the region of philosophy she had initiated if not inured me to the pursuit of truth as an end of study. The splendid integrity of Aristotle, and still more of Butler, conferred upon me an inestimable service. Elsewhere I have not scrupled to speak with severity of myself, but I declare that while in the arms of Oxford, I was possessed through and through with a single-minded and passionate love of truth, with a virgin love of truth, so that, although I might be swathed in clouds of prejudice there was something of an eye within, that might gradually pierce them.

Book II

(1832-1846)

CHAPTER I

ENTERS PARLIAMENT

(1832-1834)

I may speak of the House of Commons as a school of discipline for those who enter it. In my opinion it is a school of extraordinary power and efficacy. It is a great and noble school for the creation of all the qualities of force, suppleness, and versatility of intellect. And it is also a great moral school. It is a school of temper. It is also a school of patience. It is a school of honour, and it is a school of justice.— GLADSTONE (1878).

LEAVING home in the latter part of January (1832), with a Wordsworth for a pocket companion, Mr. Gladstone made his way to Oxford, where he laboured through his packing, settled accounts, 'heard a very able sermon indeed from Newman at St. Mary's,' took his bachelor's degree (Jan. 26), and after a day or two with relatives and friends in London, left England along with his brother John at the beginning of February. He did not return until the end of July. He visited Brussels, Paris, Florence, Naples, Rome, Venice, and Milan. Of this long journey he kept a full record, and it contains one entry of no small moment in his mental history. A conception now began to possess him, that according to one religious school kindled a saving illumination, and according to another threw something of a shade upon his future path. In either view it marked a change of spiritual course, a transformation not of religion as the centre of his being, for that it always was, but of the frame and mould within which religion was to expand.

In entering St. Peter's at Rome (March 31, 1832) he experienced his 'first conception of unity in the Church,' and first longed for its visible attainment. Here he felt 'the pain and shame of the schism which separates us from Rome—whose guilt surely rests not upon the venerable fathers of the English Reformed Church but upon Rome itself, yet whose melancholy effects the mind is doomed to feel when you enter this magnificent temple and behold in its walls the images of Christian saints and the words of everlasting truth ; yet such is the mass of intervening encumbrances that you scarcely own, and can yet more scantily realise, any bond of sympathy or union.' This was no fleeting impression of a traveller. It had been preceded by a disenchantment, for he had made his way from Turin to Pinerol, and seen one of the Vaudois valleys. He had framed a lofty conception of the people as ideal Christians, and he underwent a chill of disappointment on finding them apparently much like other men. Even the pastor, though a quiet, inoffensive man, gave no sign of energy or of what would have been called in England vital religion. With this chill at his heart he came upon the atmosphere of gorgeous Rome. It was, however, in the words of Clough's fine line from *Easter Day*, 'through the great sinful streets of Naples as he passed,' that a great mutation overtook him.

One Sunday (May 13) something, I know not what, set me on examining the occasional offices of the church in the prayer book. They made a strong impression upon me on that very day, and the impression has never been effaced. I had previously taken a great deal of teaching direct from the Bible, as best I could, but now the figure of the Church arose before me as a teacher too, and I gradually found in how incomplete and fragmentary a manner I had drawn divine truth from the sacred volume, as indeed I had also missed in the thirty-nine articles some things which ought to have taught me better. Such, for I believe that I have given the fact as it occurred, in its silence and its solitude, was my first introduction to the august conception of the Church of Christ. It presented to me Christianity under an aspect in which I had not yet known it : its ministry of symbols, its channels of grace, its unending line of teachers joining from the Head : a sublime construction, based throughout upon historic fact, uplifting the idea of the community in which we live, and of the access which it enjoys through the new and living way to the presence of the Most High. From this time I began to feel my way by degrees into or towards a true notion of the Church. It became a definite and organised idea when, at the suggestion of James Hope, I read the just published and remarkable work of Palmer. But the charm of freshness lay upon that first disclosure of 1832.

This mighty question :—what is the nature of a church and what the duties, titles, and symbols of faithful membership, which in divers forms had shaken the world for so many ages and now first dawned upon his ardent mind, was the germ of a deep and lasting pre-occupation of which we shall speedily and without cessation find abundant traces.

II

A few weeks later, the great rival interest in Mr. Gladstone's life, if rival we may call it, was forced into startling prominence

before him. At Milan he received a letter from Lord Lincoln,
saying that he was commissioned by his father, the Duke of
Newcastle, to inform him that his influence in the borough of
Newark was at Mr. Gladstone's disposal if he should be ready
to enter parliamentary life. This was the fruit of his famous
anti-reform speech at the Oxford Union. No wonder that such
an offer made him giddy. 'This stunning and overpowering
proposal,' he says to his father (July 8), 'naturally left me the
whole of the evening on which I received it, in a flutter of
confusion. Since that evening there has been time to reflect,
and to see that it is not of so intoxicating a character as it
seemed at first. First, because the Duke of Newcastle's offer
must have been made at the instance of a single person
(Lincoln), that person young and sanguine, and I may say in
such a matter partial. . . . This much at least became clear to
me by the time I had recovered my breath; that decidedly
more than mere permission from my dear father would be
necessary to authorise my entering on the consideration of
particulars at all.' And then he falls into a vein of devout
reflection, almost as if this sudden destination of his life were
some irrevocable priesthood or vow of monastic profession, and
not the mere stringent secularity of labour in a parliament.
It would be thin and narrow to count all this an overstrain.
To a nature like his, of such eager strength of equipment;
conscious of life as a battle and not a parade; apt for all
external action yet with a burning glow of light and fire in the
internal spirit; resolute from the first in small things and in
great against aimless drift and eddy,—to such an one the
moment of fixing alike the goal and the track may well have
been grave.

    Then points of doubt arose. 'It is, I daresay, in your
recollection,'—this to his father—'that at the time when Mr.
Canning came to power, the Duke of Newcastle, in the House
of Lords, declared him the most profligate minister the country
had ever had. Now it struck me to inquire of myself, does
the duke know the feelings I happen to entertain towards
Mr. Canning? Does he know, or can he have had in his mind, my
father's connection with Mr. Canning?' The duke had in fact
been one of the busiest and bitterest of Canning's enemies, and
had afterwards in the same spirit striven with might and main
to keep Huskisson out of the Wellington cabinet. Another
awkwardness appeared. The duke had offered a handsome
contribution towards expenses. Would not this tend to abridge
the member's independence? What was the footing on which
patron and member were to stand? Mr. Gladstone was
informed by his brother that the duke had neither heretofore
asked for pledges, nor now demanded them.

    After a very brief correspondence with his shrewd and
generous father, the plunge was taken, and on his return to

England, after a fortnight spent 'in an amphibious state between
that of a candidate and ἰδιώτης or private person,' he issued his
address to the electors of Newark (August 4, 1832). He did
not go actually on to the ground until the end of September.
The intervening weeks he spent with his family at Torquay,
where he varied electioneering correspondence and yachting
with plenty of sufficiently serious reading from Blackstone and
Plato and the *Excursion* down to *Corinne*. One Sunday morning (September 23), his father burst into his bedroom, with the
news that his presence was urgently needed at Newark. 'I
rose, dressed, and breakfasted speedily, with infinite disgust.
I left Torquay at 8¾ and devoted my Sunday to the journey.
Was I right? . . . My father drove me to Newton ; chaise to
Exeter. There near an hour ; went to the cathedral and heard
a part of the prayers. Mail to London. Conversation with
a tory countryman who got in for a few miles, on Sunday
travelling, which we agreed in disapproving. Gave him some
tracts. Excellent mail. Dined at Yeovil ; read a little of the
Christian Year [published 1827]. At 6½ A.M. arrived at
Piccadilly, 18½ hours from Exeter. Went to Fetter Lane,
washed and breakfasted, and came off at 8 o'clock by a High
Flyer for Newark. The sun hovered red and cold through the
heavy fog of London sky, but in the country the day was fine.
Tea at Stamford ; arrived at Newark at midnight.' Such in
forty hours was the first of Mr. Gladstone's countless political
pilgrimages.

His two election addresses are a curious starting-point for
so memorable a journey. Thrown into the form of a modern
programme, the points are these :—union of church and state,
the defence in particular of our Irish establishments ; correction of the poor laws ; allotment of cottage grounds ; adequate
remuneration of labour ; a system of Christian instruction
for the West Indian slaves, but no emancipation until that
instruction had fitted them for it ; a dignified and impartial
foreign policy. The duke was much startled by the passage
about labour receiving adequate remuneration, 'which unhappily among several classes of our fellow-countrymen is not
now the case.' He did not, however, interfere. The whig
newspaper said roundly of the first of Mr. Gladstone's two
addresses, that a more jumbled collection of words had seldom
been sent from the press. The tory paper, on the contrary,
congratulated the constituency on a candidate of considerable
commercial experience and talent. The anti-slavery men
fought him stoutly. They put his name into their black
schedule with nine-and-twenty other candidates, they harried
him with posers from a pamphlet of his father's, and they met
his doctrine that if slavery were sinful the Bible would not
have commended the regulation of it, by bluntly asking him
on the hustings whether he knew a text in Exodus declaring

that 'he that stealeth a man and selleth him, or if he be found
in his hand, he shall surely be put to death.' His father's
pamphlets undoubtedly exposed a good deal of surface. We
cannot be surprised that any adherent of these standard
sophistries should be placed on the black list of the zealous
soldiers of humanity. The candidate held to the ground he
had taken at Oxford and in his election address, and apparently
made converts. He had an interview with forty voters of
abolitionist complexion at his hotel, and according to the
friendly narrative of his brother, who was present, 'he shone
not only in his powers of conversation, but by the tact, quickness, and talent, with which he made his replies, to the
thorough and complete satisfaction of baptists, wesleyan
methodists, and I may say even, of almost every religious sect!
Not one refused their vote : they came forward, and enrolled
their names, though before, I believe, they never supported
any one on the duke's interest!'

The humours of an election of the ancient sort are a very
old story, and Newark had its full share of them. The register
contained rather under sixteen hundred voters on a scot and
lot qualification, to elect a couple of members. The principal
influence over about one-quarter of them was exercised by the
Duke of Newcastle, who three years before had punished the
whigs of the borough for the outrage of voting against his
nominee, by serving, in concert with another proprietor, forty
of them with notice to quit. Then the trodden worm turned.
The notices were framed, affixed to poles, and carried with
bands of music through the streets. Even the audacity of a
petition to parliament was projected. The duke, whose chief
fault was not to know that time had brought him into a novel
age, defended himself with the haughty truism, then just
ceasing to be true, that he had a right to do as he liked with
his own. This clear-cut enunciation of a vanishing principle
became a sort of landmark, and gave to his name an unpleasing
immortality in our political history. In the high tide of agitation for reform the whigs gave the duke a beating, and brought
their man to the top of the poll, a tory being his colleague.
Handley, the tory, on our present occasion seemed safe, and
the fight lay between Mr. Gladstone and Serjeant Wilde, the
sitting whig, a lawyer of merit and eminence, who eighteen
years later went to the woolsack as Lord Truro. Reform at
Newark was already on the ebb. Mr. Gladstone, though
mocked as a mere schoolboy, and fiercely assailed as a slavery
man, exhibited from the first hour of the fight tremendous gifts
of speech and skill of fence. His Red club worked valiantly ;
the serjeant did not play his cards skilfully ; and pretty early
in the long struggle it was felt that the duke would this time
come into his own again. The young student soon showed
that his double first class, his love of books, his religious pre-

occupations, had not unfitted him by a single jot for one of the most arduous of all forms of the battle of life. He proved a diligent and prepossessing canvasser, an untiring combatant, and of course the readiest and most fluent of speakers. Wilde after hearing him said sententiously to one of his own supporters, 'There is a great future before this young man.' The rather rotten borough became suffused with the radiant atmosphere of Olympus. The ladies presented their hero with a banner of red silk, and an address expressive of their conviction that the good old Red cause was the salvation of their ancient borough. The young candidate in reply speedily put it in far more glowing colours. It was no trivial banner of a party club, it was the red flag of England that he saw before him, the symbol of national moderation and national power, under which, when every throne on the continent had crumbled into dust beneath the tyrannous strength of France, mankind had found sure refuge and triumphant hope, and the blast that tore every other ensign to tatters served only to unfold their own and display its beauty and its glory. Amid these oratorical splendours the old hands of the club silently supplemented eloquence and argument by darker agencies, of which happily the candidate knew little until after. There was a red band and each musician received fifteen shillings a day, there happening accidentally to be among them no fewer than ten patriotic red plumpers. Large tea-parties attracted red ladies. The inns great and small were thrown joyously open on one side or other, and when the time came, our national heroes from Robin Hood to Lord Nelson and the Duke of Wellington, as well as half the animal kingdom, the swan and salmon, horses, bulls, boars, lions, and eagles, of all the colours of the rainbow and in every kind of strange partnership, sent in bills for meat and liquor supplied to free and independent electors to the tune of a couple of thousand pounds. Apart from these black arts, and apart from the duke's interest, there was a good force of the staunch and honest type, the life-blood of electioneering and the salvation of party government, who cried stoutly, 'I was born Red, I live Red, and I will die Red.' 'We started on the canvass,' says one who was with Mr. Gladstone, 'at eight in the morning and worked at it for about nine hours, with a great crowd, band and flags, and innumerable glasses of beer and wine all jumbled together; then a dinner of 30 or 40, with speeches and songs until say ten o'clock; then he always played a rubber of whist, and about twelve or one I got to bed and not to sleep.'

At length the end came. At the nomination the show of hands was against the reds, but when the poll was taken and closed on the second day, Gladstone appeared at the head of it with 887 votes, against 798 for his colleague Handley, and 726 for the fallen Wilde. 'Yesterday' (Dec. 13, 1832), he tells his

father, 'we went to the town hall at 9 A.M., when the mayor
cast up the numbers and declared the poll. While he was
doing this the popular wrath vented itself for the most part
upon Handley. . . . The serjeant obtained me a hearing, and I
spoke for perhaps an hour or more, but it was flat work, as
they were no more than patient, and agreed with but little
that I said. The serjeant then spoke for an hour and a half.
. . . He went into matters connected with his own adieu to
Newark, besought the people most energetically to bear with
their disappointment like men, and expressed his farewell with
great depth of feeling. Affected to tears himself, he affected
others also. In the evening near fifty dined here [Clinton
Arms] and the utmost enthusiasm was manifested.' The new
member began his first speech as a member of parliament as
follows :—

Gentlemen ; in looking forward to the field which is now opened
before me, I cannot but conceive that I shall often be reproached with
being not your representative but the representative of the Duke of
Newcastle. Now I should rather incline to exaggerate than to ex-
tenuate such connection as does exist between me and that nobleman :
and for my part should have no reluctance to see every sentiment which
ever passed between us, whether by letter or by word of mouth, exposed to the view of the world. I met the Duke of Newcastle upon the
broad ground of public principle, and upon that ground alone. I own
no other bond of union with him than this, that he in his exalted
sphere, and I in my humble one, entertained the same persuasion, that
the institutions of this country are to be defended against those who
threaten their destruction, at all hazards, and to all extremities. Why
do you return me to parliament ? Not because I am the Duke of Newcastle's man, simply : but because, coinciding with the duke in political
sentiment, you likewise admit that one possessing so large a property
here, and faithfully discharging the duties which the possession of that
property entails, ought in the natural course of things to exercise a
certain influence. You return me to parliament, not merely because I
am the Duke of Newcastle's man : but because both the man whom
the duke has sent, and the duke himself, are *your men*.

The election was of course pointed to by rejoicing conservatives as a proof the more of that reaction which the ministerial
and radical press was audacious enough to laugh at. This
borough, says the local journalist, was led away by the bubble
reform, to support those who by specious and showy qualification had dazzled their eyes ; delusion had vanished, shadows
satisfied no longer, Newark was restored to its high place in
the esteem of the friends of order and good government. Of
course the intimates of the days of his youth were delighted.
We want such a man as Gladstone, wrote Hallam to Gaskell
(October 1, 1832) 'in some things he is likely to be obstinate
and prejudiced ; but he has a fine fund of high chivalrous tory
sentiment, and a tongue, moreover, to let it loose with. I
think he may do a great deal.'

In the course of his three months of sojourn at Newark Mr. Gladstone paid his first visit to the great man at Clumber.

The duke received me, he tells his father, with the greatest kindness, and conversed with such ease and familiarity of manner as speedily to dispel a certain degree of awe which I had previously entertained, and to throw me perhaps more off my guard than I ought to have been in company with a man of his age and rank. . . . The utmost regularity and subordination appears to prevail in the family, and no doubt it is in many respects a good specimen of the old English style. He is apparently a most affectionate father, but still the sons and daughters are under a certain degree of restraint in his presence. . . . A man, be his station of life what it may, more entirely divested of personal pride and arrogance, more single-minded and disinterested in his views, or more courageous and resolute in determination to adhere to them as the dictates of his own conscience, I cannot conceive.

From this frigid interior Mr. Gladstone made his way to the genial company of Milnes Gaskell at Thornes and had a delightful week. Thence he proceeded to spend some days with his sick mother at Leamington. 'We have been singularly dealt with as a family,' he observes, 'once snatched from a position where we were what is called entering society, and sent to comparative seclusion as regards family establishment —and now again prevented from assuming the situation that seems the natural termination of a career like my father's. Here is a noble trial—for me personally to exercise a kindly and unselfish feeling, if amid the excitements and allurements now near me, I am enabled duly to realise the bond of consanguinity and suffer with those whom Providence has ordained to suffer.' And this assuredly was no mere entry in a journal. In betrothals, marriages, deaths, on all the great occasions of life in his circle, his letters under old-fashioned formalities of phrase yet beat with a marked and living pulse of genuine interest, solicitude, sympathy, unselfishness and union.

III

As always, he sought refreshment from turmoil that was only moderately congenial to him, in reading and writing. Among much else he learns Shelley by heart, but his devotion to Wordsworth is unshaken. 'One remarkable similarity prevails between Wordsworth and Shelley; the quality of combining and connecting everywhere external nature with internal and unseen mind. But how different are they in applications. It frets and irritates the one, it is the key to the peacefulness of the other.' Two books of *Paradise Regained*, he finds 'very objectionable on religious grounds,'—the books presumably where Milton has been convicted of Arian heresy. He still has energy enough left for more mundane things, to write a succession of articles for the *Liverpool Standard*, and he finds time to record his joy (December 7) over 'five Eton

first classes' at Oxford. Then, by and by, the election accounts
come in. The arrangement had been made that the expenses
were not to exceed a thousand pounds, of which the duke was
to contribute one half, and John Gladstone the other half. It
now appeared that twice as much would not suffice. The new
member flung himself with all his soul into a struggle with his
committee against the practice of opening public houses and
the exorbitant demands that came of it. Open houses, he protested, meant profligate expenditure and organized drunkenness ; they were not a pecuniary question, but a question of
right and wrong. In the afternoon of the second day of polling,
his agent had said to him, speaking about special constables,
that he scarcely knew how they could be got if wanted, for he
thought nearly every man in the town was drunk. It was in
vain that the committee assured him of the discouraging truth
that a certain proportion of the voters could not be got to the
poll without a breakfast ; and an observer from another planet
might perhaps have asked himself whether all this was so
remarkable an improvement on the duke doing what he liked
with his own. Mr. Gladstone still stood to it that a system
of entertainment that ended in producing a state of general
intoxication, was the most demoralising and vicious of all forms
of outlay, and the Newark worthies were bewildered and confounded by the gigantic dialectical and rhetorical resources of
their incensed representative. The fierce battle lasted, with
moments of mitigation, over many of the thirteen years of the
connection. Of all the measures that Mr. Gladstone was
destined in days to come to place upon the statute book, none
was more salutary than the law that purified corrupt practices
at elections.[1]

On his birthday at the close of this eventful year, here is
his entry in his diary :—'On this day I have completed my
twenty-third year. . . . The exertions of the year have been
smaller than those of the last, but in some respects the diminution has been unavoidable. In future I hope circumstances
will bind me down to work with a rigour which my natural
sluggishness will find it impossible to elude. I wish that I
could hope my frame of mind had been in any degree removed
from earth and brought nearer to heaven, that the habit of
my mind had been imbued with something of that spirit which
is not of this world. I have now familiarised myself with
maxims sanctioning and encouraging a degree of intercourse
with society, perhaps attended with much risk. . . . Nor do I
now think myself warranted in withdrawing from the practices
of my fellow men except when they really *involve* an encouragement of sin, in which case I do certainly rank races and
theatres. . . .' 'Periods like these,' he writes to his friend
Gaskell (January 3, 1833), 'grievous generally in many of their

[1] Sir Henry James's Act (1883).

results, are by no means unfavourable to the due growth and progress of individual character. I remember a very wise saying of Archidamus in Thucydides, that the being educated ἐν τοῖς ἀναγκαιοτάτοις brings strength and efficacy to the character.'[1]

In one of his letters to his father at this exciting epoch Mr. Gladstone says, that before the sudden opening now made for him, what he had marked out for himself was 'a good many years of silent reading and inquiry.' That blessed dream was over ; his own temperament and outer circumstances, both of them made its realisation impossible ; but in a sense he clung to it all his days. He entered at Lincoln's Inn (January 25), and he dined pretty frequently in hall down to 1839, meeting many old Eton and Oxford acquaintances, more genuine law students than himself. He kept thirteen terms but was never called to the bar. If he had intended to undergo a legal training, the design was ended by Newark. After residing for a short time in lodgings in Jermyn Street, he took quarters at the Albany (March 1833), which remained his London home for six years. 'I am getting on rapidly with my furnishing,' he tells his father, 'and I shall be able, I feel confident, to do it all, including plate, within the liberal limits which you allow. I cannot warmly enough thank you for the terms and footing on which you propose to place me in the chambers, but I really fear that after this year my allowance in all will be greater not only than I have any title to, but than I ought to accept without blushing.' He became a member of the Oxford and Cambridge Club the previous month,[2] and now was 'elected *without* my will (but not more than without it) a member of the Carlton Club.' He would not go to dinner parties on Sundays, not even with Sir Robert Peel. He was closely attentive to the minor duties of social life, if duties they be ; he was a strict observer of the etiquette of calls, and on some afternoons he notes that he made a dozen or fourteen of them. He frequented musical parties where his fine voice, now reasonably well trained, made him a welcome guest, and he goes to public concerts where he finds Pasta and Schröder splendid. His irrepressible desire to expand himself in writing or in speech found a vent in constant articles in the *Liverpool Standard*, neither better nor worse than the ordinary juvenilia of a keen young college politician. He was confident that whether estimated by their numbers, their wealth, or their respectability, the conservatives indubitably held in their hands the means and elements of permanent power. He discharges a fusillade from Roman history against the bare idea of vote

[1] Thuc. i. 84, § 7.—'We should remember that man differs little from man, except that he turns out best who is trained in the sharpest school.'

[2] Proposed by Sir R. Inglis and seconded by George Denison, afterwards the militant Archdeacon of Taunton. He was on the committee from 1834 to 1838, and he withdrew from the Club at the end of 1842.

by ballot, quotes Cicero as its determined enemy, and ascribes to secret suffrage the fall of the republic. He quotes with much zest a sentence from an ultra-radical journal that the life of the West Indian negro is happiness itself compared with that of the poor inmate of our spinning-mills. He scores a good point for the patron of Newark, by an eloquent article on the one man who had laboured to retrieve the miserable condition of the factory children, and ends with a taunting reminder to the reformers that this one man, Sadler,[1] was the nominee of a borough-monger, and that borough-monger the Duke of Newcastle.

It need not be said that his church-going never flagged. In 1840 his friend, the elder Acland, interested himself in forming a small brotherhood, with rules for systematic exercises of devotion and works of mercy. Mr. Gladstone was one of the number. The names were not published, nor did any one but the treasurer know the amounts given. The pledge to personal and active benevolence seems not to have been strongly operative, for at the end of 1845 (Dec. 7) Mr. Gladstone writes to Hope in reference to Acland's scheme :—'The desire we then both felt passed off, as far as I am concerned, into a plan of asking only a donation and subscription. Now it is very difficult to satisfy the demands of duty to the poor by money alone. On the other hand, it is extremely hard for me—and I suppose possibly for you—to give them much in the shape of time and thought, for both with me we are already tasked up to and beyond their powers . . . I much wish we could execute some plan which without demanding much time would entail the discharge of some humble and humbling office. . . . If you thought with me—and I do not see why you should not, except to assume the reverse is paying myself a compliment—let us go to work, as in the young days of the college plan but with a more direct and less ambitious purpose.' Of this we may see something later. At a great service at St. Paul's, he notes the glory alike of sight and sound as 'possessing that remarkable criterion of the sublime, a grand result from a combination of simple elements.' Edward Irving did not attract ; 'a scene pregnant with melancholy instruction.' He was immensely struck by Melvill, whom some of us have heard pronounced by the generation before us to be the most puissant of all the men in his calling. 'His sentiments,' says Mr. Gladstone, 'are manly in tone ; he deals powerfully with all his subjects ; his language is flowing and unbounded ; his imagery varied and intensely strong. Vigorous

---

[1] Sadler is now not much more than a name, except to students of the history of social reform in England, known to some by a couple of articles of Macaulay's, written in that great man's least worthy and least agreeable style, and by the fact that Macaulay beat him at Leeds in 1832. But he deserves our honourable recollection on the ground mentioned by Mr. Gladstone, as a man of indefatigable and effective zeal in one of the best of causes.

and lofty as are his conceptions, he is not, I think, less remarkable for soundness and healthiness of mind.' Such a passage
shows among other things how the diarist was already teaching himself to analyse the art of oratory. I may note one
rather curious habit, no doubt practised with a view to
training in the art of speech. Besides listening to as many
sermons as possible, he was also for a long time fond of
reading them aloud, especially Dr. Arnold's, in rather a
peculiar way. 'My plan is,' he says, 'to strengthen or qualify
or omit expressions as I go along.'

IV

In an autobiographical note, written in the late days of
his life, when he had become the only commoner left who had
sat in the old burned House of Commons, he says :—

I took my seat at the opening of 1833, provided unquestionably with
a large stock of schoolboy bashfulness. The first time that business
required me to go to the arm of the chair to say something to the
Speaker, Manners Sutton—the first of seven whose subject I have been—
who was something of a Keate, I remember the revival in me bodily of
the frame of mind in which a schoolboy stands before his master. But
apart from an incidental recollection of this kind, I found it most
difficult to believe with any reality of belief, that such a poor and
insignificant creature as I, could really belong to, really form a *part* of,
an assembly which, notwithstanding the prosaic character of its entire
visible equipment, I felt to be so august. What I may term its corporeal
conveniences were, I may observe in passing, marvellously small. I do
not think that in any part of the building it afforded the means of so
much as washing the hands. The residences of members were at that
time less distant : but they were principally reached on foot. When a
large House broke up after a considerable division, a copious dark
stream found its way up Parliament Street, Whitehall, and Charing
Cross.

I remember that there occurred some case in which a constituent
(probably a maltster) at Newark sent me a communication which made
oral communication with the treasury, or with the chancellor of the
exchequer (then Lord Althorp), convenient. As to the means of bringing this about, I was puzzled and abashed. Some experienced friend on
the opposition bench, probably Mr. Goulburn, said to me, There is Lord
Althorp sitting alone on the treasury bench, go to him and tell him
your business. With such encouragement I did it. Lord Althorp
received me in the kindest manner possible, alike to my pleasure and
my surprise.

The exact composition of the first reformed House of
Commons was usually analysed as tories, 144 ; reformers, 395 ;
English and Scotch radicals, 76 ; Irish repealers, 43. Mr. Gladstone was for counting the decided conservatives as 160, and
reckoning as a separate group a small party who had once
been tories and now ranked between conservative opposition
and whig ministers. The Irish representatives he divided

between 28 tories, and a body of 50 who were made up of ministerialists, conditional repealers, and tithe extinguishers. He heard Joseph Hume, the most effective of the leading radicals, get the first word in the reformed parliament, speaking for an hour and perhaps justifying O'Connell's witty saying that Hume would have been an excellent speaker, if only he would finish a sentence before beginning the next but one after it.

No more diligent member of parliament than Mr. Gladstone ever sat upon the green benches. He read his blue-books, did his duty by election committees, and on the first occasion when, in consequence of staying a little too long at a dinner at the Duke of Hamilton's, he missed a division, his self-reproach was almost as sharp as if he had fallen into mortal sin. This is often enough the way with virtuous young members, but Mr. Gladstone's zealous ideal of parliamentary duty lasted, and both at first and always he was a singular union of deep meditative seriousness with untiring animation, assiduity, and practical energy and force working over a wide field definitely mapped.

In the assembly where he was one day to rank among the most powerful orators ever inscribed upon its golden roll, he first opened his lips in a few words on a Newark petition (April 30) and shortly after (May 21) he spoke two or three minutes on an Edinburgh petition. A little later the question of slavery, where he knew every inch of the ground, brought him to a serious ordeal. In May, Stanley as colonial secretary introduced the proposals of the government for the gradual abolition of colonial slavery. Abolition was to be preceded by an intermediate stage, designated as apprenticeship, to last for twelve years; and the planters were to be helped through the difficulties of the transition by a loan of fifteen millions. In the course of the proceedings, the intermediate period was shortened from twelve years to seven, and the loan of fifteen millions was transformed into a free gift of twenty. To this scheme John Gladstone, whose indomitable energy made him the leading spirit of the West Indian interest, was consistently opposed, and he naturally became the mark of abolitionist attack. The occasion of Mr. Gladstone's first speech was an attack by Lord Howick on the manager of John Gladstone's Demerara estates, whom he denounced as 'the murderer of slaves,'—an attack made without notice to the two sons of the incriminated proprietor sitting in front of him. He declared that the slaves on the Vreedenhoop sugar plantations were systematically worked to death in order to increase the crop. Mr. Gladstone tried in vain to catch the eye of the Chairman on May 30, and the next day he wished to speak but saw no good opportunity. 'The emotions through which one passes, at least through which I pass, in anticipating such an effort as

this, are painful and humiliating. The utter prostration and
depression of spirit ; the deep sincerity, the burdensome and
overpowering reality of the feeling of mere feebleness and
incapacity, felt in the inmost heart, yet not to find relief by
expression, because the expression of such things goes for affectation, — these things I am unequal to describe, yet I have
experienced them now.' On June 3, the chance came. Here is
his story of the day : ' Began *le miei Prigioni*. West India meeting of members at one at Lord Sandon's. Resolutions discussed
and agreed upon ; . . . . dined early. Re-arranged my notes
for the debate. Rode. House 5 to 1. Spoke my first time, for
50 minutes. My leading desire was to benefit the cause of those
who are now so sorely beset. The House heard me very kindly,
and my friends were satisfied. Tea afterwards at the Carlton.'
The speech was an uncommon success. Stanley, the minister
mainly concerned, congratulated him with more than those
conventional compliments which the good nature of the House
of Commons expects to be paid to any decent beginner. 'I
never listened to any speech with greater pleasure,' said
Stanley, himself the prince of debaters and then in the most
brilliant part of his career ; 'the member for Newark argued his
case with a temper, an ability, and a fairness which may well
be cited as a good model to many older members of this House.'
His own leader, though he spoke later, said nothing in his
speech about the new recruit, but two days after Mr. Gladstone
mentioned that Sir R. Peel came up to him and praised Monday
night's affair. King William wrote to Althorp : 'he rejoices
that a young member has come forward in so promising a
manner, as Viscount Althorp states Mr. W. E. Gladstone to
have done.'[1]

Apart from its special vindication in close detail of the state
of things at Vreedenhoop as being no worse than others, the
points of the speech on this great issue of the time were familiar
ones. He confessed with shame and pain that cases of cruelty
had existed, and would always exist, under the system of
slavery, and that this was 'a substantial reason why the
British legislature and public should set themselves in good
earnest to provide for its extinction.' He admitted, too, that
we had not fulfilled our Christian obligations by communicating the inestimable benefits of our religion to the slaves in
our colonies, and that the belief among the early English
planters, that if you made a man a Christian you could not
keep him a slave, had led them to the monstrous conclusion
that they ought not to impart Christianity to their slaves.
Its extinction was a consummation devoutly to be desired, and
in good earnest to be forwarded, but immediate and uncon-
ditioned emancipation, without a previous advance in character,
must place the negro in a state where he would be his own worst

[1] *Memoir of Althorp*, p. 471.

enemy, and so must crown all the wrongs already done to him
by cutting off the last hope of rising to a higher level in social
existence. At some later period of his life Mr. Gladstone read
a corrected report of his first speech, and found its tone much
less than satisfactory. 'But of course,' he adds, 'allowance
must be made for the enormous and most blessed change
of opinion since that day on the subject of negro slavery.
I must say, however, that even before this time I had come
to entertain little or no confidence in the proceedings of the
resident agents in the West Indies.' 'I can now see plainly
enough,' he said sixty years later, 'the sad defects, the real
illiberalism of my opinions on that subject. Yet they were
not illiberal as compared with the ideas of the times, and as
declared in parliament in 1833 they obtained the commenda-
tion of the liberal leaders.'

It is fair to remember that Pitt, Fox, Grenville, and Grey,
while eager to bring the slave trade to an instant end,
habitually disclaimed as a calumny any intention of emancipating the blacks on the sugar islands. In 1807, when the
foul blot of the trade was abolished, even Wilberforce himself
discouraged attempts to abolish slavery, though the noble
philanthropist soon advanced to the full length of his own
principles. Peel in 1833 would have nothing to do with either
immediate emancipation or gradual. Disraeli has put his view
on deliberate record that 'the movement of the middle class
for the abolition of slavery was virtuous, but it was not wise.
It was an ignorant movement. The history of the abolition of
slavery by the English and its consequences, would be a narrative of ignorance, injustice, blundering, waste, and havoc, not
easily paralleled in the history of mankind.'[1]

A week later Lord Howick proposed to move for papers
relating to Vreedenhoop. Lord Althorp did not refuse to grant
them, but recommended him to drop his motion, as Mr. Gladstone insisted on the equal necessity of a similar return for all
neighbouring plantations. Howick withdrew his motion,
though he afterwards asserted that ministers had declined the
return, which was not true. When Buxton moved to reduce
the term of apprenticeship, Mr. Gladstone voted against him.
On the following day Stanley, without previous intimation,
announced the change from twelve years to seven. 'I spoke
a few sentences,' Mr. Gladstone enters in his diary, 'in much
confusion : for I could not easily recover from the sensation
caused by the sudden overthrow of an entire and undoubting
reliance.'

The question of electoral scandals at Liverpool, which
naturally excited lively interest in a family with local ties
so strong, came up in various forms during the session, and on
one of these occasions (July 4) Mr. Gladstone spoke upon it,

[1] *Lord George Bentinck*, chapter xviii. p. 324.

'for twenty minutes or more, anything but satisfactorily to myself.' Nor can the speech now be called satisfactory by any one else, except for the enunciation of the sound maxim that the giver of a bribe deserves punishment quite as richly as the receiver. Four days later he spoke for something less than half an hour on the third reading of the Irish Church Reform bill. 'I was heard,' he tells his father, 'with kindness and indulgence, but it is, after all, uphill work to address an assembly so much estranged in feeling from one's self.' Peel's speech was described as temporising, and the deliverance of his young lieutenant was temporising too, though firm on the necessary principle, as he called it, of which the world was before long to hear so much from him, that the nation should be taxed for the support of a national church.

Besides his speeches he gave a full number of party votes, some of them interesting enough in view of the vast career before him. I think the first of them all was in the majority of 428 against 40 upon O'Connell's amendment for repeal,—an occasion that came vividly to his memory on the eve of his momentous change of policy in 1886. He voted for the worst clauses of the Irish Coercion bill, including the court-martial clause. He fought steadily against the admission of Jews to parliament. He fought against the admission of dissenters without a test to the universities, which he described as seminaries for the established church. He supported the existing corn law. He said 'No' to the property tax and 'Aye' for retaining the house and window taxes. He resisted a motion of Hume's for the abolition of military and naval sinecures (February 14), and another motion of the same excellent man's for the abolition of all flogging in the army save for mutiny and drunkenness. He voted against the publication of the division lists. He voted with ministers both against shorter parliaments, and (April 25) against the ballot, a cardinal reform carried by his own government forty years later. On the other hand he voted (July 5) with Lord Ashley against postponing his beneficent policy of factory legislation ; but he did not vote either way a fortnight later when Althorp sensibly reduced the limit of ten hours' work in factories from the impracticable age of eighteen proposed by Ashley, to the age of thirteen. He supported a bill against work on Sundays.

v

A page or two from his diary will carry us succinctly enough over the rest of the first and second years of his parliamentary life.

July 21, 1833, *Sunday.*— . . . Wrote some lines and prose also. Finished Strype. Read Abbott and Sumner aloud. Thought for some hours on my own future destiny, and took a solitary walk to and about Kensington Gardens. *July* 23.—Read *L'Allemagne, Rape of the Lock,* and finished factory report. *July* 25.—Went to breakfast with old Mr. Wilberforce, introduced by his son. He is cheerful and serene, a beautiful picture of old age in sight of immortality. Heard him pray with his family. Blessing and honour are upon his head. *July* 30.— *L'Allemagne.* Bulwer's England. Parnell. Looked at my Plato. Rode. House. *July* 31.—Hallam breakfasted with me. . . . Committee on West India bill finished. . . . German lesson. *August* 2.—Worked German several hours. Read half of the *Bride of Lammermoor*. *L'Allemagne.* Rode. House. *August* 3.—German lesson and worked alone. . . . Attended Mr. Wilberforce's funeral; it brought solemn thoughts, particularly about the slaves. This a burdensome question. [German kept up steadily for many days.] *August* 9.—House. . . . voted in 48 to 87 against legal tender clause. . . . Read Tasso. *August* 11.—St. James's morning and afternoon. Read Bible. Abbott (finished) and a sermon of Blomfield's aloud. Wrote a paraphrase of part of chapter 8 of Romans. *August* 15.—Committee 1-3¼. Rode. Plato. Finished Tasso, canto 1. Anti-slavery observations on bill. German vocabulary and exercise. *August* 16.—2¾-3½ Committee finished. German lesson. Finished Plato, *Republic*, Bk. v. Preparing to pack. *August* 17.—Started for Aberdeen on board *Queen of Scotland* at 12. *August* 18*th*.—Rose to breakfast but uneasily. Attempted reading, and read most of Baxter's narrative. Not too unwell to reflect. *August* 19*th*.— Remained in bed. Read Goethe and translated a few lines. Also *Beauties of Shakespere*. In the evening it blew; very ill though in bed. Could not help admiring the crests of the waves even as I stood at cabin window. *August* 20.—Arrived 8½ A.M.—56½ hours.

His father met him, and in the evening he and his brother found themselves at the new paternal seat. In 1829 John Gladstone, after much negotiation, had bought the estate of Fasque in Kincardineshire for £80,000, to which and to other Scotch affairs he devoted his special and personal attention pretty exclusively. The home at Seaforth was broken up, though relatives remained there or in the neighbourhood. For some time he had a house in Edinburgh for private residence— the centre house in Atholl Crescent. They used for three or four years to come in from Kincardineshire, and spend the winter months in Edinburgh. Fasque was his home for the rest of his days. This was W. E. Gladstone's first visit, followed by at least one long annual spell for the remaining eighteen years of his father's life.

On the morning of his arrival, he notes, 'I rode to the mill of Kincairn to see Mackay who was shot last night. He was suffering much and seemed near death. Read the Holy Scriptures to him (Psalms 51, 69, 71, Isaiah 55, Joh. 14, Col. 3). Left my prayer book.' The visit was repeated daily until the poor man's death a week later. Apart from such calls of duty, books are his main interest. He is greatly delighted with Hamilton's *Men and Manners in America*. Alfieri's *Antigone* he dislikes as having the faults of both ancient and modern drama. He grinds away through Gifford's *Pitt*, and reads Hallam's *Middle Ages*. 'My method has usually been, 1, to read over regularly;

2, to glance again over all I have read, and analyse.' He was just as little of the lounger in his lighter reading. Schiller's plays he went through with attention, finding it 'a good plan to read along with history, historical plays of the same events for material illustration, as well as aid to the memory.' He read Scott's chapters on Mary Stuart in his history of Scotland, 'to enable me better to appreciate the admirable judgment of Schiller (in *Maria Stuart*) both where he has adhered to history and where he has gone beyond it.' He finds fault with the *Temistocle* of Metastasio, as 'too humane.' 'History should not be violated without a reason. It may be set aside to fill up poetical verisimilitude. If history assigns a cause inadequate to its effect, or an effect inadequate to its cause, poetry may supply the deficiency for the sake of an impressive whole. But it is too much to overset a narrative and call it a historical play.' Then came a tragic stroke in real life.

October 6, 1833. — Post hour to-day brought me a melancholy announcement—the death of Arthur Hallam. This intelligence was deeply oppressive even to my selfish disposition. I mourn in him, for myself, my earliest near friend ; for my fellow-creatures, one who would have adorned his age and country, a mind full of beauty and of power, attaining almost to that ideal standard of which it is presumption to expect an example. When shall I see his like ? Yet this dispensation is not all pain, for there is a hope and not (in my mind) a bare or rash hope that his soul rests with God in Jesus Christ. . . . I walked upon the hills to muse upon this very mournful event, which cuts me to the heart. Alas for his family and his intended bride. *October 7th.*—My usual occupations, but not without many thoughts upon my departed friend. Bible. Alfieri, *Wallenstein*, Plato, Gifford's *Pitt*, *Biographia Literaria*. Rode with my father and Helen. All objects lay deep in the softness and solemnity of autumnal decay. Alas, my poor friend was cut off in the spring of his bright existence.

December 13, *Edinburgh.*—Breakfast with Dr. Chalmers. His modesty is so extreme that it is oppressive to those who are in his company, especially his juniors, since it is impossible for them to keep their behaviour in due proportion to his. He was on his own subject, the Poor Laws, very eloquent, earnest and impressive. Perhaps he may have been hasty in applying maxims drawn from Scotland to a more advanced stage of society in England. *December* 17. — Robertson's *Charles V.*, Plato, began Book 10. Chalmers. Singing-lesson and practice. Whist. Walked on the Glasgow road, first milestone to fourth and back in 70 minutes—the returning three miles in about 33¾. Ground in some places rather muddy and slippery. *December* 26.—A feeble day. Three successive callers and conversation with my father occupied the morning. Read a good allowance of Robertson, an historian *who leads his reader on*, I think, more pleasantly than any I know. The style most attractive, but the mind of the writer does not set forth the loftiest principles. *December* 29*th, Sunday.*—Twenty-four years have I lived. . . . Where is the *continuous* work which ought to fill up the life of a Christian without intermission ? . . . I have been growing, that is certain ; in good or evil ? Much fluctuation ; often a supposed progress, terminating in finding myself at, or short of, the point which I deemed I had left behind me. Business and political excitement a tremendous trial, not so much alleviating as forcibly dragging down the soul from that temper which is fit to inhale the air of heaven. *Jan.* 8, 1834, *Edinburgh.*—Breakfast with Dr. Chalmers. Attended his lecture 2-3. . . . More than ever struck with the superabundance of Dr. C.'s gorgeous language, which leads him into repetitions, until the stores of our tongue be exhausted on each particular point. Yet the variety and magnificence of his expositions must fix them very strongly in the minds of his hearers. In ordinary works great attention would be excited by the very infrequent occurrence of the very brilliant expressions and illustrations with which he cloys the palate. His gems lie like paving-stones. He does indeed seem to be an *admirable* man.

Of Edinburgh his knowledge soon became intimate. His father and mother took him to that city, as we have seen, in 1814. He spent a spring there in 1828 just before going to Oxford, and he recollected to the end of his life a sermon of Dr. Andrew Thomson's on the Repentance of Judas, 'a great and striking subject.' Some circumstance or another brought him into relations with Chalmers, that ripened into friendship. 'We used to have walks together,' Mr. Gladstone remembered, 'chiefly out of the town by the Dean Bridge and along the Queensferry road. On one of our walks together, Chalmers took me down to see one of his districts by the water of Leith, and I remember we went into one or more of the cottages. He went in with smiling countenance, greeting and being greeted by the people, and sat down. But he had nothing to say. He was exactly like the Duke of Wellington, who said of himself that he had no small talk. His whole mind was always full of some great subject and he could not deviate from it. He sat smiling among the people, but he had no small talk for them and they had no large talk. So after some time we came away, he pleased to have been with the people, and they proud to have had the Doctor with them.' [1] For Chalmers he never lost a warm appreciation, often expressed in admirable words—'one of nature's nobles ; his warrior grandeur, his rich and glowing eloquence, his absorbed and absorbing earnestness, above all his singular simplicity and detachment from the world.' Among other memories, 'There was a quaint old shop at the Bowhead which used to interest me very much. It was kept by a book-seller, Mr. Thomas Nelson. I remember being amused by a reply he made to me one day when I went in and asked for Booth's *Reign of Grace.* He half turned his head towards me, and remarked with a peculiar twinkle in his eye, "Ay, man, but ye're a young chiel to be askin' after a book like that."'

On his way south in January 1834, Mr. Gladstone stays with relatives at Seaforth, 'where even the wind howling upon the window at night was dear and familiar' ; and a few days

[1] Report of an interview with Mr. Gladstone in 1890, in *Scottish Liberal,* May 2, 9, etc., 1890.

later finds himself once more within the ever congenial walls of Oxford.

January 19, *Sunday*.—Read the first lesson in morning chapel. A most masterly sermon of Pusey's preached by Clarke. Lancaster in the afternoon on the Sacrament. Good walk. Wrote [family letters]. Read Whyte. Three of Girdlestone's Sermons. Pickering on adult baptism (some clever and singularly insufficient reasoning). Episcopal pastoral letter for 1832. Doane's Ordination sermon, 1833, admirable, —Wrote some thoughts. *Jan.* 20. — Sismondi's *Italian Republics*. Dined at Merton, and spent all the evening there in interesting conversation. I was Hamilton's guest [afterwards Bishop of Salisbury]. It was delightful, it wrings joy even from the most unfeeling heart, to see religion on the increase as it is here. *Jan.* 23*rd*.—Much of to-day, it fell out, spent in conversation of an interesting kind, with Brandreth and Pearson on eternal punishment ; with Williams on baptism ; with Churton on faith and religion in the university ; with Harrison on prophecy and the papacy. . . . *Jan.* 24.—Began *Essay on Saving Faith*, and wrote thereon. *Jan.* 29*th*.—Dined at Oriel. Conversation with Newman chiefly on church matters. . . . I excuse some idleness to myself by the fear of doing some real injury to my eyes. [After a flight of three or four days to London, he again returns for a Sunday in Oxford.] *Feb.* 9.—Two university sermons and St. Peter's. Round the meadows with Williams. Dined with him, common room. Tea and a pleasant conversation with Harrison. Began *Chrysostom de Sacerdotio*, and Cecil's *Friendly Visit*. [Then he goes back to town for the rest of the session.] *Feb.* 12, *London*. — Finished *Friendly Visit*, beautiful little book. Finished Tennyson's poems. Wrote a paper on ἠθική πίστις in poetry. Recollections of Robert Hall. 13*th*.—With Doyle, long and solemn conversation on the doctrine of the Trinity. . . . Began Wardlaw's *Christian Ethics*. 26*th*, *London*.—A busy day, yet of little palpable profit. . . . Read two important Demerara papers. . . . Rode. At the levee. House 5½-11. Wished to speak, but deterred by the extremely ill disposition to hear. Much sickened by their unfairness in the judicial character, more still at my own wretched feebleness and fears. *April* 1.—Dined at Sir R. Peel's. Herries, Sir G. Murray, Chantrey, etc. Sir R. Peel very kind in his manner to us. *May* 29.— Mignet's *Introduction* [to 'the History of the Spanish succession,' one of the masterpieces of historical literature]. *June* 4.—Bruce to breakfast. Paper. Mignet and analysis. Burke. Harvey committee.[1] Ancient music concert. Dined at Lincoln's Inn. House 11¼-12¾. Rode. *June* 6.—*Paradise Lost*. Began Leibnitz's *Tentamina Theodiceæ*. *June* 11.—Read Pitt's speeches on the Union in January, 1799, and Grattan on Catholic petition in 1805. 15*th*.—Read some passages in the latter part of *Corinne*, which always work strongly on me. 18*th*.— Coming home to dine, found *Remains of A. H. H.* Yesterday a bridal at a friend's, to-day a sad memorial of death. 'Tis a sad subject, a very sad one to me. I have not seen his like. The memory of him reposes

---

[1] Daniel Whittle Harvey was an eloquent member of parliament whom the benchers of his inn refused to call to the bar, on the ground of certain charges against his probity. The House appointed a committee of which Mr. Gladstone was a member to inquire into these charges. O'Connell was chairman, and they acquitted Harvey, without however affecting the decision of the benchers. Mr. Gladstone was the only member of the committee who did not concur in its final judgment. See his article on Daniel O'Connell in the *Nineteenth Century*, Jan. 1889.

gently in my inmost heart, a fountain of tears which soften and fertilise it in the midst of pursuits whose tendency is to dry up the sources of emotion by the fever of excitement. I read his memoir. His father had done me much and undeserved kindness there. 20th.—Most of my time went in thinking confusedly over the university question. Very anxious to speak, tortured with nervous anticipations ; could not get an opportunity. Certainly my inward experience on these occasions ought to make me humble. Herbert's maiden speech very successful. I ought to be thankful for my *miss* ; perhaps also because my mind was so much oppressed that I could not, I fear, have unfolded my inward convictions. What a world it is, and how does it require the Divine power and aid to clothe in words the profound and mysterious thoughts on those subjects most connected with the human soul—thoughts which the mind does not command as a mistress, but entertains reverentially as honoured guests . . . content with only a partial comprehension, hoping to render it a progressive one, but how difficult to define in words a conception, many of whose parts are still in a nascent state with no fixed outline or palpable substance. *July* 2.— . . . Guizot. Cousin. Bossuet (*Hist. Univ.*). Rode. Committee and House. Curious detail from O'Connell of his interview with Littleton. 10th.—7¼ A.M.-7½ in an open chaise to Coggeshall and back with O'Connell and Sir G. Sinclair, to examine Skingley [a proceeding arising from the Harvey committee], which was done with little success.

The conversation of the great Liberator was never wholly forgotten, and it was probably his earliest chance of a glimpse of the Irish point of view at first hand.

July 11.—No news till the afternoon and then heard on very good authority that the Grey government is definitely broken up, and that attempts at reconstruction have failed. Cousin, Sismondi, Education evidence. Letters. House. 21st.—To-day not for the first time felt a great want of courage to express feelings strongly awakened on hearing a speech of O'Connell. To have so strong an impulse and not obey it seems unnatural ; it seems like an inflicted dumbness. 28th.—Spoke 30 to 35 minutes on University bill, with more ease than I had hoped, having been more mindful or less unmindful of Divine aid. Divided in 75 v. 164. [To his father next day.] You will see by your *Post* that I held forth last night on the Universities bill. The House I am glad to say heard me with the utmost kindness, for they had been listening previously to an Indian discussion in which very few people took any interest, though indeed it was both curious and interesting. But the change of subject was no doubt felt as a relief, and their disposition to listen set me infinitely more at my ease than I should otherwise have been. 29th.—Pleasant house dinner at Carlton. Lincoln got up the party. Sir R. Peel was in good spirits and very agreeable.

It was on this occasion that he wrote to his mother,—'Sir Robert Peel caused me much gratification by the way in which he spoke to me of my speech, and particularly the great warmth of his manner. He told me he cheered me loudly, and I said in return that I had heard his voice under me while speaking, and was much encouraged thereby.' He ends the note already cited (Sept. 6, 1897) on the old House of Commons,

which was burned down this year, with what he calls a curious
incident concerning Sir Robert Peel, and with a sentence or
two upon the government of Lord Grey :—

Cobbett made a motion alike wordy and absurd, praying the king
to remove him [Peel] from the privy council as the author of the act
for the re-establishment of the gold standard in 1819. The entire
House was against him, except his colleague Fielden of Oldham, who
made a second teller.[1] After the division I think Lord Althorp at
once rose and moved the expunction of the proceedings from the votes
or journals ; a severe rebuke to the mover. Sir Robert in his speech
said, 'I am at a loss, sir, to conceive what can be the cause of the
strong hostility to me which the honourable gentleman exhibits. I
never conferred on him an obligation.' This stroke was not original.
But what struck me at the time as singular was this, that notwithstanding the state of feeling which I have described, Sir R. Peel was
greatly excited in dealing with one who at the time was little more
than a contemptible antagonist. At that period shirt collars were made
with 'gills' which came up upon the cheek ; and Peel's gills were
so soaked with perspiration that they actually lay down upon his
neck-cloth.

In one of these years, I think 1833, a motion was made by some
political economist for the abolition of the corn laws. I (an absolute
and literal ignoramus) was much struck and staggered with it. But
Sir James Graham — who knew more of economic and trade matters,
I think, than the rest of the cabinet of 1841 all put together—made a
reply in the sense of protection, whether high or low I cannot now say.
But I remember perfectly well that this speech of his built me up
again for the moment and enabled me (I believe) to vote with the
government.

The year 1833 was, as measured by quantity and in part by quality,
a splendid year of legislation. In 1834 the Government and Lord
Althorp far beyond all others did themselves high honour by the new
Poor Law Act, which rescued the English peasantry from the total loss
of their independence. Of the 658 members of Parliament about 480
must have been their general supporters. Much gratitude ought to
have been felt for this great administration. But from a variety of
causes, at the close of the session 1834 the House of Commons had
fallen into a state of cold indifference about it.

He was himself destined one day to feel how soon parliamentary reaction may follow a sweeping popular triumph.

[1] See Cobbett's *Life* by Edward Smith, ii. p. 287. Attwood of Birmingham seems
to have voted for the motion.

CHAPTER II

THE NEW CONSERVATISM AND OFFICE

(1834–1845)

I consider the Reform bill a final and irrevocable settlement of a great constitutional question. . . . If by adopting the spirit of the Reform bill it be meant that we are to live in a perpetual vortex of agitation; that public men can only support themselves in public estimation by adopting every popular impression of the day, by promising the instant redress of anything that anybody may call an abuse. . . . I will not undertake to adopt it. But if the spirit of the Reform bill implies merely a careful review of institutions civil and ecclesiastical, undertaken in a friendly temper, the correction of proved abuses and the redress of real grievances, then, etc. etc.—PEEL (*Tamworth Address*).

THE autumn of 1834 was spent at Fasque. An observant eye followed political affairs, but hardly a word is said about them in the diary. A stiff battle was kept up against electioneering iniquities at Newark. Riding, boating, shooting were Mr. Gladstone's pastimes in the day; billiards, singing, backgammon, and a rubber in the evening. Sport was not without compunction which might well, in an age that counts itself humane, be expected to come oftener. 'Had to kill a wounded partridge,' he records, 'and felt after it as if I had shot the albatross. It might be said : This should be more or less.' And that was true. He was always a great walker. He walked from Montrose, some thirteen or fourteen miles off, in two hours and three quarters, and another time he does six miles in seventy minutes. Nor does he ever walk with an unobserving mind. At Lochnagar : 'Saw Highland women from Strathspey coming down for harvest with heavy loads, some with babies, over these wild rough paths through wind and storm. Ah, with what labour does a large portion of mankind subsist, while we fare sumptuously every day !' This was the ready susceptibility to humane impression in the common circumstance of life, the eye stirring the emotions of the feeling heart, that nourished in him the soul of true oratory, to say nothing of feeding the roots of statesmanship. His bookmindedness is unabated. He began with a resolution to work at least two hours every morning before breakfast, and the resolution seems to have been manfully kept, without

prejudice to systematic reading for a good many hours of the
day besides. For the first time, rather strange to say, he read
St. Augustine's *Confessions*, and with the delight that might
have been expected. He finds in that famous composition 'a
good deal of prolix and fanciful, though acute speculation, but
the practical parts of the book have a wonderful force, and
inimitable sweetness and simplicity.' In other departments
of religion, he read Archbishop Leighton's life and Hannah
More's, Arnold's Sermons and Milner's *Church History* and
Whewell's *Bridgewater Treatise*. Once more he analyses the
Novum Organum and the *Advancement of Learning*, and he
reads or re-reads Locke's *Essay*. He studies political science
in the two great manuals of the old world and the new, in the
Politics of Aristotle and the *Prince* of Machiavelli. He goes
through three or four plays of Schiller ; also Manzoni, and
Petrarch, and Dante at the patient rate of a couple of cantos
a day ; then Boccaccio, from whom, after a half-dozen of the
days, he willingly parts company, only interested in him as
showing a strange state of manners and how religion can be
dissociated from conduct. In modern politics he reads the
memoirs of Chatham, and Brougham on Colonial Policy, of
which he says that 'eccentricity, paradox, fast and loose
reasoning and (much more) sentiment, appear to have entered
most deeply into the essence of this remarkable man when he
wrote his Colonial Policy, as now ; with the rarest power of
expressing his thoughts, has he any fixed law to guide them ?'
On Roscoe's *Leo X.* he remarks how interesting and highly
agreeable it is in style, and while disclaiming any right to
judge its fidelity and research, makes the odd observation
that it has in some degree subdued the leaven of its author's
unitarianism. He writes occasional verses, including the
completion of 'some stanzas of December 1832 on "The Human
Heart," but I am not impudent enough to call them by that
name.'

In the midst of days well filled by warm home feeling, reasonable pleasure, and vigorous animation of intellect came the
summons to action. On November 18, a guest arrived with the
astonishing news that ministers were out. The king had dismissed the Melbourne government, partly because he did not
believe that Lord John Russell could take the place of Althorp
as leader of the Commons, partly because like many cleverer
judges he was sick of them, and partly because, as is perhaps
the case with more cabinets than the world supposes, the
ministers were sick of one another, and King William knew it.
Mr. Gladstone in 1875[1] described the dismissal of the whigs in
1834 as the indiscreet proceeding of an honest and well-meaning
man, which gave the conservatives a momentary tenure of office
without power, but provoked a strong reaction in favour of the

[1] *Gleanings*, i. p. 38.

liberals, and greatly prolonged the predominance which they were on the point of losing through the play of natural causes.[1] Sir Robert Peel was summoned in hot haste from Rome, and after a journey of twelve days over alpine snows, eight nights out of the twelve in a carriage, on December 9 he reached London, saw the king and kissed hands as first lord of the treasury. Less than two years before, he had said, 'I feel that between me and office there is a wider gulf than there is perhaps between it and any other man in the House.'

Mr. Gladstone meanwhile at Fasque worked off some of his natural excitement which he notes as invading even Sundays, by the composition of a political tract. The tract has disappeared down the gulf of time. December 11 was his father's seventieth birthday, 'his strength and energy wonderful and giving promise of many more.' Within the week the fated message from the new prime minister arrived; the case is apt to quicken the pulse of even the most serene of politicians, and we may be sure that Mr. Gladstone with the keen vigour of five-and-twenty tingling in his veins was something more or less than serene.

Dec. 17.—Locke, and Russell's *Modern Europe* in the morning. Went to meet the post, found a letter from Peel desiring to see me, dated 13th. All haste; ready by 4—no place! Reluctantly deferred till the morning. Wrote to Lincoln, Sir R. Peel, etc. . . . A game of whist. This is a serious call. I got my father's advice to take anything with work and responsibility. 18*th.*—Off at 7.40 by mail. I find it a privation to be unable to read in a coach. The mind is distracted through the senses, and rambles. Nowhere is it to me so incapable of continuous thought. . . . Newcastle at 9¼ P.M. 19*th.*—Same again. At York at 6¼ A.M. to 7. Ran to peep at the minster and bore away a faint twilight image of its grandeur. 20*th.*—Arrived safe, thank God, and well at the Bull and Mouth 5¾ A.M. Albany soon. To bed for 2¼ hours. Went to Peel about eleven.

He writes to his father the same day—

My interview with him was not more than six or eight minutes, but he was *extremely* kind. He told me his letter to me was among his first; that he was prompted only by his own feelings towards me and some more of that kind; that I might have a seat either at the admiralty or treasury boards, but the latter was that which he intended for me; that I should then be in immediate and confidential communication with himself; and should thereby have more insight into the general concerns of government; that there was a person very anxious for the seat at the treasury, who would go to the admiralty if I did not; but that he meant to go upon the principle of putting every one to the post for which he thought them most fit, so far as he could, and therefore preferred the arrangement he had named. As he distinctly preferred the treasury for me, and assigned such reasons for the preference, it appeared to me that

---

[1] In another place he describes it as an action done 'with no sort of reason' (*Gleanings*, i. p. 78). But the Melbourne papers, published in 1890, pp. 219-221 and 225, indicate that Melbourne had spontaneously given the king good reasons for cashiering him and his colleagues.

the question was quite settled, and I immediately closed with his offer. I expressed my gratitude for the opinions of me which he had expressed ; and said I thought it my duty to mention that the question of my re-election at Newark upon a single vacancy had never been put to my friends, and I asked whether I should consider any part of what he had said as contingent upon the answer I might receive from them.   He said no, that he would willingly take that risk.   At first, he thought I had suspicions about the Duke of Newcastle, and assured me that he would be much pleased, of which I said I felt quite persuaded.   This inquiry, however, served the double purpose of discharging my own duty, and drawing out something about the dissolution.   He said to me, 'You will address your constituents upon vacating your seat, and acquaint them of your intention to solicit a renewal of their confidence whenever they are called upon to exercise their franchise, *which I tell you confidentially*,' he added, 'will be very soon.'   I would have given a hundred pounds to be then and there in a position to express my hopes and fears !   But it is, then, you see *certain* that we are to have it, and that they will not meet the present parliament.   Most bitterly do I lament it.

Mr. Gladstone at a later date (July 25, 1835) recorded that he had reason to believe from a conversation with a tory friend who was in many party secrets, that the Duke of Wellington set their candidates in motion all over the country before Sir Robert's return.   Active measures, and of course expense, had so generally begun, so much impatience for the dissolution had been excited, and the anticipations had been permitted for so long a time to continue and to spread, as to preclude the possibility of delay.[1]

The appointment of the young member for Newark was noted at the time as an innovation upon a semi-sacred social usage.   Sir Robert Inglis said to him, 'You are about the youngest lord who was ever placed at the treasury on his own account, and not because he was his father's son.'   The prime minister, no doubt, rejoiced in finding for the public service a young man of this high promise, sprung out of the same class, and bred in the same academic traditions as his own.[2]   The youthful minister's path was happily smoothed at Newark. This time blues and reds called a grand truce, divided the honours, and returned Mr. Gladstone and Serjeant Wilde without a contest.   The question that excited most interest in the canvass was the new poor law.   Mr. Gladstone gave the fallen ministers full credit for their measure.   Most of their bills, he said, were projected from a mere craving for

[1] Lord Palmerston doubted (Nov. 25, 1834) whether Peel would dissolve. 'I think his own bias will rather be to abide by the decision of this House of Commons, and try to propitiate it by great professions of reform.   The effect of a dissolution must be injurious to the principles that he professes. . . . But he may be overborne by the violent people of his own party whom he will not be able to control.' Ashley's *Life of Palmerston* (1879), i. p. 313.

[2] Greville, on the other hand, grumbled at Peel, for taking high birth and connections as substitutes for other qualities, because he made Sidney Herbert secretary at the board of control, instead of making him a lord of the treasury, and sending 'Gladstone, who is a very clever man' to the other and more responsible post.

popularity, but in the case of the poor law they acted in
defiance of the public press and many of their own friends.
On the other hand, he defended the new government as the
government of a truly reforming party, pointing to the commercial changes made by Lord Liverpool's administration, to
the corporation and test Acts, and to catholic emancipation.
Who could deny that these were changes of magnitude settled
in peaceful times by a parliament unreformed ? Who could
deny that Sir Robert Peel had long been a practical reformer
of the law, and that the Duke of Wellington had carried out
great retrenchments ? Let them then rally round throne and
altar, and resist the wild measures of the destructives. The
red hero was drawn through the town by six greys, with
postillions in silk jackets, amid the music of bands, the clash
of bells, and the cheers of the crowd. When the red procession
met the blue, mutual congratulations took the place of the old
insult and defiance, and at five o'clock each party sat down to
its own feast. The reds drank toasts of a spirited, loyal and
constitutional character, many admirable speeches were made
which the chronicler regrets that his limits will not allow him
to report,—regrets unshared by us—and soon after eleven Mr.
Gladstone escaped. After a day at Clumber, he was speedily
on his way to London. ' Off at 10½ P.M. Missed the High
Flyer at Tuxford, broke down in my chaise on the way to
Newark ; no injury, thanks to God. Remained 2½ hours alone ;
overtaken by the Wellington at 3½ A.M. Arrived in London
(Jan. 8) before 8 P.M. Good travelling.' On reckoning up his
movements he finds that, though not at all fond of travelling
for the sake of going from place to place, he has had in 1834
quite 2400 miles of it.

Before the dissolution, Sir H. Hardinge had told him that
the conservatives would not be over 340 nor under 300, but by
the middle of the month things looked less prosperous. The
reaction against the whigs had not yet reached full flood, the
royal dismissal of the administration was unpopular, moderate
people more especially in Scotland could not stand a government where the Duke of Wellington, the symbol of a benighted
and stubborn toryism, was seen over Peel's shoulder. ' At
present,' Mr. Gladstone writes, ' the case is, even in my view,
hopeful ; in that of most here it is more. And certainly, to
have this very privilege of entertaining a deliberate and
reasonable hope, to think that notwithstanding the ten pound
clause, a moderate parliament may be returned ; in fine, to
believe that we have now *some* prospect of surviving the
Reform bill without a bloody revolution, is to me as surprising
as delightful ; it seems to me the greatest and most providential mercy with which a nation was ever visited. . . . To-
day I am going to dine with the lord chancellor [Lyndhurst],
having received a card to that effect last night.'

It was at this dinner that Mr. Gladstone had his first opportunity of making a remarkable acquaintance. In his diary he mentions as present three of the judges, the flower of the bench, as he supposes, but he says not a word of the man of the strangest destiny there, the author of *Vivian Grey*. Disraeli himself, in a letter to his sister, names 'young Gladstone,' and others, but condemns the feast as rather dull, and declares that a swan very white and tender, and stuffed with truffles, was the best company at the table. What Mr. Gladstone carried away in his memory was a sage lesson of Lyndhurst's, by which the two men of genius at his table were in time to show themselves extremely competent to profit,— ' Never defend yourself before a popular assemblage, except with and by retorting the attack ; the hearers, in the pleasure which the assault gives them, will forget the 'previous charge.' As Disraeli himself put it afterwards, *Never complain and never explain.*

II

One afternoon, a few days later, while he was grappling at the treasury with a file of papers on the mysteries of superannuation, Mr. Gladstone was again summoned by the prime minister, and again (Jan. 26) he writes to his father :—

I have had an important interview with Sir R. Peel, the result of which is that I am to be under-secretary for the colonies. I will give you a hurried and imperfect sketch of the conversation. He began by saying he was about to make a great sacrifice both of his own feelings and convenience, but that what he had to say he hoped would be gratifying to me, as a mark of his confidence and regard. ' I am going to propose to you, Gladstone, that you should be, for you know Wortley has lost his election, under-secretary of state for the colonies, and I give you my word that I do not know six offices which are at this moment of greater importance than that to which is attached the representation of the colonial department in the House of Commons, at a period when so many questions of importance are in agitation.' I expressed as well as I could, and indeed it was but ill, my unfeigned and deep sense of his kindness, my hesitation to form any opinion of my own competency for the office, and at the same time my general desire not to shrink from any responsibility which he might think proper to lay upon me. He said that was the right and manly view to take. . . . He adverted to my connection with the West Indies as likely to give satisfaction to persons dependent on those colonies, and thought that others would not be displeased. In short, I cannot go through it all, but I can only say that if I had always heard of him that he was the warmest and freest person of all living in the expression of his feelings, such description would have been fully borne out by his demeanour to me. When I came away he took my hand and said, ' *Well, God bless you, wherever you are.*'

From Sir Robert the new under-secretary made his way, in fear and trembling, to his new chief, Lord Aberdeen.

Distinction of itself naturally and properly rather alarms the young. I had heard of his high character ; but I had also heard of him as a man of cold manners, and close and even haughty reserve. It was dark when I entered his room, so that I saw his figure rather than his countenance. I do not recollect the matter of the conversation, but I well remember that, before I had been three minutes with him, all my apprehensions had melted away like snow in the sun. I came away from that interview conscious indeed of his dignity, but of a dignity so tempered by a peculiar purity and gentleness, and so associated with impressions of his kindness and even friendship, that I believe I thought more about the wonder of his being at that time so misunderstood by the outer world, than about the new duties and responsibilities of my office.[1]

Time only deepened these impressions. It is not hard for a great party chief to win the affection and regard of his junior colleague, and where good fortune has brought together a congenial pair, no friendship outside the home can be more valuable, more delightful, alike to veteran and to tiro. Of all the host of famous or considerable men with whom he was to come into official and other relations, none ever, as we shall see, held the peculiar place in Mr. Gladstone's esteem and reverence of the two statesmen under whose auspices he now first entered the enchanted circle of public office. The promotion was a remarkable stride. He was only five-and-twenty, his parliamentary existence had barely covered two years, and he was wholly without powerful family connection. 'You are aware,' Peel wrote to John Gladstone, 'of the sacrifice I have made of personal feeling to public duty, in placing your son in one of the most important offices — that of representative of the colonial department in the House of Commons, and thus relinquishing his valuable aid in my own immediate department. Wherever he may be placed, he is sure to distinguish himself.'[2]

III

Mr. Gladstone's first spell of office was little more than momentary. The liberal majority, as has so often happened, was composite, but Peel can hardly have supposed that the sections of which it was made up would fail to coalesce, and coalesce pretty soon, for the irresistible object of ejecting ministers who were liked by none of them, and through whose repulse they could strike an avenging blow against the king. Ardent subalterns like Mr. Gladstone took more vehement views. The majority at once beat the government (supported by the group of Stanleyites, fifty-three strong) in the contest for the Speaker's chair. Other repulses followed. 'The division,' writes Mr. Gladstone to his father, with the honourable warmth of the young party man, 'I need not say was a

---

[1] Lord Stanmore's *Earl of Aberdeen* (1893), p. iii.
[2] Parker's *Peel*, ii. p. 267.

disappointment to me ; but it must have been much more so
to those who have ever thought well of the parliament. Our
party mustered splendidly. Some few, but very, very few, of
the others appear to have kept away through a sense of
decency ; they had not virtue enough to vote for the man
whom they knew to be incomparably the best, and against
whom they had no charge to bring. No more shameful act I
think has been done by a British House of Commons.'

Not many days after fervently deprecating a general resignation, an ill-omened purpose of this very course actually
flitted across the mind of the young under-secretary himself.
A scheme was on the anvil for the education of the blacks in
the West Indies, and a sudden apprehension startled Mr. Gladstone, that his chief might devote public funds to all varieties
of denominational religious teaching. Any plan of that kind
would be utterly opposed to what with him, as we shall soon
discover, was then a fundamental principle of national polity.
Happily the fatal leap was not needed, but if either small men
like the government whips, or great men like Peel and Aberdeen, could have known what was passing, they would have
shaken grave heads over this spirit of unseasonable scruple at
the very start of the race in a brilliant man with all his life
before him.

Feb. 4 *or* 5.—Charles Canning told me Peel had offered him the
vacant lordship of the treasury, through his mother. They were, he
said, very much gratified with the manner in which it had been done,
though the offer was declined, upon the ground stated in the reply, that
though he did not anticipate any discrepancy in political sentiments to
separate him from the present government, yet he should prefer in some
sense deserving an official station by parliamentary conduct. . . . Peel's
letter was written at some length, very friendly, without any statesmanlike reserve or sensitive attention to nicety of style. In the last
paragraph it spoke with amiable embarrassment of Mr. Canning ; stating
that his 'respect, regard, and admiration' (I think even), apparently
interrupted by circumstances, continued fresh and vivid, and that those
very circumstances made him more desirous of thus publicly testifying
his real sentiments.

March 30.—Wished to speak on Irish church. No opportunity.
Wrote on it. A noble-minded speech from Sir J. Graham. *March* 31.—
Spoke on the Irish church—under forty minutes. I cannot help here
recording that this matter of speaking is really my strongest religious
exercise. On all occasions, and to-day, especially, was forced upon me
the humiliating sense of my inability to exercise my reason in the face
of the H. of C., and of the necessity of my utterly failing, unless God
gave me the strength and language. It was after all a poor performance,
but would have been poorer had He never been in my thoughts as
a present and powerful aid. But this is what I am as yet totally
incompetent to effect—to realise, in speaking, anything, however small,
which at all satisfies my mind. Debating seems to me less difficult,
though unattained. But to hold in serene contemplative action the

mental faculties in the turbid excitement of debate, so as to see truth clearly and set it forth such as it is, this I cannot attain to.

As regards my speech in the Irish church debate, he tells his father (April 2), it was received by the House, and has been estimated, in a manner extremely gratifying to me. As regards satisfaction to myself in the manner of its execution, I cannot say so much. Backed by a numerous and warm-hearted party, and strong in the consciousness of a good cause, I did not find it difficult to grapple with the more popular parts of the question ; but I fell miserably short of my desires in touching upon the principles which the discussion involved, and I am sure that it must be long before I am enabled in any reasonable sense to be a speaker according even to the conception which I have formed in my own mind.

A few days later, he received the congratulations of a royal personage :—

In the evening, dining at Lord Salisbury's, I was introduced to the Duke of Cumberland, who was pleased to express himself favourably of my speech. He is fond of conversation, and the common reputation which he bears of including in his conversation many oaths, appears to be but too true. Yet he said he had made a point of sending his son to George the Fourth's funeral, thinking it an excellent advantage for a boy to receive the impression which such a scene was calculated to convey. The duke made many acute remarks, and was, I should say, most remarkably unaffected and kind. These are fine social qualities for a prince, though, of course, not the most important—'My dear Sir,' and thumps on the shoulder after a ten minutes' acquaintance. He spoke broadly and freely—much on the disappearance of the bishops' wigs, which he said had done more harm to the church than anything else !

On the same night the catastrophe happened. After a protracted and complex struggle Lord John Russell's proposal for the appropriation of the surplus revenues of the Irish church was carried against ministers. The following day Peel announced his resignation.

Though his official work had been unimportant, Mr. Gladstone had left an excellent impression behind him among the permanent men. When he first appeared in the office, Henry Taylor said, ' I rather like Gladstone, but he is said to have more of the devil in him than appears.' A few weeks were enough to show him that ' Gladstone was far the most considerable of the rising generation, having besides his abilities an excellent disposition and great strength of character.' James Stephen thought well of him, but doubted if he had pugnacity enough for public life.

A few days later Mr. Gladstone dined with an official party at the fallen minister's :—

Sir R. Peel made a very nice speech on Lincoln's proposing and our drinking his health. The following is a slight and bad sketch :—' I really can hardly call you gentlemen alone. I would rather address you as my warm and attached friends in whom I have the fullest con-

fidence, and with whom it has afforded me the greatest satisfaction to
be associated during the struggle which has just been brought to a
close. In undertaking the government, from the first I have never
expected to succeed; still it was my conviction that good might be
done, and I trust that good has been effected. I believe we have shown
that even if a conservative government be not strong enough to carry
on the public affairs of this country, at least we are so strong that we
ought to be able to prevent any other government from doing any
serious mischief to its institutions. We meet now as we met at the
beginning of the session, then perhaps in somewhat finer dresses, but
not, I am sure, with kindlier feelings towards each other.'

The rest of the session Mr. Gladstone passed in his usual
pursuits, reading all sorts of books, from the correspondence
of Leibnitz with Bossuet, and Alexander Knox's *Remains*, down
to Rousseau's *Confessions*. As to the last of these he scarcely
knew whether to read on or to throw it aside, and, in fact, he
seems only to have persevered with that strange romance of a
wandering soul for a day or two. Besides promiscuous reading,
he performed some scribbling, including a sonnet, recorded in
his diary with notes of wondering exclamation. His family
were in London for most of May, his mother in bad health;
no other engagement ever interrupted his sedulous attendance
on her every day, reading the Bible to her, and telling the
news about levees and drawing-rooms, a great dinner at Sir
Robert Peel's, and all the rest of his business and recreations.
In the House he did little between the fall of the ministry and
the close of the session. He once wished to speak, but was
shut out by the length of other speeches. 'So,' he moralises,
'I had two useful lessons instead of one. For the sense of
helplessness which always possesses me in prospect of a speech
is one very useful lesson; and being disappointed after having
attained some due state of excitement and anticipation is
another.'

In June at a feast at Newark, which, terrible to relate,
lasted from four o'clock to eleven, Mr. Gladstone gave them
nearly an hour, not to mention divers minor speeches. His
father 'expressed himself with beautiful and affectionate truth
of feeling, and the party sympathised.' His own speech
deserves to be noted as indicating the political geography for
three or four years to come. The standing dish of the tory
opposition of the period was highly-spiced reproach of the
ministers for living on the support of O'Connell, and Newark
was regaled with an ample meal. Mr. Gladstone would not
enter into a detail of the exploits, character, political opinions
of that Irish gentleman; he would rather say what he thought
of him in his presence than in his absence, because he could unfortunately say nothing of him but what was bad. 'This is
not the first period in English history,' Mr. Gladstone noted
down at that time, 'in which a government has leaned on the

Roman catholic interest in Ireland for support. Under the administration of Strafford and at the time of the Scotch revolt, Charles I. was enthusiastically supported by the recusants of the sister isle, and what was the effect? The religious sympathies of the people were touched then and they were so now with the same consequence, in the gradual decline of the party to whom the suspicion attaches in popular fervour and estimation.' Half a century later he may have recalled this early fruit of historic observation. Meanwhile, in his Newark speech, he denounced the government for seeking to undo the mischief of the Irish alliance by systematic agitation. But it was upon the church question, far deeper and more vital than municipal corporations, that the fate of the government should be decided. Then followed a vindication of the church in Ireland. 'The protestant faith is held good for us, and *what is good for us is also good for the population of Ireland.'* That most disastrous of all our false commonplaces was received at Newark, as it has been received so many hundreds of times ever since all over England, with loud and long-continued cheering, to be invariably followed in after act and event with loud and long-continued groaning.[1] Four years later Mr. Gladstone heard words from Lord John Russell on this point, that began to change his mind. 'Often do I think,' he wrote to Lord Russell in 1870, 'of a saying of yours more than thirty years back which struck me ineffaceably at the time. You said: "The true key to our Irish debates was this: that it was not properly borne in mind that as England is inhabited by Englishmen, and Scotland by Scotchmen, so Ireland is inhabited by Irishmen."'[2]

[1] O'Connell paid Newark a short visit in 1836—spoke against Mr. Gladstone for an hour in the open air, and then left the town, both he and it much as they had been before his arrival.
[2] Walpole, *Life of Lord John Russell*, ii. p. 455.

CHAPTER III

PROGRESS IN PUBLIC LIFE

(1835-1838)

Les hommes en tout ne s'éclairent que par le tâtonnement de l'expérience. Les plus grands génies sont eux-mêmes entraînés par leur siècle.—TURGOT.

Men are only enlightened by feeling their way through experience. The greatest geniuses are themselves drawn along by their age.

IN September (1835), after long suffering, his mother died amid tender care and mournful regrets. Her youngest son was a devoted nurse; her loss struck him keenly, but with a sense full of the consolations of his faith. To Gaskell he writes: 'How deeply and thoroughly her character was imbued with love; with what strong and searching processes of bodily affliction she was assimilated in mind and heart to her Redeemer; how above all other things she sighed for the advancement of His kingdom on earth; how few mortals suffered more pain, or more faithfully recognised it as one of the instruments by which God is pleased to forward that restoring process for which we are placed on earth.'

Then the world resumed its course for him, and things fell into their wonted ways of indefatigable study. His scheme for week-days included Blackstone, Mackintosh, Aristotle's *Politics* —'a book of immense value for all governors and public men' —Dante's *Purgatorio*, Spanish grammar, Tocqueville, Fox's *James II.*, by which he was disappointed, not seeing such an acuteness in extracting and exhibiting the principles that govern from beneath the actions of men and parties, nor such a grasp of generalisation, nor such a faculty of separating minute from material particulars, nor such an abstraction from a debater's modes of thought and forms of expression, as he should have hoped. To these he added as he went along the *Génie du Christianisme*, Bolingbroke, Bacon's *Essays*, *Don Quixote*, the *Annals* of Tacitus, Le Bas' *Life of Laud* ('somewhat too Laudish, though right *au fond*'; unlike Lawson's *Laud*, 'a most intemperate book, the foam swallows up all the facts'), *Childe Harold*, *Jerusalem Delivered* ('beautiful in its

kind, but how can its author be placed in the same category
of genius as Dante?'), Pollok's *Course of Time* ('much talent,
little culture, insufficient power to digest and construct his
subject or his versification; his politics radical, his religious
sentiments generally sound, though perhaps hard').

In the evenings he read aloud to his father the *Faery Queen*
and Shakespeare. On Sundays he read Chillingworth and
Jewel, and, above all, he dug and delved in St. Augustine. He
drew a sketch of a project touching Peculiarities in Religion.
For several days he was writing something on politics. Then
an outline or an essay on our colonial system. For he was no
reader of the lounging, sauntering, passively receptive species;
he went forward in a sedulous process of import and export,
a mind actively at work on all the topics that passed before it.

At the beginning of the year 1836 he was invited to pay a
visit to Drayton, where he found only Lord Harrowby—a link
with the great men of an earlier generation, for he had acted as
Pitt's second in the duel with Tierney, and had been foreign
secretary in Pitt's administration of 1804; might have been
prime minister in 1827 if he had liked; and he headed the
Waverers who secured the passing of the Reform bill by the
Lords. Other guests followed, the host rather contracting in
freedom of conversation as the party expanded.[1]

I cannot record anything continuous (Mr. Gladstone writes in his
memorandum of the visit), but commit to paper several opinions and
expressions of Sir R. Peel, which bore upon interesting and practical
questions. That Fox was not a man of settled, reasoned, political
principle. Lord Harrowby added that he was thrown into opposition
and whiggism by the insult of Lord North. That his own doctrines,
both as originally declared, and as resumed when finally in office, were
of a highly toned spirit of government. That Brougham was the most
powerful man he had ever known in the H. of C.; that no one had ever
fallen so fast and so far. That the political difficulties of England might
be susceptible of cure, and were not appalling; but that the state of
Ireland was to all appearance hopeless. That there the great difficulty
lay in procuring the ordinary administration of justice; that the very
institution of juries supposed a common interest of the juror and the
state, a condition not fulfilled in the present instance; that it was quite
unfit for the present state of society in Ireland. Lord Harrowby thought
that a strong conservative government might still quell agitation. And
Sir R. Peel said Stanley had told him that the whig government were on
the point of succeeding in putting a stop to the resistance to payment of
tithe, when Lord Althorp, alarmed at the expense already incurred,
wrote to stop its collection by the military. We should probably live
to see the independence of Poland established.

The Duke of Wellington and others arrived later in the day. It was
pleasing to see the deference with which he was received as he entered
the library; at the sound of his name everybody rose; he is addressed
by all with a respectful manner. He met Peel most cordially, and

seized both Lady Peel's hands. I now recollect that it was with *glee*
Sir R. Peel said to me on Monday, 'I am glad to say you will meet the
duke here,' which had reference, I doubt not, partly to the anticipated
pleasure of seeing him, partly to the dissipations of unworthy suspicions.
He reported that government are still labouring at a church measure
without appropriation. *Jan.* 20.—The Duke of Wellington appears to
speak little ; and never for speaking's sake, but only to convey an idea,
commonly worth conveying. He receives remarks made to him very
frequently with no more than 'Ha,' a convenient, suspensive expression, which acknowledges the arrival of the observation and no more.
Of the two days which he spent here he hunted on Thursday, shot on
Friday, and to-day travelled to Strathfieldsay, more, I believe, than 100
miles, to entertain a party of friends to dinner. With this bodily
exertion he mixes at 66 or 67 a constant attention to business. Sir
R. Peel mentioned to me to-night a very remarkable example of his
[the duke's] perhaps excessive precision. Whenever he signs a draft on
Coutts's, he addresses to them at the same time a note apprising them
that he has done so. This perfect facility of transition from one class of
occupation to their opposites, and their habitual intermixture without
any apparent encroachments on either side, is, I think, a very remarkable evidence of self-command, and a mental power of singular utility.
Sir Robert is also, I conceive, a thrifty dealer with his time, but in a
man of his age [Peel now 48] this is less beyond expectation.

He said good-bye on the last night with regret. In the
midst of the great company he found time to read Bossuet on
Variations, remarking rather oddly, 'some of Bossuet's theology
seems to me very good.'

On Jan. 30th is the entry of his journey from Liverpool, '1 to 4 to
Hawarden Castle.' [I suppose his first visit to his future home.] Got
to Chester (Feb. 1) five minutes after the mail had started. Got on
by Albion. Outside all night ; frost ; rain ; arrived at Albany 11¾.
Feb. 4th.—Session opens. Voted in 243-284. A good opportunity for
speaking, but in my weakness did not use it. *Feb. 8th.*—Stanley made
a noble speech. Voted in 243 to 307 for abolition of Irish corporations.
Pendulums and Nothingarians all against us. *Sunday.*—Wrote on
Hypocrisy. On Worship. Attempted to explain this to the servants
at night. Newman's Sermons and J. Taylor. Trench's Poems. *March
2nd.*—Read to my deep sorrow of Anstice's death on Monday. His
friends, his young widow, the world can spare him ill ; so says at least
the flesh. Stapleton. *Paradiso*, VII. VIII. Calls. Rode. Wrote.
Dined at Lord Ashburton's. House. Statistical Society's *Proceedings.*
Verses on Anstice's death. *March 22nd.*—House 5¼-9¾. Spoke 50
minutes [on negro apprenticeship ; see p. 107]; kindly heard, and I
should thank God for being made able to speak even thus indifferently.[1]
March 23rd. . . . Late, having been awake last night till between 4
and 5, as usual after speaking. How useful to make us feel the habitual
unremembered blessing of sound sleep. . . . *April 7th.—Gerus. Lib.*
c. xi. . . . Dr. Pusey here from 12 to 3 about church building. Rode.
At night 11 to 2 perusing Henry Taylor's proofs of *The Statesman*, and
writing notes on it, presumptuous enough. . . . *Gerus.* xii. Re-perused

---

[1] The *Standard* marks it 'as a brilliant and triumphant argument—one of the few
gems that have illuminated the reformed House of Commons.'

Taylor's sheets. A batch of calls. Wrote letters. Bossuet. Dined at Henry Taylor's, a keen intellectual exercise, and thus a place of danger, especially as it is exercise seen. . . . *9th.*—Spedding at breakfast. *Gerus.* xiii. Finished Locke on Understanding. It appears to me on the whole a much overrated, though, in some respects, a very useful book. . . . *May* 16*th.*—Mr. Wordsworth, H. Taylor and Doyle to breakfast. Sat till 12¾. Conversation on Shelley, Trench, Tennyson; travelling, copyright, etc. 30*th.* — Milnes, Blakesley, Taylor, Cole to breakfast. Church meeting at Archbishop of Armagh's. Ancient music rehearsal. House 6-8¼ and 9¼-12. *June* 1*st.*—Read Wordsworth, . . . House 5-12. Spoke about 45 minutes [on Tithes and Church (Ireland) bill]. I had this pleasure in my speech, that I never rose more intent upon telling what I believe to be royal truth; though I did it very ill, and further than ever below the idea which I would nevertheless hold before my mind. 3*rd.*—West Indies Committee 1-4. Finished writing out my speech and sent it. Read Wordsworth. . . . Saw Sir R. Peel. Dined at Serjeant Talfourd's to meet Wordsworth. . . . 5*th.*—St. James's, Communion. Dined at Lincoln's Inn. St. Sepulchre's. Wrote. Jer. Taylor, Newman. Began Nicole's *Préjugés.* Arnold aloud. 8*th.*—Wordsworth, since he has been in town, has breakfasted twice and dined once with me. Intercourse with him is, upon the whole, extremely pleasing. I was sorry to hear Sydney Smith say that he did not see very much in him, nor greatly admire his poems. He even adverted to the London Sonnet as ridiculous. Sheil thought this of the line :

' Dear God ! the very houses seem asleep.'

I ventured to call his attention to that which followed as carrying out the idea :

' And all that mighty heart is lying still.'

Of which I may say *omne tulit punctum.*

Wordsworth came in to breakfast the other day before his time. I asked him to excuse me while I had my servant to prayers ; but he expressed a *hearty* wish to be present, which was delightful. He has laboured long ; if for himself, yet more for men, and over all I trust for God. Will he ever be the bearer of evil thoughts to any mind ? Glory is gathering round his later years on earth, and his later works especially indicate the spiritual ripening of his noble soul. I heard but few of his opinions ; but these are some. He was charmed with Trench's poems ; liked Alford ; thought Shelley had the greatest native powers in poetry of all the men of this age. In reading *Die Braut von Korinth* translated, was more horrified than enchained, or rather altogether the first. Wondered how any one could translate it or the Faust, but spoke as knowing the original. Thought little of Murillo as to the mind of painting ; said he could not have painted Paul Veronese's 'Marriage of Cana.' Considered that old age in great measure disqualified him by its rigid fixity of habits from judging of the works of young poets—I must say that he was here even over liberal in self-depreciation. He defended the make of the steamboat as more poetical than otherwise to the eye (see Sonnets[1]). Thought Coleridge admired Ossian only in

---

[1] 'Motions and Means on Land and Sea at War,' v. 248. Steamboats, Viaducts, and Railways.

youth, and himself admired the spirit which Macpherson *professes* to embody.

Serjeant Talfourd dined here to meet Wordsworth yesterday. Wordsworth is vehement against Byron. Saw in Shelley the lowest form of irreligion, but a later progress towards better things. Named the discrepancy between his creed and his imagination as the marring idea of his works, in which description I could not concur. Spoke of the *entire* revolution in his own poetical taste. We were agreed that a man's personal character ought to be the basis of his politics. He quoted his sonnet on the contested election [what sonnet is this ?], from which I ventured to differ as regards its assuming nutriment for the heart to be inherent in politics. He described to me his views ; that the Reform Act had, as it were, brought out too prominently a particular muscle of the national frame : the strength of the towns ; that the cure was to be found in a large further enfranchisement, I fancy, of the country chiefly ; that you would thus extend the base of your pyramid and so give it strength. He wished the old institutions of the country preserved, and thought this the way to preserve them. He thought the political franchise upon the whole a good to the mass—regard being had to the state of human nature ; against me. 11*th*.—Read Browning's *Paracelsus*. Went to Richmond to dine with the Gaskells. A two hours' walk home at night. 16*th*.—Wrote two sonnets. Finished and wrote out *Braut von Korinth*. Shall I ever dare to make out a counterpart ? 21*st*.—Breakfast at Mr. Hallam's to meet Mr. Wordsworth and Mr. Rogers. Wordsworth spoke much and justly about copyright. Conversation with Talfourd in the evening, partly about that subject. Began something on egotism. 24*th*.—Breakfast with Mr. Rogers, Mr. Wordsworth only there. Very agreeable. Rogers produced an American poem, the death of Bozzaris, which Wordsworth proposed that I should read to them : of course I declined, so even did Rogers. But Wordsworth read it through in good taste, and doing it justice.

Fasque in time for Aug. 12 ; out on the hill, but unlucky with a sprained ankle, and obliged to give up early. *Aug.* 15*th*.—Wrote (long) to Dr. Chalmers. Orator. *Sept.* 20*th*.—Milner, finished Vol. ii. Cic. *Acad.* Wraxall. Began Goethe's *Iphigenie.* Wrote. *Oct.* 7*th*.— Milner. Wraxall. A dinner-party. Wrote out a sketch for an essay on Justification. Singing, whist, shooting. Copied a paper for my father. 12*th*.—A day on the hill for roe. 14 guns. [To Liverpool for public dinner at the Amphitheatre.] 18*th*.—Most kindly heard. Canning's début everything that could be desired. I thought I spoke 35 minutes, but afterwards found it was 55. Read *Marco Visconti.* 21*st*.—Operative dinner at Amphitheatre. Spoke perhaps 16 or 18 minutes. 28*th*.—*Haddo* [Lord Aberdeen's]. Finished *Marco Visconti*, a long bout, but I could not let it go. Buckland's opening chapters. *On the whole* satisfactory. 30*th*.—Lord Aberdeen read prayers in the evening with simple and earnest pathos. *Nov.* 10*th*.—*Wilhelm Meister*, Book i., and there I mean to leave it, unless I hear a better report of the succeeding one than I could make of the first. Next day, recommenced with great anticipations of delight the *Divina Commedia.* 13*th*.— Finished Nicole *De l'Unité.* August. *De Civ.* [Every day at this time.] 19*th*.—Began Cicero's *Tusculan Questions.* . . . 25*th*.—Aug. *Civ. Dei.* I am now in Book xiv. Cic. *Tusc.* finished. Book ii. *Purgatorio*, iii.-v. A dose of whist. Still snow and rain. 26*th*.—Aug. Cicero. Billiards.

Purgatorio, vi.-viii.   Began Dryden's *Fables*.   My eyes are not in their
best plight, and I am obliged to consider type a little.   *Jan. 3rd*, 1837.—
Breakfasted with Dr. Chalmers.   How kind my father is in small
matters as well as great—thoughtfully sending carriage.   13*th, Glasgow.*
—The pavilion astonishing, and the whole effect very grand.   Near 3500.
Sir R. Peel spoke 1 h. 55 m.   Explicit and bold ; it was a very great
effort.   I kept within 15 min.—quite long enough.   14*th.*—7½-5½ mail
to Carlisle.   On all night.   15*th.*—Wetherby at 7½.   Leeds 10½.   Church
there.   Walked over to Wakefield.   Church there.   Evening at Thornes.
[Milnes Gaskell's.]   17*th.*—To Newark.   Very good meeting.   Spoke
¾ hour.

In this speech, after the regulation denunciation of the reckless wickedness of O'Connell, he set about demonstrating the
change that had taken place in the character of public feeling
during the last few years.   He pointed out that at the dissolution of 1831 the conservative members of the House of Commons
amounted perhaps to 50.   In 1835 they saw this small dispirited
band grow into a resolute and formidable phalanx of 300.   The
cry was : 'Resolute attachment to the institutions of the
country.'   One passage in the speech is of interest in the
history of his attitude on toleration.   Sir William Molesworth
had been invited to come forward as candidate for the representation of Leeds.   A report spread that Sir William was not a
believer in the Christian articles of faith.   Somebody wrote to
Molesworth, to know if this was true.   He answered, that the
question whether he was a believer in the Christian religion
was one that no man of liberal principles ought to propose to
another, or could propose without being guilty of a derelic-
tion of duty.   On this incident, Mr. Gladstone said that he would
ask, 'Is it not a time for serious reflection among moderate and
candid men of all parties, when such a question was actually
thought impertinent interference ?   Surely they would say with
him, that men who have no belief in the divine revelation are
not the men to govern this nation, be they whigs or radicals.'
Long, extraordinary, and not inglorious, was the ascent from
such a position as this, to the principles so nobly vindicated in
the speech on the Affirmation bill in 1883.
     At the end of January he is back in London, arranging books
and papers and making a little daylight in his chaos.   'What
useful advice might a man who has been *buon pezzo* in parliament give to one going into it, on this mechanical portion of his
business.'   The entries for 1837 are none of them especially
interesting.   Every day in the midst of full parliamentary work,
social engagements, and public duties outside of the House of
Commons, he was elaborating the treatise on the relations of
church and state, of which we shall see more in our following
chapter.   At the beginning of the session he went to a dinner
at Peel's, at which Lord Stanley and some of his friends were
present—a circumstance noted as a sign of the impending fusion

between the whig seceders of 1834 and the conservative party.
Sir Robert seems to have gone on extending his confidence
in him.

I visited Sir Robert Peel (March 4th) about the Canada question, and
again by appointment on the 6th, with Lord Aberdeen. On the former
day he said, ' Is there any one else to invite ? ' I suggested Lord Stanley.
He said, perhaps he might be inclined to take a separate view. But in
the interval he had apparently thought otherwise. For on Monday he
read to Lord Aberdeen and myself a letter from Stanley written with the
utmost frankness and in a tone of political intimacy, saying that an
engagement as chairman of a committee at the House would prevent his
meeting us. The business of the day was discussed in conversation, and
it was agreed to be quite impossible to support the resolution on the
legislative council in its existing terms, without at least a protest.
Peel made the following remark : ' You have got another Ireland growing up in every colony you possess.'

A week later he was shocked by the death of Lady Canning.
'Breakfast with Gaskell' (March 23rd), 'and thence to Lady
Canning's funeral in Westminster Abbey. We were but eleven
in attendance. Her coffin was laid on that of her illustrious
husband. Canning showed a deep but manly sorrow. May we
live as by the side of a grave and looking in.'
In the same month he spoke on Canada (March 8th) 'with
insufficient possession of the subject,' and a week later on
church rates, for an hour or more, 'with more success than the
matter or manner deserved.' He finished his translation of the
Bride of Corinth, and the episode of Ugolino from Dante, and
read Eckermann's *Conversations with Goethe*, to which he gives
the too commonplace praise of being very interesting. He
learned Manzoni's noble ode on the death of Napoleon, of which
he by-and-by made a noble translation ; this by way of sparing
his eyes, and Italian poetry not taking him nearly half the time
of any other to commit to memory. He found a 'beautiful and
powerful production' in Channing's letter to Clay, and he
made the acquaintance of Southey, 'in appearance benignant,
melancholy, and intellectual.'

II

In June King William IV. died, 'leaving a perilous legacy
to his successor.' A month later (July 14) Mr. Gladstone went
up with the Oxford address, and this was, I suppose, the first
occasion on which he was called to present himself before the
Queen, with whose long reign his own future career and fame
were destined to be so closely and so conspicuously associated.
According to the old law prescribing a dissolution of parliament
within six months of the demise of the crown, Mr. Gladstone
was soon in the thick of a general election. By July 17th he
was at Newark, canvassing, speaking, hand-shaking, and in

lucid intervals reading Filicaja. He found a very strong, angry, and general sentiment, not against the principle of the poor law as regards the able-bodied, but against the regulations for separating man and wife, and sending the old compulsorily to the workhouse, with others of a like nature. With the disapprobation on these heads he in great part concurred. There was to be no contest, but arrangements of this kind still leave room for some anxiety, and in Mr. Gladstone's case a singular thing happened. Two days after his arrival at Newark he was followed by a body of gentlemen from Manchester, with an earnest invitation that he would be a candidate for that great town. He declined the invitation, absolutely as he supposed, but the Manchester tories nominated him notwithstanding. They assured the electors that he was the most promising young statesman of the day. The whigs on the other hand vowed that he was an insulter of dissent, a bigot of such dark hue as to wish to subject even the poor negroes of his father's estates to the slavery of a dominant church, a man who owed whatever wealth and consequence his family possessed to the crime of holding his fellow-creatures in bondage, a man who, though honest and consistent, was a member of that small ultra-tory minority which followed the Duke of Cumberland. When the votes were counted, Mr. Gladstone was at the bottom of the poll, with a majority of many hundreds against him.[1]

Meantime he was already member for Newark. His own election was no sooner over than he caught the last vacant place on the mail to Carlisle, whence he hastened to the aid of his father's patriotic labours as candidate for Dundee. Here he worked hard at canvassing and meetings, often pelted with mud and stones, but encouraged by friends more buoyant than the event justified.

Aug. 1st.—My father beaten after all, our promised votes in many cases going back or going against us. . . . Two hundred promises broken. Poll closed at Parnell, 666 ; Gladstone, 381. It is not in human approbation that the reward of right action is to be sought. Left at 4½ amid the hisses of the crowd. Perth at 7¼. Left at one in the morning for Glasgow. *2nd.*—Glasgow 8½. Steamer at 11. Breeze ; miserably sick ; deck all night. *3rd.*—Arrived at 11½ ; (Liverpool), very sore. *4th.*—Out at 8¼ to vote for S. Lancashire. Acted as representative in the booth half the day. Results of election excellent. *5th.*—Again at the booths. A great victory here. *6th.*—Wrote to Manning on the death of his wife. *9th.*—*Manchester.* Public dinner at 6 ; lasted till near 12. Music excellent. Spoke 1½ hours, I am told, *proh pudor !*[2]

[1] Thomson, 4127 ; Philips, 3759 ; Gladstone, 2324.
[2] In this speech he dealt with an attack made upon him by his opponent, Poulett Thomson, afterwards Lord Sydenham, on the question of negro slavery :—
'I have had some obloquy cast upon me by Mr. Thomson, in reference to the part which I took in the question of negro slavery. Now, if there was ever a question upon which I would desire to submit all that I have ever said to a candid inquirer, it is that of negro slavery. He should try me in opposition to Lord Stanley, and did Lord

Back at Fasque, only a day too late for the Twelfth, he found the sport bad and he shot badly, but he enjoyed the healthful walks on the hill. His employments were curiously mixed. '*Sept. 8th.*—In the bog for snipe with Sir J. Mackenzie. Read *Timæus.* Began Byron's Life. My eyes refused progress. Verses. *15th.*—Snipe-shooting with F. in the bog. Began *Critias. 22nd.—Haddo.* Otter-hunting, *senz' esito.* Finished Plato's *Laws.* Hunting, too, in the library.' The mental dispersion of country-house visiting never affects either multifarious reading or multifarious writing. Spanish grammar, Don Quixote in the original, Crabbe, *Don Juan,* alternate with Augustine *de peccatorum remissione* or *de utilitate Credendi* ('beautiful and useful'). He works at an essay of his own upon Justification, at adversaria on Aristotle's *Ethics,* at another essay upon Rationalism, and to save his eyes, spins verse enough to fill a decent volume of a hundred and fifty pages. He makes a circuit of calls upon the tenants, taking a farming lecture from one, praying by the sick-bed of another.

In November he was again in London to be sworn of the new parliament, and at the end of the month he had for the first time an interview on business with the Duke of Wellington —of interest as the collocation of two famous names. 'The immediate subject was the Cape of Good Hope. His reception of me was plain but kind. He came to the door of his room. "Will you come in? How do you do? I am glad to see you." We spoke a little of the Cape. He said with regard to the war —and with sufficient modesty—that he was pretty well aware of the operations that had taken place in it, having been at the Cape, and being in some degree able to judge of those matters. He said, "I suppose it is there as everywhere else, as we had it last night about Ireland and the House of Lords. They won't use the law, as it is in Canada, as it is in the West Indies. They excite insurrection everywhere (I, however, put in an

Stanley complain? It is well known that he stated that the only two speeches which were decidedly hostile to that measure were delivered by two gentlemen who hold office under her majesty's present government, whilst, on the contrary, his lordship was pleased to express candidly his high approbation of my sentiments, and my individual exertions for the settlement of that matter. Does Mr. Thomson mean to say that the great conservative body in parliament has offered opposition to that measure? Who, I would ask, conducted the correspondence of the government office with reference to that important question? Will any man who knows the character of Lord Bathurst—will any man who knows the character of Mr. Stephen, the under-secretary for the colonies—the chosen assistant of the noble lord in that ministry of which he was no unimportant member—will any man say that Mr. Stephen, who was all along the advocate of the slaves, with his liberal and enlightened views, exercised an influence less than under Lord Stanley? Does Mr. Thomson presume to state that Lord Aberdeen was guilty of neglect to the slaves? When I add that the question underwent a considerable discussion last year, in the House of Commons, when all parties and all interests were fairly represented, and the best disposition was evinced to assist the proper working of the measure, and to alter some parts that were considered injurious to the slaves, and which had come under the immediate cognisance of the conservative party, is it fair, is it just, that a minister of the crown should take advantage, for electioneering purposes, of the fact that my connections have an interest in the West Indies, to throw discredit upon me and the cause which I advocate?'

apology for them in the West Indies), they *want to play the part
of opposition* ; they are not a government, for they don't maintain the law." He appointed me to return to him to-morrow.'

The result of the general election was a slight improvement
in the position of the conservatives, but they still mustered no
more than 315 against 342 supporters of the ministry, including
the radical and Irish groups. If Melbourne and Russell found
their team delicate to drive, Peel's difficulties were hardly less.
Few people, he wrote at this moment, can judge of the difficulty
there has frequently been in maintaining harmony between the
various branches of the conservative party. The great majority
in the Lords and the minority in the Commons consisted of
very different elements ; they included men like Stanley and
Graham, who had been authors and advocates of parliamentary
reform, and men who had denounced reform as treason to the
constitution and ruin to the country. Even the animosities
of 1829 and catholic emancipation were only half quenched
within the tory ranks.[1] It was at a meeting held at Peel's on
December 6, 1837, that Lord Stanley for the first time appeared
among the conservative members.

The distractions produced in Canada by mismanagement
and misapprehension in Downing Street had already given
trouble during the very short time when Mr. Gladstone was
under - secretary at the colonial office ; but they now broke
into the flame of open revolt. The perversity of a foolish king
and weakness and disunion among his whig ministers had
brought about a catastrophe. At the beginning of the session
(1838) the government introduced a bill suspending the constitution and conferring various absolute powers on Lord
Durham as governor general and high commissioner. It was
in connection with this proposal that Mr. Gladstone seems to
have been first taken into the confidential consultations of the
leaders of his party.

The sage marshalling and manœuvring of the parliamentary
squads was embarrassed by a move from Sir William Molesworth, of whom we have just been hearing, the editor of
Hobbes, and one of the group nicknamed philosophic radicals
with whom Mr. Gladstone at this stage seldom or never agreed.
'The new school of morals,' he called them, 'which taught that
success was the only criterion of merit,'—a delineation for
which he would have been severely handled by Bentham or
James Mill. Molesworth gave notice of a vote of censure on
Lord Glenelg, the colonial minister ; that is, he selected a
single member of the cabinet for condemnation, on the ground
of acts for which all the other ministers were collectively just
as responsible. For this discrimination the only precedent
seems to be Fox's motion against Lord Sandwich in 1779. Mr.
Gladstone's memorandum [2] completes or modifies the account

1 Parker's *Peel* ii. pp. 336-8.   2 See Appendix.

of the dilemma of the conservative leader, already known from Sir Robert Peel's papers,[1] and the reader will find it elsewhere. It was the right of a conservative opposition to challenge a whig ministry ; yet to fight under radical colours was odious and intolerable. On the other hand he could not vote for Molesworth, because he thought him unjust ; but he could not vote against him, because that would imply confidence in the Canadian policy of ministers. A certain conservative contingent would not acquiesce in support of ministers against Molesworth, or in tame resort to the previous question. Again, Peel felt or feigned an apprehension that if by aggressive action they beat the government, a conservative ministry must come in, and he did not think that such a ministry could last. Even at this risk, it became clear that the only way of avoiding the difficulty was an amendment to Molesworth's motion from the official opposition. Mr. Gladstone spoke (Mar. 7), and was described as making his points with admirable precision and force, though 'with something of a provincial manner, like the rust to a piece of powerful steel machinery that has not worked into polish.' The debate, on which such mighty issues were thought to hang, lasted a couple of nights with not more than moderate spirit. At the close the amendment was thrown out by a majority of twenty-nine for ministers. The general result was to moderate the impatience of the Carlton Club men, who wished to see their party in, on the one hand ; and of the radical men, who did not object to having the whigs out, on the other. It showed that neither administration nor opposition was in a station of supreme command.

III

At the end of March Mr. Gladstone produced the strongest impression that he had yet made in parliament, and he now definitely took his place in the front rank. It was on the old embarrassment of slavery. Reports from the colonies showed that in some at least, and more particularly in Jamaica, the apprenticeship system had led to harsher treatment of the negroes than under slavery. As it has been well put, the bad planters regarded their slave-apprentices as a bad farmer regards a farm near the end of an expiring term. In 1836 Buxton moved for a select committee to inquire into the working of the system. Mr. Gladstone defended it, and he warned parliament against 'incautious and precipitate anticipations of entire success' (March 22). Six days later he was appointed a member of the apprenticeship committee which at once began to investigate the complaints from Jamaica. Mr. Gladstone acted as the representative of the planters on the committee, and he paid very close attention to the

1 Parker, ii. pp. 352-367.

proceedings during two sessions. In the spring of 1838 a motion was made to accelerate by two years the end of the apprentice-ship system on the slave plantations of the West Indies. Brougham had been raising a tempest of humane sentiment by more than one of his most magnificent speeches. The leading men on both sides in parliament were openly and strongly against a disturbance of the settlement, but the feeling in the constituencies was hot, and in liberal and tory camp alike members in fear and trembling tried to make up their minds. Sir George Grey made an effective case for the law as it stood, and Peel spoke on the same side; but it was agreed that Mr. Gladstone by his union of fervour, elevation, and a complete mastery of the facts of the case, went deeper than either. Even unwilling witnesses 'felt bound to admit the great ability he displayed.' His address was completely that of an advocate, and he did not even affect to look on both sides of the question, expressing his joy that the day had at length arrived when he could meet the charges against the planters and enter upon their defence.

March 30th.—Spoke from 11 to 1. Received with the greatest and most affecting kindness from all parties, both during and after. Through the debate I felt the most painful depression. Except Mr. Plumptre and Lord John Russell, all who spoke damaged the question to the utmost possible degree. Prayer earnest for the moment was wrung from me in my necessity; I hope it was not a blasphemous prayer, for support in pleading the cause of justice. . . . I am half insensible even in the moment of delight to such pleasures as this kind of occasion affords. But this is a dangerous state; indifference to the world is not love of God. . . .

In writing to him upon this speech, Mr. Stephen, his former ally at the colonial office, addressed an admonition, which is worth recalling both for its own sake and because it hits by anticipation what was to be one of the most admirable traits in the mighty parliamentarian to whom it was written. 'It seems to me,' says Stephen, 'that this part of your speech establishes nothing more than the fact that your opponents are capricious in the distribution of their sympathy, which is, after all, a reproach and nothing more. Now, reproach is not only not your strength, but it is the very thing in the disuse of which your strength consists; and indulging as I do the hope that you will one day occupy one of the foremost stations in the House of Commons, if not the first of all, I cannot help wishing that you may also be the founder of a more mag-nanimous system of parliamentary tactics than has ever yet been established, in which recrimination will be condemned as unbefitting wise men and good Christians.' In an assembly for candid deliberation modified by party spirit, this is, I fear, almost as much a counsel of perfection as it would have been in a school of Roman gladiators, but at any rate it points the better way. The speech itself has a close, direct, sinewy quality, a complete freedom from anything vague or involved ; and shows for the first time a perfect mastery of the art of handling detail upon detail without an instant of tediousness, and holding the attention of listeners sustained and unbroken. It was a remonstrance against false allegations of the misbehaviour of the planters since the emancipating act, but there is not a trace of backsliding upon the great issue. 'We joined in passing the measure ; we declared a belief that slavery was an evil and demoralising state, and *a desire to be relieved from it* ; we accepted a price in composition for the loss which was expected to accrue.'

Neither now nor at any time did Mr. Gladstone set too low a value on that great dead-lift effort, not too familiar in history, to heave off a burden from the conscience of the nation, and set back the bounds of cruel wrong upon the earth. On the day after this performance, the entry in his diary is—'In the morning my father was greatly overcome, and I could hardly speak to him. Now is the time to turn this attack into measures of benefit for the negroes.' More than once in the course of the spring he showed how much in earnest he was about the negroes, by strenuously pressing his father to allow him to go to the West Indies and view the state of things there for himself. Perhaps by prudent instinct his father disapproved, and at last spoke decidedly against any project of the kind.

The question of the education of the people was rising into political prominence, and its close relations with the claims of the church sufficed to engage the active interest of so zealous a son of the church as Mr. Gladstone. From a very early stage we find him moving for returns, serving on education committees in parliament, corresponding energetically with Manning, Acland, and others of like mind in and out of parliament. Primary education is one of the few subjects on which the fossils of extinct opinion neither interest nor instruct. It is enough to mark that Mr. Gladstone's position in the forties was that of the ultra-churchman of the time, and such as no church-ultra now dreams of fighting for. We find him 'objecting to any infringement whatever of the principle on which the established church was founded—that of confining the pecuniary support of the state to one particular religious denomination.'[1]

To Dr. Hook (March 12, 1838), he speaks of 'a safe and precious interval, perhaps the last to those who are desirous of placing the education of the people under the efficient control of the clergy.' The aims of himself and his allies were to plant training schools in every diocese ; to connect these with the cathedrals through the chapters ; to license the teachers by the bishops after examination.

[1] *Hansard*, June 20, 1839.

Writing to Manning (Feb. 22, 1839), he compares control by government to the 'little lion cub in the *Agamemnon*,' which after being in its primeval season the delight of the young and amusement of the old, gradually revealed its parent stock, and grew to be a creature of huge mischief in the household.[1] He describes a divergence of view among them on the question whether the clergyman should have his choice as to 'admitting the children of dissenters without at once teaching them the catechism.' How Mr. Gladstone went he does not say, nor does it matter. He was not yet thirty. He accepted his political toryism on authority and in good faith, and the same was true of his views on church policy. He could not foresee that it was to be in his own day of power that the cub should come out full grown lion.

His work did not prevent him from mixing pretty freely with men in society, though he seems to have thought that little of what passed was worth transcribing, nor in truth had Mr. Gladstone ever much or any of the rare talent of the born diarist. Here are one or two miscellanea which must be made to serve :

April 25/38.—A long sitting and conversation with Mr. Rogers after the Milnes' marriage breakfast. He spoke unfavourably of Bulwer ; well of Milnes' verses ; said his father wished them not to be published, because such authorship and its repute would clash with the parliamentary career of his son. Mr. Rogers thought a great author would undoubtedly stand better in parliament from being such ; but that otherwise the additament of authorship, unless on germane subjects, would be a hindrance. He quoted Swift on women. . . . He has a good and tender opinion of them ; but went nearly the length of Maurice (when mentioned to him) that they had not that specific faculty of understanding which lies beneath the reason. Peel was odd, in the contrast of a familiar first address, with slackness of manner afterwards. The Duke of Wellington took the greatest interest in the poor around him at Strathfieldsay, had all of eloquence except the words. Mr. Rogers quoted a saying about Brougham that he was not so much a master of the language as mastered by it. I doubt very much the truth of this. Brougham's management of his sentences, as I remember the late Lady Canning observing to me, is surely most wonderful. He never loses the thread, and yet he habitually twists it into a thousand varieties of intricate form. He said, when Stanley came out in public life, and at the age of thirty, he was by far the cleverest young man of the day ; and at sixty he would be the same, still by far the cleverest young man of the day.

---

[1] *Agam.* 696-716.
　　Even so belike might one
　　A lion suckling nurse,
　　Like a foster-son,
　　To his home a future curse.
　　In life's beginnings mild
　　Dear to sire and kind to child . . .
　　But in time he showed
　　The habit of his blood. . . .
　　　　　　—Gladstone in *Translations*, p. 83.

June 13th.—Sir R. Peel dined at Mr. Dugdale's. After dinner he spoke of Wilberforce; believed him to be an excellent man independently of the book, or would not have been favourably impressed by the records of his being in society, and then going home and describing as lost in sin those with whom he had been enjoying himself. Upon the other hand, however, he would have exposed himself to the opposite reproach had he been more secluded, morosely withdrawing himself from the range of human sympathies. He remembered him as an admirable speaker; agreed that the results of his life were very great (and the man must be in part measured by them). He disapproved of taking people to task by articles in the papers, for votes against their party.

July 18th.—I complimented the Speaker yesterday on the time he had saved by putting an end to discussions upon the presentation of petitions. He replied that there was a more important advantage; that those discussions very greatly increased the influence of popular feeling on the deliberations of the House; and that by stopping them he thought a wall was erected against such influence—not as strong as might be wished. Probably some day it might be broken down, but he had done his best to raise it. His maxim was to shut out as far as might be all extrinsic pressure, and then to do freely what was right within doors.

This high and sound way of regarding parliament underwent formidable changes before the close of Mr. Gladstone's career, and perhaps his career had indirectly something to do with them. But not, I think, with intention. In 1838 he cited with approval an exclamation of Roebuck's in the House of Commons, 'We, sir, are or ought to be the *élite* of the people of England for mind: we are at the head of the mind of the people of England.'

Mr. Gladstone's position in parliament and the public judgment, as the session went on, is sufficiently manifest from a letter addressed to him at this time by Samuel Wilberforce, four years his senior, henceforth one of his nearest friends, and always an acute observer of social and political forces. 'It would be an affectation in you, which you are above,' writes the future bishop (April 20, 1838), ' not to know that few young men have the weight you have in the H. of C. and are gaining rapidly throughout the country. . . . I want to urge you to look calmly before you, . . . and act now with a view to *then*. There is no height to which you may not fairly rise in this country. If it pleases God to spare us violent convulsions and the loss of our liberties, you may at a future day wield the whole government of this land; and if this should be so, of what extreme moment will your *past steps* then be to the real usefulness of your high station.'

CHAPTER IV

THE CHURCH

(1838)

A period and a movement certainly among the most remarkable in the Christendom of the last three and a half centuries; probably more remarkable than the movement associated with the name of Port Royal, for that has passed away and left hardly a trace behind; but this has left ineffaceable marks upon the English church and nation.—GLADSTONE (1891).

IT was the affinity of great natures for great issues that made Mr. Gladstone from his earliest manhood onwards take and hold fast the affairs of the churches for the objects of his most absorbing interest. He was one and the same man, his genius was one. His persistent incursions all through his long life into the multifarious doings, not only of his own anglican communion, but of the Latin church of the west, as well as of the motley Christendom of the east, puzzled and vexed political whippers-in, wire-pullers, newspaper editors, leaders, colleagues; they were the despair of party caucuses; and they made the neutral man of the world smile, as eccentricities of genius and rather singularly chosen recreations. All this was, in truth, of the very essence of his character, the manifestation of its profound unity.

The quarrel upon church comprehension that had perplexed Elizabeth and Burleigh, had distracted the councils of Charles I. and of Cromwell, had bewildered William of Orange and Tillotson and Burnet, was once more aglow with its old heat. The still mightier dispute, how wide or how narrow is the common ground between the church of England and the church of Rome, broke into fierce flame. Then by and by these familiar contests of ancient tradition, thus quickened in the eternal ebb and flow of human things into fresh vitality, were followed by a revival, with new artillery and larger strategy, of a standing war that is roughly described as the conflict between reason and faith, between science and revelation. The controversy of Laudian divines with puritans, of Hoadly with non-jurors, of Hanoverian divines with deists and free-thinkers, all may seem now to us narrow and dry when compared with such a drama, of so many interesting characters, strange evolutions, and multiple and startling climax, as gradually unfolded itself to Mr. Gladstone's ardent and impassioned gaze.

His is not one of the cases, like Pascal, or Baxter, or Rutherford, or a hundred others, where a man's theological history is to the world, however it may seem to himself, the most important aspect of his career or character. This is not the place for an exploration of Mr. Gladstone's strictly theological history, nor is mine the hand by which such exploration could be attempted. In the sphere of dogmatic faith, apart from ecclesiastical politics and all the war of principles connected with such politics, Mr. Gladstone, by the time when he was thirty, had become a man of settled questions. Nor was he for his own part, with a remarkable exception in respect of one particular doctrine towards the end of his life, ever ready to re-open them. What is extraordinary in the career of this far-shining and dominant character of his age, is not a development of specific opinions on dogma, or discipline, or ordinance, on article or sacrament, but the fact that with a steadfast tread he marched along the high anglican road to the summits of that liberalism which it was the original object of the new anglicans to assault and overthrow.

The years from 1831 to 1840 Mr. Gladstone marked as an era of a marvellous uprising of religious energy throughout the land ; it saved the church, he says. Not only in Oxford but in England he declares that party spirit within the church had fallen to a low ebb. Coming hurricanes were not foreseen. In Lord Liverpool's government patronage was considered to have been respectably dispensed, and church reform was never heard of.[1] This dreamless composure was rudely broken. The repeal of the test and corporation Acts in 1828 first roused the church ; and her sons rubbed their eyes when they beheld parliament bringing frankly to an end the odious monopoly of office under the crown, all corporate office, all magistracy, in men willing to take the communion at the altar of the privileged establishment. The next year a deadlier blow fell after a more embittered fight—the admission of Roman catholics to parliament and place. The Reform bill of 1832 followed. Even when half spent, the forces that had been gathering for many years in the direction of parliamentary reform, and had at last achieved more than one immense result, rolled heavily forward against the church. The opening of parliament and of close corporations was taken to involve an opening to correspond in the grandest and closest of all corporations. The resounding victory of the constitutional bill of 1832 was followed by a drastic handling of the church in Ireland, and by a proposal

[1] Newman, *Essays*, ii. p. 428.

I

to divert a surplus of its property to purposes not ecclesiastical.
A long and peculiarly unedifying crisis ensued. Stanley and
Graham, two of the most eminent members of the reforming
whig cabinet, on this proposal at once resigned. The Grey
ministry was thus split in 1834, and the Peel ministry ejected
in 1835, on the ground of the absolute inviolability of the
property of the Irish church. The tide of reaction set slowly
in. The shock in political party was in no long time followed
by shock after shock in the church. As has happened on more
than one occasion in our history, alarm for the church kindled
the conservative temper in the nation. Or to put it in another
way, that spontaneous attachment to the old order of things
with all its symbols, institutes, and deep associations, which
the radical reformers had both affronted and ignored, made
the church its rallying-point. The three years of tortuous
proceedings on the famous Appropriation clause—proceedings
that political philosophers declared to have disgraced this
country in the face of Europe, and that were certainly an
ignominy and a scandal in a party called reforming—were
among the things that helped most to prepare the way for the
fall of the whigs and the conservative triumph of 1841. Within
ten years from the death of Canning the church transfixed the
attention of the politician. The Duke of Wellington was hardly
a wizard in political foresight, but he had often a good soldier's
eye for things that stood straight up in front of him. 'The
real question,' said the duke in 1838, 'that now divides the
country and which truly divides the House of Commons, is
church or no church. People talk of the war in Spain, and the
Canada question. But all that is of little moment. The real
question is church or no church.'

The position of the tory party as seen by its powerful recruit
was, when he entered public life, a state of hopeless defeat and
discomfiture. 'But in my imagination,' wrote Mr. Gladstone,
'I cast over that party a prophetic mantle and assigned to it a
mission distinctly religious as the champion in the state field of
that divine truth which it was the office of the Christian
ministry to uphold in the church. Neither then did I, nor now
can I, see on what ground this inviolability could for a moment
be maintained, except the belief that the state had such a
mission.' He soon discovered how hard it is to adjust to the
many angles of an English political party the seamless mantle
of ecclesiastical predominance.

The changes in the political constitution in 1828, in 1829, and
in 1832 carried with them a deliberate recognition that the church
was not the nation; that it was not identical with the parliament who spoke for the nation; that it had no longer a title to
compose the governing order; and—a more startling disclosure
still to the minds of churchmen—that laws affecting the church
would henceforth be made by men of all churches and creeds,

or even men of none. This hateful circumstance it was that inevitably began in multitudes of devout and earnest minds to produce a revolution in their conception of a church, and a resurrection in curiously altered forms of that old ideal of Milton's austere and lofty school—the ideal of a purely spiritual association that should leave each man's soul and conscience free from 'secular chains' and 'hireling wolves.'

Strange social conditions were emerging on every side. The factory system established itself on a startling scale. Huge aggregates of population collected with little regard to antique divisions of diocese and parish. Colonies over the sea extended in boundaries and numbers, and churchmen were zealous that these infant societies should be blessed by the same services, rites, ecclesiastical ordering and exhortation, as were believed to elevate and sanctify the parent community at home. The education of the people grew to be a formidable problem, the field of angry battles and campaigns that never end. Trade, markets, wages, hours, and all the gaunt and haggard economics of the labour question, added to the statesman's load. Pauperism was appalling. In a word, the need for social regeneration both material and moral was in the spirit of the time. Here were the hopes, vague, blind, unmeasured, formless, that had inspired the wild clamour for the bill, the whole bill, and nothing but the bill. The whig patricians carried away the prizes of great office, though the work had been done by men of a very different stamp. It was the utilitarian radicals who laid the foundations of social improvement in a reasoned creed. With admirable ability, perseverance, unselfishness, and public spirit, Bentham and his disciples had regenerated political opinion, and fought the battle against debt, pauperism, class-privilege, class-monopoly, abusive patronage, a monstrous criminal law, and all the host of sinister interests.[1] As in every reforming age, men approached the work from two sides. Evangelical religion divides with rationalism the glory of more than one humanitarian struggle. Brougham, a more potent force than we now realise, plunged with the energy of a Titan into a thousand projects, all taking for granted that ignorance is the disease and useful knowledge the universal healer, all of them secular, all dealing with man from the outside, none touching imagination or the heart. March-of-mind became to many almost as wearisome a cry as wisdom-of-our-ancestors had been. According to some eager innovators, dogma and ceremony were to go, the fabrics to be turned into mechanics' institutes, the clergy to lecture on botany and statistics. The reaction against this dusty dominion of secularity kindled new life in rival schools. They insisted that if society is to be improved and civilisation saved, it can only be through improvement in the character of man, and character

[1] See Sir Leslie Stephen's *English Utilitarians*, ii. p. 42.

is moulded and inspired by more things than are dreamed of
by societies for useful knowledge. The building up of the
inward man in all his parts, faculties, and aspirations, was
seen to be, what in every age it is, the problem of problems.
This thought turned the eyes of many—of Mr. Gladstone first
among them—to the church, and stirred an endeavour to make
out of the church what Coleridge describes as the sustaining,
correcting, befriending opposite of the world, the compensating
counterforce to the inherent and inevitable defects of the state
as a state. Such was the new movement of the time between
1835 and 1845.

'It is surprising,' said Proudhon, the trenchant genius of
French socialism in 1840 and onwards, 'how at the bottom of
our politics we always found theology.' It is true at any rate
that the association of political and social change with theological revolution was the most remarkable of all the influences
in the first twenty years of Mr. Gladstone's public life. Then
rose once more into active prominence the supreme debate,
often cutting deep into the labours of the modern statesman,
always near to the heart of the speculations of the theologian,
in many fields urgent in its interest alike to ecclesiastic,
historian and philosopher, the inquiry : what is a church ?
This opened the sluices and let out the floods. What is the
church of England ? To ask that question was to ask a
hundred others. Creeds, dogmas, ordinances, hierarchy, parliamentary institution, judicial tribunals, historical tradition, the
prayer-book, the Bible—all these enormous topics sacred and
profane, with all their countless ramifications, were rapidly
swept into a tornado of such controversy as had not been seen
in England since the Revolution. Was the church a purely
human creation, changing with time and circumstance, like all
the other creations of the heart and brain and will of man ?
Were its bishops mere officers, like high ministers of mundane
state, or were they, in actual historic truth as in supposed theological necessity, the direct lineal successors of the first apostles,
endowed from the beginning with the mystical prerogatives on
which the efficacy of all sacramental rites depended ? What
were its relations to the councils of the first four centuries,
what to the councils of the fifteenth century and the sixteenth,
what to the Fathers ? The Scottish presbyterians held the conception of a church as strongly as anybody ;[1] but England,
broadly speaking, had never been persuaded that there could
be a church without bishops.

In the answers to this group of hard questions, terrible
divisions that had been long muffled and huddled away burst
into view. The stupendous quarrel of the sixteenth and seven-

---

[1] 'Nowhere that I know of,' the Duke of Argyll once wrote in friendly remonstrance
with Mr. Gladstone, 'is the doctrine of a separate society being of divine foundation,
so dogmatically expressed as in the Scotch Confession ; the 39 articles are less definite
on the subject.'

teenth centuries again broke out. To the erastian lawyer the
church was an institution erected on principles of political
expediency by act of parliament. To the school of Whately
and Arnold it was a corporation of divine origin, devised to
strengthen men in their struggle for goodness and holiness by
the association and mutual help of fellow-believers. To the
evangelical it was hardly more than a collection of congregations commended in the Bible for the diffusion of the knowledge
and right interpretation of the Scriptures, the commemoration
of gospel events, and the linking of gospel truths to a well-
ordered life. To the high anglican as to the Roman catholic,
the church was something very different from this ; not a fabric
reared by man, nor in truth any mechanical fabric at all, but a
mystically appointed channel of salvation, an indispensable
element in the relation between the soul of man and its creator.
To be a member of it was not to join an external association,
but to become an inward partaker in ineffable and mysterious
graces to which no other access lay open. Such was the
Church Catholic and Apostolic as set up from the beginning,
and of this immense mystery, of this saving agency, of this in-
commensurable spiritual force, the established church of England
was the local presence and the organ.

The noble restlessness of the profounder and more penetrating minds was not satisfied, any more than Bossuet had
been, to think of the church as only an element in a scheme of
individual salvation. They sought in it the comprehensive
solution of all the riddles of life and time. Newman drew in
powerful outline the sublime and sombre anarchy of human
history.

This is the enigma, this the solution in faith and spirit, in
which Mr. Gladstone lived and moved. In him it gave to the
energies of life their meaning, and to duty its foundation.
While poetic voices and the oracles of sages—Goethe, Scott,
Wordsworth, Shelley, Byron, Coleridge—were drawing men one
way or another, or else were leaving the void turbid and formless, he in the midst of doubts, distractions, and fears, saw a
steadfast light where the Oxford men saw it ; in that concrete
representation of the unseen Power that, as he believed. had
made and guides and rules the world, in that Church Catholic
and Apostolic which alone would have the force and the stout-
ness necessary to serve for a breakwater against the deluge.
Yet to understand Mr. Gladstone's case, we have ever to
remember that what is called the catholic revival was not in
England that which the catholic counter-revolution had been on
the continent of Europe, primarily a political movement. Its
workings were inward, in the sphere of the mind, in thought
and faith, in idealised associations of historic grandeur.[1]

[1] On this, see Fairbairn's *Catholicism, Roman and Anglican*, pp. 114-5.

II

The reader has already been told how at Rome and in Naples in 1832, Mr. Gladstone was suddenly arrested by the new idea of a church, interweaving with the whole of human life a pervading and equalised spirit of religion. Long years after, in an unfinished fragment, he began to trace the golden thread of his religious growth :—

My environment in my childhood was strictly evangelical. My dear and noble mother was a woman of warm piety but broken health, and I was not directly instructed by her. But I was brought up to believe that Doyly and Mant's Bible (then a standard book of the colour ruling in the church) was heretical, and that every unitarian (I suppose also every heathen) must, as matter of course, be lost for ever. This deplorable servitude of mind oppressed me in a greater or less degree for a number of years. As late as in the year (I think) 1836, one of my brothers married a beautiful and in every way charming person, who had been brought up in a family of the unitarian profession, yet under a mother very sincerely religious. I went through much mental difficulty and distress at the time, as there had been no express renunciation [by her] of the ancestral creed, and I absurdly busied myself with devising this or that religious test as what if accepted might suffice.[1]

So, as will be seen, the first access of churchlike ideas to my mind by no means sufficed to expel my inherited and bigoted misconception, though in the event they did it as I hope effectively. But I long retained in my recollection an observation made to me in (I think) the year 1829, by Mrs. Benjamin Gaskell of Thornes, near Wakefield, a seed which was destined long to remain in my mind without germinating. I fell into religious conversation with this excellent woman, the mother of my Eton friend Gaskell, herself an unitarian like her husband. She said to me, Surely we cannot entertain a doubt as to the future condition of any person truly united to Christ by faith and love, whatever may be the faults of his opinions. Here she supplied me with the key to the whole question. At this hour I feel grateful to her accordingly, for the scope of her remark is very wide ; and it is now my rule to remember her in prayer before the altar.

There was nothing at Eton to subvert this frame of mind ; for nothing was taught us either for it or against it. But in the spring and summer of 1828, I set to work on Hooker's *Ecclesiastical Polity*, and read it straight through. Intercourse with my elder sister Anne had increased my mental interest in religion, and she, though generally of evangelical sentiments, had an opinion that the standard divines of the English church were of great value. Hooker's exposition of the case of the church of England came to me as a mere abstraction ; but I think that I found the doctrine of Baptismal Regeneration, theretofore abhorred, impossible to reject, and the way was thus opened for further changes.

In like manner at Oxford, I do not doubt that in 1830 and 1831 the study of Bishop Butler laid the ground for new modes of thought in religion, but his teaching in the sermons on our moral nature was

---

[1] A little sheaf of curious letters on this family episode survives.

not integrated, so to speak, until several years later by larger perusal of the works of Saint Augustine. I may, however, say that I was not of a mind ill disposed to submit to authority.

The Oxford Movement, properly so called, began in the year 1833, but it had no direct effect upon me. I did not see the Tracts, and to this hour I have read but few of them. Indeed, my first impressions and emotions in connection with it were those of indignation at what I thought the rash intemperate censures pronounced by Mr. Hurrell Froude upon the reformers. My chief tie with Oxford was the close friendship I had formed in 1830 with Walter Hamilton.[1] His character always loving and loved had, not very greatly later, become deeply devout. But I do not think he at this time sympathised with Newman and his friends ; and he had the good sense, in conjunction with Mr. Denison, afterwards bishop, to oppose the censure upon Dr. Hampden, to which I foolishly and ignorantly gave in, without, however, being an active or important participator.

But the blow struck by the prayer-book in 1832 set my mind in motion, and that motion was never arrested. I found food for the new ideas and tendencies in various quarters, not least in the religious writings of Alexander Knox, all of which I perused. Moreover, I had an inclination to ecclesiastical conformity, and obedience as such, which led me to concur with some zeal in the plans of Bishop Blomfield. In the course of two or three years, Manning turned from a strongly evangelical attitude to one as strongly anglican, and about the same time converted his acquaintance with me into a close friendship. In the same manner James Hope, whom I had known but slightly at Eton or Oxford, made a carefully considered change of the same kind ; which also became the occasion of a fast friendship. Both these intimacies led me forward ; Hope especially had influence over me, more than I think any other person at any period of my life.[2]

When I was preparing in 1837-8 *The State in its Relations with the Church*, he took a warm interest in the work, which, during my absence on the continent, he corrected for the press. His attitude towards the work, however, included a desire that its propositions should be carried further. The temper of the times among young educated men was working in the same direction. I had no low churchmen among my near friends, except Walter Farquhar. Anstice, a great loss, died very early in his beautiful married life. While I was busy about my book, Hope made known to me Palmer's work on the Church, which had just appeared. I read it with care and great interest. It took hold upon me ; and gave me at once the clear, definite, and strong conception of the church which, through all the storm and strain of a most critical period, has proved for me entirely adequate to every emergency, and saved me from all vacillation. I did not, however, love the extreme rigour of the book in its treatment of non-episcopal communions. It was not very long after this, I think in 1842, that I reduced into form my convictions on the large and important range of subjects which recent controversy had brought into prominence. I conceive that in the main Palmer completed for me the work which inspection of the prayer-book had begun.

Before referring further to my 'redaction' of opinions, I desire to

---

[1] Afterwards Bishop of Salisbury.
[2] Marrying Walter Scott's granddaughter (1847) he was named Hope-Scott after 1853.

say that at this moment I am as closely an adherent to the doctrines of grace generally, and to the general sense of Saint Augustine, as at the date from which this narrative set out. I hope that my mind has dropped nothing affirmative. But I hope also that there has been dropped from it all the damnatory part of the opinions taught by the evangelical school ; not only as regards the Roman catholic religion, but also as to heretics and heathens ; nonconformists and presbyterians I think that I always let off pretty easily. . . .

III

The Tractarian movement is by this time one of the most familiar chapters in our history, and it has had singular good fortune in being told by three masters of the most winning, graphic, and melodious English prose of the century to which the tale belongs.[1] Whether we call it by the ill name of Oxford counter-reformation or the friendlier name of catholic revival, it remains a striking landmark in the varied motions of English religious thought and feeling for the three-quarters of a century since the still unfinished journey first began. In its early stages, the movement was exclusively theological. Philanthropic reform still remained with the evangelical school that so powerfully helped to sweep away the slave trade, cleansed the prisons, and aided in humanising the criminal law. It was they who 'helped to form a conscience, if not a heart, in the callous bosom of English politics,' while the very foremost of the Oxford divines was scouting the fine talk about black men, because they 'concentrated in themselves all the whiggery, dissent, cant and abomination that had been ranged on their side.'[2] Nor can we forget that Shaftesbury, the leader in that beneficent crusade of human mercy and national wisdom which ended in the deliverance of women and children in mines and factories, was also a leader of the evangelical party.

The Tractarian movement, as all know, opened, among other sources, in antagonism to utilitarian liberalism. Yet J. S. Mill, the oracle of rationalistic liberalism in Oxford and other places in the following generation, had always much to say for the Tractarians. He used to tell us that the Oxford theologians had done for England something like what Guizot, Villemain, Michelet, Cousin had done a little earlier for France ; they had opened, broadened, deepened the issues and meanings of European history ; they had reminded us that history is European ; that it is quite unintelligible if treated as merely local. He would say, moreover, that thought should recognise

[margin note: Shaftesbury leader of factory + Social Refo—]

---

[1] The *Apologia* of its leader ; Froude, *Short Studies*, vol. iv. ; and Dean Church's *Oxford Movement*, 1833-45, a truly fascinating book—called by Mr. Gladstone a great and noble book. ' It has all the delicacy,' he says, ' the insight into the human mind, heart, and character, which were Newman's great endowment ; but there is a pervading sense of soundness about it which Newman, great as he was, never inspired.'

[2] See Dr. Fairbairn's *Catholicism, Roman and Anglican*, p. 292. Pusey speaks of our ' paying twenty millions for a theory about slavery' (Liddon, *Life of Pusey*, iii. p. 172).

thought and mind always welcome mind ; and the Oxford men
had at least brought argument, learning, and even philosophy
of a sort, to break up the narrow and frigid conventions of
reigning system in church and college, in pulpits and professorial chairs. They had made the church ashamed of the
evil of her ways, they had determined that spirit of improvement from within ' which, if this sect-ridden country is ever
really to be taught, must proceed *pari passu* with assault from
without.' [1]

One of the ablest of the Oxford writers talking of the non-
jurors, remarks how very few of the movements that are
attended with a certain romance, and thus bias us for a time
in their favour, will stand full examination ; they so often
reveal some gross offence against common sense.[2] Want of
common sense is not the particular impression left by the
Tractarians, after we have put aside the plausible dialectic and
winning periods of the leader, and proceed to look at the effect,
not on their general honesty but on their intellectual integrity,
of their most peculiar situation and the methods which they
believed that situation to impose. Nobody will be so presumptuous or uncharitable as to deny that among the divines
of the Oxford movement were men as pure in soul, as fervid
lovers of truth, as this world ever possessed. On the other
hand it would be nothing short of a miracle in human nature,
if all that dreadful tangle of economies and reserves, so largely
practised and for a long time so insidiously defended, did not
familiarise a vein of subtlety, a tendency to play fast and loose
with words, a perilous disposition to regard the non-natural
sense of language as if it were just as good as the natural, a
willingness to be satisfied with a bare and rigid logical consistency of expression, without respect to the interpretation
that was sure to be put upon that expression by the hearer and
the reader. The strain of their position in all these respects
made Newman and his allies no exemplary school. Their
example has been, perhaps rightly, held to account for something that was often under the evil name of sophistry suspected
and disliked in Mr. Gladstone himself, in his speeches, his
writings, and even in his public acts.

It is true that to the impartial eye Newman is no worse than
teachers in antagonistic sects ; he is, for instance, no subtler
than Maurice. The theologian who strove so hard in the name
of anglican unity to develop all the catholic elements and hide
out of sight all the calvinistic, was not driven to any hardier
exploits of verbal legerdemain, than the theologian who strove
against all reason and clear thinking to devise common formulæ
that should embrace both catholic and calvinistic explanations
together, or indeed anything else that anybody might choose
to bring to the transfusing alchemy of his rather smoky

[1] *Dissertations*, i. p. 444.   [2] J. B. Mozley's *Letters*, p. 234.

crucible. Nor was the third, and at that moment the strongest, of the church parties at Oxford and in the country, well able to fling stones at the other two. What better right, it was asked, had low churchmen to shut their eyes to the language of rubrics, creeds, and offices, than the high churchmen had to twist the language of the articles?

The confusion was grave and it was unfathomable. Newman fought a skilful and persistent fight against liberalism, as being nothing else than the egregious doctrine that there is no positive truth in religion, and that one creed is as good as another. Dr. Arnold, on the other hand, denounced Newmanism as idolatry; declared that if you let in the little finger of tradition, you would soon have in the whole monster, horns and tail and all; and even complained of the English divines in general, with the noble exceptions of Butler and Hooker, that he found in them a want of believing or disbelieving anything because it was true or false, as if that were a question that never occurred to them.[1] The plain man, who was but a poor master either of theology or of the history of the church of England, but who loved the prayer-book and hated confession, convents, priest-craft, and mariolatry, was wrought to madness by a clergyman who should describe himself, as did R. H. Froude, as a catholic without the popery, and a church of England man without the protestantism. The plain man knew that he was not himself clever enough to form any distinct idea of what such talk meant. But then his helplessness only deepened his conviction that the more distinct his idea might become, the more intense would his aversion be, both to the thing meant and to the surpliced conjuror who, as he bitterly supposed, was by sophistic tricks trying hard to take him in.

Other portents were at the same time beginning to disturb the world. The finds and the theories of geologists made men uncomfortable, and brought down sharp anathemas. Wider speculations on cosmic and creative law came soon after, and found their way into popular reading.[2] In prose literature, in subtler forms than the verse of Shelley, new dissolving elements appeared that were destined to go far. Schleiermacher, between 1820 and 1830, opened the sluices of the theological deep, whether to deluge or to irrigate. In 1830 an alarming note was sounded in the publication by a learned clergyman of a history of the Jews. We have seen (p. 42) how Mr. Gladstone was horrified by it. Milman's book was the beginning of a new rationalism within the fold. A line of thought was opened that seemed to make the history of religious ideas more interesting than their truth. The special claims of an accepted creed were shaken by disclosing an

---

[1] Stanley's *Life of Arnold*, ii. p. 56 *n*.
[2] The *Vestiges of Creation* appeared in 1844.

unmistakeable family likeness to creeds abhorred. A belief
was deemed to be accounted for and its sanctity dissolved, by
referring it historically to human origins, and showing it to be
only one branch of a genealogical trunk. Historic explanation
became a graver peril than direct attack.

IV

The first skirmish in a dire conflict that is not even now over
or near its end happened in 1836. Lord Melbourne recommended for the chair of divinity at Oxford Dr. Hampden, a
divine whose clumsy handling of nice themes had brought
him, much against his intention, under suspicion of unsound
doctrine, and who was destined eleven years later to find
himself the centre of a still louder uproar. Evangelicals and
Tractarians flew to arms, and the two hosts who were soon to
draw their swords upon one another, now for the first time, if
not the last, swarmed forth together side by side against the
heretic. What was rather an affront than a penalty was
inflicted upon Hampden by a majority of some five to one of
the masters of arts of the university, and in accord with that
majority, as he has just told us, though he did not actually
vote, was Mr. Gladstone. Twenty years after, when he had
risen to be a shining light in the world's firmament, he wrote
to Hampden to express regret for the injustice of which in this
instance 'the forward precipitancy of youth' had made him
guilty.[1] The case of Hampden gave a sharp actuality to the
question of the relations of church and crown. The particular
quarrel was of secondary importance, but it brought home to
the high churchmen what might be expected in weightier
matters than the affair of Dr. Hampden from whig ministers,
and confirmed the horrible apprehension that whig ministers
might possibly have to fill all the regius chairs and all the sees
for a whole generation to come.

Not less important than the theology of the Oxford divines
in its influence on Mr. Gladstone's line of thought upon things
ecclesiastical was the speculation of Coleridge on the teaching
and polity of a national church. His fertile book on *Church
and State* was given to the world in 1830, four years before his
death, and this and the ideas proceeding from it were the
mainspring, if not of the theology of the movement, at least
of Mr. Gladstone's first marked contribution to the stirring
controversies of the time. He has described the profound
effect upon his mind of another book, the *Treatise on the
Church of Christ*, by William Palmer of Worcester College
(1838), and to the end of his life it held its place in his mind
among the most masterly performances of the day in the

---

[1] The letter will be found at the end of the chapter.

twin hemispheres of theology and church polity.[1] Newman
applauded the book for its magnificence of design, and undoubtedly it covers much ground, including a stiff rejection
of Locke's theory of toleration, and the assertion of the strong
doctrine that the Christian prince has a right by temporal
penalties to protect the church from the gathering together
of the froward and the insurrection of wicked doers. It has
at least the merit, so far from universal in the polemics of
that day, of clear language, definite propositions, and formal
arguments capable of being met by a downright yes or no.[2]
The question, however, that has often slumbered yet never
dies, of the right relations between the Christian prince or
state and the Christian church, was rapidly passing away from
logicians of the cloister.

Note to page 123.

'*Hawarden, Chester, November* 9, 1856.—MY LORD BISHOP,—Your
lordship will probably be surprised at receiving a letter from me, as a
stranger. The simple purpose of it is to discharge a debt of the smallest
possible importance to you, yet due I think from me, by expressing the
regret with which I now look back on my concurrence in a vote of the
University of Oxford in the year 1836, condemnatory of some of your
lordship's publications. I did not take actual part in the vote ; but
upon reference to a journal kept at the time, I find that my absence
was owing to an accident.

'For a good many years past I have found myself ill able to master
books of an abstract character, and I am far from pretending to be
competent at this time to form a judgment on the merits of any propositions then at issue. I have learned, indeed, that many things which,
in the forward precipitancy of my youth, I should have condemned, are
either in reality sound, or lie within the just limits of such discussion
as especially befits an University. But that which (after a delay, due,
I think, to the cares and pressing occupations of political life) brought
back to my mind the injustice of which I had unconsciously been guilty
in 1836, was my being called upon, as a member of the Council of King's
College in London, to concur in a measure similar in principle with
respect to Mr. Maurice ; that is to say, in a condemnation couched in
general terms which did not really declare the point of imputed guilt,
and against which perfect innocence could have no defence. I resisted
to the best of my power, though ineffectually, the grievous wrong done
to Mr. Maurice, and urged that the charges should be made distinct, that
all the best means of investigation should be brought to bear on them,
ample opportunity given for defence, and a reference then made, if
needful, to the Bishop in his proper capacity. But the majority of
laymen in the Council were inexorable. It was only, as I have said,
after mature reflection that I came to perceive the bearing of the case on

---

[1] See his article in the *Nineteenth Century* for August, 1894, where he calls Palmer's
book the most powerful and least assailable defence of the position of the anglican
church from the sixteenth century downwards.
[2] See Church, *Oxford Movement*, pp. 214-6.

that of 1836, and to find that by my resistance I had condemned myself. I then lamented very sincerely that I had not on that occasion, now so remote, felt and acted in a different manner.

'I beg your lordship to accept this expression of my cordial regret, and to allow me to subscribe myself, very respectfully, your obedient and humble servant, W. E. GLADSTONE.' [1]

[1] This letter is printed in the *Life of Hampden* (1876), p. 199.

CHAPTER V

HIS FIRST BOOK

(1838-1839)

The union [with the State] is to the Church of secondary though great importance
Her foundations are on the holy hills. Her charter is legibly divine. She, if she should
be excluded from the precinct of government, may still fulfil all her functions, and
carry them out to perfection. Her condition would be anything rather than pitiable,
should she once more occupy the position which she held before the reign of Constantine. But the State, in rejecting her, would actively violate its most solemn duty,
and would, if the theory of the connection be sound, entail upon itself a curse.—
GLADSTONE (1838).

ACCORDING to Mr. Gladstone, a furore for church establishment
came down upon the conservative squadrons between 1835 and
1838. He describes it as due especially to the activity of the
presbyterian established church of Scotland before the disruption, and especially to the 'zealous and truly noble propagandism of Dr. Chalmers, a man with the energy of a giant
and the simplicity of a child.' In 1837, Mr. Gladstone says in
one of the many fragments written when in his later years he
mused over the past, 'we had a movement for fresh parliamentary grants to build churches in Scotland. The leaders
did not seem much to like it, but had. to follow. I remember
dining at Sir R. Peel's with the Scotch deputation. It included
Collins, a church bookseller of note, who told me that no
sermon ought ever to fall short of an hour, for in less time
than that it was not possible to explain any text of the Holy
Scripture.'

In the spring of 1838, the mighty Chalmers was persuaded
to cross the border and deliver in London half a dozen discourses to vindicate the cause of ecclesiastical establishments.
The rooms in Hanover Square were crowded to suffocation by
intense audiences mainly composed of the governing class.
Princes of the blood were there, high prelates of the church,
great nobles, leading statesmen, and a throng of members of
the House of Commons, from both sides of it. The orator was
seated, but now and again in the kindling excitement of his
thought, he rose unconsciously to his feet, and by ringing

phrase or ardent gesture roused a whirlwind of enthusiasm
such that vehement bystanders assure us it could not be exceeded in the history of human eloquence.[1] In Chalmers'
fulminating energy, the mechanical polemics of an appropriation clause in a parliamentary bill assume a passionate and
living air. He had warned his northern flock, 'should the
disaster ever befall us, of vulgar and upstart politicians becoming lords of the ascendant, and an infidel or demi-infidel
government wielding the destinies of this mighty empire, and
should they be willing at the shrines of their own wretched
partizanship to make sacrifice of those great and hallowed
institutions which were consecrated by our ancestors to the
maintenance of religious truth and religious liberty,—should in
particular the monstrous proposition ever be entertained to
abridge the legal funds for the support of protestantism,—let
us hope that there is still enough, not of fiery zeal, but of calm,
resolute, enlightened principle in the land to resent the outrage—enough of energy and reaction in the revolted sense of
this great country to meet and overbear it.'

The impression made by all this on Mr. Gladstone he has
himself described in an autobiographic note of 1897 :—

The primary idea of my early politics was the church. With this
was connected the idea of the establishment, as being everything except
essential. When therefore Dr. Chalmers came to London to lecture on
the principle of church establishments, I attended as a loyal hearer. I
had a profound respect for the lecturer, with whom I had had the
honour of a good deal of acquaintance during winter residences in Edinburgh, and some correspondence by letter. I was in my earlier twenties,
and he near his sixties [he was 58], with a high and merited fame for
eloquence and character. He subscribed his letters to me 'respectfully'
(or 'most respectfully') yours, and puzzled me extremely in the effort
to find out what suitable mode of subscription to use in return. Unfortunately the basis of his lectures was totally unsound. Parliament
as being Christian was bound to know and establish the truth. But
not being made of theologians, it could not follow the truth into its
minuter shadings, and must proceed upon broad lines. Fortunately
these lines were ready to hand. There was a religious system which,
taken in the rough, was truth. This was known as protestantism : and
to its varieties it was not the business of the legislature to have regard.
On the other side lay a system which, taken again in the rough, was not
truth but error. This system was known as popery. Parliament therefore was bound to establish and endow some kind of protestantism, and
not to establish or endow popery.

In a letter to Manning (May 14, 1838) he puts the case more
bluntly :—

Such a jumble of church, un-church, and anti-church principles as
that excellent and eloquent man Dr. Chalmers has given us in his recent

lectures, no human being ever heard, and it can only be compared to the state of things—

Ante mare et terras et quod tegit omnia cœlum.[1]

He thinks that the State has not cognisance of spirituals, except upon a broad simple principle like that which separates popery from protestantism, namely that protestantism receives the word of God only, popery the word of God and the word of man alike—it is easy, he says, such being the alternatives, to judge which is preferable.   He flogged the apostolical succession grievously, seven bishops sitting below him : London, Winchester, Chester, Oxford, Llandaff, Gloucester, Exeter, and the Duke of Cambridge incessantly bobbing assent ; but for fear we should be annoyed he then turned round on the cathedrals plan and flogged it with at least equal vigour.   He has a mind keenly susceptible of what is beautiful, great, and good ; tenacious of an idea when once grasped, and with a singular power of concentrating the whole man upon it.   But unfortunately I do not believe he has ever looked in the face the real doctrine of the visible church and the apostolical succession, or has any idea what is the matter at issue.

Mr. Gladstone says he could not stand the undisputed currency in conservative circles of a theory like this, and felt that the occasion ought to be seized for further entrenching the existing institution, strong as it seemed in fact, by more systematic defences in principle and theory.   He sat down to the literary task with uncommon vigour and persistency.   His object was not merely to show that the state has a conscience, for not even the newest of new Machiavellians denies that a state is bound by some moral obligations though in history and fact it is true that

Earth is sick,
And Heaven is weary, of the hollow words
Which States and Kingdoms utter when they talk
Of truth and justice.[2]

But the obligation of conscience upon a state was not Mr. Gladstone's only point.   His propositions were, that the state is cognisant of the difference between religious truth and religious error ; that the propagation of this truth and the discouragement of this error are among the ends for which government exists ; that the English state did recognise as a fundamental duty to give an active and exclusive support to a certain religion ; and finally that the condition of things resulting from the discharge of this duty was well worth preserving against encroachment, from whatever quarter encroachment might threaten.

On July 23rd, the draft of his book was at last finished, and he dispatched it to James Hope for free criticism, suggestions, and revision.   The 'physical state of the MS.,' as Mr. Gladstone calls it, seems to have been rather indefensible, and his excuse

[1] Ovid, *Met.* i. 5.—Chaos, before sea and land and all-covering skies.
[2] *Excursion*, v.

for writing 'irregularly and confusedly, considering the pressure of other engagements'—an excuse somewhat too common with him—was not quite so valid as he seems to have thought it. 'The defects,' writes Hope, 'are such as must almost necessarily occur when a great subject is handled piecemeal and at intervals ; and I should recommend, with a view to remedying them, that you procure the whole to be copied out in a good legible hand with blank pages, and that you read it through in this shape once connectedly, with a view to the whole argument, and again with a view to examining the structure of each part.'[1] Hope took as much trouble with the argument and structure of the book as if he were himself its author. For many weeks the fervid toil went on.

The strain on his eyesight that had embarrassed Mr. Gladstone for several months now made abstinence from incessant reading and writing necessary, and he was ordered to travel. He first settled with his sister at Ems (August 15th), whither the proofs of his book with Hope's annotations followed, nor did he finally get rid of the burden until the middle of September. The tedium of life in hotels was almost worse than the tedium of revising proofs, and at Milan and Florence he was strongly tempted to return home, as the benefit was problematical ; it was even doubtful whether pictures were any less trying to his eyes than books. He made the acquaintance of one celebrated writer of the time. 'I went to see Manzoni,' he says, 'in his house some six or eight miles from Milan in 1838. He was a most interesting man, but was regarded, as I found, among the more fashionable priests in Milan as a *bacchettone* [hypocrite]. In his own way he was, I think, a liberal and a nationalist, nor was the alliance of such politics with strong religious convictions uncommon among the more eminent Italians of those days.'

October found him in Sicily,[2] where he travelled with Sir Stephen Glynne and his two sisters, and here we shall soon see that with one of these sisters a momentous thing came to pass. It was at Catania that he first heard of the publication of his book. A month or more was passed in Rome in company with Manning, and together they visited Wiseman, Manning's conversion still thirteen years off. Macaulay too, now eight-and-thirty, was at Rome that winter. 'On Christmas Eve,' he says, 'I found Gladstone in the throng, and I accosted him, as we had met, though we had never been introduced to each other. We talked and walked together in St. Peter's during the best part of an afternoon. He is both a clever and an amiable man. . . .' At Rome, as the state of his eyesight forbade too close resort to picture-galleries and museums, he

---

[1] *Memoirs of J. R. Hope-Scott*, i. p. 150, where an adequate portion of the correspondence is to be found.

[2] He wrote an extremely graphic account of their ascent of Mount Etna, which has since found a place in Murray's handbook for Sicily.

listened to countless sermons, all carefully recorded in his diary. Dr. Wiseman gave him a lesson in the missal. On his birthday he went with Manning to hear mass with the pope's choir, and they were placed on the bench behind the cardinals. At St. Peter's he recalled that there his first conception of the unity of the church had come into his mind, and the desire for its attainment—'an object in every human sense hopeless, but not therefore the less to be desired, for the horizon of human hope is not that of divine power and wisdom. That idea has been upon the whole, I believe, the ruling one of my life during the period that has since elapsed.' On January 19, he bade 'a reluctant adieu to the mysterious city, whither he should repair who wishes to renew for a time the dream of life.'

A few years later Mr. Gladstone noted some differences between English and Italian preaching that are of interest :—

The fundamental distinction between English and Italian preaching is, I think, this : the mind of the English preacher, or reader of sermons, however impressive, is fixed mainly upon his composition, that of the Italian on his hearers. The Italian is a man applying himself by his rational and persuasive organs to men, in order to move them ; the former is a man applying himself, with his best ability in many cases, to a fixed form of matter, in order to *make it* move those whom he addresses. The action in the one case is warm, living, direct, immediate, from heart to heart ; in the other it is transfused through a medium comparatively torpid. The first is surely far superior to the second in truth and reality. The preacher bears an awful message. Such messengers, if sent with authority, are too much identified with, and possessed by, that which they carry, to view it objectively during its delivery, it absorbs their very being and all its energies, they *are* their message, and they see nothing extrinsic to themselves except those to whose hearts they desire to bring it. In truth, what we want is the following of nature, and her genial development. (March 20. Palm Sunday, '42.)

II

It was the end of January (1839) before Mr. Gladstone arrived in London, and by that time his work had been out for six or seven weeks.[1] On his return we may be sure that his book and its fortunes were the young author's most lively interest. Church authorities and the clergy generally, so far as he could learn, approved, many of them very warmly. The Bishop of London wrote this, and the Archbishop of Canterbury said it. It is easy to understand with what interest and delight the average churchman would welcome so serious a contribution to the good cause, so bold an effort by so skilled a hand, by lessons from history, by general principles of national probity and a national religion, and by well-digested materials gathered, as Hooker gathered his, 'from the characteristic circumstances of the time,' to support

---

1 Of the first edition some 1500 or 1750 copies were sold.

the case for ecclesiastical privilege. Anglicans of the better
sort had their intellectual self-respect restored in Mr. Gladstone's book by finding that they need no longer subsist on
the dregs of Eldonian prejudice, but could sustain themselves
in intellectual dignity and affluence by large thoughts and
sonorous phrases upon the nature of human society as a grand
whole.[1] Even unconvinced whigs who quarrelled with the
arguments admitted that the tories had found in the young
member for Newark a well-read scholar, with extraordinary
amplitude of mind, a man who knew what reasoning meant,
and a man who knew how to write.

The first chapter dealing with establishment drew forth
premature praise from many who condemned the succeeding
chapters setting out high notions as to the church. From both
universities he had favourable accounts. ‘From Scotland they
are mixed ; those which are most definite tend to show there is
considerable soreness, at which, God knows, I am not surprised ;
but I have not sought nor desired it.’ The Germans on the
whole approved. Bunsen was exuberant ; there was nobody,
he said, with whom he so loved συμφιλοσοφεῖν καὶ συμφιλολογεῖν ;
people have too much to do about themselves to have time
to seek truth on its own account ; the greater, therefore, the
merit of the writer who forces his age to decide, whether they
will serve God or Baal. Gladstone is the first man in England
as to intellectual power, he cried, and he has heard higher tones
than any one else in this land. The Crown Prince of Prussia
sent him civil messages, and meant to have the book translated.
Rogers, the poet, wrote that his mother was descended from
stout nonconformists, that his father was perverted to his
mother's heresies, and that therefore he himself could not be
zealous in the cause ; but, however that might be, of this
Mr. Gladstone might be very sure, that he would love and
admire the author of the book as much as ever. The Duke
of Newcastle expected much satisfaction ; meanwhile declared
it to be a national duty to provide churches and pastors ;
parliament should vote even millions and millions ; then
dissent would uncommonly soon disappear, and a blessing
would fall upon the land. Dr. Arnold told his friends how
much he admired the spirit of the book throughout, how he
liked the substance of half of it, how erroneous he thought the
other half. Wordsworth pronounced it worthy of all attention,
doubted whether the author had not gone too far about
apostolical descent ; but then, like the sage that he was, the poet
admitted that he must know a great deal more ecclesiastical
history, be better read in the Fathers, and read the book itself
over again, before he could feel any right to criticise.[2]

[1] *Memoirs of J. R. Hope-Scott*, i. p. 172.
[2] Carlyle wrote to Emerson (Feb. 8, 1839): One of the strangest things about these
New England Orations (Emerson's) is a fact I have heard, but not yet seen, that a
certain W. Gladstone, an Oxford crack scholar, tory M.P., and devout churchman of

His political leaders had as yet not spoken a word. On February 9th, Mr. Gladstone dined at Sir Robert Peel's. 'Not a word from him, Stanley, or Graham yet, even to acknowledge my poor book ; but no change in manner, certainly none in Peel or Graham.' Monckton Milnes had been to Drayton, and told how the great man there had asked impatiently why anybody with so fine a career before him should go out of his way to write books. 'Sir Robert Peel,' says Mr. Gladstone, 'who was a religious man, was wholly anti-church and un-clerical, and largely undogmatic. I feel that Sir R. Peel must have been quite perplexed in his treatment of me after the publication of the book, partly through his own fault, for by habit and education he was quite incapable of comprehending the movement in the church, the strength it would reach, and the exigencies it would entail. Lord Derby, I think, early began to escape from the erastian yoke which weighed upon Peel. Lord Aberdeen was, I should say, altogether enlightened in regard to it and had cast it off : so that he obtained from some the sobriquet (during his ministry) of " the presbyterian Puseyite."' Even Mr. Gladstone's best friends trembled for the effect of his ecclesiastical zeal upon his powers of political usefulness, and to the same effect was the general talk of the town. The common suspicion that the writer was doing the work of the hated Puseyites grew darker and spread further. Then in April came Macaulay's article in the *Edinburgh*, setting out with his own incomparable directness, pungency, and effect, all the arguments on the side of that popular antagonism which was rooted far less in specific reasoning than in a general anti-sacerdotal instinct that lies deep in the hearts of Englishmen. John Sterling called the famous article the assault of an equipped and practised sophist against a crude young platonist, who happens by accident to have been taught the hard and broken dialect of Aristotle rather than the deep, continuous, and musical flow of his true and ultimate master. Author and critic exchanged magnanimous letters worthy of two great and honourable men.[1] Not the least wonderful thing about Macaulay's review is that he should not have seen how many of his own most trenchant considerations told no more strongly against Mr. Gladstone's theory, than they told against that whig theory of establishment which at the end of his article he himself tried to set up in its place.

great talent and hope, has contrived to insert a piece of you (*first* Oration it must be) in a work of his own on *Church and State*, which makes some figure at present ! I know him for a solid, serious, silent-minded man ; but how with his Coleridge shovel-hattism he has contrived to relate himself to *you*, there is the mystery. True men of all creeds, it *would* seem, are brothers.—*Correspondence of Carlyle and Emerson*, i. p. 217. There is more than one reference to Emerson in Mr. Gladstone's book, *e.g.* i. pp. 25, 130.

[1] The letters are given in full in *Gleanings*, vii. p. 106. See also Trevelyan's *Macaulay*, chap. viii.

Praise indeed came, and praise that no good man could have treated with indifference, from men like Keble, and it came from other quarters whence it was perhaps not quite so welcome, and not much more dangerous. He heard (March 19) that the Duke of Sussex, at Lord Durham's, had been strongly condemning the book; and by an odd contrast just after, as he was standing in conversation with George Sinclair, O'Connell with evident purpose came up and began to thank him for a most valuable work; for the doctrine of the authority of the church and infallibility in essentials—a great approximation to the church of Rome—an excellent sign in one who if he lived, etc. etc. It did not go far enough for the Roman catholic Archbishop of Tuam; but Dr. Murray, the Archbishop of Dublin, was delighted with it; he termed it an honest book, while as to the charges against romanism Mr. Gladstone was misinformed. 'I merely said I was very glad to approximate to any one on the ground of *truth*; *i.e.* rejoiced when truth immediately wrought out, in whatever degree, its own legitimate result of unity. O'Connell said he claimed half of me. . . . Count Montalembert came to me to-day (March 23rd), and sat long, for the purpose of ingenuously and kindly impugning certain statements in my book, viz. (1) That the peculiar tendency of the policy of romanism before the reformation went to limit in the mass of men intellectual exercise upon religion. (2) That the doctrine of purgatory adjourned until after death, more or less, the idea and practice of the practical work of religion. (3) That the Roman catholic church restricts the reading of the scriptures by the Christian people. He spoke of the evils; I contended we had a balance of good, and that the idea of duty in individuals was more developed here than in pure Roman catholic countries.'

All was of no avail. 'Scarcely had my work issued from the press,' wrote Mr. Gladstone thirty years later, 'when I became aware that there was no party, no section of a party, no individual person probably, in the House of Commons, who was prepared to act upon it. I found myself the last man on a sinking ship.' Exclusive support to the established religion of the country had been the rule; 'but when I bade it live, it was just about to die. It was really a quickened, not a deadened conscience, in the country, that insisted on enlarging the circle of state support.'[1] The result was not wholly unexpected, for in the summer of 1838 while actually writing the book, he records that he 'told Pusey for himself alone, I thought my own church and state principles within one stage of being hopeless as regards success in this generation.'

Another set of fragmentary notes, composed in 1894, and headed 'Some of my Errors,' contains a further passage that points in a significant direction:—

---

[1] Chapter of Autobiography, 1868.—*Gleanings*, vii. p. 115.

Oxford had not taught me, nor had any other place or person, the value of liberty as an essential condition of excellence in human things. True, Oxford had supplied me with the means of applying a remedy to this mischief, for she had undoubtedly infused into my mind the love of truth as a dominant and supreme motive of conduct. But this it took long to develop into its proper place and function. It may, perhaps, be thought that among these errors I ought to record the publication in 1838 of my first work, *The State in its Relation with the Church.* Undoubtedly that work was written in total disregard or rather ignorance of the conditions under which alone political action was possible in matters of religion. It involved me personally in a good deal of embarrassment. . . . In the sanguine fervour of youth, having now learned something about the nature of the church and its office, and noting the many symptoms of revival and reform within her borders, I dreamed that she was capable of recovering lost ground, and of bringing back the nation to unity in her communion. A notable projection from the ivory gate,

'Sed falsa ad cœlum mittunt insomnia manes.'[1]

From these points of view the effort seems contemptible. But I think that there is more to be said. The land was overspread with a thick curtain of prejudice. The foundations of the historic church of England, except in the minds of a few divines, were obscured. The evangelical movement, with all its virtues and merits, had the vice of individualising religion in a degree perhaps unexampled, and of rendering the language of holy scripture about Mount Sion and the kingdom of heaven little better than a jargon. . . . To meet the demands of the coming time, it was a matter of vital necessity to cut a way through all this darkness to a clearer and more solid position. Immense progress has been made in that direction during my lifetime, and I am inclined to hope that my book imparted a certain amount of stimulus to the public mind, and made some small contribution to the needful process in its earliest stage.

In the early pages of this very book, Mr. Gladstone says, that the union of church and state is to the church of secondary though great importance; *her* foundations are on the holy hills and her condition would be no pitiable one, should she once more occupy the position that she held before the reign of Constantine.[2] Faint echo of the unforgotten lines in which Dante cries out to Constantine what woes his fatal dower to the papacy had brought down on religion and mankind.[3] In these sentences lay a germ that events were speedily to draw towards maturity, a foreshadowing of the supreme principle that neither Oxford nor any other place had yet taught him, 'the value of liberty as an essential condition of excellence in human things.'

This revelation only turned his zeal for religion as the paramount issue of the time and of all times into another channel. Feeling the overwhelming strength of the tide that was running against his view of what he counted vital aspects of the

[1] *Aeneid,* vi. 896. But through the ivory gate the shades send to the upper air apparitions that do but cheat us.
[2] Chapter i. p. 5.   [3] *Inferno,* xix. 115-7.

church as a national institution, he next flew to the new task
of working out the doctrinal mysteries that this institution
embodied, and with Mr. Gladstone to work out a thing in his
own mind always meant to expound and to enforce for the
minds of others. His pen was to him at once as sword and
as buckler ; and while the book on *Church and State*, though
exciting lively interest, was evidently destined to make no
converts in theory and to be pretty promptly cast aside in
practice, he soon set about a second work on *Church Principles*.
It is true that with the tenacious instinct of a born contro-
versialist, he still gave a good deal of time to constructing
buttresses for the weaker places that had been discovered by
enemies or by himself in the earlier edifice, and in 1841 he
published a revised version of *Church and State*.[1] But ecclesiastical discussion was by then taking a new shape, and the
fourth edition fell flat. Of *Church Principles*, we may say that
it was stillborn. Lockhart said of it, that though a hazy
writer, Gladstone showed himself a considerable divine, and
it was a pity that he had entered parliament instead of taking
orders. The divinity, however, did not attract. The public are
never very willing to listen to a political layman discussing the
arcana of theology, and least of all were they inclined to listen
to him about the new-found arcana of anglo-catholic theology.
As Macaulay said, this time it was a theological treatise, not
an essay upon important questions of government ; and the
intrepid reviewer rightly sought a more fitting subject for his
magician's gifts in the dramatists of the Restoration. Newman
said of it, 'Gladstone's book is not open to the objections I
feared ; it is doctrinaire, and (I think) somewhat self-confident ;
but it will do good.'

III

A few sentences more will set before us the earliest of his
transitions, and its gradual dates. He is writing about the
first election at Newark :—

It was a curious piece of experience to a youth in his twenty-third
year, young of his age, who had seen little or nothing of the world, who
resigned himself to politics, but whose desire had been for the ministry
of God. The remains of this desire operated unfortunately. They
made me tend to glorify in an extravagant manner and degree not only
the religious character of the state, which in reality stood low, but
also the religious mission of the conservative party. There was in my
eyes a certain element of Antichrist in the Reform Act, and that act
was cordially hated, though the leaders soon perceived that there would
be no step backward. It was only under the second government of Sir
Robert Peel that I learned how impotent and barren was the conservative office for the church, though that government was formed of
men able, upright, and extremely well-disposed. It was well for me
that the unfolding destiny carried me off in a considerable degree from

[1] It was translated into German and published, with a preface by Tholuck, in
1843.

political ecclesiasticism of which I should at that time have made a sad mess. Providence directed that my mind should find its food in other pastures than those in which my youthfulness would have loved to seek it. I went beyond the general views of the tory party in state churchism, . . . it was my opinion that as to religions other than those of the state, the state should tolerate only and not pay. So I was against salaries for prison chaplains not of the church, and I applied a logic plaster to all difficulties. . . . So that Macaulay . . . was justified in treating me as belonging to the ultra section of the tories, had he limited himself to ecclesiastical questions.

In 1840, when he received Manning's imprimatur for *Church Principles*, he notes how hard the time and circumstances were in which he had to steer his little bark. 'But the polestar is clear. Reflection shows me that a political position is mainly valuable as instrumental for the good of the church, and under this rule every question becomes one of detail only.' By 1842 reflection had taken him a step further :—

I now approach the *mezzo del cammin* ; my years glide away. It is time to look forward to the close, and I do look forward. My life . . . has two prospective objects, for which I hope the performance of my present public duties may, if not qualify, yet extrinsically enable me. One, the adjustment of certain relations of the church to the state. Not that I think the action of the latter can be harmonised to the laws of the former. We have passed the point at which that was possible. . . . But it would be much if the state would honestly aim at enabling the church to develop her own intrinsic means. To this I look. The second is, unfolding the catholic system within her in some establishment or machinery looking both towards the higher life, and towards the external warfare against ignorance and depravity.

In the autumn of 1843, Mr. Gladstone explains to his father the relative positions of secular and church affairs in his mind, and this is only a few months after what to most men is the absorbing moment of accession to cabinet and its responsibilities. 'I contemplate secular affairs,' he says, 'chiefly as a means of being useful in church affairs, though I likewise think it right and prudent not to meddle in church matters for any small reason. I am not making known anything new to you. . . . These were the sentiments with which I entered public life, and although I do not at all repent of [having entered it, and] am not disappointed in the character of the employments it affords, certainly the experience of them in no way and at no time has weakened my original impressions.' At the end of 1843 he reached what looked like a final stage :—

Of public life, I certainly must say, every year shows me more and more that the idea of Christian politics cannot be realised in the state according to its present conditions of existence. For purposes sufficient, I believe, but partial and finite, I am more than content to be where I am. But the perfect freedom of the new covenant can only, it seems to me, be breathed in other air ; and the day may come when God may grant to me the application of this conviction to myself.

CHAPTER VI

CHARACTERISTICS

(1840)

> Be inspired with the belief that life is a great and noble calling; not a mean and grovelling thing that we are to shuffle through as we can, but an elevated and lofty destiny.—GLADSTONE.[1]

It is the business of biography to depict a physiognomy and not to analyse a type. In our case there is all the more reason to think of this, because type hardly applies to a figure like Mr. Gladstone's, without any near or distant parallel, and composed of so many curious dualisms and unforeseen affinities. Truly was it said of Fénelon, that half of him would be a great man, and would stand out more clearly as a great man than does the whole, because it would be simpler. So of Mr. Gladstone. We are dazzled by the endless versatility of his mind and interests as man of action, scholar, and controversial athlete; as legislator, administrator, leader of the people; as the strongest of his time in the main branches of executive force, strongest in persuasive force; supreme in the exacting details of national finance; master of the parliamentary arts; yet always living in the noble visions of the moral and spiritual idealist. This opulence, vivacity, profusion, and the promise of it all in these days of early prime, made an awakening impression even on his foremost contemporaries. The impression might have been easier to reproduce, if he had been less infinitely mobile. 'I cannot explain my own foundation,' Fénelon said; 'it escapes me; it seems to change every hour.' How are we to seek an answer to the same question in the history of Mr. Gladstone?

II

His physical vitality—his faculties of free energy, endurance, elasticity—was a superb endowment to begin with. We may often ask for ourselves and others: How many of a man's days does he really live? However men may judge the fruit it bore,

[1] Hawarden Grammar School, Sept. 19, 1877.

Mr. Gladstone lived in vigorous activity every day through all
his years. Time showed that he was born with a frame of
steel. Though, unlike some men of heroic strength,—Napoleon
for example—he often knew fatigue and weariness, yet his
organs never failed to answer the call of an intense and persistent Will. As we have already seen, in early manhood his
eyes gave him much trouble, and he both learned by heart and
composed a good deal of verse by way of sparing them. He
was a great walker, and at this time he was a sportsman, as his
diary has shown. 'My object in shooting, ill as I do it, is the
invigorating and cheering exercise, which does so much for
health (1842).' One day this year (Sept. 13, '42) while out
shooting, the second barrel of a gun went off while he was re-
loading, shattering the forefinger of his left hand. The remains
of the finger the surgeons removed. 'I have hardly ever in my
life,' he says, 'had to endure serious bodily pain, and this was
short.' In 1845, he notes, 'a hard day. What a mercy that my
strength, in appearance not remarkable, so little fails me.' In
the autumn of 1853 he was able to record, 'Eight or nine days of
bed illness, the longest since I had the scarlet fever at nine
or ten years old.' It was the same all through. His bodily
strength was in fact to prove extraordinary, and was no
secondary element in the long and strenuous course now
opening before him.

Not second to vigour of physical organisation—perhaps, if
we only knew all the secrets of mind and matter, even connected with this vigour—was strength and steadfastness of
Will. Character, as has been often repeated, is completely
fashioned will, and this superlative requirement, so indispensable for every man of action in whatever walk and on whatever scale, was eminently Mr. Gladstone's. From force of will,
with all its roots in habit, example, conviction, purpose, sprang
his leading and most effective qualities. He was never very
ready to talk about himself, but when asked what he regarded
as his master secret, he always said, '*Concentration.*' Slackness
of mind, vacuity of mind, the wheels of the mind revolving
without biting the rails of the subject, were insupportable.
Such habits were of the family of faintheartedness, which he
abhorred. Steady practice of instant, fixed, effectual attention,
was the key alike to his rapidity of apprehension and to his
powerful memory. In the orator's temperament exertion is
often followed by a reaction that looks like indolence. This
was never so with him. By instinct, by nature, by constitution,
he was a man of action in all the highest senses of a phrase too
narrowly applied and too narrowly construed. The currents
of daimonic energy seemed never to stop, the vivid susceptibility to impressions never to grow dull. He was an idealist,
yet always applying ideals to their purposes in act. Toil was
his native element ; and though he found himself possessed of

many inborn gifts, he was never visited by the dream so fatal
to many a well-laden argosy, that genius alone does all.   There
was nobody like him when it came to difficult business, for
bending his whole strength to it, like a mighty archer string-
ing a stiff bow.

Sir James Graham said of him in these years that Gladstone
could do in four hours what it took any other man sixteen to
do, and he worked sixteen hours a day.   When I came to know
him long years after, he told me that he thought when in office
in the times that our story is now approaching, fourteen hours
were a common tale.   Nor was it mere mechanic industry ; it
was hard labour, exact, strenuous, engrossing, rigorous.   No
Hohenzollern soldier held with sterner regularity to the duties
of his post.   Needless to add that he had a fierce regard for
the sanctity of time, although in the calling of the politician it
is harder than in any other to be quite sure when time is well
spent, and when wasted.   His supreme economy here, like
many other virtues, carried its own defect, and coupled with
his constitutional eagerness and his quick susceptibility, it led
at all periods of his life to some hurry.   The tumult of business,
he says one year in his diary, ' follows and whirls me day and
night.'   He speaks once in 1844 of ' a day restless as the sea.'
There were many such.   That does not mean, and has nothing
to do with, ' proud precipitance of soul,' nor haste in forming
pregnant resolves.   Here he was deliberate enough, and in the
ordinary conduct of life even minor things were objects of
scrutiny and calculation, far beyond the habit of most men.
For he was lowlander as well as highlander.   But a vast
percentage of his letters from boyhood onwards contain
apologies for haste.   More than once when his course was
nearly run, he spoke of his life having been passed in 'uninter-
mittent hurry,' just as Mill said, he had never been in a hurry
in his life until he entered parliament, and then he had never
been out of a hurry.

It was no contradiction that deep and constant in him,
along with this vehement turn for action, was a craving for
tranquil collection of himself that seemed almost monastic.
To Mrs. Gladstone he wrote a couple of years after their
marriage (Dec. 13, 1841) :—

You interpret so indulgently what I mean about the necessity of
quiescence at home during the parliamentary session, that I need not
say much ; and yet I think my doctrine must *seem* so strange that I
wish again and again to state how entirely it is different from anything
like disparagement, of George for example.   It is always relief and
always delight to see and to be with you ; and you would, I am sure,
be glad to know, how near Mary [Lady Lyttelton] comes as compared
with others to you, as respects what I can hardly describe in few words,
my mental rest, when she is present.   But there is no *man* however
near to me, with whom I am fit to be habitually, when hard worked.   I

have told you how reluctant I have always found myself to detail to my father on coming home, when I lived with him, what had been going on in the House of Commons. Setting a tired mind to work is like making a man run up and down stairs when his limbs are weary.

If he sometimes recalls a fiery hero of the *Iliad*, at other times he is the grave and studious benedictine, but whether in quietude or movement, always a man with a purpose and never the loiterer or lounger, never apathetic, never a sufferer from that worst malady of the human soul—from cheerlessness and cold.

We need not take him through a phrenological table of elements, powers, faculties, leanings, and propensities. Very early, as we shall soon see, Mr. Gladstone gave marked evidence of that sovereign quality of Courage which became one of the most signal of all his traits. He used to say that he had known three men in his time possessing in a supreme degree the virtue of parliamentary courage—Peel, Lord John Russell, and Disraeli. To some other contemporaries for whom courage might be claimed, he stoutly denied it. Nobody ever dreamed of denying it to him, whether parliamentary courage or any other, in either its active or its passive shape, either in daring or in fortitude. He had even the courage to be prudent, just as he knew when it was prudent to be bold. He applied in public things the Spenserian line, '*Be bold, be bold, and everywhere be bold*,' but neither did he forget the iron door with its admonition, '*Be not too bold.*' The great Condé, when complimented on his courage, always said that he took good care never to call upon it unless the occasion were absolutely necessary. No more did Mr. Gladstone go out of his way to summon courage for its own sake, but only when spurred by duty ; then he knew no faltering. Capable of much circumspection, yet soon he became known for a man of lion heart.

Nature had bestowed on him many towering gifts. Whether Humour was among them, his friends were wont to dispute. That he had a gaiety and sympathetic alacrity of mind that was near of kin to humour, nobody who knew him would deny. Of playfulness his speeches give a thousand proofs ; of drollery and fun he had a ready sense, though it was not always easy to be quite sure beforehand what sort of jest would hit or miss. For irony, save in its lighter forms as weapon in debate, he had no marked taste or turn. But he delighted in good comedy, and he reproached me severely for caring less than one ought to do for the *Merry Wives of Windsor*. Had he Imagination ? In its high literary and poetic form he rose to few conspicuous flights—such, for example, as Burke's descent of Hyder Ali upon the Carnatic—in vast and fantastic conceptions such as arose from time to time in the brain of Napoleon, he had no part or lot. But in force of moral and political imagination, in bold, excursive range, in the faculty of illuminating practical and objective calculations with lofty ideals of the strength of states, the happiness of peoples, the whole structure of good government, he has had no superior among the rulers of England. His very ardour of temperament gave him imagination; he felt as if everybody who listened to him in a great audience was equally fired with his own energy of sympathy, indignation, conviction, and was transported by the same emotion that thrilled through himself. All this, however, did not fully manifest itself at this time, nor for some years to come.

Strength of will found scope for exercise where some would not discover the need for it. In native capacity for righteous Anger he abounded. The flame soon kindled, and it was no fire of straw; but it did not master him. Mrs. Gladstone once said to me (1891), that whoever writes his life must remember that he had two sides—one impetuous, impatient, irrestrainable, the other all self-control, able to dismiss all but the great central aim, able to put aside what is weakening or disturbing; that he achieved this self-mastery, and had succeeded in the struggle ever since he was three- or four-and-twenty, first by the natural power of his character, and second by incessant wrestling in prayer— prayer that had been abundantly answered.

Problems of compromise are of the essence of the parliamentary and cabinet system, and for some years at any rate he was more than a little restive when they confronted him. Though in the time to come he had abundant difference with colleagues, he had all the virtues needed for political co-operation, as Cobden, Bright, and Mill had them, nor did he ever mistake for courage or independence the unhappy preference for having a party or an opinion exclusively to one's self. 'What is wanted above all things,' he said, 'in the business of joint counsel, is the faculty of making many one, of throwing the mind into the common stock.'[1] This was a favourite phrase with him for that power of working with other people, without which a man would do well to stand aside from public affairs. He used to say that of all the men he had ever known, Sir George Grey had most of this capacity for throwing his mind into joint stock. The demands of joint stock he never took to mean the quenching of the duty in a man to have a mind of his own. He was always amused by the recollection of somebody at Oxford—'a regius professor of divinity, I am sorry to say'—who was accustomed to define taste as 'a faculty of coinciding with the opinion of the majority.'

Hard as he strove for a broad basis in general theory and high abstract principle, yet always aiming at practical ends he kept in sight the opportune. Nobody knew better the truth,

[1] Mr. Gladstone on Lord Houghton's *Life*; *Speaker*, Nov. 29, 1890.

so disastrously neglected by politicians who otherwise would be the very salt of the earth, that not all questions are for all times. 'For my part,' Mr. Gladstone said, 'I have not been so happy, at any time of my life, as to be able sufficiently to adjust the proper conditions of handling any difficult question, until the question itself was at the door.'[1] He could not readily apply himself to topics outside of those with which he chanced at the moment to be engrossed :—'Can you not wait? Is it necessary to consider now?' That was part of his concentration. Nor did he fly at a piece of business, deal with it, then let it fall from his grasp. It became part of him. If circumstances brought it again into his vicinity, they found him instantly ready, with a prompt continuity that is no small element of power in public business.

How little elastic and self-confident at heart he was in some of his moods in early manhood, we discern in the curious language of a letter to his brother-in-law Lyttelton in 1840 :—

It is my nature to lean not so much on the applause as upon the assent of others to a degree which perhaps I do not show, from that sense of weakness and utter inadequacy to my work which never ceases to attend me while I am engaged upon these subjects. . . . I wish you knew the state of total impotence to which I should be reduced if there were no echo to the accents of my own voice. I go through my labour, such as it is, not by a genuine elasticity of spirit, but by a plodding movement only just able to contend with inert force, and in the midst of a life which indeed has little claim to be called active, yet is broken this way and that into a thousand small details, certainly unfavourable to calm and continuity of thought.

Here we have a glimpse of a singular vein peculiarly rare in ardent genius at thirty, but disclosing its traces in Mr. Gladstone even in his ripest years.

Was this the instinct of the orator? For it was in the noble arts of oratory that nature had been most lavish, and in them he rose to be consummate. The sympathy and assent of which he speaks are a part of oratorical inspiration, and even if such sympathy be but superficial, the highest efforts of oratorical genius take it for granted. 'The work of the orator,' he once wrote, 'from its very inception is inextricably mixed up with practice. It is cast in the mould offered to him by the mind of his hearers. It is an influence principally received from his audience (so to speak) in vapour, which he pours back upon them in a flood. The sympathy and concurrence of his time, is, with his own mind, joint parent of the work. He cannot follow nor frame ideals : his choice is, to be what his age will have him, what it requires in order to be moved by him ; or else not to be at all.'[2]

Among Mr. Gladstone's physical advantages for bearing the

1 *Gleanings*, vii. p. 133.   2 *Homeric Studies*, vol. iii.

orator's sceptre were a voice of singular fulness, depth, and variety of tone ; a falcon's eye with strange imperious flash ; features mobile, expressive, and with lively play ; a great actor's command of gesture, bold, sweeping, natural, unforced, without exaggeration or a trace of melodrama. His pose was easy, alert, erect. To these endowments of external mien was joined the gift and the glory of words. They were not sought, they came. Whether the task were reasoning or exposition or expostulation, the copious springs never failed. Nature had thus done much for him, but he superadded ungrudging labour. Later in life he proffered to a correspondent a set of suggestions on the art of speaking :—

1. Study plainness of language, always preferring the simpler word. 2. Shortness of sentences. 3. Distinctness of articulation. 4. Test and question your own arguments beforehand, not waiting for critic or opponent. 5. Seek a thorough digestion of, and familiarity with, your subject, and rely mainly on these to prompt the proper words. 6. Remember that if you are to sway an audience you must besides thinking out your matter, watch them all along.—(March 20, 1875.)

The first and second of these rules hardly fit his own style. Yet he had seriously studied from early days the devices of a speaker's training. I find copied into a little note-book many of the precepts and maxims of Quintilian on the making of an orator. So too from Cicero's *De Oratore*, including the words put into the mouth of Catulus, that nobody can attain the glory of eloquence without the height of zeal and toil and knowledge.[1] Zeal and toil and knowledge, working with an inborn faculty of powerful expression—here was the double clue. He never forgot the Ciceronian truth that the orator is not made by the tongue alone, as if it were a sword sharpened on a whetstone or hammered on an anvil ; but by having a mind well filled with a free supply of high and various matter.[2] His eloquence was 'inextricably mixed up with practice.' An old whig listening to one of his budget speeches, said with a touch of bitterness, 'Ah, Oxford on the surface, but Liverpool below.' No bad combination. He once had a lesson from Sir Robert Peel. Mr. Gladstone, being about to reply in debate, turned to his chief and said : 'Shall I be short and concise ?' 'No,' was the answer, 'be long and diffuse. It is all important in the House of Commons to state your case in many different ways, so as to produce an effect on men of many ways of thinking.'

In discussing Macaulay, Sir Francis Baring, an able and unbiassed judge, advised a junior (1860) about patterns for the parliamentary aspirant :—'Gladstone is to my mind a much better model for speaking ; I mean he is happier in joining

---

[1] Book ii. § 89, 363.
[2] Non enim solum acuenda nobis neque procudenda lingua est, sed onerandum complendumque pectus maximarum rerum et plurimarum suavitate, copia, varietate. —Cicero, *De Orat.* iii. § 30.

great eloquence and selection of words and rhetoric, if you will, with a style not a bit above debate. It does not smell of the oil. Of course there has been plenty of labour, and that not of to-day but during a whole life.' Nothing could be truer. Certainly for more than the first forty years of his parliamentary existence, he cultivated a style not above debate, though it was debate of incomparable force and brilliance. When simpletons say, as if this were to dispose of every higher claim for him, that he worked all his wonders by his gifts as orator, do they ever think what power over such an assembly as the House of Commons signifies? Here—and it was not until he had been for thirty years and more in parliament that he betook himself largely to the efforts of the platform—here he was addressing men of the world, some of them the flower of English education and intellectual accomplishment; experts in all the high practical lines of life, bankers, merchants, lawyers, captains of industry in every walk; men trained in the wide experience and high responsibilities of public office; lynx-eyed rivals and opponents. Is this the scene, or were these the men, for the triumphs of the barren rhetorician and the sophist, whose words have no true relation to the facts? Where could general mental strength be better tested? As a matter of history most of those who have held the place of leading minister in the House of Commons have hardly been orators at all, any more than Washington and Jefferson were orators. Mr. Gladstone conquered the House, because he was saturated with a subject and its arguments; because he could state and enforce his case; because he plainly believed every word he said, and earnestly wished to press the same belief into the minds of his hearers; finally because he was from the first an eager and a powerful athlete. The man who listening to his adversary asks of his contention, 'Is this true?' is a lost debater; just as a soldier would be lost who on the day of battle should bethink him that the enemy's cause might after all perhaps be just. The debater does not ask, 'Is this true?' he asks, 'What is the answer to this? How can I most surely floor him?' Lord Coleridge inquired of Mr. Gladstone whether he ever felt nervous in public speaking : 'In opening a subject often,' Mr. Gladstone answered, 'in reply never.' Yet with this inborn readiness for combat, nobody was less addicted to aggression or provocation. It was with him a salutary maxim that, if you have unpalatable opinions to declare, you should not make them more unpalatable by the way of expressing them. In his earlier years he did not often speak with passion. 'This morning,' a famous divine once said, 'I preached a sermon all flames.' Mr. Gladstone sometimes made speeches of that cast, but not frequently, I think, until the seventies. Meanwhile he impressed the House by his nobility, his sincerity, his simplicity; for there is plenty of evidence besides Mr. Gladstone's

case, that simplicity of character is no hindrance to subtlety
of intellect.

Contemporaries in these opening years describe his parliamentary manners as much in his favour.   His countenance, they
say, is mild and pleasant, and has a high intellectual expression.
His eyes are clear and quick.   His eyebrows are dark and
rather prominent.   There is not a dandy in the House but
envies his fine head of jet-black hair.   Mr. Gladstone's gesture
is varied, but not violent.   When he rises, he generally puts
both his hands behind his back, and having there suffered them
to embrace each other for a short time, he unclasps them, and
allows them to drop on either side.   They are not permitted to
remain long in that locality before you see them again closed
together, and hanging down before him.[1]   Other critics say that
his air and voice are too abstract, and 'you catch the sound as
though he were communing with himself.   It is as though you
saw a bright picture through a filmy veil.   His countenance,
without being strictly handsome, is highly intellectual.   His
pale complexion, slightly tinged with olive, and dark hair, cut
rather close to his head, with an eye of remarkable depth, still
more impress you with the abstracted character of his disposition.   The expression of his face would be sombre were it
not for the striking eye, which has a remarkable fascination.
His triumphs as a debater are achieved not by the aid of the
passions, as with Sir James Graham, or with Mr. Sheil; not of
prejudice and fallacy, as with Robert Peel; not with imagination and high seductive colouring, as with Mr. Macaulay; but
—of pure reason.   He prevails by that subdued earnestness
which results from deep religious feelings, and is not fitted
for the more usual and more stormy functions of a public
speaker.'[2]

III

We are not to think of him as prophet, seer, poet, founder of
a system, or great born man of letters like Gibbon, Macaulay,
Carlyle.   Of these characters he was none, though he had
warmth and height of genius to comprehend the value of them
all, and—what was more curious—his oratory and his acts
touched them and their work in such a way that men were
always tempted to apply to him standards that belonged to
them.   His calling was a different one, and he was wont to
appraise it lower.   His field lay 'in working the institutions of
his country.'   Whether he would have played a part as splendid
in the position of a high ruling ecclesiastic, if the times had
allowed such a personage, we cannot tell; perhaps he had not
'imperious immobility' enough.   Nor whether he would have

---

[1] *The British Senate*, by James Grant, vol. ii. pp. 88-92.
[2] *Anatomy of Parliament*, November 1840. 'Contemporary Orators,' in *Fraser's
Magazine*.

made a judge of the loftier order ; perhaps his mind was to
addicted to subtle distinctions, and not likely to give a soli
adherence to broad principles of law. A superb advocate ? A
evangelist, as irresistible as Wesley or as Whitefield ? Wha
matters it ? All agree that more magnificent power of min
was never placed at the service of the British Senate.

His letters to his father from 1832 onwards show all th
interest of a keen young member in his calling, though the
contain few anecdotes, or tales, or vivid social traits. 'O
political gossip,' he admits to his father (1843), 'you always fin
me barren enough.' What comes out in all his letters to hi
kinsfolk is his unbounded willingness to take trouble in orde
to spare others. Even in prolonged and intricate money trans
actions, of which we shall see something later—transactions o
all others the most apt to produce irritation—not an accent o
impatience or dispute escapes him, though the guarded firmnes
of his language marks the steadfast self-control. We may sa
of Mr. Gladstone that nobody ever had less to repent of from
that worst waste in human life that comes of unkindness
Kingsley noticed, with some wonder, how he never allowed th
magnitude and multiplicity of his labours to excuse him from
any of the minor charities and courtesies of life.

Active hatred of cruelty, injustice, and oppression is perhap
the main difference between a good man and a bad one ; and
here Mr. Gladstone was sublime. Yet though anger burne
fiercely in him over wrong, nobody was more chary of passin
moral censures. What he said of himself in 1842, when he wa
three-and-thirty, held good to the end :—

> Nothing grows upon me so much with lengthening life as the sense o
> the difficulties, or rather the impossibilities, with which we are bese
> whenever we attempt to take to ourselves the functions of the Eterna
> Judge (except in reference to ourselves where judgment is committed t
> us), and to form any accurate idea of relative merit and demerit, goo
> and evil, in actions. The shades of the rainbow are not so nice, and th
> sands of the sea-shore are not such a multitude, as are all the subtle
> shifting, blending forms of thought and of circumstances that go t
> determine the character of us and of our acts. But there is One tha
> seeth plainly and judgeth righteously.

This was only one side of Mr. Gladstone's many silences. T
talk of the silences of the most copious and incessant speake
and writer of his time may seem a paradox. Yet in this fluen
orator, this untiring penman, this eager and most sociable talke
at the dinner-table or on friendly walks, was a singular facult
of self-containment and reserve. Quick to notice, as he wa
and acutely observant of much that might have been expecte
to escape him, he still kept as much locked up within as he s
liberally gave out. Bulwer Lytton was at one time, as is wel
known, addicted to the study of mediæval magic, occult powe
and the conjunctions of the heavenly bodies ; and among othe

figures he one day amused himself by casting the horoscope of Mr. Gladstone (1860). To him the astrologer's son sent it. Like most of such things, the horoscope has one or two ingenious hits and a dozen nonsensical misses. But one curious sentence declares Mr. Gladstone to be '*at heart a solitary man.*' Here I have often thought that the stars knew what they were about.

Whether Mr. Gladstone ever became what is called a good judge of men it would be hard to say. Such characters are not common even among parliamentary leaders. They do not always care to take the trouble. The name is too commonly reserved for those who think dubiously or downright ill of their fellow-creatures. Those who are accustomed to make most of knowing men, do their best to convince us that men are hardly worth knowing. This was not Mr. Gladstone's way. Like Lord Aberdeen, he had a marked habit of believing people; it was part of his simplicity. His life was a curious union of ceaseless contention and inviolable charity — a true charity, having nothing in common with a lazy spirit of unconcern. He knew men well enough, at least, to have found out that none gains such ascendency over them as he who appeals to what is the nobler part in human nature. Nestors of the whigs used to wonder how so much imagination, invention, courage, knowledge, diligence—all the qualities that seem to make an orator and a statesman—could be neutralised by the want of a sound overruling judgment. They said that Gladstone's faculties were like an army without a general, or a jury without guidance from the bench.[1] Yet when the time came, this army without a general won the crowning victories of the epoch, and for twenty years the chief findings of this jury without a judge proved to be the verdicts of the nation.

It is not easy for those less extraordinarily constituted, to realise the vigour of soul that maintained an inner life in all its absorbing exaltation day after day, year after year, decade after decade, amid the ever-swelling rush of urgent secular affairs. Immersed in active responsibility for momentous secular things, he never lost the breath of what was to him a diviner aether. Habitually he strove for the lofty uplands where political and moral ideas meet. Even in those days he struck all who came into contact with him by a goodness and elevation that matched the activity and power of his mind. His political career might seem doubtful, but there was no doubt about the man. One of the most interesting of his notes about his own growth is this :—

There was a singular slowness in the development of my mind, so far as regarded its opening into the ordinary aptitudes of the man of the world. For years and years well into advanced middle life, I seem to have considered actions simply as they were in themselves, and did not take into account the way in which they would be taken and understood

[1] Lord Lansdowne to Senior (1855), in Mrs. Simpson's *Many Memories*, p. 226.

by others. I did not perceive that their natural or probable effect upon
minds other than my own formed part of the considerations determining
the propriety of each act in itself, and not unfrequently, at any rate in
public life, supplied the decisive criterion to determine what ought and
what ought not to be done. In truth the dominant tendencies of my
mind were those of a recluse, and I might, in most respects with ease,
have accommodated myself to the education of the cloister. All the
mental apparatus requisite to constitute the 'public man' had to be
purchased by a slow experience and inserted piecemeal into the composition of my character.

Lord Malmesbury describes himself in 1844 as curious to see
Mr. Gladstone, 'for he is a man much spoken of as one who
will come to the front.' He was greatly disappointed at his
personal appearance, 'which is that of a Roman catholic
ecclesiastic, but he is very agreeable.'[1] Few men can have
been more perplexed, and few perhaps more perplexing, as the
social drama of the capital was in time unfolded to his gaze.
There he beheld the glitter of rank and station, and palaces,
and men and women bearing famous names; worlds within
worlds, high diplomatic figures, the partisan leaders, the constant stream of agitated rumours about weighty affairs in
England and Europe; the keen play of ambition, passions,
interests, under easy manners and fugitive pleasantry; gross
and sordid aims, as King Hudson was soon to find out, masked
by exterior refinement; so much kindness with a free spice of
criticism and touches of ill-nature; so much of the governing
force of England still gathered into a few great houses, exclusive and full of pride and yet, after the astounding discovery
that in spite of the deluge of the Reform bill they were still
alive as the directing class, always so open to political genius if
likely to climb, and help them to climb, into political power.
These were the last high days of the undisputed sway of territorial aristocracy in England. The artificial scene was gay and
captivating; but much in it was well fitted to make serious
people wonder. Queen Victoria was assuredly not of the harsh
fibre of the misanthropist in Molière's fine comedy; yet she
once said a strange and deep thing to an archbishop. 'As I
get older,' she said, 'I cannot understand the world. I cannot
comprehend its littlenesses. When I look at the frivolities and
littlenesses, *it seems to me as if they were all a little mad.*'[2]

This was the stage on which Mr. Gladstone, with 'the
dominant tendencies of a recluse' and a mind that might easily
have been 'accommodated to the cloister,' came to play his
part,—in which he was 'by a slow experience' to insert piecemeal the mental apparatus proper to the character of the public
man. Yet it was not among the booths and merchandise and
hubbub of Vanity Fair, it was among strata in the community

1 Malmesbury, *Memoirs of an Ex-Minister*, i. p. 155.
2 *Life of Archbishop Benson*, ii. p. 11.

but little recognised as yet, that he was to find the field and the sources of his highest power. His view of the secular world was never fastidious or unmanly. Looking back upon his long experience of it he wrote (1894) :—

That political life considered as a profession has great dangers for the inner and true life of the human being, is too obvious. It has, however, some redeeming qualities. In the first place, I have never known, and can hardly conceive, a finer school of temper than the House of Commons. A lapse in this respect is on the instant an offence, a jar, a wound, to every member of the assembly ; and it brings its own punishment on the instant, like the sins of the Jews under the old dispensation. Again, I think the imperious nature of the subjects, their weight and force, demanding the entire strength of a man and all his faculties, leave him no residue, at least for the time, to apply to self-regard ; no more than there is for a swimmer swimming for his life. He must, too, in retro-spect feel himself to be so very small in comparison with the themes and the interests of which he has to treat. It is a further advantage if his occupation be not mere debate, but debate ending in work. For in this way, whether the work be legislative or administrative, it is con-tinually tested by results, and he is enabled to strip away his extravagant anticipations, his fallacious conceptions, to perceive his mistakes, and to reduce his estimates to the reality. No politician has any excuse for being vain.

Like the stoic emperor, Mr. Gladstone had in his heart the feeling that the man is a runaway who deserts the exercise of civil reason.

IV

All his activities were in his own mind one. This, we can hardly repeat too often, is the fundamental fact of Mr. Glad-stone's history. Political life was only part of his religious life. It was religion that prompted his literary life. It was religious motive that, through a thousand avenues and channels stirred him and guided him in his whole conception of active social duty, including one pitiful field of which I may say something later. The liberalism of the continent at this epoch was in its essence either hostile to Christianity or else it was indifferent ; and when men like Lamennais tried to play at the same time the double part of tribune of the people and catholic theocrat, they failed. The old world of pope and priest and socialist and red cap of liberty fought on as before. In England, too, the most that can be said of the leading breed of the political reformers of that half century, with one or two most notable exceptions, is that they were theists, and not all of them were even so much as theists.[1] If liberalism had con-tinued to run in the grooves cut by Bentham, James Mill, Grote, and the rest, Mr. Gladstone would never have grown to be a liberal. He was not only a fervid practising Christian ; he

[1] The noble anti-slavery movement must be excepted, for it was very directly connected with evangelicalism.

was a Christian steeped in the fourth century, steeped in the thirteenth and fourteenth centuries. Every man of us has all the centuries in him, though their operations be latent, dim, and very various ; in his case the roots were as unmistakable as the leafage, the blossom, and the fruits. A little later than the date with which we are now dealing (May 9, 1854)—and here the date matters little, for the case was always the same—he noted what in hours of strain and crisis the Bible was to him :—

On most occasions of very sharp pressure or trial, some word of scripture has come home to me as if borne on angels' wings. Many could I recollect. The Psalms are the great storehouse. Perhaps I should put some down now, for the continuance of memory is not to be trusted. 1. In the winter of 1837, Psalm 128. This came in a most singular manner, but it would be a long story to tell. 2. In the Oxford contest of 1847 (which was very harrowing) the verse—'O Lord God, Thou strength of my health, Thou hast covered my head in the day of battle.' 3. In the Gorham contest, after the judgment : 'And though all this be come upon us, yet do we not forget Thee ; nor behave our-selves frowardly in Thy covenant. Our heart is not turned back ; neither our steps gone out of Thy way. No not when Thou hast smitten us into the place of dragons : and covered us with the shadow of death.' 4. On Monday, April 17, 1853 [his first budget speech], it was : 'O turn Thee then unto me, and have mercy upon me : give Thy strength unto Thy servant, and help the son of Thine handmaid.' Last Sunday [Crimean war budget] it was not from the Psalms for the day : 'Thou shalt prepare a table before me against them that trouble me ; Thou hast anointed my head with oil and my cup shall be full.'

In that stage at least he had shaken off none of the grip of tradition, in which his book and college training had placed him. His mind still had greater faith in things because Aristotle or Augustine said them, than because they are true.[1] If the end of education be to teach independence of mind, the Socratic temper, the love of pushing into unexplored areas—intellectual curiosity in a word—Oxford had done none of all this for him. In every field of thought and life he started from the principle of authority ; it fitted in with his reverential instincts, his temperament, above all, his education.

The lifelong enthusiasm for Dante should on no account in this place be left out. In Mr. Gladstone it was something very different from casual dilettantism or the accident of a scholar's taste. He was always alive to the grandeur of Goethe's words, *Im Ganzen, Guten, Schönen, resolut zu leben*, 'In wholeness, goodness, beauty, strenuously to live.' But it was in Dante—active politician and thinker as well as poet—that he found this unity of thought and coherence of life, not only illuminated by a sublime imagination, but directly associated with theology, philosophy, politics, history, sentiment, duty. Here are all the elements and interests that lie about the roots of the life of a man, and of the general civilisation of the world. This ever

[1] Paruta, i. p. 64.

memorable picture of the mind and heart of Europe in the great centuries of the catholic age,—making heaven the home of the human soul, presenting the natural purposes of mankind in their universality of good and evil, exalted and mean, piteous and hateful, tragedy and farce, all commingled as a living whole,—was exactly fitted to the quality of a genius so rich and powerful as Mr. Gladstone's in the range of its spiritual intuitions and in its masculine grasp of all the complex truths of mortal nature. So true and real a book is it, he once said,— such a record of practical humanity and of the discipline of the soul amidst its wonderful poetical intensity and imaginative power. In him this meant no spurious revivalism, no flimsy and fantastic affectation. It was the real and energetic discovery in the vivid conception and commanding structure of Dante, of a light, a refuge, and an inspiration in the labours of the actual world. 'You have been good enough,' he once wrote to an Italian correspondent (1883), 'to call that supreme poet "a solemn master" for me. These are not empty words. The reading of Dante is not merely a pleasure, a *tour de force*, or a lesson; it is a vigorous discipline for the heart, the intellect, the whole man. In the school of Dante I have learned a great part of that mental provision (however insignificant it may be) which has served me to make the journey of human life up to the term of nearly seventy-three years.' He once asked of an accomplished woman possessing a scholar's breadth of reading, what poetry she most lived with. She named Dante for one. But what of Dante?' 'The Paradiso,' she replied. 'Ah, that is right,' he exclaimed, 'that's my test.' In the Paradiso it was, that he saw in beams of crystal radiance the ideal of the unity of the religious mind, the love and admiration for the high unseen things of which the Christian church was to him the sovereign embodiment. The mediæval spirit, it is true, wears something of a ghostly air in the light of our new day. This attempt, which has been made many a time before, 'to unify two ages,' did not carry men far in the second half of the nineteenth century. Nevertheless it were an idle dream to think that the dead hand of Dante's century, and all that it represented, is no longer to be taken into account by those who would be governors of men. Meanwhile, let us observe once more that the statesman who had drunk most deeply from the mediæval fountains was yet one of the supreme leaders of his own generation in a notable stage of the long transition from mediæval to modern.

'At Oxford,' he records, 'I read Rousseau's *Social Contract* which had no influence upon me, and the writings of Burke which had a great deal.' Yet the day came when he too was drawn by the movement of things into the flaming circle of thought, feeling, phrase, that in romance and politics and all the ways of life Europe for a century associated with the

name of Rousseau. There was what men call Rousseau, in a
statesman who could talk of men's common 'flesh and blood' in
connection with a franchise bill. Indeed one of the strangest
things in Mr. Gladstone's growth and career is this unconscious
raising of a partially Rousseauite structure on the foundations
laid by Burke, to whom Rousseau was of all writers on the
nature of man and the ordering of states the most odious and
contemptible. We call it strange, though such amalgams of
contrary ways of thinking and feeling are more common than
careless observers may suppose. Mr. Gladstone was never an
'equalitarian,' but the passion for simplicity he had—simplicity
in life, manners, feeling, conduct, the relations of men to men ;
dislike of luxury and profusion and all the fabric of artificial
and factitious needs. It may well be that he went no further
for all this than the Sermon on the Mount, where so many
secret elements of social volcano slumber. However we may
choose to trace the sources and relations of Mr. Gladstone's
general ideas upon the political problems of his time, what he
said of himself in the evening of his day was at least true of
its dawn and noon. 'I am for old customs and traditions,' he
wrote, 'against needless change. I am for the individual as
against the state. I am for the family and the stable family
as against the state.' He must have been in eager sympathy
with Wordsworth's line taken from old Spenser in these very
days, 'Perilous is sweeping change, all chance unsound.'[1]
Finally and above all, he stood firm in 'the old Christian faith.'
Life was to him in all its aspects an application of Christian
teaching and example. If we like to put it so, he was steadfast
for making politics more human, and no branch of civilised life
needs humanising more.

Here we touch the question of questions. At nearly every
page of Mr. Gladstone's active career the vital problem stares
us in the face, of the correspondence between the rule of
private morals and of public. Is the rule one and the same
for individual and for state ? From these early years onwards,
Mr. Gladstone's whole language and the moods that it re-
produces,—his vivid denunciations, his sanguine expectations,
his rolling epithets, his aspects and appeals and points of
view,—all take for granted that right and wrong depend on
the same set of maxims in public life and private. The
puzzle will often greet us, and here it is enough to glance at
it. In every statesman's case it arises ; in Mr. Gladstone's it
is cardinal and fundamental.

V

To say that he had drawn prizes in what is called the
lottery of life would not be untrue ; but just as true is it

---

[1] 'Blest statesman he, whose mind's unselfish will' (1838).—Knight's *Wordsworth*,
viii. p. 101.

that one of those very prizes was the determined conviction that life is no lottery at all, but a serious business worth taking infinite pains upon. To one of his sons at Oxford he wrote a little paper of suggestions that are the actual description of his own lifelong habit and unbroken practice.

Strathconan, Oct. 7, 1872.—1. To keep a short journal of principal employments in each day: most valuable as an account-book of the all-precious gift of Time.

2. To keep also an account-book of receipt and expenditure ; and the least troublesome way of keeping it is to keep it with care. This done in early life, and carefully done, creates the habit of performing the great duty of keeping our expenditure (and therefore our desires) within our means.

3. Read attentively (and it is pleasant reading) Taylor's essay on Money,[1] which if I have not done it already, I will give you. It is most healthy and most useful reading.

4. Establish a minimum number of hours in the day for study, say seven at present, and do not without reasonable cause let it be less ; noting down against yourself the days of exception. There should also be a minimum number for the vacations, which at Oxford are extremely long.

5. There arises an important question about Sundays. Though we should to the best of our power avoid secular work on Sundays, it does not follow that the mind should remain idle. There is an immense field of knowledge connected with religion, and much of it is of a kind that will be of use in the schools and in relation to your general studies. In these days of shallow scepticism, so widely spread, it is more than ever to be desired that we should we able to give a reason for the hope that is in us.

6. As to duties directly religious, such as daily prayer in the morning and evening, and daily reading of some portion of the Holy Scripture, or as to the holy ordinances of the gospel, there is little need, I am confident, to advise you; one thing, however, I would say, that it is not difficult, and it is most beneficial, to cultivate the habit of inwardly turning the thoughts to God, though but for a moment in the course or during the intervals of our business; which continually presents occasions requiring His aid and guidance.

7. Turning again to ordinary duty, I know no precept more wide or more valuable than this: cultivate self-help ; do not seek nor like to be dependent upon others for what you can yourself supply ; and keep down as much as you can the standard of your wants, for in this lies a great secret of manliness, *true* wealth, and happiness ; as, on the other hand, the multiplication of our wants makes us effeminate and slavish, as well as selfish.

8. In regard to money as well as to time, there is a great advantage in its methodical use. Especially is it wise to dedicate a certain portion of our means to purposes of charity and religion, and this is more easily begun in youth .than in after life. The greatest advantage of making a little fund of this kind is that when we are asked to give, the competition is not between *self* on the one hand and charity on the other, but between the different purposes of religion and charity with

---

[1] The first chapter in Sir Henry Taylor's *Notes from Life* (1847).

one another, among which we ought to make the most careful choice. It is desirable that the fund thus devoted should not be less than one-tenth of our means ; and it tends to bring a blessing on the rest.

9. Besides giving this, we should save something, so as to be before the world, *i.e.* to have some preparation to meet the accidents and unforeseen calls of life as well as its general future.

Fathers are generally wont to put their better mind into counsels to their sons. In this instance the counsellor was the living pattern of his own maxims. His account-books show in full detail that he never at any time in his life devoted less than a tenth of his annual incomings to charitable and religious objects. The peculiarity of all this half-mechanic ordering of a wise and virtuous individual life, was that it went with a genius and power that 'moulded a mighty State's decrees,' and sought the widest 'process of the suns.'

VI

Once more, his whole temper and spirit turned to practice. His thrift of time, his just and regulated thrift in money, his hatred of waste, were only matched by his eager and minute attention in affairs of public business. He knew how to be content with small savings of hours and of material resources. He was not downcast if progress were slow. In watching public opinion, in feeling the pulse of a cabinet, in softening the heart of a colleague, even when skies were gloomiest, he was almost provokingly anxious to detect signs of encouragement that to others were imperceptible. He was of the mind of the Roman emperor, 'Hope not for the republic of Plato ; but be content with ever so small an advance, and look on even that as a gain worth having.'[1] A commonplace, but not one of the commonplaces that are always laid to heart.

If faith was one clue, then next to faith was growth. The fundamentals of Christian dogma, so far as I know and am entitled to speak, are the only region in which Mr. Gladstone's opinions have no history. Everywhere else we look upon incessant movement ; in views about church and state, tests, national schools ; in questions of economic and fiscal policy ; in relations with party ; in the questions of popular government —in every one of these wide spheres of public interest he passes from crisis to crisis. The dealings of church and state made the first of these marked stages in the history of his opinions and his life, but it was only the beginning.

'I was born with smaller natural endowments than you,' he wrote to his old friend Sir Francis Doyle (1880), 'and I had also a narrower early training. But my life has certainly been remarkable for the mass of continuous and searching experience it has brought me ever since I began to pass out of boyhood. I have been feeling my way ; owing little

[1] Marcus Aurelius, ix. p. 29.

to living teachers, but enormously to four dead ones[1] (over and above the four gospels). It has been experience which has altered my politics. My toryism was accepted by me on authority and in good faith ; I did my best to fight for it. But if you choose to examine my parliamentary life you will find that on every subject as I came to deal with it practically, I had to deal with it as a liberal elected in '32. I began with slavery in 1833, and was commended by the liberal minister, Mr. Stanley. I took to colonial subjects principally, and in 1837 was commended for treating them liberally by Lord Russell. Then Sir R. Peel carried me into trade, and before I had been six months in office, I wanted to resign because I thought his corn law reform insufficient. In ecclesiastical policy I had been a speculator ; but if you choose to refer to a speech of Sheil's in 1844 on the Dissenters' Chapels bill,[2] you will find him describing me as predestined to be a champion of religious equality. All this seems to show that I have changed under the teaching of experience.'

And much later he wrote of himself :—

The stock-in-trade of ideas with which I set out on the career of parliamentary life was a small one. I do not think the general tendencies of my mind were even in the time of my youth illiberal. It was a great accident that threw me into the anti-liberal attitude, but having taken it up I held to it with energy. It was the accident of the Reform bill of 1831. For teachers or idols or both in politics I had Mr. Burke and Mr. Canning. I followed them in their dread of reform, and probably caricatured them as a raw and unskilled student caricatures his master. This one idea on which they were anti-liberal became the master-key of the situation, and absorbed into itself for the time the whole of politics. This, however, was not my only disadvantage. I had been educated in an extremely narrow churchmanship, that of the evangelical party. This narrow churchmanship too readily embraced the idea that the extension of representative principles, which was then the essential work of liberalism, was associated with irreligion ; an idea quite foreign to my older sentiment on behalf of Roman catholic emancipation. (*Autobiographic note, July* 22, 1894.)

VII

Notwithstanding his humility, his willingness within a certain range to learn, his profound reverence for what he took for truth, he was no more ready than many far inferior men to discern a certain important rule of intellectual life that was expressed in a quaint figure by one of our old English sages. 'He is a wonderful man,' said the sage, 'that can thread a needle when he is at cudgels in a crowd ; and yet this is as easy as to find Truth in the hurry of disputation.'[3] The strenuous member of parliament, the fervid minister fighting the clauses of his bill, the disputant in cabinet, when he passed from man of action to the topics of balanced thought, nice

---

[1] Aristotle, Augustine, Dante, Butler. 'My four "doctors,"' he tells Manning, 'are doctors to the speculative man ; would they were such to the practical too ! '
[2] See below, p. 238.
[3] Glanville's *Vanity of Dogmatising.*

scrutiny, long meditation, did not always succeed in getting his
thread into the needle's eye.

As to the problems of the metaphysician, Mr. Gladstone
showed little curiosity. Nor for abstract discussion in its
highest shape—for investigation of ultimate propositions—
had he any of that power of subtle and ingenious reasoning
which was often so extraordinary when he came to deal with
the concrete, the historic, and the demonstrable. A still more
singular limitation on the extent of his intellectual curiosity
was hardly noticed at this early epoch. The scientific movement, which along with the growth of democracy and the
growth of industrialism formed the three propelling forces
of a new age,—was not yet developed in all its range. The
astonishing discoveries in the realm of natural science, and the
philosophic speculations that were built upon them, though
quite close at hand, were still to come. Darwin's *Origin of
Species*, for example, was not given to the world until 1859.
Mr. Gladstone watched these things vaguely and with misgiving; instinct must have told him that the advance of
natural explanation, whether legitimately or not, would be
in some degree at the expense of the supernatural. But from
any full or serious examination of the details of the scientific
movement he stood aside, safe and steadfast within the citadel
of Tradition.

He was once asked to subscribe to a memorial of Tyndale,
the translator of the Bible,[1] and he put his refusal upon grounds
that show one source at least of his scruple about words. He
replies that he has been driven to a determination to renounce
all subscriptions for the commemoration of ancient worthies,
as he finds that he cannot signify gratitude for services rendered,
without being understood to sanction all that they have said or
done, and thus becoming involved in controversy or imputation
about them. 'I am often amazed,' he goes on, 'at the construction put upon my acts and words; but experience has shown
me that they are commonly put under the microscope, and then
found to contain all manner of horrors like the animalcules in
Thames water.' This microscope was far too valuable an instrument in the contentions of party, ever to be put aside; and the
animalcules duly magnified to the frightful size required, were
turned into first-rate electioneering agents. Even without party
microscopes, those who feel most warmly for Mr. Gladstone's
manifold services to his country, may often wish that he had
inscribed in letters of gold over the door of the Temple of
Peace, a certain sentence from the wise oracles of his favourite
Butler. 'For the conclusion of this,' said the bishop, 'let me
just take notice of the danger of over-great refinements; of
going beside or beyond the plain, obvious first appearances

[1] See Shaftesbury's *Life*, iii. p. 495. He refused to be on a committee for a memorial
to Thirlwall (1875).

of things, upon the subject of morals and religion.'[1] Nor would he have said less of politics. It is idle to ignore in Mr. Gladstone's style an over-refining in words, an excess of qualifying propositions, a disproportionate impressiveness in verbal shadings without real difference. Nothing irritated opponents more. They insisted on taking literary sin for moral obliquity, and because men could not understand, they assumed that he wished to mislead. Yet if we remember how carelessness in words, how the slovenly combination under the same name of things entirely different, how the taking for granted as matter of positive proof what is at the most only possible or barely probable—when we think of all the mischief and folly that has been wrought in the world by loose habits of mind that are almost as much the master vice of the head as selfishness is the master vice of the heart, men may forgive Mr. Gladstone for what passed as sophistry and subtlety, but was in truth scruple of conscience in that region where lack of scruple half spoils the world.

This peculiar trait was connected with another that some-times amused friends, but always exasperated foes. Among the papers is a letter from an illustrious man to Mr. Gladstone —wickedly no better dated by the writer than 'Saturday,' and no better docketed by the receiver than 'T. B. Macaulay, March 1,'—showing that Mr. Gladstone was just as energetic, say in some year between 1835 and 1850, in defending the entire consistency between a certain speech of the dubious date and a speech in 1833, as he ever afterwards showed himself in the same too familiar process. In later times he described himself as a sort of purist in what touches the consistency of states-men. 'Change of opinion,' he said, 'in those to whose judgment the public looks more or less to assist its own, is an evil to the country, although a much smaller evil than their persistence in a course which they know to be wrong. It is not always to be blamed. But it is always to be watched with vigilance; always to be challenged and put upon its trial.'[2] To this challenge in his own case—and no man of his day was half so often put upon his trial for inconsistency—he was always most easily provoked to make a vehement reply. In that process Mr. Gladstone's natural habit of resort to qualifying words, and his skill in showing that a new attitude could be reconciled by strict reasoning with the logical contents of old dicta, gave him wonderful advantage. His adversary as he strode con-fidently along the smooth grass, suddenly found himself tread-ing on a serpent; he had overlooked a condition, a proviso, a word of hypothesis or contingency, that sprang from its ambush and brought his triumph to naught on the spot. If Mr. Glad-stone had only taken as much trouble that his hearers should understand exactly what it was that he meant, as he took

trouble afterwards to show that his meaning had been grossly
misunderstood, all might have been well. As it was, he seemed
to be completely satisfied if he could only show that two propositions, thought by plain men to be directly contradictory,
were all the time capable on close construction of being presented in perfect harmony. As if I had a right to look only to
what my words literally mean or may in good logic be made
to mean, and had no concern at all with what the people meant
who used the same words, or with what I might have known
that my hearers were all the time supposing me to mean.
Hope-Scott once wrote to him (November 24, 1841): 'We live
in a time in which accurate distinctions, especially in theology,
are absolutely unconsidered. The "common sense" or general
tenor of questions is what alone the majority of men are guided
by. And I verily believe that semi-arian confessions or any
others turning upon nicety of thought and expression, would
be for the most part considered as fitter subjects for scholastic
dreamers than for earnest Christians.' In politics at any rate,
Bishop Butler was wiser.

The explanation of what was assailed as inconsistency is
perhaps a double one. In the first place he started on his
journey with an intellectual chart of ideas and principles not
adequate or well fitted for the voyage traced for him by the
spirit of his age. If he held to the inadequate ideas with which
Oxford and Canning and his father and even Peel had furnished
him, he would have been left helpless and useless in the days
stretching before him. The second point is that the orator of
Mr. Gladstone's commanding school exists by virtue of large
and intense expression; then if circumstances make him as
vehement for one opinion to-day as he was vehement for what
the world regards as a conflicting opinion yesterday, his
intellectual self-respect naturally prompts him to insist that
the opinions do not really clash, but are in fact identical.
You may call this a weakness if you choose, and it certainly
involved Mr. Gladstone in much unfruitful and not very edify-
ing exertion; but it is at any rate better than the front of
brass that takes any change of opinion for matter-of-course
expedient, as to which the least said will be soonest mended.
And it is better still than the disastrous self-consciousness that
makes a man persist in a foolish thing to-day, because he
chanced to say or do a foolish thing yesterday.

VIII

In this period of his life, with the battle of the world still to
come, Mr. Gladstone to whose grave temperament everything,
little or great, was matter of deliberate reflection, of duty and
scruple, took early note of minor morals as well as major.
Characteristically he found some fault with a sermon of Dr.
Wordsworth's upon Saint Barnabas, for

hardly pushing the argument for the connection of good manners with Christianity to the full extent of which it is fairly capable. The whole system of legitimate courtesy, politeness, and refinement is surely nothing less than one of the genuine though minor and often unacknowledged results of the gospel scheme. All the great moral qualities or graces, which in their large sphere determine the formation and habits of the Christian soul as before God, do also on a smaller scale apply to the very same principles in the common intercourse of life, and pervade its innumerable and separately inappreciable particulars; and the result of this application is that good breeding which distinguishes Christian civilisation. (March 31, 1844.)

It is not for us to discuss whether the breeding of Plato or Cicero or the Arabs of Cordova was better or worse than the breeding of the eastern bishops at Nicæa or Ephesus. Good manners, we may be sure, hardly have a single master-key, unless it be simplicity, or freedom from the curse of affectation. What is certain is that nobody of his time was a finer example of high good manners and genuine courtesy than Mr. Gladstone himself. He has left a little sheaf of random jottings which, without being subtle or recondite, show how he looked on this side of human things. Here is an example or two :—

There are a class of passages in Mr. Wilberforce's *Journals, e.g.* some of those recording his successful speeches, which might in many men be set down to vanity, but in him are more fairly I should think ascribable to a singlemindedness which did not inflate. Surely with *most* men it is the safest rule, to make scanty records of success achieved, and yet more rarely to notice praise, which should pass us like the breeze, enjoyed but not arrested. There must indeed be some sign, a stone as it were set up, to remind us that such and such were occasions for thankfulness; but should not the memorials be restricted wholly and expressly for this purpose? For the fumes of praise are rapidly and fearfully intoxicating; it comes like a spark to the tow if once we give it, as it were, admission within us. (1838.)

There are those to whom vanity brings more of pain than of pleasure; there are also those whom it oftener keeps in the background, than thrusts forward. The same man who to-day volunteers for that which he is not called upon to do, may to-morrow flinch from his obvious duty from one and the same cause,—vanity, or regard to the appearance he is to make, for its own sake, and perhaps that vanity which shrinks is a more subtle and far-sighted, a more ethereal, a more profound vanity than that which presumes. (1842.)

A question of immense importance meets us in ethical inquiries, as follows : is there a sense in which it is needful, right, and praiseworthy, that man should be much habituated to look back upon himself and keep his eye upon himself; a self-regard, and even a self-respect, which are compatible with the self-renunciation and self-distrust which belong to Christianity? In the observance of a single distinction we shall find, perhaps, a secure and sufficient answer. We are to respect our responsibilities, not ourselves. We are to respect the duties of which we are capable, but not our capabilities simply considered. There is to be no complacent self-contemplation, beruminating upon self. When self is viewed, it must always be in the most intimate connection with its purposes. How well were it if persons would be more careful, or rather, more conscientious, in paying compliments. How often do we delude another, in subject matter small or great, into the belief that he has done well what we know he has done ill, either by silence, or by so giving him praise on a particular point as to *imply* approbation of the whole. Now it is undoubtedly difficult to observe politeness in all cases compatibly with truth ; and politeness though a minor duty is a duty still. (1838.)

If truth permits you to praise, but binds you to praise with a quali-fication, observe how much more acceptably you will speak, if you put the qualification first, than if you postpone it. For example : 'this is a good likeness ; but it is a hard painting,' is surely much less pleasing, than 'this is a hard painting ; but it is a good likeness.' The qualifi-cation is generally taken to be more genuinely the sentiment of the speaker's mind, than the main proposition ; and it carries ostensible honesty and manliness to propose first what is the less acceptable. (1835-6.)

IX

To go back to Fénelon's question about his own foundation. 'The great work of religion,' as Mr. Gladstone conceived it, was set out in some sentences of a letter written by him to Mrs. Gladstone in 1844, five years after they were married. In these sentences we see that under all the agitated surface of a life of turmoil and contention, there flowed a deep composing stream of faith, obedience, and resignation, that gave him in face of a thousand buffets, the free mastery of all his resources of heart and brain :—

To Mrs. Gladstone.

13 *C. H. Terrace, Sunday evening, Jan.* 21, 1844.—Although I have carelessly left at the board of trade with your other letters that on which I wished to have said something, yet I am going to end this day of peace by a few words to show that what you said did not lightly pass away from my mind. There is a beautiful little sentence in the works of Charles Lamb concerning one who had been afflicted : 'he gave his heart to the Purifier, and his will to the Sovereign Will of the Universe.'[1] But there is a speech in the third canto of the *Paradiso* of Dante, spoken by a certain Piccarda, which is a rare gem. I will only quote this one line :

In la sua volontade è nostra pace.[2]

The words are few and simple, and yet they appear to me to have an inexpressible majesty of truth about them, to be almost as if they were spoken from the very mouth of God. It so happened that (unless my memory much deceives me) I first read that speech on a morning early

[1] *Rosamund Gray*, chap. xi.
[2] Mr. Gladstone's rendering of the speech of Piccarda (*Paradiso*, iii. 70) is in the volume of collected translations (p. 165), under the date of 1835 :

'In His Will is our peace. To this all things
By Him created, or by Nature made,
As to a central Sea, self-motion brings.'

in the year 1836, which was one of trial. I was profoundly impressed and powerfully sustained, almost absorbed, by these words. They cannot be too deeply graven upon the heart. In short, what we all want is that they should not come to us as an admonition from without, but as an instinct from within. They should not be adopted by effort or upon a process of proof, but they should be simply the translation into speech of the habitual tone to which all tempers, affections, emotions, are set. In the Christian mood, which ought never to be intermitted, the sense of this conviction should recur spontaneously ; it should be the foundation of all mental thoughts and acts, and the measure to which the whole experience of life, inward and outward, is referred. The final state which we are to contemplate with hope, and to seek by discipline, is that in which our will shall be *one* with the will of God ; not merely shall submit to it, not merely shall follow after it, but shall live and move with it, even as the pulse of the blood in the extremities acts with the central movement of the heart. And this is to be obtained through a double process ; the first, that of checking, repressing, quelling the inclination of the will to act with reference to self as a centre ; this is to mortify it. The second, to cherish, exercise, and expand its new and heavenly power of acting according to the will of God, first, perhaps, by painful effort in great feebleness and with many inconsistencies, but with continually augmenting regularity and force, until obedience become a necessity of second nature. . . .

Resignation is too often conceived to ·be merely a submission not unattended with complaint to what we have no power to avoid. But it is less than the whole of a work of a Christian. Your full triumph as far as that particular occasion of duty is concerned will be to find that you not merely repress inward tendencies to murmur—but that you would not if you could alter what in any matter God has plainly willed. . . . Here is the great work of religion ; here is the path through which sanctity is attained, the highest sanctity ; and yet it is a path evidently to be traced in the course of our daily duties. . . .

When we are thwarted in the exercise of some innocent, laudable, and almost sacred affection, as in the case, though its scale be small, out of which all of this has grown, Satan has us at an advantage, because when the obstacle occurs, we have a sentiment that the feeling baffled is a right one, and in indulging a rebellious temper we flatter ourselves that we are merely as it were indulgent on behalf, not of ourselves, but of a duty which we have been interrupted in performing. But our duties can take care of themselves when God calls us away from any of them. . . . To be able to relinquish a duty upon command shows a higher grace than to be able to give up a mere pleasure for a duty. . . .

The resignation thus described with all this power and deep feeling is, of course, in one form of thoughts and words, of symbol and synthesis, or another, the foundation of all the great systems of life. A summary of Mr. Gladstone's interpretation of it is perhaps found in a few words used by him of Blanco White, a heterodox writer whose strange spiritual fortunes painfully interested and perplexed him. 'He cherished,' says Mr. Gladstone, 'with whatever associations, the love of God, and maintained resignation to His will, even when it appears almost impossible to see how he could have had a

dogmatic belief in the existence of a divine will at all. There
was, in short [in Blanco White], a disposition *to resist the
tyranny of self ; to recognise the rule of duty ; to maintain the
supremacy of the higher over the lower parts of our nature.*[1]
This very disposition might with truth no less assured have
been assigned to the writer himself. These three bright
crystal laws of life were to him like pointer stars guiding a
traveller's eye to the celestial pole by which he steers.

When all has been said of a man's gifts, the critical question
still stands over, how he regards his responsibility for using
them. Once in a conversation with Mr. Gladstone, some fifty
years from the epoch of this present chapter, we fell upon the
topic of ambition. 'Well,' he said, 'I do not think that I can
tax myself in my own life with ever having been much moved
by ambition.' The remark so astonished me that, as he afterwards playfully reported to a friend, I almost jumped up from
my chair. We soon shall reach a stage in his career when both
remark and surprise may explain themselves. We shall see
that if ambition means love of power or fame for the sake of
glitter, decoration, external renown, or even dominion and
authority on their own account—and all these are common
passions enough in strong natures as well as weak—then his
view of himself was just. I think he had none of it. Ambition
in a better sense, the motion of a resolute and potent genius
to use strength for the purposes of strength, to clear the path,
dash obstacles aside, force good causes forward—such a quality
as that is the very law of the being of a personality so vigorous,
intrepid, confident, and capable as his.

1 *Gleanings,* ii. p. 20, 1845.

CHAPTER VII

CLOSE OF APPRENTICESHIP

(1839–1841)

What are great gifts but the correlative of great work? We are not born for ourselves, but for our kind, for our neighbours, for our country: it is but selfishness, indolence, a perverse fastidiousness, an unmanliness, and no virtue or praise, to bury our talent in a napkin.—CARDINAL NEWMAN.

ALONG with his domestic and parliamentary concerns, we are to recognise the ferment that was proceeding in Mr. Gladstone's mind upon new veins of theology; but it was an interior working of feeling and reflection, and went forward without much visible relation to the outer acts and facts of his life during this period. As to those, one entry in the diary (Feb. 1st, 1839) tells a sufficient tale for the next two years. 'I find I have, besides family and parliamentary concerns and those of study, *ten* committees on hand: Milbank, Society for Propagation of the Gospel, Church Building Metropolis, Church Commercial School, National Schools inquiry and correspondence, Upper Canada, Clergy, Additional Curates' Fund, Carlton Library, Oxford and Cambridge Club. These things distract and dissipate my mind.' Well they might; for in any man with less than Mr. Gladstone's amazing faculty of rapid and powerful concentration, such dispersion must have been disastrous both to effectiveness and to mental progress. As it is, I find little in the way of central facts to remark in either mental history or public action. He strayed away occasionally from the Fathers and their pastures and dipped into the new literature of the hour, associated with names of dawning popularity. Carlyle he found hard to lay down. Some of Emerson, too, he became acquainted with, as we have already seen; but his mind was far too closely filled with transcendentalisms of his own to offer much hospitality to the serene and beautiful transcendentalism of Emerson. He read *Oliver Twist* and *Nicholas Nickleby*, and on the latter he makes a characteristic comment—'the tone is very human; it is most happy in touches of natural pathos. No church in the book, and the motives are not those of religion.' So with Hallam's *History of Literature*, 'Finished (Oct. 10, 1839) his theological chapter, in which I am sorry to find amidst such merits, what is even far more grievous than his anti-church sarcasms, such notions on original sin as in iv. p. 161.' He found Chillingworth's *Religion of Protestants* 'a work of the most mixed merits,' an ambiguous phrase which I take to mean not that its merits were various, but that they were much mixed with those demerits for which the puritan Cheynell baited the unlucky latitudinarian to death. About this time also he first began Father Paul's famous history of the Council of Trent, a work that always stood as high in his esteem as in Macaulay's, who liked Sarpi the best of all modern historians.

To the great veteran poet of the time Mr. Gladstone's fidelity was unchanging, even down to compositions that the ordinary Wordsworthian gives up :—

Read aloud Wordsworth's *Cumberland Beggar* and *Peter Bell*. The former is generally acknowledged to be a noble poem. The same justice is not done to the latter ; I was more than ever struck with the vivid power of the descriptions, the strong touches of feeling, the skill and order with which the plot upon Peter's conscience is arranged, and the depth of interest which is made to attach to the humblest of quadrupeds. It must have cost great labour, and is an extraordinary poem, both as a whole and in detail.

Let not the scorner forget that Matthew Arnold, that admirable critic and fine poet, confesses to reading *Peter Bell* with pleasure and edification.

In the political field he moved steadily on. Sir R. Peel spoke to him (April 19, 1839) in the House about the debate and wished him to speak after Sheil, if Graham, who was to speak about 8 or 9, could bring him up. Peel showed him several points with regard to the committee which he thought might be urged. 'This is very kind in him as a mark of confidence ; and assures me that if, as I suspect, he considers my book as likely to bring me into some embarrassment individually, yet he is willing to let me still act under him, and fight my own battles in that matter as best with God's help I may, which is thoroughly fair. It imposes, however, a great responsibility. I was not presumptuous enough to dream of following Sheil ; not that his speech is formidable, but the impression it leaves on the House is. I meant to provoke him. A mean man may fire at a tiger, but it requires a strong and bold one to stand his charge ; and the longer I live, the more I feel my own (intrinsically) utter *powerlessness* in the House of Commons. But my principle is this—not to shrink from any such respon- sibility when laid upon me by a competent person. Sheil, however, did not speak, so I am reserved and may fulfil my own idea, please God, to-night.'

We come now to one of the memorable episodes in this vexed
decade of our political history. The sullen demon of slavery
died hard. The negro still wore about his neck galling links
of the broken chain. The transitory stage of apprenticeship
was in some respects even harsher than the bondage from
which it was to bring deliverance, and the old iniquity only
worked in new ways. The pity and energy of the humane at
home drove a perplexed and sluggish government to pass an
act for dealing with the abominations of the prisons to which
the unhappy blacks were committed in Jamaica. The assembly
of that island, a planter oligarchy, resented the new law from
the mother country as an invasion of their constitutional rights,
and stubbornly refused in their exasperation, even after a local
dissolution, to perform duties that were indispensable for
working the machinery of administration. The cabinet in
consequence asked parliament (April 9th) to suspend the
constitution of Jamaica for a term of five years. The tory
opposition, led by Peel with all his force, aided by the aversion
of a section of the liberals to a measure in which they detected
a flavour of dictatorship, ran the ministers (May 6th) within
five votes of defeat on a cardinal stage.

'I was amused,' says Mr. Gladstone, 'with observing
yesterday the differences of countenance and manner in the
ministers whom I met on my ride. Ellice (their friend) would
not look at me at all. Charles Wood looked but askance and
with the hat over the brow. Grey shouted, "Wish you joy!"
Lord Howick gave a remarkably civil and smiling nod; and
Morpeth a hand salute with all his might, as we crossed in
riding. On Monday night after the division, Peel said just as
it was known and about to be announced, "Jamaica was a good
horse to start."' Of his own share in the performance, Mr.
Gladstone only says that he spoke a dry speech to a somewhat
reluctant House. 'I cannot work up my matter at all in such
a plight. However, considering what it was, they behaved
very well. A loud cheer on the announcement of the numbers
from our people, in which I did not join.'

To have won the race by so narrow a majority as five seemed
to the whigs, wearied of their own impotence and just discredit,
a good plea for getting out of office. Peel proceeded to begin
the formation of a government, but the operation broke down
upon an affair of the bedchamber. He supposed the Queen to
object to the removal of any of the ladies of her household, and
the Queen supposed him to insist on the removal of them all.
The situation was unedifying and nonsensical, but the Queen
was not yet twenty, and Lord Melbourne had for once failed
to teach a prudent lesson. A few days saw Melbourne back in
office, and in office he remained for two years longer.[1]

[1] For Mr. Gladstone's later view of this transaction, see *Gleanings*, i. p. 39. He
composed a letter on the subject, which, he says, 'will probably never see the light.'

II

In June 1839 the understanding arrived at with Miss Catherine Glynne during the previous winter in Sicily, ripened into a definite engagement, and on the 25th of the following July their marriage took place amid much rejoicing and festivity at Hawarden. At the same time and place, Mary Glynne, the younger sister, was married to Lord Lyttelton. Sir Stephen Glynne, their brother, was the ninth, and as was to happen, the last baronet. Their mother, born Mary Neville, was the daughter of the second Lord Braybrooke and Mary Grenville his wife, sister of the first Marquis of Buckingham. Hence Lady Glynne was one of a historic clan, granddaughter of George Grenville, the minister of American taxation, and niece of William, Lord Grenville, head of the cabinet of All the Talents in 1806. She was first cousin therefore of the younger Pitt, and the Glynnes could boast of a family connection with three prime ministers, or if we choose to add Lord Chatham who married Hester Grenville, with four.[1] 'I told her,' Mr. Gladstone recorded on this occasion of their engagement (June 8th), 'what was my original destination and desire in life ; in what sense and manner I remained in connection with politics. . . . I have given her (led by her questions) these passages for canons of our living :—

> 'Le fronde, onde s'infronda tutto l'orto
> Dell' Ortolano eterno, am' io cotanto,
> Quanto da lui a lor di bene è porto.'[2]

And Dante again—

> 'In la sua volontade è nostra pace :
> Ella è quel mare, al qual tutto si muove.'[3]

In few human unions have the good hopes and fond wishes of a bridal day been better fulfilled or brought deeper and more lasting content. Sixty long years after, Mr. Gladstone said, 'It would not be possible to unfold in words the value of the gifts which the bounty of Providence has conferred upon me through her.' And the blessing remained radiant and unclouded to the distant end.

At the close of August, after posting across Scotland from

---

[1] Mr. Gladstone compiled this list of the statesmen in the maternal ancestry of his children :—

Right Hon. George Grenville	. .	Great, great grandfather.
Sir W. Wyndham	. .	Great, great, great grandfather.
Lord Chatham	. .	Great, great granduncle-in-law.
Mr. Pitt	. .	First cousin thrice removed
Lord Grenville	. .	Great granduncle.
Mr. Grenville.	. .	Great granduncle.

[2] *Paradiso*, xxvi. 64-6—

> 'Love for each plant that in the garden grows,
> Of the Eternal Gardener, I prove,
> Proportioned to the goodness he bestows.'—WRIGHT.

[3] *Ibid.* iii. 85. See above, p. 160.

Greenock by a route better known now than then to every
tourist, the young couple made their way to Fasque, where
the new bride found an auspicious approach and the kindest
of welcomes. Her 'entrance into her adoptive family was
much more formidable than it would be to those who had been
less loved, or less influential, or less needed and leant upon,
in the home where she was so long a queen.' At Fasque all
went as usual. Soon after his arrival, his father communicated
that he meant actually to transfer to his sons his Demerara
properties — Robertson to have the management. 'This increased wealth, so much beyond my needs, with its attendant
responsibility is very burdensome, however on his part the
act be beautiful.'

III

The parliamentary session of 1840 was unimportant and
dreary. The government was tottering, the conservative
leaders were in no hurry to pluck the pear before it was ripe,
and the only men with any animating principle of active
public policy in them were Cobden and the League against
the Corn Law. The attention of the House of Commons was
mainly centred in the case of Stockdale and the publication
of debates. But Mr. Gladstone's most earnest thoughts were
still far away from what he found to be the dry sawdust of the
daily politics, as the following lines may show :—

March 16th, 1840.—Manning dined with us. He kindly undertook
to revise my manuscript on 'Church Principles.'

March 18th.—Yesterday I had a long conversation with James Hope.
He came to tell me, with great generosity, that he would always
respond to any call, according to the best of his power, which I might
make on him for the behalf of the common cause—he had given up all
views of advancement in his profession—he had about £400 a year, and
this, which includes his fellowship, was quite sufficient for his wants ;
his time would be devoted to church objects ; in the intermediate
region he considered himself as having the first tonsure.

Hope urged strongly the principle, 'Let every man abide in the
calling——' I thought even over strongly. My belief is that he
foregoes the ministry from deeming himself unworthy. . . . The object
of my letter to Hope was in part to record on paper my abhorrence of
party in the church, whether Oxford party or any other.

March 18th.—To-day a meeting at Peel's on the China question ;
considered in the view of censure upon the conduct of the administration,
and a motion will accordingly be made objecting to the attempts to
force the Chinese to modify their old relations with us, and to the
leaving the superintendent without military force. It was decided not
to move simultaneously in the Lords—particularly because the Radicals
would, if there were a double motion, act not on the merits but for the
ministry. Otherwise, it seemed to be thought we should carry a
motion. The Duke of Wellington said, 'God ! if it is carried, they will
go,' that they were as near as possible to resignation on the last defeat,

and would not stand it again. Peel said, he understood four ministers
were then strongly for resigning. The duke also said, our footing in
China could not be re-established, unless under some considerable naval
and military demonstration, now that matters had gone so far. He
appeared pale and shaken, but spoke loud and a good deal, much to
the point and with considerable gesticulation. The mind's life I never
saw more vigorous.

The Chinese question was of the simplest. British subjects
insisted on smuggling opium into China in the teeth of Chinese
law. The British agent on the spot began war against China
for protecting herself against these malpractices. There was
no pretence that China was in the wrong, for in fact the British
government had sent out orders that the opium-smugglers
should not be shielded ; but the orders arrived too late, and
war having begun, Great Britain felt bound to see it through,
with the result that China was compelled to open four ports, to
cede Hong Kong, and to pay an indemnity of six hundred
thousand pounds. So true is it that statesmen have no concern
with paternosters, the Sermon on the Mount, or the *vade
mecum* of the moralist. We shall soon see that this transaction
began to make Mr. Gladstone uneasy, as was indeed to be expected in anybody who held that a state should have a conscience.[1] On April 8, 1840, his journal says : ' Read on China.
House. . . . Spoke heavily ; strongly against the trade and
the war, having previously asked whether my speaking out on
them would do harm, and having been authorised.' An un-
guarded expression brought him into a debating scrape, but his
speech abounded in the pure milk of what was to be the
Gladstonian word :—

I do not know how it can be urged as a crime against the Chinese that
they refused provisions to those who refused obedience to their laws
whilst residing within their territory. I am not competent to judge
how long this war may last, nor how protracted may be its operations,
but this I can say, that a war more unjust in its origin, a war more
calculated in its progress to cover this country with disgrace, I do not
know and I have not read of. Mr. Macaulay spoke last night in
eloquent terms of the British flag waving in glory at Canton, and of
the animating effect produced upon the minds of our sailors by the
knowledge that in no country under heaven was it permitted to be
insulted. But how comes it to pass that the sight of that flag always
raises the spirits of Englishmen ? It is because it has always been
associated with the cause of justice, with opposition to oppression, with
respect for national rights, with honourable commercial enterprise, but
now under the auspices of the noble lord [Palmerston] that flag is
hoisted to protect an infamous contraband traffic, and if it were never
to be hoisted except as it is now hoisted on the coast of China, we should
recoil from its sight with horror, and should never again feel our hearts
thrill, as they now thrill, with emotion when it floats magnificently and
in pride upon the breeze. . . . Although the Chinese were undoubtedly

[1] See Lord Palmerston's speech, Aug. 10, 1842.

guilty of much absurd phraseology, of no little ostentatious pride, and of some excess, justice in my opinion is with them, and whilst they the pagans and semi-civilised barbarians have it, we the enlightened and civilised Christians are pursuing objects at variance both with justice and with religion.[1]

May 14*th.*—Consulted [various persons] on opium. All but Sir R. Inglis were on grounds of prudence against its [a motion against the compensation demanded from China] being brought forward. To this majority of friendly and competent persons I have given way, I hope not wrongfully; but I am in dread of the judgment of God upon England for our national iniquity towards China. It has been to me matter of most painful and anxious consideration. I yielded specifically to this; the majority of the persons most trustworthy feel that to make the motion would, our leaders being in such a position and disposition with respect to it, injure the cause. *June* 1*st.*—Meeting of the Society for Suppression of the Slave Trade. [This was the occasion of a speech from Prince Albert, who presided.] Exeter Hall crammed is really a grand spectacle. Samuel Wilberforce a beautiful speaker; in some points resembles Macaulay. Peel excellent. *June* 12*th.*—This evening I voted for the Irish education grant; on the ground that in its principle, according to Lord Stanley's letter, it is identical practically with the English grant of '33-8, and I might have added with the Kildare Place grant. To exclude doctrine from exposition is in my judgment as truly a mutilation of scripture, as to omit bodily portions of the sacred volume.

His first child and eldest son was born (June 3), and Manning and Hope became his godfathers; these two were Mr. Gladstone's most intimate friends at this period. Social diversions were never wanting. One June afternoon he went down to Greenwich, 'Grillion's fish dinner to the Speaker. Great merriment; and an excellent speech from Stanley, "good sense and good nonsense." A modest one from Morpeth. But though we dined at six, these expeditions do not suit me. I am ashamed of paying £2 : 10s. for a dinner. But on this occasion the object was to do honour to a dignified and impartial Speaker.' He had been not at all grateful, by the way, for the high honour of admission to Grillion's dining club this year,—'a thing quite alien to my temperament, which requires more soothing and domestic appliances after the feverish and consuming excitements of party life; but the rules of society oblige me to submit.' As it happened, so narrow is man's foreknowledge, Grillion's down to the very end of his life, nearly sixty years ahead, had no more faithful or congenial member.

July 1*st.*—Last evening at Lambeth Palace I had a good deal of conversation with Colonel Gurwood about the Duke of Wellington and about Canada. He told me an anecdote of Lord Seaton which throws light upon his peculiar reserve, and shows it to be a modesty of character, combined no doubt with military habits and notions. When Captain Colborne, and senior officer of his rank in the 21st foot, he

[1] *Hansard,* 3 S. vol. 53, p. 819.

[Lord Seaton] was military secretary to General Fox during the war. A majority in his regiment fell vacant, Gen. Fox desired him to ascertain who was the senior captain on the *command*. 'Captain So-and-so of the 80th (I think).' 'Write to Colonel Gordon and recommend him to his royal highness for the vacant majority.' He did it. The answer came to this effect: 'The recommendation will not be refused, but we are surprised to see that it comes in the handwriting of Captain Colborne, the very man who, according to the rules of the service, ought to have this majority.' General Fox had forgotten it, and Captain Colborne had not reminded him! The error was corrected. He (Gurwood) said he had never known the Duke of Wellington speak on the subject of religion but once, when he quoted the story of Oliver Cromwell on his death-bed, and said : 'That state of grace, in my opinion, is a state or habit of doing right, of persevering in duty, and to fall from it is to cease from acting right.' He always attends the service at 8 A.M. in the Chapel Royal, and says it is a duty which ought to be done, and the earlier in the day it is discharged the better. *July 24th.* — Heard [James] Hope in the House of Lords against the Chapters bill ; and he spoke with such eloquence, learning, lofty sentiment, clear and piercing diction, continuity of argument, just order, sagacious tact, and comprehensive method, as one would say would have required the longest experience as well as the greatest natural gifts. Yet he never acted before, save as counsel for the Edinburgh and Glasgow railway. If hearts are to be moved, it must be by this speech.[1] *July 27th.*—Again went over and got up the subject of opium compensation as it respects the Chinese. I spoke thereon 1½ hours for the liberation of my conscience, and to afford the friends of peace opposite an opportunity, of which they would not avail themselves.

In August he tells Mrs. Gladstone how he has been to dine with 'such an odd party at the Guizots'; Austin, radical lawyer; John Mill, radical reviewer; M. Gaskell, Monckton Milnes, Thirlwall, new Bishop of St. David's, George Lewis, poor law commissioner. Not very ill mixed, however. The host is extremely nice.' An odd party indeed ; it comprised four at least of the strongest heads in England, and two of the most illustrious names of all the century in Europe.

In March (1840) Mr. Gladstone and Lord Lyttelton went to Eton together to fulfil the ambitious functions of examiner for the Newcastle scholarship. In thanking Mr. Gladstone for his services, Hawtrey speaks of the advantage of public men of his stamp undertaking such duties in the good cause of the established system of education, 'as against the nonsense of utilitarians and radicals.' The questions ran in the familiar mould in divinity, niceties of ancient grammar, obscurities of classical construction, caprices of vocabulary, and all the other points of the old learning. The general merit Mr. Gladstone

---

[1] 'It was the common talk of Oxford how the most distinguished lawyer of the day, a literary man and a critic, on hearing the speech in question, pronounced his prompt verdict on him in the words, "That young man's fortune is made."'— Newman's Funeral Sermon on J. R. Hope - Scott in *Sermons preached on Various Occasions*, p. 269.

found 'beyond anything possible or conceivable' when he was a boy at Eton a dozen years before :—

We sit with the boys (39 in number) and make about ten hours a day in looking over papers with great minuteness. . . . Although it is in quantity hard work, it is lightened by a warm interest, and the refreshment of early love upon a return to this sweet place. It is work apart from human passion, and is felt as a moral relaxation, though it is not one in any other sense. . . . This is a curious experience to me, of jaded body and mind refreshed. I propose for Latin theme a little sentence of Burke's which runs to this effect, 'Flattery corrupts both the receiver and the giver ; and adulation is not of more service to the people than to kings.' *April 2nd.*—The statistics become excessively interesting. Henry Hallam gained, and now stands second [the brother of his dead friend]. *April 3rd.*—In, 6 hours ; out, from 4 to 5 hours more upon the papers. Vinegar, thank God, carries my eyes through so much MS., and the occupation is deeply interesting, especially on Hallam's account. Our labours were at one time anxious and critical, the two leaders being 1388 and 1390 respectively. At night, however, all was decided. *April 4th.* 12.2.—*Viva voce* for fourteen select. At 2½ Seymour was announced scholar to the boys, and chaired forthwith. Hallam, medallist. It was quite overpowering.

Henry Hallam was the second son of the historian, the junior of Arthur by some fourteen or fifteen years. Mr. Gladstone more than a generation later described a touching supplement to his Eton story. 'In 1850 Henry Hallam had attained an age exceeding only by some four years the limit of his brother's life. During that autumn I was travelling post between Turin and Genoa, upon my road to Naples. A family coach met us on the road, and the glance of a moment at the inside showed me the familiar face of Mr. Hallam. I immediately stopped my carriage, descended, and ran after his. On overtaking it, I found the dark clouds accumulated on his brow, and learned with indescribable pain that he was on his way home from Florence, where he had just lost his second and only remaining son, from an attack corresponding in its suddenness and its devastating rapidity with that which had struck down his eldest born son seventeen years before.'

At Fasque, where his autumn sojourn began in September, he threw himself with special ardour into his design for a college for Scotch episcopalians, especially for the training of clergy. He wrote to Manning (Aug. 31, 1840) :—

Hope and I have been talking and writing upon a scheme for raising money to found in Scotland a college akin in structure to the Romish seminaries in England ; that is to say, partly for training the clergy, partly for affording an education to the children of the gentry and others who now go chiefly to presbyterian schools or are tended at home by presbyterian tutors. I think £25,000 would do it, and that it might be got. I must have my father's sanction before committing myself to it. Hope's intended absence for the winter is a great blow. Were he to be at home I do not doubt that great progress might be made. In the kirk toil and trouble, double, double, the fires burn and cauldrons bubble : and though I am not sanguine as to very speedy or extensive resumption by the church of her spiritual rights, she may have a great part to play. At present she is very weakly manned, and this is the way I think to strengthen the crew.

The scheme expanded as time went on. His father threw himself into it with characteristic energy and generosity, contributing many thousand pounds, for the sum required greatly exceeded the modest figure above mentioned. Mr. Gladstone conducted a laborious and sometimes vexatious correspondence in the midst of more important public cares. Plans were mature, and adequate funds were forthcoming, and in the autumn of 1842 Hope and the two Gladstones made what they found an agreeable tour, examining the various localities for a site, and finally deciding on a spot 'on a mountain-stream, ten miles from Perth, at the very gate of the highlands.' It was 1846 before the college at Glenalmond was opened for its destined purposes.[1] We all know examples of men holding opinions with trenchancy, decision, and even a kind of fervour, and yet with no strong desire to spread them. Mr. Gladstone was at all times of very different temper ; consumed with missionary energy and the fire of ardent propagandism.

He laboured hard at the fourth edition of his book, sometimes getting eleven hours of work, 'a good day as times go,' —Montesquieu, Burke, Bacon, Clarendon, and others of the masters of civil and historic wisdom being laid under ample contribution. By Christmas he was at Hawarden. In January he made a speech at a meeting held in Liverpool for the foundation of a church union, and a few days later he hurried off to Walsall to help his brother John, then the tory candidate, and a curious incident happened :—

I either provided myself, or I was furnished from headquarters, with a packet of pamphlets in favour of the corn laws. These I read, and I extracted from them the chief material of my speeches. I dare say it was sad stuff, furbished up at a moment's notice. We carried the election. Cobden sent me a challenge to attend a public discussion of the subject. Whether this was quite fair, I am not certain, for I was young, made no pretension to be an expert, and had never opened my lips in parliament on the subject. But it afforded me an excellent opportunity to decline with modesty and with courtesy as well as reason. I am sorry to say that, to the best of my recollection, I did far otherwise, and the pith of my answer was made to be that I regarded the Anti-Corn Law League as no better than a big borough-mongering association. Such was my first capital offence in the matter of protection ; redeemed from public condemnation only by obscurity.

The letters are preserved, but a sentence or two from Mr. Gladstone's to Cobden will be enough. 'The phrases which

[1] The reader who cares for further particulars may consult the *Memoirs of J. R. Hope-Scott*, i. pp. 248, 281-8 ; and ii. p. 291.

you quote from a report in the *Times* have reference, not to the corn law, but to the Anti-Corn Law League and its operations in Walsall. Complaining apparently of these, you desire me to meet you in discussion, not upon the League but upon the corn law. I cannot conceive two subjects more distinct. I admit the question of the repeal of the corn laws to be a subject fairly open to discussion, although I have a strong opinion against it. But as to the Anti-Corn Law League, I do not admit that any equitable doubt can be entertained as to the character of its present proceedings ; and, excepting a casual familiarity of phrase, I adhere rigidly to the substance of the sentiments which I have expressed. I know not who may be answerable for these measures, nor was your name known to me, or in my recollection at the time when I spoke.' Time soon changed all this, and showed who was teacher and who the learner.

By and by the session of 1841 opened, the whigs moving steadily towards their fall, and Mr. Gladstone almost overwhelmed with floods of domestic business. He settled in the pleasant region which is to the metropolis what Delphi was to the habitable earth, and where, if we include in it Downing Street, he passed all the most important years of his life in London.[1] Though he speaks of being overwhelmed by domestic business, and he was undoubtedly hard beset by all the demands of early housekeeping, yet he very speedily recovered his balance. He resisted now and always as jealously as he could those promiscuous claims on time and attention by which men of less strenuous purpose suffer the effectiveness of their lives to be mutilated. 'I well know,' he writes to his young wife who was expecting him to join her at Hagley, 'you would not have me come on any conditions with which one's sense of duty could not be quieted, and would (I hope) send me back by the next train. These delays are to you a practical exemplification of the difficulty of reconciling domestic and political engagements. The case is one that scarcely admits of compromise ; the least that is required in order to the fulfilment of one's duty is constant bodily presence in London until the fag-end of the session is fairly reached.'

Here are a few examples of the passing days :—

March 12th, 1841.—*Tracts for the Times*, No. 90 ; ominous. *March 13th.*—Went to see Reform Club. Sat to Bradley 2½-4. London Library committee. Carlton Library committee. Corrected two proof-sheets. Conversed an hour and a half with Mr. Richmond, who came to tea, chiefly on my plan for a picture-life of Christ. Chess with C. [his wife]. *March 14th (Sunday).* — Communion (St. James's), St. Margaret's afternoon. Wrote on Ephes. v. 1, and read it aloud to

---

[1] His first house was 13 Carlton House Terrace, then his father gave him 6 Carlton Gardens. In 1856 he purchased 11 Carlton House Terrace, which was his London home until 1875. From 1876 to 1880 he occupied 73 Harley Street.

servants. *March 20th.*—City to see Freshfield. Afternoon service in Saint Paul's. What an image, what a crowd of images! Amidst the unceasing din, and the tumult of men hurrying this way and that for gold, or pleasure, or some self-desire, the vast fabric thrusts itself up to heaven and firmly plants itself on soil begrudged to an occupant that yields no lucre. But the city cannot thrust forth its cathedral; and from thence arises the harmonious measured voice of intercession from day to day. The church praying and deprecating continually for the living mass that are dead while they live, from out of the very centre of that mass; silent and lonesome is her shrine, amidst the noise, the thunder of multitudes. Silent, lonesome, motionless, yet full of life; for were we not more dead than the stones, which, built into that sublime structure witness continually to what is great and everlasting, —did priest or chorister, or the casual worshipper but apprehend the grandeur of his function in that spot,—the very heart must burst with the tide of emotions gathering within it. Oh for speed, speed to the wings of that day when this glorious unfulfilled outline of a church shall be charged as a hive with the operations of the Spirit of God and of His war against the world; when the intervals of space and time within its walls, now untenanted by any functions of that holy work, shall be thickly occupied; and when the glorious sights and sounds which shall arrest the passenger in his haste that he may sanctify his purposes by worship, shall be symbols still failing to express the fulness of the power of God developed among His people.

March 21.—Wrote on 1 Thess. v. 17, and read it to servants. Read *The Young Communicants*; Bishop Hall's *Life*. It seems as if at this time the number and close succession of occupations without any great present reward of love or joy, and chiefly belonging to an earthly and narrow range, were my special trial and discipline. Other I seem hardly to have any of daily pressure. Health in myself and those nearest me; (comparative) wealth and success; no strokes from God; no opportunity of pardoning others, for none offend me.

April 3.—Two or three nights ago Mrs. Wilbraham told Catherine that Stanley was extremely surprised to find, after his speech on the Tamworth and Rugby railway bill, that Peel had been very much annoyed with the expression he had used: 'that his right hon. friend had in pleading for the bill made use of all that art and ingenuity with which he so well knew how to dress up a statement for that House,' and that he showed his annoyance very much by his manner to him, S., afterwards. He, upon reflecting that this was the probable cause, wrote a note to Peel to set matters to rights, in which he succeeded; but he thought Peel very thin-skinned. Wm. Cowper told me the other day at Milnes's that Lord John Russell is remarkable among his colleagues for his anxiety during the recess for the renewal of the session of parliament; that he always argues for fixing an early day of meeting, and finds pleas for it, and finds the time long until it recommences.

A visit to Nuneham (April 12) and thence to Oxford brought him into the centre of the tractarians. He saw much of Hamilton, went to afternoon service at Littlemore, breakfasted in company with Newman at Merton, had a long conversation with Pusey on Tract 90, and gathered that Newman thought differently of the Council of Trent from what he had thought a year or two back, and that he differed from Pusey in thinking the English reformation uncatholic. Mr. Gladstone replied that No. 90 had the appearance to his mind of being written by a man, if in, not of, the church of England ; and would be interpreted as exhibiting the Tridentine system for the ideal, the anglican for a mutilated and *just* tolerable actual. Then in the same month he 'finished Palmer on the Articles, deep, earnest, and generally trustworthy. Worked upon a notion of private eucharistical devotions, to be chiefly compiled ; and attended a meeting about colonial bishoprics,' where he spoke but indifferently.

IV

In 1841 the whigs in the expiring hours of their reign launched parliament and parties upon what was to be the grand marking controversy of the era. To remedy the disorder into which expenditure, mainly due to highhanded foreign policy, had brought the national finance, they proposed to reconstruct the fiscal system by reducing the duties on foreign sugar and timber, and substituting for Wellington's corn law a fixed eight shilling duty on imported wheat. The wiser heads, like Lord Spencer, were aware that as an electioneering expedient the new policy would bring them little luck, but their position in any case was desperate. The handling of their proposals was curiously maladroit ; and even if it had been otherwise, ministerial repute alike for competency and for sincerity was so damaged both in the House of Commons and the country, that their doom was certain. The reduction of the duty on slave-grown sugar from foreign countries was as obnoxious to the abolitionist as it was disadvantageous to the West Indian proprietors, and both of these powerful sections were joined by the corn-grower, well aware that his turn would come next. Many meetings took place at Sir Robert Peel's upon the sugar resolutions, and Mr. Gladstone worked up the papers and figures so as to be ready to speak if necessary. At one of these meetings, by the way, he thought it worth while to write down that Peel had the tradesmen's household books upon his desk—a circumstance that he mentioned also to the present writer, when by chance we found ourselves together in the same room fifty years later.

On May 10th, his speech on the sugar duties came off in due course. In this speech he took the sound point that the new arrangement must act as an encouragement to the slave trade, 'that monster which, while war, pestilence, and famine were slaying their thousands, slew from year to year with unceasing operation its tens of thousands.' As he went on, he fell upon Macaulay for being member of a cabinet that was thus deserting a cause in which Macaulay's father had been the unseen ally of Wilberforce, and the pillar of his strength,—'a man of profound benevolence, of acute understanding, of indefatigable industry, and of that self-denying temper which is content to work in secret, and to seek for its reward beyond the grave.' Macaulay was the last man to suffer rebuke in silence, and he made a sharp reply on the following day, followed by a magnanimous peace-making behind the Speaker's chair.

Meanwhile the air was thick and loud with rumours. Lord Eliot told Mr. Gladstone in the middle of the debate that there had been a stormy cabinet that morning, and that ministers had at last made up their minds to follow Lord Spencer's advice, to resign and not to dissolve. When the division on the sugar duties was taken, ministers were beaten (May 19) by a majority of 36, after fine performances from Sir Robert, and a good one from Palmerston on the other side. The cabinet, with a tenacity incredible in our own day, were still for holding on until their whole scheme, with the popular element of cheap bread in it, was fully before the country. Peel immediately countered them by a vote of want of confidence, and this was carried (June 4) by a majority of one :—

On Saturday morning the division in the House of Commons presented a scene of the most extraordinary excitement. While we were in our lobby we were told that we were 312 and the government either 311 or 312. It was also known that they had brought down Lord —— who was reported to be in a state of total idiocy. After returning to the House I went to sit near the bar, where the other party were coming in. We had all been counted, 312, and the tellers at the government end had counted to 308 ; there remained behind this unfortunate man, reclining in a chair, evidently in total unconsciousness of what was proceeding. Loud cries had been raised from our own side, when it was seen that he was being brought up, to clear the bar that the whole House might witness the scene, and every one stood up in intense curiosity. There were now only this figure, less human even than an automaton, and two persons, R. Stuart, and E. Ellice pushing the chair in which he lay. A loud cry of 'Shame, Shame,' burst from our side ; those opposite were silent. Those three were counted without passing the tellers, and the moment after we saw that our tellers were on the right in walking to the table, indicating that we had won. Fremantle gave out the numbers, and then the intense excitement raised by the sight we had witnessed found vent in our enthusiastic (quite irregular) hurrah with great waving of hats. Upon looking back I am sorry to think how much I partook in the excitement that prevailed ; but how could it be otherwise in so extraordinary a case ? I thought Lord John's a great speech—it was delivered too under the pressure of great indisposition. He has risen with adversity. He seemed rather below par as a leader in 1835 when he had a clear majority, and the ball nearly at his foot ; in each successive year the strength of his government has sunk and his own has risen.

Then came the dissolution, and an election memorable in the history of party. Thinking quite as much of the Scotch

college, the colonial bishoprics, and Tract Ninety, as of sugar
duties or the corn law, Mr. Gladstone hastened to Newark.
He was delighted with the new colleague who had been provided for him. 'As a candidate,' he writes to his wife, 'Lord
John Manners is excellent; his speaking is popular and
effective, and he is a good canvasser, by virtue not I think
of effort, but of a general kindliness and warmth of disposition
which naturally shows itself to every one. Nothing can be
more satisfactory than to have such a partner.' In his address
Mr. Gladstone only touched on the poor law and the corn
law. On the first he would desire liberal treatment for aged,
sick, and widowed poor, and reasonable discretion to the local
administrators of the law. As to the second, the protection
of native agriculture is an object of the first economical and
national importance, and should be secured by a graduated
scale of duties on foreign grain. 'Manners and I,' he says,
'were returned as protectionists. My speeches were of absolute
dulness, but I have no doubt they were sound in the sense of
my leaders Peel and Graham and others of the party.' The
election offered no new incidents. One old lady reproached
him for not being content with keeping bread and sugar from
the people, but likewise by a new faith, the mysterious monster
of Puseyism, stealing away from them the bread of life. He
found the wesleyans shaky, partly because they disliked his
book and were afraid of the Oxford Tracts, and partly from his
refusal to subscribe to their school. Otherwise, flags, bands,
suppers, processions, all went on in high ceremonial order as
before. Day after day passed with nothing worse than the
threat of a blue candidate, but one Sunday morning (June 26)
as people came out of church, they found an address on the
walls and a dark rumour got afloat that the new man had
brought heavy bags of money. For this rumour there was no
foundation, but it inspired annoying fears in the good and
cheerful hopes in the bad. The time was in any case too short,
and at four o'clock on June 29 the poll was found to be, Gladstone 633, Manners 630, Hobhouse 391. His own election safely
over, Mr. Gladstone turned to take part in a fierce contest
in which Sir Stephen Glynne was candidate for the representation of Flintshire, but 'bribery, faggotry, abduction,
personation, riot, factious delays, landlord's intimidations,
partiality of authorities,' carried the day, and to the bitter
dismay of Hawarden, Sir Stephen was narrowly beaten. One
ancient dame, overwhelmed by the defeat of the family that
for eighty years she had idolised, cried aloud to Mrs. Gladstone,
'I am a great woman for thinking of the Lord, but O, my
dear lady, this has put it all out of my head.' The election
involved him in what would now be thought a whimsical
correspondence with one of the Grosvenor family, who complained of Mr. Gladstone for violating the sacred canons of

electioneering etiquette by canvassing Lord Westminster's tenants. 'I did think,' says the wounded patrician, 'that interference between a landlord with whose opinions you were acquainted and his tenants was not justifiable according to those laws of delicacy and propriety which I considered binding in such cases.'

At last he was able to snatch a holiday with his wife and child by the seaside at Hoylake, which rather oddly struck him as being like Pæstum without the temples. He read away at Gibbon and Dante until he went to Hawarden, partly to consider the state of its financial affairs ; as to these something is to be said later. 'Walked alone in the Hawarden grounds,' he says one day during his stay ; 'ruminated on the last-named subject [accounts], also on anticipated changes [in government]. I can digest the crippled religious action of the state ; but I cannot be a party to exacting by blood opium compensation from the Chinese.' Then to London (Aug. 18). He attended the select party meetings at Sir Robert Peel's and Lord Aberdeen's. Dining at Grillion's he heard Stanley, speaking of the new parliament, express a high opinion of Roebuck as an able man and clear speaker, likely to make a figure ; and also of Cobden as a resolute perspicacious man, familiar with all the turns of his subject ; and when the new House assembled, he had made up his mind for himself that '*Cobden will be a worrying man on corn.*' This was Cobden's first entry into the House. At last the whigs were put out of office by a majority of 91, and Peel undertook to form a government.

Aug. 31/41.—In consequence of a note received this morning from Sir Robert Peel I went to him at half-past eleven. The following is the substance of a quarter of an hour's conversation. He said : 'In this great struggle, in which we have been and are to be engaged, the chief importance will attach to questions of finance. It would not be in my power to undertake the business of chancellor of the exchequer in detail ; I therefore have asked Goulburn to fill that office, and I shall be simply first lord. I think we shall be very strong in the House of Commons if as a part of this arrangement you will accept the post of vice-president of the board of trade, and conduct the business of that department in the House of Commons, with Lord Ripon as president. I consider it an office of the highest importance, and you will have my unbounded confidence in it.'[1]

I said, 'of the importance and responsibility of that office at the present time I am well aware ; but it is right that I should say as

---

[1] 'At that period the board of trade was the department which administered to a great extent the functions that have since passed principally into the hands of the treasury, connected with the fiscal laws of the country.'—*Mr. Gladstone at Leeds,* Oct. 8, 1881. In 1880, writing to Mr. Chamberlain, then president, he says : 'If you were to look back to the records of your department thirty-five and forty years ago, you would find how much of the public trade business was transacted in it. Revenue was then largely involved : and hence, I imagine, it came about that this business was taken over in a great degree by the treasury. I myself have drawn up new tariffs in both, at the B. of T. in 1842 and 1844-5, and at the treasury in 1853 and 1860. Why and how the old B. of T. functions also passed in part to the F. O. I do not so well know.'

strongly as I can, that I really am not fit for it. I have no general knowledge of trade whatever ; with a few questions I am acquainted, but they are such as have come across me incidentally.' He said, 'The satisfactory conduct of an office of that kind must after all depend more upon the intrinsic qualities of the man, than upon the precise amount of his previous knowledge. I also think you will find Lord Ripon a perfect master of these subjects, and depend upon it with these appointments at the board of trade we shall carry the whole commercial interests of the country with us.'

He resumed, 'If there be any other arrangement that you would prefer, my value and " affectionate regard " for you would make me most desirous to effect it so far as the claims of others would permit. To be perfectly frank and unreserved, I should tell you, that there are many reasons which would have made me wish to send you to Ireland ; but upon the whole I think that had better not be done. Some considerations connected with the presbyterians of Ireland make me prefer on the whole that we should adopt a different plan.[1] Then, if I had had the exchequer, I should have asked you to be financial secretary to the treasury ; but under the circumstances I have mentioned, that would be an office of secondary importance and I am sure you will not estimate that I now propose to you by the mere name which it bears.' He also made an allusion to the admiralty of which I do not retain the exact form. But I rather interposed and said, 'My objection on the score of fitness would certainly apply with even increased force to anything connected with the military and naval services of the country, for of them I know nothing. Nor have I any other object in view ; there is no office to which I could designate myself. I think it my duty to act upon your judgment as to my qualifications. If it be your deliberate wish to make me vice-president of the board of trade, I will not decline it ; I will endeavour to put myself into harness, and to prepare myself for the place in the best manner I can ; but it really is an apprenticeship.' He said, 'I hope you will be content to act upon the sense which others entertain of your suitableness for this office in particular, and I think it will be a good arrangement both with a view to the present conduct of business and to the brilliant destinies which I trust are in store for you.' I answered, that I was deeply grateful for his many acts of confidence and kindness ; and that I would at once assent to the plan he had proposed, only begging him to observe that I had mentioned my unfitness under a very strong sense of duty and of the facts, and not by any means as a mere matter of ceremony. I then added that I thought I should but ill respond to his confidence if I did not mention to him a subject connected with his policy which might raise a difficulty in my mind. 'I cannot,' I said, 'reconcile it to my sense of right to exact from China, as a term of peace, compensation for the opium surrendered to her. . . .' He agreed that it was best to mention it ; observed that in consequence of the shape in which the Chinese affair came into the hands of the new government, they would not be wholly unfettered ; seemed to hint that under any other circumstances the vice-president of board of trade need not so much mind what was done in the other departments, but remarked that at present every question of foreign relations and many more would be very apt to mix themselves

[1] I suppose this points to incompatibility in the fevers of the hour between protestant Ulster and a Puseyite chief secretary.

with the department of trade. He thought I had better leave the question suspended.

I hesitated a moment before coming away and said it was only from my anxiety to review what I had said, and to be sure that I had made a clean breast on the subject of my unfitness for the department of trade. Nothing could be more friendly and warm than his whole language and demeanour. It has always been my hope, that I might be able to avoid this class of public employment. On this account I have not endeavoured to train myself for them. The place is very distasteful to me, and what is of more importance, I fear I may hereafter demonstrate the unfitness I have to-day only stated. However, it comes to me, I think, as a matter of plain duty ; it may be all the better for not being according to my own bent and leaning ; I must forthwith go to work, as a reluctant schoolboy meaning well.

Sept. 3.—This day I went to Claremont to be sworn in. When the council was constructed, the Duke of Buckingham and Lord Liverpool were first called in to take their oaths and seats; then the remaining four followed, Lincoln, Eliot, Ernest Bruce and I. The Queen sat at the head of the table, composed but dejected—one could not but feel for her, all through the ceremonial. We knelt down to take the oaths of allegiance and supremacy and stood up to take (I think) the councillor's oath, then kissed the Queen's hand, then went round the table shaking hands with each member, beginning from Prince Albert who sat on the Queen's right, and ending with Lord Wharncliffe on her left. We then sat at the lower end of the table, excepting Lord E. Bruce, who went to his place behind the Queen as vice-chamberlain. Then the chancellor first and next the Duke of Buckingham were sworn to their respective offices. C. Greville forgot the duke's privy seal and sent him off without it; the Queen corrected him and gave it. . . . Then were read and approved several orders in council ; among which was one assigning a district to a church and another appointing Lord Ripon and me to act in matters of trade. These were read aloud by the Queen in a very clear though subdued voice ; and she repeated ' Approved ' after each. Upon that relating to Lord R. and myself we were called up and kissed hands again. Then the Queen rose, as did all the members of the council, and retired bowing. We had luncheon in the same room half an hour later and went off. The Duke of Wellington went in an open carriage with a pair ; all our other grand people with four. Peel looked shy all through. I visited Claremont once before, 27 years ago I think, as a child, to see the place, soon after the Princess Charlotte's death. It corresponded pretty much with my impressions.

He secured his re-election at Newark on September 14 without opposition, and without trouble, beyond the pressure of a notion rooted in the genial mind of his constituency that as master of the mint he would have an unlimited command of public coin for all purposes whether general or particular. His reflections upon his ministerial position are of much biographic interest. He had evidently expected inclusion in the cabinet:—

Sept. 16.—Upon quietly reviewing past times, and the degree of confidence which Sir Robert Peel had for years, habitually I may say, reposed in me, and especially considering its climax, in my being summoned to the meetings immediately preceding the debate on the address in August,

I am inclined to think, after allowing for the delusions of self-love, that there is not a perfect correspondence between the tenor of the past on the one hand, and my present appointment and the relations in which it places me to the administration on the other. He may have made up his mind at those meetings that I was not qualified for the consultations of a government, nor would there be anything strange in this, except the supposition that he had not seen it before. Having however taken the alarm (so to speak) upon the invitation at that time, and been impressed with the idea that it savoured of cabinet office, I considered and consulted on the Chinese question, which I regarded as a serious impediment to office of that description, and I had provisionally contemplated saying to Peel in case he should offer me Ireland with the cabinet, to reply that I would gladly serve his government in the secretaryship, but that I feared his Chinese measures would hardly admit of my acting in the cabinet. I am very sorry now to think that I may have been guilty of an altogether absurd presumption, in dreaming of the cabinet. But it was wholly suggested by that invitation. And I still think that there must have been some consultation and decision relating to me in the interval between the meetings and the formation of the new ministry, which produced some alteration. . . . In confirmation of the notion I have recorded above, I am distinct in the recollection that there was a shyness in Peel's manner and a downward eye, when he opened the conversation and made the offer, not usual with him in speaking to me.

In after years, he thus described his position when he went to the board of trade :—

I was totally ignorant both of political economy and of the commerce of the country. I might have said, as I believe was said by a former holder of the vice-presidency, that my mind was in regard to all those matters a 'sheet of white paper,' except that it was doubtless coloured by a traditional prejudice of protection, which had then quite recently become a distinctive mark of conservatism. In a spirit of ignorant mortification I said to myself at the moment : the science of politics deals with the government of men, but I am set to govern packages. In my journal for Aug. 2 I find this recorded : 'Since the address meetings' (which were quasi-cabinets) 'the idea of the Irish secretaryship had nestled imperceptibly in my mind.'[1]

The vice-presidency was the post, by the way, impudently proposed four years later by the whigs to Cobden, after he had taught both whigs and tories their business. Mr. Gladstone, at least, was quick to learn the share of 'packages' in the government of men.

Sept. 30.—Closing the month, and a period of two years comprehended within this book, I add a few words. My position is changed by office. In opposition I was frequently called, or sometimes at least, to the confidential councils of the party on a variety of subjects. In office, I shall of course have to do with the department of trade and with little or nothing beyond. There is some point in the query of the *Westminster Review : Whether my appointments are a covert satire?* But they bring great advantages ; much less responsibility, much less

---

[1] Autobiographic note.

anxiety. I could not have made myself answerable for what I expect the cabinet will do in China. It must be admitted that it presents an odd appearance, when a person whose mind and efforts have chiefly ranged within the circle of subjects connected with the church, is put into office of the most different description. It looks as if the first object were to neutralise his mischievous tendencies. But I am in doubt whether to entertain this supposition would be really a compliment to the discernment of my superiors, or a breach of charity ; therefore it is best not entertained.

Paragraphs appeared in newspapers imputing to Mr. Gladstone a strong reprobation of the prime minister's opinions upon church affairs, and he thought it worth while to write to Sir Robert a strong (and most excessively lengthy) disclaimer of being, among other things, an object of hope to unbending tories as against their moderate and cautious leader.[1] 'Should party spirit,' he went on, 'run very high against your commercial measures, I have no doubt that the venom of my religious opinions will be plentifully alleged to have infused itself into your policy even in that direction, . . . and more than ever will be heard of your culpability in taking into office a person of my bigoted and extreme sentiments.' Peel replied (October 19, 1841) with kindness and good sense. He had not taken the trouble to read the paragraph ; he had read the works from which a mischievous industry had tried to collect means of defaming their author ; he found nothing in them in the most distant manner to affect political co-operation ; and he signed his name to the letter, 'with an esteem and regard, which are proof against evil-minded attempts to sow jealousy and discord.'[2]

[1] It would appear from the manuscript at the British Museum, that Macaulay's sentence about Mr. Gladstone as the rising hope of the stern and unbending tories, which later events made long so famous and so tiresome, was a happy afterthought, written in along the margin.
[2] Parker's *Peel*, ii. pp. 514-17.

CHAPTER VIII

PEEL'S GOVERNMENT

(1842-1844)

In many of the most important rules of public policy Sir R. Peel's government surpassed generally the governments which have succeeded it, whether liberal or conservative. Among them I would mention purity in patronage, financial strictness, loyal adherence to the principle of public economy, jealous regard to the rights of parliament, a single eye to the public interest, strong aversion to extension of territorial responsibilities and a frank admission of the rights of foreign countries as equal to those of their own.—Mr. GLADSTONE (1880).[1]

OF the four or five most memorable administrations of the century, the great conservative government of Sir Robert Peel was undoubtedly one. It laid the groundwork of our solid commercial policy, it established our railway system, it settled the currency, and, by no means least, it gave us a good national character in Europe as lovers of moderation, equity, and peace. Little as most members of the new cabinet saw it, their advent definitely marked the rising dawn of an economic era. If you had to constitute new societies, Peel said to Croker, then you might on moral and social grounds prefer cornfields to cotton factories, and you might like an agricultural population better than a manufacturing ; as it was, the national lot was cast, and statesmen were powerless to turn back the tide. The food of the people, their clothing, the raw material for their industry, their education, the conditions under which women and children were suffered to toil, markets for the products of loom and forge and furnace and mechanic's shop,—these were slowly making their way into the central field of political vision, and taking the place of fantastic follies about foreign dynasties and the balance of power as the true business of the British statesman. On the eve of entering parliament (September 17, 1832), Mr. Gladstone recounts some articles of his creed at the time to his friend Gaskell, and to modern eyes a curious list it is. The first place is given to his views on the relative merits of Pedro, Miguel, Donna Maria, in respect of the throne of Portugal. The second goes to Poland. The third to the affairs of Lombardy.

[1] Undated fragment of letter to the Queen. See Appendix.

Free trade comes last. This was still the lingering fashion of the moment, and it died hard.

The new ministry contained an unusual number of men of mark and capacity, and they were destined to form a striking group. At their head was a statesman whose fame grows more impressive with time, not the author or inspirer of large creative ideas, but with what is at any rate next best—a mind open and accessible to those ideas, and endowed with such gifts of skill, vigilance, caution, and courage as were needed for the government of a community rapidly passing into a new stage of its social growth. One day in February 1842, he sent for Mr. Gladstone on some occasion of business. Peel happened not to be well, and in the course of the conversation his doctor called. Sir James Graham who had come in, said to his junior in Peel's absence with the physician, 'The pressure upon him is immense. We never had a minister who was so truly a first minister as he is. He makes himself felt in every department, and is really cognisant of the affairs of each. Lord Grey could not master such an amount of business. Canning could not do it. Now he is an actual minister, and is indeed *capax imperii.*' Next to Peel as parliamentary leaders stood Graham himself and Stanley. They had both of them sat in the cabinet of Lord Grey, and now found themselves the colleagues of the bitterest foes of Grey's administration. As we have seen, Mr. Gladstone pronounces Graham to have known more about economic subjects than all the rest of the government put together. Such things had hitherto been left to men below the first rank in the hierarchy of public office, like Huskisson. Pedro and Miguel held the field.

Mr. Gladstone's own position is described in an autobiographic fragment of his last years :—

When I entered parliament in 1832, the great controversy between protection or artificial restraint and free trade, of which Cobden was the leading figure, did not enter into the popular controversies of the day, and was still in the hands of the philosophers. My father was an active and effective local politician, and the protectionism which I inherited from him and from all my youthful associations was qualified by a thorough acceptance of the important preliminary measures of Mr. Huskisson, of whom he was the first among the local supporters. Moreover, for the first six years or so of my parliamentary life free trade was in no way a party question, and it only became strictly such in 1841 at, and somewhat before, the general election, when the whig government, *in extremis,* proposed a fixed duty upon corn. My mind was in regard to it a sheet of white paper, but I accepted the established conditions in *the lump,* and could hardly do otherwise. In 1833 only, the question was debated in the House of Commons, and the speech of the mover against the corn laws made me uncomfortable. But the reply of Sir James Graham restored my peace of mind. I followed the others with a languid interest. Yet I remember being struck with the essential unsoundness of the argument of Mr. Villiers. It was this. Under the present corn law our trade, on which we depend, is doomed, for our manufacturers cannot possibly contend with the manufacturers of the continent if they have to pay wages regulated by the protection price of food, while their rivals pay according to the natural or free trade price. The answer was obvious. 'Thank you. We quite understand you. Your object is to get down the wages of your workpeople.' It was Cobden who really set the argument on its legs; and it is futile to compare any other man with him as the father of our system of free trade.

I had in 1840 to dabble in this question, and on the wrong side of it.[1] . . . The matter passed from my mind, full of churches and church matters, in which I was now gradually acquiring knowledge. In 1841 the necessities of the whig government led to a further development of the great controversy ; but I interfered only in the colonial part of it in connection with the colonies and the slave trade to Porto Rico and Brazil. We West Indians were now great philanthropists ! When Sir Robert Peel assumed the government he had become deeply committed to protection, which in the last two or three years had become the subject of a commanding controversy. I suppose that at Newark I followed suit, but I have no record. On the change of government Peel, with much judgment, offered me the vice-presidentship of the board of trade. On sound principles of party discipline, I took the office at once ; and having taken it I set to work with all my might as a worker. In a very short time I came to form a low estimate of the knowledge and information of Lord Ripon ; and of the cabinet Sir James Graham, I think, knew most. And now the stones of which my protectionism was built up began to get uncomfortably loose. When we came to the question of the tariff, we were all nearly on a par in ignorance, and we had a very bad adviser in Macgregor, secretary to the board of trade. But I had the advantage of being able to apply myself with an undivided attention. My assumption of office at the board of trade was followed by hard, steady, and honest work ; and every day so spent beat like a battering-ram on the unsure fabric of my official protectionism. By the end of the year I was far gone in the opposite·sense. I had to speak much on these questions in the session of 1842, but it was always done with great moderation.

II

The case on the accession of the new ministers was difficult. Peel himself has drawn the picture. By incompetent finance, by reckless colonial expenditure, by solving political difficulties through gifts or promises of cash from the British treasury, by war and foreign relations hovering on the verge of war and necessitating extended preparations, the whigs had brought the national resources into an embarrassment that was extreme. The accumulated deficits of five years had become a heavy incubus, and the deficit of 1842-3 was likely to be not less than two and a half millions more. Commerce and manufactures were languishing. Distress was terrible. Poor-rates were mounting, and grants-in-aid would extend impoverishment

[1] See above, p. 172.

from the factory districts to the rural. 'Judge then,' said Peel, 'whether we can with safety retrograde in manufactures.'[1]

So grave a crisis could only be met by daring remedies. With the highest courage, moral courage no less than political, Peel resolved to ask parliament to let him raise four or five millions a year by income-tax, in order to lower the duties on the great articles of consumption, and by reforming the tariff both to relieve trade, and to stimulate and replenish the reciprocal flow of export and import. That he at this time, or perhaps in truth at any time, had acquired complete mastery of those deeper principles and wider aspects of free trade of which Adam Smith had been the great exponent—principles afterwards enforced by the genius of Cobden with such admirable skill, persistency, and patriotic spirit—there was nothing to show. Such a scheme had no originality in it. Huskisson, and men of less conspicuous name, had ten years earlier urged the necessity of a new general system of taxation, based upon remission of duty on raw materials and on articles of consumption, and upon the imposition of an income-tax. The famous report of the committee on import duties of 1840, often rightly called the charter of free trade, of which Peel, not much to his credit, had at this moment not read a word,[2] laid the foundations of the great policy of tariff reform with which the names of Peel and Gladstone are associated in history. The policy advocated in 1830 in the admirable treatise of Sir Henry Parnell is exactly the policy of Peel in 1842, as he acknowledged. After all it is an idle quarrel between the closet strategist and the victorious commander ; between the man who first discerns some great truth of government, and the man who gets the thing, or even a part of the thing, actually done.

Mr. Gladstone has left on record some particulars of his own share as subordinate minister not in the cabinet, in this first invasion upon the old tory corn law of 1827. Peel from the beginning appreciated the powers of his keen and zealous lieutenant, and even in the autumn of 1841 he had taken him into confidential counsel.[3] Besides a letter of observations on the general scheme of commercial freedom, Mr. Gladstone prepared for the prime minister a special paper on the corn laws.

The ordinary business of the department soon fell into my hands to transact with the secretaries, one of them Macgregor, a loose-minded free trader, and the other Lefevre, a clear and scientific one. In that autumn I became possessed with the desire to relax the corn law, which

---

[1] Parker, ii. pp. 499, 529, 533.

[2] *Ibid.*, p. 509. Before the end of the session (Aug. 10, 1842) he had learned enough to do more justice to Hume and the committee.

[3] The editor of Sir Robert Peel's papers was allowed to print three or four of Mr. Gladstone's letters to his chief at this interesting date. The reader will find the correspondence in Parker, ii. pp. 497-517, 519, 520.

formed, I believe, the chief subject of my meditations. Hence followed an important consequence. Very slow in acquiring relative and secondary knowledge and honestly absorbed in my work, I simply thought on and on as to what was right and fair under the circumstances.

In January 1842, as the session approached, they came to close quarters. The details of all the mysteries of protectionist iniquity we may well spare ourselves. Peel, feeling the pulse of his agricultural folk, thought it would never do to give them less than a ten-shilling duty, when the price of wheat was at sixty-two shillings the quarter; while Mr. Gladstone thought a twelve-shilling duty at a price of sixty far too low a relief to the consumer. His eyes were beginning to be opened.

Feb. 2.—I placed in Sir R. Peel's hands a long paper on the corn law in the month of November, which, on wishing to refer to it, he could not find ; and he requested me to write out afresh my argument upon the value of a rest or dead level, and the part of the scale of price at which it should arrive ; this I did.

On Monday I wrote another paper arguing for a rest between 60/ and 70/ or thereabouts ; and yesterday a third intended to show that the present law has been in practice *fully* equivalent to a prohibition up to 70/. Lord Ripon then told me the cabinet had adopted Peel's scale as it originally stood—and seemed to doubt whether *any* alteration could be made. On his announcing the adoption, I said in a marked manner, '*I am very sorry for it*'—believing that it would be virtual prohibition up to 65/ or 66/ and often beyond, to the minimum ; and not being able, in spite of all the good which the government is about to do with respect to commerce, to make up my mind to support such a protection. I see, from conversations with them to-day, that Lord Ripon, Peel, and Graham, are all aware the protection is greater than is necessary.

This mood soon carried the vice-president terribly far. On Feb. 5 he met most of the members of the cabinet at Peel's house. He argued his point that the scale would operate as virtual protection up to seventy shillings, and in a private interview with Peel afterwards hinted at retirement. Peel declared himself so taken by surprise that he hardly knew what to say ; 'he was thunderstruck' ; and he told his young colleague that 'the retirement of a person holding his office, on this question, immediately before his introducing it, would endanger the existence of the administration, and that he much doubted whether in such a case he could bring it on.'

I fear Peel was much annoyed and displeased, for he would not give me a word of help or of favourable supposition as to my own motives and belief. He used nothing like an angry or unkind word, but the negative character of the conversation had a chilling effect on my mind. I came home sick at heart in the evening and told all to Catherine, my lips, being to every one else, as I said to Sir R. Peel, absolutely sealed.

'He might have gained me more easily, I think,' Mr. Gladstone wrote years afterwards, 'by a more open and supple method of expostulation. But he was not skilful, I think, in the management of personal or sectional dilemmas, as he showed later on with respect to two important questions, the Factory acts and the crisis on the sugar duties in 1844.' This sharp and unnecessary corner safely turned, Mr. Gladstone learned the lesson how to admire a great master overcoming a legislator's difficulties.

I have been much struck (he wrote, Feb. 26) throughout the private discussions connected with the new project of a corn law, by the tenacity with which Sir Robert Peel, firstly by adhering in every point to the old arrangements where it seemed at all possible, and since the announcement of the plan to parliament, by steadily resisting changes in any part of the resolutions, has narrowed the ground and reduced in number the points of attack, and thus made his measure practicable in the face of popular excitement and a strong opposition. Until we were actually in the midst of the struggle, I did not appreciate the extraordinary sagacity of his parliamentary instinct in this particular. He said yesterday to Lord Ripon and to me, ' Among ourselves, in this room, I have no hesitation in saying, that if I had not had to look to other than abstract considerations I would have proposed a lower protection. But it would have done no good to push the matter so far as to drive Knatchbull out of the cabinet after the Duke of Buckingham, nor could I hope to pass a measure with greater reductions through the House of Lords.'

When Lord John Russell proposed an amendment substituting an eight-shilling duty for a sliding scale, Peel asked Mr. Gladstone to reply to him. 'This I did (Feb. 14, 1842),' he says, ' and with my whole heart, for I did not yet fully understand the vicious operation of the sliding scale on the corn trade, and it is hard to see how an eight-shilling duty could even then have been maintained.'

III

The three centres of operations were the corn bill, then the bill imposing the income - tax, and finally the reform of the duties upon seven hundred and fifty out of the twelve hundred articles that swelled the tariff. The corn bill was the most delicate, the tariff the most laborious, the income-tax the boldest, the most fraught alike with peril for the hour and with consequences of pith and moment for the future. It is hardly possible for us to realise the general horror in which this hated impost was then enveloped. The fact of Brougham procuring the destruction of all the public books and papers in which its odious accounts were recorded, only illustrates the intensity of the common sentiment against the dire hydra evoked by Mr. Pitt for the destruction of the regicide power of France, and sent back again to its gruesome limbo after the ruin of Napoleon. From 1842 until 1874 the question of the income-tax was the vexing enigma of public finance.

It was upon Mr. Gladstone that the burden of the immense achievement of the new tariff fell, and the toil was huge. He

used afterwards to say that he had been concerned in four
revisions of the tariff, in 1842, 1845, 1853, and 1860, and that the
first of them cost six times as much trouble as the other three
put together. He spoke one hundred and twenty-nine times
during the session. He had only once sat on a committee of
trade, and had only once spoken on a purely trade question
during the nine years of his parliamentary life. All his habits
of thought and action had been cast in a different mould. It
is ordinarily assumed that he was a born financier, endowed
besides with a gift of idealism and the fine training of a scholar.
As a matter of fact, it was the other way ; he was a man of
high practical and moral imagination, with an understanding
made accurate by strength of grasp and incomparable power of
rapid and concentrated apprehension, yoked to finance only by
force of circumstance—a man who would have made a shining
and effective figure in whatever path of great public affairs,
whether ecclesiastical or secular, duty might have called for
his exertions.

It is curious that the first measure of commercial policy in
this session should have been a measure of protection in the
shape of a bill introduced by the board of trade, imposing a
duty on corn, wheat, and flour brought from the United States
into Canada.[1] But this was only a detail, though a singular
one, in a policy that was in fact a continuance of the relaxation
of the commercial system of the colonies which had been begun
in 1822 and 1825 by Robinson and Huskisson. In his present
employment Mr. Gladstone was called upon to handle a mass
of questions that were both of extreme complexity in themselves, and also involved collision with trade interests always
easily alarmed, irritated, and even exasperated. With merchants and manufacturers, importers and exporters, brokers and
bankers, with all the serried hosts of British trade, with the laws
and circumstances of international commerce, he was every day
brought into close, detailed, and responsible contact :—Whether
the duty on straw bonnets should go by weight or by number ;
what was the difference between boot-fronts at six shillings per
dozen pairs and a 15 per cent duty *ad valorem* ; how to distinguish the regulus of tin from mere ore, and how to fix the
duty on copper ore so as not to injure the smelter ; how to find
an adjustment between the liquorice manufacturers of London
and the liquorice growers of Pontefract ; what was the special
case for muscatels as distinct from other raisins ; whether 110
pounds of ship biscuits would be a fair deposit for taking out
of bond 100 pounds of wheat if not kiln-dried, or 96 pounds if
kiln-dried ; whether there ought to be uniformity between hides
and skins. He applies to Cornewall Lewis, then a poor-law

[1] In 1843 a bill was passed lowering the duty on Canadian corn imported into
England, and Mr. Gladstone says in a memo. of 1851 : 'In 1843 I pleaded strongly for
the admission of all the colonies to the privilege then granted to Canada.'

commissioner, not on the astronomy of the ancients or the truth
of early Roman history, but to find out for a certain series of
years past the contract price of meat in workhouses. He listens
to the grievances of the lath-renders ; of the coopers who complain that casks will come in too cheap; of the coal-whippers,
and the frame-work knitters ; and he examines the hard predicament of the sawyers, who hold government answerable both for
the fatal competition of machinery and the displacement of wood
by iron. 'These deputations,' he says, 'were invaluable to me,
for by constant close questioning I learned the nature of their
trades, and armed with this admission to their interior, made
careful notes and became able to defend in debate the propositions of the tariff and to show that the respective businesses
would be carried on and not ruined as they said. I have ever
since said that deputations are most admirable aids for the
transaction of public business, provided the receiver of them is
allowed to fix the occasion and the stage at which they appear.'
Among the deputations of this period Mr. Gladstone always
recalled one from Lancashire, as the occasion on which he first
saw Mr. Bright :—

> The deputation was received not by me but by Lord Ripon, in the
> large room at the board of trade, I being present. A long line of fifteen
> or twenty gentlemen occupied benches running down and at the end of
> the room, and presented a formidable appearance. All that I remember,
> however, is the figure of a person in black or dark Quaker costume,
> seemingly the youngest of the band. Eagerly he sat a little forward on
> the bench and intervened in the discussion. I was greatly struck with
> him. He seemed to me rather fierce, but very strong and very earnest.
> I need hardly say this was John Bright. A year or two after he made
> his appearance in parliament.[1]

The best testimony to Mr. Gladstone's share in this arduous
task is supplied in a letter written by the prime minister himself to John Gladstone, and that he should have taken the
trouble to write it shows, moreover, that though Peel may have
been a ' bad horse to go up to in the stable,' his reserve easily
melted away in recognition of difficult duty well done :—

Sir Robert Peel to John Gladstone.

Whitehall, June 16, 1842.—You probably have heard that we have
concluded the discussions (the preliminary discussions at least) on the
subject of the tariff. I cannot resist the temptation, if it be only for the
satisfaction of my own feelings, of congratulating you most warmly and
sincerely, on the distinction which your son has acquired, by the manner
in which he has conducted himself throughout those discussions and all
others since his appointment to office. At no time in the annals of
parliament has there been exhibited a more admirable combination of
ability, extensive knowledge, temper and discretion. Your paternal
feelings must be gratified in the highest degree by the success which has

---

[1] Bright was elected for Durham in July 1843.

naturally and justly followed the intellectual exertions of your son, and you must be supremely happy as a father in the reflection that the capacity to make such exertions is combined in his case with such purity of heart and integrity of conduct.

More than fifty years later in offering to a severe opponent magnanimous congratulations in debate on his son's successful maiden speech, Mr. Gladstone said he knew how refreshing to a father's heart such good promise must ever be. And in his own instance Peel's generous and considerate letter naturally drew from John Gladstone a worthy and feeling response :—

John Gladstone to Sir R. Peel.

June 17.—The receipt last evening of your kind letter of yesterday filled my eyes with tears of gratitude to Almighty God, for having given me a son whose conduct in the discharge of his public duties has received the full approbation of one, who of all men, is so well qualified to form a correct judgment of his merits. Permit me to offer you my most sincere thanks for this truly acceptable testimonial, which I shall carefully preserve. William is the youngest of my four sons ; in the conduct of all of them, I have the greatest cause for thankfulness, for neither have ever caused me a pang. He excels his brothers in talent, but not so in soundness of principles, habits of usefulness, or integrity of purpose. My eldest, as you are aware, has again, and in a most satisfactory manner, got into parliament. To have the third also again there, whilst the services of naval men, circumstanced as he is, who seek unsuccessfully for employment, are not required, we are desirous to effect, and wait for a favourable opportunity to accomplish. Whenever we may succeed, I shall consider my cup to be filled, for the second is honourably and usefully engaged as a merchant in Liverpool, occupying the situation I held there for so many years.

It was while they were in office that Peel wrote from Windsor to beg Mr. Gladstone to sit for his portrait to Lucas, the same artist who had already painted Graham for him. 'I shall be very glad of this addition to the gallery of the eminent men of my own time.'

It was evident that Mr. Gladstone's admission to the cabinet could not be long deferred, and in the spring of the following year, the head of the government made him the coveted communication :—

Whitehall, May 13, 1843.

MY DEAR GLADSTONE,—I have proposed to the Queen that Lord Ripon should succeed my lamented friend and colleague, Lord Fitzgerald, as president of the board of control. I, at the same time, requested her Majesty's permission (and it was most readily conceded) to propose to you the office of president of the board of trade, with a seat in the cabinet. If it were not for the occasion of the vacancy I should have had unmixed satisfaction in thus availing myself of the earliest opportunity that has occurred since the formation of the government, of giving a wider scope to your ability to render public service, and of strengthening that government by inviting your aid as a minister of the crown. For myself personally, and I can answer also for every other member of the government, the prospect of your accession to the cabinet is very gratifying to our feelings.—Believe me, my dear Gladstone, with sincere esteem and regard, most truly yours,

ROBERT PEEL.

At two to-day (May 13), Mr. Gladstone records, I went to Sir R. Peel's on the subject of his letter. I began by thanking him for the indulgent manner in which he had excused my errors, and more than appreciated any services I might have rendered, and for the offer he had made and the manner of it. I said that I went to the board of trade without knowledge or relish, but had been very happy there; found quite enough to occupy my mind, enough responsibility for my own strength, and had no desire to move onwards, but should be perfectly satisfied with any arrangement which he might make as to Lord Ripon's successor. He spoke most warmly of service received, said he could not be governed by any personal considerations, and this which he proposed was obviously the right arrangement. I then stated the substance of what I had put in my memorandum, first on the opium question, to which his answer was, that the immediate power and responsibility lay with the East India Company; he did not express agreement with my view of the cultivation of the drug, but said it was a minor subject as compared with other imperial interests constantly brought under discussion; intimated that the Duke of Wellington had surrendered his opinion (I think) upon the boundary question; and he referred to the change in his own views, and said that in future he questioned whether he could undertake the defence of the corn laws on principle. His words were addressed to a sympathising hearer. My speeches in the House had already excited dissatisfaction if not dismay.

Then came something about the preservation of the two bishoprics in North Wales.[1] To Mr. Gladstone's surprise, Peel reckoned this a more serious matter, as it involved a practical course. After much had been said on the topic, Mr. Gladstone asked for a day or two to consider the question. 'I have to consider with God's help by Monday whether to enter the cabinet or to retire altogether: at least such is probably the second alternative.' He wished to consult Hope and Manning, and they, upon discussion, urged that the point was too narrow on which to join issue with the government. This brought him round. 'I well remember,' he says of this early case of compromise, 'that I pleaded against them that I should be viewed as a traitor, and they observed to me in reply that I must be prepared for that if necessary, that (and indeed I now feel) in these times the very wisest and most effective servants of any cause must necessarily fall so far short of the popular sentiment of its friends, as to be liable constantly to incur mistrust

---

[1] The question of the Welsh bishoprics was one of a certain magnitude in its day. The union of Bangor and St. Asaph had been provided for by parliament in 1836, with a view to form a new see at Manchester. The measure was passed with the general assent of the episcopal bench and the church at large. But sentiment soon changed, and a hostile cry was raised before the death of the Bishop of St. Asaph, when its provisions would come into force. On his death in 1846 the whig ministry gave way and the sees remained separate.

and even abuse. But patience and the power of character overcome all these difficulties. I am certain that Hope and Manning in 1843 were not my tempters but rather my good angels.'[1]

Peel had been in parliament as long, and almost as long in office, as Mr. Gladstone had lived, but experience of public life enlarges the man of high mind, and Peel, while perhaps he wondered at his junior's bad sense of proportion, was the last man to laugh at force of sincerity and conscience. Men of the other sort, as he knew, were always to be had for the asking. ' He spoke again of the satisfaction of his colleagues, and even said he did not recollect former instances of a single vacancy in a cabinet, on which there was an entire concurrence. I repeated what I had said of his and their most indulgent judgment and took occasion distinctly to apologise for my blunder, and the consequent embarrassment which I caused to him in Feb. 1842, on the corn scale.'[2]

His parliamentary success had been extraordinary. From the first his gifts of reasoning and eloquence had pleased the House ; his union of sincerity and force had attracted it as sincerity and force never fail to do ; and his industry and acuteness, his steady growth in political stature, substance, and acquisition, had gained for him the confidence of the austerest of leaders. He had reached a seat in the cabinet before he was thirty-four, and after little more than ten years of parliamentary life. Canning was thirty-seven before he won the same eminence, and he had been thirteen years in the House ; while Peel had the cabinet within reach when he was four-and-thirty, and had been in the House almost thirteen years, of which six had been passed in the arduous post of Irish secretary. Mr. Gladstone had shown that he had in him the qualities that make a minister and a speaker of the first class, though he had shown also the perilous quality of a spirit of minute scruple. He had not yet displayed those formidable powers of contention and attack, that were before long to resemble some tremendous projectile, describing a path the law of whose curves and deviations, as they watched its journey through the air in wonder and anxiety for the shattering impact, men found it impossible to calculate.

Mr. Gladstone's brief notes of his first and second cabinets are worth transcribing : the judicious reader will have little difficulty in guessing the topic for deliberation ; it figured in the latest of his cabinets as in the earliest, as well as in most of those that intervened. ' *May* 15.—My first cabinet. On Irish repeal meetings. No fear of breach of the peace, grounded on reasons. Therefore no case for interference. (The duke, however, was for issuing a proclamation.) *May* 20.—Second [cabinet] Repeal. Constabulary tainted.' It would be safe to

[1] Mr. Gladstone to Lord Lyttelton, Dec. 30, 1845.   [2] See above, p. 187.

VOL. I   O

say of any half-dozen consecutive meetings of the Queen's servants, taken at random during the reign, that Ireland would be certain to crop up. Still, protection was the burning question. From one cause or another, said Mr. Gladstone looking back to these times, 'my reputation among the conservatives on the question of protection oozed away with rapidity. It died with the year 1842, and early in 1843 a duke, I think the Duke of Richmond, speaking in the House of Lords, described some renegade proceeding as a proceeding conducted under the banner of the vice-president of the board of trade.' He was not always as careful as Peel, and sometimes came near to a scrape.

In my speech on Lord Howick's motion (Mar. 10, 1843) I was supposed to play with the question, and prepare the way for a departure from the corn law of last year, and I am sensible that I so far lost my head, as not to put well together the various, and, if taken separately, conflicting considerations which affect the question. . . . It so happens that I spoke under the influence of a new and most sincere conviction, having reference to the recent circumstances of commercial legislation abroad, to the effect that it would not be wise to displace British labour for the sake of cheap corn, without the counteracting and sustaining provisions which exchange, not distorted by tariffs all but prohibitory, would supply. . . . This, it is clear, is a slippery position for a man who does not think firmly in the midst of ambiguous and adverse cheering, and I did my work most imperfectly, but I do think honestly. Sir R. Peel's manner, by negative signs, showed that he thought either my ground insecure or my expressions dangerous.

The situation was essentially artificial. There was little secret of the surrender of protection as a principle. In introducing the proposals for the reform of the customs tariff, Peel made the gentlemen around him shiver by openly declaring that on the general principle of free trade there was no difference of opinion ; that all agreed in the rule that we should buy in the cheapest market and sell in the dearest ; that even if the foreigner were foolish enough not to follow suit, it was still for the interest of this country to buy as cheap as we could, whether other countries will buy from us or no.[1] Even important cabinet colleagues found this too strong doctrine for them.

'On Tuesday night,' says Mr. Gladstone, 'Peel opened the tariff anew, and laid down in a manner which drew great cheering from the opposition, the doctrine of purchasing in the cheapest market. Stanley said to me afterwards, "Peel laid that down a great deal too broadly." Last night he (Lord S.) sat down angry with himself, and turned to me and said, "It does not signify, I *cannot* speak on these subjects ; I quite lost my head." I merely answered that no one but himself would have discovered it.' Yet it was able men, apt to

lose their heads in economics, whom Peel had to carry along
with him. 'On another night,' says Mr. Gladstone, 'I thought
Sir R. Peel appeared in an attitude of conspicuous intellectual
greatness, and on comparing notes next day with Sir J. Graham
at the palace, I found he was similarly impressed. Sheil delivered a very effective rhetorical speech. Lord Stanley had
taken a few notes and was to follow him. Sheil was winding
up just as the clock touched twelve. Lord Stanley said to Peel,
"It is twelve, shall I follow him? I think not." Peel said, "I
do not think it will do to let this go unanswered." He had been
quite without the idea of speaking that night. Sheil sat down,
and peals of cheering followed. Stanley seemed to hesitate a
good deal, and at last said, as it were to himself, "No, I won't,
it's too late." In the meantime the adjournment had been
moved ; but when Peel saw there was no one in the breach, he
rose. The cheers were still, a little spitefully, prolonged from
the other side. He had an immense subject, a disturbed House,
a successful speech, an entire absence of notice to contend
against ; but he began with power, gathered power as he went
on, handled every point in his usual mode of balanced thought
and language, and was evidently conscious at the close, of what
no one could deny, that he had made a deep impression on the
House.'

IV

Mr. Gladstone kept pretty closely in step with his leader.
From Sir Robert he slowly learned lessons of circumspection
that may not seem congenial to his temperament, though for
that matter we should remember all through that his temperament was double. He was of opinion, as he told the House of
Commons, that a sliding scale, a fixed duty, and free trade were
all three open to serious objection. He regarded the defects of
the existing law as greatly exaggerated, and he refused to admit
that the defects of the law, whatever they might be, were fatal
to every law with a sliding scale. He wished to relieve the
consumer, to steady the trade, to augment foreign commerce,
and the demand for labour connected with commerce. On the
other hand he desired to keep clear of the countervailing evils
of disturbing either vast capitals invested in land, or the
immense masses of labour employed in agriculture.[1] He noted
with some complacency, that during the great controversy of
1846 and following years, he never saw any parliamentary
speech of his own quoted in proof of the inconsistency of the
Peelites. Here are a couple of entries from Lord Broughton's
diary for 1844 :—'*June* 17. Brougham said Gladstone was a
d——d fellow, a prig, and did much mischief to the government,
alluding to his speech about keeping sugar duties. *June* 27.
Gladstone made a decided agricultural protection speech, and

[1] *Hansard*, February 14, 1842.

was lauded therefor by Miles—so the rebels were returning to their allegiance.' Gladstone's arguments, somebody said, were in favour of free trade, and his parentheses were in favour of protection.

Well might the whole position be called as slippery a one as ever occurred in British politics. It was by the principles of free trade that Peel and his lieutenant justified tariff-reform; and they indirectly sapped protection in general by dwelling on the mischiefs of minor forms of protection in particular. They assured the country gentlemen that the sacred principle of a scale was as tenderly cherished in the new plan as in the old; on the other hand they could assure the leaguers and the doubters that the structure of the two scales was widely different. We cannot wonder that honest tories who stuck to the old doctrine, not always rejected even by Huskisson, that a country ought not to be dependent on foreign supply, were mystified and amazed as they listened to the two rival parties disputing to which of them belonged the credit of originating a policy that each of them had so short a time before so scornfully denounced. The only difference was the difference between yesterday and the day before yesterday. The whigs, with their fixed duty, were just as open as the conservatives with their sliding scale to the taunts of the Manchester school, when they decorated economics by high *a priori* declaration that the free importation of corn was not a subject for the deliberations of the senate, but a natural and inalienable law of the Creator. Rapid was the conversion. Even Lord Palmerston, of all people in the world, denounced the arrogance and presumptuous folly of dealers in restrictive duties 'setting up their miserable legislation instead of the great standing laws of nature.' Mr. Disraeli, still warmly on the side of the minister, flashed upon his uneasy friends around him a reminder of the true pedigree of the dogmas of free trade. Was it not Mr. Pitt who first promulgated them in 1787, who saw that the loss of the market of the American colonies made it necessary by lowering duties to look round for new markets on the continent of Europe? And was it not Fox, Burke, Sheridan, and the minor whig luminaries, who opposed him, while not a single member of his own government in the House of Lords was willing or able to defend him? But even reminiscences of Mr. Pitt, and oracular descriptions of Lord Shelburne as the most remarkable man of his age, brought little comfort to men sincerely convinced with fear and trembling that free corn would destroy rent, close their mansions and their parks, break up their lives, and beggar the country. They remembered also one or two chapters of history nearer to their own time. They knew that Lord John had a right to revive the unforgotten contrast between Peel's rejection of so-called protestant securities in 1817 and 1825, and the total surrender of emancipation in 1829. Natural forebodings darkened their souls that protectionism would soon share the fate of protestantism, and that capitulation to Cobden was doomed to follow the old scandal of capitulation to O'Connell. They felt that there was something much more dreadful than the mere sting of a parliamentary recrimination, in the contrast between the corn bill of 1842 and Peel's panegyrics in '39, '40, and '41 on the very system which that bill now shattered. On the other side some could not forget that in 1840 the whig prime minister, the head of a party still even at the eleventh hour unregenerated by Manchester, predicted a violent struggle as the result of the Manchester policy, stirring society to its foundations, kindling bitter animosities not easy to quench, and creating convulsions as fierce as those of the Reform bill.

A situation so precarious and so unedifying was sure to lead to strange results in the relations of parties and leaders. In July 1843 the Speaker told Hobhouse that Peel had lost all following and authority ; all but votes. Hobhouse meeting a tory friend told him that Sir Robert had got nothing but his majority. 'He won't have that long,' the tory replied. 'Who will make sacrifices for such a fellow ? They call me a *frondeur*, but there are many such. Peel thinks he can govern by Fremantle and a little clique, but it will not do. The first election that comes, out he must go.' Melbourne, only half in jest, was reported to talk of begging Peel to give him timely notice, lest the Queen might take him by surprise. On one occasion Hobhouse wished a secondary minister to tell Sir Robert how much he admired a certain speech. 'I !' exclaimed the minister ; 'he would kick me away if I dared to speak to him.' 'A man,' Hobhouse observes, 'who will not take a civil truth from a subaltern is but a sulky fellow after all ; there is no true dignity or pride in such reserve.' Oddly enough, Lord John was complaining just as loudly about the same time of his own want of hold upon his party.

The tariff operations of 1842 worked no swift social miracle. General stagnation still prevailed. Capital was a drug in the market, but food was comparatively cheap.[1] Stocks were light, and there was very little false credit. In spite of all these favouring conditions, Mr. Gladstone (March 20, 1843) had to report to his chief that 'the deadness of foreign demand keeps our commerce in a state of prolonged paralysis.' Cobden had not even yet convinced them that the true way to quicken foreign demand was to open the ports to that foreign supply, with which they paid us for what they bought from us. Mr. Gladstone saw no further than the desire of making specific arrangement with other countries for reciprocal reductions of import duties.

[1] The average price of wheat per quarter in 1841 was 64 shillings, in 1842, 57 shillings, and in 1843, 50 shillings, a lower average than for any year until 1849.

In one of his autobiographic notes (1897) Mr. Gladstone describes the short and sharp parliamentary crisis in 1844 brought about by the question of the sugar duties, but this may perhaps be relegated to an appendix.[1]

V

From 1841 to 1844 Mr. Gladstone's department was engaged in other matters lying beyond the main stream of effort. 'We were anxiously and eagerly endeavouring to make tariff treaties with many foreign countries. Austria, I think, may have been included, but I recollect especially France, Prussia, Portugal, and I believe Spain. And the state of our tariff, even after the law of 1842, was then such as to supply us with plenty of material for liberal offers. Notwithstanding this, we failed in every case. I doubt whether we advanced the cause of free trade by a single inch.'

The question of the prohibition against the export of machinery came before him. The custom-house authorities pronounced it ineffective, and recommended its removal. A parliamentary committee in 1841 had reported in favour of entire freedom. The machine-makers, of course, were active, and the general manufacturers of the country, excepting the Nottingham lace-makers and the flax-spinners of the north of Ireland, had become neutral. Only a very limited portion of the trade was any longer subject to restriction, and Mr. Gladstone, after due consultation with superior ministers, proposed a bill for removing the prohibition altogether.[2] He also brought in a bill (April 1844) for the regulation of companies. It was when he was president of the board of trade that the first Telegraph Act was passed. 'I was well aware,' he wrote, 'of the advantage of taking them into the hands of the government, but I was engaged in a plan which contemplated the ultimate acquisition of the railways by the public, and which was much opposed by the railway companies, so that to have attempted taking the telegraphs would have been hopeless. The bill was passed, but the executive machinery two years afterwards broke down.'

Questions that do not fall within the contentions of party usually cut a meagre figure on the page of the historian, and the railway policy of this decade is one of those questions. It was settled without much careful deliberation or foresight, and may be said in the main to have shaped itself. At the time when Mr. Gladstone presided over the department of trade, an immense extension of the railway system was seen to be certain, and we may now smile at what then seemed the striking novelty of such a prospect. Mr. Gladstone proposed a select committee on the subject, guided its deliberations,

[1] See Appendix.   [2] See Speech, Aug. 10, 1843.

drew its reports, and framed the bill that was founded upon them. He dwelt upon the favour now beginning to be shown to the new roads by the owners of land through which they were to pass, so different from the stubborn resistance that had for long been offered; upon the cheapened cost of construction; upon the growing disposition to employ redundant capital in making railways, instead of running the risks that had made foreign investment so disastrous. It was not long, indeed, before this very disposition led to a mania that was even more widely disastrous than any foreign investment had been since the days of the South Sea bubble. Meanwhile, Mr. Gladstone's Railway Act of 1844, besides a number of working regulations for the day, laid down two principles of the widest range : reserving to the state the full right of intervention in the concerns of the railway companies, and giving to the state the option to purchase a line at the end of a certain term at twenty-five years' purchase of the divisible profits.[1]

It was during these years of labour under Peel that he first acquired principles of administrative and parliamentary practice that afterward stood him in good stead : on no account to try to deal with a question before it is ripe; never to go the length of submitting a difference between two departments to the prime minister before the case is exhausted and complete; never to press a proposal forward beyond the particular stage at which it has arrived. Pure commonplaces if we will, but they are not all of them easy to learn. We cannot forget that Peel and Mr. Gladstone were in the strict line of political succession. They were alike in social origin and academic antecedents. They started from the same point of view as to the great organs of national life, the monarchy, the territorial peerage and the commons, the church, the universities. They showed the same clear knowledge that it was not by its decorative parts, or what Burke styled 'solemn plausibilities,' that the community derived its strength ; but that it rested for its real foundations on its manufactures, its commerce, and its credit. Even in the lesser things, in reading Sir Robert Peel's letters, those who in later years served under Mr. Gladstone can recognise the school to which he went for the methods, the habits of mind, the practices of business, and even the phrases which he employed when his own time came to assume the direction of public affairs, the surmounting of administrative difficulties, the piloting of complex measures, and the handling of troublesome persons.

[1] Wordsworth wrote (Oct. 15, 1844) to implore him to direct special attention to the desecrating project of a railway from Kendal to the head of Windermere, and enclosed a sonnet. The sixth line, by the way, is a variant from the version in the books: 'And must he too his old delights disown.'— Knight's *Wordsworth* (1896 edition), viii. 166.

CHAPTER IX

MAYNOOTH

(1844-1845)

> When I consider how munificently the colleges of Cambridge and Oxford are endowed, and with what pomp religion and learning are there surrounded ; . . . when I remember what was the faith of Edward III. and of Henry VI., of Margaret of Anjou and Margaret of Richmond, of William of Wykeham and William of Waynefleet, of Archbishop Chichele and Cardinal Wolsey ; when I remember what we have taken from the Roman catholics, King's College, New College, Christ Church, my own Trinity ; and when I look at the miserable Dotheboys' Hall which we have given them in exchange, I feel, I must own, less proud than I could wish of being a protestant and a Cambridge man.—MACAULAY.

IN pursuit of the policy of conciliation with which he was now endeavouring to counter O'Connell, Peel opened to his colleagues in 1844 a plan for dealing with the sum annually voted by parliament to the seminary for the training of catholic clergy at Maynooth. The original grant was made by the Irish parliament, protestant as it was ; and was accepted even by anti-catholic leaders after 1800 as virtually a portion of the legislative union with Ireland. Peel's proposal, by making an annual grant permanent, by tripling the amount, by incorporating the trustees, established a new and closer connection between the state and the college. It was one of the boldest things he ever did. What Lord Aberdeen wrote to Madame de Lieven in 1852 was hardly a whit less true in 1845 : 'There is more intense bigotry in England at this moment than in any other country in Europe' Peel said to Mr. Gladstone at the beginning of 1845 : 'I wish to speak without any reserve, and I ought to tell you, I think it will very probably be fatal to the government.' 'He explained that he did not know whether the feeling among Goulburn's constituents [the university of Cambridge] might not be too strong for him ; that in Scotland, as he expected, there would be a great opposition ; and he seemed to think that from the church also there might be great resistance, and he said the proceedings in the diocese of Exeter showed a very sensitive state of the public mind.' During the whole of 1844 the project simmered. At a very early moment Mr. Gladstone grew uneasy. He did not condemn the policy in itself, but whatever else might be said, it was in direct antagonism to the principle elaborately expounded by him only six years before, as the sacred rule and obligation between a Christian state and Christian churches. He had marked any departure from that rule as a sign of social declension, as a descent from a higher state of society to a lower, as a note in the ebb and flow of national life. Was it not inevitable, then, that his official participation in the extension of the public endowment of Maynooth would henceforth give to every one the right to say of him, 'That man cannot be trusted'? He was not indeed committed, by anything that he had written, to the extravagant position that the peace of society should be hazarded because it could no longer restore its ancient theories of religion ; but was he not right in holding it indispensable that any vote or further declaration from him on these matters should be given under circumstances free from all just suspicions of his disinterestedness and honesty ?[1]

In view of these approaching difficulties upon Maynooth, on July 12 he made a truly singular tender to the head of the government. He knew Peel to be disposed to entertain the question of a renewal of the public relations with the papal court at Rome, first to be opened by indirect communications through the British envoy at Florence or Naples. 'What I have to say,' Mr. Gladstone now wrote to the prime minister, 'is that if you and Lord Aberdeen should think fit to appoint me to Florence or Naples, and to employ me in any such communications as those to which I have referred, I am at your disposal.' Of this startling offer to transform himself from president of the board of trade into Vatican envoy, Mr. Gladstone left his own later judgment upon record ; here it is, and no more needs to be said upon it :—

About the time of my resignation on account of the contemplated increase of the grant to the College of Maynooth, I became possessed with the idea that there was about to be a renewal in some shape of our diplomatic [relations] with the see of Rome, and I believe that I committed the gross error of tendering myself to Sir Robert Peel to fill the post of envoy. I have difficulty at this date (1894) in conceiving by what obliquity of view I could have come to imagine that this was a rational or in any way excusable proposal : and this, although I vaguely think my friend James Hope had some hand in it, seems to show me now that there existed in my mind a strong element of fanaticism. I believe that I left it to Sir R. Peel to make me any answer or none as he might think fit ; and he with great propriety chose the latter alternative.

In the autumn of 1844, the prime minister understood that if he proceeded with the Maynooth increase, he would lose Mr. Gladstone. The loss, Peel said to Graham, was serious,

[1] The letters from Mr. Gladstone to Peel on this topic are given by Mr. Parker, Peel, iii. pp. 160. 163, 166.

and on every account to be regretted, but no hope of averting it would justify the abandonment of a most important part of their Irish policy. Meanwhile, in the midst of heavy labours on the tariff in preparation for the budget of 1845, Mr. Gladstone was sharply perturbed, as some of his letters to Mrs. Gladstone show :—

Whitehall, Nov. 22, '44.—It is much beyond my expectation that Newman should have taken my letter so kindly ; it seemed to me so like the operation of a clumsy, bungling surgeon upon a sensitive part. I cannot well comment upon his meaning, for as you may easily judge, what with cabinet, board, and Oak Farm, I have enough in my head to-day—and the subject is a fine and subtle one. But I may perhaps be able to think upon it to-night, in the meantime I think yours is a very just conjectural sketch. We have not got in cabinet to-day to the really pinching part of the discussion, the Roman catholic religious education. That comes on Monday. My mind does not waver ; pray for me, that I may do right. I have an appointment with Peel to-morrow, and I rather think he means to say something to me on the question.

Nov. 23.—You will see that whatever turns up, I am sure to be in the wrong. An invitation to Windsor for us came this morning, and I am *sorry to say* one including Sunday—Nov. 30 to Dec. 2. I have had a long battle with Peel on the matters of my office ; not another syllable. So far as it goes this tends to make me think he does not calculate on any change in me ; yet on the whole I lean the other way. Manning comes up on Monday.

Nov. 25.—Events travel fast and not slow. My opinion is that I shall be out on Friday evening. We have discussed Maynooth to-day. An intermediate letter which Sir James Graham has to write to Ireland for information causes thus much of delay. I have told them that if I go, I shall go on the ground of what is required by my personal character, and not because my mind is *made up* that the course which they propose can be avoided, far less because I consider myself bound to resist it. I had the process of this declaration to repeat. I think they were prepared for it, but they would not assume that it was to be, and rather proceeded as if I had never said a word before upon the subject. It was painful, but not so painful as the last time, and by an effort I had altogether prevented my mind from brooding upon it beforehand. At this moment (6¼) I am sure they are talking about it over the way. I am going to dine with Sir R. Peel. Under these circumstances the Windsor visit will be strange enough ! In the meantime my father writes to me most urgently, desiring me to come to Liverpool. I *hope* for some further light from him on Wednesday morning. . . .

Nov. 26.—I have no more light to throw upon the matters which I mentioned yesterday. The dinner at Peel's went off as well as could be expected ; I did not sit near him. Lord Aberdeen was with me to-day, and said very kindly it *must* be prevented. But I think it cannot, and friendly efforts to prolong the day only aggravate the pain. Manning was with me all this morning ; he is well, and is to come back to-morrow.

Jan. 9, '45.—Another postponement ; but our explanations were as satisfactory as could possibly be made under such circumstances. The tone and manner as kind as at any time—nothing like murmur. At the same time Peel said he thought it right to intimate a belief that the government might very probably be shipwrecked upon the Maynooth question, partly in connection with my retirement, but also as he intimated from the uncertainty whether there might not be a very strong popular feeling against it. *He* takes upon himself all responsibility for any inconvenience to which the government may possibly be put from the delay and a consequent abrupt retirement, and says I have given him the fullest and fairest notice. . . . I saw Manning for two hours this morning, and let the cat out of the bag to him in part. Have a note from Lockhart saying the Bishop of London had sent his chaplain to Murray to express high approval of the article on Ward—and enclosing the vulgar addition of £63.

Windsor Castle, Jan. 10.—First, owing to the Spanish ambassador's not appearing, Lady Lyttelton was suddenly invited, and fell to my lot to hand in and sit by, which was very pleasant. I am, as you know, a shockingly bad witness to looks, but she appeared to me, I confess, a little worn and aged. She ought to have at least two months' holiday every year. After dinner the Queen inquired as usual about you, and rather particularly with much interest about Lady Glynne. I told her plainly all I could. This rather helped the Queen through the conversation, as it kept me talking, and she was evidently hard pressed at the gaps. Then we went to cards, and played commerce; fortunately I was never the worst hand, and so was not called upon to pay, for I had locked up my purse before going to dinner; but I found I had won 2s. 2d. at the end, 8d. of which was paid me by the Prince. I mean to keep the 2d. piece (the 6d. I cannot identify) accordingly, unless I lose it again to-night. I had rather a nice conversation with him about the international copyright convention with Prussia. . . .

Whitehall, Jan. 11.—I came back from Windsor this morning, very kindly used. The Queen mentioned particularly that you were not asked on account of presumed inconvenience, and sent me a private print of the Prince of Wales, and on my thanking for it through Lady Lyttelton, another of the Princess. Also she brought the little people through the corridor yesterday after luncheon, where they behaved very well, and she made them come and shake hands with me. The Prince of Wales has a very good countenance; the baby I should call a very fine child indeed. The Queen said, After your own you must think them dwarfs; but I answered that I did not think the Princess Royal short as compared with Willy. We had more cards last evening; Lady —— made more blunders and was laughed at as usual. . . .

Jan. 13.—I think there will certainly be at least one cabinet more in the end of the week. My position is what would commonly be called uncomfortable. I do not know how long the Maynooth matter may be held over. I may remain a couple of months, or only a week—may go at any time at twenty-four hours' notice. I think on the whole it is an even chance whether I go before or after the meeting of parliament, so that I am unfeignedly put to obey the precept of our Lord, 'Take no thought for the morrow; the morrow will take thought for the things of itself.' I am sorry that a part of the inconvenience falls on your innocent head. I need not tell you the irksomeness of business is much increased, and one's purposes unmanned by this indefiniteness. Still, having very important matters in preparation, I must not give any signs of inattention or indifference.

Cabinet Room, Jan. 14.—I have no news to give you about myself, but continue to be quite in the dark. There is a certain Maynooth bill in preparation, and when that appears for decision my time will probably have come, but I am quite ignorant when it will be forthcoming. I am to be with Peel to-morrow morning, but I think on board of trade business only. Graham has just told us that the draft of the Maynooth bill will be ready on Saturday ; but it cannot, I think, be *considered* before the middle of next week at the earliest.

Jan. 15.—The nerves are a little unruly on a day like this between (official) life and death ; so much of feeling mixes with the more abstract question, which would be easily disposed of if it stood alone. (*Diary.*)

It was February 3 before Mr. Gladstone wrote his last note from his desk at the board of trade, thanking the prime minister for a thousand acts of kindness which he trusted himself not readily to forget. The feeling of the occasion he described to Manning :—

Do you know that daily intercourse and co-operation with men upon matters of great anxiety and moment interweaves much of one's being with theirs, and parting with them, leaving them under the pressure of their work and setting myself free, feels, I think, much like dying : more like it than if I were turning my back altogether upon public life. I have received great kindness, and so far as personal sentiments are concerned, I believe they are as well among us as they can be.

One other incident he describes to his wife :—

Peel thought I should ask an audience of the Queen on my retirement, and accordingly at the palace to-day (Feb. 3) he intimated, and then the lord-in-waiting, as is the usage, formally requested it. I saw the Queen in her private sitting-room. As she did not commence speaking immediately after the first bow, I thought it my part to do so ; and I said, 'I have had the boldness to request an audience, madam, that I might say with how much pain it is that I find myself separated from your Majesty's service, and how gratefully I feel your Majesty's many acts of kindness.' She replied that she regretted it very much, and that it was a great loss. I resumed that I had the greatest comfort I could enjoy under the circumstances in the knowledge that my feelings towards her Majesty's person and service, and also towards Sir R. Peel and my late colleagues, were altogether unchanged by my retirement. After a few words more she spoke of the state of the country and the reduced condition of Chartism, of which I said I believed the main feeder was want of employment. At the pauses I watched her eye for the first sign to retire. But she asked me about you before we concluded. Then one bow at the spot and another at the door, which was very near, and so it was all over.

Feb. 4.—Ruminated on the dangers of my explanation right and left, and it made me unusually nervous. H. of C. 4½-9. I was kindly spoken of and heard, and I hope attained practically purposes I had in view, but I think the House felt that the last part by taking away the sting reduced the matter to flatness.

According to what is perhaps a questionable usage, Lord John Russell invited the retiring minister to explain his

secession from office to the House. In the suspicion, distraction, tension that marked that ominous hour in the history
of English party, people insisted that the resignation of the
head of the department of trade must be due to divergence of
judgment upon protection. The prime minister, while expressing in terms of real feeling his admiration for Mr. Gladstone's character and ability, and his high regard for his
colleague's private qualities, thought well to restate that the
resignation came from no question of commercial policy.
'For three years,' he went on, 'I have been closely connected
with Mr. Gladstone in the introduction of measures relating to
the financial policy of the country, and I feel it my duty
openly to avow that it seems almost impossible that two
public men, acting together so long, should have had so little
divergence in their opinions upon such questions.' If anybody
found fault with Mr. Gladstone for not resigning earlier, the
prime minister was himself responsible : 'I was unwilling to
lose until the latest moment the advantages I derived from
one whom I consider capable of the highest and most eminent
services.' [1]

The point of Mr. Gladstone's reply was in fact an extremely
simple and a highly honourable one. While carefully abstaining
from laying down any theory of political affairs as under all
circumstances inflexible and immutable, yet he thought that
one who had borne such solemn testimony as he had borne in
his book, to a particular view of a great question, ought not
to make himself responsible for a material departure from it,

[1] In the course of May, 1845, Peel made some remarks on resignations, of which
Mr. Gladstone thought the report worth preserving :—'I admit that there may be
many occasions when it would be the duty of a public man to retire from office,
rather than propose measures which are contrary to the principles he has heretofore
supported. I think that the propriety of his taking that course will mainly depend
upon the effect which his retirement will have upon the success of that public
measure, which he believes to be necessary for the good of his country. I think it
was perfectly honourable, perfectly just, in my right honourable friend the late
president of the board of trade to relinquish office. The hon. gentleman thinks
I ought to have pursued the same course in 1829. That was precisely the course
I wished to pursue—it was precisely the course which I intended to pursue. Until
within a month of the period when I consented to bring forward the measure for
the relief of the Roman catholics, I did contemplate retiring from office—not because
I shrank from the responsibility of proposing that measure—not from the fear of being
charged with inconsistency—not because I was not prepared to make the painful
sacrifice of private friendships and political connections, but because I believed that
my retirement from office would promote the success of the measure. I thought that
I should more efficiently assist my noble friend in carrying that measure if I retired
from office, and gave the measure my cordial support in a private capacity. I changed
my opinion when it was demonstrated to me that there was a necessity for sacrificing
my own feelings by retaining office—when it was shown to me that, however humble
my abilities, yet, considering the station which I occupied, my retiring from office
would render the carrying of that measure totally impossible—when it was proved to
me that there were objections in the highest quarters which would not be overcome
unless I was prepared to sacrifice much that was dear to me—when it was intimated
to my noble friend that there was an intention on the part of the highest authorities
in the church of England to offer a decided opposition to the measure, and when my
noble friend intimated to me that he thought, if I persevered in my intention to
retire, success was out of the question. It was then I did not hesitate to say that I
would not expose others to obloquy or suspicions from which I myself shrunk.'

without at least placing himself openly in a position to form a judgment that should be beyond all mistake at once independent and unsuspected. That position in respect of the Maynooth policy he could not hold, so long as he was a member of the cabinet proposing it, and therefore he had resigned, though it was understood that he would not resist the Maynooth increase itself. All this, I fancy, might easily have been made plain even to those who thought his action a display of overstrained moral delicacy. As it was, his anxiety to explore every nook and cranny of his case, and to defend or discover in it every point that human ingenuity could devise for attack, led him to speak for more than an hour ; at the end of which even friendly and sympathetic listeners were left wholly at a loss for a clue to the labyrinth. 'What a marvellous talent is this,' Cobden exclaimed to a friend sitting near him ; 'here have I been sitting listening with pleasure for an hour to his explanation, and yet I know no more why he left the government than before he began.' 'I could not but know,' Mr. Gladstone wrote on this incident long years after, 'that I should inevitably be regarded as fastidious and fanciful, fitter for a dreamer or possibly a schoolman, than for the active purposes of public life in a busy and moving age.'[1]

Sir Robert Inglis begged him to lead the opposition to the bill. In the course of the conversation Inglis went back to the fatal character and consequences of the Act of 1829 ; and wished that his advice had then been taken, which was that the Duke of Cumberland should be sent as lord lieutenant to Ireland with thirty thousand men. 'As that good and very kind man spoke the words,' Mr. Gladstone says, 'my blood ran cold, and he too had helped me onwards in the path before me.' William Palmer wrote that the grant to Maynooth was the sin of 1829 over again, and would bring with it the same destruction of the conservative party. Lord Winchilsea, one of his patrons at Newark, protested against anything that savoured of the national endowment of Romanism. Mr. Disraeli was reported as saying that with his resignation on Maynooth Mr. Gladstone's career was over.

The rough verdict pronounced his act a piece of political prudery. One journalistic wag observed, 'A lady's footman jumped off the Great Western train, going forty miles an hour, merely to pick up his hat. Pretty much like this act, so disproportional to the occasion, is Mr. Gladstone's leap out of the ministry to follow his book.' When the time came he voted for the second reading of the Maynooth bill (April 11) with remarkable emphasis. 'I am prepared, in opposition to what I believe to be the prevailing opinion of the people of England and of Scotland, in opposition to the judgment of my own constituents, from whom I greatly regret to differ, and in opposition to my

[1] *Gleanings*, vii. p. 118.

own deeply cherished predilections, to give a deliberate and
even anxious support to the measure.'

The 'dreamer and the schoolman' meanwhile had left behind
him a towering monument of hard and strenuous labour in the
shape of that second and greater reform of the tariff, in which,
besides the removal of the export duty on coal and less serious
commodities, no fewer than four hundred and thirty articles
were swept altogether away from the list of the customs officer.
Glass was freed from an excise amounting to twice or thrice
the value of the article, and the whole figure of remission was
nearly three times as large as the corresponding figure in the
bold operations of 1842. Whether the budget of 1842 or that
of 1845 marked the more extensive advance, we need not
discuss ; it is enough that Mr. Gladstone himself set down the
construction of these two tariffs among the principal achievements in the history of his legislative works. His unofficial
relations with the colleagues whom he had left were perfectly
unchanged. 'You will be glad to know,' he writes to his father,
'that the best feeling, as I believe, subsists between us.
Although our powers of entertaining guests are not of the first
order, yet with a view partly to these occurrences we asked
Sir R. and Lady Peel to dinner to-day, and also Lord and Lady
Stanley and Lord Aberdeen. All accepted, but unfortunately
an invitation to Windsor has carried off Sir R. and Lady Peel.
A small matter, but I mention it as a symbol of what is
material.'

Before many days were over, he was working day and night
on a projected statement, involving much sifting and preparation, upon the recent commercial legislation. Lord John
Russell had expressed a desire for a competent commentary
on the results of the fiscal changes of 1842, and the pamphlet
in which Mr. Gladstone showed what those results had been
was the reply. Three editions of it were published within
the year.[1]

This was not the only service that Mr. Gladstone had an
opportunity of rendering in the course of the session to the
government that he had quitted. 'Peel,' he says, 'had a plan
for the admission of free labour sugar on terms of favour. Lord
Palmerston made a motion to show that this involved a breach
of our old treaties with Spain. I examined the case laboriously,
and, though I think his facts could not be denied, I undertook
(myself out of office) to answer him on behalf of the government. This I did, and Peel, who was the most conscientious
man I ever knew in spareness of eulogium, said to me when
I sat down, "That was a wonderful speech, Gladstone."' The

---

[1] 'Remarks upon recent Commercial Legislation suggested by the expository statement of the Revenue from Customs, and other Papers lately submitted to Parliament,
by the Right Hon. W. E. Gladstone, M.P. for Newark.' London, Murray, 1845. Mr.
Gladstone had written on the same subject in the *Foreign and Colonial Quarterly Review*,
January 1843.

speech took four hours, and was, I think, the last that he made
in parliament for two years and a half, for reasons that we
shall presently discover.

In the autumn of 1845, Mr. Gladstone made a proposal to
Hope-Scott. 'As Ireland,' he said, 'is likely to find this country
and parliament so much employment for years to come, I feel
rather oppressively an obligation to try and see it with my own
eyes instead of using those of other people, according to the
limited measure of my means.' He suggested that they should
devote some time 'to a working tour in Ireland, eschewing all
grandeur and taking little account of scenery, compared with
the purpose of looking at close quarters at the institutions for
religion and education of the country and at the character of
the people.' Philip Pusey was inclined to join them. 'It will
not alarm you,' says Pusey, 'if I state my belief that in these
agrarian outrages the Irish peasants have been engaged in a
justifiable civil war, because the peasant ejected from his land
could no longer by any efforts of his own preserve his family
from the risk of starvation. This view is that of a very calm
utilitarian, George Lewis.'[1] They were to start from Cork and
the south and work their way round by the west, carrying with
them Lewis's book, blue books, and a volume or two of Plato,
Æschylus, and the rest. The expedition was put off by Pusey's
discovery that the *Times* was despatching a correspondent to
carry on agrarian investigations. Mr. Gladstone urged that the
Irish land question was large enough for two, and so indeed it
swiftly proved, for Ireland was now on the edge of the black
abysses of the famine.

[1] See his memorable work on Irish Disturbances, published in 1836.

CHAPTER X

TRIUMPH OF POLICY AND FALL OF THE MINISTER

(1846)

Change of opinion, in those to whose judgment the public looks more or less to assist its own, is an evil to the country, although a much smaller evil than their persistence in a course which they know to be wrong. It is not always to be blamed. But it is always to be watched with vigilance; always to be challenged and put upon its trial.—GLADSTONE.

NOT lingering for the moment on Mr. Gladstone's varied pre-occupations during 1845, and not telling over again the well-known story of the circumstances that led to the repeal of the corn law, I pass rapidly to Mr. Gladstone's part—it was a secondary part—in the closing act of the exciting political drama on which the curtain had risen in 1841. The end of the session of 1845 had left the government in appearance even stronger than it was in the beginning of 1842. Two of the most sagacious actors knew better what this was worth. Disraeli was aware how the ties had been loosened between the minister and his supporters, and Cobden was aware that, in words used at the time, 'three weeks of rain when the wheat was ripening would rain away the corn law.'[1]

Everybody knows how the rain came, and alarming signs of a dreadful famine in Ireland came; how Peel advised his cabinet to open the ports for a limited period, but without promising them that if the corn duties were ever taken off, they could ever be put on again; how Lord John seized the moment, wrote an Edinburgh letter, and declared for total and immediate repeal; how the minister once more called his cabinet together, invited them to support him in settling the question, and as they would not all assent, resigned; how Lord John tried to form a government and failed; and how Sir Robert again became first minister of the crown, but not bringing all his colleagues back with him. 'I think,' said Mr. Gladstone in later days, 'he expected to carry the repeal of

[1] Perhaps I may refer to my *Life of Cobden*, which had the great advantage of being read before publication by Mr. Bright. Chapters xiv. and xv.

the corn law without breaking up his party, but meant at all hazard to carry it.'

Peel's conduct in 1846, Lord Aberdeen said to a friend ten years later, was very noble. With the exception of Graham and myself, his whole cabinet was against him. Lyndhurst, Goulburn, and Stanley were almost violent in their resistance. Still more opposed to him, if it were possible, was the Duke of Wellington. To break up the cabinet was an act of great courage. To resume office when Lord John had failed in constructing one, was still more courageous. He said to the Queen : 'I am ready to kiss hands as your minister to-night. I believe I can collect a ministry which will last long enough to carry free trade, and I am ready to make the attempt.' When he said this there were only two men on whom he could rely. One of the first to join him was Wellington. 'The Queen's government,' he said, 'must be carried on. We have done all that we could for the landed interest. Now we must do all that we can for the Queen.'[1]

On one of the days of this startling December, Mr. Gladstone writes to his father : 'If Peel determines to form a government, and if he sends for me (a compound uncertainty), I cannot judge what to do until I know much more than at present of the Irish case. It is there if anywhere that he must find his justification ; there if anywhere that one returned to parliament as I am, can honestly find reason for departing at this time from the present corn law.' Two other letters of Mr. Gladstone's show us more fully why he followed Peel instead of joining the dissentients, of whom the most important was Lord Stanley. The first of these was written to his father four and a half years later :—

6 *Carlton Gardens, June* 30, 1849.—As respects my 'having made Peel a free trader,' I had never seen that idea expressed anywhere, and I think it is one that does great injustice to the character and power of his mind. In every case, however, the head of a government may be influenced more or less in the affairs of each department of state by the person in charge of that department. If, then, there was any influence at all upon Peel's mind proceeding from me between 1841 and 1845, I have no doubt it may have tended on the whole towards free trade. . . . But all this ceased with the measures of 1845, when I left office. It was during the alarm of a potato famine in the autumn of that year that the movement in the government about the corn laws began. I was then on the continent, looking after Helen [his sister], and not dreaming of office or public affairs. . . . I myself had invariably, during Peel's government, spoken of protection not as a thing good in principle, but to be dealt with as tenderly and cautiously as might be according to circumstances, always moving in the direction of free trade. It *then* appeared to me that the case was materially altered by events ; it was no longer open to me to pursue that cautious course. A great struggle was imminent, in which it was plain that two parties only could really find place, on the one side for repeal, on the other side for *permanent* maintenance of a corn law and a protective system generally and on

[1] Lord Aberdeen to Senior, Sept. 1856. Mrs. Simpson's *Many Memories*, p. 233.

principle. It would have been more inconsistent in me, even if consistency had been the rule, to join the latter party than the former. But independently of that, I thought, and still think, that the circumstances of the case justified and required the change. So far as relates to the final change in the corn law, you will see that no influence proceeded from me, but rather that events over which I had no control, and steps taken by Sir R. Peel while I was out of the government, had an influence upon me in inducing me to take office. I noticed some days ago that you had made an observation on this subject, but I did not recollect that it was a question. Had I adverted to this I should have answered it at once. If I had any motive for avoiding the subject, it was, I think, this—that it is not easy to discuss such a question as that of an influence of mine over a mind so immeasurably superior, without something of egotism and vanity.

So much for the general situation. The second letter is to Mrs. Gladstone, and contributes some personal details :—

13 *Carlton House Terrace, Dec.* 22, 6 P.M., 1845.—It is offensive to begin about myself, but I must. Within the last two hours I have accepted the office of secretary for the colonies, succeeding Lord Stanley, who resigns. The last twenty-four hours have been very anxious hours. Yesterday afternoon (two hours after Holy Communion) Lincoln came to make an appointment on Peel's part. I went to meet him in Lincoln's house at five o'clock. He detailed to me the circumstances connected with the late political changes, asked me for no reply, and gave me quantities of papers to read, including letters of his own, the Queen's, and Lord J. Russell's, during the crisis. This morning I had a conversation with Bonham [the party whipper-in] upon the general merits, but without telling him precisely what the proposal made to me was. Upon the whole my mind, though I felt the weight of the question, was clear. I had to decide what was best to be done *now*. I arrived speedily at the conviction that *now*, at any rate, it is best that the question should be finally settled ; that Peel ought and is bound now to try it ; that I ought to support it in parliament ; that if, in deciding the mode, he endeavours to include the most favourable terms for the agricultural body that it is in his power to obtain, I ought not only to support it, by which I mean vote for it in parliament, but likewise not to refuse to be a party to the proposal. I found from him that he entirely recognised this view, and did feel himself bound to make the best terms that he believed attainable, while, on the other hand, I am convinced that we are now in a position that requires provision to be made for the final abolition of the corn law. Such being the state of matters, with a clear conscience, but with a heavy heart, I accepted office. He was exceedingly warm and kind. But it *was* with a heavy heart. . . . I have seen Lord Stanley 'I am extremely glad to hear you have taken office,' said he. We go to Windsor to-morrow to a council—he to resign the seals, and I to receive them.

In the diary he enters :—

Saw Sir R. Peel at 3, and accepted office—in opposition, as I have the consolation of feeling, to my leanings and desires, and with the most precarious prospects. Peel was most kind, nay fatherly. We *held* hands instinctively, and I could not but reciprocate with emphasis his 'God bless you.'

I well remember,—Mr. Gladstone wrote in a memorandum of Oct. 4, 1851,—Peel's using language to me in the Duke of Newcastle's house on Sunday, Dec. 21, 1845, which, as I conceive, distinctly intimated his belief that he would be able to carry his measure, and at the same time hold his party together. He spoke with a kind of glee and complacency in his tone when he said, making up his meaning by signs, 'I have not lived near forty years in public life to find myself wholly without the power of foreseeing the course of events in the House of Commons'—in reference to the very point of the success of his government.

One thing is worth noting as we pass. The exact proceedings of the memorable cabinets of November and the opening days of December are still obscure. It has generally been held that Disraeli planted a rather awkward stroke when he taunted Peel with his inconsistency in declaring that he was not the proper minister to propose repeal, and yet in trying to persuade his colleagues to make the attempt before giving the whigs a chance. The following note of Mr. Gladstone's (written in 1851 after reading Sir R. Peel's original memoir on the Corn Act of 1846) throws some light on the question :—

When Sir R. Peel invited me to take office in December 1845 he did not make me aware of the offer he had made to the cabinet in his memorandum, I think of Dec. 2, to propose a new corn law with a lowered sliding duty, which should diminish annually by a shilling until in some eight or ten years the trade would be free. No doubt he felt that after Lord John Russell had made his attempt to form a government, and after, by Lord Stanley's resignation, he had lost the advantages of unanimity, he could not be justified in a proposal involving so considerable an element of protection. It has become matter of history. But as matter of history it is important to show how honestly and perseveringly he strove to hold the balance fairly between contending claims, and how far he was from being the mere puppet of abstract theories.

That is to say, what he proposed to his cabinet early in December was not the total and immediate repeal to which he was led by events before the end of the month.

II

The acceptance of office vacated the seat at Newark, and Mr. Gladstone declined to offer himself again as a candidate. He had been member for Newark for thirteen years, and had been five times elected. So ended his connection with the first of the five constituencies that in his course he represented. 'I part from my constituents,' he tells his father, 'with deep regret. Though I took office under circumstances which might reasonably arouse the jealousy of my friends, an agricultural constituency, the *great* majority of my committee were prepared to support me, and took action and strong measures in my favour.' 'My deep obligation,' he says, 'to the Duke of

CHAP. X. ÆT. 37   OUT OF PARLIAMENT   213

Newcastle for the great benefit he conferred upon me, not only by his unbroken support, but, far above all, by his original introduction of me to the constituency, made it my duty at once to decline some overtures made to me for the support of my re-election, so it only remained to seek a seat elsewhere.' Some faint hopes were entertained by Mr. Gladstone's friends that the duke might allow him to sit for the rest of the parliament, but the duke was not the man to make concessions to a betrayer of the territorial interest. Mr. Gladstone, too, we must not forget, was still, and for many years to come, a tory. When it was suggested that he might stand for North Notts, he wrote to Lord Lincoln :—'It is not for one of my political opinions without an extreme necessity to stand upon the basis of democratic or popular feeling against the local proprietary : for you who are placed in the soil the case is very different.'

Soon after the session of 1846 began, it became known that the protectionist petition against the Peelite or liberal sitting member for Wigan was likely to succeed in unseating him. 'Proposals were made to me to succeed him, which were held to be eligible. I even wrote my address ; on a certain day, I was going down by the mail train. But it was an object for our opponents to keep a secretary of state out of parliament during the corn law crisis, and their petition was suddenly withdrawn. The consequence was that I remained until the resignation of the government in July a minister of the crown without a seat in parliament. This was a state of things not agreeable to the spirit of parliamentary government ; and some objection was taken, but rather slightly, in the House of Commons. Sir R. Peel stood fire.' There can be little doubt that in our own day a cabinet minister without a seat in either House of parliament would be regarded, in Mr. Gladstone's words, as a public inconvenience and a political anomaly, too *dark* to be tolerated ; and he naturally felt it his absolute duty to peep in at every chink and cranny where a seat in parliament could be had. A Peelite, however, had not a good chance at a by-election, and Mr. Gladstone remained out of the House until the general election in the year following.[1] Lord Lincoln, also a member of the cabinet, vacated his seat, but, unlike his friend, found a seat in the course of the session.

Mr. Gladstone's brother-in-law, Lyttelton, was invited to represent the colonial office in the Lords, but had qualms of conscience about the eternal question of the two Welsh bishoprics. 'How could the government of this wonderful

[1] Sibthorp asked Peel in the H. of C. when Gladstone and Lincoln would appear. Peel replied that if S. would take the Chiltern Hundreds, G. should stand against him. S. retorted that the Chiltern Hundreds is a place under government, and he would never take place from Peel ; but if P. would dissolve he would welcome Gladstone to Lincoln—or P. himself ; and added privately that he would give P. or G. best bottle of wine in his cellar if he would come to Lincoln and fight him fairly.— *Lord Broughton's Diaries.*

empire,' Peel wrote to Mr. Gladstone, 'be ever constructed, if a difference on such a point were to be an obstruction to union ? Might not any one now say with perfect honour and, what is of more importance (if they are not identical), perfect satisfaction to his own conscience, "I will not so far set up my own judgment on one isolated measure against that of a whole administration, to such an extent as to preclude me from co-operation with them at a critical period." This, of course, assumes general accordance of sentiment on the great outlines of public policy.' Wise words and sound, that might prevent some of the worst mistakes of some of the best men.

III

This memorable session of 1846 was not a session of argument, but of lobby computations. The case had been argued to the dregs, the conclusion was fixed, and all interest was centred in the play of forces, the working of high motives and low, the balance of parties, the secret ambitions and antagonism of persons. Mr. Gladstone therefore was not in the shaping of the parliamentary result seriously missed, as he had been missed in 1845. 'It soon became evident,' says a leading whig in his journal of the time, 'that Peel had very much over - rated his strength. Even the expectation of December that he could have carried with him enough of his own followers to enable Lord John, if that statesman had contrived to form a government, to pass the repeal of the corn law, was perceived to have been groundless, when the formidable number of the protectionist dissentients appeared. So many even of those who remained with Peel avowed that they disapproved of the measure, and only voted in its favour for the purpose of supporting Peel's government.'[1] The tyranny of the accomplished fact obscures one's sense of the danger that Peel's high courage averted. It is not certain that Lord John as head of a government could have carried the whole body of whigs for total and immediate repeal, Lord Lansdowne and Palmerston openly stating their preference for a fixed duty, and not a few of the smaller men cursing the precipitancy of the Edinburgh letter. It is certain, as is intimated above, that Peel could not have carried over to him the whole of the 112 men who voted for repeal solely because it was his measure. In the course of this session Sir John Hobhouse met Mr. Disraeli at an evening party, and expressed a fear lest Peel having broken up one party would also be the means of breaking up the other. 'That, you may depend upon it, he will,' replied Disraeli, 'or any other party that he has anything to do with.' It was not long after this, when all was over, that the Duke of Wellington told Lord John that he thought Peel was tired of

[1] *Halifax Papers.*

party and was determined to destroy it. After the repeal
of the corn law was safe, the minister was beaten on the Irish
coercion bill by what Wellington called a 'blackguard combination' between the whigs and the protectionists. He
resigned, and Lord John Russell at the head of the whigs
came in.

'Until three or four days before the division on the coercion
bill,' Mr. Gladstone says in a memorandum written at the time,
'I had not the smallest idea, beyond mere conjecture, of the
views and intentions of Sir R. Peel with respect to himself or
to his government. Only we had been governed in all questions,
so far as I knew, by the determination to carry the corn bill
and to let no collateral circumstance interfere with that main
purpose. . . . He sent round a memorandum some days before
the division arguing for resignation against dissolution. There
was also a correspondence between the Duke of Wellington
and him. The duke argued for holding our ground and dissolving. But when we met in cabinet on Friday the 26th of
June, not an opposing voice was raised. It was the shortest
cabinet I ever knew. Peel himself uttered two or three intro-
ductory sentences. He then said that he was convinced that
the formation of a conservative party was impossible while he
continued in office. That he had made up his mind to resign.
That he strongly advised the resignation of the entire government. Some declared their assent. None objected ; and when
he asked whether it was unanimous, there was no voice in the
negative.' 'This was simply,' as Mr. Gladstone added in later
notes, 'because he had very distinctly and positively stated his
own resolution to resign. It amounted therefore to this,—no
one proposed to go on without him.' One other note of Mr.
Gladstone's on this grave decision is worth quoting :—

I must put into words the opinion which I silently formed in my
room at the colonial office in June 1846, when I got the circulation box
with Peel's own memorandum not only arguing in favour of resignation
but intimating his own intention to resign, and with the Duke of
Wellington's in the opposite sense. The duke, in my opinion, was
right and Peel wrong, but he had borne the brunt of battle already
beyond the measure of human strength, and who can wonder that his
heart and soul as well as his physical organization needed rest ?[1]

In announcing his retirement to the House (June 29), Peel
passed a magnanimous and magnificent eulogium on Cobden.[2]

---

[1] Cobden also wrote to Peel strongly urging him to hold on, and Peel replied with
an effective defence of his own view.—*Life of Cobden*, i. chap. 18.

[2] 'There is a name that ought to be associated with the success of these measures ;
it is not the name of Lord John Russell, neither is it my name. Sir, the name which
ought to be, and will be, associated with these measures is the name of a man who,
acting from pure and disinterested motives, has advocated their cause with untiring
energy, and by appeals to reason expressed by an eloquence the more to be admired
because it was unaffected and unadorned—the name which ought to be associated with
the success of these measures is the name of Richard Cobden. Without scruple, Sir,
I attribute the success of these measures to him.'

Strange to say, the panegyric gave much offence, and among others to Mr. Gladstone. The next day he entered in his diary :—

Much comment is made upon Peel's declaration about Cobden last night. My objection to it is that it did not do full justice. For if his power of discussion has been great and his end good, his tone has been most harsh and his imputation of bad and vile motives to honourable men incessant. I do not think the thing was done in a manner altogether worthy of Peel's mind. But he, like some smaller men, is, I think, very sensible of the sweetness of the cheers of opponents.

He describes himself at the time as 'grieved and hurt' at these closing sentences; and even a year later, in answer to some inquiry from his father, who still remained protectionist, he wrote : 'July 1, '47.—I do not know anything about Peel's having repented of his speech about Cobden ; but I hope that he has seen the great objection to which it is, as I think, fairly open.' Some of his own men who voted for Peel declared that after this speech they bitterly repented.

The suspected personal significance of the Cobden panegyric is described in a memorandum written by Mr. Gladstone a few days later (July 12) :—

A day or two afterwards I met Lord Stanley crossing the park, and we had some conversation, first on colonial matters. Then he said, ' Well, I think our friend Peel went rather far last night about Cobden, did he not ?' I stated to him my very deep regret on reading that passage (as well as what followed about the monopolists), and that, not for its impolicy but for its injustice. All that he said was true, but he did not say the whole truth ; and the effect of the whole, as a whole, was therefore untrue. Mr. Cobden has throughout argued the corn question on the principle of holding up the landlords of England to the people, as plunderers and as knaves for maintaining the corn law to save their rents, and as fools because it was not necessary for that purpose. This was passed by, while he was praised for sincerity, eloquence, indefatigable zeal.

On Thursday the 2nd I saw Lord Aberdeen. He agreed in the general regret at the tone of that part of the speech. He said he feared it was designed with a view to its effects, for the purpose of making it impossible that Peel should ever again be placed in connection with the conservative party as a party. He said that Peel had absolutely made up his mind never again to lead it, never again to enter office ; that he had indeed made up his mind, at one time, to quit parliament, but that probably on the Queen's account, and in deference to her wishes, he had abandoned this part of his intentions. But that he was fixed in the idea to maintain his independent and separate position, taking part in public questions as his views of public interests might from time to time seem to require. I represented that this for *him*, and in the House of Commons, was an intention absolutely impossible to fulfil ; that with his greatness he could not remain there overshadowing and eclipsing all governments, and yet have to do with no governments ; that acts cannot for such a man be isolated, they must be in series, and his view of public affairs must coincide with one body of men rather than another, and

that the attraction must place him in relations with them. Lord
Aberdeen said that Earl Spencer in his later days was Sir R. Peel's
ideal,—rare appearances for serious purposes, and without compromise
generally to the independence of his personal habits. I put it that this
was possible in the House of Lords, but only there. . . . On Saturday I
saw him again as he came from the palace. He represented that the
Queen was sorely grieved at this change ; which indeed I had already
heard from Catherine through Lady Lyttelton, but this showed that it
continued. And again on Monday we heard through Lady Lyttelton
that the Queen said it was a comfort to think that the work of that day
would soon be over. It appears too that she spoke of the kindness she
had received from her late ministers ; and that the Prince's sentiments
are quite as decided.

On Monday we delivered up the seals at our several audiences. Her
Majesty said simply but very kindly to me, ' I am very sorry to receive
them from you.' I thanked her for my father's baronetcy, and
apologised for his not coming to court. She had her glove half off,
which made me think I was to kiss hands ; but she simply bowed and
retired. Her eyes told tales, but she smiled and put on a cheerful
countenance. It was in fact the 1st of September 1841 over again as to
feelings ; but this time with more mature judgment and longer experience. Lord Aberdeen and Sir J. Graham kissed hands, but this was by
favour.

The same night I saw Sidney Herbert at Lady Pembroke's. He
gave me in great part the same view of Sir R. Peel's speech, himself
holding the same opinion with Lord Aberdeen. But he thought that
Peel's natural temper, which he said is very violent though usually
under thorough discipline, broke out and coloured that part of the
speech, but that the end in view was to cut off all possibility of reunion.
He referred to a late conversation with Peel, in which Peel had intimated his intention of remaining in parliament and acting for himself
without party, to which Herbert replied that he knew of no minister
who had done so except Lord Bute, a bad precedent. Peel rejoined
' Lord Grenville,' showing that his mind had been at work upon the
subject. He had heard him not long ago discussing his position
with Lord Aberdeen and Sir James Graham, when he said, putting
his hand up to the side of his head, ' Ah ! you do not know what I
suffer here.'

Yesterday Lord Lyndhurst called on me. . . . He proceeded to ask
me what I thought with respect to our political course. He said he
conceived that the quarrel was a bygone quarrel, that the animosities
attending it ought now to be forgotten, and the old relations of amity
and confidence among the members of the conservative body resumed.
I told him, in the first place, that I felt some difficulty in answering
him in my state of total ignorance, so far as direct communication is
concerned, of Sir R. Peel's knowledge and intentions ; that on Tuesday
I had seen him on colonial matters, and had talked on the probable
intentions of the new government as to the sugar duties, but that I did
not like to ask what he did not seem to wish to tell, and that I did not
obtain the smallest inkling of light as to his intentions in respect to
that very matter now immediately pending. He observed it was a pity
Sir R. Peel was so uncommunicative ; but that after having been so long
connected with him, he would certainly be very unwilling to do any-

thing disagreeable to him; still, if I and others thought fit, he was
ready to do what he could towards putting the party together again. I
then replied that I thought, so far as extinguishing the animosities
which had been raised in connection with the corn law was concerned, I
could not doubt its propriety, that I thought we were bound to give a
fair trial to the government, and not to assume beforehand an air of
opposition, and that if so much of confidence is due to them, much more
is it due towards friends from whom we have differed on the single
question of free trade, that our confidence should be reposed in them.
That I thought, however, that in any case, before acting together as a
party, we ought to consider well the outline of our further course,
particularly with reference to Irish questions and the church there, as
I was of opinion that it was very doubtful whether we had now a
justification for opposing any change with respect to it, meaning as to
the property. He said with his accustomed facility, 'Ah yes, it will
require to be considered what course we shall take.'[1]

I met Lord Aberdeen the same afternoon in Bond Street, and told
him the substance of this conversation. He said, 'It is stated that
Lord G. Bentinck is to resign, and that they are to have you.' That, I
replied, was quite new to me. The (late) chancellor had simply said,
when I pointed out that the difficulties lay in the House of Commons,
that it was true, and that my being there would make the way more
open. I confess I am very doubtful of that, and much disposed to
believe that I am regretted, as things and persons *absent* often are, in
comparison with the present. At dinner I sat between Graham and
Jocelyn. The latter observed particularly on the absence from Sir
R. Peel's speech of any acknowledgment towards his supporters and his
colleagues. These last, however, are named. Jocelyn said the new
government were much divided. . . . Jocelyn believes that Lord
Palmerston will not be very long in union with this cabinet.

With Sir J. Graham I had much interesting conversation. I told
him, I thought it but fair to mention to him the regret and blame which
I found to have been elicited from all persons whom I saw and conversed
with, by the passage relating to Cobden. He said he believed it was the
same on all hands; and that the new government in particular were most
indignant at it. He feared that it was deliberately preconceived and for
the purpose; and went on to repeat what Lord Aberdeen had told me,
that Sir R. Peel had been within an ace of quitting parliament, and was
determined to abjure party and stand aloof for ever, and never resume
office. I replied as before, that in the House of Commons it was impossible. He went on to sketch the same kind of future for himself.
He was weary of labour at thirteen or fourteen hours a day, and of the
intolerable abuse to which he was obliged to submit; but his habits were
formed in the House of Commons and for it, and he was desirous to continue there as an independent gentleman, taking part from time to time
in public business as he might find occasion, and giving his leisure to his
family and to books. I said, 'Are you not building houses of cards?
Do you conceive that men who have played a great part, who have
swayed the great moving forces of the state, who have led the House
of Commons and given the tone to public policy, can at their will
remain there, but renounce the consequences of their remaining, and
refuse to fulfil what must fall to them in some contingency of public

[1] See *Life of Lord Lyndhurst*, by Lord Campbell, p. 163.

affairs? The country will demand that they who are the ablest shall not stand by inactive.' He said Sir Robert Peel had all but given up his seat. I answered that would at any rate have made his resolution a practicable one.

He said, 'You can have no conception of what the virulence is against Peel and me.' I said, No; that from having been out of parliament during these debates my sense of these things was less lively and my position in some respects different. He replied, 'Your position is quite different. You are free to take any course you please with perfect honour.' I told him of Lord Lyndhurst's visit and the purport of his conversation, of the meaning of the junction on the opposition bench in the Lords, and of what we had said of the difficulties in the Commons. He said, 'My resentment is not against the new government, but against the seventy-three conservative members of parliament who displaced the late government by a factious vote ; nearly all of them believed the bill to be necessary for Ireland ; and they knew that our removal was not desired by the crown, not desired by the country. I find no fault with the new ministers, they are fairly in possession of power—but with those gentlemen I can never unite.' Later, however, in the evening he relented somewhat, and said he must admit that what they did was done under great provocation ; that it was no wonder they regarded themselves as betrayed ; and that unfortunately it had been the fate of Sir R. Peel to perform a similar operation twice. . . .

Graham dwelt with fondness and with pain on Lord Stanley ; said he had very great qualities—that his speech on the corn law, consisting as it did simply of old fallacies though in new dress, was a magnificent speech, one of his greatest and happiest efforts—that all his conduct in the public eye had been perfectly free from exception; that he feared, however, he had been much in Lord Geo. Bentinck's counsels, and had concurred in much more than he had himself done, and had aided in marking out the course taken in the House of Commons. He had called on Lord Stanley several times but had never been able to see him, he trusted through accident, but seemed to doubt.

On the Cobden eulogy, though he did not defend it outright by any means, he said, 'Do you think if Cobden had not existed the repeal of the corn law would have been carried at this moment?' I said very probably not, that he had added greatly to the force of the movement and accelerated its issue, that I admitted the truth of every word that Peel had uttered, but complained of its omissions, of its spirit towards his own friends, of its false moral effect, as well as and much more than of its mere impolicy.[1]

IV

Still more interesting is an interview with the fallen minister himself, written ten days after it took place :—

July 24.—On Monday the 13th I visited Sir R. Peel, and found him in his dressing-room laid up with a cut in one of his feet. My im-

[1] Six years later (Nov. 26, 1852), Mr. Gladstone in the House of Commons said of Cobden, with words of characteristic qualification :—'Agree you may in his general politics, or you may not ; complain you may, if you think you have cause, of the mode and force with which in the freedom of debate he commonly states his opinions in this House. But it is impossible for us to deny that those benefits of which we are now acknowledging the existence are, in no small part at any rate, due to the labours in which he has borne so prominent a share.'

mediate purpose was to let him know the accounts from New Zealand which Lord Grey had communicated to me. . . . However *I* led on from subject to subject, for I thought it my duty not to quit town, at the end possibly of my political connection with Sir R. Peel, that is if he determined to individualise himself, without giving the opportunity at least for free communication. Though he opened nothing, yet he followed unreluctantly. I said the government appeared to show signs of internal discord or weakness. He said, Yes ; related that Lord John did not mean to include Lord Grey, that he sent Sir G. Grey and C. Wood to propitiate him, that Lord Grey was not only not hostile but volunteered his services. At last I broke the ice and said, 'You have seen Lord Lyndhurst.' He said, 'Yes.' I mentioned the substance of my interview with Lord Lyndhurst, and also what I had heard from Goulburn of his. He said, 'I am *hors de combat.*' I said to him, 'Is that possible ? Whatever your present intentions may be, can it be done ?' He said he had been twice prime minister, and nothing should induce him again to take part in the formation of a government ; the labour and anxiety were too great ; and he repeated more than once emphatically with regard to the work of his post, ' No one in the least degree knows what it is. I have told the Queen that I part from her with the deepest sentiments of gratitude and attachment ; but that there is one thing she must not ask of me, and that is to place myself again in the same position.' Then he spoke of the immense accumulation. 'There is the whole correspondence with the Queen, several times a day, and all requiring to be in my own hand, and to be carefully done ; the whole correspondence with peers and members of parliament, in my own hand, as well as other persons of consequence ; the sitting seven or eight hours a day to listen in the House of Commons. Then I must, of course, have my mind in the principal subjects connected with the various departments, such as the Oregon question for example, and all the reading connected with them. I can hardly tell you, for instance, what trouble the New Zealand question gave me. Then there is the difficulty that you have in conducting such questions on account of your colleague whom they concern.'

It was evident from this, as it had been from other signs, that he did not think Stanley had been happy in his management of the New Zealand question. I said, however, 'I can quite assent to the proposition that no one understands the labour of your post ; that, I think, is all I ever felt I could know about it, that there is nothing else like it. But then you have been prime minister in a sense in which no other man has been it since Mr. Pitt's time.' He said, 'But Mr. Pitt got up every day at eleven o'clock, and drank two bottles of port wine every night.' 'And died of old age at forty-six,' I replied. 'This all strengthens the case. I grant your full and perfect claim to retirement in point of justice and reason ; if such a claim can be made good by amount of service, I do not see how yours could be improved. You have had extraordinary physical strength to sustain you ; and you have performed an extraordinary task. Your government has not been carried on by a cabinet, but by the heads of departments each in communication with you.' He assented, and added it had been what every government ought to be, a government of confidence in one another. 'I have felt the utmost confidence as to matters of which I had no knowledge, and so have the rest. Lord Aberdeen in particular said that nothing would induce him to hold office on any other principle, or to be otherwise than perfectly free as to previous consultations.' And he spoke of the defects of the Melbourne government as a mere government of departments without a centre of unity, and of the possibility that the new ministers might experience difficulty in the same respect. I then went on to say, 'Mr. Perceval, Lord Liverpool, Lord Melbourne were not prime ministers in this sense ; what Mr. Canning might have been, the time was too short to show. I fully grant that your labours have been incredible, but, allow me to say, that is not the question. The question is not whether you are entitled to retire, but whether after all you have done, and in the position you occupy before the country, you can remain in the House of Commons as an isolated person, and hold yourself aloof from the great movements of political forces which sway to and fro there ?' He said, 'I think events will answer that question better than any reasoning beforehand.' I replied, 'That is just what I should rely upon, and should therefore urge how impossible it is for you to lay down with certainty a foregone conclusion such as that which you have announced to-day, and which events are not to influence, merely that you will remain in parliament and yet separate yourself from the parliamentary system by which our government is carried on.' Then he said, (If it is necessary I will) 'go out of parliament'—the first part of the sentence was indistinctly muttered, but the purport such as I have described. To which I merely replied that I hoped not, and that the country would have something to say upon that too. . . .

No man can doubt that he is the strong man of this parliament—of this political generation. Then it is asked, Is he honest ? But this is a question which I think cannot justly be raised nor treated as admissible in the smallest degree by those who have known and worked with him. . . . He spoke of the immense multiplication of details in public business and the enormous task imposed upon available time and strength by the work of attendance in the House of Commons. He agreed that it was extremely adverse to the growth of greatness among our public men ; and he said the mass of public business increased so fast that he could not tell what it was to end in, and did not venture to speculate even for a few years upon the mode of administering public affairs. He thought the consequence was already manifest in its being not well done.

It sometimes occurred to him whether it would after all be a good arrangement to have the prime minister in the House of Lords, which would get rid of the very encroaching duty of attendance on and correspondence with the Queen. I asked if in that case it would not be quite necessary that the leader in the Commons should frequently take upon himself to make decisions which ought properly to be made by the head of the government ? He said, Certainly, and that that would constitute a great difficulty. That although Lord Melbourne might be very well adapted to take his part in such a plan, there were, he believed, difficulties in it under him when Lord J. Russell led the House of Commons. That when he led the House in 1828 under the Duke of Wellington as premier, he had a very great advantage in the disposition of the duke to follow the judgments of others in whom he had confidence with respect to all civil matters. He said it was impossible during the session even to work the public business through the medium of the cabinet, such is the pressure upon time. . . . He told me he had suffered dreadfully in his head on the left side—that twenty-two or twenty-three years ago he injured the ear by the use of a detonating tube in shooting. Since then he had always had a noise on that side, and when he had the work of office upon him, this and the pain became scarcely bearable at times, as I understood him. Brodie told him that 'as some overwork one part and some another, he had overworked his brain,' but he said that with this exception his health was good. It was pleasant to me to find and feel by actual contact as it were (though I had no suspicion of the contrary) his manner as friendly and as much unhurt as at any former period.

V

Before leaving office Peel wrote to Mr. Gladstone (June 20) requesting him to ask his father whether it would be acceptable to him to be proposed to the Queen for a baronetcy. 'I should name him to the Queen,' he said, 'as the honoured representative of a great class of the community which has raised itself by its integrity and industry to high social eminence. I should gratify also my own feeling by a mark of personal respect for a name truly worthy of such illustration as hereditary honour can confer.' John Gladstone replied in becoming words, but honestly mentioned that he had published his strong opinion of the injurious consequences that he dreaded from 'the stupendous experiment about to be made' in commercial policy. Peel told him that this made no difference.[1]

At the close of the session a trivial incident occurred that caused Mr. Gladstone a disproportionate amount of vexation for several months. Hume stated in the House that the colonial secretary had countersigned what was a lie, in a royal patent appointing a certain Indian judge. The 'lie' consisted in reciting that a judge then holding the post had resigned, whereas he had not resigned, and the correct phrase was that the Queen had permitted him to retire. Lord George Bentinck, whose rage was then at its fiercest, pricked up his ears, and a day or two later declared that Mr. Secretary Gladstone had 'deliberately affirmed, not through any oversight or inadvertence or thoughtlessness, but designedly and of his own malice prepense, that which in his heart he knew not to be true.' Things of this sort may either be passed over in disdain, or taken with logician's severity. Mr. Gladstone might well have contented himself with the defence that his signature had been purely formal, and that every secretary of state is called upon to put his name to recitals of minute technical fact which he must take on trust from his officials. As it was, he chose to take Bentinck's reckless aspersion at its highest, and the combat lasted for weeks and months. Bentinck got up the case with his usual industrious tenacity ; he insisted that the Queen's name stood at that moment in the degrading position of being prefixed to a proclamation that all her subjects knew to recite and to be founded upon falsehood ; he declared that the whole

[1] Parker, iii. pp. 434-5.

business was a job perpetrated by the outgoing ministers, to fill
up a post that was not vacant ; he imputed no corrupt motive
to Mr. Gladstone ; he admitted that Mr. Gladstone was free
from the betrayal and treachery practised by his political
friends ; but he could not acquit him of having been in this
particular affair the tool and the catspaw of two old foxes
greedier and craftier than himself. To all this unmannerly
stuff the recipient of it only replied by holding its author the
more tight to the point of the original offence ; the blood of
his highland ancestors was up, and the poet's contest between
eagle and serpent was not more dire. The affair was submitted
to Lord Stanley. He reluctantly consented (Oct. 29) to decide
the single question whether Bentinck was justified 'on the
information before him in using the language quoted.' There
was a dispute what information Bentinck had before him, and
upon this point, where Bentinck's course might in his own
polite vocabulary be marked as pure shuffling, Lord Stanley
returned the papers (Feb. 8, 1847) and expressed his deep
regret that he could bring about no more satisfactory result.
Even so late as the spring of 1847 Mr. Gladstone was only
dissuaded by the urgent advice of Lord Lincoln and others
from pursuing the fray. It was, so far as I know, the only
personal quarrel into which he ever allowed himself to be
drawn.

CHAPTER XI

THE TRACTARIAN CATASTROPHE

(1841–1846)

The movement of 1833 started out of the anti-Roman feelings of the Emancipation time. It was anti-Roman as much as it was anti-sectarian and anti-erastian. It was to avert the danger of people becoming Romanists from ignorance of church principles. This was all changed in one important section of the party. The fundamental conceptions were reversed. It was not the Roman church but the English church that was put on its trial. . . . From this point of view the object of the movement was no longer to elevate and improve an independent English church, but to approximate it as far as possible to what was assumed to be undeniable—the perfect catholicity of Rome.—Dean Church.

The fall of Peel and the break-up of his party in the state coincided pretty nearly with a hardly less memorable rupture in that rising party in the church with which Mr. Gladstone had more or less associated himself almost from its beginning. Two main centres of authority and leading in the land were thus at the same moment dislodged and dispersed. A long struggle in secular concerns had come to a decisive issue ; and the longer struggle in religious concerns had reached a critical and menacing stage. The reader will not wonder that two events so far-reaching as the secession of Newman and the fall of Sir Robert, coupled as these public events were with certain importunities of domestic circumstance of which I shall have more to say by and by, brought Mr. Gladstone to an epoch in his life of extreme perturbation. Roughly it may be said to extend from 1845 to 1852.

At the time of his resignation in the beginning of 1845, he wrote to Lord John Manners, then his colleague at Newark, a curious account of his views on party life. Lord John was then acting with the Young England group inspired by Disraeli, who has left a picture of them in *Sybil*, the most far-seeing of all his novels.

To Lord John Manners.

Jan. 30, 1845.—You, I have no doubt, are disappointed as to the working of a conservative government. And so should I be if I were to estimate its results by a comparison with the anticipations which, from a distance and in the abstract, I had once entertained of political life. But now my expectations not only from this but from any government are very small. If they do a little good, if they prevent others from doing a good deal of evil, if they maintain an unblemished character, it is my fixed conviction that under the circumstances of the times I can as an independent member of parliament, for I am now virtually such, ask no more. And I do entertain the strongest impression that if, with your honourable and upright mind, you had been called upon for years to consult as one responsible for the movements of great parliamentary bodies, if you thus had been accustomed to look into public questions at close quarters, your expectations from an administration, and your dispositions towards it, would be materially changed. . . .

The principles and moral powers of government as such are sinking day by day, and it is not by laws and parliaments that they can be renovated. . . . I must venture even one step further, and say that such schemes of regeneration as those which were propounded (not, I am bound to add, by you) at Manchester,[1] appear to me to be most mournful delusions ; and their re-issue, for their real parentage is elsewhere, from the bosom of the party to which we belong, an omen of the worst kind if they were likely to obtain currency under the new sanction they have received. It is most easy to complain as you do of *laissez-faire* and *laissez-aller* ; nor do I in word or in heart presume to blame you ; but I should sorely blame myself if with my experience and convictions of *the growing impotence of government for its highest functions*, I were either to recommend attempts beyond its powers, which would react unfavourably upon its remaining capabilities, or to be a party to proposed substitutes for its true moral and paternal work which appear to me mere counterfeits.

On this letter we may note in passing, first, that the tariff legislation did in the foundations what the Young England party wished to do in a superficial and flimsy fashion ; and second, it was the tariff legislation that drove back a rising tide of socialism, both directly by vastly improving the condition of labour, and indirectly by force of the doctrine of free exchange which was thus corroborated by circumstances. Of this we shall see more by and by.

Throughout the years of Sir Robert Peel's government, Mr. Gladstone had been keenly intent upon the progress of religious affairs at Oxford. 'From 1841 till the beginning of 1845,' he says in a fragmentary note, ' I continued a hard-working official man, but with a decided predominance of religious over secular interests. Although I had little of direct connection with Oxford and its teachers, I was regarded in common fame as tarred with their brush ; and I was not so blind as to be unaware that for the clergy this meant not yet indeed prosecution, but proscription and exclusion from advancement by either party in the state, and for laymen a vague and indeterminate prejudice with serious doubts how far persons infected in this particular manner could have any real capacity for affairs. Sir Robert Peel must, I think, have exercised much

---

[1] Some proceedings, I think, of Mr. Disraeli and his Young England friends.

self-denial when he put me in his cabinet in 1843.' The movement that began in 1833 had by the opening of the next decade
revealed startling tendencies, and its first stage was now slowly
but unmistakably passing into the second.   Mr. Gladstone has
told us[1] how he stood at this hour of crisis; how strongly
he believed that the church of England would hold her ground,
and even revive the allegiance not only of the masses, but of
those large and powerful nonconforming bodies who were supposed to exist only as a consequence of the neglect of its duties
by the national church.   He has told us also how little he foresaw the second phase of the Oxford movement—the break-up
of a distinguished and imposing generation of clergy; 'the
spectacle of some of the most gifted sons reared by Oxford for
the service of the church of England, hurling at her head the
hottest bolts of the Vatican ; and along with this strange
deflexion on one side, a not less convulsive rationalist movement on the other,—all ending in contention and estrangement,
and in suspicions worse than either, because less accessible and
more intractable.'

II

The landmarks of the Tractarian story are familiar, and I
do not ask the reader in any detail to retrace them.   The
publication of Froude's *Remains* was the first flagrant beacon
lighting the path of divergence from the lines of historical
high-churchmen in an essentially anti-protestant direction.
Mr. Gladstone read the first instalment of this book (1838)
'with repeated regrets.'   Then came the blaze kindled by
Tract Ninety (1841).   This, in the language of its author and
his friends, was the famous attempt to clear the Articles from
the glosses encrusting them like barnacles, and to bring out
the old catholic truth that man had done his worst to disfigure
and to mutilate, and yet in spite of all man's endeavour it was
in the Articles still.   Mr. Gladstone, as we have seen, regarded
Tract Ninety with uneasy doubts as to its drift, its intentions,
the way in which the church and the world would take it.
'This No. Ninety of *Tracts for the Times* which I read by
desire of Sir R. Inglis,' he writes to Lord Lyttelton, 'is like a
repetition of the publication of Froude's *Remains*, and Newman
has again burned his fingers.   The most serious feature in the
tract to my mind is that, doubtless with very honest intentions
and with his mind turned for the moment so entirely towards
those inclined to defection, and therefore occupying *their*
point of view exclusively, he has in writing it placed himself
quite outside the church of England in point of spirit and
sympathy.   As far as regards the proposition for which he
intended mainly to argue, I believe not only that he is right,
but that it is an a b c truth, almost a truism of the reign of

1 Chapter of Autobiography : *Gleanings*, vii. pp. 142-3.

Elizabeth, namely that the authoritative documents of the church of England were not meant to bind *all* men to every opinion of their authors, and particularly that they intended to deal as gently with prepossessions thought to look towards Rome, as the necessity of securing a certain amount of reformation would allow. Certainly also the terms in which Newman characterises the present state of the church of England in his introduction are calculated to give both pain and alarm; and the whole aspect of the tract is like the assumption of a new position.'

Next followed the truly singular struggle for the university chair of poetry at the end of the same year, between a no-popery candidate and a Puseyite. Seldom surely has the service of the muses been pressed into so alien a debate. Mr. Gladstone was cut to the heart at the prospect of a sentence in the shape of a vote for this professorship, passed by the university of Oxford 'upon all that congeries of opinions which the rude popular notion associates with the *Tracts for the Times*.' Such a sentence would be a disavowal by the university of catholic principles in the gross; the association between catholic principles and the church of England would be miserably weakened; and those who at all sympathised with the Tracts would be placed in the position of aliens, corporally within the pale, but in spirit estranged or outcast. If the church should be thus broken up, there would be no space for catholicity between the rival pretensions of an ultra-protestantised or decatholicised English church, and the communion of Rome. 'Miserable choice!' These and other arguments are strongly pressed (December 3, 1841) in favour of an amicable compromise, in a letter addressed to his close friend Frederic Rogers. In the same letter Mr. Gladstone says that he cannot profess to understand or to have studied the Tracts on Reserve.[1] He 'partakes perhaps in the popular prejudice against them.' Anybody can now see in the coolness of distant time that it was these writings on Reserve that roused not merely prejudice but fury in the public mind—a fury that without either justice or logic extended from hatred of Romanisers to members of the church of Rome itself. It affected for the worse the feeling between England and Ireland, for in those days to be ultra-protestant was to be anti-Irish; and it greatly aggravated, first the storm about the Maynooth grant in 1845, and then the far wilder storm about the papal aggression six years later.

Further fuel for excitement was supplied the same year (1841) in a fantastic project by which a bishop, appointed alternately by Great Britain and Prussia and with his head-

---

[1] On Reserve in Communicating Religious Knowledge—Tracts 80 and 87. (1837-40.) With the ominous and in every sense un-English superscription, *Ad Clerum*. Isaac Williams was the author.

quarters at Jerusalem, was to take charge through a somewhat miscellaneous region, of any German protestants or members of the church of England or anybody else who might be disposed to accept his authority. The scheme stirred much enthusiasm in the religious world, but it deepened alarm among the more logical of the high churchmen. Ashley and the evangelicals were keen for it as the blessed beginning of a restoration of Israel, and the king of Prussia hoped to gain over the Lutherans and others of his subjects by this side-door into true episcopacy. Politics were not absent, and some hoped that England might find in the new protestant church such an instrument in those uncomfortable regions, as Russia possessed in the Greek church and France in the Latin. Dr. Arnold was delighted at the thought that the new church at Jerusalem would comprehend persons using different liturgies and subscribing different articles,—his favourite pattern for the church of England. Pusey at first rather liked the idea of a bishop to represent the ancient British church in the city of the Holy Sepulchre ; but Newman and Hope, with a keener instinct for their position, distrusted the whole design in root and branch as a betrayal of the church, and Pusey soon came to their mind. With caustic scorn Newman asked how the anglican church, without ceasing to be a church, could become an associate and protector of nestorians, jacobites, monophysites, and all the heretics one could hear of, and even form a sort of league with the mussulman against the Greek orthodox and the Latin catholics. Mr. Gladstone could not be drawn to go these lengths. Nobody could be more of a logician than Mr. Gladstone when he liked, no logician could wield a more trenchant blade ; but nobody ever knew better in complex circumstance the perils of the logical short cut. Hence, according to his general manner in all dubious cases, he moved slowly, and laboured to remove practical grounds for objection. Ashley describes him (October 16) at a dinner at Bunsen's rejoicing in the bishopric, and proposing the health of the new prelate, and this gave Ashley pleasure, for 'Gladstone is a good man and a clever man and an industrious man.'[1] While resolute against any plan for what Hope called gathering up the scraps of Christendom and making a new church out of them, and resolute against what he himself called the inauguration of an experimental or fancy church, Mr. Gladstone declared himself ready 'to brave misconstruction for the sake of union with any Christian men, provided the terms of union were not contrary to sound principles.' With a strenuous patience that was thoroughly characteristic, he set to work to bring the details of

1 *Life of Shaftesbury*, i. p. 377.   There is a letter from Bunsen (p. 373), in which he exclaims how wonderful it is 'that the great-grandson of Anthony Earl of Shaftesbury, the friend of Voltaire, should write thus to the great-grandson of Frederick the Great, the admirer of both.'   But not more wonderful than Bunsen forgetting that Frederick had no children ?

the scheme into an order conformable to his own views, and he even became a trustee of the endowment fund. Two bishops in succession filled the see, but in the fulness of time most men agreed with Newman, who 'never heard of any either good or harm that bishopric had ever done,' except what it had done for him. To him it gave a final shake, and brought him on to the beginning of the end.[1]

In the summer of 1842 Mr. Gladstone received confidences that amazed him. Here is a passage from his diary :—

July 31, 1842.—Walk with R. Williams to converse on the subject of our recent letters. I made it my object to learn from him the general view of the ulterior section of the Oxford writers and their friends. It is startling. They look not merely to the renewal and development of the catholic idea within the pale of the church of England, but seem to consider the main condition of that devolopment and of all health (some tending even to say of all life) to be reunion with the church of Rome as the see of Peter. They recognise, however, authority in the church of England, and abide in her without love specifically fixed upon her, to seek the fulfilment of this work of reunion. It is, for example, he said, the sole object of Oakeley's life. They do not look to any defined order of proceedings in the way of means. They consider that the end is to be reached through catholicising the mind of the members of the church of England, but do not seem to feel that this can be done to any great degree in working out and giving free scope to her own rubrical system. They have no strong feeling of revulsion from actual evils in the church of Rome, first, because they do not wish to judge ; secondly, especially not to judge the saints ; thirdly, they consider that infallibility is somewhere and nowhere but there. They could not remain in the church of England if they thought that she dogmatically condemned anything that the church of Rome has defined *de fide,* but they do and will remain on the basis of the argument of Tract 90 ; upon which, after mental conflict, they have settled steadily down. They regret what Newman has said strongly against the actual system of the church of Rome, and they could not have affirmed, though neither do they positively deny it. Wherever Roman doctrine *de fide* is oppugned they must protest ; but short of this they render absolute obedience to their ecclesiastical superiors in the church of England. They expect to work on in practical harmony with those who look mainly to the restoration of catholic ideas on the foundation laid by the church of England as reformed, and who take a different view as to reunion with Rome in particular, though of course desiring the reunion of the whole body of Christ. All this is matter for very serious consideration. In the meantime I was anxious to put it down while fresh.

Now was the time at which Mr. Gladstone's relations with Manning and Hope began to approach their closest. Newman, the great enchanter, in obedience to his bishop had dropped the issue of the Tracts ; had withdrawn from all public discussion of ecclesiastical politics ; had given up his work in Oxford ; and had retired with a neophyte or two to Littlemore, a hamlet on the outskirts of the ever venerable city, there to

---

[1] See *Memoirs of J. R. Hope-Scott,* i. chapters 15-17. *Apologia,* chapter 3, *ad fin.*

pursue his theological studies, to prepare translations of Athanasius, to attend to his little parish, and generally to go about his own business so far as he might be permitted by the restlessness alike of unprovoked opponents and unsought disciples. This was the autumn of 1843. In October Manning sent to Mr. Gladstone two letters that he had received from Newman, indicating only too plainly, as they were both convinced, that the foundations of their leader's anglicanism had been totally undermined by the sweeping repudiation alike by episcopal and university authority of the doctrines of Tract Ninety. Dr. Pusey, on the other hand, admitted that the expressions in Newman's letter were portentous, but did not believe that they necessarily meant secession. In a man of the world this would not have been regarded as candid. For Newman says, 'I formally told Pusey that I expected to leave the church of England in the autumn of 1843, and begged him to tell others, that no one might be taken by surprise or might trust me in the interval.'[1] But Newman has told us that he had from the first great difficulty in making Dr. Pusey understand the differences between them. The letters stand in the *Apologia* (chapter iv. § 2) to tell their own tale. To Mr. Gladstone their shock was extreme, not only by reason of the catastrophe to which they pointed, but from the ill-omened shadow that they threw upon the writer's probity of mind if not of heart. 'I stagger to and fro like a drunken man,' he wrote to Manning, 'I am at my wits' end.' He found some of Newman's language, 'forgive me if I say it, more like the expressions of some Faust gambling for his soul, than the records of the inner life of a great Christian teacher.' In his diary he puts it thus :—

Oct. 28, 1843.—S. Simon and S. Jude. St. James's 11 A.M. with a heavy heart. Another letter had come from Manning, enclosing a second from Newman, which announced that since the summer of 1839 he had had the conviction that the church of Rome is the catholic church, and ours not a branch of the catholic church because not in communion with Rome ; that he had resigned St. Mary's because he felt he could not with a safe conscience longer teach in her ; that by the article in the *British Critic* on the catholicity of the English Church he had quieted his mind for two years ; that in his letter to the Bishop of Oxford, written most reluctantly, he, as the best course under the circumstances, committed himself again ; that his alarms revived with that wretched affair of the Jerusalem bishopric, and had increased ever since ; that Manning's interference had only made him the more realise his views ; that Manning might make what use he pleased of his letters ; he was relieved of a heavy heart ; yet he trusted that God would keep him from hasty steps and resolves with a doubting conscience ! How are the mighty fallen and the weapons of war perished !

With the characteristic spirit with which, in politics and in

1 *Story of Dr. Pusey's Life*, p. 227.

every other field, he always insisted on espying patches of blue sky where others saw unbroken cloud, he was amazed that Newman did not, in spite of all the pranks of the Oxford heads, perceive the English church to be growing in her members more catholic from year to year, and how much more plain and undeniable was the sway of catholic principles within its bounds, since the time when he entertained no shadow of doubt about it. But while repeating his opinion that in many of the Tracts the language about the Roman church had often been far too censorious, Mr. Gladstone does not, nor did he ever, shrink from designating conversion to that church by the unflinching names of lapse and fall.[1] As he was soon to put it, 'The temptation towards the church of Rome of which some are conscious, has never been before my mind in any other sense than as other plain and flagrant sins have been before it.' [2]

Two days later he wrote to Manning again :—

Oct. 30, 1843.— . . . I have still to say that my impressions, though without more opportunity of testing them I cannot regard them as final, are still and strongly to the effect that upon the promulgation of those two letters to the world, Newman stands in the general view a *disgraced man*—and all men, all principles, with which he has had to do, disgraced in proportion to the proximity of their connection. And further I am persuaded that were he not spellbound and entranced, he could not fail to see the gross moral incoherence of the parts of his two statements; and that were I upon the terms which would warrant it, I should feel it my duty, at a time when as now, *summa res agitur,* to tell him so, after having, however, tried my own views by reference to some other mind, for instance to your own. But surely it will be said that his 'committing himself again' was simply a deliberate protestation of what he knew to be untrue. I have no doubt of his having proceeded honestly ; no doubt that he can show it ; but I say that those two letters are quite enough to condemn a man in whom one has no πίστις ἠθική : much more then one whom a great majority of the community regard with prejudice and deep suspicion. . . . With regard to your own feelings believe me that I enter into them ; and indeed our communications have now for many years been too warm, free, and confiding to make it necessary for me, as I trust, to say what a resource and privilege it is to me to take counsel with you upon those absorbing subjects and upon the fortunes of the church ; to which I desire to feel with you that life, strength, and all means and faculties, ought freely to be devoted, and indeed from such devotion alone can they derive anything of true value.[3]

The next blow was struck in the summer of 1844 by Ward's *Ideal of a Christian Church,* which had the remarkable effect of harassing and afflicting all the three high camps—the historical anglicans, the Puseyites and moderate tractarians,

---

[1] This letter of October 28 is in Purcell, *Manning,* i. p. 242.
[2] Mr. Gladstone to Dr. Hook, Jan. 30, '47.
[3] It was on the fifth of November, a week after this correspondence, that Manning preached the Guy Fawkes sermon which caused Newman to send J. A. Froude to the door to tell Manning that he was 'not at home.'—Purcell, i. pp. 245-9.

and finally the Newmanites and moderate Romanisers.[1] The writer was one of the most powerful dialecticians of the day, defiant, aggressive, implacable in his logic, unflinching in any stand that he chose to take ; the master-representative of tactics and a temper like those to which Laud and Strafford gave the pungent name of Thorough. It was not its theology, still less its history, that made his book the signal for the explosion ; it was his audacious proclamation that the whole cycle of Roman doctrine was gradually possessing numbers of English churchmen, and that he himself, a clergyman in orders and holding his fellowship on the tenure of church subscription, had in so subscribing to the Articles renounced no single Roman doctrine. This, and not the six hundred pages of argumentation, was the ringing challenge that provoked a plain issue, precipitated a decisive struggle, and brought the first stage of tractarianism to a close.

It was impossible that Mr. Gladstone even in the thick of his tariffs, his committees and deputations, his cabinet duties, and all the other absorbing occupations of an important minister in strong harness, should let a publication, in his view so injurious, pass in silence.[2] With indignation he flew to his intrepid pen, and dealt as trenchantly with Ward as Ward himself had dealt trenchantly with the reformers and all others whom he found planted in his dialectic way. Mr. Gladstone held the book up to stringent reproof for its capricious injustice ; for the triviality of its investigations of fact ; for the savageness of its censures ; for the wild and wanton opinions broached in its pages ; for the infatuation of mind manifested in some of its arguments ; and for the lamentable circumstance that it exhibited a far greater debt in mental culture to Mr. John Stuart Mill than to the whole range of Christian divines. In a sentence, Ward 'had launched on the great deep of human controversy as frail a bark as ever carried sail,' and his reviewer undoubtedly let loose upon it as shrewd a blast as ever blew from the Æolian wallet. The article was meant for the *Quarterly Review*, and it is easy to imagine the dire perplexities of Lockhart's editorial mind in times so fervid and so distracted. The practical issue after all was not the merits or the demerits of Cranmer, Ridley, Latimer, nor the real meaning of Hooker, Jewel, Bull, but simply what was to be done to Ward. Lockhart wrote to Murray that he had very seriously studied the article and studied Ward's book, and not only these, but also the Articles and the canons of the church, and he could not approve of the *Review* committing itself to a

---

[1] For a full account of this book and its consequences the reader will always consult chapters xi., xii., and xiii., of Mr. Wilfrid Ward's admirably written work, *William George Ward and the Oxford Movement*.

[2] It was in the midst of these laborious employments that Mr. Gladstone published a prayer-book, compiled for family use, from the anglican liturgy. An edition of two thousand copies went off at once, and was followed by many editions more.

judgment on the line proper to be taken by the authorities of church and university, and the expression of such a judgment he suspected to be Mr. Gladstone's main object in writing. Mr. Gladstone, describing himself most truly as 'one of those soldiers who do not know when they are beat,' saw his editor; declared that what he sought was three things, first that the process of mobbing out by invective and private interpretations is bad and should be stopped; second, that the church of England does not make assent to the proceedings of the Reformation a term of communion; and third, that before even judicial proceedings in one direction, due consideration should be had of what judicial proceedings in another direction consistency might entail, if that game were once begun. As Ward himself had virtually put it, 'Show me how any of the recognised parties in the church can subscribe in a natural sense, before you condemn me for subscribing in a non-natural.'[1] The end was a concordat between editor and contributor, followed by an immense amount of irksome revision, mutilation, and re-revision, reducing the argument in some places 'almost to tatters'; but the writer was in the long run satisfied that things were left standing in it which it was well to plant in a periodical like the *Quarterly Review*.

We have a glimpse of the passionate agitation into which this great controversy, partly theologic, partly moral, threw Mr. Gladstone :—

Feb. 6.—Breakfast at Mr. Macaulay's. Conversation chiefly on Aristotle's politics and on the Oxford proceedings. I grew hot, for which *ignoscat Deus*. *Feb.* 13.—Oxford 1-5. We were in the theatre. Ward was like himself, honest to a fault, as little like an advocate in his line of argument as well could be, and strained his theology even a point further than before. The forms are venerable, the sight imposing; the act is fearful [the degradation of Ward], if it did not leave strong hope of its revisal by law.

To Dr. Pusey he writes (Feb. 7) :—

Indignation at this proposal to treat Mr. Newman worse than a dog really makes me mistrust my judgment, as I suppose one should always do when any proposal seeming to present an aspect of incredible wickedness is advanced. *Feb.* 17.—I concur with my whole heart and soul in the desire for repose; and I fully believe that the gift of an interval of reflection is that which would be of all gifts the most precious to us all, which would restore the faculty of deliberation now almost lost in storms, and would afford the best hope both of the development of the soundest elements that are in motion amongst us, and of the mitigation or absorption of those which are more dangerous.

In the proceedings at Oxford against Ward (February 13, 1845), Mr. Gladstone voted in the minority both against the condemnation of the book, and against the proposal to strip its writer of his university degree. He held that the censure

[1] *William George Ward*, p. 332.

combined condemnation of opinions with a declaration of personal dishonesty, and the latter question he held to be one 'not fit for the adjudication of a human tribunal.'

All this has a marked place in Mr. Gladstone's mental progress. Though primarily and ostensibly the concern of the established church, yet the series of proceedings that had begun with the attack on Hampden in 1836, and then were followed down to our own day by academical, ecclesiastical and legal censures and penalties, or attempts at censure and penalty, on Newman, Pusey, Maurice, Gorham, *Essays and Reviews*, Colenso, and ended, if they have yet ended, in a host of judgments affecting minor personages almost as good as nameless—all constitute a chapter of extraordinary importance in the general history of English toleration, extending in its consequences far beyond the pale of the communion immediately concerned. It was a long and painful journey, often unedifying, not seldom squalid, with crooked turns not a few, and before it was over, casting men into strange companionship upon bleak and hazardous shores. Mr. Gladstone, though he probably was not one of those who are as if born by nature tolerant, was soon drawn by circumstance to look with favour upon that particular sort of toleration which arose out of the need for comprehension. When the six doctors condemned Pusey (June 1843) for preaching heresy and punished him by suspension, Mr. Gladstone was one of those who signed a vigorous protest against a verdict and a sentence passed upon an offender without hearing him and without stating reasons. This was at least the good beginning of an education in liberal rudiments.

III

In October 1845 the earthquake came. Newman was received into the Roman communion. Of this step Mr. Gladstone said that it has never yet been estimated at anything like the full amount of its calamitous importance. The leader who had wielded a magician's power in Oxford was followed by a host of other converts. More than once I have heard Mr. Gladstone tell the story how about this time he sought from Manning an answer to the question that sorely perplexed him : what was the common bond of union that led men of intellect so different, of characters so opposite, of such various circumstance, to come to the same conclusion. Manning's answer was slow and deliberate : '*Their common bond is their want of truth.*' 'I was surprised beyond measure,' Mr. Gladstone would proceed, 'and startled at his judgment.'[1]

Most ordinary churchmen remained where they were. An erastian statesman of our own time, when alarmists ran to him with the news that a couple of noblemen and their wives had

---

[1] The story is told in Purcell, *Manning*, i. p. 318.

just gone over to Rome, replied with calm, 'Show me a couple
of grocers and their wives who have gone over, then you will
frighten me.' The great body of church people stood firm, and
so did Pusey, Keble, Gladstone, and so too, for half a dozen
years to come, did his two closest friends, Manning and Hope.
The dominant note in Mr. Gladstone's mind was clear and it
was constant. As he put it to Manning (August 1, 1845),—
'That one should entertain love for the church of Rome in
respect of her virtues and her glories, is of course right and
obligatory ; but one is equally bound under the circumstances
of the English church in direct antagonism with Rome to keep
clearly in view their very fearful opposites.'

Tidings of the great secession happened to find Mr. Gladstone
in a rather singular atmosphere. In the course of 1842, to the
keen distress of her relatives, his sister had joined the Roman
church, and her somewhat peculiar nature led to difficulties
that taxed patience and resource to the uttermost. She had
feelings of warm attachment to her brother, and spoke strongly
in that sense to Dr. Wiseman ; and it was for the purpose of
carrying out some plans of his father's for her advantage, that
in the autumn of 1845 (September 24-November 18), Mr. Gladstone passed nearly a couple of months in Germany. The duty
was heavy and dismal, but the journey brought him into a
society that could not be without effect upon his impressionable
mind. At Munich he laid the foundation of one of the most
interesting and cherished friendships of his life. Hope-Scott
had already made the acquaintance of Dr. Döllinger, and he
now begged Mr. Gladstone on no account to fail to present
himself to him, as well as to other learned and political men,
'good catholics and good men with no ordinary talent and
information.' 'Nothing,' Mr. Gladstone once wrote in after
years, 'ever so much made me anglican *versus* Roman as reading in Döllinger over forty years ago the history of the fourth
century and Athanasius *contra mundum.*' Here is his story to
his wife :—

Munich, Sept. 30, 1845.—Yesterday evening after dinner with two
travelling companions, an Italian *negoziante* and a German, I must needs
go and have a shilling's worth of the Augsburg Opera, where we heard
Mozart (*Don Juan*) *well* played and very respectably sung. To-day I
have spent my evening differently, in tea and infinite conversation with
Dr. Döllinger, who is one of the first among the Roman catholic theologians of Germany, a remarkable and a very pleasing man. His manners
have great simplicity and I am astonished at the way in which a busy
student such as he is can receive an intruder. His appearance is,
singular to say, just compounded of those of two men who are among
the most striking in appearance of our clergy, Newman and Dr. Mill.
He surprises me by the extent of his information and the way in which
he knows the details of what takes place in England. Most of our conversation related to it. He seemed to me one of the most liberal and
catholic in mind of all the persons of his communion whom I have known.

To-morrow I am to have tea with him again, and there is to be a third, Dr. Görres, who is a man of eminence among them. Do not think he has designs upon me. Indeed he disarms my suspicions in that respect by what appears to me a great sincerity. . . .

Oct. 2.—On Tuesday after post I began to look about me ; and though I have not seen all the sights of Munich I have certainly seen a great deal that is interesting in the way of art, and having spent a good deal of time in Dr. Döllinger's company, last night till one o'clock, I have lost my heart to him. What I like perhaps most, or what crowns other causes of liking towards him, is that he, like Rio, seems to take hearty interest in the progress of religion in the church of England, apart from the (so to speak) party question between us, and to have a mind to appreciate good wherever he can find it. For instance, when in speaking of Wesley I said that his own views and intuitions were not heretical, and that if the ruling power in our church had had energy and a right mind to turn him to account, or if he had been in the church of Rome I was about to add, he would then have been a great saint, or something to that effect. But I hesitated, thinking it perhaps too strong, and even presumptuous, but he took me up and used the very words, declaring that to be his opinion. Again, speaking of Archbishop Leighton he expressed great admiration of his piety, and said it was so striking that he could not have been a real Calvinist. He is a great admirer of England and English character, and he does not at all *slur* over the mischief with which religion has to contend in Germany. Lastly, I may be wrong, but I am persuaded he in his mind abhors a great deal that is too frequently taught in the church of Rome. Last night he spoke with such a sentiment of the doctrine that was taught on the subject of indulgences which moved Luther to resist them ; and he said he believed it was true that the preachers represented to the people that by money payments they could procure the release of souls from purgatory. I told him that was exactly the doctrine I had heard preached in Messina, and he said a priest preaching so in Germany would be suspended by his bishop.

Last night he invited several of his friends whom I wanted to meet, to an entertainment which consisted first of weak tea, immediately followed by meat supper with beer and wine and sweets. For two hours was I there in the midst of five German professors, or four, and the editor of a paper, who held very interesting discussions ; I could only follow them in part, and enter into them still less, as none of them (except Dr. D.) seemed to speak any tongue but their own with any freedom, but you would have been amused to see and hear them, and me in the midst. I never saw men who spoke together in a way to make one another inaudible as they did, always excepting Dr. Döllinger, who sat like Rogers, being as he is a much more refined man than the rest. But of the others I assure you always two, sometimes three, and once all four, were speaking at once, very loud, each not trying to force the attention of the others, but to be following the current of his own thoughts. One of them was Dr. Görres,[1] who in the time of Napoleon

---

[1] Joseph Görres, one of the most famous of European publicists and gazetteers between the two revolutionary epochs of 1789 and 1848. His journal was the *Rhine Mercury*, where the doctrine of a free and united Germany was preached (1814-16) with a force that made Napoleon call the newspaper a fifth great power. In time Görres became a vehement ultramontane.

edited a journal that had a great effect in rousing Germany to arms. Unfortunately he spoke more *thickly* than any of them.[1]

At Baden-Baden (October 16) he made the acquaintance of Mrs. Craven, the wife of the secretary of the Stuttgart mission, and authoress of the *Récit d'une Sœur*. Some of the personages of that alluring book were of the company. 'I have drunk tea several times at her house, and have had two or three long conversations with them on matters of religion. They are excessively acute and also full of Christian sentiment. But they are much more difficult to make real way with than a professor of theology, because they are determined (what is vulgarly called) to go the whole hog, just as in England usually when you find a woman anti-popish in spirit, she will push the argument against them to all extremes.'

It was at the same time that he read Bunsen's book on the church. 'It is dismal,' he wrote home to Mrs. Gladstone, 'and I must write to him to say so as kindly as I can.' Bunsen would seem all the more dismal from the contrast with the spiritual graces of these catholic ladies, and the ripe thinking and massive learning of one who was still the great catholic doctor. At no time in Mr. Gladstone's letters to Manning or to Hope is there a single faltering accent in respect of Rome. The question is not for an instant, or in any of his moods, open. He never doubts nor wavers. None the less, these impressions of his German journey would rather confirm than weaken his theological faith within the boundaries of anglican form and institution. 'With my whole soul I am convinced,' he says to Manning (June 23, 1850), 'that if the Roman system is incapable of being powerfully modified in spirit, it never can be the instrument of the work of God among us; the faults and the virtues of England are alike against it.'

I need spend no time in pointing out how inevitably these new currents drew Mr. Gladstone away from the old moorings of his first book. Even in 1844 he had parted company with the high ecclesiastical principles of good tories like Sir Robert Inglis. Peel, to his great honour, in that year brought in what Macaulay truly called 'an honest, an excellent bill, introduced from none but the best and purest motives.' It arose from a judicial decision in what was known as the Lady Hewley case, and its object was nothing more revolutionary or latitudinarian than to apply to unitarian chapels the same principle of prescription that protected gentlemen in the peaceful enjoyment of their estates and their manor-houses. The equity of the thing was obvious. In 1779 parliament had relieved protestant dissenting ministers from the necessity of declaring their belief in certain church articles, including especially those affecting the doctrine of the Trinity. In 1813 parliament had repealed

[1] See Friedrich's *Life of Döllinger*, ii. pp. 222-226, for a letter from Döllinger to Mr. Gladstone after his visit, dated Nov. 15, 1845.

the act of William III. that made it blasphemy to deny that
doctrine. This legislation rendered unitarian foundations legal,
and the bill extended to unitarian congregations the same
prescriptions as covered the titles of other voluntary bodies to
their places of worship, their school-houses, and their burial-
grounds. But what was thus a question of property was
treated as if it were a question of divinity; 'bigotry sought
aid from chicane,' and a tremendous clamour was raised by
anglicans, wesleyans, presbyterians, not because they had an
inch of *locus standi* in the business, but because unitarianism
was scandalous heresy and sin. Follett made a masterly
lawyer's speech, Sheil the speech of a glittering orator,
guarding unitarians by the arguments that had (or perhaps I
should say had not) guarded Irish catholics, Peel and Gladstone
made political speeches lofty and sound, and Macaulay the
speech of an eloquent scholar and a reasoner, manfully enforcing principles both of law and justice with a luxuriance of
illustration all his own, from jurists of imperial Rome, sages of
old Greece, Hindoos, Peruvians, Mexicans and tribunals beyond
the Mississippi.[1] We do not often enjoy such parliamentary
nights in our time.

Mr. Gladstone supported the proposal on the broadest
grounds of unrestricted private judgment :—

I went into the subject laboriously, he says, and satisfied myself that
this was not to be viewed as a mere quieting of titles based on lapse of
time, but that the unitarians were the true lawful holders, because
though they did not agree with the puritan opinions they adhered
firmly to the puritan principle, which was that scripture was the
rule without any binding interpretation, and that each man, or body,
or generation must interpret for himself. This measure in some
ways heightened my churchmanship, but depressed my church-and-
statesmanship.

Far from feeling that there was any contrariety between his
principles of religious belief and those on which legislation in
their case ought to proceed, he said that the only use he could
make of these principles was to apply them to the decisive
performance of a great and important act, founded on the
everlasting principles of truth and justice. Sheil, who followed
Mr. Gladstone, made a decidedly striking observation. He
declared how delighted he was to hear from such high authority
that the bill was perfectly reconcilable with the strictest and
the sternest principles of state conscience. 'I cannot doubt,'
he continued, 'that the right hon. gentleman, the champion of
free trade, will ere long become the advocate of the most unrestricted liberty of thought.' Time was to justify Sheil's acute
prediction. Unquestionably the line of argument that suggested
it was a great advance from the arguments of 1838, of which

[1] *Hansard*, June 6, 1844.

Macaulay had said that they would warrant the roasting of dissenters at slow fires.

IV

In this vast field of human interest what engaged and inflamed him was not in the main place that solicitude for personal salvation and sanctification, which under sharp stress of argument, of pious sensibility, of spiritual panic, now sent so many flocking into the Roman fold. It was at bottom more like the passion of the great popes and ecclesiastical master-builders, for strengthening and extending the institutions by which faith is spread, its lamps trimmed afresh, its purity secured. What wrung him with affliction was the laying waste of the heritage of the Lord. 'The promise,' he cried, 'indeed stands sure to the church and the elect. In the farthest distance there is peace, truth, glory ; but what a leap to it, over what a gulf.' For himself, the old dilemma of his early years still tormented him. 'I wish,' he writes to Manning (March 8, 1846) good-humouredly, 'I could get a synodical decision in favour of my retirement from public life. For, I profess to remain there (to myself) for the service of the church, and my views of the mode of serving her are getting so fearfully wide of those generally current, that even if they be sound, they may become wholly unavailable.' The question whether the service of the church can be most effectually performed in parliament was incessantly present to his mind. Manning pressed him in one direction, the inward voice drew him in the other. 'I could write down in a few lines,' he says to Manning, 'the measures, after the adoption of which I should be prepared to say to a young man entering life, If you wish to serve the church do it in the sanctuary, and not in parliament (unless he were otherwise determined by his station, and not always then ; it must depend upon his inward vocation), and should not think it at all absurd to say the same thing to some who have already placed themselves in this latter sphere. For when the end is attained of letting "the church help herself," and when it is recognised that active help can no longer be given, the function of serving the church in the state, such as it was according to the old idea, dies of itself, and what remains of duty is of a character essentially different.' Then a pregnant passage :—'It is the essential change now in progress from the catholic to the infidel idea of the state which is the determining element in my estimate of this matter, and which has, I think, no place in yours. For I hold and believe that when that transition has once been effected, the state never can come back to the catholic idea by means of any agency from within itself : that, if at all, it must be by a sort of re-conversion from without. I am not of those (excellent as I think them) who say, Remain and bear witness for the truth. There is a place where witness is ever to be borne for truth, that is to say for full and absolute truth, but it is not there.'[1]

He reproaches himself with being 'actively engaged in carrying on a process of lowering the religious tone of the state, letting it down, demoralising it, and assisting in its transition into one which is mechanical.' The objects that warrant public life in one in whose case executive government must be an element, must be very special. True that in all probability the church will hold her nationality in substance beyond our day. 'I think she will hold it as long as the monarchy subsists.' So long the church will need parliamentary defence, but in what form ? The dissenters had no members for universities, and yet their real representation was far better organized in proportion to its weight than the church, though formally not organized at all. 'Strength with the people will for our day at least be the only effectual defence of the church in the House of Commons, as the want of it is now our weakness there. It is not everything that calls itself a defence that is really such.'[2]

Manning expressed a strong fear, amounting almost to a belief, that the church of England must split asunder. 'Nothing can be firmer in my mind,' Mr. Gladstone replied (Aug. 31, 1846), 'than the opposite idea. She will live through her struggles, she has a great providential destiny before her. Recollect that for a century and a half, a much longer period than any for which puritan and catholic principles have been in conflict within the church of England, Jansenist and anti-Jansenist dwelt within the church of Rome with the unity of wolf and lamb. Their differences were not absorbed by the force of the church ; they were in full vigour when the Revolution burst upon both. Then the breach between nation and church became so wide as to make the rivalries of the two church sections insignificant, and so to cause their fusion.' Later, he thinks that he finds a truer analogy between 'the superstition and idolatry that gnaws and corrodes' the life of the Roman church, and the puritanism that with at least as much countenance from authority abides in the English church. There are two systems, he says, in the English church vitally opposed to one another, and if they were equally developed they could not subsist together in the same sphere. If puritanical doctrines were the base of episcopal and collegiate teaching, then the church must either split or become heretical. As it is, the basis is on the whole anti-puritanic, and what we should call catholic. The conflict may go on as now, and with a progressive advance of the good principle against the bad one. 'That has been on the whole the course of things during our lifetime, and to judge from present signs it is the will of God that it should so continue.' (Dec. 7, 1846.)

The following to Mr. Phillimore sums up the case as he then believed it to stand (June 24, 1847) :—

. . . The church is now in a condition in which her children may and must desire that she should keep her national position and her civil and proprietary rights, and that she should by degrees obtain the means of extending and of strengthening herself, not only by covering a greater space, but by a more vigorous organisation. Her attaining to this state of higher health depends in no small degree upon progressive adaptations of her state and her laws to her ever-enlarging exigencies ; these depend upon the humour of the state, and the state cannot and will not be in good humour with her, if she insists upon its being in bad humour with all other communions.

It seems to me, therefore, that while in substance we should all strive to sustain her in her national position, we shall do well on her behalf to follow these rules : to part earlier, and more freely and cordially, than heretofore with such of her privileges, here and there, as may be more obnoxious than really valuable, and some such she has ; and further, not to presume too much to give directions to the state as to its policy with respect to other religious bodies. . . . This is not political expediency as opposed to religious principle. Nothing did so much damage to religion as the obstinate adherence to a negative, repressive and coercive course. For a century and more from the Revolution it brought us nothing but outwardly animosities and inwardly lethargy. The revival of a livelier sense of duty and of God is now beginning to tell in the altered policy of the church. . . . As her sense of her spiritual work rises, she is becoming less eager to assert her exclusive claim, leaving that to the state as a matter for itself to decide ; and she also begins to forego more readily, but cautiously, her external prerogatives.

Book III

(1847–1852)

CHAPTER I

MEMBER FOR OXFORD

(1847)

There is not a feature or a point in the national character which has made England great among the nations of the world, that is not strongly developed and plainly traceable in our universities. For eight hundred or a thousand years they have been intimately associated with everything that has concerned the highest interests of the country.—GLADSTONE.

In 1847 the fortunes of a general election brought Mr. Gladstone into relations that for many years to come deeply affected his political course. As a planet's orbit has puzzled astronomers until they discover the secret of its irregularities in the attraction of an unseen and unsuspected neighbour in the firmament, so some devious motions of this great luminary of ours were perturbations due in fact to the influence of his new constituency. As we have seen, Mr. Gladstone quitted Newark when he entered the cabinet to repeal the corn law. At the end of 1846, writing to Lord Lyttelton from Fasque, he tells him : 'I wish to be in parliament but coldly ; feeling at the same time that I ought to wish it warmly on many grounds. But my father is so very keen in his protective opinions, and I am so very decidedly of the other way of thinking, that I look forward with some reluctance and regret to what must, when it happens, place me in marked and public contrast with him.' The thing soon happened.

'I remained,' he says, 'without a seat until the dissolution in June 1847. But several months before this occurred it had become known that Mr. Estcourt would vacate his seat for Oxford, and I became a candidate. It was a serious campaign. The constituency, much to its honour, did not stoop to fight the battle on the ground of protection. But it was fought, and that fiercely, on religious grounds. There was an incessant

242

discussion, and I may say dissection, of my character and position in reference to the Oxford movement. This cut very deep, for it was a discussion which each member of the constituency was entitled to carry on for himself. The upshot was favourable. The liberals supported me gallantly, so did many zealous churchmen, apart from politics, and a good number of moderate men, so that I was returned by a fair majority. I held the seat for eighteen years, but with five contests and a final defeat.'

The other sitting member after the retirement of Mr. Estcourt was Sir Robert Harry Inglis, who had beaten Peel by a very narrow majority in the memorable contest for the university seat on the final crisis of the catholic question in 1829. He was blessed with a genial character and an open and happy demeanour; and the fact that he was equipped with a full store of sincere and inexorable prejudices made it easy for him to be the most upright, honourable, kindly and consistent of political men. Repeal of the Test acts, relief of the catholics, the Reform bill, relief of the Jews, reform of the Irish church, the grant to Maynooth, the repeal of the corn laws—one after another he had stoutly resisted the whole catalogue of revolutionising change. So manful a record made his seat safe. In the struggle for the second seat, Mr. Gladstone's friends encountered first Mr. Cardwell, a colleague of his as secretary of the treasury in the late government. Cardwell was deep in the confidence and regard of Sir Robert Peel, and he earned in after years the reputation of an honest and most capable administrator; but in these earlier days the ill-natured called him Peel-and-water, others labelled him latitudinarian and indifferent, and though he had the support of Peel, promised before Mr. Gladstone's name as candidate was announced, he thought it wise at a pretty early hour to withdraw from a triangular fight. The old high-and-dry party and the evangelical party combined to bring out Mr. Round. If he had achieved no sort of distinction, Mr. Round had at least given no offence: above all, he had kept clear of all those tractarian innovations which had been finally stamped with the censure of the university two years before.

Charles Wordsworth, his old tutor and now warden of Glenalmond, found it hard to give Mr. Gladstone his support, because he himself held to the high principle of state conscience, while the candidate seemed more than ever bent on the rival doctrine of social justice. Mr. Hallam joined his committee, and what that learned veteran's adhesion was in influence among older men, that of Arthur Clough was among the younger. Northcote described Clough to Mr. Gladstone as a very favourable specimen of a class, growing in numbers and importance among the younger Oxford men, a friend of Carlyle's, Frank Newman's, and others of that stamp; well read in German literature and an admirer of German intellect,

but also a still deeper admirer of Dante; just now busily
taking all his opinions to pieces and not beginning to put
them together again ; but so earnest and good that he might
be trusted to work them into something better than his friends
inclined to fear. Ruskin, again, who had the year before
published the memorable second volume of his *Modern Painters*
(he was still well under thirty), was on the right side, and the
Oxford chairman is sure that Mr. Gladstone will appreciate
at its full value the support of such high personal merit and
extraordinary natural genius. Scott, the learned Grecian who
had been beaten along with Mr. Gladstone in the contest for
the Ireland scholarship seventeen years before, wrote to him :—
' Ever since the time when you and I received Strypes at the
hand of the vice-chancellor, and so you became my

$$\text{ὁμομαστιγίας}$$
$$\text{λαβὼν ἀγῶνος τὰς ἴσας πληγὰς ἐμοί,}[1]$$

I have looked forward to your being the representative of the
university.' Richard Greswell of Worcester was the faithful
chairman of his Oxford committee now and to the end, eighteen
years off. He had reached the dignity of a bachelor of divinity,
but nearly all the rest were no more than junior masters.

Routh, the old president of Magdalen, declined to vote for
him on the well-established ground that Christ Church had
no business to hold both seats. Mr. Gladstone at once met
this by the dexterous proposition that though Christ Church
was not entitled to elect him against the wish of the other
colleges, yet the other colleges were entitled to elect him if
they liked, by giving him a majority not made up of Christ
Church votes. His eldest brother had written to tell him in
terms of affectionate regret, that he could take no part in the
election ; mere political differences would be secondary, but
in the case of a university, religion came first, and there it
was impossible to separate a candidate from his religious
opinions. When the time came, however, partly under strong
pressure from Sir John, Thomas Gladstone took a more lenient
view and gave his brother a vote.

The Round men pointed triumphantly to their hero's votes
on Maynooth and on the Dissenters' Chapels bill, and insisted
on the urgency of upholding the principles of the united church
of England and Ireland in their full integrity. The backers
of Mr. Gladstone retorted by recalling their champion's career ;
how in 1834 he first made himself known by his resistance to
the admission of dissenters to the universities ; how in 1841 he

---

[1] *Frogs,* 756; the second line is Scott's own. An Aristophanic friend translates :—
    ' Good brother-rogue, we've shared the selfsame beating :
      At least, we carried off one Strype apiece.'
Strype was the book given to Scott and Gladstone as being good seconds to the winner
of the Ireland. See above, p. 46.

threw himself into the first general move for the increase of the colonial episcopate, which had resulted in the erection of eleven new sees in six years; how zealously with energy and money he had laboured for a college training for the episcopalian clergy in Scotland; how instrumental he was in 1846, during the few months for which he held the seals of secretary of state, in erecting four colonial bishoprics; how the Society for the Propagation of the Gospel, through the mouth of the Archbishop of Canterbury himself, had thanked him for his services; how long he had been an active supporter of the great societies for the spread of church principles, the propagation of church doctrines, and the erection of church fabrics. As for the Dissenters' Chapels bill, it was an act of simple justice and involved no principles at issue between the church and dissent, and Mr. Gladstone's masterly exposition of the tendency of dissent to drop one by one all the vital truths of Christianity was proclaimed to be a real service to the church. The reader will thus see the lie of the land, what it meant to be member for a university, and why Mr. Gladstone thought the seat the highest of electoral prizes.

A circular was issued impugning his position on protestant grounds. 'I humbly trust,' wrote Mr. Gladstone in reply (July 26), 'that its writers are not justified in exhibiting me to the world as a person otherwise than heartily devoted to the doctrine and constitution of our reformed church. But I will never consent to adopt as the test of such doctrine, a disposition to identify the great and noble cause of the church of England with the restraint of the civil rights of those who differ from her.' Much was made of Mr. Gladstone's refusal to vote for the degradation of Ward. People wrote to the newspapers that it was an admitted and notorious fact that a sister of Mr. Gladstone's under his own influence had gone over to the church of Rome.[1] The fable was retracted, but at once revived in the still grosser untruth, that he habitually employed 'a Jesuitical system of argument' to show that nobody need leave the church of England, 'because all might be had there that was to be enjoyed in the church of Rome.' Maurice published a letter to a London clergyman vigorously remonstrating against the bigoted spirit that this election was warming into life, and fervently protesting against making a belief in the Nicene creed into the same thing as an opinion about a certain way of treating the property of unitarians. 'One artifice of this kind,' said Maurice, 'has been practised in this election which it makes me blush to speak of. Mr. Ward called the reformation a vile and accursed thing; Mr. Gladstone voted against a certain measure for the condemnation of Mr. Ward; therefore he spoke of the reformation as a vile and accursed thing. I should not have believed it possible that

[1] *Standard*, May 29, 1847.

such a conclusion had been drawn from such premisses even by our religious press.'

The worthy Mr. Round, on the other hand, was almost impregnable. A diligent scrutiny at last dragged the dark fact to the light of day, that he had actually sat on Peel's election committee at the time of catholic emancipation in 1829, and had voted for him against Inglis. So it appears, said the mocking Gladstonians, that the protestant Mr. Round 'was willing to lend a helping hand to the first of a series of measures which are considered by his supporters as fraught with danger to the country's very best interests.' A still more sinister rumour was next bruited abroad : that Mr. Round attended a dissenting place of worship, and he was constrained to admit that, once in 1845 and thrice in 1846, he had been guilty of this backsliding. The lost ground, however, was handsomely recovered by a public declaration that the very rare occasions on which he had been present at other modes of Christian worship had only confirmed his affection and reverential attachment to the services and formularies of his own church.

The nomination was duly made in the Sheldonian theatre (July 29), the scene of so many agitations in these fiery days. Inglis was proposed by a canon of Christ Church, Round by the master of Balliol, and Gladstone by Dr. Richards, the rector of Exeter. The prime claim advanced for him by his proposer, was his zeal for the English church in word and deed, above all his energy in securing that wherever the English church went, thither bishoprics should go too. Besides all this, his master work, he had found time to spare not only for public business of the commonwealth, but for the study of theology, philosophy, and the arts.[1] Then the voting began. The Gladstonians went into the battle with 1100 promises. Northcote,[2] passing

---

[1] The proposer's Latin is succinct, and may be worth giving for its academic flavour :—'Jam inde a pueritia literarum studio imbutus, et in celeberrimo Etonensi gymnasio informatus, ad nostram accessit academiam, ubi morum honestate, pietate, et pudore nemini æqualium secundus, indole et ingenio facile omnibus antecellebat. Summis deinde nostræ academiæ honoribus cumulatus ad res civiles cum magnâ omnium expectatione se contulit ; expectatione tamen major omni evasit. In senatûs enim domum inferiorem cooptatus, eam ad negotia tractanda habilitatem, et ingenii perspicacitatem exhibebat, ut reipublicæ administrationis particeps et adjutor adhuc adolescens fieret. Quantum erga ecclesiam Anglicanam ejus studium non verba, sed facta, testentur. Is enim erat qui inter primos et perpaucos summo labore et eloquentiâ contendebat, ut ubicunque orbis terrarum ecclesia Anglicana pervenisset, episcopatus quoque eveheretur. Et quamdiu e secretis Reginæ fuit, ecclesia Anglicana apud colonos nostros plurimis locis labefactam suâ ope stabilivit, et patrocinium ejus suscepit. Neque vero publicis negotiis adeo se dedit quin theologiæ, philosophiæ, artium studio vacaret. Quæ cum ita sint, si delegatum, Academici, cooptare velimus, qui cum omni laude idem nostris rebus decus et tutamen sit, et qui summa eloquentiæ et argumenti vi, jura et libertates nostras tueri queat, hunc hodie suffragiis nostris comprobemus.'

[2] Stafford Northcote had been private secretary to Mr. Gladstone at the board of trade. On the appointment of his first private secretary, Mr. Rawson, to a post in Canada in 1842, Mr. Gladstone applied to Coleridge of Eton to recommend a successor. He suggested three names, Farrer, afterwards Lord Farrer, Northcote, and Pocock. Northcote, who looked to a political career, was chosen. 'Mr. Gladstone,'

vigilant days in the convocation house, sent daily reports to
Mr. Gladstone at Fasque. Peel went up to vote for him
(splitting for Inglis); Ashley went up to vote against him.
At the close of the second day things looked well, but there
was no ground for over-confidence. Inglis was six hundred
ahead of Gladstone, and Gladstone only a hundred and twenty
ahead of Round. The next day Round fell a little more behind,
and when the end came (August 3) the figures stood :—Inglis
1700, Gladstone 997, Round 824, giving Gladstone a majority of
173 over his competitor.

Numbers were not the only important point. When the poll
came to be analysed by eager statisticians, the decision of the
electors was found to have a weight not measured by an extra
hundred and seventy votes. For example, Mr. Gladstone had
among his supporters twenty-five double-firsts against seven
for Round, and of single first-classes he had one hundred and
fifty-seven against Round's sixty-six. Of Ireland and Hertford
scholars Mr. Gladstone had nine to two and three to one respectively ; and of chancellor's prizemen who voted he had
forty-five against twelve. Of fellows of colleges he had two
hundred and eighteen against one hundred and twenty-eight,
and his majority in this class was highest where the elections
to fellowships were open. The heads of the colleges told a
different tale. Of these, sixteen voted for Round and only four
for Gladstone. This discrepancy it was that gave its significance
to the victory. Sitting in the convocation house watching the
last casual voters drop in at the rate of two or three an hour
through the summer afternoon, the ever faithful Northcote
wrote to Mr. Gladstone at Fasque :—

Since I have been here, the contest has seemed even more interesting
than it did in London. The effect of the contest itself has apparently
been good. It has brought together the younger men without distinction
of party, and has supplied the elements of a very noble party which will
now look to you as a leader. I think men of all kinds are prepared to
trust you, and though each feels that you will probably differ from his
set in some particulars, each seems disposed to waive objections for the
sake of the general good he expects. . . .

The victory is not looked upon as 'Puseyite'; it is a victory of the
masters over the Hebdomadal board, and as such a very important one.
The Heads felt it their last chance, and are said to have expressed themselves accordingly. The provost of Queen's, who is among the dissatisfied
supporters of Round, said the other day, 'He would rather be represented
by an old woman than by a young man.' It is not as a Maynoothian
that you are dreaded here, though they use the cry against you and
though that is the country feeling, but as a possible reformer and a man
who thinks. On the other hand, the young men exult, partly in the

he wrote to a friend, June 30, 1842, 'is the man of all others among the statesmen
of the present day to whom I should desire to attach myself. . . . He is one whom
I respect beyond measure; he stands almost alone as representative of principles
with which I cordially agree; and as a man of business, and one who humanly
speaking is sure to rise, he is pre-eminent.'—Lang's *Life of Lord Iddesleigh*, i. pp. 63-67.

hope that you will do something for the university yourself, partly in
the consciousness that they have shown the strength of the magisterial
party by carrying you against the opposition of the Heads, and have
proved their title to be considered an important element of the university.
They do not seem yet to be sufficiently united to effect great things, but
there is a large amount of ability and earnestness which only wants
direction, and this contest has tended to unite them. 'Puseyism' seems
rather to be a name of the past, though there are still Puseyites of importance.   Marriott, Mozley, and Church appear to be regarded as leaders ;
but Church, who is now abroad, is looked upon as something more, and
I am told may be considered on the whole the fairest exponent of the
feelings of the place.   Stanley, Jowett, Temple, and others are great
names in what is nicknamed the Germanising party.   Lake, and perhaps
I should say Temple, hold an intermediate position between the two
parties. . . . Whatever may have been the evils attendant on the
Puseyite movement, and I believe they were neither few nor small, it
has been productive of great results ; and it is not a little satisfactory to
see how its distinctive features are dying away and the spirit surviving,
instead of the spirit departing and leaving a great sham behind it.

Of the many strange positions to which in his long and
ardent life Mr. Gladstone was brought, none is more startling
than to find him, as in this curious moment at Oxford, the
common rallying-point of two violently antagonistic sections
of opinion.   Dr. Pusey supported him ; Stanley and Jowett
supported him.   The old school who looked on Oxford as the
ancient and peculiar inheritance of the church were zealous
for him ; the new school who deemed the university an organ
not of the church but of the nation, eagerly took him for their
champion.   A great ecclesiastical movement, reviving authority
and tradition, had ended in complete academic repulse in 1845.
It was now to be followed by an anti-ecclesiastical movement,
critical, sceptical, liberal, scornful of authority, doubtful of
tradition.   Yet both the receding force and the rising force
united to swell the stream that bore Mr. Gladstone to triumph
at the poll.   The fusion did not last.   The two bands speedily
drew off into their rival camps, to arm themselves in the new
conflict for mastery between obscurantism and illumination.
The victor was left with his laurels in what too soon proved to
be, after all, a vexed and precarious situation, that he could
neither hold with freedom nor quit with honour.

Meanwhile he thoroughly enjoyed his much coveted distinction :—

To Mrs. Gladstone.

Exeter Coll., Nov. 2, 1847.—This morning in company with Sir R.
Inglis, and under the protection or chaperonage of the dean, I have
made the formal circuit of visits to all the heads of houses and all the
common-rooms.   It has gone off very well.   There was but one reception
by a head (Corpus) that was not decidedly *kind*, and that was only a
little cold.   Marsham (Merton), who is a frank, warm man, keenly
opposed, said very fairly, to Inglis, 'I congratulate you warmly' ; and

then to me, 'And I would be very glad to do the same to you, Mr.
Gladstone, if I could think you would do the same as Sir R. Inglis.' I
like a man for this. They say the dean should have asked me to dine
to-day, but I think he may be, and perhaps wisely, afraid of recognising
me in any very marked way, for fear of endangering the old Christ
Church right to one seat which it is his peculiar duty to guard.

We dined yesterday in the hall at Christ Church, it being a grand
day there. Rather unfortunately the undergraduates chose to make a
row in honour of me during dinner, which the two censors had to run
all down the hall to stop. This had better not be talked about.
Thursday the warden of All Souls' has asked me and I *think* I must
accept ; had it not been a head (and it is one of the little party of four
who voted for me) I should not have doubted, but at once have declined.

CHAPTER II

THE HAWARDEN ESTATE

(1847)

It is no Baseness for the Greatest to descend and looke into their owne Estate. Some forbeare it, not upon Negligence alone, But doubting to bring themselves into Melancholy in respect they shall finde it Broken. But wounds cannot be cured without Searching. Hee that cleareth by Degrees induceth a habit of Frugalitie, and gaineth as well upon his Minde, as upon his Estate.—BACON.

I MUST here pause for material affairs of money and business, with which, as a rule, in the case of its heroes the public is considered to have little concern. They can no more be altogether omitted here than the bills, acceptances, renewals, notes of hand, and all the other financial apparatus of his printers and publishers can be left out of the story of Sir Walter Scott. Not many pages will be needed, though this brevity will give the reader little idea of the pre-occupations with which they beset a not inconsiderable proportion of Mr. Gladstone's days. A few sentences in a biography many a time mean long chapters in a life, and what looked like an incident turns out to be an epoch.

Sir Stephen Glynne possessed a small property in Staffordshire of something less than a hundred acres of land, named the Oak Farm, near Stourbridge, and under these acres were valuable seams of coal and ironstone. For this he refused an offer of five-and-thirty thousand pounds in 1835, and under the advice of an energetic and sanguine agent proceeded to its rapid development. On the double marriage in 1839, Sir Stephen associated his two brothers-in-law with himself to the modest extent of one-tenth share each in an enterprise that seemed of high prospective value. Their interests were acquired through their wives, and it is to be presumed that they had no opportunity of making a personal examination of the concern. The adventurous agent, now manager-in-chief of the business, rapidly extended operations, setting up furnaces, forges, rolling-mills, and all the machinery for producing tools and hardware for which he foresaw a roaring foreign market.

The agent's confidence and enthusiasm mastered his principal, and large capital was raised solely on the security of the Hawarden fortune and credit. Whether Oak Farm was irrationally inflated or not, we cannot say, though the impression is that it had the material of a sound property if carefully worked ; but it was evidently pushed in excess of its realisable capital. The whole basis of its credit was the Hawarden estate, and a forced stoppage of Oak Farm would be the deathblow to Hawarden. As early as 1844 clouds rose on the horizon. The position of Sir Stephen Glynne had become seriously compromised, while under the system of unlimited partnership the liability of his two brothers-in-law extended in proportion. In 1845 the three brothers-in-law by agreement retired, each retaining an equitable mortgage on the concern. Two years later, one of our historic panics shook the money-market, and in its course brought down Oak Farm.[1] A great accountant reported, a meeting was held at Freshfield's, the company was found hopelessly insolvent, and it was determined to wind up. The court directed a sale. In April 1849, at Birmingham, Mr. Gladstone purchased the concern on behalf of himself and his two brothers-in-law, subject to certain existing interests ; and in May Sir Stephen Glynne resumed legal possession of the wreck of Oak Farm. The burden on Hawarden was over £250,000, leaving its owner with no margin to live upon.

Into this far-spreading entanglement Mr Gladstone for several years threw himself with the whole weight of his untiring tenacity and force. He plunged into masses of accounts, mastered the coil of interests and parties, studied legal intricacies, did daily battle with human unreason, and year after year carried on a voluminous correspondence. There are a hundred and forty of his letters to Mr. Freshfield on Oak Farm alone. Let us note in passing what is, I think, a not unimportant biographic fact. These circumstances brought him into close and responsible contact with a side of the material interests of the country that was new to him. At home he had been bred in the atmosphere of commerce. At the board of trade, in the reform of the tariff, in connection with the Bank act and in the growth of the railway system, he had been well trained in high economics. Now he came to serve an arduous apprenticeship in the motions and machinery of industrial life. The labour was immense, prolonged, uncongenial ; but it completed his knowledge of the customs, rules, maxims, and currents of trade and it bore good fruit in future days at the exchequer. He manfully and deliberately took up the burden as if the errors had been his own, and as if the financial sacrifice that he was called to make both now and later were matter

---

[1] For an account of the creditors' meeting held at Birmingham on Dec. 2, 1847, see the *Times* of Dec. 3, 1847.

of direct and inexorable obligation. These, indeed, are the things in life that test whether a man be made of gold or clay. 'The weight,' he writes to his father (June 16, 1849), 'of the private demands upon my mind has been such, since the Oak Farm broke down, as frequently to disqualify me for my duties in the House of Commons.' The load even tempted him, along with the working of other considerations, to think of total withdrawal from parliament and public life. Yet without a trace of the frozen stoicism or cynical apathy that sometimes passes muster for true resignation, he kept himself nobly free from vexation, murmur, repining, and complaint. Here is a moving passage from a letter of the time to Mrs. Gladstone :—

> *Fasque, Jan.* 20, 1849.—Do not suppose for a moment that if I could by waving my hand strike out for ever from my cares and occupations those which relate to the Oak Farm and Stephen's affairs, I would do so ; I have never felt that, have never asked it ; and if my language seems to look that way, it is the mere impatience of weakness comforting itself by finding a vent. It has evidently come to me by the ordinance of God ; and I am rather frightened to think how light my lot would be, were it removed, so light that something else would surely come in its place. I do not confound it with visitations and afflictions ; it is merely a drain on strength and a peculiar one, because it asks for a kind of strength and skill and habits which I have not, but it falls altogether short of the category of high trials. Least of all suppose that the subject can ever associate itself painfully with the idea of you. No persons who have been in contact with it can be so absolutely blameless as you and Mary, nor can *our* relation together be rendered in the very smallest degree less or more a blessing by the addition or the subtraction of worldly wealth. I have abundant comfort *now* in the thought that at any rate I am the means of keeping a load off the minds of others ; and I shall have much more hereafter when Stephen is brought through, and once more firmly planted in the place of his fathers, provided I can conscientiously feel that the restoration of his affairs has at any rate not been impeded by indolence, obstinacy, or blunders on my part. Nor can anything be more generous than the confidence placed in me by all concerned. Indeed, I can only regret that it is too free and absolute.

I may as well now tell the story to the end, though in anticipation of remote dates, for in truth it held a marked place in Mr. Gladstone's whole life, and made a standing background amid the vast throng of varying interests and transient commotions of his great career. Here is his own narrative as told in a letter written to his eldest son for a definite purpose in 1885 :—

To W. H. Gladstone.

Hawarden, Oct. 3, 1885.—Down to the latter part of that year (1847), your uncle Stephen was regarded by all as a wealthy country gentleman with say £10,000 a year or more (subject, however, to his mother's jointure) to spend, and great prospects from iron in a Midland estate. In the bank crisis of that year the whole truth was revealed ; and it came out that his agent at the Oak Farm (and formerly also at

Hawarden) had involved him to the extent of £250,000; to say nothing of minor blows to your uncle Lyttelton and myself.

At a conversation in the library of 13 Carlton House Terrace, it was considered whether Hawarden should be sold. Every obvious argument was in favour of it, for example the comparison between the income and the liabilities I have named. How was Lady Glynne's jointure (£2500) to be paid? How was Sir Stephen to be supported? There was *no* income, even less than none. Oak Farm, the iron property, was under lease to an insolvent company, and could not be relied on. Your grandfather, who had in some degree surveyed the state of affairs, thought the case was hopeless. But the family were unanimously set upon making any and every effort and sacrifice to avoid the necessity of sale. Mr. Barker, their lawyer, and Mr. Burnett, the land agent, entirely sympathised; and it was resolved to persevere. But the first effect was that Sir Stephen had to close the house (which it was hoped, but hoped in vain, to let); to give up carriages, horses, and I think for several years his personal servant; and to take an allowance of £700 a year, out of which, I believe, he continued to pay the heavy subvention of the family to the schools of the parish, which was certainly counted by hundreds. Had the estate been sold, it was estimated that he would have come out a wealthy bachelor, possessed of from a hundred to a hundred and twenty thousand pounds free from all encumbrance but the jointure.

In order to give effect to the nearly hopeless resolution thus taken at the meeting in London, it was determined to clip the estate by selling £200,000 worth of land. Of this, nearly one-half was to be taken by your uncle Lyttelton and myself, in the proportion of about two parts for me and one for him. Neither of us had the power to buy this, but my father enabled me, and Lord Spencer took over his portion. The rest of the sales were effected, a number of fortunate secondary incidents occurred, and the great business of recovering and realising from the Oak Farm was laboriously set about.

Considerable relief was obtained by these and other measures. By 1852, there was a partial but perceptible improvement in the position. The house was reopened in a very quiet way by arrangement, and the allowance for Sir Stephen's expenditure was rather more than doubled. But there was nothing like ease for him until the purchase of the reversion was effected by me in 1865. I paid £57,000 for the bulk of the property, subject to debts not exceeding £150,000, and after the lives of the two brothers, the table value of which was, I think, twenty-two and a half years. From this time your uncle had an income to spend of, I think, £2200, or not more than half what he probably would have had since 1847 had the estate been sold, which it would only have been through the grievous fault of others.

The full process of recovery was still incomplete, but the means of carrying it forward were now comparatively simple. Since the reversion came in, I have, as you know, forwarded that process; but it has been retarded by agricultural depression and by the disastrous condition through so many years of coal-mining; so that there still remains a considerable work to be done before the end can be attained, which I hope will never be lost sight of, namely, that of extinguishing the debt upon the property, though for family purposes the estate may still remain subject to charges in the way of annuity.

The full history of the Hawarden estate from 1847 would run to a volume. For some years after 1847, it and the Oak Farm supplied my principal employment;[1] but I was amply repaid by the value of it a little later on as a home, and by the unbroken domestic happiness there enjoyed. What I think you will see, as clearly resulting from this narrative, is the high obligation not only to keep the estate in the family, and as I trust in its natural course of descent, but to raise it to the best condition by thrift and care, and to promote by all reasonable means the aim of diminishing and finally extinguishing its debt.

This I found partly on a high estimate of the general duty to promote the permanence of families having estates in land, but very specially on the sacrifices made, through his remaining twenty-seven years of life, by your uncle Stephen, without a murmur, and with the concurrence of us all. . . .

Before closing I will repair one omission. When I concurred in the decision to struggle for the retention of Hawarden, I had not the least idea that my children would have an interest in the succession. In 1847 your uncle Stephen was only forty; your uncle Henry, at thirty-seven, was married, and had a child almost every year. It was not until 1865 that I had any title to look forward to your becoming at a future time the proprietor.—Ever your affectionate father.

The upshot is this, that Mr. Gladstone, with his father's consent and support, threw the bulk of his own fortune into the assets of Hawarden. By this, and the wise realisation of everything convertible to advantage, including, in 1865, the reversion after the lives of Sir Stephen Glynne and his brother, he succeeded in making what was left of Hawarden solvent. His own expenditure from first to last upon the Hawarden estate as now existing, he noted at £267,000. 'It has been for thirty-five years,' he wrote to W. H. Gladstone in 1882, '*i.e.*, since the breakdown in 1847, a great object of my life, in conjunction with your mother and your uncle Stephen, to keep the Hawarden estate together (or replace what was alienated), to keep it in the family, and to relieve it from debt with which it was ruinously loaded.'

In 1867 a settlement was made, to which Sir Stephen Glynne and his brother, and Mr. Gladstone and his wife, were the parties, by which the estate was conveyed in trust for one or more of the Gladstone children as Mr. Gladstone might appoint.[2] This was subject to a power of determining the settlement by either of the Glynne brothers, on repaying with interest the sum paid for the reversion. As the transaction touched matters in which he might be supposed liable to bias, Mr. Gladstone required that its terms should be referred to two men of perfect competence and probity—Lord Devon and Sir Robert Philli-

[1] To Lord Lyttelton, July 29, 1874: 'I could not devote my entire life to it; and after 1852 my attention was only occasional.'

[2] This settlement followed the lines of a will made by Sir Stephen in 1855, devising the estate to his brother for life, with the remainder to his brother's sons in tail male; and next to W. H. Gladstone and his sons in tail male, and then to W. E. Gladstone's other sons; and in default of male issue of W. E. Gladstone, then to the eldest and other sons of Lord Lyttelton, and so forth in the ordinary form of an entailed estate.

more—for their judgment and approval. Phillimore visited Hawarden (August 19-26, 1865) to meet Lord Devon, and to confer with him upon Sir Stephen Glynne's affairs. Here are a couple of entries from his diary :—

Aug. 26.—The whole morning was occupied with the investigation of S. G.'s affairs by Lord Devon and myself. We examined at some length the solicitor and the agent. Lord D. and I perfectly agreed in the opinion expressed in a memorandum signed by us both. Gladstone, as might have been expected, has behaved very well. *Sept.* 19 [*London*].—Correspondence between Lyttelton and Gladstone, contained in Lord Devon's letter. Same subject as that which Lord D. and I came to consult upon at Hawarden. *Sept.* 24.—I wrote to Stephen Glynne to the effect that Henry entirely approved of the scheme agreed upon by Lord D. and myself, after a new consideration of all the circumstances, and after reading the Lyttelton-Gladstone correspondence. I showed Henry Glynne the letter, of which he entirely approved.

In 1874 the death of Sir Stephen Glynne, following that of his brother two years before, made Mr. Gladstone owner in possession of the Hawarden estate, under the transaction of 1865. With as little delay as possible (April 1875) he took the necessary steps to make his eldest son the owner in fee, and seven years after that (October 1882) he further transferred to the same son his own lands in the county, acquired by purchase, as we have seen, after the crash in 1847. By agreement, the possession and control of the castle and its contents remained with Mrs. Gladstone for life, as if she were taking a life-interest in it under settlement or will.

Although, therefore, for a few months the legal owner of the whole Hawarden estate, Mr. Gladstone divested himself of that quality as soon as he could, and at no time did he assume to be its master. The letters written by him on these matters to his son are both too interesting as the expression of his views on high articles of social policy, and too characteristic of his ideas of personal duty, for me to omit them here, though much out of their strict chronological place. The first is written after the death of Sir Stephen, and the falling in of the reversion :—

To W. H. Gladstone.

11 *Carlton House Terrace, April* 5, 1875.—There are several matters which I have to mention to you, and for which the present moment is suitable ; while they embrace the future in several of its aspects.

1. I have given instructions to Messrs. Barker and Hignett to convert your life interest under the Hawarden settlement into a fee simple. Reflection and experience have brought me to favour this latter method of holding landed property as on the whole the best, though the arguments may not be all on one side. In the present case, they are to my mind entirely conclusive. First, because I am able thoroughly to repose in you an entire confidence as to your use of the estate during your lifetime, and your capacity to provide wisely for its future destination. Secondly,

because you have, delivered over to you with the estate, the duty and office of progressively emancipating it from the once ruinous debt ; and it is almost necessary towards the satisfactory prosecution of this purpose, which it may still take very many years to complete, that you should be entire master of the property, and should feel the full benefit of the steady care and attention which it ought to receive from you.

2. I hope that with it you will inherit the several conterminous properties belonging to me, and that you will receive these in such a condition as to enjoy a large proportion of the income they yield. Taking the two estates together, they form the most considerable estate in the county, and give what may be termed the first social position there. The importance of this position is enhanced by the large population which inhabits them. You will, I hope, familiarise your mind with this truth, that you can no more become the proprietor of such a body of property, or of the portion of it now accruing, than your brother Stephen could become rector of the parish, without recognising the serious moral and social responsibilities which belong to it. They are full of interest and rich in pleasure, but they demand (in the absence of special cause) residence on the spot, and a good share of time, and especially a free and ungrudging discharge of them. Nowhere in the world is the position of the landed proprietor so high as in this country, and this in great part for the reason that nowhere else is the possession of landed property so closely associated with definite duty.

3. In truth, with this and your seat in parliament, which I hope (whether Whitby supply it, or whether you migrate) will continue, you will, I trust, have a well-charged, though not an over-charged, life, and will, like professional and other thoroughly employed men, have to regard the bulk of your time as forestalled on behalf of duty, while a liberal residue may be available for your special pursuits and tastes, and for recreations. This is really the sound basis of life, which never can be honourable or satisfactory without adequate guarantees against frittering away, even in part, the precious gift of time.

While touching on the subject I would remind you of an old recommendation of mine, that you should choose some parliamentary branch or subject, to which to give special attention. The House of Commons has always heard your voice with pleasure, and ought not to be allowed to forget it. I say this the more freely, because I think it is, in your case, the virtue of a real modesty, which rather too much indisposes you to put yourself forward.

Yet another word. As years gather upon me, I naturally look forward to what is to be after I am gone ; and although I should indeed be sorry to do or say anything having a tendency to force the action of your mind beyond its natural course, it will indeed be a great pleasure to me to see you well settled in life by marriage. Well settled, I feel confident, you will be, if settled at all. In your position at Hawarden, there would then be at once increased ease and increased attraction in the performance of your duties ; nor can I overlook the fact that the life of the unmarried man, in this age particularly, is under peculiar and insidious temptations to selfishness, unless his celibacy arise from a very strong and definite course of self-devotion to the service of God and his fellow creatures.

The great and sad change of Hawarden [by the death of Sir Stephen] which has forced upon us the consideration of so many subjects, gave at the same time an opening for others, and it seemed to me to be best to put together the few remarks I had to make. I hope the announcement with which I began will show that I write in the spirit of confidence as well as of affection. It is on this footing that we have ever stood, and I trust ever shall stand. You have acted towards me at all times up to the standard of all I could desire. May you have the help of the Almighty to embrace as justly, and fulfil as cheerfully, the whole conception of your duties in the position to which it has pleased Him to call you, and which perhaps has come upon you with somewhat the effect of a surprise; that may, however, have the healthy influence of a stimulus to action, and a help towards excellence. Believe me ever, my dear son, your affectionate father.

In the second letter Mr. Gladstone informed W. H. Gladstone that he had at Chester that morning (Oct. 23, 1882), along with Mrs. Gladstone, executed the deeds that made his son the proprietor of Mr. Gladstone's lands in Flintshire, subject to the payment of annuities specified in the instrument of transfer; and he proceeds :—

I earnestly entreat that you will never, under any circumstances, mortgage any of your land. I consider that our law has offered to proprietors of land, under a narrow and mistaken notion of promoting their interests, dangerous facilities and inducements to this practice; and that its mischievous consequences have been so terribly felt (the word is strong, but hardly too strong) in the case of Hawarden, that they ought to operate powerfully as a warning for the future.

You are not the son of very wealthy parents; but the income of the estates (the Hawarden estates and mine jointly), with your prudence and diligence, will enable you to go steadily forward in the work I have had in hand, and after a time will in the course of nature give considerable means for the purpose.

I have much confidence in your prudence and intelligence; I have not the smallest fear that the rather unusual step I have taken will in any way weaken the happy union and harmony of our family; and I am sure you will always bear in mind the duties which attach to you as the head of those among whom you receive a preference, and as the landlord of a numerous tenantry, prepared to give you their confidence and affection.

A third letter on the same topics followed three years after, and contains a narrative of the Hawarden transactions already given in an earlier page of this chapter.

To W. H. Gladstone.

Oct. 3, 1885.—When you first made known to me that you thought of retiring from the general election of this year, I received the intimation with mixed feelings. The question of money no doubt deserves, under existing circumstances, to be kept in view; still I must think twice before regarding this as the conclusive question. I conceive the balance has to be struck mainly between these two things; on the one hand, the duty of persons connected with the proprietorship of considerable estates in land, to assume freely the burden and responsi-

bility of serving in parliament. On the other hand, the peculiar
position of this combined estate, which in the first place is of a nature
to demand from the proprietor an unusual degree of care and super-
vision, and which in the second place has been hit severely by recent
depressions in corn and coal, which may be termed its two pillars.

On the first point it may fairly be taken into view that in serving
for twenty years you have stood four contested elections, a number I
think decidedly beyond the average. . . . I will assume, for the present,
that the election has passed without bringing you back to parliament.
I should then consider that you had thus relieved yourself, at any rate
for a period, from a serious call upon your time and mind, mainly with
a view to the estate ; and on this account, and because I have constituted
you its legal master, I write this letter in order to place clearly before
you some of the circumstances which invest your relation to it with a
rather peculiar character.

I premise a few words of a general nature. An enemy to entails,
principally though not exclusively on social and domestic grounds, I
nevertheless regard it as a very high duty to labour for the conservation
of estates, and the permanence of the families in possession of them, as
a principal source of our social strength, and as a large part of true
conservatism, from the time when Aeschylus wrote

$$\dot{\alpha}\rho\chi\alpha\iota\sigma\pi\lambda\sigma\acute{\upsilon}\tau\omega\nu\ \delta\epsilon\sigma\pi\sigma\tau\hat{\omega}\nu\ \pi\sigma\lambda\lambda\dot{\eta}\ \chi\acute{\alpha}\rho\iota\varsigma.[1]$$

But if their possession is to be prolonged by conduct, not by factitious
arrangements, we must recognise this consequence, that conduct becomes
subject to fresh demands and liabilities.

In condemning laws which tie up the *corpus*, I say nothing against
powers of charge, either by marriage settlement or otherwise, for wife
and children, although questions of degree and circumstance may always
have to be considered. But to mortgages I am greatly opposed. Whether
they ought or ought not to be restrained by law, I do not now inquire.
But I am confident that few and rare causes only will warrant them,
and that as a general rule they are mischievous, and in many cases, as
to their consequences, anti-social and immoral. Wherever they exist
they ought to be looked upon as evils, which are to be warred upon and
got rid of. One of our financial follies has been to give them encouragement by an excessively low tax ; and one of the better effects of the
income-tax is that it is a fine upon mortgaging.

---

[1] *Agam.* 1043, ' A great blessing are masters with ancient riches.'

CHAPTER III

PARTY EVOLUTION—NEW COLONIAL POLICY

(1846-1850)

I shall ever thankfully rejoice to have lived in a period when so blessed a change in our colonial policy was brought about ; a change which is full of promise and profit to a country having such claims on mankind as England, but also a change of system, in which we have done no more than make a transition from misfortune and from evil, back to the rules of justice, of reason, of nature, and of common sense.—GLADSTONE (1856).

THE fall of Peel and the break up of the conservative party in 1846 led to a long train of public inconveniences. When Lord John Russell was forming his government, he saw Peel, and proposed to include any of his party. Peel thought such a junction under existing circumstances unadvisable, but said he should have no ground of complaint if Lord John made offers to any of his friends ; and he should not attempt to influence them either way.[1] The action ended in a proposal of office to Dalhousie, Lincoln, and Sidney Herbert. Nothing came of it, and the whigs were left to go on as they best could upon the narrow base of their own party. The protectionists gave them to understand that before Bentinck and his friends made up their minds to turn Peel out, they had decided that it would not be fair to put the whigs in merely to punish the betrayer, and then to turn round upon them. On the contrary, fair and candid support was what they intended. The conservative government had carried liberal measures ; the liberal government subsisted on conservative declarations. Such was this singular situation.

The Peelites, according to a memorandum of Mr. Gladstone's, from a number approaching 120 in the corn law crisis of 1846, were reduced at once by the election of 1847 to less than half. This number, added to the liberal force, gave free trade a very large majority : added to the protectionists it just turned the balance in their favour. So long as Sir Robert Peel lived (down to June 1850) the entire body never voted with the protectionists. From the first a distinction arose among Peel's

[1] *The Halifax Papers.*

adherents that widened, as time went on, and led to a long
series of doubts, perturbations, manœuvres. These perplexities
lasted down to 1859, and they constitute a vital chapter in
Mr. Gladstone's political story. The distinction was in the
nature of political things. Many of those who had stood by
Peel's side in the day of battle, and who still stood by him in
the curious morrow that combined victorious policy with
personal defeat, were in more or less latent sympathy with
the severed protectionists in everything except protection.[1]
Differing from these, says Mr. Gladstone, others of the Peelites
'whose opinions were more akin to those of the liberals,
cherished, nevertheless, personal sympathies and lingering
wishes which made them tardy, perhaps unduly tardy, in
drawing towards that party. I think that this description
applied in some degree to Mr. Sidney Herbert, and in the same
or a greater degree to myself.'[2]

Shortly described, the Peelites were all free trade conservatives, drawn by under-currents, according to temperament,
circumstances, and all the other things that turn the balance
of men's opinions, to antipodean poles of the political compass.
'We have no party,' Mr. Gladstone tells his father in June
1849, 'no organisation, no whipper-in ; and under these circumstances we cannot exercise any considerable degree of
permanent influence as a body.' The leading sentiment that
guided the proceedings of the whole body of Peelites alike was
a desire to give to protection its final quietus. While the
younger members of the Peel cabinet held that this could only
be done in one way, namely, by forcing the protectionists into
office where they must put their professions to the proof, Peel
himself, and Graham with him, took a directly opposite view,
and adopted as the leading principle of their action the vital
necessity of keeping the protectionists out. This broad difference led to no diminution of personal intercourse or political
attachment.

'Certainly this was not due,' says Mr. Gladstone, 'to any desire (at
least in Sir R. Peel's mind) for, or contemplation of, coalition with the
liberal party. It sprang entirely from a belief on his part that the chiefs
of the protectionists would on their accession to power endeavour to
establish a policy in accordance with the designation of their party,
and would in so doing probably convulse the country. As long as
Lord George Bentinck lived, with his iron will and strong convictions,
this was a contingency that could not be overlooked. But he died in
1848, and with his death it became a visionary dream. Yet I remember
well Sir Robert Peel saying to me, when I was endeavouring to stir him
up on some great fault (as I thought it) in the colonial policy of the
ministers, "I foresee a tremendous struggle in this country for the

---

[1] Among them were such men as Wilson Patten, General Peel, Mr. Corry, Lord
Stanhope, Lord Hardinge, most of whom in days to come took their places in conservative administrations.
[2] Memo. of 1876.

restoration of protection." He would sometimes even threaten us with the possibility of being "sent for" if a crisis should occur, which was a thing far enough from our limited conceptions. We were flatly at issue with him on this opinion. We even considered that as long as the protectionists had no responsibilities but those of opposition, and as there were two hundred and fifty seats in parliament to be won by chanting the woes of the land and promising redress, there would be protectionists in plenty to fill the left-hand benches on those terms.'

The question what it was that finally converted the country to free trade is not easy to answer. Not the arguments of Cobden, for in the summer of 1845 even his buoyant spirit perceived that some precipitating event, and not reasoning, would decide. His appeals had become, as Disraeli wrote, both to nation and parliament a wearisome iteration, and he knew it. Those arguments, it is true, had laid the foundations of the case in all their solidity and breadth. But until the emergency in Ireland presented itself, and until prosperity had justified the experiment, Peel was hardly wrong in reckoning on the possibility of a protectionist reaction. Even the new prosperity and contentment of the country were capable of being explained by the extraordinary employment found in the creation of railways. As Mr. Gladstone said to a correspondent in the autumn of 1846, 'The liberal proceedings of conservative governments, and the conservative proceedings of the new liberal administration, unite in pointing to the propriety of an abstinence from high-pitched opinions.' This was a euphemism. What it really meant was that outside of protection no high-pitched opinions on any other subject were available. The tenets of party throughout this embarrassed period from 1846 to 1852 were shifting, equivocal, and fluid. Nor even in the period that followed did they very rapidly consolidate.

Mr. Gladstone writes to his father (June 30, 1849) :—

I will only add a few words about your desire that I should withdraw my confidence from Peel. My feelings of admiration, attachment, and gratitude to him I do not expect to lose ; and I agree with Graham that he has done more and *suffered* more than any other living statesman for the good of the people. But still I must confess with sorrow that the present course of events tends to separate and disorganise the small troop of the late government and their adherents. On the West Indian question last year I, with others, spoke and voted against Peel. On the Navigation law this year I was saved from it only by the shipowners and their friends, who would not adopt a plan upon the basis I proposed. Upon Canada—a vital question—I again spoke and voted against him.[1] And upon other colonial questions, yet most important to the government, I fear even this year the same thing may happen again. However

---

[1] A bill to indemnify the inhabitants of Lower Canada, many of whom had taken part in the rebellion of 1837-8, for the destruction and injury of their property. Mr. Gladstone strongly opposed any compensation being given to Canadian rebels.— *Hansard*, June 14, 1849.

painful, then, it may be to me to differ from him, it is plain that my conduct is not placed in his hands to govern.

We find an illustration of the distractions of this long day of party metamorphosis, as well as an example of what was regarded as Mr. Gladstone's over ingenuity, in one among other passing divergences between him and his chief. Mr. Disraeli brought forward a motion (Feb. 19, 1850) of a very familiar kind, on the distress of the agricultural classes and the insecurity of relief of rural burdens. Bright bluntly denied that there was a case in which the fee of land had been depreciated or rent been permanently lowered. Graham said the mover's policy was simply a transfer of the entire poor rate to the consolidated fund, violating the principles of local control and inviting prodigal expenditure. Fortune then, in Mr. Disraeli's own language, sent him an unexpected champion, by whom, according to him, Graham was fairly unhorsed. The reader will hardly think so, for though the unexpected champion was Mr. Gladstone, he found no better reason for supporting the motion, than that its adoption would weaken the case for restoring protection. As if the landlords and farmers were likely to be satisfied with a small admission of a great claim, while all the rest of their claim was to be as bitterly contested as ever; with the transfer of a shabby couple of millions from their own shoulders to the consolidated fund, when they were clamouring that fourteen millions would hardly be enough. Peel rose later, promptly took this plain point against his ingenious lieutenant, and then proceeded to one more of his elaborate defences, both of free trade and of his own motives and character. For the last time, as it was to happen, Peel declared that for Mr. Gladstone he had 'the greatest respect and admiration.' 'I was associated with him in the preparation and conduct of those measures, to the desire of maintaining which he partly attributes the conclusion at which he has arrived. I derived from him the most zealous, the most effective assistance, and it is no small consolation to me to hear from him, although in this particular motion we arrive at different conclusions, that his confidence in the justice of those principles for which we in common contended remains entirely unshaken.'[1]

On this particular battle, as well as on more general matter, a letter from Mr. Gladstone to his wife (Feb. 22, 1850) sheds some light :—

To Mrs. Gladstone.

Indeed you do rise to very daring flights to-day, and suggest many things that flow from your own deep affection which, perhaps, disguises from you some things that are nevertheless real. I cannot form to myself any other conception of my duty in parliament except the simple

[1] Hansard, Feb. 21, 1850, p. 1233.

one of acting independently, without faction, and without subserviency, on all questions as they arise. To the formation of a party, or even of the nucleus of a party, there are in my circumstances many obstacles. I have been talking over these matters with Manning this morning, and I found him to be of the opinion which is deliberately mine, namely, that it is better that I should not be the head or leader even of my own contemporaries; that there are others of them whose position is less embarrassed, and more favourable and powerful, particularly from birth or wealth or both. Three or four years ago, before I had much considered the matter, and while we still felt as if Peel were our actual chief in politics, I did not think so, but perhaps thought or assumed that as, up to the then present time, I had discharged some prominent duties in office and in parliament, the first place might naturally fall to me when the other men were no longer in the van. But since we have become more disorganised, and I have had little sense of union except with the men of my own standing, and I have *felt* more of the actual state of things, and how this or that would work in the House of Commons, I have come to be satisfied in my own mind that, if there were a question whether there should be a leader and who it should be, it would be much better that either Lincoln or Herbert should assume that post, whatever share of the mere work might fall on me. I have viewed the matter very drily, and so perhaps you will think I have written on it.

To turn then to what is more amusing, the battle of last night. After much consideration and conference with Herbert (who has had an attack of bilious fever and could not come down, though much better, and soon, I hope, to be out again, but who agreed with me), I determined that I ought to vote last night with Disraeli; and made up my mind accordingly, which involved saying why, at some period of the night. I was anxious to do it early, as I knew Graham would speak on the other side, and did not wish any conflict even of reasoning with him. But he found I was going to speak, and I suppose may have had some similar wish. At any rate, he had the opportunity of following Stafford who began the debate, as he was to take the other side. Then there was an amusing scene between him and Peel. Both rose and stood in competition for the Speaker's eye. The Speaker had seen Graham first, and he got it. But when he was speaking I felt I had no choice but to follow him. He made so very able a speech that this was no pleasant prospect; but I acquired the courage that proceeds from fear, according to a line from Ariosto : *Chi per virtù, chi per paura vale* [one from valour, another from fear, is strong], and made my plunge when he sat down. But the Speaker was not dreaming of me, and called a certain Mr. Scott who had risen at the same time. Upon this I sat down again, and there was a great uproar because the House always anticipating more or less interest when men speak on opposite sides and in succession, who are usually together, called for me. So I was up again, and the Speaker deserted Scott and called me, and I had to make the best I could after Graham. That is the end of the story, for there is nothing else worth saying. It was at the dinner hour from 7 to 7¾, and then I went home for a little quiet. Peel again replied upon me, but I did not hear that part of him ; and Disraeli showed the marvellous talent that he has, for summing up with brilliancy, buoyancy, and comprehensiveness at the close of a debate. You have heard me speak of that talent before when I have been wholly

against him ; but never, last night or at any other time, would I go to
him for conviction, but for the delight of the ear and the fancy.   What
a long story !

During the parliament that sat from 1847 to 1852, Mr. Gladstone's political life was in partial abeyance. The whole burden
of conducting the affairs of the Hawarden estate fell upon him.
For five years, he said, 'it constituted my daily and continuing
care, while parliamentary action was only occasional. It supplied in fact my education for the office of finance minister.'
The demands of church matters were anxious and at times
absorbing. He warmly favoured and spoke copiously for the
repeal of the navigation laws. He desired, however, to accept
a recent overture from America which offered everything, even
their vast coasting trade, upon a footing of absolute reciprocity.
'I gave notice,' he says, 'of a motion to that effect. But the
government declined to accept it. I accordingly withdrew it.
At this the tories were much put about. I, who had thought
of things only and not taken persons into view, was surprised
at their surprise. It did not occur to me that by my public
notification I had given to the opposition generally something
like a vested interest in my proposal. I certainly should have
done better never to have given my notice. This is one of the
cases illustrating the extreme slowness of my political education.' The sentence about thinking of things only and leaving
persons out, indicates a turn of mind that partly for great
good, partly for some evil, never wholly disappeared.

Yet partially withdrawn as he was from active life in the
House of Commons, Mr. Gladstone was far too acute an
observer to have any leanings to the delusive self-indulgence
of temporary retirements. To his intimate friend, Sir Walter
James, who seems to have nursed some such intention, he
wrote at this very time (Feb. 13, 1847) :—

The way to make parliament profitable is to deal with it as a calling,
and if it be a calling it can rarely be advantageous to suspend the pursuit
of it for years together with an uncertainty, too, as to its resumption.
You have not settled in the country, nor got your other vocation open
and your line clear before you. The purchase of an estate is a very
serious matter, which you may not be able to accomplish to your satisfaction except after the lapse of years. It would be more satisfactory to
drop parliament with another path open to you already, than in order
to seek about for one. . . . I think with you that the change in the
position of the conservative party makes public life still more painful
where it was painful before, and less enjoyable, where it was enjoyable ;
but I do not think it remains less a duty to work through the tornado
and to influence for good according to our means the new forms into
which political combination may be cast.

In 1848 Northcote speaks of Mr. Gladstone as the 'patron
saint' of the coal-whippers, who, as a manifestation of their
gratitude for the Act which he had induced parliament to pass

for them, offered their services to put down the chartist mob.
Both Mr. Gladstone and his brother John served as special
constables during the troubled days of April. In his diary he
records on April 10, 'On duty from 2 to 3¾ P.M.'

II

When Mr. Gladstone became colonial secretary at the end of
1845, he was described as a strong accession to the progressive
or theorising section of the cabinet—the men, that is to say,
who applied to the routine of government, as they found it,
critical principles and improved ideals. If the church had
been the first of Mr. Gladstone's commanding interests and
free trade the second, the turn of the colonies came next. He
had not held the seals of the colonial department for more than
a few months, but to any business, whatever it might be, that
happened to kindle his imagination or work on his reflection,
he never failed to bend his whole strength. He had sat upon
a committee in 1835-6 on native affairs at the Cape, and there
he had come into full view of the costly and sanguinary nature
of that important side of the colonial question. Molesworth
mentions the 'prominent and valuable' part taken by him in
the committee on Waste Lands (1836). He served on committees upon military expenditure in the colonies, and upon
colonial accounts. He was a member of the important committee of 1840 on the colonisation of New Zealand, and voted
in the minority for the draft report of the chairman, containing
among other things the principle of the reservation of all un-
occupied lands to the crown.[1] Between 1837 and 1841 he spoke
frequently on colonial affairs. When he was secretary of state
in 1846, questions arose upon the legal status of colonial clergy,
full of knotty points as to which he wrote minutes ; questions
upon education in penal settlements, and so forth, in which he
interested himself, not seldom differing from Stephen, the chief
of the staff in the office. He composed an argumentative
despatch on the commercial relations between Canada and the
mother country, endeavouring to wean the Canadian assembly
from its economic delusions. It was in effect little better than
if written in water. He made the mistake of sending out
despatches in favour of resuming on a limited scale the trans-
portation of convicts to Australia, a practice effectually condemned by the terrible committee eight years before. Opinion
in Australia was divided, Robert Lowe leading the opposition,[2]
and the experiment was vetoed by Mr. Gladstone's successor at
the colonial office. He exposed himself to criticism and abuse
by recalling a colonial governor for inefficiency in his post ;

[1] Garnett's *Edward Gibbon Wakefield*, p. 248.   See also p. 232.
[2] See *The Gladstone Colony* by J. F. Hogan, M.P., with prefatory note by Mr.
Gladstone, April 20, 1897, and the chapter in Lord Sherbrooke's *Life*, ' Mr. Gladstone's
Penal Colony.'

imprudently in the simplicity of his heart he added to the
recall a private letter stating rumours against the governor's
personal character. These he had taken on trust from the
bishop of the diocese and others. The bishop left him in the
lurch ; the recall was one affair, the personal rumours were
another ; nimble partisanship confused the two, to the disadvantage of the secretary of state ; the usual clatter that attends
any important personage in a trivial scrape ensued ; Mr.
Gladstone's explanations, simple and veracious as the sunlight
in their substance, were over-skilful in form, and half a dozen
blunt, sound sentences would have stood him in far better stead.
'There was on my part in this matter,' he says in a fugitive
scrap upon it, 'a singular absence of worldly wisdom.'[1] To
colonial policy at this stage I discern no particular contribution, and the matters that I have named are now well covered
with the moss of kindly time.

Almost from the first he was convinced that some leading
maxims of Downing Street were erroneous. He had, from his
earliest parliamentary days, regarded our colonial connection as
one of duty rather than as one of advantage. When he had
only been four years in the House he took a firm stand against
pretensions in Canada to set their assembly on an equal footing
with the imperial parliament at home.[2] On the other hand,
while he should always be glad to see parliament inclined to
make large sacrifices for the purpose of maintaining the
colonies, he conceived that nothing could be more ridiculous, or
more mistaken, than to suppose that Great Britain had anything to gain by maintaining that union in opposition to the
deliberate and permanent conviction of the people of the
colonies themselves.[3]

He did not at all undervalue what he called the mere
political connection, but he urged that the root of such a
connection lay in the natural affection of the colonies for
the land from which they sprang, and their spontaneous desire
to reproduce its laws and the spirit of its institutions. From
first to last he always declared the really valuable tie with a
colony to be the moral and the social tie.[4] The master key
with him was local freedom, and he was never weary of protest
against the fallacy of what was called 'preparing' these new
communities for freedom : teaching a colony, like an infant,
by slow degrees to walk, first putting it into long clothes, then
into short clothes. A governing class was reared up for the
purposes which the colony ought to fulfil itself ; and, as the
climax of the evil, a great military expenditure was maintained,
which became a premium on war. Our modern colonists, he

---

[1] Stafford Northcote published an effective vindication in a 'Letter to a Friend,' 1847.
[2] Speech on affairs of Lower Canada, Mar. 8, 1837.
[3] On Government of Canada bill, May 29, 1840.
[4] See his evidence before a Select Committee on Colonial Military Expenditure,
June 6, 1861.

said, after quitting the mother country, instead of keeping their hereditary liberties, go out to Australia or New Zealand to be deprived of these liberties, and then perhaps, after fifteen or twenty or thirty years' waiting, have a portion given back to them, with magnificent language about the liberality of parliament in conceding free institutions. During the whole of that interval they are condemned to hear all the miserable jargon about fitting them for the privileges thus conferred; while, in point of fact, every year and every month during which they are retained under the administration of a despotic government, renders them less fit for free institutions. 'No consideration of money ought to induce parliament to sever the connection between any one of the colonies and the mother country,' though it was certain that the cost of the existing system was both large and unnecessary. But the real mischief was not here, he said. Our error lay in the attempt to hold the colonies by the mere exercise of power.[1] Even for the church in the colonies he rejected the boon of civil preference as being undoubtedly a fatal gift,—'nothing but a source of weakness to the church herself and of discord and difficulty to the colonial communities, in the soil of which I am anxious to see the church of England take a strong and healthy root.'[2] He acknowledged how much he had learned from Molesworth's speeches,[3] and neither of them sympathised with the opinion expressed by Mr. Disraeli in those days, 'These wretched colonies will all be independent too in a few years, and are a millstone round our necks.'[4] Nor did Mr. Gladstone share any such sentiments as those of Molesworth who, in the Canadian revolt of the winter of 1837, actually invoked disaster upon the British arms.[5]

In their views of colonial policy Mr. Gladstone was in sub-

[1] See speech on Australian Colonies bill, June 26, 1849, Colonial Administration, April 16, 1849, on the Australian Colonies, Feb. 8, 1850, March 22, 1850, and May 13, 1850. On the Kaffir War, April 5, 1852. On the New Zealand Government bill, May 21, 1852. Also speech on Scientific Colonisation before the St. Martin in the Fields Association for the Propagation of the Gospel in Foreign Parts, March 27, 1849.

[2] On the Colonial Bishops bill, April 28, 1852.

[3] Wakefield was their common teacher. In a letter as secretary of state to Sir George Grey, then governor of New Zealand (March 27), 1846, he states how the signal ability of Wakefield and his devotion to every subject connected with the foundation of colonies has influenced him.

[4] 'To Lord Malmesbury, Aug. 13, 1852. Memoirs of an Ex-Minister, by the Earl of Malmesbury, i. p. 344.

[5] 'Should a war take place, I must declare that I should more deplore success on the part of this country than defeat; and though as an English citizen I could not but lament the disasters of my countrymen, still it would be to me a less poignant matter of regret than a success which would offer to the world the disastrous and disgraceful spectacle of a free and mighty nation succeeding by force of arms in putting down and tyrannising over a free though feebler community struggling in defence of its just rights. . . . That our dominion in America should now be brought to a conclusion, I for one most sincerely desire, but I desire it should terminate in peace and friendship. Great would be the advantages of an amicable separation of the two countries, and great would be the honour this country would reap in consenting to such a step.' Mr. Gladstone spoke the same evening in an opposite sense.—Hans. 39, p. 1466, Dec. 22, 1837. Walpole, Hist. Eng. iii. p. 425.

stantial accord with radicals of the school of Cobden, Hume,
and Molesworth. He does not seem to have joined a reforming
association founded by these eminent men among others
in 1850, but its principles coincided with his own :—local
independence, an end of rule from Downing Street, the relief
of the mother country from the whole expense of the local
government of the colonies, save for defence from aggression
by a foreign power. Parliament was, as a rule, so little moved
by colonial concerns that, according to Mr. Gladstone, in nine
cases out of ten it was impossible for the minister to secure
parliamentary attention, and in the tenth case it was only
obtained by the casual operations of party spirit. Lord
Glenelg's case showed that colonial secretaries were punished
when they got into bad messes, and his passion for messes
was punished, in the language of the journals of the day, by
the life of a toad under a harrow until he was worried out
of office. There was, however, no force in public opinion to
prevent the minister from going wrong if he liked ; still less
to prevent him from going right if he liked. Popular feeling
was coloured by no wish to give up the colonies, but people
doubted whether the sum of three millions sterling a year
for colonial defence and half a million more for civil charges,
was not excessive, and they thought the return by no means
commensurate with the outlay.[1] In discussions on bills effecting the enlargement of Australian constitutions, Mr. Gladstone's views came out in clear contrast with the old school.
'Spoke 1½ hours on the Australian Colonies bill,' he records
(May 13, 1850), 'to an indifferent, inattentive House. But it is
necessary to speak these truths of colonial policy even to
unwilling ears.' In the proceedings on the constitution for
New Zealand, he delivered a speech justly described as a
pattern of close argument and classic oratory.[2] Lord John
Russell, adverting to the concession of an elective chamber
and responsible government, said that one by one in this
manner, all the shields of our authority were thrown away,
and the monarchy was left exposed in the colonies to the
assaults of democracy. 'Now I confess,' said Mr. Gladstone,
in a counter minute, 'that the nominated council and the
independent executive were not shields of authority, but
sources of weakness, disorder, disunion, and disloyalty.'[3]

[1] See, for instance, *Spectator*, Jan. 17, 1845 ; *Times*, June 8, 1849. In 1861 it was
estimated that colonial military expenditure was between three and four millions a
year, about nine-tenths of which was borne by British taxpayers, and one-tenth by
colonial contribution.

[2] *Edward Gibbon Wakefield*, p. 331. The reader will find an extract in the Appendix.
' The New Zealand Government bill of 1852, with all its errors and complications, was
a grand step in the recovery of our old colonial policy ; but perhaps its chief contribution to the re-establishment of constitutional views was Mr. Gladstone's speech on its
second reading.'—Right Hon. C. B. Adderley, *Review of Earl Grey's Colonial Policy of
Lord John Russell's Administration*, p. 135.

[3] See Mr Gladstone's speech on introducing the Government of Ireland bill, April 8,
1886.

His whole view he set out at Chester[1] a little later than the time at which we now stand :—

. . . Experience has proved that if you want to strengthen the connection between the colonies and this country—if you want to see British law held in respect and British institutions adopted and beloved in the colonies, never associate with them the hated name of force and coercion exercised by us, at a distance, over their rising fortunes. Govern them upon a principle of freedom. Defend them against aggression from without. Regulate their foreign relations. These things belong to the colonial connection. But of the duration of that connection let them be the judges, and I predict that if you leave them the freedom of judgment it is hard to say when the day will come when they will wish to separate from the great name of England. Depend upon it, they covet a share in that great name. You will find in that feeling of theirs the greatest security for the connection. Make the name of England yet more and more an object of desire to the colonies. Their natural disposition is to love and revere the name of England, and this reverence is by far the best security you can have for their continuing, not only to be subjects of the crown, not only to render it allegiance, but to render it that allegiance which is the most precious of all—the allegiance which proceeds from the depths of the heart of man. You have seen various colonies, some of them lying at the antipodes, offering to you their contributions to assist in supporting the wives and families of your soldiers, the heroes that have fallen in the war. This, I venture to say, may be said, without exaggeration, to be among the first fruits of that system upon which, within the last twelve or fifteen years, you have founded a rational mode of administering the affairs of your colonies without gratuitous interference.

As I turn over these old minutes, memoranda, dispatches, speeches, one feels a curious irony in the charge engendered by party heat or malice, studiously and scandalously careless of facts, that Mr. Gladstone's policy aimed at getting rid of the colonies. As if any other policy than that which he so ardently enforced could possibly have saved them.

III

In 1849 Mr. Gladstone was concerned in a painful incident that befell one of his nearest friends. Nobody of humane feeling would now willingly choose either to speak or hear of it, but it finds a place in books even to this day ; it has been often misrepresented ; and it is so characteristic of Mr. Gladstone, and so entirely to his honour, that it cannot be wholly passed over. Fortunately a few sentences will suffice. His friend's wife had been for some time travelling abroad, and rumours by and by reached England of movements that might be no more than indiscreet, but might be worse. In consequence of these rumours, and after anxious consultations between the husband and three or four important members of his circle, it

[1] Nov. 12, 1855. See also two speeches of extraordinary fervour and exaltation, one at Mold (Sept. 29, 1856), and the other at Liverpool the same evening, both in support of the claims of societies for foreign missions.

was thought best that some one should seek access to the lady, and try to induce her to place herself in a position of security. The further conclusion reached was that Mr. Gladstone and Manning were the two persons best qualified by character and friendship for this critical mission. Manning was unable to go, but Mr. Gladstone at the earnest solicitation of his friend, and also of his own wife who had long been much attached to the person missing, set off alone for a purpose, as he conscientiously believed, alike friendly to both parties and in the interests of both. I have called the proceeding characteristic, for it was in fact exactly like him to be ready at the call of friendship, and in the hope of preventing a terrible disaster, cheerfully to undertake a duty detestable to anybody and especially detestable to him; and again, it was like him to regard the affair with an optimistic simplicity that made him hopeful of success, where to ninety-nine men of a hundred the thought of success would have seemed absurd. To no one was it a greater shock than to him when, after a journey across half Europe, he suddenly found himself the discoverer of what it was inevitable that he should report to his friend at home. In the course of the subsequent proceedings on the bill for a divorce brought into the House of Lords, he was called as a witness to show that in this case the person claiming the bill had omitted no means that duty or affection could suggest for averting the calamity with which his hearth was threatened. It was quite untrue, as he had occasion to tell the House of Commons in 1857, that he had anything whatever to do with the collection of evidence, or that the evidence given by him was the evidence, or any part of it, on which the divorce was founded. The only thing to be added is the judgment of Sir Robert Peel upon a transaction, with all the details of which he was particularly well acquainted:

Aug. 26, 1849.

MY DEAR GLADSTONE,—I am deeply concerned to hear the result of that mission which, with unparalleled kindness and generosity, you undertook in the hope of mitigating the affliction of a friend, and conducing possibly to the salvation of a wife and mother. Your errand has not been a fruitless one, for it affords the conclusive proof that everything that the forbearance and tender consideration of a husband and the devotion of a friend could suggest as the means of averting the necessity for appealing to the Law for such protection as it can afford, had been essayed and essayed with the utmost delicacy. This proof is valuable so far as the world and the world's opinion is concerned—much more valuable as it respects the heart and conscience of those who have been the active agents in a work of charity. I can offer you nothing in return for that which you undertook with the promptitude of affectionate friendship, under circumstances which few would not have considered a valid excuse if not a superior obligation, but the expression of my sincere admiration for truly virtuous and generous conduct.—Ever, my dear Gladstone, most faithfully yours,   ROBERT PEEL.

CHAPTER IV

DEATH OF SIR ROBERT PEEL

(1850)

Famous men—whose merit it is to have joined their name to events that were brought onwards by the course of things.—PAUL-LOUIS COURIER.

IT was now that Lord Palmerston strode to a front place—one of the two conspicuous statesmen with whom, at successive epochs in his career, Mr. Gladstone found himself in different degrees of energetic antagonism. This was all the stiffer and more deeply rooted, for being in both cases as much a moral antagonism as it was political. After a long spell of peace, earnestness, and political economy, the nation was for a time in a mood for change, and Palmerston convinced it that he was the man for its mood. He had his full share of shrewd common sense, yet was capable of infinite recklessness. He was good-tempered and a man of bluff cheerful humour. But to lose the game was intolerable, and it was noticed that with him the next best thing to success was quick retaliation on a victorious adversary—a trait of which he was before long to give the world an example that amused it. Yet he had no capacity for deep and long resentments. Like so many of his class, he united passion for public business to sympathy with social gaiety and pleasure. Diplomatists found him firm, prompt, clean-cut, but apt to be narrow, teasing, obstinate, a prisoner to his own arguments, and wanting in the statesman's first quality of seeing the whole and not merely the half. Metternich described him as an audacious and passionate marksman, ready to make arrows out of any wood. He was a sanguine man who always believed what he desired ; a confident man who was sure that he must be right in whatever he chose to fear. On the economic or the moral side of national life, in the things that make a nation rich and the things that make it scrupulous and just, he had only limited perception and moderate faith. Where Peel was strong and penetrating, Palmerston was weak and purblind. He regarded Bright and Cobden as displeasing mixtures of the bagman and the preacher. In 1840 he had

brought us within an ace of war with France. Disputes about
an American frontier were bringing us at the same period
within an ace of war with the United States. When Peel and
Aberdeen got this quarrel into more promising shape, Palmerston characteristically taunted them with capitulation. Lord
Grey refused help in manufacturing a whig government in
December 1845, because he was convinced that at that moment
Palmerston at the foreign office meant an American war. When
he was dismissed by Lord John Russell in 1852, a foreign ruler
on an insecure throne observed to an Englishman, 'This is a
blow to me, for so long as Lord Palmerston remained at the
foreign office, it was certain that you could not procure a
single ally in Europe.'

Yet all this policy of high spirits and careless dictatorial
temper had its fine side. With none of the grandeur of the
highest heroes of his school — of Chatham, Carteret, Pitt—
without a spark of their heroic fire or their brilliant and steadfast glow, Palmerston represented, not always in their best
form, some of the most generous instincts of his countrymen.
A follower of Canning, he was the enemy of tyrants and foreign
misrule. He had a healthy hatred of the absolutism and reaction that were supreme at Vienna in 1815 ; and if he meddled
in many affairs that were no affairs of ours, at least he intervened for freedom. The action that made him hated at Vienna
and Petersburg won the confidence of his countrymen. They
saw him in Belgium and Holland, Spain, Italy, Greece, Portugal,
the fearless champion of constitutions and nationality. Of
Aberdeen, who had been Peel's foreign minister, it was said that
at home he was a liberal without being an enthusiast ; abroad
he was a zealot, in the sense most opposed to Palmerston.
So, of Palmerston it could be said that he was conservative
at home and revolutionist abroad. If such a word can ever
be applied to such a thing, his patriotism was sometimes not
without a tinge of vulgarity, but it was always genuine and
sincere.

This masterful and expert personage was the ruling member
of the weak whig government now in office, and he made sensible
men tremble. Still, said Graham to Peel, 'it is a choice of
dangers and evils, and I am disposed to think that Palmerston
and his foreign policy are less to be dreaded than Stanley and
a new corn law.'[1] In a debate of extraordinary force and range
in the summer of 1850, the two schools of foreign policy found
themselves face to face. Palmerston defended his various proceedings with remarkable amplitude, power, moderation, and
sincerity. He had arrayed against him, besides Mr. Gladstone,
the greatest men in the House—Peel, Disraeli, Cobden, Graham,
Bright—but in his last sentence the undaunted minister struck
a note that made triumph in the division lobbies sure. For

---

[1] Parker, iii. p. 536.

five hours a crowded house hung upon his lips, and he then wound up with a fearless challenge of a verdict on the question, 'Whether, as the Roman in days of old held himself free from indignity when he could say *Civis Romanus sum*, so also a British subject, in whatever land he may be, shall feel confident that the watchful eye and the strong arm of England will protect him against injustice and wrong?'

The Roman citizen was in this instance a Mediterranean Jew who chanced to be a British subject. His house at Athens had for some reason or other been sacked by the mob; he presented a demand for compensation absurdly fraudulent on the face of it. The Greek government refused to pay. England dispatched the fleet to collect this and some other petty accounts outstanding. Russia and France proposed their good offices; the mediation of France was accepted; then a number of Greek vessels were peremptorily seized, and France in umbrage recalled her ambassador from London. Well might Peel, in the last speech ever delivered by him in the House of Commons, describe such a course of action as consistent neither with the dignity nor the honour of England. The debate travelled far beyond Don Pacifico, and it stands to this day as a grand classic exposition in parliament of the contending views as to the temper and the principles on which nations in our modern era should conduct their dealings with one another.

It was in the Greek debate of 1850, which involved the censure or acquittal of Lord Palmerston, that I first meddled in speech with foreign affairs, to which I had heretofore paid the slightest possible attention. Lord Palmerston's speech was a marvel for physical strength, for memory, and for lucid and precise exposition of his policy as a whole. A very curious incident on this occasion evinced the extreme reluctance of Sir R. Peel to appear in any ostensible relation with Disraeli. Voting with him was disagreeable enough, but this with his strong aversion to the Palmerstonian policy Peel could not avoid; besides which, it was known that Lord Palmerston would carry the division. Disraeli, not yet fully recognised as leader of the protectionists, was working hard for that position, and assumed the manners of it, with Beresford, a kind of whipper-in, for his right-hand man. After the Palmerston speech he asked me on the next night whether I would undertake to answer it. I said that I was incompetent to do it, from want of knowledge and otherwise. He answered that in that case he must do it. As the debate was not to close that evening, this left another night free for Peel when he might speak and *not* be in Disraeli's *neighbourhood*. I told Peel what Disraeli had arranged. He was very well satisfied. But, shortly afterwards, I received from Disraeli a message through Beresford, that he had changed his mind, and would not speak until the next and closing night, when Peel would have to speak also. I had to make known to Peel this alteration. He received the tidings with extreme annoyance: thinking, I suppose, that if the two spoke on the same side and in the late hours just before the division it would convey the idea of some concert or co-operation between them, which it was evident that he was most anxious to avoid. But he could not help himself. Disraeli's speech was a very poor one, almost like a 'cross,' and Peel's was prudent but otherwise not one of his best.[1]

Mr. Gladstone had not in 1850 at all acquired such full parliamentary ascendency as belonged to the hardy veteran confronting him; still less had he such authority as the dethroned leader who sat by his side. Yet the House felt that, in the image of an ancient critic, here was no cistern of carefully collected rain-water, but the bounteous flow of a living spring. It felt all the noble elevation of an orator who transported them apart from the chicane of diplomatic chanceries, above the narrow expediencies of the particular case, though of these too he proved himself a thoroughly well-armed master, into a full view of the state system of Europe and of the principles and relations on which the fabric is founded. Now for the first time he made the appeal, so often repeated by him, to the common sentiment of the civilised world, to the general and fixed convictions of mankind, to the principles of brotherhood among nations, to their sacred independence, to the equality in their rights of the weak with the strong. Such was his language. 'When we are asking for the maintenance of the rights that belong to our fellow-subjects resident in Greece,' he said, '*let us do as we would be done by*; let us pay all respect to a feeble state and to the infancy of free institutions, which we should desire and should exact from others towards their authority and strength.' Mr. Gladstone had not read history for nothing, he was not a Christian for nothing. He knew the evils that followed in Europe the breakdown of the great spiritual power—once, though with so many defects, a controlling force over violence, anarchy, and brute wrong. He knew the necessity for some substitute, even a substitute so imperfect as the law of nations. 'You may call the rule of nations vague and untrustworthy,' he exclaimed; 'I find in it, on the contrary, a great and noble monument of human wisdom, founded on the combined dictates of sound experience, a precious inheritance bequeathed to us by the generations that have gone before us, and a firm foundation on which we must take care to build whatever it may be our part to add to their acquisitions, if indeed we wish to promote the peace and welfare of the world.'

The government triumphed by a handsome majority, and Mr. Gladstone, as was his wont, consoled himself for present disappointment by hopes for a better future. 'The majority of the House of Commons, I am convinced,' he wrote to Guizot, then in permanent exile from power, 'was with us in heart and in conviction; but fear of inconveniences attending the removal of a ministry which there is no regularly organised opposition ready to succeed, carried the day beyond all authoritative doubt, against the merits of the particular question. It remains

---

[1] Fragment of 1897.

to hope that the demonstration which has been made may not
be without its effect upon the tone of Lord Palmerston's future
proceedings.'

The conflict thus opened between Mr. Gladstone and Lord
Palmerston in 1850 went on in many changing phases, with
some curious vicissitudes and inversions. They were sometimes
frank foes, occasionally partners in opposition, and for a long
while colleagues in office. Never at any time were they in
thought or feeling congenial.[1]

On the afternoon of the day following this debate, Peel was
thrown from his horse and received injuries from which he died
three days later (July 2), in the sixty-third year of his age, and
after forty-one years of parliamentary life. When the House
met the next day, Hume, as one of its oldest members, at once
moved the adjournment, and it fell to Mr. Gladstone to second
him. He was content with a few words of sorrow and with the
quotation of Scott's moving lines to the memory of Pitt:

> Now is the stately column broke,
> The beacon-light is quench'd in smoke,
> The trumpet's silver sound is still,
> The warder silent on the hill!'

These beautiful words were addressed, said Mr. Gladstone, 'to
a man great indeed, but not greater than Sir Robert Peel.'

'Great as he was to the last,' wrote Mr. Gladstone in one of
his notes in 1851, 'I must consider the closing years of his life
as beneath those that had preceded them. His enormous
energies were in truth so lavishly spent upon the gigantic work
of government, which he conducted after a fashion quite different,
—I mean as to the work done in the workshop of his own brain,
—from preceding and succeeding prime ministers, that their
root was enfeebled, though in its feebleness it had more strength
probably remaining than fell to the lot of any other public
man.'

Peel may at least divide with Walpole the laurels of our
greatest peace minister to that date—the man who presided
over beneficent and necessary changes in national polity, that
in hands less strong and less skilful might easily have opened
the sluices of civil confusion. And when we think of Walpole's
closing days, and of the melancholy end of most other ruling
spirits in our political history—of the mortifications and dis-
appointments in which, from Chatham and Pitt down to
Canning and O'Connell, they have quitted the glorious field
—Peel must seem happy in the manner and moment of his
death. Daring and prosperous legislative exploits had marked
his path. His authority in parliament never stood higher, his
honour in the country never stood so high. His last words had
been a commanding appeal for temperance in national action

[1] Mr. Gladstone's Don Pacifico speech is still not quite out of date.—June 27,
Hansard, 1850.

and language, a solemn plea for peace as the true aim to set before a powerful people.

To his father Mr. Gladstone wrote :—

July 2, 1850.—I thought Sir R. Peel looked extremely feeble during the debate last week. I mean as compared with what he usually is. I observed that he slept during much of Lord Palmerston's speech, that he spoke with little physical energy, and next day, Saturday, in the forenoon I thought he looked very ill at a meeting which, in common with him, I had to attend. This is all that I know and that is worth telling on a subject which is one of deep interest to all classes, from the Queen downwards. I was at the palace last night and she spoke to me with great earnestness about it. As to the division I shall say little ; it is an unsatisfactory subject. The majority of the government was made up out of our ranks, partly by people staying away and partly by some twenty who actually voted with the government. By far the greater portion, I am sorry to say, of both sets of persons were what are called Peelites, and not protectionists. The fact is, that if all calling themselves liberal be put on one side, and all calling themselves conservatives on the other, the House of Commons is as nearly as possible *equally* divided.

I have already described how Mr. Gladstone thought it a great mistake in Peel to resist any step that might put upon the protectionists the responsibilities of office. In a note composed a quarter of a century later (1876), he says :—'This I think was not only a safe experiment (after 1848) but a vital necessity. I do not, therefore, think, and I did not think, that the death of Sir R. Peel at the time when it occurred was a great calamity so far as the chief question of our internal politics was concerned. In other respects it was indeed great ; in some of them it may almost be called immeasurable. The moral atmosphere of the House of Commons has never since his death been quite the same, and is now widely different. He had a kind of authority there that was possessed by no one else. Lord John might in some respects compete with, in some even excel, him ; but to him, as leader of the liberals, the loss of such an opponent was immense. It is sad to think what, with his high mental force and noble moral sense, he might have done for us in after years. Even the afterthought of knowledge of such a man and of intercourse with him, is a high privilege and a precious possession.'

An interesting word or two upon his own position at this season occur in a letter to his father (July 9, 1850) :—

The letter in which you expressed a desire to be informed by me, so far as I might be able to speak, whether there was anything in the rumours circulated with regard to my becoming the leader in parliament of the conservative party, did not come to my hands until yesterday. The fact is, that there is nothing whatever in those rumours beyond mere speculation on things supposed probable or possible, and they must pass for what they are worth in that character only. People feel, I suppose, that Sir Robert Peel's life and continuance in parliament

were of themselves powerful obstacles to the general reorganisation of
the conservative party, and as there is great annoyance and dissatisfaction with the present state of things, and a widely spread feeling that it is not conducive to the public interests, there arises in men's
minds an expectation that the party will be in some manner reconsti-
tuted. I share in the feeling that it is desirable ; but I see very great
difficulties in the way, and do not at present see how they are to be
effectually overcome. The House of Commons is almost equally divided,
indeed, between those professing liberal and those professing conservative politics ; but the late division [Don Pacifico] showed how ill the
latter could hang together, even when all those who had any prominent
station among them in any sense were united. . . .

Cornewall Lewis wrote, ' Upon Gladstone the death of Peel
will have the effect of removing a weight from a spring—he
will come forward more and take more part in discussion.
The general opinion is that Gladstone will renounce his free
trade opinions, and become leader of the protectionists. I
expect neither the one event nor the other.'[1] More interesting
still is something told by the Duke of Buccleuch. 'Very
shortly,' said the duke in 1851, ' before Sir Robert Peel's death,
he expressed to me his belief that Sidney Herbert or Gladstone
would one day be premier ; but Peel said with sarcasm, If the
hour comes, Disraeli must be made governor-general of India.
He will be a second Ellenborough.'[2]

[1] *Letters*, p. 226.   [2] Dean Boyle's *Recollections*, p. 32.

CHAPTER V

GORHAM CASE—SECESSION OF FRIENDS

(1847-1851)

It is not by the State that man can be regenerated, and the terrible woes of this darkened world effectually dealt with.—GLADSTONE (1894).

THE test case of toleration at the moment of the Oxford election of 1847 was the admission of the Jews to sit in parliament, and in the last month of 1847 Mr. Gladstone astonished his father, as well as a great host of his political supporters, by voting with the government in favour of the removal of Jewish disabilities. No ordinary degree of moral courage was needed for such a step by the member for such a constituency. 'It is a painful decision to come to,' he writes in his diary (Dec. 16), 'but the only substantive doubt it raises is about remaining in parliament, and it is truly and only the church which holds me there, though she may seem to some to draw me from it.' Pusey wrote to him in rather violent indignation, for Mr. Gladstone was the only man of that school who learned, or was able to learn, what the modern state is or is going to be. This was the third phase, so Gladstone argued, of an irresistible movement. The tory party had fought first for an anglican parliament, second they fought for a protestant parliament, and now they were fighting for a Christian parliament. Parliament had ceased to be anglican and it had ceased to be protestant, and the considerations that supported these two earlier operations thenceforth condemned the exclusion from full civil rights of those who were not Christians. To his father he explained (December 17, 1847): 'After much consideration, prolonged indeed I may say for the last two years and a half, I made up my mind to support Lord John Russell's bill for the admission of the Jews. I spoke to this effect last night. It is with reluctance that I give the vote, but I am convinced that after the civil privileges we have given them already (including the magistracy and the franchise), and after the admission we have already conceded to unitarians who refuse the whole of the most vital doctrines of the Gospel, we cannot compatibly with entire justice and fairness refuse to admit them.'

His father, who was sometimes exacting, complained of concealment. Mr. Gladstone replied that he regarded the question as one of difficulty, and he therefore took as much time as he possibly could for reflection upon it, though he never intended to run it as close as it actually came. 'I know,' he says, in a notable sentence, 'it seems strange to you that I should find it necessary to hold my judgment in suspense on a question which seemed to many so plain ; *but suspense is of constant occurrence in public life upon very many kinds of questions, and without it errors and inconsistencies would be much more frequent than even they are now.*' This did not satisfy his father. 'I shall certainly read your speech to find some fair apology for your vote : good and satisfactory reason I do not expect. I cannot doubt you thought you withheld your opinions from me under the undecided state you were in, without any intention whatever to annoy me. There is, however, a natural closeness in your disposition, with a reserve towards those who may think they may have some claim to your confidence, probably increased by official habits, which it may perhaps in some cases be worth your inquiring into.' The sentence above about suspense is a key to many misunderstandings of Mr. Gladstone's character. His stouthearted friend Thomas Acland had warned him, for the sake of his personal influence, to be sure to deal with the Jew question on broad grounds, without refining, and without dragging out some recondite view not seen by common men, 'in short, to be *as little as possible like Maurice, and more like the Duke of Wellington.*' 'My speech,' Mr. Gladstone answered, 'was most unsatisfactory in many ways, but I do not believe that it mystified or puzzled anybody.'

The following year he received the honour of a D.C.L. degree at Oxford. Mrs. Gladstone was there, he tells his father, and 'was well satisfied with my reception, though it is not to be denied that my vote upon the Jew bill is upon the whole unpalatable there, and they had been provoked by a paragraph in the *Globe* newspaper stating that I was to have the degree, and that this made it quite clear that the minority was not unfavourable to the Jew bill.'

July 5.—I went off after breakfast to Oxford. Joined the V.-C. and doctors in the hall at Wadham, and went in procession to the Divinity schools provided with a white neckcloth by Sir R. Inglis, who seized me at the station in horror and alarm when he saw me with a black one. In due time we were summoned to the theatre where my degree had been granted with some *non placets* but with no scrutiny. The scene remarkable to the eye and mind, so pictorial and so national. There was great tumult about me, the hisses being obstinate, and the *fautores* also very generous. 'Gladstone and the Jew bill' came sometimes from the gallery, sometimes more favouring sounds.

II

After the whig government was formed in 1846, Mr. Gladstone expressed himself as having little fear that they could do much harm, 'barring church patronage.' He was soon justified in his own eyes in this limitation of his confidence, for the next year Dr. Hampden was made a bishop.[1] This was a rude blow both to the university which had eleven years before pronounced him heretical, and to the bishops who now bitterly and fervidly remonstrated. Grave points of law were raised, but Mr. Gladstone, though warmly reprobating the prime minister's recommendation of a divine so sure to raise the hurricane, took no leading part in the strife that followed. 'Never in my opinion,' he said to his father (Feb. 2, 1848), 'was a firebrand more wantonly and gratuitously cast.' It was an indication the more of a determination to substitute a sort of general religion for the doctrines of the church. The next really marking incident after the secession of Newman was a decision of a court of law, known as the Gorham judgment. This and the preferment of Hampden to his bishopric produced the second great tide of secession. 'Were we together,' Mr. Gladstone writes to Manning at the end of 1849 (December 30), 'I should wish to converse with you from sunrise to sunset on the Gorham case. It is a stupendous issue. Perhaps they will evade it. On abstract grounds this would be still more distasteful than a decision of the state against a catholic doctrine. But what I feel is that as a body we are not ready yet for the last alternatives. More years must elapse from the secession of Newman and the group of secessions which, following or preceding, belonged to it. A more composed and settled state of the public mind in regard to our relations with the church of Rome must supervene. There must be more years of faithful *work* for the church to point to in argument, and to grow into her habits. And besides all these very needful conditions of preparation for a crisis, I want to see the question more fully answered, What will the state of its own free and good will do, or allow to be done, for the church while yet in alliance with it?'

The Gorham case was this: a bishop refused to institute a clergyman to a vicarage in the west of England, on the ground of unsound doctrine upon regeneration by baptism. The clergyman sought a remedy in the ecclesiastical court of Arches. The judge decided against him. The case then came on appeal before the judicial committee of the privy council, and here a majority with the two archbishops as asessors reversed the decision of the court below. The bishop, one of the most combative of the human race, flew to Westminster Hall,

[1] See above, p. 123.

tried move upon move in queen's bench, exchequer, common
pleas; declared that his archbishop had abused his high commission; and even actually renounced communion with him.
But the sons of Zeruiah were too hard. The religious world in
both of its two standing camps was convulsed, for if Gorham
had lost the day it would or might have meant the expulsion
from the establishment of calvinists and evangelicals bag and
baggage. 'I am old enough,' said the provost of Oriel, 'to remember three baptismal controversies, and this is the first in
which one party has tried to eject the other from the church.'
On the other hand the sacramental wing found it intolerable
that fundamental doctrines of the church should be settled
under the veil of royal supremacy, by a court possessed of no
distinctly church character.

The judgment was declared on March 8 (1850), and Manning
is made to tell a vivid story about going to Mr. Gladstone's
house, finding him ill with influenza, sitting down by his bedside and telling him what the court had done; whereon Mr.
Gladstone started up, threw out his arms and exclaimed that
the church of England was gone unless it relieved itself by
some authoritative act. A witty judge once observed in regard
to the practice of keeping diaries, that it was wise to keep diary
enough at any rate to prove an *alibi*. According to Mr. Gladstone's diary he was not laid up until several days later, when
he did see various people, Manning included, in his bedroom.
On the black day of the judgment, having dined at the palace
the night before, and having friends to dine with him on this
night, he records a busy day, including a morning spent after
letter-writing, in discussion with Manning, Hope, and others
on the Gorham case and its probable consequences. This slip
of memory in the cardinal is trivial and not worth mentioning,
but perhaps it tends to impair another vivid scene described
on the same authority; how thirteen of them met at Mr.
Gladstone's house, agreed to a declaration against the judgment,
and proceeded to sign; how Mr. Gladstone, standing with his
back to the fire, began to demur; and when pressed by Manning to sign, asked him, in a low voice whether he thought
that as a privy councillor he ought to sign such a protest; and
finally how Manning, knowing the pertinacity of his character,
turned and said: We will not press him further.[1] This graphic
relation looks as if Mr. Gladstone were leaving his friends in
the lurch. None of them ever said so, none of them made any
signs of thinking so. There is no evidence that Mr. Gladstone
ever agreed to the resolution at all, and there is even evidence
that points presumptively the other way: that he was taking
a line of his own, and arguing tenaciously against all the rest
for delay.[2] Mr. Gladstone was often enough in a hurry him-

[1] Purcell, *Manning*, i. pp. 528-33.
[2] See J. R. Hope's letter (undated) in Purcell, i. p. 530.

self, but there never was a man in this world more resolute
against being hurried by other people.[1]

We need not, however, argue probabilities. Mr. Gladstone
no sooner saw the story than he pronounced it fiction. In a
letter to the writer of the book on Cardinal Manning (Jan.
14, 1896) he says :—

I read with surprise Manning's statement (made first after 35 years)
that I would not sign the declaration of 1850 because I ' was a privy
councillor.' I should not have been more surprised had he written that
I told him I could not sign because my name began with G. I had
done stronger things than that when I was not only privy councillor but
official servant of the crown, nay, I believe cabinet minister. The
declaration was liable to *many* interior objections. Seven out of the
thirteen who signed did so without (I believe) any kind of sequel. I
wish you to know that I entirely disavow and disclaim Manning's statement as it *stands*. And here I have to ask you to insert two lines in
your second or next edition ; with the simple statement that I prepared
and published with promptitude an elaborate argument to show that the
judicial committee was historically unconstitutional, as an organ for
the decision of ecclesiastical questions. This declaration was entitled,
I think, 'A Letter to the Bishop of London on the Ecclesiastical
Supremacy.' If I recollect right, while it dealt little with theology, it
was a more pregnant production than the declaration, and it went much
nearer the mark. It has been repeatedly published, and is still on sale
at Murray's. I am glad to see that Sidney Herbert (a *gentleman* if ever
there was one) also declined to sign. It seems to me *now*, that there is
something almost ludicrous in the propounding of such a congeries of
statements by such persons as we were ; not the more, but certainly not
the less, because of being privy councillors.

It was a terrible time ; aggravated for me by heavy cares and
responsibilities of a nature quite extraneous : and far beyond all others
by the illness and death of a much-loved child, with great anxieties
about another. My recollections of the conversations before the declaration are little but a mass of confusion and bewilderment. I stand only
upon what I *did*. No one of us, I think, understood the actual position,
not even our lawyers, until Baron Alderson printed an excellent statement on the points raised.[1]

---

[1] On March 13, Hope writes to Mr. Gladstone from 14 Curzon Street :—' Keble and
Pusey have been with me to-day, and the latter has suggested some alterations in the
resolutions ; I have taken upon me to propose a meeting at your house at ¼ before 10
to-morrow morning. If you cannot or *do not wish* to be present, I do not doubt you
will at any rate allow me the use of your rooms.' The meeting seems to have taken
place, for the entry on March 14 in Mr. Gladstone's diary is this :—' Hope, Badeley,
Talbot, Cavendish, Denison, Dr. Pusey, Keble, Bennett, here from 9¾ to 12 on the
draft of the resolutions. Badeley again in the evening. On the whole I resolved to
try some immediate effort.' This would appear to be the last meeting, and Manning
is not named as present. On the 18th :—' Drs. Mill, Pusey, etc., met here in the
evening, I was not with them.' On the same day Mr. Gladstone had written to the
Rev. W. Maskell, ' As respects myself, I do not intend to pursue the consideration of
them with those who meet to-night, first, because the pressure of other business has
become very heavy upon me, and secondly and mainly, because I do not consider that
the time for any enunciation of a character pointing to ultimate issues will have
arrived until the Gorham judgment shall have taken effect.' No later meeting is ever
mentioned.

[2] Purcell professed to rectify the matter in the fourth edition, i. p. 536, but the
reader is nowhere told that Mr. Gladstone disavowed the original story.

III

For long the new situation filled his mind. 'The case of the church of England at this moment,' he wrote to Lord Lyttelton, 'is a very dismal one, and almost leaves men to choose between a broken heart and no heart at all. But at present it is all dark or only twilight which rests upon our future.' He busily set down thoughts upon the supremacy. He studied Cawdry's case, and he mastered Lord Coke's view of the law. He feels better pleased with the Reformation in regard to the supremacy ; but also much more sensible of the drifting of the church since, away from the range of her constitutional securities ; and more than ever convinced how thoroughly false is the present position. As to himself and his own work in life, in reply I suppose to something urged by Manning, he says (April 29, 1850), 'I have two characters to fulfil—that of a lay member of the church, and that of a member of a sort of wreck of a political party. I must not break my understood compact with the last, and forswear my profession, unless and until the necessity has arisen. That necessity will plainly have arisen for me when it shall have become evident that justice cannot, *i.e.* will not, be done by the state to the church.' With boundless exaltation of spirit he expatiated on the arduous and noble task which it was now laid upon the children of the church of England amid trouble, suspense, and it might be even agony to perform. 'Fully believing that the death of the church of England is among the alternative issues of the Gorham case,' he wrote to a clerical friend (April 9), 'I yet also believe that all Christendom and all its history have rarely afforded a nobler opportunity of doing battle for the faith in the church than that now offered to English churchmen. That opportunity is a prize far beyond any with which the days of her prosperity, in any period, can have been adorned.' He does not think (June 1, 1850) that a loftier work was ever committed to men. Such vast interests were at stake, such unbounded prospects open before them. What they wanted was the divine art to draw from present terrible calamities and appalling future prospects the conquering secret to rise through the struggle into something better than historical anglicanism, which essentially depended on conditions that have passed away. 'In my own case,' he says to Manning a little later, 'there is work ready to my hand and much more than enough for its weakness, a great mercy and comfort. But I think I know what my course would be, were there not. It would be to set to work upon the holy task of clearing, opening, and establishing positive truth in the church of England, which is an office doubly blessed, inasmuch as it is both the business of truth, and the laying of firm foundations for future union in Christendom.' If this vision of a dream had ever come to

pass, perhaps Europe might have seen the mightiest Christian
doctor since Bossuet; and just as Bossuet's struggle was
called the grandest spectacle of the seventeenth century, so
to many eyes this might have appeared the greatest of the
nineteenth. Mr. Gladstone did not see, in truth he never saw,
any more than Bossuet saw in his age, that the Time-Spirit
was shifting the foundations of the controversy. However
that may be, the interesting thing for us in the history of his
life is the characteristic blaze of battle that this case now
kindled in his breast.

On the eve of his return from Germany in the autumn of
1845, one of his letters to Mrs. Gladstone reveals the pressing
intensity of his conviction, deepened by his intercourse with
the grave and pious circles at Munich and at Stuttgart, of the
supreme interest of spiritual things :—

In my wanderings my thoughts too have had time to travel; and I
have had much conversation upon church matters first at Munich and
since coming here with Mrs. Craven and some connections of hers
staying with her, who are Roman catholics of a high school. All that
I can see and learn induces me more and more to feel what a crisis for
religion at large is this period of the world's history—how the power
of religion and its permanence are bound up with the church—how
inestimably precious would be the church's unity, inestimably precious
on the one hand, and on the other to human eyes immeasurably remote
—lastly how loud, how solemn is the call upon all those who hear and
who *can* obey it, to labour more and more in the spirit of these principles,
to give themselves, if it may be, clearly and wholly to that work. It
is dangerous to put indefinite thoughts, instincts, longings, into
language which is necessarily determinate. I cannot trace the line of
my own future life, but I hope and pray it may not always be where it
is. . . . Ireland, Ireland ! that cloud in the west, that coming storm,
the minister of God's retribution upon cruel and inveterate and but
half-atoned injustice ! Ireland forces upon us those great social and
great religious questions—God grant that we may have courage to look
them in the face, and to work through them. Were they over, were
the path of the church clear before her, as a body able to take her trial
before God and the world upon the performance of her work as His
organ for the recovery of our country—how joyfully would I retire from
the barren, exhausting strife of merely political contention. I do not
think that you would be very sorrowful ? As to ambition in its ordinary
sense, we are spared the chief part of its temptations. If it has a
valuable reward upon earth over and above a good name, it is when a
man is enabled to bequeath to his children a high place in the social
system of his country. That cannot be our case. The days are gone
by when such a thing might have been possible. To leave to Willy
a title with its burdens and restraints and disqualifications, but without
the material substratum of wealth, and the duties and means of good,
as well as the general power attending it, would not I think be acting
for him in a wise and loving spirit—assuming, which may be a vain
assumption, that the alternative could ever be before us.

The fact that in Scotland, a country in which Mr. Gladstone

passed so much time and had such lively interests, the members of his own episcopal church were dissenters, was well fitted to hasten the progress of his mind in the liberal direction. Certain it is that in a strongly-written letter to a Scotch bishop at the end of 1851, Mr. Gladstone boldly enlarged upon the doctrine of religious freedom, with a directness that kindled both alarm and indignation among some of his warmest friends.[1] Away, he cried, with the servile doctrine that religion cannot live but by the aid of parliaments. When the state has ceased to bear a definite and full religious character, it is our interest and our duty alike to maintain a full religious freedom. It is this plenary religious freedom that brings out into full vigour the internal energies of each communion. Of all civil calamities the greatest is the mutilation, under the seal of civil authority, of the Christian religion itself. One fine passage in this letter denotes an advance in his political temper, as remarkable as the power of the language in which it finds expression :—

It is a great and noble secret, that of constitutional freedom, which has given to us the largest liberties, with the steadiest throne and the most vigorous executive in Christendom. I confess to my strong faith in the virtue of this principle. I have lived now for many years in the midst of the hottest and noisiest of its workshops, and have seen that amidst the clatter and the din a ceaseless labour is going on ; stubborn matter is reduced to obedience, and the brute powers of society like the fire, air, water and mineral of nature are, with clamour indeed but also with might, educated and shaped into the most refined and regular forms of usefulness for man. I am deeply convinced that among us all systems, whether religious or political, which rest on a principle of absolutism, must of necessity be, not indeed tyrannical, but feeble and ineffective systems ; and that methodically to enlist the members of a community, with due regard to their several capacities, in the performance of its public duties, is the way to make that community powerful and healthful, to give a firm seat to its rulers, and to engender a warm and intelligent devotion in those beneath their sway.[2]

These were the golden trumpet-notes of a new time. When they reached the ears of old Dr. Routh, as he sat in wig and cassock among his books and manuscripts at Magdalen, revolving nearly a hundred years of mortal life, he exclaimed that he had heard enough to be quite sure that no man holding such opinions as these could ever be a proper member for the university of Oxford. A few months later, it was seen how the learned man found several hundreds of unlearned to agree with him.

IV

This chapter naturally closes with what was to Mr. Gladstone

---

[1] *Letter to the Right Rev. William Skinner, Bishop of Aberdeen and Primus, on the functions of laymen in the Church*, reprinted in *Gleanings*, vi. Also *Letter* to Mr. Gladstone on this letter by Charles Wordsworth, the Warden of Glenalmond. Oxford. J. H. Parker, 1852.   [2] *Gleanings*, vi. p. 17.

one of the dire catastrophes of his life. With growing dismay
he had seen Manning drawing steadily towards the edge of
the cataract. When he took the ominous step of quitting
his charge at Lavington, Mr. Gladstone wrote to him from
Naples (January 26, 1851) : — 'Without description from you,
I can too well comprehend what you have suffered. . . . Such
griefs ought to be sacred to all men, they must be sacred to
me, even did they not touch me sharply with a reflected
sorrow. You can do nothing that does not reach me, considering
how long you have been a large part both of my actual life
and of my hopes and reckonings. Should you do the act which
I pray God with my whole soul you may not do, it will not
break, however it may impair or strain, the bonds between us.'
'If you go over,' he says, in another letter of the same month,
'I should earnestly pray that you might not be as others who
have gone before you, but might carry with you a larger heart
and mind, able to raise and keep you above that slavery to a
system, that exaggeration of its forms, that disposition to rivet
every shackle tighter and to stretch every breach wider, which
makes me mournfully feel that the men who have gone from
the church of England after being reared in her and by her,
are far more keen, and I must add, far more cruel adversaries
to her, than were the mass of those whom they joined.'

   In the case of Hope there had been for some considerable
time a lingering sense of change. 'My affection for him,
during these later years before his change, was I may almost
say intense : there was hardly anything I think which he
could have asked me to do, and which I would not have done.
But as I saw more and more through the dim light what was
to happen, it became more and more like the affection felt
for one departed.' Hope, he says, was not one of those shallow
souls who think that such a relation can continue after its
daily bread has been taken away. At the end of March he
enters in his diary :—'Wrote a paper on Manning's question
and gave it him. He smote me to the ground by announcing
with suppressed emotion that he is now upon the *brink*, and
Hope too. Such terrible blows not only overset and oppress
but, I fear, demoralise me.' On the same day in April 1851,
Manning and Hope were received together into the Roman
church. Political separations, though these too have their
pangs, must have seemed to Mr. Gladstone trivial indeed, after
the tragic severance of such a fellowship as this had been.

   'They were my two props,' he wrote in his diary the next
day. 'Their going may be to me a sign that my work is gone
with them. . . . One blessing I have : total freedom from
doubts. These dismal events have smitten, but not shaken.'
The day after that, he made a codicil to his will striking out
Hope as executor, and substituting Northcote. Friendship
did not die, but only lived 'as it lives between those who

inhabit separate worlds.' Communication was not severed ;
social intercourse was not avoided ; and both on occasions
in life, the passing by of which, as Hope-Scott said, would
be a loss to friendship, and on smaller opportunities, they
corresponded in terms of the old affection. *Quis desiderio*
is Mr. Gladstone's docket on one of Hope's letters, and in
another (1858) Hope communicates in words of tender feeling
the loss of his wife, and the consolatory teachings of the
faith that she, like himself, had embraced ; and he recalls to
Mr. Gladstone that the root of their friendship which struck
the deepest was fed by a common interest in religion.[1]

In Manning's case the wound cut deeper, and for many
years the estrangement was complete.[2] To Wilberforce, the
archdeacon, Mr. Gladstone wrote (April 11, 1851) :—

> I do indeed feel the loss of Manning, if and as far as I am capable of
> feeling anything. It comes to me cumulated, and doubled, with that
> of James Hope. Nothing like it can ever happen to me again. Arrived
> now at middle life, I never *can* form I suppose with any other two men
> the habits of communication, counsel, and dependence, in which I have
> now for from fifteen to eighteen years lived with them both. . . . My
> intellect does deliberately reject the grounds on which Manning has
> proceeded. Indeed they are such as go far to destroy my confidence,
> which was once and far too long at the highest point, in the healthiness
> and soundness of his. To show that at any rate this is not from the
> mere change he has made, I may add, that my conversations with Hope
> have not left any corresponding impression upon my mind with regard
> to him.

A wider breach was this same year made in his inmost
circle. In April of the year before a little daughter, between
four and five years old, had died, and was buried at Fasque.
The illness was long and painful, and Mr. Gladstone bore his
part in the nursing and watching. He was tenderly fond of
his little children, and the sorrow had a peculiar bitterness.
It was the first time that death entered his married home.

When he returned to Fasque in the autumn he found that
his father had taken ' a decided step, nay a stride, in old age ' ;
not having lost any of his interest in politics, but grown quite
mild. The old man was nearing his eighty-seventh year. 'The
very wreck of his powerful and simple nature is full of grandeur.
. . . Mischief is at work upon his brain—that indefatigable
brain which has had to stand all the wear and pressure of his
long life.' In the spring of 1851 he finds him 'very like a spent
cannon - ball, with a great and sometimes almost frightful
energy remaining in him : though weak in comparison with

---

[1] In 1868 Mr. Gladstone urged him to produce an abridged version of Lockhart's
Life of Scott. Then Hope found that his father-in-law's own abridgment was unknown ;
and (1871) asks Mr. Gladstone's leave to dedicate a reprint of it to him as ' one among
those who think that Scott still deserves to be remembered, not as an author only,
but as a noble and vigorous man.'

[2] From 1853 to 1861 they did not correspond nor did they even meet.

what he was, he hits a very hard knock to those who come
across him.' When December came, the veteran was taken
seriously ill, and the hope disappeared of seeing him even
reach his eighty-seventh birthday (Dec. 11). On the 7th he
died. As Mr. Gladstone wrote to Phillimore, 'though with
little left either of sight or hearing, and only able to walk from
one room to another or to his brougham for a short drive,
though his memory was gone, his hold upon language even
for common purposes imperfect, the reasoning power much
decayed and even his perception of personality rather indis-
tinct, yet so much remained about him as one of the most
manful, energetic, affectionate, and simple - hearted among
human beings, that he still filled a great space to the eye,
mind, and heart, and a great space is accordingly left void by
his withdrawal.' 'The death of my father,' Mr. Gladstone
wrote to his brother John, 'is the loss of a great object of
love, and it is the shattering of a great bond of union. Among
few families of five persons will be found differences of character and opinion to the same aggregate amount as among us.
We cannot shut our eyes to this fact; by opening them, I think
we may the better strive to prevent such differences from
begetting estrangement.'

CHAPTER VI

NAPLES

(1850-1851)

It would be amusing, if the misfortunes of mankind ever could be so, to hear the pretensions of the government here [Naples] to mildness and clemency, because it does not put men to death, and confines itself to leaving six or seven thousand state prisoners to perish in dungeons. I am ready to believe that the king of Naples is naturally mild and kindly, but he is afraid, and the worst of all tyrannies is the tyranny of cowards.—TOCQUEVILLE [1850].

IN the autumn of 1850, with the object of benefiting the eyesight of one of their daughters, the Gladstones made a journey to southern Italy, and an eventful journey it proved. For Italy it was, that now first drew Mr. Gladstone by the native ardour of his humanity, unconsciously and involuntarily, into that great European stream of liberalism which was destined to carry him so far. Two deep principles, sentiments, aspirations, forces, call them what we will, awoke the huge uprisings that shook Europe in 1848—the principle of Liberty, the sentiment of Nationality. Mr. Gladstone, slowly and almost blindly heaving off his shoulders the weight of old conservative tradition, did not at first go beyond liberty, with all that ordered liberty conveys. Nationality penetrated later, and then indeed it penetrated to the heart's core. He went to Naples with no purposes of political propagandism, and his prepossessions were at that time pretty strongly in favour of established governments, either at Naples or anywhere else. The case had doubtless been opened to him by Panizzi—a man as Mr. Gladstone described him, 'of warm, large and free nature, an accomplished man of letters, and a victim of political persecution, who came to this country a nearly starving refugee.' But Panizzi had certainly made no great revolutionist of him. His opinions, as he told Lord Aberdeen, were the involuntary and unexpected result of his sojourn.

He had nothing to do with the subterranean forces at work in the kingdom of the Two Sicilies, in the States of the Church, and in truth all over the Peninsula. The protracted struggle

that had begun after the establishment of Austrian domination
in the Peninsula in 1815, and was at last to end in the construction of an Italian kingdom—the most wonderful political transformation of the century — seemed after the fatal crisis of
Novara (1849) further than ever from a close. Now was the
morrow of the vast failures and disenchantments of 1848.
Jesuits and absolutists were once more masters, and reaction
again alternated with conspiracy, risings, desperate carbonari
plots.   Mazzini, four years older than Mr. Gladstone, and
Cavour, a year his junior, were directing in widely different
ways, the one the revolutionary movement of Young Italy, the
other the constitutional movement of the Italian Resurrection.
The scene presented brutal repression on the one hand ; on the
other a chaos of republicans and monarchists, unitarians and
federalists, frenzied idealists and sedate economists, wild ultras
and men of the sober middle course.   In the midst was the
pope, the august shadow, not long before the centre, now once
again the foe, of his countrymen's aspirations after freedom and
a purer glimpse of the lights of the sun.   The evolution of this
extraordinary historic drama, to which passion, genius, hope,
contrivance, stratagem, and force contributed alike the highest
and the lowest elements in human nature and the growth of
states, was to be one of the most sincere of Mr. Gladstone's
interests for the rest of his life.

As we shall see, he was at first and he long remained untouched by the idea of Italian unity and Italy a nation. He
met some thirty or more Italian gentlemen in society at
Naples, of whom seven or eight only were in any sense liberals,
and not one of them a republican. It was now that he made
the acquaintance of Lacaita, afterwards so valued a friend of
his, and so well known in many circles in England for his
geniality, cultivation, and enlightenment. He was the legal
adviser to the British embassy ; he met Mr. Gladstone constantly ; they talked politics and literature day and night,
'under the acacias and palms, between the fountains and
statues of the Villa Reale, looking now to the sea, now to the
world of fashion in the Corso.'[1]   Here Lacaita first opened the
traveller's eyes to the condition of things, though he was able
to say with literal truth that not a single statement of fact
was made upon Lacaita's credit. Mr. Gladstone saw Bourbon
absolutism no longer in the decorous hues of conventional
diplomacy, but as the black and execrable thing it really was,
—'the negation of God erected into a system of government.'
Sitting in court for long hours during the trial of Poerio, he
listened with as much patience as he could command to the
principal crown witness, giving such evidence that the tenth
part of what he heard should not only have ended the case, but
secured condign punishment for perjury — evidence that a

[1] See Munz's *Italienische Reminiscenzen und Profile*, p. 248.

prostitute court found good enough to justify the infliction on Poerio, not long before a minister of the crown, of the dreadful penalty of four-and-twenty years in irons. Mr. Gladstone accurately informed himself of the condition of those who for unproved political offences were in thousands undergoing degrading and murderous penalties. He contrived to visit some of the Neapolitan prisons, another name for the extreme of filth and horror ; he saw political prisoners (and political prisoners included a large percentage of the liberal opposition) chained two and two in double irons to common felons ; he conversed with Poerio himself in the bagno of Nisida chained in this way ; he watched sick prisoners, men almost with death in their faces, toiling upstairs to see the doctors, because the lower regions were too foul and loathsome to allow it to be expected that professional men would enter. Even these inhuman and revolting scenes stirred him less, as it was right they should, than the corruptions of the tribunals, the vindictive treatment for long periods of time of uncondemned and untried men, and all the other proceedings of the government, 'desolating entire classes upon which the life and growth of the nation depend, undermining the foundation of all civil rule.' It was this violation of all law, and of the constitution to which King Ferdinand had solemnly sworn fidelity only a year or two before, that outraged him more than even rigorous sentences and barbarous prison practice. 'Even on the severity of these sentences,' he wrote, 'I would not endeavour to fix attention so much as to draw it off from the great fact of illegality, which seems to me to be the foundation of the Neapolitan system ; illegality, the fountain-head of cruelty and baseness and every other vice ; illegality which gives a bad conscience, creates fears ; those fears lead to tyranny, that tyranny begets resentment, that resentment creates true causes of fear where they were not before ; and thus fear is quickened and enhanced, the original vice multiplies itself with fearful speed, and the old crime engenders a necessity for new.' [1]

Poerio apprehended that his own case had been made worse by the intervention of Mr. Temple, the British minister and brother of Lord Palmerston ; not in the least as blaming him or considering it officious. He adopted the motto, 'to suffer is to do,' '*il patire è anche operare.*' For himself he was not only willing—he rejoiced—to play the martyr's part.

'I was particularly desirous,' wrote Mr. Gladstone in a private memorandum, 'to have Poerio's opinion on the expediency of making some effort in England to draw general attention to these horrors, and dissociate the conservative party from all suppositions of winking at them ; because I had had from a sensible man one strong opinion against such a course. I said to him that in my view only two modes could be thought of,—the first, amicable remonstrance through the cabinets, the

[1] For the two *Letters to Lord Aberdeen*, see *Gleanings*, iv.

second public notoriety and shame. That had Lord Aberdeen been in
power the first might have been practicable, but that with Lord
Palmerston it would not, because of his position relatively to the other
cabinets ("Yes," he said, "Lord Palmerston was *isolato*"), not because he
would be wanting in the will. Matters standing thus, I saw no way
open but that of exposure ; and might that possibly exasperate the
Neapolitan government, and increase their severity ? His reply was,
" As to us, never mind ; we can hardly be worse than we are. But
think of our country, for which we are most willing to be sacrificed.
Exposure will do it good. The present government of Naples rely on
the English conservative party. Consequently we were all in horror
when Lord Stanley last year carried his motion in the House of Lords.
Let there be a voice from that party showing that whatever government
be in power in England, no support will be given to such proceedings as
these. It will do much to break them down. It will also strengthen
the hands of a better and less obdurate class about the court. Even
there all are not alike. I know it from observation. These ministers
are the extremest of extremes. There are others who would willingly
see more moderate means adopted." On such grounds as these (I do not
quote words) he strongly recommended me to *act*.'

II

Mr. Gladstone reached London on February 26. Phillimore
met him at the station with Lord Stanley's letter, of which we
shall hear in the next chapter, pressing him to enter the government. 'I was never more struck,' says Phillimore, 'by the
earnestness and simplicity of his character. He could speak of
nothing so readily as the horrors of the Neapolitan government,
of which I verily believe he thought nearly as much as the
prospect of his own accession to one of the highest offices of
state.' He probably thought not only nearly as much, but
infinitely more of those 'scenes fitter for hell than earth,' now
many hundred miles away, but still vividly burning in the
haunted chambers of his wrath and pity. After rapidly despatching the proposal to join the new cabinet, after making
the best he could of the poignant anxieties that were stirred in
him by the unmistakable signs of the approaching secession of
Hope and Manning, he sought Lord Aberdeen (March 4), and
'found him as always, satisfactory ; kind, just, moderate,
humane' (to Mrs. Gladstone, March 4). He had come to
London with the intention of obtaining, if possible, Aberdeen's
intervention, in preference to any other mode of proceeding,[1]
and they agreed that private representation and remonstrance
should be tried in the first instance, as less likely than public
action by Mr. Gladstone in parliament, to rouse international

[1] There was a slight discrepancy between the two on this point, Mr. Gladstone
describing the position as above, Aberdeen believing that it was by his persuasion
that Mr. Gladstone dropped his intention of instant publicity. Probably the latter
used such urgent language about an appeal to the public opinion of England and
Europe, that Lord Aberdeen supposed it to be an immediate and not an ulterior
resort. Aberdeen to Castelcicala, September 15, 1851, and Mr. Gladstone to Aberdeen,
October 3.

jealousy abroad, or to turn the odious tragedy into the narrow channels of party at home.   Mr. Gladstone, at Lord Aberdeen's desire, was to submit a statement of the case for his consideration and judgment.

This statement, the first memorable Letter to Lord Aberdeen, was ready at the beginning of April.   The old minister gave it 'mature consideration' for the best part of a month.   His antecedents made him cautious.   Mr. Gladstone, ten years later, admitted that Lord Aberdeen's views of Italy did not harmonise with what was his general mode of estimating human action and the world's affairs, and there was a reason for this in his past career.   In very early youth he had been called upon to deal with the gigantic questions that laid their mighty weight upon European statesmen at the fall of Napoleon ; the natural effect of this close contact with the vast and formidable problems of 1814-15 was to make him regard the state-system then founded as a structure on which only reckless or criminal unwisdom would dare to lay a finger.   The fierce storms of 1848 were not calculated to loosen this fixed idea, or to dispose him to any new views of either the relations of Austria to Italy, or of the uncounted mischiefs to the Peninsula of which those relations were the nourishing and maintaining cause.   In a debate in the Lords two years before (July 20, 1849), Lord Aberdeen had sharply criticised the British government of the day for doing the very thing officially, which Mr. Gladstone was now bringing moral compulsion on him to attempt unofficially. Lord Palmerston had called attention at Vienna to the crying evils of the government of Naples, and had boldly said that it was little wonder if men groaning for long years under such grievances and seeing no hope of redress, should take up any scheme, however wild, that held out any chance of relief.   This and other proceedings indicating unfriendliness to the King of Naples and a veiled sympathy with rebellion shocked Aberdeen as much as Lamartine's trenchant saying that the treaties of Vienna were effete.   In attacking Palmerston's foreign policy again in 1850, he protested that we had deeply injured Austria and had represented her operations in Italy in a completely false light.   In his speech in the Pacifico debate, he had referred to the Neapolitan government without approval but in guarded phrases, and had urged as against Lord Palmerston that the less they admired Neapolitan institutions and usages, the more careful ought they to be not to impair the application of the sacred principles that govern and harmonise the intercourse between states, from which you never can depart without producing mischiefs a thousandfold greater than any promised advantage.   Aberdeen was too upright and deeply humane a man to resist the dreadful evidence that was now forced upon him.   Still that evidence plainly shook down his own case of a few months earlier, and this cannot have been pleasing.   He

felt the truth and the enormity of the indictment laid before
him ; he saw the prejudice that would inevitably be done to
conservatism both at home and on the European continent, by
the publication of such an indictment from the lips of such a
pleader ; and he perceived from Mr. Gladstone's demeanour
that the decorous plausibilities of diplomacy would no more
hold him back from resolute exposure, than they would put out
the fires of Vesuvius or Etna.

On May 2 Lord Aberdeen wrote to Schwarzenberg at Vienna,
saying that for forty years he had been connected with the
Austrian government, and taken a warm interest in the
fortunes of the empire ; that Mr. Gladstone, one of the most distinguished members of the cabinet of Peel, had been so shocked
by what he saw at Naples, that he was resolved to make some
public appeal ; then to avoid the pain and scandal of a conservative statesman taking such a course, would not his highness use his powerful influence to get done at Naples all that
could reasonably be desired ? The Austrian minister replied
several weeks after (June 30). If he had been invited, he said,
officially to interfere he would have declined ; as it was, he
would bring Mr. Gladstone's statements to the notice of his
Sicilian majesty. Meanwhile, at great length, he reminded
Lord Aberdeen that a political offender may be the worst of all
offenders, and argued that the rigour exercised by England
herself in the Ionian Islands, in Ceylon, in respect of Irishmen,
and in the recent case of Ernest Jones, showed how careful she
should be in taking up abroad the cause of bad men posing as
martyrs in the holy cause of liberty.

During all these weeks, while Aberdeen was maturely considering, and while Prince Schwarzenberg was making his
secretaries hunt up recriminatory cases against England,
Mr. Gladstone was growing impatient. Lord Aberdeen begged
him to give the Austrian minister a little more time. It was
nearly four months since Mr. Gladstone landed at Dover, and
every day he thought of Poerio, Settembrini, and the rest,
wearing their double chains, subsisting on their foul soup,
degraded by forced companionship with criminals, cut off from
the light of heaven, and festering in their dungeons. The facts
that escaped from him in private conversation seemed to him
—so he tells Lacaita—to spread like wildfire from man to man,
exciting the liveliest interest, and extending to the highest
persons in the land. He waited a fortnight more, then at the
beginning of July he launched his thunderbolt, publishing his
Letter to Lord Aberdeen, followed by a second explanation and
enlargement a fortnight later.[1] He did not obtain formal leave
from Lord Aberdeen for the publication, but from their conversation took it for granted.

[1] The mere announcement caused such a demand that a second edition was required
almost before the first was published.

The sensation was profound, and not in England only. The Letters were translated into various tongues and had a large circulation. The Society of the Friends of Italy in London, the disciples of Mazzini (and a high-hearted band they were), besought him to become a member. Exiles wrote him letters of gratitude and hope, with all the moving accent of revolutionary illusion. Italian women composed fervid odes in fire and tears to the '*generoso britanno,*' the '*magnanimo cor,*' the '*difensore d'un popolo gemente.*' The press in this country took the matter up with the warmth that might have been expected. The character and the politics of the accuser added invincible force to his accusations, and for the first time in his life Mr. Gladstone found himself vehemently applauded in liberal prints. Even the contemporary excitement of English public feeling against the Roman catholic church fed the flame. It was pointed out that the King of Naples was the bosom friend of the pope, and that the infernal system described by Mr. Gladstone was that which the Roman clergy regarded as normal and complete.[1] Mr. Gladstone had denounced as one of the most detestable books he ever read a certain catechism used in the Neapolitan schools. Why then, cried the *Times*, does he omit all comment on the church which is the main and direct agent in this atrocious instruction? The clergy had either basely accepted from the government doctrines that they were bound to abhor, or else these doctrines were their own. And so things glided easily round to Dr. Cullen and the Irish education question. This line was none the less natural from the fact that the editor of the *Univers*, the chief catholic organ in France, made himself the foremost champion of the Neapolitan policy. The Letters delighted the Paris Reds. They regarded their own epithets as insipid by comparison with the ferocious adjectives of the English conservative. On the other hand, an English gentleman was blackballed at one of the fashionable clubs in Paris for no better reason than that he bore the name of Gladstone. For European conservatives read the letters with disgust and apprehension. People like Madame de Lieven pronounced Mr. Gladstone the dupe of men less honest than himself, and declared that he had injured the good cause and discredited his own fame, besides doing Lord Aberdeen the wrong of setting his name at the head of a detestable libel. The illustrious Guizot wrote Mr. Gladstone a long letter expressing, with much courtesy and kindness, his regret at the publication. Nothing is left in Italy, said Guizot, between the terrors of governments attacked in their very existence and the fury of the beaten revolutionists with hopes more alert than ever for destruction and chaos. The King of Naples on one side, Mazzini on the other ; such, said Guizot, is Italy. Between the King of Naples and Mazzini, he

[1] *Wesleyan Methodist Magazine*, October 1851. *Protestant Magazine*, September 1851.

for one did not hesitate. This was Mr. Gladstone's first contact
with the European party of order in the middle of the century.
Guizot was a great man, but '48 had perverted his generalising
intellect, and everywhere his jaundiced vision perceived in
progress a struggle for life and death with 'the revolutionary
spirit, blind, chimerical, insatiate, impracticable.' He avowed
his own failure when he was at the head of the French government, to induce the rulers of Italy to make reforms ; and now
the answer of Schwarzenberg to Lord Aberdeen, as well as the
official communications from Naples, showed that like Guizot's
French policy the Austrian remedy was moonshine.

Perhaps discomposed by the reproaches of reactionary friends
abroad, Lord Aberdeen thought he had some reason to complain
of the publication. It is not easy to see why. Mr. Gladstone
from the first insisted that if private remonstrance did not
work 'without elusion or delay,' he would make a public appeal.
In transmitting the first letter, he described in very specific
terms his idea that a short time would suffice to show whether
the private method could be relied upon.[1] The attitude of the
minister at Vienna, of Fortunato at Naples, and of Castelcicala
in London, discovered even to Aberdeen himself how little
reasonable hope there was of anything being done ; elusion
and delay was all that he could expect. He was forced to give
entire credit to Mr. Gladstone's horrible story, and was as far
as possible from thinking it a detestable libel. He never denied
the foundation of the case, or the actual state of the abominable
facts. Schwarzenberg never consented to comply with his
wishes even when writing before the publication. How then
could Aberdeen expect that Mr. Gladstone should abandon the
set and avowed purpose with which he had come flaming and
resolved to England ?

It was exactly because the party with which Mr. Gladstone
was allied had made itself the supporter of established governments throughout Europe, that in his eyes that party became
specially responsible for not passing by in silence any course of
conduct, even in a foreign country, flagrantly at variance with
right.[2] And what was there, when at last they arrived, in
Prince Schwarzenberg's idle dissertations and recriminations,
winding up with a still more idle sentence about bringing the
charges under the notice of the Neapolitan government, that
should induce Mr. Gladstone to abandon his purpose ? He had
something else to think of than the scandal to the reactionaries
of Europe. 'I wish it were in your power,' he writes to Lacaita
in May, 'to assure any of those directly interested, in my name,
that I am not unfaithful to them, and will use every means in
my power ; feeble they are, and I lament it ; but God is strong
and is just and good ; and the issue is in His hands.' That is

---

[1] Gladstone to Lord Aberdeen, September 16, 1851.
[2] Mr. Gladstone in an undated draft letter to Castelcicala.

what he was thinking of. When he talked of 'the sacred purposes of humanity' it was not artificial claptrap in a protocol.[1]

'When I consider,' Mr. Gladstone wrote to Lord Aberdeen, 'that Prince Schwarzenberg really knew the state of things at Naples well enough independently of me, and then ask myself why did he wait seven weeks before acknowledging a letter relating to the intense sufferings of human beings which were going on day by day and hour by hour, while his people were concocting all that trash about Frost and Ernest Jones and O'Brien, I cannot say that I think the spirit of the letter was creditable to him, or very promising as regards these people.' The Neapolitan government entered the field with a formal reply point by point, and Mr. Gladstone met them with a point by point rejoinder. The matter did not rest there. Soon after his arrival at home, he had had some conversation with John Russell, Palmerston, and other members of the government. They were much interested and not at all incredulous. Lord Palmerston's brother kept him too well informed about the state of things there for him to be sceptical. 'Gladstone and Molesworth,' wrote Palmerston, 'say that they were wrong last year in their attacks on my foreign policy, but they did not know the truth.'[2] Lord Palmerston directed copies of Mr. Gladstone's Letters to be sent to the British representatives in all the courts of Europe, with instructions to give a copy to each government. The Neapolitan envoy in London in his turn requested him also to send fifteen copies of the pamphlet that had been got up on the other side. Palmerston promptly, and in his most characteristic style, vindicated Mr. Gladstone against the charges of overstatement and hostile intention; warned the Neapolitan government of the violent revolution that long-continued and widespread injustice would assuredly bring upon them; hoped that they might have set to work to correct the manifold and grave abuses to which their attention had been drawn; and flatly refused to have anything to do with an official pamphlet 'consisting of a flimsy tissue of bare assertions and reckless denials, mixed up with coarse ribaldry and commonplace abuse.' This was the kind of thing that

[1] The one point on which Lord Aberdeen had a right to complain was that Mr. Gladstone did not take his advice. As the point revives in Lord Stanmore's excellent life of his father, it may be worth while to reproduce two further passages from Mr. Gladstone's letter to Lord Aberdeen of July 7, 1851. Before publishing the second of the two Letters, he wrote to Lord Aberdeen :—'I ought perhaps to have asked your formal permission for the act of publication ; but *I thought that I distinctly inferred it from a recent conversation with you as to the mode of proceeding*' (Mr. Gladstone to Lord Aberdeen, July 7, 1851). Then he proceeds as to the new supplementary publication :—'If it be disagreeable to you in any manner to be the recipient of such sad communications, or if you think it better for any other reason, I would put the further matter into another form.' In answer to this, Lord Aberdeen seems not to have done any more to refuse leave to associate his name with the second Letter, than he had done to withdraw the assumed leave for the association of his name with the first.

[2] Ashley, *Palmerston*, ii. p. 179.

gave to Lord Palmerston the best of his power over the people of England.

In the House of Commons he spoke with no less warmth. Though he had not felt it his duty, he said, to make representations at Naples on a matter relating to internal affairs, he thought Mr. Gladstone had done himself great honour. Instead of seeking amusements, diving into volcanoes and exploring excavated cities, he had visited prisons, descended into dungeons, examined cases of the victims of illegality and injustice, and had then sought to rouse the public opinion of Europe. It was because he concurred in this opinion that he had circulated the pamphlet, in the hope that the European courts might use their influence.[1] As Lord Aberdeen told Madame de Lieven, Mr. Gladstone's pamphlet by the extraordinary sensation it had created among men of all parties had given a great practical triumph to Palmerston and the foreign office.

The immediate effect of Mr. Gladstone's appeal was an aggravation of prison rigour. Panizzi was convinced that the king did not know of all the iniquities exposed by Mr. Gladstone. At the close of 1851 he obtained an interview with Ferdinand, and for twenty minutes spoke of Poerio, Settembrini and the condition of the prisons. The king suddenly cut short the interview, saying, *Addio, terribile Panizzi*.[2] Faint streaks of light from the outside world pierced the gloom of the dungeons. As time went on, a lady contrived to smuggle in a few pages of Mr. Gladstone's first Letter; and in 1854 the martyrs heard vaguely of the action of Cavour. But it was not until 1859 that the tyrant, fearing the cry of horror that would go up in Europe if Poerio should die in chains, or worse than death, should go mad, commuted prison to perpetual exile,[3] and sixty-six of them were embarked for America. At Lisbon they were transferred to an American ship; the captain, either intimidated or bribed, put in at Queenstown. 'In setting foot on this free soil,' Poerio wrote to Mr. Gladstone from the Irish haven (March 12, 1859), 'the first need of my heart was to seek news of you.' Communications were speedily opened. The Italians made their way to Bristol, where they were received with sympathy and applause by the population. The deliverance of their country was close at hand.

Not now, nor for many years to come, did Mr. Gladstone grasp the idea of Italian unity. It was impossible for him to ignore, but he did undoubtedly set aside, the fact that every shade and section of Italian liberalism from Farini on the right, to Mazzini on the furthest left, insisted on treating Italy as a political integer, and placed the independence of Italy and the expulsion of Austria from Italian soil as the first and

[1] August 7, 1851. *Hansard*, cxv. p. 1949.
[2] Fagan's *Life of Panizzi*, ii. pp. 102-3.
[3] On the share of Mr. Gladstone's Letters in leading indirectly to this decision, see the address of Baldacchini, *Della Vita e de' Tempi di Carlo Poerio* (1867), p. 58.

fundamental article in the creed of reform. Like most of the
English friends of the Italian cause at this time, except the
small but earnest group who rallied round the powerful moral
genius of Mazzini, he thought only of local freedom and local
reforms. 'The purely abstract idea of Italian nationality,' said
Mr. Gladstone at this time, 'makes little impression and finds
limited sympathy among ourselves.' 'I am certain,' he wrote
to Panizzi (June 21, 1851), 'that the Italian habit of preaching
unity and nationality in preference to showing grievances produces a revulsion here ; for if there are two things on earth
that John Bull hates, they are an abstract proposition and the
pope.' 'You need not be afraid, I think,' he told Lord Aberdeen (December 1, 1851), 'of Mazzinism from me, still less of
Kossuth-ism, which means the other *plus* imposture, Lord
Palmerston, and his nationalities.' But then in 1854 Manin
came to England, and failed to persuade even Lord Palmerston
that the unity of Italy was the only clue to her freedom.[1]
The Russian war made it inconvenient to quarrel with Austria
about Italy. With Mr. Gladstone he made more way. 'Seven
to breakfast to meet Manin,' says the diary ; 'he too is wild.'
Not too wild, however, to work conversion on his host. 'It was
my privilege,' Mr. Gladstone afterwards wrote, 'to welcome
Manin in London in 1854, when I had long been anxious for
reform in Italy, and it was from him that, in common with
some other Englishmen, I had my first lessons upon Italian
unity as the indispensable basis of all effectual reform under
the peculiar circumstances of that country.'[2] Yet the page of
Dante holds the lesson.

III

On one important element in the complex Italian case at
this time, Mr. Gladstone gained a clear view.

'Some things I have learned in Italy,' he wrote to Manning (*January*
26, 1851), 'that I did not know before, one in particular. The temporal
power of the pope, that great, wonderful and ancient erection, is *gone.*
The problem has been worked out—the ground is mined—the train is
laid—a foreign force, in its nature transitory, alone stays the hand of
those who would complete the process by applying the match. This
seems, rather than is, a digression. When that event comes, it will
bring about a great shifting of parts—much super- and much subter-
position. God grant it may be for good. I desire it, because I see
plainly that justice requires it. Not out of malice to the popedom ; for
I cannot at this moment dare to answer with a confident affirmative, the
question, a very solemn one—Ten, twenty, fifty years hence, will there
be any other body in western Christendom witnessing for fixed dogmatic
truth ? With all my heart I wish it well (though perhaps not wholly
what the consistory might think agreed with the meaning of the term)

1 *Gleanings*, iv. pp. 188, 195. Trans. of Farini, pref. p. ix.
2 To Dr. Errera, author of *A Life of Manin*, Sept. 28, 1872. For Manin's account,
see his *Life*, by Henri Martin, p. 377.

—it would be to me a joyous day in which I should see it really doing well.'

Various ideas of this kind set him to work on the large and curious enterprise, long since forgotten, of translating Farini's volumes on the Roman State from 1815 down to 1850. According to the entries in his diary he began and finished the translation of a large portion of the book at Naples in 1850—dictating and writing almost daily. Three of the four volumes of this English translation were done with extraordinary speed by Mr. Gladstone's own hand, and the fourth was done under his direction.[1] His object was, without any reference to Italian unity, to give an illustration of the actual working of the temporal power in its latest history. It is easy to understand how the theme fitted in with the widest topics of his life ; the nature of theocratic government ; the possibility (to borrow Cavour's famous phrase) of a free church in a free state ; and above all,—as he says to Manning now, and said to all the world twenty years later in the day of the Vatican decrees,—the mischiefs done to the cause of what he took for saving truth by evil-doing in the heart and centre of the most powerful of all the churches. His translation of Farini, followed by his article on the same subject in the *Edinburgh* in 1852, was his first blast against 'the covetous, domineering, implacable policy represented in the term Ultramontanism ; the winding up higher and higher, tighter and tighter, of the hierarchical spirit, in total disregard of those elements by which it ought to be checked and balanced ; and an unceasing, covert, smouldering war against human freedom, even in its most modest and retiring forms of private life and of the individual conscience.' With an energy not unworthy of Burke at his fiercest, he denounces the fallen and impotent regality of the popes as temporal sovereigns. 'A monarchy sustained by foreign armies, smitten with the curse of social barrenness, unable to strike root downward or bear fruit upward, the sun, the air, the rain soliciting in vain its sapless and rotten boughs—such a monarchy, even were it not a monarchy of priests, and tenfold more because it is one, stands out a foul blot upon the face of creation, an offence to Christendom and to mankind.'[2] As we shall soon see, he was just as wrathful, just as impassioned and as eloquent, when, in a memorable case in his own country, the temporal power bethought itself of a bill for meddling with the rights of a Roman voluntary church.

[1] The first two volumes were published by Mr. Murray in 1852, and the last two in 1854. '*June* 17, 1851.—Got my first copies of Farini. Sent No. 1 to the Prince ; and wrote with sad feelings in those for Hope and Manning.'—*Diary.*
[2] *Gleanings*, iv. pp. 160, 176.

CHAPTER VII

RELIGIOUS TORNADO—PEELITE DIFFICULTIES

(1851-1852)

I am always disposed to view with regret the rupture of party ties—my disposition is rather to maintain them. I confess I look, if not with suspicion, at least with disapprobation on any one who is disposed to treat party connections as matters of small importance. My opinion is that party ties closely appertain to those principles of confidence which we entertain for the House of Commons.—GLADSTONE (1852).

As we have seen, on the morning of his arrival from his Italian journey (February 26, 1851) Mr. Gladstone found that he was urgently required to meet Lord Stanley. Mortified by more than one repulse at the opening of the session, the whigs had resigned. The Queen sent for the protectionist leader. Stanley said that he was not then prepared to form a government, but that if other combinations failed, he would make the attempt. Lord John Russell was once more summoned to the palace, this time along with Aberdeen and Graham—the first move in a critical march towards the fated coalition between whigs and Peelites. The negotiation broke off on the No Popery bill; Lord John was committed to it, the other two strongly disapproved. The Queen next wished Aberdeen to undertake the task. Apparently not without some lingering doubts, he declined on the good ground that the House of Commons would not stand his attitude on papal aggression.[1] Then according to promise Lord Stanley tried his hand. Proceedings were suspended for some days until Mr. Gladstone should be on the ground. He no sooner reached Carlton Gardens, than Lord Lincoln arrived, eager to dissuade him from accepting office. Before the discussion had gone far, the tory whip hurried in from Stanley, begging for an immediate visit.

'I promised,' says Mr. Gladstone, 'to go directly after seeing Lord Aberdeen. But he came back with a fresh message to go at once, and

[1] 'He had told the Queen that he thought all the offices might be filled in a respectable manner from among the members of the Peel administration. On a subsequent day both Herbert and Cardwell made out from his conversation what I did not clearly catch, namely that Lord Aberdeen himself would have acted on the Queen's wish, and that Graham had either suggested the difficulty altogether, or at any rate got it put forward into its position.'—Gladstone Memo., April 22, 1851.

hear what Stanley had to say. I did not like to stickle, and went. He told me his object was that I should take office with him—*any* office, subject to the reservation that the foreign department was offered to Canning, but if he declined it was open to me, along with others of which he named the colonial office and the board of trade. Nothing was said of the leadership of the House of Commons, but his anxiety was evident to have any occupant but one for the foreign office. I told him, I should ask no questions and make no remark on these points, as none of them would constitute a difficulty with me, provided no preliminary obstacle were found to intervene. Stanley then said that he proposed to maintain the system of free trade generally, but to put a duty of five or six shillings on corn. I heard him pretty much in silence, but with an intense sense of relief; feeling that if he had put protection in abeyance, I might have had a most difficult question to decide, whereas now I had no question at all. I thought, however, it might be well that I should still see Lord Aberdeen before giving him an answer; and told him I would do so. I asked him also what was his intention with respect to papal aggression. He said that this measure was hasty and intemperate as well as ineffective; and that he thought something much better might result from a comprehensive and deliberate inquiry. I told him I was utterly against all penal legislation and against the ministerial bill, but that I did not on principle object to inquiry; that, on general as well as on personal grounds, I wished well to his undertaking; and that I would see Lord Aberdeen, but that what he had told me about corn constituted, I must not conceal from him, "an enormous difficulty." I used this expression for the purpose of preparing him to receive the answer it was plain I must give; he told me his persevering would probably depend on me.'

Mr. Gladstone next hastened to Lord Aberdeen, and learned what had been going on during his absence abroad. He learned also the clear opinions held by Aberdeen and Graham against No Popery legislation, and noticed it as remarkable that so many minds should arrive independently at the same conclusion on a new question, and in opposition to the overwhelming majority. 'I then,' he continues, 'went on to the levee, saw Lord Normanby and others, and began to bruit abroad the fame of the Neapolitan government. Immediately after leaving the levee (where I also saw Canning, told him what I meant to do, and gathered that he would do the like), I changed my clothes and went to give Lord Stanley my answer, at which he did not show the least surprise. He said he would still persevere, though with little hope. I think I told him it seemed to me he ought to do so. I was not five minutes with him this second time.'[1]

The protectionists having failed, and the Peelites standing aside, the whigs came back, most of them well aware that they could not go on for long. The events of the late crisis had given Mr. Gladstone the hope that Graham would effectively place himself at the head of the Peelites, and that they would now at length begin to take an independent course of their

[1] Memorandum, dated Fasque, April 22, 1851.

own. 'But it soon appeared that, unconsciously I think more
than consciously, he is set upon the object of avoiding the
responsibility either of taking the government with the Peel
squadron, or of letting in Stanley and his friends.' Here was
the weak point in a strong and capable character. When
Graham died ten years after this (1861), Mr. Gladstone wrote to
a friend, 'On administrative questions, for the last twenty
years and more, I had more spontaneous recourse to him for
advice, than to all other colleagues together.' In some of the
foundations of character no two men could be more unlike.
One of his closest allies talks to Graham of 'your sombre
temperament.' 'My forebodings are always gloomy,' says
Graham himself; 'I shudder on the brink of the torrent.' All
accounts agree that he was a good counsellor in cabinet, a first-
rate manager of business, a good if rather pompous speaker,
admirably loyal and single-minded, but half-ruined by intense
timidity. I have heard nobody use warmer language of com-
mendation about him than Mr. Bright. But nature had not
made him for a post of chief command.

It by and by appeared that the Duke of Newcastle, known to
us hitherto as Lord Lincoln, coveted the post of leader, but
Mr. Gladstone thought that on every ground Lord Aberdeen
was the person entitled to hold it. 'I made,' says Mr. Gladstone,
'my views distinctly known to the duke. He took no offence.
I do not know what communications he may have held with
others. But the upshot was that Lord Aberdeen became our
leader. And this result was obtained without any shock or
conflict.'[1]

II

In the autumn of 1850 the people of this country were
frightened out of their senses by a document from the Vatican,
dividing England into dioceses bearing territorial titles and
appointing Cardinal Wiseman to be Archbishop of Westminster.
The uproar was tremendous. Lord John Russell cast fuel upon
the flame in a perverse letter to the Bishop of Durham (Nov. 4,
1850). In this unhappy document he accepted the description
of the aggression of the pope upon our protestantism as insolent
and insidious, declared his indignation to be greater even than
his alarm, and even his alarm at the aggressions of a foreign
sovereign to be less than at the conduct of unworthy sons of the
church of England within her own gates. He wound up by
declaring that the great mass of the nation looked with contempt upon the mummeries of superstition. Justified indeed
was Bright's stern rebuke to a prime minister of the Queen who
thus allowed himself to offend and to indict eight millions of
his countrymen, recklessly to create fresh discords between the
Irish and English nations, and to perpetuate animosities that

[1] Memorandum, Sept. 9, 1897.

the last five-and-twenty years had done so much to assuage.
Having thus precipitately committed himself, the minister was
forced to legislate. 'I suspect,' wrote Mr. Gladstone to his
great friend, Sir Walter James, 'John Russell has more rocks
and breakers ahead than he reckoned upon when he dipped his
pen in gall to smite first the pope, but most those who not being
papists are such traitors and fools as really to mean something
when they say, "I believe in one Holy Catholic Church."'
There was some division of opinion in the cabinet,[1] but a bill
was settled, and the temper of the times may be gauged by the
fact that leave to introduce it was given by the overwhelming
majority of 395 votes to 63.

In his own language, Mr. Gladstone lamented and disapproved
of the pope's proceeding extremely, and had taken care to say
so in parliament two and a half years before, when 'Lord John
Russell, if he had chosen, could have stopped it ; but the government and the press were alike silent at that period.'[2] His
attitude is succinctly described in a letter to Greswell, his
Oxford chairman, in 1852 : 'Do not let it be asserted without
contradiction that I ever felt or counselled indifference in
regard to the division of England into Romish dioceses. So
far is this from being the truth that shortly after I was elected,
when the government were encouraging the pope to proceed, and
when there was yet time to stop the measure (which I deplore
sincerely) by amicable means, I took the opportunity in the
House (as did Sir R. Inglis, I *think* a little later), of trying to
draw attention to it. But it was nobody's game then, and the
subject fell to the ground. Amicable prevention I desired ;
spiritual and ecclesiastical resistance I heartily approved ; but
while I say this, I cannot recede from one inch of the ground
I took in opposing the bill, and I would far rather quit parliament for ever than not have voted against so pernicious a
measure.'

Other matters, as we have seen, brought on a ministerial
crisis, the bill was stopped, and after the crisis was over the
measure came to life again with changes making it still more
futile for its ends. The Peelites while, like Mr. Bright, 'despising
and loathing' the language of the Vatican and the Flaminian
Gate, had all of them without concert taken this outburst of
prejudice and passion at its right value, and all resolved to
resist legislation. How, they asked, could you tolerate the
Roman catholic religion, if you would not tolerate its tenet of
the ecclesiastical supremacy of the pope ; and what sort of
toleration of such a tenet would that be, which forbade the
pope to name ecclesiastics to exercise the spiritual authority
exercised in any other voluntary episcopal church, Scottish,
colonial, or another ? Why was it more of a usurpation for
the pope to make a new Archbishop of Westminster, than to

---

[1] *Grey Papers.*   [2] To Phillimore, Nov. 26, 1850.

administer London by the old form of vicars apostolic? Was
not the action of the pope, after all, a secondary consideration,
and the frenzy really and in essence an explosion of popular
wrath against the Puseyites? What was to be thought of a
prime minister who, at such risk to the public peace, tried to
turn the ferment to account for the sake of strengthening his
tottering government? To all this there was no rational reply;
and even the editor of a powerful newspaper that every morning
blew up the coals, admitted to Greville that 'he thought the
whole thing humbug and a pack of nonsense!'[1]

The debate on the second reading was marked by a little
brutality and much sanctimony. Mr. Gladstone (March 25,
1851), spoke to a House practically almost solid against him.
Yet his superb resources as an orator, his transparent depth of
conviction, the unmistakable proofs that his whole heart was
in the matter, mastered his audience and made the best of
them in their hearts ashamed. He talked of Boniface VIII.
and Honorius IV.; he pursued a long and close historical
demonstration of the earnest desire of the lay catholics of
this country for diocesan bishops as against vicars apostolic;
he moved among bulls and rescripts, briefs and pastorals and
canon law, with as much ease as if he had been arguing
about taxes and tariffs. Through it all the House watched
and listened in enchantment, as to a magnificent tragedian
playing a noble part in a foreign tongue. They did not
apprehend every point, nor were they converted, but they
felt a man with the orator's quality of taking fire and kindling
fire at a moral idea. They felt his command of the whole
stock of fact and of principle belonging to his topics, as with the
air and the power of a heroic master he cleared the way before
him towards his purpose. Along with complete grasp of details,
went grasp of some of the most important truths in the policy
of a modern state. He clearly perceived the very relevant fact,
so often overlooked by advocates of the free church in a free
state, that 'there is no religious body in the world where
religious offices do not in a certain degree conjoin with temporal incidents.' But this did not affect the power of his stroke,
as he insisted on respect for the frontier—no scientific frontier
—between temporal and spiritual. 'You speak of the progress
of the Roman catholic religion, and you pretend to meet that
progress by a measure false in principle as it is ludicrous in
extent. You must meet the progress of that spiritual system
by the progress of another; you can never do it by penal
enactments. Here, once for all, I enter my most solemn,
earnest, and deliberate protest against all attempts to meet
the spiritual dangers of our church by temporal legislation
of a penal character.' The whole speech is in all its elements
and aspects one of the great orator's three or four most

[1] Greville, Part II. vol. iii. p. 369.

conspicuous masterpieces, and the reader would not forgive me if I failed to transcribe its resplendent close. He went back to a passage of Lord John Russell's on the Maynooth bill of 1845. 'I never heard,' said Mr. Gladstone, 'a more impressive passage delivered by any statesman at any time in this House.'

The noble lord referred to some beautiful and touching lines of Virgil, which the house will not regret to hear :—

> 'Scilicet et tempus veniet, cum finibus illis
> Agricola, incurvo terram molitus aratro,
> Exesa inveniet scabra rubigine pila ;
> Aut gravibus rastris galeas pulsabit inanes,
> Grandiaque effossis mirabitur ossa sepulcris.' [1]

And he said, upon those scenes where battles have been fought, the hand of nature effaces the traces of the wrath of man, and the cultivator of the soil in following times finds the rusted arms, and looks upon them with calm and joy, as the memorials of forgotten strife, and as quickening his sense of the blessings of his peaceful occupation. The noble lord went on to say, in reference to the powerful opposition then offered to the bill for the endowment of Maynooth, that it seems as if upon the questions of religious freedom, our strife is never to cease, and our arms are never to rust. Would any man, who heard the noble lord deliver these impressive sentiments, have believed not only that the strife with respect to religious liberty was to be revived with a greater degree of acerbity, in the year 1851, but that the noble lord himself was to be a main agent in its revival—that his was to be the head that was to wear the helmet, and his the hand that was to grasp the spear ? My conviction is, that this great subject of religious freedom is not to be dealt with as one of the ordinary matters in which you may, with safety or with honour, do to-day, and un-do to-morrow. This great people whom we have the honour to represent, moves slowly in politics and legislation ; but, although it moves slowly, it moves steadily.   The principle of religious freedom, its adaptation to our modern state, and its compatibility with ancient institutions, was a principle which you did not adopt in haste.   It was a principle well tried in struggle and conflict. It was a principle which gained the assent of one public man after another. It was a principle which ultimately triumphed, after you had spent upon it half a century of agonising struggle. And now what are you going to do ? You have arrived at the division of the century. Are you going to repeat Penelope's process, but without the purpose of Penelope ? Are you going to spend the decay and the dusk of the nineteenth century in undoing the great work which with so much pain and difficulty your greatest men have been achieving during its daybreak and its youth ? Surely not. Oh, recollect the functions you have to perform in the face of the world. Recollect that Europe and the whole of the civilised world look to England at this moment not less, no, but even more than ever they looked to her before, as the mistress and guide of nations, in regard to the great work of civil legislation. And what is it they

---

[1] *Georgics*, i. 493-7.   'Aye, and time will come when the husbandman with bent ploughshare upturning the clods, shall find all corroded by rusty scurf the Roman pikeheads ; shall strike with heavy rake on empty helms, and gaze in wonder on giant bones cast from their broken graves.'

chiefly admire in England? It is not the rapidity with which you form constitutions and broach abstract theories. On the contrary, they know that nothing is so distasteful to you as abstract theories, and that you are proverbial for resisting what is new until you are well assured by gradual effort, by progressive trials, and beneficial tendency. But they know that when you make a step forward you keep it. They know that there is reality and honesty, strength and substance, about your proceedings. They know that you are not a monarchy to-day, a republic to-morrow, and a military despotism the day after. They know that you have been happily preserved from irrational vicissitudes that have marked the career of the greatest and noblest among the neighbouring nations. Your fathers and yourselves have earned this brilliant character for England. Do not forfeit it. Do not allow it to be tarnished or impaired. Show, I beseech you—have the courage to show the pope of Rome, and his cardinals, and his church, that England too, as well as Rome, has her *semper eadem*; and that when she has once adopted some great principle of legislation, which is destined to influence the national character, to draw the dividing lines of her policy for ages to come, and to affect the whole nature of her influence and her standing among the nations of the world—show that when she has done this slowly, and done it deliberately, she has done it once for all; and that she will then no more retrace her steps than the river that bathes this giant city can flow back upon its source. The character of England is in our hands. Let us feel the responsibility that belongs to us, and let us rely on it; if to-day we make this step backwards, it is one which hereafter we shall have to retrace with pain. We cannot change the profound and resistless tendencies of the age towards religious liberty. It is our business to guide and to control their application; do this you may, but to endeavour to turn them backwards is the sport of children, done by the hands of men, and every effort you may make in that direction will recoil upon you in disaster and disgrace. The noble lord appealed to gentlemen who sit behind me, in the names of Hampden and Pym. I have great reverence for these in one portion at least of their political career, because they were men energetically engaged in resisting oppression. But I would rather have heard Hampden and Pym quoted on any other subject than one which relates to the mode of legislation or the policy to be adopted with our Roman catholic fellow-citizens, because, if there was one blot on their escutcheon, if there was one painful—I would almost say odious—feature in the character of the party among whom they were the most distinguished chiefs, it was the bitter and ferocious intolerance which in them became the more powerful because it was directed against the Roman catholics alone. I would appeal in other names to gentlemen who sit on this side of the House. If Hampden and Pym were friends of freedom, so were Clarendon and Newcastle, so were the gentlemen who sustained the principles of loyalty. . . . They were not always seeking to tighten the chains and deepen the brand. Their disposition was to relax the severity of the law, and attract the affections of their Roman catholic fellow-subjects to the constitution by treating them as brethren. . . . We are a minority insignificant in point of numbers. We are more insignificant still, because we are but knots and groups of two or three, we have no power of cohesion, no ordinary bond of union. What is it that binds us together against you, but the conviction that we have on our side the

principle of justice—the conviction that we shall soon have on our side
the strength of public opinion (*oh, oh !*). I am sure I have not wished
to say a syllable that would wound the feelings of any man, and if in the
warmth of argument such expressions should have escaped me, I wish
them unsaid. But above all we are sustained by the sense of justice
which we feel belongs to the cause we are defending; and we are, I trust,
well determined to follow that bright star of justice, beaming from the
heavens, whithersoever it may lead.

All this was of no avail, just as the same arguments and
temper on two other occasions of the same eternal theme
in his life,[1] were to be of no avail. Disraeli spoke strongly
against the line taken by the Peelites. The second reading
was carried by 438 against 95, one-third even of this minority
being Irish catholics, and the rest mainly Peelites, 'a limited
but accomplished school,' as Disraeli styled them. Hume
asked Mr. Gladstone for his speech for publication to circulate
among the dissenters who, he said, know nothing about
religious liberty. It was something, however, to find Mr.
Gladstone, the greatest living churchman, and Bright, the
greatest living nonconformist, voting in the same lobby.
The fight was stiff, and was kept up until the end of the
summer. The weapon that had been forged in this blazing
furnace by these clumsy armourers proved blunt and worth-
less ; the law was from the first a dead letter, and it was
struck out of the statute book in 1871 in Mr. Gladstone's
own administration.[2]

III

In the autumn (1851) a committee of the whig cabinet,
now reinforced by the admission for the first time of Lord
Granville, was named to prepare a reform bill. Palmerston,
no friend to reform, fell into restive courses that finally
upset the coach. The cabinet, early in November, settled
that he should not receive Kossuth, and he complied ; but
he received a public deputation and an address compliment-
ing him for his exertions on Kossuth's behalf. The court
at this proceeding took lively offence, and the Queen
requested the prime minister to ascertain the opinion of the
cabinet upon it. Such an appeal by the sovereign from the
minister to the cabinet was felt by them to be unconstitu-

---

[1] Affirmation bill (1883) and Religious Disabilities Removal bill (1891).

[2] One of the most illustrious of the European liberals of the century wrote to
Senior :—
  Ce que vous me dites que le bill contre les titres ecclésiastiques ne mènera à
rien, me paraît vraisemblable, grâce aux mœurs du pays. Mais pourquoi faire des
lois pires que les mœurs ? C'est le contraire qui devait être. Je vous avoue que
j'ai été de cœur et d'esprit avec ceux qui comme Lord Aberdeen et M. Gladstone,
se sont opposés au nom de la liberté et du principe même de la réforme, à ces
atteintes à la fois vaines et dangereuses que le bill a portées au moins en théorie à
l'indépendance de conscience. Où se réfugiera la liberté religieuse, si on la chasse
de l'Angleterre ?—Tocqueville, *Corr.* iii. p. 274.

tional, and though they did not conceal from Palmerston their general dissatisfaction, they declined to adopt any resolution. Before the year ended Palmerston persisted in taking an unauthorised line of his own upon Napoleon's *coup d'état* (this time for once not on the side of freedom against despotism), and Lord John closed a correspondence between them by telling him that he could not advise the Queen to leave the seals of the foreign department any longer in his hands. This dismissal of Palmerston introduced a new element of disruption and confusion, for the fallen minister had plenty of friends. Lord Lansdowne was very uneasy about reform, and talked ominously about preferring to be a supporter rather than a member of the government; and whig dissensions, though less acute in type, threatened a perplexity as sharp in the way of a stable administration, as the discords among conservatives.

Lord John (Jan. 14, 1852) next asked his cabinet whether an offer should be made to Graham. A long discussion followed; whether Graham alone would do them any good; whether the Peelites, considering themselves as a party, might join, but would not consent to be absorbed; whether an offer to them was to be a persistent attempt in good faith or only a device to mend the parliamentary case, if the offer were made and refused. Two or three of the whig ministers, true to the church traditions of the caste, made great difficulties about the Puseyite notions of Newcastle and Mr. Gladstone. 'Gladstone,' writes one of them, 'is a Jesuit, and more Peelite than I believe was Peel himself.' In the end Lord John Russell and his men met parliament without any new support. Their tottering life was short, and it was an amendment moved by Palmerston (Feb. 20) on a clause in a militia bill, that slit the thread. The hostile majority was only eleven, but other perils lay pretty thick in front. The ministers resigned, and Lord Stanley, who had now become Earl of Derby, had no choice but to give his followers their chance. The experiment that seemed so impossible when Bentinck first tried it, of forming a new third party in the state, seemed up to this point to have prospered, and the protectionists had a definite existence. The ministers were nearly all new to public office, and seventeen of them were for the first time sworn of the privy council in a single day. One jest was that the cabinet consisted of three men and a half—Derby, Disraeli, St. Leonards, and a worthy fractional personage at the admiralty.

Sending to his wife at Hawarden a provisional list (Feb. 23), Mr. Gladstone doubts the way in which the offices were distributed :—'It is not good, as compared I mean with what it should have been. Disraeli could not have been worse placed than at the exchequer. Henley could not have been

worse than at the board of trade. T. Baring, who would
have been their best chancellor of the exchequer, seems to
have declined. Herries would have been much better than
Disraeli for that particular place. I suppose Lord Malmesbury is temporary foreign secretary, to hold the place for
S. Canning. What does not appear on the face of the case
is, who is to lead the House of Commons, and about that
everybody seems to be in the dark.'

IV

The first Derby administration, thus formed and covering
the year 1852, marks a highly interesting stage in Mr.
Gladstone's career. 'The key to my position,' as he afterwards said, 'was that my opinions went one way, my lingering
sympathies the other.' His opinions looked towards liberalism,
his sympathies drew him to his first party. It was the Peelites
who had now been thrown into the case of a dubious third
party. At the end of February Mr. Gladstone sought Lord
Aberdeen, looking 'to his weight, his prudence, and his.
kindliness of disposition as the main anchor of their section.
His tone has usually been, during the last few years, that of
anxiety to reunite the fragments and reconstruct the conservative party, but yesterday, particularly at the commencement
of our conversation, he seemed to lean the other way ; spoke
kindly of Lord Derby and wished that *he* could be extricated
from the company with which he is associated ; said that
though called a despot all his life, he himself had always been,
and was now, friendly to a liberal policy. He did not, however, like the reform question in Lord John's hands ; but he
considered, I thought (and if so he differed from me), that on
church questions we all might co-operate with him securely.'
Mr. Gladstone, on the contrary, insisted that their duty plainly
was to hold themselves clear and free from whig and Derbyite
alike, so as to be prepared to take whatever of three courses
might, after the defeat of protectionist proposals, seem most
honourable — whether conservative reconstruction, or liberal
conjunction, or Peelism single-handed. The last he described
as their least natural position ; for, he urged, they might be
'liberal in the sense of Peel, working out a liberal policy
through the medium of the conservative party.' To that pro-
crastinating view Mr. Gladstone stood tenaciously, and his
course now is one of the multitudinous illustrations of his
constant abhorrence of premature committal, and the taking
of a second step before the first.

After Aberdeen he approached Graham, who proceeded to
use language that seemed to point to his virtual return to his
old friends of the liberal party, for the reader will not forget
the striking circumstance that the new head of a conservative

government, and the most trusted of the cabinet colleagues of Peel, had both of them begun official life in the reform ministry of Lord Grey. Graham said he had a very high opinion of Lord Derby's talents and character, and that Lord J. Russell had committed many errors, but that looking at the two as they stood, he thought that the opinions of Lord Derby as a whole were more dangerous to the country than those of Lord John. Mr. Gladstone said it did not appear to him that the question lay between these two ; but Graham's reception of this remark implied a contrary opinion.

Lincoln, now Duke of Newcastle, he found obdurate in another direction, speaking with great asperity against Lord Derby and his party ; he would make no vows as to junction, not even that he would not join Disraeli ; but he thought this government must be opposed and overthrown ; then those who led the charge against it would reap the reward ; if the Peelites did not place themselves in a prominent position, others would. They had a further conversation. The duke told him that Beresford, the whip, had sent out orders to tory newspapers to run them down ; that the same worthy had said 'The Peelites, let them go to hell.' Mr. Gladstone replied that Beresford's language was not a good test of the feelings of his party, and that his violence and that of other people was stimulated by what they imagined or heard of the Peelites. Newcastle persisted in his disbelief in the government. 'During this conversation, held on a sofa at the Carlton, we were rather warm ; and I said to him, "It appears to me that you do not believe this party to be composed even of men of honour or of gentlemen." . . . He clung to the idea that we were hereafter to form a party of our own, containing all the good elements of both parties. To which I replied, the country cannot be governed by a third or middle party unless it be for a time only, and on the whole I thought a liberal policy would be worked out with greater security to the country through the medium of the conservative party, and I thought a position like Peel's on the liberal side of that party preferable, comparing all advantages and disadvantages, to the conservative side of the liberal party. And when he spoke of the tories as the obstructive body I said not all of them—for instance Mr. Pitt, Mr. Canning, Mr. Huskisson, and in some degree Lord Londonderry and Lord Liverpool.'

The upshot of all these discussions was the discovery that there were at least four distinct shades among the Peelites. 'Newcastle stands nearly alone, if not quite, in the rather high-flown idea that we are to create and lead a great, virtuous, powerful intelligent party, neither the actual conservative nor the actual liberal party but a new one. Apart from these witcheries, Graham was ready to take his place in the liberal ranks ; Cardwell, Fitzroy and Oswald would I think have gone

with him, as F. Peel and Sir C. Douglas went before him.
But this section has been arrested, not thoroughly amalga-
mated, owing to Graham. Thirdly, there are the great bulk of
the Peelites from Goulburn downwards, more or less un-
disguisedly anticipating junction with Lord Derby, and
avowing that free trade is their only point of difference.
Lastly myself, and I think I am with Lord Aberdeen and
S. Herbert, who have nearly the same desire, but feel that the
matter is too crude, too difficult and important for anticipating
any conclusion, and that our clear line of duty is independence,
until the question of protection shall be settled.' (March 28,
1852.)

The personal composition of this section deserves a sentence.
In 1835, during Peel's short government, the whig phalanx
opposed to it in the House of Commons consisted of John
Russell and seven others.[1] Of these eight all were alive in
1851, seven of them in the then existing cabinet; six of the
eight still in the Commons. On the other hand, Peel's cabinet
began its career thus manned in the Commons—Peel, Stanley,
Graham, Hardinge, Knatchbull, Goulburn. Of these only the
last remained in his old position. Peel and Knatchbull were
dead; Stanley in the Lords and separated; Graham isolated;
Hardinge in the Lords and by way of having retired. Nor was
the band very large even as recruited. Of ex-cabinet ministers
there were but three commoners; Goulburn, Herbert, Gladstone. And of others who had held important offices there
were only available, Clerk, Cardwell, Sir J. Young, H. Corry.
The Lords contributed Aberdeen, Newcastle, Canning,[2] St.
Germans and the Duke of Argyll. Such, as counted off by
Mr. Gladstone, was the Peelite staff.

Graham in April made his own position definitely liberal, or
'whig and something more,' in so pronounced a way as to cut
him off from the Gladstonian subdivision or main body of the
Peelites. Mr. Gladstone read the speech in which this departure was taken, 'with discomfort and surprise.' He instantly
went to read to Lord Aberdeen some of the more pungent
passages; one or two consultations were held with Newcastle
and Goulburn; and all agreed that Graham's words were
decisive. 'I mentioned that some of them were coming to
5 Carlton Gardens in the course of the afternoon (April 20);
and my first wish was that now Lord Aberdeen himself would
go and tell them how we stood upon Graham's speech. To this
they were all opposed; and they seemed to feel that as we had
had no meeting yet, it would seem ungracious and unkind to

---

[1] Namely Palmerston, Spring-Rice, F. Baring, Charles Wood, Hobhouse, Labouchere,
Lord Howick.

[2] This, of course, was Charles John Earl Canning, third son of Canning the prime
minister, Mr. Gladstone's contemporary at Eton and Christ Church, and known to
history as governor-general of India in the Mutiny. Stratford Canning, afterwards
Lord Stratford de Redcliffe, was cousin of George Canning.

an old friend to hold one by way of ovation over his departure. It was therefore agreed that I should acquaint Young it was their wish that he should tell any one who might come, that we, who were there present, looked upon our political connection with Graham as dissolved by the Carlisle speech.'[1]

The temporary parting from Graham was conducted with a degree of good feeling that is a pattern for such occasions in politics. In writing to Mr. Gladstone (Mar. 29, 1852), and speaking of his colleagues in Peel's government, Graham says, 'I have always felt that my age and position were different from theirs : that the habits and connexions of my early political life, though broken, gave to me a bias, which to them was not congenial ; and since the death of our great master and friend, I have always feared that the time might arrive when we must separate. You intimate the decision that party connexion must no longer subsist between us. I submit to your decision with regret ; but at parting I hope that you will retain towards me some feelings of esteem and regard, such as I can never cease to entertain towards you ; and though political friendships are often short-lived, having known each other well, we shall continue, I trust, to maintain kindly relations. It is a pleasure to me to remember that we have no cause of complaint against each other.' 'I have to thank you,' Mr. Gladstone replies, 'for the unvarying kindness of many years, to acknowledge all the advantages I have derived from communication with you, to accept and re-echo cordially your expressions of good-will, and to convey the fervent hope that no act or word of mine may ever tend to impair these sentiments in my own mind or yours.'

When the others had withdrawn, Aberdeen told Mr. Gladstone that Lord John had been to call upon him the day before for the first time, and he believed that the visit had special reference to Mr. Gladstone himself. 'The tenour of his conversation,' Mr. Gladstone reports, 'was that my opinions were quite as liberal as his ; that in regard to the colonies I went beyond him ; that my Naples pamphlets could have been called revolutionary if he had written them ; and in regard to church matters he saw no reason why there should not be joint action, for he was cordially disposed to maintain the church of England, and so, he believed, was I.' Lord John, however, we may be sure was the last man not to know how many another element, besides agreement in opinion, decides relations of party. Personal sympathies and antipathies, hosts of indirect affinities having apparently little to do with the main trunk of the school or the faction, hosts of motives only half disclosed, or

[1] Graham spoke of himself as a tried reformer and as a member of the liberal party, and as glad to find himself the ally of so faithful a liberal and reformer as his fellow-candidate. He would not exactly pledge himself to support the ballot, but he admitted it was a hard question, and said he was not so blind that practical experience might not convince him that he was wrong. (Mar. 26, 1852.)

not disclosed at all even to him in whom they are at work—all
these intrude in the composition and management of parties
whether religious or political.

Grave discussions turned on new nicknames. The tories had
greatly gained by calling themselves conservatives after 1832.
The name of whig had some associations that were only less unpopular in the country than the name of tory. It was pointed
out that many people would on no account join the whigs, who
yet would join a government of which Russells, Greys, Howards,
Cavendishes, Villierses, were members On the other hand
Graham declared that Paley's maxim about religion was just
as true in politics—that men often change their creed, but not
so often the name of their sect. And as to the suggestion, constantly made at all times in our politics for the benefit of
waverers, of the name of liberal-conservative, Lord John
caustically observed that whig has the convenience of expressing in one syllable what liberal-conservative expresses in seven,
and whiggism in two syllables what conservative progress
expresses in six.

Connected with all this arose a geographical question—in
what quarter of the House were the Peelites to sit? Hitherto
the two wings of the broken tory party, protectionist and Peelite, had sat together on the opposition benches. The change
of administration in 1852 sent the protectionists over to the
Speaker's right, and brought the whigs to the natural place of
opposition on his left. The Peelite leaders therefore had no
other choice than to take their seats below the gangway, but
on which side? Such a question is always graver than to the
heedless outsider it may seem, and the Peelite discussions upon
it were both copious and vehement.[1] Graham at once resolved
on sharing the front opposition bench with the whigs: he
repeated that his own case was different from the others,
because he had once been a whig himself. Herbert, who acted
pretty strictly with Mr. Gladstone all this year, argued that
they only held aloof from the new ministers on one question,
and therefore that they ought not to sit opposite to them as
adversaries, but should sit below the gangway on the ministerial
side. Newcastle intimated dissent from both, looking to the
formation of his virtuous and enlightened third party, but
where they should sit in the meantime he did not seem to know.
Mr. Gladstone expressed from the first a decided opinion in
favour of going below the gangway on the opposition side.
What they ought to desire was the promotion of a government
conservative in its personal composition and traditions, as soon
as the crisis of protection should be over. Taking a seat, he
said, is an external sign and pledge that ought to follow upon
full conviction of the thing it was understood to betoken ; and

---

[1] The same question greatly exercised Mr. Gladstone's mind in 1886 for the same
reason, that he again hoped for the reunion of a divided party.

to sit on the front opposition bench would indicate division
from the conservative government as a party, while in fact
they were not divided from them as a party, but only on a
single question. In the end, Graham sat above the opposition
gangway next to Lord John Russell and Cardwell. The Peelite
body as a whole determined on giving the new government
what is called a fair trial. 'Mr. Sidney Herbert and I,' says
Mr. Gladstone, 'took pains to bring them together, in the
recognised modes. They sat on the opposition side, but below
the gangway, full, or about forty strong; and Sir James
Graham, I recollect, once complimented me on the excellent
appearance they had presented to him as he passed them in
walking up the House.' Considerable uneasiness was felt
among some of them at finding themselves neighbours on the
benches to Cobden and Bright and Hume and their friends on
the one hand, and 'the Irish Brass Band' on the other.

It depended entirely on the Peelites whether the new government should be permitted to conduct the business of the session
(subject to conditions or otherwise), or whether they should be
open to an instant attack as the enemies of free trade. The
effect of such attack must have been defeat, followed by dissolution forthwith, and by the ejection of the Derby government in June (as happened in 1859) instead of in December.
The tactics of giving the ministers a fair trial prevailed and
were faithfully adhered to, Graham and Cardwell taking their
own course. As the result of this and other conditions, for ten
months ministers, greatly outnumbered, were maintained in
power by the deliberate and united action of about forty
Peelites.

Lord Derby had opened his administration with a pledge, as
the Peelites understood, to confine himself during the session to
business already open and advanced, or of an urgent character.
When Mr. Disraeli gave notice of a bill to dispose of four seats
which were vacant, this was regarded by them as a manner of
opening new and important issues, and not within the definition
that had been the condition of their provisional support.[1]
'Lord John Russell came and said to me,' says Mr. Gladstone,
'"What will you do?" I admitted we were bound to act; and,
joining the liberals, we threw over the proposal by a large
majority. This was the only occasion of conflict that arose;
and it was provoked, as we thought, by the government itself.'

[1] This was a bill to assign the four disfranchised seats for Sudbury and St. Albans
to the West Riding of Yorkshire and the southern division of Lancashire. Mr. Gladstone carried the order of the day by a majority of 86 against the government.

CHAPTER VIII

END OF PROTECTION

(1852)

It is not too much to ask that now at least, after so much waste of public time, after ministries overturned and parties disorganised, the question of free trade should be placed high and dry on the shore whither the tide of political party strife could no longer reach it.—GLADSTONE.

THE parliament was now dissolved (July 1) to decide a great question. The repeal of the corn law, the ultimate equalisation of the sugar duties, the repeal of the navigation laws, had been the three great free trade measures of the last half-dozen years, and the issue before the electors in 1852 was whether this policy was sound or unsound. Lord Derby might have faced it boldly by announcing a moderate protection for corn and for colonial sugar. Or he might have openly told the country that he had changed his mind, as Peel had changed his mind about the catholic question and about free trade, and as Mr. Disraeli was to change his mind upon franchise in 1867, and Mr. Gladstone upon the Irish church in 1868. Instead of this, all was equivocation. The Derbyite, as was well said, was protectionist in a county, neutral in a small town, free trader in a large one. He was for Maynooth in Ireland, and against it in Scotland. Mr. Disraeli did his best to mystify the agricultural elector by phrases about set-offs and compensations and relief of burdens, 'seeming to loom in the future.' He rang the changes on mysterious new principles of taxation, but what they were to be, he did not disclose. The great change since 1846 was that the working-class had become strenuous free traders. They had in earlier times never been really convinced when Cobden and Bright assured them that no fall in wages would follow the promised fall in the price of food. It was the experience of six years that convinced them. England alone had gone unhurt and unsinged through the fiery furnace of 1848, and nobody doubted that the stability of her institutions and the unity of her people were due to the repeal of bad laws, believed to raise the price of bread to the toilers in order to raise rents for territorial idlers.

Long before the dissolution, it was certain that Mr. Gladstone would have to fight for his seat. His letter to the Scotch bishop (see above, p. 285), his vote for the Jews, his tenacity and vehemence in resisting the bill against the pope,—the two last exhibitions in open defiance of solemn resolutions of the university convocation itself—had alienated some friends and inflamed all his enemies. Half a score of the Heads induced Dr. Marsham, the warden of Merton, to come out. In private qualities the warden was one of the most excellent of men, and the accident of his opposition to Mr. Gladstone is no reason why we should recall transient electioneering railleries against a forgotten worthy. The political addresses of his friends depict him. They applaud his sound and manly consistency of principle and his sober attachment to the reformed church of England, and they dwell with zest on the goodness of his heart. The issue, as they put it, was simple :—'At a time when the stability of the protestant succession, the authority of a protestant Queen, and even the Christianity of the national character, have been rudely assailed by Rome on one side, and on the other by democratic associations directed against the union of the Christian church with the British constitution—at such a time, it becomes a protestant university from which emanates a continuous stream of instruction on all ecclesiastical and Christian questions over the whole empire, to manifest the importance which it attaches to protestant truth, by the selection of a *Protestant Representative.*' The teaching residents were, as always, decisively for Gladstone, and nearly all the fellows of Merton voted against their own warden. In one respect this was remarkable, for Mr. Gladstone had in 1850 (July 18) resisted the proposal for that commission of inquiry into the universities which the Oxford liberals had much at heart, and it would not have been surprising if they had held aloof from a candidate who had told the House of Commons that 'after all, science was but a small part of the business of education,'—a proposition that in one sense may be true, but applied to unreformed Oxford was the reverse of true. The non-residents were diligently and rather unscrupulously worked upon, and they made a formidable set of discordant elements. The evangelicals disliked Mr. Gladstone. The plain high-and-dry men distrusted him as what they called a sophist. Even some of the anglo-catholic men began to regard as a bad friend 'to the holy apostolic church of these realms, the author of the new theory of religious liberty' in the Scotch letter. They reproachfully insisted that had he headed a party in the House of Commons defending the church, not upon latitudinarian theories of religious liberty, not upon vague hints of a disaffected movement of the non-juring sort, still less upon romanising principles, but on the principles of the constitution, royal supremacy included, then the church would have escaped

the worst that had befallen her since 1846. The minister would
never have dared to force Hampden into the seat of a bishop.
The privy council would never have reversed the court of
arches in the Gorham case. The claim of the clergy to meet in
convocation would never have been refused. The committee of
council would have treated education very differently.[1]   All
came right in the end, however, and Mr. Gladstone was re-
elected (July 14), receiving 260 votes fewer than Sir Robert
Inglis, but 350 more than the warden of Merton.[2]   We have to
remember that he was not returned as a liberal.

II

The leaders of the sections out of office, when the general
election was over, at once fetched forth line and plummet to
take their soundings. 'The next few months,' Mr. Gladstone
wrote to Lord Aberdeen (Aug. 20), 'are, I apprehend, the crisis
of *our* fate, and will show whether we are equal or unequal to
playing out with prudence, honour, and resolution *the drama or
trilogy that has been on the stage since* 1841.' He still regarded
the situation as something like a reproduction of the position of
the previous March. The precise number of the ministerialists
could not be ascertained until tested by a motion in the House.
They had gained rather more than was expected, and some
put them as high as 320, others as low as 290. What was
undoubted was that Lord Derby was left in a minority, and
that the support of the Peelites might any hour turn it into
a majority. Notwithstanding a loss or two in the recent
elections, that party still numbered not far short of 40, and
Mr. Gladstone was naturally desirous of retaining it in connection with himself. Most of the group were disposed rather
to support a conservative government than not, unless such a
government were to do, or propose, something open to strong
and definite objection. At the same time what he described
as the difficulty of keeping Peelism for ever so short a space
upon its legs, was as obvious to him as to everybody else.
'It will be an impossible parliament,' Graham said to
Mr. Gladstone (July 15), 'parties will be found too nicely
balanced to render a new line of policy practicable without a
fresh appeal to the electors.' Before a fresh appeal to the
electors took place, the impossible parliament had tumbled into
a great war.

When the newly chosen members met in November,
Mr. Disraeli told the House of Commons that 'there was no
question in the minds of ministers with respect to the result
of that election : there was no doubt that there was not only
not a preponderating majority in favour of a change in the
laws [free trade] passed in the last few years, or even of

[1] Charles Wordsworth, *Letter to Mr. Gladstone*, 1852, p. 50.
[2] Inglis, 1368 ; Gladstone, 1108 ; Marsham, 758.

modifying them in any degree ; but that on the contrary there
was a decisive opinion on the part of the country that that
settlement should not be disturbed.' Mr. Gladstone wrote to
Lord Aberdeen (July 30) that he thought the government
absolutely chained to Mr. Disraeli's next budget, and 'I, for
one, am not prepared to accept him as a financial organ, or to
be responsible for what he may propose in his present capacity.'
Each successive speech made by Mr. Disraeli at Aylesbury he
found 'more quackish in its flavour than its predecessor.'
Yet action on his own part was unavoidably hampered by
Oxford. 'Were I either of opinion,' he told Lord Aberdeen
(Aug. 5), 'that Lord John Russell ought to succeed Lord Derby,
or prepared without any further development of the plans of
the government to take my stand as one of the party opposed
to them, the first step which, as a man of honour, I ought to
adopt, should be to resign my seat.' 'I do not mean hereby,'
he adds in words that were soon to derive forcible significance
from the march of events, 'that I am unconditionally committed
against any alliance or fusion, but that any such alliance or
fusion, to be lawful for me, must grow out of some failure of
the government in carrying on public affairs, or a disapproval
of its measures when they shall have been proposed.' He still,
in spite of all the misdeeds of ministers during the elections,
could not think so ill of them as did Lord Aberdeen.

'Protection and religious liberty,' he wrote to Lord Aberdeen
(Aug. 5), 'are the subjects on which my main complaints would
turn ; shuffling as to the former, trading on bigotry as to the
latter. The shifting and shuffling that I complain of have
been due partly to a miserably false position and the giddy
prominence of inferior men ; partly to the (surely not unexpected) unscrupulousness and second motives of Mr. Disraeli,
at once the necessity of Lord Derby and his curse. I do not
mean that this justifies what has been said and done ; I only
think it brings the case within the common limits of political
misconduct. As for religious bigotry,' he continues, 'I condemn
the proceedings of the present government ; yet much less
strongly than the unheard-of course pursued by Lord John
Russell in 1850-1, the person to whom I am now invited to
transfer my confidence.' Even on the superficial conversion
of the Derbyites to free trade, Mr. Gladstone found a *tu quoque*
against the whigs. 'It is, when strictly judged, an act of
public immorality to form and lead an opposition on a certain
plea, to succeed, and then in office to abandon it. . . . But in
this view, the conduct of the present administration is the
counterpart and copy of that of the whigs themselves in 1835,
who ran Sir Robert Peel to ground upon the appropriation
clause, worked it just while it suited them, and then cast it
to the winds ; to say nothing of their conduct on the Irish
Assassination bill of 1846.'

This letter was forwarded by Aberdeen to Lord John
Russell. Lord John had the peculiar temperament that is
hard to agitate, but easy to nettle. So polemical a reading of
former whig pranks nettled him considerably. Why, he asked,
should he not say just as reasonably that Mr. Gladstone held
up the whigs to odium in 1841 for stripping the farmer of
adequate protection ; worked the corn law of 1842 as long
as it suited him ; and then turned round and cast the corn
law to the winds ? If he gave credit to Mr. Gladstone for
being sincere in 1841, 1842, and 1846, why should not Mr.
Gladstone give the same credit to him ? As to the principle
of appropriation, he and Althorp had opposed four of their
colleagues in the Grey cabinet ; how could he concede to
Peel what he had refused to them ? As for the Irish bill on
which he had turned Peel out, it was one of the worst of all
coercion bills ; Peel with 117 followers evidently could not
carry on the government ; and what sense could there have
been in voting for a bad bill, in order to retain in office an
impossible ministry ? This smart apologia of Lord John's
was hardly even plausible, much less did it cover the ground.
The charge against the whigs is not that they took up
appropriation, but that having taken it up they dropped it
for the sake of office. Nor was it a charge that they resisted
an Irish coercion bill, but that having supported it on the
first reading ('worst of all coercion bills' as it was, even in
the eyes of men who had passed the reckless act of 1833),
they voted against it when they found that both Bentinck
and the Manchester men were going to do the same, thus
enabling them to turn Peel out.

Sharp sallies into the past, however, did not ease the
present. It was an extraordinary situation only to be
described in negatives. A majority could not be found to
beat the government upon a vote of want of confidence.
Nobody knew who could take their places. Lord John
Russell as head of a government was impossible, for his
maladroit handling of papal aggression had alienated the
Irish ; his dealings with Palmerston had offended one powerful
section of the English whigs ; the Scottish whigs hated
him as too much managed by the lights of the free church ;
and the radicals proscribed him as the chief of a patrician
clique. Yet though he was impossible, he sometimes used
language to the effect that for him to take any place save
the first would be a personal degradation, that would lower
him to the level of Sidmouth or Goderich. Lord Palmerston
represented the moderate centre of the liberal party. Even
now he enjoyed a growing personal favour out of doors,
not at all impaired by the bad terms on which he was known
to be with the court, for the court was not at that date so
popular an institution as it became by and by. Among other

schemes of ingenious persons at this confused and broken time was a combination under Palmerston or Lansdowne of aristocratic whigs, a great contingent of Derbyites, and the Peelites ; and before the elections it was true that Lord Derby had made overtures to these two eminent men. A Lansdowne combination lingered long in the mind of Lord Palmerston himself, who wished for the restoration of a whig government, but resented the idea of serving under its late head. Some dreamed that Palmerston and Disraeli might form a government on the basis of resistance to parliamentary reform. Strange rumours were even afloat that Mr. Gladstone's communications with Palmerston before he left London at the election had been intimate and frequent. 'I cannot make Gladstone out,' said Lord Malmesbury, 'he seems to me a dark horse.'

In the closing days of the autumn (September 12) Graham interpreted some obscure language of Mr. Gladstone's as meaning that if protection were renounced, as it might be, if Palmerston joined Derby and the government were reconstructed, and if Disraeli ceased to be leader, then his own relations with the government would be changed. Gladstone was so uneasy in his present position, so nice in the equipoise of his opinions that he wished to be, as he said, 'on the liberal side of the conservative party, rather than on the conservative side of the liberal party.' A little earlier than this, Lord Aberdeen and Graham agreed in thinking (August) that 'Disraeli's leadership was the great cause of Gladstone's reluctance to have anything to do with the government; . . . that even if this should be removed, it would not be very easy for him to enter into partnership with them.' Mr. Gladstone himself now and always denied that the lead in the Commons or other personal question had anything to do with the balance of his opinions at the present and later moments. Those who know most of public life are best aware how great is the need in the case of public men for charitable construction of their motives and intent. Yet it would surely have been straining charity to the point of dishonour if, within two years of Peel's death, any of those who had been attached to him as master and as friend, either Mr. Gladstone or anybody else, could have looked without reprobation and aversion on the idea of cabinet intimacy with the bitterest and least sincere of all Peel's assailants.

III

Mr. Gladstone repaired to London some weeks before the new session, and though he was not in a position to open direct relations with the government, he expressed to Lord Hardinge, with a view to its communication to Lord Derby, his strong opinion that the House of Commons would, and should, require from ministers a frank and explicit adoption of free trade

through the address, and secondly, the immediate production
of their financial measures. Lord Derby told Hardinge at
Windsor that he thought that neither expectation was far
wrong. When the Peelites met at Lord Aberdeen's to discuss
tactics, they were secretly dissatisfied with the paragraphs
about free trade.

Mr. Disraeli had laid down at the election the sonorous
maxim, that no statesman can disregard with impunity the
genius of the epoch in which he lives. And he now after the
election averred, that the genius of the age was in favour of
free exchange. Still it was pleasanter to swallow the dose
with as little public observation as possible. 'What would
have been said,' cried Lord Derby in fervid remonstrance, 'if
shortly after catholic emancipation and the reform bill had
been admitted as settlements, their friends had come down and
insisted not only that the Houses of parliament should consent
to act on the new policy they had adopted, but should expressly
recant their opinion in favour of the policy that had formerly
prevailed ? What would the friends of Sir R. Peel have said in
1835 if, when he assumed the government and when the new
parliament assembled, he had been called upon to declare that
the reform bill was wise, just, and necessary ?' The original
free traders were not disposed to connive at Derbyite operations any more than were the whigs. Notice was at once
given by Mr. Villiers of a motion virtually assailing the
ministers, by asserting the doctrine of free trade in terms
they could not adopt. 'Now,' says Mr. Gladstone, 'we came to
a case in which the liberals did that which had been done by
the government in the case of the Four Seats bill ; that is to
say, they raised an issue which placed us against them. Lord
Palmerston moved the amendment which defeated the attack,
but he did this at the express request of S. Herbert and mine,
and we carried the amendment to him at his house. He did
not recommend any particular plan of action, and he willingly
acquiesced in and adopted ours.' He said he would convey it
to Disraeli, 'with whom,' he said, 'I have had communications
from time to time.'

In the debate (Nov. 26) upon the two rival amendments—
that of Mr. Villiers, which the ministers could not accept, and
that of Palmerston, which they could—Sidney Herbert paid off
some old scores in a speech full of fire and jubilation ; Mr.
Gladstone, on the other hand, was elaborately pacific. He
earnestly deprecated the language of severity and exasperation, or anything that would tend to embitter party warfare.
His illustrious leader Peel, he said, did indeed look for his
revenge ; but for what revenge did he look ? Assuredly not
for stinging speeches, assuredly not for motions made in favour
of his policy, if they carried pain and degradation to the minds
of honourable men. Were they not celebrating the obsequies

of an obnoxious policy? Let them cherish no desire to trample on those who had fought manfully and been defeated fairly. Rather let them rejoice in the great public good that had been achieved; let them take courage from the attainment of that good, for the performance of their public duty in future. All this was inspired by the strong hope of conservative reunion. 'Nervous excitement kept me very wakeful after speaking,' says Mr. Gladstone, 'the first time for many years.' (*Diary.*)

Villiers's motion was rejected by 336 to 256, the Peelites and Graham voting with ministers in the majority. The Peelite amendment in moderated terms, for which Palmerston stood sponsor, was then carried against the radicals by 468 to 53. For the moment the government was saved.

'This evening,' Mr. Gladstone writes on the next day, Nov. 27, 'I went to Lady Derby's evening party, where Lord Derby took me a little aside and said he must take the opportunity of thanking me for the tone of my speech last night, which he thought tended to place the discussion on its right footing. It was evident from his manner, and Lady Derby's too, that they were highly pleased with the issue of it. I simply made my acknowledgments in terms of the common kind, upon which he went on to ask me what in my view was to happen next? The great object, he said, was to get rid of all personal questions, and to consider how all those men who were united in their general views of government might combine together to carry on with effect. For himself he felt both uncertain and indifferent; he might be able to carry on the government or he might not; but the question lay beyond that, by what combination or arrangement of a satisfactory nature, in the event of his displacement, the administration of public affairs could be conducted.

'To this I replied, that it seemed to me that our situation (meaning that of Herbert, Goulburn, and others, with myself) in relation to his government remained much as it was in March and April last. . . . We have to expect your budget, and the production of that is the next step. He replied that he much desired to see whether there was a possibility of any *rapprochement*, and seemed to glance at personal considerations as likely perhaps to stand in the way [Disraeli, presumably]. I said in reply, that no doubt there were many difficulties of a personal nature to be faced in conceiving of any ministerial combination when we looked at the present House of Commons: many men of power and eminence, but great difficulties arising from various causes, present and past relations, incompatibilities, peculiar defects of character, or failure in bringing them into harmony. I said that, as to relations of parties, circumstances were often stronger than the human will; that we must wait for their guiding, and follow it. . . . He said, rather decidedly, that he assented to the truth of this doctrine. He added, "I think Sidney said more last night than he intended, did he not?" I answered, "You mean as to one particular expression or sentence?" He rejoined, "Yes."[1] I said, "I

---

[1] I suppose this refers to a passage about Mr. Disraeli :—'For my part I acquit the chancellor of the exchequer, so far as his own convictions are concerned, of the charge of having ever been a protectionist. I never for one moment thought he believed in the least degree in protection. I do not accuse him of having forgotten what he said or what he believed in those years. I only accuse him of having forgotten now what he then wished it to appear that he believed.' The same speech contains a whimsical

have had no conversation with him on it, but I think it very probable
that he grew warm and went beyond his intention at that point ; at the
same time, I think I ought to observe to you that I am confident that
expression was occasioned by one particular preceding speech in the debate.''
He gave a significant assent, and seemed to express no surprise.'

IV

The respite for ministers was short. The long day of
shadowy promises and delusive dreams was over ; and the
oracular expounder of mysteries was at last gripped by the
hard realities of the taxes. Whigs and Peelites, men who had
been at the exchequer and men who hoped to be, were all ready
at last to stalk down their crafty quarry. Without delay
Disraeli presented his budget (Dec. 3). As a private member
in opposition he had brought forward many financial proposals,
but it now turned out that none of them was fit for real use.
With a serene audacity that accounts for some of Mr. Gladstone's repulsion, he told the House that he had greater
subjects to consider 'than the triumph of obsolete opinions.'
His proposals dazzled for a day, and then were seen to be a
scheme of illusory compensations and dislocated expedients.
He took off half of the malt-tax and half of the hop duty, and
in stages reduced the tea duty from two shillings and two
pence to one shilling. More important, he broke up the old
frame of the income-tax by a variation of its rates, and as for
the house-tax, he doubled its rate and extended its area. In
one of his fragmentary notes, Mr. Gladstone says :—

Having run away from protection, as it was plain from the first they
would do, they had little to offer the land, but that little their minority
was ready to accept. It was a measure essentially bad to repeal half
the malt duty. But the flagrantly vicious element in Disraeli's budget
was his proposal to reduce the income-tax on schedule D. to fivepence
in the pound, leaving the other schedules at sevenpence. This was no
compensation to the land ; but, inasmuch as to exempt one is to tax
another, it was a distinct addition to the burdens borne by the holders
of visible property. It was on Disraeli's part a most daring bid for the
support of the liberal majority, for we all knew quite well that the
current opinion of the whigs and liberals was in favour of this scheme ;
which, on the other hand, was disapproved by sound financiers. The
authority of Pitt and Peel, and then my own study of the subject, made
me believe that it was impracticable, and probably meant the disruption of the tax, with confusion in finance, as an immediate sequitur.
What angered me was that Disraeli had never examined the question.
And I afterwards found that he had not even made known his intentions
to the board of inland revenue. The gravity of the question thus raised
made me feel that the day was come to eject the government.

It was upon the increase of the house-tax that the great
battle was finally staked. Mr. Gladstone's letters to his wife

reason why the Jews make no converts, which the taste of our more democratic House
would certainly not tolerate.

at Hawarden bring the rapid and excited scenes vividly
before us.

6 *Carlton Gardens, Dec.* 3, 1852.—I write from H. of C. at 4½ just
expecting the budget. All seem to look for startling and dangerous
proposals. You will read them in the papers of to-morrow, be they
what they may. If there is anything outrageous, we may protest at
once ; but I do not expect any extended debate to-night. . . . The rush
for places in the H. of C. is immense.

Monday, Dec. 6.—On Saturday, in the early part of the day, I had a
return, perhaps caused by the damp relaxing weather, of the neuralgic
pain in my face, and in the afternoon a long sitting at Lord Aberdeen's
about the budget, during which strange to say my pain disappeared,
but which kept me past the ordinary post hour. These were the causes
of your having no letter. The said budget will give rise to serious
difficulties. It is plain enough that when its author announced something looming in the distance, he did not mean this plan but something
more extensive. Even his reduced scheme, however, includes fundamental faults of principle which it is impossible to overlook or compound
with. The first day of serious debate on it will be Friday next, and a
vote will be taken either then or on Monday.

Dec. 8.—Be sure to read Lord Derby's speech on Monday. His
reference to the cause of his quarrel with Lord George Bentinck was
most striking, and is interpreted as a rap at Disraeli.[1] I have had a
long sit with Lord Aberdeen to-day talking over possibilities. The
government, I believe, talk confidently about the decision on the house-
tax, but I should doubt whether they are right. Meantime I am convinced that Disraeli's is the least conservative budget I have ever known.

Dec. 14.—I need hardly say the vision of going down to-morrow has
been dissolved. It has been arranged that I am not to speak until the
close of the debate ; and it is considered almost certain to go on till
Monday. Ministers have become much less confident, but I understand
that some, I know not how many, of Lord John's men are not to be
relied on. Whether they win or not (I expect the latter, but my opinion
is *naught*) they cannot carry this house-tax nor their budget. But the
mischief of the proposals they have launched will not die with them.

Dec. 15.—I write in great haste. Though it is Wednesday, I have
been down at the House almost all day to unravel a device of Disraeli's
about the manner in which the question is to be put, by which he means
to catch votes ; and *I think* after full consultation with Mahon and
Wilson Patten, that this will be accomplished. The debate may close
to-morrow night. I am sorry to say I have a long speech fermenting in
me, and I feel as a loaf might in the oven. The government, it is
thought, are likely to be beaten.

Dec. 16.—I have been engaged in the House till close on post time.
Disraeli trying to wriggle out of the question, and get it put upon words
without meaning, to enable more to vote as they please, *i.e.* his men or
those favourably inclined to him. But he is beaten in this point, and
we have now the right question before us. It is not now quite certain

[1] 'The only serious misunderstanding I ever had with my noble and lamented
friend Lord George Bentinck, which I am happy to say was thoroughly removed before
his untimely death—was upon a full and frank expression of my opinion that nothing
could be more unfitting nor more impolitic than to load with terms of vituperation
those from whom we are compelled conscientiously to differ ' (*Dec.* 6).

whether we shall divide to-night ; I hope we may, for it is weary work sitting with a speech fermenting inside one.[1]

Dec. 18.—I have never gone through so exciting a passage of parliamentary life. The intense efforts which we made to obtain, and the government to escape, a definite issue, were like a fox chase, and prepared us all for excitement. I came home at seven, dined, read for a quarter of an hour, and actually contrived (only think) to sleep in the fur cloak for another quarter of an hour ; got back to the House at nine. Disraeli rose at 10.20 [Dec. 16], and from that moment, of course, I was on tenterhooks, except when his superlative acting and brilliant oratory from time to time absorbed me and made me quite *forget* that I had to follow him. He spoke until one. His speech as a whole was grand ; I think the most powerful I ever heard from him. At the same time it was disgraced by shameless personalities and otherwise ; I had therefore to begin by attacking him for these. There was a question whether it would not be too late, but when I heard his personalities I felt there was no choice but to go on. My great object was to show the conservative party how their leader was hoodwinking and bewildering them, and this I have the happiness of believing that in some degree I effected ; for while among some there was great heat and a disposition to interrupt me when they could, I could *see* in the faces and demeanour of others quite other feelings expressed. But it was a most difficult operation, and altogether it might have been better effected. The House has not I think been so much excited for years. The power of his speech, and the importance of the issue, combined with the lateness of the hour, which always operates, were the causes. My brain was strung very high, and has not yet quite got back to calm, but I slept well last night. On Thursday night [*i.e.* Friday morning] after two hours of sleep, I awoke, and remembered a gross omission I had made, which worked upon me so that I could not rest any more. And still, of course, the time is an anxious one, and I wake with the consciousness of it, but I am very well and really not unquiet. When I came home from the House, I thought it would be good for me to be mortified. Next morning I opened the *Times*, which I thought *you* would buy, and *was* mortified when I saw it did not contain my speech but a mangled abbreviation. Such is human nature, at least mine. But in the *Times* of to-day you will see a very curious article descriptive of the last scene of the debate. It has evidently been written by a man who must have seen what occurred, or been informed by those who did see. He by no means says too much in praise of Disraeli's speech. I am told he is much stung by what I said. I am very sorry it fell to me to say it ; God knows I have no wish to give him pain ; and really with my deep sense of his gifts I would only pray they might be well used.

The writer in the *Times* to whom the victorious orator here refers describes how, 'like two of Sir Walter Scott's champions, these redoubtable antagonists gathered up all their force for the final struggle, and encountered each other in mid-career ; how, rather equal than like, each side viewed the struggle of

---

[1] 'We had a preliminary debate to have the whole resolution put, instead of the preamble only, which was ultimately agreed to, and placed the question more fairly before the public, Disraeli making the extraordinary declaration that though the proposal was for doubling the house-tax, nobody was bound by that vote to do so. It was an attempt at a shuffle in order to catch votes from his own people, and to a certain extent it succeeded.'—*Halifax Papers*, 1852.

their chosen athletes, as if to prognosticate from the war
of words the fortunes of two parties so nicely balanced and
marshalled in apparently equal array. Mr. Disraeli's speech,'
he says, 'was in every respect worthy of his oratorical reputation. The retorts were pointed and bitter, the hits telling, the
sarcasm keen, the argument in many places cogent, in all
ingenious and in some convincing. The merits were counter-
balanced by no less glaring defects of tone, temper, and feeling.
In some passages invective was pushed to the limit of virulence,
and in others, meant no doubt to relieve them by contrast, the
coarser stimulants to laughter were very freely applied. Occasionally whole sentences were delivered with an artificial voice
and a tone of studied and sardonic bitterness, peculiarly painful
to the audience, and tending greatly to diminish the effect of
this great intellectual and physical effort. The speech of Mr.
Gladstone was in marked contrast. It was characterised
throughout by the most earnest sincerity. It was pitched in
a high tone of moral feeling—now rising to indignation, now
sinking to remonstrance — which was sustained throughout
without flagging and without effort. The language was less
ambitious, less studied, but more natural and flowing than
that of Mr. Disraeli ; and though commencing in a tone of
stern rebuke, it ended in words of almost pathetic expostulation. . . . That power of persuasion which seems entirely denied
to his antagonist, Mr. Gladstone possesses to great perfection,
and to judge by the countenances of his hearers, those powers
were very successfully exerted. He had, besides, the immense
advantage resulting from the tone of moral superiority which
he assumed and successfully maintained, and which conciliated
to him the goodwill of his audience in a degree never attained
by the most brilliant sallies of his adversary, and when he
concluded the House might well feel proud of him and of
themselves.'

A violent thunderstorm raged during the debate, but the
excited senators neither noticed the flashes of lightning nor
heard a tremendous shock of thunder. A little before four
o'clock in the morning (Dec. 17), the division was taken, and
ministers were beaten by nineteen (305 to 286). 'There was
an immense crowd,' says Macaulay, 'a deafening cheer when
Hayter took the right hand of the row of tellers, and a still
louder cheer when the numbers were read.'[1]

A small incident occurred a few nights later to show that it
was indeed high time to abate the passions of these six years
and more. A politician of secondary rank had been accused
of bribery at Derby, and a band of tory friends thought the
moment opportune to give him a banquet at the Carlton.
Mr. Gladstone in another room was harmlessly reading the
paper. Presently in came the revellers, began to use insulting

[1] Trevelyan, ii. p. 331.

language, and finally vowed that he ought to be pitched headlong out of the window into the Reform. Mr. Gladstone made
some courteous reply, but as the reporter truly says, courtesy
to gentry in this humour was the casting of pearls before
swine. Eventually they ordered candles in another room, and
left him to himself.[1] 'You will perhaps,' he wrote to his wife,
'see an account of a row at the Carlton in which I have taken
no harm.' The affair indeed was trivial, but it illustrates a
well-known and striking reflection of Cornewall Lewis upon
the assault perpetrated on Sumner in the Senate at Washington
by Brooks. 'That outrage,' he said, 'is no proof of brutal
manners or low morality in Americans; it is the first blow in
a civil war. . . . If Peel had proposed a law not only reducing
rents, but annihilating them, instead of being attacked by a
man of words like Disraeli, he would have been attacked with
physical arguments by some man of blows.'[2]

In point of numbers the stroke given to protection was not
tremendous, but as the history of half a century has shown, it
was adequate and sufficient, and Lord Derby at once resigned.
He did not take his defeat well. 'Strange to say,' Mr. Gladstone wrote to his wife, 'Lord Derby has been making a most
petulant and intemperate speech in the House of Lords on his
resignation ; such that Newcastle was obliged to rise after him
and contradict the charge of combination ; while nothing could
be better in temper, feeling, and judgment than Disraeli's farewell.' Derby angrily divided the combination that had overthrown him into, first, various gradations of liberalism from
'high aristocratic and exclusive whigs down to the extremest
radical theorists' ; second, Irish ultramontanes ; and lastly, a
party of some thirty or thirty-five gentlemen 'of great personal
worth, of great eminence and respectability, possessing considerable official experience and a large amount of talent—who
once professed, and I believe do still profess, conservative
opinions.'

Mr. Disraeli, on the contrary, with infinite polish and grace
asked pardon for the flying words of debate, and drew easy
forgiveness from the member whom a few hours before he had
mocked as 'a weird sibyl' ; the other member whom he would
not say he greatly respected, but whom he greatly regarded ;
and the third member whom he bade learn that petulance is
not sarcasm, and insolence is not invective. Lord John Russell
congratulated him on the ability and the gallantry with which
he had conducted the struggle, and so the curtain fell. The
result, as the great newspaper put it with journalistic freedom,
was 'not merely the victory of a battle, but of a war ; not a
reverse, but a conquest. The vanquished have no principles
which they dare to assert, no leaders whom they can venture
to trust.'

[1] *Times*, Dec. 23, 1852.   [2] *Letters*, p. 315.

Book IV

(1853–1859)

CHAPTER I

THE COALITION

(1853)

The materials necessary for a sound judgment of facts are not found in the success or failure of undertakings; exact knowledge of the situation that has provoked them forms no inconsiderable element of history.—METTERNICH.

ENGLAND was unconsciously on the eve of a violent break in the peace that had been her fortunate lot for nearly forty years. To the situation that preceded this signal event, a judicious reader may well give his attention. Some of the particulars may seem trivial. In countries governed by party, what those out of the actualities of the fray reckon trivial often count for much, and in the life of a man destined to be a conspicuous party leader, to pass them by would be to leave out real influences.

The first experiment in providing the country with a tory government had failed. That alliance between whig and Peelite which Lord John the year before had been unable to effect, had become imperative, and at least a second experiment was to be tried. The initial question was who should be head of the new government. In August, Lord Aberdeen had written to Mr. Gladstone in anticipation of the Derbyite defeat:—'If high character and ability only were required, *you* would be the person; but I am aware that for the present at least this would not be practicable. Whether it would be possible for Newcastle or me to undertake the concern, is more than I can say.' Other good reasons apart, it is easy to see that Mr. Gladstone's attitude in things eeclesiastical put him out of court, and though he had made a conspicuous mark not only, as Lord Aberdeen said, by character and ability but by liberality of view especially in the region of colonial reform,

329

still he had as yet had no good opportunity for showing an independent capacity for handling great affairs.

Not any less impossible was Lord John. Shortly before the occasion arose, a whig intimate told him plainly that reconstruction on the basis of his old government was out of the question. 'Lord John's answer was a frank acceptance of that opinion ; and he was understood to say that the composition of the next government must be mainly from the ranks of the Peelites ; he evidently looked forward to being a member of it, but not the head. When various persons were named as possible heads, Lord Aberdeen was distinctly approved, Graham was distinctly rejected, Newcastle was mentioned without any distinct opinion expressed. We [Aberdeen and Gladstone] were both alike at a loss to know whether Lord John had changed his mind, or had all along since his resignation been acting with this view. All his proceedings certainly seem to require an opposite construction, and to contemplate his own leadership.'[1]

Lord Palmerston was determined not to serve again under a minister who had with his own hand turned him out of office, and of whose unfitness for the first post he was at the moment profoundly convinced. He told a Peelite friend that Lord John's love of popularity would always lead him into scrapes, and that his way of suddenly announcing new policies (Durham letter and Edinburgh letter) without consulting colleagues, could not be acquiesced in. Besides the hostility of Palmerston and his friends, any government with the writer of the Durham letter at its head must have the hostility of the Irishmen to encounter. The liberal attitude of the Peelites on the still smouldering question of papal aggression gave Aberdeen a hold on the Irish such as nobody else could have.

Another man of great eminence in the whig party might have taken the helm, but Lord Lansdowne was seventy-two, and was supposed to have formally retired from office for ever. The leader of the Peelites visited the patrician whig at Lansdowne House, and each begged the other to undertake the uncoveted post. Lord Aberdeen gave a slow assent. Previously understanding from Lord John that he would join, Aberdeen accepted the Queen's commission to form a government. He had a harassed week. At first the sun shone. 'Lord John consents,' wrote Mr. Gladstone to his wife at Hawarden, 'and has behaved very well. Palmerston refuses, which is a serious blow. To-morrow I think we shall get to detailed arrangements, about which I do not expect extraordinary difficulty. But I suppose Palmerston is looking to become the leader of a Derby opposition ; and without him, or rather with him between us and the conservatives, I cannot but say the game will be a very difficult one to play. It is uncertain whether

1 Memo. by Mr. Gladstone of a conversation with Aberdeen.

I shall be chancellor of the exchequer or secretary for the
colonies ; one of the two I think certainly ; and the exchequer
will certainly come to Graham or me.'

Within a few hours angry squalls all but capsized the boat.
Lord John at first had sought consolation in an orthodox
historical parallel—the case of Mr. Fox, though at the head of
the largest party, leading the Commons under Lord Grenville
as head of the government. Why should he, then, refuse a
position that Fox had accepted ? But friends, often in his case
the most mischievous of advisers, reminded him what sort of
place he would hold in a cabinet in which the chief posts were
filled by men not of his own party. Lord John himself thought,
from memories of Bishop Hampden and other ecclesiastical
proceedings, that Mr. Gladstone would be his sharpest opponent.
Then as the days passed, he found deposition from first place to
second more bitter than he had expected. Historic and literary
consolation can seldom be a sure sedative against the stings of
political ambition. He changed his mind every twelve hours,
and made infinite difficulties. When these were with much
travail appeased, difficulties were made on behalf of others.
The sacred caste and their adherents were up in arms, and a
bitter cry arose that all the good things were going to the
Peelites, only the leavings to the whigs. Lord John doubtless
remembered what Fox had said when the ministry of All the
Talents was made,—'We are three in a bed.' Disraeli now
remarked sardonically, 'The cake is too small.' To realise the
scramble, the reader may think of the venerable carp that date
from Henry IV. and Sully, struggling for bread in the fish-
ponds of the palace of Fontainebleau. The whigs of this time
were men of intellectual refinement ; they had a genuine regard
for good government, and a decent faith in reform ; but when
we chide the selfishness of machine politicians hunting office in
modern democracy, let us console ourselves by recalling the
rapacity of our oligarchies. 'It is melancholy,' muses Sir James
Graham this Christmas in his journal, 'to see how little fitness
for office is regarded on all sides, and how much the public
employments are treated as booty to be divided among successful
combatants.'

From that point of view, the whig case was strong. 'Of 330
members of the House of Commons,' wrote Lord John to Aberdeen, ' 270 are whig and radical, thirty are Irish brigade, thirty
are Peelites. To this party of thirty you propose to give seven
seats in cabinet, to the whigs and radicals five, to Lord Palmerston one.' In the end there were six whigs, as many Peelites,
and one radical. The case of four important offices out of the
cabinet was just as heartrending : three were to go to the thirty
Peelites, and one to the two hundred and seventy just persons.
I am afraid,' cried Lord John, 'that the liberal party will never
stand this, and that the storm will overwhelm me.' Whig pride

was deeply revolted at subjection to a prime minister whom in their drawing-rooms they mocked as an old tory. In the Aberdeen cabinet, says Mr. Gladstone, 'it may be thought that the whigs, whose party was to supply five-sixths or seven-eighths of our supporters, had less than their due share of power. It should, however, be borne in mind that they had at this juncture in some degree the character of an used-up, and so far a discredited, party. Without doubt they were sufferers from their ill-conceived and mischievous Ecclesiastical Titles Act. Whereas we, the Peelites, had been for six and a half years out of office, and had upon us the gloss of freshness.'

Lord Palmerston refused to join the coalition, on the honourable ground that for many years he and Aberdeen had stood at the antipodes to one another in the momentous department of foreign affairs. In fact he looked in another direction. If the Aberdeen-Russell coalition broke down, either before they began the journey or very soon after, Lord Derby might come back with a reconstructed team, with Palmerston leading in the Commons a centre party that should include the Peelites. He was believed to have something of this kind in view when he consented to move the amendment brought to him by Gladstone and Herbert in November, and he was bitterly disappointed at the new alliance of that eminent pair with Lord John. With the tories he was on excellent terms. Pall Mall was alive with tales of the anger and disgust of the Derbyites against Mr Disraeli, who had caused them first to throw over their principles and then to lose their places. The county constituencies and many conservative boroughs were truly reported to be sick of the man who had promised marvels as 'looming in the future,' and then like a bad jockey had brought the horse upon its knees. Speculative minds cannot but be tempted to muse upon the difference that the supersession by Lord Palmerston of this extraordinary genius at that moment might have made both to the career of Disraeli himself, and to the nation of which he one day became for a space the supreme ruler. Cobden and Bright let it be understood that they were not candidates for office. 'Our day has not come yet,' Bright said to Graham and the representative of the radicals in the cabinet was Sir William Molesworth. In their newspaper the radicals wrote rather stiffly and jealously. In the end Lord Palmerston changed his mind and joined.

It was three days before the post of the exchequer was filled Mr. Gladstone in his daily letter to Hawarden writes:—'A headquarters I understand they say, "Mr. G. destroyed the budget, so he ought to make a new one." However we are trying to press Graham into that service.' The next day it was settled. From Osborne a letter had come to Lord Aberdeen —'The Queen hopes it may be possible to give the chancellorship of the exchequer to Mr. Gladstone, and to secure the

continuance of Lord St. Leonards as chancellor.'[1] Notwithstanding the royal wish, 'we pressed it,' says Mr. Gladstone,
'on Graham, but he refused point blank.' Graham, as we
know, was the best economist in the administration of Peel,
and Mr. Gladstone's frequent references to him in later times
on points of pure finance show the value set upon his capacity
in this department. His constitutional dislike of high responsibility perhaps intervened. Mr. Gladstone himself would cheerfully have returned to the colonial office, but the whigs
suspected the excesses of his colonial liberalism, and felt sure
that he would sow the tares of anglicanism in these virgin
fields. So before Christmas day came, Mr. Gladstone accepted
what was soon in influence the second post in the government,[2]
and became chancellor of the exchequer.

Say what they would, the parliamentary majority was
unstable as water. His own analysis of the House of Commons
gave 270 British liberals, not very compact, and the radical
wing of them certain to make occasions of combination against
the government, especially in finance. The only other party
avowing themselves general supporters of the government were
the forty Peelites—for at that figure he estimated them. The
ministry, therefore, were in a minority, and a portion even
of that minority not always to be depended on. The remainder
of the House he divided into forty Irish brigaders, bent on
mischief ; from fifty to eighty conservatives, not likely to join
in any factious vote, and not ill disposed to the government,
but not to be counted on either for attendance or confidence ;
finally, the Derby opposition, from 200 to 250, ready to follow
Mr. Disraeli into any combination for turning out the government. 'It thus appears, if we strike out the fifty conservatives
faintly favourable, that we have a government with 310
supporters, liable on occasions, which frequently arise, to
heavy deductions ; with an opposition of 290 (Derbyites and
brigaders), most of them ready to go all lengths. Such a
government cannot be said to possess the confidence of the
House of Commons in the full constitutional sense.'

The general course seemed smooth. Palmerston had gone
to the harmless department of home affairs. The international
airs were still. But a cabinet finally composed of six Peelites,
six whigs, and a radical, was evidently open to countless
internal hazards. 'We shall all look strangely at each other,'
one of them said, 'when we first meet in cabinet.' Graham
describes them as a powerful team that would need good
driving. 'There are some odd tempers and queer ways among
them ; but on the whole they are gentlemen, and they have a

---

1 The practical impossibility of retaining this learned man, the Derbyite chancellor,
upon the coalition woolsack, is an illustration of the tenacity of the modern party
system.
2 It was not until the rise of Mr. Gladstone that a chancellor of the exchequer, not
being prime minister, stood at this high level.

perfect gentleman at their head, who is honest and direct, and who will not brook insincerity in others.' The head of the new government described it to a friend as 'a great experiment, hitherto unattempted, and of which the success must be considered doubtful, but in the meantime the public had regarded it with singular favour.' To the King of the Belgians, Aberdeen wrote : 'England will occupy her true position in Europe as the constant advocate of moderation and peace'; and to Guizot, that 'the position which we desired to see England occupy among the nations of Europe, was to act the part of a moderator, and by reconciling differences and removing misunderstandings to preserve harmony and peace.'

I have seen no more concise analysis of the early position of the coalition government than that by one of the ablest and most experienced members of the whig party, not himself a candidate for office :—

'It is strong,' Sir Francis Baring wrote to his son, 'in personal talent ; none that I can remember stronger, though the head of the government is untried. It is strong in one point of view : as to public feeling. The country, I believe, wanted a moderate liberal government, and a fusion of liberal conservatives and moderate liberals. It is weak in the feelings of the component parts : Palmerston is degraded, Gladstone will struggle for power, Lord John cannot be comfortable. It is weak in the discordant antecedents of the cabinet ; they must all make some sacrifices and work uncomfortably. It is weak in the support. I do not mean the numbers, but the class of supporters. The Peelites are forty ; they will have the liberals on the one side and the conservatives on the other. The whigs of the cabinet will be anxious to satisfy the former ; the Peelites (Gladstone especially) the other. They are weak in their church views. The protestants look on those who voted against the Aggression bill with distrust ; the evangelicals on Gladstone and S. Herbert with dislike. I don't pretend to be a prophet, but it is always well to put down what you expect and to compare these expectations with results. My conjecture is that Gladstone will, before long, leave the government or that he will break it up.'[1]

Long afterwards Mr. Gladstone himself said this of the coalition :—

I must say of this cabinet of Lord Aberdeen's that in its deliberations it never exhibited the marks of its dual origin. Sir W. Molesworth, its radical member, seemed to be practically rather nearer in colour to the Peelites than to the whigs. There were some few idiosyncrasies without doubt. Lord Palmerston, who was home secretary, had in him some tendencies which might have been troublesome, but for a long time were not so. It is, for instance, a complete error to suppose that he asked the cabinet to treat the occupation of the Principalities as a *casus belli*. Lord Russell shook the position of Lord Aberdeen by action most capricious and unhappy. But with the general course of affairs this

[1] From the Baring papers, for which I am indebted to the kindness of Lord Northbrook.

had no connection ; and even in the complex and tortuous movements
of the Eastern negotiations, the cabinet never fell into two camps. That
question and the war were fatal to it. In itself I hardly ever saw a
cabinet with greater promise of endurance.

II

Acceptance of office vacated the Oxford seat, and the day
after Christmas a thunderbolt fell upon the new chancellor of
the exchequer from his friend, the militant archdeacon of
Taunton. 'I wish to use few words,' Denison wrote, 'where
every word I write is so bitterly distressing to me, and must be
little less so, I cannot doubt, to yourself and to many others
whom I respect and love. I have to state to you, as one of
your constituents, that from this time I can place no confidence
in you as representative of the university of Oxford, or as a
public man.' Mr. Gladstone's protestations that church patronage would be as safe in Lord Aberdeen's hands as in Lord
Derby's ; that his own past history dispensed with the necessity
of producing other assurances of his own fidelity ; that his
assumption of office could not shake it—all these were vain in
face of the staring and flagrant fact that he would henceforth
be the intimate and partner in council of Lord John Russell,
the latitudinarian, the erastian, the appropriationist, the de-
spoiler ; and worse still, of Molesworth, sometimes denounced
as a Socinian, sometimes as editor of the atheist Hobbes, but
in either case no fit person to dispense the church patronage of
the duchy of Lancaster.[1] Only a degree less shocking was the
thought of the power of filling bishoprics and deaneries by a
prime minister himself a presbyterian. No guarantee that the
member for Oxford might have taken against aggression upon
the church, or for the concession of her just claims, was worth
a feather when weighed against the mere act of a coalition so
deadly as this.

It was an awkward fact for Mr. Gladstone's canvassers that
Lord Derby had stated that his defeat was the result of a
concert or combination between the Peelites and other political
parties. Mr. Gladstone himself saw no reason why this should
cause much soreness among his Oxford supporters. 'No
doubt,' he said, 'they will remember that I avowed before and
during the last election a wish to find the policy and measures
of the government such as would justify me in giving them my
support. That wish I sincerely entertained. But the main
question was whether the concert or combination alleged to
have taken place for the purpose of ejecting Lord Derby's
government from office was fact or fiction. I have not the
slightest hesitation in stating to you that it is a fiction.
Evidence for the only presumption in its favour was this—
that we voted against the budget of Mr. Disraeli in strict

[1] Molesworth was ultimately made first commissioner of works.

conformity with every principle of finance we had professed through our political lives and with the policy of former finance ministers from the time of Mr. Pitt, against the "new principles" and "new policies" which Mr. Disraeli declared at Aylesbury his intention to submit to the House of Commons—a pledge which I admit that he completely redeemed.'[1]

All this was true enough, but what people saw was that the first fruits of the victory were a coalition with the whigs, who by voting with Villiers had from the first shown their predetermination against ministers. As Northcote humorously said, Mary Stuart could never get over the presumption which her marriage with Bothwell immediately raised as to the nature of her previous connection with him. It is hard to deny that, as the world goes, the Oxford tories clerical and lay might think they had a case. Lord Derby was the tory minister, and Mr. Gladstone had been a chief instrument in turning him out. That was the one salient fact, and the political flock is often apt to see a thing with a more single eye than their shepherds.

A candidate was found in Mr. Perceval, son of the tory prime minister who had met a tragic death forty years before. The country clergy were plied with instigations and solicitations, public and private. No absurdity was too monstrous to set afloat. Mr. Gladstone had seceded to the episcopal church of Scotland. He had long ceased to be a communicant. He was on close and intimate terms with Cardinal Wiseman. He had incited the pope to persecute protestants at Florence. In this vein a flight of angry articles and circulars descended on every parsonage where there was an Oxford master of arts with his name still on the university books. At the beginning the enemy by a rush were in a majority, but they were speedily beaten out of it. At the end of six days, in spite of frenzied efforts, no more than 1330 votes out of a constituency of 3600 had been recorded. Still the indomitable men insisted on the legal right of keeping the poll open for fifteen days, and learned persons even gloomily hinted that the time might be extended to forty days. In the end (Jan. 20) Mr. Gladstone had 1022 votes against Perceval's 898, or a narrow majority of 124. The tory press justly consoled themselves by calculating that such a majority was only six per cent of the votes polled, but they were very angry with the failure of the protestant electors in doing their patriotic duty against 'the pro-romanist candidate.' The organ of the Peelites, on the other hand, was delighted at the first verdict thus gained from the most influential constituency in Great Britain, in favour of the new experiment of conservative-liberalism and wise and rational progress. Graham said, and truly, that 'though Gladstone's defeat at that precise juncture would have been a misfortune, yet for his own sake hereafter, emancipation from the thraldom of that constituency would be a blessing. It is a millstone under which even Peel would have sunk.'

Was Mr. Gladstone right in his early notion of himself as a slow-moving mind? Would it be true to say that, compared with Pitt, for instance, he ripened slowly? Or can we accurately describe him as having in any department of life, thought, knowledge, feeling, been precocious? Perhaps not. To speak of slowness in a man of such magical rapidity of intellectual apprehension would be indeed a paradox, but we have seen already how when he is walking in the middle path of his years, there is a sense in which he was slow in character and motion. Slowness explains some qualities in his literary and oratorical form, which was often, and especially up to our present period, vague, ambiguous and obscure. The careless and the uncharitable set all down to sophistry. Better observers perceived that his seeming mystifications were in fact the result of a really embarrassed judgment. They pointed out that where the way was clear, as in free trade, colonial government, dissenters' chapels, Jewish disabilities, catholic bishoprics, nobody could run more straight, at higher speed, or with more powerful stride. They began to say that in spite of Russells, Palmerstons, Grahams, Mr. Gladstone, after all, was the least unlikely of them 'to turn out a thoroughgoing man of the people.' These anticipations of democracy there is no sign that Mr. Gladstone himself, in the smallest degree, shared. The newspapers, meanwhile, were all but unanimous in declaring that 'if experience, talent, industry, and virtue, are the attributes required for the government of this empire,' then the coalition government would be one of the best that England had ever seen.

III

Mr. Gladstone's dislike and distrust of the intrusion not only of the rude secular arm, but of anything temporal into the sphere of spiritual things, had been marked enough in the old days of battle at Oxford between the tractarians and the heads, though it was less manifest in the Gorham case. In 1853 he found occasion for an honourable exhibition of the same strong feeling. Maurice had got into trouble with the authorities at King's College by essays in which he was taken to hold that the eternity of the future torment of the wicked is a superstition not warranted by the Thirty-nine Articles. A movement followed in the council of the college to oust Maurice from his professorial chair. Mr. Gladstone took great pains to avert the stroke, and here is the story as he told it to his brother-in-law, Lord Lyttelton :—

To Lord Lyttelton.

Oct. 29, 1853.—I remained in town last Thursday in order to attend the council of K.C., and as far as I could, to see fair play. I was afraid of a very precipitous proceeding, and I regret to say my fears have been verified. The motion carried was the Bishop of London's, but I am bound to say he was quite willing to have waived it for another course, and the proceeding is due to a body of laymen chiefly lords. The motion carried is to the effect that the statements on certain points contained in Maurice's last essay are of a dangerous character, and that his connection with the theology of the school ought not to continue. I moved as an amendment that the bishop be requested to appoint competent theologians who should personally examine how far the statements of Mr. Maurice were conformable to or at variance with the three creeds and the formularies of the church of England, and should make a report upon them, and that the bishop should be requested to communicate with the council. For myself I find in different parts of what Maurice has written things that I cannot, and I am quite certain the council had not been able to, reconcile. This consideration alone seemed to me to show that they were not in a condition to proceed with a definite judgment. I do not feel sufficiently certain what his view as a whole may be, even if I were otherwise competent to judge whether it is within or beyond the latitude allowed by the church in this matter. And independently of all this I thought that even decency demanded of the council, acting perforce in a judicial capacity, that they should let the accused person know in the most distinct terms for *what* he was dismissed, and should show that they had dismissed him, if at all, only after using greater pains to ascertain that his opinions were in real contrariety to some article of the faith. I also cherished the hope, founded on certain parts of what he has said, that his friends might be able in the meantime to arrange some *formula concordiæ* which might avert the scandal and mischief of the dismissal. Sir J. Patteson, Sir B. Brodie, and Mr. Green supported the amendment, but the majority went the other way, and much was I grieved at it. I am not inclined to abate the dogmatic profession of the church—on the contrary, nothing would induce me to surrender the smallest fraction of it; but while jealous of its infraction in any particular, I am not less jealous of the obtrusion of any private or local opinion into the region of dogma ; and above all I hold that there should be as much rigour in a trial of this kind, irrespective of the high character and distinguished powers of the person charged in this particular case, as if he were indicted for murder.[1]

Long afterwards, when the alleged heretic was dead, Mr. Gladstone wrote of him to Mr. Macmillan (April 11, 1884) : 'Maurice is indeed a spiritual splendour, to borrow the phrase of Dante about St. Dominic. His intellectual constitution had long been, and still is, to me a good deal of an enigma. When I remember what is said and thought of him, and by whom, I feel that this must be greatly my own fault.' Some years after the affair at King's College, Maurice was appointed to Vere Street, and the attack upon him was renewed. Mr. Gladstone was one of those who signed an address of recognition and congratulation.

[1] See *Life of Maurice*, ii. p. 195 ; *Life of Wilberforce*, ii. pp. 208-218. See also Mr. Gladstone's letter to Bishop Hampden, 1856, above, p. 124.

CHAPTER II

THE TRIUMPH OF 1853

(1853)

We have not sought to evade the difficulties of our position. . . . We have not attempted to counteract them by narrow or flimsy expedients. . . . We have proposed plans which will go some way towards closing up many vexed financial questions. . . . While we have sought to do justice to intelligence and skill as compared with property —while we have sought to do justice to the great labouring community by further extending their relief from indirect taxation, we have not been guided by any desire to set one class against another.—GLADSTONE (1853).

MR. GLADSTONE began this year, so important both to himself and to the country, with what he described as a short but active and pleasant visit to Oxford. He stayed at Christ Church with Dr. Jacobson, of whom it was observed that he always looked as if on the point of saying something extremely piercing and shrewd, only it never came. He paid many calls, dined at Oriel, had a luncheon and made a speech in the hall at Balliol ; passed busy days and brisk evenings, and filled up whatever spare moments he could find or manufacture, with treasury papers, books on taxation, consolidated annuities, and public accounts, alternating with dips into Lamennais—the bold and passionate French mystic, fallen angel of his church, most moving of all the spiritual tragedies of that day of heroic idealists.

On February 3 he moved into the house of the chancellor of the exchequer in that best-known of all streets which is not a street, where he was destined to pass some two-and-twenty of the forty-one years of the public life that lay before him. He had a correspondence with Mr. Disraeli, his predecessor, on the valuation of the furniture in the official house. There was question, also, of the robe that passes down under some law of exchange from one chancellor to another on an apparently unsettled footing. The tone on this high concern was not wholly amicable. Mr. Gladstone notes especially in his diary that he wrote a draft of one of his letters on a Sunday, as being, I suppose, the day most favourable to self-control ; while Mr. Disraeli at last suggests that Mr. Gladstone should really con-

sult Sir Charles Wood, 'who is at least a man of the world.'
Such are the angers of celestial minds.

At an early cabinet (Feb. 5) he began the battle that lasted
in various shapes all the rest of his life. It was on a question
of reducing the force in the Pacific. 'Lord Aberdeen, Granville, Molesworth, and I were for it. We failed.' What was
the case for this particular retrenchment I do not know, nor
does it matter. Fiercer engagements, and many of them, were
to follow. Meanwhile he bent all the energies of his mind to
the other front of financial questions—to raising money rather
than expending it, and with unwearied industry applied
himself to solve the problem of redistributing the burdens
and improving the machinery of taxation.

For many years circumstances had given to finance a lively
and commanding place in popular interest. The protracted
discussion on the corn law, conducted not only in senate and
cabinet, but in country market-places and thronged exchanges,
in the farmer's ordinary and at huge gatherings in all the large
towns in the kingdom, had agitated every class in the community. The battle between free trade and protection, ending
in a revolution of our commercial system, had awakened men
to the enormous truth, as to which they are always so soon
ready to relapse into slumber, that budgets are not merely
affairs of arithmetic, but in a thousand ways go to the root of
the prosperity of individuals, the relations of classes, and the
strength of kingdoms. The finance of the whigs in the years
after the Reform bill had not only bewildered parliament, but
had filled merchants, bankers, shipowners, manufacturers, shopkeepers, and the whole array of general taxpayers with perplexity and dismay. Peel recovered a financial equilibrium
and restored public confidence, but Peel was gone. The whigs
who followed him after 1846 had once more laboured under an
unlucky star in this vital sphere of national affairs. They performed the unexampled feat of bringing forward four budgets
in a single year, the first of them introduced by Lord John
Russell himself as prime minister. By 1851 floundering had
reached a climax. Finance had thus discredited one historical
party; it had broken up the other. It was finance that overthrew weak governments and hindered the possibility of a
strong one.

Mr. Disraeli, the most unsparing of all the assailants of
Peel, tried his own hand in 1852. To have the genius and the
patience of a great partisan chief is one gift, and this he had ;
to grasp the complex material interests of a vast diversified
society like the United Kingdom demands powers of a different
order. The defeat of Mr. Disraeli's budget at the end of 1852
seemed to complete the circle of fiscal confusion. Every source
of public income was the object of assault. Every indirect
tax was to be reduced or swept away, and yet no two men

appeared to agree upon the principles of the direct taxes that
were to take their place. The window duty, the paper duty,
the tax on advertisements, the malt-tax, the stamp on marine
insurances, were all to vanish, but even the most zealous
reformers were powerless to fill the void. The order-book of
the House of Commons was loaded with motions about the
income-tax, and an important committee sat in 1851 to consider
all the questions connected with the possibility of its readjust-
ment and amendment. They could not even frame a report.
The belief that it was essentially unjust to impose the tax at
one and the same rate upon permanent and temporary incomes,
prevailed in the great mass, especially of the liberal party.
Discussions arose all through this period, descending not only
to the elementary principles of taxation, but, as Mr. Gladstone
said, almost to the first principles of civilised society itself.
Party distraction, ministerial embarrassment, adjournment
after adjournment of a decision upon fundamental maxims
of national taxation—such was the bewildered scene. At last
a statesman appeared, a financier almost by accident (for,
as we have seen, it was by no special choice of his own that
Mr. Gladstone went to the exchequer), but a financier endowed
with a practical imagination of the highest class, with a combination of the spirit of vigorous analysis and the spirit of
vigorous system, with the habit of unflagging toil, and above
all, with the gift of indomitable courage. If anybody suggested
the reappointment of Hume's committee, the idea was wisely
dismissed. It was evidently, as Graham said, the duty of the
executive government to lead the way and to guide public
opinion in a matter of this crucial importance. It seemed
impossible and unworthy to avoid a frank declaration about
the income-tax. He was strongly of opinion (March 15) that a
larger measure would be carried with greater certainty and
ease than simple renewal ; and that a combination of income-
tax, gradually diminishing to a fixed term of extinction, with
reduction of the interest of debt, and a review of the probate
and legacy duties, afforded the best ground for a financial
arrangement both successful and creditable. It was strong
ideas of this kind that encouraged Mr. Gladstone to build on a
broad foundation.

The nature of his proceedings he set out in one of the most
interesting of his political memoranda :—

The liberals were, to all appearance, pledged to the reconstruction of
the tax by their opinions, and the tories by their party following. The
small fraction of Peelites could probably be relied upon the other way,
and some few individuals with financial knowledge and experience. The
mission of the new government was described by Lord Aberdeen in the
House of Lords as a financial mission, and the stress of it thus lay upon
a person very ill-prepared. My opinions were with Peel ; but under such
circumstances it was my duty to make a close and searching investiga-

tion into the whole nature of the tax, and make up my mind whether there was any means of accepting or compounding with the existing state of opinion. I went to work, and laboured very hard. When I had entered gravely upon my financial studies, I one day had occasion—I know not what—to go into the city and to call upon Mr. Samuel Gurney, to whom experience and character had given a high position there. He asked me with interest about my preparations for my budget; and he said, 'One thing I will venture to urge, whatever your plan is,—let it be simple.' I was a man much disposed to defer to authority, and I attached weight to this advice. But as I went further and further into my subject, I became more and more convinced that, as an honest steward, I had no option but to propose the renewal of the tax in its uniform shape. I constructed much elaborate argument in support of my proposition, which I knew it would be difficult to answer. But I also knew that no amount of unassisted argument would suffice to overcome the obstacles in my way, and that this could only be done by large compensations in my accompanying propositions. So I was led legitimately on, and on, until I had framed the most complicated scheme ever submitted to parliament.

Truly has it been said that there is something repulsive to human nature in the simple reproduction of defunct budgets. Certainly if anything can be more odious than a living tax, it is a dead one. It is as much as is consonant to biography to give an outline of the plan that was gradually wrought out in Mr. Gladstone's mind during the first three laborious months of 1853, and to mark the extraordinarily far-reaching and comprehensive character of the earliest of his thirteen budgets. Its initial boldness lay in the adoption of the unusual course of estimating the national income roughly for a long period of seven years, and assuming that expenditure would remain tolerably steady for the whole of that period. Just as no provident man in private life settles his establishment on the basis of one year or two years only, so Mr. Gladstone abandoned hand-to-mouth, and took long views. 'I ought, no doubt,' he said afterwards, 'to have pointed out explicitly that a great disturbance and increase of our expenditure would baffle my reckonings.' Meanwhile, the fabric was planned on strong foundations and admirable lines. The simplification of the tariff of duties of customs, begun by Peel eleven years before, was carried forward almost to completion. Nearly one hundred and forty duties were extinguished, and nearly one hundred and fifty were lowered. The tea duty was to be reduced in stages extending over three years from over two shillings to one shilling. In the department of excise, the high and injurious duty on soap, which brought into the exchequer over eleven hundred thousand pounds annually, was swept entirely away. In the same department, by raising the duties on spirits manufactured in Ireland nearer to the level of England and Scotland, a step was taken towards identity of taxation in the three kingdoms—by no means an unequivocal good. Miscellaneous provisions and minor aspects of the scheme need not detain us ; but a great reform of rate and scale in the system of the assessed taxes, the reduction of the duty on the beneficent practice of life insurance from half-a-crown to sixpence on the hundred pounds, and the substitution of a uniform receipt stamp, were no contemptible contributions to the comfort and well-being of the community. Advertisements in newspapers became free of duty.[1]

The keystone of the budget in Mr. Gladstone's conception was the position to be assigned in it to the income-tax. This he determined to renew for a period of seven years,—for two years at sevenpence in the pound, for two years more at sixpence, and for the last three at fivepence. By that time he hoped that parliament would be able to dispense with it. Meanwhile it was to be extended to Ireland, in compensation for the remission of a debt owed by Ireland to the British treasury of between four and five millions. It was to be extended, also, at a reduced rate of fivepence, to incomes between a hundred and fifty and a hundred pounds—the former having hitherto been the line of total exemption. From the retention of the income-tax as a portion of the permanent and ordinary finance of the country the chancellor of the exchequer was wholly and strongly averse, and so he remained for more than twenty years to come. In order, however, to meet a common and a just objection, that under this impost intelligence, enterprise, and skill paid too much and property paid too little, he resolved upon a bold step. He proposed that the legacy duty, hitherto confined to personal property passing on death, either by will or by inheritance and not by settlement, should henceforth be extended to real property, and to both descriptions of property passing by settlement, whether real or personal. In a word, the legacy duty was to extend to all successions whatever. This was the proposal that in many senses cut deepest. It was the first rudimentary breach in the ramparts of the territorial system, unless, indeed, we count as first the abolition of the corn law.[2] Mr. Gladstone eagerly disclaimed any intention of accelerating by the pressure of fiscal enactment changes in the tenure of landed property, and the letters which the reader has already seen (pp. 255-8) show the high social value that he invariably set upon the maintenance of the old landed order. The succession duty, as we shall find, for the time disappointed his expectations, for he counted on two millions, and in fact it

[1] A curious parliamentary incident occurred. The original proposal was to reduce the duty from eighteenpence to sixpence. A motion to repeal it altogether was rejected by ten. Then a motion was made to substitute zero for sixpence in the clause. The Speaker ruled that this reversal of the previous vote was not out of order, and it was carried by nine.

[2] Some may place first the Act of 1833 making real estate liable for simple contract debts.

yielded little more than half of one. But it secured for its author the lasting resentment of a powerful class.

Such was the scheme that Mr. Gladstone now worked out in many weeks of toil that would have been slavish, were it not that toil is never slavish when illuminated by a strenuous purpose. When by and by the result had made him the hero of a glorious hour, he wrote to Lord Aberdeen (April 19) : ' I had the deepest anxiety with regard to you, as our chief, lest by faults of my own I should aggravate the cares and difficulties into which I had at least helped to bring you ; and the novelty of our political relations with many of our colleagues, together with the fact that I had been myself slow, and even reluctant, to the formation of a new connection, filled me with an almost feverish desire to do no injustice to that connection now that it was formed ; and to redeem the pledge you generously gave on my behalf, that there would be no want of cordiality and zeal in the discharge of any duties which it might fall to me to perform on behalf of such a government as was then in your contemplation.'

Thirteen, fourteen, fifteen hours a day he toiled at his desk. Treasury officials and trade experts, soap deputations and post-horse deputations, representatives of tobacco and representatives of the West India interest, flocked to Downing Street day by day all through March. If he went into the city to dine with the Lord Mayor, the lamentable hole thus made in his evening was repaired by working till four in the morning upon customs reform, Australian mints, budget plans of all kinds. It is characteristic that even this mountain load of concentrated and exacting labour did not prevent him from giving a Latin lesson every day to his second boy.

II

'Some days before the day appointed for my statement,' says Mr. Gladstone, 'I recited the leading particulars to my able and intelligent friend Cardwell, not in the cabinet but then holding office as president of the board of trade. He was so bewildered and astounded at the bigness of the scheme, that I began to ask myself, Have I a right to ask my colleagues to follow me amidst all these rocks and shoals ? In consequence I performed a drastic operation upon the plan, and next day I carried to Lord Aberdeen a reduced and mutilated scheme which might be deemed by some politicians to be weaker but safer. I put to Lord Aberdeen the question I had put to myself, and stated my readiness, if he should think it called for, to make this sacrifice to the probable inclinations of my colleagues. But he boldly and wisely said, "I take it upon myself to ask you to bring your original and whole plan before the cabinet." I thought this an ample warrant.'

At last, after Mr. Gladstone had spent an hour at the palace in explaining his scheme to the Prince Consort, the budget was opened to the cabinet (April 9) in a speech of three hours—an achievement, I should suppose, unparalleled in that line, for a cabinet consists of men each with pretty absorbing pre-occupations of his own. The exposition was 'as ingenious,' Lord Aberdeen told Prince Albert, 'as clear, and for the most part as convincing, as anything I have ever heard.' 'Gladstone,' said Lord Aberdeen later (1856) 'does not weigh well against one another different arguments, each of which has a real foundation. But he is unrivalled in his power of proving that a specious argument has no real foundation. On the Succession bill the whole cabinet was against him. He delivered to us much the same speech as he made in the House of Commons. At its close we were all convinced.'[1]

Differences that might easily become serious speedily arose upon details in the minds of two or three of them, and for some days the prime minister regarded the undertaking as not only difficult but perilous. Sir Charles Wood, in cabinet (April 11), strongly disapproved of the extension of income-tax to Ireland, and of the lowering of the exemption line. On Ireland the plan would lay more than half a million of new taxation, whereas much of the relief, such as soap and assessed taxes, would not touch her.[2] Palmerston thought it a great plan, perfectly just, and admirably put together, only it opened too many points of attack, and it could never be carried : Disraeli was on the watch, the Irish would join him, so would the radicals, while the succession duty, to which Palmerston individually had great objection, would estrange many conservatives. Lord John Russell perceived difficulties, but he did not see an alternative. Graham then fell in, disliked the twofold extension of the income-tax, and thought they should only take away half the soap-tax. Lord Lansdowne (a great Irish landlord) agreed with him. Mr. Gladstone told them that he was willing to propose whatever the cabinet might decide on, except one thing, namely, the breaking up of the basis of the income-tax : that he could not be a party to ; he should regard it as a high political offence. With this reservation he should follow their judgment, but he strongly adhered to his whole plan. Lord Aberdeen said, 'You must take care your proposals are not unpopular ones.' Mr. Gladstone replied that it was after applying the test of popularity, that he was convinced the budget would be damaged beforehand by some of the small changes that had been suggested.

At the end of a long and interesting discussion, there stood for the whole budget Lord John, Newcastle, Clarendon, Molesworth, Gladstone, with Argyll and Aberdeen more or less

[1] Mrs. Simpson's *Many Memories*, p. 237.
[2] For paper on Irish income-tax, see Appendix.

favourable ; for dropping the two extensions of income-tax and keeping half the soap duty, Lansdowne, Graham, Wood ; more or less leaning towards them, Palmerston and Granville. They agreed to meet again the next day (April 12), when they got into the open sea. Wood stuck to his text. Lansdowne suggested that an increased spirit duty and an income-tax for Ireland together would be something like a breach of faith. Palmerston thought they would be beaten, but he would accept the budget provided they were not to be bound to dissolve or resign upon such a point as the two extensions of the income-tax. Lord John said that if they were beaten on differentiating the tax, they would have to dissolve. Palmerston expressed his individual opinion in favour of a distinction for precarious incomes, and would act in that sense if he were out of the government ; as it was, he assented. Argyll created a diversion by suggesting the abandonment of the Irish spirit duty. Mr. Gladstone admitted that he thought the spirit duty the weakest point of the plan, though warrantable and tenable on the whole. At last, after further patient and searching discussion, the cabinet finding that the suggested amendments cut against one another, were for adopting the entire budget, the dissentients being Lansdowne, Graham, Wood, and Herbert. Graham was full of ill auguries, but said he would assent and assist. Wood looked grave, and murmured that he must take time.

In the course of these preliminaries Lord John Russell had gone to Graham, very uneasy about the income-tax. Graham, though habitually desponding, bade him be of good cheer. Their opponents, he said, were in numbers strong ; but the budget would be excellent to dissolve upon, and Lord John admitted that they would gain forty seats. They agreed, however, in Graham's language, that it would never do to play their trump card until the state of the game actually required it. Lord John confessed that he was no judge of figures,— somewhat of a weakness in a critic of a budget,—and Graham comforted him by the reply that he was at any rate the best judge living of House of Commons tactics.

The position of the government in the House of Commons was notoriously weak. The majority that had brought them into existence was excessively narrow. It had been well known from the first that if any of the accidents of a session should happen to draw the tories, the Irish, and the radicals into one lobby, ministers would find themselves in a minority. Small defeats occurred. The budget was only four days off. Mr. Gladstone enters in his diary : 'Spoke against Gibson ; beaten by 200—169. Our third time this week. Very stiff work this. Ellice said dissolution would be the end of it ; we agreed in the House to a cabinet to-morrow. Herbert and Cardwell, to whom I spoke, inclined to dissolve.' Next day (April 15), the cabinet met in a flutter, for the same tactics might well be repeated, whenever Mr. Disraeli should think the chances good.

Lord John adverted to the hostility of the radicals as exhibited in the tone of the debate, and hinted the opinion that they must take in a reef or two. Mr. Gladstone doubted whether the budget could live in that House, whatever form it might assume; but even with such perils he should look upon the whole budget as less unsafe than a partial contraction. Graham took the same view of the disposition of parliament : keen opposition ; lukewarm support ; the necessity of a greater party sympathy and connection to enable them to surmount the difficulties of a most unusual and hazardous operation. But he did not appear to lean to dissolution, and the older members of the cabinet generally declared themselves against it. 'In the end we went back to the position that we must have a budget on Monday, but Clarendon, Herbert, and Palmerston joined the chorus of those who said the measure was too sharp upon Ireland. The idea was then started whether we should go the length of the entire remission of the consolidated annuities[1] and impose the income-tax at sevenpence, with the augmented spirit duty. This view found favour generally ; and I felt that some excess in the mere sacrifice of money was no great matter compared with the advantage of so great an approximation to equal taxation.' Then, 'speaking with great deference,' Gladstone repeated his belief once more that the entire budget was safer than a contracted one, both for the House and the country, and his conviction that if they proposed it, the name and fame of the government at any rate would stand well. 'Wood seemed still to hang back, but the rest of the cabinet now appeared well satisfied, and we parted, each resolved and certainly more likely to stand or fall by the budget as a whole than we seemed to be on Wednesday.'

III

The decisive cabinet was on Saturday. April 16. It was finally settled that the budget should be proposed as it stood, with its essential features unaltered. On Sunday, the chancellor of the exchequer went as usual twice to church, and read the *Paradiso* ; 'but I was obliged,' he says, with an accent of contrition, 'to give several hours to my figures.' Monday brought the critical moment. 'April 18. Wrote minutes. Read Shakespeare at night. This day was devoted to working up my papers and figures for the evening. Then drove and walked with C. [Mrs. Gladstone]. Went at 4½ to the House. Spoke 4¾ hours in detailing the

[1] Loans made to Ireland for various purposes.

financial measures, and my strength stood out well, thank God. Many kind congratulations afterwards. Herberts and Wortleys came home with us and had soup and negus.'

The proceeding that figures here so simply was, in fact, one of the great parliamentary performances of the century. Lord Aberdeen wrote to Prince Albert that 'the display of power was wonderful; it was agreed in all quarters that there had been nothing like the speech for many years, and that under the impression of his commanding eloquence the reception of the budget had been most favourable.' Lord John told the Queen the speech was one of the ablest ever made in the House of Commons. 'Mr. Pitt, in the days of his glory, might have been more imposing, but he could not have been more persuasive.' Lord Aberdeen heard from Windsor the next day : 'The Queen must write a line to Lord Aberdeen to say how delighted she is at the great success of Mr. Gladstone's speech last night. . . . We have every reason to be sanguine now, which is a great relief to the Queen.' Prince Albert used the same language to Mr. Gladstone : 'I cannot resist writing you a line in order to congratulate you on the success of your speech of yesterday. I have just completed a close and careful perusal of it and should certainly have cheered had I a seat in the House. I hear from all sides that the budget has been well received. Trusting that your Christian humility will not allow you to be dangerously elated, I cannot help sending for your perusal the report which Lord John Russell sent to the Queen, feeling sure that it will give you pleasure, such approbation being the best reward a public man can have.'

On the cardinal question of the fortunes of the ministry its effect was decisive. The prime minister wrote to Mr. Gladstone himself (April 19): 'While everybody is congratulating *me* on the wonderful impression produced in the House of Commons last night, it seems only reasonable that I should have a word of congratulation for *you*. You will believe how much more sincerely I rejoice on your account than on my own, although most assuredly, if the existence of my government shall be prolonged, it will be your work.' To Madame de Lieven Aberdeen said that Gladstone had given a strength and lustre to the administration which it could not have derived from anything else. No testimony was more agreeable to Mr. Gladstone than a letter from Lady Peel. 'I know the recollections,' he replied, 'with which you must have written, and therefore I will not scruple to say that as I was inspired by the thought of treading, however unequally, in the steps of my great teacher and master in public affairs, so it was one of my keenest anxieties not to do dishonour to his memory, or injustice to the patriotic policy with which his name is for ever associated.'[1]

[1] Cavour, as Costi's letters show, took an eager interest in Mr. Gladstone's budget speech.

CHAP. II. ÆT. 44   POWER OF THE PERFORMANCE   349

Greville makes a true point when he says that the budget
speech 'has raised Gladstone to a great political elevation,
and what is of far greater consequence than the measure itself,
has given the country assurance of a *man* equal to great
political necessities and fit to lead parties and direct governments.'[1] Mr. Gladstone had made many speeches that were in
a high degree interesting, ingenious, attractive, forcible. He
now showed that besides and apart from all this, he was the
possessor of qualities without which no amount of rhetorician's
glitter commands the House of Commons for a single hour
after the fireworks have ceased to blaze. He showed that he
had precise perception, positive and constructive purpose, and
a powerful will. In 1851, he had on two occasions exhibited
the highest competency as a critic of the budget of Sir Charles
Wood. On the memorable night in the previous December,
when he had torn Mr. Disraeli's budget to pieces, he had proved
how terrifying he could be in exposure and assault. He now
triumphantly met the test that he had triumphantly applied to
his predecessor, and presented a command of even more imposing resources in the task of responsible construction than
he had displayed in irresponsible criticism. The speech was
saturated with fact; the horizons were large; and the opening
of each in the long series of topics, from Mr. Pitt and the great
war, down to the unsuspected connection between the repeal of
the soap-tax and the extinction of the slave trade in Africa,
was exalted and spacious. The arguments throughout were
close, persuasive, exhaustive; the moral appeal was in the only
tone worthy of a great minister addressing a governing
assembly—a masculine invocation of their intellectual and
political courage. This is the intrepid way in which a strong
parliament and a strong nation like to see public difficulties
handled, and they now welcomed the appearance of a new
minister, who rejected what he called narrow and flimsy expedients, of which so much had been seen in the last half-dozen
years; who was not afraid to make a stand against heedless
men with hearts apparently set on drying up one source of
revenue after another; who did not shrink from sconcing the
powerful landed phalanx like other people; and who at the
same time boldly used and manfully defended the most unpopular of all the public imposts. In politics the spectacle of
sheer courage is often quite as good in its influence and effect
as the best of logic. It was so here. While proposing that the
income-tax should come to an end in seven years, he yet produced the most comprehensive analysis and the boldest vindication of the structure of the tax as it stood. His manner was
plain, often almost conversational, but his elaborate examination of the principles of an income-tax remains to this day a
master example of accurate reasoning thrown into delightful

[1] Greville, Third Series, i. p. 59.

form. He admitted all the objections to it : the inquisition
that it entailed, the frauds to which it led, the sense in the
public mind of its injustice in laying the same rate upon the
holder of idle and secured public funds, upon the industrious
trader, upon the precarious earnings of the professional man.
It was these disadvantages that made him plan the extinction of the tax at the end of a definite period, when the
salutary remissions of other burdens now proposed would
have had time to bring forth their fruits. As was said by a
later chancellor of the exchequer, this speech not only won
'universal applause from his audience at the time, but changed
the convictions of a large part of the nation, and turned, at
least for several years, a current of popular opinion which had
seemed too powerful for any minister to resist.'[1]

The succession duty brought Mr. Gladstone into the first
conflict of his life with the House of Lords. That land should
be made to pay like other forms of property was a proposition
denounced as essentially impracticable, oppressive, unjust,
cowardly, and absurd. It was called *ex post facto* legislation.
It was one of the most obnoxious, detestable, and odious
measures ever proposed. Its author was a vulture soaring over
society, waiting for the rich harvest that death would pour into
his treasury. Lord Derby invoked him as a phœnix chancellor,
in whom Mr. Pitt rose from his ashes with double lustre, for
Mr. Gladstone had ventured where Pitt had failed. He admitted that nothing short of the chancellor's extraordinary
skill and dexterity could have carried proposals so evil through
the House of Commons.[2] Meanwhile the public counted up
their gains :—a remission on tea, good for twenty shillings a
year in an ordinary household ; a fall in the washing bill ;
a boon of a couple of pounds for the man who insured his life for
five hundred ; an easy saving of ten pounds a year in the assessed
taxes, and so forth,—the whole performance ending with 'a dissolving view of the decline and fall' of the hated income-tax.

The financial proceedings of this year included a proposal
for the redemption of South Sea stock and an attempted
operation on the national debt, by the creation of new stocks
bearing a lower rate of interest, two options of conversion
being given to the holders of old stock. The idea of the
creation of a two-and-half-per-cent stock, said Mr. Gladstone
in later years, though in those days novel, was very favourably
received.[3]

---

[1] Northcote, *Twenty Years of Financial Policy*, p. 185.

[2] Mr. Gladstone received valuable aid from Bethell, the solicitor - general. On
leaving office in 1855 he wrote to Bethell :—'After having had to try your patience
more than once in circumstances of real difficulty, I have found your kindness inexhaustible, and your aid invaluable, so that I really can ill tell on which of the two
I look back with the greater pleasure. The memory of the Succession Duty bill is to
me something like what Inkermann may be to a private of the Guards : you were the
sergeant from whom I got my drill and whose hand and voice carried me through.'

[3] The city articles of the time justify this statement.

I produced my plan. Disraeli offered it a malignant opposition. He made a demand for time; the one demand that ought not to have been made. In proposals of this kind, it is allowed to be altogether improper. In 1844 Mr. Goulburn was permitted, I think, to carry through with great expedition his plan for a large reduction of interest. When Mr. Goschen produced his still larger and much more important measure, we, the opposition, did our best to expedite the decision. There are no complications requiring time on such an occasion. It is a matter of aye or no. But when time is allowed the chapter of accidents allows an opponent to hope that a situation known to be unusually happy will deteriorate. Of this contingency Disraeli took his chance. Time as it happened was in his favour. It was no question of the substance of the plan, but a moderate change in the political barometer, which reduced to two or three millions a subscription which at the right moment would probably have been twenty or thirty.[1]

In a letter to W. R. Farquhar (March 8, 1861) he makes further remarks, which are introspective and autobiographic:—

Looking back now upon those of my proceedings in 1853 which related to interest upon exchequer bills and to the reduction of interest on the public debt, I think that there was nothing in the proposals themselves which might not have taken full and quick effect, if they had been made at a time which I may best describe as the time that precedes high-water with respect to abundance of money and security of the market. As respects exchequer bills, I am decidedly of opinion that the rates of premium current for some years before '53 were wholly incompatible with a sound state of things: and the fluctuations then were even greater than since. Still I think that I committed an error from want of sufficient quickness in discerning the signs of the times, for we were upon the very eve of an altered state of things, and any alteration of a kind at all serious was enough to make the period unfit for those grave operations. It is far from being the first or only time when I have had reason to lament my own deficiency in the faculty of rapid and comprehensive observation. I failed to see that high-water was just past; and that although the tide had not perceptibly fallen, yet it was going to fall. The truth likewise is this (to go a step further in my confessions) that almost all my experience in money affairs had been of a most difficult and trying kind, under circumstances which admitted of no choice but obliged me to sail always very near the wind, and this induced a habit of more daring navigation than I could now altogether approve. Nor will I excuse myself by saying that others were deceived like me, for none of them were in a condition to have precisely my responsibility.

Another note contributes a further point of explanation : 'I have always imagined that this fault was due to my experience in the affairs of the Hawarden and Oak Farm estates, where it was an incessant course of sailing near the wind, and there was really no other hope.'

Seven years later Mr. Gladstone, once more chancellor of the exchequer, again produced a budget. Semi-ironic cheers met his semi-ironic expression of an expectation that he would be asked the question : what had become of the calculations of

[1] Gladstone Memo. 1879.   See also Appendix.

1853? The succession duty proved a woeful disappointment, and instead of producing two million pounds, produced only six hundred thousand. A similar but greater disappointment, we must recollect, owing mainly to a singular miscalculation as to the income-tax, had marked Peel's memorable budget of 1842, which landed him in a deficiency of nearly two and a quarter millions, instead of a surplus of half a million.[1] Of the disappointment in his own case, Mr. Gladstone when the time came propounded an explanation, only moderately conclusive. I need not discuss it, for as everybody knows, the effective reason why the income-tax could not be removed was the heavy charge created by the Crimean war. What is more to the point in estimating the finance of 1853, is its effect in enabling us to meet the strain of the war. It was this finance that, continuing the work begun by Peel, made the country in 1859 richer by more than sixteen per cent than it had been in 1853. It was this finance, that by clinching the open questions that enveloped the income-tax, and setting it upon a defensible foundation while it lasted, bore us through the struggle. Unluckily, in demonstrating the perils of meddling with the structure of the tax, in showing its power and simplicity, the chancellor was at the same time providing the easiest means, if not also the most direct incentive, to that policy of expenditure—it rose from fifty to seventy millions between 1853 and 1859,—which was one of the most fatal obstacles to the foremost aims of his political life. It was twenty years from now, as my readers will see, before the effort, now foreshadowed, to exclude the income-tax from the ordinary sources of national revenue, reached its dramatic close.

[1] It may be said, however, that Peel was right about the yield of the income-tax, and only overlooked the fact that it would not all be collected within the year.

CHAPTER III

THE CRIMEAN WAR

(1853–1854)

He [Burke] maintained that the attempt to bring the Turkish empire into the consideration of the balance of power in Europe was extremely new, and contrary to all former political systems. He pointed out in strong terms the danger and impolity of our espousing the Ottoman cause.—BURKE (1791).

AFTER the session Mr. Gladstone had gone on a visit to Dunrobin, and there he was laid up with illness for many days. It was the end of September before he was able to travel south. At Dingwall they presented him (Sept. 27) with the freedom of that ancient burgh. He spoke of himself as having completed the twenty-first year of his political life, and as being almost the youngest of those veteran statesmen who occupied the chief places in the counsels of the Queen. At Inverness the same evening, he told them that in commercial legislation he had reaped where others had sown ; that he had enjoyed the privilege of taking a humble but laborious part in realising those principles of free trade which, in the near future, would bring, in the train of increased intercourse and augmented wealth, that closer social and moral union of the nations of the earth which men all so fervently desire, and which must in the fulness of time lessen the frequency of strife and war. Yet even while the hopeful words were falling from the speaker's lips, he might have heard, not in far distance but close at hand, the trumpets and drums, the heavy rumbling of the cannon, and all the clangour of a world in arms.

II

One of the central and perennial interests of Mr. Gladstone's life was that shifting, intractable, and interwoven tangle of conflicting interests, rival peoples, and antagonistic faiths, that is veiled under the easy name of the Eastern question. The root of the Eastern question, as everybody almost too well knows, is the presence of the Ottoman Turks in Europe, their possession of Constantinople,—that incomparable centre of

imperial power standing in Europe but facing Asia,—and their
sovereignty as Mahometan masters over Christian races. In
one of the few picturesque passages of his eloquence Mr. Gladstone once described the position of these races. 'They were
like a shelving beach that restrained the ocean. That beach,
it is true, is beaten by the waves; it is laid desolate; it
produces nothing; it becomes perhaps nothing save a mass
of shingle, of rock, of almost useless sea-weed. But it is a
fence behind which the cultivated earth can spread, and escape
the incoming tide, and such was the resistance of Bulgarians,
of Servians, and of Greeks. It was that resistance which left
Europe to claim the enjoyment of her own religion and to
develop her institutions and her laws.' This secular strife
between Ottoman and Christian gradually became a struggle
among Christian powers of northern and western Europe, to
turn tormenting questions in the east to the advantage of
rival ambitions of their own. At a certain epoch in the
eighteenth century Russia first seized her place among the
Powers. By the end of the century she had pushed her force
into the west by the dismemberment of Poland; she had made
her way to the southern shores of the Black Sea; and while
still the most barbaric of all the states, she had made good a
vague claim to exercise the guardianship of civilisation on
behalf of the Christian races and the Orthodox church. This
claim it was that led at varying intervals of time, and with
many diversities of place, plea, and colour, to crisis after crisis
springing up within the Turkish empire, but henceforth all of
them apt to spread with dangerous contagion to governments
beyond Ottoman limits.

England, unlike France, had no systematic tradition upon
this complicated struggle. When war began between Russia
and the Porte in 1771, we supported Russia and helped her
to obtain an establishment in the Black Sea. Towards the
end of 1782 when Catherine by a sort of royal syllogism, as
Fox called it, took the Crimea into her own hands, the whig
cabinet of the hour did not think it necessary to lend Turkey
their support, though France and Spain proposed a combination
to resist. Then came Pitt. The statesman whose qualities of
greatness so profoundly impressed his contemporaries has
usually been praised as a minister devoted to peace, and
only driven by the French Revolution into the long war.
His preparations in 1791 for a war with Russia on behalf of
the Turk are a serious deduction from this estimate. Happily
the alarms of the Baltic trade, and the vigorous reasoning of
Fox, produced such an effect upon opinion, that Pitt was
driven, on peril of the overthrow of his government, to find
the best expedient he could to bring the business to an end
without extremities. In 1853 the country was less fortunate
than it had been in 1791.

chiefly admire in England? It is not the rapidity with which you form
constitutions and broach abstract theories. On the contrary, they know
that nothing is so distasteful to you as abstract theories, and that you
are proverbial for resisting what is new until you are well assured by
gradual effort, by progressive trials, and beneficial tendency. But they
know that when you make a step forward you keep it. They know that
there is reality and honesty, strength and substance, about your proceedings. They know that you are not a monarchy to-day, a republic
to-morrow, and a military despotism the day after. They know that
you have been happily preserved from irrational vicissitudes that have
marked the career of the greatest and noblest among the neighbouring
nations. Your fathers and yourselves have earned this brilliant character for England. Do not forfeit it. Do not allow it to be tarnished or
impaired. Show, I beseech you—have the courage to show the pope of
Rome, and his cardinals, and his church, that England too, as well as
Rome, has her *semper eadem*; and that when she has once adopted some
great principle of legislation, which is destined to influence the national
character, to draw the dividing lines of her policy for ages to come, and
to affect the whole nature of her influence and her standing among the
nations of the world—show that when she has done this slowly, and
done it deliberately, she has done it once for all; and that she will then
no more retrace her steps than the river that bathes this giant city can
flow back upon its source. The character of England is in our hands.
Let us feel the responsibility that belongs to us, and let us rely on it ;
if to-day we make this step backwards, it is one which hereafter we shall
have to retrace with pain. We cannot change the profound and resistless tendencies of the age towards religious liberty. It is our business
to guide and to control their application ; do this you may, but to endeavour to turn them backwards is the sport of children, done by the
hands of men, and every effort you may make in that direction will
recoil upon you in disaster and disgrace. The noble lord appealed to
gentlemen who sit behind me, in the names of Hampden and Pym.
I have great reverence for these in one portion at least of their political
career, because they were men energetically engaged in resisting oppression. But I would rather have heard Hampden and Pym quoted
on any other subject than one which relates to the mode of legislation
or the policy to be adopted with our Roman catholic fellow-citizens,
because, if there was one blot on their escutcheon, if there was one
painful—I would almost say odious—feature in the character of the
party among whom they were the most distinguished chiefs, it was the
bitter and ferocious intolerance which in them became the more powerful
because it was directed against the Roman catholics alone. I would
appeal in other names to gentlemen who sit on this side of the House.
If Hampden and Pym were friends of freedom, so were Clarendon and
Newcastle, so were the gentlemen who sustained the principles of loyalty.
. . . They were not always seeking to tighten the chains and deepen the
brand. Their disposition was to relax the severity of the law, and
attract the affections of their Roman catholic fellow-subjects to the
constitution by treating them as brethren. . . . We are a minority
insignificant in point of numbers. We are more insignificant still,
because we are but knots and groups of two or three, we have no power
of cohesion, no ordinary bond of union. What is it that binds us
together against you, but the conviction that we have on our side the

principle of justice—the conviction that we shall soon have on our side
the strength of public opinion (*oh, oh !*). I am sure I have not wished
to say a syllable that would wound the feelings of any man, and if in the
warmth of argument such expressions should have escaped me, I wish
them unsaid. But above all we are sustained by the sense of justice
which we feel belongs to the cause we are defending; and we are, I trust,
well determined to follow that bright star of justice, beaming from the
heavens, whithersoever it may lead.

All this was of no avail, just as the same arguments and
temper on two other occasions of the same eternal theme
in his life,[1] were to be of no avail. Disraeli spoke strongly
against the line taken by the Peelites. The second reading
was carried by 438 against 95, one-third even of this minority
being Irish catholics, and the rest mainly Peelites, 'a limited
but accomplished school,' as Disraeli styled them. Hume
asked Mr. Gladstone for his speech for publication to circulate
among the dissenters who, he said, know nothing about
religious liberty. It was something, however, to find Mr.
Gladstone, the greatest living churchman, and Bright, the
greatest living nonconformist, voting in the same lobby.
The fight was stiff, and was kept up until the end of the
summer. The weapon that had been forged in this blazing
furnace by these clumsy armourers proved blunt and worth-
less; the law was from the first a dead letter, and it was
struck out of the statute book in 1871 in Mr. Gladstone's
own administration.[2]

III

In the autumn (1851) a committee of the whig cabinet,
now reinforced by the admission for the first time of Lord
Granville, was named to prepare a reform bill. Palmerston,
no friend to reform, fell into restive courses that finally
upset the coach. The cabinet, early in November, settled
that he should not receive Kossuth, and he complied; but
he received a public deputation and an address compliment-
ing him for his exertions on Kossuth's behalf. The court
at this proceeding took lively offence, and the Queen
requested the prime minister to ascertain the opinion of the
cabinet upon it. Such an appeal by the sovereign from the
minister to the cabinet was felt by them to be unconstitu-

---

[1] Affirmation bill (1883) and Religious Disabilities Removal bill (1891).

[2] One of the most illustrious of the European liberals of the century wrote to
Senior :—

Ce que vous me dites que le bill contre les titres ecclésiastiques ne mènera à
rien, me paraît vraisemblable, grâce aux mœurs du pays. Mais pourquoi faire des
lois pires que les mœurs? C'est le contraire qui devait être. Je vous avoue que
j'ai été de cœur et d'esprit avec ceux qui comme Lord Aberdeen et M. Gladstone,
se sont opposés au nom de la liberté et du principe même de la réforme, à ces
atteintes à la fois vaines et dangereuses que le bill a portées au moins en théorie à
l'indépendance de conscience. Où se réfugiera la liberté religieuse, si on la chasse
de l'Angleterre ?—Tocqueville, *Corr.* iii. p. 274.

A Russian diplomatist made a homely comparison of the Eastern question to the gout; now its attack is in the foot, now in the hand; but all is safe if only it does not fly to a vital part. In 1852 the Eastern question showed signs of flying to the heart, and a catastrophe was sure. A dispute between Greek and Latin religions as to the custody of the holy places at Jerusalem, followed by the diplomatic rivalries of their respective patrons, Russia and France, produced a crisis that was at first of no extraordinary pattern. The quarrel between two packs of monks about a key and a silver star was a trivial symbol of the vast rivalry of centuries between powerful churches, between great states, between heterogeneous races. The dispute about the holy places was adjusted, but was immediately followed by a claim from the Czar for recognition by treaty of his rights as protector of the Sultan's Christian subjects. This claim the Sultan, with encouragement from the British ambassador, rejected, and the Czar marched troops into the Danubian provinces, to hold them in pledge until the required concession should be made to his high protective claims. This issue was no good cause for a general conflagration. Unfortunately many combustibles happened to lie about the world at that time, and craft, misunderstanding, dupery, autocratic pride, democratic hurry, combined to spread the blaze.

The story is still fresh. With the detailed history of the diplomacy that preceded the outbreak of war between England, France, and Turkey on the one part and Russia on the other, we have here happily only the smallest concern. The large question, as it presented itself to Mr. Gladstone's mind in later years, and as it presents itself now to the historic student, had hardly then emerged to the view of the statesmen of the western Powers. Would the success of Russian designs at that day mean anything better than the transfer of the miserable Christian races to the yoke of a new master?[1] Or was the repulse of these designs necessary to secure to the Christian races—who, by the bye, were not particularly good friends to one another—the power of governing themselves without any master, either Russian or Turk? To this question, so decisive as it is in judging the policy of the Crimean war, it is not quite easy even now for the historian—who has many other things to think of than has the contemporary politician—to give a confident answer.

Nicholas was not without advisers who warned him that the break-up of Turkey by force of Russian arms might be to the deliverer a loss and not a gain. Brunnow, then Russian

---

[1] In 1772 Burke had said that he did not wish well to Turkey, for any people but the Turks, situated as they are, would have been cultivated in three hundred years; yet they grow more gross in the very native soil of civility and refinement. But he did not expect to live to see the Turkish barbarian civilised by the Russian.—*Corr.* i. p. 402.

ambassador at St. James's, said to his sovereign: 'The war in its results would cause to spring out of the ruins of Turkey all kinds of new states, as ungrateful to us as Greece has been, as troublesome as the Danubian Principalities have been, and an order of things where our influence will be more sharply combated, resisted, restrained, by the rivalries of France, England, Austria, than it has ever been under the Ottoman. War cannot turn to our direct advantage. We shall shed our blood and spend our treasure in order that King Otho may gain Thessaly; that the English may take more islands at their own convenience; that the French too may get their share; and that the Ottoman empire may be transformed into independent states, which for us will only become either burdensome clients or hostile neighbours.' If this forecast was right, then to resist Russia was at once to prevent her from embarrassing and weakening herself, and to lock up the Christians in their cruel prison-house for a quarter of a century longer. If sagacious calculation in such a vein as this were the mainspring of the world, history would be stripped of many a crimson page. But far-sighted calculation can no longer be ascribed to the actors in this tragedy of errors—to Nicholas or Napoleon, to Aberdeen or Palmerston, or to any other of them excepting Cavour and the Turk.

In England both people and ministers have been wont to change their minds upon the Eastern question. In the war between Russia and Turkey in 1828, during the last stage of the struggle for Greek independence, Russia as Greek champion against the Turk had the English populace on her side; Palmerston was warmly with her, regarding even her advance to Constantinople with indifference; and Aberdeen was reproached as a Turkish sympathiser. Now we shall see the parts inverted,—England and Palmerston ardent Turks, and Aberdeen falling into disgrace (unjustly enough) as Russian. Before we have done with Mr. Gladstone, the popular wheel will be found to make another and yet another revolution.

III

When Kinglake's first two volumes of his history of the Crimean war appeared (1863), Mr. Gladstone wrote to a friend (May 14): 'Kinglake is fit to be a brilliant popular author, but quite unfit to be a historian. His book is too bad to live, and too good to die. As to the matter most directly within my cognisance, he is not only not too true, but so entirely void of resemblance to the truth, that one asks what was really the original of his picture.'[1] A little earlier he had written to Sir

[1] To Mrs. Gladstone, Jan. 3, 1863 :—' In the evenings I have leisure. Much of it I have been spending in reading Kinglake's book, which touches very nearly, and not agreeably or justly, the character of Lord Aberdeen and his government. I am afraid

John Acton : 'I was not the important person in the negotiation before the war that Mr. Kinglake seems to suppose ; and
with him every supposition becomes an axiom and a dogma.'
All the papers from various sources to which I have had access
show that Mr. Gladstone, as he has just said, had no special
share in the various resolutions taken in the decisive period
that ended with the abandonment of the Vienna note in the
early autumn of 1853. He has himself told us that through
the whole of this critical stage Lord Clarendon, then in charge
of foreign affairs, was the centre of a distinct set of communications, first, with the prime minister, next, with Lord John
Russell as leader in the Commons, and third, with Lord Palmerston, whose long and active career at the foreign office had
given him special weight in that department. The cabinet
as a body was a machine incapable of being worked by anything like daily and sometimes hourly consultations of this
kind, 'the upshot of which would only become known on the
more important occasions to the ministers at large, especially
to those among them charged with the most laborious departments.'[1] This was not at all said by way of exculpating
Mr. Gladstone from his full share of responsibility for the war,
for of that he never at any time showed the least wish or
intention to clear himself, but rather the contrary. As matter
of fact, it was the four statesmen just named who were in
effective control of proceedings until the breakdown of the
Vienna note, and the despatch of the British and French
squadrons through the Dardanelles in October, opened the
second stage of the diplomatic campaign, and led directly if
not rapidly to its fatal climax.

We have little more than a few glimpses of Mr. Gladstone's
participation in the counsels of the eventful months that preceded the outbreak of the war. To Mrs. Gladstone he writes
(October 4) : 'I can hardly at this moment write about anything else than the Turkish declaration of war. This is a most
serious event, and at once raises the question, Are we to go
into it ? The cabinet meets on Friday, and you must not be
surprised at anything that may happen. The weather may be
smooth ; it also may be *very rough*.' First the smooth weather
came. 'October 7. We have had our cabinet, three hours and
a half ; all there but Graham and Molesworth,[2] who would both
have been strongly for peace. We shall have another to-morrow,
to look over our results in writing. Some startling things were
said and proposed, but I think that as far as government is

Newcastle blabbed on what took place, and that his blabbing was much coloured with
egotism. Clarendon, I hear, is very angry with the book, and Lewis too, but Lewis is
not a party concerned.'
[1] *Eng. Hist. Rev.*, No. vi. p. 289.
[2] 'Molesworth in the cabinet,' said Lord Aberdeen later, 'was a failure. Until the
war he was a mere cipher. When the war had broken out and was popular he became
outrageously warlike.'—Mrs. Simpson's *Many Memories*, p. 264 ; see also Cobden's
Speeches, ii. p. 28.

concerned, all will probably keep straight at this juncture, and as to war I hope we shall not be involved in it, even if it goes on between Russia and Turkey, which is not quite certain.' Aberdeen himself thought the aspect of this cabinet of the 7th on the whole very good, Gladstone arguing strongly against a proposal of Palmerston's that England should enter into an engagement with Turkey to furnish her with naval assistance. Most of the cabinet were for peace. Lord John was warlike, but subdued in tone. Palmerston urged his views 'persever-ingly but not disagreeably.' The final instruction was a com-promise, bringing the fleet to Constantinople, but limiting its employment to operations of a strictly defensive character. This was one of those peculiar compromises that in their sequel contain surrender. The step soon showed how critical it was. Well indeed might Lord Aberdeen tell the Queen that it would obviously every day become more and more difficult to draw the line between defensive and offensive, between an auxiliary and a principal. So much simpler is a distinction in words than in things. Still, he was able to assure her that, though grounds of difference existed, the discussions of the cabinet of the 8th were carried on amicably and in good humour. With straightforward common sense the Queen pressed the prime minister for his own deliberate counsel on the spirit and ulti-mate tendency of the policy that he would recommend her to approve. In fact, Lord Aberdeen had no deliberate counsel to proffer. Speedily the weather roughened.

Four days later (October 12) the minister repeated, that while elements of wide difference existed, still the appearance of that day was more favourable and tended to mutual agree-ment. At this cabinet Mr. Gladstone was not present, having gone on an expedition to Manchester, the first of the many triumphal visits of his life to the great industrial centres of the nation. 'Nothing,' he wrote to Lord Aberdeen, 'could have gone off better. Yesterday (October 11), I had to make a visit to the Exchange, which was crammed and most cordial. This morning we had first the "inauguration" of the Peel statue, in the presence of an enormous audience—misnamed so, inasmuch as but a portion of them could hear ; and then a meeting in the Town Hall, where there were addresses and speeches made, to which I had to reply. I found the feeling of the assemblage so friendly that I said more on the war question than I had intended, but I sincerely hope I did not transgress the limits you would think it wise for me to observe. The existence of a peace and a war party was evident, from alternate manifesta-tions, but I think the former feeling was decidedly the stronger, and at any rate I should say without the smallest doubt that the feeling of the whole meeting as a mass was unequivocally favourable to the course that the government have pursued.'

'Your Manchester speech,' Lord Aberdeen wrote to him

in reply, 'has produced a great and, I hope, a very beneficial
effect upon the public mind, and it has much promoted the
cause of peace.' This result was extremely doubtful. The
language of the Manchester speech is cloudy, but what it
comes to is this. It recognises the duty of maintaining the
integrity and independence of the Ottoman empire. Independence, however, in this case, says Mr. Gladstone, designates
a sovereignty full of anomaly, of misery, of difficulty, and it
has been subject every few years since we were born to
European discussion and interference; we cannot forget the
political solecism of Mahometans exercising despotic rule
over twelve millions of our fellow-Christians; into the
questions growing out of this political solecism we are not
now entering; what we see to-day is something different;
it is the necessity for regulating the distribution of power in
Europe; the absorption of power by one of the great potentates
of Europe, which would follow the fall of the Ottoman rule,
would be dangerous to the peace of the world, and it is the
duty of England, at whatever cost, to set itself against such a
result.

This was Mr. Gladstone's first public entry upon one of
the most passionate of all the objects of his concern for
forty years to come. He hears the desolate cry, then but
faint, for the succour of the oppressed Christians. He looks
to European interference to terminate the hateful solecism.
He resists the interference single-handed of the northern
invader. It was intolerable that Russia should be allowed
to work her will upon Turkey as an outlawed state.[1] In
other words, the partition of Turkey was not to follow the
partition of Poland. What we shortly call the Crimean war
was to Mr. Gladstone the vindication of the public law of
Europe against a wanton disturber. This was a characteristic
example of his insistent search for a broad sentiment and
a comprehensive moral principle. The principle in its present
application had not really much life in it; the formula was
narrow, as other invasions of public law within the next
dozen years were to show. But the clear-cut issues of history
only disclose themselves in the long result of Time. It was
the diplomatic labyrinth of the passing hour through which
the statesmen of the coalition had to thread their way.
The disastrous end was what Mr. Disraeli christened the
coalition war.

'The first year of the coalition government,' Lord Aberdeen
wrote to Mr. Gladstone, 'was eminently prosperous, and this
was chiefly owing to your own personal exertions, and to the
boldness, ability, and success of your financial measures. Our
second year, if not specially brilliant, might still have proved
greatly advantageous to the country, had we possessed the

courage to resist popular clamour and to avoid war ; but this calamity aggravated all other causes of disunion and led to our dissolution.'[1]

IV

On November 4, Clarendon wrote to Lord Aberdeen that they were now in an anomalous and painful position, and he had arrived at the conviction that it might have been avoided by firm language and a more decided course five months ago. 'Russia would then, as she is now, have been ready to come to terms, and we should have exercised a control over the Turks that is now not to be obtained.' Nobody, I suppose, doubts to-day that if firmer language had been used in June to Sultan and Czar alike, the catastrophe of war would probably have been avoided, as Lord Clarendon here remorsefully reflects. However that may have been, this pregnant and ominous avowal disclosed the truth that the British cabinet were no longer their own masters; that they had in a great degree, even at this early time, lost all that freedom of action which they constantly proclaimed it the rule of their policy to maintain, and which for a few months longer some of them at least strove very hard but all in vain to recover.

The Turks were driving a. war whilst we were labouring for peace, and both by diplomatic action and by sending the fleet to protect Turkish territory against Russian attack, we had become auxiliaries and turned the weaker of the two contending powers into the stronger. A few months afterwards Mr. Gladstone found a classic parallel for the Turkish alliance. 'When Aeneas escaped from the flames of Troy he had an ally. That ally was his father Anchises, and the part which Aeneas performed in the alliance was to carry his ally upon his back.' But the discovery came too late, nor was the Turk the only ally. Against the remonstrances of our ambassador the Sultan declared war upon Russia, and proceeded to acts of war, well knowing that England and France in what they believed to be interests of their own would see him through it. If the Sultan and his ulemas and his pashas were one intractable factor, the French Emperor was another. 'We have just as much to apprehend,' Graham wrote (Oct. 27), 'from the active intervention of our ally as from the open hostility of our enemy.' Behind the decorous curtain of European concert Napoleon III. was busily weaving scheme after scheme of his own to fix his unsteady diadem upon his brow, to plant his dynasty among the great thrones of western Europe, and to pay off some old scores of personal indignity put upon him by the Czar.

The Czar fell into all the mistakes that a man could.

[1] March 17 1856.

Emperor by divine right, he had done his best to sting the
self-esteem of the revolutionary emperor in Paris. By his
language to the British ambassador about dividing the inheritance of the sick man, he had quickened the suspicions of the
English cabinet. It is true the sick man will die, said Lord
John Russell, but it may not be for twenty, fifty, or a hundred
years to come ; when William III. and Louis XIV. signed their
treaty for the partition of the Spanish monarchy, they first
made sure that the death of the king was close at hand. Then
the choice as agent at Constantinople of the arrogant and
unskilful Menschikoff proved a dire misfortune. Finally, the
Czar was fatally misled by his own ambassador in London.
Brunnow reported that all the English liberals and economists
were convinced that the notion of Turkish reform was absurd ;
that Aberdeen had told him in accents of contempt and anger,
'I hate the Turks'; and that English views generally as to
Russian aggression and Turkish interests had been sensibly
modified. All this was not untrue, but it was not true enough
to bear the inference that was drawn from it at St. Petersburg.
The deception was disastrous, and Brunnow was never forgiven
for it.[1]

Another obstacle to a pacific solution, perhaps most formidable of them all, was Lord Stratford de Redcliffe, the British
ambassador at Constantinople. Animated by a vehement
antipathy to Russia, possessing almost sovereign ascendancy at
the Porte, believing that the Turk might never meet a happier
chance of having the battle out with his adversary once for all,
and justly confident that a policy of war would find hearty
backers in the London cabinet—in him the government had an
agent who while seeming to follow instructions in the narrow
letter baffled them in their spirit. In the autumn of 1853 Lord
Aberdeen wrote to Graham, 'I fear I must renounce the sanguine
view I have hitherto taken of the Eastern question ; for
nothing can be more alarming than the present prospect. I
thought that we should have been able to conquer Stratford,
but I begin to fear that the reverse will be the case, and that
he will succeed in defeating us. Although at our wit's end,
Clarendon and I are still labouring in the cause of peace ; but
really to contend at once with the pride of the Emperor, the
fanaticism of the Turks, and the dishonesty of Stratford is
almost a hopeless attempt.'[2] This description, when he saw it
nearly forty years later, seems to have struck Mr. Gladstone as
harsh. Though he agreed that the passage could hardly be
omitted, he confessed his surprise that Lord Aberdeen should
have applied the word dishonesty to Lord Stratford. He
suggested the addition of a note that should recognise the

[1] See Martens' *Recueil des Traités*, etc., published by the Russian foreign office, 1898,
vol. xii., containing many graphic particulars of these events.

[2] Stanmore, *Earl of Aberdeen*, pp. 270-71.

general character of Lord Stratford, and should point out that
prejudice and passion, by their blinding powers, often produce
in the mind effects like those proper to dishonesty.[1] Perhaps
we may find this a hard saying. Doubtless when he comes
to praise and blame, the political historian must make due
allowance for his actors ; and charity is the grandest of
illuminants. Still hard truth stands first, and amiable
analysis of the psychology of a diplomatic agent who lets
loose a flood of mischief on mankind is by no means what
interests us most about him. Why not call things by their
right names ?[2]

In his private letters (November) Stratford boldly exhibited
his desire for war, and declared that 'the war, to be successful,
must be a very comprehensive war on the part of England and
France.' Well might the Queen say to the prime minister that
it had become a serious question whether they were justified in
allowing Lord Stratford any longer to remain in a situation
that enabled him to frustrate all the efforts of his government
for peace. Yet here, as many another time in these devious
manœuvres, that fearful dilemma interposed—inseparable in
its many forms from all collective action whether in cabinet
or party ; so fit to test to the very uttermost all the moral
fortitude, all the wisdom of a minister, his sense of proportion,
his strength of will, his prudent pliancy of judgment, his power
of balance, his sure perception of the ruling fact. The dilemma
here is patent. To recall Lord Stratford would be to lose Lord
Palmerston and Lord John ; to lose them would be to break up
the government ; to break up the government would be to
sunder the slender thread on which the chances of peace were
hanging.[3] The thought, in short, of the high-minded Aberdeen
striving against hope to play a steadfast and pacific part in
a scene so sinister, among actors of such equivocal or crooked
purpose, recalls nothing so much as the memorable picture long
ago of Maria Theresa beset and baffled by her Kaunitzes and
Thuguts, Catherines, Josephs, great Fredericks, Grand Turks,
and wringing her hands over the consummation of an iniquitous
policy to which the perversity of man and circumstance had
driven her.

As the proceedings in the cabinet dragged on through the
winter, new projects were mooted. The ground was shifted to
what Lord Stratford had called a comprehensive war upon
Russia. Some of the cabinet began to aim at a transformation
of the policy. It was suggested that the moment should be
seized to obtain not merely the observance by Russia of her
treaty obligations to Turkey, but a revision and modification
of the treaties in Turkish interests. This is the well-known
way in which, ever since the world called civilised began, the

---

[1] To Sir A. Gordon, Aug. 31, 1892.　　[2] See Stanmore, p. 253.
[3] This is clearly worked out by Lord Stanmore, p. 254, etc.

area of conflict is widened.   If one plea is eluded or is satisfied, another is found ; and so the peacemakers are at each step checkmated by the warmakers.   The Powers of central Europe were immovable, with motives, interests, designs, each of their own.   Austria had reasons of irresistible force for keeping peace with Russia.   A single victory of Russia in Austrian Poland would enable her to march direct upon Vienna.   Austria had no secure alliance with Prussia ; on the contrary, her German rival opposed her on this question, and was incessantly canvassing the smaller states against her in respect to it.   The French Emperor was said to be revolving a plan for bribing Austria out of Northern Italy by the gift of Moldavia and Wallachia.   All was intricate and tortuous.   The view in Downing Street soon expanded to this, that it would be a shame to England and to France unless the Czar were made not only to abandon his demands, and to evacuate the Princi- palities, but also to renounce some of the stipulations in former treaties on which his present arrogant pretensions had been formed.   In the future, the guarantees for the Christian races should be sought in a treaty not between Sultan and Czar, but between the Sultan and the five Powers.

Men in the cabinet and men out of it, some with ardour, others with acquiescence, approved of war for different reasons, interchangeable in controversial value and cumulative in effect. Some believed, and more pretended to believe, that Turkey abounded in the elements and energies of self-reform, and insisted that she should have the chance.   Others were moved by vague general sympathy with a weak power assailed by a strong one, and that one, moreover, the same tyrannous strength that held an iron heel on the neck of prostrate Poland ; that only a few years before had despatched her legions to help Austria against the rising for freedom and national right in Hungary ; that urged intolerable demands upon the Sultan for the surrender of the Hungarian refugees.   Others again counted the power of Russia already exorbitant, and saw in its extension peril to Europe, and mischief to the interests of England.   Russia on the Danube, they said, means Russia on the Indus.   Russia at Constantinople would mean a complete revolution in the balance of power in the Mediterranean, and to an alarmed vision, a Russia that had only crossed the Pruth was as menacing as if her Cossacks were already encamped in permanence upon the shores of the Bosphorus.

Along with the anxieties of the Eastern question, ministers were divided upon the subject of parliamentary reform.   Some, including the prime minister, went with Lord John Russell in desiring to push a Reform bill.   Others, especially Palmerston, were strongly adverse.   Mr. Gladstone mainly followed the head of the government, but he was still a conservative, and still member for a tory constituency, and he followed his leader rather mechanically and without enthusiasm. Lord Palmerston was suspected by some of his colleagues of raising the war-cry in hopes of drowning the demand for reform. In the middle of December (1853) he resigned upon reform,[1] but nine days later he withdrew his resignation and returned. In the interval news of the Russian attack on the Turkish fleet at Sinope (November 30) had arrived—an attack justified by precedent and the rule of war. But public feeling in England had risen to fever ; the French Emperor in exacting and peremptory language had declared that if England did not take joint action with him in the Black Sea, he would either act alone or else bring his fleet home. The British cabinet yielded, and came to the cardinal decision (Dec. 22) to enter the Black Sea. 'I was rather stunned,' Gladstone wrote to Sidney Herbert next day, 'by yesterday's cabinet. I have scarcely got my breath again. I told Lord Aberdeen that I had had wishes that Palmerston were back again on account of the Eastern question.'

Here is a glimpse of this time :—

Nov. 23, '53.—Cabinet. Reform discussed largely, amicably, and satisfactorily on the whole. *Dec.* 16.—Hawarden. Off at 9 A.M. Astounded by a note from A. Gordon. [Palmerston had resigned the day before.] After dinner went to the admiralty, 10¼-1½, where Lord Aberdeen, Newcastle, Graham and I went over the late events and went over the course for to-morrow's cabinet. *Dec.* 21.—Called on Lord Palmerston, and sat an hour. 22.—Cabinet, 2-7½, on Eastern Question. Palmerston and reform. A day of no small matter for reflection. *Jan.* 4, 1854.—To Windsor. I was the only guest, and thus was promoted to sit by the Queen at dinner. She was most gracious, and above all so thoroughly natural.

On the decision of Dec. 22, Sir Charles Wood says :—

We had then a long discussion on the question of occupying the Black Sea, as proposed by France, and it seemed to me to be such a tissue of confusions that I advocated the simple course of doing so. Gladstone could not be persuaded to agree to this, in spite of a strong argument of Newcastle's. Gladstone's objection being to our being hampered by any engagement. His scheme was that our occupying the Black Sea was to be made dependent, in the first place, on the Turks having acceded to the Vienna proposals, or at any rate to their agreeing to be bound by any basis of peace on which the English and French governments agreed. Newcastle and I said we thought this would bind us much more to the Turks than if we occupied the Black Sea as part of our own measures, adopted for our own purposes, and without any engagement to the Turks, under which we should be if they accepted our conditions. Gladstone said he could be no party to unconditional occupation ; so it ended in our telling France that we would occupy the Black Sea, that is, prevent the passage of any ships or munitions of war by the Russians, but that we trusted she would join us in enforcing the above condition on the Turks. If they agreed, then we were to occupy the Black Sea ; if they did not, we were to reconsider the question, and

[1] Ashley's *Life of Palmerston*, ii. p. 270.

then determine what to do. Clarendon saw Walewski, who was quite satisfied.

By the middle of February war was certain. Mr. Gladstone wrote an account of a conversation that he had at this time with Lord Aberdeen :—

Feb. 22.—Lord Aberdeen sent for me to-day and informed me that Lord Palmerston had been with him to say that he had made up his mind to vote for putting off (without entering into the question of its merits) the consideration of the Reform bill for the present year. [Conversation on Reform.][1]

He then asked me whether I did not think that he might himself withdraw from office when we came to the declaration of war. All along he had been acting against his feelings, but still defensively. He did not think that he could regard the offensive in the same light, and was disposed to retire. I said that a defensive war might involve offensive operations, and that a declaration of war placed the case on no new ground of principle. It did not make the quarrel, but merely announced it, notifying to the world (of itself justifiable) a certain state of facts which would have arrived. He said all wars were called or pretended to be defensive. I said that if the war was untruly so called, then our position was false ; but that the war did not become less defensive from our declaring it, or from our entering upon offensive operations. To retire therefore upon such a declaration, would be to retire upon no ground warrantable and conceivable by reason. It would not be standing on a principle, whereas any man would require a distinct principle to justify him in giving up at this moment the service of the crown. He asked : How could he bring himself to fight for the Turks ? I said we were not fighting for the Turks, but we were warning Russia off the forbidden ground. That if, indeed, we undertook to put down the Christians under Turkish rule by force, then we should be fighting for the Turks ; but to this I for one could be no party. He said if I saw a way for him to get out, he hoped I would mention it to him. I replied that my own views of war so much agreed with his, and I felt such a horror of bloodshed, that I had thought the matter over incessantly for myself. We stand, I said, upon the ground that the Emperor has invaded countries not his own, inflicted wrong on Turkey, and what I feel much more, most cruel wrong on the wretched inhabitants of the Principalities ; that war had ensued and was raging with all its horrors ; that we had procured for the Emperor an offer of honourable terms of peace which he had refused ; that we were not going to extend the conflagration (but I had to correct myself as to the Baltic), but to apply more power for its extinction, and this I hoped in conjunction with all the great Powers of Europe. That I, for one, could not shoulder the musket against the Christian subjects of the Sultan, and must there take my stand. (Not even, I had already told him, if he agreed to such a course, could I bind myself to follow him in it.) He said Granville and Wood had spoken to him in the same sense. I added that S. Herbert and Graham probably would adhere ; perhaps Argyll and Molesworth, and even others might be added.

Ellice had been with him and told him that J. Russell and Palmerston were preparing to contend for his place. Ellice himself, deprecating

[1] See Appendix.

Lord Aberdeen's retirement, anticipated that if it took place Lord Palmerston would get the best of it, and drive Lord John out of the field by means of his war popularity, though Lord John had made the speech of Friday to put himself up in this point of view with the country.

In consequence of what I had said to him about Newcastle, he [Aberdeen] had watched him, and had told the Queen to look to him as her minister at some period or other; which, though afraid of him (as well as of me) about Church matters, she was prepared to do. I said I had not changed my opinion of Newcastle as he had done of Lord John Russell, but I had been disappointed and pained at the recent course of his opinions about the matter of the war. At my house last Wednesday he [Newcastle] declared openly for putting down by force the Christians of European Turkey. Yes, Lord Aberdeen replied; but he thought him the description of man who would discharge well the duties of that office. In this I agree.[1]

A few days later (March 3) Lord John Russell, by way of appeasing Aberdeen's incessant self-reproach, told him that the only course that could have prevented war would have been to counsel the Turks to acquiesce, and not to allow the British fleet to quit Malta. 'But that was a course,' Lord John continued, 'to which Lansdowne, Palmerston, Clarendon, Newcastle, and I would not have consented; so that you would only have broken up your government if you had insisted upon it.' Then the speaker added his belief that the Czar, even after the Turk's acquiescence and submission, if we could have secured so much, would have given the Sultan six months' respite, and no more. None of these arguments ever eased the mind of Lord Aberdeen. Even in his last interview with the departing ambassador of the Czar, he told him how bitterly he regretted, first, the original despatch of the fleet from Malta to Besika Bay (July 1853); and second, that he had not sent Lord Granville to St. Petersburg immediately on the failure of Menschikoff at Constantinople (May 1853), in order to carry on personal negotiations with the Emperor.[2]

An ultimatum demanding the evacuation of the Principalities was despatched to St. Petersburg by England and France, the Czar kept a haughty silence, and at the end of March war was declared. In the event the Principalities were evacuated a couple of months later, but the state of war continued. On September 14, English, French, and Turkish troops disembarked on the shores of the Crimea, and on the 20th of the month was fought the battle of the Alma. 'I cannot help

---

[1] Lord Blachford in his *Letters* says of Newcastle (p. 225):—'An honest and honourable man, a thorough gentleman in all his feelings and ways, and considerate of all about him. He respected other people's position, but was sensible of his own; and his familiarity, friendly enough, was not such as invited response. It was said of him that he did not remember his rank unless you forgot it. In political administration he was painstaking, clear-headed, and just. But his abilities were moderate, and he did not see how far they were from being sufficient for the management of great affairs, which, however, he was always ambitious of handling.' See also Selborne's *Memorials*, ii. pp. 257-8.

[2] Martens.

repeating to you,' Mr. Gladstone wrote to Lord Palmerston
(Oct. 4, 1854), 'which I hope you will forgive, the thanks
I offered at an earlier period, for the manner in which you
urged—when we were amidst many temptations to far more
embarrassing and less effective proceedings—the duty of concentrating our strokes upon the heart and centre of the war at
Sebastopol.'[1] In the same month Bright wrote the solid, wise,
and noble letter that brought him so much obloquy then, and
stands as one of the memorials of his fame now.[2] Mr. Gladstone
wrote to his brother Robertson upon it :—

Nov. 7, 1854.—I thought Bright's letter both an able and a manly
one, and though I cannot go his lengths, I respect and sympathise with
the spirit in which it originated.   I think he should draw a distinction
between petty meddlings of our own, or interferences for selfish purposes,
and an operation like this which really is in support of the public law
of Europe.   I agree with him in some of the retrospective part of his
letter.

Then came the dark days of the Crimean winter.
In his very deliberate vindication of the policy of the
Crimean war composed in 1887, Mr. Gladstone warmly denies
either that the ship of state drifted instead of being steered,
or that the cabinet was in continual conflict with itself at successive stages of the negotiation.[3] He had witnessed, he
declares, much more of sharp or warm argument in every
other of the seven cabinets to which he belonged.[4] In 1881
he said to the present writer :—'As a member of the Aberdeen
cabinet I never can admit that divided opinions in that cabinet
led to hesitating action, or brought on the war. I do not mean
that all were always and on all points of the same mind. But
I have known much sharper divisions in a cabinet that has
worked a great question honourably and energetically, and I
should confidently say, whether the negotiations were well or
ill conducted, that considering their great difficulty they were
worked with little and not much conflict. It must be borne in
mind that Lord Aberdeen subsequently developed opinions
that were widely severed from those that had guided us, but
these never appeared in the cabinet or at the time.' Still he
admits that this practical harmony could much less truly be
affirmed of the four ministers especially concerned with foreign
affairs ;[5] that is to say, of the only ministers whose discussions
mattered. It is certainly impossible to contend that Aberdeen
was not in pretty continual conflict, strong and marked though
not heated, with these three main coadjutors. Whether it be

1 The equivocal honour of originality seems to belong to the French, but they had
allowed the plan to slumber.—De La Gorce, *Hist. du second Empire*, i. pp. 231-3.
2 It is given in *Speeches*, i. p. 529.   Oct. 29, 1854.
3 *Eng. Hist. Rev.* April 1887. This article was submitted to the Duke of Argyll and
Lord Granville for correction before publication.
4 The cabinet of 1892 was his eighth.
5 Aberdeen, Russell, Palmerston, Clarendon.

true to say that the cabinet drifted, depends on the precise meaning of a word. It is undoubtedly true that it steered a course bringing the ship into waters that the captain most eagerly wished to avoid, and each tack carried it farther away from the expected haven. Winds and waves were too many for them. We may perhaps agree with Mr. Gladstone that as it was feeling rather than argument that raised the Crimean war into popularity, so it is feeling and not argument that has plunged it into the 'abyss of odium.' When we come to a period twenty years after this war was over, we shall see that Mr. Gladstone found out how little had time changed the public temper, how little had events taught their lesson.

CHAPTER IV

OXFORD REFORM—OPEN CIVIL SERVICE

(1854)

To rear up minds with aspirations and faculties above the herd, capable of leading on their countrymen to greater achievements in virtue, intelligence, and social well-being ; to do this, and likewise so to educate the leisured classes of the community generally, that they may participate as far as possible in the qualities of these superior spirits, and be prepared to appreciate them, and follow in their steps—these are purposes requiring institutions of education placed above dependence on the immediate pleasure of that very multitude whom they are designed to elevate. These are the ends for which endowed universities are desirable ; they are those which all endowed universities profess to aim at ; and great is their disgrace, if, having undertaken this task, and claiming credit for fulfilling it, they leave it unfulfilled.—J. S. MILL.

THE last waves of the tide of reform that had been flowing for a score of years, now at length reached the two ancient universities. The Tractarian revival with all its intense pre-occupations had given the antique Oxford a respite, but the hour struck, and the final effort of the expiring whigs in their closing days of power was the summons to Oxford and Cambridge to set their houses in order. Oxford had been turned into the battle-field on which contending parties in the church had at her expense fought for mastery. The result was curious. The nature of the theological struggle, by quickening mind within the university, had roused new forces ; the antagonism between anglo-catholic and puritan helped, as it had done two centuries before, to breed the latitudinarian ; a rising school in the sphere of thought and criticism rapidly made themselves an active party in the sphere of affairs ; and Mr. Gladstone found himself forced to do the work of the very liberalism which his own theological leaders and allies had first organised themselves to beat down and extinguish.

In 1850 Lord John Russell, worked upon by a persevering minority in Oxford, startled the House of Commons, delighted the liberals, and angered and dismayed the authorities of the powerful corporations thus impugned, by the announcement of a commission under the crown to inquire into their discipline, state, and revenues, and to report whether any action by crown and parliament could further promote the interests of

religion and sound learning in these venerable shrines. This
was the first step in a long journey towards the nationalisation
of the universities, and the disestablishment of the church of
England in what seemed the best fortified of all her strongholds.

After elaborate correspondence with both liberal and tory
sections in Oxford, Mr. Gladstone rose in his place and
denounced the proposed commission as probably against the
law, and certainly odious in the eye of the constitution. He
undertook to tear in tatters the various modern precedents
advanced by the government for their purpose; scouted the
alleged visitorial power of the crown; insisted that it would
blight future munificence; argued that defective instruction
with freedom and self-government would, in the choice of evils,
be better than the most perfect mechanism secured by parliamentary interference; admitted that what the universities had
done for learning was perhaps less than it might have been,
but they had done as much as answered the circumstances and
exigencies of the country. When we looked at the lawyers, the
divines, the statesmen of England, even if some might judge
them inferior in mere scholastic and technical acquirements,
why need we be ashamed of the cradles in which they were
mainly nurtured? He closed with a triumphant and moving
reference to Peel (dead a fortnight before), the most distinguished
son of Oxford in the present century, and beyond all other
men the high representative and the true type of the genius of
the British House of Commons.[1] In truth no worse case was
ever more strongly argued, and fortunately the speech is to be
recorded as the last manifesto, on a high theme and on a broad
scale, of that toryism from which this wonderful pilgrim had
started on his shining progress. It is just to add that the
party in Oxford who resisted the commission was also the
party most opposed to Mr. Gladstone, and further that the
view of the crown having no right to issue such a commission
in invitos was shared with him by Sir Robert Peel.[2] Of this
debate, Arthur Stanley (a strong supporter of the measure)
tells us: 'The ministerial speeches were very feeble. . . .
Gladstone's was very powerful; he said, in the most effective
manner, anything which could be said against the commission.
His allusion to Peel was very touching, and the House
responded to it by profound and sympathetic silence. . . .
Heywood's closing speech was happily drowned in the roar of
" Divide," so that nothing could be heard save the name of
" Cardinal Wolsey" thrice repeated.'[3] The final division was
taken on the question of the adjournment, when the govern-
ment had a majority of 22. (July 18, 1850.)

[1] July 18, 1850.   [2] Letter to Bishop Davidson, June 11, 1891.
                          [3] *Life*, i. p. 420.

II

In Oxford the party of 'organized torpor' did not yield without a struggle. They were clamorous on the sanctity of property; contemptuous of the doctrine of the rights of parliament over national domains; and protestant collegians subsisting on ancient Roman catholic endowments edified the world on the iniquity of setting aside the pious founder. They submitted an elaborate case to the most eminent counsel of the day, and counsel advised that the commission was not constitutional, not legal, and not such as the members of the university were bound to obey. The question of duty apart from legal obligation the lawyers did not answer, but they suggested that a petition might be addressed to the crown, praying that the instrument might be cancelled. The petition was duly prepared, and duly made no difference. Many of the academic authorities were recalcitrant, but this made no difference either, nor did the Bishop of Exeter's hot declaration that the proceeding had 'no parallel since the fatal attempt of King James II. to subject the colleges to his unhallowed control.' The commissioners, of whom Tait and Jeune seem to have been the leading spirits, with Stanley and Mr. Goldwin Smith for secretaries, conducted their operations with tact, good sense, and zeal. At the end of two years (April 1852) the inquiry was completed and the report made public—one of the high landmarks in the history of our modern English life and growth. 'When you consider,' Stanley said to Jowett, 'the den of lions through which the raw material had to be dragged, much will be excused. In fact the great work was to finish it at all. There is a harsh, unfriendly tone about the whole which ought, under better circumstances, to have been avoided, but which may, perhaps, have the advantage of propitiating the radicals.'[1]

Mr. Gladstone thought it one of the ablest productions submitted in his recollection to parliament, but the proposals of change too manifold and complicated. The evidence he found more moderate and less sweeping in tone than the report, but it only deepened his conviction of the necessity of important and, above all, early changes. He did not cease urging his friends at Oxford to make use of this golden opportunity for reforming the university from within, and warning them that delay would be dearly purchased.[2] 'Gladstone's connection with Oxford,' said Sir George Lewis, 'is now exercising a singular influence upon the politics of the university. Most of his high church supporters stick to him, and (insomuch as it is difficult to struggle against the current) he is liberalising them, instead of their torifying him. He is giving them a push forwards instead of their giving him a pull backwards.'[3]

[1] Life of Stanley, i. p. 432.

[2] Letters to Graham, July 30, 1852, and Dr. Haddan, Aug. 14 and Sept. 29, 1852.

[3] Letters, March 26, 1853, p. 261.

The originators of the commission were no longer in office, but things had gone too far for their successors to burke what had been done.[1] The Derby government put into the Queen's speech, in November (1852), a paragraph informing parliament that the universities had been invited to examine the recommendations of the report. After a year's time had been given them to consider, it became the duty of the Aberdeen government to frame a bill. The charge fell upon Mr. Gladstone as member for Oxford, and in the late autumn of 1853 he set to work. In none of the enterprises of his life was he more industrious or energetic. Before the middle of December he forwarded to Lord John Russell what he called a rude draft, but the rude draft contained the kernel of the plan that was ultimately carried, with a suggestion even of the names of the commissioners to whom operations were to be confided. 'It is marvellous to me,' wrote Dr. Jeune to him (Dec. 21, 1853), 'how you can give attention so minute to university affairs at such a crisis. Do great things become to great men from the force of habit, what their ordinary cares are to ordinary persons?' As he began, so he advanced, listening to everybody, arguing with everybody, flexible, persistent, clear, practical, fervid, unconquerable. 'I fear,' Lord John Russell wrote to him (March 27), 'my mind is exclusively occupied with the war and the Reform bill, and yours with university reform.' Perhaps, unluckily for the country, this was true. 'My whole heart is in the Oxford bill,' Mr. Gladstone writes (March 29); 'it is my consolation under the pain with which I view the character my office [the exchequer] is assuming under the circumstances of war.' 'Gladstone has been surprising everybody here,' writes a conspicuous high churchman from Oxford, 'by the ubiquity of his correspondence. Three-fourths of the colleges have been in communication with him, on various parts of the bill more or less affecting themselves. He answers everybody by return of post, fully and at length, quite entering into their case, and showing the greatest acquaintance with it.'[2] 'As one of your burgesses,' he told them, 'I stand upon the line that divides Oxford from the outer world, and as a sentinel I cry out to tell what I see from that position.' What he saw was that if this bill were thrown out, no other half so favourable would ever again be brought in.

The scheme accepted by the cabinet was in essentials Mr. Gladstone's own. Jowett at the earliest stage sent him a comprehensive plan, and soon after, saw Lord John (Jan. 6). 'I must own,' writes the latter to Gladstone, 'I was much

---

[1] Interesting particulars of this memorable commission are to be found in the *Life of Archbishop Tait*, i. pp. 156-170.

[2] Mozley, *Letters*, p. 220. Mr. Gladstone preserved 560 letters and documents relating to the preparation and passing of the Oxford University bill. Among them are 350 copies of his own letters written between Dec. 1853 and Dec. 1854, and 170 letters received by him during the same period.

struck by the clearness and completeness of his views.' The
difference between Jowett's plan and Mr. Gladstone's was on
the highly important point of machinery. Jowett, who all his
life had a weakness for getting and keeping authority into his
own hands, or the hands of those whom he could influence,
contended that after parliament had settled principles, Oxford
itself could be trusted to settle details far better than a little
body of great personages from outside, unacquainted with
special wants and special interests. Mr. Gladstone, on the
other hand, invented the idea of an executive commission with
statutory powers. The two plans were printed and circulated,
and the balance of opinion in the cabinet went decisively for
Mr. Gladstone's scheme. The discussion between him and
Jowett, ranging over the whole field of the bill, was maintained
until its actual production, in many interviews and much
correspondence. In drawing the clauses Mr. Gladstone received
the help of Bethell, the solicitor-general, at whose suggestion
Phillimore and Thring were called in for further aid in what
was undoubtedly a task of exceptional difficulty. The process
brought into clearer light the truth discerned by Mr. Gladstone
from the first, that the enormous number of diverse institutions
that had grown up in Oxford made resort to what he called
sub-legislation inevitable ; that is to say, they were too complex
for parliament, and could only be dealt with by delegation to
executive act.

It is untrue to say that Oxford as a place of education
had no influence on the mind of the country ; it had immense
influence, but that influence was exactly what it ought not
to have been. Instead of stimulating it checked, instead of
expanding it stereotyped. Even for the church it had failed
to bring unity, for it was from Oxford that the opinions had
sprung that seemed to be rending the church in twain. The
regeneration introduced by this momentous measure has been
overlaid by the strata of subsequent reforms. Enough to say
that the objects obtained were the deposition of the fossils and
drones, and a renovated constitution on the representative
principle for the governing body ; the wakening of a huge mass
of sleeping endowments ; the bestowal of college emoluments
only on excellence tested by competition, and associated with
active duties ; the reorganisation or re-creation of professorial
teaching ; the removal of local preferences and restrictions.
Beyond these aspects of reform, Mr. Gladstone was eager for
the proposed right to establish private halls, as a change
calculated to extend the numbers and strength of the university,
and as settling the much-disputed question, whether the scale
of living could not be reduced, and university education brought
within reach of classes of moderate means. These hopes
proved to be exaggerated, but they illustrate his constant
and lifelong interest in the widest possible diffusion of all

good things in the world from university training down to a
Cook's tour.

Mr. Gladstone seems to have pressed his draftsmen hard,
as he sometimes did. Bethell returning to him 'the *disjecta
membra* of this unfortunate bill,' tells him that he is too deeply
attached to him to care for a few marks of impatience, and
adds, 'write a few kind words to Phillimore, for he really loves
you and feels this matter deeply.' Oxford, scene of so many
agitations for a score of years past, was once more seized with
consternation, stupefaction, enthusiasm. A few private copies
of the draft were sent down from London for criticism. On
the vice-chancellor it left 'an impression of sorrow and sad
anticipations'; it opened deplorable prospects for the university,
for the church, for religion, for righteousness. The dean of
Christ Church thought it not merely inexpedient, but unjust
and tyrannical. Jowett, on the other hand, was convinced that
it must satisfy all reasonable reformers, and added emphatically
in writing to Mr. Gladstone, 'It is to yourself and Lord John
that the university will be indebted for the greatest boon that
it has ever received.' After the introduction of the bill by
Lord John Russell, the obscurantists made a final effort to call
down one of their old pelting hailstorms. A petition against
the bill was submitted to convocation; happily it passed by a
majority of no more than two.

At length the blessed day of the second reading came. The
ever-zealous Arthur Stanley was present. 'A superb speech
from Gladstone,' he records, 'in which, for the first time, all
the arguments from our report were worked up in the most
effective manner. He vainly endeavoured to reconcile his
present with his former position. But, with this exception, I
listened to his speech with the greatest delight. . . . To behold
one's old enemies slaughtered before one's face with the most
irresistible weapons was quite intoxicating. One great charm
of his speaking is its exceeding good-humour. There is great
vehemence but no bitterness.'[1] An excellent criticism of many,
perhaps most, of his speeches.

'It must ever be borne in mind,' Mr. Gladstone wrote to
Lord John at the outset, 'with respect to our old universities
that history, law, and usage with them form such a manifold,
diversified, and complex mass, that it is not one subject but a
world of subjects that we have to deal with in approaching
them.' And he pointed out that if any clever lawyer such as
Butt or Cairns were employed to oppose the bill systematically
debate would run to such lengths as to make it hopeless. This
was a point of view that Mr. Gladstone's more exacting and
abstract critics now, and many another time, forgot: they
forgot that, whatever else you may say of a bill, after all it is
a thing that is to be carried through parliament. Everybody

had views of his own. A characteristic illustration of Mr. Gladstone's temper in the arduous work of practical legislation to which so much of the energies of his life was devoted, is worth giving here from a letter of this date to Burgon of Oriel. Nobody answers better to the rare combination, in Bacon's words, of a 'glorious nature that doth put life into business, with a solid and sober nature that hath as much of the ballast as of the sail' :—

Sometimes it may be necessary in dealing with a very ancient institution to make terms, as it were, between such an institution and the actual spirit of the age. This may be in certain circumstances a necessary, but it can never be a satisfactory process. It is driving a bargain, and somewhat of a wretched bargain. But I really do not find or feel that this is the case now before us. In that case, my view, right or wrong, is this : that Oxford is far behind her duties or capabilities, not because her working men work so little, but because so large a proportion of her children do not work at all, so large a proportion of her resources remains practically dormant, and her present constitution is so ill-adapted to developing her real but latent powers. What I therefore anticipate is not the weakening of her distinctive principles, not the diminution of her labour, already great, that she discharges for the church and for the land, but a great expansion, a great invigoration, a great increase of her numbers, a still greater increase of her moral force, and of her hold upon the heart and mind of the country.

Pusey seems to have talked of the university as ruined and overthrown by a parricidal hand ; Oxford would be lost to the church ; she would have to take refuge in colleges away from the university. Oxford had now received its deathblow from Mr. Gladstone and the government to which he belonged, and he could no longer support at election times the worker of such evil, and must return to that inactivity in things political, from which only love and confidence for Mr. Gladstone had roused him. 'Personally,' the good man adds, 'I must always love you.' To Pusey, and to all who poured reproach upon him from this side, Mr. Gladstone replied with inexhaustible patience. He never denied that parliamentary intervention was an evil, but he submitted to it in order to avert greater evil. 'If the church of England has not strength enough to keep upright, this will soon appear in the troubles of emancipated Oxford : if she has, it will come out to the joy of us all in the immensely augmented energy and power of the university for good. If Germanism and Arnoldism are now to carry the day at Oxford (I mean supposing the bill is carried into law), they will carry it fairly ; let them win and wear her (God forbid, however) ; but if she has a heart true to the faith her hand will be stronger ten times over than it has been heretofore, in doing battle. . . . Nor am I saddened by the pamphlet of a certain Mr. —— which I have been reading to-day. It has more violence than venom, and also much more violence than strength. I often feel how hard it is on divines to be accused of treachery and baseness, because they do not, like *us*, get it every day and so become case-hardened against it.'

In parliament the craft laboured heavily in cross-seas. 'I have never known,' says its pilot, 'a measure so foolishly discussed in committee.' Nor was oil cast upon the waters by its friends. By the end of May Mr. Gladstone and Lord John saw that they must take in canvas. At this point a new storm broke. It was impossible that a measure on such a subject could fail to awaken the ever-ready quarrel between the two camps into which the English establishment, for so many generations, has so unhappily divided the life of the nation. From the first, the protestant dissenters had been extremely sore at the absence from the bill of any provision for their admission to the remodelled university. Bright, the most illustrious of them, told the House of Commons that he did not care whether so pusillanimous and tinkering an affair as this was passed or not. Dissenters, he said with scorn, are expected always to manifest too much of those inestimable qualities which are spoken of in the Epistle to the Corinthians : —'To hope all things, to believe all things, and to endure all things.'

More discredit than he deserved fell upon Mr. Gladstone for this obnoxious defect. In announcing the commission of inquiry four years before, Lord John as prime minister had expressly said that the improvement of the universities should be treated as a subject by itself, and that the admission of dissenters ought to be reserved for future and separate consideration. Writing to Mr. Gladstone (Jan. 1854) he said, 'I do not want to stir the question in this bill,' but he would support a proposal in a separate bill by which the halls might be the means of admitting dissenters. Mr. Gladstone himself professed to take no strong line either way ; but in a parliamentary case of this kind to take no line is not materially different from a line in effect unfriendly. Arthur Stanley pressed him as hard as he could. 'Justice to the university,' said Mr. Gladstone in reply, 'demands that it should be allowed to consider the question for itself. . . . Indeed, while I believe that the admission of dissenters without the breaking up of the religious teaching and the government of the university would be a great good, I am also of opinion that to give effect to that measure by forcible intervention of parliament would be a great evil. Whether it is an evil that must some day or other be encountered, the time has not yet, I think, arrived for determining.' The letter concludes with a remark of curious bearing upon the temper of that age. 'The very words,' he says to Stanley, 'which you have let fall upon your paper—"Roman catholics"— used in this connection, were enough to burn it through and through, considering we have *a parliament which, were the measure of* 1829 *not law at this moment, would I think probably refuse to make it law.'* There is no reason to think this an erroneous view. Perhaps it would not be extravagant even to-day.

What Mr. Gladstone called 'the evil of parliamentary interference' did not tarry, and on the report stage of the bill, a clause removing the theological test at matriculation was carried (June 22) against the government by ninety-one. The size of the majority and the diversified material of which it was composed left the government no option but to yield. 'Parliament having now unhappily determined to legislate upon the subject,' Mr. Gladstone writes to the provost of Oriel, 'it seems to me, I may add it seems to my colleagues, best for the interests of the university that we should now make some endeavour to settle the whole question and so preclude, if we can, any pretext for renewed agitation.' 'The basis of that settlement,' he went on in a formula which he tenaciously reiterated to all his correspondents, and which is a landmark in the long history of his dealing with the question, should be that the whole teaching and governing function in the university and in the colleges, halls, and private halls, should be retained, as now, in the church of England, but that everything outside the governing and teaching functions, whether in the way of degrees, honours, or emoluments, should be left open.' The new clause he described as 'one of those incomplete arrangements that seem to suit the practical habits of this country, and which by taking the edge off a matter of complaint, are often found virtually to dispose of it for a length of time.' In the end the church of England test was removed, not only on admission to the university, but from the bachelor's degree. Tests in other forms remained, as we shall in good time perceive. 'We have proceeded,' Mr. Gladstone wrote, 'in the full belief that the means of applying a church test to fellowships in colleges are clear and ample.' So they were, and so remained, until seventeen years later in the life of an administration of his own the obnoxious fetter was struck off.

The debates did not close without at least one characteristic masterpiece from Mr. Disraeli. He had not taken a division on the second reading, but he executed with entire gravity all the regulation manœuvres of opposition, and his appearance on the page of Hansard relieves a dull discussion. If government, he asked, could defer a reform of the constitution (referring to the withdrawal of Lord John's bill) why should they hurry to reform the universities? The talk about the erudite professors of Germany as so superior to Oxford was nonsense. The great men of Germany became professors only because they could not become members of parliament. 'We, on the contrary, are a nation of action, and you may depend upon it, that though you may give an Oxford professor two thousand a year instead

of two hundred, still ambition in England will look to public
life and to the House of Commons, and not to professors'
chairs.' The moment the revolution of 1848 gave the German
professors a chance, see how they rushed into political conventions and grasped administrative offices. Again, the principle
of the bill was the laying of an unhallowed hand upon the ark
of the universities, and wore in effect the hideous aspect of the
never-to-be-forgotten appropriation clause. If he were asked
whether he would rather have Oxford free with all its imperfections, or an Oxford without imperfections but under the
control of the government, he would reply, 'Give me Oxford
free and independent, with all its anomalies and imperfections.'
An excellently worded but amusingly irrelevant passage about
Voltaire and Rousseau, and the land that was enlightened by
the one and inflamed by the other, brought the curious performance to a solemn close. High fantastic trifling of this
sort, though it may divert a later generation to whose legislative
bills it can do no harm, helps to explain the deep disfavour
with which Disraeli was regarded by his severe and strenuous
opponent.

'The admiration of posterity,' Dr. Jeune wrote to Mr.
Gladstone, 'would be greatly increased if men hereafter could
know what wisdom, what firmness, what temper, what labour
your success has required.' More than this, it was notorious
that Mr. Gladstone was bravely risking his seat. This side of
the matter Jeune made plain to him. 'Had I foreseen in 1847,'
replied Mr. Gladstone (*Broadstairs*, Aug. 26, 1854), 'that church
controversies which I then hoped were on the decline, were
really about to assume a fiercer glare and a wider range than
they had done before, I should not have been presumptuous
enough to face the contingencies of such a seat at such a time.'
As things stood he was bound to hold on. With dauntless
confidence that never failed him, he was convinced that no
long time would suffice to scatter the bugbears, and the bill
would be nothing but a source of strength to any one standing
in reputed connection with it. To Dr. Jeune when the battle
was over he expresses 'his warm sense of the great encouragement and solid advantage which at every stage he had derived
from his singularly ready and able help.' To Jowett and Goldwin Smith he acknowledged a hardly lower degree of obligation. The last twenty years, wrote a shrewd and expert sage
in 1866, 'have seen more improvement in the temper and teaching of Oxford than the three centuries since the Reformation.
This has undoubtedly been vastly promoted by the Reform bill
of 1854, or at least by one enactment in it, the abolition of close
fellowships, which has done more for us than all the other enactments of the measure put together.'[1] 'The indirect effects,'
says the same writer in words of pregnant praise, 'in stimu-

[1] *Academical Organisation.* By Mark Pattison, p. 24.

CHAP. IV. ÆT. 45

lating the spirit of improvement among us, have been no less important than the specific reforms enacted by it.'[1]

III

Another of the most far-reaching changes of this era of reform affected the civil service. J. S. Mill, then himself an official at the India House, did not hesitate 'to hail the plan of throwing open the civil service to competition as one of the greatest improvements in public affairs ever proposed by a government.' On the system then reigning, civil employment under the crown was in all the offices the result of patronage, though in some, and those not the more important of them, nominees were partially tested by qualifying examination and periods of probation. The eminent men who held what were called the staff appointments in the service—the Merivales, Taylors, Farrers—were introduced from without, with the obvious implication that either the civil service trained up within its own ranks a poor breed, or else that the meritorious men were discouraged and kept back by the sight of prizes falling to outsiders. Mr. Gladstone was not slow to point out that the existing system if it brought eminent men in, had driven men like Manning and Spedding out. What patronage meant is forcibly described in a private memorandum of a leading reformer, preserved by Mr. Gladstone among his papers on this subject. 'The existing corps of civil servants,' says the writer, 'do not like the new plan, because the introduction of well-educated, active men, will force them to bestir themselves, and because they cannot hope to get their own ill-educated sons appointed under the new system. *The old established political families habitually batten on the public patronage*—their sons legitimate and illegitimate, their relatives and dependents of every degree, are provided for by the score. Besides the adventuring disreputable class of members of parliament, who make God knows what use of the patronage, a large number of borough members are mainly dependent upon it for their seats. What, for instance, are the members to do who have been sent down by the patronage secretary to contest boroughs in the interest of the government, and who are pledged twenty deep to their constituents?'

The foreign office had undergone, some years before, a thorough reconstruction by Lord Palmerston, who, though very cool to constitutional reform, was assiduous and exacting in the forms of public business, not least so in the vital matter of a strong, plain, bold handwriting. Revision had been attempted in various departments before Mr. Gladstone went

[1] The following speeches made by Mr. Gladstone on the Oxford bill were deemed by him of sufficient importance to be included in the projected edition of his collected speeches:—On the introduction of the bill, March 19 (1854); on the second reading, April 7; during the committee stage, April 27, June 1, 22, 23, and July 27.

to the exchequer, and a spirit of improvement was in the air. Lowe, beginning his official career as one of the secretaries of the board of control, had procured the insertion in the India bill of 1853 of a provision throwing open the great service of India to competition for all British-born subjects, and he was a vigorous advocate of a general extension of the principle.[1] It was the conditions common to all the public establishments that called for revision, and the foundations for reform were laid in a report by Northcote and Sir Charles Trevelyan (November 1853), prepared for Mr. Gladstone at his request, recommending two propositions, so familiarised to us to-day as to seem like primordial elements of the British constitution. One was, that access to the public service should be through the door of a competitive examination ; the other, that for conducting these examinations a central board should be constituted. The effect of such a change has been enormous not only on the efficiency of the service, but on the education of the country, and by a thousand indirect influences, raising and strengthening the social feeling for the immortal maxim that the career should be open to the talents. The lazy doctrine that men are much of a muchness gave way to a higher respect for merit and to more effectual standards of competency.

The reform was not achieved without a battle. The whole case was argued by Mr. Gladstone in a letter to Lord John Russell of incomparable trenchancy and force, one of the best specimens of the writer at his best, and only not worth repro-ducing here, because the case has long been finished.[2] Lord John (Jan. 20) wrote to him curtly in reply, ' I hope no change will be made, and I certainly must protest against it.' In reply to even a second assault, he remained quite unconvinced. At present, he said, the Queen appointed the ministers, and the ministers the subordinates ; in future the board of examiners would be in the place of the Queen. Our institutions would be as nearly republican as possible, and the new spirit of the public offices would not be loyalty but republicanism ! As one of Lord John's kindred spirits declared, 'The more the civil service is recruited from the lower classes, the less will it be sought after by the higher, until at last the aristocracy will be altogether dissociated from the permanent civil service of the country.' How could the country go on with a democratic civil service by the side of an aristocratic legislature ?[3] This was just the spirit that Mr. Gladstone loathed. To Graham he wrote (Jan. 3, 1854), ' I do not want any pledges as to details ; what I seek is your countenance and favour in an endeavour to introduce to the cabinet a proposal that we should give our sanction to the principle that in every case where a satisfactory

[1] Life of Lord Sherbrooke, pp. 421-2.   [2] For an extract see Appendix.
[3] Romilly, quoted by Layard, June 15th, 1855.

test of a defined and palpable nature can be furnished, the
public service shall be laid open to personal merit. . . . This
is *my* contribution to parliamentary reform.' On January 26
(1854) the cabinet was chiefly occupied by Mr. Gladstone's
proposition, and after a long discussion his plan was adopted.
When reformers more ardent than accurate insisted in later
years that it was the aristocracy who kept patronage, Mr.
Gladstone reminded the House, 'No cabinet could have been
more aristocratically composed than that over which Lord
Aberdeen presided. I myself was the only one of fifteen
noblemen and gentlemen who composed it, who could not
fairly be said to belong to that class.' Yet it was this cabinet
that conceived and matured a plan for the surrender of all
its patronage. There for the moment, in spite of all his vigour
and resolution, the reform was arrested. Time did not change
him. In November he wrote to Trevelyan : 'My own opinions
are more and more in favour of the plan of competition. I do
not mean that they can be more in its favour as a principle,
than they were when I invited you and Northcote to write the
report which has lit up the flame ; but more and more do the
incidental evils seem curable and the difficulties removable.'
As the Crimean war went on, the usual cry for administrative
reform was raised, and Mr. Gladstone never made a more terse,
pithy, and incontrovertible speech than his defence for an open
civil service in the summer of 1855.[1]

For this branch of reform, too, the inspiration had proceeded
from Oxford. Two of the foremost champions of the change
had been Temple—afterwards Archbishop of Canterbury—and
Jowett. The latter was described by Mr. Gladstone to Graham
as being 'as handy a workman as you shall readily find,' and in
the beginning of 1855 he proposed to these two reformers that
they should take the salaried office of examiners under the
civil service scheme. Much of his confident expectation of
good, he told them, was built upon their co-operation. In all
his proceedings on this subject, Mr. Gladstone showed in
strong light in how unique a degree he combined a profound
democratic instinct with the spirit of good government ; the
instinct of popular equality along with the scientific spirit
of the enlightened bureaucrat.

[1] He made three speeches on the subject at this period ; June 15th and July 10th,
1855, and April 24th, 1856. The first was on Layard's motion for reform, which was
rejected by 359 to 46.

CHAPTER V

WAR FINANCE—TAX OR LOAN

(1854)

> The expenses of a war are the moral check which it has pleased the Almighty to impose upon the ambition and lust of conquest, that are inherent in so many nations. There is pomp and circumstance, there is glory and excitement about war, which, notwithstanding the miseries it entails, invests it with charms in the eyes of the community, and tends to blind men to those evils to a fearful and dangerous degree. The necessity of meeting from year to year the expenditure which it entails is a salutary and wholesome check, making them feel what they are about, and making them measure the cost of the benefit upon which they may calculate.—GLADSTONE.

THE finance of 1854 offered nothing more original or ingenious than bluntly doubling the income tax (from seven pence to fourteen pence), and raising the duties on spirits, sugar, and malt. The draught was administered in two doses, first in a provisional budget for half a year (March 6), next in a completed scheme two months later. During the interval the chancellor of the exchequer was exposed to much criticism alike from city experts and plain men. The plans of 1853 had, in the main, proved a remarkable success, but they were not without weak points. Reductions in the duties of customs, excise, and stamps had all been followed by increase in their proceeds. But the succession duty brought in no more than a fraction of the estimated sum—the only time, Mr. Gladstone observes, in which he knew the excellent department concerned to have fallen into such an error. The proposal for conversion proved, under circumstances already described, to have no attraction for the fundholder. The operation on the South Sea stock was worse than a failure, for it made the exchequer, in order to pay off eight millions at par, raise a larger sum at three and a half per cent, and at three per cent in a stock standing at 87.[1] All this brought loudish complaints from the money market. The men at the clubs talked of the discredit into which Gladstone had fallen as a financier, and even persons not unfriendly to him spoke of him as rash, obstinate, and

[1] Northcote, *Financial Policy*, p. 242; Buxton, *Mr. Gladstone: A Study*, pp. 154-5.

injudicious. He was declared to have destroyed his prestige and overthrown his authority.[1]

This roused all the slumbering warrior in him, and when the time came (May 8), in a speech three and a half hours long, he threw his detractors into a depth of confusion that might have satisfied the Psalmist himself. Peremptorily he brushed aside the apology of his assailants for not challenging him by a direct vote of want of confidence, that such a vote would be awkward in a time of war. On the contrary, he said, a case so momentous as the case of war is the very reason why you should show boldly whether you have confidence in our management of your finances or not; if you disapprove, the sooner I know it the better. Then he dashed into a close and elaborate defence in detail, under all the heads of attack,—his manner of dealing with the unfunded debt, his abortive scheme of conversion, his mode of charging deficiency bills. This astonishing mass of dry and difficult matter was impressed in full significance upon the House, not only by the orator's own buoyant and energetic interest in the performance, but by the sense which he awoke in his hearers, that to exercise their attention and judgment upon the case before them was a binding debt imperatively due to themselves and to the country, by men owning the high responsibility of their station. This was the way in which he at all times strove to stir the self-respect of the House of Commons. Not sparing his critics a point or an argument, he drove his case clean home with a vigour that made it seem as if the study of Augustine and Dante and old divines were after all the best training for an intimate and triumphant mastery of the proper amount of gold to be kept at the bank, the right interest on an exchequer bond and an exchequer bill, and all the arcana of the public accounts.[2] Even where their case had something in it, he showed that they had taken the wrong points. Nor did he leave out the spice of the sarcasm that the House loves. A peer had reproached him for the amount of his deficiency bills. This peer had once himself for four years been chancellor of the exchequer. 'My deficiency bills,' cried Mr. Gladstone, 'reached three millions and a half. How much were the bills of the chancellor whom this figure shocks? In his first year they were four millions and a half, in the second almost the same, in the third more than five and a quarter, in the fourth nearly five millions and a half.' Disraeli and others pretended that they had foreseen the failure of the conversion. Mr. Gladstone proved that, as matter of recorded fact, they had done nothing of the sort. 'This is the way in which mythical history arises. An event happens without attracting much

---

[1] Greville, Part III. i. pp. 150, 151, 157.

[2] Not many years before (1838), Talleyrand had surprised the French institute by a paper in which he passed a eulogy on strong theological studies; their influence on vigour as well as on finesse of mind; on the skilful ecclesiastical diplomatists that those studies had formed.

notice ; subsequently it excites interest, then people look back upon the time now passed, and see things not as they are or were, but through the haze of distance—they see them as they wish them to have been, and what they wish them to have been, they believe that they were.'

For this budget no genius, only courage, was needed ; but Mr. Gladstone advanced in connection with it a doctrine that raised great questions, moral, political, and economic, and again illustrated that characteristic of his mind which always made some broad general principle a necessity of action. All through 1854, and in a sense very often since, parliament was agitated by Mr. Gladstone's bold proposition that the cost of war should be met by taxation at the time, and not by loans to be paid back by another generation. He did not advance his abstract doctrine without qualification. This, in truth, Mr. Gladstone hardly ever did, and it was one of the reasons why he acquired a bad name for sophistry and worse. Men fastened on the general principle, set out in all its breadth and with much emphasis ; they overlooked the lurking qualification ; and then were furiously provoked at having been taken in. 'I do not know,' he wrote some years later to Northcote, 'where you find that I laid down any general maxim that all war supplies were to be raised by taxes. . . . I said in my speech of May 8, revised for Hansard, it was the duty and policy of the country to make *in the first instance* a great effort from its own resources.' The discussions of the time, however, seem to have turned on the unqualified construction. While professing his veneration and respect for the memory of Pitt, he opened in all its breadth the question raised by Pitt's policy of loan, loan, loan. The economic answer is open to more dispute than he then appeared to suppose, but it was the political and moral reasons for meeting the demands of war by tax and not by loan that coloured his economic view. The passage in which he set forth the grounds for his opinion has become a classic place in parliamentary discussion, but it is only too likely for a long time to come to bear reproducing, and I have taken it as a motto for this chapter. His condemnation of loans, absolutely if not relatively, was emphatic. 'The system of raising funds necessary for wars by loan practises wholesale, systematic, and continual deception upon the people. The people do not really know what they are doing. The consequences are adjourned into a far future.' I may as well here complete or correct this language by a further quotation from the letter to Northcote to which I have already referred. He is writing in 1862 on Northcote's book on *Twenty Years of Finance*. 'I cannot refrain,' he says, 'from paying you a sincere compliment, first on the skill with which you have composed an eminently readable work on a dry subject ; and secondly, on the tact founded in good feeling and the love of

truth with which you have handled your materials throughout.'
He then remarks on various points in the book, and among the
rest on this :—

Allow me also to say that I think in your comparison of the effect of
taxes and loans you have looked (p. 262) too much to the effect on
labour at the moment. Capital and labour are in permanent competition for the division of the fruits of production. When in years of war
say twenty millions annually are provided by loan say for three, five,
or ten years, then two consequences follow.

1. An immense factitious stimulus is given to labour at the time—
and thus much more labour is brought into the market.

2. When that stimulus is withdrawn an augmented quantity of
labour is left to compete in the market with a greatly diminished
quantity of capital.

Here is the story of the *misery* of great masses of the English people
after 1815, or at the least a material part of that story.

I hold by the doctrine that war loans are in many ways a great evil :
but I admit their necessity, and in fact the budget of 1855 was handed
over by me to Sir George Lewis, and underwent in his hands little alteration unless such as, with the growing demands of the war, I should myself
have had to make in it, *i.e.* some, not very considerable, enlargement.

Writing a second letter to Northcote a few days later
(August 11, 1862), he goes a little deeper into the subject :—

The general question of loans *v.* taxes for war purposes is one of the
utmost interest, but one that I have never seen worked out in print.
But assuming as *data* the established principles of our financial system,
and by no means denying the necessity of loans, I have not the least
doubt that it is for the interest of labour, as opposed to capital, that as
large a share as possible of war expenditure should be defrayed from
taxes. When war breaks out the wages of labour on the whole have a
tendency to rise, and the labour of the country is well able to bear some
augmentation of taxes. The sums added to the public expenditure are
likely at the outset, and for some time, to be larger than the sums withdrawn from commerce. When war ends, on the contrary, a great mass
of persons are dismissed from public employment, and, flooding the
labour market, reduce the rate of wages. But again, when war comes,
it is quite certain that a large share of the war taxes will be laid upon
property : and that, in war, property will bear a larger share of our
total taxation than in peace. From this it seems to follow at once that,
up to the point at which endurance is practicable, payment by war-taxes
rather than by taxes in peace is for the interest of the people at large.
I am not one of those who think that our system of taxation, taken as a
whole, is an over-liberal one towards them. These observations are
mere contributions to a discussion, and by no means pretend to dispose
of the question.

II

In the autumn he had a sharp tussle with the Bank of
England, and displayed a toughness, stiffness, and sustained
anger that greatly astonished Threadneedle Street. In the
spring he had introduced a change in the mode of issuing

deficiency bills, limiting the quarterly amount to such a sum
as would cover the maximum of dividends payable, as known
by long experience to be called for. The Bank held this to
be illegal; claimed the whole amount required, along with
balances actually in hand, to cover the entire amount payable;
and asked him to take the opinion of the law officers. The
lawyers backed the chancellor of the exchequer. Then the
Bank took an opinion of their own; their counsel (Kelly and
Palmer) advised that the attorney and solicitor were wrong;
and recommended the Bank to bring their grievance before
the prime minister. Mr. Gladstone was righteously incensed
at this refusal to abide by an opinion invited by the Bank
itself, and by which if it had been adverse he would himself
have been bound. 'And then,' said Bethell, urging Mr. Gladstone to stand to his guns, 'its counsel call the Bank a trustee
for the public! Proh pudor! What stuff lawyers will talk.
But 'tis their vocation.' Mr. Gladstone's letters were often
prolix, but nobody could be more terse and direct when
occasion moved him, and the proceedings of the lawyers with
their high Bank views and the equivocal faith of the directors
in bringing fresh lawyers into the case at all provoked more
than one stern and brief epistle. The governor, who was his
private friend, winced. 'I do not study diplomacy in letters
of this kind,' Mr. Gladstone replied, 'and there is no sort of
doubt that I am very angry about the matter of the opinion;
but affected and sarcastic politeness is an instrument which
in writing to you I should think it the worst taste and the
worst feeling to employ. I admire the old fashion according
to which in English pugilism (which, however, I do not admire)
the combatants shook hands before they fought; only I think
much time ought not to be spent upon such salutations when
there is other work to do.'

In a letter to his wife seven years later, Mr. Gladstone says
of this dispute, 'Mr. Arbuthnot told me to-day an observation
of Sir George Lewis's when at the exchequer here. Speaking of
my controversy with the Bank in 1854, he said, "It is a pity
Gladstone puts so much heat, so much irritability into business.
Now I am as cool as a fish."' The worst of being as cool as a
fish is that you never get great things done, you effect no
improvements and you carry no reforms, against the lethargy
or selfishness of men and the tyranny of old custom.[1]

Now also his attention was engaged by the controversies on
currency that thrive so lustily in the atmosphere of the Bank
Charter Act, and, after much discussion with authorities both
in Lombard Street and at the treasury, without committal he
sketched out at least one shadow of a project of his own. He
knew, however, that any great measure must be undertaken by
a finance minister with a clear position and strong hands, and

_____
[1] See Appendix.

he told Graham that even if he saw his way distinctly to a
plan, he did not feel individually strong enough for the attempt.
Nor was there time. To reconstitute the Savings Bank finance,
to place the chancery and some other accounts on a right basis,
and to readjust the banking relations properly so-called between
the Bank and the state, would be even more than a fair share
of financial work for the session. Before the year was over he
passed a bill, for which he had laid before the cabinet elaborate
argumentative supports, removing a number of objections to
the then existing system of dealing with the funds drawn from
Savings Banks.[1]

III

The year closed with an incident that created a considerable
stir, and might by misadventure have become memorable.
What has been truly called a warm and prolonged dispute [2]
arose out of Mr. Gladstone's removal of a certain official from
his post in the department of woods and forests. As Lord
Aberdeen told the Queen that he could not easily make the
case intelligible, it is not likely that I should succeed any
better, and we may as well leave the thick dust undisturbed.
Enough to say that Lord John Russell thought the dismissal
harsh ; that Mr. Gladstone stood his ground against either the
reversal of what he had done, or any proceedings in parliament
that might look like contrition, but was willing to submit the
points to the decision of colleagues ; that Lord John would
submit no point to colleagues 'affecting his personal honour'—
to such degrees of heat can the quicksilver mount even in a
cabinet thermometer. If such quarrels of the great are painful,
there is some compensation in the firmness, patience, and
benignity with which a man like Lord Aberdeen strove to
appease them. Some of his colleagues actually thought that
Lord John would make this paltry affair a plea for resigning,
while others suspected that he might find a better excuse in the
revival of convocation. As it happened, a graver occasion
offered itself.

[1] 17 and 18 Vict., c. 50.
[2] Walpole's *Russell*, ii. p. 243 *n*.

CHAPTER VI

CRISIS OF 1855 AND BREAK-UP OF THE PEELITES

(1855)

Party has no doubt its evils; but all the evils of party put together would be scarcely a grain in the balance, when compared with the dissolution of honourable friendships, the pursuit of selfish ends, the want of concert in council, the absence of a settled policy in foreign affairs, the corruption of certain statesmen, the caprices of an intriguing court, which the extinction of party connection has brought and would bring again upon this country.—EARL RUSSELL.[1]

THE administrative miscarriages of the war in the Crimea during the winter of 1854-5 destroyed the coalition government.[2] When parliament assembled on January 23, 1855, Mr. Roebuck on the first night of the session gave notice of a motion for a committee of inquiry. Lord John Russell attended to the formal business, and when the House was up went home accompanied by Sir Charles Wood. Nothing of consequence passed between the two colleagues, and no word was said to Wood in the direction of withdrawal. The same evening as the prime minister was sitting in his drawing-room, a red box was brought in to him by his son, containing Lord John Russell's resignation. He was as much amazed as Lord Newcastle, smoking his evening pipe of tobacco in his coach, was amazed by the news that the battle of Marston Moor had begun. Nothing has come to light since to set aside the severe judgment pronounced upon this proceeding by the universal opinion of contemporaries, including Lord John's own closest political allies. That a minister should run away from a hostile motion upon affairs for which responsibility was collective, and this without a word of consultation with a single colleague, is a transaction happily without a precedent in the history of modern English cabinets.[3] It opened an intricate and unexpected chapter of affairs.

The ministerial crisis of 1855 was unusually prolonged; it was interesting as a drama of character and motive; it marked a decisive stage in the evolution of party, and it was one of the

[1] On Bute's plan of superseding party by prerogative, in the introduction to vol. iii. of the Bedford *Correspondence.*

[2] See Appendix.   [3] See Chap. x. of Lord Stanmore's *Earl of Aberdeen.*

turning-points in the career of the subject of this biography. Fortunately for us, Mr. Gladstone has told in his own way the whole story of what he calls this 'sharp and difficult passage in public affairs,' and he might have added that it was a sharp passage in his own life. His narrative, with the omission of some details now dead and indifferent, and of a certain number of repetitions, is the basis of this chapter.

I

On the day following Lord John's letter the cabinet met, and the prime minister told them that at first he thought it meant the break-up of the government, but on further consideration he thought they should hold on, if it could be done with honour and utility. Newcastle suggested his own resignation, and the substitution of Lord Palmerston in his place. Palmerston agreed that the country, rightly or wrongly, wished to see him at the war office, but he was ready to do whatever his colleagues thought best. The whigs thought resignation necessary. Mr. Gladstone thought otherwise, and scouted the suggestion that as Newcastle was willing to resign, Lord John might come back. Lord John himself actually sent a sort of message to know whether he should attend the cabinet. In the end Lord Aberdeen carried all their resignations to the Queen. These she declined to accept, and she 'urged with the greatest eagerness that the decision should be reconsidered.' It is hard at this distance of time to understand how any cabinet under national circumstances of such gravity could have thought of the ignominy of taking to flight from a motion of censure, whatever a single colleague like Lord John Russell might deem honourable. On pressure from the Queen, the whigs in the government, Lord John notwithstanding, agreed to stand fire. Mr. Gladstone proceeds :—

Lord John's explanation, which was very untrue in its general effect, though I believe kindly conceived in feeling as well as tempered with some grains of policy and a contemplation of another possible premiership, carried the House with him, as Herbert observed while he was speaking. Palmerston's reply to him was wretched. It produced in the House (that is, in so much of the House as would otherwise have been favourable) a flatness and deadness of spirit towards the government which was indescribable ; and Charles Wood with a marked expression of face said while it was going on, 'And this is to be our leader !' I was myself so painfully full of the scene, that when Palmerston himself sat down I was on the very point of saying to him unconsciously, 'Can anything more be said ?' But no one would rise in the adverse sense, and therefore there was no opening for a minister. Palmerston [now become leader in the Commons] had written to ask me to follow Lord John on account of his being a *party*. But it was justly thought in the cabinet that there were good reasons against my taking this part upon me, and so the arrangement was changed.

Roebuck brought forward his motion. Mr. Gladstone resisted it on behalf of the government with immense argumentative force, and he put the point against Lord John which explains the word 'untrue' in the passage just quoted, namely, that though he desired in November the substitution of Palmerston for Newcastle as war minister, he had given it up in December, and yet this vital fact was omitted.[1] It was not for the government, he said, either to attempt to make terms with the House by reconstruction of a cabinet, or to shrink from any judgment of the House upon their acts. If they had so shrunk, he exclaimed, this is the sort of epitaph that he would expect to have written over their remains :—'Here lie the dishonoured ashes of a ministry that found England in peace and left it in war, that was content to enjoy the emoluments of office and to wield the sceptre of power, so long as no man had the courage to question their existence : they saw the storm gathering over the country ; they heard the agonising accounts that were almost daily received of the sick and wounded in the East. These things did not move them, but so soon as a member of opposition raised his hand to point the thunderbolt, they became conscience-stricken into a sense of guilt, and hoping to escape punishment, they ran away from duty.' Such would be their epitaph. Of the proposed inquiry itself,—an inquiry into the conduct of generals and troops actually in the field, and fighting by the side of, and in concert with, foreign allies, he observed—'Your inquiry will never take place as a real inquiry ; or, if it did, it would lead to nothing but confusion and disturbance, increased disasters, shame at home and weakness abroad ; it would convey no consolation to those whom you seek to aid, but it would carry malignant joy to the hearts of the enemies of England ; and, for my part, I shall ever rejoice, if this motion is carried to-night, that my own last words as a member of the cabinet of the Earl of Aberdeen have been words of solemn and earnest protest against a proceeding which has no foundation either in the constitution or in the practice of preceding parliaments ; which is useless and mischievous for the purpose which it appears to contemplate ; and which, in my judgment, is full of danger to the power, dignity and usefulness of the Commons of England.' A journalistic observer, while deploring the speaker's adherence to 'the dark dogmatisms of medieval religionists,' admits that he had never heard so fine a speech. The language, he says, was devoid of redundance. The attitude was calm. Mr. Gladstone seemed to feel that he rested upon the magnitude of the argument, and had no need of the assistance of bodily vehemence of manner. His voice was clear, distinct, and flexible, without monotony. It was minute dis-

---

[1] 'This *suppressio veri* is shocking, and one of the very worst things he ever did.'— *Greville*, III. i. p. 232.

section without bitterness or ill-humoured innuendo. He sat down amid immense applause from hearers admiring but unconvinced. Mr. Gladstone himself records of this speech: 'Hard and heavy work, especially as to the cases of three persons: Lord John Russell, Duke of Newcastle, and Lord Raglan.' Ministers were beaten (January 29) by 325 to 148, and they resigned.

Jan. 30, 1855.—Cabinet 1-2. We exchanged friendly adieus. Dined with the Herberts. This was a day of personal light-heartedness, but the problem for the nation is no small one.

The Queen sent for Lord Derby, and he made an attempt to form a government. Without aid from the conservative wing of the fallen ministry there was no hope, and his first step (Jan. 31) was to call on Lord Palmerston, with an earnest request for his support, and with a hope that he would persuade Mr. Gladstone and Sidney Herbert to rejoin their old political connection; with the intimation moreover that Mr. Disraeli, with a self-abnegation that did him the highest credit, was willing to waive in Lord Palmerston's favour his own claim to the leadership of the House of Commons. Palmerston was to be president of the council, and Ellenborough minister of war. In this conversation Lord Palmerston made no objection on any political grounds, or on account of any contemplated measures; he found no fault with the position intended for himself, or for others with whom he would be associated. Lord Derby supposed that all would depend on the concurrence of Mr. Gladstone and Herbert. He left Cambridge House at half-past two in the afternoon, and at half-past nine in the evening he received a note from Lord Palmerston declining. Three hours later he heard from Mr. Gladstone, who declined also. The proceedings of this eventful day, between two in the afternoon and midnight, whatever may have been the play of motive and calculation in the innermost minds of all or any of the actors, were practically to go a long way, though by no means the whole way, as we shall see, towards making Mr. Gladstone's severance from the conservative party definitive.

Jan. 31.—Lord Palmerston came to see me between three and four, with a proposal from Lord Derby that he and I, with S. Herbert, should take office under him; Palmerston to be president of the council and lead the House of Commons. Not finding me when he called before, he had gone to S. Herbert, who seemed to be disinclined. I inquired (1) whether Derby mentioned Graham? (2) Whether he had told Lord Palmerston if his persevering with the commission he had received would depend on the answer to this proposal. (3) How he was himself inclined. He answered the two first questions in the negative, and said as to the third, though not keenly, that he felt disinclined, but that if he refused it would be attributed to his contemplating another result, which other result he considered would be agreeable to the country. I then argued strongly with him that though he might form a government, and though if he formed it, he would certainly start it amidst immense clapping of hands, yet he could not have any reasonable prospect of stable parliamentary support ; on the one hand would stand Derby with his phalanx, on the other Lord J. Russell, of necessity a centre and nucleus of discontent, and between these two there would and could be no room for a parliamentary majority such as would uphold his government. He argued only rather faintly the other way, and seemed rather to come to my way of thinking.

I said that even if the proposition were entertained, there would be much to consider ; that I thought it clear, whatever else was doubtful, that we could not join without him, for in his absence the wound would not heal kindly again, that I could not act without Lord Aberdeen's approval, nor should I willingly separate myself from Graham ; that if we joined, we must join in force. But I was disposed to wish that if all details could be arranged, we should join in that manner rather than that Derby should give up the commission, though I thought the best thing of all would be Derby forming a ministry of his own men, provided only he could get a good or fair foreign secretary instead of Clarendon, who in any case would be an immense loss. . . .

I went off to speak to Lord Aberdeen, and Palmerston went to speak to Clarendon, with respect to whom he had told Derby that he could hardly enter any government which had not Clarendon at the foreign office. When we reassembled, I asked Lord Palmerston whether he had made up his mind for himself independently of us, inasmuch as I thought that if he had, that was enough to close the whole question ? He answered, Yes ; that he should tell Derby he did not think he could render him useful service in his administration. He then left. It was perhaps 6.30. Herbert and I sat down to write, but thought it well to send off nothing till after dinner, and we went to Grillion's where we had a small but merry party. Herbert even beyond himself amusing. At night we went to Lord Aberdeen's and Graham's, and so my letter came through some slight emendations to the form in which it went.[1] I had doubts in my mind whether Derby had even intended to propose to Herbert and me *except* in conjunction with Palmerston, though I had no doubt that without Palmerston it would not do ; and I framed my letter so as not to assume that I had an independent proposal, but to make my refusal a part of his.

Feb. 2.—I yesterday also called on Lord Palmerston and read him my letter to Lord Derby. He said : 'Nothing can be better.'

Lord Derby knew that, though he had the country gentlemen behind him, his own political friends, with the notable and only half-welcome exception of Mr. Disraeli, were too far below mediocrity in either capacity or experience to face so angry and dangerous a crisis. Accordingly he gave up the task. Many years after, Mr. Gladstone recorded his opinion that here Lord Derby missed his one real chance of playing a high historic part. 'To a Derby government,' he said, 'now that the party had been *drubbed* out of protection, I did not in

---

[1] At Lord Aberdeen's the question seems to have been discussed on the assumption that the offer to Mr. Gladstone and Herbert was meant to be independent of Palmerston's acceptance or refusal, and the impression there was that Mr. Gladstone had been not wholly disinclined to consider the offer.

principle object ; for old ties were with me more operatively strong than new opinions, and I think that Lord Derby's error in not forming an administration was palpable and even gross. Such, it has appeared, was the opinion of Disraeli.[1] Lord Derby had many fine qualities ; but strong parliamentary courage was not among them. When Lord Palmerston (probably with a sagacious discernment of the immediate future) declined, he made no separate offer to the Peelites. Had Lord Derby gone on, he would have been supported by the country, then absorbed in the consideration of the war. None of the three occasions when he took office offered him so fine an opportunity as this ; but he missed it.'

On the previous day, Mr. Gladstone records :—'Saw Mr. Disraeli in the House of Lords and put out my hand, which was very kindly accepted.' To nobody was the hour fraught with more bitter mortification than to Mr. Disraeli, who beheld a golden chance of bringing a consolidated party into the possession of real power flung away.

II

Next, at the Queen's request, soundings in the whig and Peelite waters were undertaken by Lord Lansdowne, and he sent for Mr. Gladstone, with a result that to the latter was ever after matter of regret.

Feb. 2.—In consequence of a communication from Lord Lansdowne, I went to him in the forenoon and found him just returned from Windsor. He trusted I should not mind speaking freely to him, and I engaged to do it, only premising that in so crude and dark a state of facts, it was impossible to go beyond first impressions. We then conversed on various combinations, as (1) Lord J. Russell, premier, (2) Lord Palmerston, (3) Lord Clarendon, (4) Lord Lansdowne himself. Of the first I doubted whether, in the present state of feeling, he could get a ministry on its legs. In answer to a question from him, I added that I thought, viewing my relations to Lord Aberdeen and to Newcastle, and *his* to them also, the public feeling would be offended, and it would not be for the public interest, if I were to form part of his government (*i.e.* Russell's). Of the second I said that it appeared to me Lord Palmerston could not obtain a party majority. Aloof from him would stand on the one hand Derby and his party, on the other Lord J. Russell, who I took it for granted would never serve under him. Whatever the impression made by Russell's recent conduct, yet his high personal character and station, forty years' career, one-half of it in the leadership of his party, and the close connection of his name with all the great legislative changes of the period, must ever render him a power in the state, and render it impossible for a government depending on the liberal party to live independently of him. I also hinted at injurious effects which the substitution of Palmerston for Lord Aberdeen would produce on foreign Powers at this critical moment, but dwelt chiefly on the impossibility of his having a majority. In this Lord Lansdowne seemed to agree.

[1] Malmesbury's *Memoirs of an Ex-Minister*, i. pp. 8, 37.

Lastly, I said that if Lord Lansdowne himself could venture to risk his health and strength by taking the government, this would be the best arrangement. My opinion was that at this crisis Derby, if he could have formed an administration, would have had advantages with regard to the absorbing questions of the war and of a peace to follow it, such as no other combination could possess. Failing this, I wished for a homogeneous whig government. The best form of it would be under him. He said he might dare it provisionally, if he could see his way to a permanent arrangement at the end of a short term ; but he could see nothing of the sort at present.

An autobiographic note of 1897 gives a further detail of moment :—He asked whether I would continue to hold my office as chancellor of the exchequer in the event of his persevering. He said that if I gave an affirmative reply he would persevere with the commission, and I think intimated that except on this condition he would not. I said that the working of the coalition since its formation in December 1852 had been to me entirely satisfactory, but that I was not prepared to co-operate in its continuation under any other head than Lord Aberdeen. I think that though perfectly satisfied to be in a Peelite government which had whigs or radicals in it, I was not ready to be in a whig government which had Peelites in it. It took a long time, with my slow-moving and tenacious character, for the Ethiopian to change his skin.

In the paper that I have already mentioned, as recording what, when all was near an end, he took to be some of the errors of his life, Mr. Gladstone names as one of those errors this refusal in 1855 to join Lord Lansdowne. 'I can hardly suppose,' he says, more than forty years after that time, 'that the eventual failure of the Queen's overture to Lord Lansdowne was due to my refusal ; but that refusal undoubtedly constituted one of his difficulties and helped to bring about the result. I have always looked back upon it with pain as a serious and even gross error of judgment. It was, I think, injurious to the public, if it contributed to the substitution as prime minister of Lord Palmerston for Lord Lansdowne,—a personage of greater dignity, and I think a higher level of political principle. There was no defect in Lord Lansdowne sufficient to warrant my refusal. He would not have been a strong or very active prime minister ; but the question of the day was the conduct of the war, and I had no right to take exception to him as a head in connection with this subject. His attitude in domestic policy was the same as Palmerston's, but I think he had a more unprejudiced and liberal mind, though less of motive force in certain directions.'

III

The next day Mr. Gladstone called on Lord Aberdeen, who for the first time let drop a sort of opinion as to their duties in the crisis on one point; hitherto he had restrained himself. He said, 'Certainly the most natural thing under the circumstances, if it could have been brought about in a satisfactory form, would have been that you should have joined Derby.' On returning home, Mr. Gladstone received an important visitor and a fruitless visit.

At half-past two to-day Lord John Russell was announced ; and sat till three—his hat shaking in his hand. A communication had reached him late last night from the Queen, charging him with the formation of a government, and he had thought it his duty to make the endeavour. I repeated to him what I had urged on Lord Lansdowne, that a coalition with advantages has also weaknesses of its own, that the late coalition was I thought fully justified by the circumstances under which it took place, but at this juncture it had broken down. This being so, I thought what is called a homogeneous government would be best for the public, and most likely to command approval ; that Derby if he could get a good foreign minister would have had immense advantages with respect to the great questions of war and peace. Lord John agreed as to Derby ; thought that every one must have supported him, and that he ought to have persevered.

I held to my point, adding that I did not think Lord Aberdeen and Lord Palmerston represented opposite principles, but rather different forms of the same principles connected with different habits and temperaments. He said that Lord Palmerston had agreed to lead the House of Commons for him, he going as first minister to the Lords ; but he did not mention any other alteration. Upon the whole his tone was low and doubtful. He asked whether my answer was to be considered as given, or whether I would take time. But I said as there was no probability that my ideas would be modified by reflection, it would not be fair to him to ask any delay.

With the single exception of Lord Palmerston, none of his colleagues would have anything to do with Lord John, some even declining to go to see him. Wood came to Mr. Gladstone, evidently in the sense of the Palmerston premiership. He declared that Aberdeen was impossible, to which, says Mr. Gladstone, 'I greatly demurred.'

IV

Thus the two regular party leaders had failed ; Lord Aberdeen, the coalition leader, was almost universally known to be out of the question ; the public was loudly clamouring for Lord Palmerston. A Palmerston ministry was now seen to be inevitable. Were the Peelites, then, having refused Lord Derby, having refused Lord John, having told Lord Lansdowne that he had better form a system of homogeneous whigs, now finally to refuse Lord Palmerston, on no better ground than that they could not have Lord Aberdeen, whom nobody save themselves would consent on any terms to have ? To propound such a question was to answer it. Lord Aberdeen himself, with admirable freedom from egotism, pressed the point that in addition to the argument of public necessity, they owed much to their late whig colleagues, 'who behaved so nobly and so generously towards us after Lord John's resignation.'

'I have heard club talk and society talk,' wrote an adherent to Mr. Gladstone late one night (February 4), 'and I am sure that in the main any government containing good names in the cabinet, provided Lord John is not in it, will obtain general support. Lord Clarendon is universally, or nearly so, looked on as essential. Next to him, I think you are considered of vital importance in your present office. After all, rightly or wrongly, Lord Palmerston is master of the situation in the country ; he is looked upon as the man. If the country sees you and Sidney Herbert holding aloof from him, it will be said the Peelites are selfish intriguers.' The same evening, another correspondent said to Mr. Gladstone : 'Two or three people have come in since eleven o'clock with the news of Brooks's and the Reform. Exultation prevails there, and the certainty of Palmerston's success to-morrow. There is a sort of rumour prevalent that Lord Palmerston may seek Lord J. Russell's aid. . . . This would, of course, negative all idea of your joining in the concern. Otherwise a refusal would be set down as sheer impracticability, or else the selfish ambition of a clique which could not stand alone, and should no longer attempt to do so. If the refusal to join Palmerston is to be a going over to the other side, and a definite junction within a brief space, that is clear and intelligible. But a refusal to join Lord Palmerston and yet holding out to him a promise of support, is a half-measure which no one will understand, and which, I own, I cannot see the grounds to defend.'

We shall now find how, after long and strenuous dubitation, the Peelite leaders refused to join on the fifth of February, and then on the sixth they joined. Unpromising from the very first cabinet, the junction was destined to a swift and sudden end. Here is the story told by one of the two leading actors.

Sunday, Feb. 4.—Herbert came to me soon after I left him, and told me Palmerston had at last got the commission. He considered that this disposed of Lord Lansdowne ; and seemed himself to be disposed to join. He said *we* must take care what we were about, and that we should be looked upon by the country as too nice if we declined to join Palmerston ; who he believed (and in this I inclined to agree) would probably form a government. He argued that Lord Aberdeen was out of the question ; that the vote of Monday night was against him ; that the country would not stand him.

No new coalition ought to be formed, I said, without a prospect of stability ; and joining Lord Palmerston's cabinet would be a new coalition. He said he rather applied that phrase to a junction with Derby. I quite agreed we could not join Derby except under conditions which might not be realised ; but if we *did* it, it would be a reunion, not a coalition. In coalition the separate existence is retained. I referred to the great instances of change of party in our time ; Palmerston himself, and Stanley with Graham. But these took place when parties were divided by great questions of principle ; there were none such now, and no one could say that the two sides of the House were divided by anything more than this, that one was rather more stationary, the other more movable. He said, 'True, the differences are on the back benches.'

I said I had now for two years been holding my mind in suspense upon the question I used to debate with Newcastle, who used to argue that we should grow into the natural leaders of the liberal party. I said, it is now plain this will not be ; we get on very well with the independent liberals, but the whigs stand as an opaque body between us and them, and moreover, there they will stand and ought to stand.

Lord Palmerston came a little after two, and remained perhaps an hour. Lord Lansdowne had promised to join him if he formed an administration on a basis sufficiently broad. He wished me to retain my office ; and dwelt on the satisfactory nature of my relations with the liberal party. He argued that Lord Aberdeen was excluded by the vote on Monday night ; and that there was now no other government in view. My argument was adverse, though without going to a positive conclusion. I referred to my conversation of Wednesday, Jan. 31, in favour of a homogeneous government at this juncture.

At half-past eleven I went to Lord Aberdeen's and stayed about an hour. His being in the Palmerston cabinet which had been proposed, was, he said, out of the question ; but his *velleities* seemed to lean rather to *our* joining, which surprised me. He was afraid of the position we should occupy in the public eye if we declined. . . .

Feb. 5.—The most irksome and painful of the days ; beginning with many hours of anxious consultation to the best of our power, and ending amidst a storm of disapproval almost unanimous, not only from the generality, but from our own immediate political friends.

At 10.30 I went to Sir James Graham, who is still in bed, and told him the point to which by hard struggles I had come. The case with me was briefly this. I was ready to make the sacrifice of personal feeling ; ready to see him (Lord Aberdeen) expelled from the premiership by a censure equally applicable to myself, and yet to remain in my office ; ready to overlook not merely the inferior fitness, but the real and manifest unfitness, of Palmerston for that office ; ready to enter upon a new venture with him, although in my opinion without any reasonable prospect of parliamentary support, such as is absolutely necessary for the credit and stability of a government—upon the one sole and all-embracing ground that the prosecution of the war with vigour, and the prosecution of it to and for peace, was now the question of the day to which every other must give way. But then it was absolutely necessary that if we joined a cabinet after our overlooking all this and more, it should be a cabinet in which confidence should be placed with reference to war and peace. Was the Aberdeen cabinet without Lord Aberdeen one in which I could place confidence ? I answer, No. He was vital to it ; his love of peace was necessary to its right and steady pursuit of that great end ; if, then, *he* could belong to a Palmerston cabinet, I might ; but without him I could not.

In all this, Sir J. Graham concurred. Herbert came full of doubts and fears, but on the whole adopted the same conclusion. Lord Aberdeen sent to say he would not come, but I wrote to beg him, and he appeared. On hearing how we stood, he said his remaining in the cabinet was quite out of the question ; and that he had told Palmerston so yesterday when he glanced at it. But he thought we should incur great blame if we did not; which, indeed, was plainly beyond all dispute.

At length, when I had written and read aloud the rough draft of an answer, Lord Aberdeen said he must strongly advise our joining. I said to him, 'Lord Aberdeen, when we have joined the Palmerston cabinet, you standing aloof from it, will you rise in your place in the House of Lords and say that you give that cabinet your confidence with regard to the question of war and peace?' He replied, 'I will express my hope that it will do right, but not my confidence, which is a different thing.' 'Certainly,' I answered, 'and that which you have now said is my justification. The unswerving honesty of your mind has saved us. Ninety-nine men out of a hundred in your position at the moment would have said, "Oh yes, I shall express my confidence." But you would not deviate an inch to the right or to the left.'

Herbert and I went to my house and despatched our answers. Now began the storm. Granville met us driving to Newcastle. Sorry beyond expression; he almost looked displeased, which for him is much. *Newcastle:* I incline to think you are wrong. *Canning:* My impression is you are wrong. Various letters streaming in, all portending condemnation and disaster. Herbert became more and more uneasy.

Feb. 6.—The last day I hope of these tangled records; in which we have seen, to say nothing of the lesser sacrifice, one more noble victim struck down, and we are set to feast over the remains. The thing is bad and the mode worse.

Arthur Gordon came early in the day with a most urgent letter from Lord Aberdeen addressed virtually to us, and urging us to join. He had seen both Palmerston and Clarendon, and derived much satisfaction from what they said. We met at the admiralty at twelve, where Graham lay much knocked up with the fatigue and anxiety of yesterday. I read to him and Lord Aberdeen Palmerston's letter of to-day to me. Herbert came in and made arguments in his sense. I told him I was at the point of yesterday, and was immovable by considerations of the class he urged. *The only security worth having lies in men;* the man is Lord Aberdeen; moral union and association with him must continue, and must be publicly known to continue. I therefore repeated my question to Lord Aberdeen, whether he would in his place as a peer declare, if we joined the cabinet, that it had his confidence with reference to war and peace? He said, much moved, that he felt the weight of the responsibility, but that after the explanation and assurances he had received, he would. He was even more moved when Graham said that though the leaning of his judgment was adverse, he would place himself absolutely in the hands of Lord Aberdeen. To Herbert, of course, it was a simple release from a difficulty. Palmerston had told Cardwell, 'Gladstone feels a difficulty first infused into him by Graham; Argyll and Herbert have made up their minds to do what Gladstone does.' Newcastle joined us, and was in Herbert's sense. I repeated again that Lord Aberdeen's declaration of confidence enabled me to see my way to joining. . . .

I went to Lord Aberdeen in his official room after his return from Palmerston. It was only when I left that room to-day that I began to realise the pang of parting. There he stood, struck down from his eminence by a vote that did not dare to avow its own purpose, and for his wisdom and virtue; there he stood endeavouring to cure the ill consequences to the public of the wrong inflicted upon himself, and as to the point immediately within reach successful in the endeavour. I ventured, however, to tell him that I hoped our conduct and reliance on him would tend to his eminence and honour, and said, 'You are not to be of the cabinet, but you are to be its tutelary deity.'

I had a message from Palmerston that he would answer me, but at night I went up to him.

V

The rush of events was now somewhat slackened. Lord John called on Graham, and complained of the Peelites for having selfishly sought too many offices, alluding to what Canning had done, and imputing the same to Cardwell. He also thought they had made a great mistake in joining Palmerston. He seemed sore about Mr. Gladstone, and told Graham that Christopher, a stout tory, had said that if Gladstone joined Derby, a hundred of the party would withdraw their allegiance. At the party meeting on Feb. 21, Lord Derby was received with loud cries of 'No Puseyites; No papists,' and was much reprehended for asking Gladstone and Graham to join.

'I ought to have mentioned before,' Mr. Gladstone writes here, 'that, during our conferences at the admiralty, Lord Aberdeen expressed great compunction for having allowed the country to be dragged without adequate cause into the war. So long as he lived, he said with his own depth and force, it would be a weight upon his conscience. He had held similar language to me lately at Argyll House; but when I asked him at what point *after* the fleet went to Besika Bay it would have been possible to stop short, he alluded to the *sommation*, which we were encouraged however, as he added, by Austria to send; and thought *this* was the false step. Yet he did not seem quite firm in the opinion.'

Then came the first cabinet (Feb. 10). It did not relieve the gloom of Mr. Gladstone's impressions. He found it more 'acephalous' than ever; 'less order; less unity of purpose.' The question of the Roebuck committee was raised, on which he said he thought the House would give it up, if government would promise an investigation under the authority of the crown. The fatal subject came up again three days later. Palmerston said it was plain from the feeling in the House the night before, that they were set upon it; if they could secure a fair committee, he was disposed to let the inquiry go forward. On this rock the ship struck. One minister said they could not resign in consequence of the appointment of the committee, because it stood affirmed by a large majority when they took office in the reconstructed cabinet. Mr. Gladstone says he 'argued with vehemence upon the breach of duty which it would involve on our part towards those holding responsible commands in the Crimea, if we without ourselves condemning

them were to allow them to be brought before another
tribunal like a select committee.'

Dining the same evening at the palace, Mr. Gladstone had
a conversation on the subject both with the Queen and
Prince Albert. 'The latter compared this appointment of a
committee to the proceedings of the Convention of France ;
but still seemed to wish that the government should submit
rather than retire. The Queen spoke openly in that sense,
and trusted that she should not be given over into the hands
of those "who are the least fit to govern." Without any
positive and final declaration, I intimated to each that I did
not think I could bring my mind to acquiesce in the proposition for an inquiry by a select committee into the state
of the army in the Crimea.'

Time did not remove difficulties. Mr. Gladstone and
Graham fought with extreme tenacity, and the first of them
with an ingenuity for which the situation gave boundless
scope. To the argument that they accepted office on reconstruction with the decision of the House for a committee
staring them in the face, he replied :—'Before we were *out*,
we were *in*. Why did we go out ? Because of that very
decision by the House of Commons. Our language was :
The appointment of such a committee is incompatible with
the functions of the executive, therefore it is a censure on the
executive ; therefore we resign ! But it is not a whit *more*
compatible with the functions of the executive now than it
was then ; therefore it is not one whit less a censure ; and
the question arises, (1) whether any government ought to
allow its (now) principal duty to be delegated to a committee
or other body, especially to one not under the control of the
crown ? (2) whether *that* government ought to allow it, the
members of which (except one) have already resigned rather
than allow it ? In what way can the first resignation be
justified on grounds which do not require a second ?' He
dwelt mainly on these two points—That the proposed transfer
of the functions of the executive to a select committee of the
House of Commons, with respect to an army in the face of
the enemy and operating by the side of our French allies, and
the recognition of this transfer by the executive government,
was an evil greater than any that could arise from a total or
partial resignation. Second, that it was clear that they did
not, as things stood, possess the confidence of a majority of
the House. 'I said that the committee was itself a censure
on the government. They had a right to believe that parliament would not inflict this committee on a government which
had its confidence. I also,' he says, 'recited my having
ascertained from Palmerston (upon this recital we were agreed)
on the 6th, before our decision was declared, his intention to
oppose the committee. . . .'

Graham did not feel disposed to govern without the confidence of the House of Commons, or to be responsible for the granting of a committee which the cabinet had unanimously felt to be unprecedented, unconstitutional, and dangerous. Lord Palmerston met all this by a strong practical clincher. He said that the House of Commons was becoming unruly from the doubts that had gone abroad as to the intentions of the government with respect to the committee; that the House was determined to have it; that if they opposed it they should be beaten by an overwhelming majority; to dissolve upon it would be ruinous; to resign a fortnight after taking office would make them the laughing-stock of the country.

Mr. Gladstone, Herbert, and Graham then resigned. Of the Peelite group the Duke of Argyll and Canning remained.

Feb. 22.—After considering various *sites*, we determined to ask the Manchester school to yield us, at any rate for to-morrow, the old place devoted to ex-ministers.[1] Sir J. Graham expressed his wish to begin the affair, on the proposal of the first name [of the committee].

Cardwell came at 4 to inform me that he had declined to be my successor; and showed me his letter, which gave as his reason disinclination to step into the cabinet over the bodies of his friends. It seems that Palmerston and Lord Lansdowne, who assists him, sent Canning to Lord Aberdeen to invoke his aid with Cardwell and prevail on him to retract. But Lord Aberdeen, though he told Canning that he disapproved (at variance here with what Graham and I considered to be his tone on Monday, but agreeing with a note he wrote in obscure terms the next morning), said he could not make such a request to Cardwell, or again play the peculiar part he had acted a fortnight ago. The cabinet on receiving Cardwell's refusal were at a deadlock. Application was to be made, or had been made, to Sir Francis Baring, but it seems that he is reluctant; he is, however, the best card they have to play.

Feb. 28.—On Sunday, Sir George Lewis called on me, and said my office had been offered him. This was after being refused by Cardwell and Baring. He asked my advice as to accepting it. This I told him I could not give. He asked if I would assist him with information in case of his accepting. I answered that he might command me precisely as if instead of resigning I had only removed to another department. I then went over some of the matters needful to be made known. On Tuesday he came again, acquainted me with his acceptance, and told me he had been mainly influenced by my promise.[2]

This day at a quarter to three I attended at the palace to resign the

---

[1] On Feb. 23 he writes to Mr. Hayter, the government whip: 'We have arranged to sit in the orthodox ex-ministers' place to-night, *i.e.* second bench immediately below the gangway. This avoids constructions and comparisons which we could hardly otherwise have escaped; and Bright and his friends agreed to give it us. Might I trust to your kindness to have some cards put in the place for us before prayers?'

[2] While Lewis went to the exchequer, Sir Charles Wood succeeded Graham at the admiralty, Lord John, then on his way to Vienna, agreed to come back to the cabinet and took the colonial office, which Sir George Grey had left for the home office, where he succeeded Palmerston.

seals, and had an audience of about twenty minutes. The Queen, in taking them over, was pleased to say that she received them with great pain. I answered that the decision which had required me to surrender them had been the most painful effort of my public life. The Queen said she was afraid on Saturday night [Feb. 17, when he had dined at the palace] from the language I then used that this was about to happen. I answered that we had then already had a discussion in the cabinet which pointed to this result, and that I spoke as I did, because I thought that to have no reserve whatever with H.M. was the first duty of all those who had the honour and happiness of being her servants. I trusted H.M. would believe that we had all been governed by no other desire than to do what was best for the interests of the crown and the country. H.M. expressed her confidence of this, and at no time throughout the conversation did she in any manner indicate an opinion that our decision had been wrong. She spoke of the difficulty of making arrangements for carrying on the government in the present state of things, and I frankly gave my opinion to H.M. that she would have little peace or comfort in these matters, until parliament should have returned to its old organisation in two political parties ; that at present we were in a false position, and that both sides of the House were demoralised — the ministerial side overcharged with an excess of official men, and the way stopped up against expectants, which led to subdivision, jealousy, and intrigue ; the opposition so weak in persons having experience of affairs as to be scarcely within the chances of office, and consequently made reckless by acting without keeping it in view ; yet at the same time, the party continued and must continue to exist, for it embodied one of the great fundamental elements of English society. The experiment of coalition had been tried with remarkable advantage under a man of the remarkable wisdom and powers of conciliation possessed by Lord Aberdeen, one in entire possession too of H.M.'s confidence. They intimated that there were peculiar disadvantages, too, evidently meaning Lord J. Russell. I named him in my answer, and said I thought that even if he had been steady, yet the divisions of the ministerial party would a little later have brought about our overthrow.[1] H.M. seeming to agree in my main position, as did the Prince, asked me : But when will parliament return to that state ? I replied I grieved to say that I perceived neither the time when, nor the manner how, that result is to come about ; but until it is reached, I fear that Y.M. will pass through a period of instability and weakness as respects the executive. She observed that the prospect is not agreeable. I said, True, madam, but it is a great consolation that all these troubles are upon the surface, and that the throne has for a long time been gaining and not losing stability from year to year. I could see but one danger to the throne, and that was from encroachments by the House of Commons. No other body in the country was strong enough to encroach. This was the consideration which had led my resigning colleagues with myself to abandon office that we might make our stand against what we thought a formidable invasion. . . . I thought the effect of the resistance was traceable in the good conduct of the House of Commons last night, when another attempt at encroachment was proposed and firmly repelled. . . . I expressed my comfort at

---

[1] This seems to contradict the proposition in the article on Greville in the *Eng. Hist. Rev.* of 1887.

finding that our motives were so graciously appreciated by H.M. and withdrew.

Loud was the public outcry. All the censure that had been foretold in case they should refuse to join, fell with double force upon them for first joining and then seceding. Lord Clarendon pronounced their conduct to be actually worse and more unpatriotic than Lord John's. The delight at Brooks's Club was uproarious, for to the whigs the Peelites had always been odious, and they had been extremely sorry when Palmerston asked them to join his government.[1] For a time Mr. Gladstone was only a degree less unpopular in the country than Cobden and Bright themselves. The newspapers declared that Gladstone's epitaph over the Aberdeen administration might be applied with peculiar force to his own fate. The short truth seems to be that Graham, Gladstone, and Palmerston were none of them emphatic or explicit enough beforehand on the refusal of the committee when the government was formed, though the intention to refuse was no doubt both stated and understood. Graham admitted afterwards that this omission was a mistake. The world would be astonished if it knew how often in the pressure of great affairs men's sight proves short. After the language used by Mr. Gladstone about the inquiry, we cannot wonder that he should have been slow to acquiesce. The result in time entirely justified his description of the Sebastopol committee.[2] But right as was his judgment on the merits, yet the case was hardly urgent enough to make withdrawal politic or wise. Idle gossip long prevailed, that Graham could not forgive Palmerston for not having (as he thought) helped to defend him in the matter of opening Mazzini's letters; that from the first he was bent on overthrowing the new minister; that he worked on Gladstone; and that the alleged reason why they left was not the real one. All the evidence is the other way; that Graham could not resist the obvious want of the confidence of parliament, and that Gladstone could not bear a futile and perilous inquiry. That they both regretted that they had yielded to over-persuasion in joining, against their own feelings and judgment, is certain. Graham even wrote to Mr. Gladstone in the following summer that his assent to joining Palmerston was perhaps the greatest mistake of his public life. In Mr. Gladstone's case, the transaction gave a rude and protracted shock to his public influence.

Lord Palmerston meanwhile sat tight in his saddle. When the crisis first began, Roebuck in energetic language had urged him to sweep the Peelites from his path, and at any rate he now very steadily went on without them. Everybody took for granted that his administration would be temporary. Mr.

---

[1] *Greville*, III. i. p. 246.

[2] Mr. Gladstone projected and partly executed some public letters on all this, to be addressed, like the Neapolitan letters, to Lord Aberdeen.

Gladstone himself gave it a twelvemonth at most. As it happened, Lord Palmerston was in fact, with one brief interruption, installed for a decade. He was seventy-one; he had been nearly forty years in office; he had worked at the admiralty, war department, foreign office, home office; he had served under ten prime ministers—Portland, Perceval, Liverpool, Canning, Goderich, Wellington, Grey, Melbourne, Russell, Aberdeen. He was not more than loosely attached to the whigs, and he had none of the strength of that aristocratic tradition and its organ, the Bedford sect. The landed interest was not with him. The Manchester men detested him. The church in all its denominations was on terms of cool and reciprocated indifference with one who was above all else the man of this world. The press he knew how to manage. In every art of parliamentary sleight of hand he was an expert, and he suited the temper of the times, while old maxims of government and policy were tardily expiring, and the forces of a new era were in their season gathering to a head.

CHAPTER VII

POLITICAL ISOLATION

(1855–1856)

ἥκιστα γὰρ πόλεμος ἐπὶ ῥητοῖς χωρεῖ.—Thuc. i. 122.

War is the last thing in all the world to go according to programme.

Statesmen are invincibly slow to learn the lesson put by Thucydides long centuries ago into the mouth of the Athenian envoys at Sparta, and often repeated in the same immortal pages, that war defies all calculations, and if it be protracted comes to be little more than mere matter of chance, over which the combatants have no control. A thousand times since has history proved this to be true. Policy is mastered by events; unforeseen sequels develop novel pretexts, or grow into start-ling and hateful necessities; the minister finds that he is fastened to an inexorable chain.

Mr. Gladstone now had this fatal law of mundane things brought home to him. As time went on, he by rapid intuition gained a truer insight into the leading facts. He realised that Mahometan institutions in the Ottoman empire were decrepit; that the youthful and vigorous elements in European Turkey were crushed under antiquated and worn-out forms and forces unfit for rule. He awoke to the disquieting reflection how the occupation of the Principalities had been discussed, day after day and month after month, entirely as a question of the pay-ment of forty thousand pounds a year to Turkey, or as a viola-tion of her rights as suzerain, but never in reference to the well-being, happiness, freedom, or peace of the inhabitants. He still held that the war in its origin was just, for it had been absolutely necessary, he said, to cut the meshes of the net in which Russia had entangled Turkey. He persisted in con-demning the whole tone and policy of Russia in 1854. By the end of 1854, in Mr. Gladstone's eyes, this aggressive spirit had been extinguished, the Czar promising an almost unreserved acceptance of the very points that he had in the previous August angrily rejected. The essential objects of the war were the abolition of Russian rights in the Principalities, and the destruction of Russian claims upon Greek Christians under Ottoman sway. These objects, Mr. Gladstone insisted, were attained in January 1855, when Russia agreed to three out of the Four Points—so the bases of agreement were named—and only demurred upon the plan for carrying out a portion of the fourth. The special object was to cancel the preponderance of Russia in the Black Sea. No fewer than seven different plans were simultaneously or in turn propounded. They were every one of them admitted to be dubious, inefficient, and imperfect. I will spare the reader the mysteries of limitation, of counterpoise, of counterpoise and limitation mixed. Russia preferred counterpoise, the allies were for limitation. Was this preference between two degrees of the imperfect, the deficient, and the ineffective a good ground for prolonging a war that was costing the allies a hundred million pounds a year, and involved to all the parties concerned the loss of a thousand lives a day? Yet, for saying No to this question, Mr. Gladstone was called a traitor, even by men who in 1853 had been willing to content themselves with the Vienna note, and in 1854 had been anxious to make peace on the basis of the Four Points. In face of pleas so wretched for a prolongation of a war to which he had assented on other grounds, was he bound to silence? 'Would it not, on the contrary,' he exclaimed, 'have been the most contemptible effeminacy of character, if a man in my position, who feels that he has been instrumental in bringing his country into this struggle, were to hesitate a single moment when he was firmly convinced in his own mind that the time had arrived when we might with honour escape from it?'

The prospect of reducing Russia to some abstract level of strength, so as to uphold an arbitrary standard of the balance of power—this he regarded as mischief and chimera. Rightly he dreaded the peril of alliances shifting from day to day, like quicksands and sea-shoals—Austria moved by a hundred strong and varying currents, France drawing by unforeseen affinities towards Russia. Every war with alliances, he once said, should be short, sharp, decisive.[1]

As was to be expected, the colleagues from whom he had parted insisted that every one of his arguments told just as logically against the war in all its stages, against the first as legitimately as the last. In fact, we can never say a plain sure aye or no to questions of peace and war, after the sword has once left the scabbard. They are all matter of judgment on the balance of policy between one course and another ; and a very slight thing may incline the balance either way, even though mighty affairs should hang on the turn of the scale. Meanwhile, as the months went on, Sebastopol still stood untaken, excitement grew, people forgot the starting-point. They ceased

[1] See Appendix.

to argue, and sheer blatancy, at all times a power, in war-time is supreme. Mr. Gladstone's trenchant dialectic had no more chance than Bright's glowing appeals. Shrewd and not unfriendly onlookers thought that Graham and Gladstone were grievously mistaken in making common cause with the peace party, immediately after quitting a war government, and quitting it, besides, not on the issues of the war. Herbert was vehement in his remonstrances. The whole advantage of co-operation with the Manchester men, he cried, would be derived by them, and all the disrepute reaped by us. 'For the purposes of peace, they were the very men we ought to avoid. As advocates for ending the war, they were out of court, for they were against beginning it.'[1] If Gladstone and Graham had gone slower, their friends said, they might have preached moderation to ministers and given reasonable advice to people out of doors. As it was, they threw the game into the hands of Lord Palmerston. They were stamped as doctrinaires, and what was worse, doctrinaires suspected of a spice of personal animus against old friends. Herbert insisted that the Manchester school 'forgot that the people have flesh and blood, and propounded theories to men swayed by national feeling.' As a matter of fact, this was wholly untrue. Cobden and Bright, as everybody nowadays admits, had a far truer perception of the underlying realities of the Eastern question in 1854, than either the Aberdeen or the Palmerston cabinet, or both of them put together. What was undeniable was that the public, with its habits of rough and ready judgment, did not understand, and could not be expected to understand, the new union of the Peelites with a peace party, in direct opposition to whose strongest views and gravest warnings they had originally begun the war. 'In Gladstone,' Cornewall Lewis said, 'people ascribe to faction, or ambition, or vanity, conduct which I believe to be the result of a conscientious, scrupulous, ingenuous, undecided mind, always looking on each side of a question and magnifying the objections which belong to almost every course of action.'[2]

A foreign envoy then resident in England was struck by the general ignorance of facts even among leading politicians. Of the friends of peace, he says, only Lord Grey and Gladstone seemed to have mastered the Vienna protocols : the rest were quite astonished when the extent of the Russian concessions was pointed out to them. The envoy dined with Mr. Gladstone at the table of the Queen, and they talked of Milner Gibson's motion censuring ministers for losing the opportunity of the Vienna conferences to make a sound and satisfactory peace. Mr. Gladstone said to him that he should undertake the grave responsibility of supporting this motion, 'because in his opinion the concessions promised by Russia contain sufficient guarantees.

[1] Herbert to Gladstone, May 27, 1855.
[2] *Many Memories*, p. 229.

Those very concessions will tear to pieces all the ancient treaties which gave an excuse to Russia for interfering in the internal affairs of Turkey.'[1]

At all times stimulated rather than checked by a difficult situation, Mr. Gladstone argued the case for peace to the House during the session of 1855 in two speeches of extraordinary power of every kind. His position was perfectly tenable, and he defended it with unsurpassed force. For the hour unfortunately his influence was gone. Great newspapers thought themselves safe in describing one of these performances as something between the rant of the fanatic and the trick of the stage actor ; a mixture of pious grimace and vindictive howl, of savage curses and dolorous forebodings ; the most unpatriotic speech ever heard within the walls of parliament. In sober fact, it was one of the three or four most masterly deliverances evoked by the Crimean war. At the very same time Lord John Russell was still sitting in the cabinet, though he had held the opinion that at the beginning of May the Austrian proposal ought to have ended the war and led to an honourable peace. The scandal of a minister remaining in a government that persisted in a war condemned by him as unnecessary was intolerable, and Lord John resigned (July 16).

The hopes of the speedy fall of Sebastopol brightened in the summer of 1855, but this brought new alarms to Lord Palmerston. 'Our danger,' he said in remarkable words, 'will then begin—a danger of peace and not a danger of war.' To drive the Russians out of the Crimea was to be no more than a preliminary. England would go on by herself, if conditions deemed by her essential were not secured. 'The British nation is unanimous, for I cannot reckon Cobden, Bright, and Co. for anything.'[2] His account of the public mind was indubitably true. Well might Aberdeen recall to his friends that, with a single exception, every treaty concluded at the termination of our great wars had been stigmatised as humiliating and degrading, ignominious, hollow and unsafe. He cited the peace of Utrecht in 1713, the peace of Aix-la-Chapelle in 1748, the peace of Paris in 1763, the peace of Versailles in 1783, and the peace of Amiens in 1801. The single exception was the peace of Paris in 1814. It would have been difficult in this case, he said, for patriotism or faction to discover humiliation 'in a treaty dictated at the head of a victorious army in the capital of the enemy.'

While the storm was raging, Mr. Gladstone made his way with his family to Penmaenmawr, whence he writes to Lord Aberdeen (Aug. 9): 'It was a charitable act on your part to write to me. It is hardly possible to believe one is not the

---

[1] Vitzthum, *St. Petersburg and London*, i. p. 170. A full account of these parliamentary events from May to July, 1855, is to be found in Martin's *Prince Consort*, iii. pp. 281-307.   [2] Ashley, ii. pp. 320, 325.

greatest scoundrel on earth, when one is assured of it from
all sides on such excellent authority. . . . I am busy reading
Homer about the Sebastopol of old time, and all manner of
other fine fellows.' In another letter of the same time, written
to Sir Walter James, one of the most closely attached of all his
friends, he strikes a deeper note :—

Sept. 17.—If I say I care little for such an attack you will perhaps
think I make little of sympathy like yours and Lord Hardinge's, but
such, I beg you and him to believe, is not the case. Public life is full
of snares and dangers, and I think it a fearful thing for a Christian
to look forward to closing his life in the midst of its (to me at
least) essentially fevered activity. It has, however, some excellent
characteristics in regard to mental and even spiritual discipline, and
among these in particular it absolutely requires the habits of resisting
temper and of suppressing pain. I never allow myself, in regard to my
public life, to realise, *i.e.* to dwell upon, the fact that a thing is *painful.*
Indeed life has no time for such broodings : neither in session nor
recess is the year, the day, or the hour long enough for what it brings
with it. Nor was there ever a case in which it was so little difficult
to pass over and make little of a personal matter : for if indeed it be
true, as I fear it is, that we have been committing grave errors, that
those errors have cost many thousands of lives and millions of money,
and that no glare of success can effectually hide the gloom of thickening
complications, the man who can be capable of weighing his own fate
and prospects in the midst of such contingencies has need to take a
lesson from the private soldier who gives his life to his country at a
shilling a day.

'We are on our way back,' he writes at the end of September,
'after a month of sea-bathing and touring among the Welsh
mountains. Most of my time is taken up with Homer and
Homeric literature, in which I am immersed with great delight
up to my ears; perhaps I should say out of my depth.'
Mr. Gladstone was one of the men whom the agitations of
politics can never submerge. Political interests were what
they ought to be, a very serious part of life; but they took
their place with other things, and were never suffered, as
in narrower natures sometimes happens, to blot out 'stars
and orbs of sun and moon' from the spacious firmament
above us. He now found a shelter from the intensity of the
times in the systematic production of his book on Homer, a
striking piece of literature that became the most definite
of his pursuits for two years or more. His children observed
that he never lounged or strolled upon the shore, but when
the morning's labour was over—and nothing was ever allowed
to break or mutilate the daily spell of serious work—he would
stride forth staff in hand, and vigorously breast the steepest
bluffs and hills that he could find. This was only emblematic
of a temperament to which the putting forth of power was both
necessity and delight. The only rest he ever knew was change
of effort.

While he was on the Welsh coast Sebastopol fell, after a
siege of three hundred and fifty days. Negotiations for peace
were opened tolerably soon afterwards, ending, after many
checks and diplomatic difficulties, in the Treaty of Paris
(March 30, 1856), as to which I need only remind the reader,
with a view to a future incident in Mr. Gladstone's history,
that the Black Sea was neutralised, and all warships of every
nation excluded from its waters. Three hundred thousand
men had perished. Countless treasure had been flung into
the abyss. The nation that had won its last victory at
Waterloo did not now enhance the glory of its arms, nor the
power of its diplomacy, nor the strength of any of its material
interests. It was our French ally who profited. The integrity
of Turkey was so ill confirmed that even at the Congress of
Paris the question of the Danubian Principalities was raised
in a form that in a couple of years reduced Turkish rule over
six millions of her subjects to the shadow of smoke. Of the
confidently promised reform of Mahometan dominion there
was never a beginning nor a sign. The vindication of the
standing European order proved so ineffectual that the Crimean
war was only the sanguinary prelude to a vast subversion of
the whole system of European states.

II

Other interests now came foremost in Mr. Gladstone's mind.
The old ground so constantly travelled over since the death of
Peel was for three years to come traversed again with fatiguing
iteration. In the spring of 1856 Lord Derby repeated the
overtures that he had made in specific form in 1851 and in
1855. The government was weak, as Mr Gladstone had predicted that it would be. Lord Derby told Sir William
Heathcote, through whom he and Mr Gladstone communicated, that as almost any day it might be overturned, and he
might be sent for by the Queen, he was bound to see what
strength he might rely upon, and he was anxious to know
what were Mr Gladstone's views on the possibility of co-
operation. What was the nature of his relations with other
members of the Peel government who had also been in the
cabinet of Lord Aberdeen? Did they systematically communicate? Were they a party? Did they intend to hold and
to act together? These questions were soon answered:—

On the first point, Mr. Gladstone said, you cannot better describe my
views for present purposes than by saying that they are much like Lord
Derby's own as I understand them—there was nothing in them to prevent a further consideration of the subject, if public affairs should assume
such a shape as to recommend it. On the second, I said Graham,
Herbert, Cardwell and I communicated together habitually and confidentially; that we did not seek to act, but rather eschewed acting, as a
party; that our habits of communication were founded upon long

political association, general agreement, and personal friendship ; that they were not, however, a covenant for the future, but a natural growth and result of the past.

Then he proceeds to tell with a new and rather startling conclusion the old story of the Peelite responsibility for the broken and disorganized state of the House of Commons :—

We, the friends of Lord Aberdeen, were a main cause of disunion and weakness in the executive government, and must be so, from whichever side the government were formed, so long as we were not absolutely incorporated into one or the other of the two great parties. For though we had few positively and regularly following us, yet we had indirect relations with others on both sides of the House, which tended to relax, and so far disable, party connections, and our existence as a section encouraged the formation of other sections all working with similar effects. I carried my feeling individually so far upon the subject as even to be ready, if I had to act alone, to surrender my seat in parliament, rather than continue a cause of disturbance to any government which I might generally wish well.[1]

This exchange of views with Lord Derby he fully reported to Graham, Herbert, and Cardwell, whom Lord Aberdeen, at his request, had summoned for the purpose. Herbert doubted the expediency of such communications, and Graham went straight to what was a real point. 'He observed that the question was of the most vital consequence, Who should lead the House of Commons ? This he thought must come to me, and could not be with Disraeli. I had said and repeated, that I thought we could not bargain Disraeli out of the saddle; that it must rest with him (so far as we were concerned) to hold the lead if he pleased ; that besides my looking to it with doubt and dread, I felt he had this right ; and that I took it as one of the *data* in the case before us upon which we might have to consider the question of political junction, and which might be seriously affected by it.' Of these approaches in the spring of 1856 nothing came. The struggle in Mr Gladstone's mind went on with growing urgency. He always protested that he never at any time contemplated an isolated return to the conservative ranks, but 'reunion of a body with a body.'

Besides his sense of the vital importance of the reconstruction of the party system, he had two other high related aims. The commanding position that had first been held in the objects of his activity by the church, then, for a considerable space, by the colonies, was now filled by finance. As he put it in a letter to his sympathetic brother Robertson : He saw two cardinal subjects for the present moment in public affairs, a rational and pacific foreign policy, and second, the due reduction in our establishments, economy in administration, and finance to correspond. In 1853 he had, as he believed, given financial pledges to the country. These pledges

were by the present ministers in danger of being forgotten.
They were incompatible with Palmerston's spirit of foreign
policy. His duty, then, was to oppose that policy, and to
labour as hard as he could for the redemption of his pledges.
Yet isolated as he was, he had little power over either one of
these aims or the other. The liberal party was determined to
support the reigning foreign policy, and this made financial
improvement desperate. Of Lord Derby's friends he was not
hopeful, but they were not committed to so dangerous a leader.[1]
As he put it to Elwin, the editor of the *Quarterly* : There is a
policy going a-begging ; the general policy that Sir Robert
Peel in 1841 took office to support—the policy of peace abroad,
of economy, of financial equilibrium, of steady resistance to
abuses, and promotion of practical improvements at home,
with a disinclination to questions of reform, gratuitously
raised.[2]

His whole mind beset, possessed, and on fire with ideals of
this kind, and with sanguine visions of the road by which they
might be realised—it was not in the temperament of this born
warrior to count the lions in his path. He was only too much
in the right, as his tribulations of a later date so amply proved,
in his perception that neither Palmerston nor Palmerstonian
liberals would take up the broken clue of Peel. The im-
portunate presence of Mr. Disraeli was not any sharper obstacle
to a definite junction with conservatives, than was the personality of Lord Palmerston to a junction with liberals. As he
had said to Graham in November 1856, 'the pain and strain
of public duty is multiplied tenfold by the want of a clear and
firm ground from which visibly to act.' In rougher phrase, a
man must have a platform and work with a party. This
indeed is for sensible men one of the rudiments of practical
politics.

Of a certain kind of cant about public life and office Mr.
Gladstone was always accustomed to make short work. The
repudiation of desire for official power, he at this time and
always roundly denounced as 'sentimental and maudlin.' One
of the not too many things that he admired in Lord Palmerston
was 'the manly frankness of his habitual declarations that office
is the natural and proper sphere of a public man's ambition, as
that in which he can most freely use his powers for the common
advantage of his country.' 'The desire for office,' said Mr.
Gladstone, 'is the desire of ardent minds for a larger space
and scope within which to serve the country, and for access
to the command of that powerful machinery for information
and practice, which the public departments supply. He must
be a very bad minister indeed, who does not do ten times the
good to the country that he would do when out of office, because
he has helps and opportunities which multiply twentyfold, as

1 To Robertson Gladstone, Dec. 16, 1856.   2 To Mr Elwin, Dec. 2, 1856.

by a system of wheels and pulleys, his power for doing it.' It is true, as the smallest of men may see—and the smaller the man, the more will he make of it—that this sterling good sense may set many a snare for the politician; but then even the consecrated affectations of our public life have their snares too.

The world was not in the secret of the communications with Lord Derby, but the intrinsic probabilities of a case often give to the public a trick of divination. In the middle of December (1856) articles actually appeared in the prints of the day announcing that Mr. Gladstone would at the opening of the next session figure at the head of the opposition. The tories, they said, wanted a leader, Mr. Gladstone wanted a party. They were credulous, he was ingenious. The minority in a party must yield to a majority, and he stood almost by himself. He would be a returned prodigal in the conservative household, for unlike Sir James Graham, he had never merged himself in the ordinary ruck of liberalism. A tory peer writes to assure him that there never was such a chance for the reunion of the party. Even the nobleman who had moved Mr. Gladstone's expulsion from the Carlton said that he supposed reunion must pretty soon come off. A few, perhaps under a score, made a great noise, but if Lord Derby would only form a government, the noisy ones would be as glad as the rest. True—and here the writer came nearer to the central difficulty—'Disraeli ought *at first* to lead the Commons,' because he had been leader before; second, he had the greater number of followers ; third, because on public grounds he must desire to see Mr. Gladstone at the exchequer ; and to transfer to him both the great subject of finance and the great prize of leadership would be impossible. So easy do flat impossibilities ever seem to sanguine simpletons in Pall Mall. Another correspondent has been staying at a grand country-house, full of tory company, and the state of parties was much discussed—'There was one unanimous opinion,' he tells Mr. Gladstone, 'that nothing could save the conservative party except electing you for their leader.' The same talk was reported from the clubs. 'The difficulty was Disraeli, not so much for any damage that his hostility could do the party, as because Lord Derby had contracted relations with him which it would perhaps be impossible for him to disown.'

Meanwhile the sagacious man in the tents of the tories, whose course was so neatly chalked out for him by sulky followers not relishing his lead, was, we may be sure, entirely wide-awake, watching currents, gales, and puffs of wind without haste, without rest. Disraeli made a bold stroke for party consolidation by inviting to his official dinner at the opening of the session of 1857, General Peel, the favourite brother of the great minister and his best accredited representative. Peel consulted Mr. Gladstone on the reply to Disraeli's invitation,

and found him strongly adverse. The public, said Mr. Gladstone, views with much jealousy every change of political
position not founded on previous parliamentary co-operation
for some national object. Mr. Gladstone might have put it on
the narrower ground, that attendance at the dinner would be
an explicit condonation of Disraeli's misdeeds ten years before,
and a direct acceptance of his leadership henceforth.

Elwin believed that he had the direct sanction of Lord
Derby for a message from him to Mr. Gladstone suggesting
communication. After much ruminating and consulting, Mr.
Gladstone wrote (Dec. 13, 1856) in sufficiently circuitous language to Elwin, that though he should not be justified in
communicating with Lord Derby, considered simply as a
political leader with whom he was not in relations of party,
yet, he proceeds, 'remembering that I was once his colleague,
and placing entire reliance on his honour, I am ready to speak
to him in confidence and without reserve on the subject of
public affairs, should it be his desire.' His three friends,
Graham, Aberdeen, and Herbert, still viewed the proceeding
with entire disfavour, and no counsels were ever dictated by
sincerer affection and solicitude. Your financial scheme, says
Graham, is conceived in the very spirit of Peel; it would be
most conducive to national welfare ; you alone and in high
office can carry it ; but it must be grafted on a pacific policy
and on a moderate scale of public expenditure; it is not
under Palmerston that such blessings are to be anticipated ;
but then are they more probable under Derby and Disraeli ?
Lord Aberdeen took another line, insisting that to make any
sort of approach to Lord Derby, after joining Palmerston only
the previous year, would be unjustifiable ; the bare apprehension of a vicious policy would be no intelligible ground for
changing sides ; more tangible reasons would be needed, and
they were only too likely soon to arrive from Palmerston's
foreign policy. Then a reasonable chance might come. Herbert, in his turn, told Mr. Gladstone that though he might
infuse vigour and respectability into a party that stood much
in need of both, yet he would always be in a false position.
'Your opinions are essentially progressive, and when the
measures of any government must be liberal and progressive,
the country will prefer the men whose antecedents and mottoes
are liberal, while the conservatives will always prefer a leader
whose prejudices are with themselves.' As Graham put it to
him : 'If you were to join the tory party to-morrow, you would
have neither their confidence nor their real good-will, and they
would openly break with you in less than a year.' It all
reminds one of the chorus in Greek plays, sagely expostulating
with a hero bent on some dread deed of fate.

III

In the autumn of 1856 ecclesiastical questions held a strong place in Mr. Gladstone's interests. The condemnation of Archdeacon Denison for heresy roused him to lively indignation. He had long interviews with the archdeacon, drafted answers for him, and flung his whole soul into the case, though he was made angry by Denison's oscillations and general tone. 'Gladstone tells me,' said Aberdeen, 'that he cannot sleep for it, and writes to me volumes upon volumes. He thinks that Denison ought to have been allowed to show that his doctrine, whether in accordance or not with the articles, is in accordance with scripture. And he thinks the decision ought to have been in his case as it was in Gorham's, that the articles are comprehensive, that they admit Denison's view of the Eucharist as well as that of his opponents.' [1]

His closing entry for the year (1856) depicts an inner mood :—

It appears to me that there are few persons who are so much as I am enclosed in the invisible net of pendent steel. I have never known what tedium was, have always found time full of calls and duties, life charged with every kind of interest. But now when I look calmly around me, I see that these interests are for ever growing and grown too many and powerful, and that were it to please God to call me I might answer with reluctance. . . . See how I stand. Into politics I am drawn deeper every year ; in the growing anxieties and struggles of the church I have no less [interest] than I have heretofore ; literature has of late acquired a new and powerful hold upon me ; the fortunes of my wife's family, which have had, with all their dry detail, all the most exciting and arduous interest of romance for me now during nine years and more ; seven children growing up around us, and each day the object of deeper thoughts and feelings, and of higher hopes to Catherine and me,—what a network is here woven out of all that the heart and all that the mind of man can supply. . . .

[1] Simpson's *Many Memories*, p. 238.

CHAPTER VIII

GENERAL ELECTION—NEW MARRIAGE LAW

(1857)

No wave on the great ocean of Time, when once it has floated past us, can be recalled. All we can do is to watch the new form and motion of the next, and launch upon it to try in the manner our best judgment may suggest our strength and skill.—GLADSTONE.

IN spite of wise counsels of circumspection, Mr. Gladstone clung to the chances that might come from personal communication between himself and Lord Derby. Under pressure from his friends, he agreed with Lord Derby to put off an interview until after the debate on the address. Then, after parliament met, they took the plunge. We are now at the beginning of February.

This afternoon at three I called on Lord Derby and remained with him above three hours, in prosecution of the correspondence which had passed between us.

I told him that I deliberately disapproved of the government of Lord Palmerston, and was prepared and desirous to aid in any proper measures which might lead to its displacement. That so strong were my objections that I was content to act thus without inquiring who was to follow, for I was convinced that any one who might follow would govern with less prejudice to the public interests. That in the existing state of public affairs I did not pretend to see far, but thus far I saw clearly. I also told him that I felt the isolated position in which I stood, and indeed in which we who are called Peelites all stand, to be a great evil as tending to prolong and aggravate that parliamentary disorganization which so much clogs and weakens the working of our government; and I denounced myself as a public nuisance, adding that it would be an advantage if my doctor sent me abroad for the session.

He concurred in the general sentiments which I had expressed, but said it was material for him, as he had friends with and for whom to act, and as I had alluded to the possibility, in the event of a change, of his being invited by the Queen to form a government, to consider beforehand on what strength he could rely. He said he believed his friends were stronger than any other single section, but that they were a minority in both Houses. Weak in 1852, he was weaker now, for it was natural that four years of exclusion from office should thin the ranks of a party, and such had been his case. He described the state of feeling among his friends, and adverted to the offer he had made, in 1851 and in 1855. The fact of an overture made and not accepted had led to much bitterness or anger towards us among a portion of his adherents. He considered that in 1855 Lord Palmerston had behaved far from well either to Herbert and me, or to him.[1]

Other interviews followed; resolutions were discussed, amendments, forms of words. They met at discreet dinners. 'Nobody,' Lord Derby tells him, 'except Disraeli knows the length to which our communications have gone.' Nobody, that is to say, excepting also Mr. Gladstone's three personal allies; them he kept accurately informed of all that passed at every stage. On February 13 the government presented their budget. In introducing his plan, Cornewall Lewis rashly quoted, and adopted as his own, the terrible heresy of Arthur Young, that to multiply the number of taxes is a step towards equality of burden, and that a good system of taxation is one that bears lightly on an infinite number of points. The reader will believe how speedily an impious opinion of this sort kindled volcanic flame in Mr. Gladstone's breast. He thought moreover that he espied in the ministerial plan a prospective deficiency a year ahead. To maintain a steady surplus of income over expenditure, he reflected; to lower indirect taxes when excessive in amount, for the relief of the people, and bearing in mind the reproductive power inherent in such operations; to simplify our fiscal system by concentrating its pressure on a few well-chosen articles of extended consumption; and to conciliate support to the income-tax by marking its temporary character, and by associating it with beneficial changes in the tariff: these aims have been for fifteen years the labour of our life. By this budget he found them in principle utterly reversed. He told his friends that the shade of Peel would appear to him if he did not oppose such plans with his whole strength. When the time came (Feb. 3), 'the government was fired into from all quarters. Disraeli in front; Gladstone on flank; John Russell in rear. Disraeli and Gladstone rose at same time. Speaker called the former. Both spoke very well. It was a night of triumph for Gladstone.'[2]

There is another note of the proceedings on Lewis's budget :—

Saturday, Feb. 14.—I was engaged to meet Graham, Herbert, and Cardwell at Lord Aberdeen's, and I knew from Lord Derby that he was to see his friends at noon. So I went to him on my way, first to point out the *deficit* of between five and six millions for 1858-9 which is created by this budget, with the augmentations of it in subsequent years ; and secondly, to say that in my opinion it was hopeless to attack the scheme in detail, and that it must be resisted on the ground of deficit as a whole, to give a hope of success. I said that if among the opposition there still lingered a desire to revive and extend indirect taxation, I must allow that the government had bid high for support from those who entertained it ; that it was the worst proposition I had ever heard from a minister of finance. At Lord Aberdeen's we examined the figures of the case, and drafted two resolutions which expressed our opinions.

The more serious point, however, was that they all wished me to insist upon taking the motion into my own hands ; and announcing this to Lord J. Russell as well as to Lord Derby. As to the second I had no difficulty, could I have acceded to the first. But I did not doubt that Disraeli would still keep hold of so much of his notice of Feb. 3 as had not been set aside by the budget. I said that from motives which I could neither describe nor conquer I was quite unable to undertake to enter into any squabble or competition with him for the possession of a post of prominence. We had much conversation on political prospects : Graham wishing to see me lead the Commons under Lord John as Commons minister in the Lords ; admitting that the same thing would do under Lord Derby, but for Disraeli, who could not be thrown away like a sucked orange ; and I vehemently deploring our position, which I said, and they admitted, was generally condemned by the country.

I again went to Derby, as he had requested, at five ; and he told me that he had had with him Malmesbury, Hardwicke, Disraeli, Pakington, Walpole, Lytton. They had all agreed that the best motion would be a resolution (from Disraeli) on Monday, before the Speaker left the chair, which would virtually rest the question on deficit. I made two verbal suggestions on the resolution to improve its form.

Late in the evening Lord Derby writes, enclosing a note received at dinner from Disraeli, 'I hope I may take it for granted that there is now a complete understanding between us as to the move on Monday night.' 'My dear lord,' runs the note, 'I like the resolution as amended. It is improved. Yours ever, D.' When Monday came, the move was duly made, and Gladstone and Disraeli again fought side by side as twin champions of the cause of reduced expenditure. Time had incensed Mr. Gladstone still further, and he conducted a terrific fusillade. He recounted how between 1842 and 1853 two-and-twenty millions of taxation had been taken off without costing a farthing. 'A man may be glad and thankful to have been an Englishman and a member of the British parliament during these years, bearing his part in so blessed a work. But if it be a blessed work, what are we to say of him who begins the undoing of it ?' The proposal of the government showed a gross, a glaring, an increasing deficiency, a deficiency unparalleled in the financial history of a quarter of a century. It was deluding the people and trifling with national interests. It is certain that no financier before or since ever, in Cromwellian phrase, made such a conscience of the matter, or ever found the task more thankless.[1] Great as was the effect of the close and searching argument that accompanied all this invective, even Mr. Gladstone's friends thought it too impassioned

[1] The reader will find a candid statement of the controversy in Northcote, *Financial Policy*, pp. 306-329.

and too severe upon Lewis, in whose favour there was consequently a reaction. The cool minister contented himself with
quoting Horace's lines upon the artist skilled in reproducing
in his bronze fierce nails or flowing hair, yet who fails because
he lacks the art to seize the whole.[1]

At the end of February (1857), at a party meeting of 160
members, Lord Derby told his men that the course taken by
Mr. Disraeli upon the budget had been concerted with him and
had his entire approval; spoke with admiration of Mr. Gladstone; justified political union when produced by men finding
themselves drawn to the same lobby by identity of sentiment;
and advised them not to decline such accession of strength as
would place their party in a position to undertake the government of the country. The newspapers cried out that the long-
expected coalition had at length really taken place. In their
hearts the conservative managers were not sure that Mr.
Gladstone's adhesion would not cost them too dearly. 'He
would only benefit us by his talents' (says Lord Malmesbury)
'for we should lose many of our supporters. The Duke of
Beaufort, one of our staunchest adherents, told me at Longleat
that if we coalesced with the Peelites he would leave the party,
and I remember in 1855, when Lord Derby attempted to form
a government, and offered places to Gladstone and Herbert,
that no less than eighty members of the House of Commons
threatened to leave him.'[2] All these schemes and calculations
were destined to be rudely interrupted.

II

While he was acting with Lord Derby on the one hand, Mr.
Gladstone sought counsel from Cobden on the other, having
great confidence in his 'firmness and integrity of purpose,' and
hoping for support from him in face of a faint-hearted disposition to regard Lord Palmerston as a magician against whom it
was vain to struggle. Events were speedily to show that Lord
Palmerston had more magic at his disposal than his valiant
foe believed. The agent of the British government in the
China seas—himself, by the way, a philosophic radical—had
forced a war upon the Chinese. The cabinet supported him.
On the motion of Cobden, the House censured the proceeding.
Mr. Gladstone, whose hatred of high-handed iniquities in China
had been stirred in early days,[3] as the reader may recall, made
the most powerful speech in a remarkable debate. 'Gladstone
rose at half-past nine,' Phillimore says (Mar. 3), 'and delivered
for nearly two hours an oration which enthralled the House,
and which for argument, dignity, eloquence, and effect is unsurpassed by any of his former achievements. It won several

[1] *Ars Poetica*, 32-5.
[2] Malmesbury, *Memoirs*, ii. pp. 56-7. See above, p. 399.
[3] See above, p. 167.

votes. Nobody denies that his speech was the finest delivered
in the memory of man in the House of Commons.' Apart from
a rigorous examination of circumstance and fact in the special
case, as in the famous precedent of Don Pacifico seven years
before, he raised the dispute to higher planes and in most
striking language. He examined it both by municipal and
international law, and on 'the higher ground of natural
justice' — 'that justice which binds man to man; which is
older than Christianity, because it was in the world before
Christianity; which is broader than Christianity, because it
extends to the world beyond Christianity; and which under-
lies Christianity, for Christianity itself appeals to it. . . . War
taken at the best is a frightful scourge upon the human race;
but because it is so, the wisdom of ages has surrounded it with
strict laws and usages, and has required formalities to be
observed which shall act as a curb upon the wild passions of
man. . . . You have dispensed with all these precautions.
You have turned a consul into a diplomatist, and that meta-
morphosed consul is forsooth to be at liberty to direct the
whole might of England against the lives of a defenceless
people.' Disraeli in turn denounced proceedings which began
in outrage and ended in ruin, mocked at 'No reform, new
taxes, Canton blazing, Persia invaded,' as the programme of
the party of progress and civilisation, and reprobated a prime
minister who had professed almost every principle, and connected himself with almost every party. Palmerston replied
by a stout piece of close argument, spiced by taunts about
coalitions, combinations, and eloquent flourishes. But this
time in parliament his slender majority failed him.

March 3, '57.—Spoke on Cobden's resolutions, and voted in 263-247—
a division doing more honour to the House of Commons than any I ever
remember. Home with C. and read Lord Ellesmere's *Faust*, being excited,
which is rare with me. (*Diary.*)

The repulse was transient. The minister appealed to the
constituencies, and won a striking triumph. Nearly all the
Manchester politicians, with Bright and Cobden at their head,
were ruthlessly dismissed, and the election was a glorious
ratification not only of the little war among the Chinese
junks, but of the great war against the Czar of Russia, and
of much besides. This, said Mr. Gladstone, was not an election like that of 1784, when Pitt appealed on the question
whether the crown should be the slave of an oligarchic faction;
nor like that of 1831, when Grey sought a judgment on reform;
nor like that of 1852, when the issue was the expiring controversy of protection. The country was to decide not upon
the Canton river, but whether it would or would not have
Lord Palmerston for prime minister. 'The insolent barbarian
wielding authority at Canton who had violated the British

flag' was indeed made to play his part. But the mainspring of the electoral victory was to be sought in the profound public weariness of the party dispersions of the last eleven years; in the determination that the country should be governed by men of intelligible opinions and definite views; in the resolution that the intermediate tints should disappear; in the conviction that Palmerston was the helmsman for the hour. The result was justly compared to the plébiscite taken in France four or five years earlier, whether they would have Louis Napoleon for emperor or not. It was computed that no fewer than one-sixth, or at best one-seventh, of the most conspicuous men in the former House of Commons were thrust out. The Derbyites were sure that the report of the coalition with the Peelites had done them irreparable harm, though their electioneering was independent. At Oxford Mr. Gladstone was returned without opposition. On the other hand, his gallant attempt to save the seat of his brother-in-law in Flintshire failed, his many speeches met much rough interruption, and to his extreme mortification Sir Stephen Glynne was thrown out.

The moral of the general election was undoubtedly a heavy shock to Mr. Gladstone, and he was fully conscious of the new awkwardness of his public position. Painful change seemed imminent even in his intimate relations with cherished friends. Sidney Herbert had written to him that as for Gladstone, Graham, and himself, they were not only broken up as a party, but the country intended to break them up and would resent any attempt at resuscitation; they ought on no account to reappear as a triumvirate on their old bench. Mr. Gladstone's reply discloses in some of its phrases a peculiar warmth of sensibility, of which he was not often wont to make much display :—

To Sidney Herbert.

March 22, 1857.—I did not reply to your letter when it arrived, because it touches principally upon subjects with respect to which I feel that my mind has been wrought into a state of sensitiveness which is excessive and morbid. For the last eleven years, with the exception of only two among them, the pains of political strife have not for us found their usual and proper compensation in the genial and extended sympathies of a great body of comrades, while suspicion, mistrust, and criticism have flanked us on both sides and in unusual measure. Our one comfort has been a concurrence of opinion which has been upon the whole remarkably close, and which has been cemented by the closer bonds of feeling and of friendship. The loss of this one comfort I have no strength to face. Contrary to your supposition, I have nothing with which to replace it; but the attachments, which began with political infancy, and which have lived through so many storms and so many subtler vicissitudes will never be replaced. You will never be able to get away from me as long as I can cling to you, and if at length, urged by your conscience and deliberate judgment, you effect the operation, the result will not be to throw me into the staff of Lord Derby. I shall seek my duty, as well as consult my inclination, first, by absconding from what may be termed general politics, and secondly, by appearing, wherever I must appear, only in the ranks.

I can neither give even the most qualified adhesion to the ministry of Lord Palmerston, nor follow the liberal party in the abandonment of the very principles and pledges which were original and principal bonds of union with it. So, on the other hand, I never have had any hope of conservative reconstruction except (and that slender and remote) such as presupposed the co-operation—I am now speaking for the House of Commons only—of yourself and Graham in particular. By adopting Reform as a watchword of present political action he has certainly inserted a certain amount of gap between himself and me, which may come to be practically material or may not. If you make a gap upon this opportunity, I believe it will be a novelty in political history : it will be the first case on record of separation between two men, all of whose views upon every public question, political, administrative, or financial, are I believe in as exact accordance as under the laws of the human mind is possible. . . .

His leaning towards the conservative party seemed to become more decided rather than less. Lord Aberdeen had written to him as if the amalgamation of Peel's friends with the liberal party had practically taken place. 'If that be true,' Mr. Gladstone replies (April 4, 1857), 'then I have been deceiving both the world and my constituents, and the deception has reached its climax within the last fortnight, during which I have been chosen without opposition to represent Oxford under a belief directly contrary in the minds of the majority of my constituents.' He saw nothing but evil in Lord Palmerston's supremacy. That was his unending refrain. He tells one of his constituents, the state of things 'is likely to end in much political confusion if it is not stopped by the failure of Lord Palmerston's physical force, the only way of stopping it which I could view with regret, for I admire the pluck with which he fights against the infirmities of age, though in political and moral courage I have never seen a minister so deficient.' Cobden asked him in the course of the first session of the new parliament, to take up some position adverse to the ministers. 'I should not knowingly,' Mr. Gladstone replies (June 16, 1857), 'allow any disgust with the state of public affairs to restrain me from the discharge of a public duty; but I arrived some time ago at the conclusion, which has guided my conduct since the dissolution, that the House of Commons would sooner and more healthily return to a sense of its own dignity and of its proper functions, if let alone by a person who had so thoroughly worried both it and the country as myself.'

III

This stern resolve to hold aloof did not last. Towards the

end of the session a subject was brought before parliament that stirred him to the very depths of heart and conscience. It marked one more stage of the history of English laws in that immense process of the secularisation of the state, against which, in his book of 1838, Mr. Gladstone had drawn up, with so much weight of reading and thought, a case so wholly unavailing. The legal doctrine of marriage had been established against the theological doctrine by Lord Hardwicke's famous act of 1753, for that measure made the observance of certain requirements then set up by law essential to a good marriage. A further fundamental change had begun with the legalisation of civil marriage in 1836. The conception of marriage underlying such a change obviously removed it from sacrament, or anything like a sacrament, to the bleak and frigid zone of civil contract ; it was antagonistic, therefore, to the whole ecclesiastical theory of divorce.[1]

A royal commission issued a report in 1853, setting forth the case against the existing system of dissolving marriage, and recommending radical changes. In the following year the cabinet of which Mr. Gladstone was a member framed and introduced a bill substantially conforming to these recommendations. For one reason or another it did not become law, nor did a bill of similar scope in 1856. In the interval of leisure that followed, Mr. Gladstone was pressed, perhaps by Bishop Wilberforce, thoroughly to consider the matter. With his prepossessions, there could be little doubt that he would incline to that view of marriage, and the terms and legal effects of loosening the marriage tie, that the Council of Trent had succeeded in making the general marriage law of catholic Europe. The subject was one peculiarly calculated to interest and excite him. Religion and the church were involved. It raised at our own hearths the eternal question of rendering to Cæsar what is Cæsar's, and to the church what belongs to the church. It was wrapped up with topics of history and of learning. It could not be discussed without that admixture of legality and ethics which delights a casuistic intellect. Above all, it went to the root both of that deepest of human relations, and of that particular branch of morals, in which Mr. Gladstone always felt the vividest concern. So, in short, being once called upon for a practical purpose to consider divorce and the many connected questions of re-marriage, he was inevitably roused to a fervour on one side, not any less heated and intense than the fervour of the mighty Milton on the other side two centuries before. He began operations by an elaborate article in the *Quarterly Review*.[2] Here he flings himself upon the well-worn texts in the Bible familiar to the readers of *Tetrachordon*,

[1] It is a striking indication of the tenacity of custom against logic that in France, though civil marriage was made not merely permissive, as with us, but compulsory in 1792, divorce was banished from French law from 1816 down to 1884.
[2] July 1857. Reprinted in *Gleanings*, vi. p. 47.

—if, indeed, *Tetrachordon* have any readers,—with a dialectical acuteness and force that only make one wonder the more how a mind so powerful as Mr. Gladstone's could dream that, at that age of the world, men would suffer one of the most far-reaching of all our social problems, whatever be the right or wrong social solution, to be in the slightest degree affected by a Greek word or two of utterly disputable and unfixed significance.

I may note in passing that in another department of supposed Levitical prohibition—the case of the wife's sister— he had in 1849 strongly argued against relaxation, mainly on the ground that it would involve an alteration of the law and doctrines of the church of England, and therefore of the law of Christianity.[1] Experience and time revolutionised his point of view, and in 1869, in supporting a bill legalising these marriages, he took the secular and utilitarian line, and said that twelve or fourteen years earlier (about the time on which we are now engaged) he formed the opinion that it was the mass of the community to which we must look in dealing with such a question, and that the fairest course would be to legalise the marriage contracts in question, and legitimise their issue, leaving to each religious community the question of attaching to such marriages a religious character.[2]

The Divorce bill of 1857 was introduced in the Lords, and passed by them without effective resistance. It was supported by the Archbishop of Canterbury and nine other prelates. Authorities no less exalted than Bishop Wilberforce were violently hostile, even at one stage carrying amendments (ultimately rejected), not only for prohibiting the inter-marriage of the guilty parties, but actually imposing a fine or imprisonment on either of them. This, I fancy, is the high-water mark of the ecclesiastical theory in the century.[3] Lord Mahon in a letter to Mr. Gladstone at this date pictures Macaulay's New Zealander being taken to the House of Lords and hearing learned lords and reverend prelates lay down the canon that marriage is indissoluble by the law of England and by the law of the church. But who, he might have asked, are those two gentlemen listening so intently ? Oh, these are two gentlemen whose marriages were dissolved last year. And that other man ? Oh, he was divorced last week. And those three ladies ? Oh, their marriages may in all probability be dissolved in another year or two. Still this view of the absurdity of existing practice did not make a convert.

As soon as the bill came down to the House of Commons Mr. Gladstone hastened up to London in the dog-days. 'A companion in the railway carriage,' he wrote to Mrs. Gladstone, 'more genial than congenial, offered me his *Times*, and then

---

[1] House of Commons, June 20, 1849.
[2] *Ibid.*, July 20, 1869. See also *Gleanings*, vi. p. 50.
[3] It may be said that the exaction of damages comes to the same thing.

brandy ! This was followed by a proposal to smoke, so that he
had disabled me from objecting on personal grounds.' Tobacco,
brandy at odd hours, and the newspaper made a triple abomination in a single dose, for none of the three was ever a favourite
article of his consumption. In London he found the counsels
of his friends by no means encouraging for the great fight on
which he was intent. They deprecated anything that would
bring him into direct collision with Lord Palmerston. They
urged that violent opposition now would be contrasted with
his past silence, and with his own cabinet responsibility for the
very same proposal. Nothing would be intelligible to the
public, Lord Aberdeen said, beyond a 'carefully moderated
course.' But a carefully moderated course was the very last
thing possible to Mr. Gladstone when the flame was once
kindled, and he fought the bill with a holy wrath as vehement
as the more worldly fury with which Henry Fox, from very
different motives, had fought the marriage bill of 1753. The
thought that stirred him was indicated in a phrase or two to
his wife at Hawarden : '*July* 31.—Parliamentary affairs are
very black ; the poor church gets deeper and deeper into the
mire. I am to speak to-night ; it will do no good ; and the
fear grows upon me from year to year that when I finally
leave parliament, I shall not leave the great question of state
and church better, but perhaps even worse, than I found it.'

The discussion of the bill in the Commons occupied no fewer
than eighteen sittings, more than one of them, according to the
standard of those primitive times, inordinately long. In the
hundred encounters between Mr. Gladstone and Bethell,
polished phrase barely hid unchristian desire to retaliate and
provoke. Bethell boldly taunted Mr. Gladstone with insincerity. Mr. Gladstone, with a vivacity very like downright
anger, reproached Bethell with being a mere hewer of wood
and drawer of water to the cabinet who forced the bill into his
charge ; with being disorderly and abusing the privileges of
speech by accusations of insincerity, 'which have not only proceeded from his mouth but gleamed from those eloquent eyes of
his, which have been continuously turned on me for the last ten
minutes, instead of being addressed to the chair.' On every
division those who affirmed the principle of the bill were at
least two to one. 'All we can do,' Mr. Gladstone wrote to his
wife, 'is to put shoulder to shoulder, and this, please God, we
will do. Graham is with us, much to my delight, and much
too, let me add, to my surprise. I am as thankful to be in
parliament for this (almost) as I was for the China vote. . . .
Yesterday ten-and-a-half hours, rather angry ; to-day with
pacification, but still tough and prolonged.' An unfriendly
but not wholly unveracious chronicler says of this ten hours'
sitting (August 14) on a single clause : 'Including questions,
explanations, and interlocutory suggestions, Mr. Gladstone

made nine-and-twenty speeches, some of them of considerable length. Sometimes he was argumentative, frequently ingenious and critical, often personal, and not less often indignant at the alleged personality of others.'

He made no pretence of thinking the principle of divorce *a vinculo* anything but an immense evil, but he still held himself free, if that view were repudiated, to consider the legislative question of dissolubility and its conditions. He resorted abundantly to what Palmerston called 'the old standard set-up form of objecting to any improvement, to say that it does not carry out all the improvements of which the matter in hand is susceptible.' One of the complaints of which he made most was the inequality in the bill between the respective rights of husband and wife. 'It is the special and peculiar doctrines of the Gospel,' he said, 'respecting the personal relation of every Christian, whether man or woman, to the person of Christ, that form the firm, the broad, the indestructible basis of the equality of the sexes under the Christian law.' Again, 'in the vast majority of instances where the woman falls into sin, she does so from motives less impure and ignoble than those of the man.' He attacks with just vigour the limitation of legal cruelty in this case to the cruelty of mere force importing danger to life, limb, or health, though he was shocked in after years, as well he might be, at the grotesque excess to which the doctrine of 'mental cruelty' has been carried in some States of the American Union. In this branch of the great controversy, at any rate, he speaks in a nobler and humaner temper than Milton, who writes with a tyrannical Jewish belief in the inferiority of women to men, and wives to husbands, that was in Mr. Gladstone's middle life slowly beginning to melt away in English public opinion. His second complaint, and in his eyes much the more urgent of the two, was the right conferred by the government bill upon divorced persons to claim marriage by a clergyman in a church, and still more bitterly did he resent the obligation imposed by the bill upon clergymen to perform such marriages. Here the fight was not wholly unsuccessful, and modifications were secured as the fruit of his efforts, narrowing and abating, though not removing his grounds of objection.[1]

IV

Before the battle was over, he was torn away from the scene by a painful bereavement. Mrs. Gladstone was at

---

[1] In republishing in 1878 his article from the *Quarterly* (*Gleanings*, vi. p. 106), he says his arguments have been too sadly illustrated by the mischievous effects of the measure. The judicial statistics, however, hardly support this view, that petitions for divorce were constantly increasing, and at an accelerating rate of progression. In England the proportion of divorce petitions to marriages and the proportion of divorce decrees to population are both of them lower than they were a few years ago. Mr. Gladstone used to desire the prohibition of publicity in these proceedings, until he learned the strong view of the president of the Court that the hideous glare of this publicity acts probably as no inconsiderable deterrent.

Hagley nursing her beloved sister, Lady Lyttelton. He wrote to his wife in the fiercest hours of the fight (11 Carlton House Terrace, Aug. 15): 'I read too plainly in your letter of yesterday that your heart is heavy, and mine too is heavy along with yours. I have been in many minds about my duty to-day; and I am all but ready to break the bands even of the high obligations that have kept me here with reference to the marriage bill. You have only to speak the word by telegraph or otherwise, showing that I can help to give any of the support you need, and I come to you. As matters stand I am wanted in the House to-day, and am wanted for the Divorce bill again on Monday.' Before Monday came, Lady Lyttelton was no more. Four days after her death, Mr. Gladstone wrote to Mr. Arthur Gordon from Hagley :—

The loss suffered here is a dreadful one, but it is borne in the way which robs death and all evil of its sting. My deceased sister-in-law was so united with my wife; they so drew from their very earliest years, and not less since marriage than before it, their breath so to speak in common, that the relation I bore to her conveys little even of what I have lost; but that again is little compared to my wife's bereavement; and far above all to that of Lyttelton, who now stands lonely among his twelve children. But the retrospect from first to last is singularly bright and pure. She seemed to be one of those rare spirits who do not need affliction to draw them to their Lord, and from first to last there was scarce a shade of it in her life. When she was told she was to die, her pulse did not change; the last communion appeared wholly to sever her from the world, but she smiled upon her husband within a minute of the time when the spirit fled.

CHAPTER IX

THE SECOND DERBY GOVERNMENT

(1858)

Extravagance and exaggeration of ideas are not the essential characteristic of either political party in this country. Both of them are composed in the main of men with English hearts and English feelings. Each of them comprises within itself far greater diversities of political principles and tendencies, than can be noted as dividing the more moderate portion of the one from the more moderate portion of the other. . . . But while the great English parties differ no more in their general outlines than by a somewhat varied distribution of the same elements in each, they are liable to be favourably or unfavourably affected and their essential characteristics unduly exaggerated, by circumstances of the order that would be termed accidental.— GLADSTONE.

THE turn of the political wheel is constantly producing strange results, but none has ever been more strikingly dramatic than when, on February 20, Bright and Milner Gibson, who had been ignominiously thrown out at Manchester the year before, had the satisfaction of walking to the table of the House of Commons as victorious tellers in the division on the Conspiracy to Murder bill that overthrew Lord Palmerston. A plot to slay the French Emperor had been organised by a band of Italian refugees in London. The bombs were manufactured in England. Orsini's design miscarried, but feeling in France was greatly excited, and the French government formally drew attention at St. James's to the fact that bodies of assassins abused our right of asylum. They hinted further that the amity of the crown called for stronger law. Palmerston very sensibly did not answer the French despatch, but introduced a bill with new powers against conspiracy. He in an instant became the most unpopular man in the country, and the idol of the year before was now hooted in the Park.

Mr. Gladstone was at first doubtful, but soon made up his mind. To Mrs. Gladstone he writes (Feb. 17):—

As respects the Conspiracy bill, you may depend upon our having plenty of fight; the result is doubtful; but if the bill gets into the House of Lords it will pass. Lord Aberdeen is strong against it. From him I went to-day to Lord Lyndhurst, and I found Lord Brougham with him. A most interesting conversation followed with these two wonderful old men at 80 and 86 (coming next birthday) respectively, both in the fullest possession of their faculties, Brougham vehement, impulsive, full of gesticulation, and not a little rambling, the other calm and clear as a deep pool upon rock.   Lord Lyndhurst is decidedly against the bill, Brougham somewhat inclines to it ; being, as Lord Lyndhurst says, half a Frenchman.   [Lord Lyndhurst expounded the matter in a most luminous way from his point of view. Brougham went into raptures and used these words : 'I tell you what, Lyndhurst, I wish I could make an exchange with you. I would give you some of my walking power, and you should give me some of your brains.' I have often told the story with this brief commentary, that the compliment was the highest I have ever known to be paid by one human being to another.]¹

The debate showed a curious inversion of the parts usually played by eminent men. Palmerston vainly explained that he was doing no more than international comity required, and doing no worse than placing the foreign refugee on the same footing in respect of certain offences as the British subject. Mr. Gladstone (Feb. 19), on the other hand, 'as one who has perhaps too often made it his business to call attention to the failings of his countrymen,' contended that if national honour was not henceforth to be a shadow and a name, it was the paramount, absolute, and imperative duty of Her Majesty's ministers to protest against the imputation upon us of favour for assassination, 'a plant which is congenial neither to our soil nor to the climate in which we live.'² One of the truest things said in the debate was Disraeli's incidental observation that 'the House should remember that in ninety-nine cases out of a hundred, when there is a quarrel between two states, it is generally occasioned by some blunder of a ministry.'   Mr. Disraeli perhaps consoled himself by the pithy saying of Baron Brunnow, that if no one made any blunders, there would be no politics. The blood of the *civis Romanus*, however, was up, and Palmerston, defeated by a majority of nineteen, at once resigned.

Lord Derby, whose heart had failed him three years earlier, now formed his second administration, and made one more attempt to bring Mr. Gladstone over to the conservative ranks. Lord Lansdowne had told the Queen that no other government

¹ The portion within brackets is from a letter of Mr. Gladstone's to Lady Lyndhurst, Aug. 31, 1883, and he continues :—'I have often compared Lord Lyndhurst in my own mind with the five other lord chancellors who since his time have been my colleagues in cabinet : much to the disadvantage in certain respects of some of them. Once I remember in the Peel cabinet the conversation happened to touch some man (there are such) who was too fond of making difficulties. Peel said to your husband "That is not your way, Lyndhurst." Of all the intellects I have ever known, his, I think, worked with the least friction.'
² 'Happily for the reputation of the House, but unhappily for the ministry, the debate assumed once more, with Gladstone's eloquence, a statesmanlike character. The foremost speaker of the House showed himself worthy of his reputation . . . much as there was to lament in the too radical tone of his often fine-spun argumentation. His thundering periods were received with thundering echoes of applause.'— Vitzthum, *St. Petersburg and London*, i. p. 273.

was possible, and an hour after he had kissed hands the new prime minister applied to Mr. Gladstone. The decisions taken by him in answer to this and another application three months later, mark one more of the curious turning points in his career and in the fate of his party.

Feb. 20, 1858.—Dined at Herbert's with Graham. We sat till 12½, but did not talk quite through the crisis. Palmerston has resigned. He is down. I must now cease to denounce him. 21.—St. James's morning, and holy communion. Westminster Abbey in evening, when I sat by Sir George Grey. From St. James's I went to Lord Aberdeen's. There Derby's letter reached me. We sent for Herbert and I wrote an answer. Graham arrived and heard it; with slight modifications it went. The case though grave was not doubtful. Made two copies and went off before 6 with S. Herbert. We separated for the evening with the fervent wish that in public life we might never part.

Two or three letters exhibit the situation :—

Lord Derby to Mr. Gladstone.

St James's Square, Feb. 21, 1858.—In consequence of the adverse vote of the other night, in which you took so prominent and distinguished a part, the government, as you know, has resigned; and I have been entrusted by the Queen with the difficult task, which I have felt it my duty not to decline, of forming an administration. In doing so, I am very desirous, if possible, of obtaining the co-operation of men of eminence, who are not at this moment fettered by other ties, and whose principles are not incompatible with my own. Believing that you stand in this position, it would afford me very great satisfaction if I could obtain your valuable aid in forming my proposed cabinet; and if I should be so fortunate as to do so, I am sure there would be on all hands a sincere desire to consult your wishes, as far as possible, as to the distribution of offices. I would willingly include Sidney Herbert in this offer; but I fear he is too intimately associated with John Russell to make it possible for him to accept.

Mr. Gladstone to Lord Derby.

10 *Great George Street, Feb.* 21, 1858.—I am very sensible of the importance of the vote taken on Friday; and I should deeply lament to see the House of Commons trampled on in consequence of that vote. The honour of the House is materially involved in giving it full effect. It would therefore be my first wish to aid, if possible, in such a task; and remembering the years when we were colleagues, I may be permitted to say that there is nothing in the fact of your being the head of a ministry, which would avail to deter me from forming part of it.

Among the first questions I have had to put to myself, in consequence of the offer which you have conveyed in such friendly and flattering terms, has been the question whether it would be in my power by accepting it, either alone or in concert with others, to render you material service. After the long years during which we have been separated, there would be various matters of public interest requiring to be noticed between us; but the question I have mentioned is a needful preliminary. Upon the best consideration which the moment allows, I think it plain that alone, as I must be, I could not render you service worth your having. The dissolution of last year excluded from parliament men with whom I had sympathies ; and it in some degree affected the position of those political friends with whom I have now for many years been united through evil and (much more rarely) through good report. Those who lament the rupture of old traditions may well desire the reconstitution of a party ; but the reconstitution of a party can only be effected, if at all, by the return of the old influences to their places, and not by the junction of an isolated person. The difficulty is even enhanced in my case by the fact that in your party, reduced as it is at the present moment in numbers, there is a small but active and not unimportant section who avowedly regard me as the representative of the most dangerous ideas. I should thus, unfortunately, be to you a source of weakness in the heart of your own adherents, while I should bring you no party or group of friends to make up for their defection or discontent.

For the reasons which I have thus stated or glanced at, my reply to your letter must be in the negative.

I must, however, add that a government formed by you at this time will, in my opinion, have strong claims upon me, and upon any one situated as I am, for favourable presumptions, and in the absence of conscientious difference on important questions, for support. I have had an opportunity of seeing Lord Aberdeen and Sidney Herbert ; and they fully concur in the sentiments I have just expressed.

Mr. Gladstone had no close personal or political ties with the Manchester men at this moment, but we may well believe that a sagacious letter from Mr. Bright made its mark upon his meditations :—

Mr. Bright to Mr Gladstone.

Reform Club, Feb. 21, '58.—Coming down Park Lane just now, I met a leading lawyer of Lord Derby's party, who will doubtless be in office with him if he succeeds in forming a government. He told me that Lord Derby and his friends were expecting to be able to induce you to join them.

Will you forgive me if I write to you on this matter ? I say nothing but in the most friendly spirit, and I have some confidence that you will not misinterpret what I am doing. Lord Derby has only about one-third of the House of Commons with him—and it is impossible by any management, or by any dissolution, to convert this minority into a majority. His minority in the House is greater and more powerful than it is in the country—and any appeal to the country, now or hereafter, must, I think, leave him in no better position than that in which he now finds himself. The whole liberal party in the country dislike him, and they dislike his former leader in the Commons ; and notoriously his own party in the country, and in the House, have not much confidence in him. There is no party in the country to rally round him, as Peel was supported in 1841. A Derby government can only exist upon forbearance, and will only last till it is convenient for us and the whigs to overthrow it. Lord Palmerston may give it his support for a time, but he can give it little more than his own vote and speeches, for the liberal constituencies will not forgive their members if they support it. If you join Lord Derby, you link your fortunes with a constant minority, and with a party in the country which is every day lessening in numbers and in power. If you remain on our side of the House, you are with the majority, and no government can be formed without you. You have many friends there, and some who would grieve much to see you leave them—and I know nothing that can prevent your being prime minister before you approach the age of every other member of the House who has or can have any claim to that high office.

If you agree rather with the men opposite than with those among whom you have been sitting of late, I have nothing to say. I am sure you will follow where 'the right' leads, if you only discover it, and I am not hoping or wishing to keep you from the right. I think I am not mistaken in the opinion I have formed of the direction in which your views have for some years been tending. You know well enough the direction in which the opinions of the country are tending. The minority which invites you to join it, if honest, must go or wish to go, in an opposite direction, and it cannot therefore govern the country. Will you unite yourself with what must be, from the beginning, an inevitable failure ?

Don't be offended, if, by writing this, I seem to believe you will join Lord Derby. I don't believe it—but I can imagine your seeing the matter from a point of view very different to mine—and I feel a strong wish just to say to you what is passing in my mind. You will not be the less able to decide on your proper course. If I thought this letter would annoy you, I would not send it. I think you will take it in the spirit in which it is written. No one knows that I am writing it, and I write it from no idea of personal advantage to myself, but with a view to yours, and to the interests of the country. I may be mistaken, but think I am not. Don't think it necessary to reply to this. I only ask you to read it, and to forgive me the intrusion upon you—and further to believe that I am yours, with much respect.

Mr. Gladstone to Mr. Bright.

10 *Great George Street, Feb.* 22, '58.—Your letter can only bear one construction, that of an act of peculiar kindness which ought not to be readily forgotten. For any one in whom I might be interested I should earnestly desire, upon his entering public life, that, if possible, he might with a good conscience end in the party where he began, or else that he might have broad and definite grounds for quitting it. When neither of these advantages appears to be certainly within command, there remains a strong and paramount consolation in seeking, as we best can, the truth and the public interests ; and I think it a marked instance of liberality, that you should give me credit for keeping this object in my view.

My seeking, however, has not on the present occasion been very difficult. The opinions, such as they are, that I hold on many questions of government and administration are strongly held ; and although I set a value, and a high value, upon the power which office gives, I earnestly hope never to be tempted by its exterior allurements, unless they are accompanied with the reasonable prospect of giving effect to some at least of those opinions and with some adequate opening for public good. On the present occasion I have not seen such a prospect ; and before I received your letter yesterday afternoon I had made my choice.

This ended the first scene of the short fifth act. The new government was wholly conservative.

II

Throughout the whole of this period, Mr. Gladstone's political friends were uneasy about him. 'He writes and says and does too much,' Graham had told Lord Aberdeen (Dec. 1856), and a year and a half later the same correspondent notices a restless anxiety for a change of position, though at Gladstone's age and with his abilities he could not wonder at it. Mr. Gladstone was now approaching fifty ; Graham was nearer seventy than sixty ; and Aberdeen drawing on to seventy-five. One of the most eminent of his friends confessed that he was 'amazed at a man of Gladstone's high moral sense of feeling being able to *bear* with Dizzy. I can only account for it on the supposition, which I suppose to be the true one, that personal dislike and distrust of Palmerston is the one absorbing feeling with him. . . . I see no good ground for the violent personal prejudice which is the sole ruling motive of Gladstone's and Graham's course— especially when the alternative is such a man as Dizzy.' Then comes some angry language about that enigmatic personage which at this cooling distance of time need not here be transcribed. At the end of 1856 Lord Aberdeen told Mr. Gladstone that his position in the House was 'very peculiar.' 'With an admitted superiority of character and intellectual power above any other member, I fear that you do not really possess the sympathy of the House at large, while you have incurred the strong dislike of a considerable portion of Lord Derby's followers.'

Things grew worse rather than better. Even friendly journalists in the spring of 1858 wrote of him as 'the most signal example that the present time affords of the man of speculation misplaced and lost in the labyrinth of practical politics.' They call him the chief orator and the weakest man in the House of Commons. He has exhibited at every stage traces of an unhappy incoherence which is making him a mere bedouin of parliament, a noble being full of spirit and power, but not to be tamed into the ordinary ways of civil life. His sympathies hover in hopeless inconsistency between love for righteous national action, good government, freedom, social and commercial reform, and a hankering after a strong, unassailable executive in the old obstructive tory sense. He protests against unfair dealing with the popular voice in the Principalities on the Danube, but when the popular voice on the Thames demands higher honours for General Havelock he resists it with the doctrine that the executive should be wholly free to dis-

tribute honours as it pleases. He is loudly indignant against
the supersession of parliament by diplomacy, but when a motion
is made directly pointing to the rightful influence of the House
over foreign affairs, he neither speaks nor votes. Is it not clear
beyond dispute that his cannot be the will to direct, nor the
wisdom to guide the party of progress out of which the materials
for the government of this country will have to be chosen ?[1]

In organs supposed to be inspired by Disraeli, Mr. Gladstone's fate is pronounced in different terms, but with equal
decision. In phrases that must surely have fallen from the
very lips of the oracle itself, the public was told that 'cerebral
natures, men of mere intellect without moral passion, are quite
unsuited for governing mankind.' The days of the mere
dialectician are over, and the rulers of Christendom are no
longer selected from the serfs of Aristotle. Without the emotions that soar and thrill and enkindle, no man can attain 'a
grand moral vision.' When Mr. Gladstone aims at philosophy,
he only reaches casuistry. He reasons like one of the sons of
Ignatius Loyola. What their Society is to the Jesuit, his own
individualism is to Mr. Gladstone. He supports his own interests
as much from intellectual zeal as from self-love. A shrewd
observer is quoted : 'Looking on Mr. Gladstone and Mr. Sidney
Herbert sitting side by side, the former with his rather saturnine
face and straight black hair, and the latter eminently handsome, with his bright, cold smile and subtlety of aspect, I have
often thought that I was beholding the Jesuit of the closet
really devout, and the Jesuit of the world, ambitious, artful,
and always on the watch for making his rapier thrusts.' Mr.
Gladstone, in a word, is extremely eminent, but strangely
eccentric, 'a Simeon Stylites among the statesmen of his time.'[2]

In May an important vacancy occurred in the ministerial
ranks by Lord Ellenborough's resignation of the presidency of
the board of control. This became the occasion of a renewed
proposal to Mr. Gladstone. He tells the story in a memorandum
prepared (May 22) for submission to Aberdeen and Graham,
whom Lord Derby urged him to consult.

*Memorandum by Mr. Gladstone submitted to Lord Aberdeen and
Sir James Graham. May 22, '58.*

Secret.—Last week after Mr. Cardwell's notice but before the debate
began, Mr. Walpole, after previously sounding Sir William Heathcote
to a similar effect, called me aside in the lobby of the House of Commons
and inquired whether I could be induced to take office. I replied that
I thought that question put by him of his own motion — as he had
described it — was one that I could hardly answer. It seemed plain,
I said, that the actual situation was one so entirely belonging to the
government as it stood, that they must plainly work through it unchanged ; that the head of the government was the only person who

[1] See *Spectator*, May 8, 1858.   [2] *Press*, April 7, 1858.

could make a proposal or put a question about taking office in it ; I added, however, that my general views were the same as in February.

This morning I had a note from Walpole asking for an appointment ; and he called on me at four o'clock accordingly. He stated that he came by authority of Lord Derby to offer me the board of control or, if I preferred it, the colonial office. That he had told Lord Derby I should, he thought, be likely to raise difficulties on two points : first, the separation from those who have been my friends in public life ; secondly, the leadership of the House of Commons. I here interrupted him to say it must be in his option to speak or to be silent on the latter of these subjects ; it was one which had never been entertained or opened by me in connection with this subject, since the former of the two points had offered an absolute preliminary bar to the acceptance of office. He, however, explained himself as follows, that Mr. Disraeli had stated his willingness to surrender the leadership to Sir James Graham, if he were disposed to join the government ; but that the expressions he had used in his speech of Thursday[1] (apparently those with respect to parties in the House and to office), seemed to put it beyond the right of the government to make any proposal to him. He at the same time spoke in the highest terms not only of the speech, but of the position in which he thought it placed Sir James Graham ; and he left me to infer that there would have been, but for the cause named, a desire to obtain his co-operation as leader of the House of Commons. With respect to the proposal as one the acceptance of which would separate me from my friends, he hoped it was not so. It was one made to me alone, the immediate vacancy being a single one ; but the spirit in which it was made was a desire that it should be taken to signify the wish of the government progressively to extend its basis, as far as it could be effected compatibly with consistency in its opinions. He added that judging from the past he hoped he might assume that there was no active opposition to the government on the part of my friends, naming Lord Aberdeen, Sir James Graham, and the Duke of Newcastle.

I told him with respect to the leadership that I thought it handsome on the part of Mr. Disraeli to offer to waive it on behalf of Sir James Graham ; that it was a subject which did not enter into my decision for the reason I had stated ; and I hinted also that it was one on which I could never negotiate or make stipulations. It was true, I said, I had no broad differences of principle from the party opposite ; on the whole perhaps I differed more from Lord Palmerston than from almost any one, and this was more on account of his temper and views of public conduct, than of any political opinions. Nay more, it would be hard to show broad differences of public principle between the government and the bench opposite.

I said, however, that in my view the proposal which he had made to me could not be entertained. I felt the personal misfortune and public inconvenience of being thrown out of party connection ; but a man at the bottom of the well must not try to get out, however dis-

---

[1] I wish to state that it is by the courtesy of hon. gentlemen that I occupy a seat on this (the ministerial) side of the House, although I am no adherent of Her Majesty's government. By no engagement, express or implied, am I their supporter. On the contrary, my sympathies and opinions are with the liberal party sitting on the opposite side of the House, and from recent kind communications I have resumed those habits of friendly intercourse and confidential communication with my noble friend (Lord John Russell) which formerly existed between us.—*May* 20, 1858.

agreeable his position, until a rope or a ladder is put down to him. In this case my clear opinion was that by joining the government I should shock the public sentiment and should make no essential, no important, change in their position.

I expressed much regret that accidental causes had kept back from my view at the critical moment the real extent of Lord Derby's proposals in February; that I answered him then as an individual with respect to myself individually. . . . I could not separate from those with whom I had been acting all my life long, in concert with whom all the habits of my mind and my views of public affairs had been formed, to go into what might justly be called a cabinet of strangers, since it contained no man to whom I had ever been a colleague, with the single exception of Lord Derby, and that twelve or fourteen years ago.

While I did not conceive that public feeling would or ought to approve this separation, on the other hand I felt that my individual junction would and could draw no material accession of strength to the cabinet. He made the marked admission that if my acceptance must be without the *approval* of friends, that must undoubtedly be an element of great weight in the case. This showed clearly that Lord Derby was looking to me in the first place, and then to others beyond me. He did not, however, found upon this any request, and he took my answer as an absolute refusal. His tone was, I need not say, very cordial; and I think I have stated all that was material in the conversation, except that he signified they were under the belief that Herbert entertained strong personal feelings towards Disraeli.

Returning home, however, at seven this evening I found a note from Walpole expressing Lord Derby's wish in the following words: 'That before you finally decide on refusing to accept the offer he has made either of the colonies or of the India board he wishes you would consult Sir James Graham and Lord Aberdeen.' In order to meet this wish, I have put down the foregoing statement.

Lord Aberdeen agreed with Mr. Gladstone that on the whole the balance inclined to *no*.

Graham, in an admirable letter, truly worthy of a wise, affectionate and faithful friend, said, 'My judgment is, on this occasion, balanced like your own.' He ran through the catalogue of Mr. Gladstone's most intimate political friends; the result was that he stood alone. Fixed party ties and active official duties would conduce to his present happiness and his future fame. He might form an intimate alliance with Lord Derby with perfect honour. His natural affinities were strong, and his 'honest liberal tendencies' would soon leaven the whole lump and bring it into conformity with the shape and body of the times. As for the leadership in the Commons, Graham had once thought that for Gladstone to sit on the treasury bench with Disraeli for his leader would be humiliation and dishonour. Later events had qualified this opinion. Of course, the abdication of Disraeli could not be made a condition precedent, but the concession would somehow be made, and in the Commons pre-eminence would be Gladstone's, be the conditions what they might. In fine, time was wearing fast away, Gladstone had reached the utmost vigour of his powers, and present opportunities were not to be neglected in vain expectation of better.

III

Before this letter of Graham's arrived, an unexpected thing happened, and Mr. Disraeli himself advanced to the front of the stage. His communication, which opens and closes without the usual epistolary forms, just as it is reproduced here, marks a curious episode, and sheds a strange light on that perplexing figure :—

Mr. Disraeli to Mr. Gladstone.

Confidential.

I think it of such paramount importance to the public interests, that you should assume at this time a commanding position in the administration of affairs, that I feel it a solemn duty to lay before you some facts, that you may not decide under a misapprehension.

Our mutual relations have formed the great difficulty in accomplishing a result, which I have always anxiously desired.

Listen, without prejudice, to this brief narrative.

In 1850, when the balanced state of parties in the House of Commons indicated the future, I endeavoured, through the medium of the late Lord Londonderry, and for some time not without hope, to induce Sir James Graham to accept the post of leader of the conservative party, which I thought would remove all difficulties.

When he finally declined this office, I endeavoured to throw the game into your hands, and your conduct then, however unintentional, assisted me in my views.

The precipitate ministry of 1852 baffled all this. Could we have postponed it another year, all might have been right.

Nevertheless, notwithstanding my having been forced publicly into the chief place in the Commons, and all that occurred in consequence, I was still constant to my purpose, and in 1855 suggested that the leadership of the House should be offered to Lord Palmerston, entirely with the view of consulting your feelings and facilitating your position.

Some short time back, when the power of dissolution was certain, and the consequences of it such as, in my opinion, would be highly favourable to the conservative party, I again confidentially sought Sir James Graham, and implored him to avail himself of the favourable conjuncture, accept the post of leader in the H. of C., and allow both of us to serve under him.

He was more than kind to me, and fully entered into the state of affairs, but he told me his course was run, and that he had not strength or spirit for such an enterprise.

Thus you see, for more than eight years, instead of thrusting myself into the foremost place, I have been, at all times, actively prepared to make every sacrifice of self for the public good, which I have ever thought identical with your accepting office in a conservative government.

Don't you think the time has come when you might deign to be magnanimous ?

Mr. Canning was superior to Lord Castlereagh in capacity, in acquirements, in eloquence, but he joined Lord C. when Lord C. was Lord Liverpool's lieutenant, when the state of the tory party rendered it necessary. That was an enduring, and, on the whole, not an unsatisfactory connection, and it certainly terminated very gloriously for Mr. Canning.

I may be removed from the scene, or I may wish to be removed from the scene.

Every man performs his office, and there is a Power, greater than ourselves, that disposes of all this.

The conjuncture is very critical, and if prudently yet boldly managed, may rally this country. To be inactive now is, on your part, a great responsibility. If you join Lord Derby's cabinet, you will meet there some warm personal friends ; all its members are your admirers. You may place me in neither category, but in that, I assure you, you have ever been sadly mistaken. The vacant post is, at this season, the most commanding in the commonwealth ; if it were not, whatever office you filled, your shining qualities would always render you supreme ; and if party necessities retain me formally in the chief post, the sincere and delicate respect which I should always offer you, and the unbounded confidence, which on my part, if you choose you could command, would prevent your feeling my position as anything but a form.

Think of all this in a kindly spirit. These are hurried lines, but they are heartfelt. I was in the country yesterday, and must return there to-day for a county dinner. My direction is Langley Park, Slough. But on Wednesday evening I shall be in town.—B. DISRAELI. *Grosvenor Gate, May* 25, 1858.

None of us, I believe, were ever able to persuade Mr. Gladstone to do justice to Disraeli's novels,—the spirit of whim in them, the ironic solemnity, the historical paradoxes, the fantastic glitter of dubious gems, the grace of high comedy, all in union with a social vision that often pierced deep below the surface. In the comparative stiffness of Mr. Gladstone's reply on this occasion, I seem to hear the same accents of guarded reprobation :—

Mr. Gladstone to Mr. Disraeli.

11 *Carlton House Terrace, May* 25, '58.—MY DEAR SIR,—The letter you have been so kind as to address to me will enable me, I trust, to remove from your mind some impressions with which you will not be sorry to part.

You have given me a narrative of your conduct since 1850 with reference to your position as leader of your party. But I have never thought your retention of that office matter of reproach to you, and on Saturday last I acknowledged to Mr. Walpole the handsomeness of your conduct in offering to resign it to Sir James Graham.

You consider that the relations between yourself and me have proved the main difficulty in the way of certain political arrangements. Will you allow me to assure you that I have never in my life taken a decision which turned upon those relations ?

You assure me that I have ever been mistaken in failing to place you among my friends or admirers. Again I pray you to let me say that I have never known you penurious in admiration towards any one who had the slightest claim to it, and that at no period of my life, not even during the limited one when we were in sharp political conflict, have I either felt any enmity towards you, or believed that you felt any towards me.

At the present moment I am awaiting counsel which at Lord Derby's wish I have sought. But the difficulties which he wishes me to find means of overcoming, are broader than you may have supposed. Were I at this time to join any government I could not do it in virtue of party connections. I must consider then what are the conditions which make harmonious and effective co-operation in cabinet possible—how largely old habits enter into them—what connections can be formed with public approval—and what change would be requisite in the constitution of the present government, in order to make any change worth a trial.

I state these points fearlessly and without reserve, for you have yourself well reminded me that there is a Power beyond us that disposes of what we are and do, and I find the limits of choice in public life to be very narrow.—I remain, etc.

The next day Mr. Gladstone received Graham's letter already described. The interpretation that he put upon it was that although Graham appeared to lean in favour of acceptance, 'yet the counsel was indecisive.' On ordinary construction, though the counsellor said that this was a case in which only the man himself could decide, yet he also said that acceptance would be for the public good. 'Your affirmative advice, had it even been more positive, was not approval, nor was Lord Aberdeen's. On the contrary it would have been like the orders to Balaam, that he should go with the messengers of Balak, when notwithstanding the command, the act was recorded against him.' We may be quite sure that when a man draws all these distinctions, between affirmative advice, positive advice, approval, he is going to act without any advice at all, as Mr. Gladstone was in so grave a case bound to do. He declined to join.

Mr. Gladstone to Lord Derby.

Private.

11 *C. H. Terrace, May* 26, '58.—I have this morning received Sir James Graham's reply, and I have seen Lord Aberdeen before and since. Their counsel has been given in no narrow or unfriendly spirit. It is, however, indecisive, and leaves upon me the responsibility which they would have been glad if it had been in their power to remove. I must therefore adhere to the reply which I gave to Mr. Walpole on Saturday ; for I have not seen, and I do not see, a prospect of public advantage or of material accession to your strength, from my entering your government single-handed.

Had it been in your power to raise fully the question whether those who were formerly your colleagues, could again be brought into political relation with you, I should individually have thought it to be for the public good that, under the present circumstances of the country, such a scheme should be considered deliberately and in a favourable spirit. But I neither know that this is in your power, nor can I feel very sanguine hopes that the obstacles in the way of this proposal on the part of those whom it would embrace, could be surmounted. Lord Aberdeen is the person who could best give a dispassionate and weighty opinion on that subject. For me the question, confined as it is to myself, is a narrow one, and I am bound to say that I arrive without doubt at the result.

'I hope and trust,' said Graham, when he knew what Mr. Gladstone had done, 'that you have decided rightly ; my judgment inclined the other way. I should be sorry if your letter to Lord Derby led him to make any more extended proposal. It could not possibly succeed, as matters now stand ; and the abortive attempt would be injurious to him. The reconstruction of the fossil remains of the old Peel party is a hopeless task. No human power can now reanimate it with the breath of life ; it is decomposed into atoms and will be remembered only as a happy accident, while it lasted.'[1]

IV

In one remarkable debate of this summer the solitary statesman descended from his pillar. Now was the time of the memorable scheme for the construction of the Suez Canal, that first emanated from the French group of Saint Simonian visionaries in the earlier half of the century. Their dream had taken shape in the fertile and persevering genius of Lesseps, and was at this time the battle-ground of engineers, statesmen, and diplomatists in every country in Europe. For fifteen years the British government had used all their influence at Constantinople to prevent the Sultan from sanctioning the project. In June a motion of protest was made in the House of Commons. Lord Palmerston persisted that the scheme was the greatest bubble that ever was imposed upon the credulity and simplicity of the people of this country ; the public meetings on its behalf were got up by a pack of foreign projectors ; traffic by the railway would always beat traffic by steamer through the canal ; it would be a step towards the dismemberment of the Turkish empire ; it would tend to dismember our own empire by opening a passage between the Mediterranean and the Indian Ocean, which would be at the command of other nations and not at ours. Away, then, with such a sacrifice of the interest of Great Britain to philanthropic schemes and

---

[1] 'I wish,' said Mr. Disraeli to Bishop Wilberforce in 1862, 'you could have induced Gladstone to join Lord Derby's government when Lord Ellenborough resigned in 1858. It was not my fault that he did not : I almost went on my knees to him.'—*Life*, iii. p. 70.

Vitzthum reports a conversation with Mr. Disraeli in January 1858, of a different tenour :—'We are at all times ready,' he said, 'to take back this deserter, but only if he surrenders unconditionally.'—Vitzthum, i. p. 269.

philosophic reveries! So much for the sound practical man. Mr. Gladstone followed. Don't let us, he said, have governments and ex-governments coming down to instruct us here on bubble schemes. As a commercial project, let the Suez Canal stand or fall upon commercial grounds. With close reasoning, he argued against the proposition that the canal would tend to sever Turkey from Egypt. As to possible danger to our own interests, was it not a canal that would fall within the control of the strongest maritime power in Europe? And what could that power be but ourselves? Finally, what could be more unwise than to present ourselves to the world as the opponents of a scheme on the face of it beneficial to mankind, on no better ground than remote and contingent danger to interests of our own, with the alleged interest of Turkey merely thrust hypocritically in for the purpose of justifying a policy purely narrowminded and wholly selfish? The majority against the motion was large, as it was in the case of the seven cardinals against Galileo. Still the canal was made, with some very considerable consequences that were not foreseen either by those who favoured it or those who mocked it as a bubble. M. de Lesseps wrote to Mr. Gladstone from Constantinople that the clearness of his speech had enabled him to use it with good effect in his negotiations with the Porte. 'Your eloquent words, the authority of your name, and the consideration that attaches to your character, have already contributed much and will contribute more still to hinder the darkening and complication of a question of itself perfectly clear and simple, and to avoid the troubling of the relations between two countries of which it is the natural mission to hold aloft *together* the flag of modern civilisation.'

Mr. Gladstone took an active interest in the various measures —some of them extremely singular—proposed by Mr. Disraeli for the transfer of the government of India from the Company to the crown. Writing early in the year to Sir James Graham he argued that their object should be steadily and vigorously to resist all attempts at creating a monster military and civil patronage, and to insist upon a real check on the Indian minister. He had much conversation with Mr. Bright—not then an intimate acquaintance—on the difficulty of the problem to govern a people by a people. The two agreed strongly as to one prominent possibility of mischief: they both distrusted the discretion confided to the Indian minister in the use of the Indian army. Mr. Gladstone set a mark upon the bill by carrying a clause to provide that the Indian army should not be employed beyond the frontiers of India without the permission of parliament. This clause he privately hoped would 'afford a standingground from which a control might be exercised on future Palmerstons.'

CHAPTER X

THE IONIAN ISLANDS

(1858–1859)

> The world is now taking an immense interest in Greek affairs, and does not seem to know why. But there are very good reasons for it. Greece is a centre of life, and the only possible centre for the Archipelago, and its immediate neighbourhood. But it is vain to think of it as a centre from which light and warmth can proceed, until it has attained to a tolerable organisation, political and economical. I believe in the capacity of the people to receive the boon.—GLADSTONE (1862).

AT the beginning of October, while on a visit to Lord Aberdeen at Haddo, Mr. Gladstone was amazed by a letter from the secretary of state for the colonies—one of the two famous writers of romance then in Lord Derby's cabinet—which opened to him the question of undertaking a special mission to the Ionian islands. This, said Bulwer Lytton, would be to render to the crown a service that no other could do so well, and that might not inharmoniously blend with his general fame as scholar and statesman. 'To reconcile a race that speaks the Greek language to the science of practical liberty seemed to me a task that might be a noble episode in your career.' The origin of an invitation so singular is explained by Phillimore :—

November 2nd, 1858.—Lord Carnarvon (then under-secretary at the colonial office) sent an earnest letter to me to come to the C.O. and advise with Rogers and himself as to drawing the commission. I met Bulwer Lytton there, overflowing with civility. The offer to Gladstone had arisen as I expected from Lord C., and he had told B. L. the conversation which he (C.) and I had together in the summer, in which I told Lord C. that I thought Gladstone would accept a mission extraordinary to Naples. . . . I risked without authority from G. this communication. Lord C. bore it in mind, and from this suggestion of mine sprang in fact this offer. So Lord C. said to me.

Lord Malmesbury very sensibly observed that to send Mr. Gladstone to Naples was out of the question, in view of his famous letters to Lord Aberdeen. To the new proposal Mr. Gladstone replied that his first impulse on any call from a minister of the crown to see him on public business, would be to place himself at the minister's disposal. The interview did not occur for a week or two. Papers were sent from the colonial office to Hawarden, long letters followed from the secretary of state, and Mr. Gladstone took time to consider. The constitution of the Ionian islands had long been working uneasily, and what the colonial secretary invited him to undertake was an inquiry on the spot into our relations there, and into long-standing embarrassments that seemed to be rapidly coming to a head. Sir John Young, then lord high commissioner of the Ionian islands, had been with him at Eton and at Oxford, besides being a Peelite colleague in parliament, and Mr. Gladstone was not inclined to be the instrument of indicating disparagement of his friend. Then, moreover, he was in favour of 'a very liberal policy' in regard to the Ionian islands, and possibly the cabinet did not agree to a very liberal policy. As for personal interest and convenience, he was not disposed to raise any difficulty in such a case.

The Peelite colleagues whose advice he sought were all, with the single exception of the Duke of Newcastle, more or less unconditionally adverse. Lord Aberdeen (October 8) admitted that Mr. Gladstone's name, acquirements, and conciliatory character might operate powerfully on the Ionians ; still many of them were false and artful, and the best of them little better than children. 'It is clear,' he said, 'that Bulwer has sought to allure you with vague declarations and the attractions of Homeric propensities. . . . I doubt if Homer will be a *cheval de bataille* sufficiently strong to carry you safely through the intricacies of this enterprise.' The sagacious Graham also warned him that little credit would be gained by success, while failure would be attended by serious inconveniences : in any case to quell 'a storm in a teapot' was no occupation worthy of his powers and position. Sidney Herbert was strong that governments were getting more and more into the bad habit of delegating their own business to other people ; he doubted success, and expressed his hearty wish that we could be quit of the protectorate altogether, and could hand the islands bodily over to Greece, to which by blood, language, religion, and geography they belonged.

I have said that these adverse views were almost unqualified, and such qualification as existed was rather remarkable. 'The only part of the affair I should regard with real pleasure,' wrote Lord Aberdeen, 'would be the means it might afford you of drawing closer to the government, and of naturally establishing yourself in a more suitable position ; for in spite of Homer and Ulysses, your Ionian work will by no means be *tanti* in itself.' Graham took the same point : 'An approximation to the government may be fairly sought or admitted by you. But this should take place on higher grounds.' Thus, though he was now in fact unconsciously on the eve of his formal entry into a

liberal cabinet, expectations still survived that he might re-join
his old party.

As might have been expected, the wanderings of Ulysses and
the geography of Homer prevailed in Mr. Gladstone's mind over
the counsels of parliamentary Nestors. Besides the ancient
heroes, there was the fascination of the orthodox church, so
peculiar and so irresistible for the anglican school to which Mr.
Gladstone belonged. Nor must we leave out of account the
passion for public business so often allied with the student's
temperament; the desire of the politician out of work for
something definite to do; Mr. Gladstone's keen relish at all
times for any foreign travel that came in his way; finally, and
perhaps strongest of all, the fact that his wife's health had been
much shaken by the death of her sister, Lady Lyttelton, and
the doctors were advising change of scene, novel interests, and
a southern climate. His decision was very early a foregone
conclusion. So his doubting friends could only wish him good
fortune. Graham said, 'If your hand be destined to lay the
foundation of a Greek empire on the ruins of the Ottoman, no
hand can be more worthy, no work more glorious. *Recidiva
manu posuissem Pergama* was a noble aspiration;[1] with you it
may be realised.'

He hastened to enlist the services as secretary to his commission of Mr. Lacaita, whose friendship he had first made seven
years before, as we have seen, amid the sinister tribunals and
squalid dungeons of Naples. For dealings with the Greco-
Italian population of the islands he seemed the very man. 'As
regards Greek,' Mr. Gladstone wrote to him, 'you are one of
the few persons to whom one gives credit for knowing everything, and I assumed on this ground that you had a knowledge
of ancient Greek, such as would enable you easily to acquire
the *kind* of acquaintance with the modern form, such as
is, I presume, desirable. That is my own predicament; with
the additional disadvantage of our barbarous English pronuncia-
tion.' Accompanied by Mrs. Gladstone and their eldest daughter,
and with Mr. Arthur Gordon, the son of Lord Aberdeen, and now,
after long service to the state, known as Lord Stanmore, for
private secretary, Mr. Gladstone left England on November 8,
1858, and he returned to it on the 8th of March 1859.

II

The Ionian case was this. By a treaty made at Paris in
November 1815, between Great Britain, Russia, Austria, and
Prussia, the seven islands—scattered along the coast from
Epiros to the extreme south of the Morea—were constituted
into a single free and independent state under the name of the
United States of the Ionian Islands, and this state was placed
under the immediate and exclusive protection of Great Britain.

[1] Virg. *Aen.* iv. 344.

The Powers only thought of keeping the islands out of more dubious hands, and cared little or not at all about conferring any advantage upon either us or the Ionians. The States were to regulate their own internal organization, and Great Britain was 'to employ a particular solicitude with regard to the legislation and general administration of those states,' and was to appoint a lord high commissioner to reside there with all necessary powers and authorities. The Duke of Wellington foretold that it would prove 'a tough and unprofitable job,' and so in truth it did. A constitutional charter in 1817 formed a system of government that soon became despotic enough to satisfy Metternich himself. The scheme has been justly described as a singularly clever piece of work, appearing to give much while in fact giving nothing at all. It contained a decorous collection of chapters, sections, and articles imposing enough in their outer aspect, but in actual operation the whole of them reducible to a single clause enabling the high commissioner to do whatever he pleased.

This rough but not ill-natured despotism lasted for little more than thirty years, and then in 1849, under the influence of the great upheaval of 1848, it was changed into a system of more popular and democratic build. The old Venetians, when for a couple of centuries they were masters in this region, laid it down that the islanders must be kept with their teeth drawn and their claws clipped. Bread and the stick, said Father Paul, that is what they want. This view prevailed at the colonial office, and maxims of Father Paul Sarpi's sort, incongruously combined with a paper constitution, worked as ill as possible. Mr. Gladstone always applied to the new system of 1849 Charles Buller's figure, of first lighting the fire and then stopping up the chimney. The stick may be wholesome, and local self-government may be wholesome, but in combination or rapid alternation they are apt to work nothing but mischief either in Ionian or any other islands. Sir Charles Napier—the Napier of Scinde—who had been Resident in Cephalonia thirty years before, in Byron's closing days, describes the richer classes as lively and agreeable ; the women as having both beauty and wit, but of little education ; the poor as hardy, industrious, and intelligent—all full of pleasant humour and vivacity, with a striking resemblance, says Napier, to his countrymen, the Irish. The upper class was mainly Italian in origin, and willingly threw all the responsibility for affairs on the British government. The official class, more numerous in proportion to population than in any country in Europe, scrambled for the petty salaries of paltry posts allotted by popular election. Since 1849 they had increased by twenty-five per cent, and were now one in a hundred of the inhabitants. The clergy in a passive way took part with the demagogues. Men of ability and sense were not wanting, but being unorganized, discouraged, and saturated

with distrust, they made no effort to stem the jobbery, corruption, waste, going on around them. Roads, piers, aqueducts,
and other monuments of the British protectorate reared before
1849, were falling to pieces. Taxes were indifferently collected.
Transgressors of local law went unpunished. In ten years the
deficit in the revenue had amounted to nearly £100,000, or two-
thirds of a year's income. The cultivators of the soil figured in
official reports as naturally well affected, and only wishing to
grow their currants and their olives in peace and quietness.
But they were extremely poor, and they were ignorant and
superstitious, and being all these things it was inevitable that
they should nurse discontent with their government. Whoever
wanted their votes knew that the way to get them was to
denounce the Englishman as ἐτερόδοξος καὶ ξένος, heretic, alien and
tyrant. There was a senate of six members, chosen by the high
commissioner from the assembly. The forty-two members of
the assembly met below galleries that held a thousand persons,
and nothing made their seats and salaries so safe as round
declamations from the floor to the audience above, on the greatness of the Hellenic race and the need for union with the Greek
kingdom. The municipal officer in charge of education used
to set as a copy for the children, a prayer that panhellenic
concord might drive the Turks out of Greece and the English
out of the seven islands.

Cephalonia exceeded the rest of the group both in population and in vehemence of character, while Zante came first of
all in the industry and liveliness of its people.[1] These two
islands were the main scene and source of difficulty. In
Cephalonia nine years before the date with which we are now
dealing, an agrarian rising had occurred more like a bad white-
boy outrage than a national rebellion, and it was suppressed
with cruel rigour by the high commissioner of the day. Twenty-
two people had been hanged, three hundred or more had been
flogged, most of them without any species of judicial investigation. The fire-raisings and destruction of houses and vineyards
were of a fierce brutality to match. These Ionian atrocities
were the proceedings with which Prince Schwarzenberg had
taunted Lord Aberdeen by way of rejoinder to Mr. Gladstone's
letters on barbarous misgovernment in Naples, and the feelings
that they had roused were still smouldering. Half a dozen
newspapers existed, all of them vehemently and irreconcilably
unionist, though all controlled by members of the legislative
assembly who had taken an oath at the beginning of each
parliament to respect and maintain the constitutional rights of
the protecting sovereign. The liberty of unlicensed printing,
however, had been subject to a pretty stringent check. By
virtue of what was styled a power of high police, the lord high

[1] See Sir C. Napier's *The Colonies: treating of their value generally and of the Ionian Islands in particular.*

commissioner was able at his own will and pleasure to tear away from home, occupation, and livelihood anybody that he chose, and the high police found its commonest objects in the editors of newspapers. An obnoxious leading article was not infrequently followed by deportation to some small and barren rock, inhabited by a handful of fishermen. Not Cherubim and Seraphim, said Mr. Gladstone, could work such a system. A British corporal with all the patronage in his hands, said another observer, would get on better than the greatest and wisest statesman since Pericles, if he had not the patronage. It was little wonder that a distracted lord high commissioner, to adopt the similes of the florid secretary of state, should one day send home a picture like Salvator's Massacre of the Innocents, or Michel Angelo's Last Judgment, and the next day recall the swains of Albano at repose in the landscapes of Claude ; should one day advise his chief to wash their hands of the Ionians, and on the morrow should hint that perhaps the best thing would be by a bold *coup d'état* to sweep away the constitution.[1]

III

Immediately after Mr. Gladstone had started, what the secretary of state described as the most serious misfortune conceivable happened. A despatch was stolen from the pigeonholes of the colonial office, and a morning paper printed it. It had been written home some eighteen months before by Sir John Young, and in it he advised his government, with the assent of the contracting powers, to hand over either the whole of the seven islands to Greece, or else at least the five southern islands, while transforming Corfu and its little satellite of Paxo into a British colony. It was true that a few days later he had written a private letter, wholly withdrawing this advice and substituting for it the exact opposite, the suppression namely of such freedom as the islanders possessed. This second fact the public did not know, nor would the knowledge of it have made any difference. The published despatch stood on record, and say what they would, the startling impression could not be effaced. Well might Lytton call it an inconceivable misfortune. It made Austria uneasy, it perturbed France, and it irritated Russia, all of them seeing in Mr Gladstone's mission a first step towards the policy recommended in the despatch. In the breasts of the islanders it kindled intense excitement, and diversified a chronic disorder by a

[1] *Parliamentary Papers, relative to the mission of the Right Hon. W. E. Gladstone to the Ionian Islands in 1858.* Presented in 1861. Finlay's *History of Greece*, vii. p. 305, etc. *Letters by Lord Charles Fitzroy, etc., showing the anomalous political and financial position of the Ionian Islands.* (Ridgway, 1850.) *Le Gouvernement des Iles Ioniennes.* Lettre à Lord John Russell, par François Lenormant. (Paris, Amyot, 1861.) *The Ionian Islands in relation to Greece.* By John Gunn Gardner, Esq., 1859. *Four years in the Ionian Islands.* By Whittingham. Pamphlet by S. G. Potter, D.D. See also *Gleanings*, iv. p. 287.

sharp access of fever. It made Young's position desperate, though he was slow to see it, and practically it brought the business of the high commissioner extraordinary to nought before it had even begun.

He learned the disaster, for disaster it was, at Vienna, and appears to have faced it with the same rigorous firmness and self-command that some of us have beheld at untoward moments long after. The ambassador told him that he ought to see the Austrian minister. With Count Buol he had a long interview accordingly, and assured him that his mission had no concern with any question of Ionian annexation whether partial or total. Count Buol on his part disclaimed all aggressive tendencies in respect of Turkey, and stated emphatically that the views and conduct of Austria in her Eastern policy were in the strictest sense conservative.

Embarking at Trieste on the warship *Terrible*, Nov. 21, and after a delightful voyage down the Adriatic, five days after leaving Vienna (Nov. 24th) Mr. Gladstone found himself at Corfu—the famous island of which he had read such memorable things in Thucydides and Xenophon, the harbour where the Athenians had fitted out the expedition to Syracuse, so disastrous to Greek democracy ; where the young Octavian had rallied his fleet before the battle of Actium, so critical for the foundation of the empire of the Cæsars ; and whence Don John had sallied forth for the victory of Lepanto, so fatal to the conquering might of the Ottoman Turks. It was from Corfu that the brothers Bandiera had started on their tragic enterprise for the deliverance of Italy fourteen years before. Mr. Gladstone landed under a salute of seventeen guns, and was received with all ceremony and honour by the lord high commissioner and his officers.

He was not long in discovering what mischief the stolen despatch had done, and may well have suspected from the first in his inner mind that his efforts to undo it would bear little fruit. The morning after his arrival the ten members for Corfu came to him in a body with a petition to the Queen denouncing the plan of making their island a British colony, and praying for union with Greece. The municipality followed suit in the evening. The whole sequel was in keeping. Mr. Gladstone with Young's approval made a speech to the senate, in which he threw over the despatch, severed his mission wholly from any purpose or object in the way of annexation, and dwelt much upon a circular addressed by the foreign office in London to all its ministers abroad disclaiming any designs of that kind. He held levees, he called upon the archbishop, he received senators and representatives, and everywhere he held the same emphatic language. He soon saw enough to convince him of the harm done to British credit and influence by the severities in Cephalonia ; by the small regard and fre-

quent contempt shown by many Englishmen for the religion
of the people for whose government they were responsible; by
the diatribes in the London press against the Ionians as
brigands, pirates, and barbarians; and by the absence in high
commissioners and others 'of tact, good sense, and good feeling
in the sense in which it is least common in England, the sense
namely in which it includes a disposition to enter into and up
to a certain point sympathise with those who differ with us in
race, language, and creed.' Perhaps his penetrating eye early
discovered to him that forty years of bad rule had so embittered feeling, that even without the stolen despatch, he had
little chance.

He made a cruise round the islands. His visit shook him a
good deal with respect to two of the points—Corfu and Ithaca
—on which it has been customary to dwell as proving Homer's
precise local knowledge. The rain poured in torrents for most
of the time, but it cleared up for a space to reveal the loveliness
of Ithaca. In the island of Ulysses and Penelope he danced at
a ball given in his honour. In Cephalonia he was received by
a tumultuous mob of a thousand persons, whom neither the
drenching rains nor the unexpected manner of his approach
across the hills could baffle. They greeted him with incessant
cries for union with Greece, thrust disaffected papers into his
carriage, and here and there indulged in cries of κάτω ἡ
προστασία, down with the protectorate, down with the tyranny
of fifty years. This exceptional disrespect he ascribed to what
he leniently called the history of Cephalonia, meaning the
savage dose of martial law nine years before. He justly took
it for a marked symbol of the state of excitement at which
under various influences the popular mind had arrived. Age
and infirmity prevented the archbishop from coming to offer
his respects, so after his levee Mr. Gladstone with his suite
repaired to the archbishop. 'We found him,' says Mr. Gordon,
'seated on a sofa dressed in his most gorgeous robes of gold
and purple, over which flowed down a long white beard. . . .
Behind him stood a little court of black-robed, black-bearded,
black-capped, dark-faced priests. He is eighty-six years old,
and his manners and appearance were dignified in the extreme.
Speaking slowly and distinctly he began to tell Gladstone that
the sole wish of Cephalonia was to be united to Greece, and
there was something very exciting and affecting in the
tremulous tones of the old man saying over and over again,
"questa infelice isola, questa isola infelice," as the tears streamed
down his cheeks and long silvery beard. It was like a scene
in a play.'

At Zante (Dec. 15), the surface was smoother. A concourse
of several thousands awaited him; Greek flags were flying on
all sides in the strong morning sea-breeze; the town bands
played Greek national tunes; the bells were all ringing; the

harbour was covered with boats full of gaily dressed people; and the air resounded with loud shouts ζήτω ὁ φιλέλλην Γλάδστων, ζήτω ἡ ἕνωσις μετὰ τῆς Ἑλλάδος, Long live Gladstone the Philhellene, hurrah for union with Greece.

'Every room and passage in the residency,' Mr. Gordon writes to Lord Aberdeen, 'was already thronged. . . . Upstairs the excitement was great, and as soon as Gladstone had taken his place, in swept Gerasimus the bishop (followed by scores of swarthy priests in their picturesque black robes) and tendered to him the petition for union. But before he could deliver it, Gladstone stopped him and addressed to him and to the assembly a speech in excellent Italian. Never did I hear his beautiful voice ring out more clear or more thrillingly than when he said, "*Ecco l' inganno*." . . . It was a scene not to be forgotten. The priests, with eye and hand and gesture, expressed in lively pantomime to each other the effect produced by each sentence, in what we should think a most exaggerated way, like a chorus on the stage, but the effect was most picturesque.'

He attended a banquet one night, went to the theatre the next, where he was greeted with lusty zetos, and at midnight embarked on the *Terrible* on his way to Athens. His stay in the immortal city only lasted for three or four days, and I find no record of his impressions. They were probably those of most travellers educated enough to feel the spell of the Violet Crown. Illusions as to the eternal summer with which poets have blessed the Isles of Greece vanished as they found deep snow in the streets, icicles on the Acropolis, and snow-balling in the Parthenon. He had a reception only a shade less cordial than if he were Demosthenes come back. He dined with King Otho, and went to a *Te Deum* in honour of the Queen's birthday. Finlay, the learned man who had more of the true spirit of history than most historians then alive, took him to a meeting of the legislature; he beheld some of the survivors of the war of independence, and made friends with one valiant lover of freedom, the veteran General Church. Though, thanks to the generosity of an Englishman, they had a university of their own at Corfu, the Ionians preferred to send their sons to Athens, and the Athenian students immediately presented a memorial to Mr. Gladstone with the usual prayer for union with the Hellenic kingdom. On the special object of his visit, he came away from Athens with the impression that opinion in Greece was much divided on the question of immediate union with the Ionian islands. In truth his position had been a false one. Everybody was profoundly deferential, but nobody was quite sure whether he had come to pave the way for union, or to invite the Athenian government to check it, and when Rangabé, the foreign minister, found him without credentials or instructions, and staved off all discussion, Mr. Gladstone must have felt that though he had seen one of the two or three most wondrous historic sites on the globe, that was all.

Of a jaunt to wilder scenes a letter of Mr. Arthur Gordon's gives a pleasant glimpse :—

You will like an account of an expedition the whole party made yesterday to Albania to pay a visit to an old lady, a great proprietress, who lives in a large ruinous castle at a place called Filates. She is about the greatest personage in these regions, and it was thought that the lord high commissioner should pay her a visit if he wished to see Albania. . . . It was a lovely morning, and breakfast was laid on the balcony of the private apartments looking over the garden and commanding the loveliest of views across the strait. Gladstone was in the highest spirits, full of talk and *romping boyishly.* After breakfast the L. H. C.'s barge and the cutters of the *Terrible* conveyed us on board the pretty little gunboat.

We reached Sayada in about two hours, and were received on landing by the governor of the province, who had ridden down from Filates to meet us. We went to the house of the English vice-consul, whilst the long train of horses was preparing to start, but after a few minutes' stay there Gladstone became irrepressibly restless, and insisted on setting off to walk—I of course walked too. The old steward also went with us, and a guard of eight white-kilted palikari on foot. The rest of the party rode, and from a slight hill which we soon reached, it was very pretty to look back at the long procession starting from Sayada and proceeding along the narrow causeway running parallel to our path, the figures silhouetted against the sea. Filates is about 12 miles from Sayada, perhaps more, the path is rugged and mountainous, and commands some fine views. Our palikari guards fired off their long Afghan-looking guns in every direction, greatly to Gladstone's annoyance, but there was no stopping them.

Scouts on the hills gave warning of our approach, and at the entrance to Filates we were met by the whole population. First the Valideh's retainers, then the elders, then the moolahs in their great green turbans, the Christian community, and finally, on the top of the hill, the Valideh's little grandson, gorgeously dressed, and attended by his tutor and a number of black slaves. The little boy salaamed to Gladstone with much grace and self-possession, and then conducted us to the castle, in front of which all the townsfolk who were not engaged in receiving us were congregated in picturesque groups on the smooth grassy lawns and under the great plane trees. The castle is a large ruinous enclosure of walls and towers, with buildings of all sorts and ages within. The Valideh herself, attired in green silk and a fur pelisse, her train held by two negro female slaves, received us at the head of the stairs and ushered us into a large room with a divan round three sides of it. Sweetmeats and water and pipes and coffee were brought as usual, some of the cups and their filigree stands very handsome. We went out to see the town, preceded by a tall black slave in a gorgeous blue velvet jacket, with a great silver stick in his hand. Under his guidance we visited the khans, the bazaar and the mosque ; not only were we allowed to enter the mosque with our shoes on, but on Gladstone expressing a wish to hear the call to prayer, the muezzin was sent up to the top of the minaret to call the azan two hours before the proper time. The sight of the green-turbaned imam crying the azan for a Frank was most singular, and the endless variety of costume displayed by the crowds who thronged the verandahs which surround the mosque was most picturesque. The gateway of the castle too was a picturesque scene. Retainers and guards, slaves and soldiers, and even women, were lounging about, and a beautiful tame little pet roedeer played with the pretty children in bright coloured dresses, clustering under the cavernous archway.

We had dinner in another large room. I counted thirty-two dishes, or I may say courses, for each dish at a Turkish dinner is brought in separately, and it is rude not to eat of all! The most picturesque part of the dinner, and most unusual, was the way the room was lighted. Eight tall, grand Albanians stood like statues behind us, each holding a candle. It reminded me of the torch-bearers who won the laird his bet in the *Legend of Montrose*.

After dinner there was a long and somewhat tedious interval of smoking and story-telling in the dark, and we called upon Lacaita to recite Italian poetry, which he did with much effect, pouring out sonnet after sonnet of Petrarch, including that which my father thinks the most beautiful in the Italian language, that which has in it the 'lampeggiar del angelico riso.' This showed me how easy it was to fall into the habits of a country. Gladstone is as unoriental as any man well can be, yet his calling on Lacaita to recite was really just the same thing that every Pasha does after dinner, when he orders his tale-teller to repeat a story. The ladies meanwhile were packed off to the harem for the night, Lady Bowen acting as their interpreter. My L. H. C., his two secretaries, his three aide-de-camps, Captains Blomfield and Mandricardi, and the vice-consul, all slept in the same room, and that not a large one, and we were packed tight on the floor, under quilts of Brusa silk and gold, tucked up round us by gorgeous Albanians. Gladstone amused himself with speculating whether or no we were in contravention of the provisions of Lord Shaftesbury's lodging-house act!

After a month of cloudless sunshine it took it into its head to rain this night of all nights in the year, and rain as it only does in these regions. Gladstone and I walked down again despite of wind, rain, and mud, and our palikari guard—to keep up their spirits, I suppose— chanted wild choruses all the way. We nearly got stuck altogether in the muddy flat near Sayada, and got on board the *Osprey* wet through, my hands so chilled I could hardly steer the boat. Of course we had far outwalked the riding party, so we had to wait. What a breakfast we ate! that is those of us who could eat, for the passage was rough and Gladstone and the ladies flat on their backs and very sorry for themselves.

Mr. Gladstone's comment in his diary is brief :—'The whole impression is saddening ; it is all indolence, decay, stagnation ; the image of God seems as if it were nowhere. But there is much of wild and picturesque.' The English in the island, both civil and military, adopted the tone of unfriendly journals in London, and the garrison went so far as not even to invite Mr. Gladstone to mess, a compliment never omitted before. The Ionians, on the other hand, like people in most other badly governed countries did not show in the noblest colours. There were petitions, letters, memorials, as to which Mr. Gladstone mildly notes that he has to 'lament a spirit of exaggeration and obvious errors of fact.' There was a stream of demands from hosts of Spiridiones, Christodulos, Euphrosunes, for government employ, and the memorial survives, attested by bishop and clergy, of a man with a daughter to marry, who being too poor to find a dowry 'had decided on reverting to your Excellency's well-known philhellenism, and with tears in his eyes besought that your Excellency,' et cetera.

One incident was much disliked at home, as having the fearsome flavour of the Puseyite. It had been customary at levees for the lord high commissioner to bow to everybody, but also to shake hands with the bishops and sundry other high persons. Mr. Gladstone stooped and actually kissed the bishop's hand. Sir Edward Lytton inquired if the story were true, as a question might be asked in parliament. It is true, said Mr. Gladstone (February 7), but 'I hope Sir E. L. will not in his consideration for me entangle himself in such a matter, but as he knows nothing now, will continue to know nothing, and will say that the subject did not enter into his instructions, and that he presumes I shall be at home in two or three more weeks to answer for all my misdeeds.'[1]

The secretary of state and his potent emissary—the radical who had turned tory and the tory who was on the verge of formally turning liberal—got on excellently together. Though he was not exact in business, the minister's despatches and letters show shrewdness, good sense, and right feeling, with a copious garnish of flummery. Demagogy, he says to Mr. Gladstone, will continue to be a trade and the most fascinating of all trades, because animated by personal vanity, and its venality disguised even to the demagogue himself by the love of country, by which it may be really accompanied. The Ionian constitution should certainly be mended, for 'my convictions tell me that there is nothing so impracticable as the Unreal.' He comforts his commissioner by the reminder that a population after all has one great human heart, and a great human heart is that which chiefly exalts the Man of Genius over the mere Man of Talent, so that when a Man of Genius with practical experience of the principles of sound government comes face to face with a people whose interest it is to be governed well, the chances are that they will understand each other.

IV

Mr. Gladstone applied himself with the utmost gravity to the affairs of a pygmy state with a total population under 250,000. His imagination did its work. While you seem, he said most truly, to be dealing only with a few specks scarcely visible on the map of Europe, you are engaged in solving a problem as delicate

---

[1] This and his alleged attendance at mass, and compliance with sundry other rites, were often heard of in later times, and even so late as 1879 Mr. Gladstone was subjected to some rude baiting from doctors of divinity and others.

and difficult as if it arose on a far more conspicuous stage. The people he found to be eminently gifted by nature with that sublety which is apt to degenerate into sophistry, and prone to be both rather light-minded and extremely suspicious. The permanent officials in Downing Street, with less polite analysis, had been accustomed to regard the islanders more bluntly as a 'pack of scamps.' This was what had done the mischief. The material condition of the cultivators was in some respects not bad, but Mr. Gladstone laid down a profound and solid principle when he said that 'no method of dealing with a civilised community can be satisfactory which does not make provision for its political action as well as its social state.'[1] The idea of political reform had for a time made head against the idea of union with the Greek kingdom, but for some years past the whole stream of popular tendency and feeling set strongly towards union, and disdained contentment with anything else. Mankind turn naturally to the solutions that seem the simplest. Mr. Gladstone condemned the existing system as bad for us and bad for them. Circumstances made it impossible for him to suggest amendment by throwing the burden bodily off our shoulders, and at that time he undoubtedly regarded union with Greece as in itself undesirable for the Ionians. Circumstances and his own love of freedom made it equally impossible to recommend the violent suppression of the constitution. The only course left open was to turn the mockery of free government into a reality, and this operation he proposed to carry out with a bold hand. The details of this enlargement of popular rights and privileges, and the accompanying financial purgation, do not now concern us. Whether the case either demanded or permitted originality in the way of construction I need not discuss. The manufacture of a constitution is always the easiest thing in the world. The question is whether the people concerned will work it, and in spite of that buoyant optimism which never in any circumstances deserted him in respect of whatever business he might have in hand, Mr. Gladstone must have doubted whether his islanders would ever pretend to accept what they did not seek, as a substitute for what they did seek but were not allowed to have. Before anybody knew the scope of his plan, the six newspapers flew to arms with a vivacity that, whether it was Italian or was Greek, was in either case a fatal sign of the public temper. What, they cried, did the treaty of 1815 mean by describing the Ionian state as free and independent ? What was a protectorate, and

[1] Finlay, *History of Greece*, vii. p. 306, blames both Bulwer and Mr. Gladstone because they 'directed their attention to the means of applying sound theories of government to a state of things where a change in the social relations of the inhabitants and modifications in the tenure and rights of property were the real evils that required remedy, and over these the British government could exercise very little influence if opposed by the Ionian representatives.' But is not this to say that the real remedy was unattainable without political reform ?

what the rights of the protector? Was there no difference
between a protector and a sovereign? What could be more
arrogant and absurd than that the protector, who was not
sovereign, should talk about 'conceding' reforms to a free and
independent state? All these questions were in themselves not
very easy to answer, but what was a more serious obstacle than
the argumentative puzzles of partisans was a want of moral
and political courage; was the sycophancy of one class, and the
greediness of others.[1]

Closely connected with the recommendations of constitutional
reform was the question by whom the necessary communications
with the assembly were to be conducted. Sir John Young was
obviously impossible, though he was not at once brought to
face the fact. Mr. Gladstone upon this made to the colonial
secretary (December 27) an offer that if he had already determined on Young's recall, and if he thought reform would stand
a better chance if introduced by Mr. Gladstone himself, he was
willing to serve as lord high commissioner for the very limited
time that might be necessary. We may be sure that the
government lost not an hour in making up their minds on
a plan that went still further both in the way of bringing
Mr. Gladstone into still closer connection with them, and
towards relieving themselves of a responsibility which they
never from the first had any business to devolve upon Mr.
Gladstone or anybody else. The answer came by telegraph
(January 11), 'The Queen accepts. Your commission is being
made out.'

All other embarrassments were now infinitely aggravated by
the sudden discovery from the lawyers that acceptance of the
new office not only vacated the seat in parliament, but also
rendered Mr. Gladstone incapable of election until he had
ceased to hold the office. 'This, I must confess,' he told Sir
Edward, 'is a great blow. The difficulty and the detriment
are serious' (January 17). If some enemy on the meeting of
the House in February should choose to move the writ for the
vacant seat at Oxford, the election would necessarily take
place at a date too early for the completion of the business at
Corfu, and Mr. Gladstone still at work as high commissioner
would still therefore be ineligible. Nobody was ever by constitution more averse than Mr. Gladstone to turning backward,
and in this case he felt himself especially bound to go forward
not only by the logic of the Ionian situation at the moment,
but for the reason which was also characteristic of him, that
the Queen in approving his appointment (January 7) had
described his conduct as both patriotic and most opportune,

[1] May 7, 1861. *Hans.* 3rd Ser. 162, p. 1687. The salaries of the deputies struck
him as especially excessive, and on the same occasion he let fall the *obiter dictum*:
'For my part I trust that of all the changes that may in the course of generations
be made in the constitution of this country, the very last and latest will be the
payment of members of this House.'

and therefore he thought there would be unspeakable shabbiness in turning round upon her by a hurried withdrawal. The Oxford entanglement thus became almost desperate. Resolved not to disturb the settled order of proceeding with his assembly, Mr. Gladstone with a thoroughly characteristic union of ingenuity and tenacity tried various ways of extrication. To complete the mortifications of the position, the telegraph broke down.

The scrape was nearly as harassing to his friends at home as to himself. Politicians above all men can never safely count on the charity that thinketh no evil. Lord John Russell told Lord Aberdeen that it was clear that Gladstone was staying away to avoid a discussion on the coming Reform bill. There was a violent attack upon him in the *Times* (January 13) as having supplanted Young. The writers of leading articles looked up Greek history from the days of the visit of Ulysses to Alcinous downwards, and they mocked his respect for the countrymen of Miltiades, and his reverence for the church of Chrysostom and Athanasius. The satirists of the cleverest journal of the day admitted his greatness, the brilliance and originality of his finance, the incomparable splendour of his eloquence, and a courage equal to any undertaking, that quailed before no opposition and suffered no abatement in defeat, and they only marvelled the more that a statesman of the first rank should accept at the hands of an insidious rival a fifth-rate mission—insidious rival not named but easy to identify. The fact that Mr. Gladstone had hired a house at Corfu was the foundation of a transcendent story that Mr. Disraeli wished to make him the king of the Ionian islands. 'I hardly think it needful to assure you,' Mr. Gladstone told Lytton, 'that I have never attached the smallest weight to any of the insinuations which it seems people have thought worth while to launch at some member or members of your government with respect to my mission.' Though Mr. Gladstone was never by any means unconscious of the hum and buzz of paltriness and malice that often surrounds conspicuous public men, nobody was ever more regally indifferent. Graham predicted that though Gladstone would always be the first man in the House of Commons, he would not again be what he was before the Ionian business. They all thought that he would be attacked on his return. '*Ah*,' said Aberdeen, '*but he is terrible in the rebound.*'

After much perplexity and running to and fro in London, it was arranged between the secretary of state and Mr. Gladstone's friends, including Phillimore principally, and then Northcote and M. Bernard, that a course of proceeding should be followed, which Mr. Gladstone when he knew it thought unfortunate. A new commission naming a successor was issued, and Mr. Gladstone then became *ipso facto* liberated. Sir Henry Storks

was the officer chosen, and as soon as his commission was
formally received by him, he was to execute a warrant under
which he deputed all powers to Mr. Gladstone until his arrival.
Whether Mr. Gladstone was lord high commissioner when
he came to propose his reform, is a moot point. So intricate
was the puzzle that the under-secretary addressed a letter to
Mr. Gladstone by his name and not by the style of his official
dignity, because he could not be at all sure what that official
dignity really was. What is certain is that Mr. Gladstone,
though it was never his way to quarrel with other people's
action taken in good faith on his behalf, did not perceive the
necessity for proceeding so rapidly to the appointment of his
successor, and thought it decidedly injurious to such chances
as his reforms might have possessed.[1]

The assembly that had been convoked by Sir John Young
for an extraordinary session (January 25), at once showed that
its labours would bear no fruit. Mr. Gladstone as lord high
commissioner opened the session with a message that they had
met to consider proposals for reform which he desired to lay
before them as soon as possible. The game began with the
passing of a resolution that it was the single and unanimous *will*
(θέλησις) of the Ionian people that the seven islands should be
united to Greece. Mr. Gladstone fought like a lion for scholar's
authority to treat the word as only meaning wish or disposition,
and he took for touchstone the question whether men could
speak of the θέλησις of the Almighty ; the word in the Lord's
Prayer was found to be θέλημα. As Finlay truly says, it would
have been much more to the point to accept the word as it was
meant by those who used it. As to that no mistake was possible.
Some say that he ought plainly to have told them they had
violated the constitution, to have dissolved them, and above all
to have stopped their pay. Instead of this he informed them
that they must put their wishes into the shape of a petition to
the Queen. The idea was seized with alacrity (January 29).
Oligarchs and demagogues were equally pleased to fall in with
it, the former because they hoped it would throw their rivals
into deeper discredit with their common master, the latter
because they knew it would endear them to their constituents.

The Corfiotes received the declaration of the assembly and
the address to the Queen with enthusiasm. Great crowds
followed the members to their homes with joyous acclamations,
all the bells of the town were set ringing, there was a grand
illumination for two nights, and the archbishop ordered a *Te
Deum*. Neither te-deums nor prayers melted the heart of the
British cabinet, aware of the truth impressed at the time on

---

[1] On Feb. 7, the secretary of the treasury moved the writ, and the next day the
vice-chancellor notified that there would be an election, Mr. Gladstone having 'vacated
his seat by accepting the office of lord high commissioner of the Ionian Islands, which
he no longer holds.' He was re-elected (Feb. 12) without opposition.

Mr. Gladstone by Lytton, that neither the English public nor the English parliament likes any policy that '*gives anything up.*' The Queen was advised to reply that she could neither consent to abandon the obligations she had undertaken, nor could permit any application from the islands to other Powers in furtherance of any similar design.

Then at last came the grand plan for constitutional reconstruction. Mr. Gladstone after first stating the reply of the Queen, read an eloquent address to the assembly (February 4) in Italian, adjuring them to reject all attempts to evade by any indirect devices the duty of pronouncing a clear and intelligible judgment on the propositions now laid before them. His appeal was useless, and it was received exactly as plans for assimilating Irish administration to English used to be. The nationalists knew that reform would be a difficulty the more in the way of separation, the retrogrades knew it would be a spoke in the wheel of their own jobbery. Mr. Gladstone professed extreme and truly characteristic astonishment in respect of the address to the Queen, that they should regard the permission to ask as identical with the promise to grant, and the right to petition as equivalent to the right to demand. If the affair had been less practically vexatious, we can imagine the Socratic satisfaction with which Mr. Gladstone would have revelled in pressing all these and many other distinctions on those who boasted of being Socrates' fellow-countrymen.

From day to day anxiously did Mr. Gladstone watch what he called the dodges of the assembly. Abundant reason as there was to complain of the conduct of the Ionians in all these proceedings, it is well to record the existence of a number of sincere patriots and enlightened men like the two brothers Themistocles, Napoleon Zambelli, and Sir Peter Braila, afterwards Greek minister in London. This small band of loyal adherents gave Mr. Gladstone all the help they could in preparing his scheme of reform, and after the scheme was launched, they strained every nerve to induce the assembly to assent to it in spite of the pressure from the people. Their efforts were necessarily unavailing. The great majority, composed as usual of the friends of England who trembled for their own jobs, joining hands with the demagogues, was hostile to the changes proposed, and only flinched from a peremptory vote from doubt as to its reception among the people. Promptitude and force were not to be expected in either way from men in such a frame of mind. 'On a preliminary debate,' Mr. Gladstone wrote mournfully to Phillimore, ' without any motion whatever, one man has spoken for nearly the whole of two days.' Strong language about the proposals as cheating and fraudulent was freely used, but nothing that in Mr. Gladstone's view justified one of those high-handed prorogations after the manner of the Stuarts, that had been the usual expedient in quarrels between

the high commissioner and a recalcitrant assembly. These
doings had brought English rule over the islands to a level in
the opinion of Southern Europe with Austrian rule at Venice
and the reign of the cardinals in the pontifical states.

Sir Henry Storks arrived on the 16th of February, and the
same day the assembly which before had been working for
delay, in a great hurry gave a vote against the proposals,
which, though in form preliminary, was in substance decisive ;
there were only seven dissentients. Mr. Gladstone sums up the
case in a private letter to Sidney Herbert.

Corfu, 17th Feb. 1859.—This decision is not convenient for me
personally, nor for the government at home ; but as a whole I cannot
regret it so far as England is concerned. I think the proposals give
here almost for the first time a perfectly honourable and tenable position
in the face of the islands. The first set of manœuvres was directed to
preventing them from being made ; and that made me really uneasy.
The only point of real importance was to get them out. . . . Do not
hamper yourself in this affair with me. Let me sink or swim. I have
been labouring for truth and justice, and am sufficiently happy in the
consciousness of it, to be little distressed either with the prospect of
blame, or with the more serious question whether I acted rightly or
wrongly in putting myself in the place of L.H.C. to propose these
reforms,—a step which has of course been much damaged by the early
nomination of Sir H. Storks, done out of mere consideration for me in
another point of view. Lytton's conduct throughout has been such
that I could have expected no more from the oldest and most confiding
friend.

To Lytton himself he writes (Feb. 7, 1859) :—

I sincerely wish that I could have repaid your generous confidence
and admirable support with recommendations suited to the immediate
convenience of your government. But in sending me, you grappled
with a difficulty which you might have postponed, and I could not but
do the same. Whether it was right that I should come, I do not feel
very certain. Yet (stolen dispatch and all) I do not regret it. For my
feelings are those you have so admirably described ; and I really do not
know for what it is that political life is worth the living, if it be not
for an opportunity of endeavouring to redeem in the face of the world
the character of our country wherever, it matters not on how small a
scale, that character has been compromised.

Language like this, as sincere as it was lofty, supplies the
true test by which to judge Mr. Gladstone's conduct both in
the Ionian transaction and many another. From the point of
personal and selfish interest any simpleton might see that
he made a mistake, but measured by his own standard of
public virtue, how is he to be blamed, how is he not to be
applauded, for undertaking a mission that, but for an unforeseen accident, might have redounded to the honour and the
credit of the British power ?

V

On February 19 he quitted the scene of so many anxieties and such strenuous effort as we have seen. The *Terrible* fell into a strong north-easter in the Adriatic, and took thirty-six hours to Pola. There they sought shelter and got across with a smooth sea to Venice on the 23rd. He saw the Austrian archduke whom he found kind, intelligent, earnest, pleasing. At Turin a few days later (March 3), he had an interview with Cavour, for whom at that moment the crowning scenes of his great career were just opening. 'At Vicenza,' the diary records (Feb. 28), 'we had cavalry and artillery at the station about to march; more cavalry on the road with a van and pickets, some with drawn swords; at Verona regiments in review; at Milan pickets in the streets; as I write I hear the tread of horse patrolling the streets. Dark omens!' The war with Austria was close at hand.

I may as well in a few sentences finally close the Ionian chapter, though the consummation was not immediate. Mr. Gladstone, while he was for the moment bitten by the notion of ceding the southern islands to Greece, was no more touched by the nationalist aspirations of the Ionians than he had been by nationalism and unification in Italy in 1851. Just as in Italy he clung to constitutional reforms in the particular provinces and states as the key to regeneration, so here he leaned upon the moderates who, while professing strong nationalist feeling, did not believe that the time for its realisation had arrived. A debate was raised in the House of Commons in the spring of 1861, by an Irish member. The Irish catholics twitted Mr. Gladstone with flying the flag of nationality in Italy, and trampling on it in the Ionian islands. He in reply twitted them with crying up nationality for the Greeks, and running it down when it told against the pope. In the Italian case Lord John Russell had (1860) set up the broad doctrine that a people are the only true judges who should be their rulers—a proposition that was at once seized and much used by the Dandolos, Lombardos, Cavalieratos and the rest at Corfu. Scarcely anybody pretended that England had any separate or selfish interest of her own. 'It is in my view,' said Mr. Gladstone, 'entirely a matter of that kind of interest only, which is in one sense the highest interest of all—namely the interest which is inherent in her character and duty, and her exact and regular fulfilment of obligations which she has contracted with Europe.'[1]

But he held the opinion that it would be nothing less than a crime against the safety of Europe, as connected with the

[1] Mr. Gladstone, May 7, 1861.—*Hans.* Third Ser. 162, p. 1687.

state and course of the Eastern question, if England were at this moment to surrender the protectorate; for if you should surrender the protectorate, what were you to say to Candia, Thessaly, Albania, and other communities of Greek stock still under Turkish rule? Then there was a military question. Large sums of British money had been flung away on forti-fications,[1] and people talked of Corfu as they talked in later years about Cyprus, as a needed supplement to the strength of Gibraltar and Malta, and indispensable to our Mediterranean power. People listened agape to demonstrations that the Ionian islands were midway between England and the Persian Gulf; that they were two-thirds of the way to the Red Sea; that they blocked up the mouth of the Adriatic; Constanti-nople, Smyrna, Alexandria, Naples, formed a belt of great towns around them; they were central to Asia, Europe and Africa. And so forth in the alarmist's well-worn currency.

Lord Palmerston in 1850 had declared in his highest style that Corfu was a very important position for Mediterranean interests in the event of a war, and it would be great folly to give it up. A year later he repeated that though he should not object to the annexation of the southern islands to Greece, Corfu was too important a military and naval post ever to be abandoned by us.[2] As Lord Palmerston changed, so did Mr. Gladstone change. 'Without a good head for Greece, I should not like to see the Ionian protectorate surrendered; with it, I should be well pleased for one to be responsible for giving it up.' Among many other wonderful suggestions was one that he should himself become that 'good head.' 'The first mention,' he wrote to a correspondent in parliament (Jan. 21, 1863), 'of my candidature in Greece some time ago made me laugh very heartily, for though I do love the country and never laughed at anything else in connection with it before, yet the seeing my own name, which in my person was never meant to carry a title of any kind, placed in juxtaposition with that particular idea, made me give way.'

Meanwhile it is safe to conjecture, for the period with which in this chapter we are immediately concerned, that in conceiv-ing and drawing up his Ionian scheme, close contact with liberal doctrines as to free institutions and popular government must have quickened Mr. Gladstone's progress in liberal doctrines in our own affairs at home. In 1863[3] Lord Palmerston himself, in spite of that national aversion to anything like giving up, of which he was himself the most formidable representative,

1 Napier in his *Memoir on the Roads of Cephalonia* (p. 45) tells how Maitland had a notion of building a fort on that island, and on his boat one day asked the commanding engineer how much it would cost. The engineer talked about £100,000. 'Upon this Sir Thomas turned round in the boat, with a long and loud whistle. After this whistle I thought it best to let at least a year pass without again mentioning the subject.'

2 Ashley, ii. pp. 184, 186.

3 *Dec.* 8, 1862.—Cabinet. Resolution to surrender the Ionian protectorate. Only Lord W[estbury] opposing.

cheerfully handed the Ionians over to their kinsfolk, if kinsfolk they truly were, upon the mainland.[1]

[1] Mr. Gladstone sent home and revised afterwards three elaborate reports on the mischiefs of Ionian government and the constitutional remedies proper for them. They were printed for the use of the cabinet, though whether these fifty large pages, amounting to about a quarter of this volume, received much attention from that body, may without *scandalum magnatum* be doubted, nor do the reports appear to have been laid before parliament. The Italian war was then creating an agitation in Europe upon nationality, as to which the people of the Ionian islands were sensitively alive, and the reports would have supplied a good deal of fuel. There was a separate fourth report upon the suppression of disorder in Cephalonia in 1848, which everybody afterwards agreed that it was not expedient to publish. It still exists in the archives of the colonial office.

CHAPTER XI

JUNCTION WITH THE LIBERALS

(1859)

> Conviction, in spite of early associations and long-cherished prepossessions—strong conviction, and an overpowering sense of the public interests operating for many many years before full effect was given to it, placed me in the ranks of the liberal party.—GLADSTONE (Ormskirk, 1867).

WHEN Mr. Gladstone returned to England in March 1859, he found the conservatives with much ineffectual industry, some misplaced ingenuity, and many misgivings and divisions, trying their hands at parliamentary reform. Their infringement of what passed for a liberal patent was not turning out well. Convulsions in the cabinet, murmurs in the lobbies, resistance from the opposite benches, all showed that a ministry existing on sufferance would not at that stage be allowed to settle the question. In this contest Mr. Gladstone did not actively join. Speaking from the ministerial side of the House, he made a fervid defence of nomination boroughs as the nurseries of statesmen, but he voted with ministers against a whig amendment. His desire, he said, was to settle the question as soon as possible, always, however, on the foundation of trust in the people, that 'sound and satisfactory basis on which for several years past legislation had been proceeding.' The hostile amendment was carried against ministers by statesmen irreconcilably at variance with one another, alike in principle and object. The majority of thirty-nine was very large for those days, and it was decisive. Though the parliament was little more than a couple of years old, yet in face of the desperate confusion among leaders, parties, and groups, and upon the plea that reform had not been formally submitted as an issue to the country, Lord Derby felt justified in dissolving. Mr. Gladstone held the Oxford seat without opposition. The constituencies displayed an extension of the same essentially conservative feeling that had given Lord Palmerston the victory two years before. Once more the real question lay not so much between measures as men ; not so much between democratic change and conservative moderation, as between Palmerston and Russell on the one hand, and Derby and Disraeli on the other. The government at the election improved their position by some thirty votes. This was not enough to outnumber the phalanx of their various opponents combined, but was it possible that the phalanx should combine? Mr. Gladstone, who spoke of the dissolution as being a most improper as well as a most important measure, alike in domestic and in foreign bearings, told Acland that he would not be surprised if the government were to attempt some reconstruction on a broad basis before the new parliament met. This course was not adopted.

The chances of turning out the government were matters of infinite computation among the leaders. The liberal whip after the election gave his own party a majority of fifteen, but the treasury whip, on the other hand, was equally confident of a majority of ten. Still all was admittedly uncertain. The prime perplexity was whether if a new administration could be formed, Lord Palmerston or Lord John should be at its head. Everybody agreed that it would be both impossible and wrong to depose the tories until it was certain that the liberals were united enough to mount into their seat, and no government could last unless it comprehended both the old prime ministers. Could not one of them carry the prize of the premiership into the Lords, and leave to the other the consolation stake of leadership in the Commons? Lord Palmerston, who took the crisis with a veteran's good-humoured coolness, told his intimates that he at any rate would not go up to the Lords, for he could not trust John Russell in the other House. With a view, however, to ministerial efficiency, he was anxious to keep Russell in the Commons, as with him and Gladstone they would make a strong treasury bench. But was it certain that Gladstone would join? On this there was endless gossip. One story ran that Mrs. Gladstone had told somebody that her husband wished bygones to be bygones, was all for a strong government, and was ready to join in forming one. Then the personage to whom this was said upset the inference by declaring there was nothing in the conversation incompatible with a Derby junction. Sir Charles Wood says in his journal :—

May 22.—Saw Mrs. Gladstone, who did not seem to contemplate a junction with Palmerston but rather that he should join Derby. I stated the impossibility of that, and that the strongest government possible under present circumstances would be by such a union as took place under Aberdeen. To effect this, all people must pull the same and not different ways as of late years. I said that I blamed her husband for quitting, and ever since he quitted, Palmerston's government in 1855, as well as Lord John ; that in the quarrel between Lord John and Gladstone the former had behaved ill, and the latter well.

May 27.—Gladstone dined here. . . . He would vote a condemnation of the dissolution, and is afraid of the foreign affairs at so critical a moment being left in the hands of Malmesbury ; says that we, the opposition, are not only justified but called upon by the challenge in the Queen's speech on the dissolution, to test the strength of parties ; but that he is himself in a different position, that he would vote a condemnation of the dissolution, but hesitates as to no confidence.

Sir Robert Phillimore [1] gives us other glimpses during this month :—

May 18.—Long interview with Gladstone. He entered most fully and without any reserve into his views on the state of political parties and on the duties of a statesman at this juncture. Thought the only chance of a strong government was an engrafting of Palmerston upon Lord Derby, dethroning Disraeli from the leadership of the House of Commons, arranging for a moderate Reform bill, placing the foreign office in other hands, but not in Disraeli's. He dwelt much upon this. Foreign politics seemed to have the chief place in his mind.

May 31.—Gladstone has seen Palmerston, and said he will not vote against Lord Derby in support of Lord John's supposed motion. The government Gladstone thinks desirable is a fusion of Palmerston and his followers with Lord Derby, which implies, of course, weeding out half at least of the present cabinet. Gladstone will have to vote with government and speak against the cabinet, and violently he will be abused.

June 1.—Dined with Gladstone. He is much harassed and distressed at his position relative to the government and opposition. Spoke strongly against Lord Malmesbury. Said if the proposal is to censure the dissolution, he must agree with it, but he will vote against a want of confidence.

One important personage was quite confident that Gladstone would vote the government out. Another thought that he would be sure to join a liberal administration. Palmerston believed this too, even though he might not vote for a motion of want of confidence. Clarendon expected Gladstone to join, though he would rather see him at the foreign office than at the exchequer. At a dinner party at Lord Carlisle's where Palmerston, Lord John, Granville, Clarendon, Lewis, Argyll, and Delane were present, Sir Charles Wood in a conversation with Mrs. Gladstone found her much less inclined to keep the Derby government in. In the last week of May a party feast was planned by Lord Palmerston and the whip, but Lord John Russell declined to join the dinner. It was decided to call a meeting of the party. A confidential visitor was talking of it at Cambridge House, when the brougham came to the door to take Palmerston down to Pembroke Lodge. He was going, he said, to ask Lord John what they should say if they were asked at the meeting whether they had come to an agreement. The interview was not unsatisfactory. Four days later (June 6) a well-attended meeting of the party was held at Willis's Rooms. The two protagonists declared themselves

[1] Not, however, Sir Robert until 1862, when he was knighted on becoming Queen's advocate. He was created baronet in 1881.

ready to aid in forming a government on a broad basis, and
it was understood that either would serve under the other.
It would be for the sovereign to decide. Mr. Bright spoke in
what the whigs pronounced to be a highly reasonable vein, and
they all broke up in great spirits. The whip pored over his
lists, and made out that they could not beat the government by
less than seven. This was but a slender margin for a vote of
no confidence, but it was felt that mere numbers, though a
majority might be an indispensable incident, were in this
case not the only test of the conditions required for a solid
government. Lord Hartington, the representative of the
great house of Cavendish, was put up to move a vote of no
confidence.[1]

After three days' debate, ministers were defeated (June 11)
by the narrow figure of thirteen in a House of six hundred and
thirty-seven. Mr. Gladstone did not speak, but he answered
the riddle that had for long so much harassed the wirepullers,
by going into the lobby with Disraeli and his flock. The
general sense of the majority was probably best expressed by
Mr. Bright. Since the fall of the government of Sir Robert
Peel, he said, there had been no good handling of the liberal
party in the House : the cabinet had been exclusive, the policy
had been sometimes wholly wrong, and generally feeble and
paltering : if in the new government there should be found
men adequately representing these reconciled sections, acting
with some measure of boldness and power, grappling with the
abuses that were admitted to exist, and relying upon the moral
sense and honest feeling of the House, and the general sympathy of the people of England for improvement in our
legislation, he was bold to hope that the new government
would have a longer tenure of office than any government that
had existed for many years past.

The Queen, in the embarrassment of a choice between the
two whig veterans, induced Lord Granville, whose cabinet life
as yet was only some five years, to try to form a government.
This step Palmerston explained by her German sympathies,
which made her adverse alike to Lord John and himself. Lord
Granville first applied to Palmerston, who said that the Queen
ought to have sent for himself first ; still he agreed to serve.
Lord John would only serve under Granville on condition of
being leader in the House of Commons ; if he joined—so he
argued—and if Palmerston were leader in the Commons, this
would make himself third instead of second : on that point his
answer was final. So Lord Granville threw up a commission
that never had life in it ; the Queen handed the task over to

1 Lord Hartington's motion was—'That it is essential for the satisfactory result of
our deliberations, and for facilitating the discharge of your Majesty's high functions,
that your Majesty's government should possess the confidence of this House and of
the country ; and we deem it our duty respectfully to submit to your Majesty that
such confidence is not reposed in the present advisers of your Majesty.'

Palmerston, and in a few days the new administration was installed. (June 17, 1859.)

II

Mr. Gladstone went back to the office that he had quitted four years and a half before, and undertook the department of finance. The appointment did not pass without considerable remark. 'The real scandal,' he wrote to his Oxford chairman, 'is among the extreme men on the liberal side ; they naturally say, "This man has done all he could on behalf of Lord Derby ; why is he here to keep out one of us?"' Even some among Mr. Gladstone's private friends wondered how he could bring himself to join a minister of whom he had for three or four years used such unsparing language as had been common on his lips about Lord Palmerston. The plain man was puzzled by a vote in favour of keeping a tory government in, followed by a junction with the men who had thrown that government out. Cobden, as we know, declined to join.[1] 'I am exceedingly glad,' wrote Mr. Gladstone to his brother Robertson (July 2), 'to find that Cobden does not take office. It was in his person that there seemed to be the best chance of a favourable trial of the experiment of connecting his friends with the practical administration of the government of this country. I am very glad we have Gibson ; but Cobden would, especially as an addition to the former, have made a great difference in point of weight.'[2]

Mr. Gladstone, with no special anxiety to defend himself, was clear about his own course. 'Never,' he says, 'had I an easier question to determine than when I was asked to join the government. I can hardly now think how I could have looked any one in the face, had I refused my aid (such as it is) at such a time and under such circumstances.' 'At a moment,' he wrote to the warden of All Souls, 'when war is raging in Europe, when the English government is the only instrument through which there is any hope, humanly speaking, of any safe and early settlement, and when all parties agree that the government of the Queen ought to be strengthened, I have joined the only administration that could be formed, in concert with all the friends (setting aside those whom age excludes) with whom I joined and acted in the government of Lord Aberdeen.'

To the provost of Oriel he addressed a rather elaborate explanation,[3] but it only expands what he says more briefly

---

[1] *Life of Cobden*, ii. pp. 229-33.

[2] There is a strange story in the *Halifax Papers* of Bright at this time visiting Lord Aberdeen, and displaying much ill humour. 'He cannot reconcile himself to not being considered capable of taking office. Lord John broached a scheme for sending him as governor-general to Canada. I rather doubted the expediency of this, but Mr. Gladstone seemed to think it not a bad scheme' (June 15, 1859). Many curious things sprang up in men's minds at that moment.

[3] Reproduced in Mr. Russell's book on Mr. Gladstone, pp. 144-5.

in a letter (June 16) to Sir William Heathcote, an excellent and honourable man, his colleague in the representation of Oxford :—

I am so little sensible of having had any very doubtful point to consider, that I feel confident that, given the antecedents of the problem as they clearly stood before me, you would have decided in the way that I have done. For thirteen years, the middle space of life, I have been cast out of party connection, severed from my old party, and loath irrecoverably to join a new one. So long have I adhered to the vague hope of a reconstruction, that I have been left alone by every political friend in association with whom I had grown up. My votes too, and such support as I could give, have practically been given to Lord Derby's government, in such a manner as undoubtedly to divest me of all claims whatever on the liberal party and the incoming government. Under these circumstances I am asked to take office. The two leading points which must determine immediate action are those of reform and foreign policy. On the first I think that Lord Derby had by dissolution lost all chance of settling it ; and, as I desire to see it settled, it seems my duty to assist those who perhaps may settle it. Upon the second I am in real and close harmony of sentiment with the new premier, and the new foreign secretary. How could I, under these circumstances, say, I will have nothing to do with you, and be the one remaining Ishmael in the House of Commons ?

Writing to Sir John Acton in 1864, Mr. Gladstone said :—

When I took my present office in 1859, I had several negative and several positive reasons for accepting it. Of the first, there were these. There had been differences and collisions, but there were no resentments. I felt myself to be mischievous in an isolated position, outside the regular party organisation of parliament. And I was aware of no differences of opinion or tendency likely to disturb the new government. Then on the positive side. I felt sure that in finance there was still much useful work to be done. I was desirous to co-operate in settling the question of the franchise, and failed to anticipate the disaster that it was to undergo. My friends were enlisted, or I knew would enlist : Sir James Graham indeed declining office, but taking his position in the party. And the overwhelming interest and weight of the Italian question, and of our foreign policy in connection with it, joined to my entire mistrust of the former government in relation to it, led me to decide without one moment's hesitation. . . .

On the day on which Mr. Gladstone kissed hands (June 18) disturbing news came from Oxford. Not only was his re-election to be opposed, but the enemy had secured the most formidable candidate that he had yet encountered, in the person of Lord Chandos, the eldest son of the Duke of Buckingham. His London chairman became chairman for his new antagonist, and Stafford Northcote, who with Phillimore and Bernard had hitherto fought every election on his behalf, now refused to serve on his committee, while even Sir John Coleridge was alarmed at some reported wavering on the question of a deceased wife's sister. 'Gladstone, angry, harassed, sore,'

Phillimore records, 'as well he might be.' The provost of Oriel explains to him that men asked whether his very last vote had not been a vote of confidence in a Derby government, and of want of confidence in a Palmerston government, yet he had joined the government in which he declared by anticipation that he had no confidence. After all, the root of the anger against him was simply that the tories were out and the liberals in, with himself as their strongest confederate. A question was raised whether he ought not to go down and address convocation in person. The dean of Christ Church, however, thought it very doubtful whether he would get a hearing. 'Those,' he told Mr. Gladstone, 'who remember Sir Robert Peel's election testify that there never was a more unreasonable and ferocious mob than convocation was at that time. If you were heard, it is doubtful whether you would gain any votes at that last moment, while it is believed you would lose some. You would be questioned as to the ecclesiastical policy of the cabinet. Either you would not be able to answer fully, or you would answer in such terms as to alienate one or other of the two numerous classes who will now give you many votes.'

The usual waterspout began to pour. The newspapers asserted that Mr. Gladstone meant to cut down naval estimates, and this moved the country clergy to angry apprehension that he was for peace at any price. The candidate was obliged to spend thankless hours on letters to reassure them. 'The two assertions of fact respecting me are wholly unfounded. I mean these two:—(1) That as chancellor of the exchequer I "starved" the Crimean war : that is to say limited the expenditure upon it. There is not a shadow of truth in this statement. (2) That as soon as the war was over I caused the government to reduce their estimates, diminish the army, disband two fleets, and break faith with our seamen. When the war was over, that is in the year 1856, I did not take objection at all to the establishment or expenditure of the year. In the next year, 1857, I considered that they ought to have been further reduced : but neither a man nor a shilling was taken from them in consequence of my endeavours.' Other correspondents were uneasy about his soundness on rifle corps and rifle clubs. 'How,' he replied, 'can any uncertainty exist as to the intentions in regard to defence in a government with Lord Palmerston at its head?' He was warned that Cobden, Bright, and Gibson were odious in Oxford, and he was suspected of being their accomplice. The clamour against Puseyism had died down, and the hostility of the evangelicals was no longer keen ; otherwise it was the old story. Goldwin Smith tells him, 'Win or lose, you will have the vote of every one of heart and brain in the university and really connected with it. Young Oxford is all with you. Every year more

men obtain the reward of their industry through your legislation. But old Oxford takes a long time in dying.' In the
end (July 1), he won the battle by a majority of 191—
Gladstone, 1050, Chandos, 859.

'My conscience is light and clear,' he wrote to Heathcote
in the course of the contest. 'The interests that have
weighed with me are in some degree peculiar, and I daresay
it is a fault in me, especially as member for Oxford, that I
cannot merge the man in the representative. While they
have had much reason to complain, I have not had an over-
good bargain. In the estimate of mere pleasure and pain,
the representation of the university is not worth my having;
for though the account is long on both sides, the latter is
the heavier, and sharper. In the true estimates of good and
evil, I can look back upon the past twelve years with some
satisfaction, first, because I feel that as far as I am capable
of labouring for anything, I have laboured for Oxford;
and secondly, because in this respect at least I have been
happy, that the times afforded me in various ways a field.
And even as to the contemptible summing up between
suffering and enjoyment, my belief is that the latter will
endure, while the former will pass away.' The balance struck
in this last sentence is a characteristic fragment of Mr.
Gladstone's philosophy of public life. It lightened and
dispelled the inevitable hours of disappointment and chagrin
that, in natures of less lofty fortitude than his, are apt to
slacken the nerve and rust the sword.

III

It seems a mistake to treat the acceptance of office under
Lord Palmerston as a chief landmark in Mr. Gladstone's protracted journey from tory to liberal. The dilemma between
joining Derby and joining Palmerston was no vital choice
between two political creeds. The new prime minister and his
chancellor of the exchequer had both of them started with
Canning for their common master; but there was a generation
between them, and Mr. Gladstone had travelled along a road
of his own, perhaps not even now perceiving its goal. As we
have seen, he told Mr. Walpole in May 1858 (p. 435), that
there were 'no broad and palpable differences of opinion on
public questions of principle' that separated himself from the
Derbyite tories.[1] Palmerston on the other hand was so much
of a Derbyite tory, that his government, which Mr. Gladstone
was now entering, owed its long spell of office and power

---

[1] It is worth noticing that he sat on the ministerial side of the House without
breach of continuity from 1853 to 1866. During the first Derby government, as we
have already seen (p. 314), he sat below the gangway on the opposition side; during
the Palmerston administration of 1855 he sat below the gangway on the government
side; and he remained there after the second Derby accession to office in 1858.

to the countenance of Derby and his men. Mr. Bright had contemplated (p. 431) the possibility of a reverse process—a Derbyite government favoured by Palmerston's men. In either case, the political identity of the two leaders was recognised. To join the new administration, then, marked a party severance but no changed principles. I am far from denying the enormous significance of the party wrench, but it was not a conversion. Mr. Gladstone was at this time in his politics a liberal reformer of Turgot's type, a born lover of good government, of just practical laws, of wise improvement, of public business well handled, of a state that should emancipate and serve the individual. The necessity of summoning new driving force, and amending the machinery of the constitution, had not yet disclosed itself to him. This was soon discovered by events. Meanwhile he may well have thought that he saw as good a chance of great work with Palmerston as with Disraeli ; or far better, for the election had shown that Bright was not wrong when he warned him that a Derby government could only exist upon forbearance.

Bright's own words already referred to (p. 466) sufficiently describe Mr. Gladstone's point of view ; the need for a ministry with men in it 'acting with some measure of boldness and power, grappling with abuses, and relying upon the moral sense and honest feeling of the House, and the general sympathy of the people of England for improvement.' With such purposes an alliance with liberals of Lord Palmerston's temper implied no wonderful dislodgment. The really great dislodgment in his life had occurred long before. It was the fates that befell his book, it was the Maynooth grant, and the Gorham case, that swept away the foundations on which he had first built. In writing to Manning in 1845 (April 25) after his retirement on the question of Maynooth, Mr. Gladstone says to him, 'Newman sent me a letter giving his own explanation of my position. It was admirably done.' Newman in this letter told him that various persons had asked how he understood Mr. Gladstone's present position, so he put down what he conceived it to be, and he expresses the great interest that he feels in the tone of thought then engaging the statesman's mind :—

I say then [writes Newman, addressing an imaginary interlocutor] :— 'Mr. Gladstone has said the state *ought* to have a conscience, but it has not a conscience. Can *he* give it a conscience ? Is he to impose his own conscience on the state ? He would be very glad to do so, if it thereby would become the state's conscience. But that is absurd. He must deal with facts. It has a thousand consciences, as being in its legislative and executive capacities the aggregate of a hundred minds ; that is, it has no conscience.

'You will say, "Well the obvious thing would be, if the state has not a conscience, that he shall cease to be answerable for it." So he has—he has retired from the ministry. While he thought he could believe it had a conscience—till he was forced to give up, what it was his duty to cherish as long as ever he could, the notion that the British empire was a subject and servant of the kingdom of Christ—he served the state. Now that he finds this to be a mere dream, much as it ought to be otherwise, and as it once was otherwise, he has said, I cannot serve such a mistress.

'But really,' I continue, 'do you in your heart mean to say that he should absolutely and for ever give up the state and country? I hope not. I do not think he has so committed himself. That the conclusion he has come to is a very grave one, and not consistent with his going on blindly in the din and hurry of business, without having principles to guide him, I admit; and this, I conceive, is his reason for at once retiring from the ministry, that he may contemplate the state of things calmly and from without. But I really cannot pronounce, nor can you, nor can he perhaps at once, what is a Christian's duty under these new circumstances, whether to remain in retirement from public affairs or not. Retirement, however, could not be done by halves. If he is absolutely to give up all management of public affairs, he must retire not only from the ministry but from parliament.

'I see another reason for his retiring from the ministry. The public thought they had in his book a pledge that the government would not take such a step with regard to Maynooth as is now before the country. Had he continued in the ministry he would to a certain extent have been misleading the country.

'You say, "He made some show of seeing his way in future, for he gave advice; he said it would be well for all parties to yield something. To see his way and to give advice is as if he had found some principle to go on." I do not so understand him. I thought he distinctly stated he had not yet found a principle. But he gave that advice which facts, or what he called circumstances, made necessary, and which if followed out, will, it is to be hoped, lead to some basis of principle which we do not see at present.'

Compared to the supreme case of conscience indicated here, and it haunted Mr. Gladstone for nearly all his life, the perplexities of party could be but secondary. Those perplexities were never sharper than in the four years from 1854 to 1859; and with his living sense of responsibility for the right use of transcendent powers of national service, it was practically inevitable that he should at last quit the barren position of 'the one remaining Ishmael in the House of Commons.'

IV

Later in this year Mr. Gladstone was chosen to be the first lord rector of the university of Edinburgh under powers conferred by a recent law. His unsuccessful rival was Lord Neaves, excellent as lawyer, humourist, and scholar. In April the following year, in the midst of the most trying session of his life, he went down from the battle-ground at Westminster, and delivered his rectorial address [1]—not particularly pregnant,

---

[1] The Address is in *Gleanings*, vii.

original, or pithy, but marked by incomparable buoyancy ; enforcing a conception of the proper functions of a university that can never be enforced too strongly or too often ; and impressing in melodious period and glowing image those ever-needed commonplaces about thrift of time and thirst for fame and the glory of knowledge, that kindle sacred fire in young hearts. It was his own career, intellectual as well as political, that gave to his discourse momentum. It was his own example that to youthful hearers gave new depth to a trite lesson, when he exclaimed : ' Believe me when I tell you that the thrift of time will repay you in after life with an usury of profit beyond your most sanguine dreams, and that the waste of it will make you dwindle, alike in intellectual and in moral stature, beneath your darkest reckonings.' So too, we who have it all before us know that it was a maxim of his own inner life, when he told them : ' The thirst for an enduring fame is near akin to the love of true excellence ; but the fame of the moment is a dangerous possession and a bastard motive ; and he who does his acts in order that the echo of them may come back as a soft music in his ears, plays false to his noble destiny as a Christian man, places himself in continual danger of dallying with wrong, and taints even his virtuous actions at their source.'

Book V

(1859–1868)

CHAPTER I

THE ITALIAN REVOLUTION

(1859–1860)

Rarely, if ever, in the course of our history has there been such a mixture of high considerations, legislative, military, commercial, foreign, and constitutional, each for the most part traversing the rest, and all capable of exercising a vital influence on public policy, as in the long and complicated session of 1860. The commercial treaty first struck the keynote of the year; and the most deeply marked and peculiar feature of the year was the silent conflict between the motives and provisions of the treaty on the one hand, and the excitement and exasperation of military sentiment on the other.—GLADSTONE.[1]

THIS description extends in truth much beyond the session of a given year to the whole existence of the new cabinet, and through a highly important period in Mr. Gladstone's career. More than that, it directly links our biographic story to a series of events that created kingdoms, awoke nations, and re-made the map of Europe. The opening of this long and complex episode was the Italian revolution. Writing to Sir John Acton in 1864 Mr. Gladstone said to him of the budget of 1860, 'When viewed as a whole, it is one of the few cases in which my fortunes as an individual have been closely associated with matters of a public and even an historic interest.' I will venture to recall in outline to the reader's memory the ampler background of this striking epoch in Mr. Gladstone's public life. The old principles of the European state-system, and the old principles that inspired the vast contentions of ages, lingered but they seemed to have grown decrepit. Divine right of kings, providential pre-eminence of dynasties, balance of power, sovereign independence of the papacy,—these and the other accredited catchwords of history were giving place to the vague, indefinable, shifting, but most potent and inspir-

[1] *Eng. Hist. Rev.*, April 1887, p. 296.

ing doctrine of Nationality. On no statesman of this time did
that fiery doctrine with all its tributaries gain more commanding hold than on Mr. Gladstone. 'Of the various and important
incidents,' he writes in a memorandum, dated Braemar, July 16,
1892, 'which associated me almost unawares with foreign affairs
in Greece (1850), in the Neapolitan kingdom (1851), and in the
Balkan peninsula and the Turkish empire (1853), I will only
say that they all contributed to forward the action of those
home causes more continuous in their operation, which, without in any way effacing my old sense of reverence for the past,
determined for me my place in the present and my direction
towards the future.'

I

At the opening of the seventh decade of the century—ten
years of such moment for our western world—the relations of
the European states with one another had fallen into chaos.
The perilous distractions of 1859-62 were the prelude to conflicts
that after strange and mighty events at Sadowa, Venice, Rome,
Sedan, Versailles, came to their close in 1871. The first breach
in the ramparts of European order set up by the kings after
Waterloo, was the independence of Greece in 1829. Then
followed the transformation of the power of the Turk over
Roumanians and Serbs from despotism to suzerainty. In
1830 Paris overthrew monarchy by divine right; Belgium
cut herself asunder from the supremacy of the Dutch ; then
Italians and Poles strove hard but in vain to shake off the yoke
of Austria and of Russia. In 1848 revolts of race against alien
dominion broke out afresh in Italy and Hungary. The rise of
the French empire, bringing with it the principle or idiosyncrasy
of its new ruler, carried this movement of race into its full
ascendant. Treaties were confronted by the doctrine of
Nationality. What called itself Order quaked before something that for lack of a better name was called the Revolution.
Reason of State was eclipsed by the Rights of Peoples. Such
was the spirit of the new time.

The end of the Crimean war and the peace of Paris brought
a temporary and superficial repose. The French ruler, by
strange irony at once the sabre of Revolution and the trumpet
of Order, made a beginning in urging the constitution of a
Roumanian nationality, by uniting the two Danubian principalities in a single quasi-independent state. This was obviously
a further step towards that partition of Turkey which the
Crimean war had been waged to prevent. Austria for reasons
of her own objected, and England, still in her Turcophil
humour, went with Austria against France for keeping the
two provinces, although in fiscal and military union, politically
divided. According to the fashion of that time—called a
comedy by some, a homage to the democratic evangel by others

—a popular vote was taken. Its result was ingeniously falsified
by the sultan (whose ability to speak French was one of the
odd reasons why Lord Palmerston was sanguine about Turkish
civilisation) ; western diplomacy insisted that the question of
union should be put afresh. Mr. Gladstone, not then in office,
wrote to Lord Aberdeen (Sept. 10, 1857) :—

> The course taken about the Principalities has grieved me. I do not
> mean so much this or that measure, as the principle on which it is to
> rest. I thought we made war in order to keep Russia out, and then
> suffer life, if it would, to take the place of death. But it now seems to
> be all but avowed, that the fear of danger, not to Europe, but to Islam
> —and Islam not from Russia, but from the Christians of Turkey,—is to
> be a ground for stinting their liberties.

In 1858 (May 4) he urged the Derby government to
support the declared wish of the people of Wallachia and
Moldavia, and to fulfil the pledges made at Paris in 1856.
'Surely the best resistance to be offered to Russia,' he said, 'is
by the strength and freedom of those countries that will have
to resist her. You want to place a living barrier between
Russia and Turkey. *There is no barrier like the breast of free-
men.*' The union of the Principalities would raise up antagonists
to the ambitions of Russia more powerful than any that could
be bought with money. The motion was supported by Lord
John Russell and Lord Robert Cecil, but Disraeli and Palmerston
joined in opposing it, and it was rejected by a large majority.
Mr. Gladstone wrote in his diary :—' May 4.—H. of C.—Made
my motion on the Principalities. Lost by 292 : 114 ; and with
it goes another broken promise to a people.' So soon did the
illusions and deceptions of the Crimean war creep forth.

In no long time (1858) Roumania was created into a virtually
independent state. Meanwhile, much against Napoleon's wish
and policy, these proceedings chilled the alliance between
France and England. Other powers grew more and more
uneasy, turning restlessly from side to side, like sick men on
their beds. The object of Russia ever since the peace had been,
first to break down the intimacy between England and France,
by flattering the ambition and enthusiasm of the French
Emperor ; next to wreak her vengeance on Austria for offences
during the Crimean war, still pronounced unpardonable.
Austria, in turn, was far too slow for a moving age ; she
entrenched herself behind forms with too little heed to substance ; and neighbours mistook her dulness for dishonesty.
For the diplomatic air was thick and dark with suspicion.
The rivalry of France and Austria in Italy was the oldest of
European stories, and for that matter the Lombardo-Venetian
province was a possession of material value to Austria, for
while only containing one-eighth of her population, it contributed one-fourth of her revenue.

The central figure upon the European stage throughout the time on which we are now about to enter was the ruler of France. The Crimean war appeared to have strengthened his dynasty at home, while faith in the depth of his political designs and in the grandeur of his military power had secured him predominance abroad. Europe hung upon his words ; a sentence to an ambassador at a public audience on new year's day, a paragraph in a speech at the opening of his parliament of puppets, a pamphlet supposed to be inspired, was enough to shake Vienna, Turin, London, the Vatican, with emotions pitched in every key. Yet the mind of this imposing and mysterious potentate was the shadowy home of vagrant ideals and fugitive chimeras. It was said by one who knew him well, *Scratch the emperor and you will find the political refugee.* You will find, that is to say, the man of fluctuating hope without firm calculation of fact, the man of half-shaped end with no sure eye to means. The sphinx in our modern politics is usually something of a charlatan, and in time the spite of fortune brought this mock Napoleon into fatal conflict with the supple, positive, practical genius of Italy in the person of one of the hardiest representatives of this genius that Italy ever had ; just as ten years later the same nemesis brought him into collision with the stern, rough genius of the north in the person of Count Bismarck. Meanwhile the sovereigns of central and northern Europe had interviews at Stuttgart, at Teplitz, at Warsaw. It was at Warsaw that the rulers of Austria and Prussia met the Czar at the end of 1860,—Poland quivering as she saw the three crowned pirates choose the capital city of their victim for a rendezvous. Russia declined to join in what would have been a coalition against France, and the pope described the conference of Warsaw as three sovereigns assembling to hear one of them communicate to the other two the orders of the Emperor of the French. The French empire was at its zenith. Thiers said that the greatest compensation to a Frenchman for being nothing in his own country, was the sight of that country filling its right place in the world.

The reader will remember that at Turin on his way home from the Ionian Islands in the spring of 1859, Mr. Gladstone saw the statesman who was destined to make Italy. Sir James Hudson, our ambassador at the court of Piedmont, had sounded Cavour as to his disposition to receive the returning traveller. Cavour replied, ' I hope you will do all you can to bring such a proceeding about. I set the highest value on the visit of a statesman so distinguished and such a friend of Italy as Mr. Gladstone.' In conveying this message to Mr. Gladstone (Feb. 7, 1859), Hudson adds, ' I can only say I think your counsels may be very useful to this government, and that I look to your coming here as a means possibly of composing differences, which may, if not handled by some such calm unprejudiced statesman as yourself, lead to very serious disturbances in the European body politic.' Mr. Gladstone dined at Cavour's table at the foreign office, where, among other things, he had the satisfaction of hearing his host speak of Hudson as *quel uomo italianissimo.* Ministers, the president of the chamber, and other distinguished persons were present, and Cavour was well pleased to have the chance of freely opening his position and policy to 'one of the sincerest and most important friends that Italy had.'[1]

Among Cavour's difficulties at this most critical moment was the attitude of England. The government of Lord Derby, true to the Austrian sympathies of his party, and the German sympathies of the court, accused Italy of endangering the peace of Europe. 'No,' said Cavour, 'it is the statesmen, the diplomatists, the writers of England, who are responsible for the troubled situation of Italy ; for is it not they who have worked for years to kindle political passion in our peninsula, and is it not England that has encouraged Sardinia to oppose the propaganda of moral influences to the illegitimate predominance of Austria in Italy?' To Mr. Gladstone, who had seen the Austrian forces in Venetia and in Lombardy, he said, 'You behold for yourself, that it is Austria who menaces us ; here we are tranquil ; the country is calm ; we will do our duty ; England is wrong in identifying peace with the continuance of Austrian domination.' Two or three days later the Piedmontese minister made one of those momentous visits to Paris that forced a will less steadfast than his own.

The French Emperor in his dealings with Cavour had entangled himself, in Mr. Gladstone's phrase, with 'a stronger and better informed intellect than his own.' 'Two men,' said Guizot, 'at this moment divide the attention of Europe, the Emperor Napoleon and Count Cavour. The match has begun. I back Count Cavour.' The game was long and subtly played. It was difficult for the ruler who had risen to power by blood-stained usurpation and the perfidious ruin of a constitution, to keep in step with a statesman, the inspiring purpose of whose life was the deliverance of his country by the magic of freedom. Yet Napoleon was an organ of European revolution in a double sense. He proclaimed the doctrine of nationality, and paid decorous homage to the principle of appeal to the popular voice. In time England appeared upon the scene, and by his flexible management of the two western powers, England and France, Cavour executed the most striking political transformation in the history of contemporary Europe. It brought, however, as Mr. Gladstone speedily found, much trouble into the relations of the two western powers with one another.

The overthrow of the Derby government and the accession of the whigs exactly coincided in time with the struggle

[1] *Il Conte di Cavour. Ricordi biografici.* Per G. Massari (Turin, 1875), p. 204.

between Austria and the Franco-Sardinian allies on the bloody
fields of Magenta and Solferino. A few days after Mr. Gladstone took office, the French and Austrian emperors and King
Victor Emmanuel signed those preliminaries of Villafranca
(July 11, 1859) which summarily ended an inconclusive war by
the union of Lombardy to the Piedmontese kingdom, and the
proposed erection of an Italian federation over which it was
hoped that the pope might preside, and of which Venetia, still
remaining Austrian, should be a member. The scheme was
intrinsically futile, but it served its turn. The Emperor of the
French was driven to peace by mixed motives. The carnage of
Solferino appalled or unnerved him ; he had revealed to his
soldiers and to France that their ruler had none of the genius
of a great commander ; the clerical party at home fiercely
assailed the prolongation of a war that must put the pope
in peril ; the case of Poland, the case of Hungary, might
almost any day be kindled into general conflagration by the
freshly lighted torch of Nationality ; above all, Germany
might stride forward to the Rhine to avenge the repulse of
Austria on the Po and the Mincio.[1]

Whatever the motive, Villafranca was a rude check to Italian
aspirations. Cavour in poignant rage peremptorily quitted
office, rather than share responsibility for this abortive end of
all the astute and deep-laid combinations for ten years past,
that had brought the hated Austrian from the triumph of
Novara down to the defeat of Solferino. Before many months
he once more grasped the helm. In the interval the movement
went forward as if all his political tact, his prudence, his suppleness, his patience, and his daring, had passed into the whole
population of central Italy. For eight months after Villafranca,
it seemed as if the deep and politic temper that built up the
old Roman Commonwealth, were again alive in Bologna, Parma,
Modena, Florence. When we think of the pitfalls that lay on
every side, how easily France might have been irritated or
estranged, what unseasonable questions might not unnaturally
have been forced forward, what mischief the voice and spirit of
the demagogue might have stirred up, there can surely be no
more wonderful case in history of strong and sagacious leaders,
Cavour, Farini, Ricasoli, the Piedmontese king, guiding a people
through the ferments of revolt, with discipline, energy, legality,
order, self-control, to the achievement of a constructive revolution. Without the sword of France the work could not have
been begun ; but it was the people and statesmen of northern
and central Italy who in these eight months made the consummation possible. And England, too, had no inconsiderable
share ; for it was she who secured the principle of non-intervention by foreign powers in Italian affairs ; it was she who
strongly favoured the annexation of central Italy to the new

[1] See *L'Empire Libéral*, by Émile Ollivier, iv. p. 217.

kingdom in the north. Here it was that England directly and unconsciously opened the way to a certain proceeding that when it came to pass she passionately resented. In the first three weeks of March (1860) Victor Emmanuel legalised in due form the annexation of the four central states to Piedmont and Lombardy, and in the latter half of April he made his entry into Florence. Cavour attended him, and strange as it sounds, he now for the first time in his life beheld the famed city,— centre of undying beauty and so many glories in the history of his country and the genius of mankind. In one spot at least his musings might well have been profound—the tomb of Machiavelli, the champion of principles three centuries before, to guide that armed reformer, part fox part lion, who should one day come to raise up an Italy one and independent. The Florentine secretary's orb never quite sets, and it was now rising to a lurid ascendant in the politics of Europe for a long generation to come, lighting up the unblest gospel that whatever policy may demand justice will allow.[1]

On March 24 Cavour paid Napoleon a bitter price for his assent to annexation, by acquiescing in the cession to France of Savoy and Nice, provinces that were, one of them the cradle of the royal race, the other the birthplace of Garibaldi, the hero of the people. In this transaction the theory of the *plébiscite*, or direct popular vote upon a given question, for the first time found a place among the clauses of a diplomatic act. The *plébiscite*, though stigmatized as a hypocritical farce, and often no better than a formal homage paid by violence or intrigue to public right, was a derivative from the doctrines of nationality and the sovereignty of the people then ruling in Europe. The issue of the operation in Savoy and Nice was what had been anticipated. Italy bore the stroke with wise fortitude, but England when she saw the bargain closed for which she had herself prepared the way, took fierce umbrage at the aggrandisement of France, and heavy clouds floated into the European sky. As we have seen, the first act of the extraordinary drama closed at Villafranca. The curtain fell next at Florence upon the fusion of central with upper Italy. Piedmont, a secondary state, had now grown to be a kingdom with eleven or twelve millions of inhabitants. Greater things were yet to follow. Ten millions still remained in the south under the yoke of Bourbons and the Vatican. The third act, most romantic, most picturesque of all, an incomparable union of heroism with policy at double play with all the shifts of circumstance, opened a few weeks later.

The great unsolved problem was the pope. The French ambassador at the Vatican in those days chanced to have had

---

[1] It is a notable thing that in 1859 the provisional government of Tuscany made a decree for the publication of a complete edition of Machiavelli's works at the cost of the state.

diplomatic experience in Turkey. He wrote to his government
in Paris that the pope and his cardinals reminded him of
nothing so much as the sultan and his ulemas—the same
vacillation, the same shifty helplessness, the same stubborn
impenetrability. The Cross seemed in truth as grave a danger
in one quarter of Europe as was the Crescent in another, and the
pope was now to undergo the same course of territorial partition
as had befallen the head of a rival faith. For ten years the
priests had been maintained in their evilly abused authority by
twenty thousand French bayonets—the bayonets of the empire
that the cardinals with undisguised ingratitude distrusted and
hated.[1] The Emperor was eager to withdraw his force, if only
he were sure that no catastrophe would result to outrage the
catholic world and bring down his own throne.

Unluckily for this design, Garibaldi interposed. One night
in May (1860), soon after the annexation to Piedmont of the
four central states, the hero whom an admirer described as
'a summary of the lives of Plutarch,' sailed forth from Genoa
for the deliverance of the Sicilian insurgents. In the eyes of
Garibaldi and his Thousand, Sicily and Naples marked the
path that led to Rome. The share of Cavour as accomplice in
the adventure is still obscure. Whether he even really desired
the acquisition of the Neapolitan kingdom, or would have
preferred, as indeed he attempted, a federation between a
northern kingdom and a southern, is not established. How
far he had made certain of the abstention of Louis Napoleon,
how far he had realised the weakness of Austria, we do not
authentically know. He was at least alive to all the risks
to which Garibaldi's enterprise must instantly expose him in
every quarter of the horizon—from Austria, deeming her hold
upon Venetia at stake; from the French Emperor, with hostile
clericals in France to face; from the whole army of catholics
all over the world; and not least from triumphant Mazzinians,
his personal foes, in whose inspirations he had no faith, whose
success might easily roll him and his policy into mire and ruin.
Now as always with consummate suppleness he confronted the
necessities of a situation that he had not sought, and assuredly
had neither invented nor hurried. The politician, he used to
tell his friends, must above all things have the tact of the
Possible. Well did Manzoni say of him, 'Cavour has all the
prudence and all the imprudence of the true statesman.'
Stained and turbid are the whirlpools of revolution. Yet
the case of Italy was overwhelming. Sir James Hudson wrote
to Mr. Gladstone from Turin (April 3, 1859)—' Piedmont cannot
separate the question of national independence from the
accidental existence of constitutional liberty (in Piedmont) if

---

[1] One of the pope's chamberlains gravely assured the English resident in Rome
that he knew from a sure and trustworthy source that the French Emperor had made
a bargain with the Devil, and frequently consulted him.

she would. Misgovernment in central Italy, heavy taxation
and dearth in Lombardy, misgovernment in Modena, vacillation
in Tuscany, cruelty in Naples, constitute the famous *grido di
dolore*. The congress of Paris wedded Piedmont to the redress
of grievances.'

In August (1860) Garibaldi crossed from Sicily to the mainland and speedily made his triumphant entry into Naples.
The young king Francis withdrew before him at the head of
a small force of faithful adherents to Capua, afterwards to
Gaeta. At the Volturno the Garibaldians, meeting a vigorous
resistance, drove back a force of the royal troops enormously
superior in numbers. On the height of this agitated tide, and
just in time to forestall a fatal movement of Garibaldi upon
Rome, the Sardinian army had entered the territories of the
pope (September 11).

II

In the series of transactions that I have sketched, the
sympathies of Mr. Gladstone never wavered. From the
appearance of his Neapolitan letters in 1851, he lost no opportunity of calling attention to Italian affairs. In 1854 he
brought before Lord Clarendon the miserable condition of
Poerio, Settembrini, and the rest. He took great personal
trouble in helping to raise and invest a fund for the Settembrini family, and elaborate accounts in his own handwriting
remain. In 1855 he wrote to Lord John Russell, then starting
for Vienna, as to a rumour of the adhesion of Naples to the
alliance of the western powers :—'In any case I can conceive
it possible that the Vienna conferences may touch upon Italian
questions ; and I sincerely rely upon your humanity as well
as your love of freedom, indeed the latter is but little in
question, to plead for the prisoners in the kingdom of the two
Sicilies detained for political offences, real or pretended. I do
not ask you to leave any greater duty undone, but to bear in
mind the singular claims on your commiseration of these most
unhappy persons, if occasion offers.'

As we have already seen, it was long before he advanced to
the view of the thoroughgoing school. Like nearly all his
countrymen, he was at first a reformer, not a revolutionary.
To the Marquis Dragonetti, Mr. Gladstone wrote from Broadstairs in 1854 :—

Naples has a government as bad as anarchy ; Rome unites the evils
of the worst government and the most entire anarchy. In those
countries I can hardly imagine any change that would not be for the
better. But in the wild opinions of some of your political sectaries, I
see the best and most available defence of the existing system with its
hideous mischiefs. Almost every Italian who heartily desires the
removal from Italy and from the face of the earth of the immeasurable
evils which your country now suffers through some of its governments,

adopts Italian union and national independence for his watchwords.
. . . Do not think it presumption, for it is the mere description of a
fact, if I say, we in England cannot bring our minds to this mode of
looking at the Italian question. All our habits, all our instincts, all
our history lead us in another direction. In our view this is not building from the bottom upwards, but from the top downwards. . . . All
our experience has been to the effect that the champion of liberty should
take his ground, not upon any remote or abstract proposition, but upon
the right of man, under every law divine and human, first to good
government, and next to the institutions which are the necessary
guarantees of it. . . . We sympathise strongly, I believe, with the
victims of misgovernment, but the English mind is not shocked *in
limine* at the notion of people belonging to one race and language, yet
politically incorporated or associated with another ; and of Italian
unity, I think the language of this nation would be, We shall be glad
if it proves to be feasible, but the condition of it must be gradually
matured by a course of improvement in the several states, and by the
political education of the people ; if it cannot be reached by these
means, it hardly will be by any others ; and certainly not by opinions
which closely link Italian reconstruction with European disorganization
and general war.

So far removed at this date was Mr. Gladstone from the
glorified democracy of the Mazzinian propaganda. He told
Cobden that when he returned from Corfu in the spring of
1859, he found in England not only a government with strong
Austrian leanings, but to his great disappointment not even
the House of Commons so alive as he could have wished upon
the Italian question. 'It was in my opinion the authority and
zeal of Lord Palmerston and Lord John Russell in this question,
that kindled the country.'

While Europe was anxiously watching the prospects of war
between France and Austria, Mr. Gladstone spoke in debate
(April 18, 1859) upon the situation, to express his firm conviction that no plan of peace could be durable which failed to
effect some mitigation of the sore evils afflicting the Italian
peninsula. The course of events after the peace speedily
ripened both his opinions and the sentiment of the country,
and he was as angry as his neighbours at the unexpected preliminaries of Villafranca. 'I little thought,' he wrote to Poerio
(July 15, 1859), 'to have lived to see the day when the conclusion of a peace should in my own mind cause disgust rather
than impart relief. But that day has come. I appreciate all
the difficulties of the position both of the King of Sardinia and
of Count Cavour. It is hardly possible for me to pass a judgment upon his resignation as a political step : but I think few
will doubt that the moral character of the act is high. The
duties of England in respect to the Italian question are limited
by her powers, and these are greatly confined. But her sentiments cannot change, because they are founded upon a regard
to the deepest among those principles which regulate the inter-

course of men and their formation into political societies.' By
the end of the year, he softened his judgment of the proceedings
of the French Emperor.

The heavy load of his other concerns did not absolve him in
his conscience from duty to the Italian cause :—

Jan. 3, 1860.—I sat up till 2 A.M. with my letter to Ld. J. Russell
about Italy, and had an almost sleepless night for it. 4.—2½ hours
with the Prince Consort, *à deux reprises*, about the Italian question,
which was largely stated on both sides. I thought he admitted so
much as to leave him no standing ground. 5.—Went down to Pembroke Lodge and passed the evening with Lord John and his family.
Lord John and I had much conversation on Italy.

In a cabinet memorandum (Jan. 3, 1860), he declared himself
bound in candour to admit that the Emperor had shown,
'though partial and inconsistent, indications of a genuine
feeling for the Italians—and far beyond this he has committed
himself very considerably to the Italian cause in the face of the
world. When in reply to all that, we fling in his face the truce
of Villafranca, he may reply—and the answer is not without
force—that he stood single-handed in a cause when any moment
Europe might have stood combined against him. We gave him
verbal sympathy and encouragement, or at least criticism ; no
one else gave him anything at all. No doubt he showed then
that he had undertaken a work to which his powers were
unequal ; but I do not think that, when fairly judged, he can
be said to have given proof by that measure of insincerity or
indifference.' This was no more than justice, it is even less ;
and both Italians and Englishmen have perhaps been too ready
to forget that the freedom of Italy would have remained an
empty hope if Napoleon III. had not unsheathed his sword.

After discussing details, Mr. Gladstone laid down in his
memorandum a general maxim for the times, that 'the
alliance with France is the true basis of peace in Europe, for
England and France never will unite in any European purpose
which is radically unjust.' He put the same view in a letter
to Lacaita a few months later (Sept. 16) ;—'A close alliance
between England and France cannot be used for mischief, and
cannot provoke any dangerous counter combination ; but a
close alliance between England and other powers would
provoke a dangerous counter combination immediately, besides
that it could not in itself be trusted. My own leaning, therefore, is not indeed to place reliance on the French Emperor,
but to interpret him candidly, and in Italian matters especially
to recollect the great difficulties in which he is placed, (1)
because, whether by his own fault or not, he cannot reckon
upon strong support from England when he takes a right
course. (2) Because he has his own ultramontane party in
France to deal with, whom, especially if not well supported
abroad, he cannot afford to defy.'

As everybody soon saw, it was the relation of Louis Napoleon to the French ultramontanes that constituted the tremendous hazard of the Piedmontese invasion of the territories of the pope. This critical proceeding committed Cavour to a startling change, and henceforth he was constrained to advance to Italian unity. A storm of extreme violence broke upon him. Gortchakoff said that if geography had permitted, the Czar would betake himself to arms in defence of the Bourbon king. Prussia talked of reviving the holy alliance in defence of the law of nations against the overweening ambition of Piedmont. The French ambassador was recalled from Turin. Still no active intervention followed.

One great power alone stood firm, and Lord John Russell wrote one of the most famous despatches in the history of our diplomacy (October 27, 1860). The governments of the pope and the king of the Two Sicilies, he said, provided so ill for the welfare of their people, that their subjects looked to their overthrow as a necessary preliminary to any improvement. Her Majesty's government were bound to admit that the Italians themselves are the best judges of their own interests. Vattel, that eminent jurist, had well said that when a people for good reasons take up arms against an oppressor, it is but an act of justice and generosity to assist brave men in the defence of their liberties. Did the people of Naples and the Roman States take up arms against their government for good reasons? Upon this grave matter, her Majesty's government held that the people in question are themselves the best judges of their own affairs. Her Majesty's government did not feel justified in declaring that the people of Southern Italy had not good reasons for throwing off their allegiance to their former governments. Her Majesty's government, therefore, could not pretend to blame the King of Sardinia for assisting them. So downright was the language of Lord John. We cannot wonder that such words as these spread in Italy like flame, that people copied the translation from each other, weeping over it for joy and gratitude in their homes, and that it was hailed as worth more than a force of a hundred thousand men.[1]

The sensation elsewhere was no less profound, though very different. The three potentates at Warsaw viewed the despatch with an emotion that was diplomatically called regret, but more resembled horror. The Prince Regent of Prussia, afterwards the Emperor William, told Prince Albert that it was a tough morsel, a disruption of the law of nations and of the holy ties that bind peoples to their sovereigns.[2] Many in England were equally shocked. Even Sir James Graham, for instance, said that he would never have believed that such a document could have passed through a British cabinet or received the approval of a British sovereign; India, Ireland,

Canada would await the application of the fatal doctrine that it contained ; it was a great public wrong, a grave error ; and even Garibaldi and Mazzini would come out of the Italian affair with cleaner hands. Yet to-day we may ask ourselves, was it not a little idle to talk of the holy ties that bind nations to their sovereigns, in respect of a system under which in Naples thousands of the most respectable of the subjects of the king were in prison or in exile ; in the papal states ordinary justice was administered by rough-handed German soldiers, and young offenders shot by court-martial at the drumhead ; and in the Lombardo-Venetian provinces press offences were judged by martial law, with chains, shooting, and flogging for punishment.[1] Whatever may be thought of Lord John and his doctrine, only those who hold to the converse doctrine, that subjects may never rise against a king, nor ever under any circumstances seek succour from foreign power, will deny that the cruelties of Naples and the iniquities connected with the temporal authority of the clergy in the states of the church, constituted an irrefragable case for revolt.

Within a few weeks after the troops of Victor Emmanuel had crossed the frontier (Sept. 1860), the papal forces had been routed, and a popular vote in the Neapolitan kingdom supported annexation to Piedmont. The papal states, with the exception of the patrimony of St. Peter in the immediate neighbourhood of Rome itself, fell into the hands of the king. Victor Emmanuel and Garibaldi rode into Naples side by side (Nov. 7). The Bourbon flag after a long stand was at last lowered at the stronghold of Gaeta (Feb. 14, 1861) ; the young Bourbon king became an exile for the rest of his life ; and on February 18 the first parliament of united Italy assembled at Turin—Venice and Rome for a short season still outside. A few months before, Mr. Gladstone had written a long letter to d'Azeglio. It was an earnest exposition of the economic and political ideas that seemed to shine in the firmament above a nation now emerging from the tomb. The letter was to be shown to Cavour. 'Tell that good friend of ours,' he replied, 'that our trade laws are the most liberal of the continent ; that for ten years we have been practising the maxims that he exhorts us to adopt ; tell him that he preaches to the converted.'[2] Then one of those disasters happened that seem to shake the planetary nations out of their pre-appointed orbits. Cavour died.[3]

[1] A *General Review of the Different States of Italy* ; prepared for the Foreign Office by Sir Henry Bulwer, January 1853.

[2] Cavour to Marquis d'Azeglio, Dec. 9, 1860. *La Politique du Comte Camille de Cavour de 1852, à 1861*, p. 392.

[3] June 6, 1861.

CHAPTER II

THE GREAT BUDGET

(1860-1861)

It was said that by this treaty the British nation was about blindly to throw herself into the arms of this constant and uniform foe. . . . Did it not much rather, by opening new sources of wealth, speak this forcible language—that the interval of peace, as it would enrich the nation, would also prove the means of enabling her to combat her enemy with more effect when the day of hostility should come? It did more than this ; by promoting habits of friendly intercourse and of mutual benefit, while it invigorated the resources of Britain, it made it less likely that she should have occasion to call forth these resources.—PITT (February 12, 1787).

As we survey the panorama of a great man's life, conspicuous peaks of time and act stand out to fix the eye, and in our statesman's long career the budget of 1860 with its spurs of appendant circumstance, is one of these commanding points. In the letter to Acton already quoted (p. 474), Mr. Gladstone says :—

Before Parliament met in 1860, the 'situation' was very greatly *tightened* and *enhanced* by three circumstances. First, the disaster in China.[1] Secondly, a visit of Mr. Cobden's to Hawarden, when he proposed to me in a garden stroll, the French treaty, and I, for myself and my share, adopted it (nor have I ever for a moment repented or had a doubt) as rapidly as the tender of office two months before. Thirdly, and the gravest of all, the Savoy affair. If, as is supposed, I have Quixotism in my nature, I can assure you that I was at this juncture much more than satiated, and could have wished with Penelope that the whirlwind would take me up, and carry me to the shore of the great stream of Ocean.[2] And the wish would in this point not have been extravagant : the whirlwind was there ready to hand. In and from the midst of it was born the budget of 1860.

The financial arrangements of 1859 were avowedly pro-

[1] The disaster was the outcome of the Chinese refusal to receive Mr. Bruce, the British minister at Pekin. Admiral Hope in endeavouring to force an entrance to the Peiho river was repulsed by the fire of the Chinese forts (June 25, 1859). In the following year a joint Anglo-French expedition captured the Taku forts and occupied Pekin (Oct. 12, 1860).

[2] *Odyssey*, xx. 63.

visional and temporary, and need not detain us. The only feature was a rise in the income tax from fivepence to nine-pence—its highest figure so far in a time of peace. 'My budget,' he wrote to Mrs. Gladstone (July 16), 'is just through the cabinet, very kindly and well received, no one making objection but Lewis, who preached low doctrine. It confirms me in the belief I have long had, that he was fitter for most other offices than for that I now hold.' '*July* 21 *or rather* 22, *one a.m.*—Just come back from a long night and stiff con-tention at the House of Commons. . . . It has been rather nice and close fighting. Disraeli made a popular motion to trip me up, but had to withdraw it, at any rate for the time. This I can say, it was not so that I used him. I am afraid that the truce between us is over, and that we shall have to pitch in as before.'

The only important speech was one on Italy (August 8),[1] of which Disraeli said that though they were always charmed by the speaker's eloquence, this was a burst of even unusual brilliance, and it gave pleasure in all quarters. 'Spoke for an *oretta* [short hour],' says the orator, 'on Italian affairs ; my best offhand speech.' 'The fish dinner,' Mr. Gladstone writes, 'went off very well, and I think my proposing Lord Palmer-ston's health (without speech) was decidedly approved. I have had a warm message from Lord Lansdowne about my speech ; and Lord P. told me that on Tuesday night as he went upstairs on getting home he heard Lady P. spouting as she read by candle-light ; it turned out to be the same effusion.'

Another incident briefly related to Mrs. Gladstone, brings us on to more serious ground :—'*Hawarden, Sept.* 12.—Cobden came early. Nothing could be better than the luncheon, but I am afraid the dinner will be rather strong with local clergy. I have had a walk and long talk with Cobden who, I think, pleases and is pleased.' This was the garden walk of which we have just heard, where Cobden, the ardent hopeful sower, scattered the good seed into rich ground. The idea of a com-mercial treaty with France was in the air. Bright had opened it, Chevalier had followed it up, Persigny agreed, Cobden made an opportunity, Gladstone seized it. Cobden's first suggestion had been that as he was about to spend a part of the winter in Paris, he might perhaps be of use to Mr. Gladstone in the way of inquiry. Conversation expanded this into something more definite and more energetic. Why should he not, with the informal sanction of the British government, put himself into communication with the Emperor and his ministers, and work out with them the scheme of a treaty that should at once open the way to a great fiscal reform in both countries, and in both countries produce a solid and sterling pacification of feeling.

[1] On a motion by Lord Elcho against any participation in a conference to settle the details of the peace between Austria and France.

Cobden saw Palmerston and tried to see Lord John Russell, and though he hardly received encouragement, at least he was not forbidden to proceed upon his volunteered mission.[1] 'Gladstone,' wrote Cobden to Mr. Bright, 'is really almost the only cabinet minister of five years' standing who is not afraid to let his heart guide his head a little at times.' The Emperor had played with the idea of a more open trade for five or six years, and Cobden, with his union of economic, moral, and social elements, and his incomparable gifts of argumentative persuasion, was the very man to strike Napoleon's impressionable mind. Although, having alienated the clericals by his Italian policy, the ruler of France might well have hesitated before proceeding to alienate the protectionists also, he became a convert and did not shrink.

'Both Cobden and I,' says Mr. Gladstone, 'were keenly in favour of such a treaty (I myself certainly), without intending thereby to signify the smallest disposition to the promotion of tariff treaties in general. I had been an active party to the various attempts under Sir Robert Peel's government to conclude such treaties, and was as far as possible removed from any disposition to the renewal of labour which was in itself so profitless, and which was dangerously near to a practical assertion of a false principle, namely that the reductions of indirect taxation, permitted by fiscal considerations, are in themselves injurious to the country that makes them, and are only to be entertained when a compensation can be had for them.[2] . . . The correspondence which would in the ordinary course have been exchanged between the foreign offices of the two countries, was carried through in a series of personal letters between Mr. Cobden and myself. I remember indeed that the Emperor or his government were desirous to conceal from their own foreign minister (Walewski) the fact that such a measure was in contemplation. On our side, the method pursued was only recommended by practical considerations. I contemplated including the conditions of the French treaty in a new and sweeping revision of the tariff, the particulars of which it was of course important to keep from the public eye until they were ready to be submitted to parliament.'

At the end of 1859 the question of the treaty was brought into the cabinet, and there met with no general opposition, though some objection was taken by Lewis and Wood, based on the ground that they ought not to commit themselves by treaty engagements to a sacrifice of revenue, until they had before them the income and the charges of the year. Writing to his

---

[1] I may be forgiven for referring to my *Life of Cobden*, ii. chap. xi. For the French side of the transaction, see an interesting chapter in De La Gorce, *Hist. du Second Empire*, iii. pp. 213-32.

[2] 'I will undertake that there is not a syllable on our side of the treaty that is inconsistent with the soundest principles of free trade. We do not propose to reduce a duty which, on its merits, ought not to have been dealt with long ago. We give no concessions to France which do not apply to all other nations. We leave ourselves free to lay on any amount of internal duties and to put on an equal tax on foreign articles of the same kind at the custom-house. It is true we bind ourselves for ten years not otherwise to raise such of our customs as affect the French trade, or put on fresh ones; and this, I think, no true free trader will regret.'—*Cobden to Bright.*

wife about some invitation to a country house, Mr. Gladstone says (Jan. 11, 1860) :—

> I cannot go without a clear sacrifice of public duty. For the measure is of immense importance and of no less nicety, and here it all depends on me. Lord John backs me most cordially and well, but it is no small thing to get a cabinet to give up one and a half or two millions of revenue at a time when all the public passion is for enormous expenditure, and in a case beset with great difficulties. In *fact*, a majority of the cabinet is indifferent or averse, but they have behaved very well. I almost always agree with Lewis on other matters, but in trade and finance I do not find his opinions satisfactory. Till it is through, this vital question will need my closest and most anxious attention. [Two days later he writes :—] The cabinet has been again on the French treaty. There are four or five zealous, perhaps as many who would rather be without it. It has required pressure, but we have got sufficient power now, if the French will do what is reasonable. Lord John has been excellent, Palmerston rather neutral. It is really a great European operation. [A fortnight later (*Jan.* 28) :—] A word to say I have opened the fundamental parts of my budget in the cabinet, and that I could not have hoped a better reception. Nothing decided, for I did not ask it, and indeed the case was not complete, but there was no general [resistance], no decided objection ; the tone of questioning was favourable, Granville and Argyll delighted, Newcastle, I think, ditto. Thank God.
>
> *To Cobden, Jan.* 28.—Criticism is busy ; but the only thing really formidable is the unavowed but strong conflict with that passionate expectation of war, which no more bears disappointment than if it were hope or love. *Feb.* 6.—Cobbett once compared an insignificant public man in an important situation to the linch-pin in the carriage, and my position recalls his very apt figure to my mind.

Of course in his zeal for the treaty and its connection with tariff reform, Mr. Gladstone believed that the operation would open a great volume of trade and largely enrich the country. But in one sense this was the least of it :-

> I had a reason of a higher order. The French Emperor had launched his project as to Savoy and Nice. It should have been plain to all those who desired an united Italy, that such an Italy ought not to draw Savoy in its wake ; a country severed from it by the mountains, by language, by climate, and I suppose by pursuits. But it does not follow that Savoy should have been tacked on to France, while for the annexation of Nice it was difficult to find a word of apology. But it could scarcely be said to concern our interests, while there was not the shadow of a case of honour. The susceptibilities of England were, however, violently aroused. Even Lord Russell used imprudent language in parliament about looking for other allies. A French panic prevailed as strong as any of the other panics that have done so much discredit to this country. For this panic, the treaty of commerce with France was the only sedative. It was in fact a counter-irritant ; and it aroused the sense of commercial interest to counteract the war passion. It was and is my opinion, that the choice lay between the Cobden treaty and not the certainty, but the high probability, of a war with France. (*Undated memo.*)

II

Out of the commercial treaty grew the whole of the great financial scheme of 1860. By his first budget Mr. Gladstone had marked out this year for a notable epoch in finance. Happily it found him at the exchequer. The expiry of certain annuities payable to the public creditor removed a charge of some two millions, and Mr. Gladstone was vehemently resolved that this amount should not 'pass into the great gulf of expenditure there to be swallowed up.' If the year, in such circumstances, is to pass, he said to Cobden, 'without anything done for trade and the masses, it will be a great discredit and a great calamity.' The alterations of duty required for the French treaty were made possible by the lapse of the annuities, and laid the foundation of a plan that averted the discredit and calamity of doing nothing for trade, and nothing for the masses of the population. France engaged to reduce duties and remove prohibitions on a long list of articles of British production and export, iron the most important,—'the daily bread of all industries,' as Cobden called it. England engaged immediately to abolish all duties upon all manufactured articles at her ports, and to reduce the duties on wine and brandy. The English reductions and abolitions extended beyond France to the commodities of all countries alike. Mr. Gladstone called 1860 the last of the cardinal and organic years of emancipatory fiscal legislation; it ended a series of which the four earlier terms had been reached in 1842, in 1845, in 1846, and 1853. With the French treaty, he used to say, the movement in favour of free trade reached its zenith.

The financial fabric that rose from the treaty was one of the boldest of all his achievements, and the reader who seeks to take the measure of Mr. Gladstone as financier, in comparison with any of his contemporaries in the western world, will find in this fabric ample material.[1] Various circumstances had led to an immense increase in national expenditure. The structure of warships was revolutionised by the use of iron in place of wood. It was a remarkable era in artillery, and guns were urgently demanded of new type. In the far East a quarrel had broken out with the Chinese. The threats of French officers after the plot of Orsini had bred a sense of insecurity in our own borders. Thus more money than ever was required; more than ever economy was both unpopular and difficult. The annual estimates stood at seventy millions; when Mr. Gladstone framed his famous budget seven years before, that charge stood at fifty-two millions. If the sole object of a chancellor of the exchequer be to balance his account, Mr. Gladstone might have contented himself with keeping the

[1] The reader who wishes to follow these proceedings in close detail will, of course, read the volume of *The Financial Statements* of 1853, 1860-63, containing also the speech on tax-bills, 1861, and on charities, 1863. (Murray, 1863.)

income-tax and duties on tea and sugar as they were, meeting the remissions needed by the French treaty out of the sum released by the expiry of the long annuities. Or he might have reduced tea and sugar to a peace rate, and raised the income-tax from ninepence to a shilling. Instead of taking this easy course, Mr. Gladstone after having relinquished upwards of a million for the sake of the French treaty, now further relinquished nearly a million more for the sake of releasing 371 articles from duties of customs, and a third million in order to abolish the vexatious excise duty upon the manufacture of paper. Nearly one million of all this loss he recouped by the imposition of certain small charges and minor taxes, and by one or two ingenious expedients of collection and account, and the other two millions he made good out of the lapsed annuities. Tea and sugar he left as they were, and the income-tax he raised from ninepence to tenpence. Severe economists, not quite unjustly called these small charges a blot on his escutcheon. Time soon wiped it off, for in fact they were a failure.

The removal of the excise duty upon paper proved to be the chief stumbling-block, and ultimately it raised more excitement than any other portion of the scheme. The fiscal project became by and by associated with a constitutional struggle between Lords and Commons. In the Commons the majority in favour of abolishing the duty sank from fifty-three to nine ; troubles with China caused a demand for new expenditure ; the yield from the paper duty was wanted ; and the Lords finding in all this a plausible starting-point for a stroke of party business, or for the assertion of the principle that to reject a repealing money bill was not the same thing as to meddle with a bill putting on a tax, threw it out. Then when the Lords had rejected the bill, many who had been entirely cool about taking off the 'taxes upon knowledge'—for this unfavourable name was given to the paper duty by its foes—rose to exasperation at the thought of the peers meddling with votes of money. All this we shall see as we proceed.

This was the broad outline of an operation that completed the great process of reducing articles liable to customs duties from 1052, as they stood in 1842 when Peel opened the attack upon them ; from 466, as Mr. Gladstone found them in 1853 ; and from 419, as he found them now, down to 48, at which he now left them.[1] Simplification had little further to go. 'Why did you not wait,' he was asked, 'till the surplus came, which notwithstanding all drawbacks you got in 1863, and then

---

[1] Strictly speaking, in 1845 the figure had risen from 1052 to 1163 articles, for the first operation of tariff reform was to multiply the number in consequence of the transition from *ad valorem* to specific duties, and this increased the headings under which they were described. In 1860 Mr. Gladstone removed the duties from 371 articles, reducing the number to 48, of which only 15 were of importance—spirits, sugar, tea, tobacco, wine, coffee, corn, currants, timber, chicory, figs, hops, pepper, raisins, and rice.

operate in a quiet way, without disturbing anybody ?'[1] His answer was that the surplus would not have come at all, because it was created by his legislation. 'The principle adopted,' he said, 'was this. We are now (1860) on a high table-land of expenditure. This being so, it is not as if we were merely meeting an occasional and momentary charge. We must consider how best to keep ourselves going during a *period* of high charge. In order to do that, we will aggravate a momentary deficiency that we may thereby make a *great and permanent addition to productive power.*' This was his ceaseless refrain—the steadfast pursuit of the durable enlargement of productive power as the commanding aim of high finance.

III

At the beginning of the year the public expectation was fixed upon Lord John Russell as the protagonist in the approaching battle of parliamentary reform, and the eager partisans at the Carlton Club were confident that on reform they would pull down the ministry. The partisans of another sort assure us that 'the whole character of the session was changed by Mr. Gladstone's invincible resolution to come forward in spite of his friends, and in defiance of his foes, for his own *aristeia* or innings.' The explanation is not good-natured, and we know that it is not true ; but what is true is that when February opened, the interest of the country had become centred at its highest pitch in the budget and the commercial treaty. As the day for lifting the veil was close at hand, Mr. Gladstone fell ill, and here again political benevolence surmised that his disorder was diplomatic. An entry or two from Phillimore's journal will bring him before us as he was :—

Jan. 29.—Gladstone's emaciation in the past fortnight alarms me, as it has, I find, many other persons. *Feb.* 5.—Gladstone seriously ill ; all the afternoon in Downing Street ; a slight congestion of the lungs. Great treaty and financial speech put off till Thursday. Was to have been to-morrow. Gladstone wished to see me, but I would only stay a minute by his bedside. He looked very pale. He must not speak for ten days, or Ferguson (his doctor) said, he will meet Canning's fate. *Feb.* 6. —With Gladstone in the evening. He is still in bed, but visibly better. *Feb.* 7.—With Gladstone a long time in the morning. Found him much better though still in bed. Annoyed at the publication of the new treaty with France in the Belgian papers, it being part of the scheme of his finance measure. *Feb.* 8.—Gladstone drove out to-day ; bent on speaking the day after to-morrow. Ferguson allows him. I again protested. *Feb.* 9.—Saw Gladstone ; he is better. But I am frightened at the proposed exertion of Friday. *Feb.* 10.—Saw Gladstone in the morning, radiant with expected success, and again at night at 10 o'clock in Downing Street still more radiant with triumph. Spoke for three hours and fifty

---

[1] See an interesting letter to Sir W. Heathcote in reply to other criticisms, in Appendix.

minutes without suffering. Thinks that the House will accept all that is material in his finance scheme. *Feb.* 13.—Dined with Gladstone ; ordered not to leave the house this week. *Feb.* 25.—Called on the Gladstones at breakfast time. Found them both exceedingly happy at the immense majority of 116 which affirmed last night the principle of his grand budget.[1] His hard dry cough distresses me. Gladstone thinks he has done what Pitt would have done but for the French Revolution. With characteristic modesty he said, 'I am a dwarf on the shoulders of a giant.'

Mr. Gladstone's own entries are these :—

Feb. 10, '60.—Spoke 5-9 without great exhaustion; aided by a great stock of egg and wine. Thank God! Home at 11. This was the most arduous operation I have ever had in parliament. *March* 9.—Spoke on various matters in the Treaty debate ; voted in 282 : 56 ; a most prosperous ending to a great transaction in which I heartily thank God for having given me a share. *March* 23.—A long day of 16½ hours' work.

Of the speech in which the budget was presented everybody agreed that it was one of the most extraordinary triumphs ever witnessed in the House of Commons. The casual delay of a week had raised expectation still higher ; hints dropped by friends in the secret had added to the general excitement ; and as was truly said by contemporaries, suspense that would have been fatal to mediocrity actually served Mr. Gladstone. Even the censorious critics of the leading journal found in the largeness and variety of the scheme its greatest recommendation, as suggesting an accord between the occasion, the man, and the measure, so marvellous that it would be a waste of all three not to accept them. Among other hearers was Lord Brougham, who for the first time since he had quitted the scene of his triumphs a generation before, came to the House of Commons, and for four hours listened intently to the orator who had now acquired the supremacy that was once his own. 'The speech,' said Bulwer, 'will remain among the monuments of English eloquence as long as the language lasts.' Napoleon begged Lord Cowley to convey his thanks to Mr. Gladstone for the copy of his budget speech he had sent him, which he said he would preserve 'as a precious souvenir of a man who has my thorough esteem, and whose eloquence is of a lofty character commensurate with the grandeur of his views.' Prince Albert wrote to Stockmar (March 17), 'Gladstone is now the real leader of the House, and works with an energy and vigour almost incredible.'[2]

Almost every section of the trading and political community looked with favour upon the budget as a whole, though it was true that each section touched by it found fault with its own part. Mr. Gladstone said that they were without exception

---

[1] On Mr. Duncan's resolution against adding to an existing deficiency by diminishing ordinary revenue and against re-imposing the income-tax at an unnecessarily high rate. *Moved Feb.* 21.

[2] Martin's *Life of Prince Consort*, v. pp. 35, 37, 51.

free traders, but not free traders without exception. The magnitude and comprehensiveness of the enterprise seized the imagination of the country. At the same time it multiplied sullen or uneasy interests. The scheme was no sooner launched, than the chancellor of the exchequer was overwhelmed by deputations. Within a couple of days he was besieged by delegates from the paper makers ; distillers came down upon him ; merchants interested in the bonding system, wholesale stationers, linen manufacturers, maltsters, licensed victuallers, all in turn thronged his ante-room. He was now, says Greville (Feb. 15), '*the* great man of the day!' The reduction of duties on currants created lively excitement in Greece, and Mr. Gladstone was told that if he were to appear there he could divide honours with Bacchus and Triptolemus, the latest benefactors of that neighbourhood.

Political onlookers with whom the wish was not alien to their thought, soon perceived that in spite of admiration for splendid eloquence and incomparable dexterity, it would not be all sunshine and plain sailing. At a very early moment the great editor of the *Times* went about saying that Gladstone would find it hard work to get his budget through ; if Peel with a majority of ninety needed it all to carry his budget, what would happen to a government that could but command a majority of nine ?[1] Both the commercial treaty and the finance speedily proved to have many enemies. Before the end of March Phillimore met a parliamentary friend who like everybody else talked of Gladstone, and confirmed the apprehension that the whigs obeyed and trembled and were frightened to death. 'We don't know where he is leading us,' said Hayter, who had been whipper-in. On the last day of the month Phillimore enters : '*March* 30—Gladstone has taken his name off the Carlton, which I regret. It is a marked and significant act of entire separation from the *whole* party and will strengthen Disraeli's hands. The whigs hate Gladstone. The moderate conservatives and the radicals incline to him. The old tories hate him.' For reasons not easy to trace, a general atmosphere of doubt and unpopularity seemed suddenly to surround his name.

The fortunes of the budget have been succinctly described by its author :—

They were chequered, and they were peculiar in this, that the first blow struck was delivered by one of the best among its friends. Lord John Russell, keenly alive to the discredit of any tampering as in former years with the question of the franchise, insisted on introducing his Reform bill on March 1, when the treaty and the financial proposals of the year, numerous and complex as they were, had not proceeded beyond their early stages. This was in flat violation of a rule of Lord Bacon's, even more weighty now than in his time, which Sir James Graham was

[1] Greville, III. ii. p. 291.

fond of quoting : 'Never overlap business.' The enemies of the treaty were thus invited to obstruct it through prolonged debating on reform, and the enemies of reform to discharge a corresponding office by prolonged debating on the finance. A large majority of the House were in disguised hostility to the extension of the franchise. The discussions on it were at once protracted, intermittent, and languid. No division was taken against it. It was defeated by the pure *vis inertiæ* of the House skilfully applied : and it was withdrawn on June 11. But it had done its work, by delaying the *tail* of the financial measures until a time when the marriage effected by the treaty between England and France had outlived its parliamentary honeymoon. There had intervened the Savoy and Nice explosion ; settlement with China was uncertain ; the prospects of the harvest were bad ; French invasion was apprehended by many men usually rational. The Paper Duty bill, which would have passed the Commons by a large majority in the beginning of March, only escaped defeat on May 8 by a majority of nine.[1]

When Lord John had asked the cabinet to stop the budget in order to fix a day for his second reading, Mr. Gladstone enters in an autobiographic memorandum of his latest years [2] :—

I said to him, 'Lord John, I will go down on my knees to you, to entreat you not to press that request.' But he persevered ; and this although he was both a loyal colleague and a sincere friend to the budget and to the French treaty. When reform was at last got rid of, in order to prosecute finance we had much to do, and in the midst of it there came upon us the news of hostilities in China, which demanded at once an increase of outlay . . . sufficient to destroy my accruing balance, and thus to disorganize the finance of the year. The opposition to the Paper bill now assumed most formidable dimensions. . . . During a long course of years there had grown up in the House of Commons a practice of finally disposing of the several parts of the budget each by itself. And the House of Lords had shown so much self-control in confining itself to criticism on matters of finance, that the freedom of the House of Commons was in no degree impaired. But there was the opportunity of mischief; and round the carcass the vultures now gathered in overwhelming force. It at once became clear that the Lords would avail themselves of the opportunity afforded them by the single presentation of financial bills, and would prolong, and virtually re-enact a tax, which the representatives of the people had repealed.

On May 5 the diary reports :—'Cabinet. Lord Palmerston spoke ¾ hour against Paper Duties bill ! I had to reply. Cabinet against him, except a few, Wood and Cardwell in particular. Three wild schemes of foreign alliance are afloat ! Our old men (2) are unhappily our youngest.' Palmerston not only spoke against the bill, as he had a right in cabinet to do, but actually wrote to the Queen that he was bound in duty to say that if the Lords threw out the bill—the bill of his own cabinet—'they would perform a good public service.' [3]

Phillimore's notes show that the intense strain was telling

---

[1] *Eng. Hist. Rev.* April 1887, p. 301.   The majority in the Lords was 193 to 104.
[2] Aug. 31, 1897.   [3] Martin, v. p. 100.

on his hero's physical condition, though it only worked his resolution to a more undaunted pitch :—

May 9.—Found Gladstone in good spirits in spite of the narrow majority on the paper duty last night, but ill with a cough. *May* 15. —The whigs out of office, and perhaps in, abusing Gladstone and lauding G. Lewis. I had much conversation with Walpole. Told me he, Henley, and those who went with them would have followed Gladstone if he had not joined this government, but added he was justified in doing so. *May* 18.—Gladstone is *ill* ; vexed and *indignant* at the possible and probable conduct of the peers on Monday. Nothing will prevent him from denouncing them in the Commons, if they throw out the paper bill, as having violated in substance and practically the constitution. Meanwhile his unpopularity flows on.

IV

The rejection of the bill affecting the paper duty by the Lords was followed by proceedings set out by Mr. Gladstone in one of his political memoranda, dated May 26, 1860 :—

Though I seldom have time to note the hairbreadth 'scapes of which so many occur in these strange times and with our strangely constructed cabinet, yet I must put down a few words with respect to the great question now depending between the Lords and the English nation. On Sunday, when it was well known that the Paper Duties bill would be rejected, I received from Lord John Russell a letter which enclosed one to him from Lord Palmerston. Lord Palmerston's came in sum to this : that the vote of the Lords would not be a party vote, that as to the *thing done* it was right, that we could not help ourselves, that we should simply acquiesce, and no minister ought to resign. Lord John in his reply to this, stated that he took a much more serious view of the question and gave reasons. Then he went on to say that though he did not agree in the grounds stated by Lord Palmerston, he would endeavour to arrive at the same conclusion. His letter accordingly ended with practical acquiescence. And he stated to me his concurrence in Lord Palmerston's closing proposition.

Thereupon I wrote an immediate reply. We met in cabinet to consider the case. Lord Palmerston started on the line he had marked out. I think he proposed to use some meaningless words in the House of Commons as to the value we set on our privileges, and our determination to defend them if attacked, by way of garniture to the act of their abandonment. Upon this I stated my opinions, coming to the point that this proceeding of the House of Lords amounted to the establishment of a revising power over the House of Commons in its most vital function long declared exclusively its own, and to a divided responsibility in fixing the revenue and charge of the country for the year ; besides aggravating circumstances upon which it was needless to dwell. In this proceeding nothing would induce me to acquiesce, though I earnestly desired that the mildest means of correction should be adopted. This was strongly backed in principle by Lord John ; who thought that as public affairs would not admit of our at once confining ourselves to this subject, we should take it up the first thing next session, and send up a new bill. Practical, as well as other, objections were taken to this

mode of proceeding, and opposition was continued on the merits; Lord
Palmerston keen and persevering. He was supported by the Chancellor,
Wood, Granville (in substance), Lewis, and Cardwell, who thought
nothing could be done, but were ready to join in resigning if thought
fit. Lord John, Gibson, and I were for decided action. Argyll leaned
the same way. Newcastle was for inquiry to end in a declaratory
resolution. Villiers thought some step necessary. Grey argued mildly,
inclined I think to inaction. Herbert advised resignation, opposed any
other course. Somerset was silent, which I conceive meant inaction.
At last Palmerston gave in, and adopted with but middling grace the
proposition to set out with inquiries, and with the intention to make as
little of the matter as he could.

His language in giving notice, on Tuesday, of the committee went
near the verge of saying, We mean nothing. An unsatisfactory impression was left on the House. Not a syllable was said in recognition
of the gravity of the occasion. Lord John had unfortunately gone away
to the foreign office. I thought I should do mischief at that stage by
appearing to catch at a part in the transaction. Yesterday all was
changed by the dignified declaration of Lord John. I suggested to him
that he should get up, and Lord Palmerston, who had intended to keep
the matter in his own hands, gave way. But Lord Palmerston was
uneasy and said, 'You won't pitch it into the Lords,' and other things
of the same kind. On the whole, I hope that in this grave matter at
least we have turned the corner.

As we know, even the fighting party in the cabinet was
forced to content itself for the moment with three protesting
resolutions. Lord Palmerston and his chancellor of the exchequer both spoke in parliament. 'The tone of the two
remonstrances,' says Mr. Gladstone euphemistically, 'could
not be in exact accord; but by careful steering on my part,
and I presume on his, all occasion of scandal was avoided.'
Not altogether, perhaps. Phillimore says :—

July 6.—A strange and memorable debate. Palmerston moving
resolution condemnatory of the Lords, and yet speaking in defence
of their conduct. Gladstone most earnestly and eloquently condemning
them, and declaring that action and not resolutions became the House
of Commons, and that though he agreed to the language and spirit of
the resolutions, if action were proposed he would support the proposal,
and taunted the conservatives with silently abetting 'a gigantic innovation on the constitution.' Loudly and tempestuously cheered by the
radicals, and no one else. Yet he was the true conservative at this
moment. But ought he to have spoken this as chancellor of the
exchequer, and from the treasury bench, after the first lord of the
treasury had spoken in almost totally opposite sense ? The answer
may be that it was a House of Commons, and not a government
question. I fear he is very unwell, and I greatly fear killing himself.
17.—'I have lived,' he said, speaking of the debate on the Lords and
the paper duty, 'to hear a radical read a long passage from Mr. Burke
amid the jeers and scoffs of the so-called conservatives.'

The struggle still went on :—

July 20.—H. of C. Lost my Savings Bank Monies bill; my *first* defeat in a measure of finance in the H. of C. This ought to be very good for me ; and I earnestly wish to make it so.

Aug. 6.—H. of C. Spoke 1½ hour on the Paper duty ; a favourable House. Voted in 266-233. A most kind and indeed notable reception afterwards.

Aug. 7.—This was a day of congratulations from many kind M.P.'s.

The occasion of the notable reception was the moving of his resolutions reducing the customs duty on imported paper to the level of the excise duty. This proceeding was made necessary by the treaty, and was taken to be, as Mr. Gladstone intended that it should be, a clear indication of further determination to abolish customs duty and excise duty alike. The first resolution was carried by 33, and when he rose to move the second the cheering from the liberal benches kept him standing for four or five minutes—cheering intended to be heard the whole length of the corridor that led to another place.[1]

The great result, as Greville says in a sentence that always amused the chief person concerned, is 'to give some life to half-dead, broken-down, and tempest-tossed Gladstone.' In this rather tame fashion the battle ended for the session, but the blaze in the bosom of the chancellor of the exchequer was inextinguishable, as the Lords in good time found out. Their rejection of the Paper Duties bill must have had no inconsiderable share in propelling him along the paths of liberalism. The same proceeding helped to make him more than ever the centre of popular hopes. He had taken the unpopular side in resisting the inquiry into the miscarriages of the Crimea, in pressing peace with Russia, in opposing the panic on papal aggression, on the bill for divorce, and on the bill against church rates ; and he represented with fidelity the constituency that was least of all in England in accord with the prepossessions of democracy. Yet this made no difference when the time came to seek a leader. 'There is not,' Mr. Bright said, in the course of this quarrel with the Lords, 'a man who labours and sweats for his daily bread, there is not a woman living in a cottage who strives to make her home happy for husband and children, to whom the words of the chancellor of the exchequer have not brought hope, and to whom his measures, which have been defended with an eloquence few can equal and with a logic none can contest, have not administered consolation.'

At the end of the session Phillimore reports :—

Aug. 12.—Gladstone is physically weak, requires rest, air, and generous living. He discoursed without the smallest reserve upon political affairs, the feebleness of the government, mainly attributable to the absence of any effective head ; Palmerston's weakness in the

[1] Bright wrote to Mr. Gladstone that he was inclined 'to think that the true course for Lord John, yourself, and Mr. Gibson, and for any others who agreed with you, was to have resigned rather than continue a government which could commit so great a sin against the representative branch of our constitution.'

cabinet, and his low standard for all public conduct. He said in Peel's cabinet, a cabinet minister if he had a measure to bring forward consulted Peel and then the cabinet. Nobody thought of consulting Palmerston first, but brought his measure at once to the cabinet. Gladstone said his work in the cabinet had been so constant and severe that his work in the House of Commons was refreshing by comparison. I never heard him speak so strongly of the timidity and vacillation of his comrades. The last victory, which alone preserved the government from dropping to pieces, was won in spite of them.

V

In a contemporary memorandum (May 30, 1860) on the opinions of the cabinet at this date Mr. Gladstone sets out the principal trains of business with which he and his colleagues were called upon to deal. It is a lively picture of the vast and diverse interests of a minister disposed to take his cabinet duties seriously. It is, too, a curious chart of the currents and cross-currents of the time. Here are the seven heads as he sets them down :—

(1) The Italian question— Austrian or anti-Austrian ; (2) Foreign policy in general—leaning towards calm and peace, or brusqueness and war ; (3) Defences and expenditure—alarm and money charges on the one side, modest and timid retrenchment with confidence in our position on the other ; (4) Finance, as adapted to the one or the other of these groups of ideas and feelings respectively ; (5) Reform—ultra-conservative on the one side, on the other, no fear of the working class and the belief that something *real* though limited should be done towards their enfranchisement ; (6) Church matters may perhaps be also mentioned, though there has been no collision in regard to them, whatever difference there may be—they have indeed held a very secondary place amidst the rude and constant shocks of the last twelve months ; (7) Lastly, the *coup d'état* on the paper duties draws a new line of division.

'In the many passages of argument and opinion,' Mr. Gladstone adds, ' the only person from whom I have never to my recollection differed on a serious matter during this anxious twelvemonth is Milner Gibson.' The reader will find elsewhere the enumeration of the various parts in this complex dramatic piece.[1] Some of the most Italian members of the cabinet were also the most combative in foreign policy, the most martial in respect of defence, the most stationary in finance. In the matter of reform, some who were liberal as to the franchise were conservative as to redistribution. In matters ecclesiastical, those who like Mr. Gladstone were most liberal elsewhere, were (with sympathy from Argyll) ' most conservative and church-like.'

On the paper duties there are, I think, only three members of the cabinet who have a strong feeling of the need of a remedy for the late aggression— Lord John Russell, Gibson, W. E. G. —and Lord John

1 See Appendix.

Russell leans so much upon Palmerston in regard to foreign affairs that
he is weaker in other subjects when opposed to him, than might be
desired. With us in feeling are, more or less, Newcastle, Argyll,
Villiers. On the other side, and pretty decidedly—first and foremost,
Lord Palmerston; after him, the Chancellor, Granville, Lewis, Wood,
Cardwell, Herbert. It is easy to judge what an odd shifting of parts
takes place in our discussions. We are not Mr. Burke's famous mosaic,
but we are a mosaic in solution, that is to say, a kaleidoscope.[1] When
the instrument turns, the separate pieces readjust themselves, and all
come out in perfectly novel combinations. Such a cabinet ought not
to be acephalous.

Before he had been a year and a half in office, Mr. Gladstone
wrote to Graham (Nov. 27, '60):—'We live in anti-reforming
times. All improvements have to be urged in apologetic,
almost in supplicatory tones. I sometimes reflect how much
less liberal as to domestic policy in any true sense of the
word, is this government than was Sir Robert Peel's; and
how much the tone of ultra-toryism prevails among a large
portion of the liberal party.' 'I speak a literal truth,' he
wrote to Cobden, 'when I say that in these days it is
more difficult to save a shilling than to spend a million.'
'The men,' he said, 'who ought to have been breasting and
stemming the tide have become captains general of the
alarmists,' and he deplored Cobden's refusal of office when the
Palmerston government was formed. All this only provoked
him to more relentless energy. Well might Prince Albert call
it incredible.

VI

After the 'gigantic innovation' perpetrated by the Lords,
Mr. Gladstone read to the cabinet (June 30, 1860) an elaborate
memorandum on the paper duty and the taxing powers of
the two Houses. He dealt fully alike with the fiscal and the
constitutional aspects of a situation from which he was 'certain
that nothing could extricate them with credit, except the
united, determined, and even authoritative action of the
government.' He wound up with a broad declaration that, to
any who knew his tenacity of purpose when once roused, made
it certain that he would never acquiesce in the pretensions of
the other House. The fiscal consideration, he concluded, 'is
nothing compared with the vital importance of maintaining
the exclusive rights of the House of Commons in matter of
supply. There is hardly any conceivable interference of the
Lords hereafter, except sending down a tax imposed by
themselves, which would not be covered by this precedent.
It may be said they are wise and will not do it. Assuming

[1] 'He made an administration so checkered and speckled, he put together a piece
of joinery so crossly indented and whimsically dovetailed, a cabinet so variously
inlaid, such a piece of diversified mosaic, such a tesselated pavement without cement
. . . that it was indeed a very curious show, but utterly unsafe to touch and unsure
to stand upon.'—*Speech on American Taxation.*

that they will be wise, yet I for one am not willing that the
House of Commons should hold on sufferance in the nineteenth
century what it won in the seventeenth and confirmed and
enlarged in the eighteenth.'

The intervening months did not relax this valiant and
patriotic resolution. He wrote down a short version of the
story in the last year of his life :—

The hostilities in China reached a rather early termination, and in
the early part of the session of 1861 it appeared almost certain that
there would be a surplus for 1861-2 such as I thought would make it
possible again to operate on the paper duties. Unfortunately, the
income tax was at so high a rate that we could not reasonably hope to
carry paper duty repeal without taking a penny off the tax. The
double plan strained the probable means afforded by the budget. In
this dilemma I received most valuable aid from the shrewd ingenuity
of Milner Gibson, who said : Why not fix the repeal of the paper duty
at a later date than had been intended, say on the 10th of October,
which will reduce the loss for the year ? I gladly adopted the
proposition, and proposed a budget reducing the income tax by one
penny, and repealing the paper duties from October 10, 1861. With
this was combined what was more essential than either—the adoption
of a new practice with respect to finance, which would combine all the
financial measures of the year in a single bill. We had separate
discussions in the cabinet on the constitutional proposal [the single
bill]. It was not extensively resisted there, though quietly a good
deal misliked. I rather think the chancellor, Campbell, took strong
objection to it ; and I well remember that the Duke of Newcastle gave
valuable and telling aid. So it was adopted. The budget was the
subject of a fierce discussion, in which Lord Palmerston appeared to me
to lose his temper for the first and only time. The plan, however, to
my great delight, was adopted. It was followed by a strange and
painful incident. I received with astonishment from Lord Palmerston,
immediately after the adoption of the budget, a distinct notice that he
should not consider it a cabinet question in the House of Commons,
where it was known that the opposition and the paper makers would
use every effort to destroy the plan. I wrote an uncontroversial reply
(with some self-repression) and showed it to Granville, who warmly
approved, and was silent on the letter of Lord Palmerston. The battle
in parliament was hard, but was as nothing to the internal fighting ;
and we won it. We likewise succeeded in the plan of uniting the
financial proposals in one bill. To this Spencer Walpole gave
honourable support ; and it became a standing rule. The House of
Lords, for its misconduct, was deservedly extinguished, in effect, as to
all matters of finance.

Of the 'internal fighting' we have a glimpse in the diary :—

April 10, '61.—Saw Lord Palmerston and explained to him my plans,
which did not meet his views. A laborious and anxious day. 11.—
Cabinet. Explained my case 1-3. Chaos ! 12.—Cabinet 1-3. Very
stiff. We 'broke up' in our sense and all but in another. 13.—Cabinet
3¾-6. My plan as now framed was accepted, Lord Palmerston yielding
gracefully ; Stanley of Alderley almost the only kicker. The plan of one

bill was accepted after fighting. 15.—H. of C., financial statement for three hours. The figures rather made my head ache. It was the discharge of a long pent-up excitement. *May* 13.—Lord J. R. again sustained me most handsomely in debate. Lord P. after hearing Graham amended his speech, but said we must not use any words tending to make this a vote of confidence. 30.—H. of C. Spoke one hour on omission of clause IV [that repealing the paper duty], and voted in 296–281. One of the greatest nights in the whole of my recollection. *June* 1.—Yesterday was a day of subsiding excitement. To-day is the same. Habit enables me to expel exciting thought, but not the subtler nervous action which ever comes with a crisis. 7.—To-day's debate in the H. of L. was a great event for me.

The abiding feature of constitutional interest in the budget of 1861 was this inclusion of the various financial proposals in a single bill, so that the Lords must either accept the whole of them, or try the impossible performance of rejecting the whole of them. This was the affirmation in practical shape of the resolution of the House of Commons in the previous year, that it possessed in its own hands the power to remit and impose taxes, and that the right to frame bills of supply in its own measure, manner, time, and matter, is a right to be kept inviolable. Until now the practice had been to make the different taxes the subject of as many different bills, thus placing it in the power of the Lords to reject a given tax bill without throwing the financial machinery wholly out of gear. By including all the taxes in a single finance bill the power of the Lords to override the other House was effectually arrested.

In language of that time, he had carried every stitch of free-trade canvas in the teeth of a tempest that might have made the boldest financial pilot shorten sail. Many even of his friends were sorry that he did not reduce the war duty on tea and sugar, instead of releasing paper from its duty of excise. Neither friends nor foes daunted him. He possessed his soul in patience until the hour struck, and then came forth in full panoply. Enthusiastic journalists with the gift of a poetic pen told their millions of readers how, after weeks of malign prophecy that the great trickster in Downing Street would be proved to have beggared the exchequer, that years of gloom and insolvency awaited us,—suddenly, the moment the magician chose to draw aside the veil, the darkness rolled away ; he had fluttered out of sight the whole race of sombre Volscians ; and where the gazers dreaded to see a gulf they beheld a golden monument of glorious finance ; like the traveller in the Arabian fable who was pursued in the Valley of Shadows by unearthly imprecations, he never glanced to right or left until he could disperse the shadows by a single stroke. 'He is,' says another onlooker, 'in his ministerial capacity, probably the best abused and the best hated man in the House ; neverthe-

less the House is honestly proud of h:m, and even the
country party feels a glow of pride in exhibiting to the
diplomatic gallery such a transcendent mouthpiece of a
nation of shopkeepers. The audacious shrewdness of Lancashire married to the polished grace of Oxford is a felicitous
union of the strength and culture of liberal and conservative
England ; and no party in the House, whatever may be its
likings or antipathies, can sit under the spell of Mr. Gladstone's rounded and shining eloquence without a conviction
that the man who can talk "shop" like a tenth Muse is,
after all, a true representative man of the market of the
world.'

In describing the result of the repeal of the paper duty a
little after this,[1] he used glowing words. 'Never was there
a measure so conservative as that which called into vivid,
energetic, permanent, and successful action the cheap press
of this country.' It was also a common radical opinion of
that hour that if the most numerous classes acquired the
franchise as well as cheap newspapers, the reign of peace
would thenceforth be unbroken. In a people of bold and
martial temper such as are the people of our island, this
proved to be a miscalculation. Meanwhile there is little
doubt that Mr. Gladstone's share in thus fostering the growth
of the cheap press was one of the secrets of his rapid rise in
popularity.

[1] At Manchester, Oct. 14, 1864.

CHAPTER III

BATTLE FOR ECONOMY

(1860–1862)

The session of 1860, with its complement in the principal part of 1861, was, I think, the most trying part of my whole political life.—GLADSTONE (1897).

In reading history, we are almost tempted to believe that the chief end of government in promoting internal quiet has been to accumulate greater resources for foreign hostilities.—CHANNING.

ALL this time the battle for thrifty husbandry went on, and the bark of the watch-dog at the exchequer sounded a hoarse refrain. 'We need not maunder in ante-chambers,' as Mr. Disraeli put it, 'to discover differences in the cabinet, when we have a patriotic prime minister appealing to the spirit of the country; and when at the same time we find his chancellor of the exchequer, whose duty it is to supply the ways and means by which those exertions are to be supported, proposing votes with innuendo, and recommending expenditure in a whispered invective.'

Severer than any battle in parliament is a long struggle inside a cabinet. Opponents contend at closer quarters, the weapons are shorter, it is easier to make mischief. Mr. Gladstone was the least quarrelsome of the human race; he was no wrestler intent only on being a winner in Olympic games; nor was he one of those who need an adversary to bring out all their strength. But in a cause that he had at heart he was untiring, unfaltering, and indomitable. Parallel with his contention about budget and treaty in 1860 was persistent contention for economy. The financial crisis went on with the fortifications crisis. The battle was incessant. He had not been many months in office before those deep differences came prominently forward in temperament, tradition, views of national policy, that continued to make themselves felt between himself and Lord Palmerston so long as the government endured. Perhaps I should put it more widely, and say between himself and that vast body of excited opinion in the country, of which Lord Palmerston was the cheerful mouthpiece. The struggle soon began.

Sidney Herbert, then at the war office, after circulating a memorandum, wrote privately to Mr. Gladstone (Nov. 23, 1859), that he was convinced that a great calamity was impending in the shape of a war provoked by France. Officers who had visited that country told him that all thinking men in France were against war with England, all noisy men for it, the army for it, and above all, the government for it. Inspired pamphlets were scattered broadcast. Everything was determined except time and occasion. The general expectation was for next summer. French tradesmen at St. Malo were sending in their bills to the English, thinking war coming. 'We have to do with a godless people who look on war as a game open to all without responsibility or sin ; and there is a man at the head of them who combines the qualities of a gambler and a fatalist.'

Mr. Gladstone replied in two letters, one of them (Nov. 27) of the stamp usual from a chancellor of the exchequer criticising a swollen estimate, with controversial doubts, pungent interrogatories, caustic asides, hints for saving here and paring there. On the following day he fired what he called his second barrel, in the shape of a letter, which states with admirable force and fulness the sceptic's case against the scare. This time it was no ordinary exchequer wrestle. He combats the inference of an English from an Italian war, by the historic reminder that a struggle between France and Austria for supremacy or influence in Italy had been going on for four whole centuries, so that its renewal was nothing strange. If France, now unable to secure our co-operation, still thought the Italian danger grave enough to warrant single-handed intervention, how does that support the inference that she must certainly be ready to invade England next ? He ridicules the conclusion that the invasion was at our doors, from such contested allegations as that the Châlons farmers refused the loan of horses from the government, because they would soon be wanted back again for the approaching war with England. What extraordinary farmers to refuse the loan of horses for their ploughing and seed time, because they might be reclaimed for purposes of war before winter ! Then why could we not see a single copy of the incendiary and anti-English pamphlets, said to be disseminated broadcast among the troops ? What was the value of all this contested and unsifted statement ? Why, if he were bent on a rupture, did the Emperor not stir at the moment of the great Mutiny, when every available man we had was sent to India, and when he had what might have passed for a plausible excuse in the Orsini conspiracy, and in the deliberate and pointed refusal of parliament to deal with it ? With emphasis, he insists that we have no adequate idea of the predisposing power which

an immense series of measures of preparation for war on our
own part, have in actually begetting war. They familiarise
ideas which when familiar lose their horror, and they light
an inward flame of excitement of which, when it is habitually fed, we lose the consciousness.

This application of cool and reasoned common sense to
actual probabilities seldom avails against imaginations excited
by random possibilities ; and he made little way. Lord Palmerston advanced into the field, in high anxiety that the cabinet
should promptly adopt Herbert's proposal.[1] They soon came
to a smart encounter, and Mr. Gladstone writes to the prime
minister (Feb. 7, 1860) :—' There are, I fear, the most serious
differences among us with respect to a loan for fortifications.
. . . My mind is made up, and to propose any loan for fortifications would be, on my part, with the views I entertain, a
betrayal of my public duty.' A vigorous correspondence
between Mr. Gladstone and Herbert upon military charges
followed, and the tension seemed likely to snap the cord.

If I may judge from the minutes of the members of the
cabinet on the papers circulated, most of them stood with their
chief, and not one of them, not even Milner Gibson nor Villiers,
was ready to proceed onward from a sort of general leaning
towards Mr. Gladstone's view to the further stage of making a
strong stand-up fight for it. The controversy between him
and his colleagues still raged at red heat over the whole
ground of military estimates, the handling of the militia, and
the construction of fortifications. He wrote memorandum
upon memorandum with untiring energy, pressing the cabinet
with the enormous rate in the increase of charge ; with the
slight grounds on which increase of charge was now ordinarily
proposed and entertained ; and, most of all, with the absence
of all attempt to compensate for new and necessary expenditure by retrenchment in quarters where the scale of outlay had
either always been, or had become unnecessary. He was too
sound a master of the conditions of public business to pretend
to take away from the ministers at the head of the great
departments of expenditure their duty of devising plans of
reduction, but he boldly urged the reconsideration of such
large general items of charge as the military expenditure in
the colonies, then standing at an annual burden of over two
millions on the taxpayers of this country. He was keen from
the lessons of experience, to expose the ever indestructible
fallacy that mighty armaments make for peace.

Still the cabinet was not moved, and in Palmerston he
found a will and purpose as tenacious as his own. 'The interview with Lord Palmerston came off to-day,' he writes to the
Duke of Argyll (June 6, 1860). 'Nothing could be more kind
and frank than his manner. The *matter* was first to warn me

[1] For his letter to Mr. Gladstone, Dec. 15, 1859, see Ashley, ii. p. 375.

of the evils and hazards attending, for me, the operation of resigning. Secondly, to express his own strong sense of the obligation to persevere. Both of these I told him I could fully understand. He said he had had two great objects always before him in life — one the suppression of the slave trade, the other to put England in a state of defence. In short, it appears that he now sees, as he considers, the opportunity of attaining a long cherished object ; and it is not unnatural that he should repel any proposal which should defraud him of a glory, in and by absolving him from a duty. . . . I am now sure that Lord Palmerston entertained this purpose when he formed the government ; but had I been in the slightest degree aware of it, I should certainly, but very reluctantly, have abstained from joining it, and helped, as I could, from another bench its Italian purposes. Still, I am far indeed from regretting to have joined it, which is quite another matter.'

Now labouring hard in Paris month after month at the tariff, Cobden plied Mr. Gladstone with exhortations 'to challenge the alarmists on the facts ; to compare the outlay by France for a dozen years past on docks, fortifications, arsenals, with the corresponding outlay by England ; to show that our steam navy, building and afloat, to say nothing of our vast mercantile marine, was at least double the strength of France ; and above all, to make his colleagues consider whether the French Emperor had not, as a matter of self-interest, made the friendship of England, from the first, the hinge of his whole policy. Cobden, as always, knew thoroughly and in detail what he was talking about, for he had sat for three successive sessions on a select committee upon army, navy, and ordnance expenditure. In another letter he turned personally to Mr. Gladstone himself : ' Unconsciously,' he says, ' you have administered to the support of a system which has no better foundation than a gigantic delusion' (June 11, 1860). ' You say unconsciously,' Mr. Gladstone replies (June 13), ' I am afraid that in one respect this is too favourable a description. I have consciously, as a member of parliament and as a member of the government, concurred in measures that provide for an expenditure beyond what were it in my power I would fix. . . . But I suppose that the duty of choosing the lesser evil binds me ; *the difficulty is to determine what the lesser evil is.*'

My story grows long, and it ends as such stories in our politics usually end. A compromise was arranged on the initiative of the Duke of Somerset, keeping clear, as Mr. Gladstone supposed, of the fortification scheme as a whole, and not pledging future years.[1] ' Never at any time in my life,'

---

[1] See Appendix. ' This account, Mr. Gladstone writes, ' contains probably the only reply I shall ever make to an account given or printed by Sir Theodore Martin in his *Life of the Prince Consort*, which is most injurious to me without a shadow of founda-

Mr. Gladstone told Graham, 'have I had such a sense of mental and moral exhaustion.' The strain was not ended by the compromise, for in moving the resolution for a vote of two millions for fortifications (July 23), Lord Palmerston not only declared that he held it to be absolutely necessary to carry the whole scheme into effect—the very proposition which the compromise put aside—but defended it by a series of stringent criticisms particularly fitted to offend and irritate France. Mr. Gladstone was not present,[1] but he felt strongly that he had good grounds of complaint, and that faith had not been strictly kept. 'Much dismayed,' he wrote in his diary (*July* 24), 'at the terms of Lord Palmerston's resolution.' It was now, however, too late to draw back.[2] Mr. Bright made a weighty and masterly attack (Aug. 2), hinting plainly that the thing was 'a compromise to enable the government to avoid the rock, or get over the quicksand, which this question has interjected into their midst,' and quoting with excellent effect a pregnant passage from Peel :—'If you adopt the opinion of military men, naturally anxious for the complete security of every available point ; naturally anxious to throw upon you the whole responsibility for the loss, in the event of war suddenly breaking out, of some of our valuable possessions,—you would overwhelm this country with taxes in time of peace.' But this was a Palmerstonian parliament. The year before, a remarkable debate (July 21, 1859) had promised better things. Disraeli had opened it with emphatic declarations :—'There is no country,' he said, 'that can go on raising seventy millions in time of peace with impunity. England cannot, and if England cannot, no country can.' Bright followed with the assurance that Cobden and he might now consider Mr. Disraeli a convert to their views. Lord John Russell came next, agreeing with Bright ; and even Palmerston himself was constrained to make a peace speech.

II

In May 1861 Mr. Gladstone notes 'a day of over fourteen hours : thank God for the strength.' The atmosphere around him would have depressed a weaker man. 'At Brooks's,' says

---

tion : owing, I have no doubt, to defective acquaintance with the subject.' The passage is in vol. v. p. 148. Lord Palmerston's words to the Queen about Mr. Gladstone are a curiously unedifying specimen of loyalty to a colleague.

[1] It appears that he wrote his final opinion on the subject to the cabinet on Saturday, left them to deliberate, and went to the Crystal Palace. The Duke of Argyll joined him there and said it was all right. The Gladstones then went to Cliveden and he purposely did not return till late, twelve o'clock on Monday night, in order that Palmerston might make his speech as he pleased. I doubt the policy of his absence. It of course excited much remark, and does not in any way protect Gladstone. M. Gibson was also absent.'—*Phillimore Diary*, July 23. In his diary Mr. Gladstone records : '*July* 21. Cabinet 3½-5½. I left it that the discussion might be free and went to Stafford House and Sydenham. There I saw, later, Argyll and S. Herbert, who seemed to bring good news. At night we went off to Cliveden.'

[2] For an interesting letter on all this to the Duke of Argyll, see Appendix.

Phillimore, 'they hate Gladstone worse than at the Carlton.'
In the summer the strife upon expenditure was renewed.
Eventually Mr. Gladstone was able to write to Graham from
the cabinet room (July 20, 1861) that Castor and Pollux appeared aloft at the right moment, and the clouds had disappeared. In a letter to his close friend, Sir Walter James, in
1871 Mr. Gladstone says :—'The storm of criticism and rebuke
does not surprise nor discourage me. Doubtless much must be
just ; and what is not, is what we call in logic an "inseparable
accident" of politics. Time and reflection will, please God, enable us to distinguish between them. For my own part I *never*
was so abused as in 1860 ; but it was one of the most useful or
least useless years of my life.' The battle was as severe in 1861
as it had been the year before. In the middle of the session
(May 9) Phillimore reports : 'Found Gladstone in good spirits ;
he spoke with real greatness of mind of the attacks made
on him.'

The next year Lord Palmerston wrote to express his concern
at something that became upon in a railway journey. 'I read with
much interest,' he wrote to his chancellor of the exchequer
(April 29, 1862), 'your able and eloquent speeches at Manchester,
but I wish to submit to you some observations upon the
financial part of the second speech.' He did not agree with
Mr. Gladstone that the nation had forced the cabinet and parliament into high expenditure, but if it were so, he regarded it
not as matter of reproach, but as a proof of the nation's
superior sagacity. Panic there had been none ; governors and
governed had for a long time been blind and apathetic ; then
they awoke. There was on the other side of the channel a
people who, say what they may, hate us and would make any
sacrifice to humiliate us, and they had now at their head an
able, active, wary, counsel-keeping, but ever-planning sovereign
[Napoleon III.]. 'Have the Parliament and the nation been
wrong, and have Bright and Cobden and yourself been right ?'
All this being so, he could not but regret that Mr Gladstone
should by speeches in and out of parliament invite agitation to
force the government of which he was a member, to retrace its
steps taken deliberately and with full sense of responsibility.[1]
To Palmerston's eight quarto pages, written in one of the finest
hands of the time, Mr. Gladstone replied in twelve.

In all good humour, he said, I prefer not being classed with Mr.
Bright, or even Mr. Cobden ; first, because I do not know their opinions
with any precision ; and secondly, because as far as I do know or can grasp
them, they seem to contemplate fundamental changes in taxation which
I disapprove in principle, and believe also to be unattainable in practice,
and reductions of establishment and expenditure for which I am not
prepared to be responsible. . . . I think it a mean and guilty course to
hold out vague and indefinite promises of vast retrenchment, but I think

[1] This letter is printed in full by Mr. Ashley, ii. p. 413.

it will be a healthful day, both for the country and for the party over which you so ably preside, when the word retrenchment, of course with a due regard to altered circumstances, shall again take its place among their battle cries.

A spirited correspondence followed, for Lord Palmerston knew his business, and had abundant faculty of application; while Mr. Gladstone, for his part, was too much in earnest to forego rejoinder and even surrejoinder. 'No claptrap reductions,' cried the prime minister. 'You are feeding not only expenditure,' rejoined the chancellor of the exchequer, 'but what is worse, the spirit of expenditure.' 'You disclaim political community of opinion with Bright and Cobden, and justly,' said Lord Palmerston, 'but you cannot but be aware that owing to various accidental circumstances many people at home and abroad connect you unjustly with them, and this false impression is certainly not advantageous.'

'My dear Gladstone,' he wrote good-humouredly on another occasion, 'You may not have seen how your name is taken in vain by people with whom I conceive you do not sympathise,—Yours sincerely,   PALMERSTON.'

Enclosed was a placard with many large capital letters, notes of exclamation, italics, and all the rest of the paraphernalia of political emphasis :—

TAX PAYERS! Read Mr. Cobden's new pamphlet, the 'THREE PANICS,' and judge for yourselves. How long will you suffer Yourselves to be Humbugged by PALMERSTONIANISM, and Robbed by the 'Services,' and others interested in a War Expenditure, even in times of Peace ? . . . THE CHANCELLOR OF THE EXCHEQUER APPEALS TO YOU TO HELP HIM. You have the power in your own hands if you will only exert it. Reform the House of Commons, AND DO IT THOROUGHLY THIS TIME.

Of the continuance of the struggle in 1862, a few items from the diary give an adequate picture :—

Jan. 30, 1862. — A heavy blow in the announcement of increased military estimates from Sir George Lewis gave me a disturbed evening. 31.—Worked on the formidable subject of the estimates, and made known to the cabinet my difficulties. *Feb.* 1.—Cabinet 3½-6. It went well; the tenth penny [on the income-tax] proved to be a strong physic ; £750,000 of reductions ordered. 12.—Wrote mem. on possible reductions, etc., to dispense with income-tax. The whole question, I think, is, can we be satisfied (I think we ought and will) with 21 millions for army and navy instead of 27 ? *March* 1.—Cabinet 3¾-6¼, very stiff, on the Belgian negotiations I had to go to the ultima ratio. 31.—H. of C. The fortifications got their first blow.

By midsummer public feeling veered a little :—'The tide has turned. Lord Palmerston is now "the strong swimmer in his agony." '[1]

[1] Diary.

A candid and friendly observer has told us the situation :—
'When I was private secretary to Lord Palmerston,' he says,
'and Mr. Gladstone was his chancellor of the exchequer, it was
a constant source of sorrow to me, and a perpetual cause of
mystery, to note how they misunderstood one another, and how
evidently each mistrusted the other, though perfectly cordial
and most friendly in their mutual intercourse. . . . If the proposal was adhered to, Mr. Gladstone gave way. This seemed
to Lord Palmerston a case of gratuitous difficulties put in his
way, and attempts to thwart without the courage to resist.'[1]

In closing this chapter, let us note that in spite of Lord
Palmerston, he won no inconsiderable success. When 1866
came, and his financial administration ended, he had managed,
with the aid of the reduction of debt charge after the lapse of
the long annuities, to carry expenditure back to the level of
1857. Naval expenditure rose until 1861, and then began to
fall ; army expenditure rose until 1863, and then began to fall.
In 1859, when he went to the exchequer, the total under these
two heads was nearly twenty-six millions ; when he quitted
office in 1866 the total was twenty-four millions. In the
middle years it had swelled to twenty-eight. After half a dozen
years of panic and extravagance, all sedulously fostered by a
strong prime minister, that he should still have left the cost of
government little higher than he found it was no defeat, but an
extremely satisfactory performance. 'We must follow the
nature of our affairs,' Burke says, 'and conform ourselves to
our situation. Why should we resolve to do nothing because
what I propose to you may not be the exact demand of the
petition ? If we cry, like children, for the moon, like children
we must cry on.'[2]

III

Ruminating in the late evening of life over his legislative
work, Mr. Gladstone wrote :—'Selecting the larger measures
and looking only to achieved results, I should take the following heads : 1. The Tariffs, 1842-60. 2. Oxford University Act.
3. Post Office Savings Banks. 4. Irish Church Disestablishment. 5. Irish Land Acts. 6. Franchise Act. Although this
excludes the last of all the efforts, viz., the Irish Government
bill.' The third item in the list belongs to the period (1861) at
which we have now arrived.

The points to be noted are three. 1. The whole of my action in
1859-65 was viewed with the utmost jealousy by a large minority and a
section of the very limited majority. It was an object to me to get this
bill passed *sub silentio*, a full statement of my expectations from it
would have been absolutely fatal. I admit they have been more than
realised. 2. The Trustee Savings Banks were doubly defective, nay
trebly, for they sometimes broke. (1) Their principle was left in doubt

[1] Mr. Evelyn Ashley in *National Review*, June 1898, pp. 536-40.
[2] Plan for Economical Reform.

—were the general funds in trust, or cash at a banker's? This was vital. (2) They never got or could get within the doors of the masses, for they smelt of class. It was necessary to provide for the savings of the people with (*a*) safety, (*b*) cheapness, (*c*) convenience. The banks *cost* money to the State. The Post Office Savings Banks bring in a revenue. 3. Behind all this I had an object of first-rate importance, which has been attained: to provide the minister of finance with a strong financial arm, and to secure his independence of the City by giving him a large and certain command of money.

A sequel to this salutary measure was a bill three years later with the apparently unheroic but really beneficent object of facilitating the acquisition of small annuities, without the risk of fraud or bankruptcy.[1] An eyewitness tells how (March 7, 1864) 'Mr. Gladstone held the house for two hours enchained by his defence of a measure which avowedly will not benefit the class from which members are selected; which involves not only a "wilderness of figures," but calculations of a kind as intelligible to most men as equations to London cabdrivers; and which, though it might and would interest the nation, would never in the nature of things be made a hustings cry. The riveted attention of the House was in itself a triumph; the deep impression received by the nation on the following day was a greater one. It was felt that here was a man who really could lead, instead of merely reflecting the conclusions of the popular mind.' The measure encountered a pretty stiff opposition. The insurance companies were vexed that they had neglected their proper business, others feared that it might undermine the poor law, others again took the pessimist's favourite line that it would be inoperative. But the case was good, Mr. Gladstone's hand was firm, and in due time the bill became law amid a loud chorus of approval.

Thus he encouraged, stimulated, and facilitated private and personal thrift, at the same time and in the same spirit in which he laboured his fervid exhortations to national economy. He was deeply convinced, he said and kept saying, 'that all excess in the public expenditure beyond the legitimate wants of the country is not only a pecuniary waste, but a great political, and above all, a great moral evil. It is a characteristic of the mischiefs that arise from financial prodigality that they creep onwards with a noiseless and a stealthy step; that they commonly remain unseen and unfelt, until they have reached a magnitude absolutely overwhelming.' He referred to the case of Austria, where these mischiefs seemed to threaten the very foundations of empire.

[1] 27 and 28 Vict., chap. 43.

CHAPTER IV

THE SPIRIT OF GLADSTONIAN FINANCE

(1859-1866)

Nations seldom realise till too late how prominent a place a sound system of finance holds among the vital elements of national stability and well-being; how few political changes are worth purchasing by its sacrifice; how widely and seriously human happiness is affected by the downfall or the perturbation of national credit, or by excessive, injudicious, and unjust taxation.—LECKY.

IN finance, the most important of all the many fields of his activity, Mr. Gladstone had the signal distinction of creating the public opinion by which he worked, and warming the climate in which his projects throve. In other matters he followed, as it was his business and necessity to follow, the governing forces of the public mind; in finance he was a strenuous leader. He not only led with a boldness sometimes verging on improvidence; apart from the merits of this or that proposal, he raised finance to the high place that belongs to it in the interest, curiosity, and imperious concern of every sound self-governing community. Even its narrowest technicalities by his supple and resplendent power as orator were suffused with life and colour. When ephemeral critics disparaged him as mere rhetorician—and nobody denies that he was often declamatory and discursive, that he often over-argued and over-refined—they forgot that he nowhere exerted greater influence than in that department of affairs where words out of relation to fact are most surely exposed. If he often carried the proper rhetorical arts of amplification and development to excess, yet the basis of fact was both sound and clear, and his digressions, as when, for example, he introduced an account of the changes in the English taste for wine,[1] were found, and still remain, both relevant and extremely interesting.

One recorder who had listened to all the financiers from Peel downwards, said that Peel's statements were ingenious and able, but dry; Disraeli was clever but out of his element; Wood was like a cart without springs on a heavy road; Glad-

---

[1] *Financial Statements*, p. 151.

CHAP. IV. ÆT. 50-57 CREATION OF PUBLIC INTEREST 515

stone was the only man who could lead his hearers over the
arid desert, and yet keep them cheerful and lively and interested without flagging. Another is reminded of Sir Joshua's
picture of Garrick between tragedy and comedy, such was his
duality of attitude and expression ; such the skill with which
he varied his moods in a single speech, his fervid eloquence and
passion, his lightness and buoyancy of humour, his lambent
and spontaneous sarcasm. Just as Macaulay made thousands
read history who before had turned from it as dry and repulsive, so Mr. Gladstone made thousands eager to follow the
public balance-sheet, and the whole nation became his audience,
interested in him and his themes and in the House where his
dazzling wonders were performed. All this made a magnificent
contribution to the national spirit of his time. Such extraordinary power over others had its mainspring in the depths
and zeal of his own conviction and concern. 'For nine or ten
months of the year,' he told Sir Henry Taylor in 1864, 'I am
always willing to go out of office, but in the two or three that
precede the budget I begin to feel an itch to have the handling
of it. Last summer I should have been delighted to go out ;
now [December] I am indifferent ; in February, if I live as long,
I shall, I have no doubt, be loath ; but in April quite ready
again. Such are my signs of the zodiac.' The eagerness of his
own mind transmitted itself like an electric current through
his audience.

Interest abroad was almost as much alive as the interest felt
in England itself. We have already seen how keenly Cavour
followed Mr. Gladstone's performances. His budget speeches
were circulated by foreign ministers among deputies and
editors. Fould, one of the best of Napoleon's finance ministers,
kept up a pretty steady correspondence with the English chancellor : appeals to him as to the sound doctrine on sugar drawbacks ; is much struck by his proposals on Scotch banks ; says
mournfully to him (April 28, 1863), in a sentence that is a whole
chapter in the history of the empire :—'You are very fortunate
in being able to give such relief to the taxpayers ; if it had not
been for the war in Mexico, I should perhaps have been able
to do something of the same sort, and that would have been,
especially in view of the elections, very favourable to the
government of the Emperor.'

When Mr. Gladstone came to leave office in 1866, he said to
Fould (July 11) :—'The statesmen of to-day have a new mission
opened to them : the mission of substituting the concert of
nations for their conflicts, and of teaching them to grow great
in common, and to give to others by giving to themselves. Of
this beneficent work a good share has fallen to the departments with which we have respectively been connected.' Fould
had already deplored his loss. 'I counted,' he says, 'on the
influence of your wise doctrines in finance, to help me in

maintaining our country in that system of order and economy, of which you were setting the example.' Alas, in France and in continental Europe generally at that time, selfish material interests and their class representatives were very strong, popular power was weak ; in most of them the soldier was the master. Happily for our famous chancellor of the exchequer, England was different.

It has often been said that he ignored the social question ; did not even seem to know there was one. The truth is, that what marks him from other chancellors is exactly the dominating hold gained by the social question in all its depth and breadth upon his most susceptible imagination. Tariff reform, adjustment of burdens, invincible repugnance to waste or profusion, accurate keeping and continuous scrutiny of accounts, substitution of a few good taxes for many bad ones,—all these were not merely the love of a methodical and thrifty man for habits of business ; they were directly associated in him with the amelioration of the hard lot of the toiling mass, and sprang from an ardent concern in improving human well-being, and raising the moral ideals of mankind. In his 'musings for the good of man,' Liberation of Intercourse, to borrow his own larger name for free trade, figured in his mind's eye as one of the promoting conditions of abundant employment. 'If you want,' he said in a pregnant proposition, 'to benefit the labouring classes and to do the maximum of good, it is not enough to operate upon the articles consumed by them ; you should rather operate on the articles that give them the maximum of employment.' In other words, you should extend the area of trade by steadily removing restrictions. He recalled the days when our predecessors thought it must be for man's good to have 'most of the avenues by which the mind, and also the hand of man conveyed and exchanged their respective products,' blocked or narrowed by regulation and taxation. Dissemination of news, travelling, letters, transit of goods, were all made as costly and difficult as the legislator could make them. 'I rank,' he said, 'the introduction of cheap postage for letters, documents, patterns, and printed matter, and the abolition of all taxes on printed matter, in the catalogue of free trade legislation. These great measures may well take their place beside the abolition of prohibitions and protective duties, the simplifying of revenue laws, and the repeal of the Navigation Act, as forming together the great code of industrial emancipation.'[1]

It was not unnatural that fault should be found with him for not making a more resolute effort to lighten the burden of that heavy mortgage which, under the name of the National

[1] See his elaborate article in the *Nineteenth Century* for February 1880 on *Free Trade, Railways, and Commerce*, in which he endeavours fairly to divide the credit of our material progress between its two great factors, the Liberation of Intercourse, and the Improvement of Locomotion. Under the head of new locomotive forces he counts the Suez canal.

Debt, we have laid upon the industry and property of the nation. In 1866 he was keenly excited by Jevons's argument from the ultimate shrinkage of our coal supply, and he accepted the inference that we should vigorously apply ourselves by reduction of the debt to preparation for the arrival of the evil day. But, as he wrote to Jevons (March 16, 1866), 'Until the great work of the liberation of industry was in the main effected, it would have been premature or even wrong to give too much prominence to this view of the subject. Nor do I regard that liberation as yet having reached the point at which we might say, we will now cease to make remission of taxes a principal element and aim in finance. But we are in my judgment near it. And I am most anxious that the public should begin to take a closer and more practical view of the topics which you have done so much to bring into prominence.'

He was always thinking of the emancipation of commerce, like Peel and Cobden. His general policy was simple. When great expenditure demanded large revenue, he raised his money by high income-tax, and high rates of duty on a few articles, neither absolute necessities of life nor raw materials of manufacture. He left the income-tax at fourpence. In 1866, he told the House that the new parliament then about to be elected might dispense with the tax. 'If,' he said, 'parliament and the country preferred to retain the tax, then the rate of fourpence is the rate at which in time of peace and in the absence of any special emergency, we believe it may be most justly and wisely so retained.' While cordially embracing Cobden's policy of combining free trade with retrenchment, he could not withstand a carnal satisfaction at abundant revenue. Deploring expenditure with all his soul, he still rubs his hands in professional pride at the elasticity of the revenue under his management.

II

When it is asked, with no particular relevancy, what original contribution of the first order was made by Mr. Gladstone to the science of national finance, we may return the same answer as if it were asked of Walpole, Pitt, or Peel. It was for Adam Smith from his retreat upon the sea-beach of distant Kirkcaldy to introduce new and fruitful ideas, though he too owed a debt to French economists. The statesman's business is not to invent ideas in finance, but to create occasions and contrive expedients for applying them. 'What an extraordinary man Pitt is,' said Adam Smith ; 'he understands my ideas better than I understand them myself.' Originality may lie as much in perception of opportunity as in invention. Cobden discovered no new economic truths that I know of, but his perception of the bearings of abstract economic truths upon the actual and prospective circumstances of his country and the world, made him the most original economic statesman of his day. The

glory of Mr. Gladstone was different. It rested on the practical
power and tenacity with which he opened new paths, and
forced the application of sound doctrine over long successions
of countless obstacles.

If we probe his fame as financier to the core and marrow, it
was not his power as orator, it was not his ingenuity in device
and expedient, it was his unswerving faith in certain fixed
aims, and his steadfast and insistent zeal in pursuing them,
that built up the splendid edifice. Pitt performed striking
financial feats, especially in the consolidation of duties, in
reformed administration, and in the French treaty of 1786.
But ill-fortune dragged him into the vortex of European war,
and finance sank into the place of a secondary instrument, an
art for devising aliments, some of them desperate enough, for
feeding the war-chest of the nation. Sir Robert Walpole, Mr.
Gladstone wrote, 'had not to contend with like difficulties, and
I think his administration should be compared with the early
years of Pitt, in which way of judging he would come off
second, though a man of cool and sagacious judgment, while
morally he stood low.'[1]

In the happier conditions of his time, Mr. Gladstone was able
to use wise and bold finance as the lever for enlarging all
the facilities of life, and diffusing them over the widest area.
If men sometimes smile at his extraordinary zeal for cheap
wines and cheap books and low railway fares, if they are sometimes provoked by his rather harsh views on privileges for patents
and copyrights for authors, restrictive of the common enjoyment, it is well to remember that all this and the like came
from what was at once clear financial vision and true social
feeling. 'A financial experience,' he once said, 'which is long
and wide, has profoundly convinced me that, as a rule, the state
or individual or company thrives best which dives deepest
down into the mass of the community, and adapts its arrangements to the wants of the greatest number.' His exultation in
the stimulus given by fiscal freedom to extended trade, and
therefore to more abundant employment at higher wages, was
less the exultation of the economist watching the intoxicating
growth of wealth, than of the social moralist surveying multiplied access to fuller life and more felicity. I always remember,
in a roving talk with him in 1891, when he was a very old man
and ill, how he gradually took fire at the notion—I forget how
it arose—of the iniquities under which the poor man suffered
a generation ago. 'See—the sons and daughters went forth
from their homes; the cost of postage was so high that correspondence was practically prohibited; yet the rich all the
time, by the privilege of franking, carried on a really immense
amount of letter - writing absolutely free. Think what a

[1] From a letter to his son Herbert, March 10, 1876, containing some interesting
remarks on Pitt's finance. See Appendix.

softening of domestic exile ; what an aid in keeping warm the feel of family affection, in mitigating the rude breach in the circle of the hearth.' This vigorous sympathy was with Mr. Gladstone a living part of his Christian enthusiasm. ' If you would gain mankind,' said old Jeremy Bentham, ' the best way is to appear to love them, and the best way of appearing to love them, is to love them in reality.' When he thought of the effect of his work at the exchequer, he derived ' profound and inestimable consolation from the reflection that while the rich have been growing richer, the poor have become less poor.' Yet, as my readers have by this time found out, there never was a man less in need of Aristotle's warning, that to be for ever hunting after the useful befits not those of free and lofty soul.[1] As was noted by contemporaries, like all the followers of Sir Robert Peel, he never thought without an eye to utilitarian results, but mixed with that attitude of mind he had ' a certain refinement and subtlety of religiousness that redeemed it from the coldness, if it sometimes overshadowed the clearness, of mere statesmanlike prudence.' On the other hand, he had ' the Lancashire temperament.'

III

This thought and feeling for the taxpayer was at the root of another achievement, no less original than the peculiar interest that he was able to excite by his manner of stating a financial case. Peel was only prime minister for five years, and only four months chancellor. Mr. Gladstone was prime minister for twelve—ten years short of Sir Robert Walpole in that office, seven years short of Pitt. But he was also chancellor of the exchequer under three other prime ministers for ten years. Thus his connection with the treasury covered a longer period than was attained by the greatest of his predecessors. His long reign at the treasury, and his personal predominance in parliament and the country, enabled him to stamp on the public departments administrative principles of the utmost breadth and strength. Thrift of public money, resolute resistance to waste, rigid exactitude in time, and all the other aspects of official duty, conviction that in the working of the vast machinery of state nothing is a trifle—through the firm establishment of maxims and principles of this sort, Mr. Gladstone built up a strong and efficacious system of administrative unity that must be counted a conspicuous part of his very greatest work. ' No chancellor of the exchequer,' he once said, ' is worth his salt who makes his own popularity either his first consideration, or any consideration at all, in administering the public purse. In my opinion, the chancellor of the

[1] Τὸ ζητεῖν πανταχοῦ τὸ χρήσιμον ἥκιστα ἁρμόττει τοῖς ἐλευθέροις.
Politics, viii. 3.

exchequer is the trusted and confidential steward of the public. He is under a sacred obligation with regard to all that he consents to spend.'[1] This tone of thinking and feeling about the service of the state spread under his magisterial influence from chancellors and the permanent officers that bear unobtrusive but effective sway in Whitehall, down to tidewaiters and distributors of stamps. As Burke put the old Latin saw, he endeavoured to 'give us a system of economy, which is itself a great revenue.' The Exchequer and Audit Act of 1866 is a monument of his zeal and power in this direction. It converted the nominal control by parliament into a real control, and has borne the strain of nearly forty years.

He was more alive than any man at the exchequer had ever been before, to the mischiefs of the spirit of expenditure. As he told the House of Commons in 1863 (April 16):—'I mean this, that together with the so-called increase of expenditure there grows up what may be termed a spirit of expenditure, a desire, a tendency prevailing in the country, which, insensibly and unconsciously perhaps, but really, affects the spirit of the people, the spirit of parliament, the spirit of the public departments, and perhaps even the spirit of those whose duty it is to submit the estimates to parliament.' 'But how,' he wrote to Cobden (Jan. 5, 1864), 'is the spirit of expenditure to be exorcised? Not by my preaching; I doubt if even by yours. I seriously doubt whether it will ever give place to the old spirit of economy, as long as we have the income-tax. There, or hard by, lie questions of deep practical moment.' This last pregnant reference to the income-tax, makes it worth while to insert here a word or two from letters of 1859 to his brother Robertson, an even more ardent financial reformer than himself :—

Economy is the first and great article (economy such as I understand it) in my financial creed. The controversy between direct and indirect taxation holds a minor though important place. I have not the smallest doubt we should at this moment have had a smaller expenditure if financial reformers had not directed their chief attention, not to the question how much of expenditure and taxes we shall have, but to the question how it should be raised. . . . I agree with you that if you had only direct taxes, you would have economical government. But in my opinion the indirect taxes will last as long as the monarchy ; and while we have them, I am deeply convinced that the facility of recurring to, and of maintaining, income-tax has been a main source of that extravagance in government, which I date from the Russian war (for before that a good spirit had prevailed for some twenty-five years).

Bagehot, that economist who united such experience and sense with so much subtlety and humour, wrote to Mr. Gladstone in 1863 :—'Indirect taxation so cramps trade and heavy direct taxation so impairs morality that a large expenditure becomes a great evil. I have often said so to Sir G.

[1] Edinburgh, Nov. 29, 1879.

Lewis, but he always answered, "Government is a very rough
business. You must be content with very unsatisfactory
results.'" This was a content that Mr. Gladstone never learned.

It was not only in the finance of millions that he showed
himself a hero. 'The chancellor of the exchequer,' he said,
'should boldly uphold economy in detail ; and it is the mark
of a chicken-hearted chancellor when he shrinks from upholding
economy in detail, when because it is a question of only two
or three thousand pounds, he says that is no matter. He is
ridiculed, no doubt, for what is called candle-ends and cheese-
parings, but he is not worth his salt if he is not ready to save
what are meant by candle-ends and cheese-parings in the
cause of the country.'[1] He held it to be his special duty in
his office not simply to abolish sinecures, but to watch for
every opportunity of cutting down all unnecessary appointments. He hears that a clerk at the national debt office is at
death's door, and on the instant writes to Lord Palmerston
that there is no necessity to appoint a successor. During the
last twenty years, he said in 1863, 'since I began to deal with
these subjects, every financial change beneficial to the country
at large has been met with a threat that somebody would be
dismissed.' All such discouragements he treated with the half
scornful scepticism without which no administrative reformer
will go far.

He did not think it beneath his dignity to appeal to the
foreign office for a retrenchment in fly-leaves and thick folio
sheets used for docketing only, and the same for mere covering
despatches without description ; for all these had to be bound,
and the bound books wanted bookcases, and the bookcases
wanted buildings, and the libraries wanted librarians. 'My
idea is that it would be quite worth while to appoint an official
committee from various departments to go over the "contingencies" and minor charges of the different departments
into which abuse must always be creeping, from the nature of
the case and without much blame to any one.' Sir R. Bethell
as attorney-general insisted on the duty incumbent on certain
high officials, including secretaries of state, of taking out
patents for their offices, and paying the stamp duties of two
hundred pounds apiece thereon. 'I shall deal with these
eminent persons,' he wrote to the chancellor of the exchequer,
'exactly as I should and do daily deal with John Smith accused
of fraud as a distiller, or John Brown reported as guilty of
smuggling tobacco.' Mr. Gladstone replies (1859) :—

I rejoice to see that neither the heat, the stench, nor service in the
courts can exhaust even your superfluous vigour ; and it is most
ennobling to see such energies devoted to the highest of all purposes—
that of replenishing her Majesty's exchequer. I hope, however, that in
one point the case stands better than I had supposed. The proof of

[1] Edinburgh, Nov. 29, 1879.

absolute contumacy is not yet complete, though, alas, the *animus furandi* stands forth in all its hideous colours. I spoke yesterday to Lord Palmerston on the painful theme ; and he confessed to me with much emotion that he has not yet resorted to those mild means of exhortation — what the presbyterians call dealing with an erring brother—from which we had hoped much. The unhappy men may therefore yet come to their senses ; in any case I rejoice to think that you, in the new capacity of mad doctor, are sure to cure them and abate the mischief, if the which do not happen (I quote the new Tennyson) :—

> 'some evil chance
> Will make the smouldering scandal break and blaze
> Before the people and our Lord the King.' [1]

After a due amount of amusing correspondence, the recusant confederacy struck their colours and paid their money.

When he went to Corfu in the *Terrible* in 1858, some two or three sleeping cabins were made by wooden partitions put up round spaces taken off the deck. Thirteen years after, his unslumbering memory made this an illustrating point in an exhortation to a first lord of the admiralty not to disregard small outgoings. 'I never in my life was more astonished than upon being told the sum this had cost ; I think it was in hundreds of pounds, where I should have expected tens.' Sometimes, no doubt, this drift descended to the ludicrous. On this same expedition to Corfu, among the small pieces of economy enjoined by Mr. Gladstone on the members of his mission, one was to scratch out the address on the parchment label of the despatch bags and to use the same label in returning the bag to the colonial office in London. One day while the secretary was busily engaged in thus saving a few halfpence, an officer came into the room, having arrived by a special steamer from Trieste at a cost of between seven and eight hundred pounds. The ordinary mail-boat would have brought him a very few hours later. We can hardly wonder that the heroical economist denounced such pranks as 'profligate' and much else. Though an individual case may often enough seem ludicrous, yet the system and the spirit engendered by it were to the taxpayer, that is to the nation, priceless.

IV

One of the few failures of this active and fruitful period was the proposal (1863) that charities should pay income-tax upon the returns from their endowments. What is their exemption but the equivalent of a gift to them from the general taxpayer ? He has to make good the sum that ought in reason and equity to have been paid by them, as by other people, to the government that protects them. Why should this burden be compulsorily laid upon him ? What is the quality of an endowment

for a charitable purpose that constitutes a valid claim for such
a boon? Into this case Mr. Gladstone threw himself with full
force. The opposition to him was as heated and as vigorous as
he ever provoked, and the violence of the resistance roused an
answering vehemence in him. He speaks in his diary of his
'deadly encounter with the so-called charities.' 'I was endeavouring,' he says, 'to uphold the reality of truth and justice
against their superficial and flimsy appearances.' 'Spoke from
5.10 to 8.20, with all my might, such as it was.' This speech,
with its fierce cogency and trenchant reasoning, was counted
by good judges who heard it, to be among the two or three
most powerful that he ever made, and even to-day it may be
read with the same sort of interest as we give to Turgot's
famous disquisition on Foundations. It turns a rude search-
light upon illusions about charity that are all the more painful
to dispel, because they often spring from pity and from
sympathy, not the commonest of human elements. It affects
the jurist, the economist, the moralist, the politician. The
House was profoundly impressed by both the argument and
the performance, but the clamour was too loud, all the idols of
market-place and tribe were marched out in high parade, and
the proposal at last was dropped.

Though the idea of putting a tax on the income of charitable
endowments was rejected, the budget of 1863 was the record of
a triumph that was complete. The American civil war by
arresting the supply of cotton had half ruined Lancashire. The
same cause had diminished the export trade to America by six
millions sterling. Three bad seasons spoiled the crops. There
was distress in Ireland. Yet the chancellor had a revenue in
excess of expenditure by the noble figure of three millions and
three quarters. Mr. Gladstone naturally took the opportunity
of surveying the effects of four years of his financial policy. He
admitted that they had been four years of tension, and this
tension had been enhanced by his large remissions of duty, and
by taking in hand the completion of the great work of commercial legislation. The end of it all was a growth of wealth,
as he called it, almost intoxicating. The value of British goods
sent to France had risen from four millions and three quarters
to nearly nine millions and one quarter, in other words had
about doubled under the operations of the treaty of commerce.[1]
If to this were added foreign and colonial produce sent through
us, and acquired by us in exchange for our own produce, the
value had risen from nine and a half in 1859 to twenty-one and
three quarters in 1862. In Mr. Gladstone's own description
later, the export trade of 1860, in spite of a bad harvest, was so
stimulated by the liberating customs act, that it rose at once
from a hundred and thirty millions to a hundred and thirty-

[1] For his later views on the French treaty, see his speech at Leeds in 1881, an
extract from which is given in Appendix.

five. The next year it fell to a hundred and twenty-five, and in 1862 it fell by another million owing to the withdrawal, by reason of the American war, of the material of our greatest manufacture. In 1866 it rose to a hundred and eighty-eight millions.[1] Then under the head of income-tax, and comparing 1842 with 1862, over the same area, and with the same limitations, the aggregate amount of assessed income had risen from one hundred and fifty-six millions to two hundred and twenty-one. Other tests and figures need not detain us.

April 16, 1863.—My statement lasted three hours, and this with a good deal of compression. It wound up, I hope, a chapter in finance and in my life. Thanks to God. 17.—The usual sense of relaxation after an effort. I am oppressed too with a feeling of deep unworthiness, inability to answer my vocation, and the desire of rest. 18. To Windsor, had an audience of the Queen ; so warm about Sir G. Lewis, and she warned me not to overwork.

Lewis had died five days before (April 13), and this is Mr. Gladstone's entry :—

April 14.—Reached C. H. T. at 11¼, and was met by the sad news of the death of Sir George Lewis. I am pained to think of my differences with him at one time on finance ; however, he took benefit by them rather than otherwise. A most able, most learned, most unselfish, and most genial man.

To Sir Gilbert Lewis, he wrote (April 18) :—

Like several eminent public men of our time, he had many qualities for which the outer world did not perhaps, though it may not have denied them, ever give him full positive credit. For example, his singular courtesy and careful attention to others in all transactions great and small ; his thoroughly warm and most forthcoming and genial disposition ; his almost unconsciousness of the vast stores of his mind, and of the great facility and marvellous precision with which he used them ; and, if I may so say, the noble and antique simplicity of character which he united with such knowledge of men and of affairs.

The final budget of this most remarkable series was that of 1866, when he swept away the last of the old vexatious duties on timber. It contained another element as to which, as I have said, some thought he had not been keen enough. In the budget of 1866 he first started the scheme of a sinking fund, which, when amplified, and particularly when simplified by his successors, did so much to reduce the dead weight of debt.[2] The complication of his scheme was due to his desire to make sure of its stability, and undoubtedly he would have carried it if he had remained in office through the session. He is, however, entitled to credit for laying the foundation of an effective sinking fund.

One word more may be added on Mr. Gladstone as financier.

[1] *Nineteenth Century*, Feb. 1880, p. 381.
[2] Mr. Courtney contributes a good account of this measure to the chapter on Finance in Ward's *Reign of Queen Victoria*, i. pp. 345-7.

He was far too comprehensive in his outlook to suppose that
the great outburst of material prosperity during the years in
which he controlled the exchequer and guided parliament in
affairs of money, was wholly and without qualification due to
budgets alone. To insist on ascribing complex results to single
causes is the well-known vice of narrow and untrained minds.
He was quite alive to the effects of 'the enormous, constant,
rapid and diversified development of mechanical power, and
the consequent saving of labour by the extension of machinery.'
He was well aware of the share of new means of locomotion in
the growth of industrial enterprise. But the special cause of
what was most peculiar to England in the experience of this
period he considered to be the wise legislation of parliament,
in seeking every opportunity for abolishing restrictions upon
the application of capital and the exercise of industry and
skill.   In this wise legislation his own energetic and beneficent
genius played the master part.

CHAPTER V

AMERICAN CIVIL WAR

(1861–1863)

Then came the outbreak which had been so often foretold, so often menaced ; and the ground reeled under the nation during four years of agony, until at last, after the smoke of the battlefield had cleared away, the horrid shape which had cast its shadow over a whole continent had vanished, and was gone for ever.—John Bright.

Sir Cornewall Lewis in a memorandum printed for the use of his colleagues both truly and impressively described the momentous struggle that at this time broke upon the family of civilised nations in both hemispheres. 'It may be fairly asserted,' says the particularly competent writer of it, 'that the war in America is the greatest event that has occurred in the political world since the definitive fall of Napoleon in 1815. The expulsion of the elder branch of the Bourbons in 1830 ; the expulsion of Louis Philippe in 1848 ; the re-establishment of a republic, and the subsequent restoration of a Bonaparte to the imperial throne—were all important events, both to France and to the rest of Europe ; but (with the exception of the recent annexation of Savoy and Nice) they have not altered the boundaries of France ; and Europe still, in spite of minor changes, substantially retains the form impressed upon it by the treaty of Vienna.[1] With respect to the internal consequences of these changes, a French revolution has become a fight in the streets of Paris, in order to determine who shall be the occupant of the Tuileries. The administrative body and the army—the two great governing powers of France—remain substantially unaffected ; whereas the American civil war threatens a complete territorial re-arrangement of the Union ; it also portends a fundamental change in the constitution, by which both its federal and state elements will be recast.'

Of this immense conflict Mr. Gladstone, like most of the leading statesmen of the time, and like the majority of his countrymen, failed to take the true measure. The error that

[1] On this sentence in his copy of the memorandum Mr. Gladstone pencils in the margin as was his way, his favourite Italian corrective, ma !

lay at the root of our English misconception of the American struggle is now clear. We applied ordinary political maxims to what was not merely a political contest, but a social revolution. Without scrutiny of the cardinal realities beneath, we discussed it like some superficial conflict in our old world about boundaries, successions, territorial partitions, dynastic preponderance. The significance of the American war was its relation to slavery. That war arose from the economic, social, and political consequences that flowed from slavery—its wasteful cultivation, the consequent need for extension of slave territory, the probable revival of the accursed African trade, the constitution of slave-holders as the sole depositaries of social prestige and political power. Secession was undertaken for the purpose of erecting into an independent state a community whose whole structure was moulded on a system that held labour in contempt, that kept the labourer in ignorance and cruel bondage, that demanded a vigilant censorship of the press and an army of watchmen and spies. And this barbaric state was to set itself up on the border of a great nation, founded on free industry, political equality, diffused knowledge, energetic progress. Such was the meaning of secession. 'The rebellion,' as Charles Sumner well said to Mr. Gladstone in 1864, 'is slavery in arms, revolting, indecent, imperious.' Therefore those who fought against secession fought against slavery and all that was involved in that dark burden, and whatever their motives may at different times have been, they rendered an immortal service to humanity.[1]

At a very early period Mr. Gladstone formed the opinion that the attempt to restore the Union by force would and must fail. 'As far as the *controversy* between North and South,' he wrote to the Duchess of Sutherland (May 29, 1861) 'is a controversy on the principle announced by the vice-president of the South, viz. that which asserts the superiority of the white man, and therewith founds on it his right to hold the black in slavery, I think that principle detestable, and I am wholly with the opponents of it . . . No distinction can in my eyes be broader than the distinction between the question whether the Southern ideas of slavery are right, and the question whether they can justifiably be put down by war from the North.' To Cyrus Field he wrote (Nov. 27, 1862) :—'Your frightful conflict may be regarded from many points of view. The competency of the Southern states to secede ; the rightfulness of their conduct in seceding (two matters wholly distinct and a great

[1] Of course the literature of this great theme is enormous, but an English reader with not too much time will find it well worked out in the masterly political study, *The Slave Power*, by J. E. Cairnes (1861), that vigorous thinker and sincere lover of truth, if ever there was one. Besides Cairnes, the reader who cares to understand the American civil war should turn to F. L. Olmsted's *Journeys and Explorations in the Cotton Kingdom* (1861), and *A Journey in the Seaboard Slave States* (1856)—as interesting a picture of the South on the eve of its catastrophe, as Arthur Young's picture of France on the eve of the revolution.

deal too much confounded) ; the natural reluctance of Northern Americans to acquiesce in the severance of the union, and the apparent loss of strength and glory to their country ; the bearing of the separation on the real interests and on the moral character of the North ; again, for an Englishman, its bearing with respect to British interests ;—all these are texts of which any one affords ample matter for reflection, but I will only state as regards the last of them, that I for one have never hesitated to maintain that, in my opinion, the separate and special interests of England were all on the side of the maintenance of the old union, and if I were to look at those interests alone, and had the power of choosing in what way the war should end, I would choose for its ending by the restoration of the old union this very day.'

In a letter to the Duchess of Sutherland (Nov. 7, 1862), he says :—'A friendly correspondent writes to say he is sorry the South has my sympathies. But the South has not my sympathies, except in the sense in which the North has them also. I wish them both cordially well, which I believe is more than most Englishmen can at present say with truth. In both I see the elements of future power and good ; in both I see also the elements of danger and mischief.' To another correspondent :— 'I have never to my knowledge expressed any sympathy with the Southern cause in any speech at Newcastle or elsewhere, nor have I passed any eulogium upon President Davis. In dealing whether with South or North I have thought it out of my province to touch in any way the complicated question of praise and blame.'

At a very early stage the Duke of Argyll sent him some letter of Mrs. Beecher Stowe's, and Mr. Gladstone in acknowledging it from Penmaenmawr (Aug. 26, 1861) writes expressing all possible respect for her character and talents, but thinks that she has lost intellectual integrity :—

It seems to me that the South has two objects in view : firstly the liberation of its trade and people from the law of tribute to the North ; secondly and perhaps mainly, the maintenance of the slave system without fear or risk of Northern interference. That on the other hand it is very difficult to analyse that movement of the North which Mrs. Stowe finds sublime, but which in my eyes is tumultuous. There is the anti-slavery motive impelling with great vehemence a small section, which she rather offensively calls the Christian people of the union ; there is the spirit of protection and monopoly, unwilling to surrender future booty ; there is the unquietness in the great towns, found in America as in all countries, and ever ready for a row ; there is the fear which Mr. Motley described, that unless a firm front were shown against secession it would not stop where it had begun ; there is last and (relatively to this subject matter) best of all, the strong instinct of national life, and the abhorrence of nature itself towards all severance of an organized body. This last sentiment, as well as the first, deserve to be treated by us with great tenderness and respect. . . . As to the authority and title of the North it must be granted *prima facie*, but on examination it is subject to a good deal of doubt, and I think it seems to have been the intention of the framers of the constitution not to lay down a rule for the solution of a great question of this kind, but to leave it open. And if so, I think they were wise ; for such a question could only arise for any practical purpose at a time when the foundations of the great social deep are broken up, and when the forces brought into unrestrained play are by far too gigantic to be controlled by paper conventions.

So much for his view of the case in its general aspect.

II

At one dangerous moment in the conflict it seemed possible that Great Britain might be forced to take a part. The commander of an American man-of-war boarded the *Trent* (Nov. 8, 1861), a British mail-boat, seized two emissaries from the Southern confederacy on their way to Europe, and carried them off to his own ship, whence they were afterwards landed and thrown into prison. This act was in direct violation of those rights of neutrals of which the United States hitherto had been the strictest champion against Great Britain ; and nothing was to be gained by it, for the presence of the two commissioners was not in the least likely to effect any change in the policy of either England or France. Violent explosions of public feeling broke out on both sides of the Atlantic ; of anger in England, of exultation in America. Mr. Gladstone's movements at this critical hour are interesting. On Nov. 27, says Phillimore, 'Gladstones dined here. Gladstone, with the account in his pocket from the evening papers of the capture of the Southern envoys out of the English mail-ship.' The next two nights he was at court.

Nov. 28.—Off at 6.30 to Windsor. The Queen and Prince spoke much of the American news.

Nov. 29 (Friday).—Came up to town for the cabinet on American news. Returned to Windsor for dinner, and reported to Queen and Prince.

Of this important cabinet, Mr. Gladstone wrote an account to the Duke of Argyll, then absent from London :—

Dec. 3, '61.—The cabinet determined on Friday to ask reparation, and on Saturday they agreed to two despatches to Lord Lyons of which the one recited the facts, stated we could not but suppose the American government would of itself be desirous to afford us reparation, and said that in any case we must have (1) the commissioners returned to British protection ; and (2) an apology or expression of regret. The second of these despatches desired Lyons to come away within seven days if the demands are not complied with. *I thought and urged that we should hear what the Americans had to say before withdrawing Lyons, for I could not feel sure that we were at the bottom of the law of the case, or could judge here and now what form it would assume. But this view did not prevail.*

We may assume that Mr. Gladstone, in reporting these proceedings at Windsor, did not conceal his own arguments for
moderation which had been overruled. On the following day
the cabinet again met. ' Nov. 30 (Sat.). Left Windsor at 11.25.
Cabinet 3-5½. Lord Russell's draft softened and abridged.'
That is to say the draft was brought nearer, though not near
enough, to the temper urged upon the cabinet and represented
at court by Mr. Gladstone the day before.

The story of the first of these two critical despatches is
pretty well known ; how the draft initialled by Lord Russell
was sent down the same night to Windsor ; how the Prince
Consort—then as it proved rapidly sinking down into his fatal
illness—found it somewhat meagre, and suggested modifications
and simplifications ; how the Queen returned the draft with the
suggestions in a letter to the prime minister ; how Palmerston
thought them excellent, and after remodelling the draft in the
more temperate spirit recommended by the Prince, though
dropping at least one irritating phrase in the Queen's
memorandum,[1] sent it back to the foreign office, whence it was
duly sent on (Dec. 1) to Lord Lyons at Washington. It seems,
moreover, that a day's reflection had brought his colleagues
round to Mr. Gladstone's mind, for Lord Russell wrote to
Lord Lyons a private note (Dec. 1) in effect instructing him
to say nothing about withdrawing in seven days.[2]

The British despatches were delivered to Lord Lyons at
Washington at midnight on December 18 ; the reparation
despatch was formally read to Mr. Seward on the 23rd ; and
on Christmas Day Lincoln had a meeting of his cabinet.
Sumner was invited to attend, and he read long letters from
Cobden and Bright. 'At all hazards,' said Bright, 'you must
not let this matter grow to a war with England. Even if you
are right and we are wrong, war will be fatal to your idea of
restoring the union. . . . I implore you not, on any feeling that
nothing can be conceded, and that England is arrogant and
seeking a quarrel, to play the game of every enemy of your
country.'[3] A French despatch in the English sense was also
read. Seward and Sumner were in favour of giving up the
men. The president, thinking of popular excitement, hesitated.
In the end, partly because the case was bad on the merits,
partly because they could not afford to have a second great war
upon their hands, all came round to Seward's view.[4]

---

[1] See Nicolay and Hay, *Abraham Lincoln*, v. p. 28. Also Martin's *Life of the Prince
Consort*, v. p. 421.

[2] See Walpole's *Russell*, ii. p. 358.

[3] War with England, or the probability of it, would have meant the raising of the
blockade, the withdrawal of a large part of the troops from the Southern frontier, and
substantially the leaving of the Confederates to a *de facto* independence.—Dana's
Wheaton, p. 648.

[4] Rhodes, *History of the United States since 1850*, iii. p. 538. See also *Life of C. F.
Adams*, by his son C. F. A., Boston, 1900, chapter xii., especially pp. 223-4.

III

By the autumn of 1862 the war had lasted a year and a half. It was already entailing a cost heavier than our war with Napoleon at its most expensive period. The North had still failed to execute its declared purpose of reducing the South to submission. The blockade of the southern ports, by stopping the export of cotton, was declared to have produced worse privations, loss, and suffering to England and France than were ever produced to neutral nations by a war. It was not in Mr. Gladstone's nature to sit with folded hands in sight of what he took to be hideous and unavailing carnage and havoc. Lord Palmerston, he tells Mrs. Gladstone (July 29, 1862), 'has come exactly to my mind about some early representation of a friendly kind to America, if we can get France *and* Russia to join.' A day or two later (Aug. 3) he writes to the Duke of Argyll :—'My *opinion* is that it is vain, and wholly unsustained by precedent, to say nothing shall be done until both parties are desirous of it ; that, however, we ought to avoid sole action, or anything except acting in such a combination as would morally represent the weight of impartial Europe ; that with this view we ought to communicate with France and Russia ; to make with them a friendly representation (if they are ready to do it) of the mischief and the hopelessness of prolonging the contest in which both sides have made extraordinary and heroic efforts ; but if they are not ready, then to wait for some opportunity when they may be disposed to move with us. The adhesion of other powers would be desirable if it does not encumber the movement.'

'In the year 1862,' says Mr. Gladstone in a fragment of autobiography, 'I had emerged from very grave financial [budget] difficulties, which in 1860 and 1861 went near to breaking me down. A blue sky was now above me, and some of the Northern liberals devised for me a triumphant visit to the Tyne, which of course entailed as one of its incidents a public dinner.' Seeing a visit to Newcastle announced, Lord Palmerston wrote (Sept. 24) to Mr. Gladstone, begging him on no account to let the chancellor of the exchequer be too sympathetic with the tax-payer, or to tell the country that it was spending more money than it could afford. A more important part of the letter was to inform Mr. Gladstone that he himself and Lord Russell thought the time was fast approaching when an offer of mediation ought to be made by England, France, and Russia, and that Russell was going privately to instruct the ambassador at Paris to sound the French government. 'Of course,' Lord Palmerston said, 'no actual step would be taken without the sanction of the cabinet. But if I am not mistaken, you would be inclined to approve such a course.' The proposal would be made to both North and South.

If both should accept, an armistice would follow, and negotiations on the basis of separation. If both should decline, then
Lord Palmerston assumed that they would acknowledge the
independence of the South. The next day Mr. Gladstone
replied. He was glad to learn what the prime minister had
told him, and for two reasons especially he desired that the
proceedings should be prompt. The first was the rapid
progress of the Southern arms and the extension of the area
of Southern feeling. The second was the risk of violent
impatience in the cotton-towns of Lancashire, such as would
prejudice the dignity and disinterestedness of the proffered
mediation.[1] On September 17 Russell had replied to a letter
from Palmerston three days earlier, saying explicitly, 'I agree
with you that the time is come for offering mediation to the
United States government, with a view to the recognition of
the independence of the Confederates. I agree further, that
in case of failure, we ought ourselves to recognise the Southern
states as an independent state.'[2] So far, then, had the two
heads of the government advanced, when Mr. Gladstone went
to Newcastle.

The people of the Tyne gave him the reception of a king.
The prints of the time tell how the bells rang, guns thundered,
a great procession of steamers followed him to the mouth of
the river, ships flew their gayest bunting, the banks were
thronged with hosts of the black-handed toilers of the forges,
the furnaces, the coal-staiths, chemical works, glass factories,
shipyards, eager to catch a glimpse of the great man ; and all
this not because he had tripled the exports to France, but
because a sure instinct had revealed an accent in his eloquence
that spoke of feeling for the common people.[3]

Oct. 7, 1862.—Reflected further on what I should say about Lancashire
and America, for both these subjects are critical. . . . At two we went

[1] In the summer of 1862 he took an active part in schemes for finding employment
at Hawarden for Lancashire operatives thrown out of work by the cotton-famine.
One of the winding-paths leading through some of the most beautiful spots of the park
at Hawarden was made at this time by factory workers from Lancashire employed by
Mr. Gladstone for purposes of relief.
[2] Walpole's *Life of Russell*, ii. p. 361.
[3] In a jingle composed for the occasion, the refrain is—

'Honour give to sterling worth,
Genius better is than birth,
So here's success to Gladstone.'

In thanking a Newcastle correspondent for his reception, Mr. Gladstone writes
(Oct. 20, 1862) :—'To treat these occurrences as matter of personal obligation to those
who have taken a part in them would be to mistake the ground on which they rest.
But I must say with unfeigned sincerity that I can now perceive I have been appropriat-
ing no small share of honour that is really due to the labour of others : of Mr. Cobden
as to the French treaty, and of the distinguished men who have in our day by their
upright and enlightened public conduct made law and government names so dear to
the people of England.' 'Indeed,' says a contemporary journalist, 'if Middlesborough
did not do honour to Mr. Gladstone, we don't know who should, for the French treaty
has been a greater boon to the iron manufacturers of that young but rising seaport,
than to any other class of commercial men in the north of England.'—*Newcastle Daily
Chronicle* Oct. 11, 1862.

to Newcastle and saw the principal objects, including especially the fine church and lantern, the gem of an old castle, and Grey Street—I think our best modern street. The photographer also laid hands on me. At six we went to a crowded and enthusiastic dinner of near 500. I was obliged to make a long oration which was admirably borne. The hall is not very easy to fill with the voice, but quite practicable. 8.—Reached Gateshead at 12, and after an address and reply, embarked in the midst of a most striking scene which was prolonged and heightened as we went down the river at the head of a fleet of some 25 steamers, amidst the roar of guns and the banks lined or dotted above and below with multitudes of people. The expedition lasted six hours, and I had as many speeches as hours. Such a pomp I shall probably never again witness ; circumstances have brought upon me what I do not in any way deserve. . . . The spectacle was really one for Turner, no one else. 9.—Off to Sunderland. Here we had a similar reception and a progress through the town and over the docks and harbour works. I had to address the naval men, and then came a large meeting in the hall. Thence by rail to Middlesborough. At Darlington we were met by Lord Zetland, the mayor, and others. Middlesborough was as warm or even warmer. Another progress and steamboat procession and incessant flood of information respecting this curious place. The labour, however, is too much ; giddiness came over me for a moment while I spoke at Sunderland, and I had to take hold of the table. At Middlesborough we had an address and reply in the town hall, then a public dinner, and we ended a day of over fifteen hours at Upleatham before midnight. C. again holding out, and indeed she is a great part of the whole business with the people everywhere. I ought to be thankful, still more ought I to be ashamed. It was vain to think of reading, writing, or much reflecting on such a day. I was most happy to lie down for fifteen minutes at Mr. Vaughan's in Middlesborough. 11.—Off at 8 A.M. to take the rail at Guisbro'. At Middlesborough many friends had gathered at the station to give us a parting cheer. We came on to York, went at once to the mansion-house, and then visited the minster. At two came the 'luncheon,' and I had to address another kind of audience.

Unhappily, the slave must still go in the triumphal car to remind us of the fallibilities of men, and here the conqueror made a grave mistake. At the banquet in the town hall of Newcastle (Oct. 7), with which all these joyous proceedings had begun, Mr. Gladstone let fall a sentence about the American war of which he was destined never to hear the last :—'We know quite well that the people of the Northern states have not yet drunk of the cup—they are still trying to hold it far from their lips—which all the rest of the world see they nevertheless must drink of. We may have our own opinions about slavery ; we may be for or against the South ; but there is no doubt that Jefferson Davis and other leaders of the South have made an army ; they are making, it appears, a navy ; and they have made what is more than either, they have made a nation.'

Here the speaker was forgetful of a wholesome saying of his own, that 'a man who speaks in public ought to know, besides his own meaning, the meaning which others will attach to his words.' The sensation was immediate and profound. All the world took so pointed an utterance to mean that the government were about to recognise the independence of the South. The cotton men were thrown into a position of doubt and uncertainty that still further disturbed their trade. Orders for cotton were countermanded, and the supply of the precious material for a moment threatened to become worse than ever. Cobden and Bright were twitted with the lapse of their favourite from a central article of their own creed and commandments. Louis Blanc, then in exile here, describing the feeling of the country, compares the sympathy for the North to a dam and the sympathy for the South to a torrent, and says he fears that Gladstone at Newcastle had yielded to the temptation of courting popularity.[1] The American minister dropped a hint about passports.[2]

To the numerous correspondents who complained of his language Mr. Gladstone framed a form of reply, disclaiming responsibility for all the various inferences that people chose to draw from his language. 'And generally,' his secretary concluded, in phrases that justly provoked plain men to wrath, 'Mr. Gladstone desires me to remark that to form opinions upon questions of policy, to announce them to the world, and to take or to be a party to taking any of the steps necessary for giving them effect, are matters which, though connected together, are in themselves distinct, and which may be separated by intervals of time longer or shorter according to the particular circumstances of the case.'[3] Mr. Gladstone sent a copy of this enigmatical response to the foreign secretary, who was far too acute not to perceive all the mischief and the peril, but had his full share of that generosity of our public life that prevents a minister from bearing too hardly on a colleague who has got the boat and its crew into a scrape. Lord Russell replied from Walmer (Oct. 20) :—' I have forwarded to your private secretary your very proper answer to your very impertinent correspondent. Still, you must allow me to say that I think you went beyond the latitude which all speakers must be allowed, when you said that Jeff. Davis had made a nation. Recognition would seem to follow, and for that step I think the cabinet is not prepared. However, we shall soon meet to discuss this very topic.' A week after the deliverance at Newcastle, Lewis, at Lord Palmerston's request as I have heard, put things right in a speech at Hereford. The Southern states, he said, had not

---

[1] *Letters on England*, pp. 146-78.
[2] Adams wrote in his diary :—'*Oct.* 8. If Gladstone be any exponent at all of the views of the cabinet, then is my term likely to be very short. The animus, as it respects Mr. Davis and the recognition of the rebel cause, is very apparent. *Oct.* 9 :— We are now passing through the very crisis of our fate. I have had thoughts of seeking a conference with Lord Russell, to ask an explanation of Gladstone's position ; but, on reflection, I think I shall let a few days at least pass, and then perhaps sound matters incidentally.'—Rhodes, iv. p. 340. *Life of Adams*, pp. 286-7.
[3] Oct. 18, 1862.

de facto established their independence and were not entitled to recognition on any accepted principles of public law.

It is superfluous for any of us at this day to pass judgment. Mr. Gladstone has left on record in a fragmentary note of late date his own estimate of an error that was in truth serious enough, and that has since been most of all exaggerated by those sections of society and opinion who at the time most eagerly and freely shared the very same delusion.

'I have yet to record,' he writes (July 1896) in the fragment already more than once mentioned, ' an undoubted error, the most singular and palpable, I may add the least excusable of them all, especially since it was committed so late as in the year 1862, when I had outlived half a century. In the autumn of that year, and in a speech delivered after a public dinner at Newcastle-upon-Tyne, I declared in the heat of the American struggle that Jefferson Davis had made a nation, that is to say, that the division of the American Republic by the establishment of a Southern or secession state was an accomplished fact. Strange to say, this declaration, most unwarrantable to be made by a minister of the crown with no authority other than his own, was not due to any feeling of partizanship for the South or hostility to the North. The fortunes of the South were at their zenith. Many who wished well to the Northern cause despaired of its success. The friends of the North in England were beginning to advise that it should give way, for the avoidance of further bloodshed and greater calamity. I weakly supposed that the time had come when respectful suggestions of this kind, founded on the necessity of the case, were required by a spirit of that friendship which, in so many contingencies of life, has to offer sound recommendations with a knowledge that they will not be popular. Not only was this a misjudgment of the case, but even if it had been otherwise, I was not the person to make the declaration. I really, though most strangely, believed that it was an act of friendliness to all America to recognise that the struggle was virtually at an end. I was not one of those who on the ground of British interests desired a division of the American Union. My view was distinctly opposite. I thought that while the Union continued it never could exercise any dangerous pressure upon Canada to estrange it from the empire—our honour, as I thought, rather than our interest forbidding its surrender. But were the Union split, the North, no longer checked by the jealousies of slave-power, would seek a partial compensation for its loss in annexing, or trying to annex, British North America. Lord Palmerston desired the severance as a diminution of a dangerous power, but prudently held his tongue.

That my opinion was founded upon a false estimate of the facts was the very least part of my fault. I did not perceive the gross impropriety of such an utterance from a cabinet minister, of a power allied in blood and language, and bound to loyal neutrality ; the case being further exaggerated by the fact that we were already, so to speak, under indictment before the world for not (as was alleged) having strictly enforced the laws of neutrality in the matter of the cruisers. My offence was indeed only a mistake, but one of incredible grossness, and with such consequences of offence and alarm attached to it, that my failing to perceive them justly exposed me to very severe blame. It illustrates vividly that incapacity which my mind so long retained, and perhaps still exhibits, an incapacity of viewing subjects all round, in their extraneous as well as in their internal properties, and thereby of knowing when to be silent and when to speak.

I am the more pained and grieved, because I have for the last five-and-twenty years received from the government and people of America tokens of goodwill which could not fail to arouse my undying gratitude. When we came to the arbitration at Geneva, my words were cited as part of the proof of hostile *animus*. Meantime I had prepared a lengthened statement to show from my abundant declarations on other occasions that there was and could be on my part no such *animus*. I was desirous to present this statement to the arbitrators. My colleagues objected so largely to the proceeding that I desisted. In this I think they probably were wrong. I addressed my paper to the American minister for the information of his government, and Mr. Secretary Fish gave me, so far as intention was concerned, a very handsome acquittal.

And strange to say, *post hoc* though perhaps not *propter hoc*, the United States have been that country of the world in which the most signal marks of public honour have been paid me, and in which my name has been the most popular, the only parallels being Italy, Greece, and the Balkan Peninsula.'

Among the many calumnies poured upon him in this connection was the charge that he had been a subscriber to the Confederate Loan. 'The statement,' he wrote to a correspondent (Oct. 17, 1865), 'is not only untrue, but it is so entirely void of the slightest shadow of support in any imaginable incident of the case, that I am hardly able to ascribe it to mere error, and am painfully perplexed as to the motives which could have prompted so mischievous a forgery.'

IV

As I have already said, the American minister had hinted at passports. Ten days after Mr. Gladstone's speech Mr. Adams saw Lord Russell. Having mentioned some minor matters he came to the real object of the interview. 'If I had trusted,' he said, 'to the construction given by the public to a late speech, I should have begun to think of packing my carpet bag and trunks. His lordship at once embraced the allusion, and whilst endeavouring to excuse Mr. Gladstone, in fact admitted that his act had been regretted by Lord Palmerston and the other cabinet officers. Still he could not disavow the sentiments of Mr. Gladstone ; so far as he understood them (his meaning) was not that ascribed to him by the public. Mr. Gladstone was himself willing to disclaim that. He had written to that effect to Lord Palmerston. . . . His lordship said that the policy of the government was to adhere to a strict neutrality, and to leave this struggle to settle itself. . . . I asked him if I was to understand that policy as not now to be changed. He said, Yes.' [1]

If this relation be accurate, then the foreign secretary did

1 Rhodes, iv. p. 340. Also *Life of C. F. Adams*, p. 287.

not construe strict neutrality as excluding what diplomatists call good offices. On October 13, Lord Russell circulated a memorandum to the cabinet setting out in an argumentative tone all the adverse and confused aspects of the situation and outlook in America, and ending in the emphatic conclusion that it had now become a question for the great Powers of Europe whether it was not their duty to ask both parties to agree to a suspension of arms for the purpose of weighing calmly the advantages of peace. Cornewall Lewis (Oct. 17), while expressing an opinion that a peaceful separation between North and South would in the end have been best for the North, and while apparently believing that the war must one day end in Southern independence, met Russell's suggestion by cogent arguments against action on our part.[1] A week later (Oct. 24), Mr. Gladstone circulated a rejoinder to Lewis, arguing for representation to the two combatants from England, France, and Russia—a representation with moral authority and force, of the opinion of the civilised world upon the conditions of the case.

This pretty nearly concludes all that need be said upon the attitude taken by Mr. Gladstone in that mighty struggle. We may at least add that if, and where, it differed from that of the majority of his countrymen, it did not differ for the worse. In November (1862) the French Emperor renewed proposals of joint mediation. The Emperor had objects of his own to serve. He was entangled in the coils of the Mexican adventure that was to give the first shock to his throne and to add another to the long scroll of tragedies in the house of Hapsburg. From the first the government of the American Union had scowled upon the intervention of Europe in the affairs of Mexico, just as the same government had refused to intervene in a European protest on behalf of Poland. The civil war between North and South kept American hands tied, and Napoleon well knew that the success of the North and the consolidation of the Union would overthrow his designs in Mexico. He cast restlessly about for any combination that promised aid to the Southern confederates, who, whether they should emerge strong or weak from the struggle, would be a useful instrument for his future purposes. So now he pressed England and Russia to join him in a project of mediation. Russia declined. The London cabinet was divided.[2] Mr. Gladstone writes home in

[1] Lewis, throughout 1861, used language of characteristic coolness about the war : 'It is the most singular action for the restitution of conjugal rights that the world ever heard of.' 'You may conquer an insurgent province, but you cannot conquer a seceding state' (Jan. 21, '61). 'The Northern states have been drifted, or rather plunged into war without having any intelligible aim or policy. The South fight for independence ; but what do the North fight for, except to gratify passion or pride ?'— Letters, p. 395, etc. See also preface to his Administration of Great Britain (p. xix), where he says, in 1856, he sees no solution but separation.

[2] There is a story, not very accurate, I should suppose, about Mr. Disraeli's concurrence in the Emperor's view, told from Slidell's despatches in an article by O. F. Aldus, in North American Review, October 1879.

these important days.—'*Nov.* 11. We have had our cabinet to-day and meet again to-morrow. I am afraid we shall do little or nothing in the business of America. But I will send you definite intelligence. Both Lords Palmerston and Russell are *right.—Nov.* 12. The United States affair has ended and not well. Lord Russell rather turned tail. He gave way without resolutely fighting out his battle. However, though we decline for the moment, the answer is put upon grounds and in terms which leave the matter very open for the future. —*Nov.* 13. I think the French will make our answer about America public ; at least it is very possible. But I hope they may not take it as a positive refusal, or at any rate that they may themselves act in the matter. It will be clear that we concur with them, that the war should cease. Palmerston gave to Russell's proposal a feeble and half-hearted support. As to the state of matters generally in the cabinet, I have never seen it smoother ; and they look pretty well, I think, as regards my department, though the distress tells upon me.'

The only speech, I believe, delivered by Mr. Gladstone upon the war in parliament, while resisting the motion for the recognition of the confederacy, was curiously balanced.[1] As to the South, he said, not a few must sympathise with a resistance as heroic as ever was offered in the history of the world on the part of a weaker body against the overpowering forces of a stronger. On the other hand, the cause of the South was so connected with slavery that a strong counter-current of feeling must arise in the mind. Then again, it is impossible for any Englishman not to have a very strong feeling of sympathy with those in the North who saw exalted visions of the great future of their country, now threatened with destruction. He had never agreed with those who thought it a matter of high British interest that the old American union should be torn in pieces. He had always thought that, involved as England was both in interest and in duty and honour with Canada, the balanced state of the American union which caused the whole of American politics to turn on the relative strength of the slavery and Northern interests, was more favourable to our colonial relations in North America, than if the said union were to be divided into a cluster of Northern and a cluster of Southern states. The North would endeavour to re-establish their territorial grandeur by seeking union with the British possessions in North America. He dwelt upon the horrid incidents of war. He insisted once more that the public opinion of this country was unanimous

[1] June 30, 1863. *Hansard*, vol. 171, p. 1800. On four other occasions Mr. Gladstone gave public utterance to his opinion 'on the subject of the war and the disruption '—at Leith, Jan. 11, 1862, at Manchester, April 24, 1862, at Newcastle, Oct. 7, 1862, and once in parliament when a member spoke of the bursting of the American bubble, he says, 'I commented on the expressions with a reproof as sharp as I could venture to make it' (May 27, 1861).

that the restoration of the American union by force was unattainable. Some cries of 'No' greeted this declaration about unanimity, but he would not qualify it further than to say that at any rate it was almost unanimous. The other chief speakers that night were Mr. Forster (who played a brave and clear-sighted part throughout), Lord Robert Cecil, who attacked the 'vague and loose' arguments of the chancellor of the exchequer, and Mr. Bright, who made perhaps the most powerful and the noblest speech of his life.

CHAPTER VI

DEATH OF FRIENDS—DAYS AT BALMORAL

1861–1864)

Itaque veræ amicitiæ difficillime reperiuntur in iis qui in honoribus reque publica versantur.—CICERO.

True friendships are hard to find among men who busy themselves about politics and office.

WITHIN a few months of one another, three of Mr. Gladstone's closest friends and allies were lost to him. Lord Aberdeen died at the end of 1860. The letter written by Mr. Gladstone to the son of his veteran chief is long, but it deserves reproduction.[1] As a writer, though an alert and most strenuous disputant, he was apt to be diffuse and abstract. Partly, these defects were due to the subjects with which, in his literary performances, he mostly chose to deal. Perhaps one secret was that he forgot the famous word of Quintilian, that the way to write well is not to write quickly, but if you take trouble to write well, in time you can write as quickly as you like.[2] His character of Lord Aberdeen, like his beautiful letter in a similar vein about Hope-Scott,[3] where also his feelings were deeply moved, is very different from his more formal manner, and may claim high place among our literary portraits. It is penetrating in analysis, admirable in diction, rich in experience of life and human nature, and truly inspiring in those noble moralities that are the lifeblood of style, and of greater things than mere style can ever be.

Then, in the autumn of 1861, both Graham and Sidney Herbert died; the former the most esteemed and valued of all his counsellors; the latter, so prematurely cut off, 'that beautiful and sunny spirit,' as he called him, perhaps the best beloved of all his friends. 'Called on Gladstone,' says Phillimore on this last occasion (Aug. 3); 'found him at breakfast alone; very glad to see me. His eyes filled with

1 See Appendix.   2 x. iii. 10.
3 *Memoirs of J. R. Hope-Scott,* ii. pp. 284-293.

tears all the time he spoke to me in a broken voice about his
departed friend. The effect upon him has been very striking,
increased no doubt by recent political differences of opinion.'
'It is difficult to speak of Herbert,' Mr. Gladstone said later,
'because with that singular harmony and singular variety of
gifts—every gift of person, every gift of position, every gift
of character with which it pleased Providence to bless him—
he was one of whom we may well recite words that the great
poet of this country has applied to a prince of our early
history, cut off by death earlier than his countrymen would
have desired :—

> ' A sweeter and a lovelier gentleman,
> Framed in the prodigality of nature,
> The spacious world cannot again afford.' [1]

The void thus left was never filled. Of Graham he wrote to
the Duchess of Sutherland :—

Oct. 26.—This most sad and unexpected news from Netherby rises up
between me and your letter. I have lost a friend whom I seem to appreciate the more because the world appreciated him so inadequately ; his
intellectual force could not be denied, but I have never known a person
who had such signal virtues that were so little understood. The remainder
of my political career be it what it may (and I trust not over long) will
be passed in the House of Commons without one old friend who is *both*
political and personal. This is the gradual withdrawal of the props
preparing for what is to follow. Let me not, however, seem to complain,
for never, I believe, was any one blessed so entirely beyond his deserts in
the especial and capital article of friendships.

Not many months later (June, 1862) he had to write to Mr.
Gordon, 'We are all sorely smitten by Canning's death,' whose
fame, he said, would 'bear the scrutinizing judgment of
posterity, under whose keen eye so many illusions are doomed
to fade away.' [2]

In the December of 1861 died the Prince Consort. His last
communication to Mr. Gladstone was a letter (Nov. 19) proposing to recommend him as an elder brother of the Trinity
House in place of Graham. Of Mr. Gladstone's first interview
with the Queen after her bereavement, Dean Wellesley wrote
to him that she was greatly touched by his evidence of sympathy.
'She saw how much you felt for her, and the mind of a person
in such deep affliction is keenly sensitive and observant. Of all
her ministers, she seemed to me to think that you had most
entered into her sorrows, and she dwelt especially upon the
manner in which you had parted from her.' To the Duchess of
Sutherland Mr. Gladstone writes :—

March 20, 1862.—I find I must go out at four exactly. In any case
I do not like to trust to chance your knowing or not knowing what befell
me yesterday. Your advice was excellent. I was really bewildered, but

---

[1] *Richard III.* i. sc. ii. At Salisbury, Sept. 7, 1866.
[2] His school friend, and later, governor-general of India.

that all vanished when the Queen came in and kept my hand a moment. All was beautiful, simple, noble, touching to the very last degree. It was a meeting, for me, to be remembered. I need only report the first and last words of the personal part of the conversation. The first (after a quarter of an hour upon affairs) was (putting down her head and struggling) 'the nation has been very good to me in my time of sorrow'; and the last, 'I earnestly pray it may be long before you are parted from one another.' [1]

In the spring he took occasion at Manchester to pronounce a fine panegyric on the Prince,[2] for which the Queen thanked him in a letter of passionate desolation, too sacred in the anguish of its emotion to be printed here. 'Every source of interest or pleasure,' she concludes, 'causes now the acutest pain. Mrs. Gladstone, who, the Queen knows, is a most tender wife, may in a faint manner picture to herself what the Queen suffers.' Mr Gladstone replies :—

It may not be impertinent in him to assure your Majesty that all the words to which your Majesty refers were received with deep emotion by the whole of a very large assembly, who appeared to feel both your Majesty's too conspicuous affliction, and the solemnity of its relation to the severe and, alas! darkening circumstances of the district.[3]

In presuming to touch upon that relation, and in following the direction which his subject gave him towards very sacred ground, he was especially desirous to avoid using even a phrase or a word of exaggeration, and likewise to speak only as one who had seen your Majesty's great sorrow in no other way than as all your Majesty's subjects beheld it.

In speaking thus he knew that he must fall short of the truth ; and indeed, even were it becoming to make the attempt, he would in vain labour to convey the impression made upon his mind by the interview to which he was admitted at Windsor, and by the letter now in his hands.

More follows in the vein and on the topics that are usual in letters of mourning sympathy, and the effect was what the writer sought. From Balmoral came a note (May 6, 1862) :— 'The Queen wishes Princess Alice to thank Mr. Gladstone in her name for the kind letter he wrote to her the other day, which did her aching heart good. Kind words soothe, but nothing can lessen or alleviate the weight of sorrow she has to bear.'

Many years later he sat down to place on record his thoughts about the Prince Consort, but did not proceed beyond a scanty fragment, which I will here transcribe :—

My praise will be impartial : for he did not fascinate, or command, or attract me through any medium but that of judgment and conscience. There was, I think, a want of freedom, nature, and movement in his demeanour, due partly to a faculty and habit of reflection that never intermitted, partly to an inexorable watchfulness over all he did and said,

1 *March* 19.—Reading, conversation and survey in the house filled the morning at Cliveden. At four we went to Windsor . . . I had an audience of the Queen . . . I had the gratification of hearing, through Lady A. Bruce, that it was agreeable to H.M.—(*Diary.*)
   2 *Gleanings*, i.   3 The Lancashire cotton famine.

which produced something that was related to stillness and chillness in a manner which was notwithstanding, invariably modest, frank, and kind, even to one who had no claims upon him for the particular exhibition of such qualities. Perhaps I had better first disburden myself of what I have to set down against him. I do not think he was a man without prejudices, and this particularly in religion. His views of the church of Rome must, I think, have been illiberal. At any rate, I well remember a conversation with him at Windsor respecting the papal decree imposing the belief in the immaculate conception, somewhere about the time when it came forth. He said he was glad of it, as it would tend to expose and explode the whole system. I contended, with a freedom which he always seemed to encourage, that we all had an interest in the well being and well doing, absolute or relative, of that great Christian communion, and that whatever indicated or increased the predominance of the worse influences within her pale over the better was a thing we ought much to deplore. No assent, even qualified, was to be got.[1]

The death of the Prince Consort was a greater personal calamity to Mr. Gladstone than he could then foresee. Perhaps the disadvantage was almost as real as the death of the consort of King George II. to Sir Robert Walpole. Much as they might differ in political and religious opinion, yet in seriousness, conscience, and laborious temperament, the Prince and he were in exact accord, and it is impossible to doubt that if the Prince had survived at the Queen's right hand, certain jars might have been avoided that made many difficulties for the minister in later times.

II

I may as well here gather into a chapter some short pieces, mainly from letters to Mrs. Gladstone during the period covered by this fifth book. The most interesting of them, perhaps, are the little pictures of his life as minister in attendance at Balmoral; but there are, besides, two or three hints of a simplicity in his faculty of enjoyment in regions outside of graver things, that may shock critics of more complex or fastidious judgment. Readers will benevolently take them all as they come. He made a curious entry in his diary upon his birthday at the end of 1860 :—' *Dec.* 29. Began my fifty-second year. I cannot believe it. I feel within me the rebellious unspoken word. I will not be old. The horizon enlarges, the sky shifts, around me. It is an age of shocks ; a discipline so strong, so manifold, so rapid and whirling that only when it is at an end, if then, can I hope to comprehend it.' Yet nearly all the most conspicuous scenes still lay before him.

October 18, 1860.—I did not get to the play last night from finding *The Woman in White* so very interesting. It has no dull parts, and is far better sustained than *Adam Bede*, though I do not know if it rises quite as high. The character drawing is excellent.

Downing Street, Dec. 15.—The chancellor says (keep this from view)

[1] See the three articles on the Life of the Prince Consort in *Gleanings*, i. pp. 23-130.

that Prince Albert said to him at Windsor: 'We Germans have no boundaries; our only boundary is the Quadrilateral,' *i.e.* fortress in the heart of Italy. This, I fear, must be true, and, if so, is sad enough, because he evidently spoke his mind out unsuspiciously.

Dec. 18.—I actually went last night five mortal miles to Hoxton to see 'Eily O'Connor,' the Colleen Bawn in another shape! It was not without interest, though very inferior, and imitated in some cases with a ludicrous closeness. The theatre is a poor working man's theatre. I paid 1s. for a very aristocratic place. To-night I am going with Phillimore to the Westminster play, a Latin one, which I am afraid is rather long.

Jan. 18, 1861.—I write a few lines to you in the train, near Harrow. We shall not be in till four; all safe; and immense care evidently taken on account of the frost, though I do not feel it much in the air. I have had other matters to keep me warm. Among the letters given me this morning at Hawarden was one from Lord John, in which he quietly informs me that since the cabinet separated *he* has agreed to guarantee a loan, and for Morocco! This I mean to resist, and have managed to write a letter in the carriage to tell him so. What will come of it, I do not know. It is a very serious affair. I am afraid he has committed himself egregiously. I am very bad now; but what *shall* I be at sixty-eight?

Jan. 19.—Indeed, this is a strange world. Yesterday it seemed Lord J. Russell might go out, or more likely I might, or even the cabinet might go to pieces. To-day he writes to me that he supposes he must find a way out of his proposal! So that is over.

Jan. 23.—You seem to have taken great pains about stable affairs, and I am quite satisfied. The truth indeed, alas, is, I am not fit at this critical time to give any thought to such matters. The embarrassment of our vast public expenditure, together with the ill effects of the bad harvest, are so thick upon me, together with the arrangements for next year and the preparation of my own bills for improvements, which, though a laborious, are a healthy and delightful part of my work.

Jan. 24.—I expect Argyll to share my mutton to-night, and we shall, I dare say, have a comfortable talk. Last night I saw Herbert. I think he looks much better. He did not open the subject of estimates, nor did I, before *her*, but I told him what I am sorry to say is true, that the prospects of revenue grow much worse. Up to a certain point, I must certainly make a stand. But I think he is rather frightened about expenditure, and not so panic-stricken about France; so that we may come together.

Jan. 25.—I write from the cabinet. I am in the midst of a deadly struggle about the estimates; the only comfort this year is, that I think the conflict will be more with the navy than the army. Herbert has told me to-day, with a simplicity and absence of egotism, which one could not but remark in his graceful character, the nature of his complaint. You will quickly guess. As to cabinets, Lord John says we had better meet frequently, and it will be on Tuesday *if* I am able to come down next week, but this is full of uncertainty. I hear that the Prince is *wild* about the Danish question.

Jan. 26.—Another cabinet on Monday. It is just possible they may relax after that day. I have had two long days of hard fighting. By dint of what, after all, might be called threat of resignation, I have got the navy estimates a little down, and I am now *in* the battle about the army. About the reduction in the navy, Palmerston criticised, Lord John protested, and Cardwell ! I think went farther than either. Never on any single occasion since this government was formed has his voice been raised in the cabinet for economy. What a misfortune it is that Herbert has no nerve to speak out even in a private conversation. He told me yesterday of his reduction, but did not tell me that more than half of it was purely nominal ! The article in the *Quarterly* is clever ; and what it says, moreover, on the merits of the income-tax is true. I suspect, I might say I fear, it is written by Northcote.

Feb. 5.—Yesterday, in the carriage from Kidderminster, I heard in part a dialogue, of which I gathered so much. *First worthy,* 'I suppose we shall have to pay twopence or threepence more income-tax.' *Second worthy,* 'Gladstone seems to be a totally incompetent man.' *Third,* 'Then he always wraps himself in such mystery. But now I do not see what else he can do ; he has cut away the ground from under his feet' —with a growl about the conservative party. Such is the public opinion of Worcestershire beyond all doubt.

Hawarden, May 24.—The house looks cleanliness itself, and altogether being down here in the fresh air, and seeing nature all round me so busy with her work so beneficent and beautiful, makes me very sick of London and its wrathful politics, and wish that we were all here or hereabouts once more.

July 20.—The political storm has blown over, but I do not think it seems an evening for riding to Holly House, nor can I honestly say that a party there would be a relaxation for my weary bones, and wearier nerves and brain.

Aug. 4.—I have been at All Saints this morning. Though London is empty, as they say, it was absolutely crammed. Richards preached an excellent sermon. But I certainly should not wish to be an habitual attendant there. The intention of the service is most devout, but I am far from liking wholly the mode of execution. My neighbour in church whispered to me, ' Is the Bishop of London's jurisdiction acknowledged here ?' I think he seemed to wish it should not be.

Oct. 22.—Tell Harry [his son] he is right, Latin is difficult, and it is in great part because it is difficult that it is useful. Suppose he wanted to make himself a good jumper ; how would he do it ? By trying *first,* indeed, what was easy, but after that always what was difficult enough to make him exert himself to the uttermost. If he kept to the easy jumps, he would never improve. But the jumps that are at first difficult by and bye become easy. So the Latin lessons, which he now finds difficult, he will find easy when once his mind has been improved and strengthened by those very lessons. See if he understands this.

Dec. 29.—The strangest feeling of all in me is a rebellion (I know not what else to call it) against growing old.

Cliveden, Maidenhead, Jan. 14, 1862.—I have written to John [his brother], and if he is in town I shall go up and see him to-morrow. Meantime I have mentioned Locock, as recommended by you. I fear the dark cloud is slowly gathering over him [his wife's illness], as we have seen it lately gather over so many and then break. I am amazed at the mercy of God towards us, and towards me in particular. I think of all the children, and of their health in body and in mind. It seems as if it could not last; but this is all in God's hand.

Here are the Argylls, Lady Blantyre and a heap of young. We have been busy reading translations of Homer this morning, including some of mine, which are approved. Tennyson has written most noble lines on the Prince. Lord Palmerston is reported well.

Jan. 18.—I lifted Hayward last night back from dinner. He is full of the doctrine that Lord Palmerston is not to last another year. Johnny is then to succeed, and I to lead (as he says by the universal admission of the whigs) in the H. of C. It is rather hard before the death thus to divide the inheritance. But that we may not be too vain, it is attended with this further announcement, that when that event occurs, the government is shortly to break down.

Cabinet Room, Feb. 1.—The cabinet has gone well.[1] It is rather amusing. I am driving the screw; Lewis yields point by point. I think in substance the question is ruled in my favour. Thank God for the prospect of peace; but it will not positively be settled till Monday. Lewis's last dying speech, 'Well, we will see what can be done.'

Bowden, Wilts., Feb. 19. — The funeral is over [the wife of his brother]. Nothing could be better ordered in point of taste and feeling. It was one of the most touching, I think the most touching, scene I ever witnessed, when the six daughters weeping profusely knelt around the grave, and amidst their sobs and tears just faltered out the petitions of the Lord's Prayer in the service. John, sensible of his duty of supporting others, went through it all with great fortitude. On the whole, I must say I can wish no more for any family, than that when the stroke of bereavement comes, they meet it as it has been met here.

Nov. 18.—I have sat an hour with Lord Lyndhurst. He is much *older* than when I saw him last, but still has pith and life in him, as well as that astonishing freshness of mind which gives him a charm in its way quite unrivalled. He was very kind, and what is more, he showed, I think, a seriousness of tone which has been missed before.

Last night I saw 'Lord Dundreary.' I think it—the part and the player, not the play—quite admirable. It is a thoroughly refined piece of acting, such as we hardly ever see in England; and it combines with refinement intense fun. My face became with laughing like what Falstaff says he will make Prince Henry's face, 'like a wet cloak ill laid up'[2] (*Phillimore*).

Windsor Castle, Dec. 10.—Here I am with six candles blazing! of which I shall put out a larger proportion when no longer afraid of a visit from the great people about the passages. I got your letter this morning, but I am amazed at your thinking I have the pluck to ask the Princess of Wales! or the Queen!!! about photographs promised or not promised.

In came the Dean; after that, a summons to the Queen, with whom I have been an hour. She is well in health and in spirits, and when she speaks of the Prince does it with a free, natural, and healthy tone, that is most pleasing. I am to see the Prince of Wales after dinner. I now therefore make sure of leaving to-morrow. The Queen asked kindly about you, and I saw little Princess Beatrice.

---

[1] On the estimates for 1862-63.   [2] *2 Henry IV.*, v. sc. i.

III

Aug. 31, 1863.—Walked 24¾ miles. Found it rather too much for my stiffening limbs. My day of long stretches is, I think, gone by.

Balmoral, Sept. 26.—This place is on the whole very beautiful and satisfactory ; and Deeside at large has lost for me none of its charms, with its black-green fir and grey rock, and its boundless ranges of heather still almost in full bloom. The Queen spends a good many hours out, and looks well, but older. I had a long conversation or audience to-day, but as regards the form and mode of life here, so far as I see, it does not differ for visitors from Windsor. All meals and rooms are separate, but sometimes, it appears, some are invited to dine with the Queen. The household circle is smaller here than at Windsor, and so less formal and dull. I doubt your doctrine about your message, but I will give it if a good opportunity occurs. She talked very pleasantly and well upon many matters public and other—(Do not go on reading this aloud or give it to others). As to politics, she talked most of America and Germany ; also some Lancashire distress. She feels an immense interest in Germany, her recollections of the Prince's senti-ments being in that, as in other matters, a barometer to govern her sympathies and affections. She said (when I hoped she had received benefit from the air here) that she thought she had been better in Germany than anywhere, though it was excessively hot. She asked where I had been, and about our living at Hawarden, and where it was. I told her I thought she had been there, at least driving through from Eaton (was it not so ?) when she was Princess, and at last she seemed to remember it, and said it was thirty-one years ago. Princess Alice has got a black boy here who was given to her, and he produces a great sensation on the Deeside, where the people never saw anything of the kind and cannot conceive it. A woman, and an intelligent one, cried out in amazement on seeing him, and said she would certainly have fallen down but for the Queen's presence. She said nothing would induce her to wash his clothes *as the black would come off !* This story the Queen told me in good spirits.

She said that some people after heavy bereavement disliked seeing those whom they had known well before, and who reminded them of what had been, but with her it was exactly the opposite ; it was the greatest effort and pain to her to see any one who had [not] known *them* before, and their mode of living. As an instance, she said it cost her much to see the Emperor of Austria, whom the Prince had never known. Evidently this clinging to things old will form itself into a habit, but I am afraid it may hereafter, when more have died off, be a matter of difficulty to her. It is impossible to help seeing that she mistrusts Lord Russell's judgment in foreign affairs, indeed I have already had clear proof of this. She likes Lord Palmerston's better ; thinks he looks very old, and will not allow that it is all owing to an accident. But dinner is drawing near, so good-bye. We have had a good day, and have been up to the pyramid put on a hill-top as a memorial to the Prince, with the beautiful inscription.

Sept. 27.—I do not think Sunday is the best of days here. I in vain inquired with care about episcopal services ; there did not seem to be one within fifteen miles, if indeed so near. We had something between family prayer and a service in the dining-room at ten ; it lasted about forty minutes. Dr. Caird gave a short discourse, good in material, though over florid in style for my taste. The rest of the day I have had to myself. The Prince and Princess of Hesse I think went to the parish church. You are better off at Penmaenmawr. . . . I saw the two princes last night. They were playing billiards. The Prince of Wales asked particularly, as always, about you and Willy.

Sept. 28.—I must be brief as I have been out riding with Sir C. and Miss Phipps to Alt-na-Guisach (the Queen's cottage), and came in *late*. Be assured all is very comfortable and restful here. I think too that I feel the air very invigorating, my room is pleasant and cheerful on the ground floor, with a turret dressing-room. . . . I am pretty much master of my time. To-day I have heard nothing of the Queen. Last evening I was summoned to dine, as was Lady Churchill. It was extremely interesting. We were but seven in all, and anything more beautifully domestic than the Queen and her family it was impossible to conceive. The five were her Majesty, Prince and Princess Louis, Prince Alfred, and Princess Helena. Princess Louis (whom the Queen in speaking of still calls Princess Alice) asked about you all. I had the pleasure of hearing the good report of Lucy altogether confirmed from her lips and *the Queen's*. The Queen thinks her like her dear mother. She talked about many things and persons ; among others the Lyttelton family, and asked about the boys *seriatim*, but pulled me up at once when, in a fit of momentary oblivion, I said the New Zealander was the third. She spoke of the chancellor and of Roundell Palmer ; I had a good opportunity of speaking him *up*, and found she had his book of hymns. She spoke very freely about the chancellor ; and I heard from her that the attorney-general resigns on the score of health—of course Palmer succeeds. Prince Alfred is going to Edinburgh to study ; he is a smart fellow, and has plenty of go in him.

Sept. 29.—I have just come in at 6½ from a fine hill walk of over three hours, quite ready for another were there light and opportunity.

Sept. 30.—I am come in from a nineteen mile walk to the Lake of Lochnagar with Dr. Bekker, as fresh as a lark ! Very wet. The Queen sent me a message not to go up Lochnagar (top) if there was mist ; and mist there was, with rain to boot. I find the resemblance to Snowdon rather striking. It is 3800 feet ; we went up about 3300. You forgot to tell me for what pious object you picked Lord P.'s pocket. Nor do you distinctly tell me where to address, but as you say three nights I suppose it should be Penmaenmawr. Last night we went down to Aber-geldie to the gillies' ball. There was a dance called the perpetual jig, nearly the best fun I ever witnessed. The princes danced with great activity after deer-stalking, and very well ; Prince Alfred I thought beautifully. They were immensely amused at having passed me on the way home and offered me a lift, to which I replied (it was dark) thinking they were General Grey and a household party. The Princess did not dance—asked about you—is taking great care, and the Prince very strict about it also. She does not ride or fatigue herself. The event, accord-ing to Dr. Jenner, should take place in March or early in April. You see his authority and yours are at variance. The Queen was (according to Mrs. Bruce, who dined with her) very low last night, on account of the ball, which naturally recalled so much.

Oct. 3.—It happened oddly yesterday I was sent for while out. I had had a message from the Queen in the morning which made me think there would be no more, so I went out at a quarter past three. I am very sorry this happened. I am to see her, I believe, this evening.

Oct. 4.—The service at Ballater has made a great difference in favour of this Sunday. It was celebrated in the Free Kirk schoolroom for girls! and with a congregation under twenty, most attentive though very small, and no one left the room when we came to the Holy Communion. The Knollys family and people were one half or so. I gave Mrs. Knollys and one daughter a lift in *my* drag back to Birkhall (2½ miles which they all loyally walk to and fro) and had luncheon there. I had Thomas with me. The sermon was *extremely* good ; but the priest had a *few* antics. I believe this is about the first expedition ever made from Balmoral to an episcopal service. Perhaps encouraged by my example, Captain W. got a drag to Castleton this morning, being a Roman. There was *no* chaplain here to-day, and so no dining-room service, which for many I fear means no service at all.

I dined with the Queen again last night ; also Lady Augusta Bruce—seven, again, in all. The Crown Princess had a headache, as well she might, so they were not there. The same royalties as before, and everything quite as pleasing. The Queen talked Shakespeare, Scott, the use of the German language in England (and there I could not speak out *all* my mind), Guizot's translation of the Prince's speeches, and his preface (which the Queen has since sent me to look at), the children's play at Windsor (when Princess Alice acted a high priest, with great success—in 'Athalie,' I think), the Prussian children (the Queen says the baby is not pretty—the little boy on coming yesterday called them all Stumpfnase, pugnose), handwritings, Lord Palmerston's to wit, Mr. Disraeli's style in his letters to the Queen, the proper mode of writing, on what paper, etc., and *great* laudation of Lady Lyttelton's letters. Princess Alice declares her baby is pretty, and says she shall show it me. The Queen was very cheerful, and seemed for the time happy. A statue of the Prince is about to be set up at Aberdeen, and she is then to attend and receive an address, with Sir G. Grey present in due form. The household life is really very agreeable when one comes to know them. One way and another they have a great deal in them.

Oct. 5.—I have been riding to Invercauld House and up above it. The beauty there even surpassed my high expectations, and made everything here look quite pale in comparison. They were very kind, and offered me deer-stalking ; we drank tea and ate scones.

I have only time to tell you two things. First, the Queen is on Friday to do her first public act, to attend at the 'inauguration' of the statue of the Prince, and to receive an address. I am to be there officially. I have telegraphed for my uniform. I go on to Aberdeen and Trinity College at night, and on Saturday evening to Edinburgh. There was fear that it might be on Saturday, and that I should be kept, but this could not be, as Saturday is a 'fast' for the periodical sacrament on Sunday. I told you the Queen talked about German on Saturday at dinner, among other things Schiller's and Coleridge's *Wallenstein.* Next morning she sent me, through Lady A. Bruce, the book, with a passage of which I have hastily translated the most important part. It is easy to conceive how it answers to her feelings.

> Too well I know the treasure I have lost.
> From off my life the bloom is swept away
> It lies before me cold and colourless ;

> For he, that stood beside me like my youth,
> He charmed reality into a dream,
> And over all the common face of things
> He shed the golden glow of morning's blush ;
> And in the fire of his affection
> Dull forms, that throng the life of every day,
> Yea to mine own amazement, tow'red aloft.
> Win what I may henceforth, the Beautiful
> Is gone, and gone without return.[1]

You will say this was an opening. In reading another part of the book I found lines which I have turned as follows, no better than the others :—

> For nothing other than a noble aim
> Up from its depths can stir humanity ;
> The narrow circle narrows, too, the mind,
> And man grows greater as his ends are great.[2]

Now, I thought, can I in reply call the Queen's attention to these significant words, a noble sermon ? I asked Lady Augusta (of course I mean the German words) and she would not venture it. Had I a *viva voce* chance, I would try.

Oct. 6.—I am sorry you quitted Penmaenmawr in the sulks—I mean him in the sulks, not you. Your exploit was great ; was it not rather over-great ? I have been out to-day for a real good seven hours in the open air, going up Lochnagar. The day was glorious. We went five gentlemen, at least men. E. H. was keen to go, but the Queen would not let her. Thomas also went up with a party from here, and his *raptures* are such as would do you good. He says there is nothing it was not worth, and he has no words to describe his pleasure. Our party drove to Loch Muich, and then went up, some of us on ponies, some riding. I walked it all, and am not in the least tired, but quite ready, if there were need, to set out for it again. We saw towards the north as far as Caithness. I could not do all that the others did in looking down the precipices, but I managed a little. We had a very steep side to come down, covered with snow and very slippery ; I was put to it, and had to come very slow, but Lord C. Fitzroy, like a good Samaritan, kept me company. The day was as lovely (after frost and snow in the night) as anything could be, and the whole is voted a great success. Well, there is a cabinet fixed for Tuesday ; on the whole, this may be better than having it hang over one's head.

Oct. 7.—The Queen's talk last night (only think, she wants to read the French Jesuit—don't know this) was about Guizot's comparison of the Prince and King William, about Macaulay, America and the iron-clads, where she was very national and high-spirited ; and Schleswig-Holstein, in which she is intensely interested, because the Prince thought it a great case of justice on the side rather opposite to that of Lord Palmerston and the government policy. She spoke about this with intense earnestness, and said she considered it a legacy from him.

Princess Alice's baby lives above me, and I believe never cries. I

---

[1] *Death of Wallenstein*, Act v. Sc. 3. In Coleridge, v. 1.
[2] Denn nur der grosse Gegenstand vermag
    Den tiefen Grund der Menschheit aufzuregen,
    Im engen Kreis verengert sich der Sinn,
    Es wächst der Mensch mit seinen grössern Zwecken.
                 Prologue to Wallenstein, stanza 5.

never hear it. We have been out riding to Birkhall to-day, and I had much talk with Lady Churchill about the Queen. She (Lady C.) feels and speaks most properly about her. I told Lady Augusta last night, *à propos* to the lines I wanted to mention, that I had been a great coward, *and she too.* She was very submissive at dinner in her manner to the Queen, and I told her it made me feel I had been so impudent. Only think of this : both through her and through General Grey it has come round to me that the Queen thinks she was too cheerful on the night I last dined. This she feels a kind of sin. She said, however, to Lady Augusta she was sure I should understand it. . . . I am very glad and a little surprised that Mrs. Bruce should say I have a good name here. The people are, one and all, very easy to get on with, and Windsor, I suppose, stiffens them a little.

Oct. 8.—The Queen has had a most providential escape. The carriage, a sociable, very low and safe, was overturned last night after dark, on her way back from an expedition of seven or eight hours. Princesses Louis of Hesse and Helena were with her. They were undermost, and not at all hurt. The Queen was shot out of the carriage, and received a contusion on the temple and sprained a thumb. When she got in, I think near ten o'clock, Dr. Jenner wished her to go to bed, but she said it was of no use, and she would not. She was very confident, however, about performing the duties of the ceremonial in Aberdeen to-morrow. But now this evening it is given up, and I do not doubt this is wise, but much inconvenience will be caused by so late a postponement. I have been up to the place to-day. . . . The Queen should give up these drives after dark ; it is impossible to guarantee them. But she says she feels the hours from her drive to dinner such weary hours.

Little Princess Victoria paid me a visit in my bedroom, which is also sitting-room, to-day. She is of sweet temper, decidedly pretty, very like both the Queen and her mother. Then I went to see the three Prussian children, and the two elder ones played with my rusty old stick of twenty or twenty-five years' standing.

Holyrood, Oct. 11.—On Friday morning, as I expected, I talked to the Queen until the last moment. She did give me opportunities which might have led on to anything, but want of time hustled me, and though I spoke abruptly enough, and did not find myself timid, yet I could [not] manage it at all to my satisfaction. She said the one purpose of her life was gone, and she could not help wishing the accident had ended it. This is hardly qualified by another thing which she said to Lady Churchill, that she should not like to have died in that way. She went on to speak of her life as likely to be short. I told her that she would not give way, that duty would sustain her (this she quite recognised), that her burden was altogether peculiar, but the honour was in proportion, that no one could wonder at her feeling the present, which is near, but that the reward is *there*, though distant. . . . Then about politics, which will keep. She rowed me for writing to Lord Palmerston about her accident, and said, 'But, dear Mr. Gladstone, that was quite wrong.' The secret is kept wonderfully, and you must keep it. I hinted that it would be a very bad thing to have G. Grey away from such a cabinet on Tuesday, but all I could get was that I might arrange for any other minister (some one there certainly ought to be). I lectured her a little for driving after dark in such a country, but she said all her habits were formed on the Prince's wishes and directions, and she could not alter them.

Hawarden, Dec. 29.—I am well *past half* a century. My life has not been inactive. But of what kind has been its activity? Inwardly I feel it to be open to this general observation : it seems to have been and to be a series of efforts to be and to do what is beyond my natural force. This of itself is not condemnation, though it is a spectacle effectually humbling when I see that I have not according to Schiller's figure enlarged with the circle in which I live and move. [*Diary.*]

IV

Jan. 2, 1864.—The cabinet was on matters of great importance connected with Denmark, and has decided rightly to seek the co-opera- tion of France and other powers before talking about the use, in any event, of force.[1] Lord Palmerston has gout sharply in the hand. The Queen wrote a letter which I think did her great credit. Her love of truth and wish to do right prevent all prejudices from effectually warping her.

The Queen talked much about the Danish question, and is very desirous of a more staid and quiet foreign policy. For the first time I think she takes a just credit to herself for having influenced beneficially the course of policy and of affairs in the late controversy.

Balmoral, Sept. 28.—I thought the Queen's state of health and spirits last night very satisfactory. She looks better, more like what she used to look, and the spirits were very even ; with the little references to the Prince just as usual. Whenever she quotes an opinion of the Prince, she looks upon the question as completely shut up by it, for herself and all the world. Prince Alfred is going to Germany for nine weeks—to study at Bonn, and to be more or less at Coburg. The Queen asked for you, of course. She has not said a syllable about public affairs to me since I came, but talked pleasantly of all manner of things.

Sept. 29.—The Queen sent to offer a day's deer-stalking, but I am loth to trust my long eyesight.

Oct. 2.—At dinner last night there was a great deal of conversation, and to-day I have been near an hour with the Queen after coming back from Ballater. She was as good and as gracious as possible. I can hardly tell you all the things talked about—Prince Humbert, Garibaldi, Lady Lyttelton, the Hagley boys, Lucy, smoking, dress, fashion, Prince Alfred, his establishment and future plans, Prince of Wales's visit to Denmark, revenue, Lancashire, foreign policy, the newspaper press, the habits of the present generation, young men, young married ladies, clubs, Clarendon's journey, the Prince Consort on dress and fashion, Prince of Wales on ditto, Sir R. Peel, F. Peel, Mrs. Stonor, the rest of that family, misreading foreign names and words, repute of English people abroad, happy absence of foreign office disputes and quarrels.

Oct. 3.—I am just in from a sixteen mile walk, quite fresh, and pleased with myself ! for having in my old age walked a measured mile in twelve minutes by the side of this beautiful Dee.

1 See Walpole's *Life of Russell,* ii. p. 402.

Oct. 7.—I have just come in from a delightful twenty-five miles' ride with General Grey and another companion. I had another long interview with the Queen to-day. She talked most, and very freely and confidentially, about the Prince of Wales ; also about Lord Russell and Lord Palmerston, and about Granville and Clarendon, the latter perhaps to an effect that will a little surprise you. Also the Dean of Windsor. It was a kind of farewell audience.

CHAPTER VII

GARIBALDI—DENMARK

(1864)

There are in Europe two great questions: the question called social and the question of nationalities. . . . The map of Europe has to be re-made. . . . I affirm with profound conviction that this movement of nationalities has attained in Italy, in Hungary, in Vienna, in a great part of Germany, and in some of the Slavonian populations, a degree of importance that must at no distant period produce decisive results. . . . The first war-cry that arises will carry with it a whole zone of Europe.— MAZZINI, 1852.

'My confidence in the Italian parliament and people,' Mr. Gladstone wrote to Lacaita at the end of 1862, 'increases from day to day. Their self-command, moderation, patience, firmness, and forethought reaching far into the future, are really beyond all praise.' And a few days later, again to Lacaita— 'Your letter proves that the king has not merely got the constitutional lesson by rote—though even this for an Italian king would be much; but that the doctrine has sunk into the marrow and the bone.' The cause was won, and the work of construction went forward, but not on such lines as Cavour's master-hand was likely to have traced. Very early Mr. Gladstone began to be uneasy about Italian finance. 'I am sure,' he wrote to Lacaita in April 1863, 'that Italian freedom has no greater enemy in the Triple Crown or elsewhere, than large continuing deficits.'

As events marched forward, the French occupation of Rome became an ever greater scandal in Mr. Gladstone's eyes. He writes to Panizzi (October 28, 1862):—

My course about the Emperor has been a very simple one. It is not for me to pass gratuitous opinions upon his character or that of French institutions, or on his dealings with them. I believe him to be firmly attached to the English alliance, and I think his course towards us has been, on almost every occasion, marked by a friendliness perhaps greater and more conspicuous than we have always deserved at his hands. It is most painful to me to witness his conduct with regard to Italy. . . . He conferred upon her in 1859 an immense, an inestimable boon. He marred this boon in a way which to me seemed little worthy of France by the paltry but unkind appropriation of Nice in particular. But in the matter of Rome he inflicts upon Italy a fearful injury. And I do not know by what law of ethics any one is entitled to plead the having conferred an unexpected boon, as giving a right to inflict a gross and enduring wrong.[1]

It was in 1862 that Mr. Gladstone made his greatest speech on Italian affairs.[2] 'I am ashamed to say,' he told the House, 'that for a long time, I, like many, withheld my assent and approval from Italian yearnings.' He amply atoned for his tardiness, and his exposure of Naples, where perjury was the tradition of its kings; of the government of the pope in the Romagna, where the common administration of law and justice was handed over to Austrian soldiery; of the stupid and execrable lawlessness of the Duke of Modena; of the attitude of Austria as a dominant and conquering nation over a subject and conquered race ;—all this stamped a decisive impression on the minds of his hearers. Along with his speech on Reform in 1864, and that on the Irish church in the spring of 1865, it secured Mr. Gladstone's hold upon all of the rising generation of liberals who cared for the influence and the good name of Great Britain in Europe, and who were capable of sympathising with popular feeling and the claims of national justice.

II

The Italian sentiment of England reached its climax in the reception accorded to Garibaldi by the metropolis in April 1864. 'I do not know what persons in office are to do with him,' Mr. Gladstone wrote to Lord Palmerston (March 26), 'but you will lead, and we shall follow suit.' The populace took the thing into their own hands. London has seldom beheld a spectacle more extraordinary or more moving. The hero in the red shirt and blue-grey cloak long associated in the popular mind with so many thrilling stories of which they had been told, drove from the railway at Vauxhall to Stafford House, the noblest of the private palaces of the capital, amid vast continuous multitudes, blocking roadways, filling windows, lining every parapet and roof with eager gazers. For five hours Garibaldi passed on amid tumultuous waves of passionate curiosity, delight, enthusiasm. And this more than regal entry was the arrival not of some loved prince or triumphant captain of our own, but of a foreigner and the deliverer of a foreign people. Some were drawn by his daring as a fighter, and by the picturesque figure as of a hero of antique mould ; many by sight of the sworn foe of Giant Pope ; but what fired the hearts of most was the thought of him as the soldier who bore the sword for human freedom. The western world was in one of its generous

---

[1] A memorandum of Mr. Gladstone's of March 1863 on the Roman Question is republished in Minghetti's posthumous volume, *La Convenzione di Settembre*, Bologna, 1899.

[2] April 11, 1862. That of March 7, 1861, is also worth turning over.

moments. In those days there were idealists; democracy was conscious of common interests and common brotherhood; a liberal Europe was then a force and not a dream.

'We who then saw Garibaldi for the first time,' Mr. Gladstone said nearly twenty years after, 'can many of us never forget the marvellous effect produced upon all minds by the simple nobility of his demeanour, by his manners and his acts. . . . Besides his splendid integrity, and his wide and universal sympathies, besides that seductive simplicity of manner which never departed from him, and that inborn and native grace which seemed to attend all his actions, I would almost select from every other quality this, which was in apparent contrast but real harmony in Garibaldi—the union of the most profound and tender humanity with his fiery valour.'[1] He once described the Italian chief to me as 'one of the finest combinations of profound and unalterable simplicity with self-consciousness and self-possession. I shall never forget an occasion at Chiswick; Palmerston, John Russell, and all the leaders were awaiting him on the *perron*; he advanced with perfect simplicity and naturalness, yet with perfect consciousness of his position; very striking and very fine.' Garibaldi dined with Mr. Gladstone, and they met elsewhere. At a dinner at Panizzi's, they sat by one another. 'I remember,' said Mr. Gladstone, 'he told a story in these words:—" When I was a boy," he said, " I was at school in Genoa. It was towards the close of the great French Revolution. Genoa was a great military post—a large garrison always in the town, constant parades and military display, with bands and flags that were beyond everything attractive to schoolboys. All my schoolfellows used to run here and there all over the town to see if they could get sight of one of these military parades and exhibitions. I never went to one. It struck me then as a matter of pain and horror, that it should be necessary that one portion of mankind should be set aside to have for their profession the business of destroying others."'

Another side of Garibaldi was less congenial. A great lady wrote to Mr. Gladstone of a conversation with him. 'I talked to Garibaldi with regret that Renan was so much read in Italy. He said " *Perchè?* " and showed that he did not dislike it, and that he has also in leaving Rome left very much else. I know that woman's words are useless: the more men disbelieve, the more they think it well that women should be "superstitious." You are not likely to have *arguments* with him, but I would give much that he should take away with him some few words that would bring home to him the fact that the statesman he cares for most would think life a miserable thing without faith in God our Saviour.' To another correspondent on this point Mr. Gladstone wrote:—

[1] Speech at Stafford House. June 2, 1883.

The honour paid him was I think his due as a most singularly simple, disinterested, and heroic character, who had achieved great things for Italy, for liberty well-understood, and even for mankind. His insurrection we knew and lamented, and treated as exceptional. No Mazzinian leanings of his were known. I read the speech at the luncheon with surprise and concern.[1] As to his attenuated belief, I view it with the deepest sorrow and concern. I need not repeat an opinion, always painful to me to pronounce, as to the principal causes to which it is referable, and as to the chief seat of the responsibility for it. As to his Goddess Reason, I understand by it simply an adoption of what are called on the continent the principles of the French Revolution. These we neither want nor warmly relish in England, but they are different from its excesses, and the words will bear an innocent and even in some respects a beneficial meaning.

The diary records :—

April 12.—To Chiswick and met Garibaldi. We were quite satisfied with him. He did me much more than justice. 14.—Went by a desperate push to see Garibaldi welcomed at the opera. It was good, but not like the *people*. 17.—At Stafford House 5¼-6½ and 9¼-12½ on Garibaldi's movements. In a conversation he agreed to give up the provincial tour. 20.—In the evening the great entertainment to Garibaldi came off. Before the door at night say a thousand people all in the best of humour, the hall and stair full before dinner. A hostile demonstration invaded us at ten, but we ejected them. I settled about to-morrow with Garibaldi, the Duke of Sutherland, Lord Palmerston, and Lord Shaftesbury. My nerves would not let me—hardened as I am—sleep till after five.

Suddenly one morning the country was surprised to learn that Garibaldi was at once departing. Dark suspicions rose instantly in the minds of his more democratic friends. It had always been rather bitter to them that he should be the guest of a duke. They now insisted that the whig aristocrats were in a panic lest he should compromise himself with the radicals, and that he was being hustled out of the country against his will. This suspicion next grew into something blacker still. A story spread that the Emperor of the French had taken umbrage, and signified to the government that the reception of Garibaldi was distasteful to France. Lord Clarendon promptly denied the fable. He told the House of Lords that the Emperor (of whom he had recently had an audience) had even expressed his admiration for the feeling of which the reception was a sign. Lord Palmerston in the other House explained that Garibaldi was going away earlier than had been expected, because at home he went to bed at eight and rose at five, and to a person of these habits to dine at half past eight and to remain in a throng of admirers until midnight must necessarily be injurious. Still the fog hung heavy on the public mind. A rider was now added to the tale, that it was the chancellor of the exchequer

<hr/>

[1] Speech not discoverable by me.

who out of deference to the Emperor, or to please the whigs, or out of complaisance to the court, had induced the hero to take his hurried leave. Mr. Gladstone was forced to explain to the House of Commons, seldom reluctant to lighten its graver deliberations with a personal incident, that the Duke of Sutherland had carried him to Stafford House ; there he found that Garibaldi had accepted invitations to thirty provincial towns and that the list was growing longer every day ; the doctors declared that the general's strength would never stand the exhaustion of a progress on such a scale ; and the friends there present begged him to express his own opinion to Garibaldi. This Mr. Gladstone accordingly did, to the effect that the hero's life and health were objects of value to the whole world, and that even apart from health the repetition all over England of the national reception in London would do something to impair a unique historical event.[1] The general was taken to show excellent sense by accepting advice not to allow himself to be killed by kindness. At any rate he firmly declared that if he could not go to all the places that invited him, it was impossible for him to draw a line of preference, and therefore he would go to none. His radical friends, however, seem to have instilled some of their own suspicions into his mind, for two days later (April 23) Mr. Gladstone writes to Lord Clarendon :—' I am to see Garibaldi at Cliveden this evening, and it is possible that some occasion may offer there for obtaining from him a further declaration. But since I received your note the following circumstance has occurred. Clarence Paget has been to me, and reports that Mrs. ——, a well-known and zealous but anti-Mazzinian liberal in Italian matters, who is also a friend of Garibaldi's, has acquainted him that Garibaldi himself has made known to her that according to his own painful impression the English government do consider the prolongation of his stay in England very embarrassing, and are very anxious that he should go. What a pity, if this be so, that this simple and heroic man could not speak his mind plainly out to me, but wrapped himself in the depths of diplomatic reserve, instead of acting like Lord Aberdeen, who used to say, " I have a habit of believing people." '[2] After three or four days at Cliveden the general still held to his purpose. ' April 24.—Cliveden. Conversation with Garibaldi. The utmost I could get from him was that it would be sad if the Italian people should lose its faith.' So Garibaldi forthwith sailed away from our shores.[3]

---

[1] Hansard, April 19, 1864, pp. 1277, 1290. April 21, p. 1423.

[2] This was in reply to a letter from Lord Clarendon to Mr. Gladstone, April 23, '64, asking him : ' Do not you think that he ought in a letter to some personal friends to state frankly the reasons which have induced him to go? He alone can put a stop to all these mischievous reports. . . . He ought to say that no government, English or foreign, has to do with his departure, and that he goes solely because the state of his health does not permit him to fulfil his engagements.'

[3] The story has been told from the radical point of view by Sir James Stansfeld in Review of Reviews, June 1895, p. 512. Another account by Mr. Seely, M.P., was

When all was over, an Italian statesman wrote to Panizzi that though he thought Garibaldi one of the choicest natures ever created, — enterprising, humane, disinterested, eminent in national service, yet neither he nor any other citizen was entitled to set himself above the laws of his country, and that such a man should be officially received by the heir to the throne and by secretaries of state, was a thing to be bitterly deplored by every sensible man.[1] Still history can afford to agree with Mr. Gladstone when he said of Garibaldi—'His name is indeed illustrious, it remains inseparably connected with the not less illustrious name of the great Cavour, and these two names are again associated with the name of Victor Emmanuel. These three together form for Italians a tricolour as brilliant, as ever fresh, and I hope as enduring for many and many generations, as the national flag that now waves over united Italy.'

III

The tide of vast events in this momentous period now rolled heavily away from the Danube and the Bosphorus, from Tiber and Po and Adriatic sea, to the shores of the Baltic and the mouths of the Elbe. None of the fascination of old-world history lends its magic to the new chapter that opened in 1863. Cavour had gone. Bismarck with sterner genius, fiercer purpose, more implacable designs, and with a hand as of hammered iron, strode into the field. The Italian statesman was the author of a singular prediction. In 1861 when Cavour was deprecating angry protests from the European powers against his invasion of the Marches, he used words of extraordinary foresight to the representative of Prussia. 'I am sorry,' he said, 'that the cabinet of Berlin judges so severely the conduct of the King of Italy and his government. I console myself by thinking that on this occasion I am setting an example that probably in no long time, Prussia will be very glad to imitate.'[2] So the world speedily found out.

The torch of nationality reached material for a flame long smouldering in two duchies of the remote north, that had been incorporated in Denmark by solemn European engagements in

furnished to the *Times* (April 21, 1864). Lord Shaftesbury, who was a staunch Garibaldian, presumably on high protestant grounds, also wrote to the *Times* (April 24):— 'The solid, persevering and hearty attachment of Mr. Gladstone to the cause of Italy and General Garibaldi is as notorious as it is generous and true, and I declare in the most solemn manner and on the word of a gentleman, my firm belief that we were all of us animated by the same ardent desire (without reference to anything and anybody but the General himself) to urge that and that only, which was indispensable to his personal welfare. It was, I assert, the General's own and unsuggested decision to give up the provincial journey altogether.'

[1] Fagan's *Panizzi*, ii. p. 252. The same view was reported to be taken at the English Court, and a story got abroad that the Queen had said that for the first time she felt half ashamed of being the head of a nation capable of such follies. Mérimée, *Lettres à Panizzi*, ii. p. 25. On the other hand, the diary has this entry :—*Oct.* 1, 1864. Dined with H.M. She spoke good-humouredly of Garibaldi.

[2] *Le Comte de Cavour* : par Charles de Mazade (1877), p. 389.

1852, but were inhabited by a population, one of them wholly and the other mainly, not Scandinavian but German. Thus the same question of race, history, language, sentiment, that had worked in Italy, Poland, the Balkan states, rose up in this miniature case. The circumstances that brought that case into such fatal prominence do not concern us here. The alleged wrongs of her brethren in Schleswig-Holstein unchained such a tempest of excitement in central Germany, that the German courts could hardly have resisted if they would. Just as powerless was the Danish government in face of the Scandinavian sentiment of its subjects and their neighbours of the race. Even the liberals, then a power in Germany and Bismarck's bitter foes, were vehemently on the national side against the Danish claim; and one of the most striking of all Bismarck's feats was the skill with which he now used his domestic enemies to further his own designs of national aggrandisement. How war broke out between the small power and the two great powers of Austria and Prussia, and how the small power was ruthlessly crushed; by what infinite and complex machinations the diplomacy of Europe found itself paralysed; how Prussia audaciously possessed herself of territory that would give her a deep-water port, and the head of a channel that would unite two great seas; how all this ended in Prussia, 'the Piedmont of the north,' doing what Cavour in his Piedmont of the south had foretold that she would be glad to do; how at Sadowa (July 3, 1866) Austria was driven out of her long hegemony, and Hanover incorporated; and to what a train of amazing conflicts in western Europe, to what unexpected victories, territorial change, dynastic ruin, this so resistlessly led up—here is a narrative that belongs to the province of history. Yet it has a place in any political biography of the Palmerston administration.

In such an era of general confusion, the English cabinet found no powerful or noble part to play. Still they went far —almost too far to recede—towards embarking in a continental war on behalf of Denmark, that would have been full of mischief to herself, of little profit to her client, and could hardly have ended otherwise than in widespread disaster. Here is one of the very few instances in which the public opinion of the country at the eleventh hour reined back a warlike minister. Lord Palmerston told the House of Commons in the summer of 1863 that, if any violent attempt were made to overthrow the rights of Denmark or to interfere with its independence and integrity, he was convinced that those who made the attempt would find in the result that 'it would not be Denmark alone with which they would have to contend.'[1] This did indeed sound like a compromising declaration of quite sufficient emphasis.

[1] July 23, 1863.

' It seems,' says Mr. Gladstone,[1] ' that this statement was generally and not unnaturally interpreted as a promise of support from England. Lord Palmerston does not seem to have added any condition or reservation. Strange as it may appear, he had spoken entirely of his own motion and without the authority or knowledge of his cabinet, in which indeed, so far as my memory serves, nothing had happened to render likely any declaration of any kind on the subject. I have no means of knowing whether he spoke in concert with the foreign secretary, Earl Russell, with whom his communications, agreeably to policy and to established usage, were, I believe, large and constant. When the question was eventually disposed of by the war which Prussia and Austria waged against Denmark, there was much indignation felt against England for the breach of her engagement to give support in the case of war, to the small power so egregiously in need of it. And there was no one to raise a voice in our favour.

' As the year advanced (1863) and the prospect of war came nearer, the subject was very properly brought before the cabinet. I believe that at the time I was not even aware of Lord Palmerston's declaration, which, owing to the exhausted period of the session, had I believe attracted no great amount of attention in England. Whether my colleagues generally were as little aware of what happened as myself I do not know, but unquestionably we could not all have missed learning it. However we did not as a body recognise in any way the title of the prime minister to bind us to go to war. We were, however, indignant at the conduct of the German powers who, as we thought, were scheming piracy under cover of pacific correspondence. And we agreed upon a very important measure, in which Lord Palmerston acquiesced, when he had failed, if I remember right, in inducing the cabinet to go farther. We knew that France took the same view of the question as we did, and we framed a communication to her to the following effect. We were jointly to insist that the claim of the Duke of Augustenburg should be peacefully settled on juridical grounds ; and to announce to Prussia and Austria that if they proceeded to prosecute it by the use of force against Denmark, we would jointly resist them with all our might.[2]

' This communication was accordingly made to Louis Napoleon. He declined the proposal. He said that the question was one of immense importance to us, who had such vast interests involved, and that the plan was reasonable from our point of view ; but that the matter was one of small moment for France, whom accordingly we could not ask to join in it. The explanation of this answer, so foolish in its terms, and so pregnant with consequences in this matter, was, I believe, to be found in the pique of Louis Napoleon at a reply we had then recently given to a proposal of his for an European conference or congress.[3] We all thought that his plan was wholly needless and would in all likelihood lead to mischief. So we declined it in perfect good faith and without implying by our refusal any difference of policy in the particular matter.'

Throughout the session of 1864 the attention of the country was fixed upon this question whether England should or should not take part in the war between Germany and Denmark. The

---

[1] Memorandum of 1897.   [2] See Walpole's *Russell*, ii. pp. 402-404.
[3] For the revision of the Treaty of Vienna. See Ashley's *Palmerston*, ii. p. 424.

week before the time arrived for the minister to announce the
decision of the cabinet, it became clear that public opinion in
the great English centres would run decisively for non-intervention. Some of the steadiest supporters of government in
parliament boldly told the party whips that if war against
Germany were proposed, they would vote against it. The
cabinet met. Palmerston and Lord Russell were for war, even
though it would be war single-handed. Little support came
to them. The Queen was strongly against them. They be-
moaned to one another the timidity of their colleagues, and
half-mournfully contrasted the convenient cyphers that filled
the cabinets of Pitt and Peel, with the number of able men
with independent opinions in their own administration. The
prime minister, as I have heard from one who was present,
held his head down while the talk proceeded, and then at last
looking up said in a neutral voice, 'I think the cabinet is
against war.' Here is Mr. Gladstone's record :—

May 7, '64.—Cabinet. The war 'party' as it might be called—Lord
Palmerston, Lord Russell, Lord Stanley of Alderley, and the chancellor
(Lord Westbury). All went well. *June* 11.—Cabinet. Very stiff on
the Danish question, but went well. *June* 24.—Cabinet. A grave
issue well discussed. *June* 25.—Cabinet. We divided, and came to a
tolerable, not the best, conclusion.

It seems almost incredible that a cabinet of rational men
could have debated for ten minutes the question of going to
war with Prussia and Austria, when they knew that twenty
thousand men were the largest force that we could have put
into the field when war began, though moderate additions
might have been made as time went on—not, however, without
hazardous denudation of India, where the memories of the
mutiny were still fresh. The Emperor of the French in fact
had good reason for fearing that he would be left in the lurch
again, as he thought that he had been left before in his attempts
for Poland. Your intervention, he said to England, will be
naval ; but we may have to fight a people of forty millions on
land, and we will not intervene unless you engage to send
troops.[1] The dismemberment of Denmark was thought an
odious feat, but the localisation of the war was at least a
restriction of the evils attending it.

A high parliamentary debate followed (July 4) on a motion
made by Mr. Disraeli, 'to express to Her Majesty our great regret
that while the course pursued by the government had failed to
maintain their avowed policy of upholding the independence
and integrity of Denmark, it has lowered the just influence of
this country in the councils of Europe, and thereby diminished
the securities for peace.'[2] Cobden taunted both front benches
pretty impartially with the equivocal and most dishonourable

1 See Ollivier's *Empire Libéral*, vii. 71 ; De la Gorce, iv. 512.
2 July 4, 1864.

position into which their policy had brought the country, by encouraging a small power to fight two great ones and then straightway leaving her to get out as best she might. The government was only saved by Palmerston's appeal to its financial triumphs—the very triumphs that he had himself made most difficult to achieve. The appeal was irrelevant, but it was decisive, and ministers escaped a condemnation by no means unmerited on the special issue, by a majority of eighteen. The Manchester men agreed to help in the result, because in Cobden's words they were convinced that a revolution had been at last wrought in the mischievous policy of incessant intervention. Mr. Disraeli's case was easy, but to propound an easy case when its exposition demands much selection from voluminous blue-books is often hard, and the orator was long and over-elaborate. The excitement of an audience, aware all the time that actual danger hovered over the ministry, revived afresh when Disraeli sat down and Gladstone rose. The personal emulation of powerful rivals lends dramatic elements to disputation. Lord Palmerston had written to Mr. Gladstone beforehand—'We shall want a great gun to follow Disraeli. Would you be ready to follow him?'

July 3.—I was happy enough, aided by force of habit, to drive bodily out of my head for the whole day everything Dano-German. But not out of my nerves. I delivered during the night a speech in parliament on the Roman question.

July 4.—H. of C. Replied to Disraeli. It took an hour and thirty-five minutes. I threw overboard all my heavy armament and fought light.

Nobody who is not historian or biographer is likely to read this speech of Mr. Gladstone's to-day, but we may believe contemporary witnesses who record that the orator's weight of fact, his force of argument, his sarcastic play of personal impulse and motive, his bold and energetic refutation of hostile criticism, his defiant statement of the ministerial case, so impressed even a sceptical and doubting House that, though his string of special pleas did not amount to a justification, 'they almost reached the height of an excuse,' and they crushed the debate. The basis was the familiar refrain upon Mr. Gladstone's lips,—'The steps taken by the government, what were they but endeavours to bind together the powers of Europe for fulfilment and maintenance of an important European engagement?' Still history, even of that sane and tempered school that is content to take politics as often an affair of second-best, will probably judge that Mr. Disraeli was not wrong when he said of the policy of this era that, whether we looked to Russia, to Greece, to France, there had been exhibited by ministers a confusion, an inconsistency of conduct, a contrariety of courses with regard to the same powers and a total want of system in their diplomacy.[1] It is true, however, that just the same confusion, inconsistency, and contrariety marked Russia, France, and Austria themselves. Another speaker of the same party, as mordant as Disraeli, and destined like him to rise to the chief place in the councils of the nation, went further, and said, in following Cobden in the debate, 'If Mr. Cobden had been foreign secretary, instead of Lord Russell, I fully believe this country would occupy a position proud and noble compared to that which she occupies at this moment. She would at least have been entitled to the credit of holding out in the name of England no hopes which she did not intend to fulfil, of entering into no engagements from which she was ready to recede.'[2] Well might Mr. Gladstone enter in his diary :—

July 8.—This debate ought to be an epoch in foreign policy. We have all much to learn. Lord Palmerston's speech was unequivocally weak in the mental and the bodily sense. I think it was to-day that the Prince of Wales rode with Granville and me ; he showed a little Danism.

[1] Feb. 4, 1864.   [2] Lord Robert Cecil, July 4, 1864.

CHAPTER VIII

ADVANCE IN PUBLIC POSITION AND OTHERWISE

(1864)

The best form of government is that which doth actuate and dispose every part and member of a state to the common good. If, instead of concord and interchange of support, one part seeks to uphold an old form of government, and the other part introduce a new, they will miserably consume one another. Histories are full of the calamities of entire states and nations in such cases. It is, nevertheless, equally true that time must needs bring about some alterations. . . . Therefore have those commonwealths been ever the most durable and perpetual which have often formed and recomposed themselves according to their first institution and ordinance.—PYM.

A RAPID and extraordinary change began to take place in Mr. Gladstone's position after the year 1863. With this was associated an internal development of his political ideas and an expansion of social feeling, still more remarkable and interesting. As we have seen, he reckoned that a little earlier than this he had reached his lowest point in public estimation. He had now been more than thirty years in parliament. He had sat in three cabinets, each of a different colour and different connections from the other two. It was not until he had seen half a century of life on our planet, and more than quarter of a century of life in the House of Commons, that it was at all certain whether he would be conservative or liberal, to what species of either genus he would attach himself, or whether there might not from his progressive transmutations be evolved some variety wholly new.

I have already given his picture of the Palmerston cabinet as a kaleidoscope, and the same simile would be no bad account of his own relation to the political groups and parties around him. The Manchester men and the young radicals from the West Riding of Yorkshire were his ardent adherents when he preached economy and peace, but they were chilled to the core by his neutrality or worse upon the life and death struggle across the Atlantic. His bold and confident finance was doubted by the whigs, and disliked by the tories. But then the tories, apart from their wiser leader, were delighted by his friendly words about the Confederates, and the whigs were delighted with his unflagging zeal for the deliverance of Italy. Only, zeal for the deliverance of Italy lost him the friendship of those children of the Holy Father who came from Ireland. Then again the City was not easy at the flash of activity and enterprise at the exchequer, and the money-changers did not know what disturbance this intrepid genius might bring into the traffic of their tables. On the other hand, the manufacturers and the merchants of the midlands and the north adored a chancellor whose budgets were associated with expanding trade and a prosperity that advanced by leaps and bounds. The nonconformists were attracted by his personal piety, though repelled by its ecclesiastical apparel. The high churchmen doubtless knew him for their own, yet even they resented his confederacy with an erastian and a latitudinarian like John Russell, or a Gallio like Lord Palmerston, who distributed mitres and crown benefices at the ultra-evangelical bidding of Lord Shaftesbury. To borrow a figure from a fine observer of those days, — the political molecules were incessantly forming and re-forming themselves into shifting aggregates, now attracted, now repelled by his central force ; now the nucleus of an organized party, then resolved again in loose and distant satellites.

The great families still held ostensibly the predominance in the liberal party which they had earned by their stout and persistent fidelity to parliamentary reform. Their days of leadership, however, were drawing towards an end, though the process has not been rapid. They produced some good administrators, but nobody with the gifts of freshness and political genius. The three originating statesmen of that era, after all, were Cobden, Gladstone, Disraeli, none of them born in the purple of the directing class. A Yorkshire member, destined to a position of prominence, entered the House in 1861, and after he had been there a couple of years he wrote to his wife, that 'the want of the liberal party of a new man was great, and felt to be great ; the old whig leaders were worn out ; there were no new whigs ; Cobden and Bright were impracticable and un-English, and there were hardly any hopeful radicals. There was a great prize of power and influence to be aimed at.'[1]

This parliamentary situation was the least part of it. No man could guide the new advance, now so evidently approaching, unless he clearly united fervour and capacity for practical improvements in government to broad and glowing sympathies, alike with the needs and the elemental instincts of the labouring mass. Mr. Gladstone offered that wonderful combination. 'If ever there was a statesman,' said Mill, about this time, 'in whom the spirit of improvement is incarnate, and in whose career as a minister the characteristic

1 *Life of W. E. Forster*, i. p. 362.

feature has been to seek out things that require or admit of improvement, instead of waiting to be pressed or driven to do them, Mr. Gladstone deserves that signal honour.' Then his point of view was lofty; he was keenly alive to the moving forces of the hour; his horizons were wide; he was always amply founded in facts; he had generous hopes for mankind; his oratory seized vast popular audiences, because it was the expression of a glowing heart and a powerful brain. All this made him a demagogue in the same high sense in which Pericles, Demosthenes, John Pym, Patrick Henry were demagogues.

It is easy to see some at any rate of the influences that were bringing Mr. Gladstone decisively into harmony with the movement of liberal opinions, now gradually spreading over Great Britain. The resurrection of Italy could only be vindicated on principles of liberty and the right of a nation to choose its own rulers. The peers and the ten-pound householders who held power in England were no Bourbon tyrants; but just as in 1830 the overthrow of the Bourbon line in France was followed by the Reform bill here, so the Italian revolution of 1860 gave new vitality to the popular side in England. Another convulsion, far away from our own shores, was still more directly potent alike in quickening popular feeling, and by a strange paradox in creating as a great popular leader the very statesman who had failed to understand it. It was impossible that a man so vigilant and so impressionable as Mr. Gladstone was, should escape the influence of the American war. Though too late to affect his judgment on the issues of the war, he discerned after the event how, in his own language, the wide participation of the people in the choice of their governors, by giving force and expression to the national will in the United States, enabled the governors thus freely chosen to marshal a power and develop an amount of energy in the execution of that will, such as probably have never been displayed in an equal time and among an equal number of men since the race of mankind sprang into existence.[1] In this judgment of the American civil war, he only shared in a general result of the salvation of the Union; it reversed the fashionable habit of making American institutions English bugbears, and gave a sweeping impulse to that steady but resistless tide of liberal and popular sentiment that ended in the parliamentary reform of 1867.

The lesson from the active resolution of America was confirmed by the passive fortitude of Lancashire. 'What are the qualities,' Mr. Gladstone asked in 1864, 'that fit a man for the exercise of a privilege such as the franchise? Self-command, self-control, respect for order, patience under suffering, con-

<hr />

[1] Speech at Liverpool, April 6, 1866.

fidence in the law, regard for superiors; and when, I should
like to ask, were all these great qualities exhibited in a manner
more signal, even more illustrious, than in the conduct of the
general body of the operatives of Lancashire under the profound affliction of the winter of 1862?' So on two sides the
liberal channel was widened and deepened and the speed of
its currents accelerated.

Besides large common influences like these, Mr. Gladstone's
special activities as a reformer brought him into contact
with the conditions of life and feeling among the workmen,
and the closer he came to them, the more did his humane and
sympathetic temper draw him towards their politics and the
ranks of their party. Looking back, he said, upon the years
immediately succeeding the fall of Napoleon in 1815, he saw
the reign of ideas that did not at all belong to the old currents
of English history, but were a reaction against the excesses of
the French revolution. This reaction seemed to set up the
doctrine that the masses must be in standing antagonism to
the law, and it resulted in severities that well justified
antagonism. 'To-day the scene was transformed; the fixed
traditional sentiment of the working man had become one of
confidence in the law, in parliament, even in the executive
government.' In 1863 he was busy in the erection of the post
office savings banks. A deputation of a powerful trades union
asked him to modify his rules so as to enable them to place
their funds in the hands of the government. A generation
before, such confidence would have been inconceivable. In
connection with the Government Annuities bill a deputation
of workmen came to him, and said, 'If there had been any
suspicion or disinclination towards it on the part of the
working classes, it was due to the dissatisfaction with parliament as to suffrage.' When he replied with something about
the alleged indifference and apparent inaction of the working
classes as to suffrage, they said, 'Since the abolition of the
corn laws we have given up political agitation; we felt we
might place confidence in parliament; instead of political
action, we tried to spend our evenings in the improvement
of our minds.' This convinced him that it was not either
want of faith in parliament, or indifference to a vote, that
explained the absence of agitation.

II

The outcome of this stream of new perceptions and new
feeling in his mind was a declaration that suddenly electrified
the political world. A Yorkshire liberal one afternoon (May
11, 1864) brought in a bill for lowering the franchise, and
Mr. Gladstone spoke for the government. He dwelt upon
the facts, historic and political. The parliamentary history
of reform for the thirteen years, since Locke King's motion

in 1851 upset a government, had been most unsatisfactory, and to set aside all the solemn and formal declarations from 1851 down to the abortive Reform bill of 1860 would be a scandal. Then, was not the state of the actual case something of a scandal, with less than one-tenth of the constituencies composed of working men, and with less than one-fiftieth of the working men in possession of the franchise? How could you defend a system that let in the lower stratum of the middle class and shut out the upper stratum of the working class? In face of such dispositions as the workmen manifested towards law, parliament, and government, was it right that the present system of almost entire exclusion should prevail? Then came the sentence that, in that stagnant or floundering hour of parliamentary opinion, marked a crisis. 'I call upon the adversary to show cause, and *I venture to say that every man who is not presumably incapacitated by some consideration of personal unfitness or of political danger, is morally entitled to come within the pale of the constitution.* Of course, in giving utterance to such a proposition, I do not recede from the protest I have previously made against sudden, or violent, or excessive, or intoxicating change.'

He concluded in words that covered much ground, though when closely scrutinised they left large loopholes. 'It is well,' he said, 'that we should be suitably provided with armies and fleets and fortifications; it is well, too, that all these should rest upon and be sustained, as they ought to be, by a sound system of finance, and out of a revenue not wasted by a careless parliament or by a profligate administration. But that which is better and more weighty still is that hearts should be bound together by a reasonable extension, at fitting times and among *selected* portions of the people, of every benefit and every privilege that can be justly conferred upon them.'

The thunderbolt of a sentence about every man's moral title to a vote startled the House with an amazement, half delight and half consternation, that broke forth in loud volleys of cheering and counter-cheering. It was to little purpose that the orator in the next breath interposed his qualifications. One of the fated words had been spoken that gather up wandering forces of time and occasion, and precipitate new eras. A conservative speaker instantly deplored the absence of the prime minister, and the substitution in his stead of his 'intractable chancellor of the exchequer.' An important liberal speaker, with equal promptitude, pointed out that one effect of the speech would be, in the first place, loss of conservative support to the government, and, in the second place, a very great gain to the health and vigour of the liberal party. Two whigs ran off to tell Phillimore that Gladstone had said something that would make his hair stand on end. Speculations began to hum and buzz whether the oracular deliverance would not upset the

government. In the press a tremendous storm broke. Mr.
Gladstone was accused of ministering aliments to popular
turbulence and vanity, of preaching the divine right of multitudes, and of encouraging, minister of the crown though he was,
a sweeping and levelling democracy. They charged him with
surveying mankind in the abstract and suffrage in the abstract,
and in that kingdom of shadows discovering or constructing
vast universal propositions about man's moral rights. Mr.
Disraeli told him that he had revived the doctrine of Tom
Paine. The radicals were as jubilant as whigs and tories were
furious. They declared that the banner he had raised aloft was
not what the tories denounced as the standard of domestic
revolution, but the long-lost flag of the liberal party. 'There
is not a statesman in England of the very first rank,' said one
newspaper, 'who has dared to say as much, and Mr. Gladstone,
in saying it, has placed himself at the head of the party that
will succeed the present administration.' This was true, but
in the meantime the head of the existing administration was
still a marvel of physical vigour, and though at the moment he
was disabled by gout, somebody must have hurried to Cambridge
House and told him the desperate tidings. On the very instant
he sent down a note of inquiry to Mr. Gladstone, asking what
he had really said. A brisk correspondence followed, neither
heated nor unfriendly.

In the morning Lord Palmerston had written him a premonitory note, not to commit himself or the government to
any particular figure of borough franchise; that a six pound
franchise had gone to the bottom; that if they should ever
have to bring in a reform bill, they ought to be free from fresh
pledges; that the workmen would swamp the classes above
them; that their influx would discourage the classes above
from voting at all; and that the workmen were under the
control of trade unions directed by a small number of agitators.
All this was the good conservative common form of the time.
The speech itself, when the prime minister came to see it,
proved no sedative.

Lord Palmerston to Mr. Gladstone.

May 12, 1864.—I have read your speech, and I must frankly say,
with much regret; as there is little in it that I can agree with, and
much from which I differ. You lay down broadly the doctrine of
universal suffrage which I can never accept. I entirely deny that every
sane and not disqualified man has a moral right to a vote. I use that
expression instead of 'the pale of the constitution,' because I hold that
all who enjoy the security and civil rights which the constitution pro-
vides are within its pale. What every man and woman too has a right
to, is to be well governed and under just laws, and they who propose a
change ought to show that the present organisation does not accomplish
those objects. . . .

You did not pronounce an opinion in favour of a specified franchise;

but is there any essential difference between naming a six pound franchise and naming the additional numbers which a six pound franchise was calculated to admit? I am not going to perform the duty which White-side assigned to me of answering your speech, but, if you will not take it amiss, I would say, that it was more like the sort of speech with which Bright would have introduced the Reform bill which he would like to propose, than the sort of speech which might have been expected from the treasury bench in the present state of things. Your speech may win Lancashire for you, though that is doubtful, but I fear it will tend to lose England for you.

Mr. Gladstone to Lord Palmerston.

11 *Carlton House Terrace, May* 13, 1864.—It is not easy to take ill anything that proceeds from you; and, moreover, frankness between all men, and especially between those who are politically associated, removes, as I believe, many more difficulties than it causes. In this spirit I will endeavour to write. I agree in your denial 'that every sane and not disqualified man has a moral right to vote.' But I am at a loss to know how, as you have read my speech, you can ascribe this opinion to me. My declaration was, taken generally, that all persons ought to be admitted to the franchise, who can be admitted to it with safety. . . . I hold by this proposition. It seems to me neither strange, nor new, nor extreme. It requires, I admit, to be construed; but I contend that the interpretation is amply given in the speech, where I have declared (for example) that the admission I desire is of the same character or rather extent as was proposed in 1860. . . . I have never exhorted the working man to agitate for the franchise, and I am at a loss to conceive what report of my speech can have been construed by you in such a sense.

Having said this much to bring down to its true limits the difference between us, I do not deny that difference. I regret it, and I should regret it much more if it were likely to have (at least as far as I can see) an early bearing upon practice. In the cabinet I argued as strongly as I could against the withdrawal of the bill in 1860, and in favour of taking the opinion of the House of Commons upon that bill. I think the party which supports your government has suffered, and is suffering, and will much more seriously suffer, from the part which as a party it has played within these recent years, in regard to the franchise. I have no desire to press the question forward. I hope no government will ever again take it up except with the full knowledge of its own mind and a reason-able probability of carrying it. But such influence as argument and statement without profession of political intentions can exercise upon the public mind, I heartily desire to see exercised in favour of extension of the franchise. . . .

On the following day Lord Palmerston wrote to him, 'I have no doubt that you have yourself heard a great deal about the bad effect of your speech, but I can assure you that I hear from many quarters the unfavourable impression it has produced even upon many of the liberal party, and upon all persons who value the maintenance of our institutions.'

To others, Mr. Gladstone wrote in less formal style, for instance to an eminent nonconformist minister: 'May 14. I have unwarily, it seems, set the Thames on fire. But I have great hopes that the Thames will, on reflection, perceive that he had no business or title to catch the flame, and will revert to his ordinary temperature accordingly.' And to his brother Robertson, he writes from Brighton, three days later :—

Many thanks for all you say respecting my speech on the franchise bill. I have been astounded to find it the cause or occasion of such a row. It would have been quite as intelligible to me had people said, 'Under the exceptions of personal unfitness and political danger you exclude or may exclude almost everybody, and you reduce your declaration to a shadow.'

In the diary he says :—'*May* 11.—Spoke on the franchise bill. Some sensation. It appears to me that it was due less to me, than to the change in the hearers and in the public mind from the professions at least if not the principles of 1859.' Much against Lord Palmerston's wish, the speech was published, with a short preface that even staunch friends like Phillimore found obscure and not well written.

An address, significant of the general feeling in the unenfranchised classes, was presented to him from the workmen of York a month after his speech in parliament. They recalled his services to free trade when he stood by the side of Peel ; his budget of 1860 ; his conspicuous and honourable share in abolishing the taxes on knowledge. 'We have marked,' they said, 'your manifestations of sympathy with the down-trodden and oppressed of every clime. You have advanced the cause of freedom in foreign lands by the power and courage with which you have assailed and exposed the misdeeds and cruelties of continental tyrants. To the provident operative you have by your Post Office Savings Bank bill given security for his small savings, and your Government Annuities bill of this session is a measure which will stimulate the people to greater thrift and forethought. These acts, together with your speeches on the last named, and on the Borough Franchise bill, make up a life that commands our lasting gratitude.' Such was the new popular estimate of him. In framing his reply to this address Mr. Gladstone did his best to discourage the repetition of like performances from other places ; he submitted the draft to Lord Palmerston, and followed his advice in omitting certain portions of it. It was reduced to the conventional type of such acknowledgment.

III

In the autumn of 1864 Mr. Gladstone made a series of speeches in his native county, which again showed the sincerity and the simplicity of his solicitude for the masses of his countrymen. The sentiment is common. Mr. Disraeli and the Young Englanders had tried to inscribe it upon a party banner twenty years before. But Mr. Gladstone had given proof that he knew how to embody sentiment in acts of parliament, and he associated it with the broadest ideas of citizenship and policy. These speeches were not a manifesto or a programme ; they were a survey of the principles of the statesmanship that befitted the period.

At Bolton (Oct. 11) he discoursed to audiences of the working class upon the progress of thirty years, with such freshness of spirit as awoke energetic hopes of the progress for the thirty years that were to follow. The next day he opened a park with words from the heart about the modern sense of the beauties of nature. The Greeks, he said, however much beauty they might have discerned in nature, had no sympathy with the delight in detached natural objects—a tree, or a stream, or a hill—which was so often part of the common life of the poorest Englishman. Even a century or less ago 'communion with nature' would have sounded an affected and unnatural phrase. Now it was a sensible part of the life of the working classes. Then came moralising, at that date less trite than it has since become, about the social ties that ought to mark the relations between master and workman.

The same night at a banquet in Liverpool, and two days later at Manchester, he advanced to high imperial ground. He told them how, after an experience now becoming long, the one standing pain to the political man in England is a sense of the inequality of his best exertions to the arduous duty of government and legislation. England had undertaken responsibilities of empire such as never before lay on the shoulders or the minds of men. We governed distant millions many times outnumbering ourselves. We were responsible for the welfare of forty or forty-five separate states. Again, what other nation was charged with the same responsibility in the exercise of its moral influence abroad, in the example it is called upon to set, in the sympathy it must feel with the cause of right and justice and constitutional freedom wherever that cause is at issue ? As for our fellow subjects abroad, we had given them practical freedom. It was our duty to abstain as far as may be from interference with their affairs, to afford them the shelter and protection of the empire, and at the same time to impress upon them that there is no grosser mistake in politics than to suppose you can separate the blessings and benefits of freedom from its burdens. In other words, the colonies should pay their own way, and if the old dream of making their interests subservient to those of the mother country had passed away, it was just as little reasonable that the mother country should bear charges that in equity belonged to them, and all the more if the colonies set up against the industry and productions of England the mischiefs and obstructions of an exploded protective system. On foreign policy he enforced the principles that, after all, had

given to Europe forty years of peace, and to England forty
years of diplomatic authority and pre-eminence. 'It is impossible that to a country like England the affairs of foreign
nations can ever be indifferent. It is impossible that England,
in my opinion, ever should forswear the interest she must
naturally feel in the cause of truth, of justice, of order, and of
good government.' The final word was an admonition against
'political lethargy.' For the first time, I think, he put into the
forefront the tormenting question that was to haunt him to the
end. 'They could not look at Ireland,' he told them, 'and say
that the state of feeling there was for the honour and the
advantage of the united kingdom.'

Oct. 14, '64.—So ended in peace an exhausting, flattering, I hope not
intoxicating circuit. God knows I have not courted them. I hope I do
not rest on them. I pray I may turn them to account for good. It is,
however, impossible not to love the people from whom such manifesta-
tions come, as meet me in every quarter. . . . Somewhat haunted by
dreams of halls, and lines of people, and great assemblies.

It was observed of this Lancashire tour, by critics who
hardly meant to praise him, that he paid his hearers the
high compliment of assuming that they could both understand his arguments, and feel his appeal to their moral
sympathies. His speeches, men said, were in fact lay
sermons of a high order, as skilfully composed, as accurately
expressed, as if they were meant for the House of Commons.
This was singularly true, and what an eulogy it was for our
modern British democracy that the man whom they made
their first great hero was an orator of such a school. Lord
Lyttelton, his brother-in-law, informed him of the alarm and
odium that his new line of policy was raising. Mr. Gladstone
(April, 1865) replied :—'After all, you are a peer, and Peel
used to say, speaking of his peer colleagues, that they were
beings of a different order. Please to recollect that we have
got to govern millions of hard hands ; that it must be done
by force, fraud, or good will ; that the latter has been tried
and is answering ; that none have profited more by this
change of system since the corn law and the Six Acts, than
those who complain of it. As to their misliking me, I have
no fault to find with them for that. It is the common lot in
similar circumstances, and the very things that I have done
or omitted doing from my extreme and almost irrational
reluctance to part company with them, become an aggravation when the parting is accomplished.' 'Gladstone, I think,'
says Bishop Wilberforce (Dec. 7), 'is certainly gaining power.
You hear now almost every one say he must be the future
premier, and such sayings tend greatly to accomplish themselves.'

It was about this time that Mr. Gladstone first found himself drawing to relations with the protestant dissenters, that
were destined to grow closer as years went on. These
relations had no small share in the extension of his public
power ; perhaps, too, no small share in the more abiding work
upon the dissenters themselves, of enlarging what was narrow,
softening what was hard and bitter, and promoting a healing
union where the existence of a church establishment turned
ecclesiastical differences into lines of social division. He had
alarmed his friends by his action on a measure (April 15, 1863)
for remedying an old grievance about the burial of dissenters.
Having served on a select committee appointed in the rather
quixotic hope that a solution of the difficulty might be found
by the somewhat unparliamentary means of 'friendly conversation among candid and impartial men,' he had convinced
himself that there was a wrong to be set right, and he voted
and spoke accordingly. 'It will most rudely shake his Oxford
seat,' says Phillimore. The peril there was becoming daily
more apparent. Then in 1864 and on later occasions he met
leading nonconformist clergy at the house of Mr. Newman
Hall—such men as Binney, Allon, Edward White, Baldwin
Brown, Henry Reynolds, and that most admirable friend,
citizen, and man, R. W. Dale, so well known as Dale of Birmingham. Their general attitude was described by Mr. Newman
Hall as this : they hoped for the ultimate recognition of the
free church theory, and meditated no political action to bring
it about ; they looked for it to come as the result of influence
within the church of England, not of efforts from without.
' Many dissenters,' one of them told him (Nov. 20, 1864), 'would
enter the church whatever their theory about establishment, if
such slight modifications were made as would allow them to do
so conscientiously—holding the essentials of the faith far more
soundly than many within the established church.' Another
regretted, after one of these gatherings, that they never got to
the core of the subject, 'namely that there run through the
prayer-book from beginning to end ideas that are not accepted
by numbers who subscribe, and which cannot *all* be admitted
by any one.'

All this once more brought Mr. Gladstone into a curious
position. Just as at Oxford he had in 1847 been the common
hope of ultra-clericals on one hand and ultra-liberals on the
other, so now he was the common hope of the two antagonistic
schools of religious comprehension — the right, who looked
towards the formularies, system, discipline, and tradition either
of the Orthodox church or the Latin, and the left, who sought
reunion on the basis of puritanism with a leaven of modern
criticism. Always the devoted friend of Dr. Pusey and his

school, he was gradually welcomed as ally and political leader by men like Dale and Allon, the independents, and Spurgeon, the baptist, on the broad ground that it was possible for all good men to hold, amid their differences about church government, the more vital sympathies and charities of their common profession. They even sounded him on one occasion about laying the foundation stone of one of their chapels. The broad result of such intercourse of the nonconformist leaders with this powerful and generous mind, enriched by historic knowledge and tradition, strengthened by high political reponsibility, deepened by meditations long, strenuous, and systematic, was indeed remarkable. Dr. Allon expressed it, with admirable point, in a letter to him some fourteen years after our present date (April 15, 1878) :—

> The kind of intercourse that you have kindly permitted with nonconformists, has helped more consciously to identify them with movements of national life, and to diminish the stern feeling of almost defiant witness-bearing that was strong a generation or two ago. It is something gained if ecclesiastical and political differences can be debated within a common circle of social confidence and identity. . . . Their confidence in you has made them amenable to your lead in respect of methods and movements needing the guidance of political insight and experience.

V

A man's mind seldom moves forward towards light and freedom on a single line, and in Mr. Gladstone's case the same impulses that made him tolerant of formal differences as to church government led slowly to a still wider liberality in respect of far deeper differences. Readers may remember the shock with which in his youth he found that one person or another was a unitarian. To Mr. Darbishire, a member of the unitarian body who was for many years his friend, he wrote about some address of James Martineau's (Dec. 21, 1862) :—

> From time to time I have read works of Mr. Martineau's, or works that I have taken for his, with great admiration, with warm respect for the writer, and moreover, with a great deal of sympathy. I should greatly like to make his acquaintance. But attached as I am to the old Christian dogma, and believing it as I do, or rather believing the Person whom it sets forth, to be the real fountain of all the gifts and graces that are largely strewn over society, and in which Mr. Martineau himself seems so amply to share, I fear I am separated from him in the order of ideas by an interval that must be called a gulf. My conviction is that the old creeds have been, and are to be, the channel by which the Christian religion is made a reality even for many who do not hold it, and I think that when we leave them we shall leave them not for something better, but something worse. Hence you will not be surprised that I regard some of Mr. Martineau's propositions as unhistorical and untrue.

And to the same gentleman a year or two later (Jan. 2, 1865) :—

> I am sorry to say I have not yet been able to read Mr. Martineau's

sermon, which I mean to do with care. I am, as you know, one altogether attached to dogma, which I believe to be the skeleton that carries the flesh, the blood, the life of the blessed thing we call the Christian religion. But I do not believe that God's tender mercies are restricted to a small portion of the human family. I dare not be responsible for Dr. Newman, nor would he thank me ; but I hope he does not so believe, and this the more because I have lately been reading Dr. Manning's letter to Dr. Pusey ; and, though Dr. Manning is far more exaggerated in his religion than Dr. Newman, and seems to me almost to caricature it, yet I think even he has by no means that limited view of the mercies of God.

I have no mental difficulty in reconciling a belief in the Church, and what may be called the high Christian doctrine, with that comforting persuasion that those who do not receive the greatest blessings (and each man must believe his religion to be greatest) are notwithstanding the partakers, each in his measure, of other gifts, and will be treated according to their use of them. I admit there are schools of Christians who think otherwise. I was myself brought up to think otherwise, and to believe that salvation depended absolutely upon the reception of a particular and a very narrow creed. But long, long have I cast those weeds behind me. Unbelief may in given conditions be a moral offence ; and only as such, only like other disobedience, and on like principles, can it be punishable.

To not a few the decisive change in Mr. Gladstone's mental history is the change from the ' very narrow creed' of his youth to the 'high Christian doctrine' of his after life. Still more will regard as the real transition the attainment of this ' comforting persuasion,' this last word of benignity and tolerance. Here we are on the foundations. Tolerance is far more than the abandonment of civil usurpations over conscience. It is a lesson often needed quite as much in the hearts of a minority as of a majority. Tolerance means reverence for all the possibilities of Truth ; it means acknowledgment that she dwells in diverse mansions, and wears vesture of many colours, and speaks in strange tongues ; it means frank respect for freedom of indwelling conscience against mechanic forms, official conventions, social force ; it means the charity that is greater than even faith and hope. Marked is the day for a man when he can truly say, as Mr. Gladstone here said, ' Long, long have I cast those weeds behind me.'

CHAPTER IX

DEFEAT AT OXFORD—DEATH OF LORD PALMERSTON—
PARLIAMENTARY LEADERSHIP

(1865)

> In public life a man of elevated mind does not make his own self tell upon others simply and entirely. He must act with other men ; he cannot select his objects, or pursue them by means unadulterated by the methods and practices of minds less elevated than his own. He can only do what he feels to be second-best. He labours at a venture, prosecuting measures so large or so complicated that their ultimate issue is uncertain.—CARDINAL NEWMAN.

THE faithful steward is a chartered bore alike of the mimic and the working stage ; the rake and spendthrift carries all before him. Nobody knew better than Mr. Gladstone that of all the parts in public life, the teasing and economising drudge is the most thankless. The public only half apprehends, or refuses to apprehend at all ; his spending colleagues naturally fight ; colleagues who do not spend, have other business and prize a quiet life. All this made Mr. Gladstone's invincible tenacity as guardian of the national accounts the more genuinely heroic. In a long letter from Balmoral, in the October of 1864, he began what was destined to be the closing battle of the six years' war. To Mrs. Gladstone he wrote :—

> I have fired off to-day my letter to Lord Palmerston about expenditure. For a long time, though I did not let myself worry by needlessly thinking about it, I have had it lying on me like a nightmare. I mean it to be moderate (I shall have the copy when we meet to show you), but unless he concurs it may lead to consequences between this time and February. What is really painful is to believe that he will not agree unless through apprehension, his own leanings and desires being in favour of a large and not a moderate expenditure. . . .

Figures, details, points, were varied, but the issue was in essence the same, and the end was much the same. Lord Palmerston took his stand on the demands of public opinion. He insisted (Oct. 19) that anybody who looked carefully at the signs of the times must see that there were at present two strong feelings in the national mind—the one a disinclination to organic changes in our representative system, the other a steady determination that the country should be placed and kept in an efficient condition of defence. He pointed to the dead indifference of the workmen themselves to their own enfranchisement as evidence of the one, and to the volunteer movement as evidence of the other.

Mr. Gladstone rejoined that it was Lord Palmerston's personal popularity, and not the conviction or desire of the nation, that kept up estimates. Palmerston retorted that this was to mistake cause and effect. 'If I have in any degree been fortunate enough to have obtained some share of the goodwill and confidence of my fellow-countrymen, it has been because I have rightly understood the feelings and opinion of the nation. . . . You may depend upon it that any degree of popularity that is worth having can be obtained only by such means, and of that popularity I sincerely wish you the most ample share.' The strain was severe :—

Oct. 1, 1864.—I still feel much mental lassitude, and not only shrink from public business, but from hard books. It is uphill work. *Oct.* 21. —A pamphlet letter from Lord Palmerston about defence holds out a dark prospect. *Oct.* 22.—Wrote, late in the day, my reply to Lord Palmerston in a rather decisive tone, for I feel conscious of right and of necessity

To Mrs. Gladstone.

Nov. 9.—After more than a fortnight's delay, I received yesterday evening the enclosed very unfavourable letter from Lord Palmerston. I send with it the draft of my reply. Please to return them to-morrow by Willy—for they ought not to be even for that short time out of my custody, but I do not like to keep you in the dark. I suppose the matter may now stand over as far as debate is concerned until next month, or even till the middle of January. I fear you will not have much time for reading or writing to-morrow before you start for Chatsworth.

This *sort* of controversy keeps the nerves too highly strung. I am more afraid of running away than of holding my ground. But I do not quite forget how plentifully I am blessed and sustained, and how mercifully spared other and sorer trials.

To-morrow comes the supper of the St. Martin's Volunteers ; and after that I hope to close my lips until February. The scene last night[1] was very different from that of Monday ; but very remarkable, and even more enthusiastic. I was the only layman among five hundred lawyers ; and it made me, wickedly, think of my position when locked alone in the Naples gaol.

Jan. 19, 1865.—The cabinet has been to-day almost as rough as any of the roughest times. In regard to the navy estimates, I have had no effective or broad support ; platoon-firing more or less in my sense from Argyll and Gibson, four or five were silent, the rest hostile. Probably they will appoint a committee of cabinet, and we may work through, but on the other hand we may not. My *opinion* is manifestly in a minority ; but there is an unwillingness to have a row. I am not well

---

[1] The dinner in honour of M. Berryer.

able to write about other things—these batterings are sore work, but
I must go through. C. Paget and Childers hold their ground.

Jan. 28.—The morning went fast but wretchedly. Seldom, thank
God, have I a day to which I could apply this epithet. Last night I
could have done almost anything to shut out the thought of the coming
battle. This is very weak, but it is the effects of the constant recurrence
of these things. Estimates always settled at the dagger's point.—
(*Diary.*)

Osborne, Jan. 31.—I hope you got my note last night. The weather
here is mild, and I sit with open window while writing. The Queen
and Princess both ask about you abundantly. I have been most
pertinacious about seeing the baby prince. I tried to make the request
twice to the Princess, but I think she did not understand my words.
Determined not to be beat, I applied to the Prince, who acceded with
glee, but I don't know what will come of it. He talked with good sense
last night about Greece, Ionian Islands, and Canada ; and I was his
partner at whist. We came off quits. I dined last night, and also saw
the Queen before dinner, but only for a quarter of an hour or so. She
talked about Japan and Lord Palmerston, but there was not time to get
into swing, and nothing said of nearer matters.

The sort of success that awaited his strenuous endeavour has
been already indicated.[1]

II

In the spring Mr. Gladstone made the first advance upon
what was to be an important journey. All through February
and March he worked with Phillimore and others upon the
question of the Irish church. The thing was delicate, for his
constituency would undoubtedly be adverse. His advisers
resolved that he should speak on a certain motion from a radical
below the gangway, to the effect that the present position of
the Irish church establishment was unsatisfactory, and called
for the early attention of the government. It is hard to
imagine two propositions on the merits more indisputable, but
a parliamentary resolution is not to be judged by its verbal
contents only. Dillwyn's motion was known to mean disestablishment and nothing less. In that view, Mr. Gladstone
wrote a short but pregnant letter to Phillimore—and this too
meant disestablishment and nothing less. It was the first
tolerably definite warning of what was to be one of the two or
three greatest legislative acts of his career.

To Robert Phillimore.

Feb. 13, 1865.—I would treat the Irish church, as a religious body,
with the same respect and consideration as the church of England, and
would apply to it the same liberal policy as regards its freedom of action.
But I am not loyal to it as an establishment. It exists, and is virtually
almost unchallenged as to its existence in that capacity ; it may long (I
cannot quite say long may it) outlive me ; I will never be a party,

knowingly, to what I may call frivolous acts of disturbance, nor to the premature production of schemes of change : but still comes back the refrain of my song : '*I am not loyal to it as an Establishment.*' I could not renew the votes and speeches of thirty years back. A quarter of a century of not only fair but exceptionally fair trial has wholly dispelled hopes to which they had relation ; and I am bound to say I look upon its present form of existence as no more favourable to religion, in any sense of the word, than it is to civil justice and to the contentment and loyalty of Ireland.

Lord Palmerston got wind of the forthcoming speech, and wrote a short admonitory note. He had heard that Mr. Gladstone was about to set forth his views as an individual, and not as a member of the government, and this was a distinction that he reckoned impracticable. Was it possible for a member of a government speaking from the treasury bench so to sever himself from the body corporate to which he belonged, as to be able to express decided opinions as an individual, and leave himself free to act upon different opinions, or abstain from acting on those opinions, when required to act as a member of the government taking part in the divisions of the body ? And again, if his opinions happened not to be accepted by a colleague on the same bench, would not the colleague have either to acquiesce, or else to state in what respect his own opinion differed ? In this case would not differences in a government be unnecessarily and prematurely forced upon the public ? All this was the sound doctrine of cabinet government. Mr. Gladstone, replying, felt that ' he could not as a minister, and as member for Oxford, allow the subject to be debated an indefinite number of times and remain silent.' His indictment of the Irish church was decisive. At the same time he was careful to explain in public correspondence that the question was out of all bearing on the practical politics of the day. Meanwhile, as spokesman for the government, Mr. Gladstone deprecated the responsibility of raising great questions at a time when they could not be seriously approached. One acute observer who knew him well, evidently took a different view of the practical politics of the day, or at any rate, of the morrow. Manning wrote to Mr. Gladstone two days after the speech was made and begged to be allowed to see him :—' I read your speech on the Irish church, which set me musing and fore-casting. It was a real grapple with the question.'

III

Not many days after this speech Cobden died. To his brother, Robertson, Mr. Gladstone wrote :—

April 5.—What a sad, sad loss is this death of Cobden. I feel in miniature the truth of what Bright well said yesterday—ever since I really came to know him, I have held him in high esteem and regard as

well as admiration ; but till he died I did not know how high it was.
I do not know that I have ever seen in public life a character more truly
simple, noble, and unselfish. His death will make an echo through the
world, which in its entireness he has served so well.

April 7.—To Mr. Cobden's funeral at W. Lavington. Afterwards to
his home, which I was anxious to know. Also I saw Mrs. Cobden.
The day was lovely, the scenery most beautiful and soothing, the whole
sad and impressive. Bright broke down at the grave. Cobden's name
is great ; it will be greater. (*Diary.*)

A few months before this Mr. Gladstone had lost a friend
more intimate. The death of the Duke of Newcastle, he says
(Oct. 19, 1864), 'severs the very last of those contemporaries
who were also my political friends. How it speaks to me " Be
doing, and be done."'

To Mrs. Gladstone.

Oct. 19.—Dr. Kingsley sent me a telegram to inform me of the sad
event at Clumber ; but it only arrived two hours before the papers,
though the death happened last night. So that brave heart has at last
ceased to beat. Certainly in him more than any one I have known, was
exhibited the character of our life as a dispensation of pain. This must
ever be a mystery, for we cannot see the working-out of the purposes of
God. Yet in his case I have always thought some glimpse of them
seemed to be permitted. It is well to be permitted also to believe that
he is now at rest for ever, and that the cloud is at length removed from
his destiny.

Clumber, Oct. 26.—It is a time and a place to feel, if one could feel.
He died in the room where we have been sitting before and after dinner
—where, thirty-two years ago, a stripling, I came over from Newark in
fear and trembling to see the duke, his father ; where a stiff horseshoe
semi-circle then sat round the fire in evenings ; where that rigour melted
away in Lady Lincoln's time ; where she and her mother sang so beautifully at the pianoforte, in the same place where it now stands. The house
is full of local memories.

IV

On July 6 (1865) parliament was dissolved. Four years
before, Mr. Gladstone had considered the question of retaining
or abandoning the seat for the university. It was in contemplation to give a third member to the southern division of
Lancashire, and, in July 1861, he received a requisition begging
his assent to nomination there, signed by nearly 8000 of the
electors—a number that seemed to make success certain. His
letters to Dr. Pusey and others show how strongly he inclined
to comply. Flesh and blood shrank from perpetual strife, he
thought, and after four contested elections in fourteen years at
Oxford, he asked himself whether he should not escape the
prolongation of the series. He saw, as he said, that they
meant to make it a life-battle, like the old famous college war
between Bentley and the fellows of Trinity. But he felt his
deep obligation to his Oxford supporters, and was honourably
constrained again to bear their flag. In the same month of

1851 he had declined absolutely to stand for London in the place of Lord John Russell.

At Oxford the tories this time had secured an excellent candidate in Mr. Gathorne Hardy, a man of sterling character, a bold and capable debater, a good man of business, one of the best of Lord Derby's lieutenants. The election was hard fought, like most of the four that had gone before it. The educated residents were for the chancellor of the exchequer, as they had always been, and he had both liberals and high churchmen on his side. One feature was novel, the power of sending votes by post. Mr. Gladstone had not been active in the House against this change, but only bestowed upon it a parting malediction. It strengthened the clerical vote, and as sympathy with disestablishment was thrust prominently forward against Mr. Gladstone, the new privilege cost him his seat. From the first day things looked ill, and when on the last day (July 18) the battle ended, he was one hundred and eighty votes behind Mr. Hardy.[1]

July 16, '65. — Always in straits the Bible in church supplies my needs. To-day it was in the 1st lesson, Jer. i. 19, 'And they shall fight against thee, but they shall not prevail against thee, for I am with thee, saith the Lord, to deliver thee.'

July 17.—Again came consolation to me in the Psalms—86 : 16 ; it did the same for me April 17, 1853. At night arrived the telegram announcing my defeat at Oxford as virtually accomplished. A dear dream is dispelled. God's will be done.

His valedictory address was both graceful and sincere :— 'After an arduous connection of eighteen years, I bid you respectfully farewell. My earnest purpose to serve you, my many faults and shortcomings, the incidents of the political relation between the university and myself, established in 1847, so often questioned in vain, and now, at length, finally dissolved, I leave to the judgment of the future. It is one imperative duty, and one alone, which induces me to trouble you with these few parting words — the duty of expressing my profound and lasting gratitude for indulgence as generous, and for support as warm and enthusiastic in itself, and as honourable from the character and distinctions of those who have given it, as has in my belief ever been accorded by any constituency to any representative.'

He was no sooner assured of his repulse at Oxford, than he started for the Lancashire constituency, where a nomination had been reserved for him.

July 18.—Went off at eleven . . . to the Free Trade Hall which was said to have 6000 people. They were in unbounded enthusiasm. I spoke for 1¼ hr., and when the meeting concluded went off to Liverpool. . . . Another meeting of 5000 at the Amphitheatre, if possible more enthusiastic than that at Manchester.

<hr>

[1] Heathcote, 3236; Hardy, 1904; Gladstone, 1724.

In the fine hall that stands upon the site made historic by the militant free-traders, he used a memorable phrase. 'At last, my friends,' he began, 'I am come among you, and I am come among you "unmuzzled."' The audience quickly realised the whole strength of the phrase, and so did the people of the country when it reached them. Then he opened a high magnanimous exordium about the Oxford that had cast him out. The same evening at Liverpool, he again dwelt on the desperate fondness with which he had clung to the university seat, but rapidly passed to the contrast. 'I come into South Lancashire, and find here around me different phenomena. I find the development of industry. I find the growth of enterprise. I find the progress of social philanthropy. I find the prevalence of toleration. I find an ardent desire for freedom. If there be one duty more than another incumbent upon the public men of England, it is to establish and maintain harmony between the past of our glorious history and the future that is still in store for her.'

July 20.—Robertson and I went in early and polled. He was known, and I through him, and we had a scene of great popular enthusiasm. We then followed the polls as the returns came in, apparently triumphant, but about midday it appeared that the figures of both parties were wrong, ours the worst. Instead of being well and increasingly at the head I was struggling with Egerton at 1 P.M., and Turner gaining on me. . . . Off to Chester. In the evening the figures of the close came in and gave me the second place. The volunteers in the park cheered loudly, the church bells rung, the people came down with a band and I had to address them.

To the Duchess of Sutherland.

I am by far too sorry about Oxford to feel the slightest temptation to be angry, even were there cause. I only feel that I love her better than ever. There is great enthusiasm here, stimulated no doubt by the rejection. I have just been polling amid fervid demonstrations. The first return at nine o'clock—but you will know all when this reaches you—is as follows. . . . This of course says little as to the final issue. Ten o'clock. My majority so far increases, the others diminish. But it is hard running. Eleven. My majority increases, the others diminish. Egerton is second. One of our men third. Twelve thousand four hundred have polled. My seat looks well.

I interrupt here to say you would have been *pleased* had you heard Willy, at a moment's notice, on Tuesday night, address five thousand people no one of whom had ever seen him ; he was (forgive me) so modest, so manly, *so ready*, so judicious.

Since writing thus far everything has been overset in a chaos of conflicting reports. They will all be cleared up for you before this comes. I hope I am not in a fool's paradise. All I yet know is an apparently hard fight between Egerton and me for the head of the poll, but my seat tolerably secure. I have had *such* letters !

When the votes were counted Mr. Gladstone was third upon

the poll, and so secured the seat, with two tory colleagues above him.[1]

The spirit in which Mr. Gladstone took a defeat that was no mere electioneering accident, but the landmark of a great severance in his extraordinary career, is shown in his replies to multitudes of correspondents. On the side of his tenacious and affectionate attachment to Oxford, the wound was deep. On the other side, emancipation from fetters and from contests that he regarded as ungenerous, was a profound relief. But the relief touched him less than the sorrow.

Manning wrote :—

Few men have been watching you more than I have in these last days ; and I do not know that I could wish you any other result. But you have entered upon a new and larger field as Sir R. Peel did, to whose history yours has many points of likeness. You say truly that Oxford has failed to enlarge itself to the progress of the country. I hope this will make you enlarge yourself to the facts of our age and state—and I believe it will. Only, as I said some months ago, I am anxious about you, lest you should entangle yourself with extremes. This crisis is for you politically what a certain date was for me religiously.

Mr. Gladstone replied :—

Hawarden, July 21.—I thank you very much for your kind letter, and I should have been very glad if it had contained all that it merely alludes to. From Oxford and her children I am overwhelmed with kindness. My feelings towards her are those of sorrow, leavened perhaps with pride. But I am for the moment a stunned man ; the more so because without a moment of repose I had to plunge into the whirlpools of South Lancashire, and swim there for my life, which as you will see, has been given me.

I do not think I can admit the justice of the caution against extremes. The greatest or second greatest of what people call my extremes, is one which I believe you approve. I profess myself a disciple of Butler : the greatest of all enemies to extremes. This indeed speaks for my intention only. But in a cold or lukewarm period, and such is this in public affairs, everything which moves and lives is called extreme, and that by the very people (I do not mean or think that you are one of them) who in a period of excitement would far outstrip, under pressure, those whom they now rebuke. Your caution about self-control, however, I do accept—it is very valuable—I am sadly lacking in that great quality.

At both Liverpool and Manchester, he writes to Dr. Jacobson, I had to speak of Oxford, and I have endeavoured to make it unequivocally clear that I am here as the same man, and not another, and that throwing off the academic cap and gown makes no difference in the figure.

'Vixi, et quem dederat cursum fortuna peregi.'[2]

And when I think of dear old Oxford, whose services to me I can never repay, there comes back to me that line of Wordsworth in his incomparable Ode, and I fervently address her with it—

'Forbode not any severing of our loves.'

[1] Egerton, 9171 ; Turner, 8806 ; Gladstone, 8786 ; Legh (C.), 8476 ; Thompson (L.), 7703 ; Heywood (L.), 7653.

[2] *Aen.* iv. 653. I have lived my life, my fated course have run.

To Sir Stafford Northcote, July 21.—I cannot withhold myself from writing a line to assure you it is not my fault, but my misfortune, that you are not my successor at Oxford. My desire or impulse has for a good while, not unnaturally, been to escape from the Oxford seat; not because I grudged the anxieties of it, but because I found the load, added to other loads, too great. Could I have seen my way to this proceeding, had the advice or had the conduct of my friends warranted it, you would have had such notice of it, as effectually to preclude your being anticipated. I mean no disrespect to Mr. Hardy ; but it has been a great pain to me to see in all the circulars a name different from the name that should have stood there, and that would have stood there, but for your personal feelings.

Ibid. July 22.—The separation from friends in politics is indeed very painful. . . . I have been instructed, perhaps been hardened, by a very wide experience in separation. No man has been blessed more out of proportion to his deserts than I have in friends : in πολυφιλία, in χρηστοφιλία ; [1] but when with regard to those of old standing who were nearest to me, I ask where are they, I seem to see around me a little waste, that has been made by politics, by religion, and by death. All these modes of severance are sharp. But the first of them is the least so, when the happy conviction remains that the fulfilment of duty, such as conscience points to it, is the object on both sides. And I have suffered so sorely by the far sharper partings in death, and in religion after a fashion which practically almost comes to death, that there is something of relief in turning to the lighter visitation. It is, however, a visitation still.

To the Bishop of Oxford, July 21.—. . . Do not join with others in praising me, because I am not angry, only sorry, and that deeply. For my revenge—which I do not desire, but would baffle if I could—all lies in that little word 'future' in my address, which I wrote with a consciousness that it is deeply charged with meaning, and that that which shall come will come. There have been two great deaths or transmigrations of spirit in my political existence. One very slow, the breaking of ties with my original party. The other, very short and sharp, the breaking of the tie with Oxford. There will probably be a third, and no more. . . . Again, my dear Bishop, I thank you for bearing with my waywardness, and manifesting, in the day of need, your confidence and attachment.

The bishop naturally hinted some curiosity as to the third transmigration. 'The oracular sentence,' Mr. Gladstone replied, 'has little bearing on present affairs or prospects, and may stand in its proper darkness.' In the same letter the bishop urged Mr. Gladstone to imitate Canning when he claimed the post of prime minister. 'I think,' was the reply (July 25) 'that if you had the same means of estimating my position, jointly with my faculties, as I have, you would be of a different opinion. It is my fixed determination never to take any step whatever to raise myself to a higher level in official life, and this not on grounds of Christian self-denial which would hardly apply, but on the double ground, first, of my total ignorance of my capacity, bodily or mental, to hold such a higher level, and,

[1] Aristotle, *Rhet.* i. 5 4.

secondly—perhaps I might say especially—because I am certain that the fact of my seeking it would seal my doom in taking it.'[1]

Truly was it said of Mr. Gladstone that his rejection at Oxford, and his election in Lancashire, were regarded as matters of national importance, because he was felt to have the promise of the future in him, to have a living fire in him, a capacity for action, and a belief that moving on was a national necessity ; because he was bold, earnest, impulsive ; because he could sympathise with men of all classes, occupations, interests, opinions; because he thought nothing done so long as much remained for him to do. While liberals thus venerated him as if he had been a Moses beckoning from Sinai towards the promised land, tories were described as dreading him, ever since his suffrage speech, as continental monarchs dreaded Mazzini—' a man whose name is at once an alarm, a menace, and a prediction.' They hated him partly as a deserter, partly as a disciple of Manchester. Throughout the struggle, the phrase 'I believe in Mr. Gladstone' served as the liberal *credo*, and 'I distrust Mr. Gladstone' as the condensed commination service of the tories upon all manner of change. [2]

V

On October 18, the prime minister died at Brocket. The news found Mr. Gladstone at Clumber, in performance of his duties as Newcastle trustee. For him the event opened many possibilities, and his action upon it is set out in two or three extracts from his letters :—

To Lord Russell. Clumber, Oct. 18, 1865.—I have received to-night by telegraph the appalling news of Lord Palmerston's decease. None of us, I suppose, were prepared for this event, in the sense of having communicated as to what should follow. The Queen must take the first step, but I cannot feel uncertain what it will be. Your former place as her minister, your powers, experience, services, and renown, do not leave reason for doubt that you will be sent for. Your hands will be entirely free—you are pledged probably to no one, certainly not to me. But any government now to be formed cannot be wholly a continuation, but must be in some degree a new commencement.

I am sore with conflicts about the public expenditure, which I feel that other men would have either escaped, or have conducted more gently and less fretfully. I am most willing to retire. On the other hand, I am bound by conviction even more than by credit to the principle of progressive reduction in our military and naval establishments and in the charges for them, under the favourable circumstances which we appear to enjoy. This I think is the moment to say thus much in subject matter which greatly appertains to my department. On the general field of politics, after having known your course in cabinet for eight and

---

[1] *Life of Wilberforce*, iii. pp. 161-164. The transcriber has omitted from Mr. Gladstone's second letter a sentence about Archbishop Manning's letter—' To me it seemed *meant* in the kindest and most friendly sense ; but that the man is gone out, φροῦδος, and has left nothing but the priest. No shirt collar ever took such a quantity of starch.'

[2] See *Saturday Review*, July 29 ; *Spectator*, June 24, etc.

a half years, I am quite willing to take my chance under your banner, in the exact capacity I now fill, and I adopt the step, perhaps a little unusual, of saying so, because it may be convenient to you at a juncture when time is precious, while it can, I trust, after what I have said above, hardly be hurtful.

To Mr. Panizzi, Oct. 18.—*Ei fu!*[1] Death has indeed laid low the most towering antlers in all the forest. No man in England will more sincerely mourn Lord Palmerston than you. Your warm heart, your long and close friendship with him, and your sense of all he had said and done for Italy, all so bound you to him that you will deeply feel this loss ; as for myself I am stunned. It was plain that this would come ; but sufficient unto the day is the burden thereof, and there is no surplus stock of energy in the mind to face, far less to anticipate, fresh contingencies. But I need not speak of this great event—to-morrow all England will be ringing of it, and the world will echo England. I cannot forecast the changes which will follow ; but it is easy to see what the first step should be.

To Mrs. Gladstone, Oct. 20.—I received two letters from you to-day together. The first, very naturally full of plans, the second written when those plans had been blown into the air by the anticipation (even) of Lord Palmerston's death. This great event shakes me down to the foundation, by the reason of coming trouble. I think two things are clear. 1. The Queen should have come to London. 2. She should have sent for Lord Russell. I fear she has done neither. Willy telegraphs to me that a letter from Lord Russell had come to Downing Street. Now had he heard from the Queen, he would (so I reason) either have telegraphed to me to go up, or sent a letter hither by a messenger instead of leaving it to kick its heels in Downing Street for a day. And we hear nothing of the Queen's moving ; she is getting into a groove, out of which some one ought to draw her.

Oct. 21.—As far as political matters are concerned, I am happier this morning. Lord Russell, pleased with my letter, writes to say he has been commissioned to carry on the present government as first lord, wishes me to co-operate ' in the capacity I now fill as a principal member of the administration.' I think that I have struck a stroke for economy which will diminish difficulty when we come to estimates for the year. I *hope* from his letter that he means to ask George Grey to lead, which would be very acceptable to me. Though he does not summon me to London, I think I ought to go, and shall do so accordingly to-day. I am sorry that this is again more vexation and uncertainty for you.

Oct. 22.—I came up last night and very glad I am of it. I found that Lord Palmerston's funeral was almost to be private, not because the family wished it, but because nothing had been proposed to them. I at once sent —— down to Richmond and Pembroke Lodge with a letter, and the result is that Evelyn Ashley has been written to by Lord Russell and authorised to telegraph to Balmoral to propose a funeral in Westminster Abbey. It is now very late, and all the preparations must have been made at Romsey. But in such a matter especially, better late than never.

You will have been amused to see that on Friday the *Times* actually

[1] Ei fu ! siccome immobile, etc. First line of Manzoni's ode on the death of Napoleon.

put me up for prime minister, and yesterday knocked me down again ! There is a rumour that it was the old story, Delane out of town. I was surprised at the first article, not at the second. All, I am sorry to say, seem to take for granted that I am to lead the House of Commons. But this is not so simple a matter. First, it must be offered to Sir George Grey. If he refuses, then secondly, I do not think I can get on without a different arrangement of treasury and chancellor of exchequer business, which will not be easy. But the worst of all is the distribution of offices as between the two Houses. It has long been felt that the House of Commons was too weak and the House of Lords too strong, in the share of the important offices, and now the premiership is to be carried over, unavoidably. No such thing has ever been known as an adminis- tration with the first lord, foreign secretary, secretary for war, and the first lord of the admiralty, in the House of Lords.[1] *This* is really a stiff business.

To Lord Russell. Carlton House Terrace, Oct. 23. — You having thought fit to propose that I should lead the House of Commons, I felt it necessary first to be assured that Sir George Grey, who was in con- structive possession of that office, and under whom I should have served with perfect satisfaction, could not be induced to accept the duty. Of this your letter seemed to contain sufficient proof. Next, I felt it to be necessary that some arrangement should be made for relieving me of a considerable and singularly disabling class of business, consisting of the cases of real or supposed grievance, at all times arising in connection with the collection of the public revenue under its several heads. . . . The third difficulty which I named to you in the way of my accepting your proposal, is what I venture to call the lop-sided condition of the government, with the strain and stress of administration in the House of Commons, and nearly all the offices about which the House of Com- mons cares, represented by heads in the House of Lords. It weighs very seriously on my mind, and I beg you to *consider* it. . . . I have rather particular engagements of a public nature next week ; at Edin- burgh on the 2nd and 3rd in connection with the university business, and at Glasgow on the 1st, to receive the freedom. I am anxious to know whether I may now finally confirm these engagements ?

To Mrs. Gladstone, Oct. 23.—I think I see my way a little now. Lord Russell agrees that cabinets should be postponed after Saturday, for a good fortnight. I can therefore keep my engagements in Scotland, and write to-day to say so.

Lord Palmerston is to be buried in the Abbey on Friday ; the family are pleased. I saw W. Cooper as well as Evelyn Ashley to-day. They give a good account of Lady Palmerston. . . . Lord Russell offers me the lead—I must probably settle it to-morrow. His physical strength is low, but I suppose in the Lords he may get on. The greatest difficulty is having almost all the important offices in the Lords.

Oct. 24.—Lord Russell now proposes to adjourn the cabinets till Nov. 14th, but I must be here for the Lord Mayor's dinner on the 9th. You will therefore see my programme as it now stands. I send you a batch of eight letters, which please keep carefully to yourself, and return in their bundle forthwith. There are divers proposals on foot,

---

[1] First lord, Earl Russell ; foreign secretary, Lord Clarendon ; secretary for war, Earl de Grey : first lord of the admiralty, Duke of Somerset.

but I think little will be finally settled before Friday. Sir R. Peel will probably have a peerage offered him. I have not yet accepted the lead formally, but I suppose it must come to that. The main question is whether anything, and what, can be done to improve the structure of the government as between the two Houses.

Oct. 25.—Nothing more has yet been done. I consider my position virtually fixed. I am afraid of Lord Russell's rapidity, but we shall try to rein it in. There seems to be very little venom in the atmosphere. I wish Sir G. Grey were here. The Queen's keeping so long at Balmoral is a sad mistake.

He received, as was inevitable, plenty of letters from admirers regretting that he had not gone up higher. His answer was, of course, uniform. 'It was,' he told them, 'my own impartial and firm opinion that Lord Russell was the proper person to succeed Lord Palmerston. However flattered I may be, therefore, to hear of an opinion such as you report and express, I have felt it my duty to co-operate to the best of my power in such arrangements as might enable the government to be carried on by the present ministers, with Lord Russell at their head.'

On the other hand, doubts were abundant. To Sir George Grey, one important friend wrote (Oct. 30)—'I think you are right on the score of health, to give him [Gladstone] the lead of the House; but you will see, with all his talents, he will not perceive the difference between leading and driving.' Another correspondent, of special experience, confessed to 'great misgivings as to Gladstone's tact and judgment.' 'The heart of all Israel is towards him,' wrote his good friend Dean Church; 'he is very great and very noble. But he is hated as much as, or more than, he is loved. He is fierce sometimes and wrathful and easily irritated; he wants knowledge of men and speaks rashly. And I look on with some trembling to see what will come of this his first attempt to lead the Commons and prove himself fit to lead England.'[1] It was pointed out that Roundell Palmer was the only powerful auxiliary on whom he could rely in debate, and should the leader himself offend the House by an indiscretion, no colleague was competent to cover his retreat or baffle the triumph of the enemy. His first public appearance as leader of the House of Commons and associate premier was made at Glasgow, and his friends were relieved and exultant. The point on which they trembled was caution, and at Glasgow he was caution personified.

The changes in administration were not very difficult. Lowe's admission to the cabinet was made impossible by his declaration against any lowering of the borough franchise. The inclusion of Mr. Goschen, who had only been in parliament three years, was the subject of remark. People who asked what he had done to merit promotion so striking, did not know

1 Church's *Letters*, p. 171.

his book on foreign exchanges, and were perhaps in no case competent to judge it.[1] Something seems to have been said about Mr. Bright, for in a note to Lord Russell (Dec. 11) Mr. Gladstone writes : ' With reference to your remark about Bright, he has for many years held language of a studious moderation about reform. And there is something odious in fighting shy of a man, so powerful in talent, of such undoubted integrity. Without feeling, however, that he is permanently proscribed, I am under the impression that in the present critical state of feeling on your own side with respect to the franchise, his name would sink the government and the bill together.' When Palmerston invited Cobden to join his cabinet in 1859, Cobden spoke of Bright, how he had avoided person- alities in his recent speeches. ' It is not personalities that we complained of,' Palmerston replied ; ' a public man is right in attacking persons. But it is his attacks on *classes* that have given offence to powerful bodies, who can make their resentment felt.'[2]

Mr. Gladstone's first few weeks as leader of the House were almost a surprise. ' At two,' he says (Feb. 1, 1866), ' we went down to choose the Speaker, and I had to throw off in my new capacity. If mistrust of self be a qualification, God knows I have it.' All opened excellently. Not only was he mild and conciliatory, they found him even tiresome in his deference. Some onlookers still doubted. Everybody, they said, admired and respected him, some loved him, but there were few who understood him. ' So far,' said a conservative observer, ' Glad- stone has led the House with great good temper, prosperity, and success, but his rank and file and some of his colleagues seem to like him none the better on that account.'[3]   Mean- while, words of friendly encouragement came from Windsor. On Feb. 19 :—' The Queen cannot conclude without expressing to Mr. Gladstone her gratification at the accounts she hears from all sides of the admirable manner in which he has com- menced his leadership in the House of Commons.'

He found the speech for a monument to Lord Palmerston in the Abbey ' a delicate and difficult duty ' (Feb. 22). ' It would

---

[1] Once at Hawarden I dropped the idle triviality that Mr. Pitt, Mr. Goschen, and a third person, were the three men who had been put into cabinet after the shortest spell of parliamentary life. (They were likewise out again after the shortest recorded spell of cabinet life.) ' I don't believe any such thing,' said Mr. Gladstone. ' Well, who is your man ? ' ' What do you say,' he answered, ' to Sir George Murray ? Wel- lington put him into his cabinet (1828) ; he had been with him in the Peninsula.' On returning to London, I found that Murray had been five years in parliament, and having written to tell Mr. Gladstone so, the next day I received a summary postcard—' Then try Lord Henry Petty.' Here, as far as I make out, he was right.

' It is very unusual, I think,' Mr. Gladstone wrote to the prime minister (Jan. 6, 1866), ' to put men into the cabinet without a previous official training. Lord Derby could not help himself. Peel put Knatchbull, but that was on political grounds that seemed broad, but proved narrow enough. Argyll was put there in '52-3, but there is not the same opportunity for previous training in the case of peers.'

[2] *Life of Cobden*, ii. p. 232.

[3] *Life of Sir Charles Murray*, p. 300.

have worn me down beforehand had I not been able to exclude
it from my thoughts till the last, and then I could only feel my
impotence.' Yet he performed the duty with grace and truth.
He commemorated Palmerston's share in the extension of
freedom in Europe, and especially in Italy, where, he said,
Palmerston's name might claim a place on a level with her
most distinguished patriots. Nor had his interest ever failed
in the rescue of the 'unhappy African race, whose history is for
the most part written only in blood and tears.' He applauded
his genial temper, his incomparable tact and ingenuity, his
pluck in debate, his delight in a fair stand-up fight, his inclination to avoid whatever tended to exasperate, his incapacity
of sustained anger.

CHAPTER X

MATTERS ECCLESIASTICAL

(1864–1868)

*

ὦ γῆς ὄχημα κἀπὶ γῆς ἔχων ἕδραν,
ὅστις ποτ' εἶ σύ, δυστόπαστος εἰδέναι,
Ζεύς, εἴτ' ἀνάγκη φύσεος εἴτε νοῦς βροτῶν,
προσηυξάμην σέ· πάντα γὰρ δι' ἀψόφου
βαίνων κελεύθου κατὰ δίκην τὰ θνήτ' ἄγεις.

EUR. *Troades*, 884.

O thou, upholder of the earth, who upon earth hast an abiding place, whosoever thou art, inscrutable, thou Zeus, whether thou be necessity of nature, or intelligence of mortal men, on thee I call; for, treading a noiseless path, in righteousness dost thou direct all human things.

THE reader will have surmised that amidst all the press and strain in affairs of state, Mr. Gladstone's intensity of interest in affairs of the church never for an instant slackened. Wide as the two spheres stood apart, his temper in respect of them was much the same. In church and state alike he prized institutions and the great organs of corporate life ; but what he thought of most and cared for and sought after most, was not their mechanism, though on that too he set its value, but the living spirit within the institution. In church and state alike he moved cautiously and tentatively. In both alike he strove to unite order, whether temporal order in the state or spiritual order in the church, with his sovereign principle of freedom. Many are the difficulties in the way of applying Cavour's formula of a free church in a free state, as most countries and their governors have by now found out. Yet to have a vivid sense of the supreme importance of the line between temporal power and spiritual is the note of a statesman fit for modern times. 'The whole of my public life,' he wrote to the Bishop of Oxford in 1863, 'with respect to matters ecclesiastical, for the last twenty years and more, has been a continuing effort, though a very weak one, to extricate the church in some degree from entangled relations without shock or violence.'

· The general temper of his churchmanship on its political side during these years is admirably described in a letter to his eldest son, and some extracts from it furnish a key to his most characteristic frame of mind in attempting to guide the movements of his time :—

To W. H. Gladstone.

April 16, 1865.—You appeared to speak with the supposition, a very natural one, that it was matter of duty to defend all the privileges and possessions of the church ; that concession would lead to concession ; and that the end of the series would be its destruction. . . . Now, in the first place, it is sometimes necessary in politics to make surrenders of what, if not surrendered, will be wrested from us. And it is very wise, when a necessity of this kind is approaching, to anticipate it while it is yet a good way off ; for then concession begets gratitude, and often brings a return. The *kind* of concession which is really mischievous is just that which is made under terror and extreme pressure ; and unhappily this has been the kind of concession which for more than two hundred years, it has been the fashion of men who call (and who really think) themselves 'friends of the church' to make. . . . I believe it would be a wise concession, upon grounds merely political, for the church of England to have the law of church rate abolished in all cases where it places her in fretting conflict with the dissenting bodies. . . . I say all this, however, not to form the groundwork of a conclusion, but only in illustration of a general maxim which is applicable to political questions.

But next, this surely is a political question. Were we asked to surrender an article of the creed in order to save the rest, or to consent to the abolition of the episcopal order, these things touch the faith of Christians and the life of the church, and cannot in any measure become the subject of compromise. But the external possessions of the church were given it for the more effectual promotion of its work, and may be lessened or abandoned with a view to the same end. . . . Now we have lived into a time when the great danger of the church is the sale of her faith for gold. . . . In demanding the money of dissenters for the worship of the church, we practically invest them with a title to demand that she should be adapted to their use in return, and we stimulate every kind of interference with her belief and discipline to that end. By judiciously waiving an undoubted legal claim, we not only do an act which the understood principles of modern liberty tend to favour and almost require, but we soothe ruffled minds and tempers, and what is more, we strengthen the case and claim of the church to be respected as a religious body. . . . I am convinced that the only hope of making it possible for her to discharge her high office as stewardess of divine truth, is to deal tenderly and gently with all the points at which her external privileges *grate* upon the feelings and interests of that unhappily large portion of the community who have almost ceased in any sense to care for her. This is a principle of broad application, broader far than the mere question of church rates. It is one not requiring precipitate or violent action, or the disturbance prematurely of anything established ; but it supplies a rule of the first importance for dealing with the mixed questions of temporal and religious interest when they arise. I am very anxious to see it quietly but firmly rooted in your mind. It is connected with the dearest interests not only of my public life, but as I believe of our religion. . . . I am in no way anxious that you should take my opinions in politics as a model for your own. Your free concurrence will be a lively pleasure to me. But above all I wish you to be free. What I have now been dwelling upon is a matter higher and deeper than the region of mere opinion. It has fallen to my lot to take a share larger than that of many around me, though in itself slight, in bringing the principle I have described into use as a ground of action. I am convinced that if I have laboured to any purpose at all it has been in great part for this. It is part of that business of reconciling the past with the new time and order, which seems to belong particularly to our country and its rulers.

He then goes on to cite as cases where something had been done towards securing the action of the church as a religious body, Canada, where clergy and people now appointed their own bishop ; a recent judgment of the privy council leading to widespread emancipation of the colonial church; the revival of convocation ; the licence to convocation to alter the thirty-sixth canon ; the bestowal of self-government on Oxford. 'In these measures,' he says, 'I have been permitted to take my part ; but had I adopted the rigid rule of others in regard to the temporal prerogatives, real or supposed, of the church, I should at once have lost all power to promote them.'

'As to disruption,' he wrote in these days, 'that is the old cry by means of which in all times the temporal interests of the English church have been upheld in preference to the spiritual. The church of England is much more likely of the two, to part with her faith than with her funds. It is the old question, which is the greater, the *gold* or the altar that sanctifies the gold. Had this question been more boldly asked and more truly answered in other times, we should not have been where we now are. And by continually looking to the gold and not the altar, the dangers of the future will be not diminished but increased.' [1]

In 1866 Mr. Gladstone for the first time voted for the abolition of church rates. Later in the session he introduced his own plan, not in his capacity as minister, but with the approval of the Russell cabinet. After this cabinet had gone out, Mr. Gladstone in 1868 introduced a bill, abolishing all legal proceedings for the recovery of church rates, except in cases of rates already made, or where money had been borrowed on the security of the rates. But it permitted voluntary assessments to be made, and all agreements to make such payments on the faith of which any expense was incurred, remained enforcible in the same manner as contracts of a like character. Mr. Gladstone's Bill became law in the

[1] To Sir W. Farquhar, April 4, 1864.

course of the summer, and a struggle that had been long and
bitter ended.

In another movement in the region of ecclesiastical
machinery, from which much was hoped, though little is
believed to have come, Mr. Gladstone was concerned, though
I do not gather from the papers that he watched it with the
zealous interest of some of his friends. Convocation, the
ancient assembly or parliament of the clergy of the church
of England, was permitted in 1852 to resume the active
functions that had been suspended since 1717. To Mr. Gladstone some revival or institution of the corporate organization
of the church, especially after the Gorham judgment, was ever
a cherished object. Bishop Wilberforce, long one of the most
intimate of his friends, was chief mover in proceedings that,
as was hoped, were to rescue the church from the anarchy in
which one branch of her sons regarded her as plunged. Some
of Mr. Gladstone's correspondence on the question of convocation has already been made public.[1] Here it is enough to
print a passage or two from a letter addressed by him to
the bishop (Jan. 1, 1854) setting out his view of the real
need of the time. After a generous exaltation of the zeal
and devotion of the clergy, he goes on to the gains that
might be expected from their effective organization :—

First as to her pastoral work, her warfare against sin, she would put
forth a strength, not indeed equal to it, but at least so much less unequal
than it now is, that the good fight would everywhere be maintained, and
she would not be as she now is, either hated or unknown among the
myriads who form the right arm of England's industry and skill. As
to her doctrine and all that hangs upon it, such questions as might arise
would be determined by the deliberate and permanent sense of the body.
Some unity in belief is necessary to justify association in a Christian communion. Will that unity in belief be promoted or impaired by the free
action of mind within her, subjected to order ? If her case really were so
desperate that her children had no common faith, then the sooner that
imposture were detected the better ; but if she has, then her being provided with legitimate, orderly, and authentic channels, for expressing
and bringing to a head, as need arises, the sentiments of her people, will
far more clearly manifest, and while manifesting will extend, deepen, and
consolidate, that unity. It is all very well to sneer at councils : but who
among us will deny that the councils which we acknowledge as lawful
representatives of the universal church, were great and to all appearance
necessary providential instruments in the establishment of the Christian
faith ?

But, say some, we cannot admit the laity into convocation, as it
would be in derogation of the rights of the clergy ; or as others say,
it would separate the church from the state. And others, more
numerous and stronger, in their fear of the exclusive constitution of the
convocation, resist every attempt at organizing the church, and suffer,
and even by suffering promote, the growth of all our evils. I will not
touch the question of convocation except by saying that, in which I

1 *Life of Wilberforce*, ii. pp. 136-46 ; *Life of Shaftesbury*, ii. p. 404.

think you concur, that while the present use is unsatisfactory and even scandalous, no form of church government that does not distinctly and fully provide for the expression of the voice of the laity either can be had, or if it could would satisfy the needs of the church of England. But in my own mind as well as in this letter, I am utterly against all premature, all rapid conclusions. . . . It will be much in our day if, towards the cure of such evils, when we die we can leave to our children the precious knowledge that a beginning has been made—a beginning not only towards enabling the bishops and clergy to discharge their full duty, but also, and yet more, towards raising the real character of membership in those millions upon millions, the whole bulk of our community, who now have its name and its name alone.

II

In 1860 a volume appeared containing seven 'essays and reviews' by seven different writers, six of them clergymen of the church of England. The topics were miscellaneous, the treatment of them, with one exception,[1] was neither learned nor weighty, the tone was not absolutely uniform, but it was as a whole mildly rationalistic, and the negations, such as they were, exhibited none of the fierceness or aggression that had marked the old controversies about Hampden, or Tract Ninety, or Ward's *Ideal*. A storm broke upon the seven writers, that they little intended to provoke. To the apparent partnership among them was severely imputed a sinister design. They were styled 'the Septem contra Christum'—six ministers of religion combining to assail the faith they outwardly professed—seven authors of an immoral rationalistic conspiracy. Two of them were haled into the courts, one for casting doubt upon the inspiration of the Bible, the other for impugning the eternity of the future punishment of the wicked. The Queen in council upon appeal was advised to reverse a hostile judgment in the court below (1864), and Lord Chancellor Westbury delivered the decision in a tone described in the irreverent epigram of the day as 'dismissing eternal punishment with costs.' This carried further, or completed, the principle of the Gorham judgment fourteen years before, and just as that memorable case determined that neither the evangelical nor the high anglican school should drive out the other, so the judgment in the case of *Essays and Reviews* determined that neither should those two powerful sections drive out the new critical, rational-istic, liberal, or latitudinarian school. 'It appears to me,' Mr. Gladstone wrote to the Bishop of London (April 26, 1864), 'that the spirit of this judgment has but to be consistently and cautiously followed up, in order to establish, as far as the court can establish it, a complete indifference between the Christian faith and the denial of it. I do not believe it is in the power of human language to bind the understanding and conscience

[1] Pattison's *Tendencies of Religious Thought in England*, 1688-1750. Reprinted in his *Essays*, vol. ii.

of man with any theological obligations, which the mode of argument used and the principles assumed [in the judgment] would not effectually unloose.' To Bishop Hamilton of Salisbury, who had taken part in one of the two cases, he wrote :—

Feb. 8, 1864.—This new and grave occurrence appertains to a transition state through which the Christian faith is passing. The ship is at sea far from the shore she left, far from the shore she is making for. This or that deflection from her course, from this or that wind of heaven, we cannot tell what it is, or whether favourable or adverse to her true work and destination, unless we know all the stages of the experience through which she has yet to pass. It seems to me that these judgments are most important in their character as illustrations of a system, or I should rather say, of the failure of a system, parts of a vast scheme of forces and events in the midst of which we stand, which seem to govern us, but which are in reality governed by a hand above. It may be that this rude shock to the mere scripturism which has too much prevailed, is intended to be the instrument of restoring a greater harmony of belief, and of the agencies for maintaining belief. But be that as it may, the valiant soldier who has fought manfully should be, and I hope will be, of good cheer.

In the same connection he wrote to Sir W. Farquhar, a friend from earliest days :—

Jan. 31, 1865.—I have never been much disposed to a great exaltation of clerical power, and I agree in the necessity of taking precautions against the establishment, especially of an insular and local though in its sphere legitimate authority, of new doctrines for that Christian faith which is not for England or France but for the world ; further, I believe it has been a mistake in various instances to institute the coercive proceedings which have led to the present state of things. I remember telling the Archbishop of York at Penmaenmawr, when he was Bishop of Gloucester, that it seemed to me we had lived into a time when, speaking generally, penal proceedings for the maintenance of divine truth among the clergy would have to be abandoned, and moral means alone depended on. But, on the other hand, I feel that the most vital lay interests are at stake in the definite teaching and profession of the Christian faith, and the general tendency and effect of the judgments has been and is likely to be hostile to that definite teaching, and unfavourable also to the moral tone and truthfulness, of men who may naturally enough be tempted to shelter themselves under judicial glosses in opposition to the plain meaning of words. The judgments of the present tribunal continued in a series would, I fear, result in the final triumph (in a sense he did not desire) of Mr. Ward's non-natural sense ; and the real question is whether our objection to non-natural senses is general, or is only felt when the sense favoured is the one opposed to our own inclinations.

III

No theological book, wrote Mr. Gladstone in 1866, that has appeared since the *Vestiges of Creation* twenty years before (1844), had attracted anything like the amount of notice bestowed upon 'the remarkable volume entitled *Ecce Homo*,'

published in 1865. It was an attempt, so Mr. Gladstone
described it, to bring home to the reader the impression that
there is something or other called the Gospel, 'which whatever
it may be,' as was said by an old pagan poet of the Deity,[1] has
formidable claims not merely on the intellectual condescension,
but on the loyal allegiance and humble obedience of mankind.
The book violently displeased both sides. It used language
that could not be consistently employed in treating of Christianity from the orthodox point of view. On the other hand,
it constituted 'a grave offence in the eyes of those to whom the
chequered but yet imposing fabric of actual Christianity, still
casting its majestic light and shadow over the whole civilised
world, is a rank eyesore and an intolerable offence.' Between
these two sets of assailants Mr. Gladstone interposed with a
friendlier and more hopeful construction.[2] He told those who
despised the book as resting on no evidence of the foundations
on which it was built, and therefore as being shallow and un-
critical, that we have a right to weigh the nature of the
message, apart from the credentials of the messenger. Then
he reassured the orthodox by the hope that 'the present
tendency to treat the old belief of man with a precipitate,
shallow, and unexamining disparagement' is only a passing
distemper, and that to the process of its removal the author of
the book would have the consolation and the praise of having
furnished an earnest, powerful, and original contribution.[3]
Dean Milman told him that he had brought to life again a
book that after a sudden and brief yet brilliant existence
seemed to be falling swiftly into oblivion. The mask of the
anonymous had much to do, he thought, with its popularity,
as had happened to the *Vestiges of Creation*. Undoubtedly
when the mask fell off, interest dropped.

Dr. Pusey found the book intensely painful. 'I have
seldom,' he told Mr. Gladstone, 'been able to read much at a
time, but shut the book for pain, as I used to do with Renan's.'
What revolted him was not the exhibition of the human nature
of the central figure, but of a human nature apart from and
inconsistent with its divinity ; the writer's admiring or patron-
ising tone was loathsome. 'What you have yourself written,'
Pusey said, 'I like much. But its bearings on *Ecce Homo* I
can hardly divine, except by way of contrast.' Dr. Newman
thought that here was a case where *materiam superabat opus*,
and that Mr. Gladstone's observations were more valuable for
their own sake, than as a recommendation or defence of the
book :—

Jan. 9, 1868.—I hope I have followed you correctly, says Newman :
your main proposition seems to be, that whereas both Jew and Gentile

---

[1] See the lines from Euripides at the head of the chapter.
[2] In a series of articles published in *Good Words* in January, February, March 1868,
and reprinted in volume form the same year. Reprinted again in *Gleanings*, vol. iii.
[3] *Gleanings*, iii. p. 41.

had his own notion of an heroic humanity, and neither of them a true notion, the one being political, the other even immoral, the first step necessary for bringing in the idea of an Emmanuel into the world, was to form the human mould into which it 'might drop,' and thus to supplant both the Judaic and the heathen misconception by the exhibition of the true idea. Next, passing from antecedent probabilities to history, the order of succession of the synoptical and the fourth gospels does in fact fulfil this reasonable anticipation. This seems to me a *very great* view, and I look forward eagerly to what you have still to say in illustration of it. The only objection which I see can be made to it is, that it is a clever controversial expedient after the event for accounting for a startling fact. This is an objection not peculiar to it, but to all explanations of the kind. Still, the question remains—whether it is a fact that the sacred writers recognise, however indirectly, the wise economy which you assert, or whether it is only an hypothesis?

As to the specific principles and particular opinions in Mr. Gladstone's criticism of what we now see to have been a not very effective or deeply influential book, we may think as we will. But the temper of his review, the breadth of its outlook on Christian thought, tradition, and society, show no mean elements in the composition of his greatness. So, too, does the bare fact that under the pressure of office and all the cares of a party leader in a crisis, his mind should have been free and disengaged enough to turn with large and eager interest to such themes as these. This was indeed the freedom of judgment with which, in the most moving lines of the poem that he loved above all others, Virgil bidding farewell to Dante makes him crowned and mitred master of himself—*Perch' io te sopra te corono e mitrio.*[1]

IV

Other strong gusts swept the high latitudes, when Dr. Colenso, Bishop of Natal, published certain destructive criticisms upon the canonical Scriptures. His metropolitan at Cape Town pronounced sentence of deprivation ; Colenso appealed to the Queen in council ; and the Queen in council was advised that the proceedings of the Bishop of Cape Town were null and void, for in law there was no established church in the colony, nor any ecclesiastical court with lawful jurisdiction.[2] This triumph of heresy was a heavy blow. In 1866 Bishop Colenso brought an action against Mr. Gladstone and the other trustees of the colonial bishoprics fund, calling upon them to set aside a sum of ten thousand pounds for the purpose of securing the income of the Bishop of Natal, and to pay him his salary, which they had withheld since his wrongful deprivation. 'We,' said Mr. Gladstone to Miss Burdett Coutts, 'founding ourselves on the judgment, say there is no see of Natal in the sense of the founders of the fund, and therefore, of course, no

---

[1] *Purgatorio*, xxvii. 126-42.
[2] A concise account of this transaction is in Lord Selborne's *Memorials Family and Personal*, ii. pp. 481-7. See also Anson's *Law and Custom of the Constitution*, ii. p. 407.

bishop of such a see.' Romilly, master of the rolls, gave judgment in favour of Colenso. These perplexities did not dismay Mr. Gladstone. 'Remembering what the churches in the colonies were some forty years back, when I first began (from my father's having a connection with the West Indies), to feel an interest in them, I must own that they present a cheering, a remarkable, indeed a wonderful spectacle.' 'I quite feel with you,' he says to Miss Burdett Coutts, 'a great uneasiness at what may follow from the exercise of judicial powers by synods merely ecclesiastical, especially if small, remote, and unchecked by an active public opinion. But in the American episcopal church it has been found practicable in a great degree to obviate any dangers from such a source.' Ten years after this, in one of the most remarkable articles he ever wrote, speaking of the protestant evangelical section of the adherents of the Christian system, he says that 'no portion of this entire group seems to be endowed with greater vigour than this in the United States and the British colonies, which has grown up in new soil, *and far from the possibly chilling shadow of national establishments of religion.*' [1]

[1] 'The Courses of Religious Thought' in *Gleanings*, iii. p. 115.

CHAPTER XI

POPULAR ESTIMATES

(1868)

Die Mitlebenden werden an vorzüglichen Menschen gar leicht irre ; das Besondere der Person stört sie, das laufende bewegliche Leben verrückt ihre Standpunkte und hindert das Kennen und Anerkennen eines solchen Mannes.—GOETHE.

The contemporaries of superior men easily go wrong about them. Peculiarity discomposes people ; the swift current of life distorts their points of view, and prevents them from understanding and appreciating such men.

IT must obviously be interesting, as we approach a signal crisis in his advance, to know the kind of impression, right or wrong, made by a great man upon those who came nearest to him. Friends like Aberdeen and Graham had many years earlier foreseen the high destinies of their colleague. Aberdeen told Bishop Wilberforce in 1855 that Gladstone had some great qualifications but some serious defects. 'The chief, that when he has convinced himself, perhaps by abstract reasoning of some view, he thinks that every one else ought at once to see it as he does, and can make no allowance for difference of opinion.'[1] About the same time Graham said of him that he was 'in the highest sense of the word *Liberal* ; of the greatest power ; very much the first man in the House of Commons ; detested by the aristocracy for his succession duty, the most truly conservative measure passed in my recollection. . . . He must rise to the head in such a government as ours, even in spite of all the hatred of him.' Three years later Aberdeen still thought him too obstinate and, if such a thing be possible, too honest. He does not enough think of what other men think. Does not enough look out of the window. 'Whom will he lead?' asked the bishop.[2] 'Oh! it is impossible to say! Time must show, and new combinations.' By 1863 Cardwell confidently anticipated that Mr. Gladstone must become prime minister, and Bishop Wilberforce finds all coming to the conclusion that he must be the next real chief.[3]

[1] *Life of Bishop Wilberforce*, ii. p. 286.
[2] *Ibid.*, ii. p. 412.   [3] *Ibid.*, iii. pp. 92, 101.

On the other side Lord Shaftesbury, to whom things ecclesiastical were as cardinal as they were to Mr. Gladstone, ruefully reflected in 1864 that people must make ready for great and irrevocable changes. Palmerston was simply the peg driven through the island of Delos : unloose the peg, and all would soon be adrift. 'His successor, Gladstone, will bring with him the Manchester school for colleagues and supporters, a hot tractarian for chancellor, and the Bishop of Oxford for ecclesiastical adviser. He will succumb to every pressure, except the pressure of a constitutional and conservative policy.' 'He is a dangerous man,' was one of Lord Palmerston's latest utterances, 'keep him in Oxford and he is partially muzzled ; but send him elsewhere and he will run wild.' [1] 'The long and short of our present position is,' said Shaftesbury, 'that the time has arrived (*novus sæclorum nascitur ordo*) for the triumph of the Manchester school, of which Gladstone is the disciple and the organ. And for the nonce they have a great advantage ; for, though the majority of the country is against them, the country has no leaders in or out of parliament ; whereas they are all well provided and are equally compact in purpose and action.' [2] Somewhat earlier cool observers 'out of hearing of the modulation of his voice or the torrent of his declamation' regarded him 'in spite of his eloquence unsurpassed in our day, perhaps in our century, in spite of his abilities and experience, as one most dangerous to that side to which he belongs. Like the elephant given by some eastern prince to the man he intends to ruin, he is an inmate too costly for any party to afford to keep long.' [3]

'One great weight that Gladstone has to carry in the political race,' wrote his friend Frederick Rogers (Dec. 13, 1868), 'is a *character* for want of judgment, and every addition to that is an impediment.' And indeed it is true in politics that it often takes more time to get rid of a spurious character, than to acquire the real one. According to a letter from Lord Granville to Mr. Gladstone (Feb. 11, 1867) :—

Lowe described as perfectly unjust and unfounded the criticisms which had been made of your leadership. You had always been courteous and conciliatory with the whole House and with individual members, including himself. He had seen Palmerston do and say more offensive things every week, than you have during the whole session.

Still people went on saying that he had yet to gain the same hold over his party in parliament that he had over the party in the nation ; he had studied every branch of government except the House of Commons ; he confounded the functions of leader with those of dictator ; he took counsel with one or two individuals instead of conferring with the

[1] *Life of Lord Shaftesbury*, iii. pp. 171, 188.   [2] *Ibid.*, iii. pp. 201-2.
[3] *Edinburgh Review*, April 1857, p. 567.

party ; he proclaimed as edicts what he ought to have submitted as proposals ; he lacked 'the little civilities and
hypocrisies' of political society. Such was the common
cant of the moment. He had at least one friend who dealt
faithfully with him :—

T. D. Acland to Mr. Gladstone.

Jan. 24, 1868.—Now I am going to take a great liberty with you.
I can hardly help myself. I have heard a lot of grumbling lately about
you, and have several times asked myself whether it would be *tanti* to
tease you by repeating it. Well, what is pressed on me is, that at the
present time when every one is full of anxiety as to the future, and
when your warmest supporters are longing for cohesion, there is an
impression that you are absorbed in questions about Homer and Greek
words, about *Ecce Homo*, that you are not reading the newspapers, or
feeling the pulse of followers. One man personally complained that
when you sought his opinion, you spent the whole interview in
impressing your own view on him, and hardly heard anything he might
have to say. It is with a painful feeling and (were it not for your
generous and truly modest nature it would be) with some anxiety as
to how you would take it that I consented to be the funnel of all this
grumbling. As far as I can make out, the feeling resolves itself into
two main points :—1. Whatever your own tastes may be for literature,
and however strengthening and refreshing to your own mind and heart
it may be to dig into the old springs, still the people don't understand
it ; they consider you their own, as a husband claims a wife's devotion ;
and it gives a bad impression if you are supposed to be interested,
except for an occasional slight recreation, about aught but the nation's
welfare at this critical time, and that it riles them to see the walls
placarded with your name and *Ecce Homo*. . . . 2. (*a*) The other point
is (pray forgive me if I go too far, I am simply a funnel) a feeling that
your entourage is too confined, and too much of second-rate men ; that
the strong men and the *rising* men are not gathered round you and
known to be so ; (*b*) and besides that there is so little easy contact
with the small fry, as when Palmerston sat in the tea-room, and men
were gratified by getting private speech with their leader. But this is
a small matter compared with (*a*).

Mr. Gladstone to T. D. Acland.

Hawarden, Jan. 30, '68.—Be assured I cannot feel otherwise than
grateful to you for undertaking what in the main must always be a
thankless office. It is new to me to have critics such as those whom
you represent under the first head, and who complain that I do not
attend to my business, while the complaint is illustrated by an
instance in which, professing to seek a man's opinion, I poured forth
instead the matter with which I was overflowing. Nor do I well
know how to deal with those who take out of my hands the direction
of my own conduct on such a question as the question whether I ought
to have undertaken a mission to Sheffield to meet Roebuck on his own
ground. I am afraid I can offer them little satisfaction. I have been
for near thirty-six years at public business, and I must myself be the
judge how best to husband what little energy of brain, and time for

using it, may remain to me. If I am told I should go to Sheffield instead of writing on *Ecce Homo*, I answer that it was my Sunday's work, and change of work is the chief refreshment to my mind. It is true that literature is very attractive and indeed seductive to me, but I do not *knowingly* allow it to cause neglect of public business. Undoubtedly it may be said that the vacation should be given to reading up and preparing materials for the session. And of my nine last vacations *this one only* has in part been given to any literary work, if I except the preparation of an address for Edinburgh in 1865. But I am sincerely, though it may be erroneously, impressed with the belief that the quantity of my public work cannot be increased without its quality being yet further deteriorated. Perhaps my critics have not been troubled as I have with this plague of quantity, and are not as deeply impressed as I am with the belief that grinding down the mental powers by an infinity of detail, is what now principally dwarfs our public men, to the immense detriment of the country. This conviction I cannot yield ; nor can I say more than that, with regard to the personal matters which you name, I will do the best I can. But what I have always supposed and understood is that my business in endeavouring to follow other and better men, is to be thoroughly open to all members of parliament who seek me, while my seeking them must of necessity be limited. . . . We have before us so much business that I fear a *jumble*. Reform, Education, and Ireland each in many branches will compete ; any of these alone would be enough. The last is in my mind the imperious and overpowering subject. . . . The aspect of this letter is, I think, rather combative. It would have been much less so but that I trust entirely to your indulgence.

In a second letter, after mentioning again some of these complaints, Acland says :—' On the other hand I know you are held by some of the best men (that dear, noble George Grey I am thinking of) to have the great quality of leadership : such clear apprehension of the points in council, and such faithful exactness in conveying the result agreed on, truly a great power for one who has such a *copia verborum*, with its temptations.' He still insists that a leader should drop into the tea-room and have afternoon chats with his adherents ; and earnestly wishes him to belong to the Athenæum club, 'a great centre of intellect and criticism,' where he would be sure to meet colleagues and the principal men in the public service.

All this was good advice enough, and most loyally intended. But it was work of supererogation. The House of Commons, like all assemblies, is even less affected by immediate displays than by the standing impression of power. Mr. Gladstone might be playful, courteous, reserved, gracious, silent, but the House always knew that he had a sledge-hammer behind his back, ready for work on every anvil in that resounding forge. His sheer intellectual strength, his experience and power in affairs, the tremendous hold that he had now gained upon the general public out of doors, made the artful genialities of the tea-room pure superfluity. Of the secret of the rapidity with which his star was rising, and of the popular expectations thereby signified, an admirable contemporary account was traced by an excellent observer,[1] and it would be idle to transcribe the pith of it in words other than his own :—

Mr. Gladstone's policy is coming to be used as the concrete expression of a whole system of thought, to mean something for itself, and something widely different from either the policy pursued by whigs, or the policy attributed to Lord Palmerston. This is the more remarkable because Mr. Gladstone has done less to lay down any systematised course of action than almost any man of his political standing, has a cautiousness of speech which frequently puzzles his audience even while they are cheering his oratory, and perceives alternatives with a clearness which often leaves on his own advice an impression of indecision. . . . Those who are applauding the chancellor of the exchequer, in season and out of season, seem, however they may put their aspirations, to expect, should he lead the House of Commons, two very important changes. They think that he will realise two longings of which they are deeply conscious, even while they express their hopelessness of speedy realisation. They believe, with certain misgivings, that he can offer them a new and more satisfactory system of foreign policy ; and, with no misgivings, that he will break up the torpor which has fallen upon internal affairs. Mr. Gladstone, say his admirers, may be too much afraid of war, too zealous for economy, too certain of the status of England as a fact altogether independent of her action. But he is sure to abandon those traditional ideas to which we have adhered so long : the notion that we are a continental people, bound to maintain the continental system, interested in petty matters of boundary, concerned to dictate to Germany whether she shall be united or not, to the Christians of Servia whether they shall rebel against the Turk or obey him, to everybody whether they shall or shall not develop themselves as they can. He is sure to initiate that temporary policy of abstention which is needed to make a breach in the great chain of English traditions, and enable the nation to act as its interests or duties or dignity may require, without reference to the mode in which it has acted heretofore. Mr. Gladstone, for example, certainly would not support the Turk as if Turkish sway were a moral law, would not trouble himself to interfere with the project for cutting an Eider Canal, would not from very haughtiness of temperament protest in the face of Europe unless he intended his protests to be followed by some form of action. . . . That impression may be true or it may be false, but it exists ; it is justified in part by Mr. Gladstone's recent speeches, and it indicates a very noteworthy change in the disposition of the public mind : a weariness of the line of action called ' a spirited foreign policy.' . . . The expectation as to internal affairs is far more definite and more strong. . . . All his speeches point to the inauguration of a new activity in all internal affairs, to a steady determination to improve, if possible, both the constitution and the condition of the millions who have to live under it. Most ministers have that idea in their heads, but Mr. Gladstone has more than the idea, he has plans, and the courage to propose and maintain them. He is not afraid of the suffrage, as he indicated in his celebrated speech ; he is not alarmed at risking the treasury as his reductions have proved ; does not hesitate to apply the full power of the state to ameliorate social anomalies, as he showed by creating state banks, state insurance offices, and state annuity

[1] Mr. M. Townsend in the *Spectator.*

funds for the very poor.   He of all men alive could most easily reduce our
anarchical ecclesiastical system into something like order ; he, perhaps,
alone among statesmen would have the art and the energy to try as a
deliberate plan to effect the final conciliation of Ireland. . . .[1]

A letter from Francis Newman to Mr. Gladstone is a good
illustration of the almost passionate going out of men's hearts
to him in those days :—

Until a practical reason for addressing you arose out of . . . I did not
dare to intrude on you sentiments which are happily shared by so many
thousands of warm and simple hearts ; sentiments of warm admiration,
deep sympathy, fervent hope, longing expectation of lasting national
blessing from your certain elevation to high responsibility.   The rude,
monstrous, shameful and shameless attacks which you have endured, do
but endear you to the nation.   In the moral power which you wield, go
on to elevate and purify public life, and we shall all bless you, dear sir,
as a regenerator of England.   Keep the hearts of the people.   *They* will
never envy you and never forsake you.

Church, afterwards the dean of St. Paul's, a man who united
in so wonderful a degree the best gifts that come of culture,
sound and just sense, and unstained purity of spirit, said of
Mr. Gladstone at the moment of accession to power, 'There
never was a man so genuinely admired for the qualities which
deserve admiration—his earnestness, his deep popular sympathies, his unflinching courage ; and there never was a man
more deeply hated both for his good points and for undeniable
defects and failings.   But they love him much less in the House
than they do out of doors.   A strong vein of sentiment is the
spring of what is noblest about his impulses ; but it is a perilous
quality too.'[2]   An accomplished woman with many public interests met Mr. Bright in Scotland sometime after this.   'He
would not hear a word said against Mr. Gladstone.   He said it
was just because people were not good enough themselves to
understand him that he met such abuse, and then he quoted
the stanza in the third canto of *Childe Harold* :—

> " He who ascends to mountain-tops, shall find
>   The loftiest peaks most wrapt in clouds and snow ;
> He who surpasses or subdues mankind,
>   Must look down on the hate of those below."

I asked if he did not think sometimes his temper carried Mr.
Gladstone away.   He said, " Think of the difference between a
great cart horse, and the highest bred most sensitive horse you
can imagine, and then, under lashing of a whip, think of the
difference between them."'   After a stay with Mr. Gladstone in
a country house, Jowett, the master of Balliol, said of him, 'It
is the first time that any one of such great simplicity has been
in so exalted a station.'[3]

---

[1] *Spectator*, October 29, 1864.
[2] *Life of Dean Church*, pp. 179, 188.   [3] *Life of Jowett*, i. 406.

In one of his Lancashire speeches, Mr. Gladstone described in interesting language how he stood :—

I have never swerved from what I conceive to be those truly conservative objects and desires with which I entered life. I am, if possible, more attached to the institutions of my country than I was when, as a boy, I wandered among the sandhills of Seaforth, or frequented the streets of Liverpool. But experience has brought with it its lessons. I have learnt that there is wisdom in a policy of trust, and folly in a policy of mistrust. I have not refused to acknowledge and accept the signs of the times. I have observed the effect that has been produced upon the country by what is generally known as liberal legislation. And if we are told, as we are now truly told, that all the feelings of the country are in the best and broadest sense conservative—that is to say, that the people value the country and the laws and institutions of the country—honesty compels me to admit that this happy result has been brought about by liberal legislation. Therefore, I may presume to say that since the year 1841, when Sir Robert Peel thought fit to place me in a position that brought me into direct, immediate, and responsible contact with the commercial interests of the country, from that time onward I have never swerved nor wavered, but have striven to the best of my ability to advance in the work of improving the laws, and to labour earnestly and fearlessly for the advantage of the people.[1]

Five-and-twenty years later, when his course was almost run, and the achievements of the long laborious day were over, he said :—

I have been a learner all my life, and I am a learner still ; but I do wish to learn upon just principles. I have some ideas that may not be thought to furnish good materials for a liberal politician. I do not like changes for their own sake, I only like a change when it is needful to alter something bad into something good, or something which is good into something better. I have a great reverence for antiquity. I rejoice in the great deeds of our fathers in England and in Scotland. It may be said, however, that this does not go very far towards making a man a liberal. I find, however, that the tories when it suits their purpose have much less reverence for antiquity than I have. They make changes with great rapidity, provided they are suitable to the promotion of tory interests. But the basis of my liberalism is this. It is the lesson which I have been learning ever since I was young. I am a lover of liberty ; and that liberty which I value for myself, I value for every human being in proportion to his means and opportunities. That is a basis on which I find it perfectly practicable to work in conjunction with a dislike to unreasoned change and a profound reverence for everything ancient, provided that reverence is deserved. There are those who have been so happy that they have been born with a creed that they can usefully maintain to the last. For my own part, as I have been a learner all my life, a learner I must continue to be.[2]

[1] Liverpool, July 18, 1865.   [2] Norwich, May 16, 1890.

CHAPTER XII

LETTERS

(1859–1868)

> There is no saying shocks me so much as that which I hear very often; that a man does not know how to pass his time. 'Twould have been but ill spoken by Methusalem, in the nine hundred sixty-ninth year of his life; so far it is from us, who have not time enough to attain to the utmost perfection of any part of any science, to have cause to complain that we are forced to be idle for want of work.—COWLEY.

As I said in our opening pages, Mr. Gladstone's letters are mostly concerned with points of business. They were not with him a medium for conveying the slighter incidents, fugitive moods, fleeting thoughts, of life. Perhaps of these fugitive moods he may have had too few. To me, says Crassus in Cicero, the man hardly seems to be free, who does not sometimes do nothing.[1] In table-talk he could be as disengaged, as marked in ease and charm, as any one ; he was as willing as any one to accept topics as they came, which is the first of all conditions for good conversation. When alone in his temple of peace it was not his practice to take up his pen in the same sauntering and devious humour. With him the pen was no instrument of diversion. His correspondence has an object, and a letter with an object is not of a piece with the effusions of Madame de Sévigné, Cowper, Scott, FitzGerald, and other men and women whose letters of genial satire and casual play and hints of depth below the surface, people will read as long as they read anything.

We have to remember a very intelligible fact mentioned by him to Lord Brougham, who had asked him to undertake some public address (April 25, 1860) :—

You have given me credit for your own activity and power of work : an estimate far beyond the truth. I am one of those who work very hard while they are at it, and are then left in much exhaustion. I have been for four months overdone, and though my general health, thank God,

---

[1] ' Quid igitur? quando ages negotium publicum ? quando amicorum ? quando tuum? quando denique nihil ages? Tum illud addidi, mihi enim liber esse non videtur qui non aliquando nihil agit.'—CIC. Orat. ii. 42.

is good, yet my brain warns me so distinctly that it must not be too much pressed, as to leave me in prudence no course to take except that which I have reluctantly indicated.

We might be tempted to call good letter-writing one of 'the little handicraft of an idle man'; but then two of the most perfect masters of the art were Cicero and Voltaire, two of the most occupied personages that ever lived. Of course, sentences emerge in Mr. Gladstone's letters that are the fruits of his experience, well worthy of a note, as when he says to Dr. Pusey:—'I doubt from your letter whether you are aware of the virulence and intensity with which the poison of suspicion acts in public life. All that you say in your letter of yesterday I can readily believe, but I assure you it does not alter in the slightest degree the grounds on which my last letter was written.'

He thanks Bulwer Lytton for a volume of his republished poems, but chides him for not indicating dates :—

This I grant is not always easy for a conscientious man, for example when he has almost re-written. But I need not remind you how much the public, if I may judge from one of its number, would desire it when it can be done. For in the case of those whom it has learned to honour and admire, there is a biography of the mind that is thus signified, and that is matter of deep interest.

On external incidents, he never fails in a graceful, apt, or feeling word. When the author of *The Christian Year* dies (1866), he says :—'Mr. Liddon sent me very early information of Mr. Keble's death. The church of England has lost in him a poet, a scholar, a philosopher, and a saint. I must add that he always appeared to me, since I had the honour and pleasure of knowing him, a person of most liberal mind. I hope early steps will be taken to do honour to his pure and noble memory.'

To the relatives of a valued official in his financial department he writes in commemorative sentences that testify to his warm appreciation of zeal in public duty :—

The civil service of the crown has beyond all question lost in Mr. Arbuthnot one of the highest ornaments it ever possessed. His devotion to his duties, his identification at every point of his own feelings with the public interests, will, I trust, not die with him, but will stimulate others, and especially the inheritors of his name, to follow his bright example. . . . Nor is it with a thought of anything but thankfulness on his account, that I contemplate the close of his labours ; but it will be long indeed before we cease to miss his great experience, his varied powers, his indefatigable energy, and that high-minded loyal tone which he carried into all the parts of business.

In another letter, by the way, he says (1866) :—'I am far from thinking very highly of our rank as a nation of administrators, but perhaps if we could be judged by the post office alone, we might claim the very first place in this respect.' In time even this 'most wonderful establishment' was to give him trouble enough.

Among the letters in which Mr. Gladstone exhibits the easier and less strenuous side, and that have the indefinable attraction of intimacy, pleasantness, and the light hand, are those written in the ten years between 1858 and 1868 to the Duchess of Sutherland. She was the close and lifelong friend of the Queen. She is, said the Queen to Stockmar, 'so anxious to do good, so liberal-minded, so superior to prejudice, and so eager to learn, and to improve herself and others.'[1] The centre of a brilliant and powerful social circle, she was an ardent sympathiser with Italy, with Poland, with the Abolitionists and the North, and with humane causes at home. She was accomplished, a lover of books meritorious in aim though too often slight in work—in short, with emotions and sentiments sometimes a little in advance of definite ideas, yet a high representative of the virtue, purity, simplicity, and sympathetic spirit of the Tennysonian epoch. Tennyson himself was one of her idols, and Mr. Gladstone was another. Bishop Wilberforce too was often of the company, and the Duke of Argyll, who had married a daughter of the house. Her admiration for Gladstone, says the son of the duchess, 'was boundless, and the last years of her life were certainly made happier by this friendship. His visits to her were always an intense pleasure, and even when suffering too much to receive others, she would always make an effort to appear sufficiently well to receive him. I find in a letter from her written to me in 1863, after meeting Mr. Gladstone when on a visit to her sister, Lady Taunton, at Quantock, in Somersetshire, the following :—"The Gladstones were there ; he was quite delightful, pouring out such floods of agreeable knowledge all day long, and singing admirably in the evening. Nobody makes me feel more the happiness of knowledge and the wish for it ; one must not forget that he has the happiness of the peace which passeth all understanding."[2] The Gladstones were constant visitors at the duchess's various princely homes—Stafford House in the Green Park, Trentham, Cliveden, and Chiswick on the Thames, Dunrobin on the Dornoch Firth.

A little sheaf of pieces from Mr. Gladstone's letters to her may serve to show him as he was, in the midst of his labours in the Palmerston government—how little his native kindliness of heart and power of sympathy had been chilled or parched either by hard and ceaseless toil, or by the trying atmosphere of public strife.

1859

Aug. 30.—I am much concerned to lose at the last moment the pleasure of coming to see you at Trentham—but my wife, who was not quite well when I came away but hoped a day's rest would make her so, writes

[1] Martin's *Prince Consort*, ii. p. 245 *n.*
[2] Lord Ronald Gower, *Reminiscences*, pp. 114-15.

through Agnes to say she hopes I shall get back to-day. The gratification promised me must, therefore, I fear, stand over. I will write from Hawarden, and I now send this by a messenger lest (as you might be sure I should not fail through carelessness) you should think anything very bad had happened. Among other things, I wanted help from you through speech about Tennyson. I find *Maud* takes a good deal of trouble to understand, and is hardly worth understanding. It has many peculiar beauties, but against them one sets the strange and nearly frantic passages about war ; which one can hardly tell whether he means to be taken for sense or ravings. Frank Doyle, who is essentially a poet though an unwrought one, declares *Guinevere* the finest poem of modern times.

1860

Hawarden, Oct. 3.—We are exceedingly happy at Penmaenmawr, between Italy, health, hill and sea all taken together. I do not know if you are acquainted with the Welsh coast and interior ; but I am sure you would think it well worth knowing both for the solitary grandeur of the Snowdon group, and for the widely diffused and almost endless beauty of detail. It is a kind of landscape jewellery.

The Herberts send us an excellent account of Lord Aberdeen. I have a very interesting letter from Lacaita, fresh from Panizzi, who again was fresh from Italy, and sanguine about the Emperor. But what a calamity for a man to think, or find himself forced to be double faced even when he is not double minded ; and this is the best supposition. But Warsaw is surely the point at which for the present we must look with suspicion and aversion. To-day's papers give good hope that Garibaldi has been misrepresented and does not mean to play into Mazzini's hands.

Thanks for your condolences about the *Times.* I have had it both ways, though more, perhaps, of the one than the other. Some of the penny press, which has now acquired an enormous expansion, go great lengths in my favour, and I read some eulogies quite as wide of fact as the interpretations.

Oct. 19.—I think Mr. or Sir something Burke (how ungrateful !) has been so kind as to discover the honours of my mother's descent in some book that he has published on royal descents. But the truth is that time plays strange tricks backwards as well as forwards, and it seems hardly fair to pick the results. The arithmetic of those questions is very curious : at the distance of a moderate number of centuries everybody has some hundred thousand ancestors, subject, however, to deduction.

Nov. 1.— . . . There is one proposition which the experience of life burns into my soul ; it is this, that man should beware of letting his religion spoil his morality. In a thousand ways, some great some small, but all subtle, we are daily tempted to that great sin. To speak of such a thing seems dishonouring to God ; but it is not religion as it comes from Him, it is religion with the strange and evil mixtures which it gathers from abiding in us. This frightful evil seems to rage in the Roman church more than anywhere else, probably from its highly wrought political spirit, the virtues and the vices of a close organization being much associated with one another. That same influence which keeps the mother from her child teaches Montalembert to glorify the corruption, cruelty and baseness which in the government of the papal states put the gospel itself to shame.

1861

11 *Carlton H. Terrace, March* 5.—I dare scarcely reply to your letter, for although the scene at Trentham [the death of the Duke of Sutherland] is much upon my mind, it is, amidst this crowd and pressure of business, an image reflected in ruffled waters, while it is also eminently one that ought to be kept true. A sacred sorrow seems to be profaned by bringing it within the touch of worldly cares. Still I am able, I hope not unnaturally, to speak of the pleasure which your letter has given me, for I could not wish it other than it is.

I am not one of those who think that after a stroke like this, it is our duty to try and make it seem less than it is. It is great for all, for you it is immense, for there has now been first loosened and then removed, the central stay of such a continuation of domestic love as I should not greatly exaggerate in calling without rival or example ; and if its stay centred in him, so did its fire in you. I only wish and heartily pray that your sorrow may be a tender and gentle one, even as it is great and strong. I call it great and strong *more* than sharp, for then only the fierceness of Death is felt when it leaves painful and rankling thoughts of the departed, or when it breaks the kindly process of nature and reverses the order in which she would have us quit the place of our pilgrimage, by ravishing away those whose life is but just opened or is yet unfulfilled. But you are now yearning over a Death which has come softly to your door and gone softly from it ; a death in ripeness of years, ripeness of love and honour and peace, ripeness above all in character. . . . A part of your letter brings to my mind a letter of St. Bernard on the death of his brother (remember he was a monk and so what a brother might be to him) which when I read it years ago seemed to me the most touching and beautiful expression of a natural grief that I had ever known —I will try to find it, and if I find it answers my recollection you shall hear of it again.[1] I always think Thomas à Kempis a golden book for all times, but most for times like these ; for though it does not treat professedly of sorrow, it is such a wonderful exhibition of the Man of Sorrows. . . .

1862

April 4.—I am grateful to you and to your thoughts for the quality they so eminently possess ; the Latins have a word for it, but we have none, and I can only render it by a rude conversion into ' sequacious,' or thoughts given to following.

My labours of yesterday [budget speech] had no title to so kind a reception as they actually met with. Quiet my office in these times cannot be, but this year it promises me the boon of comparative peace, at least in the outer sphere. The world believes that this is what I cannot endure ; I shall be glad of an opportunity of putting its opinion to the test.

All words from you about the Queen are full of weight and value even when they are not so decidedly words of consolation. In her, I am even glad to hear of the little bit of symbolism. That principle like others has its place, and its applications I believe are right when they flow from and conform to what is within. I cannot but hope she will have much refreshment in Scotland. Such contact with Nature's own

[1] See Morison's *Life of St. Bernard* (Ed. 1868), ii. ch. v.

very undisguised and noble self, in such forms of mountain, wood, breeze, and water! These are continual preachers, and so mild that they can bring no weariness. They come straight from their Maker's hand, and how faithfully they speak of Him in their strength, their majesty, and their calm.

As for myself I am a discharged vessel to-day. A load of figures has a suffocating effect upon the brain until they are well drilled and have taken their places. Then they are as digestible as other food of that region; still it is better when they are off, and it is always a step towards liberty.

I must at some time try to explain a little more my reference to Thomas à Kempis. I have given that book to men of uncultivated minds, who were *also* presbyterians, but all relish it. I do not believe it is possible for any one to read that book earnestly from its beginning, and think of popish, or non-popish, or of anything but the man whom it presents and brings to us.

May 8.—Unfortunately I can give you no light on the question of time. I, a bear chained to a stake, cannot tell when the principal run will be made at me, and as I can only scratch once I must wait if possible till then. The only person who could give you *des renseignements suffisants* is Disraeli. Tennyson's note is charming. I return it, and with it a touching note from Princess Alice, which reached me this evening. Pray let me have it again.

1863

Jan. 23.—I am so sorry to be unable to come to you, owing to an engagement to-night at the admiralty. I am ashamed of being utterly destitute of news—full of figures and all manner of dulnesses. . . . I went, however, to the Drury Lane pantomime last night, and laughed beyond measure; also enjoyed looking from a third row, unseen myself, at your brother and the Blantyre party.

Bowden Park, Chippenham, Feb. 7.—I feel as if your generous and overflowing sympathies made it truly unkind to draw you further into the sorrows of this darkened house. My brother [John] closed his long and arduous battle in peace this morning at six o'clock; and if the knowledge that he had the love of all who knew him, together with the assurance that he is at rest in God, could satisfy the heart, we ought not to murmur. But the visitation is no common one. Eight children, seven of them daughters, of whom only one is married and most are young, with one little boy of seven, lost their mother last February, and now see their father taken. He dies on his marriage day, we are to bury him on the first anniversary of his wife's death. Altogether it is piteous beyond belief. It was affectionate anxiety in her illness that undermined his health; it was reluctance to make his children uneasy that made him suffer in silence, and travel to Bath for advice and an operation when he should have been in his bed. In this double sense he has offered up his life. The grief is very sharp, and as yet I am hardly reconciled to it. . . . But enough and too much. Only I must answer your question. He was the brother next above me; we were not brothers only but very intimate friends until we married, and since then we have only been separated in the relative sense in which our marriages and my public life in particular, implied. He was a man of high spirit and uncommon goodness, and for *him* I have not a thought that is not perfect confidence and peace.

March 1.—Even you could not, I am persuaded, do otherwise than think me rather a savage on Wednesday evening, for the opinion I gave about helping a bazaar for the sisters of charity of the Roman community at some place in England. Let me say what I meant by it and what I did not mean. I did not mean to act as one under the influence of violent anti-Roman feeling. I rejoice to think in community of faith among bodies externally separated, so far as it extends, and it extends very far ; most of all with ancient churches of the greatest extent and the firmest organisation. But the proselytising agency of the Roman church in this country I take to be one of the worst of the religious influences of the age. I do not mean as to its motives, for these I do not presume to touch, nor feel in any way called upon to question. But I speak of its effects, and they are most deplorable. The social misery that has been caused, not for truth, but for loss of truth, is grievous enough, but it is not all, for to those who are called converts, and to those who have made them, we owe a very large proportion of the mischiefs and scandals within our own communion, that have destroyed the faith of many, and that are I fear undermining the very principle of faith in thousands and tens of thousands who as yet suspect neither the process nor the cause. With this pernicious agency I for my own part wish to have nothing whatever to do ; although I am one who thinks lightly, in comparison with most men, of the *absolute* differences in our belief from the formal documents of the church of Rome, and who wish for that church, on her own ground, as for our own, all health that she can desire, all reformation that can be good for her. The object, however, of what I have said is not to make an argument, but only to show that if I spoke strongly, I was not also speaking lightly on such a subject.

April 20.—I am afraid I shall not see you before Wednesday—when you are to do us so great a kindness—but I must write a line to tell you how exceedingly delighted we both are with all we have seen at Windsor. The charm of the princess, so visible at a distance, increases with the increase of nearness ; the Queen's tone is delightful. All seems good, delighted, and happy in the family. As regards the Queen's physical strength, it must be satisfactory. What is more fatiguing than interviews ? Last night, however, I saw her at half-past seven, after a long course of them during the day. She was quite fresh.

May 10.—I can answer you with a very good conscience. The affair of Friday night [his speech on Italy] was on my part entirely drawn forth by the speech of Disraeli and the wish of Lord Palmerston. It is D.'s practice, in contravention of the usage of the House, which allows the minister to wind up, to lie by until Lord Palmerston has spoken, and then fire in upon him. So on this occasion I was a willing instrument ; but my wife, who was within ten minutes' drive, knew nothing.

We dined at Marlborough House last night. The charm certainly does not wear off with renewed opportunity. Clarendon, who saw her for the first time, *fully* felt it. Do you know, I believe they are actually disposed to dine with us some day. Do you think you can *then* be tempted ? We asked the Bishop of Brechin to meet you on Thursday. Another bishop has volunteered : the Bishop of Montreal, who is just going off to America. You will not be frightened. Both are rather notable men. The other guests engaged are Cobden, Thackeray, and Mr. Evarts, the new U.S. coadjutor to Adams.

July 10.—I knew too well the meaning of your non-appearance, and because I knew it, was sorry for your indisposition as well as for your absence. We had the De Greys, Granville, Sir C. Eastlake, Fechter,[1] and others, with the Comte de Paris, who is as simple as ever, but greatly developed and come on. He talked much of America. I hope we may come to-morrow, not later than by the 5.5 train, to which I feel a kind of grateful attachment for the advantage and pleasure it has so often procured me. We are glad to have a hope of you next week. All our people are charmed with Mr. Fechter.—Yours affectionately.

July 29.—I am greatly concerned to hear of your suffering. You are not easily arrested in your movements, and I fear the time has been sharp. But (while above all I trust you will not stir without free and full permission) I do not abandon the hope of seeing you . . . I have been seeing Lady Theresa Lewis. It was heartrending woe; such as makes one ashamed of having so little to offer. She dwells much upon employing herself. . . . I greatly mistrust compulsion in the management of children, and under the circumstances you describe, I should lean as you do. . . . Many thanks for the carnations you sent by my wife; they still live and breathe perfume. . . . You spoke of our difference about slavery. I hope it is not very wide. I stop short of war as a means of correction. I have not heard you say that you do otherwise.

11 *Carlton House Terrace (no date).*—I am glad my wife saw you yesterday, for I hope a little that she may have been bold enough to lecture you about not taking enough care of yourself. If this sounds rather intr. sive, pray put it down to my intense confidence in her as a doctor. She has a kind of divining power springing partly from a habitual gift and partly from experience, and she hardly ever goes wrong. She is not easy about your going to Vichy alone. The House of Commons, rude and unmannerly in its arrangements at all times, is singularly so in its last kicks and plunges towards the death of the session; but after to-morrow we are free and I look forward to seeing you on Wednesday according to the hope you give. . . . Soon after this reaches you I hope to be at Hawarden. On Wednesday I am to have luncheon at Argyll Lodge to meet Tennyson. Since I gave him my translation of the first book of the *Iliad*, I have often remembered those words of Kingsley's to his friend Mr. ——, 'My dear friend, your verses are not good but bad.' The Duc d'Aumale breakfasted with us on Thursday and I had some conversation about America. He is, I think, pleased with the good opinions which the young princes have won so largely, and seems to have come very reluctantly to the conclusion that the war is hopeless. Our children are gone and the vacant footfall echoes on the stair. My wife is waiting here only to see Lady Herbert.

Hawarden, Aug. 21.—We have had Dr. Stanley here with his sister. He was charming, she only stayed a moment. He gave a good account of the Queen. They go to Italy for September and October. When any one goes there I always feel a mental process of accompanying them. We have got Mr. Woolner here too. He took it into his head to wish to make a bust of me, and my wife accepted his offer, at least by her

---

[1] A French actor who pleased the town in those days.

authority caused me to accept it. He has worked very quickly and I
think with much success, but he bestows immense labour before closing.
He is a poet too, it seems, and generally a very good companion. . . .
My journey to Balmoral will not be for some five weeks. I am dreadfully indolent as to any exertion beyond reading, but I look forward to
it with interest. . . . Indeed your scruples about writing were misplaced. There is no holiday of mine to leave unbroken so far as post is
concerned, and well would it be with me, even in the time of an exhaustion which requires to be felt before it can pass away, if the words
of my other letters were, I will not say like, but more like, yours.
However, the murmur which I thus let escape me is ungrateful. I
ought to be thankful for the remission that I get, but treasury business
is the most odious that I know, and hence it is that one wishes that the
wheel would for a little time cease its drive altogether, instead of merely
lowering it.

Penmaenmawr, Sept. 20.—It was so kind of you to see our little
fellows on their way through town. I hope they were not troublesome.
Harry is rather oppressed, I think, with the responsibilities of his
captainship—he is the head of seven boys !

We went yesterday to visit the Stanleys, and saw the South Stack
Lighthouse with its grand and savage rocks. They are very remarkable,
one part for masses of sheer precipices descending in columns to the
sea, the other for the extraordinary contortions which the rocks have
undergone from igneous action and huge compressing forces. Our
weather has been and continues cold for the season, which draws
onwards, however, and the gliding days recall to mind the busy outer
world from which we are so well defended.

1864

Jan. 4.—Often as I have been struck by the Queen's extraordinary
integrity of mind—I know of no better expression—I never felt it more
than on hearing and reading a letter of hers on Saturday (at the cabinet)
about the Danish question. Her determination in this case as in others,
not inwardly to 'sell the truth' (this is Robert Pollok) overbears all
prepossessions and longings, strong as they are, on the German side,
and enables her spontaneously to hold the balance, it seems to me,
tolerably even.

Jan. 14.—I am glad you were not scandalised about my laxity as to
the 'public-house.' But I expected from you this liberality. I really
had no choice. How can I who drink good wine and bitter beer every
day of my life, in a comfortable room and among friends, coolly stand
up and advise hardworking fellow-creatures to take 'the pledge'?
However, I have been reading Maguire's *Life of Father Mathew*, with a
most glowing admiration for the Father. Every one knew him to be
good, but I had no idea of the extent and height of his goodness, and
his boundless power and thirst not for giving only but for loving.

June 27.—Just at this time when the press and mass of ordinary
business ought to be lessening, the foreign crisis you see comes upon us,
and drowns us deeper than ever. I fully believe that England *will* not
go to war, and I am sure she *ought* not. Are you not a little alarmed
at Argyll on this matter. Of the fate of the government I cannot speak

with much confidence or with much anxious desire ; but on the whole I *rather* think, and *rather* hope, we shall come through.

Three marriages almost in as many weeks among your own immediate kin ! I look for a dinner at Woolner's with Tennyson to-day : *a sei occhi.* Last night Manning spent three hours with me ; the conversation must wait. He is sorely anti-Garibaldian. How beautiful is the ending of Newman's *Apologia,* Part VII.

Oct. 23.—Singularly happy in my old and early political friendships, I am now stripped of every one of them. It has indeed been my good lot to acquire friendships in later life, which I could not have hoped for ; but at this moment I seem to see the spirits of the dead gathered thick around me, 'all along the narrow valley,' the valley of life, over and into which the sun of a better, of a yet better life, shines narrowly. I do not think our political annals record such a removal of a generation of statesmen before its time as we have witnessed in the last four years. I could say a great deal about Newcastle. He was a high and strong character, very true, very noble, and, I think, intelligible, which (as you know) I think rare in politicians. My relations with him will be kept up in one sense by having to act, and I fear act much, as his executor and trustee, with De Tabley, an excellent colleague, who discharged the same duty for the Duke of Hamilton and for Canning.

Dec. 28.—I cannot give you a full account of Lord Derby's translation [of the *Iliad*], but there is no doubt in my mind that it is a very notable production. He always had in a high degree the inborn faculty of a scholar, with this he has an enviable power of expression, and an immense command of the English tongue ; add the quality of dash which appears in his version quite as much as in his speeches. Undoubtedly if he *wrought* his execution as Tennyson does, results might have been attained beyond the actual ones ; but, while I will not venture to speak of the precision of the version, various passages in the parts I have read are of very high excellence. Try to find out what Tennyson thinks of it.

1865

Aug. 8.—My reading has been little, but even without your question I was going to mention that I had caught at the name of ' *L'Ami Fritz,*' seeing it was by the author of the *Conscrit,* and had read it. I can recommend it too, though the subject does not at first sight look ravishing : it tells how a middle-aged middle-class German bachelor comes to marry the daughter of his own farm bailiff. Some parts are full of grace ; there is a tax-gatherer's speech on the duty of paying taxes, which came home to *my* heart. Though it a little reminds me of a sermon which I heard preached in an aisle of the Duomo of Milan to the boys of a Sunday school (said to have been founded by St. Charles Borromeo) on the absolute necessity of paying tithes ! The golden breadths of harvest are now a most lively joy to me. But we have had great official troubles in the death of Mr. Arbuthnot, a *pillar* of the treasury, and a really notable man.

Sept. 12.—I am working off my post as well as I can with the bands playing and flags fluttering outside. By and by I am going to carve rounds of beef for some part of four hundred diners. The ladies are only allowed tea. Our *weather* anxieties are great, but all is going well. The new telegram and announcement that you will come on Friday is very welcome. Indeed, I did not say anything about the marriage, because, without knowing more, I did not know what to say, except that I most sincerely wish them all good and all happiness. The rest must keep till Friday. The characters you describe are quite, I think, on the right ground. It was the great glory of the Greeks that they had those full and large views of man's nature, not the narrow and pinched ones which are sometimes found even among Christians. Lord Palmerston's abandoning his trip to Bristol is rather a serious affair. There is more in it, I fear, than gout.

Oct. 24.—If you were well enough, and I had wings, there is nothing I should more covet at this moment than to appear at Inveraray and compare and correct my impressions of Lord Palmerston's character by yours. Death of itself produces a certain tendency to view more warmly what was before admired, and more slightly anything that was not. And by stirring the thought of the nation through the press it commonly throws lights upon the subject either new in themselves or new in their combination. *Twelve* cabinet ministers I have already reckoned in my mind, all carried off by the rude hand of death in the last five years, during which three only have been made. They are:—Lord Dalhousie, Lord Aberdeen, Lord Herbert, Sir J. Graham, Lord Canning, Lord Elgin, Sir G. Lewis, Lord Campbell, Lord Macaulay, Mr. Ellice, Lord Lyndhurst, Lord Palmerston. This, in the political world, and to me especially, is an extraordinary desolation.

I hope you are at least creeping on. It was so kind of you to think about my little neuralgic affairs; thank God, I have had no more.

1866

Hawarden, Jan. 4.—We have been pleased with some partial accounts of improvement, and I can the better speak my wish to you for a happy new year. Next Wednesday I hope to inquire for myself. I have been much laden and a good deal disturbed. We have the cattle plague in full force here, and it has even touched my small group of tenants. To some of them it is a question of life and death; and my brother-in-law, who is by nature one of the most munificent persons I ever knew, is sorely straitened in mind at not being able to do all he would like for his people. But do not let this sound like complaint from me. Few have such cause for ceaseless and unbounded thankfulness. . . . If you come across Armstrong's poems[1] pray look at them. An Irish youth cut off at twenty-four. By the by, Wortley's children have admirable acting powers, which they showed in charades very cleverly got up by his wife as stage manager. Grosvenor seconds the Speaker, and F. Cavendish moves the address. We have had divers thrushes singing here, a great treat at this season. I like them better than hothouse strawberries.

July 7.—I cannot feel unmixedly glad for yourself that you are returning to Chiswick. For us it will be a great gain. . . . Disraeli and I were affectionate at the Mansion House last night. Poor fellow,

---

[1] Edmund John Armstrong (1841-65). Republished in 1877. Sir Henry Taylor, *Edinburgh Review*, July 1878, says of this poet:—'Of all the arts poetic, that which was least understood between the Elizabethan age and the second quarter of this century was the art of writing blank verse. Armstrong's blank verse [The Prisoner of Mount Saint Michael] not otherwise than good in its ordinary fabric, affords by its occasional excellence a strong presumption that, had he lived, he would have attained to a consummate mastery of it.'

he has been much tried about his wife's health. The King of the Belgians pleases me, and strikes me more as to his personal qualities on each successive visit. God bless you, my dear duchess and precious friend, affectionately yours.

1867

Hawarden, April 29.—*We both* hope to have the pleasure of dining at Chiswick on Wednesday. We assume that the hour will be 7.30 as usual. I shall be so glad to see Argyll, and to tell him the little I can about the literary department of the *Guardian*. I write from the 'Temple of Peace.' It is a sore wrench to go away. But I am thankful to have had such a quiet Easter. The false rumour about Paris has had a most beneficial effect, and has spared me a multitude of demands. The birds are delightful here. What must they be at Cliveden.—Ever affectionately yours.

Holker Hall, Sept. 22.—We find this place very charming. It explains at once the secret of the great affection they all have for it. It has a singular combination of advantages—sea, hill, home ground, and views, access, and the house such an excellent living house ; all the parts, too, in such good keeping and proportion. We much admire your steps. The inhabitants would be quite enough to make any place pleasant. We have just been at that noble old church of Cartmel. These churches are really the best champions of the men who built them.

Nov. 23.—I cannot let the moment pass at which I would have been enjoying a visit to you after your severe illness without one word of sympathy. . . . Our prospects are uncertain ; but I cling to the hope of escaping to the country at the end of next week, unless the proposals of the government as to the mode of providing for the expense of this unhappy war should prove to be very exceptionable, which at present I do not expect. I saw Lord Russell last night. He seemed very well but more deaf. Lady Russell has had some partial failure of eyesight. Lord R. is determined on an educational debate, and has given notice of resolutions ; all his friends, I think, are disposed to regret it. I am told the exchequer is deplorably poor. Poor Disraeli has been sorely cut up ; and it has not yet appeared that Mrs. Disraeli is out of danger, though she is better. Her age seems to be at the least seventy-six. I have been to see my china exhibited in its new home at Liverpool, where it seemed pretty comfortable.

1868

31 *Bloomsbury Square, Jan.* 3.—I promised to write to you in case I found matters either bad or good. I lament to say they are bad. He [Panizzi] is weaker, more feverish (pulse to-day at 122 about noon), and very restless. The best will be a severe struggle and the issue is *likely* to be unfavourable. At the same time he is not given over. I said, I shall come to-morrow. He said, You will not find me alive. I replied that was wrong. I believe there is no danger to-morrow, but what next week may do is another matter. He is warm and affectionate as ever, and very tender. He is firm and resigned, not stoically, but with trust in God. I am very sad at the thought of losing this very true, trusty, hearty friend. I must go to-morrow, though of course I should stay if I could be of any use.[1]

---

[1] Panizzi recovered and lived for eleven years. See *Life*, ii. p. 299.

This year the end came, and a few lines from his diary show the loss it was to Mr. Gladstone :—

Oct. 28.—The post brought a black-bordered letter which announced the death of the Dowager Duchess of Sutherland. I have lost in her from view the warmest and dearest friend, surely, that ever man had. Why this noble and tender spirit should have had such bounty for me and should have so freshened my advancing years, my absorbed and divided mind, I cannot tell. But I feel, strange as it might sound, ten years the older for her death. May the rest and light and peace of God be with her ever more until *that day.* None will fill her place for me, nor for many worthier than I.

CHAPTER XIII

REFORM

(1866)

L'aristocratie, la démocratie ne sont pas de vaines doctrines livrées à nos disputes ; ce sont des puissances, qu'on n'abat point, qu'on n'élève point par la louange ou par l'injure ; avant que nous parlions d'elles, elles sont ou ne sont pas.—ROYER-COLLARD.

Aristocracy, democracy, are not vain doctrines for us to dispute about ; they are powers ; you neither exalt them nor depress them by praise or by blame ; before we talk of them, they exist or they do not exist.

MR. DENISON, the Speaker, had a conversation with Mr. Gladstone almost immediately after the death of Lord Palmerston, and he reported the drift of it to Sir George Grey. The Speaker had been in Scotland, and found no strong feeling for reform or any other extensive change, while there was a general decline of interest in the ballot :—

Gladstone said, 'Certainly, as far as my constituents go, there is no strong feeling for reform among them. And as to the ballot, I think it is declining in favour.' He spoke of the difficulties before us, of the embarrassment of the reform question. 'With a majority of 80 on the liberal side, they will expect some action.' I answered, 'No doubt a majority of 80, agreed on any point, would expect action. At the time of the first Reform bill, when the whole party was for the bill, the course was clear. But is the party agreed now ? The point it was agreed upon was to support Lord Palmerston's government. But was that in order to pass a strong measure of reform ? Suppose that the country is satisfied with the foreign policy, and the home policy, and the financial policy, and wants to maintain these and their authors, and does not want great changes of any kind ?' I was, on the whole, pleased with the tone of Gladstone's conversation. It was calm, and for soothing difficulties, not for making them. . . . I should add that Gladstone spoke with great kindness about yourself, and about your management of the House of Commons, and said that it would be his wish that you should lead it.'[1]

The antecedents of the memorable crisis of 1866-7 were curious. Reform bills had been considered by five governments since 1849, and mentioned in six speeches from the

[1] *Grey Papers*, Oct. 22, 1865.

throne. Each political party had brought a plan forward, and Lord John Russell had brought forward three. Mr. Bright also reduced his policy to the clauses of a bill in 1858. In 1859 Lord Derby's government had introduced a measure which old whigs and new radicals, uniting their forces, had successfully resisted. This move Mr. Gladstone—who, as the reader will recollect, had on that occasion voted with the tories [1]—always took to impose a decisive obligation on all who withstood the tory attempt at a settlement, to come forward with proposals of their own. On the other hand, in the new parliament, the tory party was known to be utterly opposed to an extension of the franchise, and a considerable fringe of professing liberals also existed who were quite as hostile, though not quite as willing to avow hostility before their constituents. All the leaders were committed, and yet of their adherents the majority was dubious or adverse. The necessity of passing a Reform bill through an anti-reform parliament thus produced a situation of unsurpassed perplexity. Some thought that formidable susceptibilities would be soothed, if the government were reconstructed and places found for new men. Others declared that the right course would be first to weld the party together by bills on which everybody was agreed ; to read a good Reform bill a first time ; then in the recess the country would let ministers see where they were, and the next session would find them on firm ground. But Lord Russell knew that he had little time to spare—he was now close upon seventy-four—and Mr. Gladstone was the last man to try to hold him back.

The proceedings of the new government began with a familiar demonstration of the miserable failure of English statesmen to govern Ireland, in the shape of the twentieth coercion bill since the union. This need not detain us, nor need the budget, the eighth of the series that made this administration so memorable in the history of national finance. It was naturally quite enough for parliament that the accounts showed a surplus of £1,350,000 ; that the last tax on raw material vanished with the repeal of the duty on timber ; that a series of commercial treaties had been successfully negotiated ; and that homage should be paid to virtue by the nibbling of a mouse at the mountain of the national debt. The debt was eight hundred millions, and it was now proposed to apply half-a-million a year towards its annihilation. Reform, however, was the fighting question, and fighting questions absorb a legislature.

The chancellor of the exchequer introduced the Reform bill (March 12) in a speech that, though striking enough, was less impassioned than some of his later performances in the course of this famous contest. He did not forget that ' the limbo of abortive creations was peopled with the skeletons of reform

[1] See above, p. 446.

bills'; and it was his cue in a House so constituted as the one before him, to use the language and arguments of moderation and safety. Franchise was the real question at stake, and to that branch of reform the bill was limited. The other question of redistributing seats he likened to fighting in a wood, where there may be any number of partial encounters, but hardly a great and deciding issue. The only point on which there was a vital difference was the figure of the borough franchise. In 1859 Mr. Disraeli invented a quackish phrase about lateral extension and vertical extension, and offered votes to various classes who mainly had them already, without extending downwards; but whatever else his plan might do, it opened no door for the workmen. In 1860 the Palmerston government proposed a six pound occupation franchise for boroughs, and ten pounds for counties. The proposal of 1866 was seven pounds for boroughs, and fourteen for counties. We may smile at the thought that some of the most brilliant debates ever heard in the House of Commons now turned upon the mighty puzzle whether the qualification for a borough voter should be occupancy of a ten, a seven, or a six pound house;—nay, whether the ruin or salvation of the state might not lie on the razor-edge of distinction between rating and rental. Ministers were taunted with having brought in Mr. Bright's bill. Mr. Bright replied that he could not find in it a single point that he had recommended. He was never in favour of a six pound franchise; he believed in a household franchise; but if a seven pound franchise was offered, beggars could not be choosers, and seven pounds he would take. In a fragmentary note of later years Mr. Gladstone, among other things, describes one glittering protagonist of the hour :—

Lord Russell adhered with great tenacity to his ideas, in which he was strongly supported by me as his leader in the Commons, and by Granville and others of the cabinet. Bright, the representative man of popular ideas, behaved with an admirable combination of discretion and loyalty. Lowe was an outspoken opponent, so superstitiously enamoured of the ten pound franchise as to be thrown into a temper of general hostility to a government which did not recognise its finality and sanctity. He pursued our modest Reform bill of 1866 with an implacable hostility, and really supplied the whole brains of the opposition. So effective were his speeches that, during this year, and this year only, he had such a command of the House as had never in my recollection been surpassed. Nor was there any warrant for imputing to him dishonesty of purpose or arrière-pensée. But his position was one, for the moment, of personal supremacy, and this to such an extent that, when all had been reconciled and the time for his peerage came, I pressed his viscountcy on the sovereign as a tribute to his former elevation, which, though short-lived, was due to genuine power of mind, as it seemed to me that a man who had once soared to those heights trodden by so few, ought not to be lost in the common ruck of official barons.

The first trial of strength arose upon a device of one of the greatest of the territorial whigs, seconded by a much more eminent man in the ranks of territorial tories. Lord Grosvenor announced a motion that they would not proceed with the franchise, until they were in possession of the ministerial intentions upon seats. Lord Stanley, the son of the tory leader, seconded the motion. Any other form would have served equally well as a test of conflicting forces. The outlook was clouded. Mr. Brand, the skilful whip, informed the cabinet, that there were three classes of disaffected liberals, who might possibly be kept in order; first, those who, although opposed to reform, were averse to a change of government; next, those who doubted whether ministers really intended to deal with the seats at all; and finally, those who felt sure that when they came to deal with seats, they would be under the baleful influence of Bright. The first of the three sections could best be kept right by means of a stiff line against Grosvenor and Stanley and the other two sections, by the simple production of the seats bill before taking the committee on franchise. The expert's counsels were followed. Mr. Gladstone told the House that Lord Grosvenor's motion would be treated as a vote of want of confidence, but that he would disclose the whole plan as soon as the franchise bill had passed its second reading. The mutterings only grew louder. At a great meeting in Liverpool (April 6), accompanied by some of his colleagues, Mr. Gladstone roused the enthusiasm of his audience to the utmost pitch by declaring that the government would not flinch, that they had passed the Rubicon, broken the bridges, burned their boats. Still the malcontents were not cowed.

The leader himself rose in warmth of advocacy as the struggle went on. The advocates of privilege used language about the workers, that in his generous and sympathetic mind fanned the spark into a flame. Lowe asked an unhappy question, that long stood out as a beacon mark in the controversy—whether 'if you wanted venality, ignorance, drunkenness—if you wanted impulsive, unreflecting, violent people—where do you look for them? Do you go to the top or to the bottom?' Harsh judgments like this of the conditions of life and feeling in the mass of the nation — though Lowe was personally one of the kindest of men—made Mr. Gladstone stand all the more ardently by the objects of such sweeping reproach. In a discussion upon electoral statistics, he let fall a phrase that reverberated through the discussion inside parliament and out. Some gentlemen, he said, deal with these statistics, as if they were ascertaining the numbers of an invading army. 'But the persons to whom their remarks apply are our fellow-subjects, our fellow-Christians, *our own flesh and blood*, who have been lauded to the skies for their good conduct.' [1]

[1] *Hansard*, Mar. 23, 1866, p. 873.

This was instantly denounced by Lord Cranborne[1] as sentimental rant, and inquiries soon followed why kinship in flesh
and blood should be strictly limited by a seven pound rental.
Speedily Mr. Gladstone passed from steady practical argument
in the ministerial key, to all the topics of popular enthusiasm
and parliamentary invective. His impulsiveness, said critical
observers, 'betrays him at times into exaggeration or incaution;
but there is a generous quality in it.' Mr. Bright once talked
of his own agitation for reform as no better than flogging a
dead horse. The parliamentary struggle, led by Mr. Gladstone,
brought the dead horse to life, stirred the combative instincts,
and roused all the forces of reform. Lowe was glittering,
energetic, direct, and swift. Mr. Disraeli, contented to watch
his adversaries draw their swords on one another, did not put
forth all his power. In a moment of unwisdom he taunted Mr.
Gladstone with his stripling's speech at the Oxford Union five-
and-thirty years before. As Aberdeen once said, 'Gladstone is
terrible on the rebound,'[2] and anybody less imperturbable than
Disraeli would have found his retort terrible here. His speech
on the second reading (April 27), as a whole, ranks among the
greatest of his performances. 'Spoke,' he says, 'from one to
past three, following Disraeli. It was a toil much beyond my
strength, but I seemed to be sustained and borne onwards I
knew not how.' The party danger, the political theme, the
new responsibility of command, the joy of battle, all seemed to
transfigure the orator before the vision of the House, as if he
were the Greek hero sent forth to combat by Pallas Athene,
with flame streaming from head and shoulders, from helmet
and shield, like the star of summer rising effulgent from the
sea. One personal passage deserves a biographic place :—

> My position, Sir, in regard to the liberal party, is in all points the
> opposite of Earl Russell's. . . . I have none of the claims he possesses.
> I came among you an outcast from those with whom I associated, driven
> from them, I admit, by no arbitrary act, but by the slow and resistless
> forces of conviction. I came among you, to make use of the legal phrase-
> ology, *in formâ pauperis.* I had nothing to offer you but faithful and
> honourable service. You received me, as Dido received the shipwrecked
> Æneas—
>
> > '. . . Ejectum littore, egentem
> > Excepi,'
>
> and I only trust you may not hereafter at any time have to complete the
> sentence in regard to me—
>
> > 'Et regni demens in parte locavi.'[1]
>
> You received me with kindness, indulgence, generosity, and I may even
> say with some measure of confidence. And the relation between us has

---

[1] Lord Robert Cecil had on the death of his elder brother in 1865 become Lord
Cranborne.   [2] Above, p. 456.
[3] *Aen.* iv. 373 : 'The exile on my shore I sheltered and, fool as I was, shared with
him my realm.'

assumed such a form that you can never be my debtors, but that I must for ever be in your debt.

The closing sentences became memorable :—'You cannot fight against the future,' he exclaimed with a thrilling gesture, 'time is on our side. The great social forces which move onwards in their might and majesty, and which the tumult of our debates does not for a moment impede or disturb—those great social forces are against you ; they are marshalled on our side ; and the banner which we now carry in this fight, though perhaps at some moment it may droop over our sinking heads, yet it soon again will float in the eye of Heaven, and it will be borne by the firm hands of the united people of the three kingdoms, perhaps not to an easy, but to a certain and to a not far distant victory.'

A drama, as good critics tell us, is made not by words but by situations. The same is the truth of the power of the orator. Here the speaker's trope was a sounding battle-cry, not a phrase ; it disclosed both a cause and a man. For the hour neither man nor cause prospered. Neither fervour nor force of argument prevailed against the fears and resentments of the men of what Mr. Bright called the Cave of Adullam, 'to which every one was invited who was distressed, and every one who was discontented.' After eight nights of debate (April 27) Lord Grosvenor was beaten, and ministers were saved—but only by the desperate figure of five. Some thirty of the professed supporters of government voted against their leaders. A scene of delirious triumph followed the announcement of the numbers, and Mr. Lowe believed for the moment that he had really slain the horrid Demogorgon. Two men knew much better—the leader of the House and the leader of the opposition.

The cabinet, which was not without an imitation cave of its own, hesitated for an hour or two, but the two chief men in it stood firm. Mr. Gladstone was as resolute as Lord Russell, that this time nobody should say reform was only being played with, and they both insisted on going on with the bill. The chances were bad, for this was a Palmerstonian parliament, and the Gladstonian hour had not yet struck. As an honourable leader among the conservatives admitted, not one of the divisions against the bill was taken in good faith. If Mr. Gladstone gave way, he was taunted with cringing ; if he stood his ground, it was called bullying ; if he expressed a desire to consult the views of the House, Mr. Disraeli held up ministers to scorn as unhappy men without minds of their own. In introducing the bill, says Mr. Gladstone, 'I struggled with studious care to avoid every word that could give offence.' The only effect of this was to spread the tale that he was not in earnest, and did not really care for the bill. Such was the temper in which ministers were met. And the whole operation was conducted upon the basis of a solemn, firm, and formal understanding between the regular opposition and the cave men, that were it proposed to reduce the ten pound qualification no lower than nine pounds nineteen shillings and sixpence, even that change should be resisted.

Meanwhile, for the leader of the House vexation followed vexation. 'The worst incident in the history of our reform struggle,' Mr. Gladstone wrote to the prime minister from the House, on May 28, 'has occurred to-night. A most barefaced proposal further to load the bill by an instruction to insert clauses respecting bribery has been carried against us by a majority of 10; the numbers were 248 to 238. This is extremely discouraging, and it much reduces the usual strength and authority of the government. This defeat alters our position with reference to fresh defeats.' The air was thick with ideas and schemes for getting rid of the bill and yet keeping the ministers. 'I cannot,' Mr. Gladstone says to Lord Russell (June 4), 'divest such ideas and proposals of the aspect of dishonour.' They were told, he said, to introduce an amended plan next year. How would the case be altered? They would have to introduce a plan substantially identical, to meet the same invidious opposition, made all the more confident by the success of its present manœuvres.

At length an end came. On June 18, on a question raised by Lord Dunkellin, of rateable value as against gross estimated rental for the basis of the new seven-pound franchise, ministers were beaten. The numbers were 315 against 304, and in this majority of 11 against government were found no fewer than 44 of their professed supporters. The sensation was almost beyond precedent. 'With the cheering of the adversary there was shouting, violent flourishing of hats, and other manifestations which I think novel and inappropriate,' Mr. Gladstone says. The next morning, in a note to a friend, he observed :— 'The government has now just overlived its seven years : a larger term than the life of any government of this country since that of Lord Liverpool. Many circumstances show that it was time things should come to a crisis—none so much as the insidious proceedings, and the inconstant and variable voting on this bill.'

It had been decided in the cabinet a couple of days before this defeat, that an adverse vote on the narrow issue technically raised by Lord Dunkellin was not in itself to be treated in debate as a vital question, for the rating value could easily have been adjusted to the figure of rental proposed by the government. The debate, however, instead of being confined to a narrow question raised technically, covered the whole range of the bill. Taken together with the previous attempts to get rid of the thing, and the increasing number of the disaffected, all this seemed to extinguish hope, and after what had been said

about crossing Rubicons and burning boats, most thought no
course open but resignation. They might appeal to the country.
But Mr. Brand, the expert whip, told the prime minister that
he felt so strongly on the impolicy of dissolution that he could
not bring himself to take a part in it. The proceeding would
be unpopular with their own friends, who had been put to great
expense at their election only a few months before. It would,
moreover, break the party, because at an election they would
have to bring out men of more extreme views to fight the
whigs and liberals who had deserted them on reform, and who
might thus be driven permanently to the other side. Such
were the arguments, though Mr. Gladstone seems not to have
thought them decisive. At hardly any crisis in his life, I think,
did Mr. Gladstone ever incline to surrender, short of absolute
compulsion. To yield was not his temper. When he looked
back upon this particular transaction in later years, he blamed
himself and his colleagues for too promptly acquiescing in
advice to throw down the reins.

I incline to believe that we too readily accepted our defeat by an
infinitesimal majority, as a ground for resignation. There were at least
four courses open to us : first, resignation ; secondly, dissolution ; thirdly,
to deny the finality of the judgment and reverse the hostile vote on
report ; fourthly, to take shelter under a general vote of confidence which
Mr. Crawford, M.P. for the City of London, was prepared to move. Of
these, the last was the worst, as disparaging to political character. Lord
Russell, secretly conscious, I suppose, that he had arrived at the last
stage of his political existence, and desirous that it should not be forcibly
abbreviated, inclined to adopt it. Granville and I were so decidedly set
against it that we allowed ourselves, I think, to be absorbed in its defeat,
and set up against it what was undoubtedly the readiest and simplest
expedient, namely, immediate withdrawal. To dissolve would have been
a daring act, an appeal from a shuffling parliament to an unawakened
people. Yet it is possible, even probable, that such an appeal, unhesi-
tatingly made, would have evoked a response similar, though not equal,
to that of 1831. Or again, a re-trial of the question, with a call of the
House, would in all likelihood have resulted in victory. By our retirement we opened the door for that series of curious deceptions and in-
trigues within the tory party, which undoubtedly accelerated the arrival
of household suffrage.

Lord Russell tendered their resignation to the Queen, then
far away at Balmoral. The Queen received the communication with the greatest concern, and asked them to reconsider.
'The state of Europe,' she said, 'was dangerous ; the country
was apathetic about reform ; the defeat had only touched a
matter of detail ; the question was one that could never be
settled unless all sides were prepared to make concessions.'
In London three or four days were passed in discussing the
hundred ingenious futilities by which well-meaning busy-
bodies on all such occasions struggle to dissolve hard facts
by soft words. In compliance with the Queen's request, the

cabinet reopened their own discussion, and for a day or two entertained the plan of going on, if the House would pass a general vote of confidence. Mr. Gladstone, as we have seen, was on the morrow of the defeat for resignation, and from the first he thought ill of the new plan. The true alternatives were to try either a fresh parliament or a fresh ministry. Bright—not then a member of the government—wrote to Mr. Gladstone (June 24) in strong terms in favour of having a new parliament. Mr. Brand, he says, 'makes no allowance for the force of a moral contest through the country for a great principle and a great cause. Last Easter showed how much feeling your appeals could speedily arouse. . . . I do not believe in your being beaten. Besides there is something far worse than a defeat, namely to carry on your government with a party poisoned and enfeebled by the baseness of the forty traitors [elsewhere in the same letter called the "forty thieves"]. In great contingencies something must be risked. You will have a great party well compacted together, and a great future. Mr. Brand's figures should be forgotten for the moment. . . . You must not forget the concluding passage of your great speech on the second reading of the bill. Read it again to nerve you to your great duty.' The Duke of Argyll was strong in the same sense. He saw no chance of 'conducting opposition with decent sincerity or possible success, except in a parliament in which we know who are our friends and who are our enemies on this question.' In the end resignation carried the day :—

June 25.—Cabinet 2½-4½. . . . The final position appeared to be this, as to alternatives before the cabinet. 1. Dissolution, only approved by three or four. 2. A vote of confidence with vague assurances as to future reform—desired by seven, one more acquiescing reluctantly, six opposing. *W. E. G. unable to act on it.* 3. Lord Russell's proposal to rehabilitate the clause—disapproved by seven, approved by six, two ready to acquiesce. 4. Resignation, generally accepted, hardly any strongly dissenting. I have had a great weight on me in these last days, and am glad the matter draws near its close.

This decision greeted the Queen on her arrival at Windsor on the morning of June 26. Both the prime minister and the chancellor of the exchequer had audiences the same day. 'Off at 11.30 to Windsor with Lord Russell, much conversation with him. Single and joint audiences with the Queen, who showed every quality required by her station and the time. We had warm receptions at both stations.' Mr. Gladstone's memorandum of the interview is as follows :—

Windsor Castle, June 26.—H.M. expressed her regret that this crisis could not be averted ; stated she had wished that this question could have been postponed altogether to another year ; or that upon finding the strength and tenacity of the opposition to the measure, it could have been withdrawn. I reminded H.M. that she had early expressed to me her hope that if we resumed the subject of the reform of parliament, we should prosecute it to its completion. Also, I said that in my opinion, from all the miscarriages attending the past history of this question, not ministries alone, and leaders of parties, nor parties alone, but parliament itself and parliamentary government were discredited. The Queen was impressed with this, and said there was certainly great force in it. She had previously seen Lord Russell, and spoke of his proposal further to amend the clause. Such a proposal she considered advisable, subject to two conditions : (1.) The general assent and concurrence of the cabinet ; (2.) The reasonable chance of its being carried. If the proposal were made she was quite willing it should be said, with the approval of the cabinet, that she had observed that the issue taken was on a point apparently one of detail, and that it was just to the H. of C. that it should have an opportunity of voting upon the substance. Lord Russell wished in any case to state, and H.M. approved, that the Queen had founded her hesitation to accept the resignation (1.) on the fact that the decision was on a matter of detail ; (2.) on the state of the continent [1] (and the difficulty of bringing a new ministry in such a state of things at once into the position of the old). The Queen offered to write what she had said about Lord Russell's proposed amendment. Lord Russell waived this. But thinking it desirable, I afterwards revived the question, and H.M. said she thought it would be better, and went to do it.

I said to Lord Russell, 'It is singular that the same members of the cabinet (generally speaking) who were prematurely eager for resignation after the division on Lord Grosvenor's motion, are now again eager to accept almost anything in the way of a resolution as sufficient to warrant our continuing in office.' He replied, 'Yes, but I am afraid at the root of both proceedings there is a great amount of antipathy to our Reform bill. They were anxious to resign when resignation would have been injurious to it, and now they are anxious to avoid resignation because resignation will be beneficial to it.' Lord Russell showed me a letter he had written to Clarendon justifying me for my unwillingness to accept Mr. Crawford's motion of confidence. He also said that if the Queen should desire the revival of his plan for a further vote, he thought it ought to be proposed.

'On returning,' Mr. Gladstone enters in the diary, 'we went to consult Brand and then to the cabinet, when resignation was finally decided on, and a telegram was sent to Windsor. At six I went down and made my explanation for the government. I kept to facts without epithets, but I thought as I went on that some of the words were scorching. A crowd and great enthusiasm in Palace Yard on departure.' Lord Derby was sent for, accepted the royal commission, and finding Mr. Lowe and the Adullamites not available, he formed his third administration on regular conservative lines, with Mr. Disraeli as its foremost man.

July 6.—Went to Windsor to take my leave. H.M. short but kind. H. of C. on return, took my place on the opposition bench, the first time for fifteen years.[2] . . . Finished in Downing Street. Left my

---

[1] Prussia had declared war on Austria, June 18.

[2] Mr. Gladstone had sat on the front opposition bench from 1847 to the defeat of the Russell government in Feb. 1852. See footnote, p. 470.

keys behind me. Somehow it makes a void. *July* 19.—H. of C. Made a little dying speech on reform. *Sept.* 14.—Woburn. Morning *sederunt* with Lord Russell and Brand on reform and other matters. We agreed neither to egg on the government nor the reverse.

Turbulent scenes had already occurred in the metropolis, and it speedily became evident that whatever value the workmen might set on the franchise for its own sake, they would not brook the refusal of it. They chose Mr. Gladstone for their hero, for, as a good observer remarked, he was the first official statesman who had convinced the working classes that he really cared for them. On the occasion of one popular assemblage the crowd thronged (June 28) to Carlton House Terrace, shouting for Gladstone and liberty. The head of the house was away. Police officers sent up word to Mrs. Gladstone that the multitude would speedily disperse if she would appear for a moment or two on the balcony. In compliance with their request and for the public convenience, she appeared, and all passed off. The incident was described by newspapers that ought to have known better, as the ladies of his family courting an ovation from persons of the lowest class. Mr. Gladstone was compared to Wilkes and Lord George Gordon. With characteristic tenacity he thought it worth while to contradict the story, but not in the columns where the offensive tale had been invented. In July, declining an invitation to speak at a demonstration in Hyde Park Mr. Gladstone said he believed the resignation of the government to be a fresh and important step towards final success. ' In the hour of defeat I have the presentiment of victory.'

An interesting glimpse of Mr. Gladstone in the height of these distractions is given in a passage from the diaries of Mr. Adams, still the American minister :—[1]

Thursday, 7th June 1866.—The other evening at the Queen's ball Mrs. Gladstone asked me as from her husband, to come to breakfast this morning, at the same time that Colonel Holmes,[2] was invited. . . . I decided to go. I found no cause to regret the decision, for the company was very pleasant. The Duke and Duchess of Argyll, Lord Lyttelton, Lord Houghton, Lord Frederick Cavendish with his wife, and one of his uncles, and several whom I did not know. I forgot Lord Dufferin. We sat at two round tables, thus dividing the company ; but Mr. Gladstone took ours, which made all the difference in the world. His characteristic is the most extraordinary facility of conversation on almost any topic, with a great command of literary resources, which at once gives it a high tone. Lord Houghton, if put to it, is not without aptness in keeping it up ; whilst the Duke of Argyll was stimulated out of his customary indifference to take his share. Thus we passed from politics, the House of Commons, and Mr. Mill, to English prose as illustrated from the time of Milton and Bacon down to this day, and

---

[1] *Charles Francis Adams.* By his Son, p. 368.
[2] Son of Oliver Wendell Holmes, afterwards chief justice of Massachusetts, and in 1902 appointed a judge of the United States Supreme Court.

contrasted with German, which has little of good, and with French. In the latter connection Mr. Gladstone asked me if I had read the *Conscrit* of Erckmann-Chatrian. Luckily for me, who have little acquaintance with the light current literature, I could say 'Yes,' and could contrast it favourably with the artificial manner of Hugo. It is a cause of wonder to me how a man like Gladstone, so deeply plunged in the current of politics, and in the duties of legislation and official labour, can find time to keep along with the ephemeral literature abroad as well as at home. After an hour thus spent we rose, and on a question proposed by Colonel Holmes respecting a group of figures in china which stood in a corner, Mr. Gladstone launched forth into a disquisition on that topic, which he delights in, and illustrated his idea of the art by showing us several specimens of different kinds. One a grotesque but speaking figure in Capo di Monte, another a group of combatants, two of whom were lying dead with all the aspect of strained muscle stiffening; and lastly, a very classical and elegant set of Wedgwood ware, certainly finer than I ever saw before. This is the pleasantest and most profitable form of English society.

Towards the close of the session (July 21) Mr. Gladstone presided over the annual dinner of the club founded in honour of Cobden, who had died the year before. As might have been foretold, he emphasised the moral rather than the practical results of Cobden's work. 'Public economy was with Cobden,' he said, 'nothing less than a moral principle. The temper and spirit of Mr. Cobden in respect to questions of public economy was a temper and a spirit that ought to be maintained, encouraged, and propagated in this country—a temper and spirit far more in vogue, far more honoured and esteemed and cultivated by both political parties twenty or thirty years ago than it is at the present moment.' An intense love of justice, a singleness of aim, a habit of judging men fairly and estimating them favourably, an absence of the suspicion that so often forms the bane of public life—these elements and all other such elements were to be found in the character of Cobden abundantly supplied. Mr. Cobden's was a mind incapable of entertaining the discussion of a question without fully weighing and estimating its moral aspects and results. In these words so justly applied to Cobden, the orator was doubtless depicting political ideals of his own.

II

In the autumn Mr. Gladstone determined on going abroad with his wife and daughters. 'One among my reasons for going,' he told Mr. Brand, 'is that I think I am better out of the way of politics during the recess. In England I should find it most difficult to avoid for five minutes attending some public celebration or other, especially in Lancashire. I think that I have said already in one way or other, all that I can usefully say, perhaps more than all. So far as I am concerned, I now leave the wound of the liberal party to the healing powers of nature. . . . If we cannot arrive in sufficient strength at a definite understanding with respect to the mode of handling the question of the franchise, then our line ought to be great patience and quietude in opposition. If we can, then certainly the existing government might at any time disappear, after the opening of the session I mean, with advantage.' 'The journey to Italy,' says Phillimore, 'was really a measure of self-defence, to escape the incessant persecution of correspondence, suggestions, and solicitations.'

They left England in the last week of September, and proceeded direct to Rome. The Queen had given as one good reason against a change of ministers the dangerous outlook on the continent of Europe. This was the year of the Seven Weeks' War, the battle of Sadowa (July 3), and the triumph of Prussia over Austria, foreshadowing a more astonishing triumph four years hence. One of the results of Sadowa was the further consolidation of the Italian kingdom by the transfer of Venetia. Rome still remained outside. The political situation was notoriously provisional and unstable, and the French troops who had gone there in 1849 were still in their barracks at the Castle of St. Angelo. But this was no immediate concern of his. 'Nothing can be more unlikely,' he wrote to Acton (Sept. 11), 'than that I should meddle with the prisons, or anything else of the kind. The case of Rome in 1866 is very different from that of Naples in 1850, when the whole royal government was nothing but one gross and flagrant illegality. I have seen Archbishop Manning repeatedly,' he continues, 'and my impression is that he speaks to me after having sought and received his cue from Rome. He is to put me in communication with Cardinal Antonelli and others. I consider myself bound to good conduct in a very strict sense of the word.' We now know that the archbishop took pains to warn his friends at Rome to show their visitor all the kindness possible. 'Gladstone,' he wrote, 'does not come as an enemy, and may be made friendly, or he might become on his return most dangerous.' The liberals would be very jealous of him on the subject of the temporal power of the pope. Meanwhile Gladstone fully held that the Holy Father must be independent. 'Towards us in England,' said Manning, 'and towards Ireland he is the most just and forgiving of all our public men. He is very susceptible of any kindness and his sympathies and respect religiously are all with us.'[1]

To the Duchess of Sutherland.

Rome, Oct. 13.—We had for five days together last week, I will not say a surfeit or a glut, for these imply excess and satiety, but a continuous feast of fine scenery ; all the way from Pontarlier by Neuchâtel to Lucerne, and then by the St. Gothard to Como. Since then we have had only the passage of the Apennines by the railway from Ancona to

<hr>

[1] Purcell, ii. p. 398.

Rome. This is much finer than the old road, according to my recollection. It has three grand stages, one of them rising from the north and east, the others through close defiles from Foligno to Terni, and from Spoleto to Narni, where we went close by the old bridge. As to the St. Gothard I think it the finest in scenery of all the Alpine passes I have seen, and I have seen all those commonly traversed from the Stelvio downwards (in height) to the Brenner, except the Bernardino. A part of the ascent on the Italian side may perhaps compete with the Via Mala which it somewhat resembles. We were also intensely delighted with the Lake of Lugano, which I had never seen before, and which appeared to me the most beautiful of the Italian lakes.

Here we find Rome solitary, which we wished, but also wet and dirty, which we did not. We hope it will soon be clear and dry. No scenery and no city can stand the stripping off its robe of atmosphere. And Rome, which is not *very* rich in its natural features, suffers in a high degree. We caught sight of the pope yesterday on the steps of St. Peter's, made our obeisance, and received that recognition with the hand which is very appropriate, and I imagine to him not at all troublesome. Next week I hope to see Cardinal Antonelli. We have been to-day to St. Paul's. Its space is amazing, and at particular points it seems to vie with or exceed St. Peter's. But there can be no real comparison in magnificence, and St. Peter's is the more churchlike of the two. The exterior of St. Paul's [beyond the walls] is very mean indeed, and is in glaring contrast with the gorgeousness within.

Rome, Oct. 30.—. . . I observe reserve in conversation, except with such persons as cardinals. To two of them who wished me to speak freely I have spoken without any restraint about the great question immediately pending here. And next to them my most free and open conversation has been with the pope, but of course I did not go further than he led me, and on the affairs of Italy this was nearly all the way. I have seen him twice, once in an audience *quattr' occhi*, and once with my wife and daughters, Lady A. Stanley accompanying us. Nothing can be more pleasant than the impression made by his demeanour and language. He looks well and strong, but seems to have a slight touch of deafness.[1]

You ask about our 'apartment,' and I send you (partly to inform the Argylls, in the hope that they might take one of the floors) first a sketch of our general position, nearly opposite the Europa, and secondly a rude plan of the rooms. Half a bedroom unfortunately is cut off from bad management, and the Frattina rooms are much too small. Besides three rooms which we occupy there is another which we do not. We are boarded too, which saves much trouble, and we have the Stanleys here. We go quietly about our work of seeing Rome. The Vatican has been much enriched since I was here. The sculpture gallery is really wonderful in its superiority to all others. I think if I were allowed to choose two pieces I should perhaps take the Demosthenes and the Torso. The pictures have also secured valuable additions. The Palace of the Caesars since the French *scavi*, not by any means finished yet, offers a new world to view, and we expect to see another, probably next week,

[1] Oct. 22.—Saw the pope. Oct. 28.—We went at 3 (reluctantly) to the pope. Lady Augusta Stanley accompanied us. We had a conversation in French, rather miscellaneous. He was gracious as usual. N.B. his reference to the papal coinages.—*Diary.*

in the catacombs. Among modern works seen as yet I am most pleased with Tenerani's Psyche fainting. A German, Löwenthal, has done a very good picture of Gibson, and there has come up a singularly interesting portrait believed to be of Harvey. But it is idle to attempt to write of all the beauties and the marvels. The church here is satisfactory; the new clergyman, Mr. Crowther, introduced himself on Sunday with an admirable sermon. We expect the Clarendons to-night. We do Dante every morning, and are in the sixteenth canto.

Dec. 4.— At last we have got the Argylls, and I need not say what an addition they are, even amidst the surpassing and absorbing interests that surround us. I hope for your approbation in that I have recommended to his notice a beautiful set of old Sèvres dinner plates, soft paste, which with great spirit he has purchased for little more, I believe, than half what the proprietor refused for them a while ago. I shall be much disappointed if you do not think them a valuable acquisition. I own that I should never have passed them on to a second purchaser had I not, when I first saw them, already got much too near the end of my own little tether. But Sèvres plates and all other 'objects' are of small interest in comparison with the great events that hang as great thick clouds in the heaven around us, yet tipped with broad gleams of light. To-day we are at length assured unconditionally of the departure of the French ; in which I believed already on some grounds, including this, that General Count Montebello had ordered sixteen boxes to be packed with the spoils of Rome, or his share of them. This departure of the might of France represented in the garrison, takes a weight off Roman wills and energies, which has for seventeen years bowed them to the ground. With what kind of bound will they spring up again, and what ugly knocks may be given in the process !

The trip was not in every respect successful. On Christmas day, he writes to Brand : 'We have had some discomforts. Our apartments twice on fire, a floor burnt through each time. Then I was laid down with a most severe influenza : very sore throat, a thing quite new to me. The Roman climate is as bad for me as can be.' I have been told by one who saw much of the party during the Roman visit, that Mr. Gladstone seemed to care little or not at all about wonders of archæology alike in Christian and pagan Rome, but never wearied of hearing Italian sermons from priests and preaching friars. This was consonant with the whole temper of his life. He was a collector of ivories, of china, of Wedgwood, but in architecture in all its high historic bearings I never found him very deeply interested. I doubt if he followed the controversies about French Gothic and Italian, about Byzantine and Romanesque, with any more concern than he had in the controversies of geology. He had two audiences of Pope Pius IX., as we have seen, as had others of his colleagues then in Rome ; and Mr. Gladstone used to tell with much glee in what diverse fashion they impressed the pontiff. 'I like but I do not understand Mr. Gladstone,' the pope said ; 'Mr. Cardwell I understand, but I do not like ; I both like and understand Lord Clarendon ; the Duke of Argyll I neither understand nor like.' He saw ten of the cardinals, and at Florence he had an audience of the king 'who spoke very freely'; he had two long interviews with Ricasoli; and some forty or fifty members of the Italian parliament gave him the honour of a dinner at which Poerio made a most eloquent speech. To the Duchess of Sutherland he wrote :—

Florence, Jan. 13, 1867.—Yesterday Argyll, Cardwell, and I went to the king. He spoke with an astounding freedom ; freely concerning the pope and the emperor, hopeful about Italy in general, rather feebly impressed with the financial difficulty, and having his head stuffed full of military notions which it would be very desirable to displace. We have rumours from England of reform and of no reform ; but we do not trouble ourselves overmuch about these matters. To-morrow I am to be entertained by a number of the deputies in memory especially of the Naples letters. I shrank from this, as I have long ago been much over praised and over paid for the affair, but I could not find a proper ground for refusing. The dinner is to be a private one, but I suppose some notice of it will find its way into the journals. It is a curious proof of the way in which a free and open press has taken hold here, that the newspapers are ordinarily habitually cried in the streets until near midnight !

Among other objects of his keen and active interest was the preservation for its established uses of the famous monastery founded by St. Benedict thirteen centuries before at Monte Cassino,—the first home of that great rule and institute which for long ages played so striking a part in the history of civilisation in the western world. He now visited Monte Cassino in the company of Padre Tosti. The historian of this venerable nursery of learning was his friend long before now—they met first at Naples in 1850—and he had induced Mr. Gladstone to subscribe for the reparation of the tomb of the founder. In 1863 Dean Stanley visited the monastery with a letter from Mr. Gladstone : 'It secured for me not only the most hospitable reception, but an outpouring of Padre Tosti's whole soul on pope and church, and Italy and Europe, past and present, in an almost unbroken conversation of three hours.' In 1866, it seemed as if the hand of the Italian government were about to fall as heavily on Monte Cassino as on any other monastic establishment. Mr. Gladstone besides doing his best with Ricasoli and others, wrote a letter of admirable spirit to his friend Sir James Lacaita :—

It seems, he said, as if one of the lamps of learning were put out ; much promise for the future extinguished ; and a sacred link of union with the past broken. If it be asked why Englishmen should speak and feel on this Italian subject, my answer would be this : that the foundation and history of Monte Cassino have the interest for us which the Americans of the States feel in Alfred, in Edward III., in Henry V. They are part of the great current of Italian civilisation which has been diffused and distributed over all European lands. Much of my life has been devoted to the promotion of public wealth, and of that vast exterior activity which distinguishes the age ; but I am deeply

anxious for the preservation of all those centres, not too numerous, at
which the power of thought may be cultivated, and the inner and
higher life of man maintained. It has, as you know, been pressed
upon me that I should endeavour to make a respectful appeal to the
Italian government on this subject through the medium of a discussion
in the House of Commons. But I shrink from taking such a course, as
I fear that the general effect might be to present an appearance of
intrusive and impertinent interference with the affairs of a foreign
country, and that the very country towards which I should least wish
to offer the appearance of a slight. I cannot likewise refuse to cherish
the hope that the enlightened mind of Baron Ricasoli and his colleagues
may lead them either to avert or mitigate this blow.

On his return he passed through Paris. In 1865 a signal
honour had been bestowed upon him by the illustrious Institute
of France—founded on that Academy, in which Richelieu had
crowned the fame of arms and statesmanship by honour to
purity in national language and competence in letters.[1]   In
acknowledging the election, he wrote to Mignet, the historian,
then perpetual secretary :—

11 *Carlton House Terrace, March* 9, 1865.—I have already expressed
although in an imperfect manner to your distinguished colleagues Count
Wolowski and M. Guizot, the sentiments of gratitude with which I
accept the signal and most unexpected honour of my election as a foreign
associate of the Institute of France. Even the pressure, and what I
might call the tumult, of my daily occupations do not render me insensible to the nature of this distinction, which carries with it a world-wide
fame. I will not, however, dwell further on the nature of the honour,
or on my own unworthiness to receive it : except to refer for a moment
to the gentleman whose name was placed in competition with my own.
I cannot but be aware of his superior claims. I fear that, for once, the
judgment of the Academy has erred, and that in preferring me to Mr.
Mill, its suffrages have taken a wrong direction. I am only consoled by
reflecting that such a body, with such renown, and with its ranks so
filled, can afford to suffer the detriment attaching to a single mistake.
I have the honour to be, etc.

This distinction brought with it the duty of attending the
funeral of a writer eminent among the philosophers and men
of letters of his day. It had been said of him that three days
in the week he was absurd, three days mediocre, and one day
sublime. The verdict seems to be confirmed.

Jan. 23.—From 10 to 3.45 at the successive stages of Victor Cousin's
interment, in my character of member of the Institute. It was of great
interest. I saw many most eminent Frenchmen, so many that they
remained as a cloud upon my recollection, except Berryer, Thiers, and
some whom I had known before. *Jan.* 26.—Attended the meeting of

---

[1] Mr. Gladstone was elected by 27 votes out of 29, two being cast for J. S. Mill.
The minister of instruction wrote :—'Veuillez croire, monsieur, qu'il n'est pas de
décret que j'aie contresigné avec plus de bonheur que celui qui rattache à notre Insti-
tut de France un homme dont le savoir littéraire, l'habileté politique, et l'éloquence
sont l'orgueil de l'Angleterre.'

the Institute 12-2.   Spent the rest of the afternoon with M. Jules Simon in seeing certain quarters of Paris.

'Yesterday,' he wrote to Mr. Brand (Jan. 27), 'a dinner was given to Cardwell and me at the Grand Hotel, by the Society of Political Economists of France, and I did my best to improve the occasion in terms which might imply censure on the military measures here and the new turn of affairs.   Also I am a known accomplice of M. Fould's.   So I let all this be balanced by dining with the Emperor to-day, and with Rouher to-morrow.'   Of the reception at court, he says, 'Dined at the Tuileries, and was surprised at the extreme attention and courtesy of both their majesties, with whom I had much interesting conversation.' The fates with no halting foot were drawing near.   The palace was a heap of ashes, host and hostess were forlorn exiles, before in no long span of time they met their guest again.

CHAPTER XIV

THE STRUGGLE FOR HOUSEHOLD SUFFRAGE

(1867)

First of all we had a general intimation and promise that something would be
done; then a series of resolutions, which strutted a brief hour upon the stage and
then disappeared; then there was a bill, which we were told, on the authority of a
cabinet minister, was framed in ten minutes, and which was withdrawn in very little
more than ten minutes; and lastly, there was a bill which—undergoing the strangest
transformations in its course through parliament—did, I will not say, become the law
of the land, but was altered into something like that which became the law of the
land.—GLADSTONE.

FROM Rome Mr. Gladstone kept a watchful eye for the
approaching political performances at Westminster. He had
written to Mr. Brand a month after his arrival :—

51 P. di Spagna, Oct. 30, '66.—The Clarendons are to be here this
evening to stay for a fortnight or three weeks. Dean and Lady
A. Stanley are in the house with us. I doubt if there are any other
English parties in Rome.

The reform movement is by degrees complicating the question. It is
separating Bright from us, and in one sense thus clearing our way.
But then it may become too strong for us ; or at least too strong to
be stayed with our bill of last year. I do not envy Lord Derby and
his friends their reflections this autumn on the course they have pursued.
Meanwhile I wish that our press, as far as we may be said to have one,
would write on this text : *that a bill from them, to be accepted by the
people, must be larger, and not smaller, than would have been, or even
would be, accepted from us.* For confidence, or credit, stands in politics
in lieu of ready money. If, indeed, your enemy is stronger than you
are, you must take what he gives you. But in this case he is weaker,
and not stronger. A good bill from them would save us much trouble
and anxiety. A straightforward bill, such as an £8 franchise without
tricks, would be easily dealt with. But their bill will be neither good
nor straightforward. The mind of Disraeli, as leader of the House of
Commons, and standing as he does among his compeers, will pre-
dominate in its formation. Now he has made in his lifetime three
attempts at legislation—the budget of 1852, the India bill of 1858, the
Reform bill of 1859. All have been thoroughly tortuous measures.
And the Ethiopian will not change his skin. His Reform bill of 1867
will be tortuous too. But if you have to drive a man out of a wood,

you must yourself go into the wood to drive him. We may have to meet a tortuous bill by a tortuous motion. This is what I am afraid of, and what I am, for one, above all things anxious to avoid. In 1859 the liberal party had to play the obstructive, and with evil consequences. It would be most unfortunate if they should be put into such a position again. Pray consider this. I do not like what I see of Bright's speeches. We have no claim upon him, more than the government have on us ; and I imagine he will part company the moment he sees his way to more than we would give him.

II

The general character of the operations of 1867, certainly one of the most curious in our parliamentary history, was described by Mr. Gladstone in a fragment written thirty years after. · Time had extinguished the volcanic fires, and the little outline is sketched with temper and a sort of neutrality :—

When the parliament reassembled in 1867, parties and groups were curiously distributed. The two great bodies were the regular supporters of the tory ministry, and those grouped around us who had been expelled. The first did not know what course they would have to take ; that depended on the secret counsels of another mind. To keep to the *drapeau* was the guiding motive, as it has been since the creed and practice of Peel were subverted by the opposite principles of Disraeli, who on a franchise question had his peer colleagues at his feet. Besides these, other divisions had to be recognised. The Salisbury secession from the government, supported by Sir W. Heathcote and Beresford Hope, was high in character, but absolutely insignificant in numbers. There was Lowe, so great among the Adullamites of 1866, but almost alone among them in the singleness and strength of his opposition to reform. There was the bulk of the Adullamite body, unable to place themselves in declared opposition to the liberal mass, but many of them disposed to tamper with the question, and to look kindly on the tory government as the power which would most surely keep down any enlargement of the franchise to its minimum.

It would be idle to discuss the successive plans submitted by the government to the House of Commons with an unexampled rapidity. The governing idea of the man who directed the party seemed to be not so much to consider what ought to be proposed and carried, as to make sure that, whatever it was, it should be proposed and carried by those now in power. The bill on which the House of Commons eventually proceeded was a measure, I should suppose, without precedent or parallel, as, on the other hand, it was, for the purpose of the hour, and as the work of a government in a decided minority, an extraordinary stroke of parliamentary success. Our position, on the other hand, was this : (1) We felt that if household suffrage were to be introduced into the boroughs, it ought to be a real household suffrage. (2) The existing state of our legislation, under which a large majority of the householders made no disbursement of rates, but paid them without distinction in their rent, showed that a bill professedly for household suffrage, but taking no notice of compounding, would be in the first place a lottery, and in the second an imposture. Some towns would have large enfranchisement, some none at all, and no principle but the accidental state of local law would determine on which side of the line any town was to be found.

And the aggregate result would be ludicrously small as a measure of enfranchisement. Of such a measure we could not approve. We did not wish to make at once so wide a change as that involved in a genuine household suffrage (always in our minds involving county as well as town), and we could not fairly separate ourselves from Bright on such a point. (3) So we adhered to our idea of an extension, considerable but not violent, and performing all it promised.

But the Adullamite spirit went to work, and finding that the bill had the popular recommendation of a great phrase [household suffrage], combined with the recommendation to them of a narrow sphere of practical operation, determined to support the principle of the bill and abandon our plan, although our mode of operation had been warmly approved at party meetings held at my house. The result was in a tactical sense highly damaging to us. Perhaps we ought to have recognised that the idea of household suffrage, when the phrase had once been advertised by a government as its battle-ground, was irresistible, and that the only remaining choice was whether it should be a household suffrage cribbed, cabined, and confined by the condition of personal ratepaying, or a household suffrage fairly conforming in substance and operation to the idea that the phrase conveyed. The first was in our view totally inadmissible ; the second beyond the wants and wishes of the time. But the government, it must be admitted, bowled us over by the force of the phrase ; and made it our next duty to bowl them over by bringing the reality of the bill into correspondence with its great profession. This we were able to do in some degree, when we reached the committee, for some of the restrictions included in the measure were such as the double-facing liberal fringe did not venture to uphold against the assaults of their own party. But the grand question of compound householding, which was really to determine the character of our legislation, was one on which we could not reckon upon either the conscientious or the intimidated and prudential support of our liberal fringe. The government were beyond all doubt, at least for the moment, masters of the situation. The question was raised, if not in its fullest breadth yet in a form of considerable efficiency, by a proposal from Mr. Hodgkinson, member for Newark, and a local solicitor little known in the House.[1] He went there to support it, but without an idea that it could be carried, and anticipating its defeat by a majority of a hundred. Never have I undergone a stranger emotion of surprise than when, as I was entering the House, our whip met me and stated that Disraeli was about to support Hodgkinson's motion. But so it was, and the proposition was adopted without disturbance, as if it had been an affair of trivial importance.

How it came about I partially learned at a later date. A cabinet was held after the fact, which Sir John Lambert, the great statistician of the day, was summoned to attend. The cabinet had had no idea that the Hodgkinson amendment was to be accepted ; the acceptance was the sole act of Mr. Disraeli ; and when it had been done the ministers assembled in order to learn from Sir John Lambert what was the probable addition that it would make to the constituency.

I do not suppose that in the whole history of the 'mystery-man,' this proceeding can be surpassed. The tories, having been brought to accept household suffrage on the faith of the limitation imposed by

[1] This proposal was in effect to abolish compounding in the limits of parliamentary boroughs. Carried May 27.

personal payment of the rates, found at a moment's notice that that limitation had been thrown overboard, and that their leader had given them a bill virtually far larger than any that Mr. Bright had sought to impose upon them. It was certainly no business of ours to complain, and they made it no business of theirs. I imagine that they still relied upon rectification of the bill by the House of Lords. And the Lords did rectify it largely ; but these rectifications were all rejected when the bill returned to us, except the minority [representation], which Mr. Disraeli was strong enough to secure by means of the votes of a body of liberals who approved it, and which he accepted to humour or comfort the Lords a little, while he detested it, and made, as Bright said, the best speech ever delivered against it. So came about the establishment of an effective household suffrage in the cities and boroughs of England.

III

The process effecting this wide extension of political power to immense classes hitherto without it, was in every respect extraordinary. The great reform was carried by a parliament elected to support Lord Palmerston, and Lord Palmerston detested reform. It was carried by a government in a decided minority. It was carried by a minister and by a leader of opposition, neither of whom was at the time in the full confidence of his party. Finally, it was carried by a House of Commons that the year before had, in effect, rejected a measure for the admission of only 400,000 new voters, while the measure to which it now assented added almost a million voters to the electorate.[1]

We always do best to seek rational explanations in large affairs. It may be true that 'if there were no blunders there would be no politics,' but when we have made full allowance for blunder, caprice, chance, folly, craft, still reason and the nature of things have a share. The secret of the strange reversal in 1867 of all that had been said, attempted, and done in 1866, would seem to be that the tide of public opinion had suddenly swelled to flood. The same timidity that made the ruling classes dread reform, had the compensation that very little in the way of popular demonstration was quite enough to frighten them into accepting it. Here the demonstration was not little. Riots in Hyde Park, street processions measured by the mile in the great cities from London up to Glasgow, open-air meetings attended by a hundred, two hundred, two hundred and fifty thousand people at Birmingham, Manchester, Leeds, showed that even though the workmen might not be anxious to demand the franchise, yet they would not stand its refusal. In the autumn of 1866 Mr. Bright led a splendid campaign in a series of speeches in England, Scotland and Ireland, marked by every kind of power. It is worthy of remark that not one of the main changes of that age was carried in parliament

[1] The electorate was enlarged from 1,352,970 in 1867 to 2,243,259 in 1870.

without severe agitation out of doors.   Catholic emancipation
was won by O'Connell ; the reform act of 1832 by the political
unions ; free trade by the league against the corn law.   Household suffrage followed the same rule.

It was undoubtedly true in a sense that Mr. Gladstone was
at the head of a majority in 1866, and now again in 1867.
But its composition was peculiar.   Sir Thomas Acland (April
10, 1867) describes Mr. Gladstone as hampered by three sets of
people :—' 1. Radicals, who will vote for household suffrage,
but don't want it carried.   2. Whigs (aristocrats), who won't
risk a collision with the government, and hope that very little
reform will be carried, and want to discredit Gladstone.   3. A
large body who care for nothing except to avoid a dissolution.'
' There is a fresh intrigue,' he adds, ' every twelve hours.'

The trenchant and sardonic mind of the leader of the
revolt that had destroyed the bill of 1866, soon found food
for bitter rumination.   On the eve of the session Lowe
admitted that he had very little hope of a successful end
to his efforts, and made dismal protests that the reign of
reason was over.   In other words, he had found out that
the men whom he had placed in power, were going to fling
him overboard in what he called this miserable auction
between two parties, at which the country was put up for
sale, and then knocked down to those who could produce
the readiest and swiftest measure for its destruction.

The liberal cave of the previous year was broken up,
Lowe and the ablest of its old denizens now voting with
Mr. Gladstone, but the great majority going with the
government.   The place of the empty cave was taken by
a new group of dissidents, named from their habitat the
party of the Tea-Room.   Many, both whigs above the gangway
and even radicals below, were averse to bringing Lord Russell
and Mr. Gladstone back again ; they thought a bill would
have a better chance with the tories than with the old leaders.
Insubordination and disorganization were complete.   ' I have
never seen anything like it,' says the new Lord Halifax ;[1] ' but
the state of things this year enables me to understand what
was very inexplicable in all I heard of last year.'   We can
hardly wonder that the strain was often difficult to bear.   A
friend, meeting Mr. Gladstone at dinner about this time (March
25), thought that he saw signs of irritated nerve.   ' What an
invaluable gift,' he reflects, ' a present of phlegm from the gods
would be !   If we could roll up Thompson [master of Trinity]
or Bishop Thirlwall with him and then bisect the compound,
we should get a pair as invincible as the Dioscuri.'   An
accomplished observer told his constituents that one saw
the humour of the great parliamentary chess tournament,

[1] Sir Charles Wood had been created Viscount Halifax on his resignation of the
India Office in 1866.

looking at the pieces on the board and the face of Disraeli ; its tragic side in a glimpse of the face of Gladstone ; in the mephistophelian nonchalance of one, the melancholy earnestness of the other.[1]

Everybody knew that Disraeli, as he watched the scene from behind his mask, now and again launching a well-devised retort, was neither liked nor trusted, though more than a little feared ; and that Gladstone, with his deeply lined face, his 'glare of contentious eagerness,' his seeming over-righteousness, both chafed his friends and exasperated his foes. As it was excellently put by a critic in the press,—the House was indifferent, and Mr. Gladstone was earnest ; the House was lax and he was strict ; it was cynical about popular equality, and he was enthusiastic ; it was lazy about details, he insisted upon teaching it the profoundest minutiæ.[2] About this time, Lord Russell told Lord Halifax that he had gone down to see his brother the Duke of Bedford when he was dying, and had said to him that things were drifting into the country being governed by Disraeli and Gladstone, and the Duke observed that neither of them was fit for it. And Halifax himself went on to say that Gladstone had, in truth, no sympathy or connection with any considerable party in the House of Commons. For the old whig party remembered him as an opponent for many years ; the radicals knew that on many points, especially on all church matters, he did not agree with them, and though they admired his talents, and hailed his recent exertions in favour of reform, they had no great attachment to him, nor did he seem to be personally popular with any of them.

Far away from the world of politics, we have an estimate of Mr. Gladstone at this time from the piercing satirist of his age. 'Is not he at any rate a man of principle,' said a quaker lady to Carlyle. 'Oh, Gladstone!' the sage replied, 'I did hope well of him once, and so did John Sterling, though I heard he was a Puseyite and so forth ; still it seemed the right thing for a state to ‘feel itself bound to God, and to lean on Him, and so I hoped that something might come of him. But now, he has been declaiming that England is such a wonderfully prosperous state, meaning that it has plenty of money in its breeches pocket. . . . But that's not the prosperity we want. And so I say to him, "You are not the life-giver to England. I go my way, you go yours, good morning (with a most dramatic and final bow)."'[3]   England however thought otherwise about life-givers, and made a bow of a completely different sort. Yet not at once. It was Mr. Disraeli who played the leading part in this great transaction, not by inventing the phrase

---

[1] Grant Duff, *Elgin Speeches*, p. 101.   [2] *Spectator*, April 20.
[3] *Memories, etc., of Miss Caroline Fox*, p. 339 (March 5, 1867).

of household suffrage, for that principle was Mr. Bright's ; nor
by giving his bill the shape in which it ultimately became
law, for that shape was mainly due to Mr. Gladstone, but as
the mind by whose secret counsels the arduous and intricate
manœuvre was directed. 'The most wonderful thing,' wrote
Bishop Wilberforce at the end of the session, 'is the rise of
Disraeli. It is not the mere assertion of talent. He has been
able to teach the House of Commons almost to ignore Gladstone,
and at present lords it over him, and, I am told, says that he
will hold him down for twenty years.'[1] If Mr. Disraeli said
this, he proved almost as much mistaken as when Fox was
confident of holding the young Pitt down in 1783. Still he
impressed his rival. 'I met Gladstone at breakfast,' says Lord
Houghton (May), 'he seems quite awed by the diabolical
cleverness of Dizzy.' Awe, by no means the right word, I
fancy.

IV

On April 12 the first act of the Reform question of 1867
ended in an awkward crisis for Mr. Gladstone. The details of
the story are intricate and not much to our purpose. Mr. Gladstone's version printed above discovers its general features.
Some particulars, properly biographic, will fill up his sketch.
'If you have to drive a man out of a wood,' Mr. Gladstone
said, 'you must yourself go into the wood to drive him.' The
bystander of a later time, however, may be content to keep
outside the thicket until the driver and the driven both emerge.
Mr. Disraeli began by preparing a series of resolutions—plati-
tudes with little relation to realities. He told the House that
reform should no longer be allowed to determine the fate of
cabinets, and the House laughed. Yet if Mr. Disraeli had only
at this time enjoyed the advantage of a better character—if he
had been Althorp, Russell, Peel—instead of laughing, his hearers
would perhaps have recognised good sense and statesmanship.
As he said later, whig prime ministers, coalition prime ministers,
coalition chancellors of the exchequer, had one after another
had their innings, and with a majority at their back ; was it
not well now to try something that might be carried by consent ?
Under pressure from Mr. Gladstone the government explained
their plan, dropped the resolutions, and brought in a bill.[2]
Men were to have votes who had university degrees, or were
members of learned professions, or had thirty pounds in a
savings bank, or fifty pounds in the funds, or paid a pound in
direct taxes ; but the fighting point was that every householder who paid rates should have a vote. A scheme for seats
accompanied. To comfort his party for giving so wide a
suffrage, the minister provided checks by conferring a double
vote on certain classes of citizens, and imposing strict terms

as to residence. Three members of his cabinet, of whom Lord
Cranborne was the most important, refused the unsubstantial
solace and resigned. But Mr. Disraeli saw that he would regain by disorganising his opponents more than he would lose
by dislocating his friends.

Mr. Gladstone flew down upon the plan with energy, as a
measure of illusory concessions, and securities still more illusory.
His speech was taken in some quarters in a conservative sense,
for Lowe at once wrote to him (March 21) urging him to follow
it up by resisting the second reading on the principle of fighting
rent against rating. Since Callimachus, the Athenian pole-
march, had to give the casting vote at Marathon when the
ten generals were equally divided on the question of fighting
the Persians or not fighting, ' no one,' cried Lowe, ' ever had a
weightier cause to decide ' than Mr. Gladstone now. He forgot
that the brave Callimachus was slain, and Mr. Gladstone would
in a political sense have been slain likewise if he had taken
Lowe's advice, for, as he says, Disraeli had by talk of household
suffrage ' bowled them over.' A meeting of 278 liberals was
held at his house, and he addressed them for nearly an hour,
concurring not over-willingly in the conclusion that they should
not resist the second reading.[1] He had a long conversation
with Mr. Bright two days before, whom he found ' sensible,
moderate, and firm,' and whose view was no doubt the opposite
of Lowe's. The bill was read a second time without a division
(March 26).

A few entries in Sir Robert Phillimore's journal help us
to realise the state of the case during this extraordinary
session :—

April 9.—Entire collapse of Gladstone's attack on government
yesterday. *Tea-room* schism of liberal members, including the H. of
C. Russells. Disraeli's insolent triumph. 10.—Returned to the Coppice
with Ld. Richard Cavendish. He tells me Hastings Russell and his
brother cannot bear Gladstone as their leader. 12.—In the middle of
the day saw Gladstone and Mrs. Gladstone. His *disgust* and *deep
mortification* at the defection of his party, mingled with due sense of
the loyalty of the greater number, and especially of his old cabinet.
The expression of my wish that, if deserted, he will abdicate and leave
them to find another leader fully responded to by him. 13.—Defeat of
the opposition last night ; great triumph of Disraeli ; a surprise, I
believe, to both parties ; 289 voted with Gladstone. What will he
do ? *Query.*—Ought he on account of the defection of 20 to leave so
considerable a party ?

The occasion just mentioned marked a climax. Mr. Gladstone moved an amendment to remove the personal payment
of rates as an essential qualification, and to confer the franchise

---

[1] 'Gladstone,' says Lord Selborne, ' would have been ready to oppose Disraeli's bill
as a whole, if he could have overcome the reluctance of his followers. But when a
meeting was called to take counsel on the situation, it became apparent that this could
not be done ' (*Memorials*, Part II. i. pp. 68-9).

on the householder whether he paid the rate direct or through the landlord. The next day the diary records :—*April 12.*— 'Spoke in reply and voted in 289-310. A smash perhaps without example. A victory of 21 for ministers.' A new secession had taken place, and 43 liberal members voted with the government, while nearly 20 were absent. The Cranborne secession was small, and some who had been expected to stay away voted with the government. 'Gladstone expressed himself strongly to five or six members of the late government whom he summoned to his house in the morning. He spoke of retiring to a back bench, and announcing that he would give up the ostensible post of leader of the opposition. He was dissuaded from doing this at the present moment, and went out of town, as indeed did almost everybody else.'[1] Still the notion of a back bench did lodge itself in his mind for long. The 'smash' was undoubtedly severe. As Mr. Gladstone wrote to one of the members for the City, a supporter, it showed that the liberals whose convictions allowed united action upon reform were not a majority but a minority of the House of Commons. Considering the large number who supported his proposal, he told his correspondent that though he would move no further amendment of his own, he was not less willing than heretofore to remain at the service of the party. 'The friendly critics,' he said to Brand, 'note a tone of despondency in my letter to Crawford. That is all owing to Granville and others who cut off a fine peacock's tail that I had appended.' So day after day amid surf and breakers he held to his oar. If Mr. Gladstone was much buffeted in the house of his friends, he was not without valiant backers, and among them none was more stout than Mr. Bright, the least effusive of all men in the direction of large panegyric. Speaking to his constituents at Birmingham, 'Who is there in the House of Commons,' he demanded, 'who equals Mr. Gladstone in knowledge of all political questions? Who equals him in earnestness? Who equals him in eloquence? Who equals him in courage and fidelity to his convictions? If these gentlemen who say they will not follow him have any one who is equal, let them show him. If they can point out any statesman who can add dignity and grandeur to the stature of Mr. Gladstone, let them produce him.' A deputation against the bill from some popular body came to him (May 11). Mr. Disraeli at once regretted that these 'spouters of stale sedition,' these 'obsolete incendiaries,' should have come forward to pay their homage to one who, wherever he may sit, must always remain the pride and ornament of the House—

> Who but must laugh if such a man there be ?
> Who would not weep if Atticus were he ?

[1] *Halifax Papers.*

v

To the Duchess of Sutherland Mr. Gladstone wrote (July 9):—

I do not plead guilty to the indictment for ' non-attendance.' I think that for three months I have been in the House for more hours than the Speaker. I have heard every important word that has been spoken on the Reform bill, and at least nine-tenths of all the words. True, outside the Reform bill I only attend when I think there is a chance of being useful ; and in the present state of the House these opportunities are few. I act from no personal motive. But for me to be present and interfere continuously, or so far continuously as I might in other circum- stances, would exhibit needlessly from day to day the divisions and consequent weakness of the liberal party. I admit also that time tells on a man of my age and temperament ; and my brain tells me that I want more rest and not less. Is this unreasonable ? I am against all needless waste of life or anything else. Everything should be hus- banded. I must add that more attendance would but aggravate the susceptibility which depends on nerves rather than will, and already makes my attendance less useful.

The Phillimore diary gives us one or two glimpses more:—

May 9.—Carnarvon delighted with Gladstone's speech at S.P.G. meeting. 10.—Called on Gladstone in bed at 1.30. Ill from effect of the great exertion of yesterday—S.P.G. in the morning, H₄ of C. in the evening. . . . The effect of these defeats of Gladstone in the H. of C. has been to bind the whigs closer to him. 24.—The dinner to Brand and presentation of plate deferred, ostensibly on the ground of his health and necessity of going to German waters, really because at present Gladstone refuses to take the chair at the dinner, though attached to Brand, because many who had deserted him (G.) would attend the dinner. Gladstone will not countenance the appearance of a sham union when the party is discredited. *June* 7.—Attack on Gladstone as being in debt ' hard pressed by creditors,' and therefore wishing for office. The malice against him is wonderful. 29.—Dined at Newspaper Press Fund. Gladstone in the chair, made a really faultless speech. Never did I hear his voice better, nor the flow of his eloquence more unbroken.

Two or three items more from Mr. Gladstone's diary are worth recording :—

May 6.—The underground tone of the House most unsatisfactory. *May* 9.—Spoke earnestly and long for compound householders, in vain. Beaten by 322-256. Much fatigued by heat and work. *May* 28.—Spoke (perforce) on Disraeli's astonishing declaration of consistency. *July* 15. —Third reading of Reform bill. A remarkable night. Determined at the last moment not to take part in the debate, for fear of doing mischief on our own side.

The conservative leader himself was exposed to onslaughts from his followers and confederates of the previous year as severe as have ever fallen on the head of an English party. ' Never,' cried Mr. Lowe, in desolation and chagrin, ' never was there tergiversation so complete. Such conduct may fail or not ; it may lead to the retention or the loss of office ; but it merits alike the contempt of all honest men, and the execration of posterity.' Lord Cranborne, the chief conservative seceder, described the bill in its final shape, after undergoing countless transformations, as the result of the adoption of the principles of Bright at the dictation of Gladstone. It was at Mr. Gladstone's demand that lodgers were invested with votes ; that the dual vote, voting papers, educational franchise, savings-bank franchise, all disappeared ; that the distribution of seats was extended into an operation of enormously larger scale. In his most biting style, Lord Cranborne deplored that the House should have applauded a policy of legerdemain ; talked about borrowing their ethics from the political adventurer ; regretted, above all things, that the Reform bill should have been purchased at the cost of a political betrayal that had no parallel in our parliamentary annals, and that struck at the very root of that mutual confidence which is the very soul of our party government.

Merciless storms of this kind Mr. Disraeli bore imperturbably. He complained of the intolerant character of the discussions. 'Everybody who does not agree with somebody else is looked upon as a fool, or as being mainly influenced by a total want of principle in the conduct of public affairs.' He doubted whether Mr. Bright or anybody else could show that the tory party had changed their opinions. He had not changed his own opinions ; the bill was in harmony with the general policy they had always maintained, though adapted, of course, to the requirements of the year. On Mr. Lowe's 'most doleful vaticinations that ever were heard,' about the new voters repudiating the national debt and adopting an inconvertible paper currency, he poured easy ridicule. Yet only a year before this Mr. Disraeli himself had prophesied that the end of a seven pound franchise would be a parliament of no statesmanship, no eloquence, no learning, no genius. 'Instead of these you will have a horde of selfish and obscure mediocrities, incapable of anything but mischief, and that mischief devised and regulated by the raging demagogue of the hour.'

Mr. Gladstone summed the matter up in a sentence to Dr. Pusey :—' We have been passing through a strange and eventful year : a deplorable one, I think, for the character and conduct of the House of Commons, but yet one of promise for the country, though of a promise not unmixed with evils.'

CHAPTER XV

OPENING OF THE IRISH CAMPAIGN

(1868)

'I claim not to have controlled events, but confess plainly that events have controlled me. Now at the end of three years' struggle, the nation's condition is not what either party or any man desired or expected.'—ABRAHAM LINCOLN (1864).

WRITING to his brother-in-law, Lord Lyttelton, in April 1865, Mr. Gladstone sets out pretty summarily the three incidents that had been taken to mark the line of his advance in the paths of extreme and visionary politics. When it was written, his speech on the franchise the previous year had not ripened,[1] and his speech on the Irish church was only on the eve, nor did he yet know it, of taking shape as a deliberate policy of action.

To Lord Lyttelton.

11 *Carlton House Terrace, S.W., April* 9, '65.—Our interesting conversation of Wednesday evening, which looked before and after, and for your share in which I heartily thank you, has led me to review the subject matters, a process which every man in public life as well as elsewhere ought often to perform, but which the pressure of overwork, and the exhaustion it leaves behind, sadly hinder. But I sum up in favour of a verdict of 'Not guilty,' on the following grounds.

As far as I know, there are but three subjects which have exposed me to the charge of radicalism : the Irish church, the franchise, the paper duty, and the consequent struggle with the House of Lords.

My opinions on the Irish church were, I know, those of Newcastle and Sidney Herbert twenty years ago ; and they were not radicals. Ever since Maynooth, in 1845, I have seen that resistance *in principle* was gone. That was the main reason which led me to make such a serious affair of my own case about the Maynooth grant in that year. But I held this embryo opinion in my mind as there was no cause to precipitate it into life, and waited to fortify or alter or invalidate it by the teachings of experience. At last the time for speaking, and therefore for formulating my ideas came, and I have spoken according as I believe to be the sense of all the leading men with whom I acted from Peel's death onwards, and

[1] See above, p. 569.

within the sense not only of Lord Macaulay, but of the present Lord Grey.

With respect to the franchise, my belief is that the objection taken to my speech really turned not upon the doctrine of *prima facie* title, but upon the fact that it was a speech decisively and warmly in favour of the £6 franchise or something equivalent to it. That is to say, of the very franchise which as a member of the cabinet I had supported in 1860, on the credit and promise of which Lord Derby had been put out in 1859, and which, if it did not appear in the Aberdeen Reform bill of 1852, was represented there by other concessions equally large. The truth is this, that ever since the Aberdeen Reform bill, I have remained just where it placed me ; but many seem to think that it is a subject to be played with or traded on. In thinking and acting otherwise I feel myself to be upholding principles essential to the confidence of the people in governments and parliaments, and also a measure which promises by reasonably widening the basis of our institutions to strengthen the structure above.

To the repeal of the paper duty the House of Commons, when led by the Derby government, chose to commit itself unanimously, and this at a time when the tea duty was at 17d. per lb. In 1860 and 1861 the cabinet considered the respective claims, and took the same course which the Derby government had assisted the House of Commons to take before. Upon this it was found that the measure which they had approved had become in my hands a radical one ; the House of Lords was encouraged to rescue the finance of the country from the hands of the House of Commons ; and the claims of tea were declared to be paramount to those of paper. In proposing the repeal of the last remaining excise duty upon a simple article of manufacture, I adopted a principle which had already received an unanimous acceptance. In resisting to the uttermost of my power the encroachment of the House of Lords, I acted, as I believe, on the only principle which makes it practicable to defend the true, legitimate, and constitutional powers of that House itself against encroachment from other quarters.

Now let me look at the other side of the question. On church rates, on university tests, on clerical subscription (the two last being the only two questions really of principle which, as far as I remember, have been raised), I have held my ground ; and on the two last the cabinet of which I form a part has in the main adopted a course essentially (but with a little *c*) conservative.

The question of franchise was settled, the question of the powers of the Lords in matters of taxation was settled. The Irish church held its ground. In 1865 Mr. Gladstone voted against a radical member who had moved that the case of the Irish church 'called for the early attention of the government.' He agreed with the mover on the merits, but did not believe that the time had come. In 1866, when he was leader of the House, he concurred with Lord Russell, then first minister, in meeting a motion against the Irish church with a direct negative. 'In meeting a question with a negative,' he wrote to the Irish secretary (April 7), 'we may always put it on the ground of time, as well as on the merits. To meet a motion of this

kind with the previous question only, implies almost an engagement to take it up on some early occasion, and this I take it we
are not prepared for.' In the summer of 1865 he wrote to the
warden of Glenalmond that the question was 'remote and
apparently out of all bearing on the practical politics of the
day.' So far as his own judgment went, he had told Sir
Roundell Palmer in 1863, that he had made up his mind on the
subject, and should not be able to keep himself from giving
expression to his feelings. Why did he say that he did not
then believe that the question would come on in his time? 'A
man,' he replied, 'who in 1865 completed his thirty-third year
of a laborious career, who had already followed to the grave the
remains of almost all the friends abreast of whom he had
started from the university in the career of public life ; and
who had observed that, excepting two recent cases [I suppose
Palmerston and Russell], it was hard to find in our whole
history a single man who had been permitted to reach the
fortieth year of a course of labour similar to his own within
the walls of the House of Commons ; such a man might be
excused . . . if he formed a less sanguine estimate of the
fraction of space yet remaining to him, than seems to have
been the case with his critics.'[1]

It was Maynooth that originally cut from under his feet the
principle of establishment in Ireland as an obligation of the
state. When that went, more general reflections arose in his
mind. In 1872 he wrote to Guizot :—

It is very unlikely that you should remember a visit I paid you, I
think at Passy in the autumn of 1845, with a message from Lord Aberdeen about international copyright. The Maynooth Act had just been
passed. Its author, I think, meant it to be final. I had myself regarded
it as *seminal*. And you in congratulating me upon it, as I well remember, said we should have the sympathies of Europe in the work of giving
Ireland justice—a remark which evidently included more than the
measure just passed, and which I ever after saved and pondered. It
helped me on towards what has been since done.

'I must own,' he wrote to Lord Granville (April 11, 1868),
'that for years past I have been watching the sky with a strong
sense of the obligation to act with the first streak of dawn.' He
now believed the full sun was up, and he was right. In an
autobiographic note, undated but written near to the end of his
days, he says :—

I am by no means sure, upon a calm review, that Providence has
endowed me with anything that can be called a striking gift. But if
there be such a thing entrusted to me it has been shown at certain
political junctures, in what may be termed appreciations of the general
situation and its result. To make good the idea, this must not be considered as the simple acceptance of public opinion, founded upon the
discernment that it has risen to a certain height needful for a given work,

[1] *Gleanings*, vii. p. 135.

like a tide.   It is an insight into the facts of particular eras, and their relation one to another, which generates in the mind a conviction that the materials exist for forming a public opinion and for directing it to a particular end.   There are four occasions of my life with respect to which I think these considerations may be applicable.   They are these :—1. The renewal of the Income-tax in 1853 ; 2. The proposal of religious equality for Ireland, 1868. . . .

The remaining two will appear in good time.   It is easy to label this with the ill-favoured name of opportunist.   Yet if an opportunist be defined as a statesman who declines to attempt to do a thing until he believes that it can really be done, what is this but to call him a man of common sense ?

II

In 1867 Ireland was disturbed by bold and dangerous Fenian plots and the mischief flowed over into England.   In September, at Manchester, a body of armed men rescued two Fenian prisoners from a police van, and shot an officer in charge, a crime for which three of them were afterwards hanged.   In December a Fenian rolled a barrel of gunpowder up to the wall of a prison in London where a comrade was confined, and fired it.   The explosion that followed blew down part of the wall and cost several lives.

In my opinion,—Mr. Gladstone said afterwards in parliament, and was much blamed for saying,—and in the opinion of many with whom I communicated, the Fenian conspiracy has had an important influence with respect to Irish policy ; but it has not been an influence in determining, or in affecting in the slightest degree, the convictions which we have entertained with respect to the course proper to be pursued in Ireland.   The influence of Fenianism was this—that when the habeas corpus Act was suspended, when all the consequent proceedings occurred, when the tranquillity of the great city of Manchester was disturbed, when the metropolis itself was shocked and horrified by an inhuman outrage, when a sense of insecurity went abroad far and wide . . . when the inhabitants of the different towns of the country were swearing themselves in as special constables for the maintenance of life and property—then it was when these phenomena came home to the popular mind, and produced that attitude of attention and preparedness on the part of the whole population of this country which qualified them to embrace, in a manner foreign to their habits in other times, the vast importance of the Irish controversy.[1]

This influence was palpable and undoubted, and it was part of Mr. Gladstone's courage not to muffle up plain truth, from any spurious notions of national self-esteem.   He never had much patience with people who cannot bear to hear what they cannot fail to see.   In this case the truth was of the plainest. Lord Stanley, then a member of his father's government, went to a banquet at Bristol in the January of 1868, and told his

[1] *Hansard*, May 31, 1869.

conservative audience that Ireland was hardly ever absent from
the mind of anybody taking part in public affairs. 'I mean,'
he said, 'the painful, the dangerous, the discreditable state of
things that unhappily continues to exist in Ireland.' He described in tones more fervid than were usual with him, the
'miserable state of things,' and yet he asked, 'when we look
for a remedy, who is there to give us an intelligible answer?'
The state of Ireland, as Mr. Gladstone said later,[1] was admitted
by both sides to be the question of the day. The conservatives
in power took it up, and they had nothing better nor deeper to
propose than the policy of concurrent endowment. They asked
parliament to establish at the charge of the exchequer a Roman
catholic university; and declared their readiness to recognise
the principle of religious equality in Ireland by a great change
in the status of the unendowed clergy of that country, provided the protestant establishment were upheld in its integrity.
This was the policy of levelling up. It was met by a counter
plan of religious equality; disestablishment of the existing
church, without establishing any other, and with a general
cessation of endowments for religion in Ireland. Mr. Disraeli's
was at bottom the principle of Pitt and Castlereagh and of
many great whigs, but he might have known, and doubtless
did know, how odious it would be to the British householders,
who were far more like King George III. than they at all
supposed.

III

In May, 1867, Mr. Gladstone had told the House that the
time could not be far distant when parliament would have to
look the position of the Irish church fairly and fully in the
face. In the autumn Roundell Palmer visited Mr. Cardwell,
and discovered clearly from the conversation that the next
move in the party was likely to be an attack upon the Irish
church. The wider aspects of the Irish case opened themselves
to Mr. Gladstone in all their melancholy dimensions. At
Southport (Dec. 19) he first raised his standard, and proclaimed
an Irish policy on Irish lines, that should embrace the promotion of higher education in a backward country, the reform of
its religious institutions, the adjustment of the rights of the
cultivator of the soil. The church, the land, the college, should
all be dealt with in turn.[2] It might be true, he said, that these
things would not convert the Irish into a happy and contented
people. Inveterate diseases could not be healed in a moment.

[1] At Greenwich, Dec. 21, 1868.
[2] He had also in his own mind the question of the acquisition of the Irish railways
by the state, and the whole question of the position of the royal family in regard to
Ireland. On the first of these two heads he was able to man a good commission, with
the Duke of Devonshire at its head, and Lord Derby as his coadjutor. 'But this
commission,' he says, 'did not venture to face any considerable change, and as they
would not move, I, who might be held in a manner to have appealed to them, could do
nothing.'

When you have long persevered in mischief, you cannot undo it at an instant's notice. True though this might be, was the right conclusion that it was better to do nothing at all? For his own part, he would never despair of redeeming the reproach of total incapacity to assimilate to ourselves an island within three hours of our shores, that had been under our dominating influence for six centuries.

At Christmas in 1867 Lord Russell announced to Mr. Gladstone his intention not again to take office, in other words to retire from the titular leadership of the liberal party. Mr. Gladstone did not deny his claim to repose. 'Peel,' he said, 'in 1846 thought he had secured his dismissal at an age which, if spared, I shall touch in three days' time.'[1] Lord Russell was now seventy-five. He once told Lord Granville that 'the great disappointment of his life had been Grey's refusal to join his government in December 1845, which had prevented his name going down in history as the repealer of the corn laws.' 'A great reputation,' wrote Mr. Gladstone to Granville in 1868, 'built itself up on the basis of splendid public services for thirty years; for almost twenty it has, I fear, been on the decline. The movement of the clock continues, the balance weights are gone.'[2]

A more striking event than Lord Russell's withdrawal was the accession of Mr. Disraeli to the first place in the counsels of the crown. In February 1868 Lord Derby's health compelled him to retire from his position as head of the government. Mr. Gladstone found fault with the translator of Stockmar's *Memoirs* for rendering 'leichtsinnig' applied to Lord Derby as 'frivolous.' He preferred 'light-minded' :—

The difference between frivolous and light-minded is not a broad one. But in my opinion a man is frivolous by disposition, or as people say by nature, whereas he is light-minded by defect or perversity of will; further he is frivolous all over, he may be light-minded on one side of his character. So it was in an eminent degree with Lord Derby. Not only were his natural gifts unsurpassed in the present age, but he had a serious and earnest side to his character. Politics are at once a game and a high art; he allowed the excitements of the game to draw him off from the sustained and exhausting efforts of the high art. But this was the occasional deviation of an honourable man, not the fixed mental habit of an unprincipled one.

Mr. Disraeli became prime minister. For the moment, the incident was more dramatic than important; it was plain that his tenure of office could not last long. He was five years older (perhaps more) than Mr. Gladstone; his parliamentary existence had been four or five years shorter. During the thirty-one years of his life in the House of Commons, up to now he had enjoyed three short spells of office (from 1852 to

1 Mr. Gladstone's letter to Lord Russell is given in Walpole's *Russell*, ii. p. 446.
2 Till like a clock worn out with eating time,
The wheels of weary life at last stood still.—Dryden's *Œdipus*.

1868), covering little more than as many years. He had chosen finance for his department, but his budgets made no mark. In foreign affairs he had no policy of his own beyond being Austrian and papal rather than Italian, and his criticisms on the foreign policy of Palmerston and Russell followed the debating needs of the hour. For legislation in the constructive sense in which it interested and attracted Mr. Gladstone, he had no taste and little capacity. In two achievements only had he succeeded, but in importance they were supreme. Out of the wreckage left by Sir Robert Peel twenty-two years before he had built up a party. In the name of that party, called conservative, he had revolutionised the base of our parliamentary constitution. These two extraordinary feats he had performed without possessing the full confidence of his adherents, or any real confidence at all on the part of the country. That was to come later. Meanwhile the nation had got used to him. He had culture, imagination, fancy, and other gifts of a born man of letters ; the faculty of slow reflective brooding was his, and he often saw both deep and far ; he was artificial, but he was no pharisee, and he was never petty. His magniloquence of phrase was the expression of real size and spaciousness of character ; as Goethe said of St. Peter's at Rome, in spite of all the rococo, there was *etwas grosses*, something great. His inexhaustible patience, his active attention and industry, his steadfast courage, his talent in debate and the work of parliament ; his genius in espying, employing, creating political occasions, all made him, after prolonged conflict against impediments of every kind, one of the imposing figures of his time. This was the political captain with whom Mr. Gladstone had contended for some sixteen years past, and with whom on a loftier elevation for both, he was to contend for a dozen years to come.

On a motion about the state of Ireland, proceeding from an Irish member (March 16, 1868), Mr. Gladstone at last launched before parliament the memorable declaration that the time had come when the church of Ireland as a church in alliance with the state must cease to exist. This was not a mere sounding sentence in a speech ; it was one of the heroic acts of his life. Manning did not overstate the case when he wrote to Mr. Gladstone (March 28, '68) :—'The Irish establishment is a great wrong. It is the cause of division in Ireland, of alienation between Ireland and England. It embitters every other question. Even the land question is exasperated by it. The fatal ascendency of race over race is unspeakably aggravated by the ascendency of religion over religion.' But there were many pit-falls, and the ground hid dangerous fire. The parliament was Palmerstonian and in essence conservative ; both parties were demoralised by the strange and tortuous manœuvres that ended in household suffrage ; many liberals were profoundly disaffected to their leader ; nobody could say what the majority was, nor where it lay. To attack the Irish church was to alarm and scandalise his own chosen friends and closest allies in the kindred church of England. To attack a high protestant institution 'exalting its mitred front' in the catholic island, was to run sharp risk of awaking the sleuth-hounds of No-popery. The House of Lords would undoubtedly fight, as it did, to its last ditch. The legislative task itself was in complexity and detail, apart from religious passion and the prejudice of race, gigantic.

Having once decided upon this bold campaign, Mr. Gladstone entered upon it with military promptitude, and pursued it with an intrepidity all his own among the statesmen of his day, and not surpassed by Pym in 1640, nor Chatham in 1758, nor Chatham's son in 1783, nor anybody else in days gone by. Within a week of this historic trumpet-blast, he gave notice of three resolutions to the effect that the established church of Ireland should cease to exist as an establishment. Attendant and consequential changes were appended. Within a week of giving notice, he opened the first resolution, and carried the preliminary motion by a majority of 61. The cheering at this demonstration of a united and victorious party was prodigious, both within the House and in Westminster Hall, and an enthusiastic crowd followed the leader and his two sons as they walked home to Carlton House Terrace. 'This,' he wrote to the Duchess of Sutherland, 'is a day of excitement—almost of exultation. We have made a step, nay a stride, and this stride is on the pathway of justice, and of peace, and of national honour and renown.'[1]

The first resolution was carried (April 30) by a majority of 65, and a week later the second and third went through without a division. Mr. Disraeli fought his battle with much steadiness, but did not go beyond a dilatory amendment. If Mr. Gladstone had old deliverances to reconcile with new policy, so had his tory antagonist. Disraeli was reminded of that profound and brilliant oracle of 1844, when he had described the root of mischief in Ireland as a weak executive, an absentee aristocracy, and an alien church. He wasted little time in trying to explain why the alien church now found in him its champion. 'Nobody listened,' he said, 'at that time. It seemed to me that I was pouring water upon sand, but it seems now that the water came from a golden goblet.' The sentiment may have been expressed, he said, 'with the heedless rhetoric which, I suppose, is the appanage of all who sit below the gangway ; but in my historical conscience, the sentiment of that speech was right.' The prime minister did not escape taunts from those in his own camp who thought themselves betrayed by him upon reform the year before. He repaid the

[1] Lord R. Gower, *Reminiscences*, p. 202.

taunts by sarcasm. He told Lord Cranborne that there was vigour in his language and no want of vindictiveness, what it wanted was finish. Considering that Lord Cranborne had written anonymous articles against him before and since they were colleagues—'I do not know whether he wrote them when I was his colleague'—they really ought to have been more polished. Mr. Lowe, again, he described as a remarkable man; especially remarkable for his power of spontaneous aversion; he hates the working classes of England; he hates the Roman catholics of Ireland; he hates the protestants of Ireland; he hates ministers; and until Mr. Gladstone placed his hand upon the ark, he seemed almost to hate Mr. Gladstone.

After Mr. Gladstone's first resolution was carried, the prime minister acknowledged the change in the relations of the government and the House. He and his party had conducted the business of the country though in a minority, just as Lord John Russell between 1846 and 1851 had conducted business for five or six years, though in a minority, 'but being morally supported by a majority, as we have been supported by a majority.' In this crisis he pursued a peculiar course. He advised the Queen to dissolve the parliament; but at the same time he told her Majesty that if she thought the interests of the country would be better served, he tendered his resignation. The Queen did not accept it, he said; and the ministerial decision was to dissolve in the autumn when the new constituencies would be in order. The statement was not clear, and Mr. Gladstone sought in vain to discover with precision whether the prime minister had begun by resigning, or had presented two alternatives leaving the decision to the Queen, and did he mean a dissolution on existing registers? The answer to these questions was not definite, but it did not matter.

This episode did not check Mr. Gladstone for a moment in his course; in a week after the resolutions were carried, he introduced a bill suspending the creation of new interests in the Irish church. This proof of vigour and resolution rapidly carried the suspensory bill through the Commons. The Lords threw it out by a majority of 95 (June 29). If we sometimes smile at the sanguine prediction of the optimist, the gloom of his pessimist opponent is more ludicrous. 'If you overthrow the Irish established church,' cried the Archbishop of Dublin, 'you will put to the Irish protestants the choice between apostasy and expatriation, and every man among them who has money or position, when he sees his church go will leave the country. If you do that, you will find Ireland so difficult to manage that you will have to depend on the gibbet and the sword.' The Bishop of Chester and Bishop Thirlwall, whom Mr. Gladstone described as 'one of the most masculine, powerful, and luminous intellects that have for generations

been known among the bishops of England,' were deliberately
absent from the division. The effect of the bill was not impaired, perhaps it was even heightened; for it convinced the
public that its author meant earnest and vigorous business,
and the air was instantly alive with the thrill of battle. For
it is undoubted that if the country cares for a thing, the
resistance to it of the hereditary House seems to add spice and
an element of sport.

CHAPTER XVI

PRIME MINISTER

(1868)

> Geworden ist ihm eine Herrscherseele,
> Und ist gestellt auf einen Herrscherplatz.
> Wohl uns, dass es so ist ! . . . .
>   Wohl dem Ganzen, findet
> Sich einmal einer, der ein Mittelpunkt
> Für viele Tausend wird, ein Halt.
>   SCHILLER.
>
> He is possessed by a commanding spirit,
> And his, too, is the station of command.
> And well for us it is so. . . .
> Well for the whole if there be found a man
> Who makes himself what Nature destined him,
> The pause, the central point of thousand thousands.
>   *Coleridge's Translation.*

DURING the election (Nov. 23) Mr. Gladstone published his *Chapter of Autobiography,* the history of his journey from the book of 1838 to the resolutions thirty years later.[1] Lord Granville told him frankly that he never liked nor quite understood the first book ; that the description of it in the new 'Chapter' gave him little pleasure ; that he had at first a feeling that the less a person in Mr. Gladstone's position published, the better ; and that unnecessary explanation would only provoke fresh attacks. But as he read on, these misgivings melted away ; he thought the description of a certain phase of the history of the English church one of the most eloquent and feeling passages he ever read ; the reference to the nonconformists was a graceful amend to them for being so passionate an Oxonian and churchman ; the piece of controversy with Macaulay rather an exaggeration and not easy to understand ; the closing pages admirable. In short, he was all for publication. Another close friend of Mr. Gladstone's, Sir Robert Phillimore, told him (Nov. 29) :—'I am satisfied that you have done wisely and justly both with reference to the immediate and future influence of your character as a states-

---

[1] *Gleanings,* vii.

man. It is exactly what a mere man of the world would not have done. His standard would have been the ephemeral opinion of the clubs, and not the earnest opinion of the silent but thoughtful persons to whom the moral character of their chief is a matter of real moment and concern.' Newman wrote to him from the Oratory at Birmingham, 'It is most noble, and I can congratulate you with greater reason and more hearty satisfaction upon it, than I could upon a score of triumphs at the hustings.' The man of the world and the man at the club did not hide their disgust, but Phillimore was right, and great hosts of people of the other sort welcomed in this publication a sign of sincerity and simplicity and desire to take the public into that full confidence, which makes the ordinary politician tremble as undignified and indecorous.

That Mr. Gladstone had rightly divined the state of public feeling about Ireland was shown by the result. Manning put the case in apt words when he wrote to him : 'I have been much struck by the absence of all serious opposition to your policy, and by the extensive and various support given to it in England and Scotland. It is not so much a change in men's thoughts, but a revelation of what they have been thinking.' Heart and soul he flung himself into the labours of his canvass. The constituency for which he had sat in the expiring parliament was now divided, and with Mr. H. R. Grenfell for a colleague, he contested what had become South-West Lancashire. The breadth, the elevation, the freshness, the power, the measure, the high self-command of these speeches were never surpassed by any of his performances. When publicists warn us, and rightly warn us, that rash expenditure of money extracted from the taxpayer and the ratepayer is the besetting vice and peril of democracy, and when some of them in the same breath denounce Mr. Gladstone as a demagogue pandering to the multitude, they should read the speech at Leigh, in which he assailed the system of making things pleasant all round, stimulating local cupidity to feed upon the public purse, and scattering grants at the solicitation of individuals and classes. No minister that ever lived toiled more sedulously, in office and out of office, to avert this curse of popular government. The main staple of his discourse was naturally the Irish case, and though within the next twenty years he acquired a wider familiarity with detail, he never exhibited the large features of that case with more cogent and persuasive mastery. He told the story of the transformation of the franchise bill with a combined precision, completeness and lightness of hand that made his articles of charge at once extremely interesting and wholly unanswerable. In a vein of pleasant mockery, on the accusation that he was going to ruin and destroy the constitution, he reminded them that within his own recollection it had been wholly ruined and destroyed eight times : in 1828 by the repeal of the Corporation and Test acts; in 1829 by admitting Roman catholics to parliament; in 1832 by reform; in 1846 by free trade; in 1849 by repeal of the navigation law; in 1858 when Jews were allowed to sit in parliament; in 1866 when the government of Lord Russell had the incredible audacity to propose a reform bill with the intention of carrying it or falling in the attempt.

It was a magnificent campaign. But in South-West Lancashire the church of England was strong; orange prevailed vastly over green; and Mr. Gladstone was beaten. Happily he had in anticipation of the result, and by the care of friends, already been elected for Greenwich.[1] In the kingdom as a whole he was triumphant. The liberal majority was 112. When the gross votes were added up, it was calculated that the liberals had a million and a half and the conservatives less than a million.[2] After a long era of torpor a powerful party thus once more came into being. The cause was excellent, but more potent than the cause was the sight of a leader with a resolute will, an unresting spirit of reform, and the genius of political action. This ascendency Mr. Gladstone maintained for quarter of a century to come.

II

On the afternoon of the first of December, he received at Hawarden the communication from Windsor. 'I was standing by him,' says Mr. Evelyn Ashley, 'holding his coat on my arm while he in his shirt sleeves was wielding an axe to cut down a tree. Up came a telegraph messenger. He took the telegram, opened it and read it, then handed it to me, speaking only two words, "Very significant," and at once resumed his work. The message merely stated that General Grey would arrive that evening from Windsor. This of course implied that a mandate was coming from the Queen charging Mr. Gladstone with the formation of his first government. . . . After a few minutes the blows ceased, and Mr. Gladstone resting on the handle of his axe, looked up and with deep earnestness in his voice and with great intensity in his face, exclaimed, " My mission is to pacify Ireland." He then resumed his task, and never said another word till the tree was down.'[3] General Grey reached Hawarden the next day, bringing with him the letter from the Queen.

From the Queen

December 1st, 1868.—Mr. Disraeli has tendered his resignation to the Queen. The result of the appeal to the country is too evident to require

[1] In Lancashire (Nov. 24) the numbers were—Cross, 7729; Turner, 7676; Gladstone, 7415; Grenfell, 6939. At Greenwich (Nov. 17)—Salomons, 6645; Gladstone, 6351; Parker, 4661; Mahon, 4342.

[2]		Liberal.	Conservative.	Liberal Majority.
England and Wales	. .	1,231,450	824,056	407,393
Scotland	. . .	123,410	23,391	100,019
Ireland	. . . .	53,379	36,083	17,297

[3] *National Review*, June 1898.

its being proved by a vote in parliament, and the Queen entirely agrees with Mr. Disraeli and his colleagues in thinking that the most dignified course for them to pursue, as also the best for the public interests, was immediate resignation. Under these circumstances the Queen must ask Mr. Gladstone, as the acknowledged leader of the liberal party, to undertake the formation of a new administration. With one or two exceptions, the reasons for which she has desired General Grey (the bearer of this letter) to explain, the Queen would impose no restrictions on Mr. Gladstone as to the arrangements of the various offices in the manner which he believes to be best for the public service, and she trusts that he will find no difficulty in filling them up, or at least the greater part of them, so that the council may be held before the 13th. Mr. Gladstone will understand why the Queen would wish to be spared making any arrangements of this nature for the next few days after the 13th. The Queen adds what she said on a similar occasion two years and a half ago to Lord Derby, that she will not name any time for seeing Mr. Gladstone, who may wish to have an opportunity of consulting some of his friends, before he sees her; but that, as soon as he shall have done so, and expresses a desire to see the Queen, she will be ready to receive him.

One of his first letters after undertaking to form a government was to Lord Russell, to whom he said that he looked forward with hope and confidence to full and frequent communications, and to the benefit of his friendship and advice. 'There remains, however, a question,' he went on; 'you have an experience and knowledge to which no living statesman can pretend; of the benefit to be derived from it, I am sure that all with whom I can be likely to act would be deeply sensible. Would it be too great an invasion of your independence to ask you to consider whether you could afford it as a member of the cabinet without the weight of any other responsibility?' Lord Russell replied in cordial terms, but said that the servitude of a cabinet, whether with or without a special office, was what he did not wish to encounter. 'What I should have said,' he added at a later date (Dec. 28), 'if the office of the president of the council or the privy seal had been offered me, I do not know: at all events I am personally very well satisfied to be free from all responsibility.' Sir George Grey also declined, on the ground of years: he was within one of the threescore and ten allotted to mortal man. Lord Halifax, on whose ability and experience both the Queen and Mr. Gladstone set special value. declined the Irish viceroyalty, and stood good-naturedly aside until 1870 when he joined as privy seal. The inclusion in the same cabinet of Mr. Bright, who had been the chief apostle of reform, with Mr. Lowe, its fiercest persecutor, startled the country. As for Lowe, Lord Acton said to me that he once informed Mr. Gladstone that Lowe had written the review of his *Financial Statements* in the periodical of which Acton was editor. 'He told me at Grillion's that I thereby made him chancellor of the exchequer.' With Bright he had greater difficulties. He often described how he wrestled with this admirable man from eleven

o'clock until past midnight, striving to overcome his repugnance to office. The next day Bright wrote to him (Dec. 5) :—
'Since I left you at midnight I have had no sleep, from which you may imagine the mental disturbance I have suffered from our long conversation last night. Nevertheless I am driven to the conclusion to take the step to which you invite me, surrendering my inclination and my judgment to your arguments and to the counsel of some whom I have a right to consider my friends. . . . I am deeply grateful to you for the confidence you are willing to place in me, and for the many kind words you spoke to me yesterday.' In the parched air of official politics the relation of these two towards one another is a peculiar and a refreshing element. In the case of Lord Clarendon, some difficulty was intimated from Windsor before Mr. Gladstone began his task. Mr. Gladstone says in one of his late notes :—

Clarendon had already held with credit and success for a lengthened period the seals of the foreign office, and his presumptive title to resume them was beyond dispute. He was a man of free and entertaining and almost jovial conversation in society, and possibly some remark culled from the dinner hour had been reported to the Queen with carelessness or malignity. I do not know much of the interior side of court gossip, but I have a very bad opinion of it, and especially on this ground, that while absolutely irresponsible it appears to be uniformly admitted as infallible. In this case, it was impossible for me to recede from my duty, and no grave difficulty arose. So far as I can recollect the Queen had very little to say in objection, and no keen desire to say it. Clarendon was the only living British statesman whose name carried any influence in the councils of Europe. Only eighteen or twenty months remained to him ; they were spent in useful activity. My relations with him were, as they were afterwards with Granville, close, constant, and harmonious.

Of this cabinet Mr. Gladstone always spoke as one of the best instruments for government that ever were constructed.[1] Nearly everybody in it was a man of talent, character and force, and showed high capacity for public business. In one or two cases, conformably to the old Greek saying, office showed the man ; showed that mere cleverness apart from judgment and discretion is only too possible, and that good intention only makes failure and incapacity in carrying the intention out, so much the more mortifying. The achievements of this cabinet as a whole, as we shall see, are a great chapter in the history of reform and the prudent management of national affairs. It forms one of the best vindications of the cabinet system, and of the powers of the minister who created, guided, controlled and inspired it.

'And so,' Manning, the close friend of other years, now wrote to him, 'you are at the end men live for, but not, I believe, the

[1] The reader will find the list of its members, now and at later periods of its existence, in the Appendix.

end for which you have lived. It is strange so to salute you, but very pleasant. . . . There are many prayers put up among us for you, and mine are not wanting.' At an earlier stage sympathetic resolutions had been sent to him from nonconformist denominations, and in writing to Dr. Allon who forwarded them, Mr. Gladstone said :—' I thank you for all the kind words contained in your letter, but most of all for the assurance, not the first I am happy to say which has reached me, that many prayers are offered on my behalf. I feel myself by the side of this arduous undertaking a small creature ; but where the Almighty sends us duties, He also sends the strength needful to perform them.' To Mr. Arthur Gordon, the son of Lord Aberdeen, he wrote (Jan. 29, 1869) :—

As regards my own personal position, all its interior relations are up to this time entirely satisfactory. I myself, at the period of the Aberdeen administration, was as far as the world in general could possibly be, from either expecting or desiring it. I thought at that time that when Lord Russell's career should end, the Duke of Newcastle would be the proper person to be at the head of the government. But during the government of Lord Palmerston, and long before his health broke down, I had altered this opinion ; for I thought I saw an alteration both in his tone of opinion, and in his vigour of administration and breadth of view. Since that time I have seen no alternative but that which has now come about, although I am sensible that it is a very indifferent one.

On December 29 he enters in his diary :—' This birthday opens my sixtieth year. I descend the hill of life. It would be a truer figure to say I ascend a steepening path with a burden ever gathering weight. The Almighty seems to sustain and spare me for some purpose of His own, deeply unworthy as I know myself to be. Glory be to His name.' In the closing hours of the year, he enters :—

This month of December has been notable in my life as follows : *Dec.* 1809. — Born. 1827. — Left Eton. 1831. — Classes at Oxford. 1832. — Elected to parliament. 1838. — Work on Church and State published. 1834.—Took office as lord of the treasury. 1845.—Secretary of state. 1852. — Chancellor of exchequer.—1868. — First lord. Rather a frivolous enumeration. Yet it would not be so if the love of symmetry were carried with a well-proportioned earnestness and firmness into the higher parts of life. I feel like a man with a burden under which he must fall and be crushed if he looks to the right or left or fails from any cause to concentrate mind and muscle upon his progress step by step. This absorption, this excess, this constant ἄγαν, is the fault of political life with its insatiable demands, which do not leave the smallest stock of moral energy unexhausted and available for other purposes. . . . Swimming for his life, a man does not see much of the country through which the river winds, and I probably know little of these years through which I busily work and live. . . . It has been a special joy of this December that our son Stephen is given to the church, ' whose shoe latchet I am not worthy to unloose.'

Book VI

(1869-1874)

CHAPTER I

RELIGIOUS EQUALITY

(1869)

In the removal of this establishment I see the discharge of a debt of civil justice, the disappearance of a national, almost a world-wide reproach, a condition indispensable to the success of every effort to secure the peace and contentment of that country ; finally relief to a devoted clergy from a false position, cramped and beset by hopeless prejudice, and the opening of a freer career to their sacred ministry.—GLADSTONE.

ANYBODY could pulverise the Irish church in argument, and to show that it ought to be disestablished and disendowed was the easiest thing in the world. But as often happens, what it was easy to show ought to be done, was extremely hard to do. Here Mr. Gladstone was in his great element. It was true to say that 'never were the wheels of legislative machinery set in motion under conditions of peace and order and constitutional regularity to deal with a question greater or more profound,' than when the historic protestant church in Ireland was severed from its sister church in England and from its ancient connection with the state. The case had been fully examined in parliament. After examination and decision there, it was discussed and decided in the constituencies of the United Kingdom. Even then many held that the operation was too gigantic in its bearings, too complex in the mass of its detail, to be practicable. Never was our political system more severely tested, and never did it achieve a completer victory. Every great organ of the national constitution came into active play. The sovereign performed a high and useful duty. The Lords fought hard, but yielded before the strain reached a point of danger. The prelates in the midst of anger and perturbation were forced round to statesmanship. The Commons stood firm and unbroken. The law, when at length it became law, effected the national purpose with extraordinary thoroughness and precision. And the enterprise was inspired, guided, propelled, perfected, and made possible from its inception to its close by the resource, temper, and incomparable legislative skill of Mr. Gladstone. That the removal of the giant abuse of protestant establishment in Ireland made a deeper mark on national well-being than other of his legislative exploits, we can hardly think, but—quite apart from the policy of the act, as to which there can now be scarcely two opinions—as a monument of difficulties surmounted, prejudices and violent or sullen heats overcome, rights and interests adjusted, I know not where in the records of our legislation to find its master.

With characteristic hopefulness and simplicity Mr. Gladstone tried to induce Archbishop Trench and others of the Irish hierarchy to come to terms. Without raising the cry of no surrender, they declined all approaches. If Gladstone, they said, were able to announce in the House of Commons a concordat with the Irish clergy, it would ruin them both with the laity of the Irish establishment, and with the English conservatives who had fought for them at the election and might well be expected, as a piece of party business if for no better reasons, to fight on for them in the House of Lords. Who could tell that the Gladstone majority would hold together? Though 'no surrender' might be a bad cry, it was even now at the eleventh hour possible that 'no popery' would be a good one. In short, they argued, this was one of the cases where terms could only be settled on the field of battle. There were moderates, the most eminent being Bishop Magee of Peterborough, who had an interview with Mr. Gladstone at this stage, but nothing came of it. One Irish clergyman only, Stopford the archdeacon of Meath, a moderate who disliked the policy but wished to make the best of the inevitable, gave Mr. Gladstone the benefit of his experience and ability. When the work was done, Mr. Gladstone wrote to the archdeacon more than once expressing his sense of the advantage derived from his 'thorough mastery of the subject and enlightened view of the political situation.' He often spoke of Stopford's 'knowledge, terseness, discrimination, and just judgment.'

Meanwhile his own course was clear. He did not lose a day :—

Dec. 13, 1868.—Saw the Queen at one, and stated the case of the Irish church. It was graciously received. 24.—At night went to work on draft of Irish church measure, feeling the impulse. 25.—Christmas Day. Worked much on Irish church *abbozzo.* Finished it at night. 26.—Revised the Irish church draft and sent it to be copied with notes.

The general situation he described to Bishop Hinds on the last day of the year :—

We cannot wait for the church of Ireland to make up her mind. We are bound, nay compelled, to make up ours. Every day of the existence of this government is now devoted to putting forward by some step of inquiry or deliberation the great duty we have undertaken. Our principles are already laid in the resolutions of the late House of Commons. But in the mode of applying them much may depend on the attitude of resistance or co-operation assumed by the Irish church. It is idle for the leading Irish churchmen to think 'we will wait and see what they offer and then ask so much more.' Our mode of warfare cannot but be influenced by the troops we lead. Our three *corps d'armée*, I may almost say, have been Scotch presbyterians, English and Welsh nonconformists, and Irish Roman catholics. We are very strong in our minority of clerical and lay churchmen, but it is the strength of weight not of numbers. The English clergy as a body have done their worst against us and have hit us hard, as I know personally, in the countries. Yet we represent the national force, tested by a majority of considerably over a hundred voices. It is hazardous in these times to tamper with such a force.

The preparation of the bill went rapidly forward :—

Hawarden, Jan. 13, 1869.—Wrote out a paper on the plan of the measure respecting the Irish church, intended perhaps for the Queen. Worked on Homer. We felled a lime. 14.—We felled another tree. Worked on Homer, but not much, for in the evening came the Spencers [going to Dublin], also Archdeacon Stopford, and I had much Irish conversation with them. 15.—We felled an ash. Three hours' conversation with the viceroy and the archdeacon. I went over much of the roughest ground of the intended measure ; the archdeacon able and helpful. Also conversation with the viceroy, who went before 7. Worked on Homer at night. 19.—One hour on Homer with Sir J. Acton. Whist in evening. 20.—Further and long conversations on the Irish church question and its various branches with Granville, the attorney-general for Ireland, and in the evening with Dean Howson, also with Sir J. Acton. 21.—Wrote a brief abstract of the intended bill. Woodcutting. 23.—Saw the Queen [at Osborne] on the Irish church especially, and gave H.M. my paper with explanation, which appeared to be well taken. She was altogether at ease. We dined with H.M. afterwards. 24.—Saw her Majesty, who spoke very kindly about Lord Clarendon, Mr. Bright, Mr. Lowe, the Spanish crown, Prince Leopold, Mr. Mozley, and so forth, but not a word on the Irish church. *Feb.* 4.—A letter from H.M. to-day showed much disturbance, which I tried to soothe.

In February Lord Granville thought that it might do good if the Queen were to see Bishop Magee. Mr. Gladstone said to him in reply (Feb. 7, '69) :—

The case is peculiar and not free from difficulty. On the whole I think it would be wrong to place any limit upon the Queen's communications to the Bishop of Peterborough except this, that they would doubtless be made by H.M. to him for himself only, and that no part of them would go beyond him to any person whatever.

On Feb. 12, the Queen wrote to Mr. Gladstone from Osborne :—

The Queen has seen the Bishop of Peterborough according to the suggestion made by Lord Granville with the sanction of Mr. Gladstone, and has communicated to him in the strictest confidence the correspondence which had passed between herself and Mr. Gladstone on the subject of the Irish church. She now sends Mr. Gladstone a copy of the remarks made by the bishop on the papers which she placed in his hands for perusal, and would earnestly entreat Mr. Gladstone's careful and dispassionate consideration of what he says. She would point especially to the suggestion which the bishop throws out of the intervention of the bench of English bishops. The country would feel that any negotiation conducted under the direction of the Archbishop of Canterbury would be perfectly safe, and from the concessions which the Bishop of Peterborough expresses his own readiness to make, the Queen is sanguine in her hope that such negotiations would result in a settlement of the question on conditions which would entirely redeem the pledges of the government and be satisfactory to the country. The Queen must therefore strongly deprecate the hasty introduction of the measure, which would serve only to commit the government to proposals from which they could not afterwards recede, while it is *certain* from what the bishop says, that they would not be accepted on the other side, and thus an acrimonious contest would be begun, which, however it ended, would make any satisfactory settlement of the question impossible.

He replied on the following day :—

Feb. 13.—First the bishop suggests that the endowments posterior to the Reformation should be given to the church, and those preceding it to the Roman catholics. It would be more than idle and less than honest, were Mr. Gladstone to withhold from your Majesty his conviction that no negotiation founded on such a basis as this could be entertained, or, if entertained, could lead to any satisfactory result. Neither could Mr. Gladstone persuade the cabinet to adopt it, nor could the cabinet persuade the House of Commons, nor could cabinet and House of Commons united persuade the nation to acquiesce, and the very attempt would not only prolong and embitter controversy, but would weaken authority in this country. For the thing contemplated is the very thing that the parliament was elected not to do.

Osborne, Feb. 14.—The Queen thanks Mr. Gladstone for his long letter, and is much gratified and relieved by the conciliatory spirit expressed throughout his explanations on this most difficult and important question. The Queen thinks it would indeed be most desirable for him to see the Archbishop of Canterbury—and she is quite ready to write to the archbishop to inform him of her wish and of Mr. Gladstone's readiness to accede to it, should he wish it.

' My impression is,' Mr. Gladstone wrote to Lord Granville (Feb. 14), ' that we should make a great mistake if we were to yield on the point of time. It is not time that is wanted ; we have plenty of time to deal with the Bishop of Peterborough's points so far as they can be dealt with at all. Sir R. Palmer has been here to-day with overtures from persons of importance unnamed. I think probably the Archbishop of Canterbury and others.[1] I do not doubt that on the other side they want time, for their suggestions are crude.'

On the following day (Feb. 15) the Queen wrote to the archbishop, telling him that she had seen Mr. Gladstone, 'who shows the most conciliatory disposition,' and who at once assured her 'of his readiness—indeed, his anxiety—to meet the archbishop and to communicate freely with him.' The correspondence between the Queen and the archbishop has already been made known, and most of that between the archbishop and Mr. Gladstone, and I need not here reproduce it, for, in fact, at this first stage nothing particular came of it.[2] 'The great mistake, as it seems to me,' Mr. Gladstone writes to Archdeacon Stopford (Feb. 8), 'made by the Irish bishops and others is this. They seem to think that our friends are at the mercy of our adversaries, whereas our adversaries are really at the mercy of our friends, and it is to these latter that the government, especially in the absence of other support, must look.' Meanwhile the bill had made its way through the cabinet :—

Feb. 8.—Cabinet, on the heads of Irish Church bill. 9.—Cabinet, we completed the heads of the Irish Church measure to my great satisfaction. 19.—At Lambeth, 12-1½ explaining to the archbishop. 22.—Conclave on Irish church, 2-4½ and 5½-7¾. After twenty hours' work we finished the bill for this stage.

II

On March 1, Mr. Gladstone brought his plan before a House of Commons eager for its task, triumphant in its strength out of doors, and confident that its leader would justify the challenge with which for so many months the country had been ringing. The details are no longer of concern, and only broader aspects survive. A revolutionary change was made by the complete and definite severance of the protestant episcopal church in Ireland alike from the established church of England and from the government of the United Kingdom. A far more complex and delicate task was the winding up of a great temporal estate, the adjustment of many individual and corporate interests, and the distribution of some sixteen millions of property among persons and purposes to be determined by the wisdom of a parliament, where rival claims were defended by zealous and powerful champions influenced by the strongest motives, sacred and profane, of party, property, and church. It was necessary to deal with the sums, troublesome though not considerable, allotted to the presbyterians and to the catholic seminary at Maynooth. Machinery was constructed for the incorporation of a body to represent the emancipated church, and to hold property for any of its uses and purposes. Finally,

[1] No: Archbishop Trench and Lord Carnarvon. See Selborne, *Memorials*, i. pp. 114-6.
[2] See *Life of Tait*, ii. pp. 8-14.

the residue of the sixteen millions, after all the just demands upon it had been satisfied, computed at something between seven and eight millions, was appropriated in the words of the preamble, 'not for the maintenance of any church or clergy, nor for the teaching of religion, but mainly for the relief of unavoidable calamity and suffering' not touched by the poor law.

The speech in which this arduous scheme was explained to parliament was regarded as Mr. Gladstone's highest example of lucid and succinct unfolding of complicated matter. Mr. Disraeli said there was not a single word wasted. So skilfully were the facts marshalled, that every single hearer believed himself thoroughly to comprehend the eternal principles of the commutation of tithe-rent-charge, and the difference in the justice due to a transitory and a permanent curate. Manning said that the only two legislative acts in our history that approached it in importance for Ireland were the repeal of the penal laws and the Act of Union. However this may be, it is hardly an excess to say that since Pitt, the author of the Act of Union, the author of the Church Act was the only statesman in the roll of the century, capable at once of framing such a statute and expounding it with the same lofty and commanding power.[1]

In a fugitive note, Mr. Gladstone named one or two of the speakers on the second reading:—'Ball: elaborate and impressive, answered with great power by Irish attorney general. Bright: very eloquent and striking. Young George Hamilton: a first speech of great talent, admirably delivered. Hardy: an uncompromising defence of laws and institutions as they are, with a severe picture of the character and civil conduct of the Irish population.' Mr. Disraeli's speech was even more artificial than usual. It was Mr. Hardy and Dr. Ball who gave cogent and strenuous expression to the argument and passion of the church case. When the division came, called by Mr. Gladstone 'notable and historic' (March 24), the majority in a crowded house was 118.[2] 'Our division this morning,' Mr. Gladstone wrote to Lord Granville, 'even exceeded expectations, and will powerfully propel the bill.' The size of this majority deserves the reader's attention, for it marked the opening of a new parliamentary era. In 1841 Peel had turned out the Whigs by a majority of 1. Lord John Russell was displaced in 1852 by 9. The Derby government was thrown out in December 1852 by 19. The same government was again thrown out seven years later by 13. Palmerston was beaten in 1857 by 14, and the next year by 19. In 1864 Palmerston's majority on the Danish question was only 18. The second reading of the

[1] The Irish Church bill is the greatest monument of genius that I have yet known from Gladstone; even his marvellous budgets are not so marvellous.—*Dr. Temple to Acland, March* 12, 1869.

[2] 368 against 250

Franchise bill of 1866 was only carried by 5, and ministers were afterwards beaten upon it by 11. With Mr. Gladstone's accession the ruling majority for a long time stood at its highest both in size and stability.

With invincible optimism, Mr. Gladstone believed that he would now have 'material communications from the heads of the Irish church'; but letters from Lord Spencer at Dublin Castle informed him that, on the contrary, they were angrier after they knew what the majority meant, than they were before. At the diocesan conferences throughout Ireland the bill was denounced as highly offensive to Almighty God, and the greatest national sin ever committed. The Archdeacon of Ossory told churchmen to trust in God and keep their powder dry, though he afterwards explained that he did not allude to carnal weapons. The cabinet was called a cabinet of brigands, and protestant pastors were urged to see to it that before they gave up their churches to an apostate system a barrel of gunpowder and a box of matches should blow the cherished fabrics to the winds of heaven.

Even Mr. Disraeli's astuteness was at fault. The Archbishop of Canterbury perceived from his conversation that he was bent on setting the liberals by the ears, that he looked for speeches such as would betray utter dissension amid professed agreement, that he had good hopes of shattering the enemy, and 'perhaps of playing over again the game that had destroyed Lord Russell's Reform bill of 1866.' The resounding majority on the second reading, he told the archbishop, was expected; it created no enthusiasm; it was a mechanical majority.[1]

The bill swept through the stages of committee without alteration of substance and with extraordinary celerity, due not merely to the 'brute majority,' nor to the expectation that all was sure to be undone in another place, but to the peculiar powers developed by the minister. From the speech in which he unfolded his plan, down to the last amendment on report, he showed a mastery alike of himself and of his project and of the business from day to day in hand, that routed opposition and gave new animation and ardour to the confidence of his friends. For six or seven hours a day he astonished the House by his power of attention, unrelaxed yet without strain, by his double grasp of leading principle and intricate detail, by his equal command of legal and historic controversy and of all the actuarial niceties and puzzles of commutation. 'In some other qualities of parliamentary statesmanship,' says one acute observer of that time, 'as an orator, a debater, and a

---

[1] *Life of Tait,* ii. pp. 18-19. How little he was himself the dupe of these illusions was shown by the next sentence, 'What is of importance now is the course to be pursued by the House of Lords.' Bishop Magee met Disraeli on Jan. 28, '69. 'Dizzy said very little,' he wrote to a friend, 'and that merely as a politician, on the possibilities in the House of Lords. He regards it as a lost game in the Commons.'—*Life of Archbishop Magee,* i. p. 214.

tactician he has rivals ; but in the powers of embodying principles in legislative form and preserving unity of purpose through a multiplicity of confusing minutiæ he has neither equal nor second among living statesmen.'[1] The truth could not be better summed up. He carried the whole of his party with him, and the average majority in divisions on the clauses was 113. Of one dangerous corner, he says :—

> *May* 6.—H. of C., working Irish Church bill. Spoke largely on May-nooth. [Proposal to compensate Maynooth out of the funds of the Irish church.] The final division on the pinching point with a majority of 107 was the most creditable (I think) I have ever known.

By a majority of 114 the bill was read a third time on the last day of May.

III

The contest was now removed from the constituencies and their representatives in parliament to the citadel of privilege. The issue was no longer single, and the struggle for religious equality in Ireland was henceforth merged before the public eye in a conflict for the supremacy of the Commons in England. Perhaps I should not have spoken of religious equality, for in fact the establishment was known to be doomed, and the fight turned upon the amount of property with which the free church was to go forth to face its new fortunes. 'I should urge the House of Lords,' wrote the Archbishop of Canterbury to Mr. Gladstone (June 3), 'to give all its attention to saving as large an endowment as possible.'

As at the first stage the Queen had moved for conciliatory courses, so now she again desired Archbishop Tait to com-municate with the prime minister. To Mr. Gladstone himself she wrote from Balmoral (June 3) :—'The Queen thanks Mr. Gladstone for his kind letter. She has invariably found him most ready to enter into her views and to understand her feelings.' The first question was whether the Lords should reject the bill on the second reading :—

> 'It is eminently desirable,' Mr. Gladstone wrote to the archbishop (June 4), 'that the bill should be read a second time. But if I compare two methods, both inexpedient, one that of rejection on the second reading, the other that of a second reading followed by amendments inconsistent with the principle, I know no argument in favour of the latter, except what relates to the very important question of the position and true interest of the House of Lords itself.'

At the same time he promised the archbishop that any views of his upon amendments should have the most careful attention of himself and his colleagues, and 'they would be entertained in a spirit not of jealousy but of freedom, with every desire to bring them into such a shape that they may be in furtherance, and not in derogation, of the main design of the bill.'

[1] See *Daily News*, April 26, 1869.

General Grey, the Queen's secretary, told Mr. Gladstone that she had communicated with the archbishop, 'having heard that violent counsels were likely to prevail, and that in spite of their leaders, the opposition in the House of Lords was likely to try and throw out the measure on the second reading.' Her own feeling was expressed in General Grey's letter to the archbishop of the same date, of which a copy was sent to the prime minister :—

Mr. Gladstone is not ignorant (indeed the Queen has never concealed her feeling on the subject) how deeply her Majesty deplores the necessity, under which he conceived himself to lie, of raising the question as he has done ; or of the apprehensions of which she cannot divest herself, as to the possible consequences of the measure which he has introduced. These apprehensions, her Majesty is bound to say, still exist in full force ; but considering the circumstances under which the measure has come to the House of Lords, the Queen cannot regard without the greatest alarm the probable effect of its absolute rejection in that House. Carried, as it has been, by an overwhelming and steady majority through a House of Commons, chosen expressly to speak the feeling of the country on the question, there seems no reason to believe that any fresh appeal to the people would lead to a different result. The rejection of the bill, therefore, on the second reading, would only serve to bring the two Houses into collision, and to prolong a dangerous agitation on the subject.

Mr. Gladstone replied :—

June 5.—From such information as has indirectly reached Mr. Gladstone, he fears that the leaders of the majority in the House of Lords will undoubtedly oppose the second reading of the Irish Church bill, of which Lord Harrowby is to propose the rejection. He understands that Lord Salisbury, as well as Lord Carnarvon, decidedly, but in vain, objected to this course at the meeting held to-day at the Duke of Marlborough's. Very few of the bishops were present. Lord Derby, it is said, supported the resolution. Although a division must now be regarded as certain, and as very formidable, all hope need not be abandoned that your Majesty's wise counsels through the Archbishop of Canterbury, and the sagacity of the peers themselves with reference to the security and stability of their position in the legislature, may avail to frustrate an unwise resolution.

'How much more effectually,' Mr. Gladstone wrote to Hawarden, 'could the Queen assist in the settlement of this question were she not six hundred miles off.' As it was, she took a step from which Mr. Gladstone hoped for 'most important consequences,' in writing direct to Lord Derby, dwelling on the danger to the Lords of a collision with the Commons. In a record of these proceedings prepared for Mr. Gladstone (August 4, '69), Lord Granville writes :—

Before the second reading of the Irish Church bill in the House of Lords, I was asked by the Archbishop of York to meet him and the Archbishop of Canterbury. They said it was impossible for them to vote for the second reading in any case, but before they decided to abstain from voting against it they wished to know how far the government would act in a conciliatory spirit. I made to them the same declaration that I afterwards made in the House, and after seeing you I had another interview with the Archbishop of Canterbury. I told his grace that it was impossible for the government to suggest amendments against themselves, but I gave a hint of the direction in which such amendments might be framed, and, without mentioning that the suggestion came from you, I said that if his grace would tell Dr. Ball that he only wished to propose amendments which it would be possible for the government to accept, that learned gentleman would know better than others how it could be done. The archbishop, however, seems chiefly to have made use of Dr. Ball to supply him with arguments against the government.

The result was doubtful to the very end. It was three o'clock in the morning (June 19) before the close of a fine debate — fine not merely from the eloquence of the speakers and cogency of argument on either side, but because there was a deep and real issue, and because the practical conclusion was not foregone. It was the fullest House assembled in living memory. Three hundred and twenty-five peers voted. The two English archbishops did not vote, and Thirlwall was the only prelate who supported the second reading. It was carried by a majority of 33. In 1857 Lord Derby's vote of censure on Palmerston for the China war was defeated by 36, and these two were the only cases in which the conservatives had been beaten in the Lords for twenty years. Thirty-six conservative peers, including Lord Salisbury, voted away from their party in favour of the second reading.

IV

For the moment ministers breathed freely, but the bill was soon in the trough of the sea. The archbishop wrote to the Queen that they had decided if they could not get three million pounds to float the new church upon, they would take their chance of what might happen by postponing the bill until next year. Asked by the Queen what could be done (July 10), Lord Granville, being at Windsor, answered that the cabinet would not make up their mind until they knew how far the Lords would go in resistance, but he thought it right to tell her that there was no chance of ministers agreeing to postpone the bill for another year. The day after this conversation, the Queen wrote again to the archbishop, asking him seriously to reflect, in case the concessions of the government should not go quite so far as he might himself wish, whether the postponement of the settlement for another year would not be likely to result rather in worse than in better terms for the church. She trusted that he would himself consider, and endeavour to induce others to consider, any concessions offered by the House of Commons in the most conciliatory spirit, rather than to try and get rid of the bill. 'The amendments,' said Mr. Gladstone, 'seem to mean war to the knife.'

After the second reading a tory lady of high station told Lord Clarendon and Mr. Delane that in her opinion a friendly communication might have great influence on Lord Salisbury's course.

'I therefore wrote to him,' Lord Granville says in the memorandum already referred to, 'stating why on public and personal grounds it was desirable that he should meet you. I said that although it would be difficult for us to initiate suggestions, yet from your personal regard for him such a conversation would advance matters. He consented, stating that he was in communication as to amendments with Lord Cairns and the archbishop. He was extremely desirous that no one should know of the interview. You were of opinion that the interview had done good, and I wrote to ask Lord Salisbury whether he would like me to put dots on some of your i's. He declined, and considered the interview had been unsatisfactory, but gave me an assurance of his desire to avoid a conflict. . . . On the 4th of July I wrote again suggesting a compromise on Lord Carnarvon's clause. He declined, that clause being the one thing they cared about. He ended by telling me his growing impression was, that there would be no Church bill this session.'

The general result of the operations of the Lords was to leave disestablishment complete, and the legal framework of the bill undisturbed. Disendowment, on the other hand, was reduced to a shadow. An additional sum of between three and four millions was taken for the church, and the general upshot was, out of a property of sixteen millions, to make over thirteen or fourteen millions to an ecclesiastical body wholly exempt from state control. This, Mr. Gladstone told the Queen, the House of Commons would never accept, and the first effect of persistence in such a course would be a stronger move against the episcopal seats in the House of Lords than had been seen for more than two hundred years. He ridiculed as it deserved the contention that the nation had not passed judgment on the question of disendowment, and he insisted that the government could not go further than three-quarters of a million towards meeting the extravagant claims of the Lords. Confessing his disappointment at the conduct of the episcopal body, even including the archbishop, he found a certain consolation in reflecting that equally on the great occasions of 1829 and 1831, though 'the mild and wise Archbishop Howley was its leader,' that body failed either to meet the desires of the country, or to act upon a far-sighted view of the exigencies of the church. One point obstinately contested was the plan for the future application of the surplus. A majority of the Lords insisted on casting out the words of the preamble providing that the residue should not be applied for purposes of religion, and substituting in one shape or another the principle of concurrent endowment, so hostile, as Mr. Gladstone judged it, to the peace of Ireland, and so irreconcilable with public feeling in England and Scotland.

On July 12, the bill came back to the Commons. The tension had hardly yet begun to tell upon him, but Mr. Gladstone enters on these days :—

July 11.—Formidable accounts from and through Windsor. 12.—The time grows more and more anxious. 15.—This day I received from a Roman catholic bishop the assurance that he offered mass and that many pray for me ; and from Mr. Spurgeon (as often from others), an assurance of the prayers of the nonconformists. I think in these and other prayers lies the secret of the strength of body which has been given me in unusual measure during this very trying year.

This was the day on which, amid the ardent cheers of his party, he arose to announce to the House the views of the government. He was in no compromising mood. In a short speech he went through the amendments made by men so out of touch with the feeling of the country that they might have been 'living in a balloon.' One by one he moved the rejection of all amendments that involved the principle of concurrent endowment, the disposal of the surplus, or the postponement of the date of disestablishment. He agreed, however, to give a lump sum of half a million in lieu of private benefactions, to readjust the commutation terms, and make other alterations involving a further gift of £280,000 to the church. When the Commons concluded the consideration of the Lords' amendments (July 16), Mr. Gladstone observed three things : first, that the sentiment against concurrent endowment in any form was overwhelming ; second, that not only was no disposition shown to make new concessions, but concessions actually made were sorely grudged ; and third, that the tories were eager to postpone the destination of the residuary property.

V

On July 16, the bill, restored substantially to its first shape, was again back on the table of the Lords, and shipwreck seemed for five days to be inevitable. On July 20, at eleven o'clock, by a majority of 175 to 93, the Lords once more excluded from the preamble the words that the Commons had placed and replaced there, in order to declare the policy of parliament on matters ecclesiastical in Ireland. This involved a meaning which Mr. Gladstone declared that no power on earth could induce the Commons to accept. The crisis was of unsurpassed anxiety for the prime minister. He has fortunately left his own record of its phases : [1]—

Saturday, July 17.—On the 16th of July the amendments made by the Lords in the Irish Church bill had been completely disposed of by the House of Commons. The last division, taken on the disposal of the residue, had, chiefly through mere lazy absences, reduced the majority for the government to 72. This *relative* weakness offered a temptation

[1] The memorandum is dated Aug 14, 1869.

to the opposition to make play upon the point. The cabinet met the next forenoon. We felt on the one hand that it might be difficult to stake the bill on the clause for the disposal of the residue, supposing that to be the single remaining point of difference ; but that the postponement of this question would be a great moral and political evil, and that any concession made by us had far better be one that would be of some value to the disestablished church.

By desire of the cabinet I went to Windsor in the afternoon, and represented to H. M. what it was in our power to do ; namely, although we had done all we could do upon the merits, yet, for the sake of peace and of the House of Lords, [we were willing], (a) to make some one further pecuniary concession to the church of sensible though not very large amount ; (b) to make a further concession as to curates, slight in itself ; (c) to amend the residue clause so as to give to parliament the future control, and to be content with simply declaring the principle on which the property should be distributed. The Queen, while considering that she could not be a party to this or that particular scheme, agreed that it might be proper to make a representation to the archbishop to the general effect that the views of the government at this crisis of the measure were such as deserved to be weighed, and to promote confidential communication between us. She intimated her intention to employ the Dean of Windsor as a medium of communication between herself and the archbishop, and wished me to explain particulars fully to him. I went to the deanery, and, not finding the dean, had written as much as here follows on a scrap of paper, when he came in. . . .

The object of this paper was to induce the archbishop to discountenance any plan for pressing the postponement of the provisions respecting the residue, and to deal with us in preference respecting any practicable concession to the church. When the dean came in, I explained this further, recited the purport of my interview with the Queen, and on his asking me confidentially for his own information, I let him know that the further pecuniary concession we were prepared to recommend would be some £170,000 or £180,000.

Sunday, July 18.—In the afternoon Lord Granville called on me and brought me a confidential memorandum, containing an overture which Mr. Disraeli had placed in the hands of Lord Bessborough for communication to us. [Memorandum not recoverable.] He had represented the terms as those which he had with much difficulty induced Lord Cairns to consent to. While the contention as to the residue was abandoned, and pecuniary concessions alone were sought, the demand amounted, according to our computation, to between £900,000 and £1,000,000. . . . This it was evident was utterly inadmissible. I saw no possibility of approach to it ; and considered that a further quarter of a million or thereabouts was all that the House of Commons could be expected or asked further to concede. On the same afternoon Lord Granville, falling in with Mr. Goschen, asked him what he thought the very most that could be had—would it be £500,000 ? Goschen answered £300,000, and with this Glyn agreed. Mr. Disraeli desired an answer before three on Monday.

Monday, July 19.—Those members of the government who had acted as a sort of committee in the Irish church question met in the afternoon. We were all agreed in opinion that the Disraeli overture must be rejected, though without closing the door ; and a reply was prepared in this sense, which Lord Granville undertook to send. [*Draft, in the above sense that no sum approaching* £1,000,000 *could be entertained.*]

Meantime the archbishop had arrived in Downing Street, in pursuance of the arrangements of Saturday ; and a paper was either now drawn, or sanctioned by my colleagues, I do not remember which, in order to form the basis of my communication to the archbishop. I returned from my interview, and reported, as I afterwards did to the Dean of Windsor, that his tone was friendly, and that he appeared well disposed to the sort of arrangement I had sketched.

Tuesday, July 20.—The archbishop, who had communicated with Lord Cairns in the interval, came to me early to-day and brought a memorandum as a basis of agreement, which, to my surprise, demanded higher terms than those of Mr. Disraeli.[1] I told the archbishop the terms in which we had already expressed ourselves to Mr. Disraeli. . . . Meantime an answer had come from Mr. Disraeli stating that he could not do more. Then followed the meeting of the opposition peers at the Duke of Marlborough's.

On the meeting of the Houses, a few of us considered what course was to be taken if the Lords should again cast out of the preamble the words which precluded concurrent endowment ; and it was agreed to stay the proceedings for the time, and consider among ourselves what further to do. [Lord Granville has a pencil note on the margin, 'The first order I received was to throw up the bill, to which I answered that I could not do more than adjourn the debate.'] Lord Granville made this announcement accordingly after the Lords had, upon a hot debate and by a large majority, again excluded our words from the preamble [173 : 95]. This had been after a speech from Lord Cairns, in which he announced his intention of moving other amendments which he detailed, and which were in general conformable to the proposals already made to us. The first disposition of several of us this evening, myself included, was to regard the proceeding of the opposition as now complete ; since the whole had been announced, the first stroke struck, and the command shown of a force of peers amply sufficient to do the rest.[2] . . . The idea did not, however, include an absolute abandonment of the bill, but only the suspension of our responsibility for it, leaving the opposition to work their own will, and with the intention, when this had been done, of considering the matter further. . . .

Wednesday, July 21.—The cabinet met at 11 ; and I went to it in the mind of last night. We discussed, however, at great length all possible methods of proceeding that occurred to us. The result was stated in a

[1] 1. The Lords amendment as to curates to be adopted	.	£380,000
2. The Ulster glebes	. . . .	465,000
3. The glebehouses to be free	. . .	150,000
		£995,000
Or the Bishop of Peterborough's amendment as to the tax upon livings in lieu of No. 3, would carry a heavier charge by	. . . . . .	124,000
		£1,119,000

[2] The version in society was that 'Gladstone wanted to throw up the bill after the debate of last Tuesday, when the words of the preamble were re-inserted, but he was outvoted in his cabinet ; and it is said that Lord Granville told him that if he gave up the bill he must find somebody else to lead the Lords.'—(July 22, 1869), *Memoirs of an Ex-Minister*, ii. p. 409.

letter of mine to the Queen, of which I annex a copy. [*See Appendix. He enumerates the various courses considered, and states that the course adopted was to go through the endowment amendments, and if they were carried adversely, then to drop their responsibility.*]

Most of the cabinet were desirous to go on longer ; others, myself included, objected to proceeding to the end of the bill or undertaking to remit the bill again to the House of Commons as of our own motion. It occurred to me, however, that we might proceed as far as to the end of the many amendments, about the middle of the bill ; and this appeared to meet the views of all, even of those who would have preferred doing more, or less.

Thursday, July 22.—I was laid up to-day, and the transactions were carried on by Lord Granville, in communication with me from time to time at my house. First he brought me a note he had received from Lord Cairns.

This, dated July 22, was to the effect that Lord Cairns had no right and no desire to ask for any information as to the course proposed that night ; but that if the statements as to the intention of the government to proceed with the consideration of the amendments were correct, and if Lord Granville thought any advantage likely to result from it, Lord Cairns would be ready, 'as you know I have throughout been, to confer upon a mode by which without sacrifice of principle or dignity upon either side the remaining points of difference might be arranged.' The proceedings of this critical day are narrated by Lord Granville in a memorandum to Mr. Gladstone, dated August 4 :—

After seeing you I met Lord Cairns at the colonial office. He offered me terms.[1] . . . I asked him whether, in his opinion, he, the archbishop, and I could carry anything we agreed upon. He said, 'Yes, certainly.' After seeing you I met Lord Cairns a second time in his room at the House of Lords. I asked as a preliminary to giving any opinion on his amendments, how he proposed to deal with the preamble. He said, 'to leave it as amended by the Lords.' I then proposed the words which were afterwards adopted in the 68th clause. He was at first taken aback, but admitted that he had personally no objection to them. He asked what was the opposition to be feared. I suggested some from Lord Grey. He believed this to be certain, but immaterial. I objected *in toto* to Lord Salisbury's clause or its substitute. He was unwilling to yield, chiefly on Lord Salisbury's account, but finally consented. We agreed upon the commutation clause if the 7 and the 5 per cent were lumped together. On the curates clause we could come to no agreement. He proposed to see Lord Salisbury and the archbishop, and to meet again at four at the colonial office. He spoke with fairness as to the difficulty of his position, and the risk he ran with his own party. I again saw you and asked the Irish attorney-general to be present at the

[1] They were somewhat but not very greatly improved. The Ulster glebes, however, were gone. He now demanded : 1. The acceptance of the amendment respecting curates = £380,000 ; 2. Five per cent to be added to the seven per cent on commutations = £300,000 ; 3. The glebe houses to be given to the church at ten years' purchase of the sites, a slight modification of Lord Salisbury's amendment = £140,000. From this it appeared that even in the mid hours of this final day Lord Cairns asked above £800,000.

last interview. I stated to him in Lord Cairns's presence how far we
agreed, and expressed my regret that on the last point—the curates—
our difference was irreconcilable. Lord Cairns said he hoped not, and
proceeded to argue strongly in favour of his proposal. He at last, however, at 4.30, compromised the matter by accepting five years instead of
one. I shook his hand, which was trembling with nervousness. We
discussed the form of announcing the arrangement to the House. We
at once agreed it was better to tell the whole truth, and soon settled
that it would be better for its success that he should announce the
details. I was afterwards apprehensive that this latter arrangement
might be disadvantageous to us, but nothing could be better or fairer
than his statement. I cannot finish this statement, which I believe is
accurate, without expressing my admiration at the firmness and conciliation which you displayed in directing me in all these negotiations.

'The news was brought to me on my sofa,' Mr. Gladstone
says, 'and between five and six I was enabled to telegraph to
the Queen. My telegram was followed up by a letter at 7 P.M.,
which announced that the arrangement had been accepted by
the House of Lords, and that a general satisfaction prevailed.'
To the Queen he wrote (July 22) :—

Mr. Gladstone is at a loss to account for the great change in the tone
and views of the opposition since Sunday and Monday, and even Tuesday
last, but on this topic it is needless to enter. As to the principal matters,
the basis of the arrangement on the side of the government is much the
same as was intended when Mr. Gladstone had the honour of an audience
at Windsor on Saturday ; but various minor concessions have been added.
Mr. Gladstone does not doubt that, if the majority of the House of Lords
should accede to the advice of Lord Cairns, the government will be able
to induce the House of Commons to agree on the conditions proposed.
Mr. Gladstone would in vain strive to express to your Majesty the relief,
thankfulness, and satisfaction, with which he contemplates not only the
probable passing of what many believe to be a beneficent and necessary
measure, but the undoubted and signal blessing of an escape from a
formidable constitutional conflict. The skill, patience, assiduity, and
sagacity of Lord Granville in the work of to-day demand from Mr.
Gladstone the tribute of his warm admiration.

On reviewing this whole transaction, and doing full justice
to the attitude both of the Queen and the archbishop, the
reader will be inclined to agree with old Lord Halifax :—'I
think we owe a good turn to Cairns, without whose *decision* on
Thursday I hardly think that the settlement could have been
effected. Indeed Derby's conduct proves what difficulty there
would have been, if Cairns had not taken upon himself the
responsibility of acting as he did.'

Among interesting letters was one from Manning :—(July
24) 'My joy over the event is not only as a catholic, though
that must be, as it ought to be, my highest motive, but as an
Englishman to whom, as I remember your once saying, the old
English monarchy is dear next after the catholic church. But
at this time I will only add that I may wish you joy on

personal reasons. I could hardly have hoped that you could so have framed, mastered, and carried through the bill from first to last so complete, so unchanged in identity of principle and detail, and let me add with such unwearying and sustained self-control and forbearance.'

The diary gives us a further glimpse of these agitating days :—

July 20.—Conclave of colleagues on Irish church proceedings. An anxious day, a sad evening. 21.—Cabinet 11-2¼, stiff, but good. 22.— I was obliged to take to my sofa and spent the day so in continual interviews with Granville, Glyn, West, Sullivan—especially the first—on the details and particulars of the negotiations respecting the Irish Church bill. The favourable issue left me almost unmanned in the reaction from a sharp and stern tension of mind. 23.—My attack did not lessen. Dr. Clark came in the morning and made me up for the House, whither I went 2-5 P.M., to propose concurrence in the Lords' amendments. Up to the moment I felt very weak, but this all vanished when I spoke and while the debate lasted. Then I went back to bed. 25.—Weak still. I presumed over much in walking a little and fell back at night to my lowest point.

Sir Robert Phillimore records :—

July 21.—Found Gladstone at breakfast, calm, pale, but without a doubt as to the course which the government must pursue, viz. : to maintain upon every important point the bill as sent back by the Commons, probably an autumn session, a bill sternly repeated by the Commons, too probably without the clauses favourable to the Irish church. 23.— Nothing talked or written of but the political marvel of yesterday. Gladstone in a speech universally praised proposed to the House of Commons the bill as now modified, and it passed with much harmony, broken by an Orange member. Gladstone very unwell, and ought to have been in bed when he made his speech. 24.—Gladstone still very weak but in a state of calm happiness at the unexpected turn which the Irish bill had taken. Does not now know the origin or history of the sudden resolution on the part of the leaders of the opposition. I am satisfied that Disraeli was alarmed and thoroughly frightened at the state of the House of Commons and the country, that Cairns was determined to regain what he had practically lost or was losing, the leadership of the Lords, and that many of his party were frightened at the madness and folly of Tuesday night considered after a day's reflection. . . . Above all there was a well-grounded alarm on the part of Cairns and his immediate supporters in the Lords, that their order was in imminent danger. Bluster disappeared, and a retreat, as decent as well could be expected, was made from a situation known to be untenable. They had never expected that Gladstone would drop the bill. 25.—Much conversation with Gladstone, who is still very weak. He wrote to the Archbishop of Dublin to say in effect, that as a private churchman he would be glad to assist in any way the archbishop could point out in the organizing of the voluntary church in Ireland.

Sir Thomas Acland writes, August 3, 1869 :—

I stayed at House of Commons perforce till about 1.30 or 2, and then walked away with Gladstone through the Park. It is beautiful to see his intense enjoyment of the cool fresh air, the trees, the sky, the gleaming of light on the water, all that is refreshing in contrast to the din of politics.

A month later the Archbishop of Canterbury found Mr. Gladstone at Lord Granville's at Walmer Castle :—

Reached Walmer Castle about 6.30. Found Gladstone lying in blankets on the ramparts eating his dinner, looking still very ill. . . . He joined us at night full of intelligence. His fierce vigour all the better for being a little tempered. . . . Much interesting conversation about the state of the church and morality in Wales, also about leading ecclesiastics. I gather that he will certainly nominate Temple for a bishopric.[1]

[1] *Life of Archbishop Tait*, ii. p. 45.

CHAPTER II

FIRST CHAPTER OF AN AGRARIAN REVOLUTION

(1870)

The Irish Land Act of 1870 in its consequences was certainly one of the most important measures of the nineteenth century.—LECKY.

IN the beginning of 1870 one of Mr. Gladstone's colleagues wrote of him to another, 'I fear that he is steering straight upon the rocks.' So it might well seem to any who knew the unplumbed depths on which he had to shape his voyage. Irish history has been said to resemble that of Spain for the last three centuries,—the elaboration of all those ideas of law and political economy most unsuited to the needs of the nation concerned. Such ideas, deeply cherished in Britain where they had succeeded, Mr. Gladstone was now gradually drawn forward to reverse and overthrow in Ireland where they had ended in monstrous failure. Here a pilot's eye might well see jagged reefs. The occasion was the measure for dealing with the land of Ireland, that he had promised at the election. The difficulty arose from the huge and bottomless ignorance of those in whose hands the power lay. Mr. Gladstone in the course of these discussions said, and said truly, of the learned Sir Roundell Palmer, that he knew no more of land tenures in Ireland than he knew of land tenures in the moon. At the beginning much the same might have been observed of the cabinet, of the two houses of parliament, and of the whole mass of British electors. No doubt one effect of this great ignorance was to make Mr. Gladstone dictator. Still ignorance left all the more power to prejudice and interests. We may imagine the task. The cabinet was in the main made up of landlords, lawyers, hardened and convicted economists,—not economists like Mill, but men saturated with English ideas of contract, of competitive rent, of strict rule of supply and demand. Mr. Bright, it is true, had a profound conviction that the root of Irish misery and disorder lay in the land question. Here he saw far and deep. But then Mr. Bright had made up his mind that the proper solution of the land question was the gradual transformation of the tenants into owners, and this strong preconception somewhat narrowed his vision. Even while Mr. Gladstone was in the middle of his battle on the church, Bright wrote to him (May 21, '69):—

When the Irish church question is out of the way, we shall find all Ireland, north and south alike, united in demanding something on the land question much broader than anything hitherto offered or proposed in compensation bills. If the question is to go on without any real remedy for the grievance, the condition of Ireland in this particular will become worse, and measures far beyond anything I now contemplate will be necessary. I am most anxious to meet the evil before it is too great for control, and my plan *will meet* it without wrong to any man.

'I have studied the Irish land question,' said Bright, 'from a point of view almost inaccessible to the rest of your colleagues, and from which possibly even you have not had the opportunity of regarding it. . . . I hope you are being refreshed, as I am, after the long nights in the House—long nights which happily were not fruitless. I only hope our masters in the other House will not undo what we have done.' Mr. Gladstone replied the next day, opening with a sentence that, if addressed to any one less revered than Bright, might have seemed to veil a sarcasm :—' I have this advantage for learning the Irish land question, that I do not set out with the belief that I know it already ; and certainly no effort that I can make to acquire the mastery of it will be wanting.' He then proceeds to express his doubts as to the government embarking on a very large operation of land-jobbing, buying up estates from landlords and reselling them to tenants ; and whether the property bought and sold again by the state would not by force of economic laws gradually return again to fewer hands. He then comes still closer to the pith of the matter when he says to Mr. Bright :—' Your plan, if adopted in full, could only extend to a small proportion of the two or three hundred millions worth of land in Ireland ; and I do not well see how the unprotected tenants of the land in general would take essential benefit from the purchase and owning of land by a few of their fortunate brethren.' If the land question was urgent, and Bright himself, like Mill, thought that it was, this answer of Mr. Gladstone's was irrefragable. In acknowledging the despatch of this correspondence from Mr. Gladstone, Lord Granville says to him (May 26, 1869) :—

This question may break us up. Bright is thin-skinned ; the attacks in the Lords ruffle him more than he chooses to admit. I cannot make out how far he likes office, the cabinet, and his new position. It will be particularly disagreeable to him to have this plan, of which he is so much enamoured and for which he has received so much blame and a little praise, snuffed out by the cabinet. And yet how is it possible to avoid it, even putting aside the strong opinions of Lowe, Cardwell, and others ? My only hope is that you have got the germ of some larger and more comprehensive plan in your head, than has yet been developed.

The plan ultimately adopted, after a severe struggle and with momentous consequences, did not first spring from Mr. Gladstone's brain. The idea of adapting the law to custom in all its depth and breadth, and extending the rooted notion of tenant-right to its furthest bearings, was necessarily a plant of Irish and not of English growth. Mr. Chichester Fortescue, the Irish chief secretary and an Irishman, first opened a bold expansion of the familiar principle of many tenant-right bills. He had introduced such a bill himself in 1866, and the conservative government had brought in another in 1867. It is believed that he was instigated to adopt the new and bolder line by Sir Edward Sullivan, then the Irish attorney-general. Away from Sullivan, it was observed, he had little to say of value about his plan. In the cabinet Fortescue was not found effective, but he was thoroughly at home in the subject, and his speeches in public on Irish business had all the cogency of a man speaking his native tongue, and even genius in an acquired language is less telling. What is astonishing is the magic of the rapid and sympathetic penetration with which Mr. Gladstone went to the heart of the problem, as it was presented to him by his Irish advisers. This was his way. When acts of policy were not of great or immediate concern, he took them as they came ; but when they pressed for treatment and determination, then he swooped down upon them with the strength and vision of an eagle.

II

His career in the most deeply operative portion of it was so intimately concerned with Ireland, that my readers will perhaps benignantly permit a page or two of historic digression. I know the subject seems uninviting. My apology must be that it occupied no insignificant portion of Mr. Gladstone's public life, and that his treatment of it made one of his deepest marks on the legislation of the century. After all, there is no English-speaking community in any part of the wide globe, where our tragic mismanagement of the land of Ireland, and of those dwelling on it and sustained by it, has not left its unlucky stamp.

If Englishmen and Scots had not found the theme so uninviting, if they had given a fraction of the attention to the tenure and history of Irish land, that was bestowed, say, upon the Seisachtheia of Solon at Athens, or the Sempronian law in ancient Rome, this chapter in our annals would not have been written. As it was, parliament had made laws for landlord and tenant in Ireland without well understanding what is either an Irish landlord or an Irish tenant. England has been able to rule India, Mill said, because the business of ruling devolved upon men who passed their lives in India, and made Indian interests their regular occupation. India has on the whole been governed with a pretty full perception of its differences from England. Ireland on the contrary, suffering a worse misfortune than absentee landlords, was governed by an absentee parliament. In England, property means the rights of the rent-receiver who has equipped the land and prepared it for the capital and the skill of the tenant. In Ireland, in the minds of the vast majority of the population, for reasons just as good, property includes rights of the cultivator, whose labour has drained the land, and reclaimed it, and fenced it, and made farm-roads, and put a dwelling and farm buildings on it, and given to it all the working value that it possesses. We need suppose no criminality on either side. The origin of the difference was perfectly natural. In Ireland the holdings were small and multitudinous ; no landlord who was not a millionaire, could have prepared and equipped holdings numbered by hundreds of thousands ; and if he could, the hundreds and thousands of tenants had not a straw of capital. This peculiarity in social circumstances made it certain, therefore, that if the moral foundation of modern ideas of property is that he who sows shall reap, the idea of property would grow up in the mind of the cultivator, whenever the outer climate permitted the growth in his mind of any ideas of moral or equitable right at all.

In 1845 the Devon Commission had reported that it is the tenant who has made the improvements ; that large confiscations of these improvements had been systematically practised in the shape of progressive enhancements of rent ; that crime and disorder sprang from the system ; and that parliament ought to interfere. A bill was proposed by the Peel government in 1845 for protecting the rightful interests of the tenant against the landlord. It was introduced in the House mainly composed of landlords. There it had such contumelious greeting, that it was speedily dropped. This was a crowning illustration of the levity of the imperial parliament dealing with Irish problems. The vital necessity for readjusting the foundations of social life demonstrated ; a half measure languidly attempted ; attempt dropped ; bills sent to slumber in limbo ; dry rot left quietly alone for a whole generation, until bloody outrage and murder awoke legislative conscience or roused executive fear. The union was seventy years old before the elementary feature in the agrarian condition of Ireland was recognised by the parliament which had undertaken to govern Ireland. Before the union Ireland was governed by the British cabinet, through the Irish landed gentry, according to their views, and in their interests. After the union it was just the same. She was treated as a turbulent and infected province within the larger island ; never as a community with an internal economy peculiarly her own, with special sentiments, history, recollections, points of view, and necessities all her own. Between the union and the year 1870, Acts dealing with Irish land had been passed at Westminster. Every one of these Acts was in the interest of the landlord and against the tenant. A score of Insurrection Acts, no Tenant-right Act. Meanwhile Ireland had gone down into the dark gulfs of the Famine (1846-7).

Anybody can now see that the true view of the Irish cultivator was to regard him as a kind of copyholder or customary freeholder, or whatever other name best fits a man who has possessory interests in a piece of land, held at the landlord's will, but that will controlled by custom. In Ulster, and in an embryo degree elsewhere, this was what in a varying and irregular way actually had come about. Agrarian customs developed that undoubtedly belong to a backward social system, but they sprang from the necessities of the case. The essence of such customs in Ulster was first, a fair rent to be fixed not by competition, but by valuation, and exclusive of tenant's improvements ; second, the right of the tenant to transfer to somebody else his goodwill, or whatever else we may call his right of occupancy in the holding.

Instead of adapting law to custom, habit, practice, and equity, parliament proceeded to break all this down. With well-meaning but blind violence it imported into Ireland after the famine the English idea of landed property and contract. Or rather, it imported these ideas into Ireland with a definiteness and formality that would have been impracticable even in England. Just as good people thought they could easily make Ireland protestant if only she could be got within ear-shot of evangelical truth, so statesmen expected that a few clauses on a parchment would suffice to root out at a stroke the inveterate habits and ideas of long generations. We talk of revolutionary doctrinaires in France and other countries. History hardly shows such revolutionary doctrinaires anywhere as the whig and tory statesmen who tried to regenerate Ireland in the middle of the nineteenth century. They first of all passed an Act (1849) inviting the purchase of the estates of an insolvent landlord upon precisely the same principles as governed the purchase of his pictures or his furniture. We passed the Encumbered Estates Act, Mr. Gladstone said, 'with lazy, heedless, uninformed good intentions.' The important rights given by custom and equity to the cultivator were suddenly extinguished by the supreme legal right of the rent-receiver. About one-eighth of the whole area of the country is estimated to have changed hands on these terms. The extreme of wretchedness and confusion naturally followed. Parliament thought this must be due to some misunderstanding. That there might be no further mistake, it next proceeded formally to declare (1860) that the legal relations between land-lord and tenant in Ireland were to be those of strict contract.[1] Thus blunder was clenched by blunder. The cultivators were terror-struck, and agitation waxed hot.

Oliver Cromwell had a glimpse of the secret in 1649. 'These poor people,' he said, 'have been accustomed to as much in-justice and oppression from their landlords, the great men, and those who should have done them right, as any people in that which we call Christendom. Sir, if justice were freely and impartially administered here, the foregoing darkness and corruption would make it look so much the more glorious and beautiful.' It was just two hundred and twenty years before another ruler of England saw as deep, and applied his mind to the free doing of justice.

III

Almost immediately after recovering from the fatigues of the session of 1869, Mr. Gladstone threw himself upon his new task, his imagination vividly excited by its magnitude and its possibilities. 'For the last three months,' he writes to the Duke of Argyll (Dec. 5), 'I have worked daily, I think, upon the question, and so I shall continue to do. The literature of it is large, larger than I can master; but I feel the benefit of continued reading upon it. We have before us a crisis, and a great crisis, for us all, to put it on no higher ground, and a great honour or a great disgrace. As I do not mean to fail through want of perseverance, so neither will I wilfully err through precipitancy, or through want of care and desire at least to meet all apprehensions which are warranted by even the show of reason.'

It was not reading alone that brought him round to the full measure of securing the cultivator in his holding. The crucial suggestion, the expediency, namely, of making the landlord pay compensation to the tenant for disturbing him, came from Ireland. To Mr. Chichester Fortescue, the Irish secretary, Mr. Gladstone writes (Sept. 15) :—

I heartily wish it were possible that you, Sullivan, and I could have some of those preliminary conversations on land, which were certainly of great use in the first stages of the Irish Church bill. As this is difficult, let us try to compare notes as well as we can in writing. I anticipate that many members of the cabinet will find it hard to extend their views to what the exigencies of the time, soberly considered, now require ; but patience, prudence, and good feeling will, I hope, surmount all obstacles.

Like you, I am unwilling to force a peasant proprietary into existence.

[1] When the present writer once referred to the principle of the Act of 1860 as being that the hiring of land is just as much founded on trade principles as the chartering of a ship or the hiring of a street cab, loud approbation came from the tory benches. So deep was parliamentary ignorance of Ireland even in 1887, after the Acts of 1870 and 1881.—*Hansard*, 314, p. 295.

. . . The first point in this legislation, viz., that the presumption of law should give improvements to the tenant, is now, I suppose, very widely admitted, but no longer suffices to settle the question. . . . Now as to your 'compensation for disturbance.' This is indeed a question full of difficulty. It is very desirable to prevent the using of augmentation of rent as a method of eviction. I shall be most curious to see the means and provisions you may devise, without at present being too sanguine.

Meanwhile he notes to Lord Granville (Sept. 22) how critical and arduous the question is, within as well as without the cabinet, and wonders whether they ought not to be thinking of a judicious cabinet committee :—

The question fills the public mind in an extraordinary degree, and we can hardly avoid some early step towards making progress in it. A committee keeps a cabinet quiet. It is highly necessary that we should be quite ready when parliament meets, and yet there is so much mental movement upon the question from day to day, as we see from a variety of curious utterances (that of the *Times* included), that it is desirable to keep final decisions open. Much information will be open, and this a committee can prepare in concert with the Irish government. It also, I think, affords a means of bringing men's minds together.

He tells the Irish secretary that so far as he can enter into the secretary's views, he 'enters thoroughly into the spirit of them.' But many members of the cabinet, laden sufficiently with their own labours, had probably not so closely followed up the matter :—

The proposition, that *more* than compensation to tenants for their improvements will be necessary in order to settle the Irish land laws, will be unpalatable, or new, to several, and naturally enough. You will have observed the total difference in the internal situation between this case and that of the Irish church, where upon all the greater points our measure was in a manner outlined for us by the course of previous transactions.

At the end of October the question was brought formally before the cabinet :—

Oct. 30.—Cabinet, 2-5½. . . . We broke ground very satisfactorily on the question of Irish land. *Nov.* 3.—Cabinet. Chiefly on Irish land, and stiff. 9.—To Guildhall, where I spoke for the government. The combination of physical effort with measured words is difficult. 22.— Worked six hours on my books, arranging and re-arranging. The best brain rest I have had, I think, since December last.

The brain rest was not for long. On Dec. 1 he tells Lord Granville that Argyll is busy on Irish land, and in his views is misled by 'the rapid facility of his active mind.' 'It is rather awkward at this stage to talk of breaking up the government, and that is more easily said than done.' I know no more singular reading in its way than the correspondence between Mr. Gladstone and the Duke of Argyll ; Mr. Gladstone trying to lead his argumentative colleague over one or two of the barest rudiments of the history of Irish land, and occasionally showing in the process somewhat of the quality of the superior pupil teacher acquiring to-day material for the lesson of to-morrow. Mr. Gladstone goes to the root of the matter when he says to the Duke :—'What I would most earnestly entreat of you is not to rely too much on Highland experience, but to acquaint yourself by careful reading with the rather extensive facts and history of the Irish land question. My own studies in it are very imperfect, though pursued to the best of my ability ; but they have revealed to me many matters of fact which have seriously modified my views, most of them connected with and branching out of the very wide extension of the idea and even the practice of tenant right, mostly perhaps *unrecognised* beyond the limits of the Ulster custom.'

Then Lord Granville writes to him that Clarendon has sent him two letters running, talking of the certainty of the government being broken up. 'The sky is very far from clear,' Mr. Gladstone says to Mr. Fortescue (Dec. 3), 'but we must bate no jot of heart or hope.' The next day it is Mr. Bright to whom he turns in friendly earnest admonition. His words will perhaps be useful to many generations of cabinet ministers :—

It is not the courageous part of your paper to which I now object, though I doubt the policy of the reference to feebleness and timidity, as men in a cabinet do not like what may *seem* to imply that they are cowards. It is your argument (a very overstrained one in my opinion) against Fortescue's propositions, and your proposal (so it reads) to put them back in order of discussion to the second place *now*, when the mind of the cabinet has been upon them for six weeks. . . . Had the cabinet adopted at this moment *a good and sufficient scheme for dealing with the Irish tenants as tenants*, I should care little how much you depreciated such a scheme in comparison with one for converting them into owners. But the state of things is most critical. This is not a time at which those who in substance agree, can afford to throw away strength by the *relative* depreciation of those parts of a plan of relief, to which they do not themselves give the first place in importance. It is most dangerous to discredit *propositions which you mean to adopt*, in the face of any who (as yet) do not mean to adopt them, and who may consistently and honourably use all your statements against them, nay, who would really be bound to do so. No part of what I have said is an argument against your propositions. . . . If your seven propositions were law to-day, you would have made but a very small progress towards settling the land question of Ireland. For all this very plain speech, you will, I am sure, forgive me.

A letter from Mr. Gladstone to Fortescue (Dec. 5) shows the competition between Bright's projects of purchase by state-aid, and the scheme for dealing with the tenants as tenants :—

I am a good deal staggered at the idea of any interference with present rents. But I shall not speak on this subject to others. It will be difficult enough to carry the substance of the plan you proposed, without any enlargement of it. I hope to see you again before the question comes on

in the cabinet. . . . Bright is very full of waste lands, and generally of
his own plans, considerably (at present) to the detriment of yours. He
wants the government to buy waste lands, and says it is not against
political economy, but yours is. I think he will come right. It appears
to me we might in the case of waste lands lend money (on proper conditions) to *any buyers*; in the case of other lands we are only to lend
to occupiers. What do you think of this?

At this date he was still in doubt whether anybody would
agree to interference with existing rents, but he had for himself
hit upon the principle that became the foundation of his law.
He put to Fortescue (Dec. 9) as a material point :—

Whether it is expedient to adopt, wherever it can be made available,
*the custom of the country as the basis for compensation on eviction and the
like.* I cannot make out from your papers whether you wholly dissent
from this. I hoped you had agreed in it. I have acquired a strong conviction upon it, of which I have written out the grounds ; but I shall not
circulate the paper till I understand your views more fully.

Lowe, at the other extremity, describes himself as more and
more 'oppressed by a feeling of heavy responsibility and an
apprehension of serious danger,' and feeling that he and the
minority (Clarendon, Argyll, and Cardwell—of whom he was
much the best hand at an argument)—were being driven to
choose between their gravest convictions, and their allegiance
to party and cabinet. They agreed to the presumption of law
as to the making of improvements ; to compensation for improvements, retrospective and prospective ; to the right of new
tenants at will to compensation on eviction. The straw that
broke the camel's back was compensation for eviction, where no
custom could be proved in the case of an existing tenancy.
Mr. Gladstone wrote a long argumentative letter to Lord
Granville to be shown to Lowe, and it was effectual. Lowe
thought the tone of it very fair and the arguments of the right
sort, but nevertheless he added, in the words I have already
quoted, 'I fear he is steering straight upon the rocks.'

What might surprise us, if anything in Irish doings could
surprise us, is that though this was a measure for Irish tenants,
it was deemed heinously wrong to ascertain directly from their
representatives what the Irish tenants thought. Lord Bessborough was much rebuked in London for encouraging Mr.
Gladstone to communicate with Sir John Gray, the owner of
the great newspaper of the Irish tenant class. Yet Lord
O'Hagan, the chancellor, who had the rather relevant advantage
of being of the same stock and faith as three-fourths of the
nation concerned, told them that ' the success or failure of the
Land bill depends on the *Freeman's Journal* ; if it says, We
accept this as a fixity of tenure, every priest will say the same,
and *vice versâ*.' It was, however, almost a point of honour in
those days for British cabinets to make Irish laws out of their
own heads.

Nearly to the last the critical contest in the cabinet went on. Fortescue fought as well as he could even against the prime minister himself, as the following from Mr. Gladstone to him shows (Jan. 12) :—

> There can surely be no advantage in further argument between you and me at this stage—especially after so many hours and pages of it—on the recognition of usage beyond the limit of Ulster custom as a distinct head. You pressed your view repeatedly on the cabinet, which did not adopt it. Till the cabinet alters its mind, we have no option except to use every effort to get the bill drawn according to its instructions.

How much he had his Irish plans at heart, Mr. Gladstone showed by his urgency that the Queen should open parliament. His letter to her (Jan. 15) on the subject, he told Lord Granville, 'expresses my desire, not founded on ordinary motives, nor having reference to ordinary circumstances' :—

> We have now to deal with the *gros* of the Irish question, and the Irish question is in a category by itself. It would be almost a crime in a minister to omit anything that might serve to mark, and bring home to the minds of men, the gravity of the occasion. Moreover, I am persuaded that the Queen's own sympathies would be, not as last year, but in the same current as ours. To this great country the state of Ireland after seven hundred years of our tutelage is in my opinion so long as it continues, an intolerable disgrace, and a danger so absolutely transcending all others, that I call it the only real danger of the noble empire of the Queen. I cannot refrain from bringing before her in one shape or another my humble advice that she should, if *able*, open parliament.

IV

Public opinion was ripening. The *Times* made a contribution of the first importance to the discussion, in a series of letters from a correspondent, that almost for the first time brought the facts of Irish land before the general public. A pamphlet from Mill, then at the height of his influence upon both writers and readers, startled them by the daring proposition that the only plan was to buy out the landlords. The whole host of whig economists and lawyers fell heavily upon him in consequence. The new voters showed that they were not afraid of new ideas. It was not until Jan. 25 that peril was at an end inside the government :—

> *Jan.* 25, '70.—Cabinet. The great difficulties of the Irish Land bill *there* are now over. Thank God! *Feb.* 7.—With the Prince of Wales 3¼-4¼ explaining to him the Land bill, and on other matters. He has certainly much natural intelligence. 15.—H. of C. Introduced the Irish Land bill in a speech of 3¼ hours. Well received by the House at large. *Query*, the Irish popular party ?

Lord Dufferin, an Irish landlord, watching, as he admits, with considerable jealousy exceptional legislation in respect to Ireland, heard the speech from the peers' gallery, and wrote to

Mr. Gladstone the next day :—'I feel there is no one else in the country who could have recommended the provisions of such a bill to the House of Commons, with a slighter shock to the prejudices of the class whose interests are chiefly concerned.' He adds : 'I happened to find myself next to Lord Cairns. When you had done, he told me he did not think his people would oppose any of the leading principles of your bill.'

The policy of the bill as tersely explained by Mr. Gladstone in a letter to Manning, compressing as he said eight or ten columns of the *Times*, was 'to prevent the landlord from using the terrible weapon of undue and unjust eviction, by so framing the handle that it shall cut his hands with the sharp edge of pecuniary damages. The man evicted without any fault, and suffering the usual loss by it, will receive whatever the custom of the country gives, and where there is no custom, according to a scale, besides whatever he can claim for permanent buildings or reclamation of land. Wanton eviction will, as I hope, be extinguished by provisions like these. And if they extinguish wanton eviction, they will also extinguish those demands for *unjust* augmentations of rent, which are only formidable to the occupier, because the power of wanton or arbitrary eviction is behind them.' What seems so simple, and what was so necessary, marked in truth a vast revolutionary stride. It transferred to the tenant a portion of the absolute ownership, and gave him something like an estate in his holding. The statute contained a whole code of minor provisions, including the extension of Mr. Bright's clauses for peasant proprietorship in the Church Act, but this transfer was what gave the Act its place in solid legal form.

The second reading was carried by 442 to 11, the minority being composed of eight Irish members of advanced type, and three English tories, including Mr. Henley and Mr. James Lowther, himself Irish secretary eight years later. The bill was at no point fought high by the opposition. Mr. Disraeli moved an amendment limiting compensation to unexhausted improvements. The government majority fell to 76, 'a result to be expected,' Mr. Gladstone reports, 'considering the natural leanings of English and Scotch members to discount in Ireland what they would not apply in Great Britain. They are not very familiar with Irish land tenures.' One fact of much significance he notes in these historic proceedings. Disraeli, he writes to the Duke of Argyll (April 21, 1870), 'has not spoken one word against valuation of rents or perpetuity of tenure.' It was from the house of his friends that danger came :—

April 4.—H. of C. Spoke on Disraeli's amendment. A majority of 76, but the navigation is at present extremely critical. 7.—H. of C. A most ominous day from end to end. Early in the evening I gave a review of the state of the bill, and later another menace of overturn if the motion of Mr. William Fowler [a liberal banker], which Palmer had unfortunately (as is too common with him) brought into importance, should be carried. We had a majority of only 32.

To Lord Russell he writes (April 12) :—

I am in the hurry-scurry of preparation for a run into the country this evening, but I must not omit to thank you for your very kind and welcome letter. We have had a most anxious time in regard to the Irish Land bill. . . . The fear that our Land bill may cross the water creates a sensitive state of mind among all tories, many whigs, and a few radicals. Upon this state of things comes Palmer with his legal mind, legal point of view, legal aptitude and inaptitude (*vide* Mr. Burke), and stirs these susceptibilities to such a point that he is always near bringing us to grief. Even Grey more or less goes with him.

Phillimore records a visit in these critical days :—

April 8.—Gladstone looked worn and fagged. Very affectionate and confidential. Annoyed at Palmer's conduct. Gladstone feels keenly the want of support in debate. Bright ill. Lowe no moral weight. ' I feel when I have spoken, that I have not a shot in my locker.'

As a very accomplished journalist of the day wrote, there was something almost painful in the strange phenomenon of a prime minister fighting as it were all but single-handed the details of his own great measure through the ambuscades and charges of a numerous and restless enemy—and of an enemy determined apparently to fritter away the principle of the measure under the pretence of modifying its details. ' No prime minister has ever attempted any task like it—a task involving the most elaborate departmental readiness, in addition to the general duties and fatigues of a prime minister, and that too in a session when questions are showered like hail upon the treasury bench.' [1]

Then the government put on pressure, and the majority sprang up to 80. The debate in the Commons lasted over three and a half months, or about a fortnight longer than had been taken by the Church bill. The third reading was carried without a division. In the Lords the bill was read a second time without a division. Few persons ' clearly foresaw that it was the first step of a vast transfer of property, and that in a few years it would become customary for ministers of the crown to base all their legislation on the doctrine that Irish land is not an undivided ownership, but a simple partnership.' [2]

In March Mr. Gladstone had received from Manning a memorandum of ill omen from the Irish bishops, setting out the amendments by them thought necessary. This paper included the principles of perpetuity of tenure for the tiller of the soil and the adjustment of rent by a court. The reader may judge for himself how impossible it would have been, even for Mr. Gladstone, in all the plenitude of his power, to

---

[1] *Spectator.*   [2] Lecky, *Democracy and Liberty,* i. p. 165.

persuade either cabinet or parliament to adopt such invasions of prevailing doctrine. For this, ten years more of agitation were required, and then he was able to complete the memorable chapter in Irish history that he had now opened.

V

Neither the Land Act nor the Church Act at once put out the hot ashes of Fenianism. A Coercion Act was passed in the spring of 1870. In the autumn Mr. Gladstone tried to persuade the cabinet to approve the release of the Fenian prisoners, but it was not until the end of the year that he prevailed. A secret committee was thought necessary in 1871 to consider outrages in Westmeath, and a repressive law was passed in consequence. Mr. Gladstone himself always leaned strongly against these exceptional laws, and pressed the Irish government hard the other way. 'What we have to do,' he said, 'is to defy Fenianism, to rely on public sentiment, and so provide (as we have been doing) the practical measures that place the public sentiment on our side, an operation which I think is retarded by any semblance of *severity* to those whose offence we admit among ourselves to have been an ultimate result of our misgovernment of the country. I am afraid that local opinion has exercised, habitually and traditionally, too much influence in Ireland, and has greatly compromised the character of the empire. *This* question I take to be in most of its aspects an imperial question.' The proposal for a secret committee was the occasion of a duel between him and Disraeli (Feb. 27, 1871)—'both,' said Lord Granville, 'very able, but very bitter.' The tory leader taunted Mr. Gladstone for having recourse to such a proceeding, after posing as the only man capable of dealing with the evils of Ireland, and backed by a majority which had legalised confiscation, consecrated sacrilege, and condoned high treason.

CHAPTER III

EDUCATION—THE CAREER AND THE TALENTS

(1870)

He that taketh away weights from the motions, doth the same as he that addeth wings.—PYM.

AMID dire controversies that in all countries surround all questions of the school, some believe the first government of Mr. Gladstone in its dealing with education to have achieved its greatest constructive work. Others think that, on the contrary, it threw away a noble chance. In the new scheme of national education established in 1870, the head of the government rather acquiesced than led. In his own words, his responsibility was that of concurrence rather than of authorship. His close absorption in the unfamiliar riddles of Irish land, besides the mass of business incident to the office of prime minister, might well account for his small share in the frame of the education bill. More than this, however, his private interest in public education did not amount to zeal, and it was at bottom the interest of a churchman. Mr. Gladstone afterwards wrote to Lord Granville (June 14, '74), 'I have never made greater personal concessions of opinion than I did on the Education bill to the united representatives of Ripon and Forster.' His share in the adjustments of the Act was, as he said afterwards, a very simple one, and he found no occasion either to differ from departmental colleagues, or to press upon them any proposals of his own. If they had been dealing with an untouched case, he would have preferred the Scotch plan, which allowed the local school board to prescribe whatever religious education pleased it best. Nor did he object to a strict limitation of all teaching paid for in schools aided or provided out of public money, whether rate or tax, to purely secular instruction. In that case, however, he held strongly that subject to local consent, the master who gave the secular teaching should be allowed to give religious teaching also at other times, even within the school-house.[1]

[1] Article on Mr. Forster, *Nineteenth Century*, September 1888.

What Mr. Gladstone cared for was the integrity of religious instruction. What he disliked or dreaded was, in his own language, the invasion of that integrity 'under cover of protecting exceptional consciences.' The advance of his ideas is rather interesting. So far back as 1843,[1] in considering the education clauses of the Factory bill of that year, he explained to Lord Lyttelton that he was not prepared to limit church teaching in the schools to the exposition of scripture. Ten years later, he wrote to his close friend, Bishop Hamilton of Salisbury :—

I am not friendly to the idea of constraining by law either the total or the partial suppression of conscientious differences in religion, with a view to fusion of different sects whether in church or school. I believe that the free development of conviction is upon the whole the system most in favour both of truth and of charity. Consequently you may well believe that I contemplate with satisfaction the state of feeling that prevails in England, and that has led all governments to adopt the system of separate and independent subsidies to the various religious denominations.

As for the government bill of that year (1853), he entirely repudiated the construction put upon some of its clauses, namely, 'that people having the charge of schools would be obliged to admit children of all religious creeds, as well as that having admitted them, they would be put under control as to the instruction to be given.' Ten years later still, we find him saying, 'I deeply regret the aversion to "conscience clauses," which I am convinced it would be most wise for the church to adopt. As far back as 1838 I laboured hard to get the National Society to act upon this principle permissively ; and if I remember right, it was with the approval of the then Bishop of London.' In 1865 he harps on the same string in a letter to Lord Granville :—

. . . Suppose the schoolmaster is reading with his boys the third chapter of St. John, and he explains the passage relating to baptism in the sense of the prayer book and articles—the dissenters would say this is instruction in the doctrine of the church of England. Now it is utterly impossible for you to tell the church schoolmaster or the clergyman that he must not in the school explain any passage of scripture in a sense to which any of the parents of the children, or at least any sect objects ; for *then you would in principle entirely alter the character of the religious teaching for the rest of the scholars, and in fact upset the whole system.* The dissenter, on the other hand, ought (in my opinion) to be entitled to withdraw his child from the risk (if he considers it such) of receiving instruction of the kind I describe.

Mr. Gladstone had therefore held a consistent course, and in cherishing along with full freedom of conscience the integrity of

---

[1] 'In 1843 the government of Sir R. Peel, with a majority of 90, introduced an Education bill, rather large, and meant to provide for the factory districts. The non-conformists at large took up arms against it, and after full consideration in the cabinet (one of my first acts in cabinet), they withdrew it rather than stir up the religious flame.'—*Mr. Gladstone to Herbert Gladstone, May 7, 1896.*

religious instruction, he had followed a definite and intelligible
line.   Unluckily for him and his government this was not the
line now adopted.

II

When the cabinet met in the autumn of 1869, Mr. Gladstone
wrote to Lord de Grey (afterwards Ripon) (Nov. 4) :—

I have read Mr. Forster's able paper, and I follow it very generally.
On one point I cannot very well follow it. . . . Why not adopt frankly
the principle that the State or the local community should provide the
secular teaching, and either leave the option to the ratepayers to go beyond
this *sine quâ non*, if they think fit, within the limits of the conscience
clause, or else simply leave the parties themselves to find Bible and other
religious education from voluntary sources ?

Early in the session before the introduction of the bill, Mr.
Gladstone noted in his diary, 'Good hope that the principal
matters at issue may be accommodated during the session,
but great differences of opinion have come to the surface, and
much trouble may arise.' In fact trouble enough arose to shake
his ministry to its foundations. What would be curious if he
had not had the Land bill on his hands, is that he did not fight
hard for his own view in the cabinet. He seems to have been
content with stating it, without insisting. Whether he could
have carried it in the midst of a whirlwind of indeterminate but
vehement opinions, may well be doubted.

The Education bill was worked through the cabinet by
Lord de Grey as president of the council, but its lines were
laid and its provisions in their varying forms defended in
parliament, by the vice-president, who did not reach the
cabinet until July 1870. Mr. Forster was a man of sterling
force of character, with resolute and effective power of work, a
fervid love of country, and a warm and true humanity. No
orator, he was yet an excellent speaker of a sound order, for his
speaking, though plain and even rough in style, abounded in
substance ; he always went as near to the root of the matter as
his vision allowed, and always with marked effect for his own
purposes. A quaker origin is not incompatible with a militant
spirit, and Forster was sturdy in combat. He had rather a full
share of self-esteem, and he sometimes exhibited a want of tact
that unluckily irritated or estranged many whom more suavity
might have retained. Then, without meaning it, he blundered
into that most injurious of all positions for the parliamentary
leader, of appearing to care more for his enemies than for his
friends. As Mr. Gladstone said of him, 'destiny threw him on
the main occasions of his parliamentary career into open or
qualified conflict with friends as well as foes, perhaps rather
more with friends than foes' A more serious defect of mind
was that he was apt to approach great questions—Education,
Ireland, Turkey—without truly realising how great they were,

and this is the worst of all the shortcomings of statesmanship. There was one case of notable exception. In all the stages and aspects of the American civil war, Forster played an admirable part.

The problem of education might have seemed the very simplest. After the extension of the franchise to the workmen, everybody felt, in a happy phrase of that time, that 'we must educate our masters.' Outside events were supposed to hold a lesson. The triumphant North in America was the land of the common school. The victory of Prussians over Austrians at Sadowa in 1866 was called the victory of the elementary school teacher. Even the nonconformists had come round. Up to the middle of the sixties opinion among them was hostile to the intervention of the state in education. They had resisted Graham's proposals in 1843, and Lord John Russell's in 1847; but a younger generation, eager for progress, saw the new necessity that change of social and political circumstance imposed. The business in 1870 was to provide schools, and to get the children into them.[1]

It is surprising how little serious attention had been paid even by speculative writers in this country to the vast problem of the relative duties of the State and the Family in respect of education. Mill devoted a few keen pages to it in his book upon political economy. Fawcett, without much of Mill's intellectual power or any of his sensitive temperament, was supposed to represent his principles in parliament; yet in education he was against free schools, while Mill was for them. All was unsettled; important things were even unperceived. Yet the questions of national education, answer them as we will, touch the moral life and death of nations. The honourable zeal of the churches had done something, but most of the ground remained to be covered. The question was whether the system about to be created should merely supplement those sectarian, private, voluntary schools, or should erect a fabric worthy of the high name of national. The churchman hoped, but did not expect, the first. The nonconformist (broadly speaking), the academic liberal, and the hard-grit radical, were keen for the second, and they were all three well represented in the House of Commons.

What the goverment proposed was that local boards should be called into existence to provide schools where provision was

---

[1] In 1869 about 1,300,000 children were being educated in state-aided schools, 1,000,000 in schools that received no grant, were not inspected, and were altogether inefficient, and 2,000,000 ought to have been, but were not at school at all. The main burden of national education fell on the shoulders of 200,000 persons, whose voluntary subscriptions supported the schools. 'In other words, the efforts of a handful out of the whole nation had accomplished the fairly efficient education of about one-third of the children, and had provided schools for about one-half; but the rest either went to inefficient schools, or to no school at all, and for them there was no room even had the power to compel their attendance existed.'—See Sir Henry Craik's *The State in its Relation to Education*, pp. 84, 85.

inadequate and inefficient, these schools to be supported by the
pence of the children, the earned grant from parliament, and
a new rate to be levied upon the locality. The rate was the
critical element. If the boards chose, they could make bye-laws
compelling parents to send their children to school ; and they
could (with a conscience clause) settle what form of religious
instruction they pleased. The voluntary men were to have a
year of grace in which to make good any deficiency in supply
of schools, and so keep out the boards. The second reading
was secured without a division, but only on assurances from
Mr. Gladstone that amendments would be made in committee.
On June 16, the prime minister, as he says, 'explained the
plans of the government to an eager and agitated house.'

Two days before, the cabinet had embarked upon a course
that made the agitation still more eager. Mr. Gladstone wrote
the pregnant entry : '*June* 14. Cabinet ; decided on making
more general use of machinery supplied by voluntary schools,
avoidance of religious controversy in local boards.' This meant
that the new system was in no way to supersede the old non-
system, but to supplement it. The decision was fatal to a
national settlement. As Mr. Forster put it, their object was
'to complete the voluntary system and to fill up gaps.' Lord
Ripon used the same language in the Lords. Instead of the
school boards being universal, they should only come into
existence where the ecclesiastical party was not strong enough
in wealth, influence, and liberality, to keep them out. Instead
of compulsory attendance being universal, that principle could
only be applied where a school board was found, and where the
school board liked to apply it. The old parliamentary grant
to the denominational schools was to be doubled. This last
provision was Mr. Gladstone's own. Forster had told him that
it was impossible to carry a proposal allowing school boards to
contribute to denominational schools, and the only compensation
open was a larger slice of the grant from parliament.

III

The storm at once began to rage around the helmsman's
ears. Some days earlier the situation had been defined by
Mr. Brand, the whip, for his leader's guidance. The attempt,
he said, made by Fawcett, Dilke, and others, to create a diversion
in favour of exclusively secular education has signally failed ;
the opinion of the country is clearly adverse. On the other
hand, while insisting on the religious element, the country is
just as strongly opposed to dogmatic teaching in schools aided
by local rates. 'You ask me,' said Mr. Gladstone to Mr. Brand
(May 24), 'to solve the problem in the words "to include religion, and to exclude dogma," which, as far as I know, though
it admits of a sufficient practical handling by individuals acting

for themselves, has not yet been solved by any state or parliament.' Well might he report at Windsor (June 21) that, though the auspices were favourable, there was a great deal of crude and indeterminate opinion on the subject in the House as well as elsewhere, and 'the bill, if carried, would be carried by the authority and persistence of the government, aided by the acquiescence of the opposition.' It was this carrying of the bill by the aid of the tory opposition that gave fuel to the liberal flame, and the increase of the grant to the sectarian schools made the heat more intense. The most critical point of the bill, according to Mr. Gladstone, was a proposal that now seems singularly worded, to the effect that the teaching of scriptures in rate schools should not be in favour of, or opposed to, tenets of any denomination. This was beaten by 251 to 130. 'The minority was liberal, but more than half of the liberal party present voted in the majority.'

'We respect Mr. Forster,' cried Dale of Birmingham, 'we honour Mr. Gladstone, but we are determined that England shall not again be cursed with the bitterness and strife from which we had hoped that we had for ever escaped, by the abolition of the church rate.'[1]   Writing to a brother nonconformist, he expresses his almost unbounded admiration for Mr. Gladstone, 'but it is a bitter disappointment that his government should be erecting new difficulties in the way of religious equality.' Under the flashing eye of the prime minister himself the nonconformist revolt reared its crest. Miall, the veteran bearer of the flag of disestablishment, told Mr. Gladstone (July 22) that he was leading one section of the liberal party through the valley of humiliation. 'Once bit, twice shy. We can't stand this sort of thing much longer,' he said. In a flame of natural wrath Mr. Gladstone replied that he had laboured not to gain Mr. Miall's support, but to promote the welfare of the country. 'I hope my hon. friend will not continue his support to the government one moment longer than he deems it consistent with his sense of right and duty. For God's sake, sir, let him withdraw it the moment he thinks it better for the cause he has at heart that he should do so.' The government, he said, had striven to smooth difficulties, to allay passions, to avoid everything that would excite or stimulate, to endeavour to bring men to work together, to rise above mere sectional views, to eschew all extremes, and not to make their own narrow choice the model of the measure they were presenting to parliament, but to admit freely and liberally into its composition those great influences which were found swaying the community. Forster wrote to a friend, 'it does not rest with me now whether or no the state should decree against religion —decree that it is a thing of no account. Well, with my assent the state shall not do this, and I believe I can prevent it.'[2]

[1] *Life of Dale*, p. 295.   [2] *Life of Forster*, i. p. 497.

Insist, forsooth, that religion was not a thing of no account against men like Dale, one of the most ardent and instructed believers that ever fought the fight and kept the faith ; against Bright, than whom no devouter spirit breathed, and who thought the Education Act ' the worst Act passed by any liberal parliament since 1832.'

The opposition did not show deep gratitude, having secured as many favours as they could hope, and more than they had anticipated. A proposal from the government (July 14) to introduce secret voting in the election of local boards was stubbornly contested, in spite, says Mr. Gladstone, ' of the unvarying good temper, signal ability and conciliatory spirit of Mr. Forster,' and it was not until after fourteen divisions that a few assuaging words from Mr. Gladstone brought the handful of conservative opposition to reason. It was five o'clock before the unflagging prime minister found his way homewards in the broad daylight.

It is impossible to imagine a question on which in a free government it was more essential to carry public opinion with the law. To force parents to send children to school, was an enterprise that must break down if opinion would not help to work it. Yet probably on no other question in Mr. Gladstone's career as law-maker was common opinion so hard to weigh, to test, to focus and adjust. Of the final settlement of the question of religious instruction, Mr. Gladstone said to Lord Lyttelton when the battle was over (Oct. 25, '70) :—

. . . I will only say that it was in no sense my choice or that of the government. Our first proposition was by far the best. But it received no active support even from the church, the National Society, or the opposition, while divers bishops, large bodies of clergy, the Education Union, and earliest of all, I think, Roundell Palmer in the House of Commons, threw overboard the catechism. We might then have fallen back upon the plan of confining the application of the rate to secular subjects ; but this was opposed by the church, the opposition, most of the dissenters, and most of our own friends. As it was, I assure you, the very utmost that could be done was to arrange the matter as it now stands, where the exclusion is limited to the formulary, and to get rid of the popular imposture of undenominational instruction.

At bottom the battle of the schools was not educational, it was social. It was not religious but ecclesiastical, and that is often the very contrary of religious. In the conflicts of the old centuries whence Christian creeds emerged, disputes on dogma constantly sprang from rivalries of race and accidents of geography. So now quarrels about education and catechism and conscience masked the standing jealousy between church and chapel—the unwholesome fruit of the historic mishaps of the sixteenth and seventeenth centuries that separated the nation into two camps, and invested one of them with all the pomp and privilege of social ascendency. The parent and the child, in whose name the struggle raged, stood indifferent. From the point of party strategy, the policy of this great statute was fatal. The church of England was quickened into active antagonism by Irish disestablishment, by the extinction of sectarian tests at Oxford and Cambridge, and by the treatment of endowed schools. This might have been balanced by the zeal of nonconformists. Instead of zeal, the Education Act produced refrigeration and estrangement.

We may be sure that on such a subject Mr. Gladstone looked further than strategies of party. 'I own to you,' said he to a correspondent before the battle was quite over, 'that the history of these last few months leaves upon my mind some melancholy impressions, which I hope at some fancied period of future leisure and retirement to study and interpret.' He soon saw how deep the questions went, and on what difficult ground the state and the nation would be inevitably drawn. His notions of a distinctive formula were curious. Forster seems to have put some question to him on the point whether the three creeds were formularies within the Act. It appears to me, Mr. Gladstone answered (October 17, 1870):—

It is quite open to you at once to dispose of the Nicene and Athanasian Creeds and to decline inquiring whether they are distinctive, upon the ground that they are not documents employed in the instruction of young children. . . . Obviously no one has a right to call on you to define the distinctive character of a formulary such as the Thirty-nine Articles, or of any but such as are employed in schools. With respect to the Apostles' Creed, it appears to me not to be a distinctive formulary in the sense of the Act. Besides the fact that it is acknowledged by the great bulk of all Christendom, it is denied or rejected by no portion of the Christian community; and, further, it is not controversial in its form, but sets forth in the simplest shape a series of the leading facts on which Christianity, the least abstract of all religions, is based.

Manning plied him hard (September, October, November, 1871). The state of Paris (Commune blazing that year, Tuileries and Hôtel de Ville in ashes, and the Prussian spiked helmets at the gates) was traceable to a godless education—so the archbishop argued. In England the Christian tradition was unbroken. It was only a clique of doctrinaires, Huxley at the head of them, who believing nothing trumpeted secular education. 'Delighted to see Mr. Forster attacked as playing into the hands of the clergy.' Mr. Gladstone should stimulate by every agency in his power the voluntary religious energies of the three kingdoms. 'The real crisis is in the formation of men. They are as we make them, and they make society. The formation of men is the work you have given to the school boards. God gave it to the parents. Neither you nor Mr. Forster meant this; you least of all men on your side of the House. Glad to see you lay down the broad and intelligible line that state grants go to secular education, and voluntary

efforts must do the rest.   Let us all start fair in this race.   Let
every sect, even the Huxleyites, have their grant if they fulfil
the conditions.   As for the school-rate conscience, it is a
mongrel institution of quakerism.'   How Mr. Gladstone replied
on all these searching issues, I do not find.

IV

The passing of the Act did not heal the wound.   The nonconformist revolt was supported in a great conference at
Manchester in 1872, representing eight hundred churches and
other organizations.   Baptist unions and congregational unions
were unrelenting.   We may as well finish the story.   It was in
connection with this struggle that Mr. Chamberlain first came
prominently into the arena of public life—bold, intrepid, imbued
with the keen spirit of political nonconformity, and a born
tactician.   The issue selected for the attack was the twenty-
fifth section of the Education Act, enabling school boards to
pay in denominational schools the fees of parents who, though
not paupers, were unable to pay them.   This provision suddenly
swelled into dimensions of enormity hitherto unsuspected.   A
caustic onlooker observed that it was the smallest ditch in
which two great political armies ever engaged in civil war.
Yet the possibility under cover of this section, of a sectarian
board subsidising church schools was plain, and some cases,
though not many, actually occurred in which appreciable sums
were so handed over.   The twenty-fifth section was a real error,
and it made no bad flag for an assault upon a scheme of error.

Great things were hoped from Mr. Bright's return to the
government in the autumn of 1873.   The correspondence
between Mr. Gladstone and him sheds some interesting light
upon the state into which the Education Act, and Mr. Forster's
intractable bearing in defence of it, had brought important
sections of the party :—

Mr. Bright to Mr. Gladstone.

Aug. 12, 1873.—So far as I can hear, there is no intention to get up
an opposition at Birmingham, which is a comfort, as I am not in force
to fight a contested election.   I am anxious not to go to the election,
fearing that I shall not have nerve to speak to the 5000 men who will or
may crowd the town hall.   Before I go, if I go, I shall want to consult
you on the difficult matter—how to deal frankly and wisely with the
education question.   I cannot break with my 'noncon.' friends, the
political friends of all my life ; and unless my joining you can do something to lessen the mischief now existing and *still growing*, I had better
remain as I have been since my illness, a spectator rather than an actor
on the political field. . . .   I hope you are better, and that your troubles,
for a time, are diminished.   I wish much you could have announced a
change in the education department ; it would have improved the tone
of feeling in many constituencies.

Mr. Gladstone himself had touched 'the watchful jealousy' of Bright's nonconformist friends by a speech made at the time at Hawarden. This speech he explained in writing to Bright from Balmoral (Aug. 21) :—

The upshot, I think, is this. My speech could not properly have been made by a man who thinks that boards and public rates ought to be used for the purpose of putting down as quickly as may be the voluntary schools. But the recommendation which I made might have been consistently and properly supported by any one whose opinions fell short of this, and did not in the least turn upon any preference for voluntary over compulsory means.[1]

As he said afterwards to Lord Granville, 'I personally have no fear of the secular system ; but I cannot join in measures of repression against voluntary schools.'

'There is not a word said by you at Hawarden,' Bright replied (Aug. 25), 'that would fetter you in the least in considering the education question ; but at present the general feeling is against the idea of any concession on your part. . . . What is wanted is some definite willingness or resolution to recover the goodwill and confidence of the nonconformist leaders in the boroughs ; for without this, reconstruction is of no value. . . . Finance is of great moment, and people are well pleased to see you in your old office again ; but no budget will heal the soreness that has been created—it is not of the pocket, but of the feelings. . . . I want you just to know where I am and what I feel ; but if I could talk to you, I could say what I have to say with more precision, and with a greater delicacy of expression. I ask you only to put the best construction on what I write.'

If Forster could only have composed himself to the same considerate spirit, there might have been a different tale to tell. Bright made his election speech at Birmingham, and Forster was in trouble about it. 'I think,' said the orator to Mr. Gladstone, 'he ought rather to be thankful for it ; it will enable him to get out of difficulties if he will improve the occasion. There is no question of changing the policy of the government, but of making minor concessions. . . . I would willingly change the policy of irritation into one of soothing and conciliation.' Nothing of great importance in the way even of temporary reconciliation was effected by Mr. Bright's return. The ditch of the twenty-fifth clause still yawned. The prime minister fell back into the position of August. The whole situation of the ministry had become critical in every direction. 'Education must be regarded as still to a limited extent an open question in the government.'

When the general election came, the party was still disunited. Out of 425 liberal candidates in England, Scotland, and Wales, 300 were pledged to the repeal of the 25th clause.

[1] For the rest of the letter see Appendix.

Mr. Gladstone's last word was in a letter to Bright (Jan. 27, 1874) :—

The fact is, it seems to me, that the noncons. have not yet as a body made up their minds whether they want unsectarian religion, or whether they want simple secular teaching, so far as the application of the rate is concerned. I have never been strong against the latter of these two which seems to me impartial, and not, if fairly worked, of necessity in any degree unfriendly to religion. The former is in my opinion glaringly partial, and I shall never be a party to it. But there is a good deal of leaning to it in the liberal party. Any attempt to obtain definite pledges now will give power to the enemies of both plans of proceeding. We have no rational course as a party but one, which is to adjourn for a while the solution of the grave parts of the education problem ; and this I know to be in substance your opinion.

V

The same vigorous currents of national vitality that led to new endeavours for the education of the poor, had drawn men to consider the horrid chaos, the waste, and the abuses in the provision of education for the directing classes beyond the poor. Grave problems of more kinds than one came into view. The question, What is education ? was nearly as hard to answer as the question of which we have seen so much, What is a church ? The rival claims of old classical training and the acquisition of modern knowledge were matters of vivacious contest. What is the true place of classical learning in the human culture of our own age ? Misused charitable trusts, and endowments perverted by the fluctuations of time, by lethargy, by selfishness, from the objects of pious founders, touched wakeful jealousies in the privileged sect, and called into action that adoration of the principle of property which insists upon applying all the rules of individual ownership to what rightfully belongs to the community. Local interests were very sensitive, and they were multitudinous. The battle was severely fought, and it extended over several years, while commission upon commission explored the issues.

In a highly interesting letter (1861) to Lord Lyttelton Mr. Gladstone set out at length his views upon the issue between ancient and modern, between literary training and scientific, between utilitarian education and liberal. The reader will find this letter in an appendix, as well as one to Sir Stafford Northcote.[1] While rationally conservative upon the true basis of attainments in 'that small proportion of the youth of any country who are to become in the fullest sense educated men,' he is rationally liberal upon what the politics of the time made the burning question of the sacrosanctity of endowments. 'It is our habit in this country,' he said, 'to treat private interests with an extravagant tenderness. The truth is that all laxity and extravagance in dealing with what in a large sense is

1 See Appendix.

certainly public property, approximates more or less to dishonesty, or at the least lowers the moral tone of the persons concerned.'

The result of all this movement, of which it may perhaps be said that it was mainly inspired and guided by a few men of superior energy and social weight like Goldwin Smith, Temple, Jowett, Liddell, the active interest of the classes immediately concerned being hardly more than middling—was one of the best measures in the history of this government of good measures (1869). It dealt with many hundreds of schools, and with an annual income of nearly six hundred thousand pounds. As the Endowed Schools bill was one of the best measures of the government, so it was Mr. Forster's best piece of legislative work. That it strengthened the government can hardly be said ; the path of the reformer is not rose-strewn.[1]

VI

In one region Mr. Gladstone long lagged behind. He had done a fine stroke of national policy in releasing Oxford from some of her antique bonds in 1854 ;[2] but the principle of a free university was not yet admitted to his mind. In 1863 he wrote to the vice-chancellor how entirely the government concurred in the principle of restricting the governing body of the university and the colleges to the church. The following year he was willing to throw open the degree ; but the right to sit in convocation he guarded by exacting a declaration of membership of the church of England.[3] In 1865 Mr. Goschen—then beginning to make a mark as one of the ablest of the new generation in parliament, combining the large views of liberal Oxford with the practical energy of the city of London, added to a strong fibre given him by nature—brought in a bill throwing open all lay degrees. Mr. Gladstone still stood out, conducting a brisk correspondence with dissenters. 'The whole controversy,' he wrote to one of them, 'is carried on aggressively, as if to disturb and not to settle. Abstract principles urged without stint or mercy provoke the counter-assertion of abstract principles in return. There is not power to carry Mr. Goschen's speech either in the cabinet, the parliament, or the country. Yet the change in the balance of parties effected by the elections will cast upon the liberal majority a serious responsibility. I would rather see Oxford level with the ground, than its

---

[1] In 1874 the conservative government brought in a bill restoring to the church of England numerous schools in cases where the founder had recognised the authority of a bishop, or had directed attendance in the service of that church, or had required that the masters should be in holy orders. Mr. Gladstone protested against the bill as ' inequitable, unusual and unwise,' and it was largely modified in committee.

[2] See vol. i., book iv., chap. iv. By the act of 1854 a student could proceed to the bachelor's degree without the test of subscribing to the Thirty-nine Articles. Cambridge was a shade more liberal. At both universities dissenters were shut out from college fellowships, unless willing to make a declaration of conformity.

[3] Speech on Mr. Dodson's bill, March 16, 1864.

religion regulated in the manner which would please Bishop Colenso.'

Year by year the struggle was renewed. Even after the Gladstone government was formed, Coleridge, the solicitor-general, was only allowed in a private capacity to introduce a bill removing the tests. When he had been two years at the head of administration, Mr. Gladstone warned Coleridge : ' For me individually it would be beyond anything odious, I am almost tempted to say it would be impossible, after my long connection with Oxford, to go into a new controversy on the basis of what will be taken and alleged to be an absolute secularisation of the colleges ; as well as a reversal of what was deliberately considered and sanctioned in the parliamentary legislation of 1854 and 1856. I incline to think that this work is work for others, not for me.'

It was not until 1871 that Mr. Gladstone consented to make the bill a government measure. It rapidly passed the Commons and was accepted by the Lords, but with amendments. Mr. Gladstone when he had once adopted a project never loitered ; he now resolutely refused the changes proposed by the Lords, and when the time came and Lord Salisbury was for insisting on them, the peers declined by a handsome majority to carry the fight further. It is needless to add that the admission of dissenters to degrees and endowments did not injuriously affect a single object for which a national university exists. On the other hand, the mischiefs of ecclesiastical monopoly were long in disappearing.

VII

We have already seen how warmly the project of introducing competition into the civil service had kindled Mr. Gladstone's enthusiasm in the days of the Crimean war.[1] Reform had made slow progress. The civil service commission had been appointed in 1855, but their examinations only tested the quality of candidates sent before them on nomination. In 1860 a system was set up of limited competition among three nominated candidates, who had first satisfied a preliminary test examination. This lasted until 1870. Lowe had reform much at heart. At the end of 1869, he appealed to the prime minister : ' As I have so often tried in vain, will you bring the question of the civil service before the cabinet to-day ? Something must be decided. We cannot keep matters in this discreditable state of abeyance. If the cabinet will not entertain the idea of open competition, might we not at any rate require a larger number of competitors for each vacancy ? five or seven or ten ?'

Resistance came from Lord Clarendon and, strange to say, from Mr. Bright. An ingenious suggestion of Mr. Gladstone's solved the difficulty. All branches of the civil service were to

[1] Above, p. 379.

be thrown open where the minister at the head of the department approved. Lowe was ready to answer for all the departments over which he had any control,—the treasury, the board of works, audit office, national debt office, paymaster-general's office, inland revenue, customs and post-office. Mr. Cardwell, Mr. Childers, Mr. Goschen, and Lord de Grey were willing to do the same, and finally only Clarendon and the foreign office were left obdurate. It was true to say of this change that it placed the whole educated intellect of the country at the service and disposal of the state, that it stimulated the acquisition of knowledge, and that it rescued some of the most important duties in the life of the nation from the narrow class to whom they had hitherto been confided.

CHAPTER IV

THE FRANCO-GERMAN WAR

(1870)

Of all the princes of Europe, the king of England alone seemed to be seated upon the pleasant promontory that might safely view the tragic sufferings of all his neighbours about him, without any other concernment than what arose from his own princely heart and Christian compassion, to see such desolation wrought by the pride and passion and ambition of private persons, supported by princes who knew not what themselves would have.—CLARENDON.

DURING the years in which England had been widening the base of her institutions, extending her resources of wealth and credit, and strengthening her repute in the councils of Christendom, a long train of events at which we have glanced from time to time, had slowly effected a new distribution of the force of nations, and in Mr. Gladstone's phrase had unset every joint of the compacted fabric of continental Europe. The spirit in which he thought of his country's place in these transactions is to be gathered from a letter addressed by him to General Grey, the secretary of the Queen, rather more than a year before the outbreak of the Franco-German war. What was the immediate occasion I cannot be sure, nor does it matter. The letter itself is full of interest, for it is in truth a sort of charter of the leading principles of Mr. Gladstone's foreign policy at the moment when he first incurred supreme responsibility for our foreign affairs :—

Mr. Gladstone to General Grey.

April 17, 1869.—. . . Apart from this question of the moment, there is one more important as to the tone in which it is to be desired that, where matter of controversy has arisen on the continent of Europe, the diplomatic correspondence of this country should be carried on. This more important question may be the subject of differences in the country, but I observe with joy that her Majesty approves the general principle which Lord Clarendon sets forth in his letter of the 16th. I do not believe that England ever will or can be unfaithful to her great tradition, or can forswear her interest in the common transactions and the general interests of Europe. But her credit and her power form a fund, which in order that they may be made the most of, should be thriftily used.

The effect of the great revolutionary war was to place England in a position to rely upon the aid of her own resources. This was no matter of blame to either party; it was the result of a desperate struggle of over twenty years, in which every one else was down in his turn, but England was ever on her feet; in which it was found that there was no ascertained limit either to her means, or to her disposition to dispense them; in which, to use the language of Mr. Canning, her flag was always flying 'a signal of rallying to the combatant, and of shelter to the fallen.' The habit of appeal and of reliance thus engendered by peculiar circumstances, requires to be altered by a quiet and substantial though not a violent process. For though Europe never saw England faint away, *we* know at what a cost of internal danger to all the institutions of the country, she fought her way to the perilous eminence on which she undoubtedly stood in 1815.

If there be a fear abroad that England has forever abjured a resort to force other than moral force, is that fear justified by facts? In 1853, joining with France, we made ourselves the vindicators of the peace of Europe; and ten years later, be it remembered, in the case of Denmark we offered to perform the same office, but we could get no one to join us. Is it desirable that we should go further? Is England so uplifted in strength above every other nation, that she can with prudence advertise herself as ready to undertake the general redress of wrongs? Would not the consequence of such professions and promises be either the premature exhaustion of her means, or a collapse in the day of performance? Is *any* Power at this time of day warranted in assuming this comprehensive obligation? Of course, the answer is, No. But do not, on the other hand, allow it to be believed that England will never interfere. For the eccentricities of other men's belief no one can answer; but for any reasonable belief in such an abnegation on the part of England, there is no ground whatever. As I understand Lord Clarendon's ideas, they are fairly represented by his very important diplomatic communications since he has taken office. They proceed upon such grounds as these:—That England should keep entire in her own hands the means of estimating her own obligations upon the various states of facts as they arise; that she should not foreclose and narrow her own liberty of choice by declarations made to other Powers, in their real or supposed interests, of which they would claim to be at least joint interpreters; that it is dangerous for her to assume alone an advanced, and therefore an isolated position, in regard to European controversies; that, come what may, it is better for her to promise too little than too much; that she should not encourage the weak by giving expectations of aid to resist the strong, but should rather seek to deter the strong by firm but moderate language, from aggressions on the weak; that she should seek to develop and mature the action of a common, or public, or European opinion, as the best standing bulwark against wrong, but should beware of seeming to lay down the law of that opinion by her own authority, and thus running the risk of setting against her, and against right and justice, that general sentiment which ought to be, and generally would be, arrayed in their favour. I am persuaded that at this juncture opinions of this colour being true and sound, are also the only opinions which the country is disposed to approve. But I do not believe that on that account it is one whit less disposed than it has been at any time, to cast in its lot upon any fitting occasion with the cause it believes to be right. . . . I therefore hope and feel assured her Majesty will believe that Lord Clarendon really requires no intimation

from me to ensure his steadily maintaining the tone which becomes the
foreign minister of the Queen.

Heavy banks of clouds hung with occasional breaks of
brighter sky over Europe ; and all the plot, intrigue, conspiracy,
and subterranean scheming, that had been incessant ever since
the Crimean war disturbed the old European system, and
Cavour first began the recasting of the map, was but the
repulsive and dangerous symptom of a dire conflict in the
depths of international politics.   The Mexican adventure, and
the tragedy of Maximilian's death at Queretaro, had thrown a
black shadow over the iridescent and rotten fabric of Napoleon's
power.   Prussian victory over Austria at Sadowa had startled
Europe like a thunderclap.   The reactionary movement within
the catholic fold, as disclosed in the Vatican council, kindled
many hopes among the French clericals, and these hopes
inspired a lively antagonism to protestant Prussia in the breast
of the Spanish-born Empress of the French.   Prussia in 1866
had humiliated one great catholic power when she defeated the
Austrian monarchy on the battlefields of Bohemia.   Was she
to overthrow also the power that kept the pope upon his
temporal throne in Rome ?   All this, however, was no more than
the fringe, though one of the hardest things in history is to be
sure where substance begins and fringe ends.   The cardinal
fact for France and for Europe was German unity.   Ever since
the Danish conflict, as Bismarck afterwards told the British
Government,[1] the French Emperor strove to bring Prussia to
join him in plans for their common aggrandizement.   The unity
of Germany meant, besides all else, a vast extension of the area
from which the material of military strength was to be drawn ;
and this meant the relative depression of the power of French
arms.   Here was the substantial fact, feeding the flame of
national pride with solid fuel.   The German confederation of
the Congress of Vienna was a skilful invention of Metternich's,
so devised as to be inert for offence, but extremely efficient
against French aggression.   A German confederation under the
powerful and energetic leadership of Prussia gave France a
very different neighbour.

In August 1867, the French ambassador at Berlin said to the
ambassador of Great Britain, 'We can never passively permit
the formation of a German empire ; the position of the Emperor
of the French would become untenable.'   The British ambassador
in Paris was told by the foreign minister there, that 'there was
no wish for aggrandizement in the Emperor's mind, but a
solicitude for the safety of France.'   This solicitude evaporated
in what Bismarck disdainfully called the policy of *pourboires*,
the policy of tips and pickings—scraps and slips of territory to
be given to France under the diplomatic name of compensation.

---

[1] July 28, 1870.

For three years it had been no secret that peace was at the mercy of any incident that might arise.

The small Powers were in trepidation, and with good reason. Why should not France take Belgium, and Prussia take Holland? The Belgian press did not conceal bad feeling, and Bismarck let fall the ominous observation that if Belgium persisted in that course, 'she might pay dear for it.' The Dutch minister told the British ambassador in Vienna that in 1865 he had a long conversation with Bismarck, and Bismarck had given him to understand that without colonies Prussia could never become a great maritime nation; he coveted Holland less for its own sake, than for her wealthy colonies. When reminded that Belgium was guaranteed by the European Powers, Bismarck replied that 'a guarantee was in these days of little value.' This remark makes an excellent register of the diplomatic temperature of the hour.

Then for England. The French Emperor observed (1867), not without an accent of complaint, that she seemed 'little disposed to take part in the affairs of the day.' This was the time of the Derby government. When war seemed inevitable on the affair of Luxemburg, Lord Stanley, then at the foreign office, phlegmatically remarked (1867) that England had never thought it her business to guarantee the integrity of Germany. When pressed from Prussia to say whether in the event of Prussia being forced into war by France, England would take a part, Lord Stanley replied that with the causes of that quarrel we had nothing to do, and he felt sure that neither parliament nor the public would sanction an armed interference on either side. Belgium, he added, was a different question. General non-intervention, therefore, was the common doctrine of both our parties.

After Mr. Gladstone had been a year in power, the chance of a useful part for England to perform seemed to rise on the horizon, but to those who knew the racing currents, the interplay of stern forces, the chance seemed but dim and faint. Rumour and gossip of a pacific tenour could not hide the vital fact of incessant military preparation on both sides—steadfast and scientific in Prussia, loose and ill-concerted in France. Along with the perfecting of arms, went on a busy search by France for alliances. In the autumn of 1869 Lord Clarendon had gone abroad and talked with important personages. Moltke told him that in Prussia they thought war was near. To Napoleon the secretary of state spoke of the monster armaments, the intolerable burden imposed upon the people, and the constant danger of war that they created. The Emperor agreed—so Lord Clarendon wrote to Mr. Gladstone (Sept. 18, '69)—but went on to say that during the King of Prussia's life, and as long as the present Prussian system lasted, he thought no change of importance could be effected. Still the seed by and by appeared to have fallen on good ground. For in January 1870, in a conversation with the British ambassador, the French foreign minister (Daru) suggested that England might use her good offices with Prussia, to induce a partial disarmament in order that France might disarm also. The minister, at the same time, wrote a long despatch in the same sense to the French ambassador at St. James's. Lord Clarendon perceived the delicacy of opening the matter at Berlin, in view of the Prussian monarch's idolatry of his army. He agreed, however, to bring it before the king, not officially, but in a confidential form. This would compromise nobody. The French ambassador in London agreed, and Lord Clarendon wrote the draft of a letter to Loftus in Berlin. He sent the draft to Mr. Gladstone (Jan. 31, 1870) for 'approval and criticism.' Mr. Gladstone entered eagerly into Lord Clarendon's benevolent correspondence :—

Mr. Gladstone to Lord Clarendon.

31 *Jan.* 1870.—The object of your letter on disarmament is noble, and I do not see how the terms of the draft can be improved. I presume you will let the Queen know what you are about, and possibly circumstances might arrive in which she could help?

7 *Feb.*—The answer to your pacific letter as reported by Loftus throws, I think, a great responsibility on the King of Prussia.

12 *Feb.*—I hope, with Daru, that you will not desist from your efforts, whatever be the best mode of prosecuting the good design. I thought Bismarck's case, on Loftus's letter, a very bad one. I do not think Lyons's objections, towards the close of his letter, apply in a case where you have acted simply as a friend, and not in the name and on behalf of France.

18 *Feb.*—I return Bismarck's confidential letter on disarmament. As the matter appears to me, the best that can be said for this letter is that it contains matter which might be used with more or less force in a conference on disarmament, by way of abating the amount of relative call on Prussia. As an argument against entertaining the subject, it is futile, and he ought at any rate to be made to feel his responsibility,—which, I daresay, you will contrive while acknowledging his civility.

9 *April.*—I presume you have now only in the matter of disarmament to express your inability to recede from your opinions, and your regret at the result of the correspondence. If inclined to touch the point, you might with perfect justice say that while our naval responsibilities for our sea defence have no parallel or analogue in the world, we have taken not far short of two millions off our estimates, and have not announced that the work of reduction is at an end : which, whether satisfactory or not, is enough to show that you do not preach wholly without practising.

It is a striking circumstance, in view of what was to follow, that at this moment when Mr. Gladstone first came into contact with Bismarck, — the genius of popular right and free government and settled law of nations, into contact with the genius of force and reason of state and blood and iron—the realist minister of Prussia seemed to be almost as hopeful for European peace as the minister of England. 'The political horizon,' Bismarck wrote (Feb. 22), 'seen from Berlin appears at present so unclouded that there is nothing of interest to report, and I only hope that no unexpected event will render the lately risen hope of universal peace questionable.'[1] The unexpected event did not tarry, and Bismarck's own share in laying the train is still one of the historic enigmas of our time.

II

Ever since 1868 the statesmen of revolutionary Spain had looked for a prince to fill their vacant throne. Among others they bethought themselves of a member of a catholic branch of the house of Hohenzollern, and in the autumn of 1869 an actual proposal was secretly made to Prince Leopold. The thing lingered. Towards the end of February, 1870, Spanish importunities were renewed, though still under the seal of strict secrecy, even the Spanish ambassador in Paris being kept in the dark.[2] Leopold after a long struggle declined the glittering bait. The rival pretenders were too many, and order was not sure. Still his refusal was not considered final. The chances of order improved, he changed his mind, and on June 23 the Spanish emissary returned to Madrid with the news that the Hohenzollern prince was ready to accept the crown. The King of Prussia, not as king, but as head of the house, had given his assent. That Bismarck invented the Hohenzollern candidature the evidence is not conclusive. What is undoubted is that in the late spring of 1870 he took it up, and was much discontented at its failure in that stage.[3] He had become aware that France was striving to arrange alliances with Austria, and even with Italy, in spite of the obnoxious presence of the French garrison at Rome. It was possible that on certain issues Bavaria and the South might join France against Prussia. All the hindrances to German unity, the jealousies of the minor states, the hatred of the Prussian military system, were likely to be aggravated by time, if France, while keeping her powder dry, were to persevere in a prudent abstention. Bismarck believed that Moltke's preparations were more advanced than Napoleon's. It was his interest to strike before any French treaties of alliance were signed. The Spanish crown was an occasion. It might easily become a pretext for collision if either France or Germany thought the hour had come. If the Hohenzollern candidate

[1] *Reminiscences of the King of Roumania.* Edited from the original by Sydney Whitman. 1899. P. 92.

[2] King William wrote to Bismarck (Feb. 20, 1870) that the news of the Hohenzollern candidature had come upon him like a thunderbolt, and that they must confer about it. *Kaiser Wilhelm I. und Bismarck*, i. p. 207.

[3] The story of a ministerial council at Berlin on March 15, at which the question was discussed between the king, his ministers, and the Hohenzollern princes, with the result that all decided for acceptance, is denied by Bismarck.—*Recollections*, ii. p. 89.

withdrew, it was a diplomatic success for France and a humiliation to Germany ; if not, a king from Prussia planted across the Pyrenees, after the aggrandizements of north German power in 1864 and 1866, was enough to make Richelieu, Mazarin, Louis XIV., Bonaparte, even Louis Philippe, turn in their graves.

On June 27, 1870, Lord Clarendon died, and on July 6 Lord Granville received the seals of the foreign department from the Queen at Windsor. The new chief had visited his office the day before, and the permanent under-secretary coming into his room to report, gave him the most remarkable assurance ever received by any secretary of state on first seating himself at his desk. Lord Granville told the story in the House of Lords on July 11, when the crash of the fiercest storm since Waterloo was close upon them :—

The able and experienced under-secretary, Mr. Hammond, at the foreign office told me, it being then three or four o'clock, that with the exception of the sad and painful subject about to be discussed this evening [the murders by brigands in Greece] he had never during his long experience known so great a lull in foreign affairs, and that he was not aware of any important question that I should have to deal with. At six o'clock that evening I received a telegram informing me of the choice that had been made by the provisional government of Spain of Prince Leopold of Hohenzollern, and of his acceptance of the offer. I went to Windsor the following day, and had the honour of receiving the seals of the foreign office from her Majesty. On my return I saw the Marquis de Lavalette, who informed me of the fact which I already knew, and in energetic terms remarked on the great indignity thus offered to France, and expressed the determination of the government of the Emperor not to permit the project to be carried out. M. Lavalette added that he trusted that her Majesty's government, considering its friendly relations with France and its general desire to maintain peace, would use its influence with the other parties concerned. I told M. de Lavalette that the announcement had taken the prime minister and myself entirely by surprise.[1]

Yet two days before Mr. Hammond told Lord Granville that he was not aware of anything important to be dealt with at the foreign department, a deputation had started from Madrid with an invitation to Prince Leopold. At the moment when this singular language was falling from our under-secretary's lips, the Duc de Gramont, the French foreign minister, was telling Lord Lyons at Paris that France would not endure the insult, and expressing his hope that the government of the Queen would try to prevent it. After all, as we have seen, Bismarck in February had used words not very unlike Mr. Hammond's in July.

On July 5, the Emperor, who was at St. Cloud, sent for Baron Rothschild (of Paris), and told him that as there was at that moment no foreign minister in England, he wished to send through him a message to Mr. Gladstone. He wanted Mr.

[1] *Hansard*, July 11, 1870.

Gladstone to be informed, that the council of ministers at Madrid had decided to propose Prince Leopold of Hohenzollern for the Spanish throne, that his candidature would be intolerable to France, and that he hoped Mr. Gladstone would endeavour to secure its withdrawal. The message was telegraphed to London, and early on the morning of July 6, the present Lord Rothschild deciphered it for his father, and took it to Carlton House Terrace. He found Mr. Gladstone on the point of leaving for Windsor, and drove with him to the railway station. For a time Mr. Gladstone was silent. Then he said he did not approve of the candidature, but he was not disposed to interfere with the liberty of the Spanish people to choose their own sovereign.

Lord Granville put pressure on the provisional government at Madrid to withdraw their candidate, and on the government at Berlin 'effectually to discourage a project fraught with risks to the best interests of Spain.' The draft of this despatch was submitted by Lord Granville to Mr. Gladstone, who suggested a long addition afterwards incorporated in the text. The points of his addition were an appeal to the magnanimity of the King of Prussia; an injunction to say nothing to give ground for the supposition that England had any business to discuss the abstract right of Spain to choose her own sovereign; that the British government had not admitted Prince Leopold's acceptance of the throne to justify the immediate resort to arms threatened by France; but that the secrecy with which the affair had been conducted was a ground for just offence, and the withdrawal of the prince could alone repair it.[1] Austria made energetic representations at Berlin to the same effect. In sending this addition to Lord Granville, Mr. Gladstone says (July 8), 'I am doubtful whether this despatch should go till it has been seen by the cabinet, indeed I think it should not, and probably you mean this. The Queen recollects being told something about this affair by Clarendon—without result—last year. I think Gramont exacts too much. It would never do for us to get up a combination of Powers in this difficult and slippery matter.'

Events for a week—one of the great critical weeks of the century—moved at a dizzy speed towards the abyss. Peace unfortunately hung upon the prudence of a band of statesmen in Paris, who have ever since, both in their own country and everywhere else, been a byword in history for blindness and folly. The game was delicate. Even in the low and broken estate into which the moral areopagus of Europe had fallen in these days, it was a disadvantage to figure as the aggressor.

[1] The despatch is dated July 6 in the blue-book (C. 167, p. 3), but it was not sent that day, as the date of Mr. Gladstone's letter shows. No cabinet seems to have been held before July 9. The despatch was laid before the cabinet, and was sent to Berlin by special messenger that evening. The only other cabinet meeting during this critical period was on July 14.

This disadvantage the French Empire heedlessly imposed upon itself. Of the diplomacy on the side of the government of France anterior to the war, Mr. Gladstone said that it made up 'a chapter which for fault and folly taken together is almost without a parallel in the history of nations.'[1]

On July 6 the French ministers made a precipitate declaration to their Chambers, which was in fact an ultimatum to Prussia. The action of Spain was turned into Prussian action. Prussia was called to account in a form that became a public and international threat, as Bismarck put it, 'with the hand on the sword-hilt.' These rash words of challenge were the first of the French disasters. On July 8 the Duc de Gramont begged her Majesty's government to use all their influence to bring about the voluntary renunciation by Prince Leopold of his pretensions. This he told Lord Lyons would be 'a most fortunate solution' of the question. Two days later he assured Lord Lyons that 'if the Prince of Hohenzollern should, on the advice of the King of Prussia, withdraw his acceptance of the crown the whole affair would be at an end.'

On July 10 Lord Granville suggests to Mr. Gladstone : 'What do you think of asking the Queen whether there is any one to whom she could write confidentially with a view to persuade Hohenzollern to refuse ?' Mr. Gladstone replies :—

1. I should think you could not do wrong in asking the Queen, as you propose, to procure if she can a refusal from Hohenzollern, through some private channel. 2. I suppose there could be no objection to sounding the Italian government as to the Duke of Aosta. 3. If in the meantime you have authentic accounts of military movements in France, would it not be right formally to ask their suspension, if it be still the desire of the French government that you should continue to act in the sense of procuring withdrawal ?

The ambassador at Paris was instructed to work vigorously in this sense, and to urge self-possession and measure upon the Emperor's council. On July 12, however, the prospects of peace grew more and more shadowy. On that day it became known that Prince Leopold had spontaneously renounced the candidature, or that his father had renounced it on his behalf. The French ministers made up their minds that the defeat of Prussia must be more direct. Gramont told Lyons (July 12) that the French government was in a very embarrassing position. Public opinion was so much excited that it was doubtful whether the ministry would not be overthrown, if it went down to the Chamber and announced that it regarded the affair as finished, without having obtained some more complete satisfaction from Prussia. So the Emperor and his advisers

---

[1] *Gleanings*, iv. p. 222. Modern French historians do not differ from Mr. Gladstone.

flung themselves gratuitously under Bismarck's grinding wheels by a further demand that not only should the candidature be withdrawn, but the King should pledge himself against its ever being at any time revived. Mr. Gladstone was not slow to see the fatal mischief of this new development.

Mr. Gladstone to Lord Granville.

July 12, 11.30 P.M.—I have seen, since Rothschild's telegram,[1] that of Lyons, dated 7.55 P.M. It seems to me that Lyons should be supplied with an urgent instruction by telegram before the council of ministers to-morrow. France appealed to our support at the outset. She received it so far as the immediate object was concerned. It was immediately and energetically given. It appears to have been named by the French minister in public inclusively with that of other Powers. Under these circumstances it is our duty to represent the immense responsibility which will rest upon France, if she does not at once accept as satisfactory and conclusive, the withdrawal of the candidature of Prince Leopold.

The substance of this note was despatched to Paris at 2.30 A.M. on the morning of July 13. It did not reach Lord Lyons till half-past nine, when the council of ministers had already been sitting for half an hour at St. Cloud. The telegram was hastily embodied in the form of a tolerably emphatic letter and sent by special messenger to St. Cloud, where it was placed in M. de Gramont's hand, at the table at which he and the other ministers were still sitting in council in the presence of the Emperor and the Empress.[2] At the same time Lord Granville strongly urged M. de Lavalette in London, to impress upon his government that they ought not to take upon themselves the responsibility of pursuing the quarrel on a matter of form, when they had obtained what Gramont had assured Lord Lyons would put an end to the dispute. Though Mr. Disraeli afterwards imputed want of energy to the British remonstrances, there is no reason to suppose that Lord Lyons was wanting either in directness or emphasis. What warnings were likely to reach the minds of men trembling for their personal popularity and for the dynasty, afraid of clamour in the streets, afraid of the army, ignorant of vital facts both military and diplomatic, incapable of measuring such facts even if they had known them, committed by the rash declaration of defiance a week before to a position that made retreat the only alternative to the sword? At the head of them all sat in misery, a sovereign reduced by disease to a wavering shadow of the will and vision of a man. They marched headlong to the pit that Bismarck was digging for them.

On July 14 Mr. Gladstone again writes to Lord Granville,

[1] The Rothschild telegram was:—The Prince has given up his candidature. The French are satisfied.

[2] No. 39. Correspondence respecting the negotiations preliminary to the war between France and Prussia, 1870.

suggesting answers to questions that might be asked that
night in parliament. Should they say that the candidature
was withdrawn, and that with this withdrawal we had a right
to hope the whole affair would end, but that communications
were still continued with Prussia? In duty to all parties we
were bound to hope that the subject of complaint having
disappeared, the complaint itself and the danger to the peace
of Europe would disappear also. Then he proceeds :—' What
if you were to telegraph to Lyons to signify that we think
it probable questions may be asked in parliament to-day ;
that having been called in by France itself, we cannot affect
to be wholly outside the matter ; and that it will be impossible
for us to conceal the opinion that the cause of quarrel having
been removed, France ought to be satisfied. While this might
fairly pass as a friendly notice, it might also be useful as
admonition. Please to consider. The claim in the telegrams
for more acknowledgment of the conduct of Prussia in parliament, seems to me to deserve consideration.'

On July 13 Gramont asked Lord Lyons whether he could
count upon the good offices of England in obtaining the prohibition of any future candidature, at the same time giving
him a written assurance that this would terminate the incident.
Lord Lyons declined to commit himself, and referred home for
instructions. The cabinet was hastily summoned for noon on
the 14th. It decided that the demand could not be justified by
France, and at the same time took a step of which Gramont
chose to say, that it was the one act done by the English
government in favour of peace. They suggested to Bismarck
that as the King of Prussia had consented to the acceptance by
Prince Leopold of the Spanish crown, and had thereby, in a
certain sense, become a party to the arrangement, so he might
with perfect dignity communicate to the French government
his consent to the withdrawal of the acceptance, if France
waived her demand for an engagement covering the future.
This suggestion Bismarck declined (July 15) to bring before the
King, as he did not feel that he could recommend its acceptance.
As he had decided to hold France tight in the position in
which her rulers had now planted her, we can understand why
he could not recommend the English proposal to his master.
Meanwhile the die was cast.

III

The King of Prussia was taking the waters at Ems. Thither
Benedetti, the French ambassador to his court, under instructions followed him. The King with moderation and temper
told him (July 11) he had just received a telegram that the
answer of Prince Leopold would certainly reach him the next
day, and he would then at once communicate it. Something
(some say Bismarck) prevented the arrival of the courier for

some hours beyond the time anticipated. On the morning of
the 13th the King met Benedetti on the promenade, and asked
him if he had anything new to say. The ambassador obeyed
his orders, and told the King of the demand for assurances
against a future candidature. The King at once refused this
new and unexpected concession, but in parting from Benedetti
said they would resume their conversation in the afternoon.
Meanwhile the courier arrived, but before the courier a
despatch came from Paris conveying the suggestion that the
King might write an apologetic letter to the French Emperor.
This naturally gave the King some offence, but he contented
himself with sending Benedetti a polite message by an aide-de-
camp that he had received in writing from Prince Leopold the
intelligence of his renunciation. 'By this his Majesty considered the question as settled.' Benedetti persevered in
seeking to learn what answer he should make to his government on the question of further assurances. The King replied
by the same officer that he was obliged to decline absolutely
to enter into new negotiations; that what he had said in the
morning was his last word in the matter. On July 14, the
King received Benedetti in the railway carriage on his departure for Berlin, told him that any future negotiations would
be conducted by his government, and parted from him with
courteous salutations. Neither king nor ambassador was
conscious that the country of either had suffered a shadow of
indignity from the representative of the other.

Bismarck called upon the British ambassador in those days,
and made what, in the light of later revelations, seems a
singular complaint. He observed that Great Britain 'should
have forbidden France to enter on the war. She was in a
position to do so, and her interests and those of Europe
demanded it of her.'[1] Later in the year he spoke in the same
sense at Versailles : 'If, at the beginning of the war, the
English had said to Napoleon, "There must be no war," there
would have been none.'[2] What is certain is that nobody
would have been more discomfited by the success of England's
prohibition than Count Bismarck. The sincerity and substance
of his reproach are tested by a revelation made by himself long
after. Though familiar, the story is worth telling over again
in the biography of a statesman who stood for a type alien to
policies of fraud.

Bismarck had hurried from Varzin to Berlin on July 12, in
profound concern lest his royal master should subject his
country and his minister to what, after the menace of Gramont
and Ollivier on July 6, would be grave diplomatic defeat. He
had resolved to retire if the incident should end in this shape,
and the chief actor has himself described the strange sinister

[1] *The Diplomatic Reminiscences of Lord Augustus Loftus.* Second series, i. p. 283.
[2] Busch, i. p. 312.

scene that averted his design. He invited Moltke and Roon to dine with him alone on July 13. In the midst of their conversation, 'I was informed,' he says, 'that a telegram from Ems in cipher, if I recollect rightly, of about 200 "groups" was being deciphered. When the copy was handed me it showed that Abeken had drawn up and signed the telegram at his Majesty's command, and I read it out to my guests, whose dejection was so great that they turned away from food and drink. On a repeated examination of the document I lingered upon the authorisation of his Majesty, which included a command, immediately to communicate Benedetti's fresh demand and its rejection to our ambassadors and to the press. I put a few questions to Moltke as to the extent of his confidence in the state of our preparations, especially as to the time they would still require in order to meet this sudden risk of war. He answered that if there was to be war he expected no advantage to us by deferring its outbreak. . . . Under the conviction that war could be avoided only at the cost of the honour of Prussia, I made use of the royal authorisation to publish the contents of the telegram ; and in the presence of my two guests I reduced the telegram by striking out words, but without adding or altering, to the following form : " After the news of the renunciation of the hereditary Prince of Hohenzollern had been officially communicated to the imperial government of France by the royal government of Spain, the French ambassador at Ems further demanded of his Majesty the King that he would authorise him to telegraph to Paris that his Majesty the King bound himself for all future time never again to give his consent if the Hohenzollerns should renew their candidature. His Majesty the King thereupon decided not to receive the French ambassador again, and sent to tell him through the aide-de-camp on duty that his Majesty had nothing further to communicate to the ambassador." The difference in the effect of the abbreviated text of the Ems telegram, as compared with that produced by the original, was not the result of stronger words but of the form, which made this announcement appear decisive, while Abeken's version would only have been regarded as a fragment of a negotiation still pending and to be continued at Berlin. After I had read out the concentrated edition to my two guests, Moltke remarked : " Now it has a different ring ; it sounded before like a parley ; now it is like a flourish in answer to a challenge." I went on to explain : " If in execution of his Majesty's order I at once communicate this text, which contains no alteration in or addition to the telegram, not only to the newspapers, but also by telegraph to all our embassies, it will be known in Paris before midnight, and not only an account of its contents, but also an account of the manner of its distribution, will have the effect of a red rag upon the Gallic bull. Fight we must, if we do not want to act the part of the vanquished without a battle. Success, however, essentially depends upon the impression which the origination of the war makes upon us and others ; it is important that we should be the party attacked, and that we fearlessly meet the public threats of France." This explanation brought about in the two generals a revulsion to a more joyous mood, the liveliness of which surprised me. They had suddenly recovered their pleasure in eating and drinking, and spoke in a more cheerful vein. Roon said : " Our God of old lives still, and will not let us perish in disgrace." [1]

The telegram devised at the Berlin dinner-party soon reached Paris. For a second time the 14th day of July was to be a date of doom in French history. The Emperor and his council deliberated on the grave question of calling out the reserves. The decisive step had been pressed by Marshal Lebœuf the night before without success. He now returned to the charge, and this time his proposal was resolved upon. It was about four o'clock. The marshal had hardly left the room before new scruples seized his colleagues. The discussion began over again, and misgivings revived. The Emperor showed himself downcast and worn out. Towards five o'clock somebody came to tell them it was absolutely necessary that ministers should present themselves before the Chambers. Gramont rose and told them that if they wished an accommodation, there was still one way, an appeal to Europe. The word congress was no sooner pronounced than the Emperor, seized by extraordinary emotion at the thought of salvation by his own favourite chimera, was stirred even to tears. An address to the Powers was instantly drawn up, and the council broke off. At six o'clock Lebœuf received a note from the Emperor, seeming to regret the decision to call out the reserves. On Lebœuff's demand the council was convoked for ten o'clock that night. In the interval news came that the Ems telegram had been communicated to foreign governments. As Bismarck had

---

[1] Bismarck: His Reflections and Reminiscences, 1898, ii. pp. 95-101. As I have it before me, the reader will perhaps care to see the telegram as Bismarck received it, drawn up by Abeken at the King's command, handed in at Ems, July 13, in the afternoon, and reaching Berlin at six in the evening :—' His Majesty writes to me: "Count Benedetti spoke to me on the promenade, in order to demand from me, finally in a very importunate manner, that I should authorise him to telegraph at once that I bound myself for all future time never again to give my consent if the Hohenzollerns should renew their candidature. I refused at last somewhat sternly, as it is neither right nor possible to undertake engagements of this kind à tout jamais. Naturally I told him I had as yet received no news, and as he was earlier informed about Paris and Madrid he could clearly see that my government once more had no hand in the matter." His Majesty has since received a letter from the Prince. His Majesty having told Count Benedetti that he was awaiting news from the Prince, has decided, with reference to the above demand, upon the representation of Count Eulenburg and myself, not to receive Count Benedetti again, but only to let him be informed through an aide-de-camp : That his Majesty has now received from the Prince confirmation of the news which Benedetti had already received from Paris, and has nothing further to say to the ambassador. His Majesty leaves it to your excellency whether Benedetti's fresh demand and its rejection should not be at once communicated both to our ambassadors and to the press.' (ii. p. 96.)

calculated, the affront of the telegram was aggravated by publicity. At ten o'clock the council met, and mobilisation was again considered. By eleven it was almost decided that mobilisation should be put off. At eleven o'clock a foreign office despatch arrived, and was read at the council. What was this despatch, is not yet known—perhaps from the French military agent at Berlin, with further news of Prussian preparations. It was of such a kind that it brought about an instant reaction. The orders for mobilisation were maintained.[1]

An inflammatory appeal was made to the Chambers. When a parliamentary committee was appointed, a vital document was suppressed, and its purport misrepresented. Thus in point of scruple, the two parties to the transaction were not ill-matched, but Bismarck had been watchful, provident, and well informed, while his opponents were men, as one of them said, 'of a light heart,' heedless, uncalculating, and ignorant and wrong as to their facts.[2]

On July 15 Mr. Gladstone reported to the Queen :—

> Mr. Disraeli made inquiries from the government respecting the differences between France and Prussia, and in so doing expressed opinions strongly adverse to France as the apparent aggressor. Mr. Gladstone, in replying, admitted it to be the opinion of the government that there was no matter known to be in controversy of a nature to warrant a disturbance of the general peace. He said the course of events was not favourable, and the decisive moment must in all likelihood be close at hand.

'At a quarter past four,' says a colleague, 'a cabinet box was handed down the treasury bench to Gladstone. He opened it and looking along to us, said—with an accent I shall never forget—" War declared against Prussia."'[3] 'Shall I ever forget,' says Archbishop Tait, 'Gladstone's face of earnest care when I saw him in the lobby ?'[4]

The British cabinet made a final effort for peace. Lord Granville instructed our ambassadors to urge France and Prussia to be so far controlled by the treaty of Paris that before proceeding to extremities they should have recourse to the good offices of some friendly Power, adding that his government was ready to take any part that might be desired in the matter. On the 18th Bismarck replied by throwing the onus of acceptance on France. On the 19th France declined the proposal.

Just as Bismarck said that England ought to have prevented

---

1 See Sorel, *Hist. diplomatique de la guerre franco-allemande* (1875), i. pp. 169-71.

2 In the Reichstag, on July 20, Bismarck reproached the French ministers for not yielding to the pressure of the members of the opposition like Thiers and Gambetta, and producing the document, which would have overthrown the base on which the declaration of war was founded. Yet he had prepared this document for the very purpose of tempting France into a declaration of war.

3 Grant Duff's *Diaries*, ii. p. 153. The technical declaration of war by France was made at Berlin on July 19.

4 *Life*, ii. p. 78.

the war, Frenchmen also said that we ought to have held the Emperor back. With what sanction could Mr. Gladstone have enforced peremptory counsel? Was France to be made to understand that England would go to war on the Prussian side? Short of war, what more could she have done? Lord Granville had told Gramont that he had never in despatch or conversation admitted that after the French had received satisfaction in substance, there was a case for a quarrel on pure form. The British cabinet and their ambassador in Paris had redoubled warning and remonstrance. If the Emperor and his advisers did not listen to the penetrating expostulations of Thiers, and to his vigorous and instructed analysis of the conditions of their case, why should they listen to Lord Granville? Nor was there time, for their precipitancy had kindled a conflagration before either England or any other Power had any chance of extinguishing the blaze.[1]

To Michel Chevalier Mr. Gladstone wrote a few days later :—

I cannot describe to you the sensation of pain, almost of horror, which has thrilled through this country from end to end at the outbreak of hostilities, the commencement of the work of blood. I suppose there was a time when England would have said, 'Let our neighbours, being, as they are, our rivals, waste their energies, their wealth, their precious irrevocable lives, in destroying one another : they will be the weaker, we shall be relatively the stronger.' But we have now unlearned that bad philosophy ; and the war between France and Prussia saddens the whole face of society, and burdens every man with a personal grief. We do not pretend to be sufficient judges of the merits : I now mean by 'we' those who are in authority, and perhaps in a condition to judge least ill. We cannot divide praise and blame as between parties. I hope you do not think it unkind that I should write thus. Forgive the *rashness* of a friend. One of the purposes in life dear to my heart has been to knit together in true amity the people of my own country with those of your great nation. That web of concord is too tender yet, not to suffer under the rude strain of conflicts and concussions even such as we have no material share in. I think that even if I err, I cannot be without a portion of your sympathy : now when the knell of the brave begins to toll. As for us, we have endeavoured to cherish with both the relations of peace and mutual respect. May nothing happen to impair them !

Though good feeling prevented Mr. Gladstone from dividing praise and blame between the two governments, his own judgment was clear. The initial declaration of July 6, followed by the invention of a second demand by France upon Prussia after the first had been conceded, looked to him, as it did to England

---

[1] 'Il fallait donner à l'Europe le temps d'intervenir, ce qui n'empêchait pas que vos armements continuassent, et il ne fallait pas se hâter, de venir ici dans le moment où la susceptibilité française devait être la plus exigeante, des faits qui devaient causer une irritation dangereuse. . . . Ce n'est pas pour l'intérêt essentiel de la France, c'est par la faute du cabinet que nous avons la guerre.'—*Thiers*, in the Chamber, July 15, 1870. For this line of contention he was called an ' unpatriotic trumpet of disaster,' and other names commonly bestowed on all men in all countries who venture to say that what chances for the hour to be a popular war is a blunder.

generally, like a fixed resolution to force a quarrel. In September he wrote of the proceedings of the French government:—

Wonder rises to its climax when we remember that this feverish determination to force a quarrel was associated with a firm belief in the high preparation and military superiority of the French forces, the comparative inferiority of the Germans, the indisposition of the smaller states to give aid to Prussia, and even the readiness of Austria, with which from his long residence at Vienna the Duc de Gramont supposed himself to be thoroughly acquainted, to appear in arms as the ally of France. It too soon appeared that, as the advisers of the Emperor knew nothing of public rights and nothing of the sense of Europe, so they knew nothing about Austria and the mind of the German states, and less than nothing about not only the Prussian army, but even their own.[1]

[1] *Gleanings*, iv. p. 222.

CHAPTER V

NEUTRALITY AND ANNEXATION

(1870)

The immediate purpose with which Italians and Germans effected the great change in the European constitution was unity, not liberty. They constructed not securities but forces. Machiavelli's time had come.—ACTON.

'THE war is a grievous affair,' Mr. Gladstone said to Brand, 'and adds much to our cares, for to maintain our neutrality in such a case as this, will be a most arduous task. On the face of the facts France is wrong; but as to personal trustworthiness the two moving spirits on the respective sides, Napoleon and Bismarck, are nearly on a par.' His individual activity was unsparing. He held almost daily conferences with Lord Granville at the foreign office; criticised and minuted despatches; contributed freely to the drafts. 'There has not, I think,' he wrote to Bright (Sept. 12), 'been a single day on which Granville and I have not been in anxious communication on the subject of the war.' When Lord Granville went to Walmer he wrote to Mr. Gladstone, 'I miss our discussions here over the despatches as they come in very much.' 'I hope I need not say that while you are laid up with gout at Walmer,' Mr. Gladstone wrote in October, 'I am most ready to start at a few hours' notice at any time of day or night, to join you upon any matter which you may find to require it. Indeed I could not properly or with comfort remain here upon any other terms.' Details of this agitating time, with all its convulsions and readjustments, belong to the history of Europe. The part taken by Mr. Gladstone and his cabinet was for several months in pretty close harmony with the humour of the country. It will be enough for us to mark their action at decisive moments.

On July 16 he wrote to Cardwell at the war office:—

If, unhappily, which God forbid, we have to act in this war, it will not be with six months', nor three months', nor even one month's notice. The real question is, supposing an urgent call of honour and of duty in an emergency for 15,000 or 20,000 men, what would you do? What

answer would the military authorities make to this question, those of
them especially who have brains rather than mere position ? Have you
no fuller battalions than those of 500 ? At home or in the Mediterranean ?
If in the latter, should they not be brought home ? Childers seemed to
offer a handsome subscription of marines, and that the artillery would
count for much in such a case is most probable. What I should like is to
study the means of sending 20,000 men to Antwerp with as much
promptitude as at the Trent affair we sent 10,000 to Canada.

The figures of the army and navy were promptly supplied to
the prime minister, Cardwell adding with a certain shrillness
that, though he had no wish to go either to Antwerp or anywhere else, he could not be responsible for sending an
expedition abroad, unless the army were fitted for that object
by measures taken now to increase its force.

I entirely agree with you, Mr. Gladstone replied, that *when* it is
seriously intended to send troops to Antwerp or elsewhere abroad,
'immediate measures must be taken to increase our force.' I feel, however, rather uneasy at what seems to me the extreme susceptibility on one
side of the case of some members of the cabinet. I hope it will be
balanced by considering the effect of any forward step by appeal to
parliament, in compromising the true and entire neutrality of our
position, and in disturbing and misdirecting the mind of the public and
of parliament. I am afraid I have conveyed to your mind a wrong
impression as to the state of my own. It is only a far outlook which,
in my opinion, brings into view as a possibility the sending a force to
Antwerp. Should the day arrive, we shall then be on the very edge of
war, with scarcely a hope of not passing onward into the abyss.

Cardwell sent him a paper by a high military authority, on
which Mr. Gladstone made two terse ironic comments. 'I
think the paper,' he said, 'if it proves anything proves (1)
That generals and not ministers are the proper judges of those
weights in the political scales which express the likelihood of
war and peace ; (2) That there is very little difference between
absolute neutrality and actual war. I advise that Granville
should see it.'

On July 25 the *Times* divulged the text of a projected agreement in 1869 (it was in truth 1867) between the French and
Prussian governments in five articles, including one that the
incorporation of Belgium by France would not be objected to
by Prussia. The public was shocked and startled, and many
were inclined to put down the document for a forgery and a
hoax. As a matter of fact, in substance it was neither. The
Prussian ambassador a few days before had informed Mr.
Gladstone and Lord Granville personally and in strict secrecy,
that the draft of such a project existed in the handwriting of
M. Benedetti. This private communication was taken by Mr.
Gladstone to have been made with the object of prompting him
to be the agent in producing the evil news to the world, and
thus to prejudice France in the judgment of Europe. He

thought that no part of his duty, and took time to consider it, in the expectation that it was pretty sure to find its way into print by some other means, as indeed soon happened. 'For the sake of peace,' Bismarck explained to Lord Granville (July 28, 1870), 'I kept the secret, and treated the propositions in a dilatory manner.' When the British ambassador on one occasion had tried to sound him on the suspected designs of France, Bismarck answered, 'It is no business of mine to tell French secrets.'

There were members of the cabinet who doubted the expediency of England taking any action. The real position of affairs, they argued, was not altered : the draft treaty only disclosed what everybody believed before, namely that France sought compensation for Prussian aggrandizement, as she had secured it for Italian aggrandizement by taking Savoy and Nice. That Prussia would not object, provided the compensations were not at the expense of people who spoke German, had all come out at the time of the Luxemburg affair. If France and Prussia agreed, how could we help Belgium, unless indeed Europe joined? But then what chance was there of Russia and Austria joining against France and Prussia for the sake of Belgium, in which neither of them had any direct interest? At the same time ministers knew that the public in England expected them to do something, though a vote for men and money would probably suffice. The cabinet, however, advanced a step beyond a parliamentary vote. On July 30 they met and took a decision to which Mr. Gladstone then and always after attached high importance. England proposed a treaty to Prussia and France, providing that if the armies of either violated the neutrality of Belgium, Great Britain would co-operate with the other for its defence, but without engaging to take part in the general operations of the war. The treaty was to hold good for twelve months after the conclusion of the war. Bismarck at once came into the engagement. France loitered a little, but after the battle of Wörth made no more difficulty, and the instrument was signed on August 9.

The mind of the government was described by Mr. Gladstone in a letter to Bright (August 1) :—

Although some members of the cabinet were inclined on the outbreak of this most miserable war to make military preparations, others, Lord Granville and I among them, by no means shared that disposition, nor I think was the feeling of parliament that way inclined. But the publication of the treaty has altered all this, and has thrown upon us the necessity either of doing something fresh to secure Belgium, or else of saying that under no circumstances would we take any step to secure her from absorption. This publication has wholly altered the feeling of the House of Commons, and no government could at this moment venture to give utterance to such an intention about Belgium. But neither do we think it would be right, even if it were safe, to announce that we would in any case stand by with folded arms, and see actions done which would amount to a total extinction of public right in Europe.

The idea of engagements that might some day involve resort to force made Bright uneasy, and Mr. Gladstone wrote to him again (August 4) :—

It will be a great addition to the domestic portion of the griefs of this most unhappy war, if it is to be the cause of a political severance between you and the present administration. To this I know you would justly reply that the claims of conviction are paramount. I hope, however, that the moment has not quite arrived. . . . You will, I am sure, give me credit for good faith, when I say, especially on Lord Granville's part as on my own, who are most of all responsible, that we take this step in the interest of peace. . . . The recommendation set up in opposition to it generally is, that we should simply declare *we* will defend the neutrality of Belgium by arms in case it should be attacked. Now the sole or single-handed defence of Belgium would be an enterprise which we incline to think Quixotic ; if these two great military powers combined against it— that combination is the only serious danger ; and this it is which by our proposed engagements we should I hope render improbable to the very last degree. I add for myself this confession of faith. If the Belgian people desire, on their own account, to join France or any other country, I for one will be no party to taking up arms to prevent it. But that the Belgians, whether they would or not, should go 'plump' down the maw of another country to satisfy dynastic greed, is another matter. The accomplishment of such a crime as this implies, would come near to an extinction of public right in Europe, and I do not think we could look on while the sacrifice of freedom and independence was in course of consummation.

II

By the end of the first week of August the storm of war had burst upon the world. 'On the 2nd of August, in the insignificant affair of Saarbrück, the Emperor of the French assumed a feeble offensive. On the 4th, the Prussians replied energetically at Wissemburg. And then what a torrent, what a deluge of events ! In twenty-eight days ten battles were fought. Three hundred thousand men were sent to the hospitals, to captivity, or to the grave. The German enemy had penetrated into the interior of France, over a distance of a hundred and fifty miles of territory, and had stretched forth everywhere as he went the strong hand of possession. The Emperor was a prisoner, and had been deposed with general consent ; his family wanderers, none knew where ; the embryo at least of a republic, born of the hour, had risen on the ruins of the empire, while proud and gorgeous Paris was awaiting with divided mind the approach of the conquering monarch and his countless host.'[1] This was Mr. Gladstone's description of a marvellous and shattering hour.

Talleyrand was fond in the days of 1815 at Vienna, of

applying to any diplomatist who happened to agree with him the expression, 'a good European.' He meant a statesman who was capable of conceiving the state-system of the western world as a whole. The events of August made the chief minister of Austria now exclaim, 'I see no longer any Europe.' All the notions of alliance that had so much to do with the precipitation of the war were dissipated. Italy, so far from joining France, marched into Rome. Austria ostentatiously informed England that she was free from engagements. The Czar of Russia was nephew of the Prussian king and German in his leanings, but Gortchakoff, his minister, was jealous of Bismarck, and his sympathies inclined to France, and Czar and minister alike nursed designs in the Black Sea. With such materials as these Mr. Pitt himself with all his subsidies could not have constructed a fighting coalition. Even the sons of stricken France after the destruction of the empire were a divided people. For side by side with national defence against the invader, republican and monarchic propagandism was at work, internecine in its temper and scattering baleful seeds of civil war.

'Many,' Mr. Gladstone wrote to Chevalier in September, 'seem so over-sanguine as to suppose that it is in our power at any moment, by friendly influence of reasoning, to solve the problem which has brought together in the shock of battle the two greatest military powers of Europe. . . . I do not see that it is an offence on our part not to interfere when the belligerents differ so widely, when we have not the hope of bringing them together, and when we cannot adopt without reserve the language and claims of either.' Material responsibility and moral responsibility both pointed to a rigid equity between the combatants, and to strict neutrality. The utmost to be done was to localise the war ; and with this aim, the British cabinet induced Italy, Austria, Russia, and smaller powers to come to a common agreement that none of them would depart from neutrality without a previous understanding with the rest. This league of the neutrals, though negative, was at least a shadow of collective action, from which good might come if the belligerents should some day accept or invite mediation. To this diplomatic neutrality the only alternative was an armed neutrality, and armed neutrality has not always served pacific ends.

To the German contention at one stage after the overthrow of the empire, that the Empress was still the only authority existing legally for France, Mr. Gladstone was energetically opposed. 'It embodied,' he said, 'the doctrine that no country can have a new government without the consent of the old one.' 'Ought we,' he asked Lord Granville (Sept. 20), 'to witness in silence the promulgation of such a doctrine, which is utterly opposed to the modern notions of public right, though it was

in vogue fifty years back, and though it was acted on with
most fatal consequences by the Prussians of eighty years back?'
Then as for mediation, whether isolated or in common, he saw
no hope in it. He said to the Duke of Argyll (Sept. 6), 'I would
not say a word ever so gently. I believe it would do great
mischief. As at present advised, I see but two really safe
grounds for mediation, (1) a drawn battle ; (2) the request of
both parties.' Ever since 1862, and his error in the American
war—so he now wrote to Lord Granville,—'in forming and
expressing an opinion that the Southerners had virtually
established their independence, I have been very fearful of
giving opinions with regard to the proper course for foreign
nations to pursue in junctures, of which, after all, I think they
have better means of forming a judgment than foreigners can
possess.'

In the middle of September Thiers, in the course of
his valiant mission to European courts, reached London.
'Yesterday,' Mr. Gladstone writes (Sept. 14), 'I saw Thiers
and had a long conversation with him ; he was very clear and
touching in parts. But the purpose of his mission is vague.
He seems come to do just what he can.' The vagueness of
Thiers did but mirror the distractions of France. Not even
from his ingenious, confident, and fertile mind could men hope
for a clue through the labyrinth of European confusions.
Great Britain along with four other powers recognised the
new government of the Republic in France at the beginning
of February 1871.

It was about this time that Mr. Gladstone took what was
for a prime minister the rather curious step of volunteering
an anonymous article in a review, upon these great affairs in
which his personal responsibility was both heavy and direct.[1]
The precedent can hardly be called a good one, for as anybody
might have known, the veil was torn aside in a few hours
after the *Edinburgh Review* containing his article appeared.
Its object, he said afterwards, was 'to give what I thought
needful information on a matter of great national importance,
which involved at the time no interest of party whatever. If
such interests had been involved, a rule from which I have
never as a minister diverted would have debarred me from
writing.' Lord Granville told him that, 'It seemed to be an
admirable argument, the more so as it is the sort of thing
Thiers ought to have said and did not.' The article made a
great noise, as well it might, for it was written with much
eloquence, truth, and power, and was calculated to console
his countrymen for seeing a colossal European conflict going

---

[1] To be found in *Gleanings,* iv. In republishing it, Mr. Gladstone says, 'This
article is the only one ever written by me, which was meant for the time to be in
substance, as well as in form, anonymous.' That was in 1878. Two years later he
contributed an anonymous article, 'The Conservative Collapse,' to the *Fortnightly
Review* (May 1880).

on, without the privilege of a share in it. One passage about happy England—happy especially that the wise dispensation of Providence had cut her off by the streak of silver sea from continental dangers—rather irritated than convinced. The production of such an article under such circumstances was a striking illustration of Mr. Gladstone's fervid desire—the desire of a true orator's temperament—to throw his eager mind upon a multitude of men, to spread the light of his own urgent conviction, to play the part of missionary with a high evangel, which had been his earliest ideal forty years before. Everybody will agree that it was better to have a minister writing his own articles in a respectable quarterly, than doctoring other people's articles with concomitants from a reptile fund.

III

On the vital question of the annexation of Alsace and Lorraine, Mr. Gladstone's view was easy to anticipate. He could not understand how the French protests turned more upon the inviolability of French soil, than on the attachment of the people of Alsace and North Lorraine to their country. The abstract principle he thought peculiarly awkward in a nation that had made recent annexations of her own. Upon all his correspondents at home and abroad, he urged that the question ought to be worked on the basis of the sentiments of the people concerned, and not upon the principle of inviolability. He composed an elaborate memorandum for the cabinet, but without effect. On the last day of September, he records :—' *Sept.* 30 : Cabinet 2¼-6. I failed in my two objects. 1. An effort to speak with the other neutral Powers against the transfer of Alsace and Lorraine without reference to the populations. 2. Immediate release of Fenian prisoners.'

To Mr. Bright, who was still prevented by illness from attending cabinets, and who had the second of the two objects much at heart, he wrote the next day :—

I send for your private perusal the inclosed mem. which I proposed to the cabinet yesterday, but could not induce them to adopt. It presupposes the concurrence of the neutral Powers. They agreed in the opinions, but did not think the expression of them timely. My opinion certainly is that the transfer of territory and inhabitants by mere force calls for the reprobation of Europe, and that Europe is entitled to utter it, and can utter it with good effect.

The ground taken by him in the cabinet was as follows :—

A matter of this kind cannot be regarded as in principle a question between the two belligerents only, but involves considerations of legitimate interest to all the Powers of Europe. It appears to bear on the Belgian question in particular. It is also a principle likely to be of great consequence in the eventual settlement of the Eastern question. Quite apart from the subject of mediation, it cannot be right that the neutral Powers should remain silent, while this principle of consulting the wishes of the population is trampled down, should the actual sentiment of Alsace and Lorraine be such as to render that language applicable. The mode of expressing any view of this matter is doubtless a question requiring much consideration. The decision of the cabinet was that the time for it had not yet come. Any declaration in the sense described would, Mr. Gladstone thought, entail, in fairness, an obligation to repudiate the present claim of France to obtain peace without surrendering 'either an inch of her territory or a stone of her fortresses.'

Mr. Bright did not agree with him, but rather favoured the principle of inviolability. In November Mr. Gladstone prepared a still more elaborate memorandum in support of a protest from the neutral Powers. The Duke of Argyll put what was perhaps the general view when he wrote to Mr. Gladstone (Nov. 25, 1870), 'that he had himself never argued in favour of the German annexation of Alsace and Lorraine, but only against our having any right to oppose it otherwise than by the most friendly dissuasion.' The Duke held that the consent of populations to live under a particular government is a right subject to a great many qualifications, and it would not be easy to turn such a doctrine into the base of an official remonstrance. After all, he said, the instincts of nations stand for something in this world. The German did not exceed the ancient acknowledged right of nations in successful wars, when he said to Alsace and Lorraine, 'Conquest in a war forced upon me by the people of which you form a part, gives me the *right* to annex, if on other grounds I deem it expedient, and for strategic reasons I do so deem it.'

Mr. Gladstone, notwithstanding his cabinet, held to his view energetically expressed as follows :—

If the contingency happen, not very probable, of a sudden accommodation which shall include the throttling of Alsace and part of Lorraine, without any voice previously raised against it, it will in my opinion be a standing reproach to England. There is indeed the Russian plan of not recognising that in which we have had no part ; but it is difficult to say what this comes to.

On December 20 he says to Lord Granville what we may take for a last word on this part of the case :—'While I more and more feel the deep culpability of France, I have an apprehension that this violent laceration and transfer is to lead us from bad to worse, and to be the *beginning* of a new series of European complications.'

While working in the spirit of cordial and even eager loyalty to the prime minister, Lord Granville disagreed with him upon the question of diplomatic action against annexation. Palmerston, he said to Mr. Gladstone in October, 'wasted the strength derived by England in the great war by his brag. I am afraid of our wasting that which we at present derive from moral causes, by laying down general principles when nobody will

attend to them, and when in all probability they will be
disregarded. My objection to doing at present what you propose
is, that it is impossible according to my views to do so without
being considered to throw our weight into the French scale
against Germany, with consequent encouragement on one side
and irritation on the other.'

Like Thiers, Mr. Gladstone had been leaning upon the concurrence of the neutral Powers, and active co-operation at
St. Petersburg. Russian objects were inconsistent with the
alienation of Germany, and they made a fatal bar to all schemes
for lowering the German terms. This truth of the situation was
suddenly brought home to England in no palatable way.

CHAPTER VI

THE BLACK SEA

(1870–1871)

'You are always talking to me of principles. As if your public law were anything to me; I do not know what it means. What do you suppose that all your parchments and your treaties signify to me?'—ALEXANDER I. to TALLEYRAND.

AT the close of the Crimean war in 1856, by the provisions of the treaty of Paris, Russia and Turkey were restrained from constructing arsenals on the coast of the Euxine, and from maintaining ships of war on its waters. No serious statesman believed that the restriction would last, any more than Napoleon's restraint on Prussia in 1808 against keeping up an army of more than forty-two thousand men could last. Palmerston had this neutralisation more at heart than anybody else, and Lord Granville told the House of Lords what durability Palmerston expected for it :—

General Ignatieff told me that he remarked to Lord Palmerston, 'These are stipulations which you cannot expect will last long,' and Lord Palmerston replied, 'They will last ten years.' A learned civilian, a great friend of mine, told me he heard Lord Palmerston talk on the subject, and say, 'Well, at all events they will last my life.' A noble peer, a colleague of mine, an intimate friend of Lord Palmerston, says Lord Palmerston told him they would last seven years.[1]

In 1856 Mr. Gladstone declared his opinion, afterwards often repeated, that the neutralisation of the Black Sea, popular as it might be in England at the moment, was far from being a satisfactory arrangement.[2] Were the time to come, he said, when Russia might resume aggressive schemes on Turkey, he believed that neutralisation would mean nothing but a series of pitfalls much deeper than people expected.[3] These pitfalls now came into full view. On the last day of October Prince Gortchakoff addressed a circular to the Powers, announcing

[1] House of Lords, Feb. 14, 1871.

[2] The stipulations 'were politically absurd, and therefore in the long run impossible.' 'The most inept conclusions of the peace of Paris.'—Bismarck, Reflections, ii. p. 114.

[3] Hansard, May 6, 1856. See also May 24, 1855, and Aug. 3, 1855.

that his imperial master could 'no longer consider himself bound to the terms of the treaty of March 1856, in so far as these limit his rights of sovereignty in the Black Sea.' On the merits there was very little real dispute in Europe. As Lord Granville once wrote to Mr. Gladstone: 'There was no doubt about Germany having at Paris, and subsequently, always taken the Russian view. France made an intimation to the same effect very soon after the conclusion of the treaty. And Austria later. Italy did the same, but not in so decided a manner. . . . I have frequently said in public that with the exception of ourselves and the Turks, all the co-signatories of the treaty of Paris had expressed views in favour of modifying the article, previous to Prince Gortchakoff's declaration.'[1]

To have a good case on the merits was one thing, and to force it at the sword's point was something extremely different. As Mr. Gladstone put it in a memorandum that became Lord Granville's despatch, 'the question was not whether any desire expressed by Russia ought to be carefully examined in a friendly spirit by the co-signatory powers, but whether they are to accept from her an announcement that by her own act, without any consent from them, she has released herself from a solemn covenant.'[2] Mr. Gladstone, not dissenting on the substance of the Russian claim, was outraged by the form. The only parallel he ever found to Gortchakoff's proceedings in 1870 was a certain claim, of which we shall soon see something, made by America in 1872. 'I have had half an idea,' he wrote to Lord Granville, 'that it might be well I should see Brunnow [the Russian ambassador] either with you or alone. All know the mischief done by the Russian idea of Lord Aberdeen, and the opposition are in the habit of studiously representing me as his double, or his heir in pacific traditions. This I do not conceive to be true, and possibly I might undeceive Brunnow a little.'

In this country, as soon as the news of the circular was made known, the public excitement was intense. Consols instantly dropped heavily. Apart from the form of the Russian claim, the public still alert upon the eastern question, felt that the question was once more alive. As Mr. Gladstone had said to Lord Granville (Oct. 4, 1870), 'Everybody at a time like this looks out for booty; it will be hard to convince central Europe that Turkey is not a fair prize.' From France Lord Lyons wrote to Mr. Gladstone (Nov. 14) that the Russian declaration was looked upon with complacency, because it might lead to a congress, and at all events it might, by causing a stir among the neutrals, give a check to Prussia as well as to Russia.

---

[1] Bismarck, in his *Reflections*, takes credit to himself for having come to an understanding with Russia on this question at the outbreak of the Franco-German war.

[2] 'The whole pith of the despatch was yours.'—Granville to Mr. Gladstone, Nov. 18, 1870.

Lord Granville wrote to Mr. Gladstone, who was at Hawarden (Nov. 21) :—

I am very sorry to hear that you are not well. Of course, you must run no risk, but as soon as you can you will, I hope, come up and have a cabinet. Childers has been here. He tells me there is a perfect howl about ministers not meeting. He is more quiet in his talk than I hear some of our colleagues are. But he says if there is to be war, every day lost is most injurious. I have told him that it is impossible to say that we may not be driven into it by Russia, or by other foreign powers, or by our own people; that we must take care of our dignity; but if there ever was a cabinet which is bound not to drift into an unnecessary war, it is ours.

Mr. Gladstone replied next day :—

I will frankly own that I am much disgusted with a good deal of the language that I have read in the newspapers within the last few days about immediate war with Russia. I try to put a check on myself to prevent the reaction it engenders. Your observation on drifting into war is most just : though I always thought Clarendon's epithet in this one case inapplicable as well as unadvisable. I know, however, nothing more like drifting into war than would be a resort to any military measures whatever, except with reference either to some actual fact or some well defined contingency. . . .

II

The courses open to the British Government in the face of the circular were these. They might silently or with a protest acquiesce. Or they might declare an offensive war (much deprecated by Turkey herself) against a nation that had peculiar advantages for defence, and for an object that every other signatory power thought in itself a bad object. Third, they might, in accordance with a wonderfully grand scheme suggested to ministers, demand from Germany, all flushed as she was with military pride, to tell us plainly whether she was on our side or Russia's; and if the German answer did not please us, then we should make an offensive alliance with France, Austria, Italy, and Turkey, checking Russia in the east and Germany in the west. A fourth plan was mutely to wait, on the plea that whatever Russia might have said, nothing had been done. The fifth plan was a conference. This was hardly heroic enough to please everybody in the cabinet. At least it saved us from the insanity of a war that would have intensified European confusion, merely to maintain restraints considered valuable by nobody. The expedient of a conference was effectively set in motion by Bismarck, then pre-occupied in his critical Bavarian treaty and the siege of Paris. On Nov. 12, Mr. Odo Russell left London for Versailles on a special mission to the Prussian king. The intrepidity of our emissary soon secured a remarkable success, and the episode of Bismarck's intervention in the business was important.

Mr. Odo Russell had three hours' conversation with Count

Bismarck on November 21. Bismarck told him that the Russian circular had taken him by surprise; that though he had always thought the treaty of 1856 too hard upon Russia, he entirely disapproved both of the manner and time chosen for forcing on a revision of it; that he could not interfere nor even answer the circular, but to prevent the outbreak of another war he would recommend conferences at Constantinople.[1] The conversation broke off at four o'clock in the afternoon, with this unpromising cast. At ten in the evening it was resumed; it was prolonged until half an hour beyond midnight. 'I felt I knew him better,' Mr. Russell in an unofficial letter tells Lord Granville (Nov. 30), 'and could express more easily all that I had determined to say to convince him that unless he could get Russia to withdraw the circular, we should be compelled with or without allies to go to war.' Bismarck remained long obstinate in his professed doubts of England going to war; but he gradually admitted the truth of the consequences to which a pacific acceptance of 'the Russian kick must inevitably lead. And so he came round to the British point of view, and felt that in our place he could not recede.'

It was not hard to see Bismarck's interests. The mischief to Germany of another European war before Paris had fallen; the moral support to be derived by the Tours government from a revival of the old Anglo-French alliance; the chances of Beust and other persons fishing in the troubled waters of an extended European conflict; the vital importance of peace to the reconstruction of Germany—these were the disadvantages to his own country and policy, of a war between England and Russia; these worked the change in his mind between afternoon and midnight, and led him to support the cause of England and peace against Gortchakoff and his circular. Characteristically, at the same time he strove hard to drive a bargain with the English agent, and to procure some political advantages in exchange for his moral support. 'In politics,' he said, 'one hand should wash the other' (*eine Hand die andere waschen muss*). In Mr. Odo Russell, however, he found a man who talked the language, kept the tone and was alive to all the arts of diplomatic business, and no handwashing followed. When Mr. Russell went to his apartment in the Place Hoche at Versailles that night, he must have felt that he had done a good day's work.

---

[1] Bismarck's private opinion was this:—'Gortchakoff is not carrying on in this matter a real Russian policy (that is, one in the true interests of Russia), but rather a policy of violent aggression. People still believe that Russian diplomats are particularly crafty and clever, full of artifices and stratagems, but that is not the case. If the people at St. Petersburg were clever they would not make any declaration of the kind but would quietly build men-of-war in the Black Sea and wait until they were questioned on the subject. Then they might reply they knew nothing about it, but would make inquiries and so let the matter drag on. That might continue for a long time, and finally people would get accustomed to it.'—Busch, *Bismarck: Some Secret Pages of his History*, i. pp. 312-13.

In the following year, papers were laid before Parliament,
and attention was drawn to the language used by Mr. Russell
to Bismarck, in the pregnant sentence about the question
being of a nature in its present state to compel us with or
without allies, to go to war with Russia.[1]   Mr. Gladstone,
when directly challenged, replied (Feb. 16) that the agent had
used this argument without specific authority or instruction
from the government, but that the duty of diplomatic agents
required them to express themselves in the mode in which they
think they can best support the proposition of which they
wish to procure acceptance.   Mr. Odo Russell explained to Mr.
Gladstone (Feb. 27) that he was led to use the argument about
England being compelled to go to war with or without allies
by these reasons : that we were bound by a definite treaty to
regard any retractation of the stipulations of March 30, 1856,
as a cause of war ;[2] that Gortchakoff's assumption of a right to
renounce provisions directly touching Russian interests seemed
to carry with it the assumption of a right to renounce all the
rest of the treaty ; that Mr. Gladstone's government had
declared (Nov. 10) that it was impossible to sanction the course
announced by Gortchakoff ; that, therefore, France being
otherwise engaged, and Austria being unprepared, we might
be compelled by our joint and several obligations under the
tripartite treaty, to go to war with Russia for proceedings that
we pronounced ourselves unable to sanction ; finally, that he
had never been instructed to state to Prussia, that the question
was not one compelling us ever to go to war, notwithstanding
our treaty engagements.   What was Mr. Gladstone's reply to
this I do not find, but Lord Granville had very sensibly
written to him some weeks before (Dec. 8, 1870) :—

I am afraid our whole success has been owing to the belief that we
would go to war, and to tell the truth, I think that war in some shape or
other, sooner or later, was a possible risk after our note. In any case, I
would reassure nobody now. Promising peace is as unwise as to threaten
war. A sort of instinct that the bumps of combativeness and destructive-
ness are to be found somewhere in your head, has helped us much during
the last five months.

III

Having undertaken to propose a conference, Bismarck did
the best he could for it. The British cabinet accepted on condition that the conference was not to open with any previous
assumption of Gortchakoff's declaration, and they objected to
Petersburg as the scene of operations.   Mr. Gladstone in some
notes prepared for the meeting of his colleagues (Nov. 26), was
very firm on the first and main point, that 'Her Majesty's
government could enter into no conference which should assume
any portion of the treaty to have been already abrogated by

---

[1] Correspondence respecting the treaty of March 30, 1856, No. 76, pp. 44, 45, c. 245.
[2] The tripartite treaty of England, France, Austria, of April 15, 1856.

the discretion of a single Power, and it would be wholly out of place for them, under the present circumstances, to ask for a conference, as they were not the parties who desire to bring about any change in the treaty.' Russia made difficulties, but Bismarck's influence prevailed. The conference assembled not at Petersburg but in London, and subject to no previous assumption as to its results.[1]

The close of a negotiation is wont to drop the curtain over embarrassments that everybody is glad to forget :[2] but the obstacles to an exact agreement were not easily overcome. Lord Granville told Mr. Gladstone that no fewer than thirteen or fourteen versions of the most important protocol were tried before terms were reached. In the end Lord Granville's conclusion was that, as no just rights had been sacrificed, it was a positive advantage that Russia should be gratified by the removal of restraints naturally galling to her pride.

The conference opened at the foreign office on Dec. 17, and held its final meeting on March 13. Delay was caused by the difficulty of procuring the attendance of a representative of France. Jules Favre was appointed by the government at Bordeaux, but he was locked up in Paris, and he and Bismarck could not agree as to the proper form of safe-conduct. What was even more important, the governing men in France could not agree upon his instructions ; for we must remember that all this time along with the patriotic struggle against the Prussians, there went on an internal struggle only a degree less ardent between republicans and monarchists. It was not until the final meeting of the conference that the Duc de Broglie was accredited as representative of his country.[3] At the first formal meeting a special protocol was signed recording it as 'an essential principle of the law of nations that no Power can liberate itself from the engagements of a treaty, nor modify the stipulations thereof, unless with the consent of the contracting Powers by means of an amicable arrangement.'

To give a single signatory Power the right of forbidding a change desired by all the others, imposes a kind of perpetuity on treaty stipulations, that in practice neither could nor ought to be insisted upon. For instance it would have tied fast the hands of Cavour and Victor Emmanuel in the Italian transactions which Mr. Gladstone had followed and assisted with so much enthusiasm, for Austria would never have assented. It is, moreover, true that in the ever-recurring eras when force, truculent and unabashed, sweeps aside the moral judgments of the world, the mere inscription of a pious opinion in a protocol

---

[1] Russell to Lord Granville, c. 245, No. 78, p. 46.
[2] Sorel's *Guerre Franco-Allemande*, ii. chap. 4.
[3] That this failure to take advantage of the conference was an error on the part of France is admitted by modern French historians. Hanotaux, *France Contemporaine*, i. p. 108 ; Sorel, ii. pp. 216-7. Lord Granville had himself pointed out how a discussion upon the terms of peace might have been raised.

may seem worth little trouble. Yet it is the influence of good
opinion, tardy, halting, stumbling, and broken, as it must ever
be, that upholds and quickens the growth of right. The good
rules laid down in conferences and state-papers may look tame
in the glare of the real world of history as it is. Still, if we
may change the figure, they help to dilute the poisons in the
air.

IV

In England opinion veered round after Sedan. The disappearance of the French empire had effectively dispelled
the vivid suspicions of aggression. The creation of the empire
of a united Germany showed a new Europe. The keen word
of an English diplomatist expressed what was dawning in
men's minds as a new misgiving. 'Europe,' he said, 'has lost
a mistress and got a master.' Annexation wore an ugly look.
Meetings to express sympathy with France in her struggle
were held in London and the provinces. Still on the whole
the general verdict seemed to be decisively in favour of a
resolute neutrality, for in fact, nobody who knew anything of
the state of Europe could suggest a policy of British intervention that would stand an hour of debate.

One proposal favoured by Mr. Gladstone, and also, I
remember, commended by Mill, was the military neutralisation
of Alsace and Lorraine, and the dismantling of the great
border fortresses, without withdrawing the inhabitants from
their French allegiance. The idea was worked out in a
pamphlet by Count Gasparin. On this pamphlet Mr. Max
Müller put what Mr. Gladstone called the fair question,
whether its author was likely to persuade the European
powers to guarantee border neutrality. 'I will try to give
you a fair answer,' Mr. Gladstone said (Jan. 30, 1871). 'You
will not think it less fair because it is individual and unofficial ;
for a man must be a wretch indeed, who could speak at this
most solemn juncture, otherwise than from the bottom of his
heart. First then, I agree with you in disapproving the
declaration, or reputed declaration, of Lord Derby (then
Stanley) in 1867, about the Luxemburg guarantee. I have in
parliament and in my present office, declined or expressly
forborne to recognise that declaration.[1] Secondly, as to the
main question. It is great. It is difficult. But I should not
despair. I may add I should desire to find it practicable ; for

[1] *Lord Stanley on the Luxemburg Guarantee, June* 14, 1867.—The guarantee now
given is collective only. That is an important distinction. It means this, that in
the event of a violation of neutrality, all the powers who have signed the treaty may
be called upon for their collective action. No one of those powers is liable to be
called upon to act singly or separately. It is a case so to speak of 'limited liability.'
We are bound in honour—you cannot put a legal construction upon it—to see in
concert with others that these arrangements are maintained. But if the other powers
join with us, it is certain that there will be no violation of neutrality. If they,
situated exactly as we are, decline to join, we are not bound single-handed to make
up the deficiencies of the rest.

I think it would be a condition fair to both parties, and one on which Germany would have an absolute title to insist. 'Some of the most excusable errors ever committed,' he said, in closing the letter, 'have also been the most ruinous in their consequences. The smallest in the forum of conscience, they are the greatest in the vast theatre of action. May your country, justly indignant and justly exultant, be preserved from committing one of these errors.' Three months later, when all was at an end, he repeated the same thought :—

The most fatal and in their sequel most gigantic errors of men are also frequently the most excusable and the least gratuitous. They are committed when a strong impetus of right carries them up to a certain point, and a residue of that impetus, drawn from the contact with human passion and infirmity, pushes them beyond it. They vault into the saddle ; they fall on the other side. The instance most commonly present to my mind is the error of England in entering the Revolutionary war in 1793. Slow sometimes to go in, she is slower yet to come out, and if she had then held her hand, the course of the revolution and the fate of Europe would in all likelihood have been widely different. There might have been no Napoleon. There might have been no Sedan.

The changes in the political map effected by these dire months of diplomacy and war were almost comparable in one sense to those of the treaty of Münster, or the treaty of the Pyrenees, or the treaties of Vienna, save that those great instruments all left a consolidated Europe. Italy had crowned her work by the acquisition of Rome. Russia had wiped out the humiliation of 1856. Prussia, after three wars in six years, had conquered the primacy of a united Germany. Austria had fallen as Prussia rose. France had fallen, but she had shaken off a government that had no root in the noblest qualities of her people.

CHAPTER VII

'DAY'S WORK OF A GIANT'

(1870–1872)

> We have not been an idle government. We have had an active life, and that is substantially one of the conditions of a happy life. . . . I am thankful to have been the leader of the liberal party at a period of the history of this country, when it has been my privilege and my duty to give the word of advance to able coadjutors and trusty and gallant adherents.—GLADSTONE.

THE most marked administrative performance of Mr. Glad-stone's great government was the reform and reorganisation of the army. In Mr. Cardwell he was fortunate enough to have a public servant of the first order ; not a political leader nor a popular orator, but one of the best disciples of Peel's school ; sound, careful, active, firm, and with an enlightened and independent mind admirably fitted for the effective despatch of business. Before he had been a month at the war office, the new secretary of state submitted to Mr. Gladstone his ideas of a plan that would give us an effective force for defence at a greatly reduced cost. The reorganisation of the army was one of the results of that great central event, from which in every direction such momentous consequences flowed —the victory of Prussian arms at Sadowa. The victory was a surprise, for even Lord Clyde, after a close inspection of the Prussian army, had found no more to report than that it was a first-rate militia. Sadowa disclosed that a soldier, serving only between two and three years with the colours, could yet show himself the most formidable combatant in Europe. The principle of Cardwell's plan was that short enlistment is essential to a healthy organisation of the army, and this reform it was that produced an efficient reserve, the necessity for which had been one of the lessons of the Crimean war. A second, but still a highly important element, was the reduction of the whole force serving in the colonies from fifty thousand men to less than half that number.[1] 'To this change,' said

---

[1] The number of men was reduced from 49,000 in 1868 to 20,941 in 1870 ; at the same time the military expenditure on the colonies was reduced from £3,388,023 to £1,905,538.

Mr. Cardwell, 'opposition will be weak, for the principle of colonial self-reliance is very generally assented to.' The idea, as Lord Wolseley says, that a standing army during peace should be a manufactory for making soldiers rather than either a costly receptacle for veterans, or a collection of perfectly trained fighters, 'had not yet taken hold of the military mind in England.' [1] The details do not concern us here, and everybody knows the revolution effected by the changes during Mr. Gladstone's great administration in the composition, the working, and the professional spirit of the army.

Army reform first brought Mr. Gladstone into direct collision with reigning sentiment at court. In spite of Pym and Cromwell and the untoward end of Charles I. and other salutary lessons of the great rebellion, ideas still lingered in high places that the sovereign's hand bore the sword, and that the wearer of the crown through a commander-in-chief had rights of control over the army, not quite dependent on parliament and secretary of state. The Queen had doubted the policy of disestablishing the church in Ireland, but to disestablish the commander-in-chief came closer home, and was disliked as an invasion of the personal rights of the occupant of the throne. This view was rather firmly pressed, and it was the first of a series of difficulties—always to him extremely painful, perhaps more painful than any other—that Mr. Gladstone was called upon in his long career to overcome. The subject was one on which the temper of a reforming parliament allowed no compromise, even if the prime minister himself had been inclined to yield. As it was, by firmness, patience, and that tact which springs not from courtiership but from right feeling, he succeeded, and in the June of 1870 the Queen approved an order in council that put an end to the dual control of the army, defined the position of the commander-in-chief, and removed him corporeally from the horse guards to the war office in Pall Mall. [2] This, however, by no means brought all the military difficulties to an end.

One particular incident has a conspicuous place on the political side of Mr. Gladstone's life. Among the elements in the scheme was the abolition of the practice of acquiring military rank by money purchase. Public opinion had been mainly roused by Mr. Trevelyan, who now first made his mark in that assembly where he was destined to do admirable work and achieve high eminence and popularity. An Act of George III. abolished selling of offices in other departments, but gave to the crown the discretion of retaining the practice in the army, if so it should seem fit. This discretion had been exercised by the issue of a warrant sanctioning and regulating that practice; commissions in the army were bought and sold for large sums of money, far in excess of the sums fixed by the royal warrant; and vested interests on a large scale grew up in consequence. The substitution, instead of this abusive system, of promotion by selection, was one of the first steps in army reform. No effective reorganization was possible without it. As Mr. Gladstone put it, the nation must buy back its own army from its own officers. No other proceeding in the career of the ministry aroused a more determined and violent opposition. It offended a powerful profession with a host of parliamentary friends; the officers disliked liberal politics, they rather disdained a civilian master, and they fought with the vigour peculiar to irritated caste.

The first question before parliament depended upon the Commons voting the money to compensate officers who had acquired vested interests. If that was secure, there was nothing to hinder the crown, in the discretion committed to it by the statute, from cancelling the old warrant. Instead of this, ministers determined to abolish purchase by bill. Obstruction was long and sustained. The principle of the bill was debated and re-debated on every amendment in committee, and Mr. Gladstone reported that 'during his whole parliamentary life, he had been accustomed to see class interests of all kinds put themselves on their defence under the supposition of being assailed, yet he had never seen a case where the modes of operation adopted by the professing champions were calculated to leave such a painful impression on the mind.' Credible whispers were heard of the open hostility of high military personages. In one of the debates of this time upon the army (Mar. 23, 1871), speakers freely implied that the influence of what was called the horse guards was actively adverse to reform. Mr. Gladstone, taking this point, laid it down that 'military authorities without impairing in the slightest degree the general independence of their political opinions, should be in full harmony with the executive as to the military plans and measures which it might propose; and that only on this principle could the satisfactory working of our institutions be secured.'

The correspondence with the Queen was copious. In one letter, after mentioning that parliament had been persuaded to extend the tenure of the commander-in-chief's office beyond five years, and to allow the patronage and discipline of the army to be vested in him, though the secretary of state was responsible, Mr. Gladstone proceeds:—

It would have been impossible to procure the acquiescence of parliament in these arrangements, unless they had been accompanied with the declaration of Mr. Cardwell, made in the name of the cabinet, and seen and approved by your Majesty, that 'it is of course necessary for the commander-in-chief to be in harmony with the government of the day' (Feb. 21, 1871), and with a similar declaration of Mr. Gladstone on March 23, 1871, also reported to and approved by your Majesty, that while all political action properly so called was entirely free, yet the military plans and measures of the government must always have the energetic co-operation of the military chiefs of the army.

The end was of course inevitable.[1] The bill at last passed the Commons, and then an exciting stage began. In the Lords it was immediately confronted by a dilatory resolution. In view of some such proceeding, Mr. Gladstone (July 15) wrote to the Queen as to the best course to pursue, and here he first mentioned the step that was to raise such clamour :—

As the government judge that the illegality of over-regulation prices cannot continue, and as they can only be extinguished by putting an end to purchase, what has been chiefly considered is how to proceed with the greatest certainty and the smallest shock, and how to secure as far as may be for the officers all that has hitherto been asked on their behalf. With this view, the government think the first step would be to abolish the warrant under which prices of commissions are fixed. As the resolution of the House of Lords states the unwillingness of the House to take part in abolishing purchase until certain things shall have been done, it would not be applicable to a case in which, without its interposition, purchase would have been already abolished.

Two days later (July 17) the Lords passed what Sir Roundell Palmer called 'their ill-advised resolution.' On July 18 the cabinet met and resolved to recommend the cancelling of the old warrant regulating purchase, by a new warrant abolishing purchase. It has been said or implied that this proceeding was forced imperiously upon the Queen. I find no evidence of this. In the language of Lord Halifax, the minister in attendance, writing to Mr. Gladstone from Osborne (July 19, 1871), the Queen 'made no sort of difficulty in signing the warrant' after the case had been explained. In the course of the day she sent to tell Lord Halifax, that as it was a strong exercise of her power in apparent opposition to the House of Lords, she should like to have some more formal expression of the advice of the cabinet than was contained in an ordinary letter from the prime minister, dealing with this among other matters. Ministers agreed that the Queen had a fair right to have their advice on such a point of executive action on her part, recorded in a formal and deliberate submission of their opinion. The advice was at once clothed in the definite form of a minute.

On July 20 Mr. Gladstone announced to a crowded and anxious House the abolition of purchase by royal warrant. The government, he said, had no other object but simplicity and despatch, and the observance of constitutional usage. Amid some disorderly interruptions, Mr. Disraeli taunted the government with resorting to the prerogative of the crown to get out of a difficulty of their own devising. Some radicals used the same ill-omened word. After a spell of obstruction on

---

[1] At the end of the second volume, the reader will find some interesting remarks by Mr. Gladstone on these points. See Appendix.

the ballot bill, the bitter discussion on purchase revived, and Mr. Disraeli said that what had occurred early in the evening was ' disgraceful to the House of Commons,' and denounced ' the shameful and avowed conspiracy of the cabinet ' against the House of Lords. The latter expression was noticed by the chairman of committee and withdrawn, though Mr. Gladstone himself thought it the more allowable of the two.

In a letter to his brother-in-law, Lord Lyttelton, Mr. Gladstone vindicated this transaction as follows :—

July 26, '71.—I should like to assure myself that you really have the points of the case before you. 1. Was it not for us an indispensable duty to extinguish a gross, wide-spread, and most mischievous illegality, of which the existence had become certain and notorious ? 2. Was it not also our duty to extinguish it in the best manner ? 3. Was not the best manner that which, (*a*) made the extinction final ; (*b*) gave the best, *i.e.* a statutory, title for regulation prices ; (*c*) granted an indemnity to the officers ; (*d*) secured for them compensation in respect of over-regulation prices ? 4. Did not the vote of the House of Lords stop us in this best manner of proceeding ? 5. Did it absolve us from the duty of putting an end to the illegality ? 6. What method of putting an end to it remained to us, except that which we have adopted ?

Sir Roundell Palmer wrote, ' I have always thought and said that the issuing of such a warrant was within the undoubted power of the crown. . . . It did and does appear to me that the course which the government took was the least objectionable course that could be taken under the whole circumstances of the case.'[1] I can find nothing more clearly and more forcibly said upon this case than the judgment of Freeman, the historian —a man who combined in so extraordinary a degree immense learning with precision in political thought and language, and added to both the true spirit of manly citizenship :—

I must certainly protest against the word ' prerogative ' being used, as it has so often been of late, to describe Mr. Gladstone's conduct with regard to the abolition of purchase in the army. By prerogative I understand a power not necessarily contrary to law, but in some sort beyond law—a power whose source must be sought for somewhere else than in the terms of an act of parliament. But in abolishing purchase by a royal warrant Mr. Gladstone acted strictly within the terms of an act of parliament, an act so modern as the reign of George III. He in truth followed a course which that act not only allowed but rather suggested. . . . I am not one of those who condemn Mr. Gladstone's conduct in this matter ; still I grant that the thing had an ill look. The difference I take to be this. Mr. Gladstone had two courses before him : he might abolish purchase by a royal warrant—that is, by using the discretion which parliament had given to the crown : or he might bring a bill into parliament to abolish purchase. . . . What gave the thing an ill look was that, having chosen the second way and not being able to carry his point that way, he then fell back on the first way. I believe that it was better to get rid of a foul abuse in the way in which

[1] *Memorials, Personal and Political*, vol. i. pp. 193, 194.

it was got rid of, than not to get rid of it at all, especially as the House of Commons had already decided against it. Still, the thing did not look well. It might seem that by electing to bring a bill into parliament Mr. Gladstone had waived his right to employ the royal power in the matter. . . . I believe that this is one of those cases in which a strictly conscientious man like Mr. Gladstone does things from which a less conscientious man would shrink. Such a man, fully convinced of his own integrity, often thinks less than it would be wise to think of mere appearances, and so lays himself open to the imputation of motives poles asunder from the real ones.[1]

These last words undoubtedly explain some acts and tendencies that gave a handle to foes and perplexed friends.

II

Next let us turn to reform in a different field. All the highest abstract arguments were against secret voting. To have a vote is to have power; as Burke said, 'liberty is power, when men act in bodies'; but the secret vote is power without responsibility. The vote is a trust for the commonwealth; to permit secrecy makes it look like a right conferred for a man's own benefit. You enjoin upon him to give his vote on public grounds; in the same voice you tell him not to let the public know how he gives it. Secrecy saps the citizen's courage, promotes evasion, tempts to downright lying. Remove publicity and its checks, then all the mean motives of mankind—their malice, petty rivalries, pique, the prejudices that men would be ashamed to put into words even to themselves—skulk to the polling booth under a disguising cloak. Secrecy, again, prevents the statesman from weighing or testing the forces in character, stability, persistency, of the men by whom a majority has been built up, and on whose fidelity his power of action must depend. This strain of argument was worked out by J. S. Mill[2] and others, and drew from Mr. Bright, who belonged to a different school of liberals, the gruff saying, that the worst of great thinkers is that they so often think wrong.

Though the abstract reasoning might be unanswerable, the concrete case the other way was irresistible. Experience showed that without secrecy in its exercise the suffrage was not free. The farmer was afraid of his landlord, and the labourer was afraid of the farmer; the employer could tighten the screw on the workman, the shopkeeper feared the power of his best customers, the debtor quailed before his creditor, the priest wielded thunderbolts over the faithful. Not only was the open vote not free; it exposed its possessor to so much bullying, molestation, and persecution, that his possession came to be less of a boon than a nuisance.

For forty years this question had been fought. The ballot actually figured in a clause of an early draft of the Reform

[1] E. A. Freeman, in *Pall Mall Gazette*, February 12, 1874.
[2] *Representative Government*, chap. x.

bill of 1832. Grote, inspired by James Mill whose vigorous
pleas for the ballot in his well-known article in 1830 were the
high landmark in the controversy, brought it before parliament
in an annual motion. When that admirable man quitted
parliament to finish his great history of Greece, the torch was
still borne onwards by other hands. Ballot was one of the five
points of the charter. At nearly every meeting for parliamentary reform between the Crimean war and Disraeli's bill of
1867, the ballot was made a cardinal point. General opinion
fluctuated from time to time, and in the sixties journals of
repute formally dismissed it as a dead political idea. The
extension of the franchise in 1867 brought it to life again, and
Mr. Bright led the van in the election of 1868 by declaring in
his address that he regarded the ballot as of the first importance. 'Whether I look,' he said, 'to the excessive cost of
elections, or to the tumult which so often attends them, or to
the unjust and cruel pressure which is so frequently brought
to bear upon the less independent class of voters, I am persuaded that the true interest of the public and of freedom will
be served by the system of secret and free voting.' J. S. Mill
had argued that the voter should name his candidate in the
polling booth, just as the judge does his duty in a court open
to the public eye. No, replied Bright, the jury-room is as
important as the judge's bench, and yet the jury-room is treated
as secret, and in some countries the verdict is formally given
by ballot. Some scandals in the way of electoral intimidation
did much to ripen public opinion. One parliamentary committee in 1868 brought evidence of this sort to light, and
another committee recommended secret voting as the cure.

Among those most ardent for the change from open to secret
voting, the prime minister was hardly to be included. 'I am
not aware,' he wrote to Lord Shaftesbury (Dec. 11, 1871), 'of
having been at any time a vehement opponent of the ballot. I
have not been accustomed to attach to it a vital importance,
but at any time, I think, within the last twenty or twenty-five
years I should have regarded it as the legitimate complement
of the present suffrage.'[1] In the first speech he made as prime
minister at Greenwich (Dec. 21, 1868) he said that there were
two subjects that could not be overlooked in connection with
the representation of the people. 'One of them is the security
afforded by the present system for perfect freedom in the
giving of the vote, which vote has been not only not conferred
as a favour, but imposed as a duty by the legislature on the
members of the community. I have at all times given my vote
in favour of open voting, but I have done so before, and I do
so now, with an important reservation, namely, that whether
by open voting or by whatsoever means, free voting must be
secured.'

[1] The reader may remember his stripling letters—above, pp. 73-74.

A bill providing for vote by ballot, abolishing public nominations and dealing with corrupt practices in parliamentary elections, was introduced by Lord Hartington in 1870. Little progress was made with it, and it was eventually withdrawn. But the government were committed to the principle, and at the end of July Mr. Gladstone took the opportunity of explaining his change of opinion on this question, in the debate on the second reading of a Ballot bill brought in by a private member. Now that great numbers who depended for their bread upon their daily labour had acquired the vote, he said, their freedom was threatened from many quarters. The secret vote appeared to be required by the social conditions under which they lived, and therefore it had become a necessity and a duty to give effect to the principle.

Yet after the cabinet had decided to make the ballot a ministerial measure, the head of the cabinet makes a rather pensive entry in his diary :—'*July* 27, 1870.—H. of C. Spoke on ballot, and voted in 324-230 with mind satisfied, and as to feeling, a lingering reluctance.' How far this reluctance was due to misgivings on the merits of the ballot, how far to the doubts that haunt every ministerial leader as to the possibilities of parliamentary time, we do not know. The bill, enlarged and reintroduced next year, was entrusted to the hands of Mr. Forster—himself, like Mr. Gladstone, a latish convert to the principle of secret voting—and by Forster's persistent force and capacity for hard and heavy labour, after some eighteen days in committee it passed through the House of Commons.

After obstruction had been at last broken down, other well-known resources of civilisation remained, and the Lords threw out the bill.[1] It was novel, they said ; it was dangerous, it had not been considered by the country or parliament (after eighteen days of committee and forty years of public discussion), it was incoherent and contradictory, and to enact vote by ballot was inevitably to overthrow the monarchy. Even the mightiest of American orators had said as much. 'Above all things,' Daniel Webster had adjured Lord Shaftesbury, 'resist to the very last the introduction of the ballot ; for as a republican, I tell you that the ballot can never co-exist with monarchical institutions.'

The rejection by the Lords stimulated popular insistence. At Whitby in the autumn (Sept. 2), Mr. Gladstone said the people's bill had been passed by the people's House, and when it was next presented at the door of the House of Lords, it would be with an authoritative knock. He told Lord Houghton that he was sorry to see the agitation apparently rising against the House of Lords, though he had a strong opinion about the

---

[1] In the House of Lords only 48 peers voted for the bill against 97. Many of the whigs abstained.

imprudence of its conduct on the Army bill, and especially on the Ballot bill. 'There is no Duke of Wellington in these days. His reputation as a domestic statesman seems to me to rest almost entirely on his leadership of the peers between 1832 and 1841.'

The bill was again passed through the Commons in 1872. Mr. Gladstone was prepared for strong measures. The cabinet decided that if the House of Lords should hold to what the prime minister styled 'the strange provision for optional secrecy,' the government would withdraw the bill and try an autumn session, and if the Lords still hardened their hearts, ' there would remain nothing but the last alternative to consider,'—these words, I assume, meaning a dissolution. Perhaps the opposition thought that a dissolution on the ballot might give to the ministerial Antæus fresh energy. This time the Lords gave way, satisfied that the measure had now at last been more adequately discussed,—the said discussion really consisting in no more than an adequate amount of violent language out of doors against the principle of a hereditary legislature.[1]

The results of the general election two years later as they affected party, are an instructive comment on all this trepidation and alarm. In one only of the three kingdoms the ballot helped to make a truly vital difference ; it dislodged the political power of the Irish landlord. In England its influence made for purity, freedom, and decency, but it developed no new sources of liberal strength. On this aspect of things the first parliamentary precursor of the ballot made remarks that are worth a few lines of digression. 'You will feel great satisfaction,' his wife said to Grote one morning at their breakfast, 'at seeing your once favourite measure triumph over all obstacles.' 'Since the wide expansion of the voting element,' the historian replied, ' I confess that the value of the ballot has sunk in my estimation. I don't, in fact, think the elections will be affected by it one way or another, as far as party interests are concerned.' 'Still,' his interlocutor persisted, 'you will at all events get at the genuine preference of the constituency.' 'No doubt ; but then, again, I have come to perceive that the choice between one man and another among the English people, signifies less than I used formerly to think it did. The English mind is much of one pattern, take whatsoever class you will. The same favourite prejudices, amiable and otherwise ; the same antipathies, coupled with ill-regulated though benevolent efforts to eradicate human evils, are well-nigh universal. A House of Commons cannot afford to be above its own constituencies in intelligence, knowledge, or patriotism.'[2] In all this the element of truth is profound enough. In every change of political

[1] The first parliamentary election by ballot in England was the return of Mr. Childers at Pontefract (Aug. 15, 1872) on his acceptance of the duchy.
[2] *Life of Grote*, pp. 312, 313.

machinery the reformer promises and expects a new heaven
and a new earth ; then standing forces of national tradition,
character, and institution assert their strength, our millennium
lags, and the chilled enthusiast sighs. He is unreasonable, as
are all those who expect more from life and the world than life
and the world have to give. Yet here at least the reformer has
not failed. The efficacy of secret voting is negative if we will,
but it averts obvious mischiefs alike from old privileged orders
in states and churches and from new.

III

In finance the country looked for wonders. Ministers were
called the cabinet of financiers. The cabinet did, in fact, contain as many as five men who were at one time or another
chancellors of the exchequer, and its chief was recognised
through Europe as the most successful financier of the age.
No trailing cloud of glory, as in 1853 or 1860, attended the
great ministry, but sound and substantial results were
achieved, testifying to a thrifty and skilful management,
such as might have satisfied the ambition of a generation of
chancellors. The head of the new government promised
retrenchment as soon as the government was formed. He
told his constituents at Greenwich (Dec. 21, 1868) that he was
himself responsible for having taken the earliest opportunity
of directing the public mind to the subject of expenditure at
an opening stage of the late election ; for 'although there may
be times when the public mind may become comparatively
relaxed in regard to the general principles of economy and
thrift, it is the special duty of public men to watch the very
beginnings of evil in that department. It is a very easy thing
to notice these mischiefs when they have grown to a gigantic
size ; but it commonly happens that when financial error has
arisen to those dimensions, the case has become too aggravated
for a remedy.' He reminded them of the addition that had
been made to the standing charges of the country in the
ordinary and steadily recurring annual estimates presented
to parliament. He said that he knew no reason why three
millions should have been added during the two years of tory
government to the cost of our establishments :—

It is one thing, I am very well aware, to put on three millions ; it is
another thing to take them off. When you put three millions on to the
public expenditure, you create a number of new relations, a number of
new offices, a number of new claims, a number of new expectations. And
you can't, and what is more, you ought not to, destroy all these in a
moment. And, therefore, the work of retrenchment must be a well-
considered and a gradual work. But I ask you to look at the names of
the men who have been placed in charge of the great spending departments of the country. The study, the idea that has governed the
formation of the present administration has been to place able and

upright men in charge of the public purse—men of administrative experience, men of proved ability, men, lastly, holding their seats in the House of Commons, and, therefore, immediately responsible to the representatives of the people. It would not become me to promise what we can do ; but this I can tell you, that my friends connected with the various departments most concerned in the public expenditure have, even before the early moment at which I speak, directed their very first attention to this subject, and that I, for one, shall be as deeply disappointed as you can be, if in the estimates which it will be our duty to present in February you do not already perceive some results of their opening labours.

One of Mr. Gladstone's first letters to a colleague was addressed to Mr. Lowe, containing such hints and instructions upon treasury administration as a veteran pilot might give about lights, buoys, channels, currents, to a new captain. 'No man wants so much sympathy,' he said, 'as the chancellor of the exchequer, no man gets so little. Nor is there any position so lamentable for him as to be defeated in proposing some new charge on the public conceived or adopted by himself. He is like an ancient soldier wounded in the back. Whereas even defeat in resisting the raids of the House of Commons on the public purse is honourable, and always turns out well in the end.' He sent Mr. Lowe a list of the subjects that he had tried in parliament without success, and of those that he had in his head but was not able to take in hand. They make a fine example of an active and reforming mind.[1] 'What commonly happened, in cases of this kind, in my time, was as follows :— The opposition waited for a development of discontent and resistance among some small fraction of liberal members. When this was compact in itself, or was at all stimulated by constituencies, they sent out habitually strong party whips, and either beat me, or forced me to withdraw in order to avoid beating, or exposing our men to local disadvantage. This game, I hope, will not be quite so easy now.'

The first two of Mr. Lowe's budgets were on the lines thus traced beforehand. The shilling duty on a quarter of corn was abolished—'an exceeding strong case,' as Mr. Gladstone called it—taxes on conveyances were adjusted, and the duty on fire insurance was removed. The only notable contribution to the standing problem of widening the base of taxation was the proposal to put a tax on matches.[2] This was a notion borrowed from the United States, and much approved by Mr. Wells, the eminent free-trade financier of that country. In England it was greeted with violent disfavour. It was denounced as reactionary, as violating the first principles of fiscal adminis-

---

1 See Appendix.
2 Writing to Mr. Lowe on his budget proposals, Mr. Gladstone says (April 11, 1871) : —'The lucifer matches I hope and think you would carry, but I have little information, and that old. I advise that on this Glyn be consulted as to the feeling in the House of Commons. I am sceptical as to the ultimate revenue of one million.'

tration, and as the very worst tax that had been proposed within recent memory, for is not a match a necessary of life, and to tax a necessary of life is to go against Adam Smith and the books. The money, it was said, ought to have been got either by raising the taxes on tea and sugar, or else by putting the shilling duty back on corn again, though for that matter, tea, sugar, and corn are quite as much necessaries of life as, say, two-thirds of the matches used.[1] No care, however, was given to serious argument ; in fact, the tax was hardly argued at all. Some hundreds of poor women employed at a large match factory in the east end of London trooped to protest at Westminster, and the tax was quickly dropped. It was perhaps unlucky that the proposal happened to be associated with Mr. Lowe, for his uncomplimentary criticisms on the working class four or five years before were neither forgotten nor forgiven. A Latin pun that he meant to print on the proposed halfpenny match stamp, *ex luce lucellum*, 'a little gain out of a little light,' was good enough to divert a college common room, but it seemed flippant to people who expected to see the bread taken out of their mouths.

On the other side of the national account Mr. Gladstone was more successful. He fought with all his strength for a reduction of the public burdens, and in at least one of these persistent battles with colleagues of a less economising mind than himself, he came near to a breach within the walls of his cabinet. In this thankless region he was not always zealously seconded. On Dec. 14, 1871, he enters in his diary : 'Cabinet 3-7. For two and a half hours we discussed army estimates, mainly on reduction, and the chancellor of the exchequer did not speak one word.' The result is worth recording. When Mr. Gladstone was at the exchequer the charge on naval, military, and civil expenditure had been reduced between 1860 and 1865 from thirty-eight millions to thirty-one. Under the Derby-Disraeli government the figure rose in two or three years to thirty-four millions and three-quarters. By 1873 it had been brought down again to little more than thirty-two millions and a quarter.[2] That these great reductions were effected without any sacrifice of the necessary strength and efficiency of the forces, may be inferred from the fact that for ten years under successive administrations the charge on navy and army underwent no substantial augmentation. The process had been made easier, or made possible, by the necessity under which the German war laid France, then our only rival in naval force, to reduce her expenditure upon new ships. The number of seamen was maintained, but a reduction was effected in the inefficient vessels in the foreign squadrons ; two costly and

---

[1] See *The Match Tax : a Problem in Finance.* By W. Stanley Jevons (London : Stanford, 1871). A searching defence of the impost.

[2] See a speech in the House of Commons by Mr. Childers, April 24, 1873.

almost useless dockyards were suppressed (much to the disadvantage of Mr. Gladstone's own constituents), and great abuses were remedied in the dockyards that were left. In the army reduction was made possible without lessening the requisite strength, by the withdrawal of troops from Canada, New Zealand, and the Cape. This was due to the wise policy of Lord Granville and Mr. Gladstone. In spite of the increased cost of education, of army purchase, of the rise of prices, and all the other causes that swell estimates, the country was still spending no more in 1873 than when Mr. Gladstone took office in 1868.[1] To this story we have to add that nearly thirty millions of debt were paid off in the five years. Well might men point to such a record, as the best proof that the promises of economy made at the hustings had been seriously kept.[2]

When the time came for him to take stock of his own performances, Mr. Lowe, who was apt to be cleverer than he was wise, made a speech at Sheffield, in September 1873, that almost recalls the self-laudation of Cicero over the immortal glories of his consulate. He disclaimed any share of the admirable genius for finance that had been seen in Pitt, Peel, or Gladstone, but he had read in the Latin grammar that economy was a great revenue, and he thought that he could at least discharge the humble task of hindering extravagance. 'The first thing I did as chancellor of the exchequer,' he said, 'was to issue an order that no new expenditure whatever would be allowed without my opinion first being taken upon it. . . . In an evil hour for my own peace and quietness I took upon myself—I believe it was never taken upon himself by any chancellor of the exchequer before—the duty of protecting the revenue, instead of leaving it to be done by an inferior official.' After reciting his figures, he wound up with a resounding pæan : 'So far as I am aware, up to the present time there is no one who can challenge comparison with what has been done during these years. Sir R. Peel and Mr. Gladstone routed out protection in your trade, a measure that conferred immortal honour on them, but so far as relieving you from taxation is concerned, I believe you would seek in vain in British history for anything like what has been done during these last four years.' This strange vein was more than a little distasteful to the prime minister, as a letter to Lord Granville upon it shows (Sept. 9, 1873) :—

Lowe's speech at Sheffield is really too bad, and free as it is from all evil intention, it illustrates the invariable solecisms of his extraordinary mind. . . . He says no chancellor of the exchequer before did treasury business, but left it to a subordinate official. . . . Some have done more, some less. No one, probably, as much as Lowe, but some almost as

---

[1] The estimates of 1874-5 were practically the estimates of the Gladstone government, showing a revenue of £77,995,000, or a surplus of £5,492,000. See Lord Welby's letter to Mr. Lowe in Life of Lord Sherbrooke, ii. pp. 383, 384.

[2] Economist, Feb. 8, 1873.

much. I did less, perhaps much less. But I hold that the first duties of the chancellor of the exchequer are outside the treasury. One of them is to look after and control the great expenditures and estimates. In this duty I am sorry to say he was wretchedly deficient ; yet he coolly takes to himself the credit of army and navy reductions, which is due to Cardwell and Childers (who, in his admirable speech, did not say a word, I think, for himself), and with which every member of the cabinet had almost as much to do as he had. I can speak from experience, for I know what it has been to have had cast upon my shoulders the most important and most offensive duty of the financial minister. . . . He has ample merit to stand on, in a great amount of labour done, and generally well done, and with good results for the public. Much of the unpopularity is unjust ; a little patience would set all right.

CHAPTER VIII

AUTUMN OF 1871. DECLINE OF POPULARITY

(1871–1872)

For the present at least the reformation will operate against the reformers. Nothing is more common than for men to wish, and call loudly too, for a reformation, who when it arrives do by no means like the severity of its aspect. Reformation is one of those pieces which must be put at some distance in order to please. Its greatest favourers love it better in the abstract than in the substance.—BURKE.

IN July, 1871, Mr. Gladstone paid a Sunday visit to Tennyson among the Surrey hills. They had two interesting days, 'with talk ranging everywhere.' The poet read the *Holy Grail*, which Mr. Gladstone admired. They discussed the Goschen parish council plan, and other social reforms; Lacordaire and liberal collectivism; politics and the stormy times ahead. Mr. Gladstone assured them that he was a conservative, and feared extreme measures from the opposition. 'A very noble fellow,' Tennyson called him, 'and perfectly unaffected.'[1] Mr. Gladstone, for his part, records in his diary that he found 'a characteristic and delightful abode. In Tennyson are singularly united true greatness, genuine simplicity, and some eccentricity. But the latter is from habit and circumstance, the former is his nature. His wife is excellent, and in her adaptation to him wonderful. His son Hallam is most attractive.'

After a laborious and irksome session, 'in which we have sat, I believe, 150 hours after midnight,' the House rose (Aug. 21). Mr. Gladstone spent some time at Whitby with his family, and made a speech to his eldest son's constituents (Sept. 2) on the ballot, and protesting against the spirit of 'alarmism.' Towards the end of the month he went on to Balmoral. On September 26 he was presented with the freedom of Aberdeen, and made a speech on Irish home rule, of which, as we shall see, he heard a great deal fifteen years later :—

1 *Life of Tennyson*, ii. p. 108.

To Mrs. Gladstone.

Balmoral, Sept. 28.—The time is rolling on easily at this *quiet* place. . . . We breakfast six or eight. The Prince and Princess Louis of Hesse dine most days. To-day I walked with her and her party. She is quick, kind, and well informed. I got her to-day on the subject of the religious movement in the Roman catholic church in Germany. She is imbued with her father's ideas, and, I think, goes beyond them. She quoted Strauss to me, as giving his opinion that the movement would come to nothing. She said the infallibility was the legitimate development of the Roman system. I replied that the Roman system had grown up by a multitude of scarcely perceptible degrees out of the earliest form of Christianity, and if we adopted this notion of legitimate development, we ran a risk of making Saint Paul responsible for the Vatican council. She talked much about the hospitals, in which she worked so hard while nursing her baby, a very fine one, whom she introduced to me, with two flourishing elder children. She hates war ; and is not easy as to the future.

Sept. 29.—I have had a twelve-miles stretch to-day, almost all on wild ground, and so solitary ! not a living creature except three brace of grouse all the way. I am glad to report that I came in very fresh. . . . What a mess the Bishop of Winchester has made of this Glengarry kirk business.

Sept. 30.—Last night we dined ten at Abergeldie. The Prince of Wales had his usual pleasant manners. He is far lighter in hand than the Duke of Edinburgh. After dinner he invited me to play whist. I said, 'For love, sir ?' He said, 'Well, shillings and half-a-crown on the rubber,' to which I submitted. Ponsonby and I against the Prince and Brasseur, a charming old Frenchman, his tutor in the language. The Prince has apparently an *immense* whist memory, and plays well accordingly. To-day the Queen was to have seen me at six, but sent to postpone it till to-morrow on account of expecting the Princess of Wales, who was to come over and pay her a visit from Abergeldie. I think she is nervous, and shrinks from talk ; but I do not mean to say a word that would give her trouble, as there would be no good in it at this moment.

Oct. 3.—I have seen the Queen again this morning. She conversed longer, near an hour, and was visibly better and stronger, and in good spirits. She told me much about her illness. . . . She wished me a pleasant journey.

Ballater, Oct. 4.—Here am I ensconced in the station-master's box at Ballater, after a 15 or 16 mile walk round through the hills, the regular train being postponed for an hour or more to let the couple from Mar Lodge go off special. They had two carriages laden with luggage, besides their own carriage ! I hope to be at Colwyn soon after six. These solitary walks among the hills, I think, refresh and invigorate me more than anything else. To-day the early part of the day was glorious, and the wind most bracing as it came over the mass of mountains. I bade farewell reluctantly to Balmoral, for it is as homelike as any place away from home can be, and wonderfully safe from invasions. I had all the grand mountains in view at once, with their snow caps ; the lowest, about the same as Snowdon. I came by the falls of the Muich, which, after the rain, were very fine. I had an interesting conversation with Princess Louise about the Queen this morning.

Oct. 4.—Nothing sets me up in mind and body like a mountain solitude, not even, perhaps, the sea. Walked from Balmoral to Ballater, 15 miles, in 4 hrs. 5 m. 6.—Walked 20 miles in 5 hrs. and 45 minutes. 7.—Walked 15 miles.—(*Diary.*)

To Mrs. Gladstone.

Ainslie Place, Edinburgh, Oct. 8, 1871.—I got here last night before seven, and had the most affectionate welcome from the dean that you can conceive ; a dinner-party followed, and now I have for the *first time* since the government was formed had a holiday of two whole days. Last night the lord advocate tried to talk to me about the Scotch endowed schools and I refused to have anything to say to him. I have no time to write about my walk, beyond this, that it was quite successful. The dean [Ramsay] preached at St. John's this morning about Ruth. The sermon was beautiful, and the voice and manner with his venerable age made it very striking. He put an astonishing energy into it, and his clear melodious tones rang through and through as they did when I first heard him 43½ years ago. It was altogether most touching, and he told me afterwards that he had wished to preach to me once more before he died. But I rejoice to say his life seems a very good one. I would not have missed the occasion for much.

London, Oct. 27.—Went to Sir R. Murchison's funeral, the last of those who had known me or of me from infancy. And so a step towards the end is made visible. It was a great funeral. 28.—My expedition to Greenwich, or rather, Blackheath. I spoke 1 h. 50 m. ; too long, yet really not long enough for a full development of my points. Physically rather an excess of effort. All went well, thank God !—(*Diary.*)

This speech at Blackheath was a fine illustration both of Mr. Gladstone's extraordinary power, and of the sure respect of a British audience for manful handling and firm dealing in a minister, if only the appeal be high enough. It was one of the marked scenes of his life. In the cold mist of the October afternoon he stood bareheaded, pale, resolute, before a surging audience of many thousands, few of them enthusiastically his friends, a considerable mass of them dockyard workmen, furious at discharge or neglect by an economising government. He was received with loud and angry murmurs ominous of storm, but curiosity, interest, and a sense that even a prime minister should have fair play prevailed. His rich tones and clear articulation—and Mr. Gladstone had studied all the arts for husbanding vocal resources—carried his words beyond the five or six thousand persons that are commonly understood to be the limit of possible hearers in the open air. After half an hour of struggle he conquered a hold upon them that became more intense as he went on—touching topic after topic, defending all that had been done for the reform and efficiency of the army, denouncing extreme opinions on the Education Act, vindicating the ballot bill, laughing at various prescriptions of social quackery—until at the close of a speech nearly two hours long, he retired amid sustained hurricanes of earnest applause. Well might he speak of rather an excess of physical effort, to say nothing of effort of mind.

On his return to Hawarden he had a visit from Mr. Bright, whom he earnestly hoped to bring back into the cabinet.[1]

Nov. 13.—Hawarden. Two long conversations with Mr. Bright, who arrived at one. 14.—Some five hours in conversation with Mr. Bright ; also I opened my proposal to him, which he took kindly though cautiously. My conversation with him yesterday evening kept me awake till four. A most rare event ; but my brain assumes in the evening a feminine susceptibility, and resents any unusual strain, though, strange to say, it will stand a debate in the H. of C. 15.— Forenoon with Bright, who departed, having charmed everybody by his gentleness. Began the cutting of a large beech.

To Lord Granville.

Nov. 15, 1871.—Bright has been here for forty-eight hours, of which we passed I think more than a fourth in conversation on public affairs. Everything in and everything out of the cabinet I told him as far as my memory would serve, and I think we pretty well boxed the political compass. On the whole I remained convinced of two things : first, that his heart is still altogether with us ; secondly, that his health, though requiring great care, is really equal to the moderate demands we should make upon him. The truth is I was quite as much knocked up with our conversation as he was, but then I had the more active share. In the whole range of subjects that we travelled over, we came to no point of sharp difference, and I feel confident that he could work with the cabinet as harmoniously and effectually as before. In saying this I should add that I told him, with respect to economy, that I thought we should now set our faces in that direction. I told him that we should not expect of him ordinary night attendance in the House of Commons, and that his attendance in the cabinet was the main object of our desire. He was pleased and touched with our desire, and he has not rejected the proposal. He has intimated doubts and apprehensions, but he reserves it for consideration, and seemed decidedly pleased to learn that the question *might* be held open until the meeting of parliament in case of need. . . . I did not think it fair to put to him the request by which I endeavoured to hold him in December 1868, viz. : that he would not determine in the matter without seeing me again ; but I begged and pressed that he should in no case refuse without taking the opinion of a first-rate London physician, as these are the people whose wide experience best enables them to judge in such cases. Altogether my experience of him was extremely pleasant, and he was popular beyond measure in the house, where the guests were one or two ladies and four gentlemen, Sir G. Prevost, a high church (but most excellent) archdeacon, John Murray, the tory publisher, and Hayward—whom to describe it needs not. One and all were charmed with Bright. In his character the mellowing process has continued to advance, and whatever he may have been thirty years ago, he is now a gentle and tender being. Yesterday he had five hours of conversation with me and much with others, also an hour and a half walk in the rain, which seemed to do him no harm whatever. I will add but one word. He was deeply impressed with the royalty question. . . . Details I will report to the cabinet.

[1] Mr. Bright had retired from the cabinet on account of ill-health in December 1870.

Mr. Bright did not yet feel able to return, and an important year, the third of the administration, drew to its close.

II

Two stubborn and noisy scuffles arose in the autumn of 1871, in consequence of a couple of appointments to which Mr. Gladstone as prime minister was a party. One was judicial, the other was ecclesiastical.

Parliament, authorising the appointment of four paid members of the judicial committee of the privy council, had restricted the post to persons who held at the date of their appointment, or had previously held, judicial office in this country or in India.[1] Difficulty arose in finding a fourth member of the new court from the English bench. The appointment being a new one, fell to the prime minister, but he was naturally guided by the chancellor. The office was first offered by Mr. Gladstone to Lord Penzance, who declined to move. Application was then made to Willes and to Bramwell. They also declined, on the ground that no provision was made for their clerks. Willes could not abandon one who had been 'his officer, he might say friend, for thirty years.' Bramwell spoke of the pecuniary sacrifice that the post would involve, 'for I cannot let my clerks, who between them have been with me near half a century, suffer by the change.' The chancellor mentioned to Mr. Gladstone a rumour that there was 'an actual strike among the judges' in the matter. Nobody who knew Bramwell would impute unreasonable or low-minded motives to him, and from their own point of view the judges had a sort of case. It was ascertained by the chancellor that Blackburn and Martin had said expressly that they should decline. Mr. Gladstone felt, as he told Lord Hatherley, that 'it was not right to hawk the appointment about,' and he offered it to Sir Robert Collier, then attorney-general. Collier's claim to the bench, and even to the headship of a court, was undisputed ; his judicial capacity was never at any time impugned ; he acquired no additional emolument. In accepting Mr. Gladstone's offer (Oct. 1871), he reminded him : 'You are aware that in order to qualify me it will be necessary first to make me a common law judge.' Three days later, the chancellor told Mr. Gladstone, 'It would hardly do to place the attorney-general on the common law bench and then promote him.' Still under the circumstances he thought it would be best to follow the offer up, and Collier was accordingly made a judge in the common pleas, sat for a few days, and then went on to the judicial committee. The proceeding was not taken without cabinet authority, for Lord Granville writes to Mr. Gladstone :—
'Nov. 12, '71 : The cabinet completely assented to the arrange-

[1] 34 and 35 Vict. c. 91, sect. 1.

ment. Sufficient attention was perhaps not given to the
technical point. For technical it only is. . . . I think you
said at the cabinet that Collier wished to have three months'
tenure of the judgeship, and that we agreed with you that
this would have been only a sham.'

Cockburn, the chief justice of the Queen's bench, opened
fire on Mr. Gladstone (Nov. 10) in a long letter of rather over-
heroic eloquence, protesting that a colourable appointment to
a judgeship for the purpose of getting round the law seriously
compromised the dignity of the judicial office, and denouncing
the grievous impropriety of the proceeding as a mere subterfuge
and evasion of the statute. Mr. Gladstone could be extremely
summary when he chose, and he replied in three or four lines,
informing the chief justice that as the transaction was a joint
one, and as 'the completed part of it to which you have taken
objection, was the official act of the lord chancellor,' he had
transmitted the letter for his consideration. That was all he
said. The chancellor for his part contented himself with half
a dozen sentences, that his appointment of Collier to the puisne
judgeship had been made with a full knowledge of Mr. Gladstone's intention to recommend him for the judicial committee;
that he thus 'acted advisedly and with the conviction that the
arrangement was justified as regards both its fitness and its
legality'; and that he took upon himself the responsibility of
thus concurring with Mr. Gladstone, and was prepared to
vindicate the course pursued. This curt treatment of his
Junius-like composition mortified Cockburn's literary vanity,
and no vanity is so easily stung as that of the amateur.

Collier, when the storm was brewing, at once wrote to Mr.
Gladstone (Nov. 13) proposing to retain his judgeship to the
end of the term, then to resign it, and act gratuitously in the
privy council. He begged that it might not be supposed
he offered to do this merely as matter of form. 'Though I
consider the objection to my appointment wholly baseless,
still it is not pleasant to me to hold a salaried office, my right
to which is questioned.' 'I have received your letter,' Mr.
Gladstone replied (Nov. 14), 'which contains the offer that
would only be made by a high-spirited man, impatient of
suspicion or reproval, and determined to place himself beyond
it. . . . I have not a grain of inclination to recede from the
course marked out, and if you had proposed to abandon the
appointment, I should have remonstrated.'

What Mr. Gladstone called 'a parliamentary peppering'
followed in due course. It was contended that the statute in
spirit as in letter exacted judicial experience, and that formal
passing through a court was a breach of faith with parliament.
As usual, lawyers of equal eminence were found to contend
with equal confidence that a fraud had been put upon the law,
and that no fraud had been put upon it; that the law required

judicial status not experience, and on the other hand that what it required was experience not status. Lord Hatherley and Roundell Palmer were all the virtues, whether public or private, personified; they were at the top of the legal ladder; and they agreed in Palmer's deliberate judgment, that—after other judges with special fitness had declined the terms offered by parliament—in nominating the best man at the bar who was willing to take a vacant puisne judgeship upon the understanding that he should be at once transferred to the judicial committee, the government were innocent of any offence against either the spirit or substance of the law.[1]

Yet the escape was narrow. The government only missed censure in the Lords by a majority of one. In the Commons the evening was anxious. 'You will see,' says Mr. Bruce (Feb. 20, 1872), 'that we got but a small majority last night. The fact is that our victory in the Lords made men slack about coming to town, and Glyn got very nervous in the course of the evening. However, Palmer's and Gladstone's speeches, both of which were excellent, improved the feeling, and many who had announced their intention to go away without voting, remained to support us.' At one moment it even looked as if the Speaker might have to give a casting vote, and he had framed it on these lines:—'I have concluded that the House while it looks upon the course taken by government as impolitic and injudicious, is not prepared at the present juncture to visit their conduct with direct parliamentary censure.'[2] In the end, ministers had a majority of twenty-seven, and reached their homes at three in the morning with reasonably light hearts.

III

The ecclesiastical case of complaint against Mr. Gladstone was of a similar sort. By an act of parliament passed in 1871 the Queen was entitled to present to the rectory of Ewelme, but only a person who was a member of convocation of the university of Oxford. This limitation was inserted by way of compensation to the university for the severance of the advowson of the rectory from a certain chair of divinity. The living fell vacant, and the prime minister offered it (June 15) to Jelf of Christ Church, a tory and an evangelical. By Jelf it was declined. Among other names on the list for preferment was that of Mr. Harvey, a learned man who had published an edition of Irenæus, a work on the history and theology of the three creeds, articles on judaism, jansenism, and jesuitism, and other productions of merit. As might perhaps have been surmised from the nature of his favourite pursuits, he was not a liberal in politics, and he had what was for the purposes of this preferment the further misfortune of being a Cambridge man. To him Mr. Gladstone now offered Ewelme, having been advised

[1] Selborne's *Memorials*, i. p. 200.   [2] *Brand papers.*

that by the process of formal incorporation in the Oxford convocation the requirement of the statute would be satisfied.   Mr.
Harvey accepted.   He was told that it was necessary that he
should become a member of convocation before he could be
appointed.   A little later (Aug. 1) he confessed to the prime
minister his misgivings lest he should be considered as an
'interloper in succeeding to the piece of preferment that
parliament had appropriated to bona-fide members of the
university of Oxford.'   These scruples were set aside, he was
incorporated as a member of Oriel in due form, and after forty-
two days of residence was admitted to membership of convocation, but whether to such plenary membership as the Ewelme
statute was taken to require, became matter of dispute.   All
went forward, and the excellent man was presented and insti-
tuted to his rectory in regular course.   There was no secret
about operations at Oxford ; the Oriel men were aware of his
motive in seeking incorporation, and the vice-chancellor and
everybody else concerned knew all about it.   Mr. Gladstone,
when squalls began to blow, wrote to Mr. Harvey (Feb. 26, '72)
that he was advised that the presentation was perfectly valid.

The attack in parliament was, as such attacks almost always
are, much overdone.   Mr. Gladstone, it appeared, was far worse
than Oliver Cromwell and the parliament of the great rebellion ;
for though those bad men forced three professors upon Oxford
between 1648 and 1660, still they took care that the intruders
should all be men trained at Oxford and graduates of Oxford.
Who could be sure that the prime minister would not next
appoint an ultramontane divine from Bologna, or a Greek from
Corfu ?   Such extravagances did as little harm as the false
stories about Mr. Harvey being jobbed into the living because
he had been at Eton with Mr. Gladstone and was his political
supporter.   As it happened he was a conservative, and Mr.
Gladstone knew nothing of him except that a number of most
competent persons had praised his learning.   In spite of all
this, however, and of the technical validity of the appointment,
we may wish that the rector's doubts had not been overruled.
A worthy member regaled the House by a story of a gentleman
staying in the mansion of a friend ; one morning he heard
great noise and confusion in the yard ; looking out he saw a
kitchen-maid being put on a horse, and so carried round and
round the yard.   When he went downstairs he asked what was
the matter, and the groom said, 'Oh, sir, 'tis only that we're
going to take the animal to the fair to sell, and we want to say
he has carried a lady.'   The apologue was not delicate, but it
conveyed a common impression.   'Gladstone spoke,' says Mr.
Bruce (March 9, 1872), 'with great vigour and eloquence on the
Ewelme case ; but I think that, with the best possible intentions, he had placed himself in a wrong position.'

IV

In 1872 the wide popularity of the government underwent a
marked decline. The award at Geneva caused lively irritation.
The most active nonconformists were in active revolt. The
Licensing bills infuriated the most powerful of all trade
interests. The Collier case and the Ewelme case seemed
superfluous and provoking blunders. A strong military section
thirsted for revenge on the royal warrant. Mr. Goschen's
threatened bill on local rating spread vague terrors. Individual
ministers began to excite particular odium.

As time went on, the essentially composite character of a
majority that was only held together by Mr. Gladstone's
personality, his authority in the House, and his enormous
strength outside, revealed itself in awkward fissures. The
majority was described by good critics of the time as made up
of three sections, almost well defined enough to deserve the
name of three separate parties. First were the whigs, who
never forgot that the prime minister had been for half his life
a tory ; who always suspected him, and felt no personal attachment to him, though they valued his respect for property and
tradition, and knew in any case that he was the only possible
man. Then came the middle-class liberals, who had held predominance since 1832, who were captivated by Mr. Gladstone's
genius for finance and business, and who revered his high
moral ideals. Third, there was the left wing, not strong in
parliament but with a certain backing among the workmen,
who thought their leader too fond of the church, too deferential
to the aristocracy, and not plain enough and thorough enough
for a reforming age. The murmurs and suspicions of these
hard and logical utilitarians of the left galled Mr. Gladstone as
ungrateful. Phillimore records of him at this moment :—

Feb. 21, 1872.—Gladstone in high spirits and in rather a conservative
mood. 29.—Gladstone sees that the time is fast coming when he must
sever himself from his extreme supporters. He means to take the opportunity of retiring on the fair plea that he does not like to oppose those
who have shown such great confidence in him, or to join their and his
opponents. The plea seems good for retirement, but not for refraining in
his individual capacity from supporting a government which is liberal
and conservative.

Here is a sketch from the Aberdare papers of the temper
and proceedings of the session :—

April 19.—We have had a disastrous week—three defeats, of which
much the least damaging was that on local taxation, where we defended
the public purse against a dangerous raid. There is no immediate
danger to be apprehended from them. But these defeats lower prestige,
encourage the discontented and envious, and animate the opposition.
I think that Gladstone, who behaved yesterday with consummate
judgment and temper, is personally very indifferent at the result. He
is vexed at the ingratitude of men for whom he has done such great

things which would have been simply impossible without him, and would not be unwilling to leave them for a while to their own guidance, and his feeling is shared by many of the ministry. Our measures must for the most part be taken up by our successors, and we should of course be too happy to help them. But I don't see the end near, although, of course, everybody is speculating.

Yet business was done. Progress of a certain kind was made in the thorny field of the better regulation of public-houses, but Mr. Gladstone seems never to have spoken upon it in parliament. The subject was in the hands of Mr. Bruce, the home secretary, an accomplished and amiable man of the purest public spirit, and he passed his bill; but nothing did more to bring himself and his colleagues into stern disfavour among the especially pagan strata of the population. An entry or two from Mr. Bruce's papers will suffice to show Mr. Gladstone's attitude :—

Home Office, Dec. 9, 1869.—I am just returned from the cabinet, where my Licensing bill went through with flying colours. I was questioned a great deal as to details, but was ready, and I think that Gladstone was very well pleased.

Jan. 16, 1871.—I called upon Gladstone yesterday evening. He was in high spirits and full of kindness. He said that he had told Cardwell that I must be at the bottom of the abuse the press was pouring upon him, as I had contrived to relieve myself of it. 'Some one minister,' he added, 'is sure to be assailed. You caught it in the autumn, and now poor Cardwell is having a hard time of it.' I went with him afterwards to the Chapel Royal, which he never fails to attend.

Dec. 14.—We have a cabinet to-day, when I hope to have my Licensing bill in its main principles definitely settled. Unfortunately Gladstone cares for nothing but 'free trade' [in the sale of liquor], which the House won't have, and I cannot get him really to interest himself in the subject.

This is Speaker Brand's account of the general position :—

Throughout the session the opposition, ably led by Disraeli, were in an attitude of watchfulness. He kept his eye on the proceedings of the government day by day on the Alabama treaty. Had that treaty failed, no doubt Disraeli would have taken the sense of the House on the conduct of the government. For the larger part of the session the Alabama question hung like a cloud over the proceedings, but as soon as that was settled, the sky cleared. It has been a good working session. . . . Of the two leading men, Gladstone and Disraeli, neither has a strong hold on his followers. The radicals below the right gangway are turbulent and disaffected, and the same may be said of the independent obstructives below the left gangway. . . . B., E., H., L. avowedly obstruct all legislation, and thus bring the House into discredit.

It was now that Mr. Disraeli discerned the first great opportunity approaching, and he took the field. At Manchester (April 3) he drew the famous picture of the government, one of the few classic pieces of the oratory of the century :—

Extravagance is being substituted for energy by the government. The unnatural stimulus is subsiding. Their paroxysms end in prostration. Some take refuge in melancholy, and their eminent chief alternates between a menace and a sigh. As I sit opposite the treasury bench, the ministers remind me of one of those marine landscapes not very unusual on the coasts of South America. You behold a range of exhausted volcanoes. Not a flame flickers upon a single pallid crest. But the situation is still dangerous. There are occasional earthquakes, and ever and anon the dark rumblings of the sea.

On midsummer day he essayed at the Crystal Palace a higher flight, and first struck the imperialist note. He agreed that distant colonies could only have their affairs administered by self-government. 'Self-government, when it was conceded, ought to have been conceded as part of a great policy of imperial consolidation. It ought to have been accompanied by an imperial tariff, by securities for the people of England, for the enjoyment of the unappropriated lands which belonged to the sovereign as their trustee, and by a military code which should have precisely defined the means and the responsibilities by which the colonies should have been defended, and by which, if necessary, this country should call for aid from the colonies themselves. It ought further to have been accompanied by the institution of some representative council in the metropolis which would have brought the colonies into constant and continuous relations with the home government.' He confessed that he had himself at one time been so far caught by the subtle views of the disintegrationists, that he thought the tie was broken. Opinion in the country was at last rising against disintegration. The people had decided that the empire should not be destroyed. 'In my judgment,' he said, 'no minister in this country will do his duty who neglects any opportunity of reconstructing as much as possible our colonial empire, and of responding to those distant sympathies which may become the source of incalculable strength and happiness to this land.' Toryism now sought three great objects: 'the maintenance of our institutions, the preservation of our empire, and the improvement of the condition of the people.' The time was at hand when England would have to decide between national and cosmopolitan principles, and the issue was no mean one. 'You must remember,' he concluded, 'that in fighting against liberalism or the continental system, you are fighting against those who have the advantage of power—against those who have been high in place for nearly half a century. You have nothing to trust to but your own energy and the sublime instinct of an ancient people.'

Disraeli's genius, at once brooding over conceptions and penetrating in discernment of fact, had shown him the vast tory reserves that his household suffrage of 1867 would rally to his flag. The same genius again scanning the skies read aright the signs and characteristics of the time. Nobody would seriously have counselled intervention in arms between France and Germany, yet many felt a vague humiliation at a resettlement of Europe without England. Nobody seriously objected to the opening of the Black Sea, yet many were affected by a restive consciousness of diplomatic defeat. Everybody was glad that—as I am about to describe in the following chapter —we had settled the outstanding quarrel with America, yet most people were sore at the audacity of the indirect claims, followed by the award of swingeing damages. National pride in short was silently but deeply stirred ; the steady splendour of the economic era for a season paled in uncalculating minds. This coming mood the tory leader, with his rare faculty of wide and sweeping forecast, confidently divined, and he found for it the oracle of a party cry in phrases about Empire and Social Reform. When power fell into his hands, he made no single move of solid effect for either social reform or imperial unity. When Mr. Gladstone committed himself to a policy, he brought in bills to carry it out. Forecast without a bill is interesting, but not to be trusted.

END OF VOL. I

Printed by R. & R. CLARK, LIMITED, *Edinburgh*

aright the signs and characteristics of the time. Nobody would
seriously have counselled intervention in arms between France
and Germany, yet many felt a vague humiliation at a resettlement of Europe without England. Nobody seriously objected
to the opening of the Black Sea, yet many were affected by
a restive consciousness of diplomatic defeat. Everybody was
glad that—as I am about to describe in the following chapter
—we had settled the outstanding quarrel with America, yet
most people were sore at the award of swingeing damages.
National pride in short was silently but deeply stirred: the steady splendour
of the economic era for a season paled in unaccelerating minds.
This coming mood the tory leader, with his rare faculty of wide
and sweeping forecast, confidently divined, and he found for it
the oracle of a party cry in phrases about Empire and Social
reform. When power fell into his hands he made no single
move of solid effect for either social reform or imperial unity.
When Mr. Gladstone committed himself to a policy, he brought
in bills to carry it out. Forecast without a bill is interesting,
but not to be trusted.

END OF VOL. I

RECENTLY PUBLISHED.

8vo. 7s. 6d. net.

MISCELLANIES

FOURTH SERIES

BY

JOHN MORLEY

CONTENTS

MACHIAVELLI.

GUICCIARDINI.

A NEW CALENDAR OF GREAT MEN.

JOHN STUART MILL: An Anniversary.

LECKY ON DEMOCRACY.

A HISTORICAL ROMANCE.

DEMOCRACY AND REACTION.

APPENDIX.

MACMILLAN AND CO., Ltd., LONDON.

COLLECTED EDITION

OF THE WORKS OF

JOHN MORLEY

In Fourteen Vols.   Globe 8vo.   4s. net each.

[*Eversley Series.*

VOLTAIRE.   One Vol.

ROUSSEAU.   Two Vols.

DIDEROT AND THE ENCYCLOPÆDISTS.
Two Vols.

ON COMPROMISE.   One Vol.

CRITICAL MISCELLANIES. Vol. I. CONTENTS:
Robespierre—Carlyle—Byron—Macaulay—Emerson.

CRITICAL MISCELLANIES. Vol. II. CONTENTS:
Vauvenargues—Turgot—Condorcet—Joseph de Maistre.

CRITICAL MISCELLANIES. Vol. III. CONTENTS:
On Popular Culture—The Death of Mr. Mill—Mr.
Mill's Autobiography—The Life of George Eliot—On
Pattison's Memoirs—Harriet Martineau—W. R. Greg:
A Sketch—France in the Eighteenth Century—The
Expansion of England—Auguste Comte.

MACMILLAN AND CO., LTD., LONDON.

COLLECTED EDITION

OF THE WORKS OF

JOHN MORLEY

(Continued)

BURKE. One Vol.

STUDIES IN LITERATURE. One Vol. CONTENTS:
Wordsworth—Aphorisms—Maine on Popular Govern-
ment—A Few Words on French Models—On the Study
of Literature—Victor Hugo's "Ninety-Three"—On
"The Ring and the Book"—Memorials of a Man of
Letters—Valedictory.

OLIVER CROMWELL. One Vol.

THE LIFE OF RICHARD COBDEN. Two Vols.

BURKE. By JOHN MORLEY. Crown 8vo. Library
Edition. 2s. net. Popular Edition. 1s. 6d.; sewed, 1s.
[English Men of Letters Series.

WALPOLE. By JOHN MORLEY. Crown 8vo. 2s. 6d.
[Twelve English Statesmen Series.

MACMILLAN AND CO., LTD., LONDON.

Illustrated Edition.   Extra Crown 8vo.   14s. net.

Ordinary Edition.   8vo.   10s. net.

OLIVER CROMWELL

BY

JOHN MORLEY

The Illustrated Edition contains carefully authenti-

cated Portraits in Public and Private Galleries, and

Reproductions of Contemporaneous Prints in the

British Museum and the University of Oxford.

MACMILLAN AND CO., LTD., LONDON.